HANDBOOK OF
HEALTH, HEALTH CARE,
and the
HEALTH PROFESSIONS

HANDBOOK OF
HEALTH, HEALTH CARE,
and the
HEALTH PROFESSIONS

Edited by

David Mechanic

THE FREE PRESS
A Division of Macmillan Publishing Co., Inc.
NEW YORK

Collier Macmillan Publishers
LONDON

THE FREE PRESS
A Division of Macmillan Publishing Co., Inc.
866 Third Avenue, New York, N.Y. 10022

Collier Macmillan Canada, Inc.

Printed in the United States of America

printing number
1 2 3 4 5 6 7 8 9 10

Library of Congress Cataloging in Publication Data
Main entry under title:

Handbook of health, health care, and the health
  professions.

  Includes index.
    1. Medical care—United States.   2. Social
medicine—United States.   3. Medical policy—
United States.   4. Medical care—Research.
I. Mechanic, David   [DNLM: 1. Delivery
of health care—United States—Handbooks.
2. Health services—United States—Handbooks.
3. Health occupations—United States—Handbooks.
W 84 AA1 H23]
RA395.A3H36 1982   362.1'0973   82-71149
ISBN 0-02-920690-1

FOR MOM
with love on your eightieth year

Contents

Introduction

In the past two decades there has been an extraordinary expansion of the study of health and health-care services. While impressive growth in biomedical research followed World War II, it is only in the last fifteen years that research interests have broadened with an upsurge in attention to epidemiological studies, controlled clinical trials, investigations of environmental and psychosocial factors, and health-services research of all kinds. What was once an area of study for a small group of investigators from the social sciences, public health, and occasionally medicine now occupies thousands of researchers drawn from medicine, the social, economic, and behavioral sciences, epidemiology and biostatistics, and the public health disciplines. The interdisciplinary requirements for the study of health and the provision of services to prevent and treat disease have led to a variety of new areas including medical sociology, behavioral medicine, health-services research, environmental medicine, and community medicine. Many traditional fields of study such as anthropology, economics, politics, ethics, law, and the like have developed professional subdivisions directed to problems of health and health care leading students to specialize in such fields as medical anthropology, medical economics, health politics, medical ethics, and law and medicine. In every instance, we have seen the appearance of specialized journals to bring the latest thinking and research results to the large research and professional communities involved.

The growth of the study of health and health care reflects the importance of these issues in our national life. Yearly investments in health care constitute approximately one-tenth of our gross national product, and the provision of health services has become one of the largest sources of employment in our economy. Health care is no longer an issue left to doctors and nurses, if it ever was; it involves a central contribution of a wide range of specialists from engineers and computer scientists to nutritionists, social workers, and administrators. The delivery of medical care in clinics and hospitals depends on a cast of supporting technicians and ancillary workers much larger than the physician and nurse workforce.

The hospital and clinic provide too narrow a view of the role of health care in our national life. Health-care investment is an important component of the economy not only involving massive investment in such facilities as hospitals and nursing homes but also the growth of the medical equipment industries, pharmaceutical companies, and freestanding technical supports such as hemodialysis units. Moreover, outside the formal system of health, billions of dollars are spent on health-motivated activities and products such as exercise and fitness programs, special diets and health foods, stress reduction and counseling programs, and a vast array of psychotherapies of an individual or group character, ranging from treatment to recreational experiences.

The vast investment in health, of course, occupies the attention of government at all levels and industry and labor as well. Government pays more than two-fifths of total health-care expenditures and finances; administers directly and indirectly a wide range of programs, and plays a major regulatory role in most areas of important health activity. In addition to financing, administering, and regulating the largest health program in the country—Medicare—the federal government operates two massive systems of health delivery through the Department of Defense and the Veterans' Administration. Industry and labor are involved because for most Americans health benefits and coverage come through employment-related fringe benefits, and these are bargained collectively.

The massiveness and complexity of our health efforts should suggest that there is no way of simply summarizing the state of knowledge and the range of issues. The intent of this *Handbook* is to provide the reader with a broad but technically sophisticated understanding of the determinants of health and illness and the organization and provision of care. In doing this, it was clear that we could rely on no single academic discipline, professional group, or even interdisciplinary field—such as health-services research—to provide the necessary statement of problems, issues, perspectives, methodologies, and information on the state of our knowledge. Academic disciplines of contributors are reflected in the range of relevant questions—historian, sociologist, epidemiologist, public health physician, political scientist, pediatrician, nurse, economist, internist, psychologist, anthropologist, psychiatrist, health educator, social worker, health-care administrator, etc. It should be clear from the list of contributors and their backgrounds that there is no parochialism here. The contributors represent an extraordinary wealth of knowledge, technical expertise, and firsthand experience in coping with the problems discussed. I have not only selected persons recognized for their important research contributions to health but also many who have had major responsibilities in administering federal entitlement and other major government programs, large nonprofit insurance plans, federal administrative agencies, state health agencies, foundations, and programs of direct medical and nursing care. In short, the contributors represent a mix of administrators and practitioners, researchers and scholars, thinkers and doers. The mix, I believe, gives the *Handbook* vitality and grounds it more concretely in present and future challenges.

Health care, of course, is a political issue, and how questions are viewed in no small way is affected by political philosophies. In identifying contributors, I have tried to find the most knowledgeable and technically competent authors, and they have been selected irrespective of where they stand on the political spectrum. While no attempt has been made to ensure that every political viewpoint is heard, the reader will certainly discern a wide range of perspectives, from relatively conservative to fairly radical. Indeed, given the diversity of contributors and their contrasting points of view, readers will be confronted with conflicts of opinion on many major issues. These conflicts reflect not only the values inherent in health-policy formulation but also the ambiguity and inadequacy of our knowledge in many areas. Is the fight against cancer making good scientific and practical progress? To what extent can we prevent illness and promote health? Does medical care have a major impact on health status? Is there a nurse shortage, and if so, what are its causes? Do HMOs promote health? Do we better change health risks through technological efforts or through health education? The fact that there are disagreements among distinguished contributors should surprise no one. Such differences reflect the real world and varying criteria for reading the evidence. Hopefully, these differences in perspective and interpretation will stimulate readers to pursue these in their own future studies and professional activities.

One central idea that links most chapters in this volume is the concept of viewing health, disease, treatment and rehabilitation in the context of populations including: biological and sociocultural predispositions; needs and varying lifestyles; responses to disease agents and alterations in environment; and self-selection toward risking disease and dysfunction or in seeking protections against physical and psychosocial threats. Such responses in populations occur at the biological, psychological, and sociocultural levels and involve complex adaptive patterns that epidemiological and clinical studies attempt to comprehend.

The *Handbook* is divided into six general sections. The first presents issues of health and health care in their broadest historical and sociocultural dimensions. The second then focuses more specifically on epidemiological studies, examining what we know about major health risks and problems throughout the life span and their antecedents. Section 3 then focuses on health-care delivery, examining such varied institutions as hospitals, HMOs, nursing homes, and such important policy issues as long-term care. Section 4 deals with the health occupations, exploring what we know about nurses, physicians, social workers, and allied health workers, and the issues of managing health-professional organizations. Section 5 takes a patient-oriented perspective, examining how the system looks from a client's point of view, and how patients cope and adapt. Section 6, finally, deals with a range of issues and perspectives, representing different ways of approaching problems in health varying from broad structural analyses to the nuts and bolts of multivariate health research.

Putting together such a *Handbook* is a complex task. There are many possibilities for defining relevant areas and selecting contributors. Problems of scheduling and coordination can be exceedingly frustrating. In the conception and organization of the task, I had the extraordinary assistance and enthusiastic support of Gladys Topkis. She was a joy to work with, and came through especially during difficult times. I am also very grateful to two outstanding secretaries, Linda Vignec and Kay Tranfo, who were invaluable in keeping the book on course, in attending to innumerable problems and details, and in helping coordinate the work of the various contributors. Our efforts in health-care research and health-policy analysis at Rutgers have been significantly assisted by a grant from the Robert Wood Johnson Foundation. In many ways, large and small, this grant contributed to the formulation and completion of this *Handbook*.

David Mechanic

Contributors

DAVID MECHANIC, Ph.D., is University Professor and Dean of the Faculty of Arts and Sciences at Rutgers University in New Jersey. A leading specialist in the field of medical sociology and health care organization, Dr. Mechanic is the author of numerous articles and books including *Medical Sociology, Mental Health and Social Policy, The Growth of Bureaucratic Medicine* and *Future Issues in Health Care.* Among his many professional activities, he is a member of the Institute of Medicine of the National Academy of Sciences, and has served as chairperson of a panel of the President's Commission on Mental Health and as a member of the Panel on Health Services Research and Development of the President's Science Advisory Committee. His current areas of interests are in the field of organization of medical and psychiatric care, adaptation to stress, decision-making process in medicine and psychiatry, illness behavior, and comparative medical organization.

LINDA AIKEN, Ph.D., is Vice President for Research of the Robert Wood Johnson Foundation in Princeton, New Jersey, a private philanthropy interested in improving health care in the United States. Dr. Aiken is a medical sociologist and nurse whose recent research interests include health manpower policy. She is a fellow and past president of the American Academy of Nursing. She is editor of *Health Policy and Nursing Practice* and *Nursing in the 1980s: Crises, Opportunities, and Challenges.*

ODIN W. ANDERSON, Ph.D., is Emeritus Professor at the University of Chicago and has half-time professorships in sociology at the University of Chicago and the University of Wisconsin-Madison. He received his Ph.D. in Sociology from the University of Michigan in 1948 and has devoted his professional career to teaching and research in the health services, particularly consumer behavior and delivery systems. Among his former associations was the Health Information Foundation, a private research foundation which was moved to the University of Chicago, Graduate School of Business in 1962 to become the Center for Health Administration Studies. His major interest has been in delivery systems both in this country and cross-nationally. He has published extensively and is best known for his book, *Health Care: Can There Be Equity? The United States, Sweden, and England.*

MARSHALL H. BECKER, Ph.D., M.P.H., is Professor in the Department of Health Behavior and Health Education, School of Public Health, and the Department of Pediatrics and Communicable Diseases, School of Medicine, The University of Michigan, Ann Arbor, Michigan. Dr. Becker and his colleagues have conducted a number of studies of beliefs and attitudes as determinants of health behaviors (including evaluations of intervention strategies to increase patients' cooperation with recommended therapies); of physicians' attitudes and behaviors relevant to adoption of innovations; drug-prescribing patterns, and provision of abortion-related services; and of different approaches to organizing the delivery of medical care.

DIANE BOLAY LAWRENCE, M.A., is currently Director of Health Program Evaluation, Office of Health Affairs, Department of Defense. Prior to this she was the Assistant Director, Center for Health Policy Studies, Georgetown University and has served as Director of Program Planning, Office of Research, Demonstrations and Statistics, Health Care Financing Administration. She has conducted research in health services planning, organization, financing and delivery with the Public Health Service, the Social Security Administration, and the John Hopkins Medical Institutions.

PAUL W. BRANDT-RAUF, Sc.D., M.D., M.P.H., is a resident in internal medicine at Georgetown University Medical Center. He recently completed two years as a resident in environmental pathology at Columbia-Presbyterian Medical Center. He received his doctorate in applied chemistry, his M.D. and his M.P.H. in environment sciences from Columbia University. He has consulted for academic and industrial groups and the National Academy of Sciences. His interests include occupational medicine, environmental carcinogenesis, and toxicology.

LESTER BRESLOW, M.D., M.P.H., is Professor of Public Health at the School of Public Health, University of California, Los Angeles, where he was formerly Dean. He was the founder of the Alameda County Human Population Laboratory which has contributed substantially to our knowledge of how ways of living relate to health. Dr. Breslow has been an adviser to the Surgeon-General on health promotion; chaired the Board of Health Promotion and Disease Prevention, Institute of Medicine; and served as President of the American Public Health Association, the International Epidemiological Association and the Association of Schools of Public Health.

NOEL CHRISMAN, Ph.D., is Associate Professor in the Department of Community Health Care Systems at the School of Nursing, University of Washington. He received his Ph.D. in anthropology from the University of California, Berkeley in 1966 and an M.P.H. from the University of California, Berkeley School of Public Health in 1967. His earlier work was in urban anthropology, but more recently has been concerned with describing illness behavior in the popular sector and the role played by physicians in patients' illness episodes. He and Thomas Maretzki have edited the book *Clinically Applied Anthropology* which will serve as a resource for anthropologists teaching in health science schools.

PAUL CLEARY, Ph.D., is an Assistant Professor in the Department of Social Medicine and Health Policy at the Harvard Medical School. His research interests include the epidemiology of psychiatric disorder and help seeking processes, the recognition and treatment of behavioral and psychiatric disorders in general medical care settings, and research methods and statistics. He is currently co-authoring a book on the impact of the Three Mile Island incident.

FRANCES COHEN, Ph.D., is Associate Professor of Psychology in the Department of Psychiatry, School of Medicine, at the University of California, San Francisco. Dr. Cohen received her Ph.D. degree in psychology from the University of California, Berkeley, and did a postdoctoral fellowship in the Department of Psychiatry at the Stanford University School of Medicine before joining the University of California faculty. Her research interests focus on theoretical questions concerning stress and coping issues as they relate to physical health and disease. Besides teaching in the Health Psychology Ph.D. Program, she also teaches courses in the psychological core of medicine to first-year medical students.

MARGARET DIMOND, Ph.D., is currently an Associate Professor and Director of the Family and Geriatric Nurse Clinician Program at the University of Utah. She received a B.S.N. from the University of Washington and an M.A. from the University of Iowa. Prior to her doctoral studies she worked as a staff nurse, Clinical Coordinator, and was Associate Director of Nursing in an acute care setting. She received a Ph.D. in Sociology from the University of Wisconsin-Madison. Dr. Dimond's writing and research interests are in the area of chronic illness and aging. She is currently directing a longitudinal study of bereavement and the elderly and has recently co-authored a text on *Chronic Illness Across the Life Span.*

BRUCE P. DOHRENWEND, Ph.D., has been at Columbia University since 1958, where he is the Foundations' Fund for Research in Psychiatry Professor and head of the Social Psychiatry Research Unit. In addition, he is Chief of the Department of Social Psychiatry at the New York State Psychiatric Institute and Director of the Research Training Program in Psychiatric Epidemiology at Columbia. He obtained his Ph.D. in social psychology from Cornell University in 1955. Dr. Dohrenwend has authored and edited numerous papers and several books on epidemiological studies of mental disorders in communities and the role of environmentally induced stress in various types of psychopathology—often in collaboration with his wife, Dr. Barbara Snell Dohrenwend.

ANDREW DUNHAM, Ph.D., is Assistant Professor of Political Science at Colorado College. He received his Ph.D. from the University of Chicago. His major research interests include government regulation and the politics of health. He has published articles on hospital regulation, government health policy, and health planning.

JACK ELINSON, Ph.D., is Professor, initiator, and first head of the graduate program in sociomedical sciences at Columbia University in which theory and methodology of the social sciences are applied to the problems of health and health care. His work has dealt with the quantitative estimation of community health care needs, comparison of medical and sociological perspectives in conceptualizing illness, sociometric evaluation of the quality of medical and hospital care, and the development of sociomedical health indicators. He has served as chairman of the Section on Medical Sociology of the American Sociological Association and as President of the American Association for Public Opinion Research. He is a member of the Institute of Medicine, National Academy of Sciences. Dr. Elinson is co-editor of *Health Goals and Health Indicators; Policy Planning and Evaluation* and *Sociomedical Health Indicators.*

JACOB J. FELDMAN, Ph.D., is the Associate Director for Analysis and Epidemiology, National Center for Health Statistics, USPHS. He has been working for the past three decades on measurement and other methodological problems in the realms of epidemiology, health economics, and health services research. He has participated in a great many surveys pertaining to health and medical care. He was formerly a professor of biostatistics at the Harvard School of Public Health and Director of Research, NORC, University of Chicago.

CLIFTON R. GAUS, Sc.D., is currently President of the Association for Health Services Research in Washington, D.C. and Associate Professor, Department of Community and Family Medicine, Georgetown University Medical School. He was formerly Director of the Center for Health Policy Studies. From 1977–1979 Dr. Gaus directed the policy, legislative, research and statistical functions of the Health Care Financing Administration, HEW. Prior to this he held executive positions in the Social Security Administration and the Office of the Assistant Secretary of Health, HEW, and was on the faculty of Johns Hopkins University. His background is in the field of Health Services Administration, with a Masters Degree in Hospital Administration from the University of Michigan and a Doctorate in Health Services from Johns Hopkins University.

NORMAN GEVITZ, Ph.D., is Assistant Professor of the Social Sciences at the Illinois Institute of Technology. He received his doctorate in Sociology from the University of Chicago in 1980. Dr. Gevitz is the author of the forthcoming book *The D.O.'s: Osteopathic Medicine in Ameria.*

ELI GINZBERG, Ph.D., is Director of the Conservation of Human Resources, Columbia University and a member of the Institute of Medicine. Among his many books are *Men, Money and Medicine, Limits of Health Reform,* and *Health Manpower and Health Policy.* Dr. Ginzberg's current research includes the future supply of physicians and nurses, home care, the elderly, and the future of health science centers.

LAWRENCE W. GREEN, Ph.D., is Director, Center for Health Promotion, Research and Development, University of Texas Health Science Center at Houston, Houston, Texas. Dr. Green has worked as a health educator in local, state, and federal health agencies and for the Ford Foundation in Dacca, Bangladesh. He has served on the public health faculties at Berkeley, Johns Hopkins, and Harvard and on the medical faculties at Johns Hopkins, Harvard and Texas. He established the research training programs in health education and cardiovascular risk at Johns Hopkins. His interests now are in health promotion policy.

GERALD N. GROB, Ph.D., is Professor and Chairman, Department of History, Rutgers University. He received his doctorate in American history from Northwestern University in 1958. Dr. Grob taught at Clark University from 1957 to 1969 and since that time has been a member of the Department of History at Rutgers University. Since 1959 he has been engaged in research into the history of the care and treatment of the mentally ill and the development of psychiatry in America. His previous books include *Workers and Utopia, The State and the Mentally Ill, Mental Institutions in America: Social Policy to 1875,* and *Edward Jarvis and the Medical World of Nineteenth-Century America.* Currently he is finishing a book on the history of psychiatry and the mentally ill covering the period from 1875 to the Second World War.

ROBERT J. HAGGERTY, M.D., is President of the William T. Grant Foundation, which supports research on the effects of environmental stress on the health of school age children. He is also Clinical Professor of Pediatrics at Cornell University Medical School where he administers the Robert Wood Johnson Foundation's Academic General Pediatric program which trains pediatricians for academic careers in general pediatrics. He is editor of *Pediatrics in Review,* and member of the Institute of Medicine. He was formerly Roger I. Lee Professor of Health Services at the Harvard School of Public Health and Chairman of the Department of Health Services and co-editor of *Pediatrics.*

KIM HOPPER is currently Research Associate with the Community Service Society of New York and a doctoral candidate in Sociomedical Sciences at Columbia University. He has written previously on social aspects of postwar psychiatry, problems in medical ethics, and conceptual issues on medical anthropology. He is co-author of a monograph on the homeless in New York and works as an advocate with the Coalition for the Homeless.

KATRINA W. JOHNSON, Ph.D., is presently Program Scientist at the Behavioral Medicine Branch of the National Heart, Lung and Blood Institute. She received her training in medical and family sociology at the University of Notre Dame. Dr. Johnson's current concerns include the role of sociocultural factors such as minority group membership on health, coronary prone behavior patterns, and support networks in the development, treatment, and prevention of cardiovascular disease.

ROSALIE A. KANE, D.S.W., is a social scientist at the Rand Corporation and a lecturer at the University of California, Los Angeles, School of Social Welfare. She is a social work researcher, educator and consultant. Since 1979, she has edited *Health and Social Work,* a quarterly journal published by the National Association of Social Workers. Her major interests include long-term care for the elderly, delivery of hospital social work services, and the interface among hospital, long-term care facility, and community.

STANISLAV V. KASL, Ph.D., is Professor of Epidemiology in the Department of Epidemiology and Public Health, Yale University School of Medicine. He received his Ph.D. in psychology from the University of Michigan in 1962 and worked at the Institute for Social Research before coming to Yale in 1969. His primary research interest is in social and psychological influences on health status, with a special emphasis on "stress and disease" issues.

ARTHUR KLEINMAN, M.D., M.A., is Professor of Medical Anthropology at the Harvard University, where he teaches clinically applied medical anthropology, cross-cultural psychiatry, and social science in medicine. Dr. Kleinman's books include *Patients and Healers in the Context of Culture*, *Normal and Abnormal Behavior in Chinese Culture*, co-edited with T. Y. Lin, and *The Relevance of Social Science for Medicine*, co-edited with Leon Eisenberg. His field research has been in China, Taiwan, and the United States.

RICHARD S. LAZARUS, Ph.D., is Professor of Psychology at the University of California, Berkeley. he has had thirty-four years of research experience on the dynamics of human adaptation since receiving his Ph.D. in 1948 and has published extensively on the theory of stress and coping, and on his empirical research. His current work has been extended to stress and coping in aging.

HOWARD LEVENTHAL, Ph.D., is Professor of Psychology at the University of Wisconsin-Madison. Dr. Leventhal's earlier work included studies of the impact of fear communications on health behaviors and mother's emotional responses during childbirth. His current work is focused on illness cognition and inter-relates his interests in cognitive and emotional processes. He is studying patients' reactions to cancer chemotherapy, patients' reactions to diagnosis and treatment for hypertension, and the relationship of illness cognition to self perception in studies of perceived aging.

SOL LEVINE, Ph.D., is University Professor and Professor of Sociology and Community Medicine in the University Professor Program at Boston University. Dr. Levine has written numerous articles and books on health and illness, with special emphasis on health organization, social stress, rehabilitation and health policy. He has served as Director of the Social Science Program at the Harvard School of Public Health, as Chairman of the Department of Behavioral Sciences at the Johns Hopkins School of Hygiene and Public Health, and as Chairperson of the Department of Sociology at Boston University. He is past Chairman of the Medical Sociology Section of the ASA, was a member of the Health Services Research study section and member and chairman of the NIAAA study section. Dr. Levine is a member of the Institute of Medicine of the National Academy of Sciences.

DONALD W. LIGHT, Ph.D., is Professor of sociology and community medicine at the University of Medicine and Dentistry of New Jersey, New Jersey School of Osteopathic Medicine and serves on the graduate faculty of Sociology of Rutgers University. The education of professionals and the relationship between socialization and the structure of training programs have been his major areas of interest for a number of years. These themes are central to his book, *Becoming Psychiatrists: The Professional Transformation of Self*.

HAROLD S. LUFT, Ph.D., is Associate Professor of Health Economics at the Institute for Health Policy Studies, University of California, San Francisco. Dr. Luft received his undergraduate and graduate training in economics at Harvard University. His research has covered a wide range of areas, including applications of benefit cost analysis, studies of medical care utilization, the relationship between volume of surgery in hospitals and postoperative mortality, regionalization of hospital services, duplication of health insurance coverage, competition in the medical care market, and health maintenance organizations. In addition to numerous articles in scientific journals, he has recently authored *Health Maintenance Organizations: Dimensions of Performance.*

Lois A. Maiman, Ph.D., is Assistant Professor in the Departments of Pediatrics and Preventive, Family, and Rehabilitation Medicine, School of Medicine and Dentistry, and Department of Sociology, University of Rochester. She has undertaken studies of factors influencing patients' compliance with prescribed regimes (including interventions to enhance compliance in obesity, asthma, and juvenile diabetes), perceptions of patients by health professionals, and prescribing attitudes and behaviors of physicians. With Dr. Marshall Becker, she is presently investigating the contribution of sociodemographic and attitudinal factors in mothers' independent use of medications for children.

Theodore R. Marmor, Ph.D., is Professor of Political Science and Public Health and Chairman of the Center for Health Studies at Yale University. He received his A.B. and Ph.D. from Harvard and has taught at the Universities of Minnesota, Wisconsin, Essex (England), and Chicago. His research interests are broadly subsumed in the politics and policies of the welfare state. Beyond numerous articles on welfare state issues, he has authored *The Politics of Medicare,* and served as editor of and contributor to *National Health Insurance: Conflicting Goals and Policy Choices.*

Walter J. McNerney, M.H.A., is Professor of Health Policy, J. L. Kellogg Graduate School of Management at Northwestern University. He was, until recently, chief executive officer of the Blue Cross Association and, through a joint appointment, chief executive officer of the Blue Shield Association. Prior to joining Blue Cross Association, he was Assistant Coordinator of Hospitals and Clinics, University of Pittsburgh Medical Center, and administrator of a Medical Center hospital. Later he served on the faculties of the Graduate School of Public Health, University of Pittsburgh, and the School of Business Administration, University of Michigan. Mr. McNerney is the author of numerous journal articles, monographs and books, most notably his two-volume work, *Hospitals and Medical Economics.*

Judith Richman, Ph.D., is Senior Program Analyst at St. Clare's Hospital Community Mental Health Center where she is working on the design and implementation of psychotherapy outcome research. She received her Ph.D. in sociology from Columbia in 1978 (where she was also a fellow in the Psychiatric Epidemiology Training Program), and was a postdoctoral fellow in psychiatric epidemiology at Yale from 1978–1979. Dr. Richman's interests focus on the social etiology of psychiatric disorders (particularly familial, occupational and sex role factors) and on the nature and efficacy of mental health treatment interventions. She is co-editor (with Peter Stein and Natalie Hannon) of *The Family: Functions, Conflicts and Symbols.*

Leon S. Robertson, Ph.D., is Senior Research Associate in the Center for Health Studies and Lecturer in Epidemiology, Yale University. Trained as a sociologist, he did research in medical care delivery prior to developing a sense of the neglect of injuries as a public health problem. His main work during the past ten years has focused on injury epidemiology and control.

LEE N. ROBINS, Ph.D., is Professor of Sociology at the School of Medicine, Washington University in St. Louis. Dr. Robins' main research efforts have involved follow-up studies of psychiatrically treated and general population samples of children into adulthood, a follow-up of Vietnam army veterans after their return to the United States, the design of a diagnostic interview for use in the general population, and carrying out a large survey of mental health in the general population. She is author of the well-known volume, *Deviant Children Grown Up*.

GERALD ROSENTHAL, Ph.D., is an economist who has worked on problems of health and human services since 1961. He has taught at Harvard and Brandeis Universities in the Departments of Economics and the Florence Heller Graduate School of Social Welfare, and was Director of the Wage Stabilization Program for the Health Industry and chairman of the Health Industry Wage and Salary Committee of the Cost of Living Council during Phase IV. He served as Director of the National Center for Health Services Research (NCHSR) from 1974 through 1981 and established the Intramural Research Program and NCHSR's major disemination activities. He is currently working with the Pan American Health Organization in Mexico City as Advisor to the Mexican Government in the area of research and evaluation of health services.

SAM SHAPIRO is past Director of the Health Services Research and Development Center, and Professor in the Department of Health Services Administration in the School of Hygiene and Public Health, The Johns Hopkins University. He is the author or co-author of about 150 papers and monographs based on his research in breast cancer screening, epidemiology of coronary heart disease, perinatal care, and in the utilization and quality of health services. Mr. Shapiro is a member of the Institute of Medicine, National Academy of Sciences, a fellow in several professional associations, and the recipient of national and local awards for his contributions.

ROSEMARY STEVENS, Ph.D., is Professor and Chairman of the Department of History and Sociology of Science at the University of Pennsylvania. Her primary research and public interests are in twentieth century history of American and British medicine, federal policy-making in medical care and the role of professional associations in developing health man power policies. *Medical Practice in Modern England*, *American Medicine in the Public Interest*, and *The Alien Doctors: Foreign Medical Graduates in the United States* (co-authored by Louis Wolf Goodman and Stephen S. Mick) are among her publications.

MERVYN SUSSER, M.D., is presently Gertrude H. Sergievksy Professor and Director of the Gertrude H. Sergievsky Center, Faculty of Medicine, Columbia University. Previously he was Professor and Head of the Division of Epidemiology of Columbia University's School of Public Health. He received his D.P.H. degree from the Conjoint Board of Physicians and Surgeons, London, in 1960; his medical degree from the University of Witwatersrand, Johannesburg, in 1950; and he is a Fellow of the Royal College of Physicians in Edinburgh. He is the author or co-author of five books and more than 150 articles in the fields of medical sociology and epidemiology.

BRUCE VLADECK, Ph.D., is Assistant Vice President of the Robert Wood Johnson Foundation in Princeton, New Jersey. From 1979–1982, he was Assistant Commissioner for Health Planning and Resources Development in the New Jersey State Department of Health. In that position, he directed the activities of the State Health Planning and Development Agency and played a central role in the implementation of New Jersey's hospital rate-setting system based on per-case payment employing Diagnosis Related Groups. Dr. Vladeck received his B.A. from Harvard College and M.A. and Ph.D. in Political Science from the University of Michigan. He has also worked at the New York City-Rand Institute and Columbia University. He is the author of *Unloving Care: The Nursing Home Tragedy*, and numerous articles on health policy.

HOWARD WAITZKIN, M.D., Ph.D., is an internist at North Orange County Community Clinic, Anaheim, California, and Associate Professor of Medicine and Social Sciences at the University of California, Irvine. Prior to this he was an internist at La Clinica de la Raza, Oakland, California, and Assistant Clinical Professor of Medicine at the University of California, San Francisco. He is the author of *The Exploitation of Illness in Capitalist Society* and *The Second Sickness;* his other writings have appeared in sociological, medical, and political journals. His major interests are in community medicine and the political economy of health and welfare systems.

I. BERNARD WEINSTEIN, M.D., is Professor of Medicine and Environmental Sciences at Columbia University, College of Physicians and Surgeons, and Director of the Division of Environmental Sciences of the Columbia University School of Public Health. He has published extensively in the fields of biochemical genetics, cell biology and carcinogenesis and has served on numerous national and international committees and boards concerned with these areas of research.

BEVERLY WINIKOFF, M.D., M.P.H., is a Senior Medical Associate for International Programs at the Population Council and was Assistant Director for Health Services at the Rockefeller Foundation. In her work on nutrition and nutrition policy, Dr. Winikoff has been a consultant to the Congressional Office of Technology Assessment, the Institute of Medicine, National Academy of Sciences, the White House Special Task Force on International Health, and the Senate Select Committee on Nutrition and Human Needs. Among other published work in the areas of nutrition policy and the relationship of nutrition to health, she is the editor and co-author of *Nutrition and National Policy*.

I

MACRO ISSUES IN HEALTH AND HEALTH-CARE SERVICES

Chapter 1

Disease and Environment in American History

Gerald N. Grob

AMERICANS HAVE ALWAYS BEEN CONCERNED with health and the control of disease. Each succeeding generation has sought to discover the origins of various diseases. The explanations offered varied in character. Some reflected the belief that disease and death were the consequences of immoral behavior. Others emphasized environmental determinants such as climate, occupation, degree of cleanliness, population density, and diet. In relatively recent times the belief that specific diseases were caused by individual pathogens gained widespread acceptance.

The search for a fuller understanding of disease was not a mere intellectual exercise. On the contrary, most Americans assumed that increased knowledge would lead unerringly to the control, if not the eradication, of diseases that caused disability or premature death. Implicit in this outlook was an age-old belief that disease was not a necessary concommitant of the human condition, but rather an aberration caused by certain social or individual shortcomings.

Like the ancient Greeks, Americans developed their own versions of the cult of Hygeia. Health, in effect, involved a judicious mix of morality, wisdom, and knowledge. Nowhere was this faith better expressed than in the motto chosen by Dr. Hermann Biggs for the New York Department of Health in 1900: "Public Health Is Purchaseable. Within Natural Limitations Any Community Can Determine Its Own Death Rate." The fact that Americans in 1978 allocated 9.1 percent of the gross national product to health care was evidence not only of their concerns and fears but also of their confidence that disease could be controlled and conquered by a national commitment to research and medical intervention. Similarly, the growing political and social conflicts over the health-care delivery system offered additional evidence that Americans believed that disease was amenable to control.

The optimism revealed in discussions of health-related matters arose from the modern conviction that human beings possess the ability to control their environment and to create a veritable utopia on earth. Yet there is little evidence to support such a belief. In the history of humanity, for example, individual diseases

The author wishes to acknowledge that some of the research for this paper was supported by a grant from the Public Health Service, National Library of Medicine, No. 2306.

have come and gone, but disease in general has been omnipresent. Indeed, the disappearance of one category of disease often created circumstances conducive to the appearance of other diseases. Within a broad perspective, therefore, disease is less an expression of abnormality and pathology and more a mirror of the precarious balance that exists between human beings as biological organisms and the physical world they inhabit. As in any system, a change in one sector induces corresponding changes elsewhere. "Threats to life," René Dubos has astutely observed, "are inescapable accompaniments of life" (Dubos 1959a, p. 411). So long as individuals retain those characteristics that define their humanity, so long will disease continue to exist in one form or another.

The history of disease in America illustrates this point. Popular belief notwithstanding, the changes in patterns of disease at any given time have had little to do with medical practice, or even conscious decisions by public or private health-care organizations. On the contrary, disease patterns reflected the environment in which people lived. As the environment changed, the incidence of specific diseases changed, often radically. Smallpox, cholera, tuberculosis—once the scourge of humanity—no longer pose significant threats. Their decline, however, did not mean a diminution of disease in general. In recent times diseases once relatively rare have been found with a growing frequency in the population. If disease patterns have reflected the physical and biological world in which we live, then it follows that the existence of disease will be assured so long as human beings retain their mortal character.

Disease and the Amerindian

During the High Middle Ages (c. 960–1350) Europe enjoyed a relative freedom from epidemics that in past centuries decimated the population. The result was rapid economic and population growth. This growth led to increased commercial contacts with other parts of the world and ultimately contributed to the spread of some enteric and pulmonary diseases previously confined to specific geographical areas. From central Asia came the plague, which was transmitted by an infected rodent population. The plague was followed by periodic outbreaks of smallpox, typhus, and influenza, as contacts with Asia and Africa created a dramatically wider disease pool. Moreover, the absence of any epidemic disease before the mid-fourteenth century in Europe meant that the susceptible population was not sufficiently large and concentrated to sustain recurrent outbreaks of plague and other disease (McNeill 1976).

Between 1347 and 1650, however, epidemic disease threatened the very foundations of European society. Paradoxically, halfway through this era Europeans began a migration in unprecedented numbers to the recently discovered New World. These two events—recurrent epidemics and overseas expansion—proved of vital significance to the inhabitants of the Americas, for they contributed to the destruction of millions of New World peoples by various diseases. Those Amerindians who managed to survive the ravages of epidemics, particularly smallpox, offered little or no resistance, and the result was that European settlers triumphed.

European dominance in the Americas, then, was to a large extent a function of the impact of disease upon native populations. The New World at the time of the first contacts was, biologically speaking, quite different from the Old. Thousands of years of isolation after the submergence of the Bering land bridge between Siberia and Alaska allowed the Western Hemisphere to develop in distinctive ways. The Amerindian, for example, was far more uniform in blood type than any other comparable population, and the vegetation, animal life, and social and cultural systems of the New World were unlike those of Europe or Asia. "All the trees," noted Columbus with considerable surprise, "were as different from ours as day from night, and so the fruits, the herbage, the rocks, and all things" (Crosby 1972, pp. 1–34).

Even more significant was the fact that diseases of Asia and Europe, which were overwhelmingly infectious in nature and spread by animal vectors and human contact, did not exist among the native populations of the New World. Perhaps the strenuous journey from Siberia to Alaska in a cold and harsh climate eliminated certain major infectious diseases either because the pathogen or part of the host population failed to survive. Perhaps the domesticated animals of the New World did not carry parasites common to the Old World, thereby inhibiting the spread of infectious diseases among a population sufficiently large to sustain recurrent epidemics. Whatever the reasons, the fact remains that Amerindians had never been exposed to such endemic and epidemic diseases as smallpox, measles, chicken pox, and typhus.Once the native populations were exposed to these diseases, the rates of mortality were far higher than among Old World populations where comparable diseases had long existed. In the forty-two years preceding 1723, for example, about 7 percent of the population in and around London died of smallpox. But when the same disease appeared for the first time in Iceland in 1708, it killed nearly 36 percent of the island's 50,000 inhabitants within two years (Crosby 1972, pp. 35–63; Duffy 1953, p. 20).

Lacking the immunological resistance that normally follows lengthy exposure to most diseases, the Amerindian population was decimated by infectious diseases. This human catastrophe rivaled, if it did not exceed, the ravages of the plague sweeping across Europe and Asia. Some scholars have estimated that the population of central Mexico was about 25 million on the eve of conquest, but that within a decade (1532) it had fallen to 16.8 million. Fifteen years later it dropped to 6.3 million, and by 1605 the area's total population was only 1,075,000. The Mexican experience was hardly unique, for the same pattern of depopulation occurred in Peru (Crosby 1972, pp. 35–63; Borah and Cook 1963, pp. 4, 89; Jacobs 1974).

In North America the picture was somewhat the same. The pace of depopulation, however, was much slower than in many regions of Central and South America, partly because the Indian population was less heavily concentrated and partly because the westward movement of settlers was relatively slow. Nevertheless, the North American Indian population, which at the time of Columbus may have been between 10 and 12 million, reached its nadir as late as 1930, when slightly less that half a million aborigines were alive. Modern scholars have estimated that the deaths among seventeenth-century Indians may have ranged between 75 and 95 percent (Cook 1973; Jacobs 1974).

Disease was by far the most significant cause of this extraordinary mortality rate. More than anything else, disease made it possible for a relatively small European population to emerge victorious over the more numerous native inhabitants. Traditional patterns of social and cultural life among the native population were shattered, and wholesale demoralization followed. Surviving records indicate the rapidity with which Indians died. One European, commenting on an epidemic in the Massachusetts Bay area in 1622, noted that the Indians "died on heapes, as they lay in their houses; and the living, that were able to shift for themselves, would runne away and let them dy, and let there Carkases ly above the ground without burial. . . . And the bones and skulls upon the severall places of their habitations made such a spectacle after my coming into those partes, that, as I travailed in the Forrest nere the Massachusetts, it seemed to me a new found Golgatha" (Crosby 1972, p. 42). Disease, therefore, helped to eliminate much of the Amerindian population and prepared the way for the settlement of the New World by Europeans.

The Colonial Era

Although the first settlers in the seventeenth century were somewhat immune to certain diseases that decimated the Indians in North America, they did not escape unscathed. During the initial stages of settlement in certain regions the rise in death rates was phenomenal. Embarking on crowded, filthy ships, colonists had to withstand the rigors of a long and arduous journey under unsanitary conditions. As a result, typhus and other diseases took a heavy toll. Moreover, an unbalanced diet frequently caused scurvy, and the limited food supply sometimes weakened the passengers and made them prey to other diseases. Conditions were even worse for African slaves who were transported to the New World on crowded ships without regard for their health or safety.

Those surviving the ordeal of the Atlantic passage faced equally great dangers upon landing. Inadequate food, clothing, and shelter were common, and a climate subject to extremes of heat and cold further complicated any adjustment to a new and strange environment. Under these circumstances it was not surprising that many of the early settlements faced the threat of extinction.

The Virginia colony was a case in point. Between 1606 and 1618 a total of 1,800 persons sailed to Virginia. About a hundred returned to England and no less than 1,100 died on the passage or in the colony. In the six years preceding 1625 another 4,800 immigrants arrived, but the total population at the end of this period was only 1,025. The high mortality rate was due largely to malnutrition, which in turn increased the population's susceptibility to other diseases. Physical isolation and despair over the future produced apathy, which compounded the problems of malnutrition. Group discipline and leadership might have lessened the ravages of nutritionally based diseases, but for a variety of reasons they were absent. Not until the middle of the seventeenth century did Virginians begin to adjust to their new and demanding environment—an adjustment process contemporaries often referred to as "seasoning" (Duffy 1953, pp. 3–15; Kupperman 1979).

In New England, on the other hand, a somewhat different pattern developed. The crude death rate among settlers in Plymouth at the outset was 490 per thousand, as compared with 638 at Jamestown. At Jamestown the rate remained high, while in Plymouth it dropped rapidly. In Virginia the entrepreneurial drive inhibited the growing of an adequate food supply and the development of other factors conducive to good health. Plymouth, on the other hand, was largely motivated by a religious drive, and the welfare of the group took precedence over the individual. Moreover, the Indian population of New England, unlike that of Virginia, did not pose the same military threat. This was largely so because disease destroyed many tribes and severely impaired others. The adjustment to a new environment in New England, therefore, proceeded more rapidly than in Virginia (Kupperman 1979).

Once the period of seasoning was over, most colonies began to grow rapidly. In 1630 the total population of the English North American colonies had not yet reached 5,000. Between 1650 and 1700, however, the total rose from 50,000 to 250,000, and by the time of the American Revolution there were about 2.5 million people. The annual rate of growth averaged about 3 percent a year (contrasted with a 0.5 percent growth rate in England before 1750), even though the actual rate of increase was uneven and fluctuated sharply from decade to decade (U.S. Bureau of the Census 1975, part 2. p. 1168).

The rapid increase in population in seventeenth-century America was due to a fortuitous combination of circumstances. During the early stages of settlement, the average age of marriage dropped sharply. Europeans tended to marry in their mid-twenties; Americans in their early twenties. This shift alone accounted for one to two additional births per marriage. In seventeenth-century Andover, Massachusetts, for example, the first generation produced 8.3 children per completed marriage. But the natural increase in population (excluding immigration) was due also to a low mortality rate. In Europe half of all children died before reaching adulthood, but in Andover and Plymouth nine out of ten children born before 1700 survived to the age of twenty. Indeed, age-specific life expectancy of adults in Plymouth and Andover was not fundamentally dissimilar from rates in modern-day America. Plymouth males who survived to the age of twenty-one had a life expectancy of 69.2, and women that of 62.4 At age fifty, both men and women could expect to survive to nearly seventy-four. Those who reached seventy could expect to live for another decade. The average age of death of males who settled in Andover before 1660 was 71.8 and women 70.8 (Greven 1970, pp. 21–40; Demos 1965).

Even where birth rates were similar, colonial towns grew far more rapidly than their English or European counterparts. In the century following its founding in 1636, the town of Dedham in Massachusetts had a birth rate of about 36 per 1,000 per year. This compares with figures of 37 and 26–35 for two English villages and 36–40 for a French town. Yet Dedham grew rapidly, while its counterparts remained stable. The difference was to be found in a radically different mortality pattern. English and European towns tended to experience recurrent demographic crises, which were generally related to periodic epidemics and famines. During such crises anywhere between 10 and 50 percent of the population perished. Although minor crises were by no means absent, Dedham never had to contend with major disasters. Its mortality rate rarely exceeded its birth rate, and on no occasion did 10 percent of the population die in a single year or set of years (Lockridge, 1966).

The longevity and general healthfulness of life in seventeenth-century America, once settlement was established, was the result of a unique set of conditions: low population density; relative isolation between self-contained agricultural communities; the absence of large urban centers with commercial contacts with other parts of the world; and a primitive and slow-moving internal transportation network. All of these factors combined to limit the spread of infectious diseases, which constituted the major threat to survival in most parts of the world at that time. This is not to imply that infectious diseases were absent in the seventeenth century. It is only to say that environmental conditions limited their significance and prevented them from becoming established in epidemic and endemic form. For these reasons mortality patterns in many colonies after the period of seasoning tended to approximate rates found in modern America.

Paradoxically, the mortality experiences of the seventeenth century contained within them the seeds of change for the future. As Thomas Malthus pointed out nearly two hundred years ago, there always exist checks upon unregulated population growth, including pestilence, war, and famine. In the American colonies neither famine (excluding nutritional disease such as scurvy, pellagra, and others) nor war (with certain notable exceptions) were significant in stopping the growth of population. Disease, on the other hand, tended to become more important in the eighteenth century. By that time the colonies had begun to develop economically; domestic and foreign commerce diminished the physical isolation of many communities. Economic growth was accompanied by rapid population growth and the rise of urban ports with close ties to Europe, the Caribbean, and Africa. The result was the partial recreation of the harsh disease environment so characteristic of a large part of the settled world at that time. Commercial contacts spread infectious diseases, and a growing population provided a pool of susceptible persons to sustain the infectious pathogens.

During the eighteenth century the colonists began to experience periodic epidemics that in Europe caused high mortality rates, particularly among the young. Smallpox, for example, probably originated in central Africa or India, and by the fifteenth and sixteenth centuries had spread to Europe. During the eighteenth century it was endemic in virtually every major British city. From 1731 to 1765 approximately 2,100 persons died in each year in London from smallpox. Few adults were infected, mainly because childhood exposure was virtually inevitable (Duffy 1953, pp. 20–22).

Smallpox was by no means absent from the colonies before 1700; Boston had several epidemics before the end of the century. The disease, however, tended to be localized and sporadic. After 1700 the growth of population and increase of trade changed the situation, and for the remainder of the century periodic smallpox epidemics became the norm. In 1721 a major outbreak ravaged Boston; in a population of 10,670, 5,980 were infected and 844 died. Nor did the disease remain localized; it quickly spread to adjacent areas. A similar epidemic in 1730 left 500 dead and 4,000 infected out of a total population of about 14,000 (Duffy 1953, pp. 50–54).

The New England experience was by no means unique; New York, New Jersey, and Pennsylvania rarely escaped outbreaks during any five-year period. The South was least affected because of its scattered population and its comparative isolation from centers of commerce. The periodic reappearance of the disease resulted mainly from one phenomenon: During an epidemic most susceptible persons tended to become infected, and a sufficient period of time would have to pass before the number of susceptible persons reached a level capable of sustaining a new epidemic (Duffy 1953, pp. 16–112).

Similarly, there were occasional cases of diphtheria in the colonies. The first major outbreak in epidemic form did not occur until 1735, but in that year the disease appeared in Kingston, New Hampshire, in a particularly virulent form. Normally the town averaged ten deaths per year; in 1735, 102 persons died. The disease was especially deadly among children, and more than a third of the town's youngsters died. During the course of the epidemic, 983 of New Hampshire's citizens perished, of whom 802 were under the age of ten and only 43 were over twenty. The epidemic slowly moved south, but the percentage of fatalities grew progressively smaller. For reasons that are not clear, Boston remained ouside the epidemic area. Diphtheria appeared throughout the eighteenth century, and continued to claim the young as its victims (Caulfield 1939; Duffy 1953, pp. 113–29).

Much the same pattern was true for measles. The disease was relatively insignificant during the seventeenth century. Boston, for example, experienced only two epidemics before 1700, the first in 1657 and the second thirty years later. By the eighteenth century, on the other hand, the disease occurred more frequently, and the intervals between outbreaks grew shorter. Between 1713 and 1772 there were six epidemics (one every decade). Between 1783 and 1835 there were no less than eleven epidemics, or one every 4.7 years. The increasing frequency of measles epidemics was directly related to three developments. First, sailing time between Europe and America fell during the eighteenth century. Before 1700 ships remained at sea long enough for an epidemic to run its course before arrival in the New World (measles has a brief incubation period). After 1700 many vessels arrived with epidemics still in progress. Secondly, there was a steady increase in the number of ships and passengers arriving in the colonies. Finally, a greater population density in port cities provided large numbers of susceptible individuals, and eventually the disease became established in endemic forms. Nor was the death rate from measles insignificant. Indeed, on occasion mortality assumed staggering proportions. In 1759 and 1772 the mortality rate reached 627 and 616 per 100,000, respectively, for Philadelphia, and in 1802 an outbreak in New York City resulted in a death rate of 374. Although the reasons for such high rates are obscure, it is possible that measles (which struck adults as well as children), in combination with other common diseases such as dysentery, influenza, diphtheria, and scarlet fever, caused large numbers of deaths (Caulfield 1943).

Population growth and increased domestic trade undoubtedly created conditions conducive to the spread of epidemic diseases. Moreover, foreign trade brought to the colonies diseases that were relatively insignificant in England and Europe. Such was the case of yellow fever, a disease characterized by three elements—human beings, a mosquito vector, and the causative virus. By the second half of the seventeenth century the disease was established in the West Indies, and was probably imported from the west coast of Africa in slave ships. As colonial trade with the West Indies expanded, the disease appeared in coastal cities involved in such trade. Boston experienced an outbreak in 1693, and six years later Philadelphia and Charleston were affected. Throughout the eighteenth century, ports along the east coast were visited by periodic episodes of yellow fever that generally caused a high mortality rate. Unlike other diseases, yellow fever was confined to its place of origin, a fact that puzzled contemporaries who recongnized that it could not be spread by infected persons leaving the area. For reasons unknown, the disease virtually disappeared between 1760 and 1793. But in the latter year it reappeared in Philadelphia and caused perhaps the most devastating health disaster ever experienced by an American city. Before the epidemic ran its course, about half the city's population of 48,000 fled. Of those who remained, more than 5,000 perished, and the city's political, social, and economic structures virtually ceased to function. The disease continued to visit port cities for much of the nineteenth century; the New Orleans epidemic of 1853 killed 10 percent of the 100,000 who remained during the summer and early autumn and infected at least 30,000 others (Duffy 1953, pp. 138–63; Powell 1949; Shryock 1952; Duffy 1966).

Spectacular though they were, diseases such as smallpox, diphtheria, and yellow fever were not the most significant threats to the health of colonial Americans. Statistically more important were debilitating diseases such as malaria and dysentery, which were endemic in virtually all the colonies. Although they often did not kill their victims directly, these diseases weakened them and reduced their resistance to other fatal disorders. This was especially true for recently arrived settlers. Taken together, malaria and dysentery were, without doubt, the two most significant diseases in terms of colonial mortality. Because of their endemic nature, however, they aroused less fear than did other more sporadic epidemic diseases such as smallpox (Duffy 1953, pp. 204–22, 237–38).

Whether or not malaria existed in the New World before Columbus is not known, but the disease quickly became a major factor during the seventeenth and eighteenth centuries. Americans knew the spring and autumn flareups of malaria were inevitable. Certainly environmental conditions promoted its spread, since many settlements were located adjacent to bodies of water. Moreover, the practice of clearing land upset drainage patterns and created stagnant pools, which provided the anopheles mosquito with excellent breeding grounds. As infected and susceptible persons moved into an area, the cycle that made malaria endemic began. Although the disease declined in New England throughout the eighteenth century, it became firmly entrenched in other regions. In the Carolina lowlands where rice was cultivated, mortality among white settlers remained extraordinarily high. This fact, combined with the greater degree of immunity among African blacks to malaria, contributed to the development of the institution of slavery (Childs 1940; Wood 1975; Duffy 1953, pp. 204–214).

During the second half of the eighteenth century, therefore, ecological factors responsible for relatively low morbidity and mortality rates during the preceding century changed, and the corresponding advantages enjoyed by colonials, as compared with Europeans, diminished. Mortality rates for eighteenth-century Boston (about 37 per 1,000), for example, approached those of comparable English cities. In his analysis of Boston from 1705 to 1774 by ten-year periods, Lemuel Shattuck found that the number of deaths in proportion to the total population was lowest between 1705 and 1714 (30.4 per 1,000) and peaked between 1745 and 1754 (42.6 per 1,000). A higher population density, rudimentary sanitation practices, and epidemic and endemic diseases associated with trade and commerce combined to create a harsher disease environment. The most susceptible element in the population to infectious diseases continued to be the young. In the 1780s, for example, about half of all deaths in Philadelphia were children under the age of ten. In fact, urban centers continued to grow only because of immigration from the surrounding countryside or from abroad (Shattuck 1846, p. 132; Henretta 1973, p. 13).

Mortality and morbidity in the colonial period were for the most part independent of therapeutic intervention, medical or otherwise. Variolation (transplanting pus from the pustules of a smallpox victim into an incision in the skin of a healthy person) came into widespread use in the eighteenth century, for it was recognized that the resulting infection was generally mild and the mortality rate far lower. Undoubtedly variolation diminished the death rate during epidemics, but its overall impact was minor. Many communities also adopted legislation providing for quarantines during epidemics and regulated occupations that allegedly posed a threat to health. In the aggregate, however, such public health measures had a negligible influence; morbidity and mortality were influenced by broader environmental forces (Miller 1957; Blake 1959; Duffy 1953, pp. 23–42).

Morbidity and Mortality in Nineteenth-Century America

Morbidity and mortality rates rarely remain stable for long periods of time. Indeed, the harsh disease environment of the late eighteenth century quickly passed, for forces were already emerging that ultimately made possible the transition to contemporary health patterns. During the nineteenth century, industrial, economic, social, technological, and demographic changes reshaped American society. Out of this transformation emerged a sharply different disease environment, the origins of which still remain unclear.

For one thing, Americans experienced a profound demographic revolution at the close of the eighteenth century. The high birth and mortality rates common to premodern societies slowly but surely began to decline. Mortality among infants and those under twenty first declined in the North and Middle states, and later in the South. The reasons for this development are obscure, although changes in medical practice or public health were most assuredly not an important factor. Shortly thereafter fertility rates began to fall. The decline in mortality came to an end in the early nineteenth century, while fertility rates continued on a downward trend.

At the same time, America entered a new phase of population growth. Between 1790 and 1860 the decennial growth rate remained stable (unlike the colonial era, when population growth rates fluctuated sharply), and averaged about 33 percent per decade. The distribution of the population, on the other hand, changed as urban areas grew in size and number. In 1790 there were only six cities with more than 8,000 people; by 1850 there were eighty-five such areas, containing 12.5 percent of the population. In 1790 no city had more than 50,000, and only two had more than 25,000. By 1850 the largest city contained over half a million; five had between 100,000 and 250,000; and twenty more ranged in size between 25,000 and 100,000 (Weber 1899, p. 22; U.S. Bureau of the Census 1975, part 1, p. 8). All of these new developments were to affect the relationship between human beings and disease.

The changes in diet, housing, geographical location, occupation, sanitation, and behavior patterns that accompanied the transformation of American society were paralleled by new morbidity and mortality patterns. Indeed, rapid social change worked both to limit and to maximize individual diseases, a reflection of the delicate and complex ecological balance of the biological world. Although the full import of changes in the prevailing disease environment of the nineteenth century remain for the most part unexplored by historians and other scholars, it is possible to offer a few generalizations and a series of illustrative case studies.

Infectious diseases continued to pose the greatest threat to the health of Americans throughout much of the nineteenth century. Yet the pattern of individual diseases differed sharply, depending on the environmental circumstances involved. In many instances, infectious diseases appeared and disappeared without being affected by the therapeutic methods of the medical profession. In other instances, the decline of one disease was accompanied by an increase in the virulence of another.

The complexity of the relationship between disease and environment is nowhere better illustrated than by the history of malaria in the Upper Mississippi Valley (Minnesota, Wisconsin, Iowa, Illinois, and Missouri) during the nineteenth century. Before 1800 the disease was absent from this region. Malaria made its initial appearance sometime between 1800 and 1830, and this coincided with the movement of population into this area. Between 1830 and 1870 the disease reached a high endemic-epidemic level, and then began to decline sharply. By the 1890s the disease had virtually disappeared. Interestingly enough, the malarial parasite was not identified until 1890, and R. Ross demonstrated in 1897 that the anopheles mosquito was the carrier. The first active suppressive measures within the continental United States did not begin until the second decade of the twentieth century. Nor was there any effective therapy to prevent or to cure the disease during this era. Although quinine suppressed clinical symptoms, its use did not prevent infection nor sterilize the carrier. How, then, can the appearance and disappearance of malaria be explained (Ackerknecht 1945, pp. 16–61)?

The initial appearance of malaria resulted from a combination of circumstances. In the first place, a large number of settlers arrived in the Upper Mississippi Valley early in the nineteenth century. Between 1810 and 1860 the population increased from slightly over 30,000 to about 4.5 million. These migrants included both susceptible persons as well as carriers, both of whom were required for the spread of malaria. Secondly, the movement of population was along rivers and other bodies of water that were always the original places of settlement. These areas provided excellent breeding grounds for the anopheles mosquito, particularly since the clearing of land increased stagnant pools by upsetting drainage systems that had existed previously. Third, the construction of railroads contributed to the spread of the disease, since railroad workers tended to suffer from malaria and helped to disseminate the disease. Fourth, agricultural practices, including the clearing of surplus land that was not put under cultivation immediately and the construction of dams, added to the breeding grounds of the carrier. Fifth, the proverbial log cabin used by early settlers contributed to malaria because glass, which was expensive and often not available, was not used in window openings. Consequently, early homes were poorly ventilated and dark. Mosquitoes thrived under these conditions. Finally, in the early stages of settlement living conditions and diet often posed a threat to health by lowering resistance to disease. All of these factors played a role in the appearance of malaria and contributed to its subsequent endemic-epidemic phase. By 1860 the death rate from malaria reached 7.9 per 100,000 in Iowa, 5.7 in Wisconsin, 21.6 in Minnesota, 11.8 in Illinois, and 3.6 in Missouri. These statistics do not reflect the far higher incidence of the disease, which, at times, afflicted half of the population of a given region (Ackerknecht 1945).

Similarly, the decline and virtual disappearance of the disease resulted from a changing ecological pattern. First, as mobility of the population declined, it reduced the numbers of new susceptible persons and thereby cut down on the new incoming strains of the disease. This enabled the settled population to become acclimatized to the disease. Secondly, railroad building, which began on a large scale in the 1850s and initially helped to spread malaria, began to shift population away from low-lying areas and waterways that were subject to flooding. In such new areas there were fewer breeding grounds for mosquitoes. Third, in the mature stages of settlement, problems of drainage were brought under control. The growth of urban areas with paved streets and sewer systems began to limit the breeding grounds of insects. Fourth, in time better houses began to be built. Windows brought light into previously dark interiors; rudimentary forms of screens came into use. Fifth, the introduction of cattle into the region proved of special significance, because mosquitoes in general prefer to feed off animals rather than human beings. Finally, there is no doubt that the higher standard of living during the latter part of the nineteenth century contributed to the decline and disappearance of the disease. Although each of these variables operated differently in each region, the eventual outcome was the same. By 1900 the mortality rate from malaria had fallen to 0.3 in Iowa, 0.1 in Wisconsin, 0.05 in Minnesota, and 1.0 in Illinois. Only in Missouri did levels remain high at 3.1, but by 1920 deaths from malaria had dropped to 0.4 in that state (Ackerknecht 1945, pp. 16–130).

Malaria, like yellow fever, involved human beings, an insect vector, and an invading parasite. There were, however, other kinds of infectious diseases that flourished under different conditions. Cholera was one such case. The disease is caused by a bacterium, the *Vibrio cholera*. Once this organism reached human intestines, it produced an acute disease with a mortality rate as high as 50 percent in untreated cases. The symptoms were dramatic; diarrhea, vomiting, and cramps, followed by dehydration and cynosis. Cholera (like typhoid fever) can spread in any environment that leads to contact with the human digestive tract; the more familiar mechanisms included contaminated water, food, utensils, and exposure to an infected persons. The epidemic form of the disease usually spreads rapidly through a sewage-contaminated water supply.

Before 1817 cholera had been confined largely to the Orient. Its brief incubation period and rapid course meant that there was little likelihood of its spreading to areas thousands of miles away. But by the nineteenth century more rapid means of transportation, including the steamship and railroad, led to an increase in the movement of peoples and goods, which spread epidemics to areas hitherto untouched by the disease. Crude water and sewerage systems in high-density urban areas also provided ideal conditions for epidemic outbreaks. Cholera struck the United States on a number of occasions following its initial appearance between 1832 and 1834. It reappeared in the winter of 1848–49, and was prevalent in different areas between 1849 and 1854. The disease did not surface again until 1866. The final outbreak in 1873 was confined almost exclusively to the Mississippi River Valley. Railroads, canals, and steamboats all helped to disseminate the disease, and epidemics were made possible by centralized water works in urban areas.

The elimination of cholera came not as a result of the development of any specific therapy or vaccine but rather because its etiology and modes of transmission came to be understood better. In 1849 Dr. John Snow, an English anesthetist and obstetrician to Queen Victoria, noted that cholera had its greatest incidence among Londoners who drew their water from a particular pump. From this observation, he concluded that cholera was a contagious disease caused by self-reproducing poisons found in the excreta of infected individuals, which, in turn, worked its way into water systems and infected a wider population. During the epidemic of 1854 Snow tested his theory by a geographical analysis of the disease. He demonstrated that cholera was most prevalent among those Londoners served by a company that drew its water from the lower Thames, which had been contaminated by London sewage. Those who received their water from the upper Thames were affected far less. Ultimately the adoption of new sanitary practices helped first to minimize the impact of cholera epidemics and then to prevent them. During the epidemic of 1866, for example, New York City established a metropolitan board of health whose measures helped to contain the disease. There were only a tenth as many deaths from cholera in 1866 as there had been in 1849 despite a sharp increase in population (Rosenberg 1962).

Although feared in the extreme, the occasional epidemics of cholera and yellow fever had no appreciable long-term effect on the American people. Such was not the case with tuberculosis, the most significant disease of the nineteenth century. Known as the Great White Plague, tuberculosis seemed to threaten the very survival of European society. It has been estimated that nearly half of England was infected at one time. Although precise data are lacking, there is circumstantial evidence that the mortality rate from this disease in urban areas in the United States in 1830 ranged as high as 400 per 100,000. Massachusetts, which gathered the best vital statistics, reported in 1842 that "consumption" was responsible for 22 percent of all deaths within the state. In 1861 the mortality rate from tuberculosis of the respiratory system in Massachusetts was 365 per 100,000. The highest mortality rate was found among the poor, but the rich were by no means exempt (Dubos and Dubos 1952; U.S. Bureau of the Census 1975, part 1, p. 63; Dowling 1977, pp. 70–81; Spink 1978, pp. 219–32).

The epidemiology of tuberculosis provides some curious data. During the first year of an individual's life, there was great susceptibility to tuberculosis and a high mortality rate. Children between the ages of five and fifteen, however, were remarkably resistant to the disease. The rate of infection rose in the sixteen to twenty-five age group, but declined again only to rise among the aged. The majority of infected children and young adults usually had an inactive form of the disease during their lives, and only in later years did the disease reappear. Susceptibility tended to increase in populations forced to alter their way of life. During periods of wars that involved large scale social dislocations, the incidence of tuberculosis increased sharply. Even in the absence of specific data, the evidence indicates that the increase in tuberculosis during the nineteenth century was related to certain kinds of broad social, economic, and technological changes. Diet, particularly among urban populations, probably played some role. A lowered resistance to disease, especially among certain migratory populations, and the exposure made possible by high population density also accounted for a significant percentage of cases.

Curiously enough, tuberculosis began to decline in significance during the latter half of the nineteenth century. In Massachusetts, for example, mortality from tuberculosis of the respiratory system fell sharply in the latter third of the century (Table 1.1). The first national statistics, which became available in 1900, show that the rate in that year was 194 per 100,000; by 1910 the rate was 154; and on the eve of World War II it had fallen to 46. By 1970 the disease had almost disappeared, and the rate was under 3 (U.S. Bureau of the Census, 1975, part 1, pp. 58, 63).

TABLE 1.1 Mortality Rate from Tuberculosis of the Respiratory System, Massachusetts, 1865–1970 (per 100,000 of population)

YEAR	RATE	YEAR	RATE	YEAR	RATE
1865	367.9	1900	190.3	1935	42.9
1870	343.3	1905	163.5	1940	34.6
1875	347.4	1910	138.3	1945	36.9
1880	308.1	1915	116.8	1950	20.2
1885	306.6	1920	96.8	1955	9.3
1890	258.6	1925	70.1	1960	6.0
1895	223.4	1930	57.2	1965	4.0
				1970	2.5

The decline in mortality from tuberculosis, as with many other diseases, was probably a function of external environmental changes. Medical science played a relatively minor role in containing the disease. In 1882 Robert Koch discovered the tubercle bacillus, but efforts to develop a drug or vaccine proved futile. In the late nineteenth and early twentieth century a variety of therapeutic innovations were introduced, including segregation in sanatoriums, rest, rich diets, outdoor living, surgical removal of diseased tissues, and various medications. But none of these measures proved effective. The BCG vaccine, developed during the 1920s, was not widely used in the United States, and its effectiveness was also limited. It was not until the introduction of streptomycin after World War II that physicians had a useful drug to combat the disease. Given the statistical decline of tuberculosis since the late nineteenth century, it cannot be argued that the drug played a major role. Streptomycin simply steepened the decline in mortality at a point when the disease was no longer a major threat to life. Evidence that the virulence of the tubercle bacillus diminished is also lacking. Indeed, the resurgence of tuberculosis in a number of areas in Nazi-occupied Europe during World War II would indicate that such was not the case. Finally, there is circumstantial evidence to suggest that modifications of certain environmental conditions—diet, housing, population density, and occupational practice—played by far the most significant role in the precipitous decline of the disease (Dubos and Dubos, 1952; Dowling 1977, pp. 70–81; Spink 1978, pp. 219–32; McKeown 1979, pp. 92–96).

Although infectious diseases played a dominant role in morbidity and mortality patterns through the nineteenth century, dietary diseases were by no means unknown. In the South pellagra probably existed among the slave population and may have also been responsible for the deaths of hundreds of Northern soldiers at the Andersonville prison during the summer of 1864. The typical diet of slaves included corn and fat pork, neither of which provided sufficient niacin or tryptophan (an amino acid that permits the body to manufacture its own niacin). A deficiency of one or both produced pellagra. Before 1900 the disease was not identified because of the protean nature of its symptoms, which included lassitude, diarrhea, dermatitis, and, in its final stage, death (Kipple and Kipple 1977).

By the early part of the twentieth century pellagra had been identified as a specific disease that tended to follow a seasonal pattern. The first symptoms appeared in early winter and often disappeared during the summer. The disease struck largely the poor, especially blacks, whose monotonous 3—M diet (meat, meal, and molasses) made them particularly susceptible; it had its greatest incidence in rural areas and mill towns. Between 1907 and 1911 eight southern states reported nearly 16,000 cases, with a death rate of nearly 40 percent. After being assigned by the Public Health Service to study the disease, Dr. Joseph Goldberger demonstrated that pellagra was related to the social and economic structure of the region; pellagra and poverty went hand in hand. Interestingly enough, the demonstration that a varied diet would prevent the disease did not lead to its immediate eradication. Indeed, mortality from pellagra peaked in 1928 when floods devastated part of the region's agriculture. In 1927 there were about 170,000 cases of the disease, and in the three succeeding years the annual total exceeded 200,000. About 3 percent of the total died (Etheridge 1972, chaps. 1–7; Goldberger 1964; Roe 1973).

The disappearance of pellagra came about through a fortuitous combination of circumstances. Goldberger and his colleagues demonstrated as early as 1923 that yeast possessed remarkable therapeutic qualities, and by 1930 it was distributed regularly throughout the South. During the 1930s an educational program was launched to encourage people to grow fresh vegetables in their own gardens. Although such measures helped, many southerners were loathe to alter their traditional diet. Moreover, the poverty of the region and the economic depression inhibited many from adopting new dietary habits. Nevertheless, there was a sharp reduction in the number of pellagra-related deaths between 1928 and 1940.

Success in eliminating pellagra (and beriberi as well) came during the 1940s. Between 1937 and 1945 scientific research illuminated the relationship between pellagra and niacin and tryptophen. More significant were dietary innovations introduced during World War II. Higher levels of employment and larger incomes, and the mobilization of men in the armed forces, helped to alter traditional diets that fostered pellagra. The wartime emergency also stimulated the passage of state and federal legislation that provided for mandatory enrichment of bread and flour. In addition, more efficient transportation and refrigeration together with new modes of food preservation and a shift in southern agriculture from cotton to beef, dairy products, peanuts, and vegetables completed the dietary transition. After 1945 pellagra all but disappeared (Etheridge 1972, chaps. 8–10).

Patterns of Disease in Twentieth-Century America

By the end of the nineteenth century mortality from infectious diseases declined precipitously (although unevenly). Local data, which is far more detailed for the late nineteenth and early twentieth centuries than either state or national data, offer some dramatic illustrations to support this conclusion. Between 1851 and 1920 the mortality rate from a series of infectious diseases in Baltimore fell from 1,267 to 357 (per 100,000); during this same era the mortality rate from diseases associated with aging rose from 150 to 614 (Table 1.2). The experiences of other urban areas, including New York, Boston, Philadelphia, and New Orleans, demonstrated comparable trends (Table 1.3) (Meeker 1972).

The origins of the decline in mortality from infectious diseases are somewhat more obscure than its consequences. A variety of explanations have been offered to account for this decline. Some have argued that the rise of modern scientific medicine, the success of interventionist therapies (surgery and drugs), and more accurate diagnoses reduced the death rate from infectious diseases. This hypothesis, however attractive, has relatively little basis in fact. Statistically, the decline in mortality from infectious diseases began well before the introduction of effective therapies. Mortality from tuberculosis, as we have already seen, had been falling for nearly a century before the availability of effective therapies. Similarly, by the time a vaccine to prevent measles was introduced in 1963, the disease had become an insignificant element in mortality rates. The same was true in the case of whooping cough. Even where medical interventions were demonstrably effective, their actual impact on the reduction of mortality was far less significant. Mortality from scarlet fever—a disease involving a streptococcal infection—fell well before the introduction of antibiotic therapy. Certainly medicine played a role in the decline of infectious diseases, but many medical interventions became significant only after a disease lost its fatal character. Clearly, there are exceptions to this generalization. The practice of variolation in the eighteenth century and vaccination in the nineteenth and twentieth centuries con-

TABLE 1.2   Disease-Specific Mortality Rates, Baltimore, 1851–1920 (per 100,000)

YEARS	INFECTIOUS GROUP*	OLD-AGE GROUP[†]
1851–55	1,267	150
1856–60	1,182	149
1861–65	951	146
1866–70	916	177
1871–75	1,089	213
1876–80	1,030	255
1881–85	790	314
1886–90	790	314
1891–95	684	358
1896–1900	575	398
1901–5	504	459
1906–10	460	508
1911–15	388	564
1916–20	357	614

* Infectious group includes tuberculosis of the respiratory system, diphtheria, measles, scarlet fever, diarrhea, dysentery, and typhoid.
[†]Old-age group includes heart disease, dropsy, aneuryism, arteriosclerosis, nephrites, apoplexy, and cancer.

tributed to the reduction in mortality from smallpox. The introduction of an antitoxin for diphtheria between 1885 and 1922 and the subsequent use of immunization added to the decline in mortality. Nevertheless, the fact that mortality from other infectious diseases was falling in the absence of treatment or immunization suggests that additional influences were at work.From the available evidence, one is led to a single inescapable conclusion: The contribution of medical practice in reducing deaths from infectious diseases has been greatly exaggerated, particularly for the century preceding World War II.

Others have suggested that a change both in the virulence of pathogens and the host-parasite relationship reduced mortality from infectious diseases. Such explanations, however, are difficult to verify, if only because there is no way to

TABLE 1.3   Disease-Specific Mortality Rates for New York, Philadelphia, Boston, and New Orleans, 1864–88 and 1889–1913 (per 100,000)

DISEASE	ANNUAL AVERAGE MORTALITY RATE	
	1864–88	*1889–1913*
Consumption	365	223
Stomach and intestinal	299	196
Scarlet fever	66	19
Typhoid and typhus	53	25
Smallpox	40	2
Cholera	8	0
Diphtheria	123	58
Yellow fever	14	1
Total for group	964	524
Crude death rate	2,570	1,890

determine whether genetic mutations in the past reduced the threat of particular organisms to human beings, or whether a new balance between pathogens and hosts was responsible. For many infectious diseases the data suggest that a decline in mortality was largely due to changes in the host rather than the pathogen. During war, for example, inadequate diet and shelter, combined with stress, increased susceptibility even to diseases that previously ceased to represent a threat. Indeed, a famous disaster in the 1920s in Germany demonstrated the complex nature of infectious diseases. In 1927 more than 270 infants were vaccinated with a batch of BCG that had been inadvertently mixed with a virulent strain of the tubercle bacillus. Although more than 70 died, the remainder developed only minor lesions and survived the infection.

There is little doubt that certain specific organisms undergo rapid genetic change, which in turn causes marked fluctuations in the mortality rate. Influenza is one such example. The pandemic of 1918-19 infected about a quarter of the American people and killed nearly 700,000 (as compared with a normal mortality for this disease of about 125,000). Even more significant, this particular pandemic killed a disproportionate number of persons in their twenties and thirties, in contrast to the traditional peak mortality among the very young and very old. Clearly, the severity of influenza epidemics is largely a function of variations in the types of influenza virus and has little to do with environmental influences. Indeed, the cyclical nature of influenza in modern and premodern societies suggests that its natural history is quite different from the traditional infectious diseases (Crosby 1976; Beveridge 1977; McKeown 1976, p. 83).

Still others have attributed certain mortality reductions to public health innovations. Such an explanation has some validity, but only in a qualified sense. During the latter part of the nineteenth century, there was increasing recognition that a number of infectious diseases were disseminated in urban areas by contaminated central water systems. The increase in population, introduction of water closets, and appearance of plumbing led many cities to install central water works. Within a short period of time water disposal became a major problem. Many communities began to construct sewers, most of which emptied into nearby rivers. In some areas there was a decrease in the incidence of typhoid, but in others there was a sharp increase. Between 1880 and 1890 Newark, New Jersey, nearly doubled its sewer mileage; during this same period mortality from typhoid increased from 52.7 per 100,000 to 99.5. Indeed, between 1880 and 1900 mortality from typhoid in such urban communities as Atlanta, Pittsburgh, Trenton, and Toledo reached levels as high as 100-144. Ultimately many cities began to treat their sewage and to provide for more pure water systems. Such measures contributed to a reduction—but not an end—to mortality from such infectious diseases as typhoid. The introduction of filtration in twenty urban areas, for example, reduced the mortality rate from typhoid by nearly two-thirds within five years. On the other hand, there were sharp differences between the mortality experiences of various communities from water-borne infectious diseases—an indication that the introduction of public health measures alone were insufficient to account for changes in mortality indicators. In 1900 the death rate for typhoid was 18.2 for Milwaukee and 32.9 for Oakland; the comparable rates for Manchester, New Hampshire, and Lawrence, Massachusetts, were 10.5 and 12.8, respectively. Neither Milwaukee nor Manchester treated its water; Lawrence and Oakland had filtered water systems (Meeker 1972; Ashby 1979).

Finally, some have insisted that the decline in mortality from infectious diseases was due to changes in the standard of living. Nutrition, for example, undoubtedly played a role in infection rates and the outcome of infectious diseases. In specific diseases (e.g., measles) mortality rates tended to be highest among the poor and lower among middle-and upper-class groups. Moreover, the decline in both incidence and mortality from such diseases as rheumatic fever commenced well before the introduction of antibiotic therapy. In other words, certain features of modern society may have rendered Americans more resistant to many secondary effects of infectious diseases. Indeed, Thomas McKeown has argued that improved nutrition was the single most important determinant in the reduction of mortality from infectious diseases, and that this process was under way during the second half of the nineteenth century. Such an explanation, he noted, "is consistent with present-day experience of the relationship between malnutrition and infection; it accounts for the fall of mortality and growth of populations in many countries at about the same time; and when extended to include improved hygiene and limitation of numbers, it attributes the decline of the infections to modification of the conditions which led to their predominance" (McKeown 1979, pp. 59–60).

Whatever the precise reasons, it is clear that infectious diseases posed fewer threats to the health of Americans. Yet some of the social and environmental changes that contributed to the reduction in the dangers posed by many infectious diseases magnified the importance of other such diseases. One outstanding example of this generalization is poliomyelitis—a disease, ironically enough, that may be said to be caused by cleanliness. Before the late nineteenth century, poliomyelitis was a common disease of infancy. When confined to the throat or intestinal tract, the poliovirus caused temporary symptoms (such as diarrhea and fever) and then conferred lifetime immunity upon the individual. Given the crude sanitary conditions that prevailed before the twentieth century, most individuals acquired the disease during infancy, when the incidence of the paralytic form was virtually nil.

Changes in sanitation and personal hygiene, however, altered this pattern. Poliomyelitis began then to emerge as a disease of slightly older children and young adults. Among such groups there was a greater likelihood that the poliovirus could reach the central nervous system, where the relatively innocuous virus was transformed into a deadly menace. In such cases lesions of the spinal cord caused by the virus lead to various forms of paralysis and in the bulbar form of the disease often to death. Reflecting the changing environment, poliomyelitis after 1880 also exhibited a trend toward periodic epidemicity with higher and higher attack rates among older persons. In 1916, 95 percent of all poliomyelitis cases in New York City occurred in children under the age of ten. By 1947 only 52 percent of cases involved this group; 38 percent occurred in the ten to nineteen age category, and 10 percent in the twenty and over group.

The paralytic form of the disease was also more common in rural and more remote areas, where individuals were often not exposed to disease in infancy. Indeed, the first substantial epidemic of poliomyelitis occurred in Vermont in 1894. No less than 132 cases were recorded, the largest number observed in one year anywhere in the world. Although epidemics occurred in urban areas, the incidence of the disease in its paralytic form was always lower than in rural areas. Understandably, urban populations living in close contact tended to acquire immunity during infancy and childhood at a much higher rate than their rural counterparts. Moreover, within urban areas children from lower socioeconomic backgrounds acquired infections and antibodies at an earlier age than did those in higher socioeconomic categories.

Even more striking was the fact that rates of paralytic poliomyelitis were highest in areas where sanitation and hygiene were most developed and lowest in nations with more primitive conditions. In the latter most individuals were infected in infancy and acquired lifetime immunity. As a matter of fact, the endemic character of the disease in underdeveloped countries proved dangerous to susceptible military personnel from more developed nations. This was vividly demonstrated by the American military experience between 1940 and 1948. The incidence of poliomyelitis was lowest among troops serving in the United States and Europe, and highest among those in the Philippine Islands and Korea, where crude sanitary and hygienic conditions aided dissemination of the poliovirus. Although the eventual development of a vaccine helped to eliminate the paralytic form of the disease, the history of the rise and fall of poliomyelitis illustrates the complex relationships that are involved in disease patterns (Paul 1971).

Conclusion

As more Americans survived the dangers of infancy and childhood in ever growing numbers, they began to identify the decline in infectious diseases with the measures introduced by modern medicine. At the same time, the character of the medical profession was transformed by science and technology. Taken together, both developments gave rise to the modern belief that the complete conquest of disease was within the realm of possibility. This popular belief was partly responsible for the phenomenal growth of public support of modern medicine in twentieth-century America.

Yet a retrospective analysis of disease patterns offers little evidence that this belief was justified in the past or that a utopia of health may be expected in the future. This is not to argue that medical measures have been of no consequence, for medicine has made a difference in dealing with specific diseases and conditions. Moreover, physicians traditionally filled a significant social and cultural role whose significance should not be minimized. Even premodern therapeutic systems (which are often mistakenly perceived as evidence of ignorance) must be understood both in terms of the mediating role they played in the doctor-patient relationship and as an effort by human beings to explain in a rational manner seemingly unnatural and dangerous threats to their existence. (Rosenberg 1979). But even though the control of specific diseases is possible (and perhaps likely), the control or elimination of disease in general seems a contradiction in terms. For if disease and environment are mirror images of each other, a change in one will merely reflect a change in the other.

REFERENCES

ACKERKNECHT, E. H. 1945. *Malaria in the Upper Mississippi Valley 1760–1900.* Baltimore: Johns Hopkins Press.

ASHBURN, P. M. 1947. *The ranks of death: a medical history of the conquest of America.* New York: Coward-McCann.

ASHBY, E. 1979. Reflections on the costs and benefits of environmental pollution. *Perspectives in Biology and Medicine* 23: 7–24.

BEVERIDGE, W. I. B. 1977. *Influenza: the last great plague: an unfinished story of discovery.* New York: Prodist.

BLAKE, J. B. 1959. *Public health in the town of Boston, 1630–1822.* Cambridge: Harvard University Press.

BORAH, W., and COOK, S. 1963. *The aboriginal population of Central Mexico on the eve of the Spanish conquest.* Berkeley: University of California Press.

CAULFIELD, E. 1939. *A true history of the terrible epidemic vulgarly called the throat distemper . . . 1735–1740.* New Haven: Beaumont Medical Club.

——. 1943. Early measles epidemics in America. *Yale Journal of Biology and Medicine* 15: 531–56.

CHILDS, S. J. P. 1940. *Malaria and Colonization in the Low Country, 1526–1696.* Baltimore: Johns Hopkins Press.

COOK, S. F. 1973. The significance of disease in the extinction of the New England Indians. *Human Biology* 45: 485–508.

CROSBY, A. W., JR. 1972. *The Columbian exchange: biological and cultural consequences of 1492.* Westport: Greenwood Publishing Co.

——. 1976. *Epidemic and peace, 1918.* Westport: Greenwood Publishing Co.

DEMOS, J. 1965. Notes on life in Plymouth Colony. *William and Mary Quarterly*, 3d series, 22: 264–86.

DOWLING, H. F. 1977. *Fighting infection: conquests of the twentieth century.* Cambridge: Harvard University Press.

DUBOS, R. 1959a. Medical utopias. *Daedalus* 88: 410–24.

——. 1959b. *Mirage of health: utopias, progress, and biological change.* New York: Harper and Brothers.

DUBOS, R., and DUBOS, J. 1952. *The white plague: tuberculosis, man, and society.* Boston: Little, Brown and Co.

DUFFY, J. 1953. *Epidemics in colonial America.* Baton Rouge: Louisiana State University Press.

——. 1966. *Sword of pestilence: the New Orleans yellow fever epidemic of 1853.* Baton Rouge: Louisiana State University Press.

——. 1968. *A history of public health in New York City 1625–1866.* New York: Russell Sage Foundation.

——. 1974. *A history of public health in New York City 1866–1966.* New York: Russell Sage Foundation.

ETHERIDGE, E. W. 1972. *The butterfly caste: a social history of pellagra in the South.* Westport: Greenwood Publishing Co.

GOLDBERGER, J. 1964. *Goldberger on pellagra*, ed. Milton Terris. Baton Rouge: Louisiana State University Press.

Greven, P. J., Jr. 1970. *Four generations: population, land, and family in colonial Andover, Massachusetts.* Ithaca: Cornell University Press.

HENRETTA, J. A. 1973. *The evolution of American society, 1700–1815: an interdisciplinary analysis.* Lexington: D.C. Heath and Co.

JACOBS, W. R. 1974. The tip of an iceberg: pre-Columbian Indian demography and some implications for revisionism. *William and Mary Quarterly*, 3d series, 31: 123–32.

KIPPLE, K. F., and KIPPLE, V. H. 1977. Black tongue and black men: pellagra and slavery in the antebellum South. *Journal of Southern History* 43: 411–28.

KUPPERMAN, K. O. 1979. Apathy and death in early Jamestown. *Journal of American History* 66: 24–40.

LERNER, M., and ANDERSON, O. A. 1963. *Health progress in the United States 1900–1960.* Chicago: University of Chicago Press.

LINDER, F. E., and GROVE, R. D. 1943. *Vital statistics rates in the United States 1900–1940 (sixteenth census of the United States: 1940).* Washington, D.C.: Government Printing Office.

LOCKRIDGE, K. A. 1966. The population of Dedham, Massachusetts, 1636–1736. *Economic History Review*, 2d series, 19: 318–44.

McKEOWN, T. 1976. *The modern rise of population.* London: Edward Arnold.
———. 1979. *The role of medicine: dream, mirage, or nemesis.* Princeton: Princeton University Press.
McNEILL, W. H. 1976. *Plagues and peoples.* Garden City: Anchor Press/Doubleday.
MEEKER, E. 1972. The improving health of the United States, 1890–1915. *Explorations in Economic History* 9: 353–73.
———. 1974. The social rate of return on investment in public health, 1880–1910. *Journal of Economic History* 34: 392–419.
MILLER, G. 1957. *The adoption of inoculation for smallpox in England and France.* Philadelphia: University of Pennsylvania Press.
PAUL, J. R. 1971. *A history of poliomyelitis.* New Haven: Yale University Press.
PICKARD, M. E., and BULEY, R. C. 1946. *The Midwest pioneer: his ills, cures, and doctors.* New York: Henry Schuman.
POWELL, J. H. 1949. *Bring out your dead: the great plague of yellow fever in Philadelphia in 1793.* Philadelphia: University of Pennsylvania Press.
ROE, D. A. 1973. *A plague of corn: the social history of pellagra.* Ithaca: Cornell University Press.
ROSEN, G. 1958. *A history of public health.* New York: MD Publications.
———. 1977. *Preventive medicine in the United States 1900–1975: trends and interpretations.* New York: Prodist.
ROSENBERG, C. E. 1962. *The cholera years: the United States in 1832, 1849 and 1866.* Chicago: University of Chicago Press.
———. 1979. The therapeutic revolution: medicine, meaning, and social change in nineteenth-century America. In *The therapeutic revolution: essays in the social history of American medicine,* ed. M. J. Vogel and C. E. Rosenberg, pp. 3–25. Philadelphia: University of Pennsylvania Press.
ROSENKRANTZ, B. G. 1972. *Public health and the state: changing views in Massachusetts, 1842–1936.* Cambridge: Harvard University Press.
SAVITT, T. L. 1978. *Medicine and slavery: the diseases and health care of blacks in antebellum Virginia.* Urbana: University of Illinois Press.
SCHULTZ, S. K., and McSHANE, C. 1978. To engineer the metropolis: sewers, sanitation, and city planning in late-nineteenth-century America. *Journal of American History* 65: 389–411.
SHATTUCK, L. 1846. *Report to the committee of the city council appointed to obtain the census of Boston for the year 1845.* Boston: John H. Eastburn.
SHRYOCK, R. H. 1952. The yellow fever epidemics, 1793–1905. In *America in crisis: fourteen crucial episodes in American history,* ed. D. Aaron, pp. 51–70. New York: Alfred A. Knopf.
———. 1960. *Medicine and society in America, 1660–1860.* New York: New York University Press.
SPINK, W. W. 1978. *Infectious diseases: prevention and treatment in the nineteenth and twentieth centuries.* Minneapolis: University of Minnesota Press.
STEARN, E. W., and STEARN, A. E. 1945. *The effect of smallpox on the destiny of the Amerindian.* Boston: Bruce Humphries.
U. S. Bureau of the Census. 1975. *Historical statistics of the United States: Colonial times to 1970* (Bicentennial edition, 2 parts). Washington, D.C.: Government Printing Office.
WEBER, A. F. 1899. *The growth of cities in the nineteenth century.* New York: The Macmillan Co.
WINSLOW, C. E. A. 1943. *The conquest of epidemic disease: a chapter in the history of ideas.* Princeton: Princeton University Press.
WOOD, P. H. 1975. *Black majority: Negroes in colonial South Carolina from 1670 through the Stono rebellion.* New York: Alfred A. Knopf.

Chapter 2

Society, Culture, and Health

Mervyn Susser
Kim Hopper
Judith Richman

THE STATE OF HEALTH of a population is but one of the many facets of society. The diseases that flourish or decline are social as much as biological phenomena. Health is the outcome of a continuing and reciprocal interaction between a slowly evolving biological substrate of human beings and other organisms and a rapidly evolving social environment. Society imprints its scars and favors on all those who survive to reproduce and transmit their culture and genetic heritage. Diseases too have effects on societies, and these can be powerful enough to influence their course. Dramatic plagues such as the Black Death enter legend, and epidemics of smallpox and measles have almost wiped out societies newly exposed and without immune defenses. In our own times, in developed societies, the large excess of male deaths at all ages, and the resulting imbalance of the sexes in later life, has influenced living arrangements, institutions, medical care, laws about pensions and benefits, the labor force, and economic productivity.

Complex as societies are, they can be described in terms of a limited hierarchy of elements that allow for orderly analysis. Distinctive *economies* are built upon the modes in which goods are produced and exchanged. These modes engender an ordered *social structure*, with persisting social relations that give form to social institutions. In the developed world and much of the underdeveloped world, social structure is characteristically divided into social classes. The content of the social relations within a social structure—its norms, values, sanctions, and obligations—comprises the *culture* transmitted and transmuted from generation to generation, mechanisms adapted for survival in a specific environment. Through some form of legitimized authority, *states* are the political entities that define and maintain the limits and norms of given societies (Harris 1968: Miliband 1969; Sahlins 1969, 1972; Kaplan and Manners 1972; Geertz 1973; Wolf 1974; Murphy 1979).

Each of these elements has its influence on states of health; taken together they produce the particular configuration of health and disease for a given society. The clearest effects are seen on the largest scale of analysis. States with highly developed industrial economies differ markedly from those with less-developed economies in the demographic dynamic of births, deaths, and age. This demographic dynamic is the point of convergence for the social and biological forces that become manifest in different patterns of human development and disease. On a smaller scale, within societies, the distinctive impact on health patterns of varying environments can be discerned among social classes, among ethnic groups and subcultures, among families and social networks, as well as among individuals.

The interaction of health and society involves many elements: the physical and chemical environment—the quality of air, water, food, and the nature of industry and occupations; the biological environment—the ecology of microorganisms, animal and plant life; and much more. The state of health of any group is the outcome of a process. The entire biological, social, and cultural history of a society impinges upon the present; genes, culture, and social institutions all persist, and all change, evolve, and adapt. These forces operate through Darwinian evolution and ecological adaptation and, with greater immediacy, through economic, social, and political history.

The health of any individual within a group too depends on these forces. In motion long before conception, they create the social and cultural environment and determine genetic heritage. After conception, environmental forces may have their imprint during gestation, for example, through the agency of drugs; through the agency of high technology by means of amniocentesis, tissue culture, and the elimination of anomalous fetuses; and through the agency of such commonplaces as cigarette smoking, the moderate use of alcohol, and diet.

It is after birth, however, that the imprint of the present upon the individual constitution is least mistakable. The effects of nutrition, infection, and the mere fact of survival are self-evident. Less evident, but not less pervasive, are the effects of the social environment. Socialization induces the unruly newborn infant into behavior and personality that conform with the broader culture. These cultural modes of behavior have profound effects on health and disease through such obvious channels as eating, smoking, drinking, driving, and risk-taking in general. Very probably, they also exercise effects through physiological adaptations, ways of coping with stressful events and situations, and hence, potentially, on disease.

Socialization and adaptation are processes that never stop. They bring to bear on the individual, within the group-determined macrosocial context, the microsocial agencies of family structure and function, social networks, and the assignment of roles within these milieux. Families affect the socialization process differently according to the levels of material or psychological and social support they provide. The presence or absence of the figures of the immediate family—mother, father, sibs—and of other kin and friends, and the manner in which they relate with each other, can influence many aspects of development and behavior. The acquisition of sphincter control, cognitive performance and later achievement or delinquency, emotional states including anxiety and depression, and the probability of suicide all demonstrate such influence.

A long text, let alone a chapter, might not suffice to cover all aspects of this topic. To illustrate and make concrete the links between a social variable and health, we therefore choose social class as one social dimension for study and examine its relationships first to coronary heart disease and then to mental disorder.

Briefly let us convey what is meant here by social class. The concept is clouded by contending theory, yet empirically the consensus in social science is sufficient to permit analysis and results that gain common agreement. All will agree that the division into social classes universally characterizes the capitalist mode of production and that this stratification flows from the relation of occupations to the prevalent mode of production. This much is clear from the common designation of classes as "working class," "blue collar," "white collar," and "professional." Occupations are accorded different levels of prestige and can be arranged in a hierarchy according to their prestige. Occupations are powerful determinants not only of work and prestige but of ways of life—dwelling, schooling, marriage, and mortality—but they are not the only determinants of prestige. Social prestige inheres in other social statuses. Prestige is acquired from the honor accorded families, from power and authority, and from membership in particular groups including ethnic groups (Giddens 1973; Williams 1974; Poulantzas 1975; Miliband 1977; Wright 1978).

Among these many statuses there is generally a substantial degree of congruence. Thus at a group level it is possible to allocate social class position by one or a combination of a number of indices. The first and most widely used index of social class is occupation. Education is often used as well. Income, in categories sufficiently broad to overcome imprecise and inacurrate information, is a common index, and sometimes place and type of residence classify residents of small areas. In studies of health and disease, all these indices have been applied. They have in common, despite sometimes divergent results in particular cases, the consistent demonstration of marked differences in morbidity and mortality between the classes.

Coronary Heart Disease

Coronary heart disease is an epidemic of our times that accounts for about one-third of all deaths across the United States, and up to two-thirds among middle-aged men. The disease first attained prominence as a scourge of middle-aged men of the upper classes; as early as 1897, William Osler had observed that angina pectoris was an "affection of the better classes." Until quite recently coronary heart disease remained a disorder of the privileged.

A striking social class gradient for coronary heart disease, declining from upper to lower classes, was found in the analysis of mortality by occupations in Britain for the period of 1930–32. For the most part, data from American studies in the late 1930s and the 1940s confirmed the British finding (Antonovsky 1967; Marks 1967). The marked class disparity coupled with a rising death toll from the disease spurred the intensive search for environmental causes that continues to the present.

An early study (Yerushalmy and Hilleboe 1957) found a close correlation between the increase in motor vehicle licenses, radio and television ownership and rising death rate due to coronary heart disease. This is not quite the lesson in statistical absurdity it may first appear to be: cars and modern media are indicators, admittedly crude ones, of a stage of economic development and a way of life associated with it. And coronary heart disease appears to be the most infamous of the diseases of contemporary civilization (Sigerist 1943; Ryle 1948; Dubos 1965).

Among men especially, the increase during the half-century following clinical recognition of the disease by Herrick in 1912 was sharp indeed. In the 1960s, prospective studies in the United States showed that the incidence of new events of angina, infarction, and death in men in their forties and fifties had risen about 1 percent per year; in more than a fifth, death was the first manifestation. The incidence in middle-aged women was about half that in men, and less before the menopause. In both sexes, incidence regularly increased with age (Kannel, Dawber, and McNamara 1966; Doyle 1966; Stamler et al. 1966; Stamler 1973; Kuller 1976). There is not much doubt that the increase was real and not the result merely of more accurate diagnoses, or of a shift in certification of deaths from such nonspecific diagnoses as myocardial degeneration to coronary heart disease, or of a tendency to overdiagnose this disease (Morris 1951).[1]

That societies render their members more or less vulnerable to certain forms of disease is clear in the case of coronary heart disease. The disease has been linked with an affluent way of life; the incidence is high in rich countries and low in poor ones. This disparity is not simply the result of people living longer or of more effective diagnosis. Large differences are found across developed countries with roughly equivalent life spans and degrees of technological development (Keys 1970). In Israel, marked differences in mortality from coronary disease occurred among successsive waves of Yemenite Jewish migrants. Among the early immigrants, who in the period under study had been exposed to a Western way of life for twenty years or more, the mortality rate for degenerative heart disease in middle-aged men was more than six times that of recent immigrants. The difference, 3.3/1,000 versus .49/1,000, is almost identical to the changes in coronary mortality in England and Wales over the period 1931 to 1957, when the death toll rose from .49/1,000 to .3.59/1,000 (Kagan 1960). Similar changes in disease rates with environmental change occurred among Chinese and Japanese Americans; both groups have coronary heart disease rates intermediate between those prevailing in their countries of origin and those characteristic of their country of residence (Worth et al. 1975; King 1975).

Such marked variation in coronary heart disease among different countries, at different times in the same country, and among people of the same ethnic stock with different experiences underscores the importance of ways of life in shaping the distribution of disease. Even if the mode of their operation remains obscure, the key must reside in the environment, including the social structure and cultural practices. The relation between social context and disease is a dynamic one. Societies change, their environments are modified, biological pathogens evolve, and physical agents appear or disappear; and simultaneously, the vulnerability of their peoples alters with their states of immunity and nutrition. Within industrial societies, although social classes may retain their relative positions, their size and composition fluctuate as both forms of production and the organization of the labor force change. All these changes enter into the quality and quantity of consumption, the styles of living and the activities available to the members of the various classes. They may be expected also to enter into the distribution of mortality and morbidity from coronary heart disease.

Thus in both Britain and the United States, the social class gradient for cor-

1. An analysis of mortality from nonvalvular heart disease (mainly coronary heart disease and hypertensive heart disease) minimizes the problem of misclassification. One such study (Marmot et al. 1978) showed that in postwar Britain mortality for this combination of disease categories among married women, in marked contrast to the trend among men, was actually in decline. The trend for hypertensive heart disease, however, may largly account for the finding, since mortality from this condition may well have been declining throughout that period for both sexes.

onary heart disease observed before World War II did not remain the same. By 1950, mortality was already concentrated in the lowest social class among men under forty-five years of age, although not among older men. Local mortality studies obtained similar results (Lilienfeld 1956; Kent et al. 1958; Pell and D'Alonzo 1958; Breslow and Buell 1960; Stamler et al. 1960). In Britain, and probably in the United States as well, the social class shift in mortality is now present in all age groups (Marmot et al. 1978; Office of Population Censuses and Surveys 1978). One finding, remarkable for remaining so long unobserved, is that among women the mortality gradient for nonvalvular heart disease has always favored the higher social class.

In the United States, most morbidity studies found a higher incidence of coronary heart disease in the upper social classes up to the early 1960s (Lehman 1967). At the same time, in some parts of the country conflicting trends or an absence of a class gradient began to be observed. Subsequently, in a study over time of Evans County in Georgia, high prevalence was observed in the higher social classes at the onset only to be confounded later, as the population was followed, by higher incidence in the lowest social classes (Cassel et al. 1971). The change could not be explained by differences in case-fatality rates among the classes, nor by biased diagnostic criteria, by missed cases, or by competing causes of death. A social class shift in coronary morbidity and mortality in the United States in the 1960s is further suggested by studies of mortality in rich and poor states, by the results of the National Health Interview Survey, and by studies of selected metropolitan areas (Lerner and Stutz 1977, 1978; Wilson and White 1977; Yercaris and Kim 1978; Kraus, Borhani, and Franti 1980).

The concentration of coronary heart disease in the lower social classes has taken place in the face of the recent decline in death rates from coronary heart disease in the United States—amounting to about 30 percent in the past decade (Havlik and Feinleib 1979). The meager data available suggest, therefore, that the higher social classes have been the beneficiaries of the decline in coronary heart disease mortality in the United States. In Britain, the rise in coronary death rates has begun to slow but not yet to decline. The observed social class shifts in the disease, however, suggest that a decline beginning in the higher classes will follow in Britain. In the 1970s, a decline is already apparent in the mortality rates of British physicians.

Logically, social class itself can be taken to explain disease as a *group* characteristic, or a profile or pattern of disease, but the manifestation of disease in the members of a class requires the operation of intermediate agents that impinge on *individuals*. The search for factors that could explain the social class gradient first focused on diet and body weight, and later on exercise, blood pressure, smoking, and emotional strain. These are all concomitants of ways of life that vary with social class.

Diet

In diet studies, the consumption of fats has been extensively studied (Keys 1970; Stamler 1969). Diets high in saturated fatty acids raise the levels of blood lipids, cholesterol in particular. Lipids, in turn, may be connected with coronary heart disease either through the deposit of atheroma plaques on the vessel walls, which impede blood flow, or through effects on the coagulability of blood, resulting in clots that block the vessels either acutely or through slower processes that likewise narrow the vessel walls.

Dietary habits, whether customary or enforced by poverty, together with blood cholesterol levels, have been correlated with the incidence of coronary heart disease in certain social groups. In South Africa, white, colored, and black groups show a declining gradient for fat consumption, for blood cholesterol levels, and for the incidence of coronary heart disease (Bronte-Stewart, Keys, and Brock 1955). In East Africa, similar gradients have been found between Asians and Africans (Shaper and Jones 1959). In Europe, Trappist and Benedictine monks vary in their prescribed dietary habits: Benedictines regularly eat meat; Trappists never do. As expected, the Benedictines have the higher blood cholesterol levels (Groen et al. 1962). In two other diseases, diabetes and familial hyper-cholesterolaemia, cholesterol levels are abnormally high, and the incidence of coronary heart disease among those affected is also abnormally high.

Prospective surveys of persons without coronary heart disease on recruitment have clearly established that elevated cholesterol levels put individuals at higher risk of developing the disease (Kinch, Gittelsohn, and Doyle 1964; Kannel, Dawber, and McNamara 1966; Doyle 1966; Stamler et al. 1966; Morris et al. 1966; Stamler 1973; Kuller 1976; Framingham Study 1968–78). The variability of cholesterol levels is, in the main, environmentally and not genetically determined according to recent twin studies (Feinleib et al. 1977), and the intrafamilial associations found among twins and their offspring appear to reflect the influence of mothers rather than fathers (Christian et al. 1976; Christian and Kang 1977). Refined measures of cholesterol and lipid fractions in the blood have begun to add precision to predictions of risk. An excess of low-density lipoprotein and the depletion of high-density lipoprotein are independently associated with higher risk (Castelli and Morgan 1971; Medalie et al. 1973; Hsia et al. 1975; Tyroler et al. 1975; Rhoads, Gulbrandsen, and Kagen 1976). The associations of cholesterol and lipid levels with coronary heart disease apply across societies. High levels have been shown to predict a greater likelihood of developing coronary heart disease in farflung populations: in rural Georgia and South Carolina, as well as in New York, Chicago, and San Francisco; in Hawaii, Puerto Rico, and Japan; in Yugoslavia and Israel as well as in France and Britain (Castelli and Morgan 1971; Medalie et al. 1973; Gordon et al. 1974; Hsia 1975; Marmot et al. 1975; Tyroler et al. 1975: Marmot and Syme 1976; Rhoads, Culbrandsen, and Kagan 1976; Kozarevic et al. 1976; Garcia-Palmieri et al. 1978).

Still, perplexing questions remain. Certainly factors other than cholesterol levels enhance vulnerability to coronary heart disease. The risk attached to given levels of cholesterol, for instance, is consistently higher in city than in rural dwellers. In migrants to cities, too, the risk is lower than in the urban-born, but higher than in those who stay in the country. In international comparisons, coronary mortality can be made to correlate as highly with protein intake as with fat consumption. Changes over time in mortality from nonvalvular heart disease in Britain correlate best not with fats but with sucrose and whole-meal bread (Marmot et al. 1978).

Cholesterol levels reflect dietary factors other than fat alone, and the result is not necessarily in contradicion to their association with coronary heart disease. A diet low in fat is usually low in protein, high in fiber and starch, and of variable mineral and vitamin content. Each of these components has been shown in animal studies to affect cholesterol levels; in humans, not only unsaturated fatty acids but also low-protein and low-calorie intake have been reported to reduce cholesterol levels (Yerushalmy and Hilleboe 1957; Olson 1957; Yudkin 1967).

The extent to which plasma cholesterol levels reflect lifelong dietary habits is thus an unresolved problem. The effect of current diet on cholesterol levels is not clear: the daily intake of free-living populations is difficult to measure and cholesterol levels themselves vary from day to day. Thus, an English study failed to uncover any relationship between blood cholesterol levels and dietary intake calculated from reported food consumption over a short defined period (Morris et al. 1963). The Framingham study in the United States did no better (Framingham Study 1968–78). It could be that populations surveyed in developed countries are saturated with dietary cholesterol and that, consequently, much of the variation above the threshold for saturation is due to factors other than fat in the diet. A recent follow-up of a population of male workers in Chicago suggests that the problem may rather reside in the difficulties of measuring dietary intake. In this Western Electric study, dietary intake was recorded by study subjects over a twenty-eight-day period on entry. Intake of saturated fats correlated with raised cholesterol levels, and unsaturated fats with lower levels (Shekelle et al. 1981).

Cholesterol may thus represent a link in the causal chain leading to coronary disease. The fact that efforts to lower cholesterol levels by "prudent" diets and other means have had a degree of success (Christakis et al. 1966; Leren 1966; American Heart Association 1968; Turpernen et al. 1966; Dayton et al. 1969; Stamler 1969; Bierenbaum et al. 1970; Glueck, Mattson, and Bierman 1978) strengthens this notion.[2] Alternatively, cholesterol is closely linked to some factor which is the common cause of coronary disease and of raised blood cholesterol levels. In the Chicago Western Electric study, dietary intake of saturated fats was linked to serum cholesterol levels, as noted, and serum cholesterol level to coronary deaths. There was also a weak association of saturated fats and *dietary* cholesterol with coronary mortality. This association was strengthened, however, with *serum* cholesterol controlled; this suggests that serum cholesterol is not in the direct causal sequence. The evidence of the role of dietary fats in coronary disease is neither unequivocal nor complete, and other cooperating causes must play as great a part. Nonetheless, it is reasonable to suppose that dietary differences among social classes (Morris 1979) partly explain the social class differentials in coronary heart disease.

Body Weight

Men who suffer from coronary heart disease are, on average, heavier than those who do not, and relative weight (controlled for height) is a function of diet intake and energy expenditure. Some studies show coronary patients to be literally fatter, when measured by subcutaneous fat calipers, while others do not. In multivariate analysis with cholesterol and other factors controlled, the association of weight and coronary heart disease disapppears (Sanders 1959; Damon et al. 1969; Keys et al. 1972; Ashley and Kannel 1974; Weinsier 1976). This finding is compatible, however, with a place for weight in the causal chain which is antecedent to

2. When lowered by the drug clofibrate, however, raised mortality from other causes eliminated all benefit (Research Committee 1971).

cholesterol and the other factors, which would then count as intervening variables (Susser 1973). In the Framingham study, weight changes correlated highly with changes in cholesterol levels. Obesity, one might note, varies with social class in the same manner as does coronary heart disease. Obesity once symbolized wealth and affluence, as in the unflattering cartoons of capitalists early in this century, and in parts of the underdeveloped world it still does. Now, like coronary heart disease in recent times, obesity in the developed world has become a disorder of the poorer classes (Goldblatt, Moore and Stunkard 1965; Stunkard 1972).

Exercise

Physical exercise has also been linked with blood cholesterol levels, a finding that lends indirect support to the association of exercise and coronary disease. When exercise is sufficient to prevent weight gain, high-fat diets have been found not to increase cholesterol levels as they do with less exercise (Mann et al. 1955). The extraordinary physical fitness of Masai warriors, reported to take a diet of meat and milk with relatively high fat content but at the same time to cover many miles a day following their cattle, probably accounts not only for their low average cholesterol level but also for the low frequency of coronary heart disease among them as well (Mann, Shaffer, and Rich 1965). Exercise may influence coronary disease through another pathway, for it also increases the fibrinolytic activity of the blood and thereby impedes clotting (Biggs, MacFarlane, and Pilling 1947).

Physical activity may also have been a significant factor in the earlier social class gradient. The prevalence of coronary heart disease varies with occupations demanding different degrees of activity. In a national survey of consecutive autopsies of men ages forty-five to seventy in the mid-1950s, occupations were graded as "light," "active," or "heavy." At autopsy, both fatal infarcts and fibrosis of heart muscle caused by diminution of the coronary blood flow were most common in light workers, less common in active workers, and least in heavy workers. Within these grades of occupational strenuousness the prevalence of coronary heart disease did not vary by social class (Morris and Crawford 1958). However, occupations involving heavy work were concentrated in the lower social classes and light occupations in the upper classes, consistent with the class distribution of the disease at the time of the study. A number of other studies (though not all) have been able to relate the physical demands of occupations to coronary heart disease (Paffenbarger et al. 1977; Brand et al. 1979). The changes in the social class gradient in coronary diseases are not incompatible with changes in patterns of physical activity. Many previously strenuous occupations no longer demand the heavy labor they once did. At the same time, some portions of the working population have more leisure time than ever before. Vigorous leisure-time activity appears to protect against the disease and exhibits a social class gradient compatible with it, declining from upper to lower classes (Morris et al. 1973; Morris et al 1980).

Blood Pressure

Hypertension, another attribute that puts individuals at high risk of coronary heart disease, shows a similar relationship to occupation and physical activity

(Brown et al. 1957). Indeed, in the United States hypertension has consistently higher prevalence rates among persons of low income, whether male or female, white or black. Around this relationship, however, contradictions multiply; among them is the distribution of coronary heart disease and hypertension among racial groups and between the sexes. Whites engage in sedentary occupations much more than blacks, and coronary heart disease is more common among whites than blacks. It is also far more common among men than women. Yet, although hypertension is well established as a precursor of coronary heart disease, it is far more common among blacks than among whites; and above the mid-forties (the peak ages for coronary disease), hypertension is more common among women than men. Moreover, while mortality from coronary heart disease has but recently begun to decline, mortality from hypertension has been on the decline for twenty years or more (Paffenbarger et al. 1966).

This particular problem involves a form of the "ecological fallacy" (Robinson 1950; Susser 1973). Although hypertension is positively associated with coronary heart disease in *individuals*, at the *group* level it may be so far outweighed by other factors as to give the appearance of a negative association. Among *ethnic groups* other factors may be more frequent than hypertension, making larger causal contributions to coronary heart disease, and may be distributed among the groups in a manner that obscures or even reverses the relationship of hypertension with coronary disease seen at the individual level.

Smoking

Another factor associated with coronary disease, smoking (Hammond and Horn 1954; Zukel et al. 1959), also varies with social class (Cartwright, Martin, and Thompson 1959). The risk with smoking, although not as high for coronary disease as for lung cancer, is not negligible; middle-aged men who smoke more than twenty cigarettes a day have a risk compared with nonsmokers of between 2 and 4 to 1 for coronary disease (Advisory Committee 1964). Coronary disease is much more common than lung cancer, however, and the death toll from coronary disease attributable to smoking—the attributable risk—is actually greater than that from lung cancer. Among women, despite their lower incidence of coronary heart disease, social class patterns of smoking habits are likely to be more strikingly associated with heightened risk than among men, owing to the conjoint effect of oral contraceptives. In one study, premenopausal women with acute myocardial infarction were 7 times more likely to have smoked heavily, 4 times more likely to have used oral contraceptives in the past month, and 39 times more likely to have done both. Other studies are congruent (Shapiro et al. 1979; Oliver 1970; Mann et al. 1976). Both smoking and oral contraceptive use have varied markedly among social classes over time.

Stress and Coping

Emotional factors must also be considered as a possible cause of the social class gradient in coronary disease. In an early uncontrolled series of 100 young coronary patients, emotional strain was found to precede the attack in 91 cases (Russek and Zohman 1958). Many of these men were described as ambitious, conscientious, and obsessional. They tended to work to exhaustion and to be restless and nagged by guilt during their leisure time. Men of this type, particularly those beset by a sense of time urgency and competitiveness, were found to have higher cholesterol levels than unambitious men in less exacting occupations (Friedman and Rosenman 1959). When men are under pressure, cholesterol levels have been found to rise and whole-blood clotting times to accelerate, as shown in a study of accountants conducted over a period of five months during which work demands varied greatly (Friedman, Rosenman, and Carroll 1958).

Many relevant studies of stressors in coronary heart disease are of the retrospective case-control type. Histories of stressful states obtained after the fact of the acute coronary event are subject to unmeasurable bias on recall as compared with controls; measures of mental state taken after the event are likewise always assailable because their existence prior to the event can be no more than a supposition. Thus the causal sequence remains an open question. Prospective studies have identified a number of stress factors as the precursors not so much of acute myocardial infarction as of angina pectoris. Thus, anxiety, depression, and various neurotic habits and interpersonal problems have been related to angina in most studies (Ostfeld et al. 1964; Medalie et al. 1973; FlØderus, 1974; Medalie et al. 1975; Jenkins 1976) and only in some studies to myocardial infarction (FlØderus 1974; Bruhn et al. 1974). Among the latter, a recent Swedish study has added "work load" (a composite measure of job-related stress) to the list of contributing factors (Theorell and FlØderus-Myrhed 1977).

Personality types, too, have been further investigated since the early studies mentioned above. Thus, in a two-way classification of behavioral patterns into Types A and B, only Type A was found to be "coronary prone." In a predictive study, the coronary-prone complex carried a higher risk of coronary heart disease than did either a raised cholesterol or blood pressure level (Rosenman et al. 1970). An eight-and-a-half-year follow-up of the Western Collaborative Group Study, which controlled for the influence of the traditional risk factors of age, cholesterol, blood pressure, and smoking, showed that subjects classified as Type A were at twice the risk of developing coronary heart disease as their Type B counterparts (Roseman et al. 1976). A number of other studies have confirmed that the coronary-prone complex is largely independent of other risk factors (Friedman and Rosenman 1959; Rosenman et al. 1970; Jenkins et al. 1971; Jenkins 1976; Jenkins, Zyzanski, and Rosenman 1976; Haynes et al. 1978a; Haynes et al. 1978b). In the Framingham study, however, daily stresses, "age-worries," and other tensions associated with coronary heart disease tended not to be independent of age, blood pressure, cholesterol, and smoking. The causal sequence among these variables, or their independent contributions, thus remained opaque.

Two pathophysiological mechanisms have been suggested as modes through which Type A behavior engenders coronary risk: hyper-responsiveness—as measured by increased blood pressure and noradrenaline output—to challenging situations (Dembroski, MacDongall, and Shields 1977); and some unknown process leading to atherosclerosis and obstructed coronary arteries as shown on angiography (Blumenthal, Kong, and Rosenman 1975; Zyzanski et al. 1976; Frank et al. 1978).

The hard-driving, competitive, Type A man, wedded to his job and always rushing, describes an exteme if not atypical profile of a member of the "achieving society" (McClellan 1961). That the Type A pattern is environmentally induced seems not improbable: Identical twins have been found to be no more concordant for the typical repertoire of behavior than are fraternal twins (Glass 1977). The question naturally arises whether this personality configuration is a specific response to the demands of societies that induce the disease, and perhaps more particularly of modern American society. The coronary-prone behavior pattern was first described, after all, among white, middle-aged, upper-middle-class Californians, and the self-administered questionnaire most often used in surveys was standardized among them. The discovery of the Type A woman, though less common than her male counterpart, may illustrate the adaptive value of this behavioral style in fulfilling the demands of occupational roles once the preserve of males alone (Waldron 1978).

Among men in European countries the behavior pattern seems to be less common than in the United States (Zyzanski 1978). Among black Americans, too, the typical behavior pattern seems seldom to be found (Waldron et al. 1977). Not only its frequency varies across cultures but also the degree of risk associated with it. Among Japanese Americans, the Type A behavior pattern was found to be relatively rare, and was not in itself associated with significantly elevated risk for coronary disease. Indeed, the typical traits were combined in different and distinctive clusters that seemed to reflect the orientation and the values of their subculture (Cohen 1978). Only those men who exhibited the modified Type A pattern and at the same time led a highly Westernized way of life were found to be at heightened risk of coronary heart disease. Particular traits of the Type A pattern, it seems possible, may be associated with specific clinical manifestations of coronary disease (Jenkins, Zyzanski and Rosenman 1978).

In short, Type A behavior patterns may be a mode of response to particular emotional and social demands. The assembled evidence suggests that both emotional strain and the manner of coping with it could be related to the social class distribution of coronary heart disease. Although the amount and the type of strain in each social class are not easily measured, for each class, the external sources of stress and the resources for dealing with it are manifestly dissimilar (Pearlin and Radabaugh 1976; Brown and Harris 1978). Common observation and several anthropological studies suggest that behavior patterns and coping styles are also distinctive by class. Studies in the United States have shown repeatedly that in both men and women Type A behavior is characteristic of higher social class position, as measured either by education or occupation (Keith, Lown, and Stare 1965; Mettlin 1976; Shekelle, Schoenberger, and Stamler 1976; Waldron et al. 1977; Waldron 1978; Zyzanski 1978). For this distribution there are several possible reasons. In a competitive market economy, Type A behavior can be expected to be an advantage. Aggression, competitiveness, and intense commitment to job demands boost production and are likely to facilitate upward mobility. Social class differences in child-rearing practices may also play a part. The values emphasized by parents reflect the realities of their occupational positions. In Italy and the United States, for example, middle-class fathers emphasized self-control above obedience, working-class fathers the reverse. The difference between them was accounted for by the degree of independence in the father's occupation (Kohn 1969). In the United States, middle-class parents are more likely than working-class parents to embody Type A characteristics themselves, tend to have higher, more open-ended ambitions for their children, and may actively encourage certain Type A behaviors by their high performance standards (Butensky et al. 1976). In continuing the socialization process, some have suggested, the American school system, with its emphasis on competitive achievement and rapid performance of tasks, may induce in its "successful" students the typical behavior pattern (Johnson and Johnson 1974; Bowles and Gintis 1976).

In contrast with personality factors, the latter-day concentration of most other risk factors among lower-class people suggests that, as individuals, the working class lack the skill and especially the resources to protect themselves against those forces of commerce, industry, and mass communication that promote unhealthy practices which the upper classes are learning to avoid. Self-esteem and the sense of control and autonomy in shaping the course of one's life, like education and knowledge about health (Feldman 1968), diminish with the social class gradient (Pearlin and Radabaugh 1976). At the same time, many attitudes and values prevalent among the working classes are likely to reinforce their vulnerability to coronary heart disease and to most other diseases as well (Susser and Watson 1971). By paths still ill-understood, the psychosocial complex characteristic of each class engenders risks peculiar to it.

The reasons for the social class distribution of coronary heart disease, and for changes in that distribution, plainly could be manifold. Epidemiologists concern themselves first with immediate causes, and must labor at length, painstakingly and with rigor, to establish the uncontaminated contribution of single factors, to measure interaction among them, and to recognize confounding. Yet the broader context within which these factors operate equally needs to be understood.

The ways in which both good and harm are distributed are not simply in the hands of affected individuals. In industrial capitalist societies, with the coming of mass communications media and near-universal literacy, a generic culture is ever more widely shared: the same processed foods and tobaccos are available to the large body of the people, and generated power and motor transport are at the ready command of the humble as well as the rich. Jobs of low prestige that once were physically strenuous are no longer so, and a multitude of new occupations are sedentary. On the other hand, jobs of high prestige that once were emotionally strenuous may have become less so, as more men have moved into large and ever-growing organizational structures in the wake of the vanguard who have defined and formalized the roles within them. It is in accord with such changes that recent studies of morbidity among employees of large corporations show lower rates of coronary heart disease among high-level executives than among those of lower level (Pell and D'Alonzo 1963; Lehman, Schulman, and Hinkle 1967). Similarly, the Type A pattern appears to be more prevalent among business managers and lower-order professionals than among executives and higher-order professionals (Williams 1968).

Mental Disorders

The search for social and cultural factors in the genesis and course of mental disorders was kindled early on by the recognition of the uneven distribution of those disorders in society. Aside from age and sex, social class is the social variable with the most marked and consistent relation to mental disorders (Dohrenwend 1966, 1975; Dohrenwend and Dohrenwend 1969, 1974). In 1855, Edward Jarvis reported that "the pauper class furnishes, in ratio of its numbers, sixty-four times as many cases of insanity as the independent class" (Jarvis 1855). More recent twentieth-century studies continue to find striking disparities between the social classes. Understanding the class relationship is complicated, however, by the unresolved problems of selecting reliable and valid methods for identifying and classifying disorders and measuring their frequency.

Variability in the extent and nature of the social class gradient occurs with the particular mode of case finding (Weissman and Klerman 1978). Taking a global view of all types of disorders, including undifferentiated psychological distress or "demoralization" (Frank 1961; Dohrenwend et al. 1980), studies of "true prevalence" conducted largely since World War II show a gradient of rates increasing markedly at the bottom of the social scale. Incidence studies, throughout the century and a quarter during which studies are on record, also show the highest rates of psychiatric disorders in the lowest social class (Hollingshead and Redlich 1958). When attention shifts to specific disorders, however, a limited group appears to account for the social class gradient: schizophrenia and personality disorders are most frequent in the lowest social class; manic-depressive psychoses, senility, and organic brain syndrome are more evenly distributed (Adelstein et al. 1968; Susser 1968; Dohrenwend and Dohrenwend 1969, 1974; Dohrenwend 1975). When psychiatric cases are further differentiated on the basis of inception and duration of disorders, chronic disability measured by extended failure in social role performance manifests a particularly high concentration at the lower end of the class structure (Susser 1968; Susser et al. 1970a, 1970b).

Much debate has followed, not about the findings, which have proved consistent, but about their interpretation. The debate revolves around two questions. First, are the main determinants of the class relationship psychosocial or genetic? And second, within the social realm of explanation, what particular aspects of culture and society are pathogenic? Since this chapter focuses on society and culture, we shall do no more than note the gradual accumulation of evidence suggesting a complex interplay between genetic and social factors in the class relationship of mental disorders. Multicausal models seem most appropriate, but the relative contributions of specific etiologic factors remain to be demonstrated (Susser and Watson 1971; Dohrenwend 1975; Weissman and Klerman 1978; Wheaton 1978).

What then is it about the nature of societal arrangements and the corresponding cultural attitudes, behaviors, and symbolic meanings that produce high levels of generalized distress and particular mental disorders at the bottom of the class structure? Diverse aspects of society and culture differentiate the lives and experiences of groups at a social advantage from those at a disadvantage in a manner that could affect the occurrence of mental disorders among them. Hypotheses about causes range from the material conditions and consequences of poverty such as dilapidated and overcrowded housing (Booth and Edwards 1976; Gove, Hughes, and Galle 1979) and poor physical health (Thoits 1981) to such social concomitants of low economic status as job loss (Cobb and Kasl 1977), unrewarding conditions of work (Kornhauser 1965), disrupted relations with primary groups such as separation and divorce (Goode 1956), and harsh socialization experiences in childhood (Rutter 1968; Kohn 1969).

During the past decade, many investigators have focused on stressful life experiences as a source of mental disorders and of their social class distribution in particular. A progression of experimental and clinical studies had earlier demonstrated a connection between noxious physical and emotional stimuli and consequent physiological and/or psychological dysfunction (Lindemann 1944; Wolf and Wolff 1947; Selye 1950; Meyer 1951; Grinker 1953; Hill 1956; Engel

1962). These findings led epidemiologists to study the physical and mental consequences of stressful experiences in large populations.

Despite a host of methodological difficulties, these studies of stressful life
events showed that lower-class persons were indeed heavily bombarded by environmental stressors. Yet more than the frequency of stressful life events was involved. For the same frequency of events, more mental distress was generated
among lower- than higher-class persons (Brown and Harris 1978; Langner and
Michael 1963; Brown, Ni Bhrolchain, and Harris 1975; Kessler 1979; Kessler and
Cleary 1980).

The unequal response to stressors among social classes appears to have its
origin in resources that enhance or inhibit vulnerability. Resources may be external or environmental on the one hand, and internal or intrapsychic on the other
(Brown and Harris 1978; Kessler and Cleary 1980). External resources encompass
such things as finances and the support to be found in the person's network of
social relationships (Dohrenwend and Dohrenwend 1969; Susser and Watson
1971; Myers, Lindenthal, and Pepper 1975; Cobb 1976). Internal or intrapsychic
resources, by contrast, reside in the personality structure out of which flows an
individual's adaptability both in the interpretation of experiences and in the repertoire of behavior deployed in response (Susser and Watson 1971; Brown and Harris 1978; Pearlin and Schooler 1978). In the terms of the classic epidemiologic
"agent-host-environment" triad, noxious life experiences would constitute the
agent component, while external and internal resources would constitute the
environment and host components respectively. Thus, psychological damage in-
flicted by psychosocial agents will vary in magnitude with intrapsychic susceptibility or resistance to particular stressors, and with the environmental social
supports which buffer or cushion the consequences of exposure to stressors (Cobb
1976; Cassel 1976).

To illustrate the relationship between social class and mental disorders, we
turn to two discrete psychiatric conditions: depression and schizophrenia.

Depression

Both depressive symptomatology in the population at large and episodes of
clinical depression predominate among women. The prevalence of depressive
symptomatology in the population at large is also inversely related to social class
(Srole et al. 1962; Leighton et al. 1963; Weissman and Myers 1978), though the incidence of psychotic depression appears to be more evenly distributed across the
class structure (Hare 1956; Adelstein et al. 1968). A diverse set of risk factors have
been identified for episodes of clinical depression as well as for depressive symptomatology in the community at large. These include stressful life events such as
the loss of an accustomed role or relationship (Paykel 1974), or childhood emotional deprivation, often, though not always, involving disruption in early at-
tachments (Jacobsen, Fasman, and DiMascio 1975; Brown, Harris, and Copeland
1977; Rutter 1979; Bowlby 1980). They also include situations such as marital
roles in which housewives perform unskilled and unrewarding tasks, or, if working, experience "role-overload" from dual family and occupational demands
(Gove and Tudor 1973; Richman 1978). Maternal roles, too, are often combined
with isolation from other adults (Gove and Geerken 1977; Richman 1978).

Research on women in Camberwell, London (Brown and Harris 1978), points to a complex relationship between the varied sociocultural factors, social class, and clinical depression. In comparisons of psychiatric inpatients and outpatients with a diagnosis of primary depression and women chosen at random from the same community, working-class women manifested a higher incidence and prevalence of clinical depression than middle-class women. Working-class women, especially those with children at home, were also subject to a greater onslaught of severe environmental stressors (particularly those involving losses). But environmental stressors did not completely explain these social class differences in the incidence of depression. Thus, the incidence of clinical depression in women with children at home was four times as high in working-class women as in middle-class women given the same severity of stressful life events. Along with the burden of child care (in part because they are more likely to have three or more children under fourteen at home), two other factors increased the vulnerability of working-class women: They tended to lack close, intimate relationships with a spouse or lover, and they were more likely to have suffered the loss of a mother through death before the age of eleven. Only in relation to one risk factor for depression—lack of employment outside the home—were working-class women more favorably placed than middle-class women.

These results have been used to suggest a sociocultural model of depression involving a combination of stressful experiences, the absence of environmental supports, and internal psychological vulnerability (Brown and Harris 1978). Stressful life events are likely to induce certain women to feel helpless, or to perceive themselves as unable to control their world, and thus they fail to cope with the losses they experience. This state of helplessness is a consequence, first, of a lack of external resources for coping with stressors—namely, support from a close significant relationship, and the means for overcoming the burdens imposed by young children at home—and second, of low self-esteem. This perceptual state often arises in childhood in response to emotional trauma, such as the loss of significant adult figures. These sociocultural conditions conducive to clinical depression have their greatest impact on women in general, and working-class women in particular.

Schizophrenia

The epidemiologic evidence that schizophrenia is concentrated in the lowest social class is stronger and more consistent than the evidence with regard to social class and depresssion (Faris and Dunham 1939; Adelstein et al. 1968; Dohrenwend and Dohrenwend 1969; Dohrenwend 1975). Both inceptions (that is, first episodes) and overall incidence (all reported episodes) occur more frequently at the bottom of the class structure. However, the most sizable social class gradient occurs with the total number of episodes (Susser 1968). These findings suggest a social class component to the genesis of schizophrenia, and an even more powerful class component in the subsequent course of schizophrenia such as chronic disability.

Schizophrenia has been found to occur more than expected among first-degree relatives of those affected—that is, in parents, offspring, and sibs. The cause of the distribution may be either genetic or environmental; more likely it is both. The genetic transmission of schizophrenia has been well documented over the past decade by studies of adoptive children and their biological and social parents and relatives. For example, a higher rate of schizophrenia and schizophrenia-related disorders has been found in adopted children born to schizophrenic parents than in adopted children born to nonschizophrenic parents (Rosenthal and Kety 1968; Rosenthal et al. 1971). However, genetically oriented investigations do not account for all the variability in schizophrenia and the search for relevant sociocultural factors continues.

Early investigations found environments characterized by poverty and social isolation to be breeding grounds for schizophrenia. A pioneering study in the late 1930s in Chicago took first admissions to mental hospitals and related them by diagnoses to the social ecology in the areas from which the patients came (Faris and Dunham 1939). Depressive psychosis was evenly distributed across the city, but schizophrenia was concentrated in the deteriorated center. This result has been consistent in other American cities, and in Bristol, England, as well (Clark 1949; Hare 1956; Stein 1957; Adelstein et al. 1968). This study gave rise to the initial hypothesis that schizophrenia was the consequence of situations of social isolation and alienation from society. Subsequent studies uncovered associations with schizophrenia that could be seen as potentiating factors in lower-class situations. Schizophrenic patients had occupations of low prestige that frustrated any aspirations they might have shared with the dominant culture to upward social mobility (Clark 1949). In the areas they lived in, isolated single-room lodgings and tenements predominated (Gerald and Houston 1953; Hare 1956; Adelstein et al. 1968). Finally, the schizophrenic patients in such areas lived separated from the domestic support and personal relations that families could afford them. The additive and joint effects of all these factors together could be reflected in the poor prognosis and prolonged course of schizophrenia (Brown et al. 1966). Thus, a cumulative process appears progressively to exaggerate the alienating attributes of schizophrenia. After the inception of psychiatric care, patients who have repeated episodes, those who are admitted to hospitals, and those whose sickness eventually becomes chronic move progressively into more alienated situations. Thus they are more often in lower-class occupations, unemployed, or unmarried, and more often living away from families (Susser et al. 1970a, 1970b).

However, all these characteristic features of schizophrenia could come about through drift and social selection, as well as have their genesis in social situations. Thus, individuals already predisposed to schizophrenia, or manifesting early symptoms, may drift into the occupations of the lower social classes. The social correlates of schizophrenia could therefore arise, in part, from the intrinsic nature of the illness and its effects on social performance. A British study, by an ingenious method which linked mental hospital records and registrations of birth, succeeded in establishing that drift did in fact occur. Occupations of schizophrenic patients drawn from a national sample were compared with the occupations of their fathers as recorded on their birth certificates. Most patients belonged to lower occupational categories than their fathers, and since the occupations of the fathers were normally distributed at the time of the patient's birth, downward drift between the generations had taken place. Moreover, further detailed study of a sample in a field survey produced evidence of downward drift in the patient's occupational histories as well as in relation to the social and educational status of their families (Goldberg and Morrison 1963). Other studies have also produced support for the drift hypothesis (Dunham 1965; Turner and Wagenfeld 1967).

One debated model for the etiology of schizophrenia articulated in the early 1970s (Kohn 1972a, 1972b; Mechanic 1972) includes the combination of genetic susceptibility, stressful life experiences, and maladaptive coping patterns determined by the lack of adequate external and internal resources for coping. Each of the social components of the model, moreover, is linked to lower-class status. First, social stressors have been associated with both the onset and subsequent episodes of schizophrenia (Birley and Brown 1970) and, as we have seen, the frequency of stressors is greater at the bottom of the class structure. Second, some researchers argue that people in the lower class tend to lack both the external supports for coping with these stressors and the wide range of cognitive experience that could contribute to the mastery of environmental complexity. A belief in conformity with external authority and a fatalistic view of the world may be inculcated by early socialization and reinforced by an occupational environment characterized by simple repetitive work schedules and limited responsibility. From research on families of schizophrenics and psychoneurotics across social classes, some investigators have suggested that lower-class subculture could produce schizophrenia (Myers and Roberts 1959).

The family-oriented research of the past two decades, in attempting to establish a convincing causal link between disturbed patterns of socialization, resulting coping styles, and schizophrenic outcomes, has been plagued by methodological difficulties. Family dynamics, in which there is so much fluidity and reciprocity in the pattern of cognitive and affective communication and role relationships, are difficult to measure. It is not surprising that such studies have failed to establish that typical family patterns are antecedent in time to schizophrenia (Liem 1980).

In sum, many factors appear to be implicated in the onset and course of schizophrenia: genetic susceptibility, stressful life experiences, the lack of social resources, and maladaptive ways of coping learned through disturbed family socialization experiences may all contribute. Most important in understanding the sociocultural contribution is the class structure of society. This structure places lower-class persons at higher risk for the onset of schizophrenia and especially of the persistence of the condition by virtue of their location in an environment conducive to such outcomes.

Conclusion

We have tried to show that health is one facet of the social system, and that few indices illustrate better than health the inequalities that reside in class societies. In early phases of capitalist economic development, the working class and the poor carry the main burden of disease and death. Under bad conditions of housing and nutrition and wretched conditions of work, they are more susceptible to infection as well as more frequently attacked. At later stages of capitalist development in Europe and with the effective domination and exploitation of the Third World, resources, technology, productive systems and wealth expanded. Technical and environmental advances made possible control of many of the old infectious and epidemic diseases. Increased productivity improved the food supply and probably enhanced host resistance. While the overall toll of disease and mortality is as a result much less than in earlier phases, in a seeming paradox the affluence of the developed world has not dispelled the disparities in health among the social classes. The persistence of such disparities makes more apparent than ever the social determination of the distribution of disease.

Western culture can be considered a shared set of norms, values, and standards of behavior, but only to an extent. Each social class within such societies encounters a different structure of opportunities and is subject to different exigencies of daily life. These realities are reflected in the culture of classes, embodied in parental values and behavior, and, in turn, transmitted to children as part of their world view. Where productive systems are characterized by relations of domination and subordination, not only labor but also culture—forms of consumption, patterns of family life, modes of recreation and release, images of self and the shape of things hoped for, the entire body of practices and expectations that make up social life—will be affected in subtle and intricate ways.

Although this pervasive presence in everyday from the workplace to the home is experienced as natural and inevitable (Gramsci 1970; Williams 1977), it stems from a particular political-economic order. Thus, to the extent that inequalities in health reflect material deprivation—economic hardship, loss of job, poor housing and diet—they can be considered as vestiges of the exploitative character of the early stages of capitalist development. To the extent that they result from stressful conditions at work, the disruption of family and community life and consequent loss of support, maladaptive patterns of coping, and hazardous forms of consumption, inequalities in health can be seen to reflect the molding of cultural life by contemporary capitalist development (Navarro 1976; Stark 1977; Waitzkin 1978; Working Group 1980). In the absence of data, we may speculate that the health configuration across the strata of societies founded on other economic systems will equally reflect their underlying economic forms. For epidemiologists concerned with changing patterns of morbidity and mortality, "structural" explanations of the distribution of health patterns cannot be ignored.

The authors would like to acknowledge the assistance of Robert Peter Montera in the preparation of this chapter.

This material will appear in modified form in Susser and Walton, *Sociology in Medicine*, 3d ed., Oxford University Press, in preparation.

REFERENCES

ADELSTEIN, A. M.; DOWNHAM, D. Y.; STEIN, Z. A.; and SUSSER, M. W. 1968. The epidemiology of mental illness in an English city. *Social Psychiatry* 3:47–59.

Advisory Committee to the Surgeon General of the Public Health Service. 1964. *Smoking and health*. Public Health Service Publication No. 1103. Washington, D.C.

American Heart Association. 1968. *The national heart study: final report*. Monograph No. 18. New York.

ANTONOVSKY, A. 1967. Social class and the major cardiovascular diseases. *Journal of Chronic Diseases* 21:65–106.

ASHLEY JR., F. W., and KANNEL, W. B. 1974. Relation of weight change to change in atherogenic traits: the Framingham Study. *Journal of Chronic Diseases* 27:103–14.

BIERENBAUM, M. L.; FLEISCHMAN, A. I.; GREEN, D. P.; et al. 1970. The 5 year experience of modified fat diets on younger men with coronary heart disease. *Circulation* 42:943–52.

BIGGS, R.; MACFARLANE, R. G.; and PILLING, J. 1947. Observations on fibrinolysis—experimental activity produced by exercise or adrenaline. *Lancet* i:402–5.

BIRLEY, J. L. T., and BROWN, G. W. 1970. Crisis and life change preceding the onset or relapse of acute schizophrenia: clinical aspects. *British Journal of Psychiatry* 116:327–33.

BLUMENTHAL, J. A.; KONG, Y.; and ROSENMAN, R. H. 1975. Type A behavior pattern and angiographically documented coronary disease. Presented at the meeting of the American Psychosomatic Society. New Orleans. March 21, 1975.

Booth, A., and Edwards, J. N. 1976. Crowding and family relations. *American Sociological Review* 41:308–21.

Bowlby, J. 1980. *Attachment and loss.* Vol. 3. New York: Basic Books.

Bowles, S., and Gintis, H. 1976. *Schooling in capitalist America.* New York: Basic Books.

Brand, R. J.; Paffenbarger, R. S.; Sholtz, R. I., and Kamport, J. B. 1979. Work activity and fatal heart attack studied by multiple logistic risk analysis. *American Journal of Epidemiology* 110:52–62.

Breslow, L., and Buell, P. 1960. Mortality from coronary heart disease and physical activity of work in California. *Journal of Chronic Diseases* 2:421–44.

Bronte-Stewart, B.; Keys, A.; and Brock, J. F. 1955. Serum cholesterol, diet and coronary heart disease. *Lancet* ii:1103–7.

Brown, G. W.; Bone, M.; Dalison, B.; and Wing, J. K. 1966. *Schizophrenia and social care.* London: Oxford University Press.

Brown, G. W., and Harris T. 1978. *Social origins of depression: a study of psychiatric disorders in women.* New York: Free Press.

Brown, G. W.; Harris, T.; and Copeland, J. R. 1977. Depression and loss. *British Journal of Psychiatry* 130:1–18.

Brown, G. W.; Ni Bhrolchain, M.; and Harris, T. O. 1975. Social class and psychiatric disturbance among women in an urban population. *Sociology* 9:225–54.

Brown, R. G.; Davidson, L. A. G. F.; McKeown, T.; and Whitfield, A. G. W. 1957. Coronary artery disease, influences affecting its incidence in males in the seventh decade. *Lancet* ii:1073–77.

Bruhn, J. G.; Peredes, A.; Adsett, C. A.; et al. 1974. Psychological predictors of sudden death in myocardial infarction. *International Journal of Psychosomatic Research* 18:187–91.

Butensky, A.; Faralli, V.; Heebner, D.; and Waldron, I. 1976. Elements of the coronary prone behavior pattern in children and teen-agers. *Journal of Psychosomatic Research* 20:439–44.

Cartwright, A.; Martin, F. M.; and Thomson, J. G. 1959. Distribution and development of smoking habits. *Lancet* ii:725–27.

Cassel, J. 1976. The contribution of the social environment to host resistance. *American Journal of Epidemiology* 104:107–123.

Cassel, J.; Heyden S.; Bartel, A. G.; et al. 1971. Incidence of coronary heart disease by ethnic group, social class and sex. *Archives of Internal Medicine* 128:901–7.

Castelli, W. P., and Morgan, R. F. 1971. Lipid studies for assessing the risk of cardiovascular disease and hyperlipidemia. *Human Pathology* 2:153–64.

Christakis, G.; Rinzler, S. H.; Archer, M.; et al. 1966. The anti-coronary club: a dietary approach to the prevention of coronary heart disease—a seven-year report. *American Journal of Public Health* 56:299–314.

Christian, J. C.; Feinleib, M.; Hulley, S. B.; et al. 1976. Genetics of plasma cholesterol and triglycerides: a study of adult male twins. *Acta Genetica Medicae et Gemellologiae* (Roma) 25:145–49.

Christian, J. C., and Kang, K. W. 1977. Maternal influence on plasma cholesterol variation. *American Journal of Human Genetics* 29:462–67.

Clark, R. E. 1949. Psychoses, income and occupational prestige: schizophrenia in American cities. *American Journal of Sociology* 54:433–40.

Cobb, S. 1976. Social support as a moderator of life stress. *Psychosomatic Medicine* 38:300–14.

Cobb, S., and Kasl, S. V. 1977. *Termination: the consequences of job loss.* Washington D.C.: National Institute of Occupational Safety (Division of Biomedical and Behavioral Science) DHEW-77-224.

COHEN, J. B. 1978. The influence of culture on coronary-prone behavior. In *Coronary-prone behavior*, ed. T. M. Dembroski et al., pp. 191–98. New York: Springer-Verlag.

DAMON, A.; DAMON S. T.; HARPENDING, H. C.; and KANNEL, W. B. 1969. Predicting coronary heart disease from body measurements of Framingham males. *Journal of Chronic Diseases* 21:781–802.

DAYTON, S.; PEARCE, M. L.; HASHIMOTO, S.; ET AL. 1969. A controlled clinical trial of a diet high in unsaturated fat in preventing complications of atherosclerosis. *Circulation* 40 (supp. 2):1–63.

DEMBROSKI, T. M.; MACDONGALL, J. M.; and SHIELDS, J. L. 1977. Physiologic reactions to social challenge in persons evidencing the Type A Coronary-prone Behavior Pattern. *Journal of Human Stress* 3(3):2–9.

DOHRENWEND, B. P. 1966. Social status and psychological disorders: an issue of substance and an issue of method. *American Sociological Review* 31:14–34.

———. 1975. Sociocultural and socio-psychological factors in the genesis of mental disorders. *Journal of Health and Social Behavior* 16:365–92.

DOHRENWEND, B. P., and DOHRENWEND, B. S. 1969. *Social status and psychological disorder.* New York: Wiley-Interscience.

———. 1974 Social and cultural influences on psychopathology. *Annual Review of Psychology.* 25:417–52.

DOHRENWEND, B. P.; SHROUT, P.; EGRI, G.; and MENDELSOHN, F. S. 1980. Nonspecific psychological distress and other dimensions of psychopathology. *Archives of General Psychiatry* 37:1229–36.

DOYLE, J. T. 1966. Etiology of coronary disease: risk factors influencing coronary disease. *Modern Concepts of Cardiovascular Disease* 35:81–86.

DUBOS, R. 1965. *Man Adapting.* New Haven: Yale University Press.

DUNHAM, H. W. 1965. *Community and schizophrenia, an epidemiologic analysis.* Detroit: Wayne State University Press.

ENGEL, G. L. 1962. *Psychological development in health and disease.* Philadelphia: Saunders.

FARIS, R. E. L., and DUNHAM H. W. 1939. *Mental disorders in urban areas: an ecological study of schizophrenia and other psychoses,* Chicago: University of Chicago Press.

FEINLEIB, M.; GARRISON, R. J.; FABSITZ, R.; et al. 1977. The NHLBI twin study of cardiovascular disease risk factors: Methodology and summary of results. *American Journal of Epidemiology* 106:284–95.

FELDMAN, J. 1968. *The dissemination of health information, a case study in adult learning.* Chicago: Aldine.

FLØDERUS, B. 1974. Psychosocial factors in relation to coronary heart disease and associated risk factors. *Nordisk Hygiensk Tidskrift* supp. 6.

The Framingham Study. An epidemiological investigation of cardiovascular disease. 1968–78. Sections 1–33. W. B. Kannel, and T. Gordon, eds. U.S. DHEW.

FRANK, J. D. 1961. *Persuasion and healing.* Baltimore: Johns Hopkins Press.

FRANK, K. A.; HELLER, S. S.; KORNFELD, D. S.; SPORN, A. A.; et al. 1978. Type A behavior and coronary angiographic findings. *Journal of the American Medical Association* 240:761–63.

FRIEDMAN, M., and ROSENMAN, R. H. 1959. Association of specific behavior patterns with blood cholesterol. *Journal of the American Medcial Association* 169:1286–96.

FRIEDMAN, M.; ROSENMAN, R. H.; and CARROLL, V. 1958. Changes in the serum cholesterol and blood clotting time in men subjected to cyclic variation of occupational stress. *Circulation* 17:852–61.

GARCIA-PALMIERI, M. R.; COSTAS, R., JR.; CRUZ-VIDAL, M.; et al. 1978. Urban rural differences in coronary heart disease in a low incidence area, the Puerto Rico Heart Study. *American Journal of Epidemiology* 107:206–15.

GEERTZ, C. 1973. *The interpretation of cultures.* New York: Basic Books.

GERALD, D. L., and HOUSTON, L. G. 1953. Family setting and the social ecology of schizophrenia. *Psychoanalytic Quarterly* 27:90–101.

GIDDENS, A. 1973. *The class structure of the advanced societies.* New York: Barnes and Noble Books.

GLASS, D. C. 1977. *Behavior patterns, stress, and coronary disease.* Hillsdale, N.J.: Lawrence Erlbaum Associates.

GLUECK, C. J.; MATTSON, F.; and BIERMAN, E. L. 1978. Diet and coronary heart disease: Another view. *New England Journal of Medicine* 298:1471–74.

GOLDBERG, E. M., and MORRISON, S. L. 1963. Schizophrenia and social class. *British Journal of Psychiatry* 109:785–802.

GOLDBLATT, P. B.; MOORE, M. E.; AND STUNKARD, A. J. 1965. Social factors in obesity. *Journal of the American Medical Association* 192:1035–44.

GOODE, W. 1956. *After divorce.* New York: Free Press.

GORDON, T.; GARCIA-PALMIERI, M. R.; KAGAN, A.; et al. 1974. Differences in coronary heart disease in Framingham, Honolulu and Puerto Rico. *Journal of Chronic Diseases* 27:329–44.

GOVE, W., and GEERKEN, M. 1977. The effect of children and employment on the mental health of married men and women. *Social Forces* 56:66–76.

GOVE, W., and TUDOR, J. 1973. Adult sex roles and mental illness. *American Journal of Sociology* 77:812–35.

GOVE, W.; HUGHES, M.; and GALLE, O. R. 1979. Overcrowding in the home: an empirical investigation of its possible pathological consequences. *American Sociological Review* 44:59–80.

GRAMSCI, A. 1970. *Prison notebooks.* London: International Publishing.

GRINKER, R. 1953. *Psychosomatic research,* New York: Norton.

GROEN, J. J.; TIJONG, K. B.; KOSTER, M.; WILLEBRANDS, A. F.; VERDEOUCK, G.; and PEIRLOOT, M. 1962. The influence of nutrition and ways of life on blood cholesterol and the prevalence of hypertension and coronary heart disease among Trappist and Benedictine monks. *American Journal of Clinical Nutrition* 10:456–70.

HAMMOND, E. C., and HORN, D. 1954. The relationship between human smoking habits and death rates. *Journal of the American Medical Association* 155:1316–28.

HARE, E. H. 1956. Mental illness and social conditions in Bristol. *Journal of Mental Science* 102:349–57.

HARRIS, M. 1968. *The rise of anthropological theory.* New York: Crowell.

HAVLICK, R., and FEINLEIB, M., eds. 1979. Proceedings of the Conference on the decline in coronary heart disease mortality. USDHSS, PHS, NIH Publ. No. 79–1610.

HAYNES, S. G.; FEINLEIB, M.; LEVINE, S.; et al. 1978a. The relationship of psychosocial factors to coronary heart disease in the Framingham study. II. Prevalence of coronary heart disease. *American Journal of Epidemiology* 107:384–402.

HAYNES, S. G.; LEVINE, S.; SCOTCH, N.; et al. 1976b. The relationship of psychosocial factors to coronary heart disease in the Framingham study. I. Methods and risk factors. *American Journal of Epidemiology* 107:362–83.

HILL, S. R., JR. 1956. Studies on adreno-cortical and psychological response to stress in man. *Archives of Internal Medicine* 97:269–298.

HOLLINGSHEAD, A., and REDLICH, F. 1958. *Social class and mental illness.* New York: Wiley.

HSIA, S. L.; CHAO, Y.; HENNEKENS, C. H.; et al. 1975 Decreased serum-cholesterol binding reserve in premature myocardial infarction. *Lancet* ii:1000–4.

JACO, E. 1960. *Social epidemiology of mental disorders: a psychiatric survey of Texas.* New York: Russell Sage Foundation.

JACOBSEN, S.; FASMAN, F.; and DiMASCIO, A. 1975. Deprivation in the childhood of depressed women. *Journal of Nervous and Mental Disease* 160:5–14.

JARVIS, E. 1855. *Insanity and idiocy in Massachusetts: report of the commission on lunacy.* Cited in B. P. Dohrenwend (1975).

JENKINS, C. E. 1976. Recent evidence supporting psychologic and social risk factors for coronary disease. *New England Journal of Medicine* 295:987–94;1033–38.

JENKINS, C. D.; ZYZANSKI, S. J.; ROSENMAN, R. H. 1976. Risk of new myocardial infarction in middle-aged men with manifest coronary heart disease. *Circulation* 53:342–47.

JENKINS, C. D.; ZYZANSKI, S. J.; ROSENMAN, R. H.; and CLEVELAND, G. I. 1971. Association of coronary-prone behavior scores with recurrence of coronary heart disease. *Journal of Chronic Diseases* 24:601–11.

———. 1978 Coronary-prone behavior: one pattern or several? *Psychosomatic Medicine* 40:25–43.

JOHNSON, D. W., and JOHNSON, R. T. 1974. Goal structures and open education. *Journal of Research and Educational Development* 8:30–46.

KAGAN, A. 1960 Atherosclerosis of the coronary arteries—epidemiological considerations. *Proceedings of the Royal Society of Medicine* 53:18–22.

KANNEL, W. B.; DAWBER, T. R.; and McNAMARA, P. M. 1966. Detection of the coronary-prone adult: the Framingham Study. *Journal of the Iowa State Medical School* 56:26–34.

KAPLAN, D., and MANNERS, R. A. 1972. *Culture theory.* Englewood Cliffs, N.J.: Prentice-Hall.

KEITH, R. A.; LOWN, B.; and STARE, F. J. 1965. Coronary heart disease and behavior patterns. *Psychosomatic Medicine* 27:424–34.

KENT, A. P.; McCARROLL, J. R.; SCHWEITZER, M. D.; and WILLARD H. N. 1958. A comparison of coronary artery disease (arteriosclerotic heart disease) deaths in health areas of Manhattan, New York City. *American Journal of Public Health* 48:200–7.

KESSLER, R. C. 1979. Stress, social status, and psychological distress. *Journal of Health and Social Behavior* 20:100–108.

KESSLER, R. C., and CLEARY P. D. 1980. Social class and psychological distress. *American Sociological Review* 45:463–78.

KEYS, A., ed. 1970. *Coronary heart disease in seven counties.* American Heart Assoc. Monograph No. 29. New York: American Heart Association.

KEYS, A.; ARAVANIS, C.; BLACKBURN, H.; et al. 1972. Coronary heart disease: overweight and obesity as risk factors. *Annals of Internal Medicine* 77:15–27.

KINCH, S. A.; GITTELSOHN, A. M.; and DOYLE, J. T. 1964. Application of a life table analysis in a prospective study of degenerative cardiovascular disease. *Journal of Chronic Diseases* 17:503–14.

KING, H. 1975. Selected epidemiologic aspects of major diseases and causes of death among Chinese in the United States and Asia. In *Medicine in Chinese cultures: comparative studies of health care in Chinese and other societies,* ed. A. Kleinman, et al., pp. 487–550. DHEW Pub No. (NIH) 75–653.

KOHN, M. 1969. *Class and conformity.* Homewood, Ill.: Dorsey Press.

———. 1972a. Class, family and schizophrenia: a reformulation. *Social Forces* 50:295–304.

———. 1972b. Rejoinder to David Mechanic. *Social Forces* 50:310–13.

KORNHAUSER A. 1965. *Mental health of the industrial worker.* New York: Wiley

KOZAREVIC, D.; PIRC, B.; RACIC, Z.; et al. 1976. The Yugoslavia cardiovascular disease study. II. Factors in the incidence of coronary heart disease. *American Journal of Epidemiology* 104:133–40.

KRAUS, J. F.; BORHANI, N. O.; and FRANTI, C. E. 1980. Socioeconomic status, ethnicity, and risk of coronary heart disease. *American Journal of Epidemiology* 111:407–14.

KULLER, L. H. 1976. Epidemiology of cardiovascular diseases: current perspectives. *American Journal of Epidemiology* 104:425–56.

LANGNER, T. S., and MICHAEL, S. T. 1963. *Life stress and mental health.* New York: Free Press.

LEHMAN, E. W. 1967. Social class and coronary heart disease. A sociological assessment of the medical literature. *Journal of Chronic Diseases* 20:381–91.

LEHMAN, E. W.; SCHULMAN, J.; and HINKLE, L. E. 1967. Coronary deaths and organizational mobility. *Archives of Environmental Health* 15:455–61.

Leighton, D. C.; Harding, J. S.; Macklin, D. B.; MacMillan, A. M.; and Leighton, A. H. 1963. *The character of danger*. New York: Basic Books.

Leren, P. 1966. The effect of plasma cholesterol lowering diet in male survivors of myocardial infarction: a controlled clinical trial. *Acta Medica Scandinavica (supp.)* 466:5–92.

Lerner, M., and Stutz, R. N. 1977. Have we narrowed the gaps between the poor and the nonpoor? Part 2. Narrowing the gaps, 1959–61 to 1969–71: mortality. *Medical Care* 15:620–35.

———. 1978. Mortality by socioeconomic status, 1959–61 and 1969–71. *Md. State Med. J.* 35–42.

Liem, J. H. 1980. Family studies of schizophrenia: an update and commentary. *Schizophrenia Bulletin* 6:429–55.

Lilienfeld, A. M. 1956. Variation in mortality from heart disease. *Public Health Reports* 71:545–52.

Lindemann, E. 1944. Symptomatology and management of acute grief. *American Journal of Psychiatry* 101:141–48.

Mann, G. V.; Shaffer, R. D.; and Rich A. 1965. Physical fitness and immunity to heart disease in Masai. *Lancet* ii:1308–10.

Mann, G. V.; Teel, K.; Hayes, O.; McNally, A.; and Bruno, D. 1955. Exercise in the disposition of dietary calories. *New England Journal of Medicine* 253:349–55.

Mann, J. I.; Doll, R.; Thorogood, M.; et al. 1976. Risk factors for myocardial infarction in young women. *British Journal of Preventive Social Medicine* 30:94–100.

Marks, R. 1967. A review of empirical findings. In Social stress and cardiovascular disease. *Milbank Memorial Fund Quarterly* 45 (no. 2, pt. 2):51–108.

Marmot, M. G.; Adelstein, A. M.; Robinson, N.; and Rose, G. A. 1978. Changing social class distribution of heart disease. *British Medical Journal* 2:1109–12.

Marmot, M. G.; Syme, S. L.; Kagan, A.; et al. 1975. Epidemiological studies of coronary heart disease and stroke in Japanese men living in Japan, Hawaii and California: Prevalence of coronary and hypertensive heart disease and associated risk factors. *American Journal of Epidemiology* 102:514–25.

Marmot, M. G., and Syme, S. L. 1976. Acculturation and coronary heart disease in Japanese-Americans, *American Journal of Epidemiology* 104:225–47.

McClelland, D. 1961. *The achieving society*. Toronto: Van Nostrand.

Mechanic, D. 1972. Social class and schizophrenia: some requirements for a plausible theory of social influence. *Social Forces* 50:305–9.

Medalie, J. H.; Kahn, H. A.; Neufield, H. N.; et al. 1973. Myocardial infarction over a five-year period. I. Prevalence, incidence and mortality experience. *Journal of Chronic Diseases* 26:63–84.

Medalie, J. H.; Kahn, H. A.; Neufield, H. N.; et al. 1973. Five-year myocardial infarction incidence. II. Association of single variables to age and birth place. *Journal of Chronic Diseases* 26:329–49.

Medalie, J. H.; Snyder, M.; Groen, J. J.; et al. 1973. Angina pectoris among 10,000 men: 5 year incidence and univariate analysis. *American Journal of Medicine* 55:583–94.

Mettlin, C. 1976. Occupational careers and the prevention of coronary-prone behavior. *Social Science and Medicine* 10:367–72.

Meyer, A. 1951. The life chart and the obligation of specifiying postive data in psychopathological diagnosis. In *The collected papers of Adolf Meyer*, ed. E. E. Winters, vol. 3. *Medical teaching*. Baltimore: Johns Hopkins Press.

Miliband, R. 1969. *The state in capitalist society*. London: Basic Books.

———. 1977. *Marxism and politics*. New York: Oxford University Press.

Morris, J. N., 1951. Recent history of coronary disease. *Lancet* i:69–73.

———. 1979. Social inequalities undiminished. *Lancet* i:87–90.

Morris, J. N.; Adam, C.; Chave, S. P. W.; et al. 1973. Vigorous exercise in leisure-time and the incidence of coronary heart disease. *Lancet* i:333–37.

Morris, J. N., and Crawford, M. D. 1958. Coronary heart disease and physical activity of work. *British Medical Journal* 2:1485–96.

Morris, J. N.; Kagan, A.; Pattison, D. C.; Gardner, M. J.; and Raffle, P. A. B.1966. Incidence and prediction of ischaemic heart disease in London busmen. *Lancet* ii:553–59.

Morris, J. N.; Marr, J. W.; Heady, J. A.; Mills, G. L., and Pilkington, T. R. E. 1963. Diet and plasma cholesterol in 99 bank men. *British Medical Journal* 1:571–76.

Morris, J. N.; Pollard, R.; Everitt, M. G.; et al. 1980. Vigorous exercise in leisure-time: Protection against coronary heart disease. *Lancet* ii:1207–10.

Murphy, R. F. 1979. *An overture to social anthropology.* Englewood Cliffs, N.J.: Prentice-Hall.

Myers, J. K.; Lindenthal, J. J., and Pepper, M. P. 1975. Life events, social integration and psychiatric symptomatalogy. *Journal of Health and Social Behavior* 16:421–27.

Myers, J. K., and Roberts, B. H. 1959. *Family and class dynamics in mental illness,* New York: Wiley.

Navarro, V. 1976. *Medicine under capitalism.* New York: Prodist.

Office of Population Censuses and Surveys. 1978. *Occupational mortality, the registrar general's decennial supplement for England and Wales 1970–1972.* Series DS No. 1. London: HMSO.

Ostfeld, A. M.; Lebovits, D. Z.; Shekelle, R. B.; et al. 1964. A prospective study of the relationship between personality and coronary heart disease. *Journal of Chronic Diseases* 17:265–76.

Oliver, M. F. 1970. Oral contraceptives and myocardial infarction. *British Medical Journal* 2:210–213.

Olson, R. E. 1957. Dietary fat in human nutrition. *American Journal of Public Health* 47:1537–41.

Paffenbarger, R. S.; Hale, W. E.; Brand, R. J., and Hyde, R. T. 1977. Work-energy level, personal characteristics, and fatal heart attack: a birth-cohort effect. *American Journal of Epidemiology* 105:200–13.

Paffenbarger, R. S.; Milling, R. N.; Poe, N. D.; et al. 1966. Trends in death rate from hypertensive disease in Memphis, Tennessee, 1920–60. *Journal of Chronic Diseases* 19:847–56.

Paykel, E. S. 1974. Life stress and psychiatric disorders. In *Stressful life events,* ed. B. S. Dohrenwend and B. P. Dohrenwend, pp. 135–50. New York: Prodist.

Pearlin, L. I., and Radabaugh, C. W. 1976. Economic strains and the coping functions of alcohol. *American Journal of Sociology* 82:652–63.

Pearlin, L. I., and Schooler, C. 1978. The structure of coping. *Journal of Health and Social Behavior* 19:2–21.

Pell, S., and D'Alonzo, C. A. 1958. Myocardial infarction in a 1-year industrial study. *Journal of the American Medical Association* 166:332–37.

Pell, S., and D'Alonzo, A. 1963. Acute myocardial infarction in a large industrial population. *Journal of the American Medical Association* 185:31–38.

Poulantzas, N. 1975. *Classes in contemporary capitalism.* London: New Left Books.

Research Committee of the Scottish Society of Physicians. 1971. Ischaemic heart disease: a secondary prevention trial using clofibrate. *British Medical Journal* 4:775–84.

Rhoads, G. G.; Gulbrandsen, C. L.; Kagan, A. 1976. Serum lipoproteins and coronary heart disease in a population study of Hawaii Japanese men. *New England Journal of Medicine* 294:293–98.

Richman, J. 1978. "Psychological and psychophysiological distress in employed women and housewives: class, age, and ethnic differences." Ph.D. dissertation, Columbia University, New York.

Richman, N. 1978. Depression in mothers of young children. *Journal of the Royal Society of Medicine* 71:489–93.

Robinson, W. S. 1950. Ecological correlates and the behavior of individuals. *American Sociological Review* 15:351–57.

ROSENMAN, R. H.; FRIEDMAN, M.; STRAUSS, R.; WURM, M.; JENKINS, D., and MESSINGER, H. B. 1970. Coronary heart disease in the Western Collaborative Group Study. *Journal of Chronic Diseases* 23:173–90.

ROSENMAN, R. H.; BRAND, R. J.; SHOLTE, R. I., and FRIEDMAN, M. 1976. Multivariate prediction of coronary heart disease during 8.5 year follow-up in the Western Collaborative Group Study. *American Journal of Cardiology* 37:902–910.

ROSENTHAL, D., and KETY, S. S., eds. 1968. *The transmission of schizophrenia.* Oxford: Pergammon Press.

ROSENTHAL, D.; WENDER, P. H.; KETY, S. S.; WELNER, J.; and SCHULSINGER, F. 1971. The adopted-away offspring of schizophrenics. *American Journal of Psychiatry* 128:307–10.

RUSSEK, H. I., and ZOHMAN, B. L. 1958. Relative significance of heredity, diet and occupational stress in coronary heart disease of young adults. *American Journal of Medical Science* 235:266–77.

RUTTER, M. 1979. Maternal deprivation, 1972–1978: new findings, new concepts, new approaches. *Child Development* 50:283–305.

RUTTER, M. 1968. *Children of sick parents: an environmental and psychiatric study.* London: Oxford University Press.

RYLE, J. A. 1948. *The natural history of disease.* 2d ed. London: Oxford University Press.

SANDERS, K. 1959. Coronary artery disease and obesity. *Lancet* ii:432–35.

SELYE, H. 1950. *The physiology and pathology of exposure to stress.* Montreal: Acta.

SAHLINS, M. 1969. Economic anthropology and anthropological economics. *Social Science Information* 8(5):13–33.

SAHLINS, M. 1972. *Stone-Age economics.* Chicago: Aldine.

SHAPER, A. G., and JONES, K. W. 1959. Serum cholesterol, diet and coronary heart disease in Africans and Asians in Uganda. *Lancet* ii:534–37.

SHAPIRO, S.; SLONE, D.; ROSENBERG, L.; et al. 1979. Oral-contraceptive use in relation to myocardial infarction. *Lancet* i:743–47.

SHEKELLE, R. B., SCHOENBERGER, J. A., and STAMLER, J. 1976. Correlates of the JAS Type A behavior pattern score. *Journal of Chronic Diseases* 29:381–94.

SHEKELLE, R. B.; SHRYOCK, A. M.; PAUL, O.; et al. 1981. Diet, serum cholesterol, and deaths from coronary heart disease. The Western Electric Study. *New England Journal of Medicine* 304:65–70.

SIGERIST, H. E. 1943. *Civilization and disease.* Chicago: University of Chicago Press.

SROLE, L.; LANGNER, T. S.; MICHAEL, S. T.; OPLER, M. K., and RENNIE, T. A. C. 1962. *Mental health in the metropolis.* Vol. 1. New York: McGraw-Hill.

STAMLER, J. 1969. Prevention of atherosclerotic coronary heart disease. In *Trends in cardiology 2,* ed. A. M. Jones, pp. 88–132.

———. 1973. Epidemiology of coronary heart disease. *Medical Clinics of North America* 57:5–46.

STAMLER, J.; BERKSON, D. M.; et al. 1966. Coronary risk factors. *Medical Clinics of North America* 50:229–54.

STAMLER, J.; LINDBERG, H. A.; BERKSON, D. M.; SHAFFER, A.; MILLER, W., and POINDEXTER, A. 1960. Prevalence and incidence of coronary heart disease in strata of the labour force of a Chicago industrial corporation. *Journal of Chronic Diseases* 2:405–20.

STARK, E. 1977. The epidemic as a social event. *International Journal of Health Services* 7:681–705.

STEIN, L. 1957. Social class gradient in schizophrenia. *British Journal of Preventive Social Medicine* 11:181–95.

STUNKARD, A.; D'AGUILI, E.; FOX, S.; et al. 1972. Influence of social class on obesity and thinness in children. *Journal of the American Medical Association* 221:579–84.

SUSSER, M. W. 1968. *Community psychiatry: epidemiological and social themes.* New York: Random House.

———. 1973. *Causal thinking in health sciences: concepts and strategies of epidemiology.* New York: Oxford University Press.

Susser, M. W.; Stein, Z. A.; Mountney, G. H., and Freeman, H. L. 1970a. Chronic disability following mental illness in an English city. Part I: total prevalence in and out of mental hospital. *Social Psychiatry* 5:63–69.

Susser, M. W.; Stein, Z. A.; Mountney, G. H., and Freeman, H. L. 1970b. Chronic disability following mental illness in an English city. Part II: the location of patients in hospital and community. *Social Psychiatry* 5:69–76.

Susser, M., and Watson, W. 1971. *Sociology in medicine*. 2d ed. New York: Oxford University Press.

Theorell, T., and Fløderus-Myrhed, B. 1977. Workload and risk of myocardial infarction. A prospective psychosocial analysis. *International Journal of Epidemiology* 6:17–21.

Thoits, P. A. 1981. Undesirable life events and psychophysiological distress: a problem of operational confounding. *American Sociological Review* 46:97–109.

Turner, R. J., and Wagenfeld, M. 1967. Occupational mobility and schizophrenia: an assessment of the social causation and social selection hypothesis. *American Sociological Review* 32:104–113.

Turpeinen, O.; Miettinen, M.; Karvonen, M. J.; et al. 1968. Dietary prevention of coronary heart disease: long-term experiment. *American Journal of Clinical Nutrition* 21:255–76.

Tyroler, H. A.; Hames, C. G.; Krishan, I.; et al. 1975. Black-white differences in serum lipids and lipoproteins in Evans County. *Preventive Medicine* 4:541–49.

Waitzkin, H. 1978. A Marxist view of medical care. *Annals of Internal Medicine* 89:264–78.

Waldron, I. 1978. The coronary-prone behavior pattern, blood pressure, employment and socio-economic status in women. *Journal of Psychosomatic Research* 22:79–87.

Waldron, I.; Zyzanski, S.; Shekelle, R. B.; et al. 1977. The coronary-prone behavior pattern in employed men and women. *Journal of Human Stress.* 3 (4):2–18.

Weinsier, R. L.; Fuchs, R. J.; Kay, T. D.; et al. 1976. Body fat: its relationship to coronary heart disease, blood pressure, lipids and other risk factors measured in a large male population. *American Journal of Medicine* 61:815–24.

Weissman, M. M., and Klerman, G. L. 1977. Sex differences and the epidemiology of depression. *Archives of General Psychiatry* 34:98–111.

———. 1978. Epidemiology of mental disorders. *Archives of General Psychiatry* 35:705–12.

Weissman, M. M., and Myers, J. K. 1978. Rates and risks of depressive symptoms in a United States urban community. *Acta Psychiatrica Scandinavica* 57:219–31.

Wheaton, B. 1978. The sociogenesis of psychological disorder: reexamining the causal issues with longitudinal data. *American Sociological Review* 43:383–403.

Williams, C. A. 1968. The relationship of occupational change to blood pressure serum cholesterol, a specific overt behavior pattern and coronary heart disease. Ph.D. thesis, Dept. of Epidemiology, University of North Carolina, Chapel Hill. As cited by Waldron et al. 1977.

Williams, R. 1974. *Keywords*. New York: Oxford University Press.

———. 1977. *Marxism and literature*. London: Oxford University Press.

Wilson, R. W., and White, E. L. 1977. Changes in morbidity, disability, and utilization differentials between the poor and the nonpoor: data from the Health Interview Survey: 1964 and 1973. *Medical Care* 15:636–46.

Wolf, E. 1974. *Anthropology*. New York: Norton.

Wolf, S., and Wolff, H. G. 1947. *Human gastric function*. London: Oxford University Press.

Working Group on Inequalitites in Health. 1980. *Inequalities in health*. Department of Health and Social Security. London: HMSO.

Worth, R. M.; Kato, K.; Rhoads, G. G.; et al. 1975. Epidemiologic studies of coronary heart disease and stroke in Japanese men living in Japan, Hawaii, and California: mortality. *American Journal of Epidemiology* 102:481–501.

Wright, E. O., 1978. *Class, crisis and the state*. London: New Left Books.

YERCARIS, C. A., and KIM, J. H. 1978. Socioeconomic differentials in selected causes of death. *American Journal of Public Health* 68:342-51.

YERUSHALMY, J., and HILLEBOE, H. E. 1957. Fat in the diet and mortality from heart disease. *New York Medical Journal* 57:2343-54.

YUDLKN, J. 1967. Diet and coronary thrombosis. *Lancet,* ii: 115-62.

ZUKEL, W. J.; LEWIS, R. H.; ENTERLINE, P. E.; PAINTER, R. C.; RALSTON, L. S.; FAWCETT, R. M.; MEREDITH, A. P.; and PETERSON, B. 1959. A short-term community study of the epidemiology of coronary heart disease. *American Journal of Public Health* 49:1630-9.

ZYZANSKI, S. J. 1978. Coronary-prone behavior pattern and coronary heart disease: epidemiological evidence. In *Coronary-prone behavior,* ed. T. M. Dembroski et al., pp. 25-40. New York: Springer-Verlag.

ZYZANSKI, S. J.; JENKINS, C. D.; RYAN, T. J.; FLESSAS, A.; and EVERIST, M. 1976. Psychological correlates of coronary angiographic findings. *Archives of Internal Medicine* 136:1234-37.

Chapter 3

The Potential of
Health Promotion

Lester Breslow

DURING RECENT YEARS concern about health in the industrialized nations of the world has focused largely on what is called health care, particularly on the amount that is being provided and its cost. To a lesser extent there has been attention to what can be accomplished by it. The context of the term *health care,* however, usually means not care for health but care for people with a health problem. Typically these are people who have lost some degree of health from disease or injury and seek to have their health restored.

The latter approach to health is much needed and increasingly justified by advances in medical science and technology which in many cases permit cures of diseases that were formerly almost invariably fatal. For example, childhood leukemia and Hodgkin's disease can now often be treated successfully, although just a few decades ago their prognoses were dismal. The ability of modern therapeutic medicine to save lives, to mimimize disability, to relieve pain, and to provide other benefits tends to make people look upon it as the main force for health.

In reality, of course, the principal advances in health have come about through health promotion and disease prevention rather than through diagnosis and therapy. Furthermore, the potential of health promotion and disease prevention for further improvement of health is vast and growing. That fact, however, does not have much influence on thinking and decisions by people who have a particular health problem. Nor, unfortunately, does it have much influence as yet on physicians who have been trained in complaint-response medicine, or on people in government and elsewhere who must deal with the economic aspects of health care. But health promotion is receiving increased attention in many quarters.

Health promotion consists of all the measures that enhance the possibility of a full life, in both extent and quality. The goal has been expressed by the World Health Organization as "physical, mental and social well-being, not merely the absence of disease or infirmity." It encompasses, but is not limited to, specific disease prevention. For example, it includes the avoidance of diphtheria through immunization and the early detection of cervical malignancy, when it can be readily overcome. Health promotion, however, means more than prevention of specific diseases. It embraces steps to maintain and expand function generally and to build reserves against forces adverse to health. Thus, appropriate exercise and good nutrition may both enhance physical fitnesss and curtail the risk of heart disease.

Promotion of health means strengthening the anatomical, physiological, chemical, immunological, genetic, and behavioral parameters of living that are sometimes called health indicators, as illustrated in Table 3.1.

It also means adopting measures that will minimize the risk of specific health problems. Table 3.2 outlines three approaches to health promotion, applicable to some common conditions. It illustrates how major identifiable health problems may often be attacked by all three of these approaches: preventive medical, environmental, and behavioral. Health promotion, in fact, typically involves all three.

Preventive medical measures consist of personal health services, i.e., those provided by or under direction of health professionals, aimed usually at the primary or secondary prevention of disease. These latter terms were first used in the report of the Commission on Chronic Illness in 1957 to broaden the concept of prevention, adapting it to the health problems prominent in the latter part of the twentieth century and the available means of dealing with them. Primary prevention means avoiding the occurrence of disease, for example, by immunization or by not smoking cigarettes. Secondary prevention means detection of disease early in its course when medical intervention can be most effective, illustrated by finding and treating hypertension. In broader view, preventive medicine (perhaps a more accurate term would be health-maintenance medicine) implies preserving and enlarging the capacity for a full life. The goal is fitness, i.e., more than the primary or secondary prevention of specific diseases.

Environmental measures for health promotion are directed mainly toward those physical conditions of life that are adverse to health. In former times bacterial and other microbic agents of disease constituted the main target of envi-

TABLE 3.1 Examples of Health Indicators to Be Sought by Health Promotion

Anatomical	Optimum weight/height ratio Normal epithelial tissue throughout body
Physiological	Blood pressure approximately 120/80 No electrocardiographic abnormalities
Chemical	Blood cholesterol level 200–210 Glucose tolerance
Bacterial	Freedom from bacteriuria Absence of tuberculosis infection
Immunological	Immunity to current strains of influenza Immunity to poliomyelitis
Genetic	Absence of trisomy 21 in fetus No Tay-Sachs affected fetuses
Behavioral	No cigarette smoking Moderate if any use of alcohol

TABLE 3.2   Three Approaches to Promotion of Health

HEALTH PROBLEM	PREVENTIVE MEDICAL MEASURES	ENVIRONMENTAL MEASURES	INFLUENCES ON BEHAVIOR
Infant deaths	Prenatal and pediatric care	Home hygiene; reduce exposure to toxic agents	Support healthful life-styles; parent education
High blood pressure	Detect hypertension and treat it vigorously	Reduce fat and salt in processed foods	Heighten public awareness of significance of overweight, salt
Loss of teeth	Repair caries; remove calculus	Fluoridation; reduce production and promotion of refined sugars	Encourage tooth brushing and flossing; prudent diet
Lung cancer	Detect and treat disease early	Curtail promotion of cigarettes; reduce occupational exposures to pulmonary carcinogens	Encourage no cigarette smoking

ronmental health measures. Now the chemical and physical agents of disease have become relatively more prominent in countries like the United States. Expanding industrial civilization has produced a host of new substances, such as the petrochemicals; and it has increased the availability of others, such as fat in food, which pose hazards to health. Some of these substances heighten the harm of others. For example, cigarettes and asbestos act synergistically to cause lung cancer. Consciousness of the need for a systematic approach to health protection through environmental control is growing rapidly. It is apparent that this should include attention to the production of healthful food; safeguarding air, water and soil from pollution that threatens health; and assuring safe housing and workplaces. Beyond this defensive aspect of environmental measures for health promotion, however, there is increasing opportunity to enhance the environment for health, as in optimizing the fluoride content of drinking water where that element is deficient.

Perhaps the greatest current opportunity to advance health in such countries as the United States, however, is through influencing behavior. The major factors involved in the principal fatal diseases of our time are controlled by personal behavior. Cigarette smoking, excessive use of alcohol, and too much fat in the diet exemplify these factors and the problems of dealing with them. Obviously individual behavior regarding these consumable substances is largely determined by the circumstances of life, including specific health-promotional efforts in contest with specific commercial-promotional efforts. The latter contest is now raging throughout the industrially advanced nations, and it is rising in the developing nations, with respect to cigarette smoking. Other consumable goods may soon be caught up in this contest which seems to accompany industrialization, whether under capitalist or socialist forms of society. Seeking immediate economic advantage and seeking immediate personal gratifications can jeopardize health in the long run. Those concerned with public health are gradually coming to grips with personal behavior as a health factor and how to influence it favorably.

Comprehensive health promotion thus includes all three modalities: preventive medical measures, environmental measures, and influences on behavior that are favorable to health. The goal for all three, separately and in combination, is not only to avoid specific diseases but also to achieve "physical, mental, and social well-being."

Health Accomplishments

Twentieth-century industrial civilization has brought the greatest health advance in the history of mankind. In the United States, longevity increased from forty-seven years in 1900 to seventy-three years in 1977 (U.S. Dept. of Health and Human Services 1981). Until very recent years, however, this striking improvement has been achieved largely through control of infant deaths and the communicable disease.

Infant mortality began declining in the nineteenth century, to about 100 per 1,000 live births in the United States at the turn of the century. The downward trend continued until 1955 when it plateaued at 25 per 1,000 live births for the period 1955 to 1965, for reasons that are not clear. During the last fifteen years the infant mortality rate has again dropped sharply, to about half of what it was in 1965 (U.S. Dept. of Health and Human Services 1981).

Important communicable diseases that formerly affected hundreds of thousands of people and caused thousands of deaths each year have been vastly reduced, as shown in Table 3.3. While that achievement is now taken for granted, it could scarcely have been foreseen only a few decades ago. Much of the science and technology underlying the present situation was not available. Although microbic agents had been confirmed as causing disease and some artificial immunization agents were being used, the specific scientific bases for poliomyelitis and measles vaccines were still to be established. There can be no doubt that application of immunizing agents has been the main factor in the recent control of the diseases listed in Table 3.3. It should be noted, however, that the achievement has entailed more than the essential scientific advances and consequent technology. It has included organizing the necessary personal health services, especially for the

TABLE **3.3**   Decline of Selected Communicable Diseases, U.S., 1920–77

	SMALLPOX		DIPHTHERIA		POLIOMYELITIS		MEASLES	
YEAR	Cases	Deaths	Cases	Deaths	Cases	Deaths	Cases	Deaths
1920	102,128	508*	147,991	13,395*	2,338	NA	469,924	7,712*
1930	48,907	165*	66,576	5,822*	9,220	NA	419,465	3,820*
1940	2,795	14	15,536	1,457	9,804	NA	291,162	706
1950	39	1	5,796	410	33,300	1,904	319,124	408
1960	—		918	69	3,190	230	442,000	380
1970	—		435	30	33	7	47,351	89
1977	—		84	5	18	16	57,345	15

Source: U.S. Department of Health, Education and Welfare 1979a.
* Registration area only.

substantial segment of the American people largely excluded from the predominant medical-care pattern in the country. It also required widespread public as well as professional education.

In taking satisfaction from what has been accomplished, it is appropriate to recall that applying the means available for communicable disease control has been considerably less than perfect. Measles vaccine was licensed for sale in 1963, but for years thereafter tens of thousands of cases and dozens of deaths from the disease occurred annually in the United States as reported by the Centers for Disease Control in 1979. The number of reported cases fell below 50,000 first in 1968, but rose above that level in 1971 and again in 1977. Poliomyelitis and measles continue to affect children in several parts of the developing world essentially as though vaccines for these diseases had never been developed.

Other specific health advances should be noted. Physician leaders were disturbed by the fact that maternal mortality continued at a high rate into the first part of the present century. They were possibly aroused also by federal government action in 1921 to provide direct financial support for medical services to women and children. As a result, medical societies in the 1930s formed maternal-mortality committees to deal with the problem. In reviewing maternal deaths with the physicians and other involved, these medical society committees found that two-thirds of the deaths were preventable. Probably both the favorable influence on physicians' practices from such work and the availability of new drugs brought about a sharp decline in maternal deaths. The rate dropped from 60 per 10,000 live births in 1933, to 8 in 1950, and to 1 in 1975 (U.S. Dept. of Health and Human Services 1980). That improvement, however, did not overcome certain disadvantages to health inherent in life among certain segments of American society. The maternal death rate among nonwhite women continued at four times the rate among white women. Put another way, the nonwhite rate lagged about a decade throughout the decline. The potential for accomplishment may be seen in a vigorous program for American Indian women which brought their maternal mortality rate down from a level 2.2 times higher than the total United States rate, in 1958, to a point only 1.2 times that for the United States as a whole, by 1975 (U.S. Dept. of Health, Education and Welfare 1978).

While the vast health improvement in this century, and especially the first half of the century, is attributable mainly to advances against infant mortality and the communicable diseases, progress of other kinds has also been under way. By 1950 it was clear that the cardiovascular diseases, cancer, and other chronic diseases would constitute the major health problems of the second half of the century. These were now the leading causes of death, rather than influenza and pneumonia, tuberculosis, and diarrheal disease, which headed the list in 1900.

In attacking post–World War II health problems epidemiologists and other health scientists have achieved enough understanding of the major current diseases to guide substantial control efforts. Though we do not have as full a grasp of the causative processes as we now possess for communicable diseases, we have come to realize that cancer and heart disease grow mainly out of the conditions of life. These "modern plagues" are not simply aspects of aging, as was commonly believed only a few decades ago. Just as exposure of those vulnerable to microorganisms caused previous epidemics, access of those vulnerable to cigarette smoking, high-fat diets, and other common features of life in the twentieth century have resulted in the current epidemics. The latter appear as lung cancer and coronary heart disease in epidemics extending over several decades rather than the few months typical of acute communicable disease outbreaks. Acquiring knowledge about these diseases and beginning to apply it has been called "the second epidemiologic revolution." That revolution has facilitated both the primary and secondary prevention of chronic disease. For example, avoiding exposure to certain amino dyes in industry prevents bladder cancer that would otherwise occur; finding and treating cervix cancer in its early stages prevents its spread and ultimate fatality from it.

Environmental measures undertaken to protect workers against cancer-causing chemicals in the modern workplace exemplify primary prevention, i.e., avoiding the onset of disease by stopping exposure to the causative agents. The approach is analogous to curtailing cholera, typhoid, and other enteric diseases by constructing water supplies that minimize exposure to their causative agents.

Attacking diphtheria by giving antitoxin to those in the incubation stage of that disease constitutes, in retrospect, an example of what we now call secondary prevention, i.e., applying technology at an early stage of a disease process to minimize damage that would otherwise occur. Using the Papanicolaou smear against cervix cancer is a modern analogue. In the latter case technology is used for determining which individuals are in the early stages of developing one form of cancer so that treatment can be applied to interrupt the disease's progress and damage. The Papanicolaou smear for cervix-cancer control illustrates several features of secondary prevention. Established in 1941 as an effective means of discovering cervix cancer at a time in the course of the disease when treatment would be effective, the Papanicolaou smear took its place in medical practice slowly. By the early 1960s, only one-half the adult women in a reasonably typical American community had received the test even once, and that half consisted mainly of relatively affluent women who were least likely to develop the disease. Those in poorer socioeconomic circumstances and at higher risk for cervix cancer had been tested to a much lesser extent (Breslow and Hochstim 1964). It was not until the 1970s, thirty years after cervical cytology was developed, that its use extended to more than 90 percent of the women in the country; and even then, those most likely to have the disease had received its benefit the least (U.S. Dept. of Health and Human Services 1981).

Meanwhile mortality from uterine cancer including the cervix was declining; in fact, a downward trend had been recorded since the 1930s. Separating the trend of cervix cancer from that of uterine cancer as a whole became reasonably possible about 1960; before that time statistics on cancer of the uterus did not permit very clear differentiation. Cervix cancer typically develops through a phase called dysplasia to an in-situ lesion, which usually becomes manifest about age thirty to thirty-five and lasts for about ten years; then the malignancy invades the organ and spreads beyond to ultimate death. Based on that understanding of the natural history of cervix cancer and assuming no change in the incidence of the disease process, one would expect increasingly extensive use of the Papanicolaou smear, especially among younger women, to have a certain pattern of effect: (1) acceleration of the long-term decline in mortality; (2) decrease in the incidence of invasive cervical cancer, especially at the younger ages; and (3) reported incidence of in-situ lesions continuing at the same level, with some relative increase at the younger ages. Table 3.4 shows what has actually occurred in a rather typical American community, Alameda County, California, where the rate of having had at least one Papanicolaou smear increased from 51 percent in 1962 to 91 percent in 1974 (California Department of Health, unpublished).

TABLE 3.4 Average Annual Incidence and Mortality, Cervical Cancer, Alameda County, California, 1960-75

	AGE-ADJUSTED	AGE-SPECIFIC		
		25-34	*35-44*	*55-64*
Incidence, in situ				
1960-63	53	126	131	33
1964-67	50	130	113	37
1968-71	51	159	99	24
1972-75	51	163	99	22
Incidence, invasive				
1960-63	23		43	58
1964-67	21		36	44
1968-71	17		29	34
1972-75	14		23	29
Mortality				
1960-63	8.6		11.7	25.8
1964-67	6.0		7.6	18.8
1968-71	6.0		7.8	21.9
1972-75	4.6		3.6	14.8

Source: California Tumor Registry, California Department of Health.

Further evidence of recent advance against the diseases of adult and later life comes from comparative increases in longevity: 3.5 years at birth during the period 1960-77, and 2.0 years at age sixty-five during the same period of time (U.S. Dept. of Health and Human Services 1981).

Potential Health Improvement, Using Available Knowledge

Further gains in health during the remainder of this century, and beyond, depend largely on: (1) the systematic use of available knowledge that can demonstrably benefit health; and (2) the development, testing, and application of further knowledge likely to benefit health.

Failure to use available knowledge systematically may be illustrated by "the other side of the coin" in the history of the Papanicolaou smear. As noted above, the lag in use of that technique delayed achieving its potential, particularly among low-income women who are most affected by the disease. During the twenty-five years following demonstration of the Papanicolaou smear's value, approximately 10,000 women died annually from cervix cancer—more than 250,000 in all. Only during the 1970s did the annual number of deaths from that disease drop below 10,000 and even into the first part of the 1980s the number remains at about 7,000 a year. This experience shows that it is not enough to develop an effective preventive health-care technique. Systematic use of such a technique must be achieved in order to maximize the gains.

Defective application of technology may also be seen in the current approach to breast cancer (National Cancer Institute, 1978). More than 35,000 American women are dying annually from that disase at the start of the 1980s. Important knowledge on which breast cancer can be attacked with considerable effectiveness came from the Health Insurance Plan (of New York) population study. Its results showed that intensive effort to detect breast cancer early, using mammography among other modalities, yielded a substantial saving of lives. The benefit clearly was limited to women over fifty years of age (Table 3.5). Subsequently, nationally prestigious organizations sponsored demonstration programs that extended such detection efforts to women in twenty-seven centers across the country, including women under fifty years of age. Then data were presented showing that mammography in women under fifty carried a risk of inducing breast cancer, with no established benefit. The ensuing professional and public concern about the issue tended to disrupt systematic breast cancer detection in women for whom its value was well established—i.e., women over fifty years of age—and it is among the latter that approximately 80 percent of breast cancer deaths occur.

The two examples presented thus far illustrate the potential for further health improvement by more systematic use of specific preventive medical measures: the Papanicolaou smear for cervix cancer detection and means for detecting breast cancer. Deaths that might be avoided each year by these techniques number several thousand.

Cessation of cigarette smoking in the United States, however, carries the potential for curtailing the more than 300,000 deaths each year that are attributable to that habit. Of these deaths, the ones due to lung cancer are probably the best known (U.S. Dept. of Health, Education and Welfare 1979b). That single form of cancer accounts for about 100,000 deaths each year, and at least 80 percent of them are caused by cigarette smoking. The latter habit contributes also to the occurrence of cancer in other sites, such as the bladder. Not so fully appreciated is the fact that cigarette smoking is a causative factor in even more deaths from coronary heart disease than from all forms of cancer. Furthermore, it constitutes the major element in mortality from chronic obstructive lung disease.

Since the 1964 report, *Smoking and Health,* by the advisory committee to the Surgeon General, cigarette smoking has declined substantially among men. Among women the trend has not been so favorable. In 1964 more than half of all men in the United States, 53 percent of those over twenty-one years of age, smoked cigarettes. By 1978 the percentage had dropped to less than 40 percent. Those still smoking tended to be men with lower levels of education and income, and to be heavier smokers. Over the same time period, 1964–78, the percentage of women smoking cigarettes declined only from 33 to 30 percent.

Meanwhile, the frequency of lung cancer among men had apparently reached a peak and possibly started downward. Also the death rate from coronary heart disease had declined 25 percent, in part attributable to the drop in cigarette smoking. At the same time, 1964–78, lung cancer was rising sharply among women. That re-

TABLE **3.5** Breast Cancer Deaths after 7 Years in HIP Screening Study

AGE AT DEATH	CONTROL GROUP	STUDY GROUP
Total	108	70
40–44	2	1
45–49	14	16
50–54	28	17
55–59	31	15
60+	33	21

Source: S. Shapiro. Personal communication. See Breslow et al. 1977.

flected widespread cigarette smoking by women, starting about the time of World War II.

In addition to cigarette smoking several other common habits are known to be related to health status and to mortality: excessive consumption of calories, especially in the form of animal fat; alcohol abuse; and too little exercise. Various physical conditions of the body likewise constitute risks for health. Data are rapidly accumulating, in fact, to form the basis for systematic health monitoring. Table 3.1 illustrates the range of bodily status and behavioral factors that can and should be kept under routine surveillance for health.

Prudent interpretation of current evidence concerning how specific features of bodily status or behavior relate to health provides the basis for a lifetime health monitoring program. Rather than the former, vague "annual checkup," or the occasional mass screening for particular diseases, it is now possible to establish systematic health surveillance throughout life based on rapidly accumulating knowledge. This health surveillance would build on the medical-practice model already established for care of pregnant women and infants. Obstetrics and pediatrics have long focused on maintaining and promoting health through the particular periods of life with which they are concerned. Routine procedures in those aspects of medicine, established and conducted at intervals in accord with growth and development, have emerged by professional consensus. They now seem quite well understood and followed by the general public. Beyond these two periods of life, further procedural routines are being designed on the same principle of health promotion: for adolescence, early and middle adult life, and the later years. Thus, an internist or family physician for a man fifty years of age will commonly determine height, weight, blood pressure, blood cholesterol and glucose levels, vision, hearing, cigarette and alcohol consumption, and other features of health status and health-related behavior. Consensus is still building as to the appropriate periodicity and content of such examinations at the various times of life and for both sexes. The principle of establishing a new focus for medical practice, however—moving from a complaint-response to a health-maintenance focus—is increasingly accepted. It is taking such forms as the Know Your Body program for children, and Health Hazard Appraisal for adults.

According to one view of the matter a distinct set of health goals and professional services can be established for each of ten periods of life (Breslow and Somers 1977). In adolescence (ages twelve to seventeen) health goals would be to continue optimal physical, mental, and social growth and development; and to reinforce healthy behavior patterns and discourage negative ones in respect to physical fitness, nutrition, exercise, study, work, recreation, sex, individual personal relations, driving, smoking, alcohol, and drugs. Professional services would consist of mandatory school health education and individual counseling as needed for the above subjects; one professional visit with attention to emotional status, vision and hearing, skin, blood pressure, blood cholesterol and contraception; and annual dental examination and prophylaxis. For persons sixty to seventy-four years of age the health goals would be to prolong the period of optimum physical, mental, and social capacity; to minimize handicaps and discomfort from chronic conditions; and to prepare for retirement. Professional services would include biannual visits with tests for hypertension, heart disease, cancer, and diabetes as well as vision, dental, and hearing impairments; counseling regarding life-style; annual immunization against influenza and dental prophylaxis; and periodic podiatry care as needed.

Consistent with this approach to health, in 1979 the U.S. Department of Health, Education and Welfare published *Healthy People: The Surgeon General's Report on Health Promotion and Disease Prevention* (1979), which identified fifteen priority areas for the 1980s. It also established broad national goals expressed as reductions in death rates or days of disability for health improvement during five major life stages:

- To continue to improve infant health, and , by 1990, to reduce infant mortality by at least 35 percent, to fewer than 9 deaths per 1,000 live births.
- To improve child health, foster optimal childhood development, and, by 1990, reduce deaths among children ages one to fourteen years by at least 20 percent, to fewer than 34 per 100,000.
- To improve the health and health habits of adolescents and young adults, and, by 1990, to reduce deaths among people ages fifteen to twenty-four by at least 20 percent, to fewer than 93 per 100,000.
- To improve the health of adults, and, by 1990, to reduce deaths among people ages twenty-five to sixty-four by at least 25 percent, to fewer than 400 per 100,000.
- To improve the health and quality of life for older adults and, by 1990, to reduce the average annual number of days of restricted activity due to acute and chronic conditions by 20 percent, to fewer than thirty days per year for people aged sixty-five and older.

A second publication in this series from DHHS appeared in fall 1980, *Promoting Health and Preventing Disease: Objectives for the Nation.* It set forth specific and quantifiable objectives, necessary for the attainment of these broad goals, in each of the fifteen priority areas identified in the Surgeon General's report. The latter include high blood pressure control; family planning; pregnancy and infant health; immunization; sexually transmitted diseases; toxic agent control; occupational safety and health; accident prevention and injury control; fluoridation and dental health; surveillance and control of infectious diseases; smoking and health; misuse of alcohol and drugs; physical fitness and exercise; and control of stress and violent behavior.

A specific objective with respect to high blood pressure control is to attain by 1990 or earlier successful long-term blood pressure control, i.e., a blood pressure at or below 140/90 for two or more years, for at least 60 percent of the estimated 35,000,000 persons in the United States who now have definite high blood pressure (160/95). Intermediate objectives are to reduce the average sodium ingestion for adults at least to the three- to six-gram range, compared with the estimated 1979 range of four to ten grams; to reduce significant overweight (120 percent of optimum weight) among the U.S. adult population to no more than 10 percent of men and 17 percent of women, compared with corresponding figures of 14 and 24 percent in 1971–74; along with specific similar quantitative objectives in respect to public/professional awareness, such as knowledge of one's own blood pressure and of risk factors for coronary heart disease and stroke (for which 50 percent of adults should be able to state the principal ones); improved services/protection, including effective public programs in all geopolitical areas to identify persons with high blood pressure and to follow up on their treatment, and labeling at least 50 percent of processed food sold in grocery stores to inform the consumer of sodium and caloric content; and improved surveillance/evaluation systems, for example, to determine the incidence of high blood pressure, coronary heart disease, congestive heart failure, and hemorrhagic and occlusive strokes.

A comparable set of objectives is proposed for toxic agent control. As a measure of improved health status, lead toxicity among less than 500 per 100,000 children would be sought for 80 percent of communities, rather than the estimated prevalence of 1,000 per 100,000 estimated in 1980. Other objectives are: reduced risk factors, such as virtually no preventable contamination of ground water, surface water, or soil from industrial toxins associated with waste-water management systems established after 1980; increased public/professional awareness, such as at least 75 percent of all city council members in urban communities being able to report accurately whether the quality of their air and water has improved or worsened over the decade, and to identify the principal substances of concern; improved services/protection, such as having purchasers of a potentially toxic product protected by clear labeling as to content, proper use, and disposal; and establishing a broad-scale monitoring system to discern and measure known environmental hazards.

It is thus clear that available knowledge, if systematically applied, carries great potential for health improvement. That knowledge is sufficient for the establishment of individual lifetime health monitoring to guide the promotion of health and curtail risk factors for the important diseases of our time. It is also sufficient for the projection of national goals for health and specific objectives for achieving them during the 1980s.

To achieve the objectives for the nation in promoting health and preventing disease, the 1980 report outlines in considerable detail the precise measures needed (U.S. Dept. of Health and Human Services 1980). The strategy includes education and information, services, technologic measures, legislation and regulation, and economic measures directed specifically toward attaining each of the objectives listed.

Potential Health Improvement, Based on Developing New Knowledge

While much can be accomplished for health with existing knowledge, the potential for even further improvement is also discernible. It lies in the development, testing, and application of additional knowledge which seems likely to promote health. That potential extends over the range of measures already identified and, to a varying extent, being used to advance health, including: medical, environmental, and behavioral.

For example, vitamins have long been standardized for their health-promotive and disease-preventive qualities. Yet only recently the recommended minimum daily allowance for vitamin C was increased one-third in response to new understanding of its significance for health. Also, early in 1981 a flurry of excitement and activity concerning vitamin A could be sensed in the relevant scientific community. It arose from sudden, widespread appreciation that persons with higher levels of vitamin A had considerably less likelihood of developing lung cancer than did persons with lower levels of vitamin A (Wald, Idle, and Boreham, 1980). Other sites of cancer may be similarly affected. This knowledge, accumulating over a period of years and consistent with laboratory and animal investigations, has opened up the possibility of large-scale trials of vitamin A or vitamin A-like substances as a possible means of reducing cancer.

Excessive animal fat in the diet has been firmly associated in studies over the past several decades with cardiovascular disease. Now investigations are under way to ascertain its possible relationship to cancer of certain sites, especially breast and colon. Interestingly, if confirmed, this developmental order (first cardiovascular disease, then cancer) would reverse the sequence in discovering the relationship of cigarette smoking to cancer and cardiovascular disease. Also, the result would be to establish two common exogenous agents, cigarette smoking and excessive fat consumption, as jointly responsible in considerable part for two major categories of disease, cardiovascular and cancer.

Sodium is increasingly accepted as an important factor in high blood pressure. It may also be involved in the development of other forms of cardiovascular disease. Meanwhile other mineral elements, such as selenium and potassium, are attracting scientific attention as possibly more significant for health than previously realized.

From these examples of knowledge about vitamins, fat, and minerals it is evident that we may have only scratched the surface in using nutrition more deliberately for health.

Beyond the many opportunities in the biomedical and environmental fields, however, probably even greater potential for health improvement in the immediate future lies in dealing with behavioral factors. One of the earliest major contributions to understanding the health consequences of behavior in industrial civilization came from the experience of life insurance companies that found a big market during the second quarter of this century. Actuaries working for these companies noted that obesity predicted early mortality. They prepared tables to quantify the relationship, popularized them, and adjusted premiums upward for overweight persons. Thus, moderate rather than excessive eating was identified and accepted as a key factor in maintaining health.

Excessive consumption of alcohol has long been known to be associated with poor health. After Prohibition was repealed, the increase in liver cirrhosis and other adverse effects of too much alcohol drew renewed attention to its effects on health.

During the 1950s and 1960s a large series of research reports identified cigarette smoking as a causative factor not only for lung cancer but also for coronary heart disease and chronic obstructive lung disease.

These three types of behavior—excessive consumption of calories, too much alcohol, and cigarette smoking—produced large mortality consequences. Age-standardized death rates were 844 per 100,000 for persons of "normal" weight; 1,027 among persons 5–14 percent overweight; 1,215 for those 15–24 percent overweight; and 1,472 for persons 25 or more percent overweight (Dublin, Lotka, and Spiegelman 1949). A Canadian study disclosed that approximately one-fifth of all mortality before age seventy was attributable to cigarette smoking and excessive alcohol (Ouellet, Romeder, and Lance 1977).

A series of investigations in the Human Population Laboratory, conducted in Alameda County by the California State Department of Public Health during the 1960s and 1970s, showed an association between seven habits (including the three mentioned above) and physical health status (Belloc and Breslow 1972). Initiated for the purpose of measuring health and its relationship to ways of living, the first

Human Population Laboratory studies were based on a survey of 7,000 persons representing the adult population of Alameda County. The questionnaire covered things that people do (or don't do) daily as an indication of life-style, and several items to indicate health status. Results indicated that those who eat breakfast; eat regular meals rather than snacking; and eat moderately; exercise some; do not smoke cigarettes; drink alcohol moderately, if at all; and sleep seven to eight hours a night had better physical health status than persons who did not maintain these habits. At every age from twenty to seventy years those who followed all seven habits had better physical health than those who followed six, six better than five, five better than four, four better than three, and three better than two or fewer. Persons fifty to seventy years of age who followed all seven of the habits had approximately the same physical health status as that of persons thirty years younger who followed fewer than three. Association of the habits with physical health status persisted not only for person of all ages and both sexes but also at all income levels.

Further investigation revealed a similarly strong association between the seven habits and subsequent mortality (Belloc, 1973). Based on mortality experience during the five and a half years after the survey, the average expectation of life of forty-five-year-old men who were following three or fewer of the habits was to age sixty-seven. Those forty-five-year-old men following four to five habits had a life expectancy of seventy-three years; and those with six to seven of the habits, seventy-eight years. That eleven-year difference, sixty-seven to seventy-eight, may be compared with the gain of only four years in longevity from 1900 to 1970 among U.S. men at age forty-five. For women of comparable age in the Alameda study, the longevity contrast in respect to health habits was seven years.

To determine whether the habits and their relationship to mortality persisted over time, the population was studied again nine and a half years after the original survey (Breslow and Enstrom 1980). The data showed considerable stability in the pattern. Among men following zero to three of the habits in 1965, 72 percent of the survivors were in the zero to four group in 1974; among those following six to seven of the habits in 1965, 63 percent were still in the same group and another 27 percent had changed only to five. Among women the findings were essentially the same.

While the mortality gradient was somewhat higher in the first two and a half years than subsequently, the association persisted strongly not only through the next three years but through the following four years. Also, at nine and a half years, the mortality follow-up revealed a continuing association with the seven habits into the later years of life. That was particularly true for men among whom it persisted beyond the age of seventy-five years (Table 3.6).

The Human Population Laboratory provided, in addition, an opportunity to study how social network relates to physical health and mortality. In the original HPL concept social well-being was defined as the extent and strength of a person's connection with his social milieu: family, close friends, and relatives; work-situation; church and other social groups; and general citizenry. Based on items from that part of the questionnaire a social network index was constructed for each person in the sample, using measures of family and other close ties and church and other group membership. Table 3.7 indicates the mortality gradient between those with the weakest social network (S.N.I. 1) and those with the strongest (S.N.I. 8–12) among persons thirty to seventy years of age. It is quite consistent for persons of both sexes and with various habit patterns. Of considera-

TABLE 3.6   Percentage Dying in 9½ Years by Health Practice Score

HEALTH PRACTICE SCORE	AGE-ADJUSTED*	UNDER 45	45–54	55–64	65–74	75+
		MEN (AGE IN 1965)				
0–3	20	5	19	38	63	88
4	14	2	11	20	49	95
5	13	1	10	27	49	75
6	11	2	8	19	37	62
7	6	0	2	9	23	47
Total	13	2	10	22	44	72
		WOMEN (AGE IN 1965)				
0–3	12	3	7	20	43	75
4	11	2	6	18	35	69
5	8	2	2	12	33	57
6	8	2	7	9	24	57
7	5	0	2	8	7	75
Total	9	2	5	13	27	59

Source: Adapted from Breslow and Enstrom 1980.
* Age-adjusted by the direct method to the total 1965 survey sample.

ble interest is the combined effect of habits and social network. Only 4.4 percent of women who both had a strong social network and followed six to seven of the habits died within nine and a half years, whereas 15.2 percent of those at the other end of the scale died during the same time period. Among men the difference was even greater; the death rate of men with the weakest social network and who followed only four or fewer habits was five times higher than the rate among men who had the strongest social networks and who also followed six to seven of the habits.

TABLE 3.7   Age-Adjusted Mortality Rates from All Causes (Per 100) among Persons Ages 30–69 at 9½ Years by Social Network Index and Health Habits Scale

MEN S.N.I.	HEALTH HABITS			
	0–4 POS (N)	5 POS (N)	6–7 POS (N)	Total
1	21.5 (73)	9.9 (48)	10.5 (37)	15.6 (158)
2–5	14.6 (251)	11.7 (162)	9.9 (192)	12.2 (605)
6–7	10.3 (229)	9.9 (215)	6.6 (258)	8.6 (702)
8–12	7.8 (230)	9.5 (239)	4.2 (295)	6.2 (764)
Total	12.3 (783)	10.2 (664)	6.7 (782)	9.5 (2229)

WOMEN S.N.I.	0–4 POS (N)	5 POS (N)	6–7 POS (N)	Total
1	15.2 (123)	8.5 (83)	10.0 (70)	12.1 (276)
2–5	10.4 (323)	7.5 (272)	4.0 (265)	7.2 (860)
6–7	5.8 (202)	4.7 (189)	4.3 (211)	4.9 (602)
8–12	6.5 (191)	2.4 (234)	4.4 (333)	4.3 (758)
Total	9.3 (839)	5.6 (770)	4.7 (879)	6.4 (2496)

Source: Berkman and Syme 1979.

Current Trends and Issues

Encouragement to health promotion in the 1980s is coming from recent favorable trends both in mortality and health-risk factors. Following the plateau in mortality statistics during the period around 1960, the years since 1965 have brought substantial improvement. Infant mortality has dropped by half and coronary heart disease mortality by one-fourth from their levels in 1965, and longevity beginning at age sixty-five has increased two years since 1960. Large-scale health advances have been occurring. While the explanation for these is not clear, one can note concomitant improvement in regard to several health-risk factors: decline in proportion of infants with low birth weight; drop in cigarette smoking, especially among men; somewhat lower cholesterol levels; and much improved high blood pressure control.

Meanwhile, public attitudes are becoming more favorable to health maintenance. In 1978, a Louis Harris Associates national poll disclosed that two-fifths of the general public believed our health-care system should give more emphasis to preventive, less to curative, medicine. Only one-tenth believed the reverse; the rest thought the balance about right or were not sure. The same poll showed even stronger support for greater emphasis on preventive medicine and less on curative medicine among business leaders (four-fifths) and union leaders (nine-tenths). These favorable attitudes are relatively new and growing. Compared with five years previously, half of the general public and three-fourths of both business and union leaders said they were more concerned about "preventive health" today, and practically all the remainder reported they were just as concerned. More than nine-tenths of all three groups—general public, business and labor leaders—believed that "if we Americans lived healthier lives, ate more nutritious food, smoked less, maintained our proper weight, and exercised regularly, it would do more to improve our health than anything doctors and medicine could do for us."

The California Medical Association in February 1976 reported similar views among medical students and young physicians. During the 1970s an increasing majority of medical students and recent graduates from California schools expressed agreement that "medical education should place more emphasis on preventive and less on curative aspects of medical practice."

Now shaping up is the question whether the "medical model" or the "community model" or some combination offers the greater potential in health promotion. The medical model, epitomized by the Multiple Risk Factor Intervention Trial (MRFIT) sponsored by the National Heart Lung Blood Institute, consists of medically identifying persons at high risk of coronary heart disease and then trying to lower their risk factors through medical means. The community model consists of using mass media and other means to lower risk factors in the population as a whole (Farquhar et al. 1977). Investigations of these two approaches are under way.

Incorporating health promotion into the American health-care system has been frustrated by several factors in addition to past medical education. Probably an important element has been the fee-for-service payment mechanism which emphasizes surgery and other therapeutic actions and diagnostic procedures but does not generally pay for health-maintenance services. Some important shifts in that regard may be occurring. For example, Blue Cross in southern California is assisting development of prepaid health maintenance organizations.

It seems likely that health-promotion efforts will grow in the immediate future, with the aim of realizing the potential in that approach to health. In these efforts it will be important to avoid exaggerated claims and to base action on evidence that benefit will accrue, and prudent interpretation of that evidence. For more effective measures directed toward medical services, the environment and behavior as means of promoting health, scientific advances are still very much needed. Hence, devoting substantial resources to the development of such knowledge should continue. At the same time it seems wise to proceed on the basis of knowledge that has already been well established. Clearly, while we need to ascertain more about the causation of health problems and how to deal with them, we still fail to do what is now in our power to do in the promotion of health. Community, state, and national mobilization of available resources, together with motivating individuals toward a more healthful life-style to the extent of our present understanding, would extend and enlarge twentieth-century health achievements through the balance of this century and into the next.

REFERENCES

BELLOC, N. B. 1973. Relationship of health practices and mortality. *Preventive Medicine* 2: 67–81.

——, and BRESLOW, L. 1972. Relationship of health status and health practices. *Preventive Medicine* 1: 409–21.

BERKMAN, L. F., and SYME, S. L. 1979. Social networks, host resistance, and mortality. *American Journal of Epidemiology* 109:186–204.

BRESLOW, L., and ENSTROM, J. E. 1980. Persistence of health habits and their relationship to mortality. *Preventive Medicine* 9: 469–83.

BRESLOW, L.; HENDERSON, B.; MASSEY, F.; PIKE, M.; and WINKELSTEIN, W. 1977. Report of NCI ad hoc working group on the gross and net benefits of mammography in mass screening for the detection of breast cancer. *Journal of the National Cancer Institute* 59: 475–78.

BRESLOW, L., and HOCHSTIM, J. R. 1964. Sociocultural aspects of cervical cytology in Alameda County, California. *Public Health Reports* 79: 107–12, 1964.

BRESLOW, L., and SOMERS, A. 1977. The lifetime health monitoring program. *New England Journal of Medicine* 296: 601–8.

California Department of Public Health. *Human population laboratory.* Unpublished data.

California Medical Association. 1976. *The survey of attitudes of medical students and recent graduates.* February 1976.

Commission on Chronic Illness. 1957. *Prevention of chronic illness.* Vol. 1. Cambridge: Harvard University Press.

DUBLIN, L. I.; LOTKA, A. J.; and SPIEGELMAN, M. 1949. *Length of life.* New York: Ronald Free Press Co.

FARQUHAR, J. W., et al. 1977. Community education for cardiovascular health. *Lancet*, pp. 1192–95.

Louis Harris Associates. 1978. *Health maintenance.* Results of a survey commissioned by Pacific Mutual Life Insurance Company.

Multiple Risk Factor Intervention Trial (MRFIT). 1976. *Journal of the American Medical Association* 235: 825–27.

National Cancer Institute. 1978. Concensus development meeting on breast cancer screening, September 14–16, 1977. DHEW Publication No. (NIH) 78–1257.

OUELLET, B. L.; ROMEDER, J. M.; and LANCE, J. M. 1977. *Premature mortality attributable to smoking and hazardous drinking in Canada.* Canada: Department of Health and Welfare.

U.S. Department of Health, Education and Welfare. 1978. *Indian health trends and services. DHEW Publication No. (HSA) 78-12009.*

———. 1979a. Public Health Service, Centers for Disease Control.

———. 1979b. *Smoking and health: A report of the surgeon general.* DHEW Publication No.(PHS) 79-50066.

———. 1979c. *Healthy people: The surgeon general's report on health promotion and disease prevention.* DHEW (PHS) Publication No. 79-55071.

U.S. Department of Health and Human Services. 1980a. Public Health Service, Office of Maternal and Child Health.

———. 1980b. *Promoting health and preventing disease: objectives for the nation.* DHHS (PHS) U.S. Government Printing Office.

———. 1981. *Health: United States 1980. DHHS Publication No. (PHS) 81-1232.*

WALD, N.; IDLE, M.; and BOREHAM, J. 1980. *Low serum vitamin-A and subsequent risk of cancer. Lancet,* pp. 813-15.

Chapter 4

The Politics of Health

T. R. Marmor
Andrew Dunham
with the assistance of Julie Greenberg

IT IS ALMOST OBLIGATORY for articles on American medical care to begin with an incantation on the soaring social investment in medicine. Most readers are now aware that expenditures on medical care have risen from 4.6 percent of GNP in 1950 to 8.8 percent in 1977 (*Special analyses,* 1979, p. 242). Astounding as this increase may be, it would be mistaken to construe it as the key to the character of political struggles affecting the health industry.

Health is not a very useful category for political analysis. It implies the existence of a single structure of government activity affecting this substantive area. It further implies that because programs affect health, they are the products of a similar political process with similar actors and outcomes. This is not the case. Some programs affect financing of care, others investment in medical-care resources, and still others, regulation of medical-care systems. Some programs that affect health are highly controversial, others have low visibility. Simply knowing that a program is a health program does not tell us who will be concerned, what position they will take, or what outcome is likely.

The recent changes in the politics of health lie not in the basic character of these struggles but in their increasing stakes and diversity. The political battles range widely, with instances of special pleading for resources, regulatory strife, and broad national debate over the proper role of the government, each quite akin to policy struggles in education, energy production and distribution, or other domestic policy areas. But because the health-care industry is so large, the broad spectrum of struggles will include many that are politically salient.

Despite continuing controversy about government's proper role in medicine, the federal government has been extraordinarily active in recent decades. In 1967, health-care expenditures accounted for 6.8 percent of total federal outlays; in 1979, they had grown steadily to 12.7 percent (*Special analyses* 1979, p. 242). Our focus here will be on federal health programs, despite the extensive role states play in medical regulation and finance and the salience of local health controversies.

Federal Health-Care Programs and Politics

There are, of course, various approaches to explaining the recent changes in the federal role in medical care. It is useful to start by saying how not to characterize federal health activity. One should not regard the expansion of federal activity as a consequence of a deliberate federal health policy, for there is no such policy. There are various federal policies that affect health, not a health policy per se. Federal action consists of a multitude of programs with differing histories, politics, goals, and results. After analyzing the circumstances surrounding the notable absence of one particular program—national health insurance—this essay will examine both the major federal programs of the last several decades and the politics relevant to those programs. Discussion of the programs' histories and characteristics will not be comprehensive, since the aim is to highlight features of special political significance.

With many federal health programs slated by the new Reagan administration for reduction, if not complete elimination, the reader may wonder about their inclusion in this discussion. First, the political forces and ideologies that have created our present mix of policies and that will continue to shape debate about health can be most concretely described if they are linked to particular programs, regardless of those programs' projected life expectancies. Second, there is both a resiliency of health programs and an iterative nature to many forms of administrative arrangements that together make the stability of the basic structure of government health programs very likely, despite surges of clamor for revolutionary reform and reform "at the margin."

Financing Programs

NATIONAL HEALTH INSURANCE. The most important feature of federal health financing in the past decade has been a continued stalemate over national health insurance legislation. In this respect, the United States is idiosyncratic, alone among the industralized nations in not having a national health insurance program.

The national health insurance stalemate involves the stable, long-term efforts of large national pressure groups, many unconcerned with most health issues. Argument over national health insurance is markedly ideological, with positions reflecting deeply rooted views of the proper role of the national government in a public/private and federal/state mix of authority and responsibility. There is little room for compromise over such issues. Despite countless reports, congressional hearings, academic studies, and warnings of medical-care crisis, there is little or no adjustment of positions from an ideological perspective. The particular policy *expression* of stable ideological elements may change of course; such a change can be seen in the development of the "procompetitive" approaches to health-care reform that will be discussed later. But the pro- and anti-government themes continue to dominate.

There is no agreement on which problems are most pressing, let alone on the merits of proposed responses. Solutions to one problem conflict with solutions to another. As the AMA has pointed out, "any system of medical care depends basically on balancing three strong and competing dynamics: the desire to make medical care available to all, the desire to control cost, and the desire for high quality care "(AMA statement on national health insurance 1971, p. 1951). Any two of these goals work against the third.

Even the one issue that all sides view with alarm—cost—is composed of three separate problems: cost to the consumer, cost to the government, and cost to the nation. Consumers worry about high out-of-pocket costs and the possibility of catastrophic medical expenses. Government-sponsored insurance could reduce the cost to the consumer at point of use and could protect against financial catastrophe, but such programs would fuel inflationary tendencies. This would exacerbate the third cost problem: the high percentage of the nation's resources that is devoted to medical care. While a national health insurance program like that proposed in various bills introduced by Edward Kennedy, which would federalize virtually all medical expenses, provides at least the potential to control the total social outlays on health, it would also vastly increase government expenditures. Thus responses to the three cost problems also work against each other.

The struggle over national health insurance continues with the same stable stalemate of national forces that has been noted in other redistributive policy debates. In the meantime, United States financing programs continue as a series of discrete programs aimed at specific clientele. Indeed, so strong is the clientele orientation that many of the programs will continue even if a comprehensive national health insurance program is enacted. All of the major NHI plans of the 1970s retained veterans' medical benefits, for example. This point again illustrates that each public health-care program must be examined individually to understand its operation, impact, and political peculiarities.

MEDICARE AND MEDICAID. The different treatment of expenditures for Medicare (which finances medical care for the aged) and Medicaid (which finances medical care for the indigent) is politically instructive. While total expenditures for the two programs have grown at about the same pace since their inception in 1965, Medicaid has been subject to extensive criticism and reduction in benefits and eligibility, while Medicare has been neither seriously attacked nor cut back. The Reagan administration's earliest budget proposals are the latest illustration of this different treatment. Medicare, as a national program symbolizing redistributive themes, stimulates the same political forces that have generated stalemate over NHI. While that stalemate has prevented the initiation of a national health insurance program, it has also prevented any cutbacks of Medicare. Expenditures have risen, but the benefits and beneficiaries have not fundamentally changed since its advent. Further, since Medicare is largely financed through social security taxes, it has been partly insulated from state and local struggles over budget distribution and attempts to control expenditure through program retrenchment.

The contrast to Medicare is striking. Part of the different treatment, of course, is due to the fact that the elderly are a more popular clientele than the poor. But the nature of program beneficiaries alone cannot explain the different political reactions to Medicare and Medicaid. Medicaid, after all, also pays for the elderly's care since many of them are poor. In fact, a larger proportion of Medicaid expenditures have historically gone to the elderly than to recipients of Aid to Families with Dependent Children (AFDC) (Holahan, 1975, p. 13).

The key difference between Medicare and Medicaid is not their different clientele but the different political markets they face. Medicaid is a state-run program, and the depth and breadth of coverage is therefore a state and local rather than a national issue. Support for the program is fragmented in smaller, statewide constituencies, making political mobilization difficult. The effective coalition of national organizations that support Medicare is less active at the state level.

While support for Medicaid is diffuse, the opposition is intense since the state portion of Medicaid is financed out of general revenues. Any increase in benefits, beneficiaries, utilization, or medical-care prices must be met by an increase in state expenditures. The strain on state budgets generated by increased welfare rolls and medical inflation has produced continued demands for state fiscal relief. States have "solved" problems of high Medicaid expenditures by cutting back on benefits and eligibility.

OTHER FEDERAL HEALTH FINANCING PROGRAMS. A number of other programs emerged or were expanded in the 1960s: Neighborhood Health Centers; Maternal and Child Health Programs; the Early and Periodic Screening, Diagnosis and Treatment Program (EPSDT); and Community Mental Health Centers.

None of these programs can muster even as much political support as was behind Medicaid. For example, a program like the Neighborhood Health Centers produced distributive benefits to particular communities. With the erosion of support at the national level for the War on Poverty, and with stricter budget constraints, these centers depended for existence on the support they could generate in the communities they were to serve. But centers basically only served their poor, unorganized, and powerless clientele, and could not easily enlist the support of other major and politically more significant groups.

Medicaid at least serves important economic interests, since payments go directly to providers. While it is true that some providers will not serve Medicaid clients, the fact remains that many doctors, hospitals, and nursing homes receive substantial funds from Medicaid. In contrast, such groups had no real stake in a Neighborhood Health Center, and, in fact, it may actually have reduced their own business.

In addition to the Great Society initiatives aimed at expanding the medical care received by the poor and underserved, there are a number of traditional distributive programs aimed at providing benefits to specific clienteles. These programs, all of which preceded the initiation of redistributive programs, do not share the political salience and conflict of Medicare or Medicaid. Nor have they faced the same concern about expenditures, and indeed several of the programs have actually been expanded in recent years. The programs have not escaped controversy because they are fiscally insignificant. The Veterans Administration and the Department of Defense, for example, had a total combined health budget of $9.8 billion in 1979 for programs providing direct services to veterans and servicemen and for those financing care in the civilian sector (CHAMPVA and CHAMPUS). (*Special analyses* 1979, p. 247).

The basis of the stability they exhibit lies not in their size but in the character and distribution of their beneficiaries: These distributive programs enlist the support of organized, concerned groups and a committed federal bureaucracy.

The federal government also provides direct care for Indians and native Alaskans, subsidizes the purchase of private insurance through the tax system, allows medical tax deductions, and helps pay for the health insurance benefits of its employees.

These various federal programs that finance or provide medical care offer a bewildering variety of beneficiaries and programmatic fates. Their development cannot be understood in terms of the health or medical needs of the beneficiaries. However, some ordering of the programs can be imposed if we look at government action as a response to forces in the political market rather than to medical needs. Imbalanced political markets explain much of the uneven development of federal programs.

The political market approach begins by asking who has an interest in a government action (pro or con), how intense the interest is, and how effectively that interest can be expressed. This requires an examination of the organization, available resources, and the size and geographical dispersal of the affected constituencies. Put simply, those programs that have the backing of powerful organizations and constituencies with significant stakes in the program, and with sufficient resources to express their demands, will tend to prosper. Thus veterans' medical benefits have expanded since veterans are an organized clientele group and have a supportive bureaucracy, while Neighborhood Health Centers stagnated with a clientele of limited political resources. In general, programs for the poor fare poorly. One exception is the treatment of Indians and native Alaskans, but those groups have an established federal bureaucracy to support both their claims and its own organizational maintenance.

MORE ON THE NATURE OF HEALTH-CARE FINANCING PROGRAMS. The theory of imbalanced political markets cannot provide a complete explication of the development of federal financing and delivery programs, although it does provide a fair first approximation. It certainly is more powerful than explanations based on the health and medical needs of program recipients. And, unlike an approach that looks for a singular "politics of health," it can account for variations between programs. What it cannot do is explain some of the very largest and smallest programmatic changes of postwar American health politics.

For example, if one takes an international perspective, the structures of political market do not easily explain why the United States is different from other industrialized countries in its approach to financing medical care. Nor do they explain why the United States initiated programs for the underserved *at all*, and why such initiatives came when they did. That explanation lies in a shift in political forces at the national level, particularly with the Johnson landslide, that allowed an old statemate to be broken and brought many major new initiatives in health and other areas. Thus the politically less influential did acquire programs that were designed to benefit them, although the political-market approach would suggest that such groups seldom get their way.

The structure of the political market also cannot account for outcomes whose causes were idiosyncratic. For example, in 1972 amendments to the Social Security Act extended Medicare coverage to the disabled and to persons with chronic kidney disease, regardless of age. These are not insignificant additions; the latter addition alone added an estimated cost of $1.2 billion in 1979 (Rettig 1980, p. vii). There is no systematic explanation for why they occurred, however. The kidney amendment passed Congress almost by chance. Certainly it is hard to understand why end-stage renal disease was covered and why hemophilia, heart disease, or other "catastrophic" illnesses were not. The explanation almost surely requires detailed facts about specific actors, such as the skills of the promoters of kidney coverage who did extensive lobbying and arranged demonstrations by dialysis patients in front of a congressional committee.

The establishment of this program is an example of the different politics of programs dealing with identifiable lives and statistical lives. The political response in the former case is to a specific group who can be readily identified as beneficiaries. They have an obvious and intense stake in the outcome. By contrast, a program for, say, automobile safety may well save more lives at less cost, but it has only potential beneficiaries who cannot be identified in advance.

The absence of a single political market for health means that struggles over initiation and administration differ sharply. A national coalition forged to get a program enacted is seldom unified enough to monitor the implementation of the program. Thus Medicare passed over the opposition of the providers, but many of the key administrative decisions (e.g., how to pay the providers) escaped the detailed review of the national coalition that prompted the bill's enactment. This pattern of change in interest group efficacy produces cyclical program development. National legislation amid crisis is followed by implementation problems, which in turn create pressures for new reforms.

From a comparative perspective, the most striking feature of American health-financing policies is the relative weakness of government authority in health. Provider opposition delayed significant government financing of medical care for the poor, and indeed still prevents full coverage. What is more, even when the federal government implements programs, it has seldom challenged the fundamental interests of providers. This may now be changing in some areas. But it is still true that governmental coercion of providers is minimized. The liberal tradition in America leads to a limited exercise of government authority vis-à-vis the dominant health interest groups. The liberal ideology, coupled with the weakness of party government, particularly of a party based on a working-class movement, results in policy development on a program-by-program basis and policies that vary depending on the political market each faces.

Federal Programs Related to Medical Resources

FACILITIES. It is now generally agreed that there is a surplus of hospital beds in many parts of the country. The federal government, which for years was involved in the construction of health facilities (mostly hospitals) through the Hill-Burton program, has virtually eliminated direct funding of general construction. Indeed, federal regulatory programs are now designed to restrict facility growth.

The elimination of facility construction subsidies represents an unusual political occurrence: the end of a "pork barrel" program. However, the direct subsidy of construction has been replaced by an indirect federal contribution to capital expenditures through programs that finance medical services. The Social Security Administration's concern over obtaining provider participation in the Medicare program led to generous depreciation and interest allowances in cost-based reimbursements. As a consequence, the federal government now pays for expansion and modernization through reimbursement mechanisms, but it has less direct control over the amount of capital investment and its location than when the Hill-Burton subsidies were line items in the federal budget. Indeed, this indirect subsidy is much greater than Hill-Burton ever was (*Special analyses* 1978, p. 215).

Even this more subtle subsidy to health facilities is now being challenged. The Carter administration proposed a national limit on total capital expenditures by hospitals. Along with other regulatory programs, it represented pressure by the federal government to restrict the growth of hospital facilities (and hence expenditures) and demonstrated that the political market in this area is now partly balanced. While the hospitals still have a concentrated stake in maintaining federal payments and control over their investment decisions, it is countered by the stake the federal government now has in the level of the nation's medical expenditures. The pressure on federal health officials to control government health expenditures in turn results in attempts to restrict both subsidies to health-care providers and providers' decision-making autonomy.

MANPOWER. Federal health manpower policy is moving from a voluntary approach, emphasizing incentives for the appropriate production or distribution of personnel, toward a more regulated system. Until recently, federal policy was aimed at simply increasing the quantity of physicians, nurses, and other medical personnel. The problems of geographic and specialty distribution, it was believed, could be solved through the operations of the market. An increased supply was also expected to help ease the problem of the rapidly rising cost of physicians' services.

The supply of health manpower has indeed increased in the last decade. Yet as of 1976 this increased supply did not seem to have appreciably affected the problems of distribution. The disparity in the physician-to-population ratio, both across states and between rural and urban areas, worsened between World War II and 1976. And increased supply also does not seem to have reduced the phenomenon of increased specialization; while the total number of physicians is increasing nationally, the proportion of practicing general practitioners is falling (Hadley 1980, p. 190). Additionally, increasing the number of physicians has not reduced physicians' fees.

In 1965 Congress attacked geographic maldistribution by forgiving loans to medical graduates willing to practice in underserved areas. In 1971 Congress addressed specialty maldistribution by providing incentives to medical schools to emphasize family practice. In 1976 medical schools were required to have a minimum proportion of residencies in family medicine. The schools are also supposed to reserve a portion of their enrollment for students who will practice in underserved areas. Federal capitation grants are tied to compliance with provisions designed to achieve these goals. The 1976 manpower bill also restricted the entry of "foreign medical graduates" into the United States.

But manpower problems remain. A controversial 1980 report of the Graduate Medical Education National Advisory Committee (GMENAC) making numerous recommendations aimed at averting a physician surplus by the year 2000 may stimulate further legislation. It is likely that the political debate on such legislation will be encompassed in a broader dispute over competition in the health industry. The issue then will be the connection between health manpower and medical-care competition and, in particular, the question of whether physician surpluses will not only increase competition among physicians but lower their fees as well.

Regulation

The medical industry is a complex mix of public and private action. Precisely because of public financing of much medical care, the private actions of patients, physicians, and other professionals dramatically affect governmental expenditures. The relatively recent efforts of the federal and state governments to control medical-care outlays is but the latest regulatory connection between the state and the medical professions. Earlier, it was concern about the quality of care provided that justified the role of the government as the source of license to practice; today, the most powerful pressures for governmental regulation arise in connection with the relative inflation in medical care generally and the rise in public medical budgets in particular. During the 1970s these pressures resulted in four regulatory initiatives that we will now discuss.

RATE REGULATION. There are basically three types of federal policies to control the rate of payment to providers. First, federal financing programs restrict payment to cover "reasonable costs." Usually this has meant that the government has prohibited hospitals from spreading the costs of treating private patients to federal programs. The government has also refused to pay for other than "allowable costs," meaning that certain items (e.g., a new parking lot) or outrageously high charges have not been covered. However, since virtually unlimited revenues can be absorbed in the categories for which reimbursement is certain (new services, more intensive care, fancier technology), this has been neither an effective cost-control mechanism nor a major impetus to medical reform.

In 1972 Congress attempted to prevent federal payments from contributing to the unnecessary expansion of facilities. The legislation enacted—Section 1122 of the Social Security Act—stated that the costs associated with construction (depreciation and interest) would not be considered allowable costs if the hospital did not get a "certificate of need" from a state agency. It should be noted that the federal government could reduce payments only after the state government denied the certificate of need; the federal government could not initiate action.

The second major approach to rate regulation has been to place limits on increases in prices or charges. The prime example of this is the Economic Stabilization Program (ESP), which between 1971 and 1974 placed controls first on the cost increases that could be passed on in charges and then, in Phase IV, on the total charge per admission. ESP had a very definite short-term impact on hospital costs and lowered the inflation rate in the medical sector. But after the program ended there were "catch up" attempts and very sharp price increases.

The Carter administration proposed a ceiling on increases in hospital revenues. This approach is administratively easy, at least compared to the complex forms of incentive or prospective reimbursement. But ceilings have a tendency to become floors, so that the "Limit" in effect becomes the norm for rate increases. And such ceilings do not provide direct incentives for changing behavior toward increased efficiency; since the existing operation is the base on which the increase is calculated, existing inefficiences are perpetuated.

Finally, rate regulation can involve incentive or prospective reimbursement. In essence, in this form of regulation determination of rate or revenue levels is no longer made exclusively by the provider. Levels of charges or revenues are set, and the provider is given incentives to provide care at costs within those limits. There are an immense number of different approaches possible (e.g., based on costs per admission, per patient day, per service; global, departmental, or line item budget review), but each has theoretical drawbacks and is difficult to administer.

FACILITIES REGULATION AND PLANNING. The 1974 National Health Planning and Resources Development Act requires health-care facilities to obtain prior approval from the state—in the form of a "certificate of need"—before undertaking any major capital investments. The rationale for this regulation of investments is that there is a surplus of hospital facilities in this country. Since beds tend to be used whether needed or not, excess supply has a significant impact on medical costs. Health Systems Agencies (described below) must review all investment proposals in their area and recommend approval or disapproval to the state certificate-of-need agency. But it is that agency which finally decides whether to issue a certificate of need and allow new projects. The federal government does not make the decision.

The 1974 act also provided authorization for over two-hundred local health planning agencies. These Health Systems Agencies (HSAs) replace a network of planning agencies established by the Comprehensive Health Planning Act of 1967. The old planning agencies never had adequate funding. By 1974, one-fifth of the country still had no established planning agencies. Of the established agencies, over one-third were still in the "developmental phase" (U. S. Senate 1974, p. 10). Planning agencies were often dependent on medical providers for operating funds and had been accused of being subservient to them.

The new HSAs were provided with more federal funding and were forbidden to use provider contributions. Although more federal funds are now available, the establishment of planning agencies continues to be a slow process. There has been a great deal of conflict over the drawing of the HSA boundaries and over the designation of the operating agency. At the local level political squabbles have centered on HSA board membership.

HSAs are supposed to identify local health resources and needs, produce a local plan establishing the goals for the area, and develop an "implementation plan" describing projects and priorities to meet the goals. In particular, HSAs are supposed to encourage cheaper forms of care (e.g., ambulatory rather than inpatient), increase the continuity of care, and prevent unnecessary duplication of facilities. However, one study of state and local planning agencies found local health plans were not detailed or concrete enough to be used in determining the need for new medical facilities (Comptroller General 1974, p. 18). Another study found that there were no significant differences in medical-care systems between local areas that had operating planning agencies and areas that did not (May 1974, p. 48). In short, the federal government has provided funds for planning agencies, but there is little evidence that effective planning actually takes place.

UTILIZATION REGULATION. A third method of reforming the medical industry involves regulation of the utilization of medical services. The original Medicare/Medicaid bill required hospital-based "utilization review" committees to review cases to see if treatment was medically necessary. However, this provision was not seriously enforced. In 1972 amendments to the Social Security Act (PL92-103) authorized the establishment of a network of Professional Standards Review Organizations (PSROs) to review the quality and necessity of services provided to all Medicare, Medicaid, and Maternal and Child Health patients. PSROs would review services when a hospital did not have an acceptable utilization review program.

PSROs are organizations of practicing physicians. However, resistance and criticism from doctors and hospitals in some areas greatly delayed the establishment of operating PSROs. Even in the areas that have operating organizations, now the majority, the review process has not been extensive.

Ironically, recent proposals to reduce funding for or entirely scrap the organizations met with protest from the American Medical Association. Clearly, organized medicine now fears that stronger government measures to control utilization would follow in the wake of the elimination of PSROs.

It is interesting that no other industrial nation has tried to control utilization through direct regulation and review of physician decisions. We have resorted to this partly because the dominant payment method in the United States—fee-for-service with no limits on total expenditures—creates incentives for excessive utilization. Yet Canada has similar payment mechanisms but has not attempted to directly regulate physician decisions.

It is ironic that the United States, where professional dominance is so striking, has also legislated what appears to be a striking intervention into doctors' prerogatives. On the other hand, utilization regulation as it now exists affects physicians who do not conform to the established practices of the profession; it does not constrain the behavior of the majority of physicians.

Health Maintenance Organizations.   Another attempt to control indirectly the utilization of medical services has received a great deal of political attention in recent years. There is evidence that Health Maintenance Organizations (HMOs) are less costly than the traditional method of organizing the delivery of medical services. HMOs provide comprehensive medical services for a fixed payment. The organization must keep the cost of the services it provides within a fixed budget. Therefore, HMOs, unlike private physicians and hospitals, have incentives to provide care as cheaply as possible.

In 1970 the Nixon administration declared that HMOs were the centerpiece of its health policy. HMOs were popular in the conservative administration since they were potentially less costly, they promoted competition and free enterprise (patients could choose whether to enroll or not, so each HMO had to sell its product to consumers), and an HMO strategy could theoretically restructure the medical industry with a minimum of government regulation and interference. It was not until 1973, however, that Congress finally passed the Health Maintenance Act authorizing $375 million to promote the expansion of HMOs.

Many physicians and insurance companies have strongly opposed the development of HMOs. American physicians have always fought any threat to the fee-for-service standard, and they continued to oppose HMO development even after the HMO definition was expanded to include fee-for-service doctors in medical foundations. Some insurance companies saw HMOs as competitors for consumers choosing between purchases of prepaid medical care or insurance.

While the bill authorized subsidies to HMOs to help in their start-up costs, it also placed strict conditions on eligibility. HMOs had to provide a basic package of services, have periodic open enrollment when anyone could join, and charge the same premium to people whether they joined individually or in groups. These restrictions made it very difficult for HMOs to be competitive. People with costly medical problems have incentives to join HMOs and have all their care covered without coinsurance, deductibles, or benefit ceilings. Since the act did not allow

HMOs either to reject such people or to charge them extra premiums, the average subscriber premium was made less attractive relative to commercial insurance.

Also, the level of federal grants and loans to HMOs remained low for some time. From 1974 to 1977, HEW disbursed only $70 million to HMOs. Since subsidies were too small to make up for the costly eligibility requirements, a year and a half after passage of the HMO Act, only 11 of the nation's 173 HMOs had even applied to qualify for federal support (Spitz 1977, p. 1956).

Although this slow start on HMO assistance may not have been permanently crippling—by 1978, 79 of the nation's 203 health plans were federally qualified (Altman and Williams 1981, p. 32)—and 1976 and 1978 amendments to the original legislation reduced the burden of requirements for federal qualification and subsidy, HMOs were not given a great boost by initial forms of government promotion.

The HMO strategy continues to get vocal support, and liberals and conservatives alike see HMOs as a desirable method of delivering medical care. But the development of prepaid group practices is hindered by the high start-up costs (physicians, staff, and facilities must be available before subscribers will join). Rapid development of HMOs would require increased federal subsidies, and that is made unlikely by budget constraints and physician and insurance industry opposition. Though the number of organizations and of subscribers is growing, HMOs will not become the dominant delivery mode in the immediate future.

CONCLUSION ON REGULATION. Federal attempts to regulate and restructure the medical system exhibit certain uniformities. Perhaps the most striking is the gap between legislative action on the one hand and implementation and results on the other.

The HSAs probably best exemplify this gap. The announced aims of the legislation are ambitious: to produce "scientific planning with teeth" and to cut the costs of, rationalize access to, and improve the quality of medical care. HSA authority is highly qualified, however. Though HSAs must review major capital investment proposals, state governments retain the power to issue required certificates of need. HSAs must review the "appropriateness" of all health-care facilities in their areas, but the sanctions for inappropriateness are unclear—indeed the regulations guiding this task remain unpublished. HSAs are simply not equipped to achieve their prescribed aims.

Additionally, in health planning the federal government has delegated authority over issues with national implications to local decision-makers. There is reason to believe that national goals will not be served. HSAs, with a local constituency, will make decisions in the local interest. Even their highly touted requirements for consumer representation will not particularly alter that likelihood, since consumers as well as providers are interested in increasing the supply of medical facilities and services in their locality. A few states and localities may actually restrict facility growth, but the federal government has no control over those that do not.

In general, the federal government mandates that regulatory agencies exist; it does not usually perform the regulation itself. Rate, facility, and utilization regulation have largely been delegated to state or regional organizations. (Medicare reimbursement is governed primarily by federal authorities.) The federal government has little control over how (and so far, whether) the regulatory organizations actually perform.

Finally, it should be stressed that the regulatory efforts of the federal government are in a state of flux. Compared to the federal role of a decade ago, the intervention is dramatic. As expenditures continue to rise, the interest in controlling providers in order to control expenditures also rises. As the political market for regulation becomes more balanced, we can expect still greater efforts to control the medical industry or, alternatively, to stimulate the market forces that some believe would rationalize health-care expenditures and obviate the need for regulation.

The Next Decade

At the outset of the 1960s, the health agenda was dominated by the politics of expansion: to whom would health care be provided, under what auspices, and with what sort of public assistance and private control. By 1980, it was the politics of scarcity that dominated the politics of health. Whether in classic welfare state issues—like national health insurance—or highly visible attacks on medical inflation—like the proposed cost-containment bills of the Carter administration—medicine was on the defensive and the corporate rationalizers in government, business, and the planning profession were on the verbal ascendancy. Yet in all these areas, there has been choice without change, continued "experimentation," legislative stalemate, and very little alteration in underlying arrangements.

There is a less well-known agenda for medical care issues, just as we find in every area of pork barrel and regulatory politics. Hospital expansions now join highways and commercial expansion as disputed local matters; HSAs monitor and try to affect these developments just as downtown councils struggle with the direction of urban building. And, wherever possible, the locals try to externalize the costs and internalize the benefits of expansion or retrenchment. In 1980, New York City's effort to get federal funds to bail out its Brooklyn Jewish Hospital and avoid closing down two Harlem hospitals was hardly notable, though it was extreme. Likewise, the administrative implementation of Medicare and Medicaid sets the affected parties in contests very much like those in other parts of the American administrative state.

For governments, the costs of public programs for medical-care financing drive out opportunities for political adjustment. For reformers, the high stakes mean an endless search for panaceas, whether the HMOs of the early 1970s, the older dream of national health insurance, or the newer contest between the reinvigorated champions of competition and the dispersed regulatory bodies that try to cope with the industry.

It is the procompetitive approach that is likely to generate the most political attention in the coming decade. Rising governmental budgets, coupled with increasingly frequent charges of waste and inefficiency in governmental bureaucracies, have led some to propose that social service delivery systems be structured to accommodate market incentives. In medical care, these procompetitive proponents promise that a "return" to the market will lead to cost containment, more equitable allocation of scarce medical resources, the creation of more rational delivery systems, and the delivery of more appropriate and perhaps better medical care.

While all are labeled procompetitive, the positions advanced under this banner are in fact diverse and distinguishable. They vary in degree of change proposed for

American medicine, the rationale for such change, and their mechanisms, feasibility of implementation, and effects. There are in fact three separable threads of procompetitive logic, though all have interrelated elements.

First, there are those who would enhance consumer sovereignty. Advocates of this approach hold that the market for medical care is no different from other markets; if consumers face incentives that encourage sensible decisions about the amount of care and level of insurance needed, they will change their consumption patterns and consequently alter the medical-care system. Second, there is the view that nonprice competition exists within fee-for-service medicine, whereas price-related competition between fee-for-service and other delivery and financing models would be preferable. From this view, sensible reforms would encourage the establishment of groups of physicians, primarily in prepaid group practices who could compete with physicians offering services on a fee-for-service basis. Third, the proponents of antitrust initiatives hope to reduce the market power of medical-care providers.

The corollary to these proposals, though often unspoken, is that most if not all of the present health-care regulatory apparatus should be dismantled as procompetitive reforms are implemented (Marmor, Boyer, and Greenberg 1981).

The procompetitive reform proposals that directly affect the industry rather than consumers could only be enacted if a powerful political personality acted as an "entrepreneur," creating the political pressure to counterbalance concentrated interests and create a public policy seen to generate public goods. After all, if market mechanisms accomplish all that their proponents promise, consumers will benefit and most providers will suffer. Even if they do not succeed in reducing the medical-care inflation rate and ultimately the proportion of the nation's resources devoted to medical care, they would redirect resources. For example, in reform of the first type, enhancing consumer sovereignty, the insurance industry might suffer; in the second and third approaches, which focus on stimulation of competition, fee-for-service practice would be on the defensive. Additionally, one must remember that parts of the health-care industry have adapted to regulation and benefited thereby. For example, some hospitals have increased their market share through regulatory interference with their competitors' expansion, and others have learned to manipulate their charges to maximize regulated reimbursement rates. These actors will not welcome all forms of procompetitive reform.

The banner of procompetitive reform could be used to cloak a variety of changes in financing or regulatory programs that make at best nominal improvements in the competitive positions of alternatives to fee-for-service practice, and at worst simply reduce government expenditures by forcing consumers to bear greater proportions of the cost of their medical care. The latter "reform" is the most politically feasible in a climate of public retrenchment.

Procompetitive reforms will be proposed with a flourish of ideological slogans that conjure up notions of a medical-care marketplace to which few other industrialized nations in the world subscribe. What the reform proposals will not be accompanied by is the detailed implementation analysis that will show how the proposed change will affect the relevant portions of this gigantic sector of the economy which provides services unlike all others.

Some would argue that in recent procompetitive reform of the transportation and communication industries the rhetoric of reform proposals and those proposals' actual impacts were related in a straightforward fashion. They infer that the same could happen in other industries, including health care. What is forgotten in making this inference is that the government's present impact on the health-care industry is much more complex than it has been on airlines or communication networks and that the market for travel between Topeka and Atlanta or telecommunication lines between San Francisco and Seattle is of simpler construction than that for kidney dialysis or chemotherapy. While competitive health plans, multiple health plan choice, and antitrust activity all have some place in a sensible plan to reorder the medical-care system, their proper roles are not apt to emerge in the antigovernment "mood" politics of the early 1980s.

Despite the new tone of health-care debate, it would be wrong to suggest that this coming decade will witness a change in the political landscape so dramatic that the politics of our present health programs and policies will soon be past history. The programs that have proved to have such resilience in the past—Medicare, Medicaid, veterans' medical care—will maintain themselves long into the impending political struggle between the procompetitive and regulative camps, ensuring that the politics of health will not quickly transformed.

REFERENCES

ALTMAN, S., and WILLIAMS, J. 1981. Federal involvement in the development of Health Maintenance Organizations: competition in the health-care industry. In *Federal health programs: problems and prospects,* ed. S. Altman and H. Sapolsky, pp. 25–39. Lexington, Mass.: Lexington Books.

AMA statement on national health insurance (by Dr. Max Parrot). 1971. *Hearings on national health insurance.* Ways and Means Committee (October–November 1971). Washington, D.C.: Government Printing Office.

Comptroller General of the United States. 1974. *Comprehensive health planning as carried out by states and areawide agencies in three states.* Washington, D.C.: Government Printing Office.

HADLEY, J. Physician supply and distribution. 1980. In *National Health Insurance: conflicting goals and policy choices,* ed. J. Feder, J. Holahan, and T. R. Marmor, pp. 181–267. Washington, D.C.: Urban Institute.

HOLAHAN, J. 1975. *Financing health care for the poor.* Boston: D. C. Heath, 1975.

MARMOR, T. R.; BOYER, R.; and GREENBERG, J. 1981. Medical care and pro-competitive reform. *Vanderbilt Law Review* 34:1003–1028.

MAY, J. 1974. The planning and licensing agencies. In *Regulating health facilities construction,* ed. C. Havighurst, pp. 47–68. Washington, D.C.: American Enterprise Institute.

RETTIG, R. 1980. *Implementing the end-stage renal disease program of Medicare.* R-2505-HCFA/HEW. Santa Monica, Calif.: Rand Corporation.

Special analyses, budget of the United States. Fiscal year 1978. Executive Office of the President, Office of Management and Budget. Washington, D.C.: Government Printing Office.

Special analyses, budget of the United States. Fiscal Year 1979. Executive Office of the President, Office of Management and Budget. Washington, D.C.: Government Printing Office.

SPITZ, B. 1977. HMO reimbursement and regulation. In *Altering Medicaid provider reimbursement methods,* ed. J. Holahan, B. Spitz, W. Polack, and J. Feder. Washington, D.C.: Urban Institute.

U. S. Senate. 1974. National Health Planning and Resources Development Act of 1974. Labor and Public Welfare Committee Senate Report No. 93-1285, pp. 5–7. Washington, D.C.: Government Printing Office.

Chapter 5

Nutritional Patterns, Social Choices, and Health

Beverly Winikoff

Nutrition and Individual Risk

IF IT IS TRUE, as has been said, that "we are what we eat," it is also in some measure the case that we eat as we do *because* of who we are, where we live, when we live, and how our society is structured. Foods available to us are an important part of our social, cultural, and health (or illness-producing) environment. Yet, the individual is not a free agent in regard to dietary choices: important aspects of the diet and the ability to meet nutritional needs without major risks of illness are socially and economically conditioned. Just as both genes and environment determine an individual's health prospects, so both individual choices and environment determine the extent and magnitude of exposure to risk factors for disease. Depending upon the range of choices in the environment, individual behaviors can be more or less successful in modifying exposure to risks. This is as true for nutrition as it is for exposure to industrial carcinogens or air pollution.

Clearly, major health risks associated with inappropriate nutrition are modifiable, but only by a combination of action at the individual and societal levels. Where the nutritional environment is narrowly defined by economic, legal, or social restraints or narrow choices in the marketplace, the individual's ability to manipulate dietary choices is also constrained. Only where a wide range of suitable choices at a reasonable price is available to most individuals can each assume some responsibility for the dietary decisions that affect health. In addition, rational behaviors can be expected only if all individuals are well informed about both the risks associated with different dietary choices and the constituents of different food products as well as the means to obtain them. Any free-market, laissez-faire approach to the "nutrition delivery" system thus requires, as an adjunct, an effective method of guaranteeing wide dissemination of appropriate information to ensure ability of consumers to choose more desirable food items.

Because of the close link between nutrition and other social systems, any discussion of health that defines "nutrition" as the area of primary interest risks obscuring the fact that some problems that can be labeled "nutritional" might also be seen as problems of poverty, housing, marketing, or agriculture, and not necessarily problems of eating. Of course, it is easier to discuss health issues in terms of the relationship of individual behaviors to individual health outcomes, and eating patterns are the behavioral results of a host of more general social forces. Life-styles, including eating patterns, are very responsive to the total range of choices available. The availability of choices, in turn, depends very heavily on government policy, social hierarchies, economic systems, agricultural, industrial, and transportation networks, and even import and export policies. Thus, there are large forces at work creating the immediate nutritional environment in which most people operate; the available "buffet," from which each individual can make dietary choices, is not randomly set, nor does it include the total range of edibles.

In combination with the constitutional susceptibilities of individuals, nutrition has a strong influence on the probability of developing disease: patterns of diet in groups of individuals are strongly linked to patterns of disease. The relative weight of diet and genetic susceptibility in producing disease is complex and, in many ways, illustrates the problem of determining causality in science. For example, the development of scurvy is normally viewed as the result of an environmental deficiency—lack of vitamin C in the diet. However, since man is one of the few mammals that cannot synthesize vitamin C and requires it to be provided in the diet, one could say that humans suffer from a genetic metabolic disorder which can be prevented from becoming manifest by manipulating the environment appropriately, i.e., ingesting vitamin C synthesized by other organisms. In fact, it is a combination of circumstances, a superimposition of environmental factors on physiological processes that results in nutrition-related health disorders.

When nutritional sciences were in their infancy, researchers focused on the relationship of single compounds in the diet, especially vitamins or minerals, to specific disease states. Usually, the emphasis was on the syndromes that developed as a result of dietary deficiencies. Lately, it has become clear that it is important to link whole diet patterns to ill-health. Those researchers who wish to understand the relationships between nutrition and health must now look at broader aspects of diet than single compounds. It has also become apparent that not only dietary deficiency but dietary excess of certain types is important in disease causation.

Before turning to specific examples of diet/health interactions, it is necessary to clarify some key concepts. Perhaps the most important is risk. In a purely technical sense, level of risk is a definition of the closeness of association between certain diet patterns and certain health outcomes. In fact, the idea of risk is basic to much of the information about nutrition that is imparted to individuals. Perceptions of the extent of personal risk determine responses from the public and also are important to policymakers in deciding how to address the health problems associated with national dietary patterns.

There is likely to be a wide range of evidence on the precise level of risk any given eating pattern entails. In part, this is because evidence is gleaned from different types of studies. Some information may come from epidemiologic studies of large populations with wide variations in diet and from different historical periods. Other evidence may be derived from laboratory studies on animals, which may or may not be closely representative of human responses, and still other evidence may be derived from clinical studies on healthy or sick individuals.

Such different techniques are likely to produce very different types of risk calculations. In addition, within each type of study, there is an expected variation in findings due to different methodologies, different sample sizes, different populations studied, and/or different statistical treatment of data.

Both individuals and policymakers, therefore, are forced to make decisions about diet on the basis of evidence that contains much uncertainty. In particular, even where the direction of effect is ascertainable, it may not be possible to quantify levels of risk. It has been pointed out (Payne and Thomson 1979) that rational responses to diet information cannot be expected unless the true relationship of risk to various levels of intake is known for different groups in the population. The relationship between intake and risk may be linear, with higher levels of intake creating proportionately greater risks, or there may be some curvilinearity to the relationship in which no appreciable risk is noted until a threshold level of intake occurs. For many dietary substances which have been related to health issues, the nature of the relationship has not been outlined specifically enough to know how to decide on tolerable intake levels. This has important implications for informed behavior by individuals and for policymaking by governments. Often, it is not clear whether individuals benefit in proportion to the reduction of a potentially harmful substance in the food supply or whether a certain level of intake can occur without major harm to most individuals.

An appropriate response to risks is usually thought to include either conscious or unconscious risk versus benefit calculations. In practice, this can become a very strange tally because such calculations are made by summing effects, good and bad, throughout all society. Calculations do not specify that the groups by whom the risks are borne need be the same as those to whom the benefits accrue. If risks and benefits do apply to the same individuals, then the mathematical exercise may be also an equitable one. But if risks and benefits are distributed unevenly throughout society, it hardly seems appropriate to make social decisions on the basis of the sum of each and a comparison of two grand totals.

As an example of this problem, the saccharin issue presents interesting complexities. The major risk of saccharin seems to be that it is a weak carcinogen. This means that a small number of those exposed to this artificial sweetener may develop malignancies that might not have occurred had they not been exposed. According to most experts, risks would be highest for those exposed to the greatest doses over the longest period of time. Evidence from animals suggests that there may be increased risks after exposure in utero and some epidemiological evidence indicates that males may be at higher risk than females. Since this substance is relatively new to the food supply, there are no data on males exposed from intrauterine life through adulthood, when adverse effects might be expected to occur.

The benefits of saccharin, on the other hand, are related to its properties as a noncaloric sweetener. There is little scientific evidence to prove that saccharin aids in weight reduction or in diabetic control, but it is clear that a large number of users are psychologically dependent on its availability for a certain sense of well-being. The issue is complicated by the fact that other noncaloric sweeteners have not been licensed or have been withdrawn from use in the U.S. food supply, leaving saccharin as the only alternative compound. Those who feel that they need a noncaloric sweetener, therefore, have no other choice. This group is made up mainly of adults, particularly the obese and the diabetic. The problem in decision-making is not only that the *level* of risk is controversial but that the highest risk groups are quite different from the highest benefit groups. Social decision-making in such a milieu is exceedingly complicated, and the concept of risk/benefit is not totally satisfactory in addressing the difficulties.

The application of risk statistics to individuals is also complex. It is clear that risks are conditioned by the variable genotypes of individuals. Since the population is heterogenous in regard to innate susceptibilities and since actual level of susceptibility cannot be known exactly for any individual, dietary recommendations are made for "prudent" rather than "optimal" diets. But even here, there is often disagreement among nutrition scientists about what level of prudence to recommend. For example, it has been noted (Hegsted 1980) that the risk of heart attacks is related to level of serum cholesterol, with those whose cholesterol levels are over 280 mg/100 ml bearing approximately twice the risk of those with average levels. It also appears, however, that the average male does not bear the minimal level of risk. An unusually low level of cholesterol, below 180mg/100 ml, is associated with approximately half the normal risk. What level, then, should physicians recommend to their patients? What level is achievable, given the current nutritional milieu of the average American? A similar situation applies to blood pressure. Normalizing blood pressure clearly reduces the risk of stroke and coronary disease. But blood pressure that is even lower than normal seems to carry with it even less risk of these major illnesses (Stamler 1978). Obviously, it is problematic to aim for a policy of "least" or "no" risk, yet there has been no medical, scientific, or social consensus on what constitutes "acceptable" risk.

Finally, understanding the nature of risks and the implications of associated behavioral modification poses interesting problems. Although it has frequently been stated that better nutrition education will allow individuals to make more appropriate dietary choices, it seems that even good information, clearly presented and assimilated, is often partially understood or simply misconstrued. In a study of public awareness about risks of drinking alcohol during pregnancy (Little et al. 1981), 90 percent of respondents to a survey mentioned alcoholic beverages consumed by the mother as possibly harmful to the fetus. Yet only 13 percent of all respondents who felt that alcohol could be harmful advocated total abstention during pregnancy. Seventy-five percent of the sample felt that an average safe level of daily alcohol intake would be approximately *three drinks*. The authors conclude that awareness of risk is no guarantee that the public will, in fact, understand how to avoid risk.

Equally disturbing are data published by the Harris organization of a poll conducted in Chicago. A vast majority of people were concerned about the relationship of nutrition to health. Seventy-five percent were concerned about cholesterol and felt it important to limit the amount in their diets, and close to one-half of the sample recognized that too much salt in the diet is related to hypertension. On the other hand, people greatly underestimated the chances that they themselves would contract any of the diseases commonly associated with excess cholesterol or salt. A clear majority viewed it unlikely that they would *ever* have diabetes, heart disease, stroke, high blood pressure, or any of the major types of cancer, which will in fact kill about 65 to 70 percent of the population. In addition, people in this sample seriously misunderstood the implications of major illnesses and often believed that cures existed where none did and that medical science could be profoundly more helpful than is, in fact, the case (Harris Poll 1977).

The relationship of risks to patterns of eating can be understood better by examining some of the specifics of dietary practices and the ways in which they have been related to health issues. The issues may be different in poor communities than in rich ones, in developing countries and those already industralized, and for children as compared to adults. The following sections outline some of the issues of concern in each of these areas.

Infant Nutrition

Concern about the health of children and about morbidity and mortality in the early part of life have long been central for public health workers. Only recently, however, has it become clear how important nutritional patterns are in determining health risks for this age group. Good nutrition begins in utero, and adequate birth weight is the most important indicator of good nutritional status at birth. Low birth weight is a major risk factor for death in the first year of life, and it is becoming clear that maternal nutrition is an extremely important determinant of birth weight. The Dutch famine of 1944–45 provided startling evidence that exposure to inadequate diet in the last part of pregnancy produces a decrease in mean birth weight and a sharp rise in infant mortality in the first three months of life (Stein et al. 1975). Moreover, it has been demonstrated in populations in developing countries that simply feeding mothers additional calories during pregnancy may be capable of reducing infant mortality by up to 50 percent (Lechtig et al. 1975).

Malnutrition in the early years of life is related to nutritional state at birth, to incidence of infectious disease, and to dietary patterns. Infection worsens nutritional status by causing depletion of body protein, depressing appetite, and producing diarrhea and vomiting. Acute infectious disease may precipitate acute nutritional disorders such as kwashiorkor and xerophthalmia, and depleted nutritional status is well known to increase the susceptibility to and severity of further bouts of infection. Malnutrition itself alters host body defenses by impairing antibody formation and the activity of phagocytic cells as well as disrupting tissue integrity.

An investigation of early mortality in the Americas showed that more than 50 percent of all deaths had malnutrition as either an underlying or associated cause (Puffer and Serrano 1973). When the proximate cause of death was diarrheal disease, malnutrition was generally associated in 60 to 75 percent of the deaths. Infectious diseases in malnourished populations carry a much higher probability of fatality. For example, measles in developing countries has a case fatality rate of up to four hundred times that in industrial nations (Scrimshaw et al. 1969). Fully half of all children may die before the age of five in parts of Africa, with protein and calorie malnutrition either the major or secondary cause of most of these deaths (Morley 1973).

Early feeding patterns are important determinants of health during infancy and childhood and inadequate patterns of eating are responsible for major public health problems. In particular, very early weaning or lack of initiation of breast-feeding are associated with increased risks of morbidity and mortality. These risks have been documented for over a hundred years and seem to be higher in conditions where environmental sanitation and medical care are poor.

Over time, as conditions of environmental sanitation and availability of effective medical intervention improve, the death rates associated with early weaning are decreased. Nonetheless, risks persist even into modern times. In fact, in the United States, in a middle-class community in the 1970s, it was shown that babies not breast-fed or weaned before six weeks had increased chances of hospitalization and illness even when parents' levels of education, smoking habits, and socioeconomic status were controlled (Cunningham 1977, 1979).

Breast milk seems to be protective in at least two ways. In the first place, breast milk itself is clean, always fresh and nutritionally adequate in contrast to the substitutes for it which may be over- or under-diluted, prepared with contaminated water or utensils, or stored in unhygienic conditions. In addition, breast milk has protective substances in it which increase a baby's ability to fight disease. These substances include secretory IgA, living immune cells, antiviral factors, and antibacterial substances such as lactoferrin. Offering babies substitutes for human milk deprives them of these important protections in the earliest months of life when infection may pose a particular peril to nutritional and health status.

The timing and type of solid or semisolid foods added to an infant's diet also have implications for health. If babies are started too late on solid foods, the calories in breast milk or formula may become inadequate and growth retardation may result. On the other hand, if babies are started too early on supplementary food, they may be subjected to contaminated foods, or, in conditions of good environmental sanitation, they simply may be given too many calories and may run a higher risk of obesity. There is evidence that early obesity is a risk factor for adult obesity, and adult obesity entails serious health risks including high blood pressure, hyperglycemia, and elevated serum cholesterol. It would seem wise, therefore, to attempt to curb tendencies toward obesity in infancy. A study in the Caribbean (Antrobus 1971) demonstrated that the best growth of infants occurred in those children who were breast-fed for more than nine months and started on supplementary feedings no earlier than four months of age.

Health Risks and Diet in Modern America

The modern American diet and equivalent dietary patterns in other industrialized parts of the world have been associated with a long list of debilitating chronic diseases. Many of these diseases have fatal outcomes, and all of them are unable to be cured by modern medicine. These diseases include hypertension, ischemic heart disease, stroke, adult onset diabetes, certain common cancers, and dental caries. One of the pathways through which dietary indiscretion is translated into health risk is excess weight. Obesity is fairly common in the adult population of the United States. Thirty percent of all men between fifty and fifty-nine have been rated at least 20 percent overweight (Mayer 1974, p. 144); about 30 percent of middle-aged women are overweight. By age fifty, 40 percent of white females and close to 55 percent of black females have been rated obese (USDHEW 1970). Where incomes are below the poverty level, rates are higher.

In addition to the risks of illness which are exacerbated by obesity, specific items in the diet have been linked with increased risks of specific diseases. High levels of consumption of fats, saturated fats, and cholesterol are linked to increased risk of coronary heart disease. High levels of meat and fat consumption and low levels of dietary fiber have been associated with high rates of colon cancer and breast cancer. Diets which are high in sodium have been linked to increased blood pressure, and sugar consumption has been shown to lead to dental caries.

In order to understand better how diet patterns are related to risk of disease, it is useful to note alterations in food consumption patterns over time. Data from the

U. S. Department of Agriculture demonstrate in general an increase in the percentage of calories derived from fat, an increase in refined carbohydrate consumption (mainly sugar), an increase in the amount of protein from animal sources, and
a decrease in consumption of foods containing crude fiber.

These trends are not new and have been identified as starting from at least the
last century. Since 1909, data on diet patterns have been collected periodically by
the Department of Agriculture. These data are based on food "disappearance,"
i.e., the food produced and sold. They are not based on calculations of food eaten
and include a certain portion destined to be lost to spoilage and waste.
Nonetheless, trends in the data do permit an understanding of shifts in food consumption patterns. The amount of fat in the American diet has increased by a full
25 percent since 1909. Furthermore, much of this increase in fat consumption
comes from increases in the consumption of red meat, and the saturated fat found
in these meats is implicated in the causation of elevated serum cholesterol levels
and coronary heart disease. Currently, fats contribute over 40 percent of the total
caloric intake of Americans, whereas most recommended patterns emphasize that
no more than 30 to 35 percent of calories should be derived from fats.

A second significant trend in food consumption in the recent past has been a
decrease in consumption of complex carbohydrates. While total consumption of
carbohydrates per capita has fallen about 25 percent, the truly startling change is
in the balance between simple and complex carbohydrates. In 1909, over 50 percent of the carbohydrates consumed in America were derived from starch and less
than 33 percent from sugar. By 1976, only about 33 percent came from starches
and over 50 percent from sugar (Brewster and Jacobson 1978). Since total sugar in
the diet is now approximately 680 calories per person per day, one can calculate
that, for some individuals, sugar could represent approximately one-third of the
total calories ingested in twenty-four hours. In general, these trends have been
caused by a decrease in consumption of vegetables, flour, cereal, fruits, and
potatoes and a huge increase in consumption of soft drinks. Between 1960 and
1976 alone per capita consumption doubled so that in the year 1976 Americans
drank enough soft drinks to provide five hundred glasses to each. It is no surprise, therefore, that one-fourth of total sugar consumption comes from soft
drinks alone.

Changes in diet patterns have occurred, in part, in response to changes in other
aspects of American life. Specifically, at least three important trends have combined to make eating patterns what they are today. First, Americans have become
more and more sedentary in their life-styles and therefore consume fewer calories
in total. Second, Americans have taken more and more of their meals away from
home. Up to one-third of all meals are estimated to be prepared outside the home.
Finally, more and more of the American food supply has been processed industrially between the farm and the dining table. As a result, there have been more
and more alterations to the intrinsic characteristics of food consumed by
Americans. Each of these trends has important implications for diet patterns.

Because we consume fewer calories and are less physically active, the burden
of providing all the vitamins, minerals, and other micronutrients necessary to
maintain health falls on less and less food. Meals must, therefore, become more
"nutrient dense" if they are to supply all nutritional needs. Yet, in a worrisome
trend, the diet is composed of greater amounts of sugar and fats, both of which
tend to be devoid of many of the necessary nutrients. Thus, there is less leeway to
choose a diet capable of providing all necessary nutrients. Furthermore, as more of
the diet is prepared and consumed away from home, the individual is less capable

of knowing exactly what is in the foods being eaten. In fact, even the statistical tables used to calculate dietary constituents may fail in the face of this profound diet change: standard food tables have been constructed using the nutritional content of foods as prepared in the home. It is less clear what substances are included—and what nutrients are available—in foods prepared in restaurants or sold in fast-food outlets.

Finally, food processing has made enormous changes in the American national diet. While, in 1929, each American ate over four hundred pounds of unprocessed fruits and vegetables and under a hundred pounds of processed produce, in 1971, each consumed less than two hundred and fifty pounds of unprocessed and over three hundred pounds of processed fruits and vegetables (Brewster and Jacobson 1978). The potential effect of processing on the national nutrient intake can be illustrated by a rather simple example. Potatoes can be eaten in many different forms. The raw produce has 0.5 percent of its calories as fat, and 11 percent of its calories as protein. When french-fried, the same potato has 42 percent of its calories as fat and 6 percent as protein. When made into a potato chip, on the other hand, 60 percent of the calories are fat and only 3.6 percent are protein. In addition, the chip carries with it a large dose of salt. It is obvious, then, that the consumption of "potato" may mean vastly different things depending on the form in which it is eaten. In addition, industry has made available a virtual explosion of new foods and food products on shelves. In 1928, large supermarkets offered only about 867 items, but by 1979 an estimated 12,000 different products were offered in large supermarkets—up 3,000 in just the five years since 1974 (Molitor 1980). When one realizes that each of these items is a complex mixture of different nutrients and additives, the enormity of the task of calculating an individual's dietary intake becomes apparent.

In a fundamental way, the extensive use of processing has meant that Americans have lost control over their diets. Not only are they at the mercy of commercial food preparation and handling when they eat outside the home, but even when they eat at their own tables they are often unaware of the constituents of the foods they eat since much of it has been industrially processed. Food labeling only goes part way toward solving this problem; many items are not labeled for nutritional content and those that are usually only make available a standard breakdown of fats, protein, carbohydrates, and a few selected vitamins and minerals. Other items extremely important to an individual's assessment of health risk are usually not included on the labels. Such items as saturated fat, sodium, and cholesterol content or percentage of calories from simple sugar most often remain unknown—and unknowable—to the consumer. As the individual moves further and further from control over his diet, it is increasingly difficult for nutrition education to be effective. It is necessary to provide a way in which the individual can gain control over dietary choices before information can be translated into changes in dietary behavior.

Responses to Nutritional Risk

In designing ways to avoid risk-laden diet patterns, policymakers can proceed in two directions. They can attempt to change the environment to lessen risks universally or they can attempt to change individual behaviors so that people make better choices and avoid dietary risks on their own. The first approach has been advocated by many who see the current nutritional environment as too complex and difficult for the individual to negotiate. Because of the centrally determined nature of much of the food supply, it has been suggested that altering the pattern of availability is the most realistic response to dietary risk. This may be an effort to apply a lesson learned from attempts to design other preventive interventions: measures distant from the individual are usually the easiest to implement and most successful. For example, it is far easier to purify a water supply for the community than to teach each person to boil household water. Interventions that require consistent, repeated behavioral change on the part of consumers (such as taking medication or making dietary changes without changing the nutritional environment) are probably the least successful in achieving compliance.

On the other hand, those who want to avoid any governmental tampering with dietary choices advocate increased education of consumers in order that they, individually, make better choices within the current system. A difficulty of this strategy is that it requires intensive and continuing public education on a large number of nutritional issues. People must not only understand risk factors but must understand how those risk factors apply to them personally, which dietary factors are implicated, which food choices increase or decrease risks, and how to make alternative choices in the current market context. The strategy is appealing to those who advocate free market principles but presents great challenges in the effective dissemination of appropriate information to all segments of society. Without such an educational component, the market would remain "free," but the public could hardly be said to have informed "freedom of choice."

Obviously, if such a strategy succeeded, it would have very much the same effect on the market as a strategy in which regulations changed the availability of certain food choices; for if individuals altered their diets by choosing more risk-free products, the market would respond appropriately and the range of available choices would also change. Curiously, many who have advocated nutrition education as the proper route for changing public diet have also complained loudly when educational messages pointed to specific foods as most likely to be risk-laden. They advocate, instead, very general messages which do not tell people that potato chips have excess salt or that dairy products and marbled beef are a potential source of dietary risk. Instead, they hold that general principles of nutrition are sufficient for consumer education. It is because of such contentions that nutrition education has sometimes become suspect as an activity that is designed not to meddle seriously with current dietary patterns.

Opposition to systematic intervention in national dietary patterns has been based on several arguments. First, it is claimed that knowledge adequate to make recommendations for the general public does not exist. Yet it is recognized that science never creates definitive answers and policymakers never wait until absolute proof is achieved before making decisions. On the contrary, by not doing anything about national diet patterns, very definite policy choices are made implicitly. Clearly, the information now available is not the final word on many subjects; new evidence will become available and changes undoubtedly will be made in recommendations, particularly in regard to specific quantities of dietary substances. But this need not deter action, for similar problems exist with all categories of public information. Dietary recommendations need not be settled absolutely before their general direction can be offered for public information and action. It is particularly encouraging, therefore, that current evidence about various health risks lead to similar conclusions about appropriate diet changes. Whether one believes that it is better to eat less saturated fats to avoid heart disease or more complex carbohydrates to avoid diseases of the colon, the same basic prescription is offered: the percentage of calories derived from fats should be reduced and the percentage derived from other sources, most logically complex carbohydrates, will increase.

Second, those who advocate inaction on dietary matters are asking the public to accept an implied assessment of risk. If diet is related to the most common debilitating and fatal diseases, and over two-thirds of the American public can be expected to die of such causes, the risk is not trivial. On the contrary, it affects most of the public. In contrast, there is no reason to suppose that replacement of fats and refined sugars with complex carbohydrates would have any damaging effects on health. In fact, there are several long-term natural experiments in other cultures—in Japan and the Mediterranean, for example—in which the low-fat, high-starch diets advocated have been eaten for centuries with no apparent ill effects and a low incidence of heart disease.

Finally, some have claimed that dietary recommendations to the public interfere with the doctor/patient relationship. The implication is that dietary advice is a medical subject that can be addressed only in the context of individual medical care. While it is true that certain special disease states require special dietary advice, there is no reason to suppose that most individuals need to resort to medical practitioners for advice on everyday diet. In fact, a host of other factors closely related to health risks are acted upon every day without resort to medical advice. Few doctors advise their patients to use seat belts or to obey speed laws or to drink alcohol in moderation, for example. There is no reason to suppose that one is any more in need of a physician's advice to decide whether to eat a tuna sandwich or a cheeseburger for lunch.

Many of the issues involved in diet and diet changes are related to basic social tenets. To take a stand on nutrition policy involves consideration of issues of freedom of choice, the proper role of government intervention in everyday life, the obligation of society to reduce risks associated with the environment, the extent to which free enterprise serves social goals, and women's status in society. To illustrate this, one can look at three very different issues in which nutrition and social policy have recently become intricately interwined.

The Intersection of Medical, Nutritional, and Social Issues

Salt and Hypertension

The relationship of salt—or, more precisely, sodium—in the diet to the development of hypertension illustrates many of the problems of identifying dietary risks and applying that knowledge to appropriate policy initiatives. A great deal of evidence has accumulated to indicate that consumption of high levels of sodium is implicated in the etiology of essential hypertension in susceptible individuals. There is epidemiologic evidence that demonstrates an extremely high level of hypertension in areas, such as northern Japan, where there is high salt consumption and, conversely, an absence of the usual rise of blood pressure with age in societies in which salt intake is essentially nil. Stamler has cited at least eighteen separate locations in which this second association has been demonstrated

(Stamler 1978). There is also laboratory evidence on the relationship between sodium consumption and hypertension. Rats can be bred so that they are either genetically susceptible to inducement of hypertension by dietary sodium or essentially resistant to hypertension at all levels of sodium consumption. Finally, there is clinical evidence that reduction of sodium intake in hypertensive individuals lowers blood pressure.

The relationship of sodium intake to the development of hypertension is considered relatively strong by nutritional scientists. In a poll of nine distinguished nutritional scientists convened by the American Society for Clinical Nutrition, there was a high level of agreement that evidence on the association was quite solid. The salt/hypertension relationship rated a mean score of 74 out of a possible 100. Only the relationship between sugar and dental caries and alcohol and liver disease (87 and 88) ranked higher (American Journal of Clinical Nutrition 1979).

Once the existence of a diet/disease relationship is confirmed, as in the case of salt and hypertension, it then becomes necessary to evaluate the extent of the risk this relationship poses for the population. Although it has been claimed that approximately 15 percent of the population is susceptible to hypertension (National Academy of Sciences 1980), this figure seems to be excessively low. In fact, several surveys of the general adult population that screened for hypertension found closer to 30 percent to be hypertensive in such screening (Stamler 1978). This, too, is an underestimate of the total percentage of the population genetically *susceptible*, because some people in the group have not yet manifested expression of the susceptible genotype. In fact, above age sixty-five approximately three-quarters of the population has definite or borderline hypertension (USNCHS 1977), and two-thirds of this has been said to be essential hypertension, the type related to dietary sodium. Since the probability of living to age sixty-five is quite good, it might be closer to the truth to calculate that at least half the population is genetically susceptible to sodium-induced hypertension. Furthermore, although family history of hypertension suggests increased likelihood of susceptibility, there is no way to know exactly who is a salt-sensitive individual and who is not. As a result, individualized preventive interventions are quite difficult. If one uses screening programs to discover who is susceptible, the chance for prevention has already been missed: those identified have already crossed the threshold from susceptibility to overt disease.

Even with adequate information regarding family history, the scientific basis for the link between sodium consumption and hypertension, and the need to limit salt in the diet, an individual may have considerable difficulty in purchasing food appropriate for a low-salt diet. Salt is intrinsic to the food supply currently available to the American public. The average intake of salt in the United States today has a wide range but a mean around ten grams. This represents approximately twenty times the total nutritional requirement for sodium. Though it is clear that there is much room for reduction in salt consumption without any nutritional risk, it is notably difficult for individuals to reduce salt consumption on their own because of the nature of the U.S. food supply.

Approximately half of the salt consumed is added to foods *before* they are brought into the home (Stamler 1978). Salt has been included in the GRAS (Generally Recognized As Safe) list of food additives by the Food and Drug Administration and, therefore, its addition to the food supply is not regulated. There is no requirement for labeling the sodium content of processed food, and the individual, therefore, cannot make informed choices by reading food labels carefully. Here, then, is a situation in which information and understanding can be plentiful but the individual is handicapped in trying to manage dietary intakes to avoid a specific item of risk. Interventions aimed at reduction of sodium intake, therefore, must include central as well as individual initiative. For example, removing salt from the GRAS list has been proposed and is under consideration by the FDA. It is certainly possible that standards for added salt could be constructed and the amount added to processed foods could be drastically reduced without loss of market appeal. Salt labeling could be required, and then individuals could be expected to make better choices after receiving good information. Finally, food served in institutions, such as the army, jails, schools, government offices, food programs, etc., could conform to standards for sodium content. It seems highly unlikely that the individual acting alone in the current nutritional environment can be expected reasonably to regulate food intake so as to reduce substantially the risk associated with excess sodium consumption.

Self-medication and Vitamin Therapy

Issues concerning the proper roles of individual choice and government regulation also arise in connection with preventive and therapeutic self-medication by lay citizens. Those who advocate megadoses of vitamins or special, unrecognized therapies for serious diseases claim that it is the individual's right to decide for himself the risks versus benefits of such treatment. It is emphasized that the chosen therapies should be freely available to all who wish them. Some of the substances advocated for self-therapy, such as vitamins, are, in fact, widely available, while others, such as Laetrile, are not. One reason for this may be that vitamins have traditionally been viewed as nutritional supplements and not as drugs; their use usually has been advocated more in preventive than in curative aspects of self-care, although this may have changed somewhat in recent years. Substances such as Laetrile, on the other hand, are advocated largely for the treatment of certain serious diseases, in much the same manner as any other therapeutic pharmaceutical agent.

In fact, large-dose vitamin therapy might also properly be considered a type of pharmacological intervention because the doses advocated are so much higher then the levels normally used by human tissues. Any benefits of this therapy must be due to the chemical—or druglike — properties of excess vitamin intake. The utility of most of these therapies in either preventive or curative aspects of self-care remains to be proven. Most attempts to establish a scientific basis for megavitamin therapies have failed in the past. Controlled trials do not substantiate either therapeutic or preventive effects of super doses of any vitamins on the course of disease in most patients.

A short summary of both the claims and clinical investigations of one of these substances—vitamin C—is instructive as an example of the type of issues and information available to the public. Linus Pauling has made famous the contention that vitamin C is a preventive and/or cure for the common cold. In fact, there is no evidence that vitamin C prevents the common cold, and advocates of vitamin C therapy now often claim that large doses of the vitamin ameliorate common-cold symptoms. Yet, one of the most reliable studies done on this subject, which originally showed that vitamin C reduced cold symptoms, was refuted by its own authors who repeated the study and found that, with adequate scientific controls, the effect of vitamin C was no longer substantiated (Coulehan, Relsinger, and Rogers 1974; Coulehan et al. 1976). A recent study looked at the effects of large doses of vitamin C versus placebos in Marine recruits and concluded that there was no difference between the two groups in incidence or duration of colds (Pitt and Costrini 1979). According to this study, no benefit was measurable at a consumption level of two grams of vitamin C per day. This level of intake is more than thirty-three times the current Recommended Daily Allowance of the vitamin.

It should be noted further that large doses of vitamin C have been associated with some deleterious side effects. So, even as the drug may not live up to the claims of its advocates, it may also pose some important medical hazards. The following problems have all been attributed to the ingestion of megadoses of vitamin C:

—the destruction of dietary vitamin B_{12}
—kidney stones
—the destruction of blood cells in patients with certain genetic enzyme deficiencies
—sickle-cell crises in persons with sickle-cell disease
—deficiency of vitamin C (scurvy) itself due to withdrawal in persons who have accustomed themselves to large doses
—severe similar withdrawal effects in infants born to mothers who have taken megadoses of vitamin C
—increase in aspirin-induced gastrointestinal irritation

Furthermore, it has been noted that large doses of vitamin C can interfere with important medical tests, such as those designed to test for glucose in urine or for blood in stool.

The complexity of the scientific information surrounding the subject of megadoses of vitamin C—and the fact that much of the evidence is only suggestive and not proven—demonstrates how difficult the issue of "informed consent" may be in lay assessment of risks and benefits. This underscores the dilemma of the individual who attempts to make personal risk/benefit decisions about consumption without guidance from either scientific or offical policy sources. Since the medical profession is often uninterested in nutrition and frequently resists therapies with a nutritional basis as well as patient self-medication, solid clinical research in these areas has lagged. The result is that there is a relative lack of good, clinically relevant information for consumers. On the other hand, the matter is further complicated by the fact that much of the information that *is* available to the public about these different therapeutic and preventive modalities comes from promotional sources with vested interests in convincing people of the benefits of their advocated therapies. Sometimes these sources have emotional and philosophical investments in promoting a particular therapy; sometimes the investment in the product is financial as well. Thus, it is very difficult to ensure that the public receives valid information—the basis of any truly free choice.

Even when discussing vitamins, then, one gets quickly to fundamental political issues such as personal freedom of choice and the necessary environmental conditions for individuals to make free choices. The question of the proper locus of responsibility for protecting the public from harm due to diet practices arises not only in discussions of the pattern of the national food supply but also in regard to more personal, individual choices, such as how much of what vitamin to take, when, and for what.

Breast Milk

It is clear that early nutrition is closely related to health status and therefore, patterns of infant feeding and their determinants are of concern to individual parents, to health workers, and to society at large. A strongly worded endorsement of breast-feeding as the optimal form of nutrition for almost all infants in the first months of life was published by the American Academy of Pediatrics in 1978. In addition, the scientific literature on lactation has increased massively, with over a hundred and fifty papers published in 1976 alone. It would seem, then, that breast-feeding is noncontroversial. Yet despite recent increases in breast-feeding incidence, about half of U.S. babies never have the chance to consume human milk. The question of how to encourage breast-feeding and the possible risks and benefits of doing so immediately confronts other important social issues.

BREAST-FEEDING AND THE ENVIRONMENT. Environmental pollution has literally spilled over into breast milk. Many of the organic residues, such as those from pesticides, have been found in samples of human breast milk. The threat this might pose for nursing babies is not yet clear, but the fact that contaminants have been detected in mother's milk has aroused strong emotional reaction. The issue is similar to, if perhaps more dramatic than, contamination of other parts of the food supply by environmental pollutants.

The contaminants found in breast milk are those which are stored in body fat and which, therefore, may persist in the human body for a lifetime. These substances, often added to the environment through their use in argicultural or industrial processes, are concentrated in human tissues by the process of biomagnification: contaminants enter the food chain at a relatively low level, i.e., through plants exposed to pesticides or contaminated water; these plants, containing residues, are then ingested by animals or fish; the residues are transferred to the animals and stored at higher concentrations; these animals, in turn, are eaten by man, in whom the residues are again stored, often at even higher concentrations than in the lower animals. Since the chemicals may persist in the body over a lifetime and since little evidence has been collected on long-term effects in humans, there is no way to assess risk from ingestion of most of these contaminants. In fact, however, some of them are well-known carcinogens.

The most important contaminants of the food supply can be divided into two groups: (1) chemicals used in agricultural processes and their metabolites, such as dieldrin and DDT, along with its common human storage form, DDE; and (2) chemicals used in industrial processes, of which the most well known are PCBs and PBBs. The human body has only two ways to rid itself of these fat-stored chemicals, and both involve loss of fat: (1) weight loss; and (2) lactation, in which body fat is secreted by the mother into her milk. Thus, mother's milk reflects a woman's lifetime history of dietary intake, with more contamination likely in those who have eaten a lot of animal or fish products from areas where there has been environmental pollution.

Perhaps no single finding could be expected to create as highly charged an emotional atmosphere as the possibility that mother's milk might be "poison" for her baby. The Environmental Defense Fund has reviewed the evidence on contamination of human milk and concludes that the known benefit of breast-feeding must be compared with the unknown risk posed by chemical contamination of some mother's milk. The balance still weighs in favor of breast-feeding. Similar conclu-sions were reached by Wickizer, Brilliant, Copeland, and Tilden (1981).

Some, including the infant formula industry, have taken the position that one might solve the problem simply by avoiding human milk. Others suggest that pollution of human milk may not be a serious problem because: (1) it may not have any real health effects; and (2) there are acceptable, if not optimal, substitutes available. Environmentalists, physicians, and women's rights leaders have suggested, however, that the proper response is increased vigilance and surveillance of the environment, strengthened regulations against pollution, and a protected supply of human milk. Environmental regulations, in fact, can have an important effect in reducing contamination of breast milk. A recent survey, for ex-ample, showed much lower levels of DDT contamination of human milk obtained after the Environmental Protection Agency's 1972 ban on the use of DDT than of samples analyzed before that ban. Obviously, the larger social choices determine, in part, the quality of the food supply offered to the youngest citizens.

BREAST-FEEDING AND THE BEHAVIOR OF AMERICAN CORPORATIONS ABROAD. The growing popularity of breast-milk substitutes in the developing countries of the world and the changing patterns of infant feeding among the poor in these coun-tries has led to considerable publicity. It appears that, often, breast-feeding is abandoned in the very places where its protective effects are most important: where poverty is common, where sanitation is poor, where illiteracy is the norm, and where contraceptive services are nonexistent. In such circumstances, mothers may find that they cannot purchase enough artificial formula to supply the infant's nutritional needs as it grows. It is also frequently impossible in these environments to prepare powdered formula in a hygienic manner. Contamination is introduced from impure water supplies and from storage of bottles without refrigeration. Finally, where there is much illiteracy, mothers may not be able to read the direc-tions on the can and may often prepare the formulas improperly, using wrong dilutions or unsanitary techniques that result in further health risks to their in-fants. Finally, lactation is, in many places, the only contraceptive available to poor families. Early abandonment of breast-feeding increases the likelihood of closely spaced pregnancies, large family size, and higher levels of maternal and in-fant mortality. A vicious cycle of poverty and poor health is thus reinforced.

Some, particularly among the professionals, have offered the opinion that in-fant feeding is another issue best left to medical decision-making: the advice of physicians should predominate. In the situation of most developing countries, however, few have access to the advice of physicians and, frequently, physicians are, in fact, not the group best prepared to understand the psychological, scien-tific, and economic issues involved in choices between breast and bottle for the poorest of the poor. In any case, many medical personnel have had long and inten-sive exposure to the glossy advertisements of the formula companies, have attended conferences sponsored by those companies, and have received free books, instruments, and hospital supplies from them. In some circumstances, in fact, availability of modern medical care does not reach as far into the countryside as the distribution efforts of infant formula salesmen.

A proposed solution has been to turn to government regulation and legislation to control the activities of infant formula companies. Stringent regulation and monitoring of the importation and distribution of milk by developing countries themselves has been advocated, and some, such as Algeria, have taken initial steps in this direction. Other advocates concerned about trends away from breast-feeding in the developing world have attempted to make the practices and performance of American companies abroad an issue for attention by American regulatory agencies. Still others have tried to mobilize public opinion and consumer pressure within the United States to control the actions of American corporations. Again, the issue seems to involve a wide range of social, medical, and nutritional choices—all with important implications for health.

BREAST-FEEDING AND WOMEN'S LIBERATION. The issue of breast-feeding also has a complex relationship to issues of women's rights and the status of women in society. On the one hand, women have viewed breast-feeding as a traditional right and privilege, providing the best source of nutrition for babies. On the other hand, breast-feeding has been associated with other nonmodern traditional practices and, as such, has at times been viewed by women's rights advocates as part of a system in which women are socially and economically oppressed and are prevented from achieving any nontraditional goals.

Because of the deep historical relationship of breast-feeding to traditional women's roles and the emotional responses which both mothering and traditional status of females evoke among advocates of women's rights, some have stated that advocacy of breast-feeding will limit the horizons of women who have children but wish to pursue other career or educational goals. Even in developing countries where the abandonment of breast-feeding is closely linked to infant mortality, resistance to the message that breast-feeding is best for the baby has been voiced by women's groups.

The underlying political issue is the conflict imposed by current socioeconomic patterns, in which women's full participation in creative and productive work can be made inconsistent with optimal early mothering and nourishment of infants. In certain favored environments, breast-feeding and career advancement are not incompatible, but for others, a life-style which permits both is difficult to achieve. There is, however, no *intrinsic* reason why women's roles as mothers and creative, economically productive persons need be in conflict. Instead of arguing that breast-feeding is a symbol of female oppression or that it inhibits women from larger goals of professional and educational achievement, the focus of analysis might be placed on how society decides what choices to provide to women and what nutritional patterns are, therefore, offered to infants.

Conclusion

In sum, patterns of nutrition are clearly linked to health and risk of illness. But the underlying determinants both of nutritional patterns and their health outcomes may reach deeper into the structures of society and the choices that are made in political and economic spheres. There is no way to divorce nutritional choices from other social choices. Even the proper education of the individual can compensate only partially for strong environmental influences. Finally, the access to appropriate information and the ability to act on it are distributed in the population in much the same way as other social goods. The more advantaged segments of society have more contact with sources of information, receive it first, and are able to understand and use it more effectively. In fact, there is evidence that cholesterol levels have declined recently in some of the most privileged groups of the population, probably due to changes in patterns of eating.

Diet and health risks are not, however, distributed in the same way as diet and health information. Most at risk seem to be the less-educated, the less-affluent, and members of minority groups, and for some risks, particularly the women in these groups. Those who have less access to information are the same groups who also have less access to health care, less economic freedom to change their dietary habits, and lower life expectancy. Those who are best able to receive and use information seem to have lower-risk health and nutritional environments. A public health task for the immediate future is to develop strategies so that health risks and benefits are more equitably distributed in the population and so that nutritional patterns do not become a means of reinforcing social inequities.

REFERENCES

ANTROBUS, A. C. K. 1971. Child growth plus related factors in a rural community in St. Vincent. *Environmental Child Health* 17: 188–210.

American Journal of Clinical Nutrition. 1979. 32 (no. 12, suppl.).

BREWSTER, H., and JACOBSON, M. 1978. *The changing American diet.* Washington, D.C. Center for Science in the Public Interest.

COULEHAN, J. L.; EBERHARD, S.; KAPNER, L.; ET AL. 1976. Vitamin C and acute illness in Navajo school children. *New England Journal of Medicine* 295:973–77.

COULEHAN, J. L.; REISINGER, K. S.; and ROGERS, K. D. 1974. Vitamin C prophylaxis in a boarding school. *New England Journal of Medicine* 290: 6–10.

CUNNINGHAM, A. S. 1977. Morbidity in breast-fed and artificially fed infants. *Journal of Pediatrics* 90 (no. 5): 726–729.

———. 1979. Morbidity in breast-fed and artificially fed infants II. *Journal of Pediatrics* 95 (no. 5, part I): 685–689.

HARRIS POLL. 1977. Public unrealistic about medicine's power to cure effects of poor health habits, hospital study finds. Press release from Mount Sinai Hospital Medical Center, Chicago, 5 January 1977.

HEGSTED, D. M. 1980. Dietary guidelines: where do we go from here? *Journal of Nutrition Education* 12 (no. 2, suppl.): 100–2.

LECHTIG, A., et al. 1975. Influences of maternal nutrition on birth weight. *American Journal of Clinical Nutrition* 28: 1223–33.

LITTLE, R. E.; GRATHWOHL, H. L.; STREISSGUTH, A. P.; and McINTYRE, C. 1981. Public awareness and knowledge about the risks of drinking during pregnancy in Multnomah County, Oregon. *American Journal of Public Health* 71 (no. 3): 312–14.

MAYER, J. 1974. *Health.* New York: Van Nostrand.

MOLITOR, G. T. T. 1980. The food system in the 1980's. *Journal of Nutrition Education* 12 (no. 2, suppl.): 103–111

MORLEY, D. 1973. *Pediatric priorities in the developing world.* London: Butterworth Press.

National Academy of Sciences. 1980. *Toward healthful diets.* Washington, D.C.: Food and Nutrition Board, National Academy of Sciences.

PITT, H. A., and COSTRINI, A. M. 1979, Vitamin C prophylaxis in marine recruits. *Journal of American Medical Association* 241 (no. 9): 908–11.

PAYNE, P., and THOMSON, A. 1979. Food health: individual choice and collective responsibility. *Royal Society of Health Journal,* October 1979, pp. 12–16.

PUFFER, R. R., and SERRANO, C. V. 1973. *Patterns of mortality in childhood.* Washington, D.C.: Pan American Health Organization, Science Publication 262.

SCRIMSHAW, N. S.; BEHAR, M.; GUZMAN, M. A.; and GORDON, J. E. 1969. Nutrition and infection field study in Guatemalan villages, 1959–64: IX. An evaluation of medical, social, and public health benefits, with suggestions for future field study. *Archives of Environmental Health* 18; 51–62.

STAMLER, J. 1978. Epidemiology and treatment of hypertension. In *Future directions in health care: a new public policy*, ed. R. J. Carlson and R. Cunningham. Cambridge, Mass.: Ballinger Publishing Co.

STEIN, Z.; SUSSER, M.; SAENGER, G.; and MAROLLA, F. 1975. *Famine and human development: the Dutch hunger winter of 1944–45.* New York: Oxford University Press.

U.S. Department of Health, Education, and Welfare, Health Services and Mental Health Administration. 1970. *Ten-state nutrition survey: 1968–1970.* Vol. 3: *Clinical, Anthropometry, dental.* DHEW pub. no. (HSM) 72-8131, figure 10B. Washington, D.C.: Government Printing Office.

U.S. National Center for Health Statistics. 1977. *Vital and health statistics: blood pressure levels of persons 6–74 years,* United States, 1971–1974. Series 11, no. 203. DHEW pub. no. [HRA] 78-1648). Washington D.C.: Government Printing Office.

WICKIZER, T.; BRILLIANT, L. B.; COPELAND, R.; and TILDEN, R. 1981. Polychlorinated biphenyl contamination of nursing mothers' milk in Michigan. *American Journal of Public Health* 71 (no. 2): 132–37.

II

EPIDEMIOLOGY AND
CLINICAL ISSUES

Chapter 6

Epidemiology of Childhood Disease

Robert J. Haggerty

IN THE SEMINAL BOOK *Uses of Epidemiology*, Morris (1964) discusses several uses of the discipline of epidemiology, in addition to the traditional one of identifying environmental agents that contribute to disease. In this chapter I will place greater emphasis upon these other uses proposed by Morris: (1) to make a community diagnosis and to provide the *intelligence* to plan health services by defining the prevalence of health problems in different populations; and (2) *to complete the clinical picture*, especially to document the presence of signs or symptoms of illness in people who do not consider themselves ill or come to the attention of doctors. Determination of the natural history of chronic disease and its frequent asymptomatic precursors is especially important in prevention and early diagnosis.

The first use—to make a community diagnosis in order to plan services—must deal with the frequency of diseases, their distribution in different populations, and also with the impact of these illnesses (Rice, Feldman, and White 1976). Organization of services should take these facts into account, although all too often the way we organize and deliver services is based upon implicit clinical experiences, traditions, and political pressure rather than explicit information on the distribution of illness. Completing the clinical picture is of importance to the clinician searching for clusters of findings that will suggest precursors of later disease.

Burden of Illness in Children: Measurement of Determinants

Difficulties in Definition

It would be logical to think that after a century of scientific medicine the amount of illness in children would be a simple thing to determine and be well known. But, depending on the precision needed, such information is still not fully available.

Most practitioners feel that they know quite well what diseases cause illness in patients within their practices, but even pediatricians with large practices of 2,000 to 4,000 children (usually from a limited geographical, ethnic, and socioeconomic groups), may see a quite biased sample of illness as compared to the total population. In addition, the number of patients in this practice will yield reliable estimates for only the most common problems. For instance, it would be expected that in the average practice there would be only one child with cystic fibrosis, a disorder occurring in about 1 in 2,000 children. Because of early death from this disease, concentration of identified children in special clinics, and chance variation, many practitioners have never had a child with this relatively common chronic disease of childhood appear among their own patients. Individual practitioner estimates then are highly variable, except for the most common illnesses. Grouping data from many practices improves these estimates, but it is also clear that not all patients with illness go to physicians, and practice estimates seriously underestimate many problems. Therefore, household surveys are needed to gain a broader view of the distribution of illness in the community.

But surveys of random samples also have problems. The largest surveys (USDHEW 1964) obtain self-reports (for children by their parents) and define well only the most common and easily perceived (by the parent) illnesses at one point in time. The largest examination surveys (National Health Examination Surveys) yield data from careful physical and laboratory examinations, but can study only a few thousand children and miss even fairly common chronic diseases. Longitudinal studies following the same children are very important but are possible to complete on only a few hundred children and are even less likely to yield data on chronic illness. They do very well in demonstrating the frequent acute illnesses and the continuity (or discontinuity) of these over time. If estimates are made from interviews, there are variations due to memory loss or season of the year (if survey is taken in the winter, there will be more respiratory illness), and changes over decades (surveys done in the 1950s show poliomyelitis and measles, while these diseases are virtually nonexistent today) add to the difficulties of giving precise, stable definitions of the amount of illness among children.

All these caveats sound like weak excuses, but it is important to recognize that a simple definition of community diagnosis for the precise burden of illness among children is difficult.

Levels of Illness

Illnesses produce different degrees of impact. A useful way to consider impact is the easily remembered five Ds: death, disease, disability, discomfort, and dissatisfaction (Patrick and Ellison 1979). Generally, we have better data for the first level (causes of death) and least satisfactory data for the last (dissatisfaction). While death, especially premature death (which most deaths in childhood could be labeled), is of great importance, it is relatively rare in childhood today. The great bulk of illness in children, for which they and their parents seek medical attention, involves the other four levels of illness.

Sources and Types of Epidemiologic Data

Deaths are registered routinely by death certificates with reasonable precision in most developed countries, and the major causes are generally known, although a fairly recent example of mislabeling of a major cause of death in infancy (Sudden

Infant Death Syndrome) impaired research and effective intervention for years. Nearly 7,000 infants in the United States die suddenly and unexpectedly during their first year of life. These are from the 3.5 million births each year, making the rate relatively low (2/1,000). Until very recently, these were labeled "crib deaths," the implication being that these deaths were due to suffocation or "overlaying" by the mother, and were classified among accidental causes of death. This resulted in considerable parental guilt, for the parents felt they were negligent or in some way responsible. With the relabeling of this group as Sudden Infant Death Syndrome (SIDS) in the late 1960s, a new wave of research was begun, much of it epidemiological. Parental guilt was diminished, and we are now beginning to understand some of the underlying associations (low birth rate, poor growth, low-grade infections of the amniotic fluid, anemia in the mother, use of cigarettes and barbiturates by the mother during pregnancy, etc.) and possible pathophysiologic causes (chronic underventilation of the baby due to the respiratory center in the brain being less responsive to lack of oxygen) (Naeye 1980).

Morbidity (presence of defined illness) is reported routinely for only a few contagious diseases in children, and even for these there is a vast underreporting. Therefore, to know the amount of nonfatal illness or morbidity, it is necessary to carry out special surveys. The largest of these in the United States is the National Health Survey (USDHEW 1964), a continuing household interview in a representative sample of communities. In addition, special national health examinations are done on occasion to determine illnesses that can be detected only by examining the patient.

These surveys give a good picture of morbidity at the national and regional levels but not at the local community level. Among the few local community-wide studies of childhood illness are the Rochester Child Health Studies (Haggerty, Roghmann, and Pless, 1975), the Buffalo Chronic Disease Study (Sultz et al. 1972), the Isle of Wight Study (Rutter, Tizzard, and Whitmore 1970), the Newcastle-Upon-Tyne Study (Miller, et al. 1974), and the Genesee County (Flint) Michigan Study (Gortmaker, et al. 1980). These are very useful as research studies, but are too expensive to be mounted in many communities. With the exception of the Newcastle-Upon-Tyne Study, these are all cross-sectional studies, that is, even when repeated surveys are done (as in Rochester and Flint) the same person is not studied repeatedly. Thus, one cannot tell the natural history of a disease in a given person. There are only a few, but very important, longitudinal studies on the same children that have been completed that allow one to study the factors in early life leading to subsequent adult illnesses. In the United States, the Cleveland Family Study (Dingle, Badger, and Jordan 1964), the Harvard Growth Study (Valadian, Stuart, and Reed 1959), the Hagerstown, Maryland Study (Tucker and Downes 1953), and the Kauai Study (Werner, Bierman, and French 1971) all used very small numbers of subjects and often dealt with only a limited range of problems. There are a limited number of other longitudinal studies in the United States, focusing entirely upon the behavioral-developmental problems, but they are of great importance (Block 1969; MacFarlane, Allen, and Honzik 1954). In Great Britain the Newcastle-Upon-Tyne 1000 Family Study (Miller et al. 1974) and the Birthday Studies (Douglas, Ross, and Simpson 1968) are important because they studied the same children repeatedly over many years and are representative of all children in the community (Newcastle) and country (Birthday).

Different methods of measurement also produce different results. Strikingly different rates of the mild acute illnesses are obtained from the National Health Survey (i.e., 1.24 acute respiratory infections per child under age six, per year, when parents were questioned about the number in the past year at an interview) as compared to the data obtained in longitudinal studies with detailed daily diaries, such as the Cleveland Family Studies (i.e., twelve acute respiratory infections per child per year). This can be explained by the different wording of the questions in different studies, as well as loss of memory for minor illnesses the further in the past they occurred.

There is then considerable difference in the amount of reported illness (morbidity) in children from different studies. Very large samples are needed to detect infrequent, but more severe, illness. These large studies must be rather superficial and use a fairly long recall period. They, therefore, miss less severe illness. Detailed studies of small populations are necessary to determine the frequency of common, but mild, illnesses or special problems, but these intensive small-scale studies will miss rare illness. It is only from a composite of different types of studies that one can gain a realistic picture of the epidemiology of childhood illness.

Disability, Discomfort, and Dissatisfaction

With all of these caveats we can produce a reasonably accurate picture of the frequency of most of the illnesses that cause death or disease in children for the United States as a whole today. We can do much less well in detailing the impact on children or the level of disability or the performance and level of discomfort of children who have these illnesses; only in a few instances do we have data on dissatisfaction with services, even though level of satisfaction has been shown to be an important indicator of how people use the health-care system and whether they comply with recommendations.

Stability of Health

While the most reliable data on a national cross section of children are available from the National Health Survey, this source cannot tell us what happens to individual children during the subsequent years of their life. Does the child with more frequent than average respiratory illness during one year continue to have more than expected respiratory infections in later years? In general, the answer is yes, at least over a short two- or three-year period (Tucker and Downes 1953). One of the best long-term studies of children, the Newcastle-Upon-Tyne Study (Miller et al. 1974) followed about 1,000 children born in 1946 through to age fifteen. Of those with more frequent than average respiratory infections during the first five years, 50 percent continued at age fifteen to have more than the average number of infections, while of those children at average risk during the first five years, only 12 percent classified at age fifteen had more than the average number of infections. This is a fourfold increase in risk. Whether this increased risk is due to genetic susceptibility or to environmental factors is not known. Traditional medical opinion would probably argue that genetic factors are more important, but the physical environment (crowding; nutrition; exposure to air pollution, including tobacco smoke) and social stress (Meyer and Haggerty 1962) have also been shown to be important factors in some children with more frequent than expected respiratory infections. If the only consequence of this increased susceptibility is more frequent, but self-limited, acute respiratory infections, the impact would be relatively minor. But of greater long-term importance is whether the risk of chronic, obstructive, lung disease in adult life is greater in these children. It does seem that the risk of developing chronic lung disease is higher in adult life if one had frequent respiratory symptoms as a child; this risk is increased by smoking and by coming from a lower class family (Kiernan et al. 1976; Burrows, Lebowitz, and Knudson 1977).

The data are not so clear for many other problems. For instance, in one study of behavior problems in preschool children (Chamberlin 1977) it was found that while roughly the same percentage of children had behavior problems at seven as at three years of age, there was about an equal chance that it would not be the same child as had shown problems at an earlier time. In another study (Kronstadt et al. 1979), persistence of difficult behavior in children was determined through interviews of 147 mothers. There was considerable variation in the number who considered their children difficult between the ages of five weeks and six months. These maternal perceptions are somewhat at variance with studies of infant temperament (Carey and McDevitt 1978) where description by the parent of the dominant behavior of the infant was found to be quite stable over the years.

In one of the few studies conducted among youths followed from mid-teens to early adulthood (Brunswick 1980), considerable shifts in prevalence of illness were found. Males at twelve to seventeen years of age had 50 percent less reported illness than females, while at eighteen to twenty-three years of age the frequency of illness was about the same. In addition, there was considerable shift or turnover in individuals who reported health problems (Table 6-1).

The issues of stability of health or illness and the childhood antecedents of adult disease are among the most interesting and important issues facing pediatric epidemiology today. It will require long-term studies of large groups of children to determine which illnesses and precursors of illness seen in children are important. In a comprehensive review (Starfield and Pless 1980, pp. 272–334), the implica-

TABLE 6.1   Prevalence of Selected Health Problems in Black Adolescents

| | PERCENT | |
PROBLEM	*12–17 Years*	*18–23 Years*
Teeth and gums	32	44
Skin problems	18	30
Overweight	28	28
Musculoskeletal	14	28
Headaches	19	27
Menstrual problems*	89	30
Nervous or emotional	18	26
Underweight	30	25
Frequent colds	22	24
Vision problems	24	20
Indigestion	4	18
Chest pains	12	18

Adapted from Brunswick 1980.
* Female only.

tions for health services are well stated. "Because it is not possible [today] to predict exactly which children are at risk, highly targeted interventions are rarely feasible. Instead, a system of discriminating services is essential. The design of these services must stress early recognition of risk states and must provide for continuity of care over long periods of time. This approach will not only abort serious clinical problems early, but will provide better knowledge about the natural progression of disease and its determinants that is so evidently lacking at the present."

Causes of Illness

Illness is due to a small number of basic causes or etiologies. These causes manifest themselves in turn through a small number of mediating processes to produce illness, as the following illustrates.

CAUSES	MEDIATING PROCESS TO ILLNESS	OUTCOMES/DISEASE
Genetic	Metabolic disturbances	Diabetes
Environmental	Hypersensitivity	Allergy
Toxins–radiation	Neoplastic	Tumor
Infectious	Accidents	Tissue-organ damage
Traumatic	Poisons	Psychological illness
Psychosocial	Stress	
Health habits		
Exercise		
Diet		
Unknown		

We are only now beginning to understand the precise mechanisms by which a certain cause leads to a disease. People vary in their genetic makeup and life experiences and, therefore, in their susceptibility to illness. As individuals pass through life, they are exposed to agents and environments (physical and psychological stress) that produce illness in some but not in others. Some of these processes can be both cause and effect (e.g., people have different psychological makeups or susceptibility and are exposed to various levels of psychological stress. The interaction may produce physical or psychological illness or both). This is an interaction process between exposure to agent and environment and the individual host's susceptibility to both physical and psychological illness.

For the past century, most attention in epidemiology has been placed upon identifying single causes of illness—a bacterium or environmental toxin that once identified could then be removed. Great success followed this approach, but in recent years it has been recognized that many illnesses are caused by an *interaction* between two or more causes. Many people will be exposed to a bacterium, such as streptococcus, but only a few become ill. Some are resistant because of previous experience with the organism and resultant immunity, but most have a subclinical infection without symptoms, and only a few have serious illness. All of the reasons for this variation are not known, but there are recognized genetic variations in individual resistance. There are also variations in the amount or number of germs to which one is exposed, variations in the environment (amount of air pollution or psychological stress) that alter resistance, and variations in the individual's response to exposure to the toxins and psychological stress due to past experience. The balance between these multiple factors results in the final equation of whether a given individual becomes ill or not.

During various epochs of medicine, one or another of these factors has been regarded as dominant. Fads in conceptions of causation of disease come and go. Before the discovery of microorganisms, in the late nineteenth century, the environment (miasmas) and host resistance were dominant concerns. Prevention was aimed at environmental control (fresh air) and individual immunity (good diet and rest). These factors were all but forgotten in the early twentieth century as the microbiologic era unfolded, especially after antimicrobial agents were discovered and immunizing agents became available. It was then felt that most diseases could be prevented by immunization, cured by drugs, or prevented by isolation from the germ.

This phase has begun to be replaced today by recognition that multiple and interacting factors cause most illness (Susser 1973). The holistic health movement, concern for a safe environment, healthy life-styles, and interest in stress reduction represent swings of opinion today back to an emphasis on the importance of the individual and a healthy environment in preventing some illness. While the precise causal role of these various factors can rarely be stated, it is clear that *interaction of multiple factors* is the rule rather than the exception in the cause of human illness. Even most genetic disorders require a certain type of environment to produce disease (e.g., phenylketonuria [PKU], an inborn error of metabolism, requires milk in the diet to produce the illness).

The appropriate strategy for prevention or cure need not necessarily be multifactorial, however. It may be more efficient to immunize against polio virus then to eliminate all of the polio viruses from the environment, or to eliminate milk from the diet of a child with PKU, than to change the child's genes. For other illnesses, it may be necessary to reduce two or more of these factors below some threshold and, thereby, prevent or cure the illness when none of the etiologic factors can be completely eliminated. Asthma is often an example of this, although not a fully understood one. Factors such as infection, environmental allergens, psychological stress, and genetic susceptibility all contribute to the cause of asthma. Prevention or treatment may need to include reduction of environmental dust, treatment or prevention of the infection, reduction of stress—or increasing the individual's resistance to stress—immunization with environmental allergens, and reduction of the lung's asthmatic response to drugs.

The importance of the multiple causation theory of illness is that it allows for multiple rather than single attacks upon a problem. Most of the health problems that remain in Western societies must be tackled from a multiple cause approach if we are to improve health in the years to come. Most of the easy victories over illness have probably been won by the single cause approach. In the future, more attention to the combined approach of increasing the resistance of populations to physical and psychological stress and reducing environmental exposures (including substance abuse) will be necessary.

One of the most pervasive environmental factors associated with increased incidence and prevalence of many acute and chronic diseases is lower social class. For children, poverty may well be the most *potent* force, producing an increase in most illnesses. But, clearly, poverty influences this through some mechanism— either increased exposure to infectious agents and environmental toxins or reduced host resistance (poor diet, increased stress, etc.)—or through the *interaction* of multiple factors. Study of the precise means by which low social class causes illness should be a high priority for research, especially since it now appears that we will be less successful in eliminating poverty than was thought in the 1960s. In spite of the important role of environment in causing disease, it is important to recognize the boundaries or limits of the health-care system to deal with some of these (Haggerty 1972). Some health problems must be dealt with by society or not at all.

Prevalence and Incidence of Disease

Children, in contrast to adults, are characterized by rapidly changing incidence of disease at different ages.

Causes of Death (see Figure 6.1)

NEWBORN. In developed countries, more babies die during the first week of life than during the remainder of childhood. The major causes are special to this period of life. The euphemism "certain causes of mortality in early infancy" refers primarily to Respiratory Distress Syndrome, a disease limited to the first few days of life. Other major causes of death are congenital and hereditary disorders, infections acquired from the mother in the perinatal period, and a few other rare conditions. Together they cause over 80 percent of all deaths during the first year of life. Dramatic improvement has occurred in the United States in the past fifty years in reducing infant mortality (deaths during the first year) from nearly 100 to only 13 per 1,000 live born babies today. Improved perinatal care, highly technical care of babies born with immature lungs in intensive-care nurseries, and reduction in

Figure 6.1   Major Causes of Infant Deaths, 1950 and 1978 (Age Group Less than 1 Year)

Sources: USNCHS 1950, 1980.

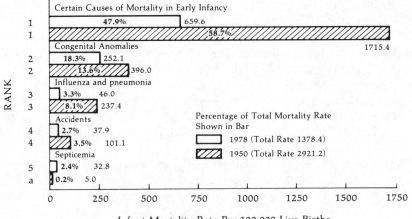

Infant Mortality Rate Per 100,000 Live Births

(a) Not Ranked in First 10 Leading Causes of Death.

deaths from diarrhea and infection from one month to twelve months have been largely responsible. After one month of age, sudden infant death, congenital anomalies, and accidents are now the leading causes of death in infancy, and the death rates from these causes have not changed much over the past twenty-five years. The causes of these deaths are largely unknown or due to multiple factors. Reducing this residual group of deaths will be more difficult than the earlier triumphs. Most of these residual causes are more common in lower social class patients. Some equalization of social class differences might be more effective in reducing this residual group of deaths than providing more technical care once the disease appears. This equalization of social class may well be the major reason some countries in Europe have so much lower infant mortality rates than the United States.

CHILDHOOD AND ADOLESCENCE (see Figure 6.2). For the rest of childhood, accidents are the leading causes of death, reaching the point where in adolescence 50 percent of all deaths are accidental. Indeed, in adolescence, violent deaths (accidents, homicide, and suicide) are three of the top four causes of death (Figure 6.3). Cancer and leukemia are the fourth cause and have by no means been conquered. However, death has been reduced, especially for acute leukemia; now over half of all children survive more than five years from a disease formerly universally fatal. Trends in death rates from accidents in children (Figure 6.4) and adolescents (Figures 6.5 and 6.6) show decreases for children and increases for adolescents over the past three decades.

Causes of Morbidity

These can be divided into acute episodic illnesses and chronic or recurrent illnesses (defined as lasting more than three months).

Figure 6.2 Major Causes of Childhood Deaths, 1950 and 1978 (Age Group 1–14 Years)
Sources: USNCHS 1950, 1980.

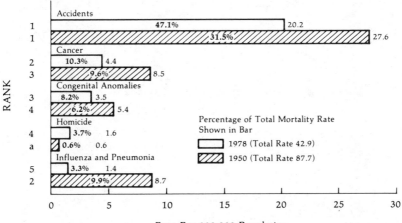

(a) Not Ranked in First 10 Leading Causes of Death.

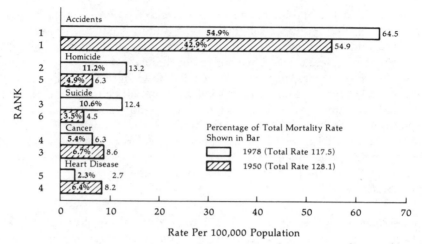

Figure 6.3 Major Causes of Adolescent Deaths, 1950 and 1978 (Age Group 15–24 Years)

Sources: USNCHS 1950, 1980.

ACUTE ILLNESS. Upper-respiratory infections are the most common cause of illness in childhood, exceeding all other causes during the preschool years (Figure 6.7). In the National Health Survey in 1974–75, there were 124 such episodes per year per 100 children under age six and 72 per 100 children per year from age six through sixteen in the United States (USNCHS 1977). These respiratory infections include a variety of different syndromes, including the common cold, sore throat, laryngitis, and otitis media. Lower-respiratory infections such as bronchitis and pneumonia are less common. The vast majority of respiratory infections are caused by viruses and generally have a benign outcome without any specific therapy. It has been estimated that each child acquires about a hundred such viral infections by the age of ten to twelve years, many of which are mild or asympto-

Figure 6.4 Trends in Accidental Death Rates for Children, from Selected Causes: Selected Years, 1950–1978 (1–14 Years Old)

Source: USNCHS various dates.

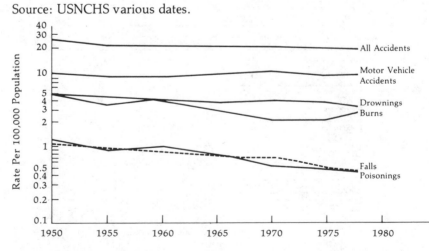

Note: The Selected Years are 1950, 1955, 1960, 1975 and 1978.

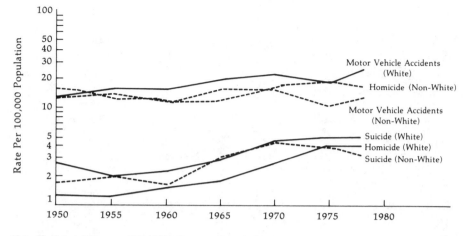

Note: The Selected Years are 1950, 1955, 1960, 1970, 1975 and 1978.

Figure 6.5   Trends in Death Rates for Suicide, Homicide, and Motor Vehicle Accidents among Adolescent Females, by Color: Selected Years, 1950–1978 (15–24-Year-Old Females, White and Nonwhite)

Source: USNCHS various dates.

matic. Only a minority of the total respiratory-infection group are caused by bacteria, but these include the important streptococcal infections, many instances of otitis media, and a few instances of croup, pneumonia, sepsis, and meningitis. These bacterial infections are important to differentiate from the large number caused by viruses; bacterial infections are usually very effectively treated with antibiotics, and if untreated have serious outcomes such as meningitis, sepsis, and other disseminated infections. A major task of clinical medicine is to make this distinction. This is often difficult in the individual at the time the patient is initially seen because diagnosis usually requires culture of the organism, which takes from

Figure 6.6   Trends in Death Rates for Suicide, Homicide, and Motor Vehicle Accidents among Adolescent Males, by Color: Selected Years, 1950–1978 (15–24-Year-Old Males, White and Nonwhite)

Source: USNCHS various dates.

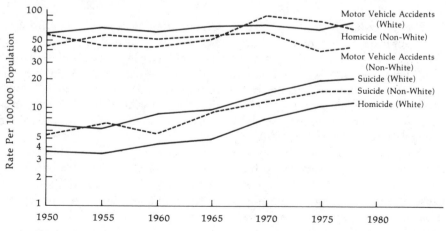

Note: The Selected Years are 1950, 1955, 1960, 1970, 1975 and 1978.

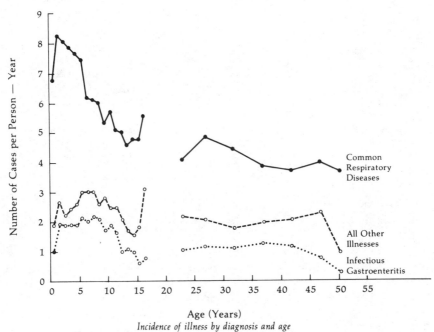

Incidence of illness by diagnosis and age

Figure 6.7   Incidence of Illness in Adults and Children

Source: Dingle, Badger, and Jordan 1964. These data demonstrate the high incidence of acute illness in children compared to adults, and that the bulk of illnesses are the common respiratory diseases, which are two to four times more common than *all* other diseases.

one to three days. Recent advances in diagnostic tests to identify antigens or antibodies in blood or urine at the time of presentation of the illness show great promise in helping to make this important distinction.

Dramatic successes have resulted from introduction of effective immunizations against many of the common contagious diseases of childhood. Poliomyelitis, tetanus, diphtheria, and whooping cough have almost been eliminated. Measles, mumps, and rubella are well on the way to being eliminated. Of the common contagious diseases, only chicken pox remains to be prevented by vaccine, and one is now being developed in Japan.

The remaining diseases are less common but often more severe. For instance, infectious hepatitis is a common illness which if acquired in early childhood rarely results in severe complications, but when acquired later in life can lead to chronic progressive liver disease. Children in day-care centers have been found to be infected but asymptomatic, yet are the source of the spread of infection to their older siblings and parents, who may develop the serious forms of the disease. Fortunately, for this problem there is also optimism that a successful vaccine will be available soon (Storch et al. 1979).

Accidents are the next most common acute health problem in children and cause an enormous amount of morbidity as well as mortality. There has been some reduction in mortality due to improved medical care of the victim and, for some causes, moderate reduction in morbidity due to managerial or regulatory approaches (e.g., the fifty-five-mile-an-hour speed limit, or safety caps on medicine bottles), but much less than for other causes of ill health. For most accidents there are from 100 to 1,000 times as many nonfatal as fatal accidents. The acute morbidity (days lost from school, pain and suffering, cost) and the late chronic complications (from brain injury, paralysis and loss of sight, disfiguring scars, or limitation of function) make the burden from accidents enormous. Accidents are the number-one child-health problem today, but the solution is more likely to be achieved by public health measures (e.g., population approaches through education and regulation) than by the medical-care system.

CHRONIC DISEASE. As acute illness has been reduced (at least the severe life-threatening complications) by pure water and food, immunizations, and effective therapy for infections, chronic illness has become more important. Chronic illnesses make up a very large number of often quite rare or special diseases. These range from those which medical care can treat effectively with no physical sequelae (e.g., adrenal insufficiency, which can be controlled by replacement hormones, or congenital heart disease that can be cured with surgery) to those where only paliation is possible (e.g., degenerative neurological disorders such as Tay-Sachs disease or thalassemia major, where life expectancy has been extended into adulthood, but with major physical limitations). Most chronic illnesses fall somewhere in between.

The frequency of chronic physical illnesses in childhood varies with the methods used to determine them. In large-scale community surveys, only visual and hearing problems, asthma, and developmental delay are found to occur in over 1 percent of children. All others are less common. It takes special surveys to determine the less frequent illnesses (Sultz et al. 1972) (Table 6.2) Overall, the approximately three thousand chronic disorders of childhood result in some 10 percent of children having one or more chronic physical disorders.

Behavioral disorders are common (10 to 30 percent of children are found with such problems), but they are less often diagnosed, and therapy has generally been felt to be less effective than in the case of the traditional physical disorders.

Mental and behavioral disorders are not limited to the developed world. In a recent study of the prevalence rates of behavioral symptoms or problems in four developing countries, 5 to 10 percent of the preadolescents and 10 to 20 percent of the adolescents were found to be suffering from behavioral disorders. Of these, only 10 to 20 percent were recognized by primary-care workers—not too dissimilar from experience in developed countries. The most common behavioral problems in this four-country study were frequent headaches, nervousness, sleep disturbance, backwardness, wetting or soiling, speech disturbances, running away, stealing, and social isolation (Giel et al. 1982).

TABLE 6.2 Cumulative Prevalence of Selected
Long-term Medical Diseases in Childhood

Endocrine disease	65/100,000
Blood dyscrasias	50/100,000
Collagen disease	21/100,000
Kidney diseases	21/100,000
Inborn errors of metabolism	16/100,000
Peptic ulcer	16/100,000
Neuromuscular genetic conditions	8/100,000
Bronchiectasis	4/100,000

Source: Sultz et al. 1972.

In addition to the high prevalence of behavioral disorders in children, it is now recognized that many children with serious physical disorders suffer additional disruption in their daily functioning because of the associated behavioral disturbance.

In my view, the dichotomy between mental and physical illness is a misleading one, for emotional factors can cause physical illness, and physical illness may cause emotional disturbances. This is one reason we need better measures of the prevalence of disability, no matter what the cause or causes, rather than more studies of the frequency of each separate illness.

We have called the changing causes of illness in children "the new morbidity" (Haggerty, Roghmann, and Pless 1975). The problems of school learning difficulties (seen in 20 to 30 percent of children), emotional problems (fears, nightmares, aggressive acts, etc.), substance abuse (including tobacco and alcohol), and teenage pregnancy are clearly not new. What is new is their prominence today and the concern they cause children and their families. Some of these problems may be increasing in frequency (e.g., substance abuse), some are brought to medical attention more often today because of the faith the public has in the ability of medical science to cure all problems, and some of the prominence may be relative, due to the decline in many traditional medical problems, leaving these more visible. In putting the name "new morbidity" on them, we sought to bring attention to a group of problems not being adequately addressed by the health professions. I am pleased to see that some are being more extensively studied, and with time and more research, we may be able to define how best to prevent or cure these problems and to determine the appropriate role of medicine in this process.

Function vs. Prevalence

In considering the five levels of the outcome of illness (death, disease, disability, discomfort, and dissatisfaction), the use of the term *disability* may seem peculiar. When one has an illness (morbidity) most of us would think that he/she should have some disability. This is especially the case with the spectrum of illness seen by the physician. After all, most people come to the doctor because they feel sick and cannot function as well as they normally do in their daily life. But medicine is now recognizing that the presence of disease and degree of disability are not directly related. Medicine's role is to improve function, not merely to cure disease. It is not enough to diagnose and even successfully correct the heart of a child with congenital heart disease, if the child is so disturbed or thinks himself so ill that he cannot go to school or relate to peers.

We have no really good data on the frequency of disability, as contrasted with disease (morbidity), and research is only now addressing the best ways of measuring and improving function. It is a major future task of epidemiology to move from assessing mortality and morbidity to assessing function.

Adolescent Health

Special mention needs to be made of adolescent health. It has generally been assumed that adolescents are healthy because respiratory infection rates are lower than in early childhood as a result of immunity acquired during childhood. Also contributing to the neglect of adolescents has been their relative resistance to seeing a physician (especially one of their parents') and even the definition of what ages constitutes adolescence. The precise age span covered by this term varies but, in general, from onset of teens to the early twenties should be considered adolescence, since these ages generally are characterized by similar illnesses. Rapid growth and development continues into the early twenties. For many children, graduation from college marks a transition that ends adolescence. It is frequently only then that the adolescent leaves the care of his/her pediatrician.

Adolescents are the one group in society who have increasing mortality, largely from accidents, homicide, and suicide. It is also clear that there is also considerable morbidity among this group (Brunswick 1980) (Table 6.1). In addition, it is during this period of life that health habits are formed that are likely to persist. Development of healthy habits among adolescents constitutes one of the greatest challenges to the health professions and society. A measure of the high frequency of potentially unhealthy behavior was shown by a recent study (Kovar 1979). The majority of adolescents have used alcohol and cigarettes, one-fourth have tried marijuana (although there is a slight decline in this in the past year), nearly half of the unmarried girls have had intercourse by the age of seventeen, and in spite of a dramatic increase in the availability of contraceptives, only 36 percent of adolescent girls, or their partners, used contraceptives during this first intercourse.

Most of our data are available only for the age groupings one to fourteen and fifteen to twenty-four years. It would help to advance our knowledge of adolescence and the development of appropriate services if data of health and behavior were broken down by developmental age periods or, at least, by year of age rather than by such large (ten-year) aggregate age groups; in adolescence rapid change from year to year and the relation of many illnesses to age of onset are more important than the chronological age. By lumping all adolescents together, we obscure many dynamic developments. For instance, it is now clear that most teenagers who smoke begin in the sixth to eighth grades (eleven to fourteen years of age). It is to this age group that antismoking efforts should be directed, yet reports of smoking behavior often are given starting with fifteen-year-olds. Suicide is becoming more common, but it is difficult to determine for precisely which age group, since broad age groups are combined in the statistics. We need statistics on adolescence that are broken down by one- or two-year age groups, rather than by ten-year clusters.

Prevention through Modification of Health Habits

Several workers have demonstrated that change in a few health behaviors would do more to improve health than the provision of medical care (Haggerty 1977). The major health behaviors involved are smoking, exercise, diet, dental hygiene, sexual promiscuity, coping with stress, risk-taking regarding accidents, and, perhaps, amount of sleep. To date, efforts to change these behaviors by education have met with only limited success. Most success has come from managerial or legal regulations or as a result of group pressure (social learning, such as current diet and exercise fads among certain groups). Changing health behavior, especially among adolescents, constitutes a major task for the health profession today.

Implication for Provision of Health Services for Children

Studies in Sweden of all children in certain communities at age four and again at ten to twelve years of age have yielded important information on the prevalence of health problems and their significance. These studies stressed the importance of identifying illness for which treatment was efficacious before symptoms appeared.

In these Swedish studies, 24.6 percent of children at four years of age were found to have some health problems. Of these, 14.7 percent were newly detected, but only 0.29 percent of these were classed as severe (Sundelin and Vuille 1975). The most frequent health problems detected were vision (6.7 percent), hearing (1.6 percent), speech (1.8 percent), developmental (0.9 percent), behavioral (3 percent), neurological (0.7 percent), and all other physical (9.9 percent). In all, 60 percent of health problems present among four-year-olds were first detected at the screening, but only 19 percent of these were identified as severe. In other words, traditional medical problems (heart disease, orthopedic problems, etc.) were being identified in large part by the regular medical-care system. Previously unrecognized problems in vision, hearing, speech, and emotional disorders were found.

It is still unclear who should screen for abnormalities. Continuous care by a sensitive and skilled physician should be optimal, but the high frequency of new diagnoses at age four in Sweden, a country where most children have access to continuing medical care, is worrisome. Society cannot afford a special cadre of "screeners" for each age of risk (and the probability of getting children found to have a defect into care with such impersonal screeners is probably low). But the performance of physicians who serve as the "medical home" for children needs to improve if we are to trust entirely to continuity of care to detect problems.

Twenty-six to 30 percent of ten- to twelve-year-olds had health problems, but six out of seven of these were previously known. The most common problems found at this age were obesity, scoliosis, eczema, asthma, and dental, hearing, vision, and mild orthopedic disorders (Kornfald, Jonsson, and Roslund 1979). Nurses were able to detect almost all these problems, thus providing more evidence confirming the inefficient nature of health screenings by physicians of children in the primary grades.

In a study of children three to eighteen years of age (Sturner et al. 1980), experienced pediatricians found 38 percent to have significant developmental or psychological problems, nearly 90 percent of these previously unknown. The implications for pediatric practice are considerable: "The routine health examination has less than one chance in 100 of uncovering significant physical problems, but three chances in ten of identifying a psychologic problem. Given these odds, each physician should decide on what is the best way of spending his time during such health supervision encounters" (Oski 1981, p. 400).

Conclusions about the implications of epidemiologic research for the provision of health services have been scattered throughout the chapter. To summarize:

1. One purpose of epidemiology is to define the burden of illness in the community in order to allow us to develop health services appropriately.

2. Health services for children in the 1980s in the United States give less attention to social-psychological causes of illness than the prevalence of those factors warrant. They pay too little attention to adolescent health problems, and too much attention to screening for physical disease in well-baby, well-child care and

school health contexts where the positive findings are very infrequent. A corollary of this finding is that what screening is done in school-age children can be done as well by nurse clinicians and other professionals as by physicians. Screening for psychological disturbances will yield a far higher prevalence of children with dysfunctions than screening for physical disease. Whether therapy is effective for those children found to have psychological disturbances is less well established.

3. The "at-risk" concept is very attractive for it could allow one to target resources to those at risk and save precious resources by not serving those at low risk. However, a study in Czechoslovakia (World Health Organization 1980) demonstrates that the proportions of children who were labeled at risk at different stages were: 5 percent during gestation, 8 percent during birth, 10 percent in the neonatal period, and 20 percent at three years of age. The children labeled at risk represented only about 25 percent of the problems encountered by these groups. Thus, these risk groups predicted poorly.

In spite of these figures, there are certain age groups where the at-risk concept has some use and there are certain ages and captive populations where screening of all children is useful. It seems wise to detect women who are at high risk during pregnancy, monitor their progress with special care, and refer them to hospitals when necessary where full technical and supportive services are available. Every newborn should be evaluated and certain screening tests performed (PKU, thyroid status, visual and hearing status). Children should then be monitored for growth (height, weight, and head circumference) and development. Special focus should be on the low socioeconomic groups and children with established illnesses, where risk of health problems and resistance to care are highest. This often requires considerable outreach efforts. Completion of immunizations on schedule is important to health, and absence of this is a proxy for other health problems. Immunization can be done in special clinics or schools. Before entry to schools, children should have a comprehensive health assessment, including special efforts to assess behavior and development.

4. Although some special attention to high-risk groups and screening at certain times is warranted, the epidemiology of child health has demonstrated that one cannot identify all children who are at high risk ahead of time. Therefore, all children should be in some type of continuing-care setting.

5. Health services and society need to develop more effective ways to teach and reinforce healthy life-styles if further major advances in health are to occur.

6. The life-span concept of human development is fairly recent. (Baltes and Brim 1980). It emphasizes the ability of the human organism to change throughout life and also recognizes the sociohistorical and cultural forces that affect behavior. This concept is optimistic—since it demonstrates that humans can change throughout life—and yet challenging. It takes away some of the guilt many parents have that they may have irreversibly damaged their children. But it is challenging because it places a burden on the helping professions to intervene effectively throughout the life span.

7. Life-span development emphasizes that individual development is not complete at the end of childhood or adolescence. But with this recognition also comes the realization that human development is very complicated and that we should be suspicious of formulations that simplify. Developmental changes depend on the historical context in which one's life occurs. Children growing up in the 1960s with the revolution in attitudes towards sex and drugs, developed quite differently than those of the 1940s.

Child health services must recognize these changes and modify services depending upon the historical, cultural, and social context. Much of the current debate about how to organize and deliver child health services stem from the changed circumstances of life for today's children, and the changes in their problems. Epidemiology is a science that helps to develop the intelligence about current problems in order to define needs and make services more relevant to the times.

REFERENCES

BALTES, P. B., and BRIM, O. G., JR., eds. 1980. *Life span development and behavior.* New York: Academic Press.

BLOCK, J. 1969. *Lives through time.* Berkeley, Calif.: Bancroft Bowles.

BRUNSWICK, A. F. 1980. *Health, stability and change: a study of urban black youth. American Journal of Public Health* 70: 504–13.

BURROWS, B.: LEBOWITZ, M.; and KNUDSON, R. 1977. Epidemiologic evidence that childhood problems predispose to airways disease in the adult. (an association between adult and pediatric respiratory disorders). *Pediatric Research* 11:218–20.

CAREY, W. B., and McDEVITT, S. C. 1978. Infant temperament questionnaire. *Pediatrics* 61:735.

CHAMBERLIN, R. W. 1977. "Can we identify a group of children at ages two who are at high risk for the development of behavior or emotional problems in kindergarten and first grade? *Pediatrics* 59 (suppl.): 971–81.

DINGLE, J. H.; BADGER, G. F.; and JORDAN, W. S., JR. 1964. *Illness in the home: a study of 25,000 illnesses in a group of Cleveland families.* Cleveland, Ohio: Case Western Reserve University Press.

DOUGLAS, J. W.; ROSS, J. M.; and SIMPSON, H. R. 1968. *All our future: a longitudinal study of secondary education.* London: Peter Davies.

GIEL, R.; DEARANGO, M. V.; CLIMENT, C. E.; et al. 1982. Childhood mental disorders in primary health care: results of observations in four developing countries. *Pediatrics* in press.

GORTMAKER, S. L., et al. 1980. *Access to and utilization of child health services in Genesee County, Michigan.* Cambridge, Mass.: Harvard University Press.

HAGGERTY, R. J. 1972. The boundaries of health care. *Pharos of Alpha Omega Alpha* 35:106.

———. 1977. Teaching healthy lifestyles. *Preventive Medicine* 6:276.

HAGGERTY, R. J.; ROGHMANN, K. J.; and PLESS, I. B. 1975. *Child health and the community.* New York: Wiley.

KIERNAN, K. E.; CALLEY, J. R. J.; DOUGLAS, J. W. B.; and RIED, D. D. 1976. Chronic cough in young adults in relation to smoking habits, childhood environment and chest illness. *Respiration* 33:236–44.

KORNFALD, R.; JÖNSSON, B.; and ROSLUND, I. 1979. Physical health screening of school children: extended health care responsibilities for school nurses. *Acta Paediatr. Scandinavia* 68:879–85.

KOVAR, M. G. 1979. Some indicators of health related behavior among adolescents in the United States. *Public Health Reports* 94:109–18

KRONSTADT, D.; OBERKLAID, F., FERB, T. E.; and SWARTZ, J. P. 1979. Infant behavior and maternal adaptations in first six months of life. *American Journal of Orthopsychiatry* 49:454–64.

MACFARLANE, J. W.; ALLEN, L.; and HONZIK, M. P. 1954. *A developmental study of the behavior problems of normal children between 21 months and 14 years.* Berkeley, Calif.; University of California Press.

MEYER, R. J., and HAGGERTY, R. J. 1962. Streptococcal infections in families: factors altering individual susceptibility. *Pediatrics* 29:539.

MILLER, F. J. W.; COURT, S. D. M.; KNOX, E. G.; and BRANDON, S. 1974. *The school years in Newcastle-Upon-Tyne.* London: Oxford University Press.

MORRIS, J. N. 1964. *Uses of epidemiology.* 2d ed. Baltimore, Md.:Williams and Wilkins.

NAEYE, R. L. 1980. Sudden infant death. *Scientific American* 242: 56–62.

OSKI, F. 1981. Comment on article by Sturner et al. *Year book of pediatrics.* Chicago: Year Book Publishing, Inc.

PATRICK, D., and ELINSON, J., 1979. "Methods of Sociomedical Research" Chapter 21, N. Freeman, H. E. Levine, L. G. Reeder, eds. *Handbook of Medical Sociology,* 3rd edition, pp. 440–442. Englewood Cliffs, N.J.: Prentice-Hall.

RICE, D. P.; FELDMAN, J. J.; and WHITE, K. K. 1976. The current burden of illness in the United States. An occasional paper of the Institute of Medicine, National Academy of Science.

ROGHMANN, K. J., and HAGGERTY, R. J. 1973. Daily stress and use of health services in young families. *Pediatric Research* 7:520

RUTTER, M.; TIZARD, J.; and WHITMORE, K. 1970. *Education, health and behavior.* London: Longman Group Ltd.

STARFIELD, B.; GROSS, E.; WOOD, M.; PANTELL, R.; ALLEN, C.; GORDON, I. B.; MOFFATT, P.; DROCHMAN, R.; and KATZ, H. 1980. Psychosocial and psychomatic diagnoses in primary care of children. *Pediatrics* 66:159.

STARFIELD, B., and PLESS, I. B. 1980. Physical health. In *Constancy and changes in human development,* ed. O. G. Brim and J. Kagan. Cambridge, Mass.: Harvard University Press.

STORCH, G.; MCFARLAND, L. M.; KELSO, K.; HEILMAN, C. J.; and CARAWAY, C. J. 1979. Viral hepatitis associated with day-care centers. *Journal of the American Medical Association* 242: 1514–18.

STURNER, R. A.; GRANGER, R. N.; KLATSKIN, E. H.; and FERHALT, J. B. 1980. The routine "well child" examination: a study of its value in discovery of significant psychologic problems. *Clinical Pediatrics* 19:251–60.

SULTZ, H. A.; SCHLESINGER, E. R.; MOSHER, W.; and FELDMAN, J. G. 1972. *Longterm childhood illness.* Pittsburgh: University of Pittsburgh Press.

SUNDELIN, C., and VUILLE, J. C. 1975. Health screening of four year olds in a Swedish Country. II. Effectiveness in detecting problems. *Acta Paediatr. Scandinavia* 64:801–6.

SUSSER, M. 1973. *Causal thinking in the health sciences: concepts and strategy in epidemiology.* New York: Oxford University Press.

TUCKER, D., and DOWNES, J. 1953. Disability from respiratory illness. *Milbank Memorial Fund Quarterly* 31:141–48.

U.S. Department of Health Education and Welfare. 1964. *Health survey procedure: concepts, questionnaire, development and definitions in the health interview survey.* PHS pub. 1,000, ser. 2, no. L. Washington, D.C.: Government Printing Office.

U.S. National Center for Health Statistics. 1950. *Vital statistics—special report—national summaries,* vol. 37. Washington, D.C.: Government Printing Office.

———. 1977. *Health interview survey: methods.* Ser. 10, no. 114. Washington, D.C.: Government Printing Office.

———. 1980. Final mortality statistics, 1978. *Monthly Vital Statistics Report* 29, (no. 6, suppl. 2).

———. Various dates. *Vital statistics of the United States.* Vol 2: Mortality. Selected years, published and unpublished data. Washington, D.C.: Government Printing Office.

VALADIAN, I.; STUART, H.; and REED, R. 1959. Patterns of illness experiences. *Pediatrics* 24:941–71.

WERNER, E. E.; BIERMAN, J. M.; and FRENCH, F. E. 1971. *The children of Kauai.* Honolulu, Hawaii: University of Hawaii Press.

World Health Organization Working Group. 1980. *Early detection of handicap in children.* Faro (Portugal), May 1979. EURO Reports and Studies 30.

Chapter 7

Epidemiology of Ischemic Heart Disease and Cancer

Sam Shapiro

THIS CHAPTER IS CONCERNED with the epidemiology of ischemic heart disease (a condition manifested by heart attacks and angina pectoris) and cancer. Combined, these conditions account for about half of all deaths that occur during the year in the United States and for a large majority of the deaths starting with the middle years of adult life. Morbidity is high and, measured from first diagnosis, it often extends over long periods of time. With few exceptions, the underlying physiological or biochemical changes are in process substantially before the state of clinical detectability; the date of biological onset is usually indeterminate and the timing of detection varies with the individual's response to signal events in the development of the disease and with the level of diagnostic capability that is available. Accordingly, there are circumstances external to the natural history of the condition that affect when it becomes known for epidemiologic investigations and these may vary in time and place.

A major objective of epidemiologic studies is to identify risk factors which might be modified and thereby prevent the occurrence of the disease (primary prevention) or alter favorably the course of the disease by early detection and treatment (secondary prevention). Data from such studies on levels and distribution of diseases are also important for developing policy and planning measures directed at meeting needs for ambulatory and institutional health services.

There are two broad types of risk factors: (1) biological (e.g., age, sex, race, age at menarche) and social characteristics (e.g., fertility patterns, income), which cannot be changed or are dependent on large societal forces; and (2) other factors, personal (e.g., smoking, diet) and environmental (e.g., occupational hazards), which interact with the first set and can become the target for change.

Knowledge is sought on both types of risk factors to establish the extent to which a characteristic elevates risk (relative risk) and how much of the incidence of the disease is due to the presence of the characteristic (attributable risk). It is possible for the relative risk associated with a characteristic to be high, but because it affects few people, the attributable risk is low. The reverse can also occur. These relationships are based mainly on associations, and questions arise about the certainty that they represent cause and effect. When supporting laboratory evidence becomes available or effects are demonstrated in well-controlled experiments, the significance of these questions is reduced. Also, replication of associations in studies of widely different populations increases confidence in drawing conclusions about causality.

The body of knowledge that has accumulated on risk factors is impressive for ischemic heart disease and many cancer sites. This subject is considered in the chapter along with efforts to test the efficacy of primary and secondary preventive actions. It is not intended to be all-inclusive and there are gaps in the information; for example, variations among geographic areas within the United States and among countries are not dealt with, except incidentally.

Both mortality and incidence are addressed. Mortality reflects the combined effect of the incidence of disease and the rate at which those who have the disease die from the condition. In the case of a rapidly fatal chronic disease, the level of the death rate reasonably approximates that of the incidence of the disease; the longer the average duration of survival, the greater the discrepancy is likely to be. When there is reason to believe that the course of the disease has not changed, trends in death rates parallel those for incidence except for the effect of changes in mortality from other conditions. Where there is minor variation among population subgroups in the prognosis of the condition, relationships based on mortality and incidence data follow similar patterns.

All of these relationships are subject to considerable variation depending on the disease. Nevertheless, the starting point for the discussion of ischemic heart disease and cancer that follows is mortality. Death rates derived from vital statistics provide the means for identifying changes over long periods of time in losses attributable to these conditions and for assessing the magnitude and distribution of this loss within the population. They serve as indicators for allocation of resources to programs of research on causation, disease detection and treatment, and as measures of success in primary and secondary control of the disease. However, it is well understood that there is no completely satisfactory substitute for knowledge about incidence and associated risk factors or the impact of the diseases on the functional status of those affected.

Source of Cause of Death Data and Rate Calculation

National mortality statistics are provided through annual tabulations by the U.S. National Center for Health Statistics (USNCHS) of death certificate information on underlying cause of death, age, sex, race, and geographic area of residence of the decedent (USNCHS 1977). An important strength of this data series is its continuity over many years—since 1933 for the country as a whole and back to 1900 for a subset of areas which met standards established for completeness of registration of deaths. An issue of some consequence which has received attention concerns the comparability of the cause of death information over extended periods of time (Klebba and Scott 1980). Changes may occur in the reporting of causes of death on the certificate due to advances in knowledge about disease processes and to recording practices. For some diseases of even greater significance are the changes made decennially in the International Classification of Diseases and in the accompanying coding rules. Studies conducted periodically to determine the influence of these changes on assignment of deaths to the various causes indicate that ischemic heart disease has been significantly affected, cancer has not. Accordingly, long-term trends of mortality due to ischemic heart disease need to be interpreted cautiously; greater attention should be given to changes in rates within ten-year periods during which the classification rules remain the same than across such periods. The importance of this issue is reduced when diseases are combined into broad categories.

Major emphasis in mortality statistics is given to rates that are age specific because of the strong relationship between the age variable and mortality. When the data combine the experience for all ages, age adjustment is introduced to take into account changes in time and differences between subgroups of the population in their age distributions. The convention has been to use the age distribution of the population enumerated in the 1940 Decennial Census as the standard: the age-adjusted rate is calculated by applying age-specific rates for a cause of death in a particular year and subgroup to the age composition of the 1940 population, aggregating the derived numbers of deaths and dividing this total by the number of persons in the 1940 population (multiplied by 1,000, 10,000, and 100,000 to express the rate in terms of per 1,000, etc., population).

Ischemic Heart Disease (IHD)

In 1980, 566,930—close to 30 percent—of the estimated 1,986,000 deaths in the United States were due to ischemic heart disease, with the deaths almost equally divided between acute myocardial infarction and chronic ischemic heart disease (USNCHS 1981). The death rate for all causes combined was 892.6 per 100,000; age adjusted, the rate was considerably lower, 594.1 per 100,000, reflecting the aging of the population since 1940. The corresponding rate for IHD was 152.4 per 100,000. Other diseases of the heart are important causes of death but in the aggregate they represent a much smaller proportion of total deaths, about 10 percent.

The social and economic burden of IHD is seen in measures of medical-care utilization and impairment of function (Rice, Feldman and White 1976). A ranking of sixteen major diagnostic categories, in which IHD is subsumed under the broader heading "diseases of the circulatory system," shows this diagnostic group as ranking first or second in person years of life lost, total economic costs, inpatient days, physician office visits, and disability or limitations in major activity during the year.

IHD Mortality by Age, Sex, and Color

The latest year for which national data by age, sex, and race were available at this writing was 1978 (USNCHS 1978). Statements regarding relationships involving these variables are expected to be applicable to more recent years.

Age is the most important determinant of mortality from IHD. In young adult ages, it is a rare occurrence. As age increases, the annual death rate from IHD rises sharply. In 1978, the rate was 454.7 per 100,000 among those fifty-five to sixty-four years and more than doubled in each successive ten-year age group. The risk of mortality from IHD is far greater among men than women at every age. In the white population, IHD mortality rates under fifty-five years of age are four to five times higher among males than females. The excess in IHD death rates for males decreases with increasing age but even at ages over seventy-five years men have substantially higher rates than women. Among nonwhites, the margin between the two sexes in their age-specific IHD death rates is smaller than among whites.

Differentials between the nonwhite and white populations in IHD mortality are sex and age related. Under age sixty-five, nonwhites in both sexes are at higher risk than whites. The magnitude of the relative risk differs greatly between men and women. Among men, the nonwhite IHD death rate is about 1.5 times the corresponding white rate at ages thirty-five to forty-four years; the ratio decreases with increasing age to 1:1 at sixty to sixty-four years. Among women, there is a similar pattern of decreasing race differentials as age advances, but here the order of magnitude of the relative risk is far greater than among men; nonwhite women have two to four times the IHD mortality of the white women. Above age sixty-five, there are also differences in patterns: white men have higher mortality rates than the nonwhite; nonwhite women's unfavorable status persists into the more advanced older ages.

Changes in Mortality from IHD

Major decreases in mortality from IHD have been under way since the mid-1960s, the first such sustained decreases that have been documented (Rosenberg and Klebba 1979; USDHHS 1981). When allowance is made for changes in classification of causes of death over the decades, three patterns emerge. Between 1950 and 1963, the age-adjusted death rates for arteriosclerotic heart disease—including coronary disease, the single most nearly comparable category to IHD—increased by almost 20 percent from 185.2 to 220.3 per 100,000. The nonwhite population experienced almost twice as large an increase as the white population. For several years, the death rate from arteriosclerotic heart disease appeared to remain stationary but it is universally accepted that a downward trend started thereafter.

Between 1968 and 1978, the age-adjusted rate dropped by almost 25 percent from 241.6 per 100,000 to 180.9 per 100,000. The decrease accounts for almost half of the reduction that occurred in the age-adjusted death rate from all causes (from 743.8 to 606.1 per 100,000).

An extraordinary feature of the decline is its breadth. Men and women, whites and nonwhites, at every age level experienced a reduction in mortality. Relatively, the IHD death rate dropped more at ages under forty-five years than at older ages, and women, particularly the nonwhite, showed a larger decline than the men.

A matter that has been the subject of intensive scrutiny concerns the factors responsible for the decline in mortality from IHD. The context for this consideration later in the chapter is the role of personal and health characteristics identified as risk factors for the incidence and prognosis of coronary heart disease. These consist of immutable characteristics, i.e., those not subject to modification through intervention programs (e.g., demographic status) and mutable characteristics, i.e., those subject to such modifications (e.g., smoking).

Risk Factors for Incidence of Coronary Heart Disease (CHD)

DEMOGRAPHIC CHARACTERISTICS. The influence of age and sex on the incidence (first occurrence) of a myocardial infarction (MI) and angina pectoris parallels the patterns in mortality from ischemic heart disease. This has been demonstrated in a wide variety of investigations involving local communities, employment groups, and populations insured for health care.

For example, the study conducted during the 1960s in the Health Insurance Plan (HIP) of Greater New York, a prepaid comprehensive group practice program, among men and women aged thirty-five to sixty-four years, showed that men had an annual incidence rate of first myocardial infarction that was five times the rate among women (5.2 per 1,000 vs 1.0 per 1,000) (Shapiro et al. 1969). Among men, the incidence rate for angina (2.0 per 1,000) was far below the MI rate whereas among women the risk of having first clinical evidence of angina (0.9 per 1000) was about the same as for having an MI.

For each manifestation of CHD, the incidence rate rose sharply with increasing age between thirty-five and sixty-four years, the ages covered in the study. The rate of increase was greater among women than men past age forty-four, but the incidence of both manifestations remained higher among the men throughout this age range.

Departures from these relationships in other studies are relatively minor despite differences in methodology. The HIP study, because of the composition of its insured population, had the capability of examining the role of race as a risk factor for incidence of CHD among men. Here it was found that the rates among white men were higher than among the nonwhite men. This runs counter to differentials in mortality rates which indicate nonwhite men have the higher rates under age sixty-five. The reason may lie in variation between local and national situations or, and more likely, poorer prognosis among the nonwhite men with CHD.

A wide range of social characteristics were investigated but differentials were relatively small in the incidence of CHD, after taking into account other risk factors. This applies to educational attainment, type of occupation, and marital status. Women in the labor force tended to have a lower incidence rate than other women. It should be noted that studies of these characteristics have not produced consistent results (Hinkle et al. 1968; Marks 1967; Shekelle 1969). Differences can arise, depending on several factors including whether mortality is at issue and whether the experience covers persons over age sixty-five years, in contrast to the HIP study which was restricted to those under sixty-five.

CHARACTERISTICS SUBJECT TO MODIFICATION. Three risk factors that have become targets for extensive intervention programs are high blood pressure, elevated blood cholesterol levels, and cigarette smoking (Stamler and Epstein 1972). The largest body of information available for all three of these factors comes from several long-term prospective studies, the first of which started in Framingham, Massachusetts, during the late 1940s (Dawber, Moore, and Mann 1957; Kannel and Gordon 1977). Basic elements in common among these investigations, in addition to their longitudinality, are: (1) baseline examinations and history to identify for follow-up individuals with no prior CHD and to determine their medical, laboratory, and personal characteristics; (2) periodic observations over many years to detect the first occurrence of CHD and identify deaths from any cause; and (3) similar diagnostic criteria.

Findings from each have been reported extensively in the literature and these have been sufficiently consistent to lead to the pooling of the data for detailed analysis of the influence of specific risk factors, particularly those subject to modification. Principal output from this effort, titled the Pooling Project (Pooling Project Research Group 1978), is derived from data for samples of the populations in two communities (Framingham, containing several large industries, and Tecumseh, Michigan, a small town with a single large industry) and three employment groups (a Chicago gas company, a Chicago electrical equipment manufacturer, and New York State employees in Albany). Observations reported from the pooled data cover major coronary events, i.e., nonfatal and fatal myocardial infarction and sudden death, during approximately ten years of follow-up. These data relate to white middle-aged men (forty to sixty-four years) at time of entry.

The data extend observations regarding a number of the previously identified risk factors to provide more complete insights into their strengths, singly and in combination, as predictors of a first major coronary event. One of the more important findings is that increases in blood pressure levels, serum cholesterol levels, and cigarette smoking, starting at quite low points, are associated with increases in risk of a first such event. In the case of both systolic and diastolic blood pressures there is a twofold range in risks between high and low levels; high is defined as a reading close to the value used in clinical practice as definitely abnormal (systolic, 150 mm Hg; diastolic, 95 mm Hg) and low extends well into "normal" values (systolic, below 130 mm Hg; diastolic, below 80 mm Hg).

Serum cholesterol is also consistently and strongly related to CHD with risk more than doubling as cholesterol values increase from below 200 mg/dl to above 270 mg/dl. Within this range are levels often designated as "normal" in clinical practice. Risk associated with cigarette smoking is dose-related to the number smoked per day. Compared to the risk of a first major coronary event among those not smoking, men who smoke more than a pack per day have three times the risk; those smoking about a pack per day have more than twice the risk; and those smoking half a pack have almost twice the risk. Men who quit smoking cigarettes have approximately the same risk for CHD as nonsmokers. Small numbers of cigar and pipe smokers in the Pooling Project preclude the possibility of determining with reasonable confidence what their relative risk for CHD is but available observations suggest that the risk, while appreciably below even moderate cigarette smokers, is higher than among nonsmokers.

Relative weight (ratio of observed weight to desirable weight for height as obtained from the Metropolitan Life Insurance Company desirable weight tables) is not as clearly related to risk of CHD; it is associated with increased risk at ages under fifty years but not at older ages. However, being overweight and a gain in weight are implicated in hypertension, which, as discussed above, is a major risk factor for CHD.

When the three risk factors—blood pressure, serum cholesterol, and cigarette smoking—are considered jointly in a multivariate statistical model, it is found that the relationship of each to a first major coronary event is independent of the others and when combined they identify an exceptionally wide range in risk (6:1) between high and low. Further, by utilizing these risk factors, it is shown that among white middle-aged men, the 20 percent who are at highest risk account for about 40 percent of those who will have a first major coronary event over the next ten years. Corresponding percentages involving groups at or near the highest risk levels indicate the ability to identify with considerable confidence a large majority of the men in the Pooling Project who subsequently had such an event. The statistical measures of risk derived in the project have been demonstrated to have high predictive power for first coronary events among middle-aged men followed in three other study populations, the data for which were available to the Pooling Project. Further, the relationships are found in many other independent, prospective, and cross-sectional investigations in communities and subpopulation groups in the United States, in other countries and in cross-national studies (Keys 1980).

OTHER RISK FACTORS. Other risk factors have been implicated for coronary heart disease. Evidence has cumulated regarding the negative effect of physical inactivity. In the HIP study, men whose overall level of physical activity, on and off the job, was rated as "least active" had twice as high a rate of myocardial infarction as "moderately active" men, who, in turn, showed no advantage over men rated as "most active" (Shapiro et al. 1969). Furthermore, the sedentary men with no prior MI appeared to be at particularly high risk for a rapidly fatal MI; the risk of a non-fatal first MI was only moderately greater among the inactive men. The HIP study findings have become part of a substantially larger set of observations that started to appear twenty to twenty-five years ago and pointed to the importance of physical inactivity as a risk factor for CHD (Breslow and Buell 1960; Morris and Crawford 1958). A source of disagreement concerns how vigorous the physical activity has to be before risk is lowered; the HIP study suggested moderate activity was adequate, but others indicate that the activity needs to be strenuous (Paffenbarger and Hale 1975). Accordingly, while physical activity seems to be a significant risk factor, there are many aspects that are unclear. It can be concluded that marked, sedentary life elevates the risk, but there is no agreement about the relationship between increasing levels of activity or types of activity and reduction in risk.

Psychosocial variables have been less thoroughly investigated for their influence on the incidence of CHD than those already discussed. However, evidence has been produced on adverse risk associated with personality characterized by hard-driving, compulsive behavior (Rosenman et al. 1975). On the other hand, as already noted, educational attainment, marital status, and other indicators of socioeconomic status which may be related to stress have not shown a consistent relationship to risk for CHD. This may simply reflect the complexity of the issues involved, when this set of variables is considered, rather than a lack of importance.

The possible role of alcohol consumption in CHD has been the subject of a wide variety of studies. A recent review of the evidence suggests that moderate alcohol consumption appears negatively associated with a lower risk of heart disease than either nondrinking or heavy drinking (LaPorte, Gresanta, and Kuller 1980). It is pointed out that the complexity of interpreting the low risk among moderate drinkers lies in the fact that alcohol consumption is a risk factor for cirrhosis, accidents, and homicide, and any negative association with CHD mortality may, in part, be the result of competing risks. Also, classification of what constitutes moderate and heavy drinking is not standardized, and the confounding effects, especially of cigarette smoking, which is highly associated with drinking, have not been sorted out well enough to reach hard conclusions about the independent effect of different levels of alcohol consumption.

EFFORTS TO CHANGE RISK FACTORS. A gratifying feature of the investment of epidemiologic research in CHD is that it has produced information necessary to undertake inquiries concerned with primary prevention. The exceptionally strong roles of blood pressure, serum cholesterol, and smoking placed prevention of CHD in a relatively favorable position because of the potential that existed to modify the effect of these risk factors through changes in diet and medication (blood pressure), diet (serum cholesterol), and smoking practices (Stamler 1978). Building on behavioral science theory and on the experience and knowledge already gained in investigations to change diet and smoking habits and to control high blood pressure through antihypertensive drugs, the National Heart, Lung and Blood Institute (NHLBI) initiated the multiple-risk factor intervention trial (MRFIT) in the early 1970s (Benfari and Sherwin 1981). Twenty-two clinical centers widely distributed throughout the country joined in this cooperative activity, which required rigorous adherence to a protocol, a central aspect of which was a randomized clinical trial.

The primary purpose of MRFIT has been to determine "whether a special risk factor intervention program directed at the reduction of elevated serum cholesterol, elevated diastolic blood pressure, and cigarette smoking in men (aged thirty-five to fifty-seven years) at high risk of death from CHD (but still free of clinical evidence of CHD) would result in a significant reduction in . . . death from CHD, combined fatal and nonfatal MI, death from all cardiovascular disease and death from all causes." Accordingly, two issues are involved: (1) the ability to introduce interventions to which the experimental groups will adhere and (2) the effect of the changes on risk of CHD and mortality. The latter was still an open question despite consistency in the associations previously discussed between the three factors included in the trial and incidence of CHD. Veterans Administration studies had demonstrated the efficacy of antihypertensive drugs (Veterans Administration Cooperative Study Group 1967, 1970), but the generalizability of the results to men in the age group covered in the MRFIT project, with moderate elevation in blood pressure and living in highly varied environments, had not yet been established. In fact, a separate trial (the Hypertension Detection and Follow-up Program) specifically directed at this question was started concurrently with MRFIT (Hypertension Detection and Follow-up Program Cooperative Group 1979). While there was evidence that cholesterol and lipoprotein concentrations could be changed in volunteers through modification of diets to reduce saturated fat consumption, the extent to which reductions in cholesterol levels could be sustained and how much of a reduction would result in a detectable decrease in CHD mortality were uncertain. Analogous questions existed about changes in cigarette smoking habits. An additional question concerned the possibility that other aspects of living might be affected. The existence of these imponderables, in the presence of overwhelming evidence that elevated blood pressure, high cholesterol, and cigarette smoking increase CHD risk severalfold, justified a costly, randomized trial.

An important issue faced in MRFIT is that the very circumstances that provide compelling reasons for conducting the research have created strong pressures for spreading knowledge about the importance of changing dietary and smoking practices and of early detection and treatment of high blood pressure. Changes have resulted, perhaps most markedly, in the extent to which those with elevated blood pressure are aware of their condition and are under treatment. This may account for current indications that there has been less of a differential between the experimental and control groups in risk reduction than originally projected, although the investigators interpret the results as reason for "cautious optimism" regarding decreases in CHD. The Hypertension Detection and Follow-up Program faced the same situation and is demonstrating reductions in mortality.

In addition to the randomized trial of MRFIT, research has been conducted to test the effectiveness of health education programs in modifying risk factors in total communities. The most extensive in the United States was the Stanford Heart Disease Prevention Program during the 1970s, involving three communities, two of which were exposed to mass media campaigns directed at cigarette smoking, blood cholesterol levels, and high blood pressure; the third had no special campaign (Farquhar et al. 1977). One of the experimental communities also had face-to-face counseling for a sample of high-risk individuals. The results have demonstrated the feasibility of achieving reductions in risk of cardiovascular disease, although the duration of the project (two years) was too brief to demonstrate persistence of the effect. End-point measures of incidence of coronary heart disease and mortality which represent key observations in MRFIT were not included in the design because of the small populations in the three communities; but the risk reductions through educational methods are interpreted as achievements of sufficient promise to justify further experimentation with mass media programs. Similar trials have been underway in other countries (World Health Organization 1974).

Factors Related to Prognosis of Coronary Heart Disease

The concentration on primary prevention measures, encouraged by the identification of risk factors for the occurrence of a first major coronary event which are amenable to control, has overshadowed but not excluded the search for personal, biochemical, and physiological factors affecting the course of coronary heart disease (Honey and Truelove 1957; Hrubec and Zukel 1971; Juergens et al. 1960; Kannel and Gordon 1970). One of the more comprehensive, population-based investigations concerned with this issue was the previously referred to HIP study; it had as its main objective determining the course and prognosis of myocardial infarction and angina pectoris among men and women under sixty-five years of age, followed up to five years after first diagnosis (Weinblatt, Shapiro, and Frank 1973).

Age, a characteristic that strongly influences the incidences of CHD, was found in both sexes to be an important predictor of mortality in the early period after an MI attack but not for subsequent mortality. Other similarities between men and women in the prognosis of CHD were identified. Among both men and women, large proportions, about 37 percent, died within one month of onset of a first coronary attack, with two-thirds of the deaths occurring before the patient reached the hospital, illustrating the significance of the problem of sudden death in secondary prevention programs. Almost one out of five who did reach the hospital succumbed within a month. Hypertension prior to onset of the attack was associated with nearly a doubling of the risk of early mortality in both sexes.

Mortality subsequent to recovery from a first MI remained high over the subsequent five months, about 9 percent on an annualized rate among men and women. This rate dropped to half or less over the next four and a half years. Women had a lower death rate than men, but the ratio was similar to that found in general mortality rates for men and women free of CHD at start of observation, when age differences were taken into account. The risk of mortality was approximately the same among men following recovery from the acute phase of an MI as among those who were followed after a first clinical diagnosis of angina. But among women the prognosis for those after first diagnosis of angina was appreciably more favorable than among those recovering from MI.

Prognosis differed between men and women in other respects. Hypertension among men with MI (one month postattack) or angina was a long-term high-risk factor. Among women, hypertension did not appear an important discriminating factor, although hypertension cannot be dismissed as a "benign" condition for women in view of the high proportion who have hypertension and the risk this imposes for mortality during the first month after the coronary attack. Elevated serum cholesterol also shows a different relationship in longer term prognosis for men and women; it represents a persistent high-risk factor for women but not for men. It is speculated that following onset of clinical CHD in women, the rate of atherosclerosis may continue at a faster rate than in men, and this rate, related to the serum cholesterol level, may be of prime importance in the prognosis of CHD in women.

More detailed information available on the course of CHD for men showed that physical inactivity prior to a first MI was an especially high-risk factor for early mortality but not subsequently (Frank et al. 1966; Weinblatt et al. 1968). Cigarette smoking before the onset of the MI, while imposing a major risk for having an attack, provided no additional mortality risk after the attack. But major changes in smoking patterns occurred among men with an MI and this may have influenced prognosis. A group that showed a relatively high risk for mortality well after the coronary attack was the blue-collar men who had elevated blood pressure (Shapiro et al. 1970). There was a suggestion that these men were less likely to have taken antihypertensive drugs than post-MI hypertensive white-collar men. Other studies have also pointed to an increased risk of mortality from CHD among low socioeconomic classes (Kitagawa and Hauser 1973). Consistent with these observations is the finding in the HIP study that following a first MI non-white men had a higher risk of dying than white men soon after the MI and in subsequent years.

Prognosis is influenced, to a large extent, by a number of physiological conditions. Persistence of ECG abnormalities among post-MI patients represents an adverse risk (Coronary Drug Project Research Group 1972). Certain types of ventricular premature beats (electrical instability in heart beat) substantially elevate the risk of sudden death among men who have recovered from the acute phase of an MI (Ruberman et al. 1977); at particularly high risk within this group are men with relatively low educational attainment, further implicating social and economic factors in mortality from CHD (Weinblatt et al. 1978).

Factors Responsible for the Reduction in Ischemic Heart Disease Mortality

It is uncertain how long the recent downward trend in IHD mortality will continue, but there is no question that it is not explained by artifacts of classification or changes in reporting causes of death. Based on incidence regarding the strength of well-established risk factors for coronary heart disease, estimates can be made of the reduction in death rates from CHD that might be achieved through their control, and this is significant. Actually, the MRFIT project is designed to make such an assessment through a deliberate attempt to modify major risk factors. It would be important to know, however, what was responsible for the decrease in ischemic heart disease mortality during the 1968–78 decade. That this is not a simple matter is indicated by inconsistencies between trends in CHD mortality over long periods of time, for age-sex groups, and geographic areas and by what is known about general changes in risk factors and medical care (Stallones 1980). Further, there is uncertainty about the magnitude and specific effects of recent changes in risk factors including cigarette smoking, high blood cholesterol levels and lipid protein concentrations, elevated blood pressure, and low levels of physical activity.

These issues were the subject of a conference held in 1979 by the National Heart, Lung, Blood Institute (NHLBI) (Havlik and Feinleib 1979). In a summary of the evidence currently available, the following conclusions were emphasized.

CIGARETTE SMOKING. The percentage of smokers and the amount of tar and nicotine in cigarettes have dropped since the release of the first Surgeon General's Report in 1964. However, the proportion who are heavy cigarette smokers, an especially high-risk group, has apparently not decreased. In addition, women, a subgroup which has had the greatest decline in mortality, have not shown changes in smoking habits across all ages consistent with predictions in mortality.

CHOLESTEROL AND SATURATED FATS. There have been nutritional changes over recent years with decreases in consumption of cholesterol and saturated fats, especially in the form of less egg and butter consumption and increases in intake of polyunsaturated fats. However, overall meat consumption has increased as has total fat intake, and an increasing frequency of obesity in certain groups suggests excess calorie consumption. The net effect on blood cholesterol levels cannot be determined accurately but it appears that there may have been an overall reduction in blood cholesterol levels of up to 5 percent. This change is consistent with the overall effect of the observed dietary changes. Depending on the assumptions that are made, such a change could translate into about a 5 percent or greater decrease in coronary heart disease deaths in middle-aged men.

HYPERTENSION. There is substantial evidence that the awareness and effective treatment of hypertension have increased dramatically over the last few years. Improved therapy of hypertension is advanced as an explanation of some of the decline in mortality. On the other hand, mortality from hypertensive heart disease and stroke began to decline some years before effective medical therapy for hypertension was available and during a time when coronary heart disease mortality was increasing.

EXERCISE. Exercise and, in particular, jogging have increased in frequency in the United States, but this trend has been a recent development and has involved only certain groups in the population. Its effect on a decline in mortality across a wide diversity of subgroups beginning in the mid-1960s must be minimal, although a future impact is possible.

It is generally accepted that fundamental and clinical research leading to better medical care had an impact on the decline, although the magnitude cannot be clearly ascertained. The exploration by the NHLBI conference of the contributions made by coronary care units, emergency medical services, and improvements in diagnosis and therapy indicates the issues involved.

CORONARY CARE UNITS. In 1963 the first coronary care unit was organized in the United States. Specialized hospital care including monitoring, prevention, and treatment of cardiac arrhythmias has become the standard form of treatment for individuals with acute myocardial infarction. The reported mortality occurring from acute coronary heart disease treated in hospitals has decreased. However, to conclude that a causal relationship between coronary care units and the continuing decline in coronary heart disease mortality exists, one must assume that each year more hospitals are adopting such treatment principles and that therapy continues to improve. Information to measure this diffusion is not available. But the impact is limited by the fact that a high proportion of coronary heart disease deaths occur out of the hospital.

EMERGENCY MEDICAL SERVICES. Care to heart attack victims in the community has changed through the use of emergency medical services personnel and other citizens trained in resuscitation techniques and through the use of mobile intensive coronary care units. The latter can provide electrocardiographic monitoring in the field, antiarrhythmic therapy, and defibrillation in the vital first hour after a heart attack, before the individual arrives at a hospital. Although such systems are increasingly applied in urban areas, delay times in rural areas prevent maximum utility. There may be a future potential for an impact. However, they could not have had a major effect on the reported decline in the past decade or two.

DIAGNOSIS AND THERAPY. There have been improvements in diagnosis and therapy, especially for patients with angina pectoris, but the specific impact of these advances on the decline in mortality cannot be estimated. The same is true of surgical care. The use of coronary bypass surgery has increased greatly in this country. It is accepted that for some specific coronary artery lesions longevity has increased; controversy exists on its effects on all lesions. However, the utilization of this surgical procedure has relatively recently been introduced and, thus, could not account for the decline in mortality starting in the 1960s.

The emphasis in this discussion has been on the reasons for uncertainty about how much of the reduction in IHD mortality can be credited to particular factors. It does not detract from the more general conclusion that changes in many of these factors did contribute to the decline in mortality or that high-risk factors need attention. However, our expectations from program action for future decline in mortality would be enhanced through a clearer identification of the separate and synergistic roles of changes in such factors and medical care. New research is starting on this issue.

Cancer

Cancer is exceeded only by ischemic heart disease in the number of deaths that occur each year in the United States. In 1980, about 414,000 of the 1,986,000 deaths were due to cancer. (USNCHS 1981). The age-adjusted death rate from cancer has been slowly increasing; in 1960, the rate was 125.8 per 100,000; in 1968, it was 129.2 per 100,000; in 1978, it was 133.8 per 100,000; and two years later, 1980, the preliminary rate stood at 134.2 per 100,000 (USNCHS 1982).

The extent to which cancer affects the population is even more clearly indicated by estimates which show that close to one out of three people will have a diagnosis of cancer during their lifetime. This places cancer second only to circulatory diseases in potential years of life lost and economic loss (Rice, Feldman and

White 1976). Other measures of the burden of illness, including hospital and primary-care utilization and limitations of activity during the year, do not rank cancer as high as many other disease categories. This is primarily due to the relatively low case survival rates among cancer patients, a circumstance which reduces the prevalence of the disease in the population at any point in time as compared with the less lethal chronic conditions.

As in the case of ischemic heart disease, age, sex, and race are important correlates of cancer mortality. Mortality rises with increasing age, although, unlike ischemic heart disease, cancer is not a rare cause of death among children and young adults; it accounts for 5 to 10 percent of all the deaths in these groups. At ages thirty-five to forty-four years, the proportion increases to 20 percent of all deaths and between ages forty-five and seventy-four years, it is responsible for twenty-five to thirty percent of the deaths. Thereafter, as a consequence of increasing dominance of ischemic heart disease, the proportion of all deaths due to cancer decreases, despite high mortality from this cause.

Paralleling relationships found for ischemic heart disease, cancer mortality is greater among men than among women. In the white population, the ratio between male and female cancer rates (age-adjusted) is almost 1:5; among the non-white, the ratio is 1:8. These ratios have been slowly increasing. Actually, almost the entire increase that has occurred in the overall death rate from cancer can be traced to increases in the rate among men.

A common characteristic of all cancers is the uncontrolled growth and spread of abnormal cells accompanied by destruction of normal cells. But cancer is not a single disease; cancers of different sites are marked more by dissimilarities than similarities in their trends in incidence and mortality, relationships to age, sex, race, and other risk factors, and prognosis of the patient. This is reflected by the mortality information in Table 7.1 for major subgroups of cancer.

TABLE 7.1   Changes in Death Rates, 1968–1978

CANCER SITE*	Death Rate[†] in 1978	Change Since 1968	Relationship to Age	RATIO BETWEEN DEATH RATES[‡]	
				Male/ Female	Non-white/ White
Digestive system (150–159)	33.4	–1%	Low rates under 45 years; large increases extend through very advanced ages.	1.50	1.22
Respiratory system (160–163)	35.4	+29%	Among men, rates exceptionally high at ages 45–64 years compared with other cancers; in both sexes, rate increases with age through 65–74 years.	3.53	1.19

TABLE 7.1   (cont.)

CANCER SITE*	Death Rate[†] in 1978	Change Since 1968	Relationship to Age	RATIO BETWEEN DEATH RATES[‡]	
				Male/ Female	Non-white/ White
Breast (female) (174)	23.1	0	Rates highest of all cancers among women at ages 25–54 years; increases with age through advanced years.	—	0.97
Male genital organs (185–187)	15.2	+5%	Rates at comparatively high level at ages 65 and over; large increases with age among older men.	—	1.80
Female genital organs (180–184)	14.6	–21%	At ages 35–54 years, rates close to those for lung and digestive system; substantially below only breast cancer's rate; rate increases into older ages.	—	1.39
Urinary organs (188, 189)	5.5	–4%	Very low rates under age 55 years; large increases through advanced ages.	2.77	0.91
Leukemia (204–207)	5.3	–10%	Rate low among children but a significant factor compared with other cancers; marked increases in rate starting at 35–44 years.	1.66	0.87
Other lymph and blood tissues (200–203, 208, 209)	7.4	–3%	Rare among children and young adults; age gradient starts in middle adult years.	1.52	0.96

* Numbers below cancer site are rubrics in the eighth *Revision of International Classification of Diseases*, adapted. Excluded from the table are cancers of buccal cavity and pharynx (death rate in 1978, 3.0 per 100,000; no change since 1968) and "malignant neoplasms of all other and unspecified sites" (death rate in 1978, 17.1 per 100,000; 9 percent increase since 1968).

[†] Death rates per 100,000 age adjusted to 1940 population.

[‡] Ratios based on 1978 age-adjusted death rates.

Selected for detailed discussion are several organ sites that have become the targets for primary or secondary prevention. These include colorectal cancer (colon and rectum), which ranks high among causes of death from cancer in both sexes; cancer of the lung and bronchus, which ranks first among causes of death from cancer among men and is on the increase among women; cancer of the breast which is by far the most common cancer among women; and cancer of the uterus, still a significant cause of death despite reductions and secondary prevention programs that screen for cervical cancer. Also included is cancer of the stomach, mortality from which has been decreasing in the absence of program efforts.

Source of Data

Mortality information comes from the vital statistics reports of the U.S. National Center for Health Statistics. Incidence information comes from publications by the staff of the National Cancer Institute on the results of the Third National Cancer Survey for 1969–71 (Cutler and Young 1975) and for later years from the Surveillance Epidemiology and End Results Program (SEER) supported in part by NCI in eleven areas (Young, Asire, and Pollack 1973–76). Other resource material used extensively includes the comprehensive analytical reviews available on the epidemiology of specific cancer sites; in selected cases reports by the investigators who conducted the research are drawn upon directly.

Case survival information is derived from reports of the National Cancer Institute based on the experience of a subset of the areas in the SEER program and its predecessor, the End Results cooperative program (Axtell, Asire, and Myers 1976: Myers and Hankey 1980). The data provide the unusual opportunity to examine long-term trends as well as the influence of age, sex, and race on case survival among cancer patients. For this chapter, the experience relates to cancers diagnosed from 1950 to 1973. There are restrictions in generalizing to the country as a whole; also, changes in completeness of reporting qualify small differentials over time and among subgroups. The data are from cancer registries in four areas, the entire state of Connecticut, about a fifth of the patients in California, and all patients in two teaching hospitals, Charity Hospital in New Orleans and the University of Iowa Hospital. Assessment of characteristics of the patients has led NCI to conclude there is no strong evidence of bias which precludes use of the data as indicators of the situation in the more general population. The case survival rates explain incongruities that appear between incidence and death rates, despite substantial differences in population coverage.

Colorectal Cancer

An estimated 114,000 new cases of colorectal cancer were diagnosed in 1980 in the United States (American Cancer Society 1979); the number of deaths was about 53,000 (age-adjusted death rate in 1978 was 16.4 per 100,000). Four out of five colorectal deaths are from cancer of the colon; the remainder from cancer of the rectum. Particularly for long-term trends, figures and other data that distinquish between cancer of the colon and cancer of the rectum are subject to some qualification because of differences and changes in diagnostic and reporting practices. To avoid distortions arising from such artifacts, information for these two sites is often combined. Nevertheless, relationships involving variables of interest differ sufficiently between the sites to justify examining them separately for each site.

Increases in risk of mortality that accompany increasing age are greater for cancer of the colon than cancer of the rectum. Men have a substantially higher risk than women of mortality from cancer of the rectum; the difference between the two sexes in the case of cancer of the colon is relatively small. There is now little difference between the white and nonwhite population in their mortality from cancer of the colon. However, the lack of difference results from offsetting age patterns: under age sixty-five, nonwhites have the higher mortality rates; after this age, and especially at very advanced ages, the relationship is reversed.

Although subject to reservation because of the possible effect of changes in differentiating between cancers of the colon and rectum, trends in the death rate appear to be substantially different for the two sites. Mortality reported for rectal cancer has decreased among white and nonwhite men and women. In contrast, there has been a slight increase in mortality from colon cancer in the total population. However, this obscures the fact that nonwhite men and women have experienced a marked increase in risk of death from colon cancer. When colon and rectal cancers are combined, the picture that emerges is one of virtually no change in mortality over many years.

INCIDENCE AND RISK FACTORS. Incidence rates are substantially greater at every age than death rates. In colon cancer, incidence is almost double the mortality rate; in rectal cancer, it is three times as high, reflecting more favorable case survival than for colon cancer. Also, the elevation in risk among whites compared with nonwhites is more pronounced in the incidence of these cancers than in mortality. Differentials between men and women are about the same for both of these measures.

At this time, there is considerable uncertainty about the extent to which environmental, personal, and dietary factors impose risks for colorectal cancer. However, there is suggestive evidence that they are involved, particularly diet (Schottenfeld and Winawer 1982, pp. 703–27). Migration studies indicate that people who migrate from low colon cancer countries develop colon cancer at a rate closer to the rates in the new country than in the country of origin (Lee 1976). Colorectal cancer has not been implicated consistently with socioeconomic status or occupational exposure, but some studies of industries that use dyes, solvents, and metallic compounds have raised questions about the possible association of such substances with cancer of the colon and rectum.

The role of diet as a risk factor has attracted most of the attention (Armstrong and Doll 1975; Modan 1977). International studies indicate that cancer of the colon in males and females is correlated with per capita meat and animal fat consumption. Cereal consumption is negatively correlated with colon cancer and to a lesser degree with rectal cancer. From these observations and case-control studies in a number of countries, there has developed a strong hypothesis that low-fiber, high fat diets are significant factors in elevating the risk of cancer of the colon in particular. Animal studies and investigations of the chemical and bacterial content of feces in high risk and low risk populations tend to support this hypothesis. Colon and rectal cancer mortality has been reported to be correlated with beer consumption; the ingredient implicated is ethanol (McMichael, Potter, and Hetzel 1979). It has been observed, however, that no specific carcinogen associated with the production or preservation of food has been identified.

The situation then is that diet is implicated as the most important source of risk for colorectal cancer, but our knowledge about specific causes is too incomplete to serve as a basis for a major program to alter diets.

PATIENT SURVIVAL. The probability of survival from cancer at any site is far greater when the diagnosis is made while the disease is in a localized stage. Among patients with colon or rectal cancers, the proportion surviving five years (relative to survival in the general population) varies between 60 percent and 75 percent, depending on the localized site, and race of the patient. Survival drops to almost half these figures when the cancer has spread regionally; distant metastases are associated with very low five-year survival, less than 10 percent. Relative survival rates decrease only slightly after the first five years, a circumstance that has led to the reference to five-year survival rates as the "cure" rate for cancers of the colon and rectum as well as for cancers of other sites.

Five-year survival rates have increased for patients with cancers of the colon and rectum diagnosed between the 1950s and the early 1970s; this was the most recent period for which the information was available when this chapter was prepared. Contributing to the improvement has been small increases in the proportion of cases diagnosed while localized and in survival among both localized and regional cancers.

There are major differences between white and black patients in the stage of disease at time of diagnosis and survival after diagnosis. The proportions with localized disease detected in 1970–73 were 41 percent for cancer of the colon and 47 percent for cancer of the rectum among white patients; the corresponding figures for black patients were 30 percent and 34 percent. Five-year survival rates among patients have been substantially higher in the white group: 46 percent and 43 percent for colon and rectum cancer patients respectively compared with 35 percent and 30 percent among black patients. This disparity is only partially due to the greater likelihood that cancer is diagnosed earlier in the white population. Among both localized cases and those diagnosed after the cancer had spread, survival was greater in the white group. Differences between male and female patients in proportions with localized disease at diagnosis and subsequent survival were negligible among white patients; in the black group, women had a clearly more favorable experience for cancer of the rectum.

Observed five-year survival rates decreased moderately with increasing age. However, when general mortality is taken into account, increasing age among white patients showed no consistent pattern of an increase or decrease in the five-year relative survival rates over the broad age span forty-five to seventy-four years. Patients under forty-five years had a more favorable relative survival rate than those who were older. Age relationships are less clear for black patients because of small numbers of patients in the SEER program; this makes the survival rates subject to high chance variation.

From the preceding, it can be concluded that for cancers of the colon and rectum the sharp increase in death rates which accompany advancing age are largely due to increases in incidence rather than decreases in survival.

Stomach Cancer

MORTALITY. One of the bright spots in cancer incidence and mortality in the United States is the sustained reductions in these rates for stomach cancer over a long period. During the 1930s, stomach cancer was one of the most common cancers among men and women. Now the frequency of diagnosis of stomach cancer and death from this cause are a small fraction—20 to 25 percent—of the figures for colorectal cancer. The estimates for 1980 are 23,000 new cases of stomach cancer and 14,000 deaths from the condition (age-adjusted death rate in 1978 was 4.6 per 100,000).

There has been no slowdown in the rate of decrease in mortality from stomach cancer with the rate dropping by about 25 percent between 1968 and 1978. The favorable trend reflects improvement in both sexes and in the white and nonwhite populations. There are differences, however, in the relative magnitude of the reductions. Mortality from stomach cancer has decreased more rapidly among women than men in both racial groups and the reduction has been larger among whites than nonwhites. A point of interest is that the rate of decrease was greater among population subgroups at lower risk of stomach cancer mortality (i.e., women and whites) and differentials have widened. The mortality rate among men is now double the rate among women; nonwhites have twice the rate for whites.

Every age group shared in the decrease in stomach cancer mortality with the relative amount of change differing only slightly by age. The older age groups had marginally greater decreases than those under sixty-five years, thus leaving the pattern of sharp increases in mortality risk as age rises unchanged. Analysis of the changes in stomach cancer mortality based on age-specific death rates for individuals born in successive time periods showed that each ten-year cohort experienced a major decrease in risk of mortality, age by age, than the next earlier one. This reinforces the view that the decline in stomach cancer mortality has been influenced by factors that appear in the early decades of life. Studies on migrant populations have also suggested that some determinants of stomach cancer risk start to exert their effect at ages when mortality is still very low.

INCIDENCE AND RISK FACTORS. There is close correspondence between incidence and mortality patterns for stomach cancer. The downward trend in mortality reflects entirely the pattern for incidence; the same age, sex, and race relationships are found whether incidence or mortality is at issue.

Studies of social and ethnic groups in local communities in the United States and investigations in other countries—particularly in Japan, where the death rate from stomach cancer is the highest in the world (about eight times the rate in the United States)—have pointed more clearly to dietary factors as a source of risk for stomach cancer than to any other circumstance (Haas and Schottenfeld 1978; Hirayama 1972; Nomura 1982). A socioeconomic gradient, with the poor having the highest rate, has been noted (Hammond and Seidman 1974); some degree of familial aggregation of stomach cancer cases has been found (Graham and Lilienfeld 1958); and certain occupations in mining industries have been implicated. However, dietary differences could explain socioeconomic gradients, occupational, ethnic, and cultural variations (Creagan, Hoover, and Fraumeni 1974). A complicating factor in reaching hard conclusions from diet studies is that the most important patterns may be those in early years of life, and this often becomes difficult to reconstruct reliably. Studies of immigrants from a country with a high stomach cancer incidence who migrate to a low incidence country and of their children born in the new environment support the following hypothesis: the effect of change in diet habits is slow and starts to appear in later generations (Haenszel et al. 1972; Waterhouse et al. 1976).

Generally, diet studies suggest that high intake of complex carbohydrates, smoked or salted foods may elevate risks; fresh fruits and vegetables may decrease risks. Also, there is some evidence of a possible association between nitrates used as preservatives and stomach cancer; these chemicals have the potential to form carcinogenic nitrosamines after ingestion. It is speculated that with the widespread availability of refrigeration over the past fifty years, the use of these preservatives has lessened and this may have contributed to the reduction in stomach cancer incidence. (Nomura 1982). It needs to be emphasized that the factors involved in the downward trend in stomach cancer are, in fact, still poorly understood since there are no specific substances in the diet or in the environment which have been definitively established as risk factors.

PATIENT SURVIVAL. The persistence of an extremely poor probability of survival represents the negative aspect of trends in stomach cancer. Only a third of the patients survive one year after the diagnosis; 12–13 percent survive five years. About 20 percent of the cases are diagnosed in a localized stage, and even in this stage, five-year survival is relatively low: 40 percent. There are no differences of any consequence in prognosis related to sex, race, or age of the patient. Further, no improvement in survival rates occurred over the 1950–73 period covered by the SEER data.

It is clear from this negative picture of patient survival that the large reductions in the rate of deaths from stomach cancer in the total population and in every subgroup has been due exclusively to the decrease in incidence.

Cancer of the Lung and Bronchus

MORTALITY. Lung cancer is the most frequent cause of death from cancer, accounting for about 101,000 deaths in 1980 (about the same number of new cases was diagnosed), or one-fourth of all deaths from cancer. The dominance of lung cancer results from an unprecedented high rate of increase that, during the 1960s, averaged 5 percent per year. Increases in lung cancer mortality have continued, but at less than half this rate, to reach 33.7 per 100,000 in 1978 (age adjusted).

Mortality risk is three to four times higher among men than women (59.1 per 100,000 and 16.0 per 100,000 respectively in 1978), but while there has been a slowdown during the 1970s in the rate of increase in the death rate from lung cancer among men, the increase among women has been extraordinarily large, averaging 9 to 10 percent per year in the 1960s and 1970s. The nonwhite population has about a 25 percent higher lung cancer death rate than the white population, an excess that is concentrated among men; the difference for women is negligible.

Lung cancer as a cause of death becomes a factor beginning at ages thirty-five to forty-four. The rate increases five-fold between the ages of thirty-five and fifty-four. It continues to increase, though not as sharply, through the ages sixty-five to seventy-four after which it levels off and then decreases among the very old.

INCIDENCE AND RISK FACTORS. The relationship between lung cancer and age, sex, and race and the changes since 1960 in the incidence of lung cancer mirror those patterns in the death rates for lung cancer due to the very poor prognosis of patients with this disease. As discussed below, there are differences in survival rates among various subgroups of the population but these variations involve small proportions of the patients.

Epidemiologic studies have, without exception, found a strong association between cigarette smoking and lung cancer: nonsmokers have an exceedingly low rate; risk increases sharply with the amount smoked, reaching a relative risk of over twenty times for heavy smokers (i.e., more than twenty cigarettes per day) compared with nonsmokers (USDHHS 1971; Hammond and Horn 1958; Kahn 1966). Also cigarette smoking among those exposed occupationally to asbestos has been shown to increase the likelihood of lung cancer several times (Hammond, Selikoff, and Seidman 1979). This provides support for the hypothesis that a markedly deleterious effect results from interaction of cigarette smoking and exposure to industrial substances such as uranium and chromium and to pollutants in the atmosphere of urban areas, all of which are independently implicated as risk factors.

There is some evidence that long-term smokers of filter cigarettes, with their generally low tar content, have a somewhat lower risk of lung cancer than nonfilter cigarette smokers. Risk remains elevated, however, compared with noncigarette smokers and the public health emphasis is on not starting the smoking habit; further, smoking cessation appears to be associated with a reduction in risk of mortality from lung cancer, after several years of cessation (Doll and Peto 1976; Hammond 1975; Wynder and Stellman 1979).

The sharp increase among women in lung cancer incidence and mortality over the past two decades is consistent with the spread of the smoking habit among them. The proportion of adult women who regularly smoked has as always been lower than the figure for men, but the margin has narrowed considerably and in 1978, 38 percent of men and 30 percent of women smoked regularly. For men, the 1978 level was well below the 1955 level of 53 percent; for women it was somewhat above the 1955 level of 25 percent (USDHHS 1980a). It is less certain why lung cancer rates have been increasing more rapidly among nonwhites. The likelihood that increased access to medical care may have led to improved diagnosis and reporting changes can not be dismissed. However, a more important factor may be related to environmental changes; nonwhites have moved to densely populated urban areas that have especially high lung cancer rates.

PATIENT SURVIVAL. Lung cancer presents an extremely poor prognostic picture. At time of diagnosis, among both white and black patients, fewer than 20 percent of the cases are in a localized stage; about half have metastasized widely. Only about 30 percent survive one year after diagnosis; less than 10 percent survive for five years. Survival rates are slightly higher among white patients than black patients. Among white patients, women have a somewhat higher five-year survival rate than men. All of the differences involve low percentages, and the general situation is one of rapid mortality following detection of the disease. Further, in the twenty years of SEER data, there has been no improvement in survival.

Breast Cancer

MORTALITY. Breast cancer is a rare disease among men and therefore attention is concentrated on its occurrence among women, for whom this is the most frequent type of cancer in the United States. In 1980, there were about 110,000 new cases diagnosed among women, and an estimated 35,000 deaths were recorded from this condition. The age-adjusted death rate (1978) was 23.1 per 100,000, or close to 20 percent of the death rate for all cancers combined.

Breast cancer mortality becomes a significant factor at fairly early adult ages; at ages forty to forty-four it is the leading cause of death from any condition among women. The death rate from breast cancer rises rapidly at ages up to sixty years; it remains stationary between sixty and sixty-nine years and then resumes an upward trend but at a slower rate than in the young and middle years of life.

About two-fifths of those who die from breast cancer before eighty years of age are diagnosed at ages thirty-five to forty-nine. Another measure of the seriousness of breast cancer is that about 9 percent of women have a diagnosis of this condition during their lifetime, and a quarter to one-third of all women eventually have a biopsy to determine whether they have breast cancer. White and nonwhite women have similar age-adjusted death rates from breast cancer (23.1 and 22.3 per 100,000 in 1978, respectively).

There has been little change in the age-adjusted death rate from breast cancer, all races combined, in at least the past forty years. This lack of change masks the fact that among nonwhite women the death rate was at one time well below the rate in the white group; increases in the rate have brought their risk of mortality from breast cancer to the same level as found among whites.

INCIDENCE AND RISK FACTORS. The constancy in the breast cancer death rate results from two counteracting trends; the incidence of diagnosed breast cancer has apparently increased and survival rates have also increased, thereby producing the static picture in mortality. White women have been in the more favored position than nonwhites in the sense that the rise in incidence has been less and the increase in survival greater.

Incidence of breast cancer is appreciably higher among white women than black: in the SEER program areas, the excess was 22 percent during 1973–76; the Third National Cancer Survey showed more than twice this margin for 1969–71. The geographic coverage in these two sources differs but it is highly likely that they reflect a true decrease in the differential between the racial groups, although the extent of the decrease may not be as great as indicated by this comparison.

Incidence rates increase sharply with age before menopause, after which the rate of increase is slowed. This explains the changes in trends in the death rate as age increases. There are differences in incidence levels and relationship with age between white and black women. Actually, in the national cancer survey, the incidence rates were fairly similar under age forty-five after which they diverged because of smaller increases among black women. The similarity of the rates at younger ages and the later dissimilarity suggests that there may be a generational change under way among black women. This would forecast decreases in the gap between whites and blacks, all ages combined, as seems to have begun.

Periodic reviews have been made of the state of knowledge regarding risk factors for breast cancer, with updates and reassessments of the available evidence from a large number of investigations (Lilienfeld 1963; MacMahon, Cole, and Brown 1973; Shapiro et al. 1968; Wynder, Bross, and Hirayama 1960). A principal conclusion reached at a meeting in 1980 of the participants in the Multidisciplinary Project on Breast Cancer of the International Union Against Cancer was that "breast cancer is hormonally mediated and estrogens are the prime agents in tumor expression (Miller and Bulbrook 1980)." The following covers many of the specific risk factors considered, all of which are discussed in the review articles (additional references that appeared later are cited on a selected basis).

The association of a twofold to threefold increase in risk with a family history of breast cancer in first-degree relatives is well recognized. Risk increases if two first-degree relatives are involved, especially if the disease occurred before menopause and was bilateral.

Early menarche, late menopause, nulliparity, and giving birth to the first child after the age of 30 years all increase risk. Having the first child before the age of 20 and artificial menopause are protective. Age at menarche seems to be nutritionally mediated in that improvements in nutrition correlate with younger age at menarche. A two to threefold increase in risk is found for women with a history of benign breast disease.

A role for dietary factors in breast cancer has been suggested by experiments with animals, by circumstantial epidemiologic evidence, by studies correlating international and intranational incidence and mortality rates with dietary factors, and by a small number of case-control studies. However, it is difficult to unravel the relative importance of the dietary and other variables (e.g., total calories, gross national product, and socioeconomic status) because they are so highly correlated. Nevertheless, it is concluded that diet may have a role in breast cancer and the issue requires further investigation. [Armstrong and Doll 1975]

Cohort and case-control studies indicate that no overall increase in risk of breast cancer results from use of oral contraceptives. The increased risk reported in certain subgroups in some studies has not been consistently found after detailed analysis within strata. More work is required because the women who have been exposed to oral contraceptives are only now reaching the age of maximal risk of breast cancer or exceeding the possible latency period of 15 years or more. [Vessey, Doll, and Jones 1975]

There is evidence that after a 10 to 15 year latency period, there is an increased risk of breast cancer in women who have used noncontraceptive estrogens at the time of menopause. Use for more than two to five years does not seem to be required for enhanced risk to occur. The relationships are complex and research on the issues is still in an early stage (Brinton et al. 1981).

PATIENT SURVIVAL. Detection of breast cancer occurs in a localized stage more often than is true for most other cancers. Four out of five patients with early breast cancer survive five years after diagnosis and the five-year survival rates for all cases combined are among the highest for cancer. Further, there has been a slow increase in the proportion of breast cancers diagnosed earlier, which has led to some improvement in the overall survival rates.

Age does not influence survival rates; old and young patients have the same relative survival rates. There are, however, major differences between white and black women in when the disease is diagnosed and in survivial rates. On both scores, the situation is poorer for black women: in 1970–73, the proportions of cases detected while localized were 48 percent and 33 percent for white and black women respectively; five-year relative survival rates were 68 percent and 51 percent, a differential only partially explained by earlier detection among whites.

A disturbing aspect of breast cancer is that the survival rate relative to general mortality among all women continues to decrease fifteen to twenty years after diagnosis. This indicates a long duration of increased risk for mortality among breast cancer patients.

Cancer of the Uterus

MORTALITY. Consideration of mortality and incidence of cancer of the uterus is most meaningful when information can be examined separately for the cervix and corpus (principally endometrium, the lining of the uterine cavity). This is so because of differences in the epidemiologic characteristics of these two parts of the uterus and the more advanced state of preventive measures in the case of cancer of cervix uteri. However, reports of cause of death quite often leave unspecified which part of the uterus was affected, and data on unspecified uterine cancer are usually combined with corpus data in order to reduce the effect of lack of specificity of the reports. A small proportion of the unspecified may actually refer to cervix, and some ambiguity exists regarding rates of change and magnitude of differentials in mortality from cancer of the cervix and corpus. To simplify terminology, from this point, corpus plus unspecified is referred to as *corpus*. A useful starting point, then, is to assess levels and trends in the death rates for cancer of the uterus, all parts combined, thereby obviating the problem.

In 1980, there were an estimated 54,000 new cases of cancer of the uterus diagnosed and close to 11,000 deaths. The death rate has been declining for a long time, and in the years since 1960, it has been cut in half, to reach 7.0 per 100,000 women in 1978 (age-adjusted).

Questions have been raised about the extent to which the decrease in the level of the death rate is a function of the number of women at risk for developing uterine cancer. Total hysterectomies have increased, and this results in a reduction in the number of women who could have cancer of the uterus. The proportion of women affected increases with age, and it has been estimated that being at risk becomes an important factor at older ages—particularly for cancer of the cervix—with perhaps as many as a third of the women eventually affected. If data were available to introduce a correction factor for age, the rate of decrease would be reduced, but there is general agreement that we would still see a decline in the mortality rate for all ages combined. Changes in rates for women under age forty-five would be influenced only slightly.

Compared with other cancer sites, death rates from cancer of the uterus are among the highest for women under forty-five years of age. Mortality from cancer of the uterus rises with increasing age but at a slower rate than is found for other high-risk cancer sites, and the death rate for uterine cancer is well below the figures for other sites at advanced ages.

Nonwhite women have more than twice as high a death rate from cancer of the uterus as do white women (13.2 per 100,000 compared with 6.3 per 100,000 in 1978). Relatively, the decrease over the period 1960–78 was about the same in the two racial groups. In the early part of this period the decrease in mortality among the nonwhite women lagged behind the decrease among white women. Later, this situation was reversed, thereby making the decrease in the rate over the entire eighteen-year interval comparable for the two groups of women.

In 1960, cancer of the cervix accounted for about 60 percent of the deaths from cancer of the uterus, but now the mortality rates for cancers of the cervix and corpus are similar due to the substantially greater rate of decrease for cancer of the cervix. One factor was a slowdown in the rate of decline for cancer of the corpus that started in the late 1960s. In contrast, mortality from cancer of the cervix has been dropping at an accelerated rate over this period with especially large reductions among women in their middle and younger years.

The present closeness of the rates, all ages combined, results from quite different age relationships. At younger ages, risk of mortality is far greater for cancer of the cervix; above sixty-five years of age, the death rate for cancer of the corpus is twice the rate for cancer of the cervix.

Nonwhite women are at considerably higher risk than white women of mortality from cancer of each of the uterine sites, but the margin is relatively greater for cancer of the cervix. For this site, the nonwhite rate is 2.6 times the white rate, the differential being greater at younger than older ages. For cancer of the corpus, the ratio between nonwhite and white rates is about 1:6, overall and for most age groups. Both racial groups have experienced reductions in mortality from cancer of the cervix and corpus, leaving virtually unchanged the gap between the rates for white and nonwhite women.

Controversy exists regarding the reasons for the reductions in mortality from cancer of the cervix and corpus. As mentioned, increasing rates of hysterectomy are believed to be a factor, but this is far from the entire explanation. Hygienic improvements and changes in fertility patterns might have contributed to the decline in mortality from cancer of the cervix. In communities where aggressive programs of periodic screening with the Papanicolaou smear have been introduced, rates of decrease in mortality from cancer of the cervix have been particularly high, and the widespread promotion of this examination to detect in-situ cancer is believed to be an important contributor to the reduction in the death rate on a national scale. Specific reasons for the reduction in mortality from cancer of the corpus have not been identified.

INCIDENCE AND RISK FACTORS. Reports for "unspecified parts" of the uterus are more frequent in mortality statistics, so we can have greater confidence in incidence data in distinguishing between cervix and corpus cancers. Further, all investigations of risk factors that go beyond age and race are specific for each part of the uterus, and the discussion that follows deals with each separately. Relationships considered below for cancer of the cervix are confined to invasive cancer; in situ cancer, which most often progresses to invasive cancer if untreated, is not included. The subject is further discussed in the section on prevention.

CANCER OF THE CERVIX UTERI. The significance of cancer of the cervix for young women is clearer in the incidence rates than in the mortality rates. Data from the Third National Cancer Survey of 1969–71 show that at ages twenty-five to thirty-nine between a fifth and a quarter of the incidence rate for all cancers combined is accounted for by cancer of the cervix. The rate increases very slowly with age, and at ages over sixty-five years the rate is only moderately higher than the rates among middle-aged women. This is the picture for white women. Among black women, the incidence rate is more than twice the rate in the white group, all ages combined. Large excesses are found at every age but because the increase in the rate with age is steeper for black than white women, the rates among black women are 2.5 to 3 times the figures for white women at older ages.

A substantial amount of information has accumulated over a long period on risk factors for cancer of the cervix that extends beyond the age and color variables. Risks are found to be elevated for women whose sexual activity starts at young ages, for those with multiple male partners, for women with many pregnancies, and for those with a history of venereal disease (Rotkin 1973). Some of these variables are highly correlated and are consistent with the hypothesis that cancer of the cervix is caused by a venereally transmitted infectious agent, such as herpes virus type 2 (Kessler 1974). Past studies have suggested that a carcinogenic agent or other factors associated with penile hygiene might be implicated, but the evidence has not been strong. For purposes of identifying high-risk women in the population who should have frequent examinations to detect cancer in situ, the dominant personal characteristic is early start of sexual activity, especially when multiple partners are involved.

CANCER OF THE CORPUS UTERI. For both racial groups, incidence of cancer of the corpus increases sharply among young and middle-aged women and then levels off at older ages, similar to what is seen in the mortality rates. There is, however, a major difference in the comparative levels for white and nonwhite women when incidence rates, and not mortality rates, are at issue. Based on the 1969–71 experience, the incidence rate for cancer of the corpus is twice as high among white women as black; the mortality rate is higher among nonwhites than whites, reflecting poorer case survival rates in the nonwhite female population following diagnosis of cancer of the corpus.

Obesity, impaired fertility, and late menopause have been implicated as risk factors for cancer of the corpus (endometrium) (MacMahon 1974), but research in recent years has concentrated on determining whether there is an association between the use of estrogen therapy in the menopause and subsequent development of cancer at this site (Antunes et al. 1979; Mack et al. 1976). Results have convinced many investigators and clinicians that there is a severalfold increase in risk for estrogen users compared with nonusers, and that long-term users are subject to a very large increase in risk. Support for these hypotheses has been found in studies which showed an increase in incidence of endometrial cancer in a period of more frequent use of estrogen therapy and a drop in the incidence soon after estrogen use declined; this was apparently due to more conservative approaches by clinicians in estrogen therapy following publicity about the associated risks (Jick et al. 1979; Weiss, Szekely, and Austin 1976). However, the causal relationship between exogenous estrogen and endometrial cancer is not universally accepted. Critics have raised questions about bias in the detection of endometrial cancer—a bias that would lead to a distortion in the number of reports of cancer caused by estogen use (Horwitz and Feinstein 1978). At this point, the more prevalent view is that such use is an important risk factor.

PATIENT SURVIVAL. Cancer of the cervix is diagnosed in a localized stage less than half the time (in-situ cases are excluded). Among white women 45 percent of the cases were diagnosed in this stage during 1970–73, and 40 percent when the disease had already spread regionally. The situation was poorer for black women: 39 percent of the cases were localized and 47 percent had spread regionally. The five-year case survival rate was higher among the white women (57 percent vs 48 percent) for all stages combined. This differential results from the more favorable stage in which cancer of the cervix is diagnosed among white women and from the higher survival rates of white women in each stage.

Changes in the proportion of cases diagnosed in a localized stage have been small for both racial groups and five-year case survival rates were stable for cases diagnosed in the 1950s and 1960s. Increases in survival rates appear to be under way among cases diagnosed in more recent years.

Substantially larger differences between white and black women exist for cancer of the corpus than for cancer of the cervix. In the early 1970s, the proportion of cases diagnosed with cancer of the corpus in a localized stage was 80 percent for white women and 50 percent for black women. This is one of the widest margins found for any cancer site. Five-year case survival rates reflect this situation: the rates for the two racial groups (cases diagnosed 1970–73) were 81 percent and 44 percent respectively; even when stage of disease is taken into account, black women with cancer of the corpus had lower survival rates than white women. It is not clear whether the far poorer situation among black women results from differences in response to symptoms or in medical care.

Improvements have occurred among white women in early diagnosis of cancer of the corpus; there has been no change among black women. Five-year case survival rates among both white and black patients have improved.

The relationship between age at diagnosis and survival rates is very different for cancers of the cervix and corpus than for many other cancers. The survival rates for women who have cancer of the cervix and corpus relative to rates among women without cancer is strongly influenced by age. For example, among white women, those under thirty-five years of age with cancer of the cervix have a relative survival rate of 79 percent as compared with a survival rate of only 48 percent for women over sixty-five years of age. The gradient varies with race and site of the cancer but the general picture is one of decreasing relative survival with increasing age.

Prevention

Primary prevention of cancer has concentrated on promoting smoking cessation and on the identification of other carcinogenic agents in the environment. Evidence regarding the deleterious effect of cigarette smoking has been so strong that discouragement of smoking is a matter of official policy of the U.S. Public Health Service; reductions in cigarette smoking can be credited to the campaigns that have been carried out since the 1960s. Results from animal experimentation and epidemiologic studies of human populations have led to the proscription of certain substances in foods and medicines and to the institution of protective measures for workers in industry. However, for some cancer sites, the risk factors are either so poorly understood or so difficult to alter that attention has been directed at the potential for reducing mortality through secondary prevention procedures; i.e., the detection of cancer at a point in its natural history when its progression can be delayed or even stopped.

More specifically, the interest has been in assessing the value of screening for early detection. Cancers of the lung, colon and rectum, breast, and cervix have been targeted as likely candidates for this approach in the United States. In the case of cancer of the lung, the emphasis is still on smoking prevention as the most important control measure, but secondary prevention has been of interest for those who continue to smoke.

Screening seems at first glance to be an attractive and benign method but when examined it becomes apparent that rigorous investigation is needed; its efficacy and efficiency must be established to justify expenditure of large resources required for its application to wide segments of the population. The issues involved can be clarified through an examination of the principles adopted for determining the state of readiness for introducing screening.

Screening was defined about twenty-five years ago as "the presumptive identification of unrecognized disease or defect by the application of test, examinations, or other procedures which can be applied rapidly. Screening tests sort out apparently well persons who probably have a disease from those who probably do not" (Commission on Chronic Illness 1957). This definition covers both "presymptomatic" individuals and those whose symptoms had previously been unrecognized.

Screening on a community-wide basis or in selected high-risk groups needs to be distinguished from early case finding in clinical practice. In routine medical practice, a physician may examine an individual, suggest a diagnostic examination, and recommend treatment on the basis of the patient's symptoms and signs of disease. In carrying out this function, the physician is required to do his best with his knowledge under the circumstances of the encounter between him and his patient. To advocate screening of populations is a different matter, and it is generally agreed that the following conditions should be met before proceeding (Wilson and Jungren 1968):

- The natural history of the disease is sufficiently well known, treatments are sufficiently effective, risks resulting from the screening are low enough, and efficacy in reducing morbidity, disability, or mortality is high enough to conclude that detection of the disease through screening will lead to a net benefit to the target population. Further, the resources required to administer the tests under screening conditions are justified in terms of the net benefit.
- The tests must have high levels of sensitivity and specificity; sensitivity is defined as the proportion who have the disease who show up positive on the test, and specificity is the proportion who do not have the disease who show up negative on the test.
- The tests must be acceptable to the target population and their physicians. Appropriate follow-up of positive findings must be assured.

Even after the above conditions have been satisfied, personal choices and individual priorities concerning the expenditure of private resources may not coincide with the community's assessment of the benefits and risks of a population screening programs where community-wide public health improvement is the goal. Finally, it must be recognized that there are no absolute standards to determine when each of the conditions has been met or how to combine them to reach a decision. Value judgments play a crucial role in reaching a decision about the relative importance of these conditions; they represent a framework for defining the information required in order to weigh whether or not screening for a particular disease should be advocated and under what circumstances.

Large efforts have been made in the United States and other Western countries to establish whether available screening modalities are effective in reducing mortality from cancer of the lung, colon and rectum, breast, and cervix. In Japan, attention has been directed at cancer of the stomach, which is at an exceptionally high rate. The discussion that follows concerns the sites that are screening targets in the United States.

COLORECTAL CANCER. Two procedures, digital rectal examination and sigmoidoscopy, have long been used in general physical examinations for detection of early cancer or of polyps which, in some instances, might develop into cancer if not removed. More attention has been directed at investigating the efficacy of sigmoidoscopy because of its greater potential for an early diagnosis, its higher cost, and the greater discomfort it causes the patient (Gilbertsen 1974). The studies conducted have not had adequate controls and definitive conclusions cannot be reached from them. However, the results have suggested a favorable effect, and the American Cancer Society is advocating that periodic examinations conducted over the age of fifty should include sigmoidoscopy; at ages forty and over, the recommendation is that rectal digital examination be performed (American Cancer Society 1980).

Widespread use of the stool guaiac slide test (smearing stool on a piece of filter paper for microscopic examination) has gained adherents; it is a screening procedure that can rapidly be adopted for large proportions of the population. Others see this test as an adjunct to sigmoidoscopy. Studies are under way to test the efficacy of the stool guaiac test alone and in combination with sigmoidoscopy. Results are not available at this time (Bond and Gilbertsen 1977; Schottenfeld, Winawer, and Miller 1978; Winawer et al. 1977). Nevertheless, because of its low cost and evidence that it can detect cancer in an earlier stage, the American Cancer Society (ACS) guidelines for the cancer-related checkup include this test as a useful procedure, though this policy will be subject to review when information is obtained from the research under way.

LUNG CANCER. Starting with the late 1950s, several studies have been conducted to determine whether periodic chest Xrays lead to reductions in mortality. The results have been either negative or inconclusive (Boucot and Weiss 1973). A new study was started early in the 1970s based on a randomized trial methodology at the Johns Hopkins Medical Institutions, the Mayo Clinic, and Memorial Sloan-Kettering Cancer Center (Baker et al. 1979; Taylor et al. 1980). The effectiveness of periodic chest Xrays and sputum cytology is being tested. Although the programs are detecting lung cancer in an earlier stage than is usually the case, it will take several more years before it can be determined whether the experimental group's mortality is lower than the control groups. It cannot be concluded from the earlier detection that mortality is reduced; screening may only move the date of diagnosis closer to the onset of disease and not change the course of the disease. Further, it is important to determine how much of a gain in saving lives or postponing death is made in view of the invasive procedures that are required to reach a definitive diagnosis.

CANCER OF THE BREAST. This is the only cancer site for which evidence on efficacy of screening is now available from a randomized control trial. In late 1963, two systematic random samples, each consisting of 31,000 women aged forty to sixty-four years, were selected from members of the Health Insurance Plan of Greater New York—a comprehensive, prepaid group practice (Shapiro 1981). Women in the experimental group were offered an initial screening examination and three additional examinations at annual intervals; two-thirds of the women appeared for their initial examination and a large majority of these women returned for reexamination. Screening consisted of a clinical examination of the breast and a mammography, a soft-tissue Xray. Women in the control group continued to receive their usual medical care.

Results have shown that this type of screening program leads to a reduction in breast cancer mortality of almost a third after ten years. The study established that the effect was most convincing for women aged fifty and over when screening was offered. The investigators conclude that the study provides no evidence of benefit from screening for women aged forty to forty-nine at entry. The evidence of a lack of efficacy of mammography in the 1960s may reflect the small number of cases involved. Other analysts have interpreted the findings as consistent with screening benefits for the forty-to forty-nine-year age group (Prorok, Hankey, and Bundy 1981; Dubin 1979).

The questions that remain have been well defined. A high-priority question concerns the necessity of mammography: Will repetitive physical examinations that include instruction in breast self-examination achieve most of the effects found in screening that also utilizes mammography? Here, reduced costs for screening and elimination of radiation exposure, although very low under controlled conditions, are at stake.

Mammography has improved in two ways since the HIP study; the quality of the image is superior, and the radiation dose is a small fraction of what it had been. All calculations on the risk of cancer resulting from mammography indicate that at ages fifty to sixty-four the benefits of screening outweigh the risk. Unless a new study demonstrates benefits for women under age fifty, the risk-benefit ratio for screening with mammography in that age group would be unfavorable.

Observations from the Breast Cancer Detection Demonstration Projects (BCDDP) (a quarter of a million women) started in the 1970s under ACS and National Cancer Institute (NCI) have shown convincingly that modern mammography has increased the ability to detect very early breast cancer among both young and older women (Beahrs, Shapiro, and Smart 1979). This raises the possibility that screening may be beneficial for women under the age of fifty years. Reluctance to accept the BCDDPs experience as a basis for promoting screening for all women ages forty to forty-nine rests on the fact that women selected themselves to participate, and most importantly there is no suitable control group with which to make comparisons. A randomized trial was recently begun in Canada to address two issues: (1) the efficacy of screening at ages forty to forty-nine; (2) the extent to which benefits at ages fifty to fifty-nine are affected when screening is limited to breast palpation in contrast to screening that includes both palpation and mammography (Miller, Howe, and Wall 1981).

Until new evidence is produced, screenings with mammography of asymptomatic women in the general population are advocated for those fifty years of age and over. For those aged forty to forty-nine, the recommendation for periodic checkups with mammography is restricted to women with a familial history (mother, sisters) of breast cancer. At ages thirty-five to thirty-nine, the recommendation for such examinations is limited to women with a personal history of breast cancer.

Monthly breast self-examination after instruction on how to do this competently is widely supported. However, there is also agreement that the practice needs to be studied carefully to determine whether it does lead to a significant reduction in breast cancer mortality and, if the benefit is small, whether it justifies an increased number of medical-care visits and psychological problems (Moore 1978).

CANCER OF THE CERVIX. The most widely applied screening test for early detection of cancer is the Pap smear. The procedure, which became available in the early 1940s, has a relatively low cost. When properly performed and interpreted, it has a high probability of detecting cancer of the cervix in a preinvasive stage (in situ) with a cure rate believed to be close to 100 percent. These factors led to the start of major screening programs twenty to thirty years ago in Jefferson County, Kentucky (Christopherson et al. 1970), Toledo, Ohio (Burns et al. 1968) and British Columbia, Canada (Fidler and Boyes 1965). The purpose was to involve a large majority of the women in the general population, usually covering ages from early twenties through the fifties, in annual Pap testing. Provisions were made for close monitoring of the results. In the United States, following reports of reductions in the incidence of invasive cancer of the cervix and mortality, annual Pap testing rapidly became part of the national and local cancer control programs sponsored by the United States Public Health Service and the American Cancer Society. Today, a large majority of the women between twenty and sixty years of age have had a Pap test and many adhere to a schedule of either annual or biennial examination.

Concurrent with the enthusiastic support for Pap testing, challenges appeared concerning the efficacy of this procedure. There were two main issues: the absence of evidence on effects from a suitable control trial (Cochrane and Holland 1971) and questions concerning the significance of cancer in situ (e.g., does regression to a nonmalignant condition occur and if so, how often; is invasive cancer always preceded by an in-situ stage?). The possibility of dealing with these and related issues through a randomized controlled trial is no longer open because of the breadth of acceptance of the efficacy of the Pap test under screening conditions. Accordingly it has become necessary to seek information on benefits from several of the long-term programs which, while not definitive, would be sufficiently convincing for policy decisions. The most extensively studied program for this purpose has been carried out in British Columbia, Canada (Walton Report 1976).

A basic aspect of the approach was to determine whether the trends in incidence of invasive cancer of the cervix and mortality from cancer of the uterus in the various provinces of Canada are related to the intensity of screening. Initial analyses suggested that the trends in British Columbia, where the heaviest screening had taken place, did not differ substantially from the trends elsewhere, thereby raising serious questions about efficacy of Pap testing. More recent analyses taking into account socioeconomic variations among the provinces have dispelled these doubts through the demonstration of a direct relationship between benefits and the extent to which screening reached the population (Miller, Lindsay, and Hill 1976). In addition, studies in other areas such as Aberdeen, Scotland, Ireland, and Finland (Johannesson, Geirsson, and Day 1978; MacGregor and Teper 1974; Timonen, Nieminen, and Kauraniemi 1974) have produced results that are consistent with those for British Columbia, and there is now wide acceptance that Pap testing is efficacious. Another conclusion is that the available data on the natural history of precancerous lesions of the cervix support the view that they are largely progressive, if not treated.

Many issues remain (Miller 1978; Foltz and Kelsey 1978). The more important ones include the periodicity of and efficiency of alternatives for applying the procedures under screening conditions and identifying where the problem is still significant. The increased knowledge about the long latency period of carcinoma in situ and the relationship between age and in-situ cancer have led to recent revisions in recommendations for screening for this condition among women in the United States; these revisions depart from the routine annual testing dogma and put this country in accord with other countries that have adopted policies of screening less often than annually. The recommendations of the American Cancer Society are that all asymptomatic women aged twenty and over, and those under twenty who are sexually active, have a Pap test annually for two negative examinations and then at least every three years until the age of sixty-five. Women at high risk for cervical cancer may need to be tested more frequently.

A Perspective

Cancer has, for years, received a greater share of public and private investment in basic and applied research and in detection and treatment than any other disease. The nature and complexity of the diseases involved have made it a certainty that progress in controlling them would be slow. Nevertheless, some gains have been made. We have increased our understanding of the epidemiology and, in a number of instances, the etiology of specific cancers. However, a major breakthrough which would radically reduce the incidence of cancer still eludes us—except in our understanding of the effects of smoking. A sharp downward trend in the proportion of the population that smokes would, in the absence of any other change, be reflected in a large decline in the incidence and mortality from cancer during the next ten to fifteen years. We are on quite certain grounds with respect to smoking. But an extensive analytical assessment of avoidable cancer risks in the United States speculated that the largest risk may be due to dietary factors not yet reliably identified (Doll and Peto 1981).

Clearly, primary prevention which extends beyond the single agent—cigarette smoking—will continiue to attract a great deal of attention in the 1980s. Also, campaigns to reach large segments of the population with the secondary prevention measures discussed above appear to be gaining momentum, and community oncology programs are aimed at reducing differentials in the stage of disease at the time of detection among population subgroups. Finally, it needs to be recognized that many environmental, social, and medical-care changes are under way that may be influencing the incidence of and survival from cancer which were not apparent from the information available at the writing of this chapter.

REFERENCES

References to sources that are frequently used in the chapter are asterisked (*) below; the text is annotated only the first time the source is utilized in a major section. The symbol (†) indicates reports with extensive literature citations; the symbol (‡) indicates analytical reviews.

* American Cancer Society. 1979. *Cancer facts and figures, 1980.* New York: American Cancer Society.
* ——. 1980. Guidelines for the cancer-related checkup Ca. *A Cancer Journal for Clinicians* 30 (no. 4).
ANTUNES, C. M.; STOLLEY, P. D.; ROSENSHEIN, N. B.; DAVIES, J. L.; TONASCIA, J. A.; BROWN, C.; BARNETT, L.; RUTLEDGE, A.; POKEMANER, M.; and GARCIA, R. 1979. Endometrial cancer and estrogen use. *New England Journal of Medicine* 300 (no. 1):9–13.
ARMSTRONG, B., and DOLL, R. 1975. Environmental factors and cancer incidence and mortality in different countries with special reference to dietary practices. *International Journal of Cancer* 15:617–31.
* AXTELL, L. M.; ASIRE, A. J.; and MYERS, M. H., eds. 1976. *Cancer patient survival report no. 5.* End Result Section, Biometry Branch, Division of Cancer Cause and Prevention, NCI. DHHS pub. no. (NIH) 77–992.
BAKER, R. R.; TOCKMAN, M. S.; MARSH, B. R.; et al. 1979. Screening for bronchogenic carcinoma: the surgical experience. *Journal of Thoracic Cardiovascular Surgery* 78:876–82.
BEAHRS, O. H.; SHAPIRO, S., and SMART, C. 1979. Report of the working group to review the National Cancer Institute-American Cancer Society breast cancer detection demonstra-

tion projects. March 1979. Division of Cancer Control and Rehabilitation, *Journal of the National Cancer Institute* 62:(no. 3):641–707.

† BENFARI, R. C., and SHERWIN, R., eds. 1980. Forum: the Multiple Risk Factor Intervention Trial (MRFIT). The methods and impact of intervention over four years. *Preventive Medicine* 10 (no. 4). Articles include:

Zukel, W. J.; Paul, O.; and Schnaper, H. W. The Multiple Risk Factor Intervention Trial (MRFIT). I. Historical perspectives, pp. 387–401.

Sherwin, R.; Kaelber, C. T.; Kezdi, P.; Kjelsberg, M. O.; and Thomas, H. E., Jr. The Multiple Risk Factor Intervention Trial (MRFIT). II. The development of the protocol, pp. 402–25.

Benfari, R. C. The Multiple Risk Factor Intervention Trial (MRFIT). III. The model for intervention, pp. 426–42.

Caggiula, A. W.; Christakis, G.; Farrand, M.; Hulley, S. G.; Johnson, R.; Lasser, N. L.; Stamler, J.; and Widdowson, G. The Multiple Risk Factor Intervention Trial (MRFIT). IV. Intervention on blood lipids, pp. 443–75.

Hughs, G. H.; Hymowitz, N.; Ockene, J. K.; Simon, N.; and Vogt, T. M. The Multiple Risk Factor Intervention Trial (MRFIT). V. Intervention on smoking, pp. 476–500.

Cohen, J. D.; Grimm, R. H., Jr.; and Smith, W. McF. The Multiple Risk Factor Intervention Trial (MRFIT). VI. Intervention on blood pressure, pp. 501–18.

Neaton, J. D.; Broste, S.; Cohen, L.; Fishman, E. L.; Kjelsberg, M.; and Schoenberger, J. The Multiple Risk Factor Intervention Trial (MRFIT). VII. A comparison of risk factor changes between the two study groups, pp. 519–43.

Benefari, R. C., and Sherwin, R. The Multiple Risk Factor Intervention Trial after 4 years: a summing-up, pp. 544–46.

BOND, J. H., and GILBERTSEN, V. A. 1977. Early detection of colonic carcinoma by mass screening for occult stool blood (preliminary report). *Gastroenterology* 72:2. 1031.

BOUCOT, K. R., and WEISS, W. 1973. Is curable lung cancer detected by semi-annual screening? *Journal of American Medical Association* 224:1361–65.

BRESLOW, L., and BUELL, P. 1960. Mortality from coronary heart disease and physical activity of work in California. *Journal of Chronic Diseases* 11:421–44.

BRINTON, L. A.; HOOVER, R. N.; SZKLO, M.; FRAUMINI, J. F. 1981. Menopausal estrogen use and risk of breast cancer. *Cancer* 47:2517–22.

BURNS, E. L.; HAMMOND, E. C.; PERCY, C.; et al. 1968. Detection of uterine cancer. Results of a community program of 17 years. *Cancer* 22:1108.

CHRISTOPHERSON, W. M.; PARKER, J. E.; MENDEZ, W. M.; et al. 1970. Cervix cancer death rates and mass cytologic screening. *Cancer* 26:808.

COCHRANE, A. L., and HOLLAND, W. W. 1971. Validation of screening procedures. *British Medical Bulletin* 27:3–8.

Commission on Chronic Illness. 1957. *Chronic Illness in the United States*, vol. 1. Cambridge, Mass.: Harvard University Press.

Coronary Drug Project Research Group. 1972. The prognostic importance of the electrocardiogram after myocardial infarction experience in the Coronary Drug Project. *Annals of Internal Medicine* 77:677–89.

CREAGAN, E. T.; HOOVER, R. M.; and FRAUMENI, J. F. 1974. Mortality from stomach cancer in coal mining regions. *Archives of Environmental Health* 28:28–30.

* CUTLER, S. J., and YOUNG, J. L., eds. 1975. *Third national cancer survery: incidence data.* National Cancer Institute. DHHS pub. no. (NIH) 75-787, monograph 41.

DAWBER, T. R.; MOORS, F. E.; and MANN, G. V. 1957. Coronary heart disease in the Framingham study. *American Journal of Public Health* 47 (no. 4, pt. 2):4–24.

† DOLL, R., and PETO, R. 1976. Mortality in relation to smoking 20 years observations on male British doctors. *British Medical Journal* 2:1525–36.

——. 1981. The causes of cancer: quantitative estimates of avoidable risks of cancer in the United States today. *Journal of National Cancer Institute* 66 (no. 6): 1193–1308.

DUBIN, N. 1979. Benefits of screening for breast cancer: application of a probabilistic model to a breast cancer detection project. *Journal of Chronic Diseases* 32:145–51.

FARQUHAR, J. W.; MACCOBY, N.; WOOD, P. D.; ALEXANDER, J. K.; BREITROSE, H.; BROWN, B. W., JR.; HASKELL, W. L.; MCALISTER, A. L.; MEYER, A. J.; NASH, J. D.; and STERN, M. P. 1977. Community education for cardiovascular health. *Lancet* 1 (no. 8023): 1192–95.

FIDLER, H. K., and BOYES, D. A. 1965. The cytology program in British Columbia. *Canadian Journal of Public Health* 56:109.

FOLTZ, A. M., and KELSEY, J. L. 1978. The annual pap test: a dubious policy success. *Milbank Memorial Fund Quarterly, Health and Society* 56:(no. 4); 426–62.

FRANK, C. W.; WEINBLATT, E.; SHAPIRO, S.; and SAGER, R. V. 1966. Myocardial infarction in men: role of physical activity and smoking in incidence and mortality. *Journal of American Medical Association* 198 (no. 12):1241–45.

GILBERTSEN, V. A. 1974. Proctosigmoidoscopy and polypectomy in reducing the incidence of rectal cancer. *Cancer* 34:936–39.

GRAHAM, S., and LILIENFELD, A. M. 1958. Genetic studies of gastric cancer in humans: an appraisal. *Cancer* 11:945–58.

‡HAAS, J. F. and SCHOTTENFELD, D. 1978. Epidemiology of gastric cancer. In *Gastrointestinal tract cancer*, ed. M. Lipkin, and R. A. Good, pp.173–206. New York: Plenum.

HAENSZEL, W.; KURIHARA, M.; SEGI, M.; and LEE, R. K. C. 1972. Stomach cancer among Japanese in Hawaii. *Journal of the National Cancer Institute* 49:969–88.

HAMMOND, E. C. 1975. Persons at high risk of cancer, an approach to cancer etiology and control. In *Cancer*, ed. J. F. Fraumani, chap. 8, New York: Academic Press.

HAMMOND, E. C. and HORN, D. 1958. Smoking and death rates—report on forty-four months of follow-up of 187,783 men. II. Death rates by cause. *Journal of American Medical Association* 166 (no. 11):1294–1308.

HAMMOND, E. C., and SEIDMAN, H. 1974. Epidemiology of gastric cancer. In *Cancer detection and prevention, proceedings of the second international symposium on cancer detection and prevention, Bologna 1973*, ed. C. Maltoni, pp. 70–80. New York: American Elsevier.

HAMMOND, E. C.; SELIKOFF, I. J.; SEIDMAN, H. 1979. Asbestos exposure, cigarette smoking, and death rates. *Annals of the New York Academy of Science* 330:473–90.

HAVLIK, R. J., and FEINLEIB, M., ed. 1979. Proceedings of the conference on the decline in coronary heart disease mortality. NHLBI. PHS pub. no. (NIH) 79–1610. Selected papers related to changes in *CHD risk factors:*
   Kleinman, J. C.; Feldman, J. J.; and Monk, M. A. Trends in smoking and ischemic heart disease mortality.
   Page, L., and Marston, R. M. Food consumption patterns.
   Beaglehold, R.; LaRosa, J. C.; Heiss, G. E., et al. Secular changes in blood cholesterol and their contribution to the decline in coronary mortality.
   Borhani, N. O. Mortality trend in hypertension, United States, 1950–1976.
   Paffenbarger, T. S. Countercurrents of physical activity and heart attack trends.
      Selected papers related to changes in *CHD care* follow:
   Killip, T. Impact of coronary care on mortality from ischemic heart disease.
   Nagel, E. L. Prehospital care as a cause for coronary heart disease mortality decline.
   McIntosh, H. D. Long-term medical care of patients with coronary artery disease.

HINKLE, L. E., JR.; WHITNEY, L. H.; LEHMAN, E. W.; et al. 1968. Occupation, education, and coronary heart disease. *Science* 161:238–46.

HIRAYAMA, T. 1972. Epidemiology of stomach cancer. *GANN*, 1972, monograph 11: *Early gastric cancer*, ed. T. Murakami, pp. 13–19. Tokyo, Japan: University Park Press.

HONEY, G. E., and TRUELOVE, S. C. 1957. Prognostic factors in myocardial infarction: Long-term prognosis. *Lancet* 272 (no. 1):1209–12.

HOROWITZ, R. I., and FEINSTEIN, A. R. 1978. Alternative analytic methods for case-control studies of estrogens and endometrial cancer. *New England Journal of Medicine* 299 (no. 20):1089–94.

HRUBEC, Z., and ZUKEL, W. J. 1971. Socioeconomic differentials in prognosis following episodes of coronary heart disease. *Journal of Chronic Diseases* 23:881–89.

Hypertension Detection and Follow-up Program Cooperative Group. 1979. Five-year findings of the Hypertension Detection and Follow-up Program: I. Reduction in mortality of persons with high blood pressure, including mild hypertension. *Journal of the American Medical Association* 242 (no. 23):2572-77.

JICK, H.; WATKINS, R. N.; HUNTER, J. R.; DINAN, R. N.; MADSEN, S.; ROTHMAN, K. J.; and WALKER, A. M. 1979. Replacement estrogens and endometrial cancer. *New England Journal of Medicine* 300:5, 218-22.

JOHANNESSON, G.; GEIRSSON, G.; and DAY, N. 1978. The effect of mass-screening in Iceland 1965-74 on incidence and mortality of cervical carcinoma. *International Journal of Cancer* 21 (no. 4):418-25.

JUERGENS, J. L.; EDWARDS, J. E.; ACHOR, R. W. P.; and BURCHELL, H. G. 1960. Prognosis of patients surviving first clinically diagnosed myocardial infarction. *American Medical Association Archives of Internal Medicine* 105:444-50.

KAHN, H. A. 1966. The Dorn study of smoking and mortality among U.S. veterans: report on 8½ years of observation. In *Epidemiological approaches to the study of cancer and other chronic diseases*, ed. W. Haenszel, USPHS, NCI monograph no. 19, pp. 1-125. Bethesda, Md.

KANNEL, W. B., and GORDON, T., eds. 1970. *The Framingham study: an epidemiological investigation of cardiovascular disease.* Section 25: J. Schiffman. Survival following certain cardiovascular events. Washington, D.C.: Government Printing Office.

†———. 1977. The Framingham study: an epidemiological investigation of cardiovascular disease. DHEW pub. no. (NIH) 74-478.

KESSLER, I. I. 1974. Perspectives on the epidemiology of cervical cancer with special reference to the herpes virus hypothesis. *Cancer Research* 34:1091.

KEYS, A. 1980. *Seven countries, a multivariate analysis of death and coronary heart disease.* Cambridge, Mass., and London, England: Harvard University Press.

KITAGAWA, E. M., and HAUSER, P. M. 1973. *Differential mortality in the United States: a study in socioeconomic epidemiology. Cambridge, Mass., and London, England: Harvard University Press.*

KLEBBA, A. J., and SCOTT, J. H. 1980. Estimates of selected comparability ratios based on dual coding of 1976 death certificates by the eighth and ninth revisions of the International Classification of Disease. NCHS, PHS, *Monthly Vital Statistics Report* 28 (no. 11, suppl.).

‡LAPORTE, R. E.; GRESANTA, J. L.; and KULLER, L. H. 1980. The relationship of alcohol consumption to atherosclerotic heart disease. *Preventive Medicine* 9:22-40.

LEE, J. A. H. 1976. Recent trends of large bowel cancer in Japan compared to United States, England, and Wales. *International Journal of Epidemiology* 5:187-94.

LILIENFELD, A. M. 1963. The epidemiology of breast cancer. *Cancer Research* 23:1503-13.

MACGREGOR, J. E., and TEPER, S. 1974. Screening for cervical cancer. *Lancet,* 1 (no. 7868):1221.

MACK, T. M.; PIKE, M. C.; HENDERSON, B. E.; et al. 1976. Cancer risk from estrogen intake. *New York State Journal of Medicine* 294:1262-67.

†MACMAHON, B. 1974. Risk factors for endometrial cancer. *Gynecologic Oncology* 2:122-29.

‡MACMAHON, B.; COLE, P.; and BROWN, J. 1973. Etiology of human breast cancer. *Journal of the National Cancer Institute* 50 (no. 1):21-42.

‡MARKS, R. U. 1967. Social stress and cardiovascular disease. Factors involving social and demographic characteristics. A review of empirical findings. *Milbank Memorial Fund Quarterly* 45 (pt. 2):51-108.

MCMICHAEL, A. J.; POTTER, J. D.; and HETZEL, B. S. 1979. Time trends in colorectal cancer mortality in relation to food and alcohol consumption: United States, United Kingdom, Australia, and New Zealand. *International Journal of Epidemiology* 8:295-303.

MILLER, A. B. 1978. Screening for cancer of the cervix in Canada, Post Walton. In Report of the UICC International Workshop, ed. A. B. Miller. Technical Report Series, vol. 40. Geneva: UICC.

MILLER, A. B., and BULBROOK, R. D. 1980. The epidemiology and etiology of breast cancer, A Special Report. *New England Journal of Medicine* 303 (no. 21):1246–48.

MILLER, A. B.; LINDSAY, J.: and HILL, G. B. 1976. Mortality from cancer of the uterus in Canada and its relationship to screeening for cancer of the cervix. *International Journal of Cancer* 17:602–612.

MILLER, A. B.; HOWE, G. R.; and WALL, C. 1981. The national study of breast cancer screening. *Clinical and Investigative Medicine* 4 (nos 3/4):227–258.

MODAN, B. 1977. Dietary role in cancer etiology. *Cancer* 40:1887–91.

MOORE, F. D. 1978. Breast self-examination. *New England Journal of Medicine* 299 (no. 6): 304.

MORRIS, J. N., and CRAWFORD, M. D. 1958. Coronary heart disease and physical activity of work. *British Medical Journal* 2:1485–96.

*MYERS, M. H., and HANKEY, B. F. 1980. Cancer patient survival experience. Biometry Branch, Division of Cancer Cause and Prevention, NCI. DHHS Pub. no. (NIH) 80–2148.

‡NOMURA, A. 1982. Stomach. In *Cancer epidemiology and prevention*, ed. D. Schottenfeld, and J. F. Fraumeni, Jr. pp. 624–37. Philadelphia, Pa.: W. B. Saunders.

PAFFENBARGER, R. S., JR., and HALE, W. E. 1975. Work activity and coronary heart mortality. *New England Journal of Medicine* 292 (no. 11):545–50.

†Pooling Project Research Group. Relationship of blood pressure, serum cholesterol, smoking habit, relative weight and ECG abnormalities to incidence of major coronary events. *Journal of Chronic Diseases* 31 (no. 4).

PROROK, P. C.; HANKEY, B. F.; BUNDY, B. N. 1981. Concepts and problems in the evaluation of screening programs. *Journal of Chronic Diseases* 34:159–71.

RICE, D. P., FELDMAN, J. J., and WHITE, K. L. 1976. The current burden of illness in the United States. An occasional paper of the Institute of Medicine, National Academy of Sciences, Washington, D.C., 27 October 1976.

ROSENBERG, H. M. and KLEBBA, A. J. 1979. Trends in cardiovascular mortality with a focus on ischemic heart disease: United States, 1950–1976. *Proceedings of the conference on the decline in coronary heart disease mortality*, May 1979. PHS pub. no. (NIH) 79–1610. Bethesda, Md.

ROSENMAN, R. H.; BRAND, R. J.; JENKINS, C. D.; et al. 1975. Coronary heart disease in the Western Collaborative Group Study: final follow-up experience of 8½ years. *Journal of the American Medical Association* 233:872–77.

‡ROTKIN, I. D. 1973. A comparison review of key epidemiological studies in cervical cancer related to current searches for transmissible agents. *Cancer Research* 33:1353.

RUBERMAN, W.; WEINBLATT, E.; GOLDBERG, J. D.; FRANK, C. W.; SHAPIRO, S.; and CHAUDHARY, B. S. 1977. Ventricular premature beats and mortality after myocardial infarction. *New England Journal of Medicine* 297:15,750–57.

‡SCHOTTENFELD, D., and WINAWER, S. J. 1982. Large intestine. In *Cancer epidemiology and prevention*, ed. D. Schottenfeld and J. F. Fraumeni, Jr., pp. 703–727. Philadelphia, Pa.: W. B. Saunders.

SCHOTTENFELD, D.; WINAWER, S. J.; and MILLER, D. G. 1978. Screening and early diagnosis of large bowel cancer. *Report of the UICC International Workshop*, ed. A. G. Miller. Technical Report Series, vol. 40. Geneva: UICC.

SHAPIRO, S. 1981. Breast cancer screening. In *Breast Cancer*, ed. B. Hoogstraten and R. W. McDivitt. pp. 53–85. Boca Raton, Fl.: CRC Press.

SHAPIRO, S.; STRAX, P.; VENET, L.; and FINK, R. 1968. The search for risk factors in breast cancer. *American Journal of Public Health* 58:820–35.

†SHAPIRO, S.; WEINBLATT, E.; FRANK, C. W.; and SAGER, R. V. 1969. Incidence of coronary heart disease in a population insured for medical care (HIP). *American Journal of Public Health* 59 (no. 6, suppl.):1–101.

———. 1970. Social factors in the prognosis of men following first myocardial infarction. *Milbank Memorial Fund Quarterly* 48 (no. 1):37–50.

SHEKELLE, R. B. 1969. Educational status and risk of coronary heart disease. *Science* 163:97–98.

STALLONES, R. A. 1980. The rise and fall of ischemic heart disease. *Scientific American* 243 (no. 5):53–59.

STAMLER, J. 1978. Lifestyles, major risk factors, proof, and public policy. *Circulation* 58:3–19.

STAMLER, J., and EPSTEIN, F. H. 1972. Coronary heart disease: risk factors as guides to preventive action. *Preventive Medicine* 1:27–48.

TAYLOR, W. F.; FONTANA, R. S.; UHLENHOPP, M. A.; et al. 1980. Screening for early lung cancer. Presented at the American Cancer Society National Conference on Cancer Prevention and Detection, Chicago, Illinois, 17–19 April 1980.

TIMONEN, S.; NIEMINEN, U.; and KAURANIEMI, T. 1974. Cervical screening (C). *Lancet* 1 (no. 7854):401–02.

†U.S. Department of Health and Human Services. 1971. PHS. The health consequence of smoking: a report to the surgeon general: 1971. *Cancer*, pp.231–384. Washington, D.C.: Government Printing Office.

———. 1980. PHS. *Promoting health preventing disease: objectives for the nation*, pp. 61–65. Washington D.C.: Government Printing Office.

*U.S. National Center for Health Statistics. 1960–1982. *Vital statistics of the United States.* vol. II, PHS, DHHS.

* ———. 1981. Annual summary of births, deaths, marriages, and divorces: United States, 1980. *Monthly vital statistics report* 29 (no. 13). PHS, DHHS.

VESSEY, M. P.; DOLL, R.; and JONES, K. 1975. Oral contraceptives and breast cancer. Progress report of an epidemiological study. *Lancet* 1 (no. 7913):941–44.

Veterans Administration Cooperative Study Group on Antihypertensive Agents. 1967. Effects of treatment on morbidity in hypertension: I. Results in patients with diastolic blood pressure averaging 115 through 129 mm Hg. *Journal of American Medical Association* 202:1028–34.

———. 1970. Effects of treatment on morbidity in hypertension: II. Results in patients with diastolic blood pressure averaging 90 through 114 mm Hg. *Journal of American Medical Association* 213:1143–52.

†Walton Report: Cervical cancer screening programs 1976. *Canadian Medical Association Journal.* 114 (no. 11):1–32.

WATERHOUSE, J.; CORREA, P.; MURI, C.; POWELL, J., eds. 1976. Cancer incidence in five continents, vol. 3, pp. 320–23. Lyon, France: International Agency for Research on Cancer, Scientific Publication no. 15.

WEINBLATT, E.; RUBERMAN, W.; GOLDBERG, J. D.; FRANK, C. W.; SHAPIRO, S.; and CHAUDHARY, B. S. 1978. Relation of education to sudden death after myocardial infarction.*New England Journal of Medicine* 299 (no. 2):60–65.

WEINBLATT, E.; SHAPIRO, S.; and FRANK, C. W. 1973. Prognosis of women with newly diagnosed coronary heart disease—a comparison with course of disease among men. *American Journal of Public Health* 63:(no. 7):577–93.

WEINBLATT, E.; SHAPIRO, S.; FRANK, C. W.; and SAGER, V. 1968. Prognosis of men after first myocardial infarction: mortality and first recurrence in relation to selected parameters. *American Journal of Public Health* 58 (no. 8):1329–47.

WEISS, N. S.; SZEKELY, D. R.; and AUSTIN, D. F. 1976. Increasing incidence of endometrial cancer in the United States. *New England Journal of Medicine* 294 (no. 23):1259–62.

WILSON, J. M. G., and JUNGREN, G. 1968. Principles and practice of screening for disease. *Public Health Papers*, no. 34. Geneva: World Health Organization.

WINAWER, S. J.; LEIDNER, S. D.; MILLER, D. G.; SCHOTTENFELD, D.; et al. 1977. Results of a screening program for the detection of early colon cancer and polyps using fecal occult blood testing. *Gastroenterology* 72 (no. 2):1150.

World Health Organization European Collaborative Group 1974. An international controlled trial in the multifactorial prevention of coronary heart disease. *International Journal of Epidemiology* 3 (no. 3):219–24.

WYNDER, E. L.; BROSS, I. J.; and HIRAYAMA, T. 1960. A study of the epidemiology of cancer of the breast. *Cancer* 13:559–601.

†WYNDER, E. L., and STELLMAN, S. D. 1979. Impact of long-term filter cigarette usage on lung and larynx cancer risk: a case control study. *Journal of the National Cancer Institute* 62 (no. 3):471–77.

*YOUNG, J. L., JR.; ASIRE, A. J.; and POLLACK, E. S. 1973–76. *SEER program: cancer incidence and mortality in the United States, 1973–76.* Biometry Branch, Division of Cancer Cause and Prevention, NCI. DHHS pub. no. (NIH) 78–1837.

Chapter 8

The Epidemiology of
Mental Disorder

Bruce P. Dohrenwend

EPIDEMIOLOGY IS GENERALLY DEFINED as the study of the occurrence (incidence and prevalence), distribution, and determinants of states of health in a population (e.g., McMahon and Pugh 1960; Mausner and Bahn 1974). The ultimate goals of epidemiology are to contribute to our understanding of the etiology of these states and to their control. Concern with populations distinguishes epidemiology from medical studies of the health of individuals. Concern with states of health distinguishes epidemiological investigations from research, including social research, focusing on other characteristics of populations (cf. Susser 1968). Within the framework of these general distinctions, the epidemiology of mental disorders investigates the kinds of health and behavior problems that are described for example, in the *Diagnostic and Statistical Manual of the American Psychiatric Association* (Committee on Nomenclature and Statistics 1952, 1968; Task Force on Nomenclature and Statistics, 1980).

With very few exceptions, the epidemiological studies of mental disorders with which we will be dealing report prevalence rates for adults in community populations. These rates usually refer to the presence of disorders regardless of their time of onset and duration and are for current cases of disorder in general and/or for particular types whether or not the individuals involved have been in treatment with members of the mental health professions. For this reason, they have come to be known as "true prevalence" studies as opposed to studies of treated prevalence. Although there is strong need for prospective studies that would provide data on the duration of disorders and permit calculations of rates of new cases, such studies of "true incidence" are extremely rare and discussion of them will be

Much of this chapter is based on analyses of the literature on epidemiological studies conducted in collaboration with Barbara Snell Dohrenwend and with fellows in the Research Training Program in Psychiatric Epidemiology at Columbia University supported by Grant T32 MH13043 from the National Institute of Mental Health, U.S. Public Health Service. It also draws on part of a presentation by the author and Barbara Snell Dohrenwend on the occasion of their receiving jointly the 1981 Rema Lapouse Mental Health Epidemiology Award from the American Public Health Association (Dohrenwend and Dohrenwend, 1982). The present work was supported by Research Scientist Award K05-MH14663 and Research Grants MH10328 and MH30710 from the National Institute of Mental Health and by the Foundations' Fund for Research in Psychiatry.

restricted to future gains that could be realized through prospective epidemiological research on mental disorders.

Most of the mental disorders are defined in terms of constellations or syndromes of symptoms. Interviews are the main procedures for identifying and describing them. While there is considerable consensus about some of the symptoms of some disorders, the boundaries for a particular disorder such as schizophrenia tend to vary with the nature of the samples with which theorists, clinicians, and researchers have been familiar; for example, whether their focus has been mainly on chronic inpatients of mental hospitals or on broader treatment contexts that have included outpatients in clinics or private practice (cf. Gruenberg 1974, p. 455). When clinical experience has been extended beyond both hospital and outpatient clinic to include samples of nonpatients, as in Selective Service screening and combat during World War II, not only have the boundaries of particular disorders widened, but also new disorders have been added to psychiatric nomenclatures. As Raines wrote in his foreword to the 1952 *Diagnostic and Statistical Manual* of the American Psychiatric Association which reflected the military experience:

> Only about 10% of the total cases fell into any of the categories ordinarily seen in public mental hospitals. Military psychiatrists, induction station psychiatrists and Veterans Administration psychiatrists, found themselves operating within the limits of a nomenclature not designed for 90% of the cases handled. [Committee on Nomenclature and Statistics 1952, p. vi]

It is thus a broader, more varied, and more complex terrain that one encounters when the concern is with the general population, as is the case with psychiatric epidemiology—a field whose most rapid growth to date has occurred following World War II. Only small minorities of the "cases" of mental disorder found in these studies have ever been in treatment with members of the mental health professions (Link and Dohrenwend 1980a).

The epidemiological investigators to whose studies I will be referring have tended to differ in their methods of research and in their concepts and beliefs about the etiology of the various mental disorders. Such differences have led to great variations in the prevalence they report, with some studies finding overall rates of 50 percent and more while others report rates of under 1 percent (Dohrenwend and Dohrenwend 1974a). Nevertheless, most of the investigators present their findings in terms of similar broad nosological distinctions. Thus many of them provide data on at least some of the following major types of "functional" mental disorders, that is, disorders with no known organic basis: schizophrenia involving behaviors that come closest to the lay person's stereotype of what is insane or crazy; affective psychoses characterized by severe depression; neuroses, whose hallmark is extreme anxiety and the panic, rituals, and phobias that can accompany it; and personality disorders, especially those that manifest themselves in persistent irresponsible and antisocial behavior and that include problems in the abuse of alcohol and drugs. Moreover, there appears to be considerable agreement among the epidemiological investigators as to the nature of these vividly contrasting symptom complexes or syndromes despite sharp differences in where the investigators draw the boundaries among the different types and between all types and "normality." The reason for inferring such agreement is that, despite the differences in concepts and methods, there are, as will be shown later on, strong consistencies from study to study in relationships reported between various types of mental disorder and such important demographic variables as gender, social class, and rural-urban location (Dohrenwend and Dohrenwend 1974a, 1974b). It is difficult to see how such consistent relationships can occur unless cores of common meaning are being tapped despite differences in the methods used by the different investigators.

Since the turn of the century, and continuing at least until 1980, when the American Psychiatric Association published its new and markedly different third edition of the *Diagnostic and Statistical Manual* (DSM-III) (Task Force on Nomenclature and Statistics 1980), there have been what I would like to describe as two generations of epidemiological studies aimed at investigating the true prevalence of mental disorders in communities all over the world (Dohrenwend and Dohrenwend 1982). The first generation consists of sixteen studies, all of which took place before World War II; the second generation consists of the more than sixty studies that were conducted for the most part following World War II (Dohrenwend and Dohrenwend 1974a, p. 425). The third generation has just barely begun to make an appearance in the last two or three years with a handful of studies that are as yet too few, too diverse, and too incomplete to provide a firm basis for predicting how this new generation will develop. Much of what the third generation of epidemiological studies could be, however, is foreshadowed in the problems, findings, and issues arising out of the first and, especially, the second.

My purpose in this paper will be to describe briefly the nature of the first- and second-generation studies and some of the key problems and issues that they pose. I will then try to discern directions that might be taken in the future generation of research that would lead to markedly increased understanding of etiology and opportunities for control. For other quite recent reviews of this field, the reader is referred to Robins (1978) and to Weissman and Klerman (1978).

The First Generation of Studies

In 1855 Edward Jarvis, a physician and epidemiologist in Massachusetts, submitted a report of what was probably the most complete and influential attempt to investigate the true prevalence of mental disorder conducted in the nineteenth century (Jarvis 1971). This was almost half a century before the beginning of the Kraepelinian era in psychiatry and Jarvis's main nosological distinction was between "insanity" and "idiocy." Jarvis was well aware of the inadequacy of treated rates for estimating either the amount or the distribution of disorder in communities; he had, in fact, published a classic study showing that such rates varied inversely with geographic distance from treatment facilities (Jarvis 1850). His procedure, therefore, was not to rely on such statistics. Rather, he conducted a survey of general practitioners supplemented by reports of other key informants such as clergymen where sufficient information from general practitioners was not available. These informant reports were checked against the records of mental hospitals and other official agencies and the resulting data analyzed according to such demographic variables as gender, place of birth, and economic status.

Like Jarvis, the first generation of epidemiological investigators tended to rely on key informants and agency records to supply the information that would enable them to identify cases in the sixteen community studies conducted prior to World War II (Dohrenwend and Dohrenwend 1974a, p. 425). Such procedures are, of course, likely to underestimate untreated cases of disorders that are characterized mainly by subjective distress that would be more likely to be revealed in direct interviews or self-report questionnaires (e.g., Cawte 1972). Direct interviews with all subjects were used in only six of these investigations.

Even in this group of interview studies, where rates tended to be higher than in studies using key informants and agency records, the median for all types of disorders was only 3.6 percent compared to a median of close to 20 percent in second-generation interview studies that were conducted after World War II (Dohrenwend and Dohrenwend 1974a, p. 425). The difference is a dramatic illustration of the effect of the change in nomenclatures following World War II on the rates of mental disorders counted in communities.

The Second Generation of Studies

Unlike the first generation of studies, most of the investigators in the more than sixty second-generation studies conducted after World War II relied on direct interviews with all subjects (Dohrenwend and Dohrenwend 1974a, p. 425). Only rarely in these studies were the interviews supplemented systematically by data from key informants and official records, although such information is extremely useful for identifying or confirming some types of psychopathology such as substance abuse and antisocial behavior (e.g., Leighton et al. 1963; Mazer 1974). Two different types of interview have been used.

First, in most of the European and Asian research, a single psychiatrist or a small team headed by a psychiatrist personally interviewed community residents and recorded diagnostic judgments on the basis of these interviews. As a rule, the interview procedures were not made explicit in this type of approach (e.g., Bash 1967; Hagnell 1966; Kato 1969; Lin 1953).

In the second type, by contrast, standard and explicit data-collection procedures were used. Although the interviews were sometimes done by psychiatrists and clinical psychologists and sometimes by lay interviewers, in all instances case identification depended on psychiatrists' evaluations of protocols compiled from the interview responses and, sometimes, from ancillary data from key informants, official records, and interviewers' observations (e.g., D. C. Leighton et al. 1963). The Midtown study and the Stirling County study (Srole et al. 1962; Leighton et al. 1963) pioneered this approach, and some more recent studies have adopted their procedures (Gillis, Lewis, and Slabbert 1965; Rin, Chu, and Lin 1966; Shore et al. 1973).

This type of approach is relatively economical when, as in the Midtown and Stirling County studies, lay interviewers rather than clinicians are used to collect the data to be evaluated. More important, the written protocols that form the basis of the evaluation can be edited to remove direct clues to social and cultural background factors such as social class that could bias the clinical judgments (cf. Phillips and Draguns 1971). On the other hand, the procedure has a distinct disadvantage since it makes a difference whether the clinicians actually see the individuals; clinicians tend to be overimpressed by pathology when working from written records alone (Buehler 1966; Dohrenwend, Egri, and Mendelsohn 1971; Gottheil et al., 1966; Shader et al., 1971). The question of what information is required to make an informed clinical judgment and the question of what information is likely to bias such judgment are two horns of a dilemma that has received considerably less attention in the epidemiological studies and in the field of assessment based on clinical judgments in general than it deserves (e.g., Dohrenwend, Egri, and Mendelsohn 1971).

Even more economical than having clinicians rate protocols constructed from data collected by lay interviewers is dispensing with clinical judgments altogether and using objectively scored measures of psychopathology. A number of the investigators in this second generation of studies have taken this route (e.g., Meile 1972; Phillips 1966). Unfortunately, however, their decisions to use objective rather than judgmental measures were based on considerations of practicality and cost rather than on tests of the relative accuracy of mechanical versus nonmechanical modes of combining data (Meehl 1954; Sawyer 1966).

The objective measure used most often is a twenty-two-item screening instrument developed by the Midtown study researchers on a purely actuarial basis to provide an approximation of their Mental Health Rating of psychiatric impairment (Langner 1962). A similar although less widely used measure consisting of twenty Health Opinion Survey questions was developed by the Stirling County study researchers as well (Macmillan 1957). Both have as their core a portion of the items from the Psychosomatic Scale of the Neuropsychiatric Screening Adjunct, developed as an aid to Selective Service screening during World War II (Star 1950).

As would be expected from the source of many of them in the NSA, almost half of the questions in these instruments are physiological in content while the others appear on their face to touch on aspects of anxiety and depression. Such structured questions with fixed alternative response categories are easy to administer and have been subject, unlike the judgmental measures, to a considerable amount of methodological investigation. As a result, they have their proponents (e.g., Shader et al. 1971; Spiro et al. 1972; Summers et al. 1971) and their critics (e.g., Crandell and Dohrenwend 1967; B. P. Dohrenwend 1966; B. S. Dohrenwend 1973; Dohrenwend and Crandell 1970; Manis, Brawer, Hunt, and Kercher 1963; Phillips and Clancy 1972; Phillips and Segal 1969).

Their proponents are impressed that these instruments have been shown to be reliable, to relate strongly to a host of demographic variables, and to discriminate between nonpatients and psychiatric patients, especially when a large portion of the latter were diagnosed as neurotic. Their critics worry about their lack of face validity as a representative sample of the range and variety of symptoms described in diagnostic manuals, their tendency to overrepresent distress in some groups, the possibility that the more physiological items among them may be confounded with physical illness, and their susceptibility to response styles—in short, an all-too-familiar catalog of assets and liabilities for personality measures constructed on actuarial bases.

There exists by now a small family of these brief screening scales that appear highly similar in content and have been used in between a quarter and a third of the second generation of epidemiological studies to measure such things as "mental health," "mental illness," "psychiatric disorders," "emotional adjustment," "symptoms of stress," and "psychophysiological symptoms" (Seiler 1973. p. 257). They show good internal consistency reliability (typically between .80 and .85) and tend to correlate with each other as highly as their reliabilities permit (Link and Dohrenwend 1980b). They are clearly all measures of the same thing. It is not readily apparent, however, what this might be from looking at the items in these scales in relation to concepts such as those listed above. The certainly do not, for example, contain symptoms of all varieties of "mental illness" or "psychiatric disorders"; nor are they limited to "psychophysiological symptoms"; nor do they exhaust the variety of stress reactions. Moreover, while whatever they measure frequently converges with diagnosable mental disorders, it occurs with at least equal frequency in the absence of such disorders (Link and Dohrenwend 1980b). It is intriguing to inquire, therefore, into what it is that they are in fact measuring.

We have found that these brief screening scales have an extremely high correlation with measures of self-esteem, helplessness-hopelessness, dread, anxiety, sadness, and confused thinking (Dohrenwend, Shrout, Egri, and Mendelsohn 1980), all of which are major facets of what Jerome Frank (1973) has called "demoralization." In Frank's theoretical formulation as well as in relevant research that we have reviewed with regard to the screening scales (Dohrenwend, Oksenberg, Shrout, Dohrenwend, and Cook 1979), this type of nonspecific psychological distress is likely to occur in response to a variety of predicaments: severe physical illnesses, especially those that are chronic; a buildup of recent stressful life events; attempts to cope with psychotic symptoms; and being from the lower social class. It is thus something like physical temperature in that when it is elevated you know that something is wrong but not what is wrong until you learn more about the context. Thus, while these measures of nonspecific distress that I prefer to call "demoralization" are interesting in their own right, they are often very indirectly related to diagnosable mental disorders.

Legacy from First and Second Generation of Studies for Future Epidemiological Research

The legacy from the first and second generations of epidemiological studies comes in four parts: (1) host of methodological problems centering on how to conceptualize and measure mental disorders in communities whether or not these disorders have been detected by treatment agencies; (2) a set of results bearing on questions about cultural similarities and differences; (3) data relevant to estimating the amount of various types of mental disorder in communities; and (4) findings on their distribution. Let us describe the four parts of the legacy before going on to some of the main issues they raise.

Methodological Problems

As mentioned earlier, the different concepts and methods used by different investigators in the first- and second-generation studies led to rates that ranged from under 1 percent in some studies to 50 percent and more in others. Even within the second generation of post–World War II studies that, generally, reported much higher rates than the prewar first generation there tend to be subgroups of low-rate, medium-rate and high-rate studies with a range in overall prevalence from 1.2 percent to 69 percent. There is no way to account for the variability in terms of substantive differences in the persons and places studied. Rather, methodological differences tended to produce great variability in rates in both the first and second generation of studies (Dohrenwend and Dohrenwend 1974a).

Such methodological differences were marked by the use of new terms like *caseness* (Leighton et al. 1963) and *impairment* (Srole et al. 1962) to describe ratings made by psychiatrists in some studies in lieu of traditional diagnoses; and, as mentioned above, they were marked by the use of cutoffs on symptom scales purporting to measure a variety of things ranging from global notions of "mental health" to "psychophysiological symptoms." In neither the first generation of studies nor the second did a consensus occur across investigators as to the best concepts and methods to use.

It would be fortunate for future research if, in retrospect, we could simply pick out the study or studies that used the best concepts and measurement strategies and adopt their approach. Unfortunately, the investigators in the first generation and second generations of studies gave little attention to providing evidence for the validity of their methods that would permit us to make choices among them on a rational basis (Dohrenwend and Dohrenwend 1969, 1974a). I will undertake a detailed analysis of this problem in light of new developments in measurement and diagnosis later on in discussing the third and future generation of epidemiological research.

Cultural Similarities and Differences

None of the first- and second-generation epidemiological studies have been conducted in the cultures that differ most sharply from our own modern, technological society. The most important omissions are investigations of nomadic hunter and gatherer societies that not only differ greatly from our own in their social organization but have been less influenced by contact with modern society than have most other non-Western, nonindustrialized groups (Nee and DeVore 1976).

Moreover, the diversity of methods of case identification and diagnosis used in the first- and second-generation epidemiological studies makes it hazardous to compare results obtained by different investigators in most of the different cultural settings that have been studied. Sparse and problematic as they are, however, the first- and second-generation studies provide the only data that go beyond anecdotal accounts of cultural differences.

Wherever psychiatric epidemiologists have attempted studies in non-Western societies with distinctively different traditions and the relative absence of modern technology, one of their main goals has been to learn whether Western psychiatric classifications are applicable. They have presented ample evidence that individual symptoms can take on distinctive content and color from the culture (cf. Beiser, Ravel, Collomb, and Egelhoff 1972; Chance 1962; Field 1960; Katz, Gudeman, and Sanborn 1969; Leighton 1969; Phillips and Draguns 1971; Yoo 1961); for example, cows and witchs occupy a more important place in the symptoms of mental disorder in rural Ghana (Field 1960) than in midtown Manhattan (Srole et al. 1962). Such differences in the coloration of symptoms, however, are superficial. I know of no instance where epidemiological investigators have attempted to use the broader Western classifications of mental disorders in non-Western societies and found them to be inapplicable (e.g., Beiser et al. 1972; Field 1960; Leighton 1969; Yoo 1961).

There appears, therefore, to be no intrinsic bar to systematic cross-cultural research in psychiatric epidemiology—in the future. For now we must be content with what can be learned from a few studies that fall into one of three categories: (1) they are of particularly unusual communities; (2) they provide comparisons of contrasting cultural settings all studied by the same team of investigators using the same methodology; (3) they employ data that, though imperfect, cover long periods of time.

One of the most important studies of an unusual community was conducted in the 1950s by Eaton and Weil (1955) of a group called the Hutterites. An ethnic enclave that has been remarkably successful in preserving its traditions in the face of contact with modern mass society, the Hutterites had, on the basis of a number of anecdotal accounts, a strong reputation for excellent mental health. At the time they were studied by Eaton and Weil, the Hutterities consisted of about 8,500 persons who had lived for over seventy-five years in over ninety small communities in west-central portions of the United States and Canada. They comprised a religiously oriented and self-sufficient communal society with a secure agrarian economy. The authors convincingly estimate that less than 5 percent of the males had left their communities never to return, and that the rate among females was much lower. There was a record of only one divorce and four separations in the history of the group. And no Hutterite had ever been allowed to become a public charge as long as he or she remained a member of this community. This extraordinarily stable society had been highly effective in providing cradle-to-grave support for its members. Did it also protect them from developing psychopathology?

Eaton and Weil's expectation when the study was initiated was "that few cases of mental disorder would be found" (1953, p. 229). If these investigators had restricted their study to treated rates, they would have confirmed their hypothesis since there were no Hutterites in mental hospitals or under treatment by psychiatrists in other settings at the time their fieldwork was done.

On the basis of direct interviews with subjects or key informant reports from members of the Hutterite population, however, Eaton and Weil arrived at a rate of psychosis that ranked the Hutterites as third highest in ten populations for whom they computed age-sex adjusted rates—higher, for example, than the urban and far from affluent Eastern Health District of Baltimore. The researchers were aware, however, that population comparisons are difficult to make across these studies, and they suspected that if the other studies had used comparable procedures, the Hutterite rate would have ranked relatively much lower. Be this as it may, given the initial expectations with which Eaton and Weil began their research, it is difficult to argue with their conclusion that the "findings do not confirm the hypothesis that a simple and relatively uncomplicated way of life provides virtual immunity from mental disorders" (1955, p. 209). It would seem that the burden of proof is on those who would locate a symptom-free utopia in the real world.

We are fortunate in having a series of studies in which similar methodology was used in differing cultural settings. These were conducted among the Yoruba, the Eskimo, and residents of a maritime county in Canada by A. H. Leighton and his colleagues (Murphy 1976). Their striking finding is that of remarkable similarity not only in prevalence rates of schizophrenia but also in rates of all disorders combined, despite the differences in cultural setting.

We have few comparable data on rates of disorders over long periods of time, and the data that do exist are restricted to treated rates. Nevertheless, they hold some surprises for those who would expect rates to increase over time with the increasing stresses and strains of modern technological society. Goldhamer and Marshall (1953), for example, found no evidence that the treated incidence of functional psychosis in the early and middle years had increased between 1840 and 1940 in Massachusetts—despite the improvements in treatment facilities.

Comparisons such as these we have been reviewing give evidence of more consistency than contrast in rates of mental disorders across time and place. Nevertheless, there is strong evidence not so much for differences in overall amounts of disorders as for the relative predominance of different types of mental disorder in different cultural settings.

Vivid examples are provided in Eaton and Weil's (1955) study of the Hutterites. While the Hutterite society clearly did not immunize its citizens against the development of mental disorders, the types of disorder that involve persistent antisocial behavior were close to being absent from this group. Only four Hutterites were diagnosed as having personality disorders, and only two of these involved antisocial behavior that posed persistent problems to the community. Even here the problems were relatively mild, taking the form of property thefts in one case and misuse of colony funds in the other. Beyond this there were only minor law violations by Hutterites, usually on a one-time-only basis. These results are especially remarkable in that the key informant techniques of data collection that Eaton and Weil used should be especially effective in securing adequate coverage of this kind of psychopathology.

Moreover, the rates of the different subtypes of functional psychosis that Eaton and Weil found—if not a function of some form of idiosyncratic diagnostic procedure—showed an unusual distribution. By contrast with the high ratio of schizophrenia to manic-depressive psychosis usually reported, the cases of manic-depressive psychosis far outnumbered cases of schizophrenia among the Hutterites. The Hutterite rate for the latter, in fact, was among the four lowest we found in the thirty-nine studies we reviewed that reported "true" prevalence rates for schizophrenia (Dohrenwend, Dohrenwend, Gottesman, Link, and Neugebauer 1979). The Hutterites do not appear to be an isolated instance of unusually low rates of schizophrenia. Murphy and Taumoepeau (1980) recently reported evidence that rates of schizophrenia are probably also unusually low in the Kingdom of Tonga in the South Pacific.

Taken together, such findings suggest that while contrasting cultural settings may not differ sharply in aggregated amounts of mental disorders, they do appear to differ in the relative amounts of different types of mental disorders. We shall find more such evidence when we look at different groups within communities in particular cultural settings, groups that differ in subcultural background. What accounts for contrasts in types of disorders in varying cultural and subcultural groups is, of course, another matter since the populations of such communities and groups can differ in genes as well as environment.

Amounts of Various Types of Mental Disorder in Communities

Despite methodological problems stemming from lack of concensus about how to conceptualize and measure mental disorders, it is possible to get a very rough estimate of the extent of psychopathology in communities by looking at the aggregated results of past first- and second-generation epidemiological studies. It is

TABLE 8.1   Medians and Ranges of Percents of Functional Psychiatric Disorders Reported in Epidemiological Studies of "True" Prevalence Published in 1950 or Later

Type of Disorder	Median	Range	Number of Studies
Schizophrenia	0.76	0.0023 - 1.95	17
Affective psychosis	0.43	0.0000 - 1.59	12
Neurosis	5.95	0.305 - 75.0*	25
Personality disorders	4.19	0.23 - 14.5*	19
Overall functional disorders	14.05	1.25 - 63.5	27
"Demoralization"	27.5	3.4 - 69.0	17

Source: Dohrenwend 1979, p. 2.
* Includes Stirling County study "symptom patterns" that are not necessarily considered "cases" in that study (D. C. Leighton et al. 1963).
Note: All percents adjusted for gender differences except for rates of "Demoralization." Medians and ranges calculated from detailed tables and bibliography prepared to supplement B. P. Dohrenwend and B. S. Dohrenwend 1974, 1976.

probably best, however, to consider such estimates as hypotheses about what investigators might find on the average if they studied a representative sample of communities with a composite of the methods of case identification and classification used in the past. We have formulated such hypotheses on the basis of analyses of results from second-generation studies which have tended to be based on the more inclusive nomenclatures introduced following World War II (Dohrenwend 1979; Dohrenwend, Dohrenwend, Gould, Link, Neugebauer, and Wunsch-Hitzig 1980) and will summarize them here.

Table 8.1 presents the medians and ranges of current prevalence rates for each major classification of functional mental disorder from second-generation studies conducted all over the world. The overall median of about 14 percent for the diagnosable functional disorder suggests that these are not rare in community populations.

The median of more than 25 percent "demoralized" in Table 8.1 suggests that even larger proportions of community populations show a level of distress that is characteristic of mixed samples of psychiatric outpatients and inpatients (Dohrenwend, Oksenberg, Shrout, Dohrenwend, and Cook 1979; Link and Dohrenwend 1980b). These "demoralized" persons are those screened by various symptom scales that measure the type of nonspecific psychological distress that we are terming "demoralization" (Dohrenwend, Oksenberg, Shrout, Dohrenwend, and Cook 1979). As noted earlier, there is only partial correspondence between a high score on screening scale measures of demoralization and diagnosable mental disorders. Figure 8.1 illustrates this point with results from three studies that provide both a diagnostic assessment, in two of the three studies by psychiatrists, and screening scale results (Link and Dohrenwend 1980b). On the basis of such findings, we estimate that at least half of those showing severe demoralization do not have diagnosable mental disorders.

Taken together, these results suggest that it would not be unusual to find 14 or 15 percent of a sample of adults from the general population suffering from some type of functional mental disorder plus about that many who were showing severe nonspecific psychological distress. The figures would be slightly higher if we restricted our sample of second-generation studies to those conducted in North America and Western Europe (Dohrenwend et al. 1980) due, in all likelihood, to

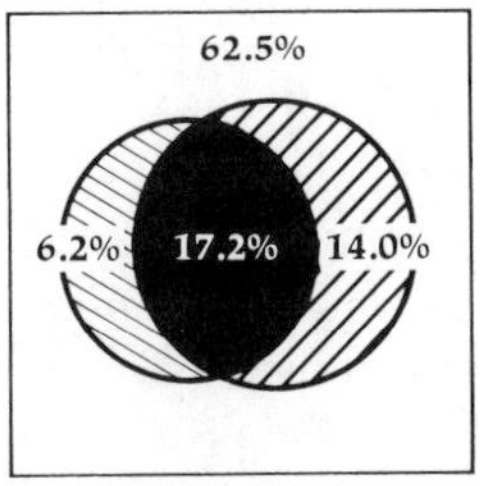

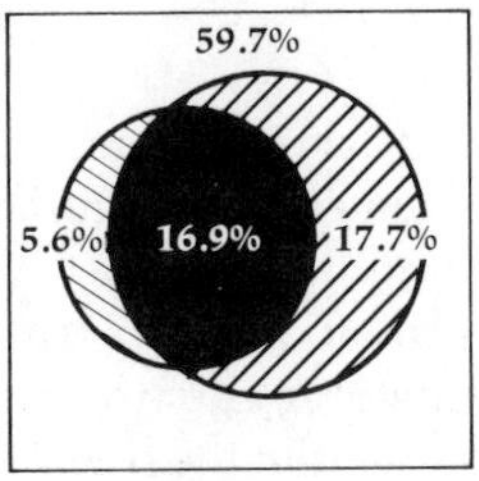

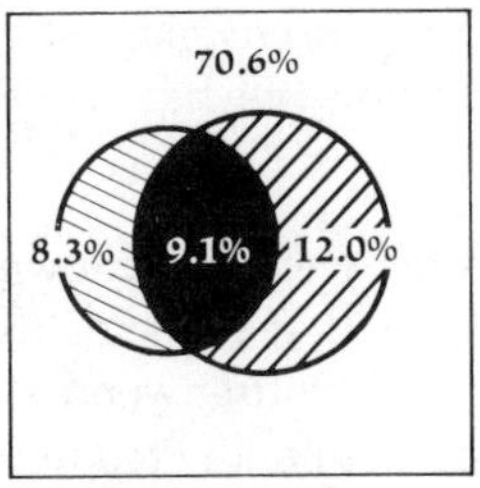

		Clinical Disorder	Screened as a Case	N	%
Study 1	62.5% / 6.2% / 17.2% / 14.0%	YES	YES	286	17.2
		NO	YES	233	14.0
		YES	NO	103	6.2
		NO	NO	1,038	62.5
Study 2	59.7% / 5.6% / 16.9% / 17.7%	YES	YES	21	16.9
		NO	YES	22	17.7
		YES	NO	7	5.6
		NO	NO	74	59.7
Study 3	70.6% / 8.3% / 9.1% / 12.0%	YES	YES	46	9.1
		NO	YES	61	12.0
		YES	NO	42	8.3
		NO	NO	358	70.6

Screened & Clinical ■   Screened Only ▨   Clinical Only ▧   Neither ☐

Figure 8.1 Relation of Clinical Mental Disorder to Screening Scale Results Source: Link and Dohrenwend 1980b, p. 116. Study 1, Langner 1962; Study 2, Dohrenwend 1973; Study 3, Myers and Weissman 1977.

the greater reliance on expanded nomenclatures by Western investigators. The figures would also be higher if we focused on adults over age sixty or sixty-five among whom an additional minority of perhaps 3.5 to 5.5 percent on the average suffer from organic psychoses (Neugebauer 1980). For children, where questions about how to describe and classify disorders are even more controversial than for adults, we are pretty much confined to studies of "clinical maladjustment" among school-age youngsters for purposes of estimating the amount of disorder and distress (Gould, Wunsch-Hitzig, and Dohrenwend 1980). Such rates are likely to average around 12 percent or so in U.S. communities (Gould et al. 1980).

Distribution of Various Types of Mental Disorder in Communities

Returning to studies mainly of adults in community populations, let us look at the distribution of mental disorders according to such important demographic variables as gender, social class, and urban-rural location. Somewhat surprisingly, in view of the methodological problems involved in these studies, there are strong consistencies, even between the relatively low rate first-generation of studies conducted before World War II and the relatively high rate second generation that followed (Dohrenwend and Dohrenwend 1969, 1974a, 1974b, 1976, 1981). These are the kinds of consistencies one might expect to find between, say, height and weight even when different investigators were using scales that were biased to register higher or lower than the true weights in a population and rulers that were biased to represent people as taller or shorter than they are. Such consistencies are probably the nearest we will come to "truth" in the past epidemiological studies of the true prevalence of mental disorders. Let us summarize these findings.

SOCIAL CLASS. The most striking finding that Jarvis reported in his landmark epidemiological study in 1855 was that "the pauper class furnishes, in ratio of its numbers, sixty-four times as many cases of insanity as the independent class" ([1855] 1971, pp. 52–53). The association of mental disorders with social class has proved not to be limited to psychotic symptomatology nor to particular times and places. Rather, it has proved remarkably persistent in the true prevalence studies conducted since the turn of the century, and holds for all of the most important subtypes of mental disorder (Dohrenwend and Dohrenwend 1981). In our various analyses of these first- and second-generation studies we have observed the following trends for rates of current prevalence:

- The highest overall rates of mental disorder were in the lowest social class in twenty-eight out of the thirty-three studies that reported data according to indicators of social class (Dohrenwend and Dohrenwend 1974a).
- This relationship was strongest in the studies conducted in urban settings or mixed urban and rural settings (nineteen out of twenty studies) (Dohrenwend and Dohrenwend 1974a).
- The inverse relationship with class was consistent for schizophrenia (five out of seven studies) (Dohrenwend and Dohrenwend 1974a), a finding further supported by most studies of relations between social class and treated rates of schizophrenia (Eaton 1974).
- It holds as well for personality disorders characterized mainly by anti-social behavior and substance abuse (eleven out of fourteen studies) (Dohrenwend and Dohrenwend 1974a).
- The two studies that provide the relevant data (Brown and Harris 1978; Weissman and Myers 1978) both indicate that the current prevalence of major depression as defined by Feighner criteria (Feighner et al. 1972) and Research Diagnostic Criteria (Spitzer, Endicott, and Robins 1978) is inversely related to social class, though perhaps only for women, who appear to show higher rates of depression than males (Weissman and Klerman 1977). Note that these two studies use criteria for affective disorder that are similar to those contained in the newly adopted third edition of the American Psychiatric Association Diagnostic and Statistical Manual (DSM-III). They might best be considered as forerunners of a new, third generation of epidemiological studies about which we will have more to say later on.
- Finally, rates of the severe, nonspecific psychological distress that we are calling demoralization are consistently highest in the lowest social class (eight out of eight studies) (Link and Dohrenwend 1980a).

In summary, then, all of the major types of functional mental disorders and nonspecific psychological distress that have been investigated in epidemiological field studies, possibly excepting bipolar affective disorder (by contrast with unipolar affective disorder or major depression), appear to show an inverse relationship with social class in either males or females or in both sexes. These class relationships are especially strong in urban settings.

GENDER. The majority of the first- and second-generation studies provided at least some data on mental disorders according to gender—though often as was the case with social class, not in the same detail on the various types of disorder from study to study. With time since the turn of the century specified as first-generation pre–World War II studies by contrast with second-generation post–World War II studies, and with place specified as rural versus urban settings in selected North American and European communities by contrast with selected communities in the rest of the world, the firm facts that we have been able to extract can be summarized as follows (Dohrenwend and Dohrenwend 1974a, pp. 436–39; Dohrenwend and Dohrenwend 1976):

- There are no consistent gender differences in rates of functional psychoses in general (thirty-four studies) or in relation to one of the two major subtypes, schizophrenia (twenty-six studies); rates of the other main subtype, manic-depressive psychosis (as defined prior to DSM-III), are generally higher among women (eighteen out of twenty-four studies).
- Rates of neurosis are consistently higher for women regardless of time or place (twenty-eight out of thirty-two studies).
- By contrast, rates of personality disorder are consistently higher for men regardless of time or place (twenty-two out of twenty-six studies).

RURAL VERSUS URBAN SETTINGS. The differences in concepts and methods used in identifying cases in the first- and second-generation studies preclude meaningful comparisons of rate differences across studies done in rural and urban settings by different investigators. Fortunately, however, at least eight investigators reported data for both a rural and an urban setting, with two reporting data for two settings each (Dohrenwend and Dohrenwend 1974b). In one comparison, the total rate for all mental disorders combined is higher in the rural setting; there is one tie; and in the remaining eight comparisons, the urban rate is higher than the rural rate. Although quite consistent, the differences are not large. The reason is that, while some types of mental disorder were found to be more prevalent in the urban setting, others were found more frequently in the rural setting. Thus:

- Total rates for all functional psychoses combined were found to be more prevalent in the rural settings (five out of seven studies) and this appears to be so for the manic-depressive subtype (three out of four studies), though not for schizophrenia (higher in the urban area in three out of five studies).
- Rates of neurosis were higher in the urban settings (five out of six studies).
- Rates of personality disorder were higher in the urban settings (five out of six studies).

Issues Raised by the First- and Second-Generation Studies

Some major theoretical, methodological, and practical issues have grown out of these epidemiological studies. These issues are related to the sheer amount of psychopathology that appears to be present in community populations, the fact that only small percents of the persons showing severe psychopathology have ever been in treatment with members of the mental health professions, and the further findings that psychopathology in general and its major subtypes are not randomly distributed within community populations.

What Are the Selective Factors in Treatment?

While only minorities of those judged to be cases of mental disorder in these epidemiological studies have ever received treatment from members of the mental health professions (Link and Dohrenwend 1980a), it is highly likely that substantial proportions of them have sought help from other sources such as clergymen and general practitioners (Gurin, Veroff, and Feld 1960; Kulka, Veroff, and Douvan 1979; Goldberg and Huxley 1980). There seems to be a kind of screen of public attitudes and reactions that sorts and sifts individuals showing deviant behavior. In the sorting process, the majority of those that would qualify as cases by psychiatric criteria are propelled to a variety of destinations, many different help sources, and various agencies of social control.

Over twenty years ago, Hollingshead and Redlich (1958) termed the attitudes and reactions that form the basis of the sorting process "lay appraisals" and pointed out that they formed the public counterpart of clinical diagnoses by psychiatrists. We still know very little about how these screens of lay appraisals operate in general populations despite the fact that we know quite a lot about public attitudes (Rabkin 1975), the utilization of mental health services (Greenley and Mechanic 1976; Kramer 1976; Regier, Goldberg, and Taube 1978; Tishler, Henisz, Myers, and Boswell 1975) and the groups at highest risk for various types of mental disorder and distress. The reason is that studies of the attitudes of people with mental disorders and the reactions of others to them and studies of actual use of mental health services as compared with, for example, use of general practitioners have not been combined with studies of the true prevalence and true incidence of mental disorders in communities. Thus we do not know the answers to such important questions as to what extent the screen of lay appraisal processes works at cross purposes with goals of delivering services as efficiently and as effectively as possible to the individuals and groups in greatest need.

There are plans developed at the U. S. National Institute of Mental Health for new research programs that should help to remedy this situation by combining studies of service utilization with epidemiological research (Regier 1980). These plans suggest that this issue, or part of it, is already on the agenda for the third and future generation of epidemiological studies. Meanwhile, we do not have compelling evidence on such basic questions as to whether it makes any difference that a person with one or another type of mental disorder is under the care of his or her family doctor, minister or rabbi, or psychiatrist.

To What Extent Is the Psychopathology Observed in the General Population Similar to That Observed in Psychiatric Patients?

Studies of extreme situations such as combat during wartime indicate that a wide variety of psychological symptomatology often appears as quite specific reactions to the stressful circumstances. This includes even the most severe symptomatology described, for example, as the "pseudo" or "three-day psychoses" (Kolb 1973, p. 438) or the "five-day" schizophrenias (Kormos 1978, p. 4). The prognosis for persons developing such symptomatology in extreme situations is generally good, in marked contrast to that of so many psychiatric patients presenting with similar symptoms.

Note that the first and second generations of epidemiological studies that we have been discussing were, with very few exceptions, conducted at one point in time. They provide a cross-sectional view of the symptomatology in community populations. We have no way to know the extent to which such symptomatology is situationally specific, as in the above examples, or to what extent such symptoms are persistent or episodically recurrent over time, as in the more usual picture from studies of the long-term careers of psychiatric patients (cf. Dohrenwend and Dohrenwend 1965, 1969). Nor do we know whether the symptomatology has the same strong relationship with disability in social functioning as in patients, especially patients in mental hospitals (Gruenberg 1967). During World War II and the Korean War, military psychiatrists seemed overly impressed with the consequences of symptomatology for disability in functioning (Ginzberg et al. 1959).

Clearly, we need to know more about the situational and familial contexts in which symptom constellations occur in community populations, the relation of these syndromes to role functioning, and the course of the psychopathology over time. A host of questions are involved: about the role of stressful events; the part played by genetic vulnerability that may be manifest in a family history of disorder; and the question of possible iatrogenic effects of psychiatric treatment through processes of labeling and/or secondary gain (Gove 1970; Gruenberg 1967; Sartorius, Jablensky, and Shapiro 1978; Scheff 1966). A major challenge for the third generation of epidemiological research is to design prospective studies that will provide an opportunity to answer such questions.

Issues of Etiology

We now know a great deal from the first and second generations of epidemiological studies about how various types of mental disorder are distributed according to such important variables as gender, social class, and rural-urban location. We have evidence that types of mental disorders vary with cultural and subcultural differences. Speculation about the implications of this information has raised important issues for further research on etiology.

GENDER DIFFERENCES. Findings that males have higher rates of the acting-out types of personality disorder while women have higher rates of the types of disorder characterized by depression (Dohrenwend and Dohrenwend 1976) raise interesting questions. Males and females in all societies differ in their social roles and their biology. The persistent problems in interpreting behavioral differences between males and females center on questions of how to unconfound the biological and social factors involved in these differences so that the relative importance of the two sets of factors and the nature of their interaction can be evaluated. Progress is most likely to come first with the identification of significant and theoretically meaningful contrasts within as well as between sex roles over time and place; and second, with investigation of the implications of these contrasts for the types of psychopathology that consistently vary by gender.

Changes in sex roles over time and the contrasts in these roles provided by different cultural settings offer opportunities to develop quasi experiments that will provide major clues to the etiological role of gender differences in psychopathology.

SOCIAL CLASS DIFFERENCES. No issues in psychiatric epidemiology have proved more persistent or compelling than those raised by the differences in rates according to social class. Jarvis had an explanation for such a finding from his 1855 study that the highest rates of "insanity" were in the "Pauper" class:

> Men of unbalanced mind and uncertain judgment do not see the true nature and relation of things, and they manifest this in mismanagement of their common affairs. They do not adapt the means which they possess or use to the ends which they desire to produce. Hence they are unsuccessful in life; their plans of obtaining subsistence for themselves or their families, or of accumulating property, often fail; and they are consequently poor, and often paupers....the cause of....their mental derangement lies behind, and is anterior to, their outward poverty. [(1855) 1971 pp. 55–56]

This interpretation by Jarvis is an early example of what has come to be known as "social selection" explanations of relationships between social position and mental disorders. It follows from the assumption that constitutional or genetic factors are more important than social environmental factors in etiology (cf. Clausen 1957, especially pp. 102–103) and has been more often advanced by European epidemiologists (e.g., Ødegaard 1956; Strömgren 1950) than by U.S. researchers since the 1930s.

Jarvis's social selection explanation contrasts sharply with the explanation that Faris and Dunham (1939) favored for their not dissimilar finding that the highest rates of mental hospital first admissions were in the central slum sections of Chicago in the 1930s:

> In these most disorganized sections of the city and, for that matter of our whole civilization, many persons are unable to achieve a satisfactory conventional organization of their world. The result may be a lack of any organization at all, resulting in a confused, frustrated, and chaotic personality. [Faris and Dunham 1939, p. 159]

This view that social location is a cause of psychopathology is reflected in the theoretical explanations supplied in most of the best-known epidemiological studies conducted by U.S. investigators since the work of Faris and Dunham. For example, Hollingshead and Redlich's (1958) study of treated rates of mental disorders in New Haven was motivated by, and the findings explained in terms of, a view that "psychiatrists work with phenomena that are essentially social in origin" (1958, p. 11). The central hypothesis of the Stirling County study (D.C. Leighton et al. 1963) and the Yoruba study (A. H. Leighton et al. 1963) was that "sociocultural disintegration" is causally related to mental disorders, and the results of the studies were interpreted as being consistent with this hypothesis. Similarly, the Midtown study investigators' "most fundamental postulate" was the proposition that "sociocultural conditions....have measurable consequences reflected in the mental health differences to be observed within a population" (Srole et al. 1962, pp. 12–13) and these researchers interpreted their main findings as reflecting the pathogenic consequences of a "poverty complex," and of processes of "stigmatize-rejection" and "role discontinuity" (1962, pp. 336–71), further elaborated in terms of a theory of environmentally induced "stress" and "strain" (Langner and Michael 1963). These explanations are examples of social causation orientations to etiology. In each, psychopathology is portrayed as mainly a consequence of the impact of adverse socioenvironmental conditions on individuals occupying positions of low status in the community. These social causation explanations are diametric opposites of social selection explanations such as Jarvis's in which psychopathology is seen as a cause rather than a consequence of adverse social circumstances.

The times had changed from Jarvis's day to the period when Faris and Dunham published their research and the major U.S. epidemiological studies described above were conducted. The United States had experienced the Great Depression, and it was clear to most by then that people could become poor for reasons quite other than inherited disabilities. The focus was shifting from the disruptive effect of sick individuals on society to the effects of a "sick society" on individuals (Frank 1936). And research during World War II unmistakably showed that situations of extreme environmental stress arising out of combat and imprisonment could produce severe psychopathology in previously normal persons (cf. Dohrenwend and Dohrenwend 1969; Dohrenwend 1979), some of it long-lasting (Beebe 1975; Eitinger 1964).

Early critics of Faris and Dunham argued, however, that downward social drift of previously ill persons could plausibly explain the concentration of cases in the slums of Chicago (e.g., Myerson, 1940). Moreover, a finding in the New Haven study that most lower class cases of psychopathology had originated in that class rather than having drifted down to it does not resolve the problem. As Gruenberg (1961) pointed out, in a society such as ours where upward mobility over succeeding generations is the norm, it is quite possible that the healthy members of the lower class have been selected upward, leaving behind a "residue" of ill. Both downward "drift" and this notion of "residues" are major varieties of what was designated above in broader terms as the social selection hypothesis. None of the studies that focused on social causation following the research of Faris and Dunham was able to rule out such alternative explanations (cf. Dohrenwend and Dohrenwend 1981). The fact of the matter is that the Zeitgeist changed far more than the epidemiological findings on social class had from Jarvis's day to the decades including the Great Depression and continuing with the major epidemiological studies conducted in the 1950s after World War II. The opposing social selection and social causation explanations remained equally plausible—their plausibility depending on point of view rather than facts.

Consider by way of illustration of the difficulties in resolving this issue research conducted since World War II on relations between social mobility and schizophrenia. The results of these studies tend to indicate that social selection processes play a role in producing the consistent finding of the highest rate of this disorder in the lowest social class (cf. Eaton and Lasry 1978; Turner 1968). These results leave room for argument, however, as to whether the social selection processes are strong enough to rule out an important role for environmental factors associated with social class (Dohrenwend and Dohrenwend 1969, pp. 41–48; Eaton 1980; Goldberg and Morrison 1963; Kohn 1972, 1972b; Mechanic 1972; Turner 1968). Grounds for such argument are especially strong when the results show that a substantial proportion of schizophrenics come from lower-class backgrounds in contrast to drifting down from a higher class. For example, Turner and Wagenfeld (1967) randomly sampled white males diagnosed as schizophrenic and with no history of prior hospitalization from the unusually comprehensive Monroe county psychiatric case register (Babigian 1972). Interviews with these subjects enabled them to compare the patients' intergenerational and intragenerational occupational mobility patterns with patterns for males in the general population. The investigators found that social selection processes clearly operated, mainly in the form of failure to rise in occupational level; that is, a larger proportion of the schizophrenics by contrast with males in the general population were born into lower-class families and they tended to remain in that class. How are these results to be explained? A vicious circle has evidently been created, but is environmental or genetic transmission involved (cf. Dohrenwend and Dohrenwend 1969, especially p. 42)?

The social causation-social selection issue has been remarkably resistant to resolution over the years. Multigeneration prospective studies that would directly trace the processes of transmission by providing data on both social mobility and the distribution of the various types of psychopathology in first degree relatives have not been undertaken (Dohrenwend and Dohrenwend 1969, especially pp. 41–48; Dohrenwend and Dohrenwend 1981). Major progress on this issue is most likely to come when innovative research strategies are brought to bear on the problem. While forerunners of such studies now exist and provide valuable data, the main hope for definitive evidence lies with the future, third generation of epidemiological research; and this hope, I shall try to show, is a bright one.

The Third and Future Generation of Epidemiological Research

First- and second-generation epidemiological studies have given rise to important theoretical and methodological issues for further research. In addition, their results permit us to develop hypotheses about the magnitude of mental health problems that should be useful for planning services. How will the third and future generation build on these achievements?

An Example of A Quasi-Experimental Strategy to Investigate the Role of Socioenvironmental Factors in Etiology

Given the practical and ethical obstacles that confront direct approaches to such important theoretical problems as the stress-selection issue raised by class differences, it is our belief that progress is most likely to come from indirect approaches that permit deductions on the basis of carefully thought out investigations of experimentallike contrasts provided by nature. Examples are the twin and adoption strategies so successfully employed to demonstrate a genetic factor in the causation of schizophrenia (e.g., Gottesman and Shields 1972; Heston 1966; Kety et al 1976). Consider what might be done to investigate the stress-selection issue.

ETHNIC BACKGROUND, SOCIAL CLASS, AND MENTAL DISORDERS. Where relations between social class and various types of psychopathology are concerned, social stress and social selection hypotheses both make the same prediction about an inverse relationship. The problem, therefore, is to find a set of circumstances in which the two contrasting theoretical orientations lead to different predictions. We have argued that the assimilation of ethnic groups into the class structures of relatively open class urban societies can be viewed as a quasi-experiment that provides such an opportunity (Dohrenwend 1966; Dohrenwend and Dohrenwend 1969; Dohrenwend 1975; Dohrenwend and Dohrenwend 1981). The opportunity arises out of the contrast between ethnic status and class status and the relationship between the two.

The most important difference between class and ethnic status for our purposes is that, unlike social class, an individual's ethnicity cannot even in small part be a function of the person's prior psychopathology. Ethnic status (being black, Puerto Rican, Mexican, Jewish, or WASP in the United States, for example, or of European, North African, or Asian origin in Israel) is ascribed at birth on the basis of such immutable characteristics as skin color, national origins, or family religion. Other things constant, such factors as prejudice and discrimination and lack of material resources place some ethnic groups, usually the most recent to arrive, at a disadvantage with respect to other ethnic groups. By contrast, class status, given among other things certain advantages or disadvantages of ethnic background, is more or less a function of individual choice, training, and performance. In multiethnic urban settings in modern democratic societies, the majority of individuals in advantaged ethnic groups have achieved middle-class status over succeeding generations; the majority of individuals in disadvantaged ethnic groups are in lower-class positions with the road to assimilation to middle-class status still stretching before them, studded with obstacles.

The crucially important point is that one's view of the contribution of ethnic status to the relationship between social class and various types of psychopathology differs greatly depending on whether one holds a social causation theory such as Faris and Dunham's or a social selection theory such as Jarvis's to explain why class is inversely related to various types of psychopathology in the first place. Let us spell out the contracts between predictions that can be derived from the two contrasting theoretical orientations when ethnic status is considered along with class status.

THE SOCIAL CAUSATION PREDICTION ABOUT CLASS AND ETHNIC DIFFERENCES. The social causation theorist would see the greater downward social pressure stemming, for example, from prejudice and discrimination, producing an increment in environmental adversity and stress on members of disadvantaged ethnic groups, over and above that stemming from class membership. Accordingly, if the rate of a particular type of psychopathology in a particular class is a function of the amount of adversity and stress induced by the social environment, as such a theorist would maintain, then one should expect to find higher rates of the psychopathology among persons from disadvantaged than among persons from advantaged ethnic groups in the same social class. This social causation prediction is diagrammed in the top half of Figure 8.2.

THE SOCIAL SELECTION PREDICTION ABOUT CLASS AND ETHNIC DIFFERENCES. The social selection theorist, by contrast, would predict just the opposite. Such a theorist would expect that the rate of psychopathology in a given social class is a function of sorting and sifting processes whereby the healthy and able tend to rise to or maintain high status and the unhealthy and disabled to drift down from high status or fail to rise out of low status. Since the downward social pressure is greater on members of disadvantaged ethnic groups, the social selection theorist would expect that many of the healthier members of the disadvantaged ethnic groups would be kept down in lower-class positions. This would thereby dilute the rate of

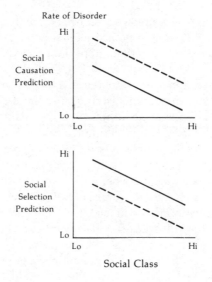

Figure 8.2 Summary of Social Causation Versus Social Selection Predictions (For Any Type of Psychopathology that is Inversely Related to Social Class in the General Population)
Source: B. P. Dohrenwend and B. S. Dohrenwend 1981, p. 135.

disorder among lower-class members of disadvantaged ethnic groups, with only the very healthiest and most able members rising against great obstacles to higher-class positions. With less pressure to block them, the tendency of healthier members of more advantaged ethnic groups to rise would leave a residue of disabled among lower class members. The more advantaged the ethnic group, the more purely homogeneous in the characteristic of disabling psychopathology would be its lower-class members, inflating the rate of disorder. Moreover, the more advantaged the ethnic group, the more individuals suffering from psychopathology it would support at higher-class levels. Thus social selection should function to give a higher rate of psychopathology among members of advantaged ethnic groups than among members of disadvantaged ethnic groups from the same social class. This outcome is diagrammed in the bottom half of Figure 8.2.

THE JOINT OPERATION OF SOCIAL CAUSATION AND SOCIAL SELECTION PROCESSES. Please note that we believe that both social causation and social selection processes operate and interact to produce the various inverse relations with class reported in the literature. It is likely that social causation factors will prove more important in some types of disorders and distress as they relate to social class; social selection factors will be more important in others. To the extent that social causation processes and social selection processes are of equal strength in determining the inverse relation between social class and any particular type of psychopathology, we would expect the solid and dotted lines in Figure 8.2 to converge.

EXPANSION OF THE QUASI-EXPERIMENTAL STRATEGY TO PROVIDE MORE DIRECT TESTS: THE EXAMPLES OF SCHIZOPHRENIA AND MAJOR DEPRESSION. Thus far, we have encountered two main problems in obtaining data for such comparisons from previous research on the types of disorders that are inversely related to class: schizophrenia, major depression, substance abuse, antisocial personality, and demoralization. The first stems from the fact that class status and ethnic status are confounded in modern urban societies; the reason, of course, is that disadvantaged ethnic groups are composed mainly of lower-class individuals and advantaged ethnic groups mainly of middle- and upper-class people. Epidemiological studies have tended to rely on random sampling procedures that leave the two factors intermixed, impairing our ability to compare advantaged and disadvantaged ethnic groups from the same social class. The second major problem has been that of securing unbiased estimates of some important types of disorder, such as schizophrenia and antisocial personality, that are both rare and, given the tendency to hospitalize and imprison persons with such disorders, likely to be underrepresented in the cross-sectional samples of community populations that typify most epidemiological research. The sparse data available thus far have been summarized elsewhere and suggest that socioenvironmental factors related to social class may indeed be important in schizophrenia, antisocial personality, and substance abuse (Dohrenwend and Dohrenwend 1981). Unfortunately, no comparisons for major depression are as yet available and those on demoralization give mixed results.

There are also data from other types of research that not only suggest that environmentally induced stress may be important in the etiology of some of these disorders but that also provide clues as to how the quasi-experimental strategy might be expanded to include more direct tests. Let us consider some findings on the role of environmentally induced stress in schizophrenia and major depression.

There is considerable evidence from twin, adoption, and family studies that genetic factors play a causal role in schizophrenia (cf. Gottesman and Shields 1972). Investigators who have used these strategies to demonstrate an etiological role for genetic factors do not suggest that they have ruled out a role for environment factors. Quite the contrary. Kety, Rosenthal, Wender, and Schulsinger (1976) and Gottesman and Shields (1972) have concluded that the genetic findings strongly imply that environmental factors are also important. Moreover, there is direct evidence suggesting what these environmental factors may be. Such evidence comes from several case-control studies conducted in London (Brown and Birley 1968; Leff et al. 1973) and New Haven (Jacobs and Myers 1976) indicating that recent stressful life events play a part in the occurrence of acute schizophrenic episodes. On the basis of further analysis of these studies, we have concluded that such events may do more than precipitate disorders that would have soon occurred in any case (Dohrenwend and Egri 1981).

There is also accumulating evidence that some types of environmentally induced stress play an important role in *major depression,* especially in women. Brown and Harris (1978) have found that death of one's mother before age eleven predisposes to clinical depression in their sample of London women; Langner and Michael (1963) reported a similar finding on the impact of death of mother before age seven on later psychiatric impairment that would include both demoralization and major affective disorder; and Dohrenwend and deFigueiredo (in press) discovered that both death of mother before age six and/or death of father at ages six to ten appear to make one vulnerable to demoralization in the face of recent losses later in life.

And probably more so than with schizophrenia, recent stressful life events have been found to play a part in clinical depression (Paykel 1979; Brown and Harris 1978), possibly including manic episodes (Ambelas 1979), as well as in depressive symptoms (e.g., Warheit 1979) and demoralization (e.g., Myers, Lindenthal, and Pepper 1974). Events involving loss appear to be particularly important (Jacobs, Prusoff, and Paykel 1974), especially those that carry implications of long-term threat to the individual (Brown and Harris 1978); it is not clear from the research to date, however, whether this is specific to depression or occurs as well in other types of disorders such as schizophrenia (cf. Leff and Vaughn 1980).

One of the most influential hypotheses in the recent literature on life stress states that social support mitigates the effects of stressful events (e.g., Caplan and Killilea 1976; Cobb 1976). Its importance for depression is suggested by Brown and Harris's (1978) finding that women who had a "close, intimate, and confiding relationship with a husband or boyfriend" (p. 174) were far less likely than those without such a relationship to develop an episode of depression in response to experience with stressful life events; an additional factor found to predispose to depression is having to cope with three or more children under age fourteen in the home.

The general interest in social support as a buffer against stress implies a concern as well with its opposite, lack of support. With the decline of the asylum and with the occurrence of what some have called "dumping," one of the most striking facts concerning treatment of the mentally ill is the plight of expatients who have no support. Such lack of support tends to be accompanied by other processes, such as negative family reactions that play a part in the occurrence of episodes of disorder (Leff and Vaughan 1980) and the negative effects of a label that may increase the likelihood of social disability (Link 1982).

Much has been learned in the last two decades from clinical observations, observations in natural settings, and experimental studies about effective psychological defense and coping responses (e.g., Lazarus 1966; Hamburg and Adams, 1967; Horwitz 1976; Pearlin and Schooler 1978). At the same time several hypotheses have been developed concerning the nature of individual differences in disposition that contribute to depression. Such hypotheses center on concepts such as self-esteem (e.g., Brown and Harris 1978; Lewinsohn 1974), helplessness (Seligman 1975), external locus of control (Rotter 1966; Lefcourt 1976), and obsessive symptoms and traits (Hirschfeld and Klerman 1979). The first three of these show interesting convergences with Frank's (1973) emphasis on helplessness, hopelessness, and low self-esteem as central to his concept of demoralization. With regard to locus of control, there has been a tendency in some studies to virtually equate internal control expectancy with competence, coping ability, and relative invulnerability to debilitating effects of stressful life events (e.g., Campbell, Converse, and Rogers 1976, pp. 59–60). The possible importance of obsessive-compulsive characteristics is also intriguing in their convergence with Type A personality features that have been implicated as risk factors in myocardial infarction (cf. Task Force on Nonmenclature and Statistics 1980, p. 327).

On the basis of such additional evidence and argument it is possible to envision expansions of the quasi-experimental strategy summarized in Figure 8.2 above to include more direct tests of the role of environmentally induced stress as compared with personal vulnerability, especially genetic vulnerability. For example, social selection explanations of inverse relations between social class and various types of psychopathology imply a genetic etiology while social causation explanations imply that stressful environmental conditions are the more important factors. It is reasonable to expect that quasi-experimental outcomes in accord with the social causation theoretical orientation would be accompanied by evidence of unusually harsh remote and/or recent environmental stress in the lives of those showing the disorder. By contrast, with a social selection outcome, we should expect the role of genetic factors to be manifested by an unusually high rate of disorder in their first degree relatives. Table 8.2 summarizes these expanded predictions which are spelled out in more detail elsewhere (B. P. Dohrenwend and B. S. Dohrenwend 1981; B. S. Dohrenwend and B. P. Dohrenwend 1981).

Research that would enable us to fill in strong evidence for each element of the quasi-experimental strategy summarized in Table 8.2 would be a major step toward resolving the venerable social causation-social selection issue raised by class differences. The reason for the qualification is that this is a quasi-experimental strategy rather than a laboratory experiment. Alternative explanations for a given outcome are always more difficult to rule out when random assignment to the contrasting experimental conditions (in this case, advantaged and disadvantaged ethnic status) is not possible. The extension of the quasi-experimental strategy, however, provides direct tests of the role of remote and recent stressful circumstances for social causation outcomes and genetic vulnerability for social selection outcomes, in a manner that increases our opportunity to rule out alternative explanations. It is extremely difficult, for example, to find a parsimonious alternative explanation for the full array of outcomes shown in each column of Table 8.2 other than those postulated in the quasi-experimental strategy. In addition, use of the quasi-experimental strategy in a different cultural setting with different ethnic groups should further help us to rule out idiosyncratic

TABLE **8.2**   Summary of Expanded Predictions Following From Social Causation by Contrast with Social Selection Explanations of Inverse Relations Between Social Class and Various Types of Psychopathology

	EXPLANATION OF CLASS RELATIONSHIP	
SUBJECT MATTER OF PREDICTION	*Social Causation*	*Social Selection*
Relative rates of disturbance in advantaged and disadvantaged ethnic groups within a social class	Disadvantaged > advantaged	Advantaged > disadvantaged
Remote and recent environmental stress	Unusually severe in cases by contrast with matched noncases of the disturbance	Not unusually severe in cases by contrast with matched noncases of the disturbance
Prevalence of disturbance in first degree relatives	No higher in cases than in matched noncases of the disturbance	Higher in cases than in matched noncases of the disturbance

Source: B. P. Dohrenwend and B. S. Dohrenwend 1981, p. 137.

cultural-historical factors and/or idiosyncratic genetic factors that could provide alternative explanations for some of the findings we get in applications of the quasi-experimental strategy in the United States.

Innovations in Procedures for Case Identification and Diagnosis

The value of the past first- and second-generation studies of the epidemiology of mental disorders comes mainly from their cumulative results. Each new study for the immediate future, whatever its theoretical or applied focus, will have to be able to stand on its own if new ground is to be broken. To do so, such new studies will have to come to terms with the central unsolved methodological problem of case identification and classification that is such a large part of the legacy from the first- and second-generation of epidemiological studies. To do so convincingly will involve supplying credible evidence for the adequacy of the measurement approach used in any particular new study. Such evidence would have to involve demonstrating: (1) the reliability and validity with which the basic data on symptoms were measured; and (2) the reliability and validity of the procedures for combining the symptoms into diagnoses, syndromes, or profiles of different types of disorder. How might this be done?

Two Contrasting Interview Approaches. In the absence of laboratory tests to establish the presence of the functional mental disorders, main reliance for measuring them has been placed on interviews. These have been of two main types. One of these has been similar to clinical interviews conducted for diagnostic purposes by expert clinicians with psychiatric patients in treatment settings. It is more typical of the first and, especially, the second generation of epidemiological studies conducted by European and Asian researchers than those by North American investigators. However, the actual interview procedures used were not made explicit in the first and second generation studies using this approach.

In the type of interview more often used in first and second generation studies on this side of the Atlantic, by contrast, far less reliance has been placed on expert clinicians for eliciting data on symptoms. Rather, standard and explicit interview schedules were administered, usually by trained interviewers who were not clinicians. To facilitate their administration by lay interviewers, the interview schedules included batteries of questions with fixed alternative response categories (e.g., Yes–No; Often–Sometimes–Never), minimized the need for probes by the interviewer, and eliminated clinical judgments by the interviewer as to what types of psychopathology were indicated by the answers. The specific questions involved were usually drawn from published psychological tests, especially, as was mentioned earlier, the Neuropsychiatric Screening Adjunct, the Cornell Medical index (Brodman et al. 1952) and the MMPI (Dahlstrom and Welsh 1960).

The clinical and psychometric traditions from which these two contrasting interviewing approaches come rely on very different procedures for dealing with measurement error. In the first- and second-generation studies, the investigators using the two interview approaches took little advantage of these procedures and the opportunity to maximize their effectiveness for research purposes. Let us, therefore, review the different procedures for dealing with error and illustrate how new developments in clinical interviewing and clinical rating approaches on the one hand, and in psychometric theory and methods on the other, offer opportunities to improve the quality of measurement in future, third-generation studies.

In the clinical interview, main reliance is placed on the experience and skill of the clinician to reduce measurement error. Meehl (1972) put it this way:

> One stage of data collection and data processing at which the skilled clinician will be indispensable for at least the foreseeable future (and perhaps longer) is the level of the diagnostic interview. Such "simple" things as noticing a patient's rigidly smiling facial expression, or sociopathoid "animal grace," or the "quasi-sleepy" voice texture of some schizotypes, cannot be discriminated by a computer or a clinically unskilled clerk or interviewer. Furthermore the elicitation of certain kinds of diagnostic behavior requires the skilled interviewer to know when to interrupt, what to say and how to say it....[pp. 135-136]

Here the clinician is both the person who elicits the information and interprets its significance as a sign or symptom. The procedure for reducing error is the application of the clinical experience and interviewing skill of the examiner. (cf. Wing, Cooper, and Sartorius 1974, especially p. 13).

In sharp contrast is the interview or questionnaire that relies on closed questions, fixed alternative response categories, and takes as its basic data the self-reports of the subjects of the research. It is an approach that grows out of the psychometric tradition in personality assessment (cf. Wiggins 1973, pp. 380-440) which has quite a different way of dealing with measurement error.

It has long been known that responses to individual test questions in the measurement of personality in general and psychopathology in particular tend to be overdetermined (cf. Fiske 1971, pp. 228–32; Nunnally 1967, pp. 56–58). Thus, for example, a positive response to a particular question is all too frequently given by different individuals for different reasons that have less to do with the presence of the characteristic being measured than such extraneous factors as differences in how the individuals understand the meaning of such words as "depressed" and "anxious." This is the problem Wing and his colleagues (1974) are concerned about in their stress on the need for cross-examination in the clinical interview. Another way of dealing with the problem of the ambiguity of responses to an individual question, one that does not rely on the expert clinician's cross-examination, is to sum conceptually related items to form scale scores. Here "truth" is seen to lie in the consistency among the responses to a series of questions as they tap a particular facet or dimension of psychopathology despite the error in responses to any particular question. When this approach is taken, there are mathematical procedures for estimating the degree of internal consistency reliability achieved with such a scale (e.g., Cronbach 1951). Moreover, there is a powerful body of test theory about the nature of measurement error and procedures for dealing with it than can be drawn upon (e.g., Cronbach et al. 1972; Lord and Novick 1968). The hallmark of this theory of measurement is its reliance on the need to define the universe of indicators of the phenomenon (here symptoms or types of psychopathology) to be measured and to systematically sample that universe.

NEW DEVELOPMENTS WITHIN THE TWO CONTRASTING INTERVIEW APPROACHES. Neither of the two interview approaches discussed above was developed in ways that maximize the strengths of each in the first and second generation of epidemiological studies. For example, the batteries of self-report questions were not systematically sampled, tested for internal consistency, and scaled to represent meaningful dimensions or facets of psychopathology; and the questioning procedures and definitions of the symptoms and syndromes to be judged in the clinical examination approaches were not spelled out so that they could be used by different investigators in further studies. Moreover, since there was little concern with evidence for validity there was, as I emphasized earlier, no firm basis for choosing the approach used in one study over that used in another.

Fortunately, there have been a number of new developments. Several instruments that were based on and designed for research with patients during the past ten to fifteen years have begun to be used with samples from the general population. Some of these are of the self-report variety. A notable example is the multidimensional and content-meaningful Johns Hopkins Symptom Checklist which, in its most recent edition, is called the SCL-90 (Derogatis 1977); a variation of it has been used with a sample of Chicago adults (Ilfeld 1978). Others are out of the clinical examination tradition: one is the Wing, Cooper, and Sartorious Present State Examination (PSE) (1974), which has been employed in important cross-national investigations of psychiatric patients (Cooper et al. 1972; Sartorius, Jablensky, and Shapiro 1978); another is the Spitzer, Endicott, Fleiss, and Cohen Psychiatric Status Schedule (PSS) (1970), an earlier version of which has also been used in an investigation of patients in different national settings (Cooper et al. 1972). Wing, Mann, Leff, and Nixon (1978), as well as Brown, Harris, and Copeland (1977), have used the Present State Examination (PSE) with general population samples, and our own group has tested the Psychiatric Status Schedule (PSS) on such a sample (Dohrenwend, Yager, Egri, and Mendelsohn 1978). Moreover, new interview instruments of these two types have been developed and used with general population samples. One of them is the Psychiatric Epidemiology Research Interview (PERI) that we constructed largely out of structured questions with fixed alternative response formats like most self-report instruments (Dohrenwend, Shrout, Egri, and Mendelsohn 1980). It provides twenty-five symptom scales, all content-meaningful and all with demonstrated internal consistency reliabilities in different demographic groups in samples from the general population as well as from psychiatric patients (Dohrenwend, Shrout, Egri and Mendelsohn 1980; Dohrenwend, Levav, and Shrout, in press; Vernon and Roberts 1981). Another, the Schedule for Affective Disorders and Schizophrenia (SADS), was constructed in the tradition of the clinical examination by Endicott and Spitzer (1978) and has much in common with the Psychiatric Status Schedule (PSS) and with the Present State Examination (PSE). A brief version of SADS, called SADS-L, has been used with a sample from the general population (Weissman, Myers, and Harding 1978).

Finally, there is an instrument now being developed that is called the Diagnostic Interview Schedule (DIS) (Robins et al. 1981). It is a hybrid based on some elements of each tradition. It has drawn in part from the clinical examination tradition but does not rely on skilled clinicians and clinical ratings; it has drawn in part from the self-report tradition, but does not rely on the dominant psychometric theories of measurement error. Its development and use in several large-scale studies aimed at integrating epidemiologic and health services research has been sponsored by the Division of Biometry and Epidemiology of the U.S. National Institute of Mental Health (Regier 1980). This program is called the NIMH Epidemiologic Catchment Area, or ECA program, and studies funded under it are in process at four or five different locations in the United States. Simultaneously, investigations are under way comparing results obtained with the Diagnostic Interview Schedule (DIS) by lay interviewers with those obtained by clinicians

(Robins et al. 1981). Related studies are being made with the rather different Present State Examination (PSE) (Sturt et al. 1981).

Strengths and Weaknesses of the Two Contrasting Approaches. In our experience with the two broad types of interview approaches described above, they have proved to have different strengths and weaknesses (Dohrenwend, Yager, Egri, and Mendelsohn 1978; Dohrenwend, Shrout, Egri, and Mendelsohn 1980; Dohrenwend, Levav, and Shrout, in press). We have a situation in which an instrument like the Psychiatric Epidemiology Research Interview (PERI), which is in the psychometric tradition and was developed through research with samples from the general population, can yield scales with high internal consistency reliabilities and cover a wide variety of dimensions of psychopathology; but PERI does not provide psychiatric diagnoses. By contrast, we have diagnostic interviews such as the Psychiatric Status Schedule (PSS) and the Present State Examination (PSE) that were developed with psychiatric patients and yield reliable diagnoses for such patients but are unlikely to provide reliable measures over the whole range of various dimensions of psychopathology in samples from the general population and can yield misleading results in such samples (Dohrenwend, Egri, Mendelsohn 1971; Dohrenwend, Yager, Egri, and Mendelsohn 1978, 1980). A likely reason is that the expertise of the clinician that helps reduce measurement error in the use of such instruments as the PSS and PSE with patients is more limited than has been recognized. It may not extend to the full range and variety of symptomatology that are found in groups from contrasting social and cultural background in the general population.

The Need for Multimethod Strategies. How might this apparent dilemma be resolved? Our suggestion is the use of multimethod strategies of case identification and diagnosis. For example, a self-report interview like the Psychiatric Epidemiology Research Interview (PERI), based on a psychometric approach to measuring dimensions of psychopathology, could be used to economically screen samples from the general population. Such screening would be designed to yield subsamples of individuals with various types of severe symptomatology. Individuals screened by high scores on the screening scales could then be followed up in a second stage of the research and interviewed by experienced clinicians with diagnostic instruments like the Schedule for Affective Disorder and Schizophrenia (SADS) or the Present State Examination (PSE) to provide rates for particular types of disorder. Results with the Psychiatric Epidemiology Research Interview (PERI) from a study in Israel lend credence to the possibility that it could with no more than seven of the twenty-five symptom scales, with a total of only seventy-three items, perform the first-stage screening function (Dohrenwend, Levav, and Shrout, in press). Such a two-stage procedure could capitalize on the ability of a psychometric instrument to provide reliable measurement over the full range of important dimensions of psychopathology and on the ability of a clinical examination to provide reliable diagnoses in groups where the types of symptomatology involved are not rare.

While the potential practical advantages of two-stage procedures such as this have long been evident (cf. Cooper and Morgan 1973), there have been only a handful of systematic attempts to use them for case identification and classification in psychiatric epidemiology. Notable among them is the approach of Rutter and his colleagues in their research on children (e.g., Rutter, Tizard, and Whitmore 1970). Duncan-Jones and Henderson (1978) have speculated that use of two-stage procedures is so rare because of fear of loss of respondents between the first screening stage and the follow-up diagnostic interview. They themselves found, however, that with careful planning, they were able to conduct interviews with 91 percent of the respondents designated for follow-up on the basis of initial screening.

The most important advantage of two-stage procedures, however, is not their practicality but rather the fact that they can be designed to bring two different methods (e.g., the psychometric screening scales and the clinical examination) rather than just one to bear. In fact, rather than thinking in terms of a two-stage procedure whose virtues are mainly those of economy, it is more useful to think in terms of multimethod procedures that offer an opportunity to establish validity. As Galen and Gambino (1975, p. 42) point out, it is rare in all of medicine to base a final decision on the result of a single test. And where, as in psychiatric epidemiology, measures are less than wholly reliable and most of the mental disorders in which we are interested have relatively low population rates, Shrout and Fleiss (1981) have shown that multimethod procedures become mandatory if accurate counts are to be made. Compelling tests of the construct validity of multimethod procedures, moreover, are available (cf. Campbell and Fiske 1959). If powerful multimethod procedures can be developed and tested, then a likely byproduct would be a practical and effective two-stage procedure. We have set forth in more detail elsewhere how this might be done, including how different first- and later-stage instruments might be tested against each other (Dohrenwend and Shrout 1981). Let us summarize a simpler case here that involves just one first-stage instrument and two later-stage instruments as shown in Figure 8.3. At Stage 1, the first method might consist of screening scales with the screened positives followed up at Stage 2 by a second method—clinical examination. When there is a divergence, categorization by a third method—perhaps a composite of official records and key informant reports—would be sought. The approach would be similar for screened negatives. "Truth" in Figure 8.3 would be defined as a convergence across at least two out of three different methods of measuring the same thing—in the instance above, the diagnoses or other classifications dictated by the nomenclature or other theoretical constructs being used.

CLASSIFICATION AND DIAGNOSIS. The validity achieved by such multimethod procedures would be relative to the validity of the particular diagnostic or classification systems that dictate how the data on symptoms are to be combined. Further tests of the validity of such systems are in order: prospective studies to check on whether there is stability of particular classes or types of psychopathology; family studies to test whether the disorders "breed true" as a function of either genetic or environmental transmission; and outcome studies of the effectiveness of therapeutic trials (cf. Woodruff, Goodwin, and Guze 1974).

Fortunately, there has been considerable interest over the past few years in this country in the neglected topic of psychiatric diagnosis. This interest has been translated into the development of far more detailed and explicit classificatory criteria in psychiatric nomenclatures (Feighner et al. 1972; Spitzer, Endicott, and Robins 1978; Task Force on Nonmenclature and Statistics 1980). The Schedule for Affective Disorder and Schizophrenia (SADS) and the Diagnostic Interview Schedule (DIS) were explicitly designed to operationalize such diagnostic criteria. The Present State Examination (PSE) is linked to the groupings of mental disorders contained in the International Classification of Diseases (ICD 9) (1977, pp. 177–212). There have also been major advances in psychometric theory and

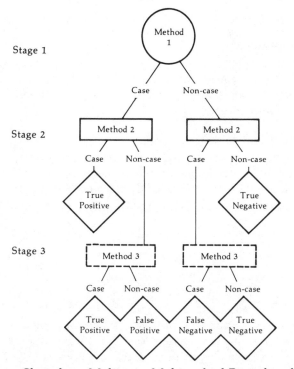

Figure 8.3 Flow Chart for a Multistage-Multimethod Procedure for Case Identification and Classification
Source: B. P. Dohrenwend and B. S. Dohrenwend 1982, p. 1276.

methods that should greatly improve opportunities to combine well-measured dimensions of psychopathology in meaningful and useful ways, some more and some less related to existing psychiatric nomenclatures (e.g., Bentler 1980; Bock and Wood 1971; Jöreskog 1973).

There are enough differences, enough unanswered questions, enough controversies so that no one classification system, on the basis of the evidence so far, can be said to have proved itself. Nor is any one of them likely to until greater knowledge of etiology and/or definitive cures are at hand. In this state of affairs, it seems best to avoid what is likely to be the premature closure of adopting one classification or diagnostic system. Rather, it would seem to make most sense to ensure that the important symptoms of a wide variety of psychopathology are well-measured. They can then be combined in a number of different ways—those dictated by psychometric methods as well as by the a priori rules of various diagnostic nomenclatures. This would make it possible to test the validity of various diagnostic and other classification procedures as they bear on particular problems, questions, or issues of interest.

Prospects for the Third Generation

What, then, should we look for in the new generation of epidemiological studies? Here are my nominations:

1. Innovative sampling plans to maximize relevant environmental and genetic contrasts and provide adequate representation of types of mental disorder that are rare in the general population. Here "relevant" would be defined in

terms of theoretical or applied considerations growing mainly out of the findings from first- and second-generation studies but not excluding leads from other research.

2. Multimethod approaches to case identification and classification.
3. Multiple measurements over time to investigate stability of psychopathology and social functioning in changing circumstances and to derive figures on incidence.

My hope is that these will be defining characteristics of such studies. They should be second only to the development of the research in terms of imaginative ideas about how to resolve important theoretical issues, define important needs, and test the efficacy of promising practical procedures aimed at the prevention and control of mental disorders in community populations.

Summary

Two generations of epidemiological studies of the "true" prevalence of mental disorders have been conducted since the turn of the century. The first and smaller in number took place prior to World War II and was characterized by use of records and key informants to define "cases" of mental disorders. The second, utilizing the greatly expanded nomenclatures that followed World War II, were based for the most part on personal interviews with all subjects or samples thereof in communities all over the world. In total, more than eighty different communities were studied by more than sixty different investigators or teams of investigators in these first- and second-generation studies.

The legacy from these studies comes in four parts: A Pandora's box of problems centering on the question of how to conceptualize and measure mental disorders independently of treatment status; a set of substantive findings about cultural similarities and differences; findings on the amounts of various types of mental disorder; and findings on their distribution according to gender, rural versus urban location, and social class. These raise important theoretical, methodological, and practical issues. In this chapter, analyses of this legacy from first- and second-generation studies have been summarized and expanded with a view to developing informed speculations about what we might hope for in the future from a vastly different third generation of studies in this field.

REFERENCES

AMBELAS, A. 1979. Psychologically stressful events in the precipitation of manic episodes. *British Journal of Psychiatry* 135: 15–21.

BABIGIAN, H. M. 1972. The role of psychiatric case registers in the longitudinal study of psychopathology. In *Life history research in psychopathology*, ed. M. Roff, L. N. Robins, and E. Pollack. vol. 2, Minneapolis, Minn.: University of Minnesota Press.

BASH, K. W. 1975. Untersuchungen ueber die Epidemiologie neuropsychiatrischer Erkrankungen unter der Landbevoelkerung der Provinz Fars, Iran. *Aktuelie Fragender Psychiatrie Neurologie* 5: 162.

BEEBE, G. W. 1975. Follow-up studies of World War II and Korean prisoners. II. Morbidity, disability, and maladjustments. *American Journal of Epidemiology* 10: 400–22.

BENTLER, P. M. Multivariate analysis with latent variables. *Annual Review of Psychology* 31: 419–56.

BEISER, M.; RAVEL, J. L.; COLLUMB, H.; and EGELHOFF, C. 1972. Assessing psychiatric disorder among the Serer of Senegal. *Journal of Nervous and Mental Disease* 154: 141–51.

BRODMAN, K.; ERDMAN, A. J.; LORGE, J.; GERSHENSEN, C. P.; and WOLFF, H. G. 1952. The Cornell Medical Index—health questionnaire II: the evaluation. *Journal of Clinical Psychology* 8: 119–24.

BROWN, G. W.; and BIRLEY, J. L. T. 1968. Crises and life changes and the onset of schizophrenia. *Journal of Health and Social Behavior* 9: 203–14.

BROWN, G. W., and HARRIS, T. 1978. *Social origins of depression*. New York: Free Press.

———; and COPELAND, J. R. 1977. Depression and loss. *British Journal of Psychiatry* 130: 1.

BOCK, R. D.; and WOOD, R. 1971. Test theory. *Annual Review of Psychology* 22: 193–224.

BUEHLER, J. A. 1966. Two experiments in psychiatric interrater reliability. *Journal of Health and Social Behavior* 7: 192–202.

CAMPBELL, A.; CONVERSE, P. E.; and ROGERS, W. L. 1976. *The quality of American life.* New York: Russell Sage Foundation.

CAMPBELL, D. T., and FISKE, D. W. 1959. Convergent and discriminant validation by the multitrait-multimethod matrix. *Psychological Bulletin* 56: 81–105.

CAPLAN, G., and KILLILEA, M., eds., 1976. *Support systems and mutual help: multidisciplinary explorations.* New York: Grune and Stratton.

CAWTE, J. 1972. *Cruel, poor and brutal nations.* Honolulu: University of Hawaii Press.

CHANCE, N. A. 1962. Conceptual and methodological problems in cross-cultural health research. *American Journal of Public Health* 52: 410–17.

CLAUSEN, J. A. 1957. The ecology of mental disorders. In Walter Reed Army Institute of Research, Walter Reed Army Medical Center and the National Research Council (sponsors). *Symposium on preventive and social psychiatry*, pp. 97–108. Washington, D.C.: Government Printing Office.

COBB, S. 1976. Social support as a moderator of life stress. 1976. *Psychosomatic Medicine* 38: 300–14.

Committee on Nomenclature and Statistics. 1952. *Diagnostic and statistical manual of mental disorders.* Washington, D.C.: American Psychiatric Association.

———. 1968. *Diagnostic and statistical manual of mental disorders.* 2nd ed. Washington, D.C.: American Psychiatric Association.

COOPER, B., and MORGAN, H. G. 1973. *Epidemiological psychiatry.* Springfield, Ill.: C. C. Thomas.

COOPER, J. E.: KENDELL, R. E.; GURLAND, B. J.; SHARPE, L.; COPELAND, J. R. M.; and SIMON, R. 1972. *Psychiatric diagnosis in New York and London.* London: Oxford University Press.

CRANDELL, D. L., and DOHRENWEND, B. P. 1967. Some relations among psychiatric symptoms, organic illness, and social class. *American Journal of Psychiatry* 123: 1527–538.

CRONBACH, L. J. 1951. Coefficient alpha and the internal structure of tests. *Psychometrics* 16: 297–334.

———; GLESER, G. C.; NANDA, H.; and RAJARATNAM, N. 1972. *The dependability of behavioral measurements: theory of generalizability for scores and profiles,* New York; Wiley.

DAHLSTRON. W. G., and WELSH, G. S. 1960. *An MMPI handbook.* Minneapolis, Minn.: University of Minnesota Press.

DEROGATIS, L. R. 1977. *SCL-90.R. (revised) version manual I.* Baltimore, Md.: Clinical Psychometrics Research Unit, Johns Hopkins University School of Medicine.

DOHRENWEND, B. P. 1966. Social status and psychological disorder: an issue of substance and an issue of method. *American Sociological Review* 31: 14–35.

———. 1973. Some issues in the definition and measurement of psychiatric disorders in the general population. In *Proceedings of the 14th National National Meeting of the Public Health Conference on Records and Statistics:* Washington D.C.: U.S. Government Printing Office, DHEW publication no. 74-1214.

——. 1975. Sociocultural and social-psychological factors in the genesis of mental disorders. *Journal of Health and Social Behavior* 16: 365–92.

——. 1979. Stressful life events and psychopathology: some issues of theory and method. In *Stress and mental disorder*, J. F. Barrett, R. M. Rose, and G. L. Klerman, pp. 1–15. New York: Raven Press.

——, and CRANDELL, D. L. 1970. Psychiatric symptoms in community, clinic, and mental hospital groups. *American Journal of Psychiatry* 126: 1611–21.

DOHRENWEND, B. P., and DOHRENWEND, B. S. 1965. The problem of validity in field studies of psychological disorder. *Journal of Abnormal Psychology* 70: 52–69.

——. 1969. *Social status and psychological disorder: a causal inquiry*. New York: Wiley.

——. 1974a. Social and cultural influences on psychopathology. *Annual Review of Psychology* 25: 417–52.

——. 1974b. Psychiatric disorders in urban settings. In *American handbook of psychiatry*, 2nd ed., vol. 2: *Child and adolescent psychiatry, socio-cultural and community psychiatry*, S. Arieti, editor-in-chief, and G. Caplan, ed. New York: Basic Books.

——. 1976. Sex differences and psychiatric disorders. *American Journal of Sociology* 81: 1447–54.

——. 1981. Socioenvironmental factors, stress, and psychopathology—Part 1: Quasi-experimental evidence on the social causation-social selection issue posed by class differences. *American Journal of Community Psychology* 9: 146–59.

——. 1982. Perspectives on the past and future of psychiatric epidemiology. *American Journal of Public Health* 72: 1271–79.

——; SCHWARTZ GOULD, M.: LINK, B.; NEUGEBAUER, R.; and WUNSCH-HITZIG, R. 1980. *Mental illness in the United States: epidemiologic estimates*. New York: Praeger.

DOHRENWEND, B. P., and EGRI, G. 1981. Recent stressful life events and episodes of schizophrenia. *Schizophrenia Bulletin* 7: 12–23.

——; and MENDELSOHN, F. 1971. Psychiatric disorder in general populations: a study of the problem of clinical judgment. *American Journal of Psychiatry* 127: 1304–12.

DOHRENWEND, B. P., and DE FIGUEIREDO, J. M. Remote and recent life events and psychopathology. In *Origins of psychopathology: research and public policy*, ed. D. L. Ricks and B. S. Dohrenwend. New York: Cambridge University Press, in press.

DOHRENWEND, B. P.; LEVAV, I.; and SHROUT, P. E. Screening scales from the psychiatric epidemiology research interview (PERI). In *Epidemiologic community surveys*, ed. J. K. Myers and M. M. Weissman. New York: Neale Watson Academic Publication, in press.

DOHRENWEND, B. P.; OKSENBERG, L.; SHROUT, P. E.; DOHRENWEND, B. S.; and COOK, D. 1979. What brief psychiatric screening scales measure. In *Health survey research methods: third biennial research conference*, National Center for Health Services Research. Washington, D.C.: U.S. Department of Health and Human Services, DHHS pub. no. (PHS) 81-3268.

DOHRENWEND, B. P., and SHROUT, P. E. 1981. Toward the development of a two-stage procedure for case identification and classification in psychiatric epidemiology. In *Research in community and mental health*, vol. 2, ed. R. G. Simmons. Greenwich, Conn.: JAI Press.

——; EGRI, G.; and MENDELSOHN, F. S. 1980. Nonspecific psychological distress and other dimensions of psychopathology: measures for use in the general population. *Archives of General Psychiatry* 37: 1229–36.

DOHRENWEND, B. P.; YAGER, T. J.; EGRI, G.; and MENDELSOHN, F. S. 1978. The Psychiatric Status Schedule (PSS) as a measure of dimensions of psychopathology in the general population. *Archives of General Psychiatry* 35: 731–39.

——. 1980. Some problems of validity with the Psychiatric Status Schedule as an instrument for case identification and classification in the general population (letter to the editor). *Archives of General Psychiatry* 37: 720–21.

DOHRENWEND, B. S. 1973. Social status and stressful life events. *Journal of Personality and Social Psychology* 28: 225–35.

——, and DOHRENWEND, B. P. 1981. Socioenvironmental factors, stress, and psychopathology—Part 2: Hypotheses about stress processes linking social class to various types of psychopathology. *American Journal of Community Psychology* 9: 146–59.

———; GOTTESMAN, I. I.; LINK, B.; and NEUGEBAUER, R. 1979. Epidemiology and genetics of schizophrenia. *Social Biology* 26: 142–53.

DUNCAN-JONES, P. and HENDERSON, S. 1978. The use of a two-phase design in a prevalence survey. *Social Psychiatry* 13: 231–37.

EATON, J. W., and WEILL, R. J. 1955. *Culture and mental disorders.* Glencoe, Ill.: Free Press.

EATON, W. W. 1974. Residence, social class, and schizophrenia. *Journal of Health and Social Behavior* 15: 289–99.

———. 1980. A formal theory of selection for schizophrenia. *American Journal of Sociology* 86: 149–58.

———, and LASRY, J. C. 1978. Mental health and occupational mobility in a group of immigrants. *Social Science and Medicine* 12: 53–58.

EITINGER, L. 1964. *Concentration camp survivors in Norway and Israel.* London: Allen and Unwin.

ENDICOTT, J., and SPITZER, R. L. 1978. A diagnostic interview: The schedule for affective disorders and schizophrenia. *Archives of General Psychiatry* 35:837–44.

FARIS, R. E. L., and DUNHAM, H. W. 1939. *Mental disorders in urban areas: an ecological study of schizophrenia and other psychoses.* Chicago: Chicago University Press.

FEIGHNER, J. P.; ROBINS, E.; GUZE, S. B.; WOODRUFF, R. A.; WINOKUR, G.; and MUNOZ, R. 1972. Diagnostic criteria for use in psychiatric research. *Archives of General Psychiatry* 26: 57–63.

FIELD, M. J. 1960. *Search for security.* Evanston, Ill.: Northwestern University Press.

FISKE, D. W. 1971. *Measuring the concepts of personality.* Chicago: Aldine.

FRANK, J. D. 1973. *Persuasion and healing.* Baltimore, Md: Johns Hopkins University Press.

FRANK, L. K. 1936. Society as the patient. *American Journal of Sociology* 42: 335–44.

GALEN, R. S., and GAMBINO, S. R. 1975. *The predictive value and efficiency of medical diagnoses.* New York: Wiley.

GILLIS, L. S.; LEWIS, J. B.; and SLABBERT, M. 1965. *Psychiatric disturbance and alcoholism in the coloured people of the Cape Peninsula.* Cape Town: University of Cape Town Department of Psychiatry.

GINZBERG, E.; ANDERSON, J. K.; GINSBURG, S. W.; and HERMA, J. L. 1959. *The lost divisions.* New York: Columbia University Press.

GOLDBERG, D., and HUXLEY, P. 1980. *Mental illness in the community: the pathway to Psychiatric care.* London and New York: Tavistock.

GOLDBERG, E. M.; and MORRISON, S. L. 1963. Schizophrenia and social class. *British Journal of Psychiatry* 109: 785–802.

GOLDHAMER, H., and MARSHALL, A. W. 1953. *Psychoses and civilization.* New York: Free Press.

GOTTESMAN, I. I., and SHIELDS, J. 1972. *Schizophrenia and genetics: a twin study vantage point.* New York: Academic Press.

GOTTHEIL, E.; KRAMER, M.; and HURWICH, M. S. 1966. Intake procedures and psychiatric decisions. *Comprehensive Psychiatry* 7: 207–15.

GOULD, M. S.; WUNSCH-HITZIG, R.; and DOHRENWEND, B. P. 1980. Formulation of hypotheses about the prevalence, treatment and prognostic significance of psychiatric disorders in children in the United States. In *Mental illness in the United States: epidemiological estimates,* B. P. Dohrenwend et al., pp. 9–44. New York: Praeger.

GOVE, W. 1970. Societal reaction as an explanation of mental illness: an evaluation. *American Journal of Sociology* 35: 873–84.

GREENLEY, J. R., and MECHANIC, D. 1976. Social selection in seeking help for psychological problems. *Journal of Health and Social Behavior* 17: 249–62.

GRUENBERG, E. M. 1961. Comments on social structures and mental disorders: competing hypotheses of explanation by H. W. Dunham. In *Causes of mental disorders, a review of epidemiological knowledge, 1959.* New York: Milbank Memorial Fund.

190   EPIDEMIOLOGY AND CLINICAL ISSUES

————. 1967. The social breakdown syndrome—some origins. *American Journal of Psychiatry* 123: 1–124.

————. 1974. The epidemiology of schizophrenia. In *American handbook of psychiatry,* vol. 2, ed. S. Arieti and G. Caplan, pp. 448–63. New York: Basic Books.

GURIN, G.; VEROFF, J.; and FELD, S. 1960. *Americans view their mental health.* New York: Basic Books.

HAGNELL, O. 1966. *A prospective study of the incidence of mental disorder.* Stockholm: Svenska Bokförlaget Norstedts-Bonniers.

HAMBURG, D., and ADAMS, J. 1967. A perspective on coping behavior, seeking and utilizing information in major transitions. *Archives of General Psychiatry* 17: 277–84.

HELGASON, T. 1964. Epidemiology of mental disorders in Iceland. *Acta Psychiatrica Scandinavica Supplement* 173: 258.

HESTON, L. L. 1966. Psychiatric disorders in foster home reared children of schizophrenic mothers. *British Journal of Psychiatry* 112: 819–25.

HIRSCHFELD, R. M. A., and KLERMAN, G. L. 1979. Personality attributes and affective disorder. *American Journal of Psychiatry* 136: 67–70.

HOLLINGSHEAD, A. B., and REDLICH, F. C. 1958. *Social class and mental illness.* New York: Wiley.

HOROWITZ, M. J. 1976. *Stress response syndromes.* New York: Jason Aronson.

International Classification of Diseases. 1977. *Manual of the international statistical classification of diseases, injuries, and causes of mental disorders.* 9th rev. Geneva: World Health Organization.

JACOBS, S. C., and MYERS, J. K. 1976. Recent life events and acute schizophrenia psychosis: a controlled study. *Journal of Nervous and Mental Disease* 162: 75–87.

JACOBS, S. C.; PRUSOFF, B. A.; and PAYKEL, E. S. 1974. Recent life events in schizophrenia and depression. *Psychological Medicine* 4: 444–53.

JARVIS, E. 1850. The influence of distance from and proximity to an insane hospital, on its use by any people. *Boston Medical and Surgical Journal* 42: 209–22.

————. 1855 (1971). *Insanity and idiocy in Massachusetts: report of the Commission on Lunacy, 1855.* Cambridge, Mass.: Harvard University Press.

JÖRESKOG, K. A. 1973. A general method for estimating a linear structural equation. In *Structural equation models in the social sciences,* ed. A. S. Goldberger and O. D. Duncan, pp. 85–112. New York: Academic Press.

KATZ, M. M. 1970. The classification of depression: normal, clinical and ethno-cultural variations. In *Depression in the 70's,* ed. R. R. Fieve, pp. 31–40.

KATO, M. 1969. Psychiatric epidemiological surveys in Japan: the problem of case finding. *In Mental health research in Asia and the Pacific,* ed. W. Caudill and T. Lin, pp. 92–104.

KETY, S. S.; ROSENTHAL, D.; WENDER, P. H.; and SCHULSINGER, F. 1976. Studies based on a total sample of adopted individuals and their relatives: why they were necessary, what they demonstrated and failed to demonstrate. *Schizophrenia Bulletin* 2: 413–28.

KOHN, M. L. 1972. Class, family, and schizophrenia: a reformulation. *Social Forces* 50: 295–304.

KOLB, L. C. 1973. *Modern clinical psychiatry.* Philadelphia, Pa.: W. B. Saunders.

KORMOS, H. R. 1978. The nature of combat stress. In *Stress disorders among Vietnam veterans: theory, research and treatment,* ed. C. R. Figley, pp. 3–22. New York: Brunner/Mazel.

KRAMER, M. 1976. Issues in the development of statistical and epidemiological data for mental health services research. *Psychological Medicine* 6: 185–215.

KULKA, R. A.; VEROFF, J.; and Douvan, E. 1979. Social class and the use of professional help for personal problems: 1957–1976. *Journal of Health and Social Behavior* 20: 2–17.

LANGNER, T. S. 1962. A twenty-two item screening score of psychiatric symptoms indicating impairment. *Journal of Health and Human Behavior* 3: 269–76.

————, and MICHAEL, S. T. 1963. *Life stress and mental health.* New York: Free Press.

LAZARUS, R. S. 1966. *Psychological stress and the coping process.* New York: McGraw-Hill.

LEE, R. B., and DeVORE I., eds. 1976. *Kalahari hunter-gatherers.* Cambridge, Mass.: Harvard University Press.

LEFCOURT, H. M. 1976. *Locus of control: current trends in theory and research.* New York: Lawrence Erlbaum Associates.

LEFF, J. P.; HIRSCH, S. R.; GAIND, R.; ROHDE, P. D.; and STEVENS, B. S. 1973. Life events and maintenance therapy in schizophrenic relapse. *British Journal of Psychiatry* 123: 659–60.

LEFF, J., and VAUGHN, C. 1980. The interaction of life events and relatives' expressed emotion in schizophrenia and depressive neurosis. *British Journal of Psychiatry* 136: 146–53.

LEIGHTON, A. H. 1969. Cultural relativity and the identification of psychiatric disorders. In *Mental health research in Asia and the Pacific,* ed. W. Caudill and T. Lin, pp. 448–62. Honolulu: East-West Center Press.

——; LAMBO, T. A.; HUGHES, C. C.; LEIGHTON, D. C.; MURPHY, J. M., and MACKLIN, D. B. 1963. *Psychiatric disorder among the Yoruba.* Ithaca N.Y.: Cornell University Press.

LEIGHTON, D. C.; HARDING, J. S.; MACKLIN, D. B.; MACMILLAN, A. M.; and LEIGHTON, A. H. 1963. *The character of danger.* New York: Basic Books.

LEWINSOHN, P. 1974. A behavioral approach to depression. In *The psychology of depression,* ed. R. Friedman and M. M. Katz, pp. 157–85. New York: Winston-Wiley.

LIN, T. 1953. A study of the incidence of mental disorder in Chinese and other cultures. *Psychiatry* 16: 313–36.

LINK, B. 1982. Mental patient status, work and income: an examination of the effects of a psychiatric label. *American Sociological Review* 47:202–15.

——, and DOHRENWEND, B. P. 1980a. Formulation of hypotheses about the ratio of untreated to treated cases in the true prevalence studies of functional psychiatric disorders in adults in the United States. In *Mental illness in the United States: epidemiological estimates,* B. P. Dohrenwend et al., pp. 133–49. New York: Praeger.

——. 1980b. Formulation of hypotheses about the true prevalence of demoralization in the United States. In *Mental illness in the United States: epidemiological estimates,* B. P. Dohrenwend et al., pp. 114–32. New York: Praeger.

LORD, F. M., and NOVICK, M. R. 1968. *Statistical theories of mental test scores.* Reading, Mass.: Addison-Wesley.

MACMILLAN, A. M. 1957. The health opinion survey: technique for estimating prevalence of psychoneurotic and related types of disorder in communities. *Psychological Reports* 3: 325–29.

MANIS, J. G.; BRAWER, M. J.; HUNT, C. L.; and KERCHER, L. C. 1963. Validating a mental health scale. *American Sociological Review* 28: 108–16.

MAUSNER, J. S., and BAHN, A. K. 1974. Epidemiology: an introductory text. Philadelphia, Pa.: W. B. Saunders.

MAZER, M. 1974. People in a predicament: a study in psychiatric and psychosocial epidemiology. *Social Psychiatry* 9: 85–90.

MacMAHON, B., and PUGH, T. F. 1960. *Epidemiologic methods,* Boston: Little, Brown.

MECHANIC, D. 1972. Social class and schizophrenia: some requirements for a plausible theory of social influence. *Social Forces* 50: 305–9.

MEEHL, P. E. 1954. *Clinical vs. statistical prediction.* Minneapolis: University of Minnesota Press.

MEILE, R. L., and HAESE, P. A. 1969. Social status, status incongruence and symptoms of stress. *Journal of Health and Social Behavior.* 10: 237–44.

MURPHY, H. B. M., and TAUMOEPEAU, B. M. 1980. Traditionalism and mental health in the South Pacific: a reexamination of an old hypothesis. *Psychological Medicine* 10: 471–82.

MURPHY, J. M. 1976. Psychiatric labeling in cross-cultural perspective. *Science* 191: 1019–28.

MYERS, J. K.; LINDENTHAL, J. J.; and PEPPER, M. P. 1974. Social class, life events, and psychiatric symptoms: a longitudinal study. In *Stressful life events: their nature and effects,* ed. B. S. Dohrenwend and B. P. Dohrenwend, pp. 191–205. New York: Wiley.

MYERS, J. K., AND WEISSMAN, M. M. 1977. Results from a community study in New Haven. Personal communication.

MYERSON, A. 1940. Review of mental disorder in urban areas: an ecological study of schizophrenia and other psychoses. *American Journal of Psychiatry* 96: 995–97.

NEUGEBAUER, R. 1980. Formulation of hypotheses about the true prevalence of functional and organic psychiatric disorders among the elderly in the United States. In *Mental illness in the United States: epidemiological estimates*, B. P. Dohrenwend et al., pp. 45–94. New York: Praeger.

NUNNALLY, J. C. 1967. *Psychometric theory.* New York: McGraw-Hill.

ØDEGAARD, Ø. 1956. The incidence of psychoses in various occupations. *International Journal of Social Psychiatry* 2: 85-104.

PAYKEL, E. S. 1979. Causal relations between clinical depression and life events. In *Stress and mental disorder*, ed. J. E. Barrett, R. M. Rose, and G. L. Klerman, pp. 71–86. New York: Raven Press.

PEARLIN, L. I., and SCHOOLER, C. 1978. The structure of coping. *Journal of Health and Social Behavior* 19 no. 1: 2–21.

PHILLIPS, D. L. 1966. The "true prevalence" of mental illness in a New England state. *Community Mental Health Journal* 2: 35–40.

PHILLIPS, D. L., and CLANCY, K. J. 1972. Some effects of "social desirability" in survey studies. *American Journal of Sociology* 77: 921–40.

PHILLIPS, D. L., and SEGAL, B. E. 1969. Sexual status and psychiatric symptoms. *American Sociological Review* 34: 58–72.

PHILLIPS, L., and DRAGUNS, J. G. 1971. Classification of the behavior disorders. *Annual Review of Psychology* 22: 447–82.

RABKIN, J. 1975. The role of attitudes toward mental illness in evaluation of mental health programs. In *Handbook of evaluation research*, vol. 2, ed. M. Guttentag and E. L. Struening, pp. 431–82. Beverly Hills, Calif.: Sage Publication.

REGIER, D. A. 1980. Research on the social effects of mental disorders. *The social consequences of psychiatric illness*, ed. L. N. Robins, P. J. Clayton, and J. K. Wing, pp. 3-10. New York. Bruner/Mazel.

————; GOLDBERG, I. D.; and TAUBE, C. A. 1978. The de facto U.S. mental health services system. *Archives of General Psychiatry* 35: 685–93.

RIN, H.; CHU, H.; and LIN, T. 1966. Psychological reactions of a rural and suburban population in Taiwan. *Acta Psychiatrica Scandinavica* 42: 410–72.

ROBINS, L. N. 1966. *Deviant children grown up.* Baltimore, Md.: Williams and Wilkins.

————. 1978. Psychiatric epidemiology. *Archives of General Psychiatry* 35: 697–702.

————; Helzer, J. E.; Crougham, R.; and RATCLIFF, K. S. 1981. National Institute of Mental Health Diagnostic Interview Schedule: Its history, characteristics, and validity. *Archives of General Psychiatry* 38: 381–89.

ROBINS, L. N.; MURPHY, G. E.; WOODRUFF, R. A.; and KING, L. J. 1971. Adult psychiatric status of black schoolboys. *Archives of General Psychiatry* 24:338–45.

ROTTER, J. B. 1966. Generalized expectancies for internal versus external control of reinforcement. *Psychological Monographs* 80 (Whole no. 609).

RUTTER, M.; TIZARD, J.; and WHITMORE, K. 1970. *Education, health and behavior.* London: Longman.

SARTORIUS, N.; JABLENSKY, A.; and SHAPIRO, R. 1978. Cross-cultural differences in the short-term prognosis of schizophrenic psychoses. *Schizophrenia Bulletin* 4: 102–13.

SAWYER, J. 1966. Measurement and prediction, clinical and statistical. *Psychological Bulletin* 66: 178–200.

SCHEFF, T. J. *Being mentally ill.* Chicago: Aldine.

SEILER, L. H. 1973. The 22-item scale used in field studies of mental illness: a question of method, a question of substance, and a question of theory. *Journal of Health and Social Behavior* 14:252–64.

SELIGMAN, M. E. P. 1975. *Helplessness: on depression, development, and death.* San Francisco, Calif.: W. H. Freeman.

SHADER, R. I.; EBERT, M. H., and HARMATZ, J. S. 1971. Langer's psychiatric impairment scale: a short screening device. *American Journal of Psychiatry* 128: 596–601.

SHORE, J. H.; KINZIE, J. D.; HAMPSON, J. L.; and PATTISON, E. M. 1973. Psychiatric epidemiology of an Indian village. *Psychiatry* 36: 70–81.

SHROUT, P. E., and FLEISS, J. L. 1981. Reliability and case detection. In *What is a case: the problem of definition in psychiatric community surveys*, ed. J. K. Wing and P. Bebbington, pp. 117–28. London: Grant-McIntyre.

SPIRO, H. R.; SIASSI, I.; and CROCETTI, G. M. 1972. What gets surveyed in a psychiatric survey? *Journal of Nervous Mental Disorder.* 154: 105–114.

SPITZER, R. L.; ENDICOTT, J.; FLEISS, J. L.; and COHEN, J. 1970. The Psychiatric Status Schedule: a technique for evaluating psychopathology and impairment in role functioning. *Archives of General Psychiatry* 23: 41–55.

SPITZER, R. L.; ENDICOTT, J.; and ROBINS, E. 1978. Research diagnostic criteria: rationale and reliability. *Archives of General Psychiatry* 35: 773–82.

SROLE, L.; LANGNER, T. S.; MICHAEL, S. T.; OPLER, M. K.; and RENNIE, T. A. C. 1962. *Mental health in the metropolis.* New York: McGraw-Hill.

STAR, S. A. 1950. The screening of psychoneurotics in the army: technical development of tests. *Measurement and prediction*, vol. 4, ed. S. A. Stouffer et al. Princeton: Princeton University Press.

STRÖMGREN, E. 1950. Statistical and genetic population studies within psychiatry: methods and principal results. In *Actualités scientifiques et industrielles.* Congres International de Psychiatrie, vol. 6: Psychiatrie sociale. Paris: Herman.

STURT, E.; BEBBINGTON, P.; HURRY, J.; and TENNANT, C. 1981. The Present State Examination used by interviewers from a survey agency: report from the MRC Camberwell Community Survey. *Psychological Medicine* 11: 185–92.

SUMMERS, G. F.; SEILER, L. H.; and HOUGH, R. L. 1971. Psychiatric symptoms: cross-validation with a rural sample. *Rural Sociology* 36: 367–78.

SUSSER, M. W. 1968. *Community psychiatry: epidemiologic and social themes.* New York: Random House.

Task Force on Nomenclature and Statistics. 1980. *Diagnostic and statistical manual of mental disorders.* 3rd ed. Washington, D.C.: American Psychiatric Association.

TISCHLER, G. L.; HENISZ, J. E.; MYERS, J. K.; and BOSWELL, P. C. 1975. Utilization of mental health services: I. Patienthood and the prevalence of symptomatology in the community. *Archives of General Psychiatry* 32: 411–15.

TURNER, R. J. 1968. Social mobility and schizophrenia. *Journal of Health and Social Behavior* 9: 194–203.

———, and WAGENFELD, M. O. 1967. Occupational mobility and schizophrenia: an assessment of the social causation and social selection hypotheses. *American Sociological Review* 32: 104–13.

VERNON, S. W., and ROBERTS, R. E. 1981. Further observations on the problem of measuring nonspecific psychological distress and other dimensions of psychopathology. *Archives of General Psychiatry* 38: 1239–47.

WARHEIT, G. J. 1979. Life events, coping, stress, and depressive symptomatology. *American Journal of Psychiatry* 136: 502–7.

WEISSMAN, M. M., and KLERMAN, G. L. 1977. Sex differences and the epidemiology of depression. *Archives of General Psychiatry*, 34: 98–111.

———. 1978. Epidemiology of mental disorders. *Archives of General Psychiatry* 35: 705–12.

WEISSMAN, M. M., and MYERS, J. K. 1978. Affective disorders in a U.S. urban community: the use of research diagnostic criteria in an epidemiological survey. *Archives of General Psychiatry* 35: 1304–11.

———; and HARDING, P. S. 1978. Psychiatric disorders in a U.S. urban community: 1975–1976. *American Journal of Psychiatry* 135: 459–62.

WIGGINS, J. S. 1973. *Personality and prediction: Principles of personality assessment.* Reading, Mass: Addison-Wesley.

WING, J. K.; COOPER, J. E.; and SARTORIUS, N. 1974. *The measurement and classification of psychiatric symptoms.* London: Cambridge University Press.

WING, J. K.; MANN, S. A.; LEFF, J. P.; and NIXON, J. M. 1978. The concept of a "case" in psychiatric population surveys. *Psychological Medicine* 8: 203–217.

WOODRUFF, R. A.; GOODWIN, D. W.; and GUZE, S. B. 1974. *Psychiatric diagnosis.* New York and London: Oxford University Press.

YOO, P. S. 1961. Mental disorder in Korean rural communities. In *Proceedings of the Third World Congress of Psychiatry,* vol. 2, pp. 1305–9. Montreal: McGill University Press.

Chapter 9

Continuities and Discontinuities in the Psychiatric Disorders of Children

Lee Robins

PSYCHIATRIC DISORDERS IN CHILDREN are of double concern: for the distress they create currently for the child and his family, and for the implications they hold for his future. While no one would argue that current distress is trivial, it is clearly of even greater moment if the current symptoms can be expected to last for years, perhaps even into adulthood, and particularly if they are likely to be handed on to the next generation.

Over the last thirty years, a series of longitudinal studies of children's behavior problems—following children in treatment, or identified through school surveys, or in general population surveys—have taught us a great deal about what symptoms and syndromes in children are likely to be short-lived and which are particularly ominous.

Disorders that appear in childhood and last through adolescence have implications that are much broader than the implications for disorders of comparable length occurring in adult life, because the long-lasting disorders of childhood can interfere not only with the child's current health and function, but can drastically interfere with his total life chances. If they prevent certain kinds of learning at the usual ages—not only topics taught in school but also social skills and affectional relationships—this learning may never be recapturable, even if recovery occurs later on. Thus, even self-limited childhood disorder may lead to permanent impairment. Handicaps may occur in areas not generally thought of as health-related, such as marriage and its stability, procreation, and job level and earnings. The continuities to be considered, therefore, must encompass much more than subjective psychiatric symptoms.

Continuity between generations is termed *transmission*. This word is used rather than *inheritance* because it does not imply that there is a genetic explanation for the similarity between the two generations. The reasons for the similarity may

This work was supported in part by PHS grants MH 00334, DA 00259, AA 03539, MH 31302.

be genetic, environmental, or both. One learns whether transmission between generations is likely to be genetic only when one locates certain critical cases: identical twins showing more similarity than fraternal twins; children adopted away at birth resembling their biological parents more than their adoptive parents; and resemblance well above chance between relatives never reared together. Resemblances in behavior between parents and the children they have reared provide no such information because there are so many plausible explanations other than a genetic one for that resemblance.

What Are Childhood Disorders?

Adult consequences of childhood psychiatric disorder are broader than the scope usually assigned to health. The definitions of emotional and behavioral problems of childhood also extend beyond those limits set for adult psychiatric disorders, and the boundaries are often ill-defined. It is not clear when fears, developmental delays, and disobedience should be considered "abnormal" and when they are simply a normal part of growing up (i.e., merely "childish") or trivial, temporary deviations from the normal. Some children's behaviors that seem outside acceptable limits of normality might be acceptable within the particular subculture in which the child was reared, and so "normal" for him. If not even his own subculture condones his behavior, does it indicate a "mental disorder," or is it merely evidence that his family, community, or school has failed to teach him certain acceptable behaviors or useful ways of coping with stress? Or is it a matter of personality type rather than an illness? Perhaps he is unusually resistant to authority or unusually timid.

One suggested solution, which makes the decision easy as to what is a mental disorder, if not intellectually satisfying, is to say "psychiatric disorders are the kinds of problems that are sometimes brought to psychiatrists, and which they agree belong in their field of expertise." Note that this definition does not require that a particular case *must* have been seen by a psychiatrist. This definition is not sufficiently restrictive, however, since psychiatrists treat some children they themselves do not regard as having mental disorders—those with problems adjusting to their own physical illness or to the illness or death of a family member.

An additional problem is that traditions differ for children and adults as to what is treated by psychiatrists. In part this is because there is an extra layer of professionals who deal with children's behavioral and emotional problems. Added to the medical, paramedical, religious, and legal professionals who are called upon to handle unusual behaviors and emotional states in adults are the educational professionals with whom children all have contact, and who act as a referral system that channels learning problems and behavior problems into psychiatric or pediatric facilities if the problems are not understood as due to limited capacity or willful disobedience. Parallel problems in adults (i.e., poor job functioning or illegal behaviors) would rarely be viewed as a reason for referral to health professionals, although such problems are recognized as possible consequences of physical or mental disorders.

Learning disability and delinquency then belong within a classificatory scheme based on the criterion that "psychiatric disorders are what psychiatrists (or psychologists) treat." Calling children mentally disordered when they have problems that would *not* be treated by psychiatrists if they were adults is particularly disturbing to critics of the "medicalization" of children's behavior problems.

Attempts to define children's psychiatric disorders less pragmatically have generally included one of two requirements: (1) that there be a disturbance of behavior or a feeling of subjective discomfort not entirely explained by demonstrated physical illness and disproportionate to any provoking environmental factors; or (2) that confusion and misperceptions of reality must be a prominent feature, whether or not explained by physical causes.

Further, these disorders have to fulfill the same requirements with respect to pattern of symptoms and course as do all medical disorders—that there be a cohesive picture which includes a *pattern* of intercorrelated symptoms and a recognizable natural history including, at least potentially, a known cause, a characteristic distribution of vulnerability in the population, and typical age of onset, duration, and course (acute with complete recovery, episodic, stable, or deteriorating). In practice, there is usually too little knowledge to flesh out the whole syndrome and its natural history. Consequently, any diagnostic scheme must be provisional, ready for reorganization when more data become available. The history of psychiatric diagnosis, like the history of the rest of medicine, is a history of improvements in nomenclature as new knowledge divides disorders previously thought to be unitary or unites into a single disorder sets of symptoms that seemed phenomenologically disparate until a common cause was discovered.

Arguments about whether this "medical model" fits children's emotional and behavioral problems seem to focus principally on issues of whether there is an *internal physical* cause for the symptoms. This seems an idle preoccupation on two grounds. First, since there is no known physical cause for many illnesses accepted as "physical," it seems inappropriate to require that the cause of patterns of behavioral and emotional problems be known before they can be considered a disorder; second, it is not clear that a physical cause of a medical disorder need be internal.

Causes of permanent physical defects can be external. A patch worn over a healthy eye can lead to permanent blindness; a healthy person confined to a small space or to bed will develop physical disease. Clearly such effects of lack of physical stimulation and constraints on activity are not very distinct from the contribution of understimulation to mental retardation among the underprivileged or from the possible contribution of restricted or unusual upbringing to other forms of psychopathology.

Because attempts to define criteria for psychiatric disorder in children either as "what comes to a psychiatrist" or according to rigorous criteria for distinguishing psychiatric disorders from brain diseases or everyday problems of maturation and behavior lead us into such impasses, we will probably do better to rely on traditional categories rather than to attempt definitional rigor.

Classification

To discuss the differential continuity of childhood disorders, we obviously require a classificatory system for those disorders. No system yet devised is acceptable to everyone. In this chapter, we will rely on the system which appeared in the American Psychiatric Association's *Diagnostic and Statistical Manual, Third Edition (DSM-III)*, published in 1980.

DSM-III divides disorders into those "Usually First Evident in Infancy, Childhood, or Adolescence" and all others. The broad headings of those specifically identified as beginning before the end of adolescence are:

- mental retardation;
- attention deficit disorder [also known as hyperactivity, hyperkinesis, minimal brain dysfunction];
- conduct disorder;
- anxiety disorders of childhood and adolescence [including anxiety, avoidant disorder (excessive shyness), and overanxious];
- other disorders of infancy, childhood, or adolescence [including reactive attachment disorder (formerly marasmus), schizoid (lack of interest in social relationships), elective mutism, oppositional (persistent disobedience without aggressiveness), and identity disorder (distress because undecided about values and goals)];
- eating disorders [including anorexia (starving oneself), bulimia (binge eating), pica (eating nonfoods), and rumination (regurgitation)];
- stereotyped movement disorders [including tics, head-banging, and other repetitive movements];
- other disorders with physical manifestations [including stuttering, enuresis, encopresis, sleepwalking, and night terrors];
- pervasive developmental disorders [including infantile autism];
- specific developmental disorders [including reading, arithmetic, language, and speech disorders]; and
- gender identity disorder of childhood.

This categorization of disorders associated with childhood and adolescence omits some "adult" disorders that in fact almost always begin before the end of adolescence—particularly sexual identification disorders, phobias, and substance abuse. Finally, disorders that usually have an adult onset occasionally begin before the end of adolescence. Among these are depression, mania, schizophrenia, and obsessive-compulsive disorder.

These categories will serve as a basis for discussing continuities and discontinuities of childhood disorders. We will not try to cover them exhaustively because little is known about the prognosis of some. We will need to be tolerant of variations in their definitions across studies, since categorizations in existing studies do not match DSM-III criteria precisely. However, the DSM-III categories are generally translatable into older terminology without doing severe violence to them.

Assessing Continuity

To understand fully the outcome of a childhood disorder, one would like to select a representative sample of children with that disorder and follow them until their own children are as old as the sample members themselves were at the time they were selected. At the same time, one would follow an appropriate comparison group for the same duration, from whom one can estimate expected outcomes if the affected sample had *not* had the disorder in question. With this design, one can learn how long a disorder typically lasts, whether it forecasts any adult disorders, whether it interferes with family formation and adult achievement, and whether it is passed on to the next generation. Such long-lasting, real-time prospective studies have been done only a few times, for they are, of course, expensive and require waiting a very long time for answers. Due to their expense, the sample of children followed has often been small, and over time it tends to become unrepresentative as cases are lost.

The surest way to get a representative sample of children with a particular disorder, as well as an appropriate comparison group, is to sample from the entire child population. The cases of the selected disorder found in a sample representative of the general population will also be representative of all children with that disorder, and the remainder of the sample will provide a representative comparison group of unaffected children. Selecting cases identified in a sample of the general population is a feasible way of studying outcomes of *common* disorders, but not of rare ones. The huge samples from a general population required to find enough cases of children with rare disorders to provide stable estimates of outcome are prohibitively expensive.

Less expensive designs for rare disorders use samples of children obtained either from treatment facilities or by teacher nomination. Control groups may be patients from the same treatment setting with other disorders—orthopedic patients are a favorite—or unnominated classmates of affected children. Selecting children with a particular diagnosis from a treatment facility biases the sample toward children with more severe forms of the disorder, those who do not recover rapidly, and those whose parents for one reason or another are predisposed to seek professional help. Using treated children with other diagnoses as the control group raises questions about whether their outcomes will not be affected by whatever brought them into treatment. It is for this reason that orthopedic cases have been popular—most are accident victims who were recently healthy. They were thought to be in treatment only by chance. However, since we have learned that accidents are more common in children with certain psychiatric problems, they now appear to be less than an ideal comparison group.

Teacher nominations provide a broader selection of cases, but obviously omit children whose problems are manifest chiefly away from the schoolroom. For instance, teacher nominations cannot identify infantile autism(which rarely allows school attendance) or night terrors (which are not apparent in daytime hours), although they are the best source for identifying cases of reading or language disorders.

To shorten the waiting time before learning the outcome, cases to follow have often been selected from old records of children's clinics after the children are already adult. The shortcomings of treated cases noted above apply to this design. In addition, the researcher must then rely on the completeness and accuracy of assessments over which he had no control.

A third technique is to select adult patients with psychiatric disorders that one suspects have their roots in childhood and study these patients' childhood histories. The childhood history of problems can be obtained from retrospective interviews with patients or their informants, or by seeking early records in schools and clinics to learn whether the patients had distinctive early histories. There are two ways of choosing a comparison group—either from among adult contemporaries or from childhood contemporaries. If the controls are adult contemporaries—either adult patients with other diagnoses or normal adults—we have a case-control study. If the controls are childhood contemporaries—perhaps classmates selected from the problem adults' elementary schools—we have a follow-back study.

If a case-control study relies on retrospective interviewing, faulty memories are an obvious potential source of error. If forgetting were equally a problem for cases and controls, the only cost would be the possibility of missing childhood differences that truly distinguished the groups. A more serious problem is that the amount and kind of forgetting is likely to be biased by the current disorder. The "case" may more often recall childhood problems that seem to be logical antecedents of his current problems. For this reason, control patients with *other* psychiatric diagnoses seem attractive—then both groups will be motivated to recall past problems that might be antecedents to their current illness. However, this design also raises problems: different theories about the prodromal stages of their respective disorders may trigger their recall only for those problems they think would have predicted their current disorder, providing false data about differences between the groups. Again, without data for normal controls, it will be impossible to say that there was a higher rate of a particular childhood problem in the index cases than expected.

Even if there is no distortion of recall, reported differences between cases and controls may be misleading. The childhood problem that is found more frequently in cases than in patient controls may not be more common in cases than in a normal population, but rather is negatively correlated with the adult disorder from which patient controls suffer. To avoid this possibility, it is generally advisable to select patient controls with diverse diagnoses rather than a diagnostically homogeneous group.

The follow-back study avoids both the problem of selective memory and controls selected for disorders different from that of the cases, but the researcher must then rely on records produced by other hands.

A fourth technique is to make no attempt to follow the same individuals across time, but instead to study persons of different ages cross-sectionally. If the study is interested in short-term outcomes, the ages studied can be confined to childhood; if adult outcomes are of interest, the age span must be greater. By noting differences in prevalence rates in persons of different ages, one can infer from such studies which problems last and which do not. For instance, since enuresis is common in seven-year-olds but rare in eighteen-year-olds, it *must* be usually confined to childhood. And if demographic characteristics of the enuretics differ at different ages, one can guess which enuretic children are more likely to recover; for example, if the sex ratio of males to females increases with age, then girls probably recover more quickly than boys do.

Inferring developmental changes from cross-sectional studies can be misleading if risks of getting a disorder have undergone historical changes. Looking at illicit drug use in a cross-sectional analysis, for instance, we would think that it almost always remits by age thirty-five. That is in part because few persons over thirty-five were ever exposed to the "drug revolution." A future follow-up into middle age of persons who reached late adolescence since the mid-1960s might present a very different picture. Misleading results are also obtained if the disorder is associated with a high mortality rate or, in studies in a restricted geographical setting, if mobility out of or into the study area is associated with having the disorder.

Noting differences in prevalence with age also leaves another important question unanswered that longitudinal studies can provide an answer to: Does the disappearance of a target symptom indicate recovery, or has it been transformed into another symptom? A childhood symptom might be a sign of an underlying disorder that is expressed by different symptoms later on. Only by following the decline and emergence of symptom patterns in the same persons at different ages can the presence of such underlying disorders with mutable symptoms be discovered. Suppose that fears of the dark are common in six-year-old girls and rare in fifteen-year-olds, while depression is rare in the former but common in the latter. Without longitudinal studies, we will not know whether these are two unrelated disorders with different ages of risk, or whether childhood fears predict the onset of adolescent depression.

We will, of necessity, make use of studies based on a variety of designs to learn about the continuities and discontinuities of childhood disorders. While none of these designs is without drawbacks, there is enough consistency of findings across designs, eras, and samples to make us reasonably confident in the findings.

In discussing what we know about continuity of disorders, we will discuss the major children's disorders for which longitudinal data exist, and divide the information into prediction about early to late childhood, childhood to adulthood, and transmission between generations. Finally, we will ask what is known about factors that affect chances for continuity.

Mental Retardation

Mental retardation is sometimes considered more a neurological than a psychiatric disorder—that is, a disorder of the brain itself rather than a disorder of behavior or emotion. While there is no question that brain disease (encephalitis) and genetic abnormalities (Down's syndrome, phenylketonuria) can cause mental subnormality, most mildly retarded children have no demonstrable physical cause for their learning problems. For them the issue is not whether they have a neurological disease, but rather whether they have any disorder at all—are they not simply within the range of normal variation from the mean? There would be evidence that they are *not* necessarily part of the "natural order of things" if their IQs could be markedly improved by intervention. That is not to say that inborn intellectual capacity would not still have a normal distribution even if every child had an excellent educational environment. But if there are many now below the mean because of lack of adequate environmental opportunities, the true population mean might rise considerably, and being two standard deviations below the new mean might be less strongly associated with coming from a lower social class family than is now the case. The striking finding is that *severe* mental retardation is associated with physical causes but *not* with social status, while the reverse is true for mild mental retardation.

In an excellent article, Stein and Susser (1969) reported on their follow-up at age twenty to twenty-four of 106 children identified as educationally subnormal in school. They interviewed all at home and gave clinical and psychological tests to a subsample of fifty-two. They discovered that the few children from middle-class or upper-lower-class families all had a physical abnormality or an IQ so low that brain damage had to be assumed. In contrast, few children from lower-lower-class (demotic) families had demonstrable lesions. They discovered that mild mental retardation had very different consequences from severe mental retardation. The latter (defined as having an IQ below 50) often resulted in permanent institutionalization, and improvement in IQ was rare. Mild subnormality (IQs of 50 to 79), in contrast, usually showed improvement after school age, with IQs rising an average of eight points over the follow-up period, and social improvement even more marked than the improvement in IQ. While mild subnormality affected the amount of formal education received, which in turn affected job level, it appeared to have little effect on job stability, family formation, or physical health—each of which was profoundly affected by severe retardation. For the severely retarded, death rates were high and parenthood extremely rare.

Despite their generally good outcomes, a few mildly mentally retarded did show adult impairment, and 10 percent ended in institutions for the retarded. These adverse outcomes were more closely related to social background factors, such as having an unstable nuclear family, than to the precise IQ level. Almost all of the minority who ended in institutions got there as a consequence of having been arrested and therefore tested. Apparently, their unstable families were predictive of criminality, which led to ascertainment and hospitalization as an alternative to incarceration. Similar conclusions result from Clarke and Clarke's review of outcome studies of mental retardation (1974). The performance of mildly subnormal persons often spontaneously improves in adolescence or early adulthood.

Stein and Susser's follow-up ended too early to allow studying the transmission of mild mental retardation between generations, but Reed and Reed (1965) did a large study on the lineages of the mentally retarded. They found that the profoundly retarded seldom reproduced, and among the mildly retarded the reproduction of males was more depressed than that of females. About 15 percent of the offspring of the mentally retarded were retarded, or about 5 times the expected rate in the general population. The elevated risk of low IQs in the children of mentally subnormal parents was in part explained by assortative matings: 9 percent of the spouses were retarded (three times the population rate). When both parents were retarded, almost half (40 percent) of the children were. The effect of parents' IQ on children's IQ seems to be in part genetic and in part environmentally determined. Adoption into families of normal IQs substantially raises the IQ of the child above that of the mother (Skeels 1966), although a correlation remains between the biological mother's IQ and that of her adopted-away children.

There has been considerable argument of late as to whether educational opportunities modify the outcomes of the mildly mentally retarded. While programs offered in elementary schools have not been able to make profound differences, children in special education programs do achieve better reading and arithmetic scores than do retardates not offered special programs (Stein and Susser 1969). Head Start programs offered at ages two to four are associated with gains in mean IQ for the group, but it is not known whether the gain is accounted for by children who start below or above the group average. In any case, without continuing enrichment programs, these gains diminish or evaporate in the first school years (Ryan 1975; Miller and Dyer 1975). Programs offered in infancy (Heber and Garber 1974) may offer more durable gains, but they have not yet been substantially tested.

In sum, for severe subnormality, there is continuity from early childhood through adult life, but little opportunity for transmission to the next generation. Mild retardation, by contrast, is usually not detected until school age, and is most commonly diagnosed in adolescence, as IQs of the lower class tend to drop over the school years. However, in adult life there is typically amelioration unless there is an associated physical handicap.

Since marriage formation and fecundity of the mildly retarded is normal, there is the opportunity for transmission of handicap into the next generation. Whether that transmission occurs appears to depend on whether the offspring are reared in the impoverished environment typically provided by parents of low intelligence. Since there tends to be assortative mating by IQ, the child of a retardate is likely to receive a double dose of both genetic and environmental determinants. Adoption or exposure to good child-care facilities in early life both seem to be able to overcome at least some of the tendency toward transmission.

The absence of demonstrable physical handicap in mildly subnormal children of lower-class backgrounds, the response to enriched environments, and the stronger correlations between IQs for siblings than between parents and offspring all suggest that among poor children, environmental factors play a major causal role. There are also clearly genetic contributions or at least contributions from the perinatal environment as well, since parent-child correlations remain even when children are removed from their parents by early adoption.

Pervasive Developmental Disorders (Infantile Autism)

Infantile autism is a disorder that affects its victims so profoundly that there is no doubt that it constitutes a mental disorder. Luckily, it is also very rare. It usually appears in the first two years of life, and sometimes seems to have been present from birth. Autistic children have serious defects in language, ranging from inability to speak at all to stereotyped "robot like" speech with odd rhythms. They also show stereotyped, repetitive behaviors, sometimes including rocking, head-banging, and self-mutilation. They seem to lack a desire for interpersonal contact, preferring to play alone, and do not seek attention from or give affection to others. Some are severely mentally retarded, while a few are of normal or even superior intelligence. Like severe mental retardation, autism is *not* more frequent in the lower class and has even been reported to occur disproportionately in upper-class families (Rutter 1970).

Information about the outcomes of autistic children comes from follow-ups into adulthood of children treated for the disorder (Rutter 1970). The diagnosis of autism is reserved for children so severely ill early in life that they are very likely to be referred to specialists. Consequently, following children seen in treatment provides a reasonable sample of persons presenting that diagnosis. It may be, of course, that there are unrecognized mild forms of the same disorder in children who seem slightly distant, compulsive, or odd.

Recovery is rare in those without speech or with low IQs at the time of assessment. Many remain institutionalized for life. Almost half of those with higher IQs are able to complete school and hold a job as adults, but their social life usually continues to be restricted, their speech and behavior improved but not normal. It is rare for them to marry, and thus there is little opportunity to learn whether the disorder can be transmitted from parents to children.

Since milder forms seen in care do much better than the more severe, if still milder untreated cases exist, they may recover completely. Indeed, some gifted adults recall that in early childhood they were solitary, often silent, and played strange games that they resented interference with, suggesting that some of the pathognomonic traits were present but temporary.

The severity of the child's withdrawal from others probably accounts for the fact that this disorder was formerly referred to as "childhood schizophrenia." It is worth emphasizing that this was a misnomer. The characteristic hallucinations and delusions of schizophrenia are no more common an outcome in these children than in the general population.

Neurological abnormalities occur in a minority in infancy, and those with low IQs are likely to develop seizures later in childhood or in adolescence, suggesting a neurological basis for the disorder, although the cause is not known. For many years there was a search for environmental factors, based on theories of how mothers' treatment of their infants might engender the disorder. Those theories are currently believed by very few, since it was noted that other children of the same mothers had no excess of psychological damage, and it was recognized that the mothers' failure to interact as much with the autistic child as with his normal siblings had to do with the affected infant's lack of demands for or response to cuddling and play. Further, the complete resistance of the disorder to the most intense therapeutic efforts aimed at providing the theorized missing maternal affection suggested that the defect is entirely internal to the child (Eaton and Menolascino 1967).

Conduct Disorder

Children who repeatedly violate a large number of societal rules as evidenced by disobeying parents or teachers, early drinking, leaving school early, getting into trouble with the law by stealing and vandalism, and running away from home are included under the diagnosis of conduct disorder. In addition to these diagnostic symptoms, they tend to have learning and emotional problems. They perform academically much more poorly than one would expect on the basis of their slightly low IQs. In adolescence they are found to suffer from low self-esteem (Kaplan 1974). The low self-esteem of children with conduct problems shows that the costs of conduct disorders are not exclusively society's, although the victims of their violence, stealing, and thefts perhaps suffer even more.

In contrast to infantile autism, conduct disorder is a diagnosis subject to extensive discussion as to whether it truly constitutes a mental disorder or is simply a failure of the child's social milieu to teach him moral values and to instill in him an ability to postpone gratification, or whether he may not be a member of a subculture that teaches him a set of behaviors and attitudes that are not acceptable in the larger society. There is also considerable discussion as to whether the essential criteria are the variety of rule-breaking and aggressive *behaviors* displayed or the underlying attitudes of callousness and hostility.

Evidence in favor of these behaviors constituting a syndrome includes the fact that the variety of behaviors used to make the diagnosis typically emerge in a reasonably predictable order (Robins and Wish 1977); are all intercorrelated with each other; have strong familial predictors; and each predicts the adult diagnosis of antisocial personality. Thus, conduct disorder does appear to be a cohesive syndrome with a well-structured natural history. Further, this same pattern of behaviors has been found in every culture in which it has been studied. At the present state of knowledge, when a group of undesirable behaviors or feeling states meet all these criteria, this is usually taken as sufficient grounds to postulate a psychiatric disorder.

Children with conduct disorder are predominantly male, and typically first come to official attention in their early school years. Their IQs average slightly below 100, but in the normal range. They often, but not exclusively, come from broken homes and from the lower social classes.

Physical correlates have been sought, but to date results are inconclusive. Certainly physical insult to the brain can produce antisocial behavior in children. Clinical cases have developed subsequent to encephalitis, brain damage following head injury, and temporal lobe epilepsy. However, histories of brain disease and trauma are found in only a tiny proportion of all children with conduct disorder. Searches for distinctive physical attributes in the majority without known brain disease or trauma have produced studies claiming that antisocial children are more mesomorphoric and athletic than others (Glueck and Glueck 1968), while other studies have suggested that they tend to be small and clumsy (Farrington and West 1980), and to show "soft" neurological signs (Rutter et al. 1970). Psychophysiological studies have suggested that they condition poorly to sound and light stimuli because of low reactivity and rapid recovery (Siddle et al. 1977).

Studies of the long-term outcome of children with conduct disorder are very similar in design and results to studies of the outcomes of juvenile delinquency. Delinquency is not, of course, a psychiatric disorder, but most juvenile delinquents would meet criteria for conduct disorder. Long before their first arrest or referral to court, they have displayed resistance to parents' and teachers' authority, played truant, stolen objects, and performed so poorly in school that most delinquents are two to three years retarded academically. On the other hand, generally only the most severe cases of conduct disorder become delinquent. Follow-up studies of children with behavior problems or delinquency have been carried out in several countries of Western Europe and in the United States. When these studies were made in clinical populations, the children were defined as showing conduct disorder. In other studies they have been described as "predelinquent" or behavior problem children. However, the behaviors described are those used in making a diagnosis of conduct disorder. The large number of such studies reflects both how common behavior problems of childhood are and how disturbing to schools and to the legal system in all Western cultures they can be.

Many of these studies attempted to predict juvenile delinquency on the basis of behavior problems reported by teachers or parents' reports of behavior problems (Tait and Hodges 1962; Craig and Glick 1963; Conger and Miller 1966; West and Farrington 1973; Powers and Witmer 1951; Wadsworth 1975). Others began with juvenile delinquents and attempted to assess recidivism and later psychiatric history (Glueck and Glueck 1968; Healy and Bronner 1936; Henn et al. 1980; Wolfgang et al. 1972). Studies with an explicitly psychiatric orientation followed children referred to psychiatric hospitals (Morris et al. 1956) or child guidance clinics for antisocial behavior (Robins 1974; Roff 1974; Michael et al. 1957), lower-class schoolchildren identified as aggressive or truant (Robins et al. 1971; Kellam et al., in press), and welfare and household samples (Gersten et al. 1976; Rutter et al. 1976).

Some of these follow-up samples have been selected from ordinary schools serving a lower-class area; others were from household samples. The continuity of conduct disorder can be studied in such general population samples because it is so common. Conduct disorder constituted the major portion of the disorders identified in a general survey of children in England (Rutter et al. 1970) and accounts for a large part of child guidance clinic populations (Rosen et al. 1968).

Onset in the first school years is marked by resistance to teacher's authority, truancy, school performance well below that expected on the basis of their IQs, fighting, stealing, early drinking, and early sex experience (West and Farrington 1973; Tait and Hodges 1962; Conger and Miller 1966). In adolescence, official delinquency, heavy drug abuse, and being a school dropout may be added (West and Farrington 1973; Robins and Wish 1977).

Only about half of the adolescents with conduct disorders still have a markedly abnormal level of antisocial behavior in their early twenties. Despite the large proportion who improve, conduct disorder in childhood remains the leading predictor of severe adolescent and adult antisocial behavior. Even those whose antisocial behavior diminishes often have a long-lasting impairment because of the strong association between antisocial activity and poor school success. They are often left handicapped in the job market by having dropped out of school early and being functionally illiterate.

Those who continue antisocial behavior from adolescence into adult life change their repertoire of behaviors as they age. For women, the stealing and fighting of childhood may be replaced by sexual promiscuity, prostitution, and child neglect (Robins 1974). Heavy drinking is a common part of the adult picture for both men and women, as is erratic work behavior, including absenteeism, impulsive quitting of jobs, and getting fired. Marital relationships are usually stormy, with frequent separations and divorce.

Despite this high rate of marital breakup, conduct disorder cases who continue their antisocial behavior into adulthood have normal fecundity. Their fecundity is sustained by early marriage and by children born out of wedlock.

The offspring they produce clearly have a greatly increased risk of themselves developing conduct disorder. It is estimated that about half of the children of antisocial parents will develop conduct disorder, and about half of all children with conduct disorder have a parent with serious antisocial behavior (Robins 1974; Rutter and Madge 1976).

The transmission of childhood conduct problems between generations has been demonstrated for school performance, including truancy and high school dropout (Robins et al. 1979), and for delinquency (Robins et al. 1975). Transmission of arrest history is greater when the parents' arrests are continued into adulthood. It is not clear why this is so. Adult arrests may indicate that the parents had had a particularly virulent form of conduct disorder, and severe forms of any disease are probably more likely to be transmitted than are milder forms. It does not appear to be necessary that children personally experience their parents' arrests: parents' arrests prior to the child's birth have as great an influence as later arrests (Farrington et al. 1975), and children adopted from biological parents with a criminal record have an increased risk of arrest even when they have never lived with the criminal parent (Hutchings and Mednick 1975). Nor is the explanation that the loss of biological parents is psychologically equivalent to living with an antisocial parent, since adopted boys whose biological parents were antisocial show more antisocial behavior themselves than do other adopted boys (Cadoret 1975). Nonetheless, improved family environments do reduce the risk, as shown by the fact that illegitimate children (often the offspring of antisocial parents) who were adopted away have fewer school problems than do those who remain with the parent (Crellin et al. 1971; Seglow et al. 1972).

Families of children with conduct disorder often have at least three generations with marked antisocial behavior. There is concentration of antisocial behavior into particular family lines because of the assortative mating between antisocial persons (Gershon 1973). Assortative mating is particularly frequent among men with antisocial parents (Robins and Lewis 1966). It is not surprising, then, that two-generation antisocial families are especially likely to produce a third generation with conduct disorder.

Since many children with early conduct problems do not become juvenile delinquents and many juvenile delinquents do not become adult criminals, there has been great interest in learning what factors might favor discontinuity. Those cases whose early behavioral problems disappear are distinguished from those whose problems continue into adolescence by a less frequent family history of criminal or otherwise antisocial parents, higher IQ, smaller sibships, and less severe early antisocial behavior (Farrington and West 1980). These factors, plus avoiding contact with the juvenile justice system, also predict discontinuity between adolescent conduct disorders and antisocial behavior in adult life.

It is not surprising that the worse the child's own problems and those of his family and the fewer the child's intellectual resources, the higher his risk of later antisocial behavior will be. It is not so clear why family size should show so regular an effect. Among plausible hypotheses are: (1) having more children than they can afford is simply one more indicator that the parents are impulsive, and their impulsivity is transmitted to their children; (2) large sibships strain the meager resources of poor and incompetent parents; or (3) the more siblings, the greater the risk that at least one of them will be a delinquent model for the remainder (Robins et al. 1975). Nor is it clear why contact with the juvenile court—an institution established to protect children from the harshness of the adult judicial system and to handle conduct problems therapeutically rather than punitively—has repeatedly been shown to make children worse rather than better (Robins 1974; Farrington and West 1980). In part, the association between referral to juvenile court and poor outcome can probably be explained by the fact that, when apprehended by police, children with the more severe current crimes, with previous arrests, who are not deferential to the arresting police officer, and whose parents are known to be criminal or clearly inadequate are the ones most likely to be referred to juvenile court rather than diverted from the criminal justice system.

Other types of intervention have generally been found as ineffective as court referral in creating discontinuities in antisocial behavior. Among methods tried have been special education programs (Ahlstrom and Havighurst 1971), athletic programs, and various types of psychotherapy. A follow-up of one experiment in prevention—the Cambridge-Somerville study—suggests that, like court referral, treatment might actually be harmful (McCord 1978). Other evaluations of treatment have rarely shown positive results (Robins 1973). Despite the failure of these attempts at prevention and intervention, a large proportion of children with conduct disorders do recover spontaneously, suggesting that there may be environmental settings that favor recovery. One consistent finding is that exposure to well-structured discipline may be helpful.

Attention Deficit Disorder (Hyperkenesis, Hyperactivity, Minimal Brain Dysfunction)

Children given a diagnosis of attention deficit disorder are distinguished by their difficulty in completing school assignments, restlessness in the classroom, inability to pay attention to the teacher, and generally poorer academic achievement than their IQ suggests. At home they are overexcited, hard to control, and sleep little. This diagnosis is currently given to a very large minority of children referred to child mental health services. It is a diagnosis made much more frequently in the United States than elsewhere. This, plus the fact that restlessness and distractibility are in a sense synonymous with being a child, has led some to suggest that rather than being a real disorder, attention deficit disorder is merely a medicalization of the normal resistance of active young children, particularly boys, to being confined to a schoolroom. Others consider it simply an early stage or mild form of conduct disorder in which the illegal and aggressive aspects are not yet prominent.

One important contribution that studies of continuities can make is to settle such arguments. If the restlessness and distractibility that support the diagnosis of attention deficit disorder disappear when children leave the classroom, one can argue that it is only a reaction to confinement. If they often progress into conduct disorder, and have the same adverse consequences for adolescent and adult life, one can argue that it is only an early form of that disorder. If adults with a history of attention deficit disorder have offspring with an elevated rate of conduct disorder, one can suspect that the parents' disorder was only a mild form of conduct disorder.

For many years it was thought that these behaviors were self-limited—that the problem disappeared in adolescence. However, follow-up studies have found that although the obvious restlessness tends to disappear, problems persist and new problems emerge, certainly into late adolescence and perhaps into adult life (Menkes et al. 1967). As compared with control subjects matched to them for sex, IQ, age, and family social status, hyperactive children are found at age nineteen to have had much poorer academic success, more delinquency, to be more restless in interview, to use more illicit drugs, and to have had more automobile accidents (Weiss et al. 1975). Those who come to psychiatric care as adults show more alcoholism, more violence, more trouble with the law, but less depression than other patients (Morrison 1980). Thus, problems do *not* all end when confinement to classrooms ends, and the outcomes are similar to those of conduct disorders.

Nor can these results be understood as a fortuitous association deriving from the fact that attention deficit disorder tends to occur in lower class children who are also at risk of developing various forms of deviant behavior later in life. Young men diagnosed in childhood as hyperactive when compared to their own brothers reared in the same households have as adults more antisocial behavior, poorer school grades, and more occupational instability (Borland and Heckman 1976). Further, like conduct disorder, attention deficit disorder is associated with having antisocial parents (Cantwell 1972, 1975).

These follow-up studies then support the possibility that attention deficit disorder might be a mild variety of conduct disorder. Not only do hyperactive children often have behavior problems early in school, but later on they show an elevated rate of the classic symptoms of dropout and deliquency. Yet many children with attention deficit disorder seem genuinely perplexed and distressed by their inability to listen and sit still in class, and willingly seek treatment to get help—attitudes one does not associate with conduct disorder. It may be that at least two distinct disorders frequently are confused. It is difficult indeed to distinguish the effects of a deficit in the *ability* to attend and to persist at tasks from a more general resistance to discipline and authority figures. Both are associated with poor school performance and creating disturbance in the classroom.

Milich and Loney (1979) have noted that among boys with attention deficit disorders, the presence of conduct problems predicts outcome better than does the degree of hyperactivity. This finding is consistent both with the view that attention deficit disorder is a mild form of conduct disorder and with the view that there are two disorders and that conduct disorder is the one with the greater continuity.

We do not yet have information about whether children of parents with attention deficit disorders have an increased risk of conduct disorder. However, we do know that the reverse is true—children of antisocial parents do have an increased risk of attention deficit disorder. At the present time, then, there are two viable interpretations: (1) that conduct disorder and attention deficit disorder are two forms of the same disorder; or (2) that they are distinct, but that differential diagnosis is sufficiently difficult that some mild conduct disorders get misdiagnosed as attention deficit disorder.

Treatment of attention deficit disorder has consisted of two main types: drug treatment and behavior modification. Both stimulant drugs and behavioral treatments have been shown to improve classroom behavior. However, follow-up studies show no long-term effects of either on long-term outcome (Weiss et al. 1975), and even the short-term effects seem confined to behavior rather than to learning (Sleator et al. 1974). While these methods have not been successful, there are many who improve without treatment. As for conduct disorders, chances for spontaneous improvement are improved when discipline at home is firm (Werner and Smith 1977).

Specific Development Disorders: Learning Disabilities

Learning-disabled children are those who, despite normal IQs, find it impossible to learn to read, spell, or do arithmetic. The diagnosis is usually made in the first years of school. Many of the children so diagnosed also qualify for a diagnosis of hyperactivity or conduct disorder (Ackerman et al. 1977); however, some children with learning disabilities are as wellbehaved as normal school children, and some are even hypoactive and withdrawn, rather than hyperactive and aggressive. Learning difficulties that cannot be explained in terms either of general intelligence level or of behavior problems and are confined to one small life area fit the ordinary picture of a medical disorder comfortably; it is often assumed that these problems indicate some underlying nervous system pathology. There *is* some evidence for an excess of soft neurological signs in children with learning disabilities, but of course this is also true for children diagnosed as being hyperactive or having a conduct disorder.

Learning-problem cases have been followed for periods of up to five years (Rutter et al. 1976; Ackerman et al. 1977; Gersten et al. 1976). Each study shows a failure of most to recover, and indeed problems generally worsen over the school years. In one five-year study (Ackerman et al. 1977), only 14 percent were performing normally in school at follow-up. The best predictors of outcome were IQ and the severity of the original problem. As compared with control children, learning-disabled children had an excess of behavior problems at follow-up. However, these were confined to children whose learning disorders were *initially* associated with hyperactivity and conduct disorder. Thus, poor school performance alone did not seem to cause antisocial behavior, although children who failed *did* develop low opinions of themselves and their abilities. The observation that cases of antisocial behavior did not appear for the first time during the follow-up period is important because the association between learning disorders and conduct disorder had raised the possibility that the learning disorder might be the primary problem, and the conduct problems a response to the low self-esteem engendered by school failure. Since learning-disabled children without conduct problems initially did *not* develop them during the follow-up interval, this explanation for conduct disorders seems unlikely to be correct.

Schools generally offer special classrooms or tutoring as treatment for learning disabilities. When there is associated hyperactivity, the children are often given stimulant drugs. Controlled follow-up studies have failed to show that either type of treatment enables learning-disabled children to catch up with their peers (Ackerman et al. 1977; Kraus 1973). In fact, the disabled children get further and further behind their classmates as they continue through school.

The absence of follow-up studies into adulthood makes it impossible to say whether learning problems eventually are self-correcting. However, there is anecdotal evidence of very successful persons who report delays in learning to read or do arithmetic in elementary school, suggesting that despite the failure to demonstrate statistically that recovery is common, it does occur. Again, anecdotally, there are reports of transmission of learning disabilities from parents to offspring, but the frequency with which this occurs is not known.

Substance Abuse Disorders:
Alcohol and Drug Abuse and Dependence

Drinking, smoking, and use of marijuana are commonplace in adolescents. Before high school graduation, 93 percent have had a drink, 71 percent have smoked tobacco, and 60 percent have smoked marijuana (Johnston et al. 1980). In contrast, *problem* or *heavy* use of these substances is relatively rare. In 1980, only 6 percent of high school seniors were daily drinkers, 17 percent daily smokers, and 11 percent daily marijuana users. Less than 1 percent were daily users of any illicit drug other than marijuana.

There is no information as yet about the frequency of diagnosable abuse or dependence in adolescents. However, it is known that alcoholism and drug dependence seldom occur in adults who have not already used psychoactive substances heavily in adolescence. If children do *not* drink or use drugs heavily, they are unlikely ever to develop substance abuse problems (Robins et al. 1970). Late onset alcoholism in the absence of heavy teenage drinking probably occurs chiefly in two types of persons: those not previously exposed to alcohol because they were reared in a teetotaling environment, and those suffering from a depressive or manic episode.

As Kandel has shown (1975), in youth of high school age, there is an orderly sequence of experimentation with psychoactive substances, beginning with cigarettes, beer and wine, progressing to hard liquor and marijuana, and only then to other illicit drugs. Many children achieving each of these stages never thereafter go on to the next. Consequently, each earlier stage serves as a *necessary* but not a *sufficient* condition for progression to the next stage.

Since drinking and illicit drug use are socially disapproved for adolescents, it is not surprising that adolescent substance abuse overlaps to some extent with conduct disorder. The overlap is closer for drinking than for illicit drug use. Early drinkers tend to have the same early school problems that children with conduct disorder do, and to come from even lower class families. Illicit drug users are *not* distinguished by poor early school success, low IQs, or lower class status, but they do show many of the adolescent signs of conduct disorder: poor attendance at school, underachievement, delinquency, and early sexual experience (Robins 1980; Jessor 1976; Jessor and Jessor 1975; Kandel 1980). Serious drug dependency is also more concentrated in minority ethnic groups than is alcohol dependence, although that concentration is restricted to particular classes of drugs: heroin dependence is heavy in blacks and Hispanics, while abuse of hallucinogens is more common among whites (Johnston et al. 1980). Like conduct disorder, adolescent substance abuse is disproportionately a male phenomenon, although cigarette dependence is now about as common in girls as boys.

As adolescent heavy drinking and drug abuse resemble adolescent conduct disorder, so do their outcomes. Like delinquency, heavy substance abuse in childhood predicts high mortality rates, low occupational status, much unemployment, marital break-up and a high risk of arrest (Robins 1980). These problems are especially prominent in early adulthood, with amelioration later.

The earlier the use of these substances begins, the greater is the likelihood of adverse outcomes (Joe 1975). Early drug and alcohol use are, therefore, of special concern, particularly since the age of initiation of illicit drugs has been dropping steadily over the last few years.

Adolescent males who are heavily involved in drugs and alcohol appear to have a somewhat lower rate of offspring than expected. This is probably in part because of the high rate of marital breakup, but there is also some evidence for a direct biological explanation. In men, these substances appear to affect testosterone levels (Cicero 1980), which may decrease sex drive. In women, heavy cigarette use during pregnancy results in an increased risk of miscarriage and premature delivery, which in turn increases the risk of perinatal death. The direct effects of other drugs on birth rates have been difficult to study because most heavy drug and alcohol users are also heavy smokers. However, animal experiments make it clear that heavy alcohol administration during pregnancy interferes with nutrition and results in reduced litter sizes.

Offspring of alcoholics and drug abusers probably show some increased risk of mental deficiency (Jones et al. 1974) associated with the posited fetal alcohol syndrome and with poor general perinatal health status. They also later show an increased risk of attention deficit disorder, conduct disorder, learning disabilities, and substance abuse, both of alcohol itself and of other drugs. The transmission of alcoholism apparently does *not* depend on being reared by the alcoholic parent, since an increased risk is found in children of alcoholic fathers reared apart from the father (Schuckit et al. 1972) and in adoptees (Bohman 1978).

Gender Identity Disorder

Early in childhood, some children show a strong affinity for wearing clothing of the opposite sex and playing with toys that are traditionally designed for the opposite sex. Some state a desire to be a member of the opposite sex, while others insist that they actually *are* members of the opposite sex. Parents much more often refer cross-dressing of effeminate boys for psychiatric evaluation than cross-dressing of tomboyish girls—probably because the behavior is less socially acceptable in boys.

Follow-up studies of effeminate boys show that they rarely achieve normal heterosexual roles by adolescence or early adulthood (Zuger 1978). Some are essentially asexual as adults, while most are homosexuals, transvestites, or transsexuals. It is not known how frequent such problems in sexual identity are, nor whether all adult cases of homosexuality, transvestism, or transsexuality begin in childhood. However, retrospective interviews with adult homosexuals (Saghir and Robins 1973) found about two-thirds of each sex had sufficient cross-sex behavior early in childhood to be considered "sissies" or "tomboys." In contrast, this occurred in only 3 percent of heterosexual males and 16 percent of heterosexual females.

There have been no attempts to ascertain whether these children can be predicted to have any adult problems other than gender identity. Studies of adult homosexuals have found increased rates of depression and substance abuse, but these may be responses to the social and religious difficulties of living as an adult homosexual and to a failure to approve one's own gender identification, rather than to problems predicted directly from the childhood disorder.

The very early appearance of gender identity problems in some children raises the possibility of an inborn propensity to identify with the opposite sex. Family attitudes and expectations are also frequently hypothesized to be the critical factor. Homosexual men report their fathers to have been uninvolved with them during childhood, but it is not known to what extent the fathers' lack of involvement may have been caused by revulsion toward the effeminate behavior of their sons, rather than having caused it. Contrariwise, homosexual women report having gotten along better with their fathers than with their mothers, in part because they shared their fathers' interests in sports and outdoor activity (Saghir and Robins 1973).

For both male and female homosexuals, the early homes were much more often broken or full of parental strife and heavy drinking than were the childhood homes of control cases. Again it is uncertain to what extent the discord between the parents was caused by the children's behavior rather than being responsible for the children's behavior.

When children with gender identity disorders act in accord with their preferences, obviously they do not have offspring. Some do marry and have children in order to conform to social pressures or because they want to be parents, but overall their fertility rate is severely reduced. Despite evidence from twin studies of a genetic factor in homosexuality (Kallman 1952), one study of children raised by their lesbian mothers found no cases of gender identity disorder in the offspring (Green 1978). This suggests that the pattern of inheritance is not through a single dominant gene and that if environmental factors play a role, they are not a simple modeling of the child's behavior on the parent's.

Anxiety Disorders

The anxiety disorders of childhood are notable both for their frequency and their transiency. Many young children go through periods of nightmares or fearing strangers, animals, the dark, and being left by their mothers. Some of these fears seem an exaggeration of normal development, which requires that children learn to trust their parents and distrust strangers, to discriminate edible from dangerous things to eat or drink, and to be cautious about approaching dangerous animals. The anxious children seem to learn these cautions *too* thoroughly and take them so to heart that it interferes with normal functioning. Most of these symptoms begin to disappear long before adolescence. When the Langner group interviewed parents about a random sample of New York children aged six to eighteen (Gersten et al. 1976), they found anxiety symptoms not to be statistically associated with impaired functioning, and when they followed the children five years later, they found that anxiety symptoms identified in the earlier interview were of no help in predicting later adjustment, except among those already adolescent at first assessment. The Berkeley Growth Study (MacFarlane et al 1954), which began with infants and nursery-school-aged children and followed them until age fourteen (and then again in adulthood), found that anxiety did not begin to show stability from one follow-up wave to the next until children reached age six. Rutter began with ten-year-olds on the Isle of Wight, and followed them to age fourteen. He found a high rate of recovery from neurotic symptoms: half affected at age ten were free of them by age fourteen, twice as high a proportion as recovered from conduct symptoms (Rutter 1976).

When anxious children are followed for longer periods, into late adolescence or adulthood, the results are similar. Roff (1974) followed boys seen in a child guidance clinic who later served in the military to learn whether their juvenile problems predicted difficulties in service. He found no increase in psychiatric discharges among those seen for neurotic problems as compared with normal controls. A follow-up into adult life of children treated at a child guidance clinic for neurotic problems (Robins 1974) found little disadvantage for these children as compared with a control group chosen from contemporary elementary schools. A follow-up study of shy child guidance clinic patients found the neurotic children had *not* developed schizophrenia, as had been anticipated. Instead, they were somewhat shy but psychiatrically healthy adults (Michael et al. 1957).

Some studies show actual advantages for "neurotic" children. In Kellam et al.'s follow-up (in press) of black first-graders, teachers' notation of them as excessively shy predicted conforming behavior at age seventeen: they were less likely to smoke, drink, and use illicit drugs than children seen as well-adjusted in the first grade. These behaviors are typically initiated in concert with the peer group, and shyness may have made it difficult for these children to enter fully into peer activities. Nor did these shy children show an excess of other forms of psychopathology at seventeen.

It is perhaps not surprising, since spontaneous recovery is so frequent among anxious children, that treatment is often reported to be successful with them. The only difficulty is in demonstrating that the treatment produces better results than does time alone. However, it seems clear that therapy can help children to abandon fears more quickly than they might otherwise (Bandura 1971).

There is one disorder usually grouped with other fears and shyness that does not seem to have such an excellent prognosis—school phobia (Waldron 1976). At age 22, school phobics previously seen in a child guidance clinic before age thirteen had more school dropout, more somatic symptoms, and were more dependent than other mildly ill patients or matched control cases.

While most childhood neurotic symptoms disappear with time, when adults with complaints of phobias are asked about their childhoods, they generally recall early fears (Marks and Gelder 1966). It is possible that adult phobias generally do begin in childhood, even though childhood fears do not significantly predict later psychiatric disorder. A failure to find a significant association may occur just because adult phobias are so rare relative to children's fears.

There has been little effort to learn anything about the child-bearing of anxious children grown up, or the degree to which their childhood fearfulness reappears in their offspring. This is an area still awaiting investigation.

Disorders Usually Appearing First in Adulthood

A number of adult disorders typically have their first onset in adulthood, but can on occasion be found in children. One can include here schizophrenia, major depressive disorder, mania, and panic disorder. Onset of these disorders is very rare in early childhood, but becomes more frequent as the child approaches adulthood.

Perhaps because there has been more resistance to classifying psychiatric problems in children than in adults, these disorders in children have often been called "adjustment reactions," rather than being given the same names used when they occur in adults. This appears to be a mistake. They are *not* signs of "adolescent turmoil" which will pass (Masterson 1968). This misinterpretation has been possible because depression and mania are episodic illnesses, and there is apparent "recovery," but an increased risk of later episodes persists. Still, among children affected, many will never again have such an episode.

Because of their rarity in childhood and arguments over diagnostic issues, the predictors and prognosis of these disorders in children have not been well studied. However, there have been a number of "follow-back" studies of adult patients with schizophrenia to learn whether there had been prognostic signs in childhood, even if the diagnosis of schizophrenia was not made. These studies have sought evidence in child guidance clinic records, school records, and hospital records. In each, control cases were selected from the same childhood source. School records and clinic records of men who later became schizophrenic (Watt and Lubensky 1976; Roff et al. 1976) have shown them to have an elevated rate of antisocial behavior in childhood, rather than being shy and withdrawn as anticipated. Girls, on the other hand, more closely approximate the expected shy, withdrawn pattern. A similar study (Lewine et al. 1978), combining the sexes, found schizophrenics described by teachers as more maladjusted, less sociable, less popular and pleasant, more misbehaving, more isolated, and more disorganized than their peers, while depressives differed from their peers in being more mature and more likely to be leaders. Adult neurotics were indistinguishable from controls as children. Schizophrenics as children also have slightly low IQs, and their IQs are less highly correlated with siblings' IQs than are normals' (Lane and Albee 1965).

Summary

Follow-up studies of children with psychiatric problems reveal no simple story concerning their future psychiatric health. With the exception of the severely retarded and the autistic who have considerable communication problems, children with diagnosable disorders frequently are psychiatrically well through much of their adult lives. On the other hand, except perhaps for those whose difficulties are limited to neurotic complaints, the risk of continuing or recurring disorder in adult life is clearly elevated in children who have had psychiatric problems.

While childhood disorders should raise concerns for the future, a childhood free of psychiatric disorder, unfortunately, is no guarantee of future mental health. There was a period when psychiatry made the claim that preventive services for children would greatly reduce the prevalence of adult psychiatric disorder. This promise has clearly not been fulfilled. Some adult disorders, such as the affective and anxiety disorders, are not typically foreshadowed by any detectable premorbid difficulties in childhood. Therefore, it would be difficult to select children at high risk for these disorders for whom one might propose preventive efforts. Further, efforts at preventing the appearance of childhood disorders have been singularly unsuccessful (Cowen et al. 1973). This is no reason, of course, to stop trying to identify children at risk of a particular disorder or a group of childhood disorders, and then to attempt to forestall the appearance of those disorders. Nor is there reason not to attempt to treat the disorder when it appears in childhood, in hopes that it will not then be carried on into later childhood or adulthood. But we will need considerable further research before we can claim to be able either to prevent or to treat childhood disorders successfully.

While any contribution to the prevention or treatment of childhood disorders will be welcome, those adult disorders which always begin in childhood would seem to demand our greatest attention, both in prevention and treatment, because success in avoiding or aborting them would have enormous benefit to the children who will have a lifetime of suffering as a result of them, to the families of those children, and to society as a whole.

REFERENCES

ACKERMAN, P. T.; DYKMAN, R. A.; and PETERS, J. E. 1977. Teenage status of hyperactive and nonhyperactive learning disabled boys. *American Journal of Orthopsychiatry* 47:577-96.

AHLSTROM, W. M., and HAVIGHURST, R. J. 1971. *400 losers*. San Francisco, Calif.: Jossey Bass.

ANNESLEY, P. T. 1961. Psychiatric illness in adolescence: presentation and prognosis. *Journal of Mental Science* 107:268-78.

BANDURA, A. 1971. Psychotherapy based upon modeling principles. In *Handbook of psychotherapy and behavior change*, ed. A. E. Bergin and S. L. Garfield, pp. 653-708. New York: Wiley.

BOHMAN, M. 1978. Some genetic aspects of alcoholism and criminality. *Archives of General Psychiatry* 35:269-76.

BORLAND, B. L., and HECKMAN, H. K. 1976. Hyperactive boys and their brothers. *Archives of General Psychiatry* 33:669-75.

CADORET, R. J. 1975. Studies of adoptees from psychiatrically disturbed biologic parents II: Temperament, hyperactive, antisocial, and developmental variables. *Pediatrics* 87:301-6.

CANTWELL, D. P. 1972. Psychiatric illness in the families of hyperactive children. *Archives of General Psychiatry* 27:414-17.

——. 1975. Genetic studies of hyperactive children. In *Genetic research in psychiatry*, ed. R. Fieve, D. Rosenthal, and H. Brill, pp. 273-80. Baltimore, Md.: Johns Hopkins University Press.

CICERO, T. J. 1980. Common mechanisms underlying the effects of ethanol and narcotics on neuroendocrine function. In *Advances in substance abuse*, ed. N. K. Mello, pp. 201–54. Greenwich, Conn.: JAI.

CLARKE, A. D. B. and CLARKE, A. M. 1974. Mental retardation and behavioral change. *British Medical Bulletin* 30:179–85.

CONGER, J. J. and MILLER, W. C. 1966. *Personality, social class and delinquency*. New York: Wiley.

COWEN, E. L.; PEDERSON, A.; BABIGIAN, H.; IZZO, L. D. and TROST, M. A. 1973. Long-term follow-up of early detected vulnerable children. *Journal of Consulting and Clinical Psychology* 41:438–46.

CRAIG, M. M., and GLICK, S. J. 1963. Ten years' experience with the Glueck Social Prediction Table. *Crime and Delinquency* 9:249–61.

CRELLIN, E.; KELLMER PRINGLE, M. L.; and WEST, P. 1971. *Born illegitimate*. London: National Foundation for Education Research in England and Wales.

EATON, L., and MENOLASCINO, F. J. 1967. Psychotic reactions of childhood: a follow-up study. *American Journal of Orthopsychiatry* 37:521–29.

FARRINGTON, D. P.; GUNDRY, G.; and WEST D. J. 1975. The familial transmission of criminality. *Medicine, Science and the Law* 15:177–86.

FARRINGTON, D. P., and WEST, D. J. 1980. The Cambridge study in delinquent development. In *Survey of prospective longitudinal research in Europe*, ed. S. A. Mednick, and A. E. Baert. Copenhagen: World Health Organization.

GERSHON, E. S.; DUNNER, D. L.; STUART, L.; and GOODWIN, F. K. 1973. Assortative mating in the affective disorders. *Biological Psychiatry* 7:63–74.

GERSTEN, J. C.; LANGNER, T. S.; EISENBERG, J. G.; SIMCHA-FAGAN, O.; and McCARTHY, E. D. 1976. Stability and change in types of behavioral disturbance of children and adolescents. *Journal of Abnormal Child Psychology* 4:111–27.

GLUECK, S., and GLUECK, E. 1968. *Delinquents and nondelinquents in perspective*. Cambridge, Mass.: Harvard University Press.

GREEN, R. 1978. Sexual identity of 37 children raised by homosexual or transsexual parents. *American Journal of Psychiatry* 135:692–97.

HEALY, W., and BRONNER, A. F. 1936. *New light on delinquency and its treatment*. New Haven, Conn.: Yale Univeristy Press.

HEBER, R., and GARBER, H. 1974. Progress report III: an experiment in the prevention of cultural-familial retardation. In *Proceedings of the Third International Congress of the International Association for the Scientific Study of Mental Deficiency*.

HENN, F. A.; BARDWELL, R.; and JENKINS, R. L. 1980. Juvenile delinquency revisited: adult criminal activity. *Archives of General Psychiatry* 37:1160–63.

HUTCHINGS, B., and MEDNICK, S. A. 1975. Registered criminality in the adoptive and biological parents of registered male criminal adoptees. In *Genetic research in psychiatry*, ed. R. Fieve, D. Rosenthal, H. Brill. Baltimore, Md.: Johns Hopkins University Press.

JESSOR, R. 1976. Predicting time of onset of marijuana use: a developmental study of high school youth. *Journal of Consulting and Clinical Psychology* 44:125–34.

————, and JESSOR, S. L. 1975. Adolescent development and the onset of drinking: a longitudinal study. *Journal of Studies in Alcoholism* 36:27–51.

JOE, G. W., and HUDIBERG, R. 1975. Behavioral correlates of age at first marijuana use (ms).

JOHNSTON, L. 1981. *Drugs and American youth*. Ann Arbor, Mich.: Institute for Social Research.

JOHNSTON, L. D.; BACHMAN, J. G.; and O'MALLEY, P. M. 1980. *Student drug use in America, 1975-1980*. DHHS pub. no. (ADM) 81–1066. Rockville, Md.: National Institute on Drug Abuse.

JONES, K. L.; SMITH, D. W.; STREISSGUTH, A. P.; and MYRIANTHOPOLOUS, N. C. 1974. Outcome in offspring of chronic alcoholic women. *Lancet*: 7866:1076–78.

KALLMAN, F. J. 1952. Twin and sibship study of overt male homosexuality. *American Journal of Human Genetics* 4:136–46.

KANDEL, D. 1975. Stages in adolescent involvement in drug use. *Science* 190:912–14.

————. 1980. Convergences in prospective longitudinal surveys of drug use in normal popu-lations. In *Human functioning in longitudinal perspective*, ed. S. B. Sells, R. Crandall, M. Roff, J. S. Strauss, W. Pollin. Baltimore, Md.: Williams and Wilkins.

KAPLAN, H. B. 1974. Self-attitudes and the adoption of deviant response patterns (ms).

KELLAM, S.; BROWN, C. H.; and FLEMING, J. P. Longitudinal community epidemiological studies of drug use: early aggressiveness, shyness, and learning problems. In *Studying drug abuse*, ed. L. Robins, in press.

KELLAM, S.; SIMON, M. B.; and ENSMINGER, M. E. Antecedents of teenage drug use and psychological well-being: a ten-year community wide prospective study. In *Origins of psychopathology: research and public policy*, ed. D. Ricks and B. S. Dohrenwend. New York: Cambridge University Press in press.

KRAUS, P. E. 1973. *Yesterday's children*. New York: Wiley.

LANE, E. A., and ALBEE, G. W. 1965. Childhood intellectual differences between schizo-phrenic adults and their siblings. *American Journal of Orthopsychiatry* 35:747–53.

LEWINE, R. R. J.; WATT, N. F.; PRENTKY, R. A.; and FRYER, J. H. 1978. Childhood behavior in schizophrenia, personality disorder, depression, and neurosis. *British Journal of Psychiatry* 133:347–57.

MACFARLANE, J.; ALLEN, J.; and HONZIK, M. 1954. *A developmental study of the behavior problems of normal children between 21 months and 14 years*. Berkeley, Calif.: Univer-sity of California Press.

MARKS, I. M., and GELDER, M. G. 1966. Different ages of onset in varieties of phobia. *Amer-ican Journal of Psychiatry* 123:218–21.

MASTERSON, J. F., 1968. The psychiatric significance of adolescent turmoil. *American Jour-nal of Psychiatry* 124:107–12.

MCCORD, J. 1978. A thirty-year follow-up of treatment effects. *American Psychologist* 33:284–89.

MCCORD, W., and MCCORD, J. 1959. *Origins of crime*. New York: Columia University Press.

MENKES, M.; ROWE, J.; MENKES, J. 1967. A 25-year follow-up study on the hyperkinetic child with minimal brain dysfunction. *Pediatrics* 39:393–99.

MICHAEL, C. M.; MORRIS, D. P.; and SOROKER, E. 1957. Follow-up studies of shy withdrawn children. *American Journal of Orthopsychiatry* 27:331–37.

MILICH, R., and LONEY, J. 1979. The role of hyperactive and aggressive symptomatology in predicting adolescent outcome among hyperactive children. *Journal of Pediatric Psy-chology* 4:93–112.

MILLER, L., and DYER, J. L. 1975. Four pre-school programs: their dimensions and effects. *Monographs of the Society for Research in Child Development* 40:1–170.

MORRIS, H. H.; ESCOLL, J. P.; and WEXLER, R. 1956. Agressive behavior disorders of child-hood: a follow-up study. *American Journal of Psychiatry* 112:991–97.

MORRISON, J. R. 1980. Childhood hyperactivity in an adult psychiatric population: Social factors. *Journal of Clinical Psychiatry* 41:40–43.

POWERS, E., and WITMER, H. 1951. *An experiment in the prevention of delinquency*. New York: Columbia University Press.

REED, E. W., and REED. S. C. 1965. *Mental retardation*. Philadelphia, Pa: W. B. Sanders.

ROBINS, L. N. 1973. Evaluation of psychiatric services for children in the United States. In *Roots of evaluation*; ed. J. K. Wing and H. Hafner. London: Oxford University Press.

————. 1974. *Deviant children grown up*. Huntington, N. Y.: Krieger.

————. 1980. Epidemiology of adolescent drug use and abuse. In *Psychopathology of chil-dren and youth: a cross-cultural perspective*, ed. E. F. Purcell. New York: Josiah Macy, Jr., Foundation.

————; DARVISH, H. and MURPHY G. E. 1970. The long-term outcome for adolescent drug users. In *Psychopathology of adolescence*, ed. J. Zubin and A. Freedman. New York: Grune and Stratton.

ROBINS, L. N., and LEWIS, R. G. 1966. The role of the antisocial family in school completion and delinquency: a three-generation study. *Sociological Quarterly* 7:500–14.

ROBINS, L. N.; MURPHY, G. E.; WOODRUFF, R. A., JR.; and KING, L. J. 1971. The adult psychiatric status of black school boys. *Archives of General Psychiatry* 24:338–45.

ROBINS, L. N.; RATCLIFF, K. S.; and West, P. A. 1979. School achievement in two generations: a study of 88 urban black families. In *New directions in children's mental health,* ed. S. J. Shamsie. New York: Spectrum.

ROBINS, L. N.; WEST, P. A.; and HERJANIC, B. 1975. Arrest and delinquency in two generations: A study of black urban families and their children. *Journal of Child Psychology and Psychiatry* 16:125–40.

ROBINS, L. N.; and WISH, E. 1977. Childhood deviance as a developmental process: a study of 223 urban black men from birth to 18. *Social Forces* 56:448–73.

ROFF, J.; KNIGHT, R.; and WERTHEIM, E. 1976. A factor-analytic study of childhood symptoms antecedent to schizophrenia. *Journal of Abnormal Psychology* 85:543–49.

ROFF, M. 1974. Childhood antecedents of adult neurosis, severe bad conduct, and psychological health. In *Life history research in psychopathology,* ed. D. Ricks, A. Thomas, and M. Roff. Minneapolis, Minn.: University of Minnesota Press.

ROSEN, B. M.; KRAMER, M.; REDICK, R. W.; and WILLNER, S. G. 1968. *Utilization of psychiatric facilities by children: current status, trends, implications.* HEW (PHS) pub. no. 1868. Washington, D. C.: Government Printing Office.

RUTTER, M. 1970. Autistic children: infancy to adulthood. *Seminars in Psychiatry.* 2:435–50.

———, and MADGE, N. 1976. *Cycles of disadvantage.* London: Heinemann.

RUTTER, M.; TIZARD, J.; and WHITMORE, K. 1970. *Education, health, and behavior.* London: Longman.

RUTTER, M.; TIZARD, J.; YULE, W.; GRAHAM, P.; and WHITMORE, K. 1976. Research report: Isle of Wight studies 1964–1974. *Psychological Medicine* 6:313–32.

RYAN, S. 1974. *A report on longitudinal evaluations of preschool programs.* DHEW pub. no. (OHD) 75-24. Washington, D.C.: Government Printing Office.

SAGHIR, M. T., and ROBINS, E. 1973. *Male and female homosexuality: a comprehensive investigation.* Baltimore, Md.: Williams and Wilkins.

SCHUCKIT, M. A.; GOODWIN, D. W.; and WINOKUR, G. A study of alcoholism in half-siblings. *American Journal of Psychiatry* 128:122–26.

SEGLOW, J.; KELLMER PRINGLE, M. L.; WEDGE, P. 1972 *Growing up adopted.* London: National Foundation for Educational Research in England and Wales.

SIDDLE, D. A. T.; MEDNICK, S. A.; NICHOL, A. R.; and FOGGITT, R. H. 1977. Skin conductance recovery in antisocial adolescents. In *Biosocial bases of criminal behavior,* ed. S. Mednick and K. O. Christiansen. New York: Gardner.

SKEELS, H. M. 1966. Adult status of children with contrasting early life experiences. *Monographs of the Society for Research in Child Development* 31, no. 105.

SLEATOR, E. K.; VON NEUMANN, A.; and SPRAGUE, R. L. 1974. Hyperactive children: A continuous long-term placebo-controlled follow-up. *Journal of the American Medical Association* 229:316–17.

STEIN, Z. A., and SUSSER, M. 1969. Mild mental subnormality: social and epidemiological studies. In *Social psychiatry,* ed. F. C. Redlich. New York: Williams and Wilkins. *Research Publication of the Association for Nervous and Mental Disease* 47:62–85.

TAIT, C. D., and HODGES, E. F. 1962. *Delinquents, their families, and the community.* Springfield, Ill.: Thomas.

WADSWORTH, M. E. J. 1975. Delinquency in a national sample of children. *British Journal of Criminology* 15:167–74.

WALDRON, S. 1976. The significance of childhood neurosis for adult mental health: a follow-up study. *American Journal of Psychiatry* 133:532–38.

WATT, N. F., and LUBENSKY, A. W. 1976. Childhood roots of schizophrenia. *Journal of Consulting and Clinical Psychology* 44:363–75.

WEISS, G.; HECHTMAN, L.; and PERLMAN, T. 1978. Hyperactives as young adults: school, employer, and self-rating scales obtained during 10-year follow-up examination. *American Journal of Orthopsychiatry* 48:438–45.

————; KRUGER, E.; DANIELSON,U.; and ELMAN, M. 1975. Effect of long-term treatment of hyperactive children with methylphenidate. *Canadian Medical Association Journal* 112:159–65.

WERNER, E. and SMITH, S. 1977. *Kuai's children come of age.* Honolulu: University of Hawaii Press.

WEST, D. J., and FARRINGTON, D. P. 1973. *Who becomes delinquent?* London: Heinemann.

————. 1977. *The delinquent way of life.* London: Heinemann.

WOLFGANG, M. E.; FIGLIO, R. M.; and SELLIN, T. 1972. *Delinquency in a birth cohort.* Chicago: University of Chicago Press.

ZUGER, B. 1978. Effeminate behavior present in boys from childhood: ten additional years of follow-up. *Comprehensive Psychiatry* 19:363–69.

Chapter 10

Injury Epidemiology and the Reduction of Harm

Leon S. Robertson

DEATH FROM INJURIES is the modern-day plague of the young. While cardiovascular diseases and malignant neoplasms each kill larger numbers of people, injuries are by far the leading contributions to loss of what are usually considered the preretirement years of life. If one subtracts from sixty-five the age of death of each person who dies before sixty-five and totals the number of preretirement years of life lost, injuries account for about the same number of those younger years lost as cardiovascular diseases and malignant neoplasms combined. The reason, of course, is that injuries are the leading killers of children and young adults, while cardiovascular diseases and malignant neoplasms are the leading killers in middle to old age, particularly in the postretirement years.

Harm to human beings (whether called disease or injury) is viewed by epidemiologists as an interaction of an agent that can do harm, a vehicle or vector that conveys the agent to the person, and the person, often called the host. The interaction of these factors may also be influenced by the environment, both physical and social, in which the interaction occurs. The incidence of harm and the extent of the harm can be a result of characteristics of the agent, the vehicle, the host individual, and the environment. And appropriately, prevention of the harm or its extent may be accomplished by changing the agent, the vehicle, the host, or the environment, depending on the individual or society's ability and willingness to change one or another of these factors.

In contrast to disease prevention—in which consideration of agents (e.g., bacteria) and vectors (e.g., insect carriers) became prominent in the late nineteenth and early twentieth centuries—until recent years injury control was almost exclusively thought of as prevention of events called "accidents," which were largely believed to be the result of human action or error, luck, or "acts of God." In this chapter, some major characteristics of agents, vehicles, hosts, and environments in processes that kill and disable by injury will be examined. Of particular interest is the degree to which the identified characteristics can be changed to prevent injuries in the environments of free societies with private enterprise market economies.

Preparation of this chapter was supported by a grant from the Henry J. Kaiser Family Foundation.

Injurious Agents and Their Vehicles

The terms we commonly use to describe injurious events (accidents, homicide, suicide) are the descriptors of blame assignment rather than descriptors of agents and vectors. The legalistic orientation toward determining intent and fault in injurious events, for purposes of meting punishment or compensation, for decades retarded the scientific approach to injury control.

The necessary and specific agent of injury is energy transfer (Haddon et al., 1964, p. 28). The energy may be in one or more of a number of forms: electrical, ionizing, mechanical, or thermal (Gibson 1961). The extent of injury to a particular host depends to some degree on host tolerance but mostly on the rate and amount of energy transfer to the host, which is often determined by characteristics of the vehicle. For example, mechanical energy is the agent common to most of the deaths from injuries, which are often thought to be very different in cause (e.g., car crashes, falls, gunshot wounds). In each of these cases it is the rate and amount of the energy at the contact surfaces and the energy-absorbing capabilities of the contact surfaces that determine the extent of injury. Although much of the physics of these characteristics has been known for more than two centuries, it has been applied more often in injury-enhancing ways (e.g., the design and manufacture of more lethal weapons, particularly those of war) than in injury-reducing ways (e.g., energy-absorbing surfaces on and in motor vehicles, floors, playgrounds, and the like). The sharp points and edges commonly seen on table corners, playground equipment, and motor vehicle interiors and front ends are not very different from those on the most ancient of weapons such as stone axes and arrows. They have been recognized for thousands of years as the characteristics of harmful instruments of battle but are not seen as the hazards that they really are in everyday modern use (Haddon 1971).

Since many of the agents of injury go unrecognized as such, it is difficult to classify injuries by the agents and vehicles involved using categories available in compiled statistics. Table 10.1 presents a very crude attempt to do so using fatal injury counts for 1975 from the National Center for Health Statistics (1976). The question marks in the table indicate that some proportion of the total to the far right should be included under the agent specified but the exact number is unknown. Homicides and suicides are included in the table in categories for firearms (29,168), solid or liquid chemicals (3,731), cutting and piercing materials (3,362), strangulation materials (3,661), and unspecified (5,420).

Despite the crudity of the classifications, Table 10.1 is striking in terms of the concentration of large numbers of deaths in a few categories. Mechanical energy accounts for about two-thirds of the deaths, due substantially to motor vehicles. Transportation deaths occur mainly because of mechanical energy transfers in crashing road vehicles or when such vehicles strike pedestrians; however, fuel and other flammable materials are a factor in some of these and other transportation-related deaths.

Describing injuries according to the agents and vehicles involved may appear at this point to be an unnecessary circumlocution. Why not just say that about 46,100 people were killed by motor vehicles, almost 15,000 fell to their deaths, and so on? In much of the remainder of this chapter those more familiar descriptions will be used. But the value of thinking about the common characteristics of the agents and vehicles cannot be overly emphasized. It was the recognition of the

TABLE 10.1 Numbers of People Killed by Violent Energy Transfer and Vehicles* Involved

TYPE OF ENERGY TRANSFER—U.S. 1975

VEHICLES	Mechanical	Thermal	Chemical	Radiation	Electrical	Lack of oxidation	Total
Road vehicles	46,108						46,108
Aircraft	1,552	?					1,552
Railway vehicles	608	?					608
Water vehicles	1,507	?					1,507
Heightened structures (Falls)	14.896						14,896
Firearms and explosives	31,548	?					31,548
Explosives	389	?					389
Miscellaneous cutting and piercing materials	3,502						3,502
Flammable materials		6,071	?				6,071
Drugs and medicaments			3,132				3,132
Other solid or liquid chemicals			5,293				5,293
Gases and vapors			4,272				4,272
Hot substances, corrosive liquid, steam, radiation		?	?	?			209
Electric conductors					1,224		1,224
Water (drowning)						6,640	6,640
Ingested material blocking breathing						3,106	3,106
Other strangulation materials						3,661	3,661
Surgical and medical materials	?	?		?	?	?	3,184
Unspecified	?	?		?	?	?	18,940
							155,842

*Vehicle here is used in the epidemiologic sense to mean the carrier of a potentially harmful agent. These are the latest data available at this writing from the National Center for Health Statistics. Motor Vehicle fatalities increased to more than 50,000 per year by 1978 (National Highway Traffic Safety Administration 1980).

necessary and specific agent common to vehicle crashes and falls—mechanical energy transfer—that led to accelerated work in ways to manage the energy to reduce harm (De Haven 1942). It is the lack of such recognition by those in positions to use the principles of energy management to reduce harm that partly explains why the knowledge is not put to greater use. Lengthy dissertations could be written on how the hazards of electrical energy were recognized and largely controlled while those of mechanical energy have remained a major problem.

We know that if unshielded electrical wiring is touched by someone injury will result; so we require protective shielding on electrical wiring. We should know by now that motor vehicles with designed speed capabilities of more than 100 miles per hour will be driven at high speeds—greatly increasing the hazard to pedestrians and vehicle occupants. Kinetic energy increases exponentially as speed increases linearly. Yet, there are no restrictions on the maximum speed capabilities of motor vehicles. We know that cars with more space for deceleration in crashes are more protective of occupants. Cars with wheel bases (front to rear axle) of 120 inches or more have half the occupant fatalities of cars with wheel bases of 100 inches or less (Robertson and Baker 1976). Yet, much of the reduction in vehicle weights to increase fuel economy has been done by "downsizing" rather than by using lightweight, energy-absorbing materials in vehicles that would save fuel and reduce injuries (O'Neill, Joksch, and Haddon 1974).

The rate at which materials burn and the amount of smoke and toxic gases created in combustion are important factors in fire-related injuries. Consideration of these characteristics has too often been neglected when materials are selected for dwellings, clothing, and transportation vehicles. We know that earthquakes are going to occur on fault lines in geologic structures, but we often ignore that information in designing and constructing multilevel buildings, dams upstream from populated areas, and nuclear reactors in such areas. The resulting disasters are considered to be "natural." Yet, the fact that we have controlled other hazardous agents and vehicles as we have learned their nature should suggest that such disasters are not inevitable.

Host Characteristics and Behavioral Factors

Some host factors are known to increase the severity of injury and the likelihood of survival. And a greater number of behavioral factors (though not necessarily the behavior of the host) may increase or decrease the likelihood of injurious energy transfers.

Although physical conditions such as hemophilia greatly increase the consequences of injury, such conditions are relatively rare and account for a small fraction of the deaths from injuries. Age is a much more important factor. Increase in falls with age among the elderly is thought to be caused by a number of factors: impaired postural reflexes and vision, unstable hip and knee joints, changes in blood pressure or occlusion of arteries affected by certain movements, and brief cessation of heart contractions (Brocklehurst 1978). The ability of certain bones to withstand impacts is less in postmenopausal women (Alfram and Bauer 1962), and the general ability to recuperate from injuries decreases with age. An older person is less likely to survive than the younger person (Baker et al. 1974). The high injury disability and death rates of the young are more a result of quantity and quality of exposure to hazardous agents than a result of relative tolerance of such agents.

Table 10.2 documents the very different age-related patterns of the leading categories of deaths from injuries. The late-teen and young-adult age groups have much higher motor vehicle and firearm death rates than the other groups. In contrast, deaths from injuries that occurred in falls are found mainly among those in their retirement years and increase dramatically among those more than seventy-five years old. Drownings and fire deaths tend to occur more often among the very young and the very old.

Males are more frequently injured than females. This is partially due to differences in exposure, e.g., men travel more than women. However, exposure is not the total explanation of sex differences. Even among very young children, males are more likely to be injured. No doubt cultural norms that encourage greater risk-taking by males are important factors, but the possibility that biological factors contribute to differences in male and female behavior cannot be ruled out (Mazur and Robertson 1972).

The theory that some people are more psychologically prone to behaviors that increase their risk of injury has led to various attempts at identifying higher risk individuals through psychological testing. The results have been disappointing. Correlations with psychological characteristics are so weak and inconsistent that they are of no practical use in screening persons at potentially higher risk (Arbous and Kerrich 1953). Specific conditions that limit performance, such as senility, impaired vision, and neuromuscular problems, may be grounds for limiting certain activities or requiring corrective measures where possible, but these conditions account for a small proportion of the injury problem. The most injury-involved group of the population—young males—is not one that commonly suffers from performance-limiting maladies. Indeed that group is, on average, the most physically well coordinated and skilled in commonly hazardous activities such as driving motor vehicles.

The often heard notion that the driving population is made up of "good drivers" and "bad drivers," the latter group being the problem, is not supported by the evidence. Studies since the 1930s have found that if the 11 percent of all drivers who are in a crash in a two-year period were successfully prohibited from driving in the subsequent two years, 82 percent of the crashes in the subsequent period would nevertheless occur (e.g., Forbes 1939; Stewart and Campbell 1972). The slightly greater involvement of those with previous crashes could simply occur, at least in part, because they drive more, not necessarily because they are "bad drivers." Even if greater than an 18 percent crash reduction could be achieved, practically, 11 percent of drivers could not be removed from the road for two years. Most people who drive are involved, at one time or another, in a crash. About one in fifty to sixty people in the United States each year will be injured in or by a motor vehicle, which means that the lifetime probability of such an injury is very high (National Center for Health Statistics 1979).

Rather than permanent traits, various temporary psychological and physical states—most notably impairment or aggressiveness associated with alcohol—are the major known behavioral contributors to injury. About half the drivers fatally injured in crashes have blood alcohol concentrations of 0.10 percent by weight or higher compared to less than 5 percent of drivers at the same sites, on the same day of the week, at the same time of day, and traveling in the same direction as the fatally injured drivers (McCarroll and Haddon 1962). Similarly, 42 percent of

TABLE 10.2 Deaths Per 100,000 Population by Groups of Injuries and Age—U.S., 1975

	AGE OF DEATH								
	0–4	5–14	15–24	25–34	35–44	45–54	55–64	65–74	75+
Motor vehicles	10.0	5.8	38.7	24.4	19.1	17.2	18.1	22.0	30.7
Firearms									
Unintentional	0.4	1.2	1.9	1.1	1.1	0.9	0.7	0.8	0.5
Homicide	0.4	0.6	9.6	13.4	11.4	7.7	4.8	3.3	1.6
Suicide	0.0	0.2	6.9	8.6	9.2	11.0	11.1	11.0	10.8
Falls	1.2	0.4	1.2	1.4	2.3	4.5	7.1	15.6	59.5
Drowning	4.9	3.2	5.5	2.6	2.1	1.9	1.7	1.8	1.9
Fire	4.7	1.7	1.3	1.6	2.1	3.2	4.3	5.8	10.3

Source: National Center for Health Statistics 1976.

adult pedestrians killed by motor vehicles have such blood alcohol concentrations compared to 8 percent of pedestrians with similarly matched exposure (Haddon et al. 1961). Evidence on adult homicide victims whose behavior probably contributed to their being assaulted (Baker et al. 1971) and adults injured in a variety of other ways (Waller 1972) implicates alcohol as a contributing factor.

Drugs other than alcohol that alter psychological states and motor abilities are likely contributors to injury. Commonly prescribed drugs such as Valium and commonly used nonprescription drugs such as marijuana are know to impair abilities needed in operating motor vehicles (Moskowitz and Burns 1977; Rafaelson et al. 1973). Reliable measures of temporary psychological states, such as stress, preoccupation with matters other than the task at hand, anger (and scores of others), are difficult to obtain reliably and thus have not been adequately investigated. In comparisons of persons who were drivers injured in car crashes and persons who had undergone appendectomies, psychiatrists found no difference in suicidal tendencies. Apparently motor vehicles are not often used in suicide attempts (Tabachnick et al. 1973).

Injury Control Programs

Injury control programs have been mainly directed at changing individual behavior, either by various types of education and persuasion or by laws and administrative rules prohibiting or requiring certain behavior. More recently, some injury control efforts have been aimed at the vehicles of energy transfers and the environment. The relative failures and successes of these programs have led to the specification of some principles that can serve as a guide to future injury control efforts.

The belief that most problems can be solved by educating people in the nature of the problems and by their abilities to handle them is a basic presumption in our culture. Unfortunately, the research evidence sometimes does not support the presumption. While it is evident that certain skills can be taught, such as how to operate a motor vehicle normally and perhaps under emergency conditions, the evidence from high school driver education programs indicates that they have little or no effect on individual risk of crash involvement. However, they increase greatly the numbers of teenagers driving and thus contribute to greater numbers of total crashes that accompany the increased exposure.

Comparisons of people who have had driver training courses in high schools with those who were taught by parents or friends reveal somewhat lower crash rates, a fact that contributed to the widespread adoption of such courses. However, researchers in the 1960s discovered that when statistical controls for miles driven and other factors were examined, the differences in crashes of those with and without high school driver education were greatly reduced (Conger et al. 1977; McGuire and Kersh 1979). Apparently, the people who subsequently drove less and were less likely to crash were the ones who took the course and the course itself had little or no effect.

In the 1970s the adverse effect of driver education was discovered. Researchers in England conducted the first controlled experiment in high school driver education. Rather than being allowed to elect the course, sixteen- and seventeen-year-olds were assigned to the course or to a control group. It was found that those who had the course drove earlier and, although their crashes per mile driven were the same as those who had learned to drive outside school, their total number of crashes was greater (Shaoul 1975). In other words, high school driver education placed greater numbers of young drivers on the roads, earlier than they would ordinarily have driven, without reducing the crashes per mile driven.

Comparisons of fatal crash rates across states in the United States revealed a similar result. The fatal crashes per licensed drivers of sixteen to seventeen years were unrelated to the proportion who had high school driver education, but the fatal crashes per population of sixteen to seventeen year-olds increased greatly as the proportion of that population taking driver education in high school increased. This occurred because increases in licensure of sixteen- to seventeen-year-olds accompanied increases in the proportion who took the high school course (Robertson and Zador 1978). In Connecticut, when state funds for high school driver education were eliminated (for cost cutting, not injury control), about 75 percent of the sixteen- to seventeen-year-olds who were being licensed after taking high school driver education waited until their eighteenth birthday or later to obtain a license in the communities that had dropped the course from the high school curricula. Commensurate reductions in crashes of sixteen- to seventeen-year old drivers were observed (Robertson 1980).

Although not as thoroughly researched, alcohol and drug education in high schools may have contributed to increased use of these substances and to the higher injury rates associated with their use. Comparisons of self-reported drug use and drug selling between students assigned to drug education courses and control groups found greater use of alcohol, marijuana and LSD and more selling of the latter two drugs among those who had the course. Evidence from the research indicated that the education had increased knowledge and, in doing so, had reduced the fear of use of the substances (Stuart 1974).

It is now clear that increasing knowledge or skills does not necessarily reduce risk to the individual and that, to the extent that increased knowledge or skills leads to increased exposure to hazardous or impairing agents and environments, the net effect is to increase rather than reduce injuries. Probably less serious, but troubling because of wasted resources, is the widespread dependence on advertising that is presumed to be effective in changing behavior to decrease risk. The belief that behavioral change can be marketed like soap is not supported by evidence.

The discovery that seat belts properly worn would greatly reduce the severity of injuries in crashes of transportation vehicles (e.g., Stapp 1957) led first to a long struggle to have them routinely installed in vehicles and second, to a variety of attempts to persuade or coerce people into wearing them. Prominent among the attempts at persuasion was the use of advertising in various media. Until the 1970s, enormous amounts of money were expended to develop and distribute such "public service" ads with no attempt to investigate adequately whether or not they were effective. In the early 1970s two independent research projects found advertising ineffective in increasing belt use.

In one study, television ads that were based on factors related to belt use were shown on one cable of a two-cable television system used for marketing studies. The two cables are distributed on a grid in a community so that observed differences in behavior of those exposed to the ads compared to people on the other cable can be attributed to the advertising. In the case of seat-belt use, however, the advertising produced no difference in observed use among those who were exposed to the ads and those who were not in the nine months that the ads were shown or in the month afterward. The ads were shown in prime time some nine hundred times during the nine-month period (rather than the early morning or late at night showing of much public service advertising). The campaign would have cost more than $7 million if done nationally (Robertson et al. 1974b). A second study used a multimedia campaign of varying intensity in two communities and a third community with no advertising. It also revealed no differences in observed belt use among those exposed to the advertising compared to those in the control community (Fleischer 1972).

Advertising is sometimes effective in persuading people to use brand A rather than brand X when there is an existent demand for the product, although the extent of its effectiveness even in such cases is overrated. However, it is quite a different matter to persuade people to do something they would not ordinarily do, particularly when the advertising and the suggested action reveal a vulnerability to hazard that many people do not acknowledge (Robertson 1977a). A more personalized approach—which has had some success in persuading people to obtain immunizations for their children (Robertson et al. 1974a), examinations for cancer (Kegeles 1969), and to reduce heart disease risk factors (Maccoby 1976)—has not been successful in convincing people to use seat belts or other restraining devices in motor vehicles.

A program that included discussions by a health educator with mothers of newborns of the importance of placing infants in protective restraints before they left the hospital had little effect on the correct use of such restraints when the children were observed in vehicles upon return visits to an outpatient clinic. Even when parents were given free infant carriers and literature describing their use, actual use increased only a few percentage points compared to a control group who received no infant carriers or communication (Riesinger and Williams 1978). Attempts by pediatricians during office visits to instruct parents with newborns in the correct use of restraints had substantial initial effect, but after four months the use of the restraints was little more than that of a control group that received no instructions (Riesinger et al 1981).

Laws requiring the use of seat belts by adults and child restraints by small children have had mixed results. Countries such as Australia and New Zealand have been able to maintain high percentages (80 percent or so) of belt use since the countries enacted belt use laws in the early 1970s (Robertson 1978). However, in Ontario, Canada, after the adoption of such a law, belt use increased to more than 70 percent but declined to about 50 percent use within six months. Belt use by teenagers in Ontario didn't increase at all. The relative lack of use among populations that are more frequently involved in severe crashes explains why the death reductions in jurisdictions with belt-use laws have not been as substantial as predicted from the known effectiveness of belts when used voluntarily. Australia experienced a 20 percent reduction in occupant deaths in urban areas and a 10 percent reduction in rural areas associated with the belt-use law (Foldvary and Lane 1974). While that is a significant accomplishment, it is less than half of the expected reduction based on the known effectiveness of properly used belts (Robertson 1976a).

In the case of child-restraint use laws, the first U.S. state to enact such a law—Tennessee—included an exemption that would allow a child riding on the lap of an adult to travel unrestrained. This law has the potential for increasing childhood injuries in crashes. In a frontal crash the weight of the adult's body adds to the force of the child's striking interior surfaces, but, thus far, there has been little change in on-lap travel. Child restraint use, however, increased from 8 percent before to twenty-nine percent two years after the Tennessee law (Williams and Wells 1981.)

The effectiveness of a law depends on its enforceability, its actual enforcement, and the ability of the social system to retain the law if it provokes strong opposition. Laws regarding behavior that is easily observed are more enforceable than laws regarding behavior that is difficult to observe. Police officers can easily observe motorcycle-helmet use, and airline attendants can easily observe seat-belt use; enforcement of laws in these instances results in virtually 100 percent usage. Enforcement of belt-use laws for cars and trucks requires more careful observation and use is less. In contrast, amount of alcohol use by drivers can only be detected accurately by analysis of blood or breath samples. This partially explains the fact that even in areas of special enforcement, only about one in two thousand drivers impaired by alcohol by legal definition is actually arrested for the offense (National Highway Traffic Safety Administration 1974). Special "crackdowns" on alcohol use may produce temporary reductions in fatal crashes, as did the British Road Safety Act of 1968, but when drivers learn that the probability of being arrested has not been increased nearly to the extent claimed by authorities, the death rate soon returns to previous levels (Ross 1973). The threat of severe penalties, such as jail sentences for drunk driving in the Scandinavian countries, has had no discernible effect on death rates in those countries (Ross 1975), at least partially because of the problem of detection that precedes judicial processing.

In the United States enforcement of drunk driving laws has been retarded by widespread plea bargaining that often leads to convictions for "reckless driving" and less severe penalties than those for driving while impaired (DWI) by alcohol. Many police officers, jaded by observing such processes, soon learn that it is useless to charge a driver with DWI.

Even when laws directed at individuals are effective, political action by those affected by the laws may result in their repeal. Motorcycle helmet use laws resulted in a 30 percent reduction in motorcyclists' deaths in states that enacted such laws compared to states without them (Robertson 1976b). Most U.S. states adopted such laws in the 1960s in response to federal safety standards that required these laws in order for states to receive certain funds. However, when a few remaining states resisted the standards, the Congress removed the requirement rather than allow the Department of Transportation to withhold the funds. Subsequently, a minority of motorcyclists in more than half the states persuaded their state legislatures to repeal the laws (Baker 1980), despite the fact that public opinion surveys found that the majority of the public in general and motorcyclists in particular were in favor of the retention of the laws (Insurance Institute for Highway Safety 1978). In those states that repealed the laws, motorcyclists' deaths increased, on average, to about the same degree as they had declined when the laws were adopted (Watson et al. 1980).

Notable exceptions to this litany of failure of behavioral control strategies to reduce injuries have occurred in organizations that have substantial administrative control over individuals. A program using information on alcohol, along with administrative review and psychiatric referral, for airmen in alcohol-related crashes at an air force base resulted in reduced injury rates compared to those at a base without such a program (Barmack and Payne 1961). In workplaces, frequent management and union attention to practices that reduce injuries has had some apparent success (Cohen, Smith, and Anger 1979). Particularly impressive is the use of information feedback to workers. For example, demonstrating to workers their amount of hearing loss in a noisy environment resulted in greatly increased use of earplugs compared to the use of earplugs by groups that were not provided such feedback (Zohar, Cohen, and Azar 1980). However, studies of the prevention of injury to the lower back caused by lifting concluded that neither special selection of workers for lifting tasks nor special training in lifting heavy objects were effective in injury reduction. "Designing the job to fit the worker" was found to be the effective strategy (Snook, Campanelli, and Hart 1978).

Engineering for people rather than engineering of people by changing their behaviors has the better record of success. Injury control programs that automatically protect people without their having to take any special action (Haddon and Goddard 1962) are the most successful. In the 1960s the federal government adopted performance standards for vehicles sold to the federal government, and beginning with the 1968 models, these and some additional standards were applied to all new cars sold in the United States. Among these initial standards were requirements that steering assemblies absorb energy on impact rather than spearing drivers in the chests as they commonly did in frontal crashes of prior models. Improvements in the energy-absorbing capability of windshields and some other interior surfaces and in door latches to reduce ejection in crashes were among other important standards. Comparisons of occupant death rates in vehicles that met the initial standards with those that did not revealed a 23 percent reduction in deaths associated with the standards (Robertson 1977b). Children's falls from windows in multilevel dwellings decreased by 50 percent when New York City required landlords to install devices on windows that make it difficult for young children to crawl out the windows (Spiegel and Lindeman 1977).

Recent research has found that rear-end vehicle crashes that occur when the front vehicle has its brakes applied were reduced 50 percent by placing a rear brake light on top of the trunk more centrally in the sight of the following driver (Reilly, Kurke, and Buckenmaier 1980). This suggests that subtle aspects of the environment contribute to perceptual problems and that the environment can be changed to reduce those problems.

Even in instances where injury is intentional, the reduction in lethality of the agent prior to its use can be successful. In Birmingham, England, the reduction of carbon monoxide in coal gas used for cooking and heating (and sometimes for suicide) resulted in a reduction of suicides without commensurate increases by other methods (Hassel and Trethowan 1972). Changing the environment to automatically protect people from current leading forms of energy damage is analogous to approaches used successfully for decades in other areas of public health (e.g., pasteurized milk, water treatment) and in other areas of potential injury (e.g., preuse insulation on electrical wiring and fuses that automatically break electrical circuits when they are overloaded). The success of these approaches in reducing human damage is based on three factors: recognition of the damaging agent involved; effectiveness of the technology in reducing the damage of the agent; and just as important, recognition that many of the people exposed to the hazard will not be sufficiently aware of the hazard or mentally, physically or physiologically in a position to avoid it at a crucial moment. Control of injuries that continue to plague us will depend on recognition of these factors by people in the position to systematically survey the options available and adopt those that are shown by competent research to be effective in injury reduction.

Injury Control Strategies

Specification of hazardous energy transfers and their vehicles has led to the identification of a rich variety of strategies to reduce not only injuries but all hazardous conditions. William Haddon, Jr., has enumerated ten such strategies (Haddon 1970, 1973, 1975, 1980) and their possible use has been elaborated by a number of writers (e.g., Feck, et al. 1977; Baker and Dietz 1979).

The following is a list of the Haddon strategies and some illustrations regarding their application to leading categories of injury:

1. "Prevent the creation of the hazard in the first place."
   - Do not manufacture handguns.
   - Do not use flammable materials in dwelling units, furniture, and clothing.
2. "Reduce the amount of the hazard brought into being."
   - Alter transportation from cars, trucks, and vans to less hazardous buses, trains, and commercially scheduled airplanes.
   - Reduce the designed top speed capability of motor vehicles.
   - Reduce the hardness of playground surfaces.
   - Reduce the temperatures to below scalding levels in water heaters.
3. "Prevent the release of the hazard that already exists."
   - Increase road skid resistance.
   - Keep all guns locked up at supervised hunting and target ranges.
   - Use childproof matches and lighters.
4. "Modify the rate or spatial distribution of release of the hazard from its source."
   - Increase the use of child restraints and seat belts in transportation vehicles.
   - Build or modify storm drains to make them adequate to prevent the accumulation of water.
   - Make containers for hot liquids (cups, coffee, and tea pots, etc.) with large bottoms and centers of gravity arranged so that likelihood of spillage is minimized.
5. "Separate, in time or in space, the hazard and that which is to be protected."
   - Build pedestrian overpasses and underpasses on roads that are convenient to use.
   - Designate separate roads for travel by cars and heavier vehicles.
   - Build playgrounds at a distance from streams or reroute streams from play areas.
6. "Separate the hazard and that which is to be protected by interposition of a material barrier."
   - Install air bags that automatically inflate between vehicle occupants and interior surfaces in motor vehicle crashes of injurious severity.
   - Install energy-absorbing material around fixed objects on roadsides where vehicles most commonly leave roadsides and hit the objects.
   - Install fences around swimming pools with gates that cannot be opened by children. Similarly, cover wells, irrigation and drainage ditches and culverts in ways that children cannot enter them.

7. "Modify basic qualities of the hazard."
   • Use utility and light poles along roadsides that "break away" when struck by motor vehicles.
   • Prohibit hard surfaces, sharp points, and edges on interiors of transportation vehicles and on bicycles, stairs, furniture, toys, sports equipment, playground equipment, and the like.
   • Develop emetic coatings for appropriate drugs in amounts that have no effect at prescribed doses but induce vomiting at poisonous doses.
8. "Make that to be protected more resistant to damage from the hazard."
   • Provide blood clotting factors to persons with hemophilia.
   • Install gas tanks and containers that do not rupture in crashes for hazardous materials in transport.
   • Perform warm-up exercises before vigorous exercise and athletic competition, and prohibit schools from allowing those in athletic competition to play when hurt or out of condition.
9. "Counter damage already done by environmental hazard."
   • Provide for strategically placed quick rescue and emergency medical response.
   • Increase emergency roadside telephones.
   • Restore severed limbs.
10. "Stabilize, repair, and rehabilitate the object of the damage."
   • Increase special job training for the disabled.
   • Provide for rehabilitative and cosmetic surgery.
   • Make burn centers accessible to those who need them.

It should be clear from the discussion of the necessary and specific causes of injury, i.e., energy transfers, and the variety of strategies to prevent the harm associated with them, that the continued injury and disability toll is not for lack of knowing what can be done about it.

Choices to Reduce Harm

The adoption of effective means to reduce injury does not immediately follow from the identification of the general strategy or a specific tactic to implement it. Most of the hazardous energy transfers that produce injury involve products and processes that, in many industrialized societies, are bought and sold in relatively free market economies. Both the general ideology supporting individual responsibility for market decisions and the interests of the producers and processors in maintaining exclusive control over their business decisions contribute to substantial resistance and sometimes recalcitrance in adopting changes to make the products and processes less hazardous.

Some economists and others argue that consumers decide by their choices in the marketplace what they are willing to pay for the amount of risk they are willing to take and that governmental or other intervention should be limited to informing consumers of the risks associated with particular products (Mills 1978). This assumes that those who make the purchases are the same individuals who are taking the risks and that the marketplace will always provide the less hazardous processes and products so that consumers have the choice. Neither of these assumptions is valid.

Even if they could be taught the hazards involved; children are often not party to the purchase of their cribs, toys, or the vehicles in which they will ride. One study of people in car crashes estimated that about 80 percent of the people of all ages injured as drivers and passengers were not the original purchasers (Baker 1979), and certainly the pedestrians and bicyclists struck by motor vehicles seldom had a say in the hardness or shape of the vehicle surfaces that determine the severity of their injuries.

And even in the face of consumer demand, some companies have refused to use less hazardous products or processes. For example, air bags that inflate automatically in moderate to severe front and front angle crashes, reducing severe and fatal injuries to front seat occupants by 40 percent, were developed and tested in the 1960s and were available for production in the early 1970s. Edward N. Cole, then president of General Motors, promised the government that air bags would be standard equipment on all 1975 GM cars. However, they were offered only on a few of the most expensive Buicks, Cadillacs, and Oldsmobiles during 1974–76 with virtually no advertising of their availability. Consumers attempting to purchase them experienced substantial dealer resistance and delays in delivery (Karr 1976). Despite this, about 10,000 air-bag-equipped cars were sold to the public in addition to the 1,750 sold to private fleets previously. Following Cole's retirement, air bag production was phased out.

One possible reason for Cole's interest in the air bag was marketing research by GM that indicated that consumer demand for the air bag would be high. That research done in 1971 did not come to public light until 1979. New car buyers were shown air bags and automatic belts in cars, films showing air bags in crash tests, and favorable and adverse publicity on air bags. The marketing report states that "consumers are *overwhelmingly in favor of some kind of occupant restraint system*...., (are) not scared of the Air Cushion concept and that *the Air Cushion Restraint concept is a viable one* to the consumers....After seeing prices quoted—which were higher than those which respondents expected, and had a slight dampening effect—the Air Cushion still maintained half of all preference votes" (General Motors Corporation 1971, emphasis theirs).

Why Cole's successors ignored that research and GM executives phased out the air bag is not known publicly but it was most certainly not because of lack of consumer demand. Marketing research by GM throughout the 1970s found results similar to the original study. Yet GM announced in 1980 that automatic seat belts would be the only means used to meet a federal crash protection standard for 1982 in larger model cars, despite the fact that its own marketing research found these belts less acceptable to many consumers than air bags and despite the fact that benefits of airbags would greatly exceed their costs (U.S. Department of Transportation 1976).

It is evident that markets are imperfect in protecting the public's health and this imperfection is justification for government intervention in the marketplace. But considerable dispute is generated over justification of particular interventions in cost-benefit terms. Theoretically, benefit/cost analysis is a comprehensive accounting of the effects of any action, including noneconomic as well as economic costs and benefits. Partly because many health benefits are intangible, use of so-called benefit/cost analysis by governmental and corporate technocrats in regulatory proceedings is often narrowed to whether the costs to the economy to withdraw or modify a product will be offset by a return to the economy resulting from reduced disease and injury. The assumption prevalent in those proceedings that costs should not exceed such benefits is a value judgment that denies the American people the right, if they so choose, to contribute more through their government or marketplace purchases to the reduction of disease and injury than the diseased and injured would return to the economy. If that value judgment were uniformly applied, there would be no public funds expended for medical care of persons who suffer spinal cord injuries (Kraus, et al 1975) or permanent brain damage (Annegers and Kurland 1979) serious enough that their economic productivity, if any, would not produce a net return to the economy.

The fact that public monies are expended to care for those who will not provide an economic return is evidence that the society does not demand that the measurable benefits of such care exceed the costs, at least when the persons affected are readily identifiable. However, in the case of most injuries, the affected lives are called "statistical lives" by economists, meaning that the individuals who will be affected are not identifiable before the fact. Since it is difficult to deny treatment after a person is harmed, a disproportionate share of resources may be allocated to treatment when prevention could have been accomplished at less cost.

Even if the analysis is focused only on the more easily measured costs and benefits, the estimates in common dollar terms have not been very successful. Government and business estimates of the cost of modification of injurious processes and products to make them less hazardous sometimes differ manyfold. By using accounting methods that amortize certain costs over unreasonably short periods—as automobile manufacturers did in estimating costs of increased automatic crash protection (U.S. Department of Transportation 1976)—a strategy can be made to look much less cost beneficial than it actually would be if implemented. The estimates of dollar value of benefits are even more questionable because they require the placement of dollar values on a life, an eye, or an arm and the discounting of those dollars over time based on various assumptions.

In use, benefit/cost analysis has become a part of the costs, and delays in ameliorative action have been fostered by requirements for such analyses. For example, more than one-third of motor vehicle fatalities and severe injuries occur when vehicles leave the road and strike rigid objects such as trees, utility poles, and bridge abutments that are often only a few inches or feet from roadsides; this situation would not be tolerated if the objects were on airport runways. Removal of the objects, changing those that can be modified to break away on impact, or the placement of energy absorbing materials between them and the road would greatly reduce the human damage. However, known principles for selecting sites for ameliorative action have not been widely applied. Research has established that severe fixed object crashes are many times more likely within five hundred feet of curves greater than six degrees on downhill grades of greater than 2 percent on nonlocal roads, and that such sites are only a small proportion of such roads (Wright and Robertson 1976). Rather than use that information to arrive at an estimate of average costs and benefits for modification of groupings of sites with common characteristics, highway departments have expended substantial sums for roadside surveys of all fixed objects and a benefit/cost analysis of fixing *each site* that is considered. Thus, there are fewer dollars in the budget for actual ameliorative modifications.

Rather than such uses of benefit/cost analysis, more emphasis on the effect of current government expenditures on health and the effect of government policy on private expenditures for health could possibly result in a more rational allocation of resources and commensurate improvements in health. Such analyses would undoubtedly reveal great differences in the cost per life saved among various governmental life-saving efforts. Sometimes economic or other conditions prevent the expansion of the funds available. In such instances the expenditure of funds in areas that would save the most lives per dollars allocated would be rational. However, the legislative and bureaucratic tendencies to avoid transfer of funds from established programs contributes to the continuing irrationality in resource allocation.

There is, of course, an upper limit on the resources that can be used to prevent or treat injury and disease without severely reducing other human needs. And where alterations in the structure and use of goods might result in chronic unemployment or other undesirable consequences, planning for retraining or appropriate compensation of those adversely affected may be, in itself, a necessary health measure.

However, injury control is seldom a zero sum game in which one person can benefit only at the expense of others. Many changes to make products and processes less hazardous can be made as part of periodic redesign that would occur in any case. Indeed the cost may be less if, for example, a car has a lightweight steering assembly that absorbs energy in frontal crashes rather than a heavy, rigid steel pole that spears drivers in the chest. Health and safety regulations can lead to increased employment and profits in industries that design, tool, manufacture, and sell an altered or new product. There is no adverse effect of such changes in an expanding economy where sales are growing, although there will be some redistribution in size of the pieces of the expanding pie. A survey of new-car buyers indicated that they would be willing to add much more to their new-car payments to save certain numbers of statistical lives than the added protection would cost. This willingness was not related to their own perception of personal vulnerability in a crash (Robertson 1977a). In fact, the savings in car insurance premiums for personal injury and liability would offset the additional costs of currently proposed improvements during the lifetime of the average vehicle (*Federal Register* 1977). Who pays what costs and who benefits are the major questions that make health and safety regulation a matter of controversy.

Roles for Health Professionals

The major emphasis in this chapter on automatic, technological amelioration of injurious hazards and the role of government in inducing the use of such approaches is not intended to relieve the health professional from roles in injury reduction. Greater care should be exercised in prescribing psychoactive or other possibly impairing drugs. Although the effectiveness of emergency medical response and physical repair and rehabilitation is often limited by the severity of the trauma, there is evidence that probability of survival is related to quickness of response and diagnostic and treatment skill (Gertner, et al 1972). One obvious role for the health professional is to push for improved medical emergency systems and organizational arrangements that increase the frequency of treatment of particular types of injuries by those most skilled to handle them (Franklin and Boelp 1980).

Although the effect of patient education has been found limited, it may be possible to influence those behaviors that must occur only once or infrequently to be effective. Such behaviors include turning water heater thermostats to less than scalding temperatures, installing smoke detectors in houses, and purchasing a more crashworthy motor vehicle.

Less obvious are the substantial roles that health professionals can occupy in the political process necessary to reduce hazards in the environment. Health professionals enjoy an almost unique prestige in their communities and in the nation. That prestige coupled with solid information can be a powerful force in bringing to the attention of politicians and regulatory agencies the need for ameliorative changes. Working individually and through professional associations, health professionals have increasingly brought recognition to injuries as a major threat to public health and some of the strategies available to reduce them.

REFERENCES

ALFRAM, P., and BAUER, G. C. H. 1962. Epidemiology of fractures of the forearm: a biomechanical investigation of bone strength. *Journal of Bone and Joint Surgery* 44: 105.

ANNEGERS, J. F., and KURLAND, L. T. 1979. The epidemiology of central nervous system trauma. In *Central nervous system trauma research report*, ed. G. L. Odom, Bethesda, Md.: National Institute of Neurological and Communicative Disorders and Stroke.

ARBOUS, A. G., and KERRICH, J. E. 1953. The phenomenon of accident proneness. *Industrial Medicine and Surgery* 22: 141–48.

BAKER, S. P. 1979. Who bought the cars in which people are injured? An exploratory study. *American Journal of Public Health* 69: 76–77.

———. 1980. On lobbies, liberty, and the public good. *American Journal of Public Health* 70: 573–75.

———, and DIETZ, P. E. 1979. Epidemiology and prevention of injuries. In *Management of trauma* (3d ed.), ed. G. D. Zuidema et al. Philadelphia, Pa.: W. B. Saunders.

BAKER, S. P., et al. 1971. Tattoos, alcohol, and violent death. *Journal of Forensic Sciences.* 16: 219–25.

BAKER, S. P., et al. 1974. The injury severity score: a method for describing patients with multiple injuries and evaluating emergency care. *Journal of Trauma* 14: 187.

BARMACK, J. E., and PAYNE, D. E. 1961. The Lackland accident countermeasure experiment. *Highway Research Board Proceedings* 40: 513–22.

BROCKLEHURST, J. 1978. Aging and health. In *The social challenge of aging*, ed. D. Hobman. New York: St. Martin's Press.

COHEN, A.; SMITH, M. J.; and ANGER, W. K. 1979. Self-protective measures against workplace hazards. *Journal of Safety Research* 11: 121–31.

CONGER, J. J., et al. 1966. Effects of driver education: the role of motivation, intelligence, social class and exposure. *Traffic Safety Research Review* 10:67–71.

DE HAVEN, H. 1942. Mechanical analysis of survival in falls from heights of fifty to one hundred and fifty feet. *War Medicine* 2: 586–96.

FECK, G., et al. 1977. *An epidemiologic study of burn injuries and strategies for prevention.* New York: New York State Department of Health. *Federal Register.* 1977. 42: 34290–99.

FLEISCHER, G. A. 1972. *An experiment in the use of broadcast media in highway safety.* Los Angeles, Calif.: University of California, Department of Industrial and Systems Engineering.

FOLDVARY, L. A., and LANE, J. C. 1974. The effectiveness of compulsory wearing of seat belts in casualty reduction. *Accident Analysis and Prevention* 6: 59–81.

FORBES, T. W. 1939. The normal automobile driver as a traffic problem. *Journal of General Psychology* 20: 471–74.

FRANKLIN, J., and BOELP, A. *Shocktrauma.* New York: St. Martin's Press.

General Motors Corporation. 1971. *Consumer opinions relative to automotive restraint systems.* Advertising and Merchandising Section, Report #71-27p.

GERTNER, H. R., et al. 1972. Evaluation of the management of vehicular fatalities secondary to abdominal injuries. *Journal of Trauma* 12: 425.

GIBSON, J. J. 1961. The contribution of experimental psychology to the formulation of the problem of safety: a brief for basic research. In *Behavioral approaches to accident research.* New York: Association for the Aid of Crippled Children.

HADDON, W., JR. 1970. On the escape of tigers: an ecologic note. *American Journal of Public Health* 60: 2229–34.

――――. 1971. Testimony in *Hearings on automobile insurance reform and cost savings* (pt. 1), 92d Cong. 1st sess.

――――. 1973. Energy damage and the ten countermeasures strategies. *Journal of Trauma* 13: 321–31.

――――. 1975. Reducing the damage of motor vehicle use. *Technology Review* 77: 53–59.

――――. 1980. Advances in the epidemiology of injuries as a basis for public policy. *Public Health Reports* 95: 411.

――――, et al. 1961. A controlled investigation of the characteristics of adult pedestrians fatally injured by motor vehicles in Manhattan. *Journal of Chronic Diseases* 14: 655–678.

――――, and GODDARD, J. L. 1962. An analysis of highway safety strategies. In *Passenger car design and highway safety.* New York: Association for the Aid of Crippled Children and Consumer's Union of the U.S.

――――; SUCHMAN, E. A.; and KLEIN, D., eds. 1964. *Accident research: methods and approaches.* New York: Harper and Row.

HASSEL, C., and TRETHOWAN, W. H. 1972. Suicide in Birmingham. *British Medical Journal* 1: 717.

Insurance Institute for Highway Safety, Michigan motorcyclists favor helmet use. 1978. *The highway loss reduction status report,* 30 October, 1978.

KARR, A. R. 1976. Saga of the air bag, or the slow deflation of a car-safety idea. *Wall Street Journal* 11 November, 1976.

KEGELES, S. S. 1969. A field experimental attempt to change beliefs of women in an urban ghetto. *Journal of Health and Social Behavior* 10: 115.

KRAMER, L. 1978. Automakers under pressure to become innovative again. *Washington Post,* November 26, 1978, Fl.

KRAUS, J. F., et al. 1975. Incidence of traumatic spinal cord lesions. *Journal of Chronic Diseases* 28: 471–92.

McCARROLL, J. R., and HADDON, W., JR. 1962. A controlled study of fatal automobile accidents in New York City. *Journal of Chronic Diseases* 15: 811.

MACCOBY, N. 1976. The Stanford heart disease prevention program. In *Consumer behavior in the health marketplace,* ed. I. M. Newman. Lincoln, Nebr.: University of Nebraska Center for Health Education.

McGUIRE, F. L., and KERSH, R. C. 1969. *An evaluation of drivers education.* Berkeley, Calif., University of California Press.

MAZUR, A., and ROBERTSON, L. S. 1972. *Biology and social behavior.* New York: Free Press.

MILLS, E. S. 1978. *The economics of environmental quality.* New York: Norton.

MOSKOWITZ, H., and BURNS, M. 1977. The effects of alcohol and Valium, singly and in combination, upon driving related skills performance. *Proceedings of the Twenty-first Conference of the American Association for Automotive Medicine.* Morton Grove, Ill.: American Association for Automotive Medicine.

National Center for Health Statistics. 1976 *Vital statistics of the United States, 1975.* Vol. 2: *Mortality.* Washington, D.C.: U.S. Department of Health, Education, and Welfare.

――――. 1979. *Acute conditions, incidence and associated disability—U.S. 1977-78.* Washington, D. C.: U.S. Department of Health, Education, and Welfare.

National Highway Traffic Safety Administration. 1974. *Alcohol safety action projects, evaluation of operations.* Vol. 2: *Detailed analysis.* Washington, D.C.: U.S. Department of Transportation.

———. 1980. *Fatal accident reporting system: 1978 annual report.* Washington, D.C.: U.S. Department of Transportation.

O'NEILL, B.; JOKSCH, H.; and HADDON, W., JR. 1974. Relationships between car size, car weight and crash injuries in car-to-car crashes. *Proceedings of the Third International Congress on Automotive Safety.* Washington, D.C.: Government Printing Office.

PERLMAN, J. 1978. Pinto trial: complex plan spelled success. *Los Angeles Times,* section X, p. 1, 17 September, 1978.

RAFAELSON, O. J., et al. 1973. Cannabis and alcohol: effects on simulated car driving. *Science* 179: 920–23.

REILLY, R. E.; KURKE, D. S.; and Buckenmaier, C. C., Jr. 1980. *Validation of the reduction of rear-end collisions by a high-mounted auxilliary stop lamp.* Washington, D.C.: U.S. Department of Transportation.

RIESINGER, K. S., and WILLIAMS, A. F. 1978. Evaluation of programs designed to increase the protection of infants in cars. *Pediatrics* 62: 280–87.

RIESINGER, K. S., et al. 1981. The effect of pediatricians counseling on infant restraint use. *Pediatrics* 67: 201–6.

ROBERTSON, L. S. 1976a. Estimates of motor vehicle seat belt effectiveness and use: implications for occupant crash protection. *American Journal of Public Health* 66: 859–64.

———. 1976b. An instance of effective legal regulation: motorcyclist helmet and daytime headlamp laws. *Law and Society Review* 10: 467–477.

———. 1977a. Car crashes: perceived vulnerability and willingness to pay for crash protection. *Journal of Community Health* 3: 136–41.

———. 1977b. State and federal new-car safety regulation: effects on fatality rates. *Accident Analysis and Prevention* 9: 151–56.

———. 1978. Automobile seat belt use in selected countries, states, and provinces with and without laws requiring belt use. *Accident Analysis and Prevention* 10: 5–10.

———. 1980. Crash involvement of teenaged drivers when driver education is eliminated from high school. *American Journal of Public Health* 70: 599–603.

———, et al. 1974a. *Changing the medical care system.* New York: Praeger.

———. 1974b. A controlled study of the effect of television messages on safety belt use. *American Journal of Public Health* 64: 1071–80.

ROBERTSON, L. S., and BAKER, S. P. 1976. Motor vehicle sizes in 1,440 fatal crashes. *Accident Analysis and Prevention* 8:167–75.

ROBERTSON, L. S., and ZADOR, P. L. 1978. Driver education and fatal crash involvement of teenaged drivers. *American Journal of Public Health* 68: 959–65.

ROSS, H. L. 1973. Law, science, and accidents: the British Road Safety Act of 1967. *Journal of Legal Studies* 2: 1–78.

———. 1975. The Scandinavian myth: the effectiveness of drinking and driving legislation in Sweden and Norway. *Journal of Legal Studies* 4: 285–310.

SHAOUL, J. 1975 *The use of accidents and traffic offenses as criteria for evaluating courses in driver education.* Salford, England: University of Salford.

SNOOK, S. S.; CAMPANELLI, M. S.; and HART, J. W. 1978. A study of three preventive approaches to low back injury. *Journal of Occupational Medicine* 20: 478–81.

SPIEGEL, C. N., and LINDEMAN, F. C. 1977. Children can't fly: a program to prevent childhood morbidity and mortality from window falls. *American Journal of Public Health* 67: 1143–47.

STAPP, J. P. 1957. Human tolerance to deceleration. *American Journal of Surgery* 93: 734–40.

STEWART, J. R., and CAMPBELL, B. J. 1972. *The statistical association between past and future accidents and violations.* Chapel Hill, N.C.: University of North Carolina Highway Safety Research Center.

STUART, R. B. 1974. Teaching facts about drugs: pushing or preventing? *Journal of Educational Psychology* 66: 189–201.

TABACHNICK, N., et al. 1973. *Accident or suicide?* Springfield, Ill.: Thomas.

U.S. Department of Transportation. 1976. *The secretary's decision concerning motor vehicle occupant protection.* Washington, D.C.: U.S. Department of Transportation.

WALLER, J. A. 1972. Nonhighway injury fatalities—1. The roles of alcohol and problem drinking, drugs and medical impairment. *Journal of Chronic Diseases* 25: 33–45.

WATSON, G. F., et al. 1980. The repeal of helmet laws and increased motorcyclist mortality in the United States, 1975-1978. *American Journal of Public Health* 70:579–85.

WILLIAMS, A. F., and WELLS, J. K. 1981. The Tennessee child restraint law in the third year. *American Journal of Public Health* 71: 163.

WRIGHT, P., and ROBERTSON, L. S. 1976. Priorities for roadside hazard modification: a study of 300 fatal roadside object crashes. *Traffic Engineering* 46: 24–30.

ZOHAR, D.; COHEN, A.; and AZAR, N. 1980. Promoting increased use of ear protectors in noise through information feedback. *Human Factors* 22: 69–79.

Chapter 11

Environment and Disease

Paul W. Brandt-Rauf
I. Bernard Weinstein

OVER THE PAST CENTURY there has been a significant shift in the pattern of disease in the industrialized areas of the world. Morbidity and mortality due to acute episodes of infectious disease have given way largely to the noninfectious, chronic, or degenerative disorders such as arteriosclerotic cardiovascular disease, cancer, and chronic obstructive pulmonary disease. This shift may be partially attributed to advances in public health and the medical sciences—for example, improved hygiene and nutrition as well as identification and treatment of infections. The complex interactions involved in the process of modernization and industrial development have apparently also contributed to the increased incidence and mortality of the chronic diseases. One significant way in which this development has altered the pattern of disease is via the effect of industrialization on the environment in which we live—the pollution of the air we breathe and the water we drink, the materials we come in contact with at home or work (drugs, foods, cosmetics, solid wastes, pesticides, noise, radiation and energy-related hazards, consumer products, industrial chemicals), alterations in diet (fat content, etc.) and the way we live (social contacts, behavioral changes, urbanization, psychological stresses). This chapter focuses on the way this new environment has contributed to human disease states. It is difficult in a brief review to be all-inclusive. In general, we have concentrated on the chemical and physical hazards around us and omitted or mentioned only in passing other environmental aspects such as general nutrition, microbes, and personal and psychosocial factors.

The significance of these hazards can be better appreciated when one considers that each year hundreds of new chemicals in commercial quantities are being added to the tens of thousands already in our environment and the fact that the vast majority of these have been inadequately tested for their effect on human health. However, adequate testing of a new chemical to determine whether it may present a health hazard is easier said than done. In-vitro and animal testing can be questioned as to their relevance to human exposure situations. Epidemiologic studies of human populations are plagued by confounding variables and limited

The authors are indebted to the Institute of Medicine of the U.S. National Academy of Sciences for permission to publish Tables 11.1 - 11.8. These are taken intact from a report, *Costs of Environment-related Health Effects*, Institute of Medicine, Washington, D.C., 1981.

sensitivity, not to mention time and cost constraints. Time constraints can be particularly vexing. For instance, when dealing with an acute, high-dose exposure to a toxic material, the response usually follows rapidly, facilitating the detection of the cause-effect linkage. However, many environmental exposures occur at low dosages and over long periods of time and may produce delayed toxic effects with a long latent period. This tends to obfuscate the cause-effect relationship and delay the evaluation of potential health hazards. Furthermore, only rarely in environmental medicine is one dealing with a single, isolated exposure that leads to a unique disease entity. Usually the disease under consideration results from complex interactions between environmental and host factors, and the patient under consideration has been exposed to a multitude of potentially contributory toxins that can interact in a variety of ways. Thus, some hazardous materials can substitute equally for others producing approximately the same toxic effect. Some factors have an additive effect when combined exposure occurs; others can act synergistically producing an effect in combination that is greater than that produced with either alone; still others can act antagonistically. Such multifactor interactions can have more than scientific or medical significance. Consider, for example, the legal assessment of liability in the case of an asbestos worker who smokes cigarettes and develops lung cancer in light of the fact that there is a synergistic relationship between asbestos exposure and smoking in the causation of lung cancer. There are still other complicating variables that need to be considered. There are variables related to the material itself including: the physical form (e.g., mercury vapor is more dangerous than the liquid); the chemical form (e.g., organic mercury is more dangerous than inorganic); and the concentration and total amount. There are variables related generally to the environment such as duration and frequency of exposure, route of contact and alterations in transit (e.g., absorption; chemical reaction as in the oxidation and hydration of sulfur dioxide to sulfuric acid). Then there are variables related to the exposed individual that affect susceptibility. These include: absorption and distribution mechanisms; metabolism; routes of excretion; and variation in age, sex, nutritional status, activity status, immunologic status, hormonal status, reproductive status, behavior, psychological status, genetic factors, preexisting disease and previous exposure.

With these constraints in mind, this chapter will review environmental factors which have been associated, with varying degrees of certitude, with specific pathological conditions. We discuss these aspects with respect to specific organ systems and disease states. An alternative approach is to consider a given chemical or physical agent and list its effects on various organ systems and diseases. For the latter approach the reader is referred to the tables at the end of this chapter. The last section of the chapter deals in some detail with a disease of immense importance: cancer. This disease cuts across organ system boundaries in its significance and pathologic mechanisms and is becoming increasingly recognized as having a major environmental component in its etiology.

Environment and Pulmonary Disease

Of all the organ systems, the respiratory tract is probably the best studied in terms of environmentally related disease. This is understandable when one considers the lungs' unique interface between internal and external environments: the huge alveolar surface area (70m²); the thinness (less than 1 μm) of the alveolar wall which allows for efficient gas exchange but presents a relatively ineffective barrier to inhaled toxins; and the exposure to 10,000 to 20,000 liters of respired air per day (Lee 1972). It is small wonder that this system is the most common route of entry for hazardous substances in the workplace and also a major route of exposure for the general population. The result is a major burden of disease ranging from asthma (affecting about 2 percent of the U.S. population) to chronic bronchitis (afflicting an estimated 20 percent of adult males) to lung cancer (the most common malignancy in the U.S. male). Extensive information has accumulated linking cigarette smoke, occupational inhalants, and air pollution to the pulmonary disease process (U.S. Department of Health, Education and Welfare 1964, 1972; Morgan and Seaton 1975; Aharonson, Ben-David, and Klingberg 1976). Thus, for example, it is generally accepted that cigarette smoking is linked to lung cancer and chronic obstructive pulmonary disease and that dust exposure in the workplace can lead to pneumoconioses such as silicosis and asbestosis. The data on general air pollution are more difficult to interpret, but the increased mortality rates during air pollution disasters in the Meuse Valley, Donora, Pennsylvania, and London certainly provide incriminating evidence (Bouhuys 1974).

There are several ways of classifying respiratory toxins and diseases. One useful method is by mechanism of pulmonary injury. However, first it is necessary to consider those agents that do not produce direct injury to the lungs, but that subvert lung function by depriving body tissues of oxygen. They may do this directly by occupying space like the simple asphyxiants, carbon dioxide and certain aliphatic hydrocarbons. Alternately, agents can be chemical asphyxiants such as carbon monoxide, which displaces oxygen from hemoglobin, or cyanide, which interferes with cytochrome oxidase.

Many agents of acute lung injury produce irritation, inflammation and/or increased vascular permeability. They can produce rhinitis, pharyngitis, laryngitis, tracheobronchitis, pneumonitis, and pulmonary edema; their site of action generally is dependent upon their solubility. This category includes chlorine, ammonia, nitrogen oxides, sulfur dioxide, ozone, phosgene, and hydrogen chloride (Brain 1977; Said 1978).

Agents of acute disease can also act via an allergic mechanism and produce an asthmatic airway obstruction. Thus, "industrial asthma" has been noted in workers exposed to proteases of the bacterium *Bacillus subtilis* in enzyme detergents and to toluene diisocyanate used in the manufacture of polyurethane plastics (Gibson et al. 1976). Besides the common plant and animal allergens, general air pollution also apparently contains components that can initiate or exacerbate bronchoconstrictive disease as, for example, in "Tokyo-Yokohama asthma" (Lopez, Wessels, and Salvaggio 1977).

Allergic mechanisms can also contribute to more chronic lung disease. For example, extrinsic allergic alveolitis may follow exposure to a broad range of bacterial and fungal products found on various organic dusts. This is the mechanism of disease in farmer's lung, bagassosis, mushroom picker's lung, maple bark stripper's lung, and cheese washer's lung, to name a few (Pepys 1969). A similar reaction to antigenic or nonantigenic histamine stimulators in cotton, flax, and hemp dust probably explains byssinosis, a bronchoconstrictive syndrome that progresses to chronic lung disease (Hitchcock, Piscitelli, and Bouhuys 1973).

Chronic lung injury can also arise from factors that produce persistent inflammation or proteolysis. This can lead to the cellular hyperplasia and increased mucus production of chronic bronchitis or the dissolution of elastin and collagen and destruction of lung architecture characteristic of emphysema. For example, certain compunds in cigarette smoke suppress elastase inhibitors and may contribute to emphysema (Carp and Janoff 1978). Other offenders may include oxides of sulfur and nitrogen (Bouhuys 1974).

Another class of agents produces increased connective tissue and scarring possibly by stimulating the release of mediators from macrophages (Allison 1974). These produce the fibrosing alveolitides or pneumonoconioses primarily due to exposure to inorganic dusts in an occupational setting. Included are coal, kaolin, talc, silica, and asbestos. A special case is beryllium, which produces chronic inflammation in the form of granulomata and eventual fibrosis (Morgan and Seaton 1975).

Many environmental agents have been implicated as causes of human lung cancer. These include cigarette smoke, asbestos, chromates, nickel, cobalt, uranium, arsenic, acrylonitrile, bischloromethyl ether (BCME), chloroprene, coke oven emissions, cadmium, and vinyl chloride (Brain 1977; U.S. Department of Health, Education and Welfare 1979a). The most important of these is, of course, cigarette smoking, which accounts for about 40 percent of all deaths from cancer in American males. With the rapid increase in cigarette smoking in American women there is currently an alarming increase in lung cancer in women. The marked increase in lung cancer in asbestos workers who are also cigarette smokers, provides a striking example of synergy in the interaction between two environmental agents.

Inhalation of environmental contaminants can produce a variety of other effects. For example, zinc and copper vapors can produce a febrile syndrome with mild pneumonitis referred to as metal fume fever. Altered susceptibility to infection due to diminished macrophage function and mucociliary transport may be produced by inhalants such as tobacco smoke, nitrogen oxide, and ozone. Lung injury can also result from agents that are not inhaled; exposure to X rays can cause radiation pneumonitis and fibrosis and ingestion of paraquat can cause pulmonary edema (Lee 1972).

Environment and Skin Disease

Consonant with its primary role as a barrier and mediator of exchanges between the body's internal milieu and the external surroundings, the skin occupies a uniquely important position with regard to environmentally related disease. Despite its multiple adaptive mechanisms and defenses, the skin remains quite vulnerable to assault due to its large surface area, which is in constant and direct contact with the environment. For this reason, environmental skin disease continues to be a major public health problem. For example, dermatoses initiated by occupational exposure alone account for 25 to 80 percent of all occupational diseases according to workmen's compensation statistics, resulting in a total cost of over $100 million a year in the United States (Suskind 1977; Sauer 1980). Environmental exposure to ultraviolet radiation is the single most important factor in the pathogenesis of skin cancer, which is the most common form of cancer among Caucasian populations (Emmett 1975). Thus, environmental skin conditions represent a significant disease burden for the American population. These diseases cover a wide range of dermatologic problems including: direct mechanical or physical injury; primary irritant dermatitis; allergic dermatitis; systemic disorders with dermatologic manifestations; cancers; and miscellaneous disorders like chloracne, alopecia, and pigmentary changes.

Mechanical and physical agents that cause environmental skin disease include friction, pressure, vibration, electricity, heat and cold, moisture, radiation, and certain fibrous materials. For instance, heat can produce thermal burns directly, or it can injure indirectly by stimulating eccrine sweat glands leading to prickly heat or miliaria rubra. Cold can cause frostbite and in combination with moisture can lead to pernio and immersion foot. Radiation can produce numerous skin changes including erythema, hyperpigmentation, atrophy, telangiectasia, and tumors. When asbestos spicules penetrate the skin they can produce so-called asbestos warts, and fiberglass can cause mechanical irritation and pruritus (Moschella, Pillsbury, and Hurley 1975).

Many chemicals have a primary irritant effect on the skin. These agents can produce their effect by direct corrosion, dissolution of fat and keratin, desiccation, denaturation of protein, hydrolysis, oxidation and inflammation. They produce a reaction in 100 percent of the population on first exposure if applied in high enough concentration and for a long enough period of time. Included in this category are strong acids and alkalis, phenol, ammonia, kerosene, turpentine, carbon tetracholoride, mercury and chromium salts, soaps and detergents, cutting oils, styrene, paints and solvents, to name a few (Moschella, Pillsbury, Hurley 1975).

Allergic reactions to environmental chemicals are differentiated from primary irritant effects by the fact that they do not occur in all exposed individuals. In addition, because there is a latent period for the development of immunologic response, there is no immediate reaction on first exposure. Cutaneous allergic conditions can be mediated by humoral antibodies. This is usually the case when the antigen gains access to the body by the respiratory or gastrointestinal route, for example with certain foods, drugs, pollens, and danders. Alternatively, an allergic contact dermatitis can develop when the antigen is absorbed through the skin, conjugates with protein and stimulates a cell-mediated (T lymphocytes) rather than a humoral (circulating antibody) immunologic response. Included in this category are: metal compounds like chromium salts, beryllium, mercury salts, nickel and cobalt; plant products like poison ivy, cashew shell oil used in the manufacture of plastics and wood products; dye products such as the derivatives of paraphenylenediamine in photographic developers; plastic and resin products such as the butyl catechol stabilizer in polystyrene and aliphatic amines used as epoxy resin hardeners; and agricultural chemicals like the carbamate pesticides (Fisher 1973; Moschella, Pillsbury, and Hurley 1975; Suskind and Majeti 1976).

Certain environmental agents produce systemic disease with dermatologic manifestations. For example, Yusho disease, caused by ingestion of PCB-contaminated rice oil, is charcterized by neurologic, hepatic, and teratologic effects along with acne and hyperpigmentation (Kuratsune et al. 1972). Porphyria cutanea tarda is a hepatic disease associated with uroporphyrinuria and skin changes including dermal fragility, pigmentary alteration and hypertrichosis. It has been associated with occupational exposure to chlorinated phenols, ingestion of hexachlorobenzene contaminated wheat, and exposure to polychlorinated biphenyls and dioxins (Cam and Nigogosyan 1963; Bleiberg et al. 1964).

Skin tumors, including keratoacanthomas, basal cell carcinomas, squamous cell carcinomas and melanomas, have been associated with ultraviolet radiation primarily from excessive sunlight exposure (Giese 1970; Emmett 1973, 1975). Polycyclic aromatic hydrocarbons, inorganic arsenic compounds, and ionizing radiation have also been linked to human skin cancer (Suskind 1977).

Chloracne results from chemical stimulation of the epithelium of the sebaceous duct which proliferates clogging the orifice and leading to the production of comedones. Chemicals implicated include chlorinated naphthalenes, diphenyls and dioxins, cutting oils and coal tar fractions. Chloracne is an important diagnostic marker of toxicity from these agents. Other chemicals that attack the pilosebaceous unit can cause hair loss by altering the metabolism of the follicular epithelium. Examples are thallium and dimers of chloroprene found in the rubber industry (Suskind 1977). Lastly, there are environmental disturbances of pigmentation. Hyperpigmentation can be caused by radiation especially in conjunction with coal tar products or certain essential oils. Hypopigmentation can occur from exposure to monobenzyl ether of hydroquinone, an antioxidant in rubber, or to some phenol-detergent germicides (Kahn 1970; Suskind 1977). Altered skin color can also be caused by the dermal deposition of extraneous materials as occurs in silversmiths with argyria.

Environment and Disease of the Digestive System

The digestive system encompasses the alimentary canal (oral cavity, pharynx, esophagus, stomach, small intestine, colon, and rectum) as well as the accessory organs (salivary glands, gall bladder and bile ducts, liver, and pancreas). Along with the skin and the respiratory system, the alimentary canal is a major site of contact and absorption of environmental agents. The lumen of the canal may be considered an extension of the external environment in intimate contact with the body's internal environment, with access via ingestion. The anatomic and physiologic mechanisms that make the digestive system ideally suited for the absorption of food stuffs and essential nutrients also allow for considerable uptake of potentially toxic materials. These mechanisms include: (1) an enormous absorptive surface area (due to the valvulae conniventes, the villi and the microvilli, the small intestinal area alone is about 250 square meters); (2) the systems for facilitated or active transport which carry nutrients as well as toxins from the lumen of the intestine into the blood stream; and (3) the rich supply of blood vessels and lymphatics in the gut wall for transporting absorbed materials. There are several other important factors that affect the relationship of environmental exposures to digestive disease. For example, substances that are inhaled may interact with the gastrointestinal tract after muco-ciliary transport and swallowing. The enzyme content or acidity of gastrointestinal secretions can influence absorption; acids are generally absorbed in the stomach and bases in the small intestine due to the effect of pH on ionization, with unionized and nonpolar substances passing more easily across the cell membranes. The acidity of the contents of the stomach has also been implicated in the endogenous formation of nitrosamine carcinogens from dietary nitrite and secondary amines. The status and activity of enteric flora can also have profound effects on toxic interactions. Many environmental agents are excreted by the liver into the bile in the form of nonresorptive glucuronide conjugates; however, bacterial glucuronidase can hydrolyze the conjugates to absorbable forms establishing an enterohepatic circulation of the agent, prolonging its action and enhancing its toxicity. Bacterial action can have a direct effect on ingested substances converting innocuous materials into toxins, as in the case of nitrate conversion to nitrite. Transit time through the gut, which depends in part on dietary factors such as fiber content, is important in terms of limiting contact time and absorption of environmental agents and may play a role in colonic cancer and diverticular disease (Schedl 1977).

There are several specific disease states of the alimentary canal that have been linked to environmental factors. These include: acute esophagitis from ingestion of corrosives; peptic ulcer disease from stress; acute gastritis from alcohol or smoking; nontropical sprue from the gliadin fraction of wheat gluten; and diverticular disease and spastic colon and stress. The most important single condition related to environmental exposure is cancer.

Cancers of the alimentary tract make up approximately 25 percent of all cancers and account for about eighty thousand deaths per year in this country, the majority being from cancer of the colon and rectum. Many factors ranging from diet to occupation have been implicated. For example, increased dietary fat has been associated with colo-rectal cancer in human populations and increases the induction of colon cancer in rodents. The fact that within a few generations Japanese who immigrate to the United States lose the high incidence of gastric cancer characteristic of Japan and acquire the high incidence of colon cancer characteristic of the United States strongly implies environmental factors, probably dietary, in the causation of these two diseases. Alterations in gastrointestinal microflora may play a role by metabolizing bile acids or ingested materials into carcinogens. Mutagens have been detected in human feces and may play a role in colon cancer. Vitamin A levels may be crucial to epithelial differentiation. The role of food additives and chemical residues in food, such as artificial coloring agents, hormones, and pesticides, has been questioned. Nitrosamines, formed by the interaction of nitrites and amines in the stomach, are known to be potent carcinogens. Other factors that have been implicated include: personal habits such as smoking and drinking, occupational exposures such as asbestos and acrylonitrile, broiling foods at high temperatures that can produce mutagenic substances from the pyrolysis of amino acids, and radiation.

There are many other environmental agents that do not produce particular disease states of the digestive tract but that do contribute to nonspecific syndromes of gastrointestinal upset. The symptoms produced may include abdominal pain, distention, nausea, vomiting, diarrhea or constipation, and malabsorption. Several metals can produce these effects. For example, mercury can produce excess salivation and inflammation along the whole length of the alimentary canal. Cadmium can cause nausea, vomiting, salivation, diarrhea, cramps, and depression of the absorption of calcium, phosphorus, copper, glucose, and alanine. Lead poisoning is known to produce a characteristic colic along with nausea, vomiting, and constipation. Organophosphorus insecticides can increase salivation, muscle tone, and peristalsis via cholinergic stimulation causing nausea, vomiting, cramps, diarrhea, tenesmus, and involuntary defecation. Other offenders include biological toxins, for example, dinoflagellate-contaminated shellfish, methanol, ethanol, and radiation (Krawitt 1977; Schedl 1977; Hammond and Beliles 1980; Murphy 1980).

Of the accessory organs of digestion, the liver is clearly the most important in terms of environmental interactions. Besides its role in biliary excretion and the enterohepatic circulation noted above, the liver is anatomically situated such that most of the venous drainage of the gut along with its absorbed nutrients and toxins must traverse the liver before gaining access to the systemic circulation. This, along with the liver's key role in intermediary metabolism via its inducible enzymatic processing systems, grants this organ a unique position in the human environmental response that includes both toxification and detoxification of absorbed substances. Hepatotoxins can produce a variety of acute and chronic malfunctions of the liver. Some compounds produce disease by interfering with the hepatic blood circulation. Beryllium and dimethylnitrosamine cause hemorrhagic necrosis, and the pyrrolizidine alkaloids of Crotalaria used in "bush tea" cause a characteristic veno-occlusive lesion. Most environmental agents that affect liver cells produce zonal hepatocellular alterations without an inflammatory reaction; the alterations may be accumulation of lipids (fatty change), degeneration (necrosis), or both. For example, ethionine and cerium produce fatty change; tannic acid, Amanita toxin, beryllium, and urethane produce necrosis; carbon tetrachloride, chloroform, trichloroethylene, aflatoxin, and phosphorus produce both. Other forms of acute hepatotoxic injury include intrahepatic cholestasis with jaundice and hepatic necrosis with an inflammatory reaction reminiscent of viral hepatitis. These reactions are different from the former group in that incidence after exposure is low, dose dependency does not exist, and the lesions are not reproduced in experimental animals. Environmental agents in these categories are almost exclusively therapeutic drugs and range from antipsychotics and antimicrobials to diuretics and anesthetics. Other potential acute hepatotoxins that operate by various mechanisms include vinyl bromide, methyl mercury, manganese, arsenic, chromium, cadmium, antimony, selenium, and flame retardants. The two most significant forms of chronic liver injury are cirrhosis and cancer. The chronic morphological alteration of the liver seen in cirrhosis can be produced in animals by a variety of toxins including carbon tetrachloride and aflatoxin; however, the single most important cause of this condition in man is ethanol consumption. Cancers of the liver, including malignant hepatomas and hemangiosarcomas, have been linked by animal data or epidemiologic studies to a variety of environmental agents, namely, aflatoxin, arsenic, cycasin, safrole, dialkyl nitrosamines, organochlorine pesticides, PCBs, vinyl chloride, and thorium. Finally, it should be noted that there are many substances that are not directly hepatotoxic but that alter the physiologic response of the organism to toxins and carcinogens via the induction of hepatic enzymes; these include drugs, DDT, benzene and toluene (Reynolds 1977; Plaa 1980). Current studies strongly implicate chronic infection with hepatitis virus as playing a causal role, perhaps in association with aflatoxin or other chemical toxins, in the causation of liver cancer in parts of Asia and Africa. This may provide an interesting example of viral-chemical interaction in disease causation.

Due to the excretion of toxins in the bile and the role of the gallbladder in the concentration and storage of bile, it might be expected that the extrahepatic biliary system would be an important site for toxic interactions. However, very little attention has been paid to the role of environmental agents in common biliary disease states, such as gallstone formation and cholecystitis, aside from drugs and dietary factors that may be lithogenic. Epidemiologic surveys have indicated that work in particular industries increases the risk of developing gallbladder cancer (automotive, rubber, textile, and metal-fabricating industries) and bile duct cancer (aircraft, automotive, chemical, rubber, and wood-finishing industries), but the particular carcinogens involved remain to be identified (Krain 1972; Fraumeni 1975).

Similarly, much work needs to be done in elucidating the role of the environment in pancreatic disease. It is well known that alcohol ingestion is an important contributing factor to the development of pancreatitis, but a third of cases of acute pancreatitis are of unknown etiology, and it is reasonable to suspect that some of these are environmentally induced. Numerous chemicals, including acetylaminofluorene, aflatoxin, carbon tetrachloride, and cobalt, have been shown to produce acinar cell damage in animals, and several drugs are known to cause pancreatitis in humans. Carcinoma of the pancreas may also have a significant environmental contribution. Workers exposed to naphthylamine or benzidine, workers in certain metal industries, chemists, and cigarette smokers all have an increased risk of death from pancreatic cancer. Dietary factors, particularly fat intake, have also been implicated in this disease (Fraumeni 1975; Longnecker 1977). Further studies on the etiology of pancreatic cancer are urgently needed because of the recent increased incidence of this disease and its generally very poor prognosis. Little is known of environmental influences on the salivary glands, although cancer of the salivary glands has a suspected link to radiation exposure and work in the rubber industry (U.S. Department of Health, Education and Welfare 1979a).

Environment and Renal Disease

Although not directly exposed to environmental assaults like the skin or lungs, the kidneys and the urinary tract are particularly susceptible to damage by environmental toxins once they gain access to the circulation. This is due to several factors. First, although making up less than 1 percent of the body weight, the kidneys receive 20 to 25 percent of the resting cardiac output; this means that a large fraction of any toxin in the circulation can reach the kidneys rapidly. Second, the normal renal functions of filtration, reabsorption, and secretion can lead to the accumulation of substances in the renal parenchyma or tubular lumen until very high toxic levels are reached. Third, other normal tubular functions such as acid-base balancing can cause toxic interactions. Finally, since the kidneys have a high metabolic activity, they tend to be sensitive to metabolic poisons (Foulkes and Hammond 1975; Finn 1977). Thus it is not surprising that environmental toxins have been implicated in many forms of renal damage from acute tubular necrosis to chronic glomerulonephritis. Toxins have been noted to act at all levels of the nephron including the vasculature, the glomerulus, the proximal and distal tubules, the collecting system and the renal interstitium; in addition, renal damage can be produced indirectly as a result of injury to other parts of the body.

The first class of environmental renal toxins has, as one mechanism of injury, an effect on the renal vasculature and blood supply. For example, one way mercury compounds may produce kidney damage is by increasing renal resistance to blood flow, leading in some cases to renal shut down; experimental administration of mercuric chloride has been shown to produce preglomerular vasoconstriction and/or postglomerular vasodilatation in rats, lending support to this hypothesis (Flanigan and Oken 1965; Valek, Broulik, and Taborsky 1969). Other agents that can affect renal blood flow include cadmium, carbon tetrachloride, and radiation.

Certain types of renal toxins can influence the filtering mechanism of the nephron by attacking the glomerulus. Thus, the disease Goodpasture syndrome has been noted in humans following inhalation exposure to various hydrocarbons. It is hypothesized that the mechanism of action is via alteration of the antigenicity of the glomerular basement membrane proteins, thus leading to fixation of immunoglobulin and complement and resultant inflammatory damage (Beirne and Brennan 1972). Other agents, for example bismuth tartrate and mercuric chloride (Karelitz and Freedman 1951; Troen, Kaufman, and Katz 1951) may impair glomerular permeability, presumably at the level of the basement membrane, leading to a nephrotic syndrome characterized by proteinuria, hypoproteinemia, hypercholesterolemia, and edema.

A wide variety of substances can affect the renal tubules by several different mechanisms. In some cases remote injury in the body can produce a toxic effect on the tubules. For example, occupational exposure to arsine gas can cause severe hemolysis, hemoglobinuria, tubular obstruction by hemoglobin casts, acute renal failure, and death (Fowler and Weissberg 1974). Similarly, epidemic myoglobinuria (called Haff disease) due to the ingestion of fish contaminated by industrial toxins can cause kidney damage (Berlin 1948). Tubular obstruction can also occur by more direct mechanisms as in the case of calcium oxalate crystallization in the tubules following exposure to and metabolism of ethylene glycol (Friedman et al. 1962). The most common site of action of renal toxins is the tubular epithelium. Substances implicated include: organic solvents like carbon tetrachloride, toluene, and trichlorethylene; heavy metals like mercury, antimony, arsenic, bismuth, cadmium, lead, and uranium; pesticides like parathion, chlordane, and paraquat; and diagnostic and therapeutic agents like iodinated dyes, antibiotics, and ionizing radiation (Finn 1977). Several different disease states in addition to acute renal failure can occur with exposure to a wide variety of toxins. Thus, proximal tubule poisons like lead, uranium, mercury, cadmium, or bismuth can produce aminoaciduria, glucosuria, and phosphaturia in a Fanconi-type syndrome by blocking reabsorptive transport. Blockage of proximal tubule secretion of uric acid by lead or cadmium may be linked to gout. Cadmium can also cause a low molecular weight proteinuria possibly by altering proximal tubule reabsorption or metabolism of protein. Distal tubule syndromes include failure of sodium conservation in lead intoxication and failure of water balancing in uranyl exposure (Adams, Harrison, and Scott 1969; Emmerson, Mirosch, and Douglas 1971; Foulkes and Gieske 1973; Foulkes and Hammond 1975).

The distal urinary collecting system including the renal pelves, ureters, and bladder are targets for certain important environmental carcinogens. Occupational exposure to a number of aromatic amines has been associated with the development of such cancers probably due to the high concentrations of these substances achieved by the excretion process (Foulds 1975). Lastly, it should be noted that diseases of the renal interstitium like chronic interstitial nephritis can be produced by several environmental agents including lead and X rays and kidney cancer has been linked to exposure to coke oven emissions (U.S. Department of Health, Education and Welfare 1979a).

Environment and Disease of the Nervous System

The importance of environmental insults to the nervous system cannot be overemphasized due to the crucial functions performed by this system. Although the neurologist's view that all other organs exist only to support the central nervous system (CNS) may be somewhat limited, society's increasing acceptance of brain death as the point at which life ceases lends credence to the notion of placing great value on the preservation of nervous system function. Furthermore, the fact that neurons are postmitotic, and thus once lost are not replaceable, underscores this theme. Even though the nervous system can exhibit recovery from tissue loss on the basis of plasticity of organization and redundancy of function, the loss of neurons represents at the minimum a permanent decrement in functional reserve capacity. Also, although in some ways more protected than other organ systems by the presence of a blood-brain barrier, there are many toxins that can cross the barrier, the barrier varies in permeability from area to area in the brain and the nervous system has its own particular sensitivity, being highly dependent on blood supply and the delivery of nutrients and oxygen for example. In addition, a number of environmental toxins are lipophilic and might therefore concentrate in lipid-rich areas of the brain. For these reasons there has been increasing concern over the role of environmental agents in disorders of the nervous system. This interest has extended beyond specific toxic states to include more subtle behavioral alterations and the possible contribution to more common conditions such as cerebrovascular disease and presenile dementia; for example, the role of aluminum in Alzheimer's disease, a major public health problem, is expected to receive increased attention in the future (Paulson 1977).

No single classification scheme of environmental nervous system toxins is entirely satisfactory. Agents can affect sensory, motor, or integrative functions or combinations; the central nervous system or peripheral nervous system or both; white matter, gray matter or both; neurons, glial elements or both. One useful method is based on primary toxic action and includes agents causing anoxia, agents damaging myelin, agents causing peripheral axonopathies, agents damaging peripheral perikarya, agents affecting the neuromuscular junction, and agents causing localized CNS lesions (Norton 1980).

Anoxic damage to the nervous system has several subtypes. Anoxic anoxia indicates primary oxygen deficiency with adequate blood supply and usually leads to damage in area H_1 of the hippocampus. This is relatively rare since prolonged anoxia eventually interferes with cardiac function leading to poor perfusion. However, anoxic anoxia can be seen in high-altitude low-oxygen exposures, in barbiturate coma, with simple asphyxiants, and in carbon monoxide poisoning. In addition, the latter can produce ischemic anoxia when blood flow is compromised. This has also been termed pallidal toxicity because of primary damage to the globus pallidus as well as the subthalamus, fascia dentata and area H_2 of the hippocampus. Furthermore, repeated or prolonged anoxia, as can occur in carbon monoxide coma, may damage the blood-brain barrier causing a leukencephalopathy with demyelination and diffuse sclerosis of the white matter. Clinically, this is usually a delayed fatal toxicity occurring as a relapse more than five days after recovering from acute carbon monoxide poisoning. It may represent a severe autoimmune status spongiosus and is characterized by sudden confusion, disorientation, ataxia, incoordination, fever, and weakness (Lapresle and Fardeau 1967). Anoxia can occur by interference with cell metabolism when both oxygen supply and perfusion are adequate. This is called cytotoxic anoxia or striatal toxicity since damage is primarily to the corpora striata as well as the cortical gray matter, area H_1 of the hippocampus, thalamus, and substantia nigra. Unlike other forms of anoxia, which have greater effects on the neurons, cytotoxic anoxia usually damages the oligodendroglia first. Cyanide and azide produce this effect by inhibiting cytochrome oxidase (Miyoshi 1967; Bass 1968).

Demyelinating agents selectively injure the oligodendroglia of the central nervous system and/or the Schwann cells of the peripheral nervous system. Peripheral myelin loss predominantly of motor fibers to the upper extremities is characteristic of chronic adult lead poisoning. Lead can also cause central demyelination, encephalopathy, and permanent cerebral damage, particularly in children. Thallium poisoning in man produces damage to myelin sheaths resembling lead neuropathy with resultant ataxia, painful paresthesias, and weakness (Cavanagh et al. 1974). Other demyelinating agents that can affect man, producing both central and peripheral effects, include isoniazid, triethyltin, and tellurium. Hexachlorophene has been shown to affect myelin in experimental animals, and, because of its wide use as an antiseptic, concern has been raised about possible human effects (Norton 1980).

Environmental agents can produce neuropathies not only by damaging myelin but also by direct injury to the axon. Damage to axons usually propagates back toward the cell body and hence these are called dying-back neuropathies, and they characteristically have a delayed onset dependent upon dose. Chronic ethanol consumption and occupational exposure to acrylamide or carbon disulfide have been shown to produce this type of defect. Two industrial solvents, n-hexane and methyl-n-butyl ketone, produce an identical axonopathy via a common metabolite, 2,5-hexanedione, that affects peripheral sensory and motor fibers and the long ascending and descending pathways of the spinal cord (Norton 1980). Organophosphorus compounds, including triorthocresyl phosphate, diisopropyl fluorophosphate, leptofos and mipafox, produce a delayed axonopathy possibly by phosphorylation of a neurotoxic esterase (Johnson 1975).

Although it is not always possible to be certain because of the complex relationship between perikarya and axon, it seems likely that primary damage to the cell body with centrifugal propagation down the axon is much less common than the dying-back injury noted above. However, it probably does occur with certain environmental insults. Organomercurials cause this type of injury primarily to the sensory cell bodies of the dorsal root ganglia, perhaps due to a defective blood barrier at this point (Cavanagh 1977).

The neuromuscular junction is particularly vulnerable to assault by environmental toxins. This is the site of action of many biological agents, including: botulinum toxin; tetrodotoxin, which comes from improperly prepared puffer fish; ciguatoxin from contaminated fish; and saxitoxin, which poisons man when he consumes shellfish contaminated by the offending dinoflagellate. Lead can also affect the neuromuscular junction (Manalis and Cooper 1973; Oehme, Brown, and Fowler 1980).

Certain toxins produce lesions in a limited anatomic distribution due to, among other things, variations in the blood-brain barrier or biochemical specialization of the cells in the area. For example, organic mercury produces necrosis of the granule cell layer of the cerebellum and focal atrophy of the cortex with sensory disturbances, ataxia, and dysarthria. Inorganic mercury produces erethismus mercurialis affecting the cerebral and cerebellar cortex and the autonomic nervous system leading to tremor, salivation, and psychological disturbances (Norton 1980). Manganese is another classic example causing neuronal degeneration in the basal ganglia and cerebellum producing the extrapyramidal signs of parkinsonism and the emotional changes of pseudobulbar palsy (Cotzias 1958).

Some environmentally related disorders of the nervous system are not encompassed by this classification scheme. An example is provided by effects on the special senses, especially sight and hearing. Practically every part of the eye is adversely affected by some environmental insult. Examples include: the lacrimator effect of peroxyacetyl nitrate in photochemical smog; the corrosion of the cornea by acids and alkalis; effects on the aqueous outflow system, e.g., the open-angle glaucoma of epidemic dropsy caused by contamination of cooking oil by argemone seeds; alteration of the autonomic activity of the iris, e.g., in "corn-picker's pupil," a mydriasis caused by working in cornfields containing jimson weed with subsequent parasympatholytic exposure; cataracts of the lens from drugs, radiation and thallium; changes of the retina and choroid such as occur in retrolental fibroplasia from high oxygen tension exposures in neonates; and damage to the ganglion cell layer and optic nerve as occurs with methanol, carbon disulfide and thallium (Potts and Gonasun 1980). Hearing ability can be permanently compromised by exposure to noisy environments; organic mercury compounds affect the eighth cranial nerve causing loss of hearing and vestibular function. Organic mercury exposure can also have sensory effects on smell and taste. Heavy industrial exposure to cadmium can cause anosmia (Hammond and Beliles 1980). So-called general depression of the CNS is a functional state normally associated with general anesthetics that can be closely mimicked by overexposure to many industrial solvents via ingestion or inhalation. Symptoms include loss of concentration, sleepiness, disorientation and unconsciousness. Alcohol abuse and its usually concomitant dietary insufficiencies represent a major environmental public health problem with multiple serious nervous system effects ranging from peripheral neuropathy to cerebellar deterioration. The list of other, less well known environmental influences on the nervous system is too extensive to consider in entirety, but includes: seizure disorders from chronic borax intoxication; marijuana amotivational syndrome; hypervitaminosis A and cerebral edema; vibration and entrapment neuropathies; radiation myelitis; trichloroethylene and polyneuritis cranialis; methyl bromide and myoclonus; the multiple effects of kepone and various halogenated polycyclic compounds; and, finally, the association of brain tumors with experimental nitrosourea and occupational vinyl chloride exposures (Paulson 1977).

Environment and Reproductive Dysfunction

The barriers to successful reproduction are enormous. For example, it has been estimated that 10 to 20 percent of married couples are absolutely infertile, up to 70 percent of fertilized eggs perish and at least 6 percent of all newborns demonstrate a genetic or developmental abnormality, a third of which are major malformations accounting for 20 percent of all neonatal deaths (Witschi 1970; Persaud 1977; Berg 1979). Compounding these problems are the more subtle defects that contribute to behavioral changes or increased susceptibility to cancer or other diseases in the offspring. The health burden is staggering. For instance, the cost of genetic disease alone has been placed at 25 percent of the national expenditure for health services in the United States (Lederberg 1971). The loss in life years due to birth defects has been placed at greater than 35 million, dwarfing other major diseases (U.S. Department of Health, Education and Welfare 1974). Environmental agents have been shown to act deleteriously at all the various steps in the reproductive process. Thus, they can diminish libido, promote impotence, or decrease fertility;

they can increase pregnancy wastage through implantation defects, abortions, or stillbirths; they can be mutagenic or teratogenic, causing structural, functional or metabolic defects; they can act as transplacental carcinogens, influence behavioral development, or increase disease susceptibility. The exact contribution of environmental agents to the overall burden is not clear. Estimates for developmental defects place the contribution from environmental causes at 4 to 7 percent. However, the etiology of about two-thirds of cases is unknown, and the contribution of the environment to this large fraction is obviously unknown as well (Berg 1979). Furthermore, the significance of reproductive effects from environmental agents is heightened by the risk they pose to future as well as present generations through mutation and chromosome alteration, thus representing a progressive accumulation of morbidity and mortality in our progeny.

The first category of agents that impair reproduction, i.e., those that decrease fertility or potency, include many environmental factors from stress and infections to drugs and radiation. Only a few examples can be considered here. For instance, organochlorines can decrease fertility in animals, and similar effects may explain reproductive dysfunctions of operating room personnel exposed to trichlorethylene. Occupational exposure to synthetic estrogens diminish libido and fertility in males (Stellman 1979). Sperm abnormalities have occurred in lead, chloroprene, and DBCP workers (Lancranjan et al. 1975; Sanotskii 1976; Whorton et al. 1979).

Several environmental agents have been noted to cause pregnancy wastage. Nutritional deficiencies and excesses, thermal stress, physical trauma, and ionizing radiation have been implicated in this category. Pregnancy failure can apparently be caused by various drugs and chemicals, including anticancer agents, hypoglycemics, and carbon monoxide, the latter possibly being responsible for increased pregnancy loss in heavy smokers (Wilson and Fraser 1977). Anesthetic gases, chloroprene, vinyl chloride, and other hydrocarbons may increase the miscarriage rate; even if the exposure is to the male there may be an increased spontaneous abortion rate among unexposed wives (Infante et al. 1976; Stellman 1979).

The distinction between mutagen and teratogen and between this category and the others is often unclear since teratogenesis can arise from mutation, and both mutations and teratogenic changes can, for example, increase pregnancy wastage. In addition, teratogenesis can probably also occur through nonmutational mechanisms. A multitude of environmental mutagens have been identified (Vogel and Rohrborn 1970). Perhaps the best studied has been ionizing radiation (BEIR 1972). Other classes include: agricultural chemicals, industrial compounds, food and feed additives, naturally occurring substances, drugs and pollutants (Wilson and Fraser 1977). The list of potential environmental teratogens is also long. Ionizing and nonionizing radiation, air pollutants, temperature extremes, and nutritional imbalances from vitamin A to zinc have all been implicated. Drugs have been extensively studied. Other suspected environmental chemicals include: natural substances, insecticides, herbicides, fungicides, metals, solvents, detergents, food additives, tobacco smoke, PBBs, PCBs, and others (Nishimura and Tanimura 1976; Wilson and Fraser 1977).

The last group are the agents that increase disease susceptibility in the offspring such as transplacental carcinogens. The classic example is DES, which causes an increase in vaginal cancer in the daughters of mothers who took it (Herbst, Ulfelder, and Pozkanzer 1971). The incidence of cancer may be increased in the children of male hydrocarbon workers (Fabia and Thuy 1974). In fact, it has been suggested that a person's lifetime risk of developing cancer may be conditioned by prenatal exposures (Berg 1979). Much research remains to be done on the role of such exposures in the development of cancer and other chronic disease states. It should also be noted that environmental agents can directly cause cancers in adults in organs related to reproduction. Thus, for example, cadmium has been linked to prostatic malignancy and radiation to breast cancer (U.S. Department of Health, Education and Welfare 1979a).

Environment and Hematologic Disorders

The blood and the bone marrrow, which is the site of formation of the circulating cellular elements of the blood in the adult, are important in environmental toxicology for several reasons. First, the blood is the transport system of the body. Once an environmental agent is absorbed, the blood, including the plasma fluid, dissolved proteins and cells, plays a crucial role in distributing the agent around the body to target organs and sites of storage, metabolism, and excretion. Second, the blood serves several vital physiologic functions that can be altered by environmental influences. This is particularly true of the formed elements of the blood. Thus, specific agents acting on the bone marrow or in the circulation can affect erythrocytes, interfering with the transport of oxygen to the tissues and carbon dioxide back to the lungs, leukocytes, interfering with the body's defense mechanisms directed against foreign organisms or other extraneous environmental materials, and thrombocytes, interfering with clotting. Finally, the hematopoetic cells of the bone marrow are subject to neoplastic changes that can lead to the development of various types of leukemia.

It is convenient to divide environmental hematologic toxins into those that act on the precursor cells in the bone marrow and those that act on the formed elements in the peripheral circulation. The former category produces effects by either increasing or decreasing the production of circulating cells. A few substances that act on the marrow are relatively specific, selectively depressing only one of the cell lines, erythrocytes, leukocytes or thrombocytes. Lead, for example, inhibits the synthesis of hemoglobin by a complex mechanism producing anemia (Hammond and Beliles 1980). The anticancer drug cytosine arabinoside is said to preferentially depress platelet production. By and large, however, toxins that affect the bone marrow will act on all three major cell lines resulting in pancytopenia. The marrow may be of normal appearance but unresponsive, failing to introduce formed elements into the blood, producing bone marrow failure. On the other hand, the damage may cease cellular proliferation causing so-called aplastic anemia. Common agents linked to the development of pancytopenia are ionizing radiation, benzene, arsenic, trinitrotoluene and certain drugs including antimetabolites, nitrogen mustard, chloramphenicol, gold, hydantoin derivatives, and phenylbutazone (Harris and Kellermeyer 1970). Other agents increase the production of formed elements. Polycythemia occurs in cobalt toxicity due to its effect of increasing renal release of erythropoietin (Gosselin et al. 1976). Leukemia, especially acute myelogenous leukemia, has been associated with certain environmental influences. These include radiation, benzene, chloramphenicol, and phenylbutazone (Smith 1980).

Peripheral destruction of formed elements can also be environmentally mediated. For example, arsine, naphthalene, saponin, and phenylhydrazine produce direct hemolysis of red blood cells. Autoimmune hemolytic anemia may be induced by acetanilid exposure. Primaquine produces hemolysis of glucose-6-phosphate dehydrogenase deficient cells. Immunologic interactions with aminopyrine, phenylbutazone, and methyluracil can lead to peripheral destruction of granulocytes. Autoimmune thrombocytopenic purpura has been linked to quinidine and phenacetin exposure (Beutler 1969; Smith 1980).

Environmental agents can produce peripheral hematologic effects not only by destruction of cells but also by interference with their functions. Thus, aspirin interferes with prostaglandin synthesis and inhibits platelet aggregation. Halogenated biphenyls may interfere with white cell function and produce immunosuppression. The classic instances of altered red cell function are carboxyhemoglobinemia, methemoglobinemia, and sulfhemoglobinemia. Carbon monoxide is a well-known red cell toxin. It has a high avidity for hemoglobin (220 times that of oxygen) and is therefore dangerous at low concentrations. It not only occupies potential oxygen binding sites on the hemoglobin but it alters the allosteric cooperativity of the molecular subunits shifting the oxyhemoglobin dissociation curve to the left and making it more difficult to deliver the oxygen load to the tissues (Bartlett 1973). Methemoglobin, formed by the oxidation of the heme iron from the ferrous to the ferric state, is hazardous for the same reasons, albeit to a lesser degree; it cannot bind oxygen and it shifts the dissociation curve to the left. Environmental causes of methemoglobin include nitrite, hydroxylamine, aniline, and nitrobenzene (Kiese 1974). Sulfhemoglobin refers to a denatured protein formed in vitro from hemoglobin and sulfides and an incompletely characterized pigment formed in vivo when hemoglobin is exposed to certain oxidant stresses; the two are probably unrelated and it is the latter that is of interest toxicologically. These irreversibly altered hemoglobin molecules may form disulfide bonds to the erythrocyte membrane thiol groups and coalesce to form the dark, refractile granules called Heinz bodies. In so doing, they impair membrane ion transport functions, which may eventually lead to hyperpermeability and osmotic hemolysis. Alternately, the distorted red cells may be removed from the circulation by premature splenic sequestration. Agents that produce sulfhemoglobin include sulfite, aniline, nitrobenzene, phenols, ascorbic acid, dichromate, arsine, stibine, hydroxylamine, and chlorate salts (Smith 1980).

Environment and Cardiovascular Disease

The diseases of the cardiovascular system, such as hypertension, coronary heart disease, and cerebrovascular disease, remain one of the major public health problems in the United States despite the recent downturn in overall cardiovascular mortality. A considerable amount of information has accrued regarding the contribution of various personal environmental factors to the development of these disorders. For example, the roles of diet, hypertension, hypercholesterolemia, smoking, personality type, family history, and physical activity in cardiovascular disease have been fairly well documented (American Heart Association 1968), and they will not be considered further here. The data on general environmental factors are more sketchy, yet several specific potential hazards have been identified including: water hardness, trace elements, physical stressors, carbon monoxide, and certain inhalant occupational exposures (Rosenman 1979; American Heart Association 1979). Although it is widely suspected that the former category of personal environmental factors contributes much more to the development of cardiovascular disorders than general environmental factors, given the huge overall death rate from these diseases in this country, a relatively small fraction attributable to general environmental factors could still represent a considerable burden of morbidity and mortality.

Several nationwide U.S. studies have demonstrated a significant inverse association between hardness of drinking water in the area as defined by calcium carbonate equivalent and cardiovascular mortality rates (Comstock 1979). The relative risk for cardiovascular mortality between states with zero hardness and states with 200 mg $CaCO_3$ equivalent/L has been estimated as 1.24. However, this issue is far from resolution due to conflicting studies restricted to smaller geographic units (Comstock 1971; Allwright, Coulson, and Detels 1974), the suspicion of confounding variables including the role of magnesium (Anderson et al. 1975), and the lack of plausible biochemical explanations. Thorough studies in Great Britain seemingly provided strong support for the connection (Gardner et al. 1969), but when rainfall distribution is factored in, the statistical significance of the correlation is apparently erased (Roberts and Lloyd 1972). These inconsistencies tend to suggest that water hardness is only indirectly related to the pathogenesis of cardiovascular disease, and its effect may be mediated by other as yet undefined factors.

An issue related to water hardness is the role of trace elements in the etiology of cardiovascular disease. The data in this case are also somewhat confusing, but several materials have been implicated, including: antimony, arsenic, cadmium, cobalt, and lead (Rosenman 1979). It has also been suggested that a high zinc to copper ratio in the myocardium may be important in the development of coronary heart disease (Klevay 1975).

Much has been written about psychosocial stresses and cardiovascular disease, but much less attention has been paid to physical stressors. The effects of hot and cold environments have been examined, and there is no evidence of increased cardiovascular mortality from these stresses. However, the acclimatization response may be critical for patients with preexisting cardiovascular disease, and a deterioration in clinical status can occur (American Heart Association 1979). Vibratory stresses delivered to the upper extremities in certain occupations can lead to vascular spasm and a resultant Reynaud-like syndrome (Taylor and Pelmear 1975). The effects of noise on the cardiovascular system are regarded generally as being mediated through the stress response. Noise has been shown to increase catecholamines, cholesterol, triglycerides, free fatty acids, cortisol, and blood pressure (Ortiz et al. 1974). The significance of these findings to the role of chronic noise exposure in the development of cardiovascular disease remains to be elucidated.

Exposure to carbon monoxide, primarily through smoking or in the workplace, can apparently affect the cardiovascular system by several mechanisms. Carbon monoxide decreases oxygen delivery to the tissues via its effect on hemoglobin. Normal individuals can compensate, for example, with increased coronary blood flow, but coronary heart patients cannot; this could clearly exacerbate the symptoms of coronary heart disease (U.S. Department of Health, Education and Welfare 1975). Carbon monoxide may even play a role in the in-

duction of atherosclerosis by increasing endothelial permeability, cholesterol uptake, and platelet adhesiveness (Astrup and Kjeldsen 1973). Shinshu myocarditis
and other occupational heart disease have been attributed to carbon monoxide exposure (Rosenman 1979).

Inhalant exposures in the workplace other than carbon monoxide can also produce cardiovascular disease. It is well established that fibrogenic dusts such as
silica and asbestos can produce severe pulmonary disease with subsequent right-
sided heart failure. Likewise, much data have accumulated linking occupational
exposure to carbon disulfide with an increased risk of death from coronary artery
disease (Davidson and Feinleib 1972). Exposure to nitrates used in the explosives
industry has caused sudden cardiac deaths from withdrawal and rebound
vasospasm (Morton 1977). Miscellaneous other compounds, especially halogenated hydrocarbons, have been linked to adverse cardiovascular effects such as
arrhythmia production (Rosenman 1979).

Finally, mention should be made of the possible role of genotoxic agents
and/or agents that stimulate cell proliferation in the pathogenesis of atherosclerosis. Recent theories of atherosclerosis have postulated that atherosclerotic plaques
may have their primary origin in the inappropriate proliferation of smooth-muscle
cells located within the innermost layer of the artery wall, the intima (Benditt
1978; Ross, Glomset, and Harker 1979). If this theory is correct, then environmental agents that might induce this process, either directly or indirectly, play a
critical part in the development of this most important cardiovascular disease.

Environment and Musculoskeletal Disease

In the past the relationship of environmental influences to disorders of the muscles
and bone was largely ignored. This was at least partially attributable to the limited
physiologic conception of this system, which, for example, viewed the skeleton
merely as an inert mechanical scaffolding of the body. However, with the growth
in knowledge concerning the dynamics of bone remodeling, skeletal ion exchange
reactions and the electrical-chemical-mechanical operations of muscles, there has
been increasing interest in the various ways in which the environment impinges
upon and alters these processes. Several interesting examples have been uncovered. Unfortunately, much remains to be elucidated, and it would be impossible at this time to estimate what the overall contribution of the environment to
musculoskeletal disease might be.

Particular dietary influences on bone including calcium and vitamins A, C,
and D have been extensively studied, but these are outside our present scope and
will not be considered further. More specific environmental toxins that are at
times related to diet have also achieved certain notoriety. In particular, bone-
seeking radioisotopes that exchange for calcium in the mineral crystal of bone or
bind ionically to the proteins of the bone matrix produce damage by acting as a
source of internal ionizing radiation. External radiation can produce similar effects. These include indirect injury due to damage of blood vessels, direct killing of
osteocytes, increased fibrosis and alteration of the osteoblasts and osteoclasts with
resultant irregular new bone formation and in some cases malignancy, particularly osteogenic sarcomas (Vaughan 1971; Budy 1975). For example, the in-
advertent ingestion of radioisotopes by radium dial painters led to an increased

incidence of bone tumors in this group of workers (Martland and Humphries 1929). Concern over the accumulation of strontium 90 in bone followed the above-ground testing of nuclear weapons two decades ago. Strontium and its decay product yttrium are known to produce malignant tumors of bone in laboratory animals (McLean and Budy 1964). Nonradioactive environmental toxins of bone that promote, inhibit, or alter calcification mechanisms have also been described. The accumulation of lead in the bones is well known as are the bone and teeth abnormalities of fluorosis. Likewise, human ingestion of foods high in selenium has been noted to cause decay and discoloration of teeth. Itai-itai, an environmental disease related to chronic cadmium poisoning, includes a susceptibility to fractures and resultant skeletal deformities probably via a renal calcium-losing mechanism (Beliles 1975). An interesting and distinctive example of occupational bone disease is acroosteolysis. The syndrome consists primarily of osteolysis of the distal phalanges and Raynaud's phenomenon and has been associated with hand cleaning of polyvinyl chloride polymerization reactors (Dinman et al. 1971).

Environmentally related disease of the joints is an area that has received little attention. Outside of occupational traumatic injuries to the joints, only a couple of examples have been noted. For instance, it is known that prolonged dietary exposure of cattle and sheep to molybdenum can produce teart, a disease that includes joint deformation. The classic human example of an environmental joint disorder is Kaschin-Beck, or Uvov, disease. It is endemic to eastern Siberia and northern China and Korea and is characterized by chronic, disabling, degenerative osteoarthritis of the peripheral joints and spine during childhood. It has been variously attributed to the ingestion of cereals contaminated by toxic products of the fungus Fusaria sporotrichiella and/or to the consumption of drinking water of excessive iron content (Nesterov 1964; Beliles 1975; McCarty 1979).

Aside from direct mechanical injury as in crush syndromes or strenuous physical exertion, skeletal muscle has generally been regarded to be particularly resistant to environmental insult. However, certain drugs including plasmocid, succinylcholine, heroin, and ethanol have been implicated in muscle necrosis. Malayan sea snake poison apparently injures skeletal muscle directly by attacking the cell membrane. Lead intoxication may damage myofibrils both by an indirect effect on peripheral nerves and by a direct fibrillary degeneration (Rowland and Penn 1972; Adams 1975). Finally, Haff disease, an epidemic myoglobinuria, has been attributed to muscle necrosis due to the consumption of industrial contaminants in fish from polluted Baltic waters (Berlin 1948).

Environment and Immunologic and Endocrine Diseases

There are other environmentally related pathological states that either have not been mentioned above or have been cursorily considered under several different organ systems. Disease of the immune system is a prime example of the latter. Immune reactions are by and large mediated via the mononuclear white blood cells and their products. Such reactions are therefore subject to some of the environmental agents already noted that affect the bone marrow and circulating formed elements of the blood. Immune reactions are themselves important mediators of disease states in certain organs including, for example, the contact dermatitides and the extrinsic allergic alveolitides. The immune system is also the body's primary discriminator of self-nonself choices, which can be regarded as key to many environmental interactions; this includes response to infectious agents, response to toxic foreign materials, and possibly surveillance and control of incipient tumors.

Environmental hazards generally affect the immune system either by producing immunodeficiency, with a concomitant lapse of these important defenses, or by causing immunopathologic responses in which the immune mechanisms react to the detriment of the health of the organism. Agents producing immunodeficient states include ionizing radiation, chemicals like benzene, and drugs. The drugs include those in which immunosuppression is an unintentional side effect (e.g., anticancer drugs) and those in which it is the desired therapeutic effect, in dealing with autoimmune diseases for instance. There is evidence that chronic exposure to heavy metals or halogenated hydrocarbons may alter the immune system and increase infectious disease susceptibility. This may also be true of psychological stresses and social factors such as overcrowding. Immunopathological reactions have traditionally been divided into four mechanistic classes: reaginic allergy-anaphylaxis, cytotoxic, immune complex, delayed hypersensitivity (Gell and Coombs 1968). Environmental factors have been implicated in all classes. In fact, a single agent, for example, penicillin, may be capable of producing any or all of these responses. Other substances implicated in the production of immuno-pathological reactions include: natural allergens such as pollens, danders, poison ivy resin, insect venoms, foods, parasites, and infectious agents; occupational allergens such as organic dusts, detergent enzymes, heavy metal salts, toluene diisocyanate, phthalic acid anhydride, piperazines, epoxy resins, soldering flux, and polyvinyl chloride fumes; drugs ranging from anesthetics to antibiotics; cosmetics and perfume ingredients; and food additives and preservatives (Adkinson 1977). Besides the circulating cells, the immune system consists of the important sites of production, alteration and maturation of these cells, namely the bone marrow, thymus, spleen, and other parts of the reticuloendothelial system including the lymph nodes and aggregates of lymphoid tissue around the body. Environmental influences on the bone marrow have already been considered. Unfortunately, very little is known about effects on the rest of the system other than a few scattered examples, such as radiation producing premature involution of the thymus or thymic tumors, selenium exposure effecting damage to the spleen and chemicals like arsenic, anesthetic gases and vinyl chloride being linked to lymphoid and reticuloendothelial malignancies (Luckey 1973; U.S. Department of Health, Education and Welfare 1979a; Hammond and Beliles 1980).

The endocrine system is another site where interactions between the organism and the environment have received little attention, except those produced by drugs. Undoubtedly, several of the examples of reproductive dysfunction previously noted are due to environmental effects on the gonadal-hypothalamic-pituitary axis. However, the exact mechanisms remain to be elucidated. Animal experiments indicate that changes in light, temperature, food, social contacts, noise, odors, altitude, and stress can affect pituitary processes and sexual functioning, but the significance of these observations to human pathology is largely unexplored. Perhaps the best-studied environment-endocrine interaction involves the release of ACTH and adrenal hormones in response to various physical and emotional stresses. Such stresses may also play a role in the pituitary secretion of growth hormone and thyroid stimulating hormone and possibly even in the development of some cases of Graves disease (Harris and Donovan 1966; Behrman and Kistner 1968; Turner and Bagnara 1976). Thyroid goiters are associated with iodine deficiency in the diet, natural goiterogens in certain foods, and exposures to cobalt and arsenic in areas where these compounds are concentrated in the water and soil (Hammond and Beliles 1980). Occupational exposure to polybrominated biphenyls has been linked to hypothyroidism, and cancer of the thyroid has been linked to radiation exposure (U.S. Department of Health, Education and Welfare 1979a; Bahn et al. 1980). Degenerative changes of the adrenals have been reported in man after chronic ingestion of thallium, and DDT has been reported to cause adrenal necrosis of the zonae fasciculata and reticularis and adrenal atrophy in dogs. In lead intoxication, the abnormally low capacity of patients to conserve sodium even with dietary restriction has been attributed to a reduction in adrenal aldosterone secretion. Cadmium is known to cause hyperglycemia and glucose intolerance in animals that may be attributable to inhibition of pancreatic islet beta cell activity; beta cells are also subject to destruction by other drugs and chemicals such as alloxan, streptozotocin, and cyproheptadine. Alpha cells of the pancreatic islets may be toxicologically damaged by exposure to cobalt (Longnecker 1977; Doull et al. 1980).

Environment and Cancer

One of the most important environmentally related diseases in cancer. In the United States alone there are approximately 700,000 new cases of cancer (not counting skin cancer and cervical carcinoma in situ) and 400,000 deaths attributable to the disease each year. This makes cancer the second leading cause of death in this country representing 20 percent of the overall mortality. Furthermore, it has been estimated that up to 80 percent of human cancers are caused by exogenous environmental influences rather than endogenous heritable factors. Although the exact percentage of adscititious carcinogenesis is debatable, the burden of cancer ascribable to the environment, whether general environmental factors like chemical pollutants and radiation or personal environmental factors like smoking and diet, is most likely quite significant. Besides the specific epidemiologic and experimental associations between various exposures and cancers noted above, there are several other evidentiary threads that lend credence to this notion. One of these has to do with global variations in incidence for particular forms of cancer. For example, the incidence of carcinoma of the colon and rectum is much higher in the United States than in Japan, whereas the incidence of gastric cancer is much higher in Japan than here. Furthermore, Japanese immigrants to the Unites States acquire the high endemic incidence of colonic cancer and the low endemic incidence of gastric cancer within a generation or two even without intermarriage. This reinforces the notion that for these two cancers environmental influences are more important than heredity. Analysis of time trends can also be revealing. The most striking example is provided by the rise of lung cancer over the last fifty years paralleling the preceding increase in cigarette smoking with a lag period of approximately two decades. The rapidity of the change in incidence of lung cancer virtually precludes a genetic basis, and the striking temporal association with smoking along with copious other suggestive evidence indicates a highly incriminating relationship of cause and effect (Hiatt, Watson, and Winsten 1977; Cairns 1978; Weinstein 1980).

The field of environmental oncology can be considered to be two centuries old, dating from the clinical observation by Sir Percival Pott of an increased incidence of scrotal skin cancer among chimney sweeps. However, it was not until the current century and primarily the last few decades that any real progress was made in elucidating the role environmental chemicals play in cancer production. Indeed even today there is much that remains unanswered about the mechanisms of chemical carcinogenesis. Nevertheless, certain unifying concepts can be identified. First, there is an apparent dose-response relationship for chemical carcinogens with no discernible safe threshold level; increasing doses can increase tumor incidence and/or shorten the latency period. This latter concept of latency is also important, indicating a typically long delay, generally proportional to the species life span, between exposure and disease appearance. This in turn may be at least partially attributed to the apparent multistep nature of the carcinogenic process. This may depend on the interaction between initiating agents, which produce a stable, irreversible change in cells on a single exposure, and promoting agents, which with continual, prolonged application following initiation somehow stimulate the gradual expression of this change culminating in malignancy. Furthermore, if the cells are proliferating carcinogenesis is enhanced. However, the tumors that are generated, even with the same chemical in the same tissue, are remarkable for their antigenic and phenotypic diversity, suggesting some degree of randomness to the process. Another important point about diversity is the great structural variety displayed by chemical carcinogens; they range from complex natural products and polycyclic aromatic hydrocarbons to metals and asbestos. Many of the potential chemical carcinogens require metabolic activation to exhibit their detrimental effects. These metabolites are generally highly electrophilic species that covalently bind to cellular nucleophiles such as proteins and nucleic acids. Carcinogens that bind to DNA can induce mutations (mismatched bases, frame shifts, deletions, and chromosome breaks) that may lead to cancer. Perhaps as important as these mutational changes in DNA replication for carcinogenesis may be the distortions in gene transcription and translation and the pattern of gene regulation and expression produced by these chemicals. Thus, carcinogens may act at an epigenetic level as well, reprogramming cells into patterns of aberrant differentiation. Still other possible effects of chemical carcinogens may include influence over cell selection via suppression of immunologic surveillance or augmentation of activity of oncogenic viruses (Weinstein 1976, 1978, 1980).

In summary, it can be said of environmental carcinogenesis and environmental disease in general that encouraging advances have been made in the identification of hazardous exposures and the mechanisms of action whereby they produce disease. Future advances will build on this knowledge base extending our ability to identify environmental hazards and understand how they work and how to prevent their deleterious health effects through a combination of epidemiologic, clinical, and laboratory research. One key to these advances will be the refinement of simple and convenient bioassays for potential toxins that will allow the prediction of their influence on health and the degree of risk they pose prior to any human exposure (Weinstein 1981). However, the control of environmental disease will require more than scientific and medical progress in the field. Success will ultimately depend in large measure on effective public education as to the avoidance and prevention of these health hazards and a vigorous societal commitment in the form of new legislation and better enforcement of existing law in this area before environmental disease can be controlled and ameliorated.

TABLE 11.1 The Work Environment

Agent, Pollutant, or Source	Disease, Effect, Illness or Injury	Types of Workers Affected
Acrylonitrile	Lung cancer, colon cancer	Manufacturers of apparel, carpeting, blankets, draperies, synthetic furs, and hair wigs
4-aminobiphenyl	Bladder cancer	Chemical workers
Anesthetic gases	Miscarriages, birth defects, decreased alertness, increased reaction time, reticuloendothelial cancer, lymphoid cancer	Physician-anesthetists, nurse-anesthetists, other operating room personnel
Arsenic	Poorly differentiated epidermoid bronchogenic carcinoma, skin cancer, scrotal cancer, cancer of the lymphatic system, hemangiosarcoma of the liver	Workers in the metallurgical industries, sheep-dip workers, pesticide production, copper smelters workers, children living near copper smelters, people living where arsenical insecticide was sprayed, vineyard workers, insecticide makers and sprayers, tanners, miners (gold miners)
Asbestos	Asbestosis (pneumoconiosis), cancer of lung, GI tract, larynx, mesothelioma	Asbestos factory workers, textile workers, relatives of asbestos workers, people who live near asbestos factories, rubber-tire manufacturing industry workers, miners, insulation workers, shipyard workers
Auramine	Bladder cancer	Dyestuffs manufacturers, rubber workers, textile dyers, paint manufacturers
Benzene	Aplastic or hypoplastic anemia, leukemia	Rubber-tire manufacturing industry workers, painters, shoe manufacturing workers, rubber cement workers, glue and varnish workers, distillers, shoemakers, plastics workers, chemical workers

Substance	Health effects	Workers at risk
Benzidine	Bladder cancer, pancreatic cancer	Dyeworkers, chemical workers
Beryllium	Berylliosis (pneumoconiosis)	Beryllium workers, electronics workers, missile parts producers
Bis-chloromethyl ether (BCME)	Bronchogenic cancer	Workers in plants producing anion-exchange resins (chemical workers)
Cadmium	Lung cancer, prostatic cancer	Cadmium production workers, metallurgical workers, electroplating industry workers, chemical workers, jewelry workers, nuclear workers, and pigment workers
Carbon disulfide	EKG changes, hypertension, neurological abnormalities, decreased sperm counts, menstrual disorders, increased spontaneous abortions	Rayon manufacturers, textile workers, paint industry workers
Carbon monoxide	Neurological and behavioral disturbances	Miners, workers in the iron and steel industry and in gas plants and tunnel workers
Carbon tetrachloride	Liver and kidney damage	Plastic workers, dry cleaners
Chloromethyl methyl ether (CMME)	Lung cancer	Chemical workers, workers in plants producing ion exchange resin
Chloroprene	Central nervous system depression, lung, liver, kidney injuries, lung and skin cancer, miscarriages	Workers in rubber-producing plants
Chromium	Bronchogenic cancer	Chromate-producing industry workers, acetylene and aniline workers, bleachers, glass, pottery, pigment, and linoleum workers
Coal dust	Pneumoconiosis	Miners, gashouse workers, stokers and producers
Coal tar pitch volatiles	Lung cancer, scrotal cancer	Steel industry workers, aluminum potroom workers, foundry workers
Coke oven emissions	Lung cancer, kidney cancer	Steel industry workers, coke plant workers, children born of female steel industry workers

TABLE 11.1 (cont.)

AGENT, POLLUTANT, OR SOURCE	DISEASE, EFFECT, ILLNESS OR INJURY	TYPES OF WORKERS AFFECTED
Cold temperatures	Chilblains, erythrocyanosis, immersion foot, frostbite, general hypothermia	Farmworkers, sailors, fishermen, telephone linemen
Cotton dust	Byssinosis ("brown lung disease")	Textile workers
Decaborane	Neurological and behavioral disturbances	
Dibromo-3-chloropropane	Sterility, impotence	Pesticide production workers/applicators
Hair spray		Hairdressers
Heat	Decreased alertness, decreased psychomotor coordination	Steelworkers, railroad workers, foundrymen
Hematite	Lung cancer	Miners
Inadequate lighting	Eye strain, fatigue, headache, eye pain, lachrymation, congestion around the cornea, "miner's nystagmus"	Miners, office workers
Kepone	Weakness, tremors, numbness, tingling, blurred vision, temporary memory loss, loss of balance	Kepone (insecticide) plant workers, agricultural workers
Lead	Miscarriage, birth defects; defects in hearing, eye-hand coordination; anemia, acute encephalopathy, "lead colic" (abdominal pain), decreased male fertility, decreased muscular strength and endurance, end stage renal disease, wrist drop, hostility, depression, anxiety	Lead production workers, lead battery plant workers, smelter workers, firing range attendants, welders, solderers
Leptophos	Weakness, tremors, numbness, tingling, blurred vision, temporary memory loss, loss of balance	Insecticide production workers, agricultural workers

264

Manganese	Neurological and behavioral disturbances	Steel workers, ceramic makers, electric arc welders, battery makers, drug makers, food additive makers, foundry workers, glass makers, match, paint, and varnish makers, ink makers, water treaters
Mercury	Nephrosis, pneumonitis, bronchitis, chest pain, shortness of breath, coughing, neurological and behavioral disturbances	Dental assistants, dental hygienists, chemical workers
Methyl butyl ketone	Peripheral neuropathy	Solvent workers, varnish and stain makers, wax makers, adhesive makers, dope (glue) workers, explosive makers, garage mechanics, celluloid makers, dyemakers, oil and lacquer processors, shoemakers
2-naphthylamine	Bladder cancer, pancreatic cancer	Dyeworkers, rubber-tire manufacturing industry workers, chemical workers, manufacturers of coal gas, nickel refiners, copper smelters, electrolysis workers
Noise	Headaches, hearing losses	Factory workers, construction workers, textile workers
Radiation	Cancer of paranasal and mastoid sinuses, cancer of the: skin, pancreas, brain, stomach, breast, salivary glands, thyroid, GI organs, bronchus, lymphoid tissue; leukemia, multiple myeloma	Uranium miners, radiologists, radiographers, luminous dial painters
Silica	Silicosis (pneumoconiosis)	Workers in mines and quarries, steelworkers; workers in iron foundries, glass and ceramics industries
Thorium dioxide	Angiosarcoma of the liver	Chemical workers, steel workers, ceramic makers, incandescent lamp makers, nuclear reactor workers, gas mantle makers, metal refiners, vacuum tube makers

TABLE 11.1 (cont.)

Agent, Pollutant, or Source	Disease, Effect, Illness or Injury	Types of Workers Affected
Tin	Neurological and behavioral disturbances	Aluminum and steel workers, welders, solderers
Toluene diisocyanate (TDI)	Pulmonary sensitization	Adhesive workers, isocyanate resin workers, organic chemical synthesizers, insulation workers, paint sprayers, lacquer workers, polyurethane makers, rubber workers, textile processors, wire coating workers
Trichloroethylene	Neurological and behavioral disturbances	Operating room personnel
Ultraviolet radiation	Conjunctivitis, keratitis, skin cancer	Farmers, sailors, arc welders
Vinyl chloride	Angiosarcoma of the liver, chromosome aberrations, cancer of the lung, brain lymphatic and hematopoietic systems, gall bladder, and liver; lymphoma, miscarriages, birth defects	Plastics factory workers, vinyl chloride polymerization plant workers, pregnant women living in communities near PVC plants
Polybrominated Biphenyls (decabromobiphenyl) Polybrominated Biphenyl Oxides (decabromobiphenyl oxide)	Hypothyroidism	Chemical plant workers where PBB and PBBO are manufactured

Sources: Bahn, Mills, Snyder et al. 1980; Lehmann and Kalmar 1979; Landrigan, n.d.

TABLE 11.2   The Housing and Nonoccupational Indoor Environment

AGENT, POLLUTANT, OR SOURCE	DISEASE, EFFECT, ILLNESS, OR INJURY
Heating, cooking, and refrigeration	Acute fatalities from carbon monoxide, fires and explosions, and discarded refrigerators, burns; increase in diseases of the respiratory tract in infants
Fumes and dust	Acute illness from fumes, aggravation of asthma; increase in chronic respiratory disease
Crowding	Spread of acute and contribution to chronic disease morbidity and mortality, stress
Structural factors (including electrical wiring, stoves, and thin walls)	Accidental fatality, accidental injury, morbidity and mortality from lack of protection from heat or cold, morbidity due to fire or explosion
Paints and solvents	Childhood lead-poisoning, associated with mental impairment, anemia, and some fatalities; renal and hepatic toxicity, fatalities from ingestion
Household equipment and supplies (including pesticides)	Fatalities from fire and injury, morbidity from fire and injury, fatalities and morbidity from poisoning
Toys, beads, and painted objects	Morbidity and mortality from swallowing small objects, lead poisoning from paint
Urban design	Increased accident risks, contribution to mental illness, stress
Tobacco combustion products from smoke-filled atmospheres	Minor eye and throat irritations; during first year of life, children of smoking parents may be more likely to have bronchitis and pneumonia; effects on fetus; possible long-term effects on the physical and intellectual development of children; possible accelerated loss of pulmonary vital capacity
Formaldehyde from insulation	Eye and respiratory tract irritation

Sources: Task Force on Theory 1976; U.S. National Committee on Vital and Health Statistics 1977.

TABLE 11.3   The Community Environment: Food

AGENT, POLLUTANT, OR SOURCE	DISEASE, EFFECT, ILLNESS, OR INJURY
PBB in dairy products and other foods (1973, Michigan)	Fatigue, headache, muscular pains, raises serum triglycerides and cholesterol levels. Can be mutagenic and carcinogenic in laboratory animals
PCB (Polychlorinated biphenyl	Yusho disease
Methyl mercury	Birth defects, central nervous system damage, death
Alkyl mercury	Chromosome breaks in lymphocytes, central nervous system damage
Lead	Nervous system affected; kidney affected
Intentional food additives, for example, saccharin	Carcinogenic in experimental animals

Sources: Food 1972; Office of Technology Assessment 1979; Second Task Force 1977; U.S. National Committee on Vital and Health Statistics 1977; Waldbott 1978.

TABLE 11.4 The Community Environment: Water

AGENT, POLLUTANT, OR SOURCE	DISEASE, EFFECT, ILLNESS, OR INJURY
Bacteria	Epidemic and endemic gastrointestinal infections (typhoid, cholera, shigellosis, salmonellosis, leptospirosis, etc.); secondary interaction with nitrates in water
Viruses	Epidemic hepatitis and other viral infections; eye and skin inflammation from swimming
Soft water areas	Possibility of cardiovascular disease, mental retardation in children. The water may leach lead out of old plumbing
Sulfates and/or phosphates	Gastrointestinal hypermotility
Fluorides when in excess	Fluorosis of teeth
Organic chemical contaminants	Reproductive failures in laboratory animals
Rain water acidity	Undetermined in man
Nitrate contamination	Nitrite intoxication; in young—nitrite cyanosis and methemoglobinemia possible
Oil spills	Threat to marine life; illness from direct consumption of contaminated water or through food chain
Chlorination	May result in carcinogenic byproducts

Sources: Cheh, Skochdopole, Koski, and Cole 1980; Second Task Force 1977; U.S. National Committee on Vital and Health Statistics 1977; Waldbott 1978.

TABLE 11.5 The Community Environment: Air

AGENT, POLLUTANT, OR SOURCE	DISEASE, EFFECT, ILLNESS, OR INJURY
Sulfur dioxide (effects of sulfur oxides may be due to sulfur dioxide, sulfur trioxide, sulfuric acid, or sulfate salts)	Aggravation of asthma and chronic bronchitis, impairment of pulmonary function, sensory irritation
Sulfur oxides and particulate matter from combustion sources	Short-term increase in morbidity and mortality, aggravation of bronchitis and cardiovascular disease, contributory role in etiology of chronic bronchitis and emphysema, contributory role in respiratory disease in children, contributory role in etiology of lung cancer
Nonspecific particulate matter	Increase in chronic respiratory disease
Oxidants	Aggravates emphysema, asthma, and bronchitis, impairs lung function in patients with bronchitis-emphysema; eye and respiratory irritation and impairment in performance of athletes
Ozone	Impairs lung function, acceleration of aging (possibly due to lipid peroxidation and related processes)
Carbon monoxide	Impairs exercise tolerance in patients with cardiovascular disease, increased general mortality and coronary mortality rates, impairment of central nervous system function, causal factor in atherosclerosis
Nitrogen dioxide	Factor in pulmonary emphysema, impairment of lung defenses such as mast cells and macrophages or altered lung function

TABLE 11.5 (*cont.*)

AGENT, POLLUTANT, OR SOURCE	DISEASE, EFFECT, ILLNESS, OR INJURY
Lead	Increased storage in body, impairment of hemoglobin and porphyrin synthesis; developmental or behavior problems
Hydrogen sulfide	Increased mortality from acute exposures, causes sensory irritation
Mercaptans	Headache, nausea, and sinus afflictions
Asbestos	Produces pleural calcification, malignant mesothelioma, asbestosis, contributes to chronic pulmonary disease (lung cancer)
Organophosphorus pesticides	Acute fetal poisoning, acute illness, impaired cholinesterase activity
Beryllium	Berylliosis with pulmonary impairment
Airborne microorganisms	Airborne infections

Sources: Second Task Force 1977; Silverman 1979; U.S. Department of Health, Education, and Welfare 1979b; U.S. National Committee on Vital and Health Statistics 1977; Waldbott 1978.

TABLE 11.6 The Community Environment: Land

AGENT, POLLUTANT, OR SOURCE	DISEASE, EFFECT, ILLNESS, OR INJURY
Human excreta	Schistosomiasis, taeniasis, hookworm, and other parasitic and nonparasitic infections
Sewage	Typhus, plague, leptospirosis, and other infectious diseases possible
Industrial and radioactive waste (Example, PCBs)	Storage within the body; effects from toxic metals and other substances through food chains, seepage, etc.

Source: U.S. National Committee on Vital and Health Statistics 1977.

TABLE 11.7 The Community Environment: Influences on Mental Health

AGENT, POLLUTANT, OR SOURCE	DISEASE, EFFECT, ILLNESS, OR INJURY
Population density (overcrowding)	Some epidemiologic studies show high rates of schizophrenia, crime, suicide, alcoholism, and drug abuse; increased risk of epidemics; stress*
Isolated populations	May show higher rates of mental disorders, e.g., mental retardation—presumably from inbreeding
Technological change and industrialization	Modifies psychological attitudes, rapid shifts in values, fragmentation of personal services, loss of self-sufficiency, stress*
Poverty and economic dislocation crises	Psychosomatic disorders, stress*

Sources: Dohrenwend 1979; Environmental influences 1972; U.S. Department of Health, Education and Welfare 1979b.
* Stressful life events exacerbated by such factors as lack of social supports or inadequate stress-coping skills can promote excessive alcohol and drug use, violence, reckless behavior, depression, hypertension, cardiovascular disease, gastrointestinal disorders, complications of pregnancy or delivery, increased susceptibility to physical agents, "demoralization," neurosis.

TABLE 11.8 Physical Factors in the Environment*

Agent, Pollutant, or Source	Disease, Effect, Illness, or Injury	Populations Exposed
Ionizing radiation (high energy particles and electromagnetic radiation); medical diagnosis and treatment; nuclear energy; consumer products	Tissue injury; genetic effects; cancer	Whole populations; special and occupational groups
Visible light; artificial lighting, lasers; communications, industrial and medical applications	Retinal burns, photosensitization; effects on circadian rhythms	Special and occupational groups
Environmental heat and humidity; infrared radiation, heat lamps; exposure to cold weather, cold and wet conditions	Thermal stress death in susceptible individuals (elderly, very young and cardiovascular disease); Infrared damage to eyes (cataracts); Cold stress, hypothermia in susceptible individuals (inadequately clad, very young, elderly and those with cardiovascular disease)	Whole populations (summer heat and winter cold); special and occupational groups
Microwaves: radio frequencies; radar and other communications; ovens; industrial and medical applications	Thermal effects at high power levels; affects heart pacemakers and metal prosthetic devices; possible behavioral effects at low levels	Potentially large proportion of population

Source	Effects	Populations affected
Power lines: fusion power; industrial and research laboratories; magnetic and electrostatic fields. Electric power: communications systems; extremely low radio frequencies	Behavioral and psychologic effects reported	Small occupational groups
Noise: Occupational sources, community and home; transportation (airports, highways)	Possible central nervous system effects; electrical shock	Relatively small occupational groups; possibly local inhabitants
Vibration: occupational sources; transportation	Hearing loss; psychologic reactions; effects on performance, general welfare and health	Special occupational groups, urban populations
Ultrasonics: occupational medical diagnosis and treatment	Peripheral vascular disease; neuromuscular effects; motion sickness; behavioral effects; kidney problems	Occupational groups; truck and large machine operations
Barometric pressure: Hypo - (Altitudes over 1300 m; air transportation)	Potential molecular, cellular and organ effects	Occupational groups, patients
	Hypoxia, congenital malformation, fetal wastage, synergistic with other factors; high altitude pulmonary edema; cardiovascular symptoms	Large populations at high altitudes; special recreational groups; aircraft passengers and personnel
Barometric pressure: Hyper - (underwater operations especially at 2 to 60 atmospheres absolute)	Bends, oxygen toxicity; nitrogen narcosis; osteonecrosis	Occupational and recreational divers

Source: Second Task Force 1977.
*See also The Work Environment for more details on cold temperatures, heat, noise, radiation.

271

TABLE 11.9 Chemicals and Industrial Processes That Are Carcinogenic for Humans*

Group 1:

4-Aminobiphenyl	Diethylstilboestrol
Arsenic and certain arsenic compounds	Underground haematite mining
Asbestos	Manufacture of isopropyl alcohol by the strong acid process
Manufacture of auramine	Melphalan
Benzene	Mustard gas
Benzidine	2-Naphthylamine
N,N-bis (2-chloroethyl)-2-napthylamine (chlornaphazine)	Nickel refining
Bis(chloromethyl)ether and technical grade chloromethyl methyl ether	Soots, tars and mineral oils
Chromium and certain chromium compounds	Vinyl chloride
Cigarette smoke	Industrial processes associated with cancer in humans

Group 2:

Group (A)

Aflatoxins	Cyclophosphamide
Cadmium and certain cadmium compounds	Nickel and certain nickel compounds
Chlorambucil	Tris(1-aziridinyl)phosphine sulphide (thiotepa)

Group (B)

Acrylonitrile	Dimethylsulphate
Amitrole (aminotriazole)	Ethylene oxide
Auramine	Iron dextran
Beryllium and certain beryllium compounds	Oxymetholone
Carbon tetrachloride	Phenacetin
Dimethylcarbamoyl chloride	Polychlorinated biphenyls

*For the 19 chemicals in Group 1 there appears to be convincing epidemiologic evidence of carcinogenicity in humans. The evidence for the 18 in Group 2 indicates that they are *probably* carcinogenic in humans. The evidence for compounds in Group A is stronger than that for compounds in Group B.
Ionizing and ultraviolet radiation are also recognized carcinogens in humans.

REFERENCES

ADAMS, R. D. 1975. *Diseases of muscles.* Hagerstown, Md.: Harper and Row.

ADAMS, R. G.; HARRISON, J. F.; and SCOTT, P. 1969. The development of cadmium-induced proteinuria, impaired renal function and osteomalacia in alkaline battery workers. *Quarterly Journal of Medicine* 38: 425–43.

ADKINSON, N. F., JR. 1977. Environmental influences on the immune system and allergic reactions. *Environmental Health Perspectives* 20: 97–103.

AHARONSON, E. F.; BEN-DAVID, A.; and KLINGBERG, M. A. 1976. *Air pollution and the lung.* New York: Wiley.

ALLISON, A. C. 1974. Pathogenic effects of inhaled particles and antigens. *Annals of the New York Academy of Sciences* 221: 299–308.

ALLWRIGHT, S. P. A.; COULSON, A.; AND DETELS, R. 1974. Mortality and water-hardness in three matched communities in Los Angeles. *Lancet* 2:860–64.

American Heart Association. Central Committee for Medical and Community Program

1968. Risk factors and coronary disease: a statement for physicians. New York: American Heart Association.

———. Task Force on Environment and Cardiovascular Disease 1979. The impact of the environment on cardiovascular disease. New York: American Heart Association.

ANDERSON, T. W.; NERI, L. C.; SCHREIBER, G. B.; TALBOT, F. D. F.; and ZDROJEWSKI, A. 1975. Ischemic heart disease, water hardness and myocardial magnesium. *Journal of the Canadian Medical Association* 113: 199–203.

ASTROP, P., and KJELDSEN, K. 1973. Carbon monoxide, smoking, and atherosclerosis. *Medical Clinics of North America* 58: 323–50.

BAHN, A. K.; MILLS, J. L.; SNYDER, P. J.; GANN, P. H.; HOUTEN, L.; BIALIK, O.; HOLLMANN, L.; and UTIGER, R. D. 1980. Hypothyroidism in workers exposed to polybrominated biphenyls. *New England Journal of Medicine* 302: 31–33.

BARTLETT, D., JR. 1973. Effects of carbon monoxide in human physiological processes. In *Proceedings of the conference on health effects of air pollutants*, serial 93-15. Washington, D.C.: Government Printing Office.

BASS, N. H. 1968. Pathogenesis of myelin lesions in experimental cyanide encephalopathy. *Neurology* 18: 167–77.

BEHRMAN, S. J., and KISTNER, R. W. 1968. *Progress in infertility.* Boston: Little, Brown.

BEIR Report. Advisory Committee on the Biological Effects of Ionizing Radiation 1972. *The effects on populations of exposure to low levels of ionizing radiation.* NAS-NRC, Washington, D.C.

BEIRNE, G. J., and BRENNAN, J. T. 1972. Glomerulonephritis associated with hydrocarbon solvents. *Archives of Environmental Health* 25: 365–69.

BELILES, R. P. 1975. Metals. In *Toxicology: the basic science of poisons.* New York: Macmillan.

BENDITT, E. P. 1978. The monoclonal theory of atherogenesis. In *Atherosclerosis reviews*, ed. R. Paoletti and A. M. Gotto, Jr., vol. 3, p. 77. New York: Raven Press.

BERG, K., ed. 1979. *Genetic damage in man caused by environmental agents.* New York: Academic Press.

BERLIN, R. 1948. Haff disease in Sweden. *Acta Medica Scandinavica* 129:560–72.

BEUTLER, E. 1969. Drug-induced hemolytic anemia. *Pharmacological Review* 21: 73–103.

BLEIBERG, J.; WALLEN, M.; BRODKIN, R.; and APPLEBAUM, I. L. 1964. Industrially acquired porphyria. *Archives of Dermatology* 89: 793–97.

BOUHUYS, A. 1974. *Breathing, physiology, environment and lung disease.* New York: Grune and Stratton.

BRAIN, J. D. 1977. The respiratory tract and the environment. *Environmental Health Perspectives* 20: 113–26.

BRUCE, R.; VARGHESE, A. J.; FURRER, R.; and LANE, P. C. 1977. In *Origins of human cancer*, ed. H. H. Hiatt, J. D. Watson, and J. A. Winsten, vol. A, pp. 1641-48. New York: Cold Spring Harbor Laboratory.

BUDY, A. 1975. Toxicology of the skeletal system. In *Toxicology: the basic science of poisons.* New York: Macmillan.

CAIRNS, J. 1978. *Cancer: science and society.* San Francisco, Calif.: W. H. Freeman.

CAM, C., and NIGOGOSYAN, G. 1963. Acquired toxic porphyria cutanea tarda due to hexachlorobenzene. *Journal of the American Medical Association* 183: 88–91.

CARP, H., and JANOFF, A. 1978. Possible mechanisms of emphysema in smokers. *American Review of Respiratory Diseases* 118: 617–21.

CAVANAUGH, J. B. 1977. Metabolic mechanisms of neurotoxicity caused by mercury. In *Neurotoxicology.* New York: Raven Press.

———; FULLER, N. H.; JOHNSON, H. R. M.; and RUDGE, P. 1974. The effect of thallium salts with particular reference to the nervous system changes. *Quarterly Journal of Medicine* 43: 293–319.

Center for Disease Control. 1979. Involuntary smoking. In *Smoking and health. A report of the surgeon general*, chap. 11. DHEW Government Printing Office.

CHEH, A. M.; SKOCHDOPOLE, J.; KOSKI, P.; and COLE, L. 1980. Nonvolatile mutagens in drinking water: production by chlorination and destruction by sulfite. *Science* 207: 90–92.

Committee on Toxicology, Assembly of Life Sciences, National Research Council. 1976. *Recommendations for the prevention of lead poisoning in children.* Washington, D.C.: National Academy of Sciences.

COMSTOCK, G. W. 1971. Fatal arteriosclerotic heart disease, water hardness at home, and socioeconomic characteristics. *American Journal of Epidemiology* 94: 1–10.

———. 1979. Water hardness and cardiovascular diseases. *American Journal of Epidemiology* 110: 375–400.

COTZIAS, G. C. 1958. Manganese in health and disease. *Physiology Review* 38: 503–32.

DAVIDSON, M., and FEINLEIB, M. 1972. Carbon disulfide poisoning: a review. *American Heart Journal* 83: 100–14.

DINMAN, B. D.; COOK, W. A.; WHITEHOUSE, W. M.; MAGNUSON, H. J.; and DITCHECK, T. 1971. Occupational acroosteolysis. *Archives of Environmental Health* 22: 61–91.

DOHRENWEND, B. P. 1979. Stressful life events and psychopathology: some issues of theory and method. In *Stress and mental disorder.* ed. J. E. Barrett et al. New York: Raven Press.

DOULL, J.; KLAASSEN, C. D.; and AMDUR, M. O. 1980. *Toxicology: the basic science of poisons.* New York: Macmillan.

EMMERSON, B. T.; MIROSCH, W.; and DOUGLAS, J. B. 1971. The relative contributions of tubular reabsorption and secretion to urate excretion in lead nephropathy. *Australian and New Zealand Journal of Medicine* 1: 353–62.

EMMETT, E. A. 1973. Ultraviolet radiation as a cause of skin tumors. *Critical Review of Toxicology* 2: 211–55.

———. 1975. Occupational skin cancer: a review. *Journal of Occupational Medicine* 17: 44–49.

Environmental influences on mental health. 1972. In *Health hazards of the human environment,* chap. 10. Geneva: World Health Organization.

FABIA, J., and THUY, T. D. 1974. Occupation of father at time of birth of children dying of malignant diseases. *British Journal of Preventive and Social Medicine* 28: 98–100.

FINN, W. F. 1977. Renal response to environmental toxins. *Environmental Health Perspectives* 20: 15–26.

FISCHER, A. A. 1973. *Contact dermatitis.* Philadelphia, Pa.: Lea and Febiger.

FLANIGAN, W. J., and OKEN, D. E. 1965. Renal micropuncture study of the development of anuria in the rat with mercury-induced acute renal failure. *Journal of Clinical Investigation* 44: 449–57.

Food. 1972. In *Health hazards of the human environment,* pp. 72–93. Geneva: World Health Organization.

FOULDS, L. 1975. Neoplasia of the urinary tract. In *Neoplastic development.* London: Academic Press.

FOULKES, E. C., and GIESKE, T. H. 1973. Specificity and metal sensitivity of renal amino acid transport. *Biochimica et Biophysica Acta* 318: 439–45.

———, and HAMMOND, P. B. 1975. Toxicology of the kidney. In *Toxicology: the basic science of poisons.* New York: Macmillan.

FOWLER, B. A., and WEISSBERG, J. B. 1974. Arsine Poisoning. *New England Journal of Medicine* 291: 1171–74.

FRAUMENI, J. F. 1975. Cancers of the pancreas and biliary tract: epidemiologic considerations. *Cancer research* 35: 3437–46.

FRIEDMAN, E. A.; GREENBERG, J. B.; MERRILL, J. P.; and DAMMIN, G. J. 1962. Consequences of ethylene glycol poisoning. *American Journal of Medicine* 32: 891–902.

GARDNER, M. J.; CRAWFORD, M. D.; and MORRIS, J. N. 1969. Pattern of mortality in middle and early old age in the county boroughs of England and Wales. *British Journal of Preventive and Social Medicine* 23: 133–40.

GELL, P. G. H., and COOMBS, R. R. A. 1968. *Clinical aspects of immunology.* Oxford: Blackwell.

Giese, A. C., ed. 1970. *Photophysiology.* New York: Academic Press.

Gilson, J. R.; Juniper, C. P.; Martin, R. B.; and Weill, H. 1976. Biological effects of proteolytic enzyme detergents. *Thorax* 31: 621–34.

Gosselin, R. E.; Hodge, H. C.; Smith, R. P.; and Gleason, M. N. 1976. *Clinical toxicology of commercial products. Acute poisoning.* Baltimore, Md.: Williams and Wilkins.

Hammond, P. B., and Beliles, R. P. 1980. Metals. In *Toxicology: the basic science of poisons.* New York: Macmillan.

Harris, G. W., and Donovan, B. T. 1966. *The pituitary gland,* vol. 2. Berkeley, Calif.: University of California Press.

Harris, J. W., and Kellermeyer, R. W. 1970. *The red cell production, metabolism, destruction: normal and abnormal.* Cambridge, Mass.: Harvard University Press.

Herbst, A. L.; Ulfelder, H.; and Pozkanzer, D. C. 1971. Adenocarcinoma of the vagina. *New England Journal of Medicine* 284: 878–81.

Hiatt, H. H.; Watson, J. D.; and Winsten, J. A. 1977. *Origins of human cancer.* Cold Spring Harbor, N.Y.: Cold Spring Harbor Laboratory.

Hitchcock, M.; Piscitelli, D. M.; and Bouhuys, A. 1973. Histamine release from human lung by a component of cotton bracts. *Archives of Environmental Health* 26: 177–82.

IARC Monographs on the Evolution of the Carcinogenic Risk of Chemicals to Humans, Chemicals and Industrial Processes Associated with Cancer in Humans. IARC suppl. 1. International Agency for Research on Cancer, Lyon, 1979.

Infante, P. F.; Wagoner, J. K.; McMichael, A. J.; Waxweiler, R. J.; and Falk, H. 1976. Genetic risks of vinyl chloride. *Lancet* 1: 734–35.

Johnson, M. K. 1975. The delayed neuropathy caused by some organophosphorous esters. *Critical Review of Toxicology* 3: 289–316.

Kahn, G. 1970. Depigmentation caused by phenolic detergent germicides. *Archives of Dermatology* 102: 177–87.

Karelitz, S., and Freedman, A. D. 1951. Hepatitis and nephrosis due to soluble bismuth. *Pediatrics* 8: 772–77.

Kiese, M. 1974. *Methemoglobinemia: a comprehensive treatise.* Cleveland, Ohio: CRC Press.

Klevay, L. M. 1975. Coronary heart disease: the zinc/copper hypothesis. *American Journal of Clinical Nutrition* 28: 764–74.

Krain, L. S. 1972. Gall bladder and extrahepatic bile duct carcinoma. *Geriatrics* 27: 111–17.

Krawitt, E. L. 1977. Ethanol and development of disease and injury to the alimentary tract. *Environmental Health Perspectives* 20: 71–73.

Kuratsune, M.; Yoshimura, T.; Matsuzaka, J.; and Yamaguchi, A. 1972. Epidemiologic study on yusho, a poisoning caused by ingestion of rice oil contaminated with a commercial brand of polychlorinated biphenyls. *Environmental Health Perspectives* 1: 119–28.

Lancranjan, I.; Popescu, H.; Gavanescu, O.; Klepsch, I.; and Sarbanescu, M. 1975. Reproductive ability of workmen occupationally exposed to lead. *Archives of Environmental Health* 30: 396–401.

Landrigan, P. (NIOSH.) Personal communication.

Lapresle, J., and Fardeau, M. 1967. The central nervous system and carbon monoxide poisoning. *Progress in Brain Research* 24: 31–74.

Lederberg, J. 1971. In *The mutagenicity of pesticides: concepts and evaluations.* Cambridge, Mass.: M.I.T. Press.

Lee, D. H. K. 1972. *Environmental factors in respiratory disease.* New York: Academic Press.

Lehmann, P. E., and Kalmar, V. K. 1979. Improving the quality of the work environment. In *Healthy people. The surgeon general's report on health promotion and disease prevention. Background papers,* pp. 387-407. DHEW publ. no. (PHS) 79-55071A. Washington, D.C.: Government Printing Office.

Longnecker, D. S. 1977. Environmental factors and diseases of the pancreas. *Environmental Health Perspectives* 20: 105–12.

Lopez, M.; Wessels, F.; and Salvaggio, J. E. 1977. In *Bronchial asthma: mechanisms and therapeutics*. Boston: Little, Brown.

Luckey, T. D. 1973. *Thymic hormones*. Baltimore, Md.: University Park Press.

Manalis, R. S., and Cooper, G. P. (1973). Presynaptic and postsynaptic effects of lead at the frog neuromuscular junction. *Nature* 243: 354–55.

Martland, H. S., and Humphries, R. E. 1929. Osteogenic sarcoma in dial painters using luminous paint. *Archives of Pathology* 7: 406–17.

McCarty, D. J. 1979. *Arthritis and allied conditions*. Philadelphia, Pa.: Lea and Febiger.

McLean, F. C., and Budy, A. M. 1964. *Radiation, isotopes, and bone*. New York: Academic Press.

Miyoshi, K. 1976. Experimental striatal necrosis induced by sodium azide. *Acta Neuropathologica* 9: 199–216.

Morgan, W. K. C., and Seaton, A. 1975. *Occupational lung disease*. Philadelphia, Pa.: W. B. Saunders.

Morton, W. E. 1977. Occupational habituation to aliphatic nitrates and the withdrawal hazards of coronary disease and hypertension. *Journal of Occupational Medicine* 19: 197–200.

Moschella, S. L.; Pillsbury, D. M.; and Hurley, H. J., Jr., eds. 1975. *Dermatology*. Philadelphia, Pa.: W. B. Saunders.

Murphy, S. D. 1980. Pesticides. In *Toxicology: the basic science of poisons*. New York: Macmillan.

National Institute of Child Health and Human Development. 1979. Pregnancy and infant health. In *Smoking and health. A report of the surgeon general*, chap. 8. DHEW pub. no. (PHS) 79-50066. Washington, D.C.: Government Printing Office.

Nesterov, A. I. 1964. The clinical course of Kashin-Beck disease. *Arthritis and Rheumatism* 7: 29–40.

Nishimura, H., and Tanimura, T. 1976. *Clinical aspects of the teratogenicity of drugs*. New York: Elsevier.

Norton, S. 1980. Toxic responses of the central nervous system. In *Toxicology: the basic science of poisons*. New York: Macmillan.

Oehme, F. W.; Brown, J. F.; and Fowler, M. E. 1980. Toxins of animal origin. In *Toxicology: the basic science of poisons*. New York: Macmillan.

Office of Technology Assessment. 1979. *Environmental contaminants in food. Summary*. Washington, D.C.: Government Printing Office.

Ortiz, G. A.; Arguelles, A. E.; Crespin, H. A.; Sposari, G.; and Villafañe, C. T. 1974. Modifications of epinephrine, nor-epinephrine, blood lipid fractions and cardiovascular system produced by noise in an industrial medium. *Hormone Research* 5: 57–64.

Paulson, G. W. 1977. Environmental effects on the central nervous system. *Environmental Health Perspectives* 20: 75–96.

Pepys, J. 1969. *Hypersensitivity disease of the lung due to fungi and organic dusts*. Basel: S. Karger.

Persaud, T. V. N., ed. 1977. *Problems of birth defects*. Baltimore, Md.: University Park Press.

Plaa, G. L. 1980. Toxic responses of the liver. In *Toxicology: the basic science of poisons*. New York: Macmillan.

Potts, A. M., and Gonasun, L. M. 1980. Toxic responses of the eye. In *Toxicology: the basic science of poisons*. New York: Macmillan.

Reynolds, E. S. 1977. Environmental aspects of injury and disease: liver and bile ducts. *Environmental Health Perspectives* 20: 1–13.

Roberts, C. J., and Lloyd, S. 1972. Association between mortality from ischaemic heart-disease and rainfall in South Wales and in the county boroughs of England and Wales. *Lancet* 1: 1091–93.

Rosenman, K. D. 1979. Cardiovascular disease and environmental exposure. *British Journal of Industrial Medicine* 36: 85–97.

Ross, R.; Glomset, J.; Harker, L. 1978. The response to injury and atherogenesis: the role of endothelium and smooth muscle. In *Atherosclerosis reviews,* ed. R. Paoletti and A. M. Gotto, Jr., vol. 3., p. 77. New York: Raven Press.

ROWLAND, L. P., and PENN, A. S. 1972. Myoglobinuria. *Medical Clinics of North America* 56: 1233–56.

SAID, S. I. 1978. Environmental injury of the lung. *Federation Proceedings* 37: 2504–7.

SANOTSKII, I. V. 1976. Aspects of the toxicology of chloroprene: immediate and long-term effects. *Environmental Health Perspectives* 17: 85–93.

SAUER, G. C. 1980. *Manual of skin diseases.* Philadelphia, Pa.: Lippincott.

SCHEDL, H. P. 1977. Environmental factors and the development of disease and injury in the alimentary tract. *Environmental Health Perspectives* 20: 39–54.

Second Task Force for Research Planning in Environmental Health Science. 1977. *Human health and the environment—some research needs.* DHEW pub. no. (NIH) 77-1299. Washington, D.C.: Government Printing Office.

SILVERMAN, F. 1979. Asthma and respiratory irritants (ozone). *Environmental Health Perspectives* 29: 131–36.

SMITH, R. P. 1980. Toxic responses of the blood. In *Toxicology: the basic science of poisons.* New York: Macmillan.

STELLMAN, J. M. 1979. The effects of toxic agents on reproduction. *Occupational Health and Safety* 48: 36–43.

SUSKIND, R. R. 1977. Environment and the skin. *Environmental Health Perspectives* 20: 27–37.

———, and MAJETI, V. A. 1976. Occupational and environmental allergic problems of the skin. *Journal of Dermatology* 3: 3–13.

Task Force on Theory, Practice and Application of Prevention in Environmental Health. 1976. In *Preventive medicine USA,* pp. 529–615. New York: Prodist.

TAYLOR, W., and PELMEAR, P. L., eds. 1975. *Vibration white finger in industry.* New York: Academic Press.

TROEN, P.; KAUFMAN, S. A.; and KATZ, K. H. 1951. Mercuric bichloride poisoning. *New England Journal of Medicine* 244: 459–63.

TURNER, C. D., and BAGNARA, J. T. 1976. *General endocrinology.* Philadelphia, Pa.: W. B. Saunders.

U.S. Department of Health, Education and Welfare. 1964. *Smoking and health. Report of the advisory committee to the surgeon general of the Public Health Service.* Pub. no. (PHS) 1103.

———. 1972. *The health consequences of smoking. A report of the surgeon general.* Pub. no. (HSM) 72-7516.

———. 1974. *What are the facts about genetic disease.* Pub. no. 75-370.

———. 1975. *The health consequences of smoking,* pp. 230–367. Pub. no. (NIH) 76-1221.

———. 1979a. *Surgeon general's report on health promotion and disease prevention. Background papers.* Pub. no. (PHS) 79-55071A.

———. 1979b. *Healthy people. The surgeon general's report on health promotion and disease prevention.* DHEW pub. no. (PHS) 79-55071. Washington, D.C.: Government Printing Office.

U.S. National Committee on Vital and Health Statistics. 1977. *Statistics needed for determining the effects of the environment on health.* DHEW pub. no. (HRA) 77-1457. Washington, D.C.: Government Printing Office.

VALEK, A.; BROULIK, P.; and TABORSKY, J. 1969. Changes of renal hemodynamics following acute intoxication with mercury compounds. *Casopis Lekaru Ceskych* 108: 860–63.

VAUGHAN, J. M. 1971. The effects of radiation on bone. In *The biochemistry and physiology of bone,* vol. 3. New York: Academic Press.

VOGEL, F., and ROHRBORN, G., eds. 1970. *Chemical mutagenesis in mammals and man.* New York: Springer-Verlag.

WALDBOTT, G. L. 1978. *Health effects of environmental pollutants.* St. Louis: C. V. Mosby.

WEINSTEIN, I. B. 1976. Cancer biology, II. Etiology and therapy. In *Advances in pathobiology,* vol. 4. New York: Stratton Intercontinental Medical Book Corp.

————. 1978. Current concepts on mechanisms of chemical carcinogenesis. *Bulletin of the New York Academy of Medicine* 54: 366–83.

————. 1980. Molecular and cellular mechanisms of chemical carcinogenesis. In *Cancer and chemotherapy.* New York: Academic Press.

————. 1981. The scientific basis for carcinogen detection and primary cancer prevention. *Cancer* 47: 1133–41.

WHORTON, D.; MILBY, T. H.; KRAUSS, R. M.; and STUBBS, H. A. 1979. Testicular function in DBCP exposed pesticide workers. *Journal of Occupational Medicine* 21: 161–66.

WILSON, J. G., and FRASER, F. C., eds. 1977. *Handbook of teratology.* New York: Plenum Press.

WITSCHI, E. 1970. In *Proceedings of the Third International Conference on Birth Defects.* New York: Excerpta Medica.

III

HEALTH–CARE
DELIVERY
AND MANAGEMENT

Chapter 12

Comparisons in Health Care: Britain as Contrast to the United States

Rosemary Stevens

Why Compare?

BRITAIN, like many other countries of the world, has a government-run national health service system. Virtually all medical costs are paid for through taxation. Almost all hospitals are government-owned and physicians and other health professionals receive most of their income through the National Health Service. Medical benefits are universal and comprehensive: that is, the whole population is covered under the National Health Service, irrespective of individual contributions or individual income, and services include a wide spectrum of medical care, from family planning to kidney dialysis, with no specified limit on the number of days or types of care. There are some charges to patients for prescriptions, dental care and eye-glasses—1978–79 charges paid by National Health Service patients met 3.4 percent of general pharmaceutical costs, 19.1 percent of general dental costs, and 34.4 percent of general ophthalmic costs of the National Health Service—otherwise services are provided free at the time of use (Royal Commission 1979a, p. 340).

The nearest parallel to the National Health Service in the United States is the Veterans' Administration medical service, which provides tax-supported care to veterans through a chain of government facilities. But the parallel is limited. The VA system, vast though it is, covers only a subsection of the population; moreover it is based not on comprehensive health care but on recognized disabilities. Other government-run systems, such as the Indian Medical Service, are also limited in serving population subsections. A clearer parallel in terms of function, if not of scale, is the health maintenance organization (HMO), for here, as in the National Health Service, specified sums of money are paid for relatively comprehensive medical care to a defined general population; but, here too, the parallel is inexact and misleading. HMOs are not government-run. Indeed, they are being pressed in the United States as a major alternative to greater government intervention. It is reasonable to ask, why then compare Britain and the United States?

From the point of view of developing health policy in the United States there are at least three persuasive reasons for examining the British system in the 1980s. The first, and most obvious, derives from their contrasting political and ideological bases. The National Health Service (NHS) is built on—and has strengthened—an assumption that health services are a national resource which should be shared across the population so that services are, as far as possible, apportioned on the basis of medical need rather than the ability to pay. Various cracks in this position will be described, notably in the continuation of private practice and in recognition of continuing differences in health status by social class. Nevertheless the NHS has been, and remains, egalitarian in intent. That government is the necessary vehicle for achieving a reasonable social distribution of health care has been a corollary tenet of the NHS.

The National Health Service was enacted in 1946 (it came into effect in 1948) as a plank in the post–World War II welfare state. Health services were included as a necessary part of a "comprehensive policy of social progress," to be achieved by "cooperation between the State and the individual," in the sweeping Beveridge report on social insurance and allied services of 1942 (Beveridge Report 1942, pp. 6, 158–63). While the movement toward government health services had a long history and was supported by all three political parties, the replacement of the wartime coalition government by a Labour government in the 1945 elections made the drive for a national health service explicitly socialist. This view was reinforced by the placing of Aneurin Bevan as British minister of health in 1945, for not only did he support the role of government as guaranteeing a wide range of social services, but he also was instrumental in nationalizing the nation's uncoordinated network of voluntary and local government hospitals, at one stroke, in the health service legislation of 1946. The rejection in the 1940s of proposals for national health insurance in the United States appeared to affirm fundamentally different political philosophies underlying health services in Britain and the United States. In the one country was "socialized medicine" (an American term); in the other a predominantly private system. In Britain government was director, financier, and producer of services; its role was central and managerial. In the United States, government's role was residual and regulatory.

Contrasting the United States as a system subject to public regulation and Britain as a system of public management remains useful. However, the dilemmas of health policy in both countries are quite similar. In the past two or three decades the lines between "public" and "private" systems have become blurred in both countries. The advent of Medicare and Medicaid and other social programs of the 1960s transformed the American system into a mixed, or pluralistic, system, highly sensitive to government fiat, funding, and incentives. In Britain, meanwhile, the NHS, though operated and funded by government, is being seen, increasingly, as a multi-interest system, fragmented into occupational groups, divided by the perceived needs of different areas and populations, and conflicted by loyalties and vested interests. Conservative party spokemen are now advocating greater involvement of the "private sector" in providing services for the NHS and for an expansion of the still small role of private health insurance. (At the end of September 1980 the three major insurance schemes, the British/United Provident Association, Private Patients Plan, and Western Provident Association had 1,550,000 subscribers, covering a total insured population of 3,366,000, the equivalent of 6 percent of the population of the United Kingdom.) In these and other ways British and American policy-making for health care can be seen as parallel, if not as converging processes (cf. Anderson 1977; Stevens 1977). Clearly, the fact that Britain has a government health system has had a critical, continuing impact on thinking about the nature, purposes, and goals of health services in Britain, as the service has evolved since 1948. Yet it makes only partial sense to compare the American and British systems in the 1980s as if their sole or most important distinctions were questions of public or private interest. A second reason for comparison is to identify common organizational and policy themes.

Finally, the NHS is worth looking at as a huge, managerial system. As the equivalent of an HMO serving 55 million people, NHS budgets have been predetermined and constricted. Priorities have to be determined at a more conscious level—certainly in a more publicized context—than in the United States. This chapter shows the continuing struggles in the NHS to realize goals of equity, of efficiency, of responsiveness to community needs and other legitimate interests through major changes within the NHS in the 1970s and 1980s. For reasons both of philosophy and of structure the NHS experience is germane to developing debates in the United States.

The following two sections provide background on the similarities and differences in American and British health care, and on the organization of the NHS. The chapter then turns to contemporary perceptions of health policy in the NHS in England and, finally, to their relevance to the United States.

The Two Health Services: Some Statistics

The British National Health Service serves more than 55 million people in the United Kingdom (England, Wales, Scotland, Northern Ireland), 46 million of whom live in England. The United Kingdom has a population about one-fourth that of the United States, concentrated in a much smaller land area. There are approximately sixty persons, on average, per square mile in the United States, about six hundred persons per square mile in the United Kingdom (Table 12.1). Population density and geographical territory are important in considering national versus local policies for health services—for a region of (say) 4 million persons in England is more geographically compact than an average region of such population in the United States.

In each country the population over sixty-five years of age has been increasing steadily in the past decades. In the United Kingdom one of every seven persons is now over sixty-five years of age. Given the existence of the NHS one would expect the health problems of the elderly to be particularly evident and services for the elderly to be given special attention. Indeed, since 1976 NHS policies have singled out the elderly, as well as the mentally ill, the mentally handicapped, and children as priorities for service development over the expansion of acute hospital care. The number of geriatric patients served by the health service has been growing rapidly. The number of geriatric patients discharged from NHS hospitals increased by 29 percent between 1970 and 1976, outpatient and day-care attendances rose by 64 percent, and day hospital attendances by 102 percent (Royal Commission 1979a, p. 60).

National birth rates, infant mortality rates, and maternal death rates are sim-

TABLE 12.1   Selected Statistical Comparisons, United Kingdom and United States, 1978

	UNITED KINGDOM	UNITED STATES
Resident population (1000)	55,835	218,059
Land area, square miles	94,251	3,618,467
Population per square mile of land area	592.4	60.3
Percent of the population under 5 years old	6.1%	7.0%
Percent of the population 65 years and over	14.5%	11.0%
Birth rate (births per 1,000 population)	11.8*	15.3
Infant mortality rate (deaths under 1 year per 1,000 live births)	13.3	13.6
Maternal death rate (maternal deaths per 1,000 live births)	0.13*	0.11
Marriages per 1,000 population	14.4*	10.3
Divorces per 1,000 population	2.6†	5.1
Legal termination of pregnancy per 1,000 women 15–44 years	10.2‡	26.9*
Births to unmarried women as percent of all live births	9.6*	15.5*
Death rate per 1,000 population	12.0	8.8

Sources: Great Britain, Central Statistical Office 1980a, 1980b; U. S. Department of Commerce 1979.

* 1977.

† Figures for England and Wales only, 1977.

‡ Figures exclude Northern Ireland, 1977.

ilar in the two countries. In both countries, however, there is concern about systematic variation in the mortality rates for different population groups. Infant mortality in Britain continues to hold a straight-line association with social class as measured by parental occupation. Thus a recent British report on *Inequalities in Health* (1980 pp. 35, 37) notes with concern that at birth and during the first month of life the risk of death in social class V (unskilled manual workers) is twice the risk in class I (professional workers), and that the risk of mortality continues to be closely correlated with class up to the age fourteen, despite the fact that health services are available to all members of the population. The report suggests, inter alia, that there is "severe underutilization" of preventive services by the working class and that working-class parents are less likely to seek medical attention for their children when they are sick . Discussion of class as a measure of social equality has been given particular emphasis in Britain, although the increasing population of immigrants (and racial tension) in Britain suggests an increasing attention in the future to differences by race (cf. Terry, Condie, Settatree 1980). In the United States, in contrast, the overriding concern about social inequalities relates to race and ethnicity, although clearly race and social class are in many ways interwoven (Institute of Medicine, 1981). Again one would expect these concerns to be built into and reflected from the organizational arrangements for medical care. In Britain questions of equality are defined in terms of spreading health services resources as equally as possible over all social groups and geographical areas. Since there is a unified centralized management structure for health services this policy of "equalization" translates—as will be shown—into operational definitions for resource allocation.

Table 12.1 suggests other cultural and social characteristics of the two countries which form a necessary backdrop to organizational considerations in medical care. Figures on marriage, divorce, and abortion suggest different family structures, social attitudes, and life choices, which may be important to individual health experiences and expectations of a health-care system. Comparative mortality rates reflect a higher overall mortality in Britain, but a higher prevalence of violence in the United States. Cochrane has shown, for example, that death rates for men aged fifteen to twenty-four in England and Wales and the United States in 1970 show the United States to have an "excess" of 98 deaths per 100,000 population over England and Wales: however, almost all of these additional deaths are attributable to violence: accidents, suicide and homicide. When these causes are removed, the comparative death rates for this group are quite similar (Cochrane 1978, p. 5). While the theme of this section is the interrelationship between the goals of health services and the structure and management of the health-care system, rather than cultural factors affecting health, cultural factors obviously form a necessary context to decisions implicit in and arising out of structure.

Table 12.2 gives selected figures on the resources devoted to health services in

TABLE 12.2   Health Services Resources in the United Kingdom and United States, 1978

	UNITED KINGDOM (NHS ONLY)	UNITED STATES
Percent of GNP spent on health services	5.5%	9.1%
Per capita expenditures	£120 ($264)	$863
Hospital Admissions or Discharges per 1,000 population (all types of hospitals)	116.0*	171.7[†]
Nonpsychiatric beds per 1,000 population	5.5	5.3
Average length of stay in acute specialties (days)	9.5[‡]	8.3[†]
Psychiatric beds per 1,000 population	3.0	1.1[§]
Outpatient attendances, excluding emergency patients, per 1,000 population	718.0[‡]	828.8
Accident and emergency outpatient visits per 1,000 population	288.2[‡]	380.0
Physicians in active practice per 100,000 population	122"	177[†]
Percent of physicians in active practice who are general practitioners	64.6%[#]	19.6%[**]

Sources: American Hospital Association 1979, Table 1; Great Britain, Central Statistical Office 1980a, 1980b; U. S. Department of Commerce 1979.

*Discharges or deaths in NHS hospitals, England and Wales. All figures for hospitals in the United Kingdom exclude the (small) role of hospitals outside the NHS.

[†] 1977.

[‡] England, 1977.

[§] Nonfederal psychiatric beds.

"NHS only, Great Britain. There were 66,474 physicians (or full-time equivalents) working in the NHS in Great Britain in 1978.

[#] Figures for Great Britain (excluding Northern Ireland). Exclude physicians in training positions. In Great Britain in 1978 there were 13,820 hospital specialists and 25,247 unrestricted general practitioner principals.

[**] Percent of office-based practitioners who were general practitioners, 1977.

the United Kingdom and the United States. Several striking features are evident. First, the United Kingdom spends relatively less on health services than the United States. The percentage spent on the National Health Service rose from less than 4 percent GNP in 1960 to 5.6 percent by 1975 and has since then been held at approximately the same level. Private expenditures on services provided outside the NHS are not included in this total, but private expenditures are estimated at only 3 percent of total health-care expenditures (Royal Commission 1979a, p. 289). The relatively small role of private hospital care is illustrated in Table 12.3. United States figures show a much greater commitment of the GNP to health-service expenditures; moreover the percentage has been rising steadily over the past decade.

The NHS is funded each year through government appropriation; in 1978–79, 88 percent of the cost was raised through general taxation, less than 10 percent from national insurance contributions, 2 percent from prescription and other charges, and the remainder from miscellaneous sources, including the sale of land. The health service competes with other demands on taxation, such as defense, environment, or employment, and more directly with other government-funded social benefits: notably with education, personal social services, school meals, milk and welfare foods, social security benefits, and government housing programs. The proportion spent on health services has been kept in line with the expansion of domestic social expenditures in general. Thus in 1978–79 NHS expenditures represented 19.4 percent of government expenditures on health, education, housing, and social services, virtually the same proportion as in 1968–69 (Great Britain, Central Statistical Office 1980a, p. 54).

A third observation on Table 12.2 relates to the continuing predominance of general or family practitioner care in the United Kingdom. Government policy of the last fifteen years has been to encourage and stimulate primary care, including the narrowing or abolition of the wide income gap between general practitioners and specialists that existed into the mid-1960s. The number of general practitioners rose slowly in the 1970s; by 1978 there were approximately 27,000 family practitioners in the United Kingdom.

Following traditional British patterns, general or family practitioners work out of offices or health centers in the community, usually in group practices of three or

TABLE 12.3 Public and Private Hospital Care, England, 1977–78

Public Sector	
NHS hospital beds (1977)	375,900
Beds per 1,000 population (1977)	8.1
Number of patients discharged (1977)	5,345,000
Private Sector	
Acute beds in private hospitals (1977)	3,698
Pay beds in NHS hospitals (1978)	2,896
Pay beds in private and NHS hospitals per 1,000 population (1977–78)	0.14
Patients treated in pay beds (England and Wales, 1977)	93,877

Sources: Royal Commission 1979a, pp. 285, 292, 428; Great Britain, Central Statistical Office 1980b; p. 70. The figure for the number of patients treated in pay beds, cited in the Royal Commission report, is drawn in turn from Lee 1978.

more physicians. Members of the population select and register with a family physician for primary care. When necessary the physician refers the patient to a hospital-based specialist for consultation or hospital admission. This separation of functions between family doctor and specialist care has a long history and is an intrinsic part of the British professional, as well as organizational, system, incorporated into the structures of the NHS in 1948 (Stevens 1966; Honigsbaum 1979). Family doctors are, technically, independent contractors with the NHS, reimbursed on a complicated per capita formula for each person registered in the practice; on average there are approximately 2,300 patients per doctor. In many cases family practices include additional NHS professional staff, including district nurses and health visitors (nurses with special training in health education and preventive care who work primarily with families, young children and the elderly). Medical specialists, in contrast, are employed by the NHS on salary and based on hospitals. The salary scale is uniform across specialties from pediatrics to neurosurgery, although additional "distinction awards" are given to selected individuals on the basis of merit, as judged by special professional committees.

If all doctors are counted, including those in hospital residency positions, physicians in Britain are based on hospitals in approximately a 3:2 ratio. The number of senior specialist positions is limited, however, by the number of salaried positions made available in the NHS. When trainees are excluded, as Table 12.2 indicates, family practitioners greatly outnumber fully recognized specialists.

Out of more than one million staff working in the National Health Service, fewer than 7 percent are physicians. Physicians play a similarly minor role, numerically, in the health-care system of the United States. Table 12.4 shows the array of staff employed in health care in the United Kingdom. Notable is the dependence of health services on the two largest groups of workers identified in the table: nurses and ancillary workers. While the proportions and diversity of staff are characteristic of all major health-service systems, representing the growing complexity of services and organizations rather than government activity per se, the sheer numbers of personnel in different groups create clearly defined power groups within the system. The NHS employs, for example, more than 430,000 nurses and more than 200,000 ancillary workers (in jobs such as catering, laundry, domestic work, portering). Strikes by one group can cause disruptions throughout the system. Widespread strikes of ancillary workers occurred in 1972–73 (cf. Bosanquet 1979), although recent figures show little industrial action: eight days lost per thousand NHS staff in 1977 (Royal Commission 1979a, p. 163). Constant adjustments and readjustments are required of all workers as the number and types of workers have grown, as unionization is developed at all levels, as roles need constantly to be renegotiated; and industrial relations have become of increasing importance throughout the NHS. Because health services are centralized, such activities are more visible than in similar labor disputes in the United States. Moreover, the organizational prominence of different occupational groups creates questions of "equity" in decision-making, challenging the traditional dominance of physicians.

Tables 12.1 through 12.4 suggest some fundamental distinctions in the context and provision of health services in the United Kingdom and United States. In part these distinctions are cultural, in part based on the political decisions underlying the NHS as a publicly funded social service, in part organizational. Cultural, political, and organizational factors are of course mutually interdependent. Britain was more attuned in the 1940s to the idea of a welfare state than was the United States;

TABLE 12.4   NHS Staff:UK 1977

CATEGORY OF STAFF	UNIT	NUMBER/WTES OF STAFF (ROUNDED)	PERCENTAGE OF THE TOTAL
Total	number/ wte	1,003,000	
Doctors*			
Hospital, community and school health medical staff and locums †	wte	39,500	3.9
General medical practitioners	number	27,700	2.8
Dentists*			
Hospital, community and school health dental staff and locums ‡	wte	3,200	0.3
General dental practitioners	number	13,900	1.4
Other practitioners*			
Hospital pharmacists and opticians	wte	3,000	0.3
Ophthalmic and dispensing opticians in the GOS, ophthalmic medical practitioners and pharmacists in the GPS#	number	24,800	2.5
Nursing and midwifery Staff			
Hospital, community, school health, blood transfusion service and agency staff	wte	430,500	43.0
Professional and technical (excluding works) Staff			
Scientific, technical, dental ancillary and remedial staff	wte	64,700	6.5
Ancillary staff and others			
Catering, laundry, domestic, portering etc staff	wte	219,700	21.9
Ambulance service staff			
Ambulance officers, control assistants and ambulancemen §	wte	20,900	2.1
Administrative and clerical staff			
Administrators, clerical staff, support services managers etc	wte	123,200	12.3
Works and maintenance staff			
Regional, area and district works staff and hospital maintenance staff	wte	31,600	3.2

Source: Royal Commission 1979a, p. 178.
* The addition of numbers and whole-time equivalents involves an element of duplication as some practitioners are included in both categories.
† GPs holding hospital appointments are excluded.
‡ Dentists holding hospital appointments are excluded.
§ Other ambulance service staff are included under the respective staff category.
#GOS stands for General Ophthalmic Services, GPS for General Practitioner Services.

British political decision-making allowed for the act's passage; the organizational structures developed for health services reflected cultural expectations, traditions and ideologies of preexisting institutions, as well as political expediencies.

Yet to assume that organization is merely an expression of culture and politics draws a line that is too constricting. Organizations take on their own lives, make accommodations, acquire personalities, develop their own patterns of inertia and momentum. In order to explore the working assumptions of the NHS more clearly we need to know more about the special characteristics of the NHS as an organization which has evolved and changed over more than three decades.

The System of Health-Care Delivery in England

In the early 1980s, the NHS was in the throes of its third organizational change since 1946. The acceptance of a national policy for health care has put a continuing pressure on the infrastructure.

The original structure was tripartite. Hospitals, general practitioner, and public health services were served by three parallel organizations, formally combined only at national level by the Ministry of Health. Hospitals were organized as part of a national hospital service, subdivided into university-based hospital regions, with hospitals grouped for administrative purposes within each region. General practitioners, already used to the preexisting, much more limited scheme of national health insurance, were paid their capitation fees by an entirely separate network of organizations (executive councils). Public health services, including ambulance, home nursing services, and some mental health services, together with other nonhospital services, were organized through local government under the direction of Medical Officers of Health. Strategically there was much to be said for this arrangement; it allowed for implementation with a minimum of fuss. In each of the three branches of the service change was incremental rather than revolutionary. The most radical change was nationalizing the hospitals, which (with very few exceptions) became government-owned on 5 July 1948. But while rational in terms of implementation, by the 1960s there was widespread criticism of gaps in communication among the three branches at the local level. The NHS had moved into a second phase. Given a service already in place, the debate was no longer about broad national values and policies for medical care—these were accepted—but about organizational results and administrative procedures.

Notable problems in the tripartite structure were perceived in maternity services and psychiatric care, pieces of which were provided in all three branches of the service. A given patient, for example, might seek obstetrical care from a general practitioner, attend a local government maternity clinic, and enter hospital for delivery. None of these services was connected. Coordination of all three branches at the local level seemed essential to meet the needs of special services or population groups. A major report from the medical profession in 1962 (the Porritt Report 1962) came out strongly for recognition of one health authority, responsible for all health services, in an area. From that date until 1974, when the health services were reorganized into an area-wide pattern of comprehensive care, the development of a unified, integrated service at the local level appeared increasingly inevitable.

Before 1974 the NHS looked, structurally, like a highly centralized bureaucracy, particularly with respect to hospitals, with power and budgetary allocations flowing downward from the Ministry of Health to regions and through them to local hospital management committees, each responsible for several hospitals. But appearances can be deceiving. Critics of the NHS observed that the apparent center, the ministry, was distinguished by lack of initiative rather than by strong authority or direction (Brown 1979, pp. 10–13). The purpose of the ministry, as it had evolved through the first two decades of the NHS, was to respond to requests coming up from health authorities and to provide money to the regions rather than to develop detailed national service goals, prescribe guidelines, and supervise implementing them. Central statistical and reporting systems were weak. With budgets developed at local and regional level on the basis of services already in place, preexisting imbalances in the quality and supply of services in different areas of the country continued, notably in hospital care. General practitioner services were reasonably evenly spread across the country. However, the fact that the poorest hospital region in 1950 (Sheffield) remained the poorest region in 1971, with per capita revenue allocation for hospitals of only 84 percent the national average, was regarded by the 1970s as a major organizational deficiency (Cooper 1975, p. 65). Discussion had shifted from minimal access to health services for the whole population (goal of the NHS first phase) to perceived maldistribution of resources. There had been a shift in ideas of equity. While there were broad national entitlements to comprehensive care and a well-seasoned national structure for health services, there was no real history of a *national* health service in terms of explicit national priorities or expected outcomes.

The relationship between a national program and egalitarian aims—equal entitlements, access, and results of health care—was to emerge as a topic for debate in the mid 1970s. While egalitarian in intent, the NHS in the early 1970s was not strictly egalitarian in effect. Priorities were ill-defined or not defined. Management of an increasingly expensive and complex system appeared to be deficient as real resources stabilized or promised to dwindle. This background is important in understanding the reasons for, and implications of, structural change in 1974 and—the third major reorganization—the further modifications begun in 1980, with expected completion in 1982.

But organizational change is rarely simple and by the early 1970s there were other potent pressures for reform. Social services were scrutinized in a major government report (Seebohm Committee 1968), which recommended a unified, professionally directed social service department within each major local authority, instead of the scattering of services among health, welfare and child-care departments. This meant the removal from the NHS of nonmedically directed social services, such as home helps, hostels, or day-care centers (it would also mean the reassignment of medical and psychiatric social workers to social service departments when the health services, too, were reorganized in 1974); and the need to rethink, in turn, what was an appropriate scope for community *health* services. Local government boundaries were also in the process of being redrawn in a major reorganization of local government functions and areas, achieved by the Local Government Act of 1972. Discussion of the need to link health services with social services, now reorganized and unified in major departments in the new local government areas, emphasized as logical the unification and integration of health services to correspond with local government areas. An explicit policy assumption was that health and social services ought indeed to be closely linked.

As a separate, but connected movement, concern over management of health services was evident. Management terminology pervaded the NHS, as well as U.S. health services, by the early 1970s; words such as *planning, rationalization, priorities,* and *efficiency* heralded the arrival of management experts. The movement toward reorganization of the NHS was assisted, inter alia, by management consultants McKinsey and Company, and the Health Services Organization Research Unit of Brunel University, whose advice was given to the committee on management arrangements for the reorganized health service. By 1972, when this committee reported, reorganization was supported by both major political parties, though with somewhat different proposals. The National Health Service Reorganization Act of 1973 stipulated the pattern for a major reorganization of the NHS, effective 1 April 1974.

The nature and implementation of the 1974 changes have been analyzed by numerous students of the health-care scene (Abel-Smith 1978; Brown 1979; Levitt 1979, 1980; Watkin 1978). The general aim of reorganization was to integrate health services locally and to provide "maximum decentralization and delegation of decision making . . . within policies established at national, regional and area levels" ("Grey Book" p. 16). Health services were reorganized into fourteen regions in England, conforming more or less to the old hospital service regions. Present regional populations range from less than 2 million (East Anglia) to over 5 million (West Midlands). On the assumption that health service and social service boundaries should coincide, the 1974 changes mandated (within the regions) ninety area health authorities, with responsibility for providing health services in areas conforming to the new local government areas. However, in order to meet the concurrent goal of maximum decentralization, 205 districts were also established within the health areas, run by district management teams responsible to area health authorities. Finally, the functions of management and those of consumer representation were seen to be different. To provide community participation at the local level, new community health councils were also established at district level; and to ensure adequate professional advice from major groups, a network of advisory committees was developed.

It was evident from 1974 that the reorganization, in trying to meet a variety of goals, had invented a profusion of administrative structures, a conclusion confirmed by the Royal Commission on the National Health Service in 1979. The question was which tier should be removed—region, area, or district? In the event, the principle of conformity to local government boundaries lost out to the principle of maximum decentralization. The 1980–82 reorganization retains the regions but abolishes area health authorities in favor of reorganized and strengthened districts. District health authorities are being established for the "smallest geographical areas within which it is possible to carry out the integrated planning, provision and development of primary care and other community health services, together with those services normally associated with a district general hospital [a hospital of 750–1,100 beds or its equivalent on several sites], including those for the elderly, mentally ill and mentally handicapped" (Department of Health and Social Security 1980). The authorities are not expected to be self-sufficient in all services. Nevertheless, the basic outline of the health service, now being restructured, is of a federation of districts, each serving less than 500,000 population, grouped into regions of 2 to 5 million population.

Responsibility for the NHS at the national level is vested in the secretary of state for social services, head of the Department of Health and Social Security, who is, in turn, responsible to Parliament. (The Ministries of Health and Social Security were merged in 1968). The department (DHSS) was reorganized and strengthened in the early 1970s to take a stronger central role in managing health services. In 1971, for example, DHSS began to allocate NHS funds to the regions according to a formula that took into account local populations and variations in apparent need. Between 1972 and 1974 DHSS took a major role in the details of health-service reorganization. After 1974, DHSS developed a system of strategic planning to be undertaken at all NHS management levels (the first strategic plans filtered back to DHSS in 1977); and in 1976 DHSS introduced a modified method of resource allocation to the regions based on recommendations of the Resource Allocation Working Party (RAWP).

Regional health authorities form the next level of administration from a budgetary point of view. The health authorities themselves are management boards with a paid chairman and members who serve as volunteers. The staff is run by a consensus management team of six, including a regional medical officer and regional nursing officer. Regions vary both in population and in resources; the average population is 3.3 million. The number of NHS staff and practitioners ranges from less than 28,000 in the smallest region (East Anglia) to over 80,000 in the largest (West Midlands). NHS expenditures within each regional area ranged in 1977–78 from less than £200 million to over £500 million, but the proportional distribution of funds is similar in each region. Approximately 60 percent goes to hospital-based services, including medical specialists and hospital laboratory and X-ray services to family practitioners; 21 percent to family practitioner services (family doctors, dentists, opticians, and retail pharmacists), 6 percent to community health services (community nursing, maternal and child welfare clinics, school health services, family planning, psychology, chiropody, speech therapy, physiotherapy, vaccination and immunizations), 6 percent for capital expenditures, 4 percent for headquarters administration, and 3 percent for miscellaneous services (Great Britain, Central Statistical Office 1980b).

Regions are responsible for strategic planning, for major building and for specialized clinical services which have to be provided for large populations. In the North East Thames region, for example, regional specialties include cardiothoracic surgery and cardiology, neurosurgery and associated neurology, radiotherapy, hemodialysis and renal transplantation, plastic surgery (including burns), neonatal intensive care, communicable diseases, psychiatric medium secure care, and child and adolescent psychiatry, and other fields are being considered (North East Thames 1980, B36). Regions also employ consultants (medical specialists) and senior registrars (senior residents), each assigned to specific hospitals within districts in the region, organize blood transfusion services, and provide some management services to districts on a regional basis.

Since they control the purse strings for hospitals and community health services (family practitioner services are reimbursed through a separate network of family practitioner committees), the regions are theoretically powerful organizations. However, their role is limited by three practical constraints. The first is the momentum of the existing system. Regional health authorities, like other planning agencies, can have most apparent effect when the system is expanding—by offering monetary incentives to districts. However, in real terms, total annual expenditures of the NHS barely changed between 1972 and 1979, and no major expansions are foreseen.

Nationally defined priorities for certain services form a second set of constraints. The Labour Government document *Priorities for Health and Social Services in England* (Department of Health and Social Security 1976a) laid out areas in which there was to be expansion—even in a period of minimal or no growth in resources—and specified target increases in the costs of these "essential national priorities." These include primary-care and the so-called Cinderella services (services to the elderly, mentally ill, mentally handicapped, and for children). Initially the money for such increases had to be diverted from general hospital care. Implementing these national shifts at the margin of medical expenses imposes a general discipline on all regions, and on authorities within the regions, in order to meet national goals.

A third constraint on regional decision-making is government commitment to decentralized local decision-making, reinforced in the Conservative government's paper *Patients First* (1979): "We are determined to see that as many decisions as possible are taken at the local level—in the hospital and in the community. We are determined to have more local health authorities, whose members will be encouraged to manage the Service with a minimum of interference by any central authority, whether at region or in central government departments" (Department of Health and Social Security 1979, p. 2). Regions are thus caught in a peculiar tension—between demands for national goals for national services and policies of local responsibility. Inevitably these two philosophies conflict; they must be held in pragmatic equilibrium.

District health authorities are now being established within the regions to meet the aim of decentralization. The target size for district, as envisaged in the 1974 changes, was a population of 250,000, although there are considerable variations from place to place. Taking the target as a guide, a region of 3 million would include twelve districts, each now to be the responsibility of a district health authority. The existence of an authority and a management team parallels the structure at region. Each authority appoints a district management team to formulate advice to the authority on district-wide policies, priorities, and program and determine how decisions will be implemented. The team itself follows the pattern established in 1974: a consensus team of six including a district administrator, district treasurer, district nursing officer, district community physician, a consultant (specialist) physician, and a general medical practitioner. Consensus, it is pointed out, does not mean seeking unanimity at all costs; where there are significant differences of view, these will be reported to the authority. Below the DMT each district is to have wide discretion in determining its management arrangements.

The DHAs are responsible for hospital and community services, but not directly for family practitioner services, which continue to be run by separate family practitioner committees (a concession won by family practitioners themselves). Community health councils (CHCs) will continue, one council for each district, to represent the consumer view. Apart from professional advisory committees, there are thus three collectivities at district level, the authority, management team, and the CHC.

In some respects these structures can be seen as providing a participatory role for specific interests: providers, workers and consumers. However, the lines are not clear. By creating the CHC, the function of public representation has been rather oddly divorced from the function of management of public service (Levitt 1980, p. 41). This structure does, however, allow for the formulation of specific health-care interests. The fact that voluntary associations, trade unions, local government, professional groups, and others are consulted in forming CHCs and DHAs reflects a recognition of the pluralism and the complexity of interests in health services over and above the collective interests of all taxpayers.

At the same time the structure highlights the fact that there are also multiple interest groups wanting to influence aspects of the NHS, and thus multiple concepts of what the NHS should be. A report to the Royal Commission on the working of the NHS noted that the rationale for reorganization—the need for a "rational, allocative, equitable, accountable and participative system"—endorsed abstract collective assumptions which may conflict with individualist assumptions about health care. Moreover, some of the aims may be only "superficially compatible" (Royal Commission 1978, p. 223). Thus decision-making must assume a continuing conflict of expectations among participants.

In summary, the NHS is, in structure, nationally organized, with certain priorities specified on a national basis; divided into regions with planning and budgetary responsibilities; and further divided into districts of approximately a quarter of a million population with planning and operational responsibilities. Each level has a fixed budget and must meet this budget within strict cash limits. But a neat structure does not necessarily imply general agreement about goals and objectives. The process of definition continues.

Functional Definitions of Health Policy in England

No country has a clear-cut goal for health or health services. In Britain, as in the United States, health-care policies are in a constant process of negotiation, reappraisal, reinvention. The secretary of state's duty in each section of the United Kingdom—England and Wales, Scotland, Northern Ireland—is to secure improvement in physical and mental health and in the prevention, diagnosis, and treatment of illness, but these are vague goals, to say the least. The recent Royal Commission on the National Health Service (1979) attempted more concrete definitions of objectives: to encourage and assist individuals to remain healthy; to provide equality of entitlements to health services, a broad range of services of a high standard, equality of access and a service free at the time of use; to satisfy the reasonable expectations of its users; to remain a national service responsive to local needs (Royal Commission 1979a, pp. 8–9). But these goals, too, require refinement and ratification within a given organizational setting. Goals shift, depending on available resources, organizational behavior, and political contexts.

An important set of goals, reiterated by the Royal Commission, concern equality in health-services provision: including equality of entitlements and of access to care. But equality—and its softer American cousin *equity*—is a slippery term at best. Translation into functional meanings may require accommodations and adjustments among groups whose notions of equality are quite different, as well as recognition that constrained resources may limit, and organizational rigidities may channel, the implementation of ideals in an operating system.

Discussion in the NHS about equity has centered recently on four points: (1) how far the NHS has provided equal access to medical care; (2) how far equality of results has been attained, given the different needs of different population groups; (3) how far the distribution of tax funds is fair, with respect to the relative amount of money flowing into different areas and regions; and (4) what is the appropriate balance of authority for decision-making in a national service which is, at one and the same time, committed both to national entitlements and to decentralized local administration.

Equal access to health services was implied, in theory, from the beginning of the NHS with the removal of cost barriers to medical care. But there are obvious difficulties in how equal access is to be measured. Are we to deal, for example, with the experiences of large groups (and if so, which?) or with the experiences or perceptions of individuals? Values for equal access are still emerging in the NHS. The 1980 report, *Inequalities in Health*, focused on differences in apparent need and utilization of care by social class. While marked differences in health continue to be observed in Britain by social class, receipt of care under the NHS appears to be reasonably equitable if it is assumed that services should be either equally utilized by all classes or that individuals in higher social classes, being relatively healthier than average, should show a lower than average utilization. There is, for example, no significant class gradient in hospital outpatient vists for specialist consultations, and the use of hospitals by inpatients rises inversely with social class. (*Inequalities in Health* 1980, pp. 102, 104). The report suggests that there may be systematic differences in the quality of care received within the hospital by social class; however there is little evidence one way or another. (Moreover, it also assumes that hospital care is an unmitigated good.) The report finds the most notable differences in the health needs of children and in underutilization of preventive services by the working classes.

Table 12.5 shows a relationship between perception of illness and the actual use of services in the NHS, by occupational class for men aged forty-five to sixty-four years.These data suggest that some degree of equitable access has been achieved, if social class differences in health are taken into account. Another study, based on the findings of the British General Household Survey, concludes that the NHS has achieved equity in terms of primary care (Collins and Klein 1980). There is no consistent bias against lower socioeconomic groups once use has been standardized for self-reported morbidity; indeed, there is some suggestion that lower socioeconomic groups have higher rates than might otherwise be expected. A study of access to primary care undertaken for the Royal Commission on the National Health Service found the availability of general practitioners apparently adequate, as reported from a survey of patients, as well as a high degree of satisfaction; their greatest problems related to transportation (Royal Commission 1979b, pp. 1149–58). Others, however, disagree. The Royal Commission also notes general satisfaction with hospital services.

Different notions and evaluations of equal entitlements are clearly evident in these appraisals. The Royal Commission noted "significant geographical and social inequity," but implied that social equality would not be achieved until actual measures of *health* were broadly similar by social class; it noted the absence of evidence (in available mortality and morbidity data) to show that social inequalities in health had decreased since the NHS came into being: "The position of

TABLE 12.5   Sickness and Medical Consultation by Social Class, Men Aged 45–64, Rates per 1,000 Population, Great Britain

Socioeconomic Group	Long-standing Illness	Restricted Activity	Medical Consultation
1. Professional	229	71	76
2. Managerial	257	75	75
3. Intermediate	368	98	122
4. Skilled Manual	358	103	112
5. Semiskilled Manual	388	101	125
6. Unskilled Manual	486	120	146
All	349	97	110
Ratio 6/All	1.39	1.24	1.32

Source: Data from the British General Household Survey, 1974–76, reported in *Inequalities in Health* 1980, Table 2:14, p. 53.

those in social classes IV and V appears to have worsened relative to those in social classes I and II, though it should be remembered that all social classes are healthier than they were thirty years ago" (Royal Commission 1979a, pp. 18–19). However, the commission also recognized that inequality in personal health can only partly be attributed to health service and cited Brotherston's conclusion that some degree of inequality may be expected to arise out of the fact that the NHS is a "self-help" system in which those most in need do not necessarily seek care (Brotherston 1976). This disagreement about whether equal entitlements have been achieved in Britain points up the general fuzziness of "equality" as a functional definition.

British concern about continuing social class differences will undoubtedly mean continuing concern about morbidity differences under the general rubric of vertical or social equity. From the managerial perspective, however, horizontal or geographical equity is easier to measure. Presumably an equitable health service does not penalize or favor its participants according to where they happen to live. Table 12.6 shows the distribution of primary care personnel across broad geographical regions of England. One notable feature of the NHS has been a relatively even distribution of general medical practitioners across the country. The table shows that primary care nurses are also available to a comparable degree across the regions; dentists (whose role in the NHS is more akin to private practice) are less evenly spread.

Consideration of access on both a social and a geographical basis underlines the strong relationships that exist between notions of equity, the role of planning and priorities in a health care system, and the distribution of available resources across different health care locations. The Royal Commission came out squarely with the statement that "a fundamental purpose of a national service must be equality of provision so far as this can be achieved without an unacceptable sacrifice of standards" (Royal Commission 1979a, p. 10). A corollary is equity in financing such provision. "Equalization" as a distributional fiscal doctrine appeared in the 1970s as a deliberate attempt to establish geographical equity in the distribution of funding to NHS regions.

TABLE 12.6 Regional Distribution of General Medical and Dental Services, England, 1978

	GMP Average List*	Persons per Primary Care Nurse[†]	Persons per Dentist	Prescriptions per Person
North	2,377	1,728	5,277	7.1
Yorkshire and Humberside	2,362	2,016	4,658	7.2
East Midlands	2,400	1,920	5,212	6.4
East Anglia	2,214	2,064	4,417	6.6
South East	2,277	2,071	3,127	6.2
South West	2,156	1,959	3,391	6.8
West Midlands	2,371	1,936	4,814	6.8
North West	2,370	1,742	4,369	7.6
England	2,312	1,962	3,871	6.7
United Kingdom	2,252	1,849	3,960	6.8

Source: Great Britain, Central Statistical Office 1980b, from Tables 2.1, 5.2, 5.9.

* Persons registered for services with NHS general medical practitioners (family physicians).

[†] Registered nurses employed in primary care as midwives, health visitors and home nurses.

The principle of equitable distribution of funds to populations served by a large-scale health system is one barely discussed in the United States, but one that may become more important in the future as discrepancies in major public programs, such as in Medicare or Medicaid, become more evident by geographical region. In Britain policies of geographical equalization of funds have been made explicit. The 1970 Labour party Green Paper included a statement that financial allocations for services would eventually be based on populations served, differences in morbidity, the state of capital plant and the special needs of teaching and research. In the same year DHSS introduced its resource allocation formula for nonuniversity teaching hospitals, designed to produce an equitable distribution of funds geographically within ten years; but there was dissatisfaction with the formula, based as it was in part on the existing number of beds and cases served in the various NHS regions rather than on definitions of "need." A new formula was developed by the Resource Allocation Working Party (1976) aimed deliberately at "equal opportunity for access to health care for people at equal risk" (Department of Health and Social Security 1976b, p. 25). Formula allocations are based on age and sex, standard mortality ratios and differential bed use for age, sex, and selected conditions (actual differences in bed use in the regions were removed from the formula). Target allocations for NHS funding by region theoretically permit a much higher growth of spending in some regions than others. However, the target of geographical equalization of funds has coincided with a period of general economic retrenchment, making the target a long-term philosophy rather than a short term program.

The concept of geographical equity in funding is not new, either in Britain or the United States. (It was on this basis, indeed, that federal old-age assistance grants were first given to the states through the 1935 social security legislation, in a formula favoring the poorer over the richer states; and more recently in federal grants to states for Medicaid.) Ensuring that funds for medical care are broadly similar across geographical areas remains an appealing distributional principle. When translated into equivalent block grants for each geographical entity, an overall rationing of funds may be achieved while discretionary spending in local areas remains.

Equality in funding, per capita, does not, however, necessarily lead to equality of access to service, to similar quality of care, nor to social equity; indeed, fiscal "equalization" may lead to noticeable discrepancies in service from place to place. Two health authorities may be given equivalent amounts of money with respect to population; the more efficient will presumably provide more effective services based, inter alia, on preexisting quality and stock of resources, demands of the population, managerial abilities, and efficiencies due to economies of scale. (In the United States, a leading health plan proposal designed to stimulate private sector competition, Alain Enthoven's consumer choice plan, assumes that if price per capita for an array of services is fixed, qualitative differences will appear from one health plan to the next.) Given the variations that exist among districts in the NHS, differential value-for-money may be expected. Thus, while the principle of equalization endorsed in Britain on a geographic basis is far from full implementation, the nature of "equality" implied in "equalization" is different from the egalitarian notions implicit in equal access or equality of care.

How far the results of medical care (equal outcomes) are comparable among individuals in different areas or different institutions, it is difficult to say, for British doctors see suggestions for medical audit or outcome measures as unnecessarily

authoritarian. One of the characteristics of the American system of public regulation of private industry is a tacit acceptance of standardization of processes, in-
spections, and required statistical reports. Hence the readier acceptance in the
United States of health-planning norms and PSROs. In Britain, in industries where
public management is accepted, ironically there is much less accountability by individuals within the system. British medical groups are frequently assured by their
leaders that they are not advocating the development of a "corps of inspectors,"
and participants at meetings on possible medical audit systems make comments
such as: "Compulsion could only be bulldozed through over many dead bodies in
last ditches" ("Audit in General Practice" 1980; Reynell 1981.) In this case, as in
other aspects of health management in Britain, physicians' attitudes are taken
seriously.

This observation leads to more general considerations of the participation of
different interests in decision-making in the NHS. The medical profession and
other professional organizations are heavily involved in managing the health service through representatives on management teams at district and regional levels,
as well as through advisory committees. Professional associations such as the British Medical Association develop managerial policy positions. In late 1980, for example, the BMA was developing a document on the future of primary care, and
discussing the role of community nurses in inner-city areas with the Royal College
of Nursing.

This partial incorporation of the major health-care occupations within the
NHS structure, a further heritage of the organizational experience of the health
service, raises (1) notions of equity with respect to the responsibilities and roles of
health professionals, and (2) questions of *whose* attitudes about fairness (and
other aspects of policy) should be structured into decision-making. In Britain
physicians and other independent professionals are both captives of a system
which is a virtual monopoly and essential to the operation of that system. Physicians, for example, are at one and the same time more effectively unionized in Britain than in the United States (the BMA is registered as a trade union and affiliated
with the TUC, the equivalent of the AFL-CIO), and organized into representative
organizations which connect with the advisory and management structure of the
NHS. More broadly, the notion that the health professions have a right to participate in major NHS decisions has been accepted on both sides of the table. This notion of occupational participation, as well as notions of consumer participation
implicit in the community health councils, provides an important element in decisions and definitions of service goals.

National priorities for the development of services for selected population
groups provide a further dimension to contemporary debates about equity in Britain. A national health service sounds, by its very nature, like a planned service.
Yet before 1974 there was little effective planning in the NHS. Planning was
mainly through a process of historical accident. In 1976 in a consultative document, *Priorities for Health and Personal Social Services in England*, serious efforts
were made by government to establish "rational and systematic priorities
throughout the health and personal social services" (Department of Health and
Social Security 1976a, p. 1). It was in this document that national priority was
given to services used mainly by the elderly, services for the mentally ill, services
for the handicapped, and services for children. The concurrent developments of
equalization and rationalization as policies provided two interweaving attempts
to rechannel resources in the NHS: first to deprived areas and, second, to improve

care to neglected populations. As yet, it is too early to assess the results of these policy shifts. Both may turn out to be unrealistic.

While it has been stressed that the national priorities are designed as goals for broad national changes rather than specific targets to be reached by declared dates in any particular locality, and that the pattern and pace of change will vary from place to place, a series of departmental guidelines have been set. For example, the 1977 guidelines for acute inpatient beds were to reduce such beds from the 1975–76 level of 3.4 per thousand to 2.8 per thousand in the future. It is difficult to have a nationally managed system (or even a nationally regulated system) without some precise overall objectives; but how precise—and how mandatory—should these be? A general answer is no clearer in Britain than in the United States, yet the issues are important in both countries. How far, for example, are the perceptions of local communities—and which communities?—to be taken into account in the development of services at a time when potential demand for care outstrips the resources available? How far is variation in services among different communities fair? And on what basis?

The inevitable tension between national goals and local initiative forms the final strand considered here in the discussions of policy in Britain. Both the 1974 and the 1980s reorganizations have, as an important goal, decentralization of responsibility. Patrick Jenkin, Conservative secretary of state for social services, speaks of local health systems having the "minimum of interference by any central authority" (Department of Health and Social Security 1979, p. 2). The establishment, in the early 1980s, of district health authorities follows the same goal of decentralizing service to the local level. Decentralization is an appealing concept in government-operated, as well as in government-regulated, systems. For a service faced with no real increases in funds and with statements of national priorities which can only be met by reducing acute hospital care, delegation of tough decisions to the district level makes administrative sense. Decisions not to open new hospitals because of additional costs, or to close old ones because of more pressing needs—both essentially political activities—have to be played out within a given budget for comprehensive services at the local level. Yet district management teams have shown themselves to be remarkably varying in their capacity to develop consensus and change, and decentralization of its very nature assumes the promotion of local variations (Stewart et al. 1980). Variations may be expected on two counts: first, because of different local decisions, for example, to promote mental health services over geriatrics, or vice versa; second, because of the relative success of district authorities and management teams in forming consensus at the local level.

The development of policies for decentralization in Britain will be interesting to watch from American as well as British perspectives, if only to assess the degree of similarity or difference that emerges in health services in different areas in a period of years. But there are more general questions. If local agencies make all decisions about priorities in health care, national policies become less relevant. Conversely, if there are too many national norms, local autonomy is an illusion (cf. Lee 1977). To some extent the dilemma has been avoided in Britain since there has been little money since 1974 to press for major distinctions at the local level. Nevertheless, the balance between national (system) norms and local (subsystem) initiative remains a critical question for any large-scale health service. Perhaps the NHS will go through a cycle of swings—from increasing local variation to national norms, and vice versa, as a form of continuing self-correction.

Relevance to the United States

The continuation of both philosophical and structural problems in the NHS has direct relevance for health-policy debates in the United States. First, it is evident that choices in health services go far beyond the choices implicit in adopting the political rhetoric of a "socialized" versus a "private" system. Britain is, indeed, flirting with the idea of increasing involvement of private enterprise in health care, if only at the margin. But the real philosophical problems, of egalitarianism, for example, exist within (and beyond) the confines of the NHS; for they are problems in large part of organizational complexity, of differences of opinion, points of view, clarity of expression, or lack of evidence. It is salutary to appreciate that even in Britain, with more than thirty years of a national system, "equity" has no single meaning. Discussions about social class are not necessarily linked to debates about equal access to care; the lack of outcome measures makes it virtually impossible to generalize about equality of results (equal outcomes of care or quality) in the health system. The "equalization" policy for the distribution of funds on a geographical basis does not necessarily connect with other definitions, and there are continuing questions of the appropriate emphasis to be placed on local decision-making versus national norms for care.

There are, indeed, multiple concepts of what a health service should be. Given that the NHS has formalized, in its structure, a whole range of administrative, professional, and social interests, conflicts over goals are to be expected. But it is difficult to see how such interests could *not* be recognized in any organized health system. Problems of how control and authority will be exercised in a complex system (which includes the control of work of specific professionals and of a large bureaucratic organization) have yet to be fully acknowledged, let alone thought through even in Britain (Royal Commission 1978, pp. 223–27). More generally, it must be accepted that there are inherent tensions and ambiguities in health systems, that choices have to be made when there is no perfect solution, and that policies cannot be developed in any simple, nonconflictual decision-making structure.

There is, in short, no one rational system for health care—in the United States or in Britain—which will meet the perceived ideals of all participants. As a large, complex set of enterprises, health services will develop goals out of a continuing process of accommodation among a variety of interests: notably among political, professional, and consumer representatives. It follows, too, that goals will shift, both over time and as an expression of economic constraints and of the relative dominance of given interests.

The tight economies and political conservatism of the 1980s raise other questions for debate in the United States. While the United States has been able to expand health expenditures far more than the British system, there seems little question that rationing of one sort or another will become an increasingly important question here: assuming rationing to mean deliberate attempts by public or private groups to share out resources according to articulated values and priorities. As the political focus in the United States turns in the 1980s toward a more explicit emphasis on private enterprise, a concomitant slackening of government regulation over private industry, and a commitment by the Reagan administration to shift responsibility away from national government to the states, British efforts to define appropriate structures and definitions of equity become curiously relevant.

The innate sense of egalitarianism that pervades the British NHS—the sense that limited resources for health care should be shared out, as far as possible across the whole population, may never be part of the larger system of health services in the United States. Egalitarian goals of health and other social services which distinguished the Great Society programs of the 1960s have long given way to acceptance of, or apathy toward, social differences. Holders of well-endowed Blue Cross plans feel little sense of solidarity with Medicaid beneficiaries or those with no insurance protection. Notions of equality implicit in Medicaid's initial goal of bringing the poor into the "mainstream of medicine" (care by private practitioners) rested in large part on the simultaneous assumption that medical care was an expanding market, i.e., that tax money for the program would be available. Current debates on welfare, including Medicaid, as a "safety net" assume both minimal protection for the poor and distinctions between the care available to the poor and middle-class medicine. Only the incorporation of all social groups into systems with egalitarian expectations—and these could be HMOs—will change this basic two-class system.

If equity is defined as rationing limited resources equally across all social groups, socialized or quasi-governmental medicine is probably the only answer. (Quasi-governmental means, for example, a system in which resources continue in private ownership but government regulates health insurance and resource distribution.) Britain has gone a long way in its health system to remove potential cost barriers and to spread services (particularly primary care) more equally. Moreover, while efforts are being made to maintain high-technology hospital care, national priorities for care also favor the medically and socially disadvantaged—the old, the mentally ill, the mentally retarded—in ways which are inconceivable in the United States, at least at present. Medicare and Medicaid are much more likely to be cut back than to be expanded in the 1980s. Indeed, the signs are already evident.

Such cuts highlight other aspects of British policy-making which will become increasingly relevant here. The geographical distribution of tax funds is likely to become a more central aspect of health-policy debates in the United States. The British policies of "equalization" and "rationalization" of tax funds deserve fuller exploration. Given limited tax funds, both through social security (Medicare) and general taxation (Medicaid), on what distributional principle should these be expended? Is it fair that Medicare beneficiaries in one part of the country get a better deal in terms of money spent on care than those elsewhere? Or, for that matter, that a Medicare beneficiary needing major surgery (covered by Medicare) is favored over an elderly person lacking teeth (not covered)? As Medicaid programs retrench in different states, under both federal and state tax squeezes, differences among state Medicaid programs will become more pronounced. States with a relatively generous tradition of care (and states which are richer) will try to maintain programs at current levels; other states will cut. As programs change, the philosophies underlying American health service provision—the implicit goals—will demand a clearer articulation. It will be sad if the structured inequalities that promise to result are attributed solely to the existence of a "private" health-care system.

Managerially, too, the United States has much to learn from comparisons with Britain. Consensus management and the increasing involvement of occupational and consumer groups are already evident in large-scale American systems such as hospital chains or HMOs. More managerially conscious medical and nursing professionals promise to emerge in the 1980s, if only as a result of the development of educational programs in cost-containment. Both movements are important. Perhaps the most important question is, however, the proper division of responsibility for decision-making between government and local services, whether these services are technically in the "public" or the "private" sector. In the United States debates on these questions are still rudimentary.

The 1980s reorganization of the British health service is designed to do what contemporary American politics also suggests: to take central government, as far as possible, out of the picture and to encourage local initiative. The British mixture of broad national priorities, some national programs (such as heart transplantation or kidney dialysis), some programs reserved for regional decision (such as plastic surgery), and distribution of budgets to local areas on a formula basis (designed to equalize resources geographically) works only in a comprehensively organized service; although it could work for private national or regional medical-care systems in the United States. In many respects, then, there are apparently parallel moves in the two countries, although perhaps more parallel in intent than in potential execution.

The dilemmas of government's role in the regulation of health services and regulation at which level—national, state, or local—have not yet been faced in the United States. The granting of tax funds without detailed accountability is also alien to the American tradition. The recent history of Medicare and Medicaid show quite clearly that Congress is reluctant to delegate decisions to private organizations or to the states. Detailed regulation, probably at the national level, will also be necessary if, indeed, competition in health services is to be encouraged in the United States. Obviously competition requires standardized information on the basis of which consumer choices can be made. How, otherwise, will rational consumers of health care know which are best buys for health insurance, which the most efficient institutions?

The critical level of management in Britain in the next decade is the relatively small district. In this country the critical level is the state, where action will be required, if federal decision-making is to be downplayed. Decentralization as an issue in the United States is thus partial and relative—like delegating health services in Britain only to the regions. State and local experience in regulating health services will have to be effective in the United States if decentralized decision-making is to be achieved. It is possible that, lacking initiative in the states, or, more likely, with mixed experience of standard-setting from state to state, the United States may turn back in the future to detailed national regulation of health-care provision, at least for tax-supported services and possibly for all forms of care. Indeed, it is possible that government regulation of medical care in the United States, in terms of specification of detailed procedures and standards, may eventually become much more detailed than in Britain. Paradoxically, we may yet see a health service in this country which is subject to a greater degree of national control than in Britain.

In both countries, the experiment continues. Differences in the function of government as provider or regulator of medical care, and comparison between the NHS, a vast health-service organization, and large-scale health systems in the United States, will continue to provide rich fruit for comparison. But the hardest questions on both sides of the Atlantic are, in the end, social value judgements. How do we wish to measure the success of a health service? Whose attitudes about fairness are to be taken most seriously?

REFERENCES

ABEL-SMITH, B. 1978. *National Health Service: the first thirty years,* London: HMSO.

American Hospital Association. 1979. *Hospital Statistics.* Chicago: American Hospital Association.

ANDERSON, O. W. 1977. Are national health systems converging? Predictions for the United States. *Annals, American Academy of Political and Social Science* 434:24–38.

"Audit in General Practice." 1980. *British Medical Journal* 281:1375.

Beveridge Report. 1942. *Social insurance and allied services.* Report by Sir William Beveridge, Cmd. 6404. London: HMSO.

BOSANQUET, N., ed. 1979. *Industrial relations in the NHS: the search for a system.* London: King Edward's Hospital Fund.

BROTHERSTON, J. 1976. Inequality: is it inevitable? In *Equalities and inequalities in health,* ed. C. O. Carter and J. Peel, p. 97. London: Academic Press.

BROWN, R. G. S. 1979. *Reorganising the National Health Service.* Oxford: Blackwell and Martin Robertson.

COCHRANE, A. L. 1978. 1931–1971: a critical review with particular reference to the medical profession. In *Medicine for the year 2000,* symposium held at the Royal College of Physicians, London, ed. G. Teeling-Smith and N. Wells. London: Office of Health Economics.

COLLINS, E., and R. KLEIN, 1980. Equity and the NHS: self-reported morbidity, access, and primary care. *British Medical Journal* 281:1111–15.

COOPER, M. H. 1975. *Rationing health care.* New York: Wiley.

Department of Health and Social Security. 1976a. *Priorities for health and personal social services in England: a consultative document.* London: HMSO.

———. 1976b. *Sharing resources for health in England. Report of the Resource Allocation Working Party.* London: HMSO.

———. 1979. *Patients first: consultative paper on the structure and management of the National Health Service in England and Wales.* London: HMSO.

———. 1980. *Health Service development, structure and management,* Health Circular HC (80), 8. London: DHSS, July 1980.

Great Britain, Central Statistical Office. 1980a. *Annual abstract of statistics,* 1980 ed. London: HMSO.

———. 1980b. *Regional statistics,* no. 15, 1980 ed. London: HMSO.

"Grey Book." 1972. *Management arrangements for the reorganised Health Service.* London: HMSO.

HONIGSBAUM, F. 1979. *The division in British Medicine: a history of the separation of general practice from hospital care 1911–1968.* New York: St. Martin's Press.

Inequalities in Health. 1980. Report of a research working group (Chairman: Sir Douglas Black). London: Department of Health and Social Security.

Institute of Medicine, National Academy of Sciences. 1981. *Health care in a context of civil rights,* chap. 2. Washington, D. C.: National Academy of Sciences.

KLEIN, R. 1978. Ideology, class and the National Health Service. *Journal of Health Politics, Policy and Law* 4:464–90.

LEE, K. 1977. Public expenditure, planning and local democracy. In *Conflicts in the National Health Service,* ed. K. Barnard and K. Lee, pp. 200–31. London: Croom Helm.

LEE, M. 1978. *Private and National Health Services.* London: Policy Studies Institute.

LEVITT, R. 1979. *The reorganised National Health Service.* London: Croom Helm, 2d ed. rev.

———. 1980. *The people's voice in the NHS: community health councils after five years.* London: King Edward's Hospital Fund.

North East Thames Regional Health Authority. 1980. *Regional strategic plan 1978–1988.* London.

Porritt Report. 1962. *A review of the medical services in Great Britain.* Report of a committee sponsored by the Royal College of Physicians of London et al. London.

REYNELL, P. C. 1981. Conference report. *Lancet* 1:286.

Royal Commission on the National Health Service. 1978. *The working of the National Health Service.* Research Paper no. 1. London: HMSO.

——. 1979a. *Report,* Cmnd. 7615. London: HMSO. Chairman, Sir Alex Merrison.

——. 1979b. *Access to primary care.* Research Paper no. 6, London: HMSO.

Seebohm Committee. 1968. *Report of the committee on local authority and allied personal social services,* Cmnd., 3703. London: HMSO.

STEVENS, R. 1966. *Medical practice in modern England: the impact of specialization and state medicine.* New Haven, Conn.: Yale University Press.

——. 1977. Governments and medical care. In *Medical education and medical care,* ed. G. McLachlan, pp. 155–75. London: Oxford University Press for the Nuffield Provincial Hospitals Trust.

STEWART, R.; SMITH, P.; BLAKE, J.; and WINGATE, P. 1980. *The district administrator in the National Health Service.* London: King Edward's Hospital Fund.

TERRY, P. B.; CONDIE, R. G.; and SETTATREE, R. S. 1980. Analysis of ethnic differences in perinatal statistics. *British Medical Journal* 281:1307.

U.S. Department of Commerce, Bureau of the Census, 1979. *Statistical Abstract of the United States, 1979,* 100th ed. Washington, D.C.: Government Printing Office.

WATKIN, B. 1978. *The National Health Service: the first phase, 1948–74 and after.* London: Allen and Unwin.

Chapter 13

The General Hospital: A Social and Historical Perspective

Odin W. Anderson
Norman Gevitz

THE HOSPITAL CURRENTLY SERVES three major interrelated social functions: as a center for patient care, a site for medical education, and a locus for ongoing clinical research. However, for most of its history, it has also operated as a vehicle for spiritual salvation, a hotel for travelers, and a custodial institution for perceived deviants and defectives. The particular goals of the hospital have been dependent on and are reflective of the dominant values of the larger social order. A generally felt need to perform good works as a means of achieving grace certainly bears consequences different from those where a high premium is put upon the advancement of scientific knowledge. In addition, such issues as the number, average size, financing, staffing, organization, and orientation of the hospital are related to a range of other macrosociological variables, among these the degree of urbanization, the form and condition of the economy, and of course the political environment.

The Evolution of the Hospital

One of the earliest and most important antecedents of the hospital in the Western world emerged in ancient Greece out of the cult of Aesculapius, which gained prominence in the area by the beginning of the fourth century B.C. Temples were established in the healing god's name where supplicants gathered for a cure of their assorted ailments. After offering prayers, the individual would spend at least one night at the base of a statue of the deity, awaiting a dream in which Aesculapius himself would appear either to directly eliminate the affliction or to offer advice as to how it might be cured. In return, grateful patients provided testimonials, donated money, and offered golden, silver, or marble representations of the bodily part successfully restored to normal function. Gradually, physicians became affiliated with the temples, thereby serving to introduce physical modalities into overall patient management, though the continued reliance upon super-

305

natural intervention as part of the regimen was not in strict accord with the image of the rational, experience-based approach more generally associated with the Hippocratic tradition.

The Romans, who succeeded the Greeks as the masters of the Mediterranean, relied heavily upon the medical knowledge of their predecessors. Their own contributions came in the field of public health—the building of aqueducts to provide a continuous and relatively pure water supply; the establishment of an efficient sewage system to eliminate the wastes that left unattended provide the breeding ground for epidemic disease; the creation of public baths for the cleansing and relaxation of its citizens; and last, but certainly not least, the hospital. The first Roman hospitals, or *valetudinaria*, were run for the military. Due to the breadth of the empire, soldiers would be separated from their families for extended periods. Thus, when sick they often had to be boarded in the homes of strangers where the nursing significantly varied in its quality and devotion. By the first century A.D. some Roman generals made provision for a separate barracks to be erected in their camps for the ill and temporarily disabled. With a centralized treatment facility, the men were more easily kept track of, medical care was standardized, and costs reduced. Furthermore, ailing soldiers felt less isolated receiving continuous social support in a familiar setting, surrounded by friends and peers. Soon this system was adopted throughout the army and extended to the care of gladiators and slaves.

With the rise and spread of Christianity across the Roman world, the nature and purpose of the hospital was transformed. The instrumental objective of providing facilities for special categories of individuals whose recovery was deemed in the best interests of the state gave way to a more sacred mission. Among the teachings of the new religion was the value of charity. The Christian was told that aid to the less fortunate members of society, including the sick, was a duty. This commitment was strengthened by the widespread belief that salvation of one's soul would be vouchsafed by regular alms-giving. In ministering to and providing for the ill and infirm, the benefactor, it was argued, could later gain entry into heaven.

The virtual political and cultural bifurcation of the empire beginning in the third century resulted in two different paths toward hospital development within Christendom. The East was marked by considerable specialization. In terms of charity services, separate facilities were established for pilgrims and travelers (*xenodocia*); the aged (*gerocomia*); orphans (*orphanotrophia*); and the sick (*noscomia*). The various functions and operations of the latter institution were highly compartmentalized. For example, one *noscomia* at Constantinople built in 1136 had five separate divisions, each for a different class of diseases plus an outpatient department. It was administered by two physicians, and under their direction were two chief clinicians who supervised the rest of the medical staff. This pattern, which was a fusion of Roman organization and rational Greek medical practice, was well suited to the needs of a highly centralized government overseeing a large urban population.

While the internal structure of Byzantine hospitals influenced the development of similar facilities in the Islamic world, its impact upon Europe was negligible. In the West, the decline and ultimate dissolution of the empire in the latter part of the fifth century made for diffuse and weak political centers. The cities—the transmitters of learning—suffered badly. Rome, once boasting of approximately a million people, sank to a population of a mere twenty thousand. Occupational specialization also diminished with medicine becoming a part-time calling of the clergy. Almost all medical charity institutions established in the West would be undifferentiated, serving as a combination hospital, orphanage, hotel, and workhouse.

The first facilities sprang from monasteries—two of the earliest being the Hôtel-Dieu of Lyons (542) and the Hôtel-Dieu of Paris (650)—literally translated, hotels of God. This movement was accelerated by the action of the Council of Aachen in 816, making it church policy for bishops and abbots to create refuges for the poor. During the next three centuries, hundreds of such hospitals were founded in connection with religious communities, while still others were built along the various routes taken during the Crusades. Not only did these institutions serve as gateways to paradise, they created considerable goodwill among the public here on earth. This in turn stimulated certain nonecclesiastical groups —royalty, merchant associations, guilds, fraternities, and city governments—to establish their own facilities, although the actual care of the sick and other dependents was left to monks and nuns. Much of the goodwill, however, would evaporate as growing corruption within the church during the fourteenth and fifteenth centuries was reflected in hospital management. Money and other benefices meant for the poor and afflicted were diverted to personal use with some institutions engaging in the noncharitable business of catering to paying boarders.

With the Reformation and the rise of the national state the doctrine that medical care for the poor was a community rather than a church responsibility was firmly laid down; however, as Rosen (1963) notes, hospitals in Protestant countries suffered a continuing decline in the quality of care. Under secular control the charitable impulse in these facilities faded. Devout nursing sisters serving their God were replaced by women whose commitment to patients was minimal and whose motivation was pecuniary. Furthermore, where the church perceived the poor and sick as objects through which good works might be performed, civil authorities regarded them largely in terms of a financial burden—one which they preferred to reduce as much as possible.

During the eigthteenth and early nineteenth centuries, Western European hospitals went through two significant changes. First, they became more socially specialized, this a by-product of increased urbanization. The traditional approach of lumping all types of dependents into the same facility was gradually discarded as hospitals became repositories for the poor sick. Not all the medically incapacitated were admitted, though—only the "worthy poor," i.e., those lower-class individuals adjudged by administrators and sponsors to be potentially useful citizens capable of making a contribution to the commonweal. Others, namely the aged, the very young, the physically handicapped, and the mentally deficient—all of whom the prevailing mercantilist philosophy regarded as having little social value—were confined to abysmally kept poorhouses, irrespective of whether they were in need of medical attention. The second change was that hospitals became more medically specialized. Wards were established for different illness categories with separate facilities founded for handling smallpox, mental illness, eye disorders, orthopedic afflictions, and obstetrical cases. This phenomenon may be attributed in part to a renewed desire for medical knowledge. Though formally trained doctors began to be associated with hospitals in the 1400s, it was not until the seventeenth century that physicians were recognizing that the healing arts could progress only through direct observation. By keeping patients with the same or seemingly related ailments together, one could readily make far more detailed comparisons and thus advance learning.

The Rise of the American Hospital

Hospital development started late in America, as could be expected of an outpost of European society. Though some military hospitals were built in the seventeenth and eighteenth centuries, and a number of pesthouses and lazarettos to prevent the spread of infectious disease were periodically maintained, the need for ongoing facilities to serve the civilian sick was not so apparent. Low population densities and extended kinship ties favored home-centered medical care. Nevertheless, with the steady growth of the cities and the increasing geographical mobility of the people, colonial legislatures were obliged to make some provision for the poor, the sick, the criminal, and infirm. To this end, the multipurpose almshouse was the logical choice—differentiation being too expensive for the community to support.

The first inpatient institution in the colonies to serve the exclusive function of treating disease was the Pennsylvania Hospital. Benjamin Franklin, who led the campaign to have this facility built, believed that the existing Philadelphia almshouse, which operated in part as a prison, was simply not a suitable environment to place the physically ill and emotionally disturbed if they were to become "useful to themselves, their families, and the public for many years after." Appealing to the self-interest of his middle- and upper-class audience, he argued that the hospital could be a training ground for physicians so that the fruits of their acquired experience with the poor could be put to good use in treating private patients. In response, the provincial assembly agreed to set aside £2,000 if the public contributed a matching amount. To the surprise of many legislators, this figure was quickly met and the facility opened in 1751. The idea, however, did not spread immediately. The general hospital was not ready technically to complement and replace the health-caring functions of the family. It was a repository for those without close relatives and without means, i.e., the residuals of society. Seventy-five years later, there were but three similar institutions operating in this country—New York Hospital (1791); Massachusetts General (1821); and New Haven Hospital (1826)—though some existing almshouses were increasingly focusing their attention on the ill. Nevertheless, as the century unfolded and as the previously mentioned trends continued, the number of general hospitals increased substantially. By the early 1870s, the figure had surpassed one hundred.

The building of facilities for the emotionally disturbed was initially sporadic as well. These institutions were parallel to and separate from the hospitals for the sane and destitute sick with separate staffs and career lines. The mental hospitals protected society from those individuals manifesting unpredictable and frequently violent behavior, while the general hospital protected society from its inability to manage the poor in the prevailing informal caring structure of the time.

The first mental hospital to be founded was the state-run Public Lunatic Hospital at Williamsburg, Virginia, in 1773; the second opened nearly forty-five years later in Lexington, Kentucky. However, beginning in the 1820s, there was a sustained pattern of development, and by 1860, twenty-eight of the then thirty-three states were maintaining separate public facilities for the insane and in addition, a number of private asylums were accepting patients. The care that was provided in these early hospitals reflected the Enlightenment doctrine of "moral treatment," consisting of minimal restraint, kindness, and individual attention as a means of teaching the patient order, discipline, and self-control—habits, argued asylum superintendents, which could only be inculcated away from the demands and pressures of family and business.

After the Civil War and through the early decades of the twentieth century, the capacity of most state hospitals grew tremendously. The effects of rapid population increases, industrialization, and immigration, combined with the perception of greater personal and social disorganization among more recently settled immigrants, made for higher rates of admission. Once an active treatment center, the state asylum became predominantly custodial in function by virtue of its size, limited personnel, and budget. On the other hand, due to their smaller census and better staffing, private mental hospitals serving the more affluent social classes would allow for greater therapeutic intervention and more interpersonal contact, and partly as a consequence achieve far higher rates of discharge and long-term remission.

Throughout the greater part of the nineteenth century, the general hospital did not enjoy an enviable reputation among the public nor did it deserve one. The upper and middle classes viewed it as an institution exclusively for the poor, while the lower strata, which it served, regarded hospitalization as stigmatizing—a sign of family breakdown and economic failure. More important, most people, rich and poor, considered hospitals to be death houses. Indeed, mortality was high even for seemingly minor ailments—this the result of the constant threat of infection passed from patient to patient with the physician often serving as a transmitter. Ironically, anesthesia, discovered in the mid-1840s, had the immediate effect of making surgeons far bolder in the operations they were willing to undertake, and without sterile conditions, the chances for recovery were rather dubious.

In the decades following the Civil War, the prevailing perception of the hospital gradually changed with the institution becoming a treatment center for all social classes for the first time in its history. This radical transformation into the modern hospital may be attributed largely to scientific and technological innovations of the period. European bacteriological research helped to place medicine upon a firmer foundation, making possible antisepsis (1867) and asepsis (1888), which dramatically reduced postoperative infection and mortality. Given the new recognition of the need for absolute cleanliness, the hospital now became the only suitable place where major surgery could be performed. Futhermore, microscopic examination of bodily fluids and tissues and the growing of cultures could be more conveniently and efficiently performed in a specially equipped laboratory, and the sheer bulk and expense of the new Xray (1895) and EKG (1903) militated against office use. In short, the most sophisticated medical care was found in the hospital—a point of view increasingly shared by physicians and patients alike.

Wide-scale social and economic factors also contributed to this utilization pattern and image-altering process. As Vogel (1980) has shown in the case of Boston, the extended family was declining toward the end of the century. The practice of several generations living under one roof grew unfashionable as couples and single people took to apartment life. When ill, one no longer had several attendants at hand, nor was there room for separate accommodations for the sick. Indeed, these considerations were used as selling points by hospitals as they tried to attract more private patients—a need occasioned by the rising cost of the free care they provided and one that could not be met through voluntary contributions alone. That the institution was successful in changing its role is reflected in the fact that the total number of hospitals rose from 178 with 35,608 beds in 1873 to 4,359 with 421,065 beds in 1909—more than seven times the growth expected on the basis of population alone. The great majority of these new hospitals were voluntary; this in contrast to the pattern outside the United States, where most facilities were being erected and maintained by their governments.

Hospitals bulit largely by private funds and philanthropy are quite peculiar to the American experience. The tremendous industrial and economic expansion after the Civil War produced a great many millionaires whose quest for upward social mobility found expression in considerable donations to general hospitals. This was free capital. There was no interest, nor did it have to be paid back. Thus was created the backbone of the American hospital system. Physicians in private practice, particularly surgeons, began to make arrangements with individual facilities for admission privileges for which they, in turn, provided free care for the poor, a continuing obligation of the hospitals given their charter.

The rapid expansion of medical knowledge would have a significant impact on the growth of the educational function of the hospital. In the period following the Civil War, most American physicians received their degrees from poorly equipped proprietary medical colleges. Courses were characterized by didactic lectures with laboratory experience and patient contact kept to a minimum—a program not all that different from that offered at more prestigious schools. Many graduates who felt limited by this approach decided to continue their studies in Europe—principally in Germany and Austria. What they returned home with was a recognition of the need for university affiliated colleges where the undergraduate years would be spent immersed in the basic sciences and hospital training. This orientation became the driving force behind the creation of the Johns Hopkins University Medical School (1893), which quickly became acknowledged as the leading center of medical education in the United States, and whose program other reputable institutions began to copy. As for the proprietary colleges, this problem was finally attacked by the AMA Council on Medical Education (1901), which began setting accreditation standards and making ratings that were accepted by state licensing boards. Its continuing effort—supplemented by Abraham Flexner's Carnegie Commission Report (1910), which for the first time made the general public aware of the sad state of a majority of the schools—served to eliminate inferior colleges while also placing the hospital at the core of the curriculum in those institutions that remained open. Naturally, the cost of medical education increased, but an expanding economy was willing to afford it.

Improved and expanded hospital training occurred on the postdoctoral level as well. The ongoing information explosion in medicine was encouraging a greater number of graduates to receive further instruction and specialize in circumscribed fields—a trend which led the AMA to establish rules governing hospital-based internships (1919) and residencies (1928). In 1930 approximately 15 percent of all M.D.'s were full-time specialists; by 1962 this figure had topped 50 percent, and in 1980 it stands at over 75 percent.

Changing Roles and Relationships

Over the past one hundred years, the functions of the principal actors within the American hospital have undergone significant modifications—a fact illustrated by the changing contributions of the board of trustees. Although not surprising, it should be pointed out that board members for community hospitals were drawn from the upper-level business, industry, and professional cadres of American society. They were unpaid and carried on the traditional volunteer and public custodial role inherited from England. They legitimized the hospital for the community and forestalled government intervention and ownership by their interest and presence. Unlike public education, health services were viewed as a personal responsibility, a conception that has since undergone modification.

Initially, trustees played a dominant role in managing all facets of hospital operations. They decided what patients were to be admitted to the wards, the conditions of medical instruction, autopsy policies, questions relating to staff discipline and performance, and they even had input over the range of therapeutics to be employed. However, as Rosenberg (1979) notes, this pattern of stewardship became inappropriate as hospitals grew in size and complexity. What time individual board members had available to devote to their institutions was simply not enough to provide comprehensive financial and administrative leadership. Furthermore, with the knowledge of physicians becoming more esoteric, laymen felt less competent and were thus more reluctant to intervene in medical decision-making. As a consequence, in recent decades most boards have limited their active role to fund raising and long-term planning—leaving day-to-day business responsibilities to full-time paid administrators and patient care to medical staff. This division has come to be known as the dual authority structure, a bureaucratic anomaly, but one suited to the division of functions in the hospital given the need for discretionary authority on the part of the medical staff.

The earliest hospital administrators were supervisory nurses and physicians, the latter serving part time except in the very large hospitals. Later, lay administrators would be brought in, drawn from the world of industry and commerce in the belief that their organizational experience and knowledge would be readily transferable. However, the American hospital of the twentieth century did not emerge as a typical business since, for the most part, it was a not-for-profit enterprise, nor did it operate as a standard bureaucracy by virtue of its two lines of authority. Also, given the unique type of service it rendered its clients, the orientation, information and methods garnered outside this environment did not always appear to be applicable or sufficient. Therefore, given the special background required, masters' level programs in hospital administration were begun with the first successful ongoing school founded at the University of Chicago (1934). Such university programs are currently structured to provide the student with both a theoretical understanding and practical on-site training to handle those economic, personnel, and physical plant problems peculiar to the hospital as well as to cope with the increasingly important function of dealing with external authorities.

The hospital itself is composed of several interest groups, each with its own demands and power. To function effectively, there must be some degree of give and take, which has led to considerable research on the hospital system as a negotiated order. The greatest challenge to administrators is forging a cooperative working relationship with the medical staff. Historically, both groups have maintained an adversary position as the goals of each tend to conflict. Ideally the administrator is the custodian of resources, and the physician the advocate for the patient. Purchasing the latest equipment and technology, ordering a host of diagnostic procedures on a routine basis, and seeing as many "interesting" charity cases as possible may further the research, prestige, and educational aims of the staff, but it also puts a tremendous strain on the financial resources of the institution. Administrators who try to contain costs by limiting these practices are commonly perceived by physicians as impediments to progress and good medical care, while they in turn are likely to view their physicians as extravagant and unmindful spenders. Consequently, the successful administrator is one who can satisfy most of the demands of the staff and patients while keeping the institution economically viable. In this regard it is important to observe that in most other nations there is no dual authority system in that the head of the hospital is a physician responsible for both administrative and medical affairs. Also, unlike the United States, most of the doctors are salaried employees whose advancement is based on some form of merit selection process. These structural arrangements help make for a situation where the needs of individual doctors and groups are more easily contained within available financial resources.

Originally, staff appointments in many American voluntary hospitals were few and rather prestigious. However, in the late nineteenth century, as they began to compete for private patients, hospitals, particularly newer ones, adopted an "open staff" policy, i.e., every licensed M.D. in the community was granted admitting and attending privileges. One consequence was that poorly trained graduates were placed on an equal footing with those holding superior academic credentials—a situation which not surprisingly bred discontent among the latter. Following World War I, the American College of Surgeons, as part of its effort to raise the standards of U.S. hospitals, started placing pressure on institutions to differentiate between the types of privileges extended, and to restrict staff physicians to the fields in which they were competent. These principles, which were later endorsed by the AMA and are now embodied in the requirements of the Joint Commission on the Accreditation of Hospitals (1952), have provided more explicit criteria governing the quality of patient care. Still, American institutions, except for university hospitals, continue by and large to be "open staff" in comparison with those of European countries where there is a far sharper distinction between office and hospital-based practitioners.

Nursing is another hospital role that has been transformed over time. With advances in medical knowledge, the traditional surrogate-mother approach, combining basic housekeeping and emotional support, gave way to a more technical role stressing objectivity in one's work. In past decades, most American R.N.'s were trained in hospital-based schools, but recently the trend has been toward an academically oriented curriculum in universities and junior colleges, with the former program being phased out. Unlike most U.S. physicians, nurses are salaried employees of the hospital and as such owe their allegiance to the administration. Nevertheless, since they have a duty to carry out the orders of physicians they owe them loyalty as well. Accordingly, the nurse is caught in a dilemma if a doctor's directive, however medically justifiable, violates the hospital's formal rules and regulations. The most pressing problem facing nursing, though, is contradictory role expectations. While R.N.'s conceive of themselves as professionals, many do not feel that their talents are being fully utilized or appreciated. Some also become torn between the bedside nurse model and the medical-technical model. Furthermore, their relationship to physicians is generally not collegial. Nurses who have recommendations to make regarding patient care are often obliged to transmit these in such a way so as not to challenge the doctor's superior position. This circumstance, particularly in an era of increasing social equality for women, appears to be a major reason, along with blocked occupational mobility, why growing numbers of R.N.'s are quitting the hospital and changing careers—a phenomenon not characteristic of their counterparts in nations where submissiveness is more widely accepted by women.

Interestingly, the social position of the American nurse is quite different from that of the academically trained technician. With the recent growth and application of computer science and electronics to medicine, engineers have emerged as more important figures within the hospital. Their knowledge is esoteric and, unlike that of the nurse, is not ordinarily possessed by the physician. Therefore, while they are also under the direction of M.D.'s, their specialized skills and backgrounds are permitting them a greater degree of autonomy which will undoubtedly allow them ultimately to achieve a higher level of professionalization and power.

The Costs of the Modern General Hospital

By 1930, the delivery pattern that had emerged at the end of the nineteenth century was fully in place. A majority of beds in voluntary hospitals were filled with paying patients admitted by private physicians with the remainder occupied by the poor, whose expenses were either covered by government and philanthropy or absorbed by the institutions themselves. Fiscally, the general hospital was still an autonomous unit manipulating such funding sources as were available and staying out of the red. During the depression of the 1930s, however, the pattern began to change as the broad middle class found they could ill afford to get sick, let alone bear the expense of hospitalization. Private facilities, recognizing the danger to their solvency should the bulk of their clients be unable to pay and seeing a threat to their independence by the growing specter of socialized medicine, decided to act, helping to evolve the hospital and medically dominated private insurance plans of Blue Cross and Blue Shield which covered institutional costs and physicians' fees respectively. With the inauguration of these programs, private hospitals began to exchange much of their original autonomy for financial security.

Between 1930 and 1965 the general hospital became the most expensive component of all personal health services, moving from 20 percent to 40 percent of all such expenditures, with per diem charges within the institution rising by approximately 900 percent. One reason for this was that hospitals were moving beyond the bricks and mortar, bed, board, and general nursing-care elements to become major purchasers of costly medical equipment which needed long-term amortization. Another factor was the lack of effective controls. The period following the depression was so affluent and the desire for more health services so great that expenditures were based more on the willingness and capacity of third parties to spend than on institutional performance. Indeed, there seemed to be an indifference to costs by labor unions and industry, who were responsible for a large share through payroll and tax-deductible business contributions.

Adding to the cost of care during this era was hospital expansion. In the 1940s the supply of general hospital beds in America was regarded by many critics as grossly inadequate, or at least inadequately distributed. To correct for this, Congress passed the Hospital Survey and Construction Act (Hill-Burton) in 1946 to provide federal start-up funds matched by money raised by local communities for new or existing facilities. As a consequence, the number of beds increased from 3.5 to 4.5 per 1,000 population, and many small rural hospitals were built where there were no institutions before. By the early 1960s, however, it was becoming apparent through a reading of daily hospital census figures that some areas had too many beds, thus creating unnecessary duplications of services. Nevertheless, hospital construction in these communities went on largely unchecked. This situation was temporarily eased in the mid-1960s by the passage of Medicare for the aged and Medicaid for the poor. These acts made access to the hospital by each group far easier and had the immediate effect of helping to fill otherwise empty beds and provide yet another regular and dependable source of income to the institution. The underlying problem, however, remained.

By 1970 the per diem charges of the general hospital were exceeding $250 a day with an annual increase of 15 percent. The public did not loudly complain because the rising costs were not being felt, unless personal insurance was inadequate for truly expensive episodes. It was instead the clamor of third-party payers, who were now beginning to feel the pinch on their respective pocketbooks, that set the stage for a cost-containment movement. Indeed, concern on the part of government had become sufficiently intense that even in a Republican administration under President Nixon a short-lived price control measure was implemented in 1971, unsuccessful possibly because it was complicated and difficult to enforce as it left other segments of the economy untouched.

In the last ten years hospitals have been besieged from all sides, but mainly by regulatory agencies. The Professional Standards Review Organization (PSRO) amendment to the Medicare Act of 1972 mandated the creation of over two hundred areas in which there was to be systematic surveillance of hospital admissions and length of stay by committees of physicians. This constituted an attempt to make decision-making more rational by setting up norms which in turn might justify the costs of hospital care. Furthermore, state after state has set up independent bodies that oversee hospital charges, and has passed "certificate of need" legislation to control the supply of new hospital beds and the purchasing of new medical equipment.

One problem facing hospital administrators is that they can actually control only a portion of their institutions' costs. They can have major input over so-called hotel services, but even here they have less to say than hotel managers, for hotels house well clients merely looking for pleasant accommodations and a good time, compared with inpatients looking for relief from pain and seeking a cure. The administrator has no real power over the professional prerogatives of the medical staff, nor is such control seen as advisable. Physicians' decisions for laboratory tests, length of stay, and so on are in effect open ended. The administrator must ride the cost tide as well as possible and not antagonize either the patient or the attending physician.

What many hospitals have been able to do on their own is to set up joint purchasing agreements for supplies and joint laundry services to take advantage of lower unit costs through mass buying. More fundamental, however, has been the trend toward multihospital conglomerates, horizontal reorganization, and the creation of diversified health services under one corporation to include prepayment plans, physicians' offices, salaried department heads, outpatient departments for walk-in patients, and emergency departments with specialized staffs to triage individuals. One knowledgeable observer (DeVries 1978), commenting on these trends, has argued that the era of the independent, autonomous hospital is coming to a close.

While it may be claimed that all these cost-containment efforts have been successful to a degree, hospital expenses have nonetheless continued to mount. One not previously mentioned factor behind this problem is the skyrocketing premiums for liability insurance due to a proliferation of malpractices claims—not apparently connected to any lessening of competence but to a new willingness on the part of the public to sue. Huge dollar judgments on successfully brought cases over the last decade have in turn given hospital physicians an incentive to order more comprehensive diagnostic workups, which only serve to jack up overall costs. An additional factor has been the recent efforts by nurses and nonprofessional personnel to organize unions and bargain for better salaries and benefit packages. Most significant, however, is the general condition of the economy. Double-digit inflation has been generating spiraling costs for goods and services, and higher interest rates to finance capital improvements. Indeed, if inflation throughout the marketplace is not addressed, no visible stabilization of hospital costs can realistically be expected.

The Future of the General Hospital

Despite all the rhetoric to deemphasize it relative to other elements in the health services spectrum, the general hospital will remain a pivotal component. This is inherent in the technological imperative of medicine and society in general. There are and will be attempts to shrink the system through planning and certificate of need, and possibly even rate review to squeeze out "inefficient" institutions. It seems, however, that the system will be shrunk not by closing hospitals, but by holding the bed supply constant as population continues to increase. Even without certificate of need, other regulatory devices, and planning, it is likely the system will contract anyway because of its cost compared to other services (i.e., free-standing clinics and hospices) which can be substituted. Economics is forcing the hospital into treating patients who "really need to be there," which means that it will return to the patient-diagnostic mix of fifty years ago when only the very sick were admitted.

American hospitals, it appears, will continue to evolve toward more corporate types of conglomerates, vertically and horizontally. Indeed, hospital administrators have already become financial managers, and a greater percentage of private office-based physicians have also adopted the corporate model of operation. Because the health-services sector will be seeking management skills and less of the more general type of training applicable to small institutions and nursing homes, it is likely that the hospital and health-services industry will be drawing more heavily upon graduates from schools of business and management and less from those programs in schools of public health and university medical centers. To survive in an ongoing struggle for resources, the hospital will have to take on more corporate characteristics, but should emulate the industrial model only insofar as it needs it for financial management, personnel handling, and planning.

For the patient, the hospital of the future will probably be characterized by increasingly effective and dazzling technological care but decreasing one to one attention. Job differentiation and the so-called team approach, where no one takes on total responsibility, will make personal care difficult, as both patients and hospital staff become interchangeable parts of a "curing and management machine." Modern bureaucratic structures simply do not facilitate individualization. In recent years, one can see a popular reaction toward overspecialization and impersonality in the form of "holistic medicine," but this movement appears to be merely making minor adjustments rather than fundamentally altering the direction in which medicine is seemingly headed. If a radically different picture of hospital structure and interpersonal relations does emerge, it would logically have to involve a society-wide change in thinking about our positively held values toward science, technology, and organization. While this possibility may not appear to be all that likely in the near future, it is nonetheless instructive to keep in mind the transformation of the *valetudinaria* wrought by the advent of Christianity. The hospital, after all, has been, to a considerable extent, a mirror of the world around it.

REFERENCES

DeVries, R. A. 1978. Health care delivery: strength in numbers. *Hospitals* 52:81–84.

Rosen, G. 1963. The hospital: historical sociology of a community institution. In *The hospital in modern society*, ed. E. Freidson. New York: Free Press.

Rosenberg, C. E. 1979. Inward vision and outward glance: the shaping of the American hospital, 1880–1914. *Bulletin of the History of Medicine* 53:346–91.

Vogel, M. 1980. The invention of the modern hospital. Chicago: University of Chicago Press.

BIBLIOGRAPHY

Abel-Smith, B. 1963. *The hospitals 1800-1948: a study in social administration in England and Wales*. Cambridge: Harvard University Press.

Belknap, I., and Steinle, J. G. 1963. *The community and its hospitals: a comparative analysis*. Syracuse, N.Y.: Syracuse University Press.

Berry, R. E., Jr. 1974. Cost and efficiency in the production of hospital services. *Health and Society* 52:291–313.

Blankenship, L. V., and Elling, R. H. 1962. Organizational support and community power structure: the hospital. *Journal of Health and Human Behavior* 3:257–269.

Brown, M. 1976. Contract management: latest development in the trend towards regionalization of hospital and health services. *Hospital and Services Administration* 21:40-59.

———, and Lewis, H. L. 1976. *Hospital management systems: multi-unit organizations and delivery of health care*. Germantown, Md.: Aspen Systems Corp.

Burling, T.; Lentz, E. M.; and Wilson, R. N. 1956. *The give and take in hospitals*. New York: G.P. Putnam's Sons.

Commission on Hospital Care. 1947. *Hospital care in the United States*. New York: Commonwealth Fund.

Commission on Public General Hospitals. *Report on the future of the public general hospital; an agenda for transition*. Chicago: Hospital Research and Educational Trust.

Corwin, E. H. L. 1946. *The American hospital*. New York: Commonwealth Fund.

Davis, K. 1972. Economic theories of behavior in nonprofit private hospitals. *Economic and Business Bulletin* 24:1–13.

Dowling, W. L., and Armstrong, P. A. 1980. The Hospital. In *Introduction to health services*, ed. S. J. Williams and P. R. Torrens. New York: Wiley.

Eaton, L. K. 1957. *New England hospitals 1790–1833*. Ann Arbor, Mich.: University of Michigan Press.

Feder, J., and Spitz, B. 1979. The politics of hospital payment. *Journal of Health Politics, Policy and Law* 4:455–463.

Foster, R. W. 1974. Economic models of hospitals. *Hospital Administration* 19:87–93.

Freidson, E., ed. 1963. *The hospital in modern society*. Glencoe, Ill.: Free Press of Glencoe.

Georgopoulos, B. S. 1964. Hospital organization and administration: prospects and perspectives. *Hospital Administration* 9:23–35.

———, and Mann, F. C. 1962. *The community general hospital.* New York: Macmillan.

———, and Matijko, A. 1967. The American general hospital as a complex social system. *Health Services Research* 2:76–111.

Gibson, R. M., and Fisher, C. R. 1978. National health expenditures, fiscal year 1977. *Social Security Bulletin* 41:11.

Glaser, W. A. 1970. *Social settings and medical organization: a cross national study of the hospital.* New York: Atherton Press.

Grob, G. N. 1970. The state mental hospital in mid-nineteenth century America: a social analysis. In *Social psychology and mental health,* ed. H. Wechsler, L. Solomon, and B. M. Kramer. New York: Holt, Rinehart and Winston.

Gross, E. 1971. Incentive and the structure of organizational motivation. *Hospital Administration* 16:8–20.

Hofmann, P. B. 1979. Can hospitals afford to do less. *Hospitals* 53:80–82.

Holloway, R. G.; Artis, J. W.; and Freeman, W. E. The participation patterns of "economic influentials" and their control of a hospital board of trustees. *Journal of Health and Human Behavior* 4:88–99.

Jaeger, B. J., ed. 1977. *The impact of collective action on hospitals—a report of the 1976 National Forum on Hospital and Health Affairs.* Durham, N.C.: Department of Health Administration.

Kaufman, K.; Shortell, S.; Becker, S.; and Neuhauser, D. 1979. The effect of board composition and structure on hospital performance. *Hospital and Health Services Administration* 24:37–62.

Lave, J. R., and Lave, L. B. 1974. *The Hospital Construction Act: an evaluation of the Hill-Burton program, 1948–1973.* Washington, D.C.: American Enterprise Institute for Public Policy Research.

Longest, B. B. 1980. A conceptual framework for understanding the multihospital approach strategy. *Health Care Management Review* 5:17–24.

Neuhauser, D. 1972. The hospital as a matrix organization. *Hospital Administration* 17:8–25.

Roemer, M. I., and Friedman, J. W. 1971. *Doctors in hospitals: medical staff organization and hospital performance.* Baltimore, Md.: Johns Hopkins University Press.

Rothman, D. 1971. *The discovery of the asylum: social order and disorder in the new republic.* Boston: Little, Brown.

Russell, L. B. 1979. *Technology in hospitals; medical advances and their diffusion.* Washington, D.C.: Brookings Institute.

Salkever, D. S. 1978. Competition among hospitals. In *Competition in the health care sector; past, present, and future,* ed. W. Greenberg, pp. 149–61. Germantown, Md.: Aspen Systems Corp.

Smith, D. B. and Kaluzny, A. D. 1975. *The white labyrinth; understanding the organization of health care.* Berkeley, Calif.: McCutchan.

Southwick, A. F. *The law of hospital and health care administration.* Ann Arbor, Mich.: Health Administration Press.

Stevens, C. M. 1970. Hospital market efficiency: the anatomy of the supply response. In *Empirical studies in health economics: proceedings of the second conference on the economics of health,* ed. H. E. Klarman, pp. 229–48. Baltimore, Md.: Johns Hopkins Press.

Stevens, R. 1971. *American medicine and the public interest.* New Haven, Conn.: Yale University Press.

Stewart, D. A. 1973. The history and status of proprietary hospitals. *Blue Cross Reports* Research Series 9. Chicago: Blue Cross Association.

Strauss, A.; Schatzman, L.; Ehrlich, D.; Bucher, R.; and Salshin, M. 1963. The hospital and its negotiated order. In *The Hospital in Modern Society,* ed. E. Freidson. New York: Free Press.

Taylor, E. 1977. Participation in shared programs up sharply. *Hospitals* 51:192–98.

Vogel, M. 1980. *The invention of the modern hospital.* Chicago: University of Chicago Press.

Chapter 14

Health-Maintenance Organizations

Harold S. Luft

HEALTH-MAINTENANCE ORGANIZATIONS, or HMOs, represent a marked departure from the conventional U.S. system of medical care of third-party insurance with fee-for-service payment to providers. Moreover, HMOs are now viewed not just as a curious aberration but as a potential solution to the rising cost of medical care and therefore they have acquired substantial policy importance.

This chapter will begin with a definition of the HMO concept and a brief historical overview of HMO growth and development. This is followed by a discussion of some of the major questions people ask concerning HMO performance and the difficulties one encounters in deriving answers to those questions. The next two sections address the primary questions of whether HMOs save money and whether there are differences in quality, consumer satisfaction, and physician satisfaction between HMOs and traditional providers. The fifth section examines the organizational and environmental factors influencing HMO performance. The sixth section discusses the potential role of HMOs in addressing the larger public policy issues of meeting the needs of the underserved, reducing the rate of growth in medical care costs, and the competitive impact of HMOs on other providers. A final section outlines directions for further research.

A Definition of the HMO Concept and an Historical Perspective

Definition of the HMO Concept

The term *health-maintenance organization* is used to refer to a variety of organizational entities. It may refer to prepaid group practices that have existed for decades, to consumer-sponsored programs, or to plans under medical society,

Parts of this chapter have appeared in the Executive Summary of "A Synthesis of Research Findings on the Operations and Performance of Health Maintenance Organizations," prepared by Harold S. Luft and Applied Management Sciences for the National Center for Health Services Research, and are used with permission. Both documents draw upon the author's *Health Maintenance Organizations: Dimensions of Performance*, New York: Wiley-Interscience, 1981. I am indebted to Nancy Blustein, Theodore Goldberg, Edward F. X. Hughes, David Lairson, Susan C. Maerki, Alfred Meltzer, and Joan B. Trauner for comments on earlier drafts.

labor union, university, insurance company, or employer control. Under the Federal HMO Act of 1973, federally qualified HMOs are strictly defined as group practice, staff model, or individual practice associations that conform to a specific set of federal standards. However, in certain settings state licensing requirements vary from federal standards, and, as a result, some HMOs have chosen not to seek federal qualification.

Because of the variation in the use of the term health-maintenance organization, this chapter will specify the following essential characteristics for purposes of providing a generic definition of an HMO:

1. The HMO assumes a *contractual responsibility* to provide or assure the delivery of a stated range of health services, including at least physician and hospital services;
2. The HMO serves an *enrolled, defined* population;
3. The HMO has *voluntary enrollment* of subscribers;
4. The HMO requires a *fixed periodic payment* to the organization that is independent of use of services. (There may be small charges related to utilization, but these are relatively insignificant.); and
5. The HMO assumes at least part of the *financial risk* and/or gain in the provision of services, *unlike* a fiscal intermediary.

This definition purposely allows considerable latitude in HMO organizational characteristics. It does not specify any restrictions on methods of physician reimbursement or on practice setting. The definition encompasses two major types of plans: (1) group or staff model plans that generally pay physicians on a salary or capitation basis, often referred to as prepaid group practices (PGPs); and (2) individual practice associations (IPAs), which are composed of physicians in private offices who generally bill the HMO on a fee-for-service basis. There are, however, exceptions to these generalizations—some group practices have physicians paid essentially on a fee-for-service basis, while some IPAs use capitation payments for primary-care physicians.

Fee-for-service payment generates incentives to provide more services while salary and capitation generate incentives to provide fewer services. Simultaneously, group and solo practice by physicians implies differences in work settings and in style. Thus, prepaid group practices with salaried physicians are likely to be most different from solo, fee-for-service basis, are most similar to the conventional medical-care model.

Health-maintenance organizations also vary in the extent to which they meet the five criteria of the overall HMO definition. The comprehensiveness of guaranteed services varies widely among plans and beneficiaries. Federally qualified HMOs must offer a basic benefit package, but additional services may be tailored to the enrollee group. HMO enrollments range from a few thousand to over a million and range from homogeneous populations, such as university faculty and staff, to a cross-section of the area's population. The wide range of possible HMO configurations and their influence on HMO performance are discussed in the section on organizational and environmental factors.

A Historical Overview

Prepaid medical service plans have existed in this country since the nineteenth century. In urban settings, early plans were primarily under the sponsorship of fraternal lodges and benevolent societies, while those in rural areas were developed largely by the railroad, mining, and lumber industries to serve their employees. At the onset of the twentieth century, private hospitals began to market prepaid plans, and gradually community hospitals and medical group clinics began to experiment with this system of health-care delivery. Most plans operated in relative obscurity until the early 1930s, when the Committee on the Costs of Medical Care (1928–32) began to popularize the concept of prepaid health services. Recognizing that most Americans were without any form of health or disability insurance and that a vast segment of the population was unable to afford private medical care, the committee recommended that organized groups of health professionals furnish health care on a group prepayment basis.

During the late 1920s and in the depression years, several well-known prepaid group practice plans were established. These include Ross-Loos, Group Health Association of Washington, D.C., and the precursors to the Kaiser-Permanente plans. Additional plans such as the Health Insurance Plan (HIP) of Greater New York and Group Health Cooperative of Puget Sound were established in the early postwar period and a slow, but steady growth continued through the 1960s. Some plans developed to fill the needs of particular population groups. Others, such as the individual practice associations or foundations for medical care, developed as a response to prepaid groups. By the early 1970s, health insurance had become widely available to most Americans, and third-party payors assumed major responsibility for most health bills. National health expenditures rose precipitously, from 4.0 percent of the Gross National Product in 1935 to 9.0 percent in 1979 (Gibson 1979; Freeland, Calat, and Schendler 1980). In response to an ever-increasing health budget, the emphasis of national health policy in the 1970s shifted from guaranteeing accessibility of health services to cost containment. Once again, prepaid health services became a focus of national attention.

In the early 1970s, the prepaid health plan concept was labeled the health-maintenance organization, or HMO. This concept has been promoted by a variety of interest groups concerned with such divergent goals as cost containment, consumer action, and limiting government involvement in the health-care system. HMOs have been viewed as more cost efficient than traditional fee-for-service forms of coverage, and they are considered to provide medical care of comparable or better quality. They have also been seen as having the potential to stimulate competition within the health industry by encouraging traditional providers to adopt cost-containment programs and develop new premium and benefit structures. Since 1973, federal policy has encouraged the development and growth of HMOs through a program of grants, loan guarantees, and mandated access to employer groups. As of July 1980, HMO enrollment was 9.03 million in some 234 plans, of which 111 with an enrollment of 6.2 million had been qualified according to federal standards ("HMO Enrollment Update," 29 July 1980).

Major Questions Concerning HMO Performance

This chapter is oriented around a series of questions concerning HMO performance. The first question many people ask about HMOs is whether they save money for their enrollees, and if so, how? Addressing the "how" question leads to further questions: Are "savings" achieved through increased efficiency resulting from a substitution of ambulatory for hospital services? Is the lower hospital use by HMO members a result of more preventive services? Does self-selection by enrollees result in a membership mix that explains the lower HMO costs? Another set of explanations examines alternative reasons for the lower costs to HMO enrollees: poorer quality care and unsatisfied members, or conversely, more efficient production of given types of medical and hospital services.

To answer the above questions, one must draw on a wide variety of data from many different HMOs. However, not all HMOs perform equally well and certain factors may consistently influence HMO performance. Some of these factors are internal, such as the HMO's organizational structure, its financial incentives, facilities, and the like. Other factors are external, such as the regulatory climate, local acceptability, the health insurance market, and the presence of competing providers.

These questions focus on performance only with respect to HMO enrollees, and there are a number of larger issues that must also be addressed. HMOs enroll only 4 percent of the population, and the current public interest in prepayment systems stems from their potential role in solving some pressing social problems. For instance, can HMOs provide access to medically underserved groups, such as the poor, the aged, and rural populations? Do HMOs lower the rate of growth in medical care expenditures? Does HMO growth and competition lead conventional insurers and providers to become more cost conscious? Can HMOs be made sufficiently attractive to physicians? Although this chapter does not provide conclusive answers to all the above questions, it reviews what is known and not known and it may serve as a framework for guiding and informing future policy and research.

Cautionary Notes

In evaluating the evidence on HMO experience, four important cautionary notes must be considered. The *first* stems from the diversity of HMOs. To understand the published findings, one must view each HMO as a unique entity. Yet to be useful for policymakers, results must be generalizable, and thus the findings of multiple studies may have to be combined. While obvious differences among studies may be explained, more subtle, but nonetheless important, differences may escape scrutiny.

The *second* caution relates to the data available for analysis. A recent comprehensive review of the published evidence on HMO performance indicates that available data vary in depth, breadth, and quality (i.e., reliability and validity) (Luft 1981). For example, there are more than fifty comparisons of hospitalization, but for some dimensions of performance only a single study is available. In some cases data are drawn from well-designed studies and in other cases only anecdotal evidence is available.

The *third* caution relates to the source of published findings on HMO performance. The vast majority of the existing studies relate to a handful of large, well-established plans. Many of these are hospital-based prepaid group practices in large metropolitan areas, and most all were developed prior to the advent of the federal HMO program. Research on these mature HMOs may not be directly applicable to new, developing plans.

Fourth, there have been no randomized, controlled experiments that involve the assignment of a representative group of people to a wide range of health maintenance organizations and traditional health insurance plans. The ongoing Rand Health Insurance Experiment includes the randomization of people to one HMO. Results of this study are not yet available. Therefore, while we can say that costs (or utilization, or satisfaction) are lower in one situation than another, we cannot determine if the differences are attributable to general characteristics of the plans, to unique features of the providers and administrators, or to subtle differences among the people selecting the plan, that is, the potential for self-selection. Whenever people have a choice of plans, they can be expected to choose the plan they think is best for themselves. Sometimes, this choice may affect the enrollees' subsequent utilization. Moreover, selection may or may not be controllable by the HMO.

Because HMOs have often been perceived as an answer to current problems in the health-care system by serving their own enrollees and providing a stimulus for change within the health system, these cautions have often been ignored or downplayed in reviewing data on HMO performance. Some advocates have made uncritical use of certain evidence on HMO performance to oversell the HMO concept, and some HMO opponents have used certain evidence to attack the concept. As will be seen, there are crucial areas of HMO performance about which almost nothing is known. The last section of this chapter will outline some of the areas most in need of further research and discuss some of the strategic problems in carrying out the necessary studies.

Do HMOs Save Money?

Health-maintenance organizations appear attractive as a means for cost control because they alter the usual economic incentives in medical care and give providers a stake in restraining costs; this is in distinct contrast to the prevailing system of extensive third-party reimbursement for providers. A review of all substantive research on health-care expenditures leads to the general conclusion that HMO enrollees have lower total expenditures for medical care (premium plus out-of-pocket expenditures) than comparable people with conventional insurance coverage (Luft 1978b; Wersinger and Sorensen 1980). Further, the lowest expenditures are for enrollees in prepaid group practices, where they range from 10 to 40 percent below expenditures for conventional insurance enrollees. Total expenditures for enrollees in medical-society–sponsored individual practice associations do not appear significantly lower than those of enrollees in conventional plans (Luft 1978b). Unfortunately, there are only seven published studies of comparative costs between HMOs and fee-for-service settings and only two of these include data on IPAs.

Total expenditures for medical care are composed of premiums, which may be paid by the employer (or agency, such as a Medicaid program), the individual, or both, and out-of-pocket expenses paid directly by the individual. Out-of-pocket expenses include copayments for covered services, expenses for services not offered through the plan, and services offered by the plan but obtained from other providers. For many years, HMO premiums exceeded premiums of conventional plans because of the more comprehensive benefits offered by HMOs, but some HMO premiums have recently become less expensive than conventional coverage. Out-of-pocket expenditures for HMO enrollees have consistently been below those of enrollees having conventional coverage (Luft 1978b). Furthermore, because of their comprehensive coverage, HMO enrollees are less likely to be faced with large costs not covered by their plan (Luft 1981).

Despite this evidence, the question remains: Do HMOs save money? There are a great many observational studies concerning HMO enrollees and comparable populations in the conventional system. The review of such studies allows for a discussion of *differences* in performance, but we do not yet know precisely what causes these differences. By carefully examining possible reasons for lower expenditures among HMO enrollees, we can reject some explanations and focus attention of future studies on more promising areas.

Savings in HMOs Through Increased Efficiency

Given the different economic incentives for HMOs and the conventional medical-care system, we might expect HMOs to save money by being more efficient. Improved efficiency may occur at two major levels:

1. The production of specific types of services; for example, might HMOs be large enough to achieve economies of scale, or share services among several facilities to avoid costly duplication?
2. The number and mix of services used to care for a given population; for example, might an HMO discourage certain types of marginally useful services, such as tonsillectomies, or substitute outpatient services for more costly inpatient care?

Within the second level of efficiency, it may be easier for HMOs to save money by reducing the use of hospital services, which are far more expensive, and access to these services is much more controllable than ambulatory visits. The patient can initiate an office visit, while only a physician can arrange hospital admission. Moreover, the much more extensive coverage of ambulatory care in HMOs lowers financial barriers for office visits.

Do HMOs Produce Specific Medical Services More Efficiently?

As noted above, HMOs might achieve certain efficiencies by changing the number and mix of services they use to care for their enrollees. Other efficiencies might occur through changes in the production process that lower the cost of specific procedures. Because HMOs generally pay the going rate for employee salaries and their physicians have hourly earnings comparable to those in fee-for-service practice, attention must be focused on the issue of HMO efficiency as related to physician productivity, use of ancillary and alternative health personnel, administrative services, and avoidance of duplication of facilities.

The question of whether group practice leads to economies of scale has long been a subject of debate. It appears that economies of scale occur as practice size increases, but these economies peak at a relatively small practice size, between two and five practitioners. Whether productivity per physician remains constant or even declines beyond that point is hard to evaluate. Thus there is no real support for the claim that large prepaid group practices realize substantial economies of scale in ambulatory care (Held and Reinhardt 1979). More precisely, potential economies may be offset by diseconomies, such as additional layers of administration, and the fact that in large groups savings are shared by a great many partners, thereby reducing the incentives to be efficient (Newhouse 1973; Sloan 1974).

A hospital controlled by an HMO might be a more efficient producer of inpatient care than a hospital operating largely on a cost reimbursement basis. A comparison of HMO-controlled hospitals with nearby community hospitals of the same size shows no consistent differences in cost per day, but since length of stay is shorter in the HMOs, costs per case are lower. However, this comparison did not control for case mix (i.e., the severity of the cases treated) (Luft 1981). For example, hospitals with more severely ill patients would experience a higher cost per case. An examination of costs for people hospitalized in Group Health Cooperative of Puget Sound and those in a comprehensive Blue Cross/Blue Shield plan in Seattle indicates that hospital costs per admission for the HMO members are about 25 percent lower. However, as stated previously, almost all this difference is attributable to shorter lengths of stay; unit costs for drugs, X rays, laboratory tests, and other services are comparable (McCaffree et al. 1976). (Hospital costs *per enrollee year* were 57 percent lower for Group Health enrollees, reflecting a lower admission rate.)

Health-maintenance organizations also may increase their relative efficiency by avoiding duplication of facilities. Kaiser-Permanente hospitals appear to centralize their services and to have somewhat less duplication of highly specialized facilities than the conventional health-delivery system (Luft and Crane 1980).

Ambulatory Care Use by HMO Enrollees

The expected effects of HMOs on ambulatory care are composed of several parts: higher office visit rates because of better coverage; substitution of outpatient for inpatient care; and lower visit rates because of the HMO's incentive to economize. The evidence is consistent on one point—when compared to people in conventional plans, a larger proportion of HMO enrollees have at least one visit per year. This is often used as an indicator of improved access to care. Data for matched groups with the same ambulatory coverage (e.g., Medicaid enrollees) suggest that this general finding is largely the result of better coverage in HMOs (Luft 1981).

In nearly two-thirds of the twenty-nine comparisons with credible data, HMO enrollees have a larger number of ambulatory visits per year. In six of seven IPAs with published data, enrollees had more visits than comparison non-HMO populations, while PGP enrollees had about the same chance of having more or fewer visits as their comparison non-HMO populations (Luft 1978b; Luft 1981). When comparing HMO enrollees to people with comprehensive fee-for-service ambulatory coverage, some studies show comparable utilization of ambulatory services while others show lower use by HMO enrollees (Luft 1981). Moreover, the mix of ambulatory services is similar for HMO enrollees and patients with traditional coverage, a finding which results from the great variability among physicians' practice patterns in all settings. Thus, there are few striking differences in the use of ambulatory services between HMO and non-HMO populations.

Hospital Utilization by HMO Enrollees

A broad range of observations over a twenty-five-year period almost unanimously support the claim that PGP enrollees have lower hospital admission rates than people with conventional insurance (Luft 1978b). Results for IPA enrollees are mixed. While most comparisons show lower hospital utilization by IPA enrollees, a substantial minority show higher use. Average differences in hospital utilization between HMO enrollees and people who rely on fee-for-service medical care are substantial, with about 30 percent fewer hospital days for PGP enrollees and 20 percent fewer days for IPA enrollees (Luft 1978b). HMO enrollees experience somewhat shorter average lengths of stay than do people in conventional plans, but length of stay is difficult to evaluate without careful adjustment for differences in case mix. Because HMOs try to eliminate discretionary hospital admissions, they may perform certain tests and procedures on an outpatient basis that would otherwise be performed in the hospital. Because many of those admissions would have been for just one or two days, the HMO case mix may be shifted (i.e., HMOs would have a sicker mix of patients). Simultaneously, the HMO has incentives to discharge patients from the hospital as soon as possible.

Two initial explanations occur for the lower hospital admission rates in HMOs: (1) HMOs identify and screen out groups of cases that do not require hospitalization; and (2) HMOs achieve a lower admission rate without any apparent discrimination among diagnostic categories according to obvious "necessity." The best available data from a broad range of HMOs tend to support the second explanation rather than the first (Luft 1978b). Lower admission rates are not achieved by disproportionately reducing surgical as opposed to medical cases. Instead, admissions seem to be lower in general. Similarly, although admissions for certain discretionary procedures, such as hernia repair and hysterectomy, are lower in HMOs than in conventional plans, the figures for discretionary procedures examined do not appear disproportionately lower than the figures for all surgical procedures. One must immediately point out, however, that the measures for discretionary cases are very rough approximations that may mask the fine distinctions in patient care. It is highly likely that many admissions in categories labeled discretionary are actually essential, and that many admissions in categories labeled nondiscretionary are actually optional.

Having recognized that the lower hospital admission rates in HMOs cannot be explained simply by a reduction of only obviously discretionary cases, we find four possible, but not mutually exclusive, explanations for lower hospital admissions in HMOs:

1. Rather than reducing admissions for broad categories of patients identified by researchers as discretionary, HMOs have an incentive to eliminate admissions that individual case management reveals as discretionary. In other words, physicians may evaluate patients on an individual basis and decide who really needs admission and who can be treated on an ambulatory basis.
2. HMOs may provide preventive care that reduces the occurrence of health problems requiring hospital admission.
3. Self-selection by HMO enrollees may result in lower admission rates. That is, better health or greater aversion to hospital admissions among HMO

enrollees may contribute to the differences between HMO and fee-for-service admission rates.

4. HMOs may undertreat, or traditional providers may overtreat, nondiscretionary cases. This suggests differences in the quality of care between HMOs and conventional providers.

The first and fourth of these imply that differences in quality of care explain lower hospital admission rates in HMOs. The topic of quality of care is handled in the next section of this chapter. The second and third possible explanations for lower admission rates are discussed below.

Does Increased Use of Preventive Services Account for Lower Hospitalization Rates by HMO Enrollees?

Although increased use of preventive services seems to be implied by the term health-maintenance organization, the evidence is mixed. While a majority of studies show that HMO enrollees use more preventive services, such as routine physical examinations and checkups, than do people in conventional plans, a substantial minority of studies show the opposite result (Luft 1978a). The explanation for the conflicting results lies in the better coverage of such services in HMOs. If HMOs are compared with conventional plans covering preventive services, there seems to be no difference in use or even somewhat less use by HMO enrollees (Luft 1978a).

More crucial to this discussion, however, is the fact that, with the exception of certain immunizations, there is little clinical evidence that mass screening and frequent physical examinations have any measurable effect on health status or hospital use (Sagel et al. 1974; Foltz and Kelsey 1978; Chamberlain 1975; Kaiser Foundation Health Plan 1976; Sackett 1975). Recently, because of the low benefits relative to costs, Kaiser and other HMOs have discouraged the annual physical exam and, instead, intervals for checkups are scaled to the age of the enrollee (Kaiser Foundation Health Plan 1976; Thompson 1979). Thus while better coverage of preventive services for HMO enrollees may lead to more use of such services, evidence is lacking that this practice results in substantially better health or lower hospital use.

The Role of Self-selection

People are not randomly assigned to HMOs and conventional medical care plans; enrollees generally choose (self-select) HMO membership over other delivery options. The literature about self-selection is not conclusive. The theory of consumer preference (often identified as the risk-vulnerability hypothesis) argues that people most concerned about expected medical-care expenditures will choose the HMO option, and HMOs have been concerned that open enrollment requirements will leave them with the sickest subscribers. Conversely, it is sometimes argued that low HMO hospital utilization rates prove that HMO members are inherently healthier. Sociological factors (e.g., attitudes toward illness and medical care) and demographic factors (e.g., age, sex, and marital status) also influence the HMO choice. However, various empirical studies fail to provide consistent evidence of differences in sociological and sociodemographic factors related to underlying health status or in perceived health status (Berki and Ashcraft 1980; Blumberg 1980).

What advantages does an HMO offer individuals already covered by conventional insurance? Conventional coverage offered in dual-choice situations usually includes reasonably comprehensive hospitalization benefits which, with the possible exception of maternity coverage, are somewhat comparable to HMO protection. The major financial advantage provided by HMOs is their coverage of ambulatory visits. HMO enrollment is, therefore, most likely among people who anticipate a large number of ambulatory visits, either because of poor health status or because of a desire for complete maternity and pediatric coverage. Whereas the first category works to the disadvantage of HMOs, the second tips the scale in favor of a relatively young, healthy population.

Studies of enrollment when people have the choice between HMOs and conventional insurance plans (dual or multiple choice) indicate that people having good relationships with their fee-for-service physicians are unlikely to give them up to join a prepaid group practice (Berki et al. 1977). Patients undergoing treatment also are not likely to switch physicians. (This is not an issue if the choice is between a conventional insurer and coverage of the same physicians through an IPA or fee-for-service group switching to prepayment.) Moreover, numerous studies show that having a "usual physician" is closely associated with medical-care use in both HMO and conventional settings. Among employed people with "no usual physician," the major reason given for not having a personal physician is that none is needed. In studies of enrollment patterns when people were offered the choice of comprehensive coverage at the same price through either an IPA-type plan or a PGP, those joining the PGP were lower utilizers of hospital care prior to enrollment (Luft 1981; Roghmann, Sorensen, and Wells 1980; Richardson et al. 1976). Sometimes preenrollment utilization differences appear in spite of similar measures on scales of health status (Richardson et al. 1976). This may account for part of the lower observed admission rates in PGPs. It is crucial to point out that differential selection is likely to be most important when a population is first offered a multiple choice option with a prepaid group practice and other plans. It is likely that over time some of the people who lacked physician ties when they joined the PGP will develop ties to PGP physicians. Following this logic, the selection effect may be more important in a new plan than in an older plan whose enrollees have established ties to their HMO physicians. Over time both HMO and non-HMO populations will age and their health will deteriorate, thereby reducing this selection effect. For instance, in California where many enrollees have maintained HMO membership for a number of years, there are no substantial health status differences between HMO members and people with conventional coverage (Blumberg 1980). Moreover, while we can say that a selection effect occurs in certain circumstances, we do not know whether it accounts for a large or small fraction of the observed differences in any particular study.

In summary, all the available published evidence indicates lower costs for enrollees in PGPs. The lower costs do not stem from substantial efficiencies in the production of specific medical services, such as a hospital day or a physician office visit. Instead, they are largely due to changes in the number and mix of services provided. Enrollees in both PGPs and IPAs experience somewhat more ambulatory or office visits than people with conventional coverage. This is largely a result of the better HMO coverage for such services and is reflected in a higher proportion of people in HMOs seeing a physician at least once a year. The major source of the cost difference is in hospital use, with markedly lower hospital admission rates for PGPs and somewhat less clear differences for IPAs. The admission differences cannot be attributed simply to a few obvious disease or procedure categories. Nor can the lower hospitalization be explained by increased emphasis in HMOs on annual checkups and screening programs. Finally, there may be some selection into PGPs by people who prefer less reliance on medical care even though they may be no healthier than their counterparts using conventional providers.

Are There Differences In Quality, Consumer Satisfaction, and Physician Satisfaction Between HMOs and Traditional Providers?

Proponents of fee-for-service practice sometimes attribute lower HMO costs to a product of inferior quality. Therefore, one must ask whether the quality of care in HMOs is poorer than in the fee-for-service sector. (Some HMO advocates claim it is better.) Quality of medical care, however, is only one aspect of performance; the broader issue of consumer and provider satisfaction with HMOs must also be examined.

Quality of Care in HMOs

Quality assessment measures can be grouped under the headings of structure, process, and outcome. Although each is a more or less crude approximation of what is implicitly understood by most people as quality, they represent the state-of-the-art and are at the core of present discussions about quality.

Structural measures, such as the proportion of board-certified physicians, are furthest removed from true quality, but they are the most visible indices. The available structural data generally support the contention that HMOs are at least as good as the conventional system. They tend to have higher proportions of board-certified physicians and are more likely to use accredited hospitals than the community at large (Shapiro, Weiner, and Densen 1960; Hastings et al. 1973; Mechanic 1975). However, there are a number of important exceptions: Some HMOs have not been able to obtain access to the better hospitals; others apparently have downplayed the use of specialists or have contracted with nonaccredited facilities (LoGerfo et al. 1976; Gibbens 1973; Columbia University School of Public Health and Administrative Medicine 1962). HMOs also seem to provide better quality than fee-for-service settings in terms of other structural measures, such as informal consultations, peer-review systems, and continuing education.

Process measures—for instance, whether appropriate therapy was instituted for an upper-respiratory infection—are primarily designed to evaluate the technical quality of medical care. Most process studies suggest that the average HMO offers care that is comparable or superior to the "average" fee-for-service practitioner but not better than that of the "better" non-HMO settings (Cunningham and Williamson 1980; Luft 1981). Large multispecialty group practices seem to have a quality advantage over small groups (three to five physicians) and solo practitioners (Payne and Lyons 1972). (This may well be due to the type of physician who joins groups, rather than to a "groupness" factor.) Thus large PGPs exhibit higher quality relative to the average fee-for-service provider but not relative to large fee-for-service groups.

Outcome measures in quality evaluation usually focus either on narrowly defined mortality/morbidity measures or on broad, self reported outcomes, such as disability days. The early studies of Health Insurance Plan (HIP) of Greater New York showed lower prematurity and mortality rates for HMO enrollees (Shapiro, Weiner, and Densen 1960; Shapiro et al. 1960; Shapiro et al. 1967). Few studies as extensive or thorough have been carried out since then. In general, the available data suggest that outcomes in HMOs are much the same as or somewhat better than those in conventional practice (Luft 1981; Cunningham and Williamson 1980).

In summary, while the quality question is only partially resolved, we can tentatively reject the notion that HMOs reduce hospital utilization and achieve cost savings by offering a substantially lower quality of care than the fee-for-service system, and there is even some suggestion of higher quality in HMOs.

Consumer Satisfaction

The most important features of HMOs for which consumer satisfaction evidence is available are access, financial coverage, continuity of care, doctor-patient communication, and perceived quality. PGPs offer shorter in-office waiting times but longer waiting periods to obtain an appointment (Anderson and Sheatsley 1956; Dozier et al. 1973; DeFriese 1975; Tessler and Mechanic 1975; Ashcraft et al. 1978; Hetherington, Hopkins, and Roemer 1975; Richardson, Shortell, and Diehr 1976). The relative value of these two measures of access varies among individuals. The PGP pattern would probably be more satisfactory for people with routine problems that can be scheduled, such as checkups and periodic visits for chronic conditions, while the typical fee-for-service pattern may be more satisfactory for people with urgent problems and wanting to see their usual physician.

PGPs and fee-for-service arrangements also seem to differ with respect to doctor-patient relationships (Mechanic 1975). Prepaid group practices offer less continuity of care in terms of patient identification with a single physician, but there is more institutional continuity. While PGP enrollees express less satisfaction with their physicians than do people in conventional plans, the doctor-patient relationship may be less important than improved financial coverage for people who have chosen prepaid groups (Luft 1981). There are few studies of IPA enrollee satisfaction, but these few indicate that they are as happy with their care as are people with conventional insurance. HMO members almost universally express greater satisfaction with their financial coverage than do people with fee-for-service coverage.

Another approach to measuring consumer satisfaction focuses on the use of services outside the plan. Between 5 and 20 percent of PGP enrollees are regular out-of-plan users, and a comparable proportion of other members use an occasional service outside the plan. Overall, outside use accounts for 7 to 14 percent of all services purchased by HMO enrollees (Luft 1981). This is comparable to the proportion of members reporting substantial dissatisfaction in interviews, but we don't know if these are the same people. To some degree, out-of-plan use may reflect duplicate coverage, as some PGP enrollees have access to conventional third-party coverage through family members (Blumberg 1980).

Dual-choice arrangements available to most HMO enrollees probably offer the best *objective* measure of overall consumer satisfaction. The impressive record of long-term growth in the HMO market share within given enrollee groups implies that enrollee dissatisfaction has an insignificant effect on membership. A small proportion of new enrollees, perhaps 5 to 10 percent, may eventually become dissatisfied for one reason or another and leave. Others may become more satisfied as they grow accustomed to the system and its providers. In addition, there is also a large number of individuals who disenroll due to job turnover. However, these withdrawals are more than offset by new members who leave conventional plans.

Physician Satisfaction

By tradition, physicians are the pivotal element in medical-care delivery in our society. HMOs must be able to attract physicians in sufficient number and with suitable training and qualifications to compete effectively with the fee-for-service system. A national sample of pediatricians and general practitioners, in solo, group, and prepaid group practice, has shown that physicians in prepaid practice earn less per year but work fewer hours, so earnings per hour are comparable (Mechanic 1975). Most prepaid groups have some form of income sharing that results in a general leveling of income differences across specialties—an occasional source of physician dissatisfaction.

HMO physician dissatisfaction with work overload has been reported in several studies (Freidson 1973; McElrath 1961). This often appears to be dissatisfaction with the intensity of work while seeing patients, even though more time is available for leisure. In contrast, national surveys of physicians in general show substantial dissatisfaction with a lack of free time (*American Medical News* 1980; Owens 1977, 1978). Some of the dissatisfaction of HMO-based physicians may be attributed to the contractual nature of prepaid systems; whereas fee-for-service physicians can refer out or refuse to treat patients they perceive as neurotic or overly demanding, HMO subscribers have the right to receive medical care within the system. On the other hand, it is claimed that HMO coverage allows physicians to practice high-quality medical care without having to be concerned about a patient's ability to pay (Cook 1971; Hetherington, Hopkins, and Roemer 1975).

Physician satisfaction with HMOs can be measured in terms of the ability of plans to recruit new physicians and to keep turnover to a reasonable level. Whereas prepaid groups had difficulty recruiting physicians in the 1950s and early 1960s, the situation has changed and most positions are now readily filled. Turnover rates for physicians who have achieved partnership status tend to be quite low.

To date, physician satisfaction has largely been measured within well-established prepaid groups. The attitudes of physicians in newly formed groups or IPAs—particularly during the start-up stages—need to be examined, since the incentives, workload, and income base of the new plans may vary significantly from the older plans.

Organizational and Environmental
Factors Influencing HMO Performance

The factors that influence how a particular HMO develops, grows, and performs can roughly be classified into two groups: those reflecting the internal organizational characteristics of the plan and those reflecting the environment in which the HMO is located. No single factor can be pinpointed to account for the differential growth rate among HMOs. A useful analogy is to think about the factors which make flowers grow and bloom. Some combinations of soil, light, and moisture produce environments conducive to certain species while others are hostile to the same plants. Some strains of the same species thrive better than others because of subtle genetic characteristics. And, within any batch of seeds, some will do poorly because of various injuries, lack of attention, or overcrowding. Similarly, HMOs have not thrived to date in all environments. For instance, as of June 1979, fifteen states were without even one operational HMO while California alone had thirty-one plans. Equally important, plans under similar sponsorship or with similar organizational characteristics may flourish in one area but fail in another; examples can be seen in the case histories of IPAs affiliated with medical societies.

To evaluate factors affecting HMO performance, the following discussion will be divided into two major sections. The first addresses internal organizational factors such as sponsorship and goals, administrative structure, financial incentives, professional staffing, control of hospital services, and marketing of services. The second deals with the external or environmental factors such as professional acceptability to the medical profession, the legal and regulatory environment, sociodemographic characteristics of the local population, and the nature of the local medical care market.

Internal Organizational Factors

The factors that make for the running of a successful business are equally important in the management of an HMO. Qualities such as the "integrity" of key personnel, "commitment or drive," "business acumen," and the "goodwill" in the community are acknowledged by the HMO Program and researchers as key ingredients for a successful HMO (Jurgovan and Blair, Inc. 1979; *American Medical News* 1980). However, specific studies detailing their impact on HMO performance are lacking. Therefore, HMOs tend to be evaluated according to the organizational categories described below.

SPONSORSHIP AND GOALS. Discussions about the success or failure of HMOs usually begin by grouping plans into staff, group, or IPA models and then looking at the sponsorship of the plan. Sources of HMO sponsorship include medical societies, teaching hospitals, universities, labor unions, industrial firms, entrepreneurs, commercial insurers, consumer cooperatives, municipal agencies, and health centers. HMO performance is conditioned, in turn, by the underlying motives of the plan sponsors. For instance, consumer-sponsored plans embracing the "service ideal" of the HMO concept will operate differently from plans which may be attempting to fill empty hospital beds, to earn a sizable profit, or to drive out competitors within the local area.

There is some direct evidence that sponsorship does influence HMO performance. Strumpf and Garramone (1976) examined sixty-six HMO development projects that terminated after receiving federal funds and concluded that their demise was related to insufficient sponsor commitment. IPAs with a medical society or foundation affiliation often suffer from a lack of direction and an inability to control utilization of services (Sorensen, Saward, and Wersinger 1980; Physician Health Plan of Minnesota Staff, n.d.). HMOs that affiliate with large commercial insurers to gain access to employers may find that their plans are poorly marketed because of a conflict of interest on the part of the insurers (Pollack 1979). Union-sponsored plans may encounter resistance from management, as was the case when Rhode Island Group Health Association (RIGHA) first tried to market its coverage (Brown, n.d.). University-sponsored HMOs may experience financial difficulties if the faculty gives preference to the educational aspects of diagnosing and treating patients rather than cost-conscious practice (Zelten 1977). Consumer-based plans may encounter excessive costs because of job creation, high wages, and board interference in administrative operations (Goldstein 1978).

Another issue directly related to sponsorship and goals is whether for-profit or nonprofit status influences HMO performance. To date, the evidence is mixed, largely because nonprofit status often reflects a legal technicality rather than an organizational goal. For instance, in the early and mid-1970s, prepaid health plans in California which contracted with MediCal (Medicaid) were required to have a nonprofit status; however, profits could readily be siphoned off into affiliated entities. Today, while the abuses of the program have ended, many California plans with proprietary or commercial sponsorship still continue to be licensed as nonprofit entities, even though state law, effective 1 January 1980, has permitted health plans to operate on a for-profit basis. The availability of federal funds to for-profit plans is severely restricted, but access to capital markets is more readily accomplished than for nonprofit plans. In most situations, for-profit or nonprofit status appears to be less important in terms of HMO performance than management capability and goals (Starkweather 1970).

Similarly, consumer involvement in HMOs appears to have little direct effect on HMO performance. While the federal qualification process requires consumer participation on HMO policymaking bodies (a minimum of one-third of the seats), HMOs can control the actual selection process. Federal law also requires formal complaint and grievance procedures but professional staff tends to be relatively isolated from such procedures (Kornfield 1979; Barr and Steinberg 1979). HMOs may have consumer councils but they, too, often have relatively little influence (Harrelson and Donovan 1975; Steinberg 1976; Goldstein 1978). The most extensive form of consumer control is achieved in cooperatives that are owned by the membership and employ salaried physicians. Group Health Cooperative of Puget Sound is a highly successful model of this type, while Group Health Association of Washington, D.C., has experienced major difficulties between the consumer board and the physician staff (Meyer 1978; Cohn 1976; Peck 1978).

ORGANIZATIONAL AND ADMINISTRATIVE STRUCTURE. All HMOs have three major functions: marketing benefits and enrolling subscribers; delivering physician and ancillary services; and providing for hospital care. The corporate HMO entity may handle all three functions, or it may contract out to separate entities for medical and hospital services. For instance, state law may prohibit an HMO from employing physicians, so an HMO may contract with a medical group which may be organized as a partnership or a professional corporation. The plan or medical group may control or own a hospital, or the facility may become a third legal entity which then contracts with either the health plan, the medical group, or both. However, HMOs need not be structured around a group practice. Some use a central HMO contracting with individual physicians (either independently or through a physicians association) to provide services to enrollees at agreed-upon rates and using the physicians' customary hospitals, which the HMO reimburses as does any insurer (Zelten 1977). One must examine carefully the true organizational structure that may lie behind a superficial classification. Some HMOs are classified as IPAs when, in fact, they function as PGPs. An independently sponsored HMO contracting at arm's length with a hospital may perform very differently from one sponsored by the hospital. Research is only now beginning on the role of various organizational factors in HMO performance (National Center for Health Services Research 1980).

All forms of medical practice, from a solo, fee-for-service office to a large prepaid group plan, require some degree of administration. In HMOs, administrative authority will be divided generally between the medical director, who oversees the activities of the professional staff, and the executive director who is involved in the day-to-day operations of the health plan. If the plan operates its own facilities (e.g., an outpatient clinic or a hospital), there may be another line of administrative authority. Because HMOs must ultimately balance operational costs against premium income, they tend to be more cost conscious and to exert more administrative controls than traditional fee-for-service providers. However, within HMOs there may be great variation. Some large prepaid group practices are highly centralized, while others allow substantial autonomy on a regional basis (Kaiser) or on a medical group basis (HIP).

Administrative costs vary widely across new plans, but mature HMOs tend to operate in a relatively narrow 7 to 10 percent range (National Association of Employees on Health Maintenance Organizations 1979). The time required for new plans to break even tends to reflect structural differences. HMOs using preexisting medical groups tend to break even in two years or less with an enrollment of ten-thousand or less, whereas plans that require establishment of new medical staffs take more than two years and enrollments above ten-thousand (Ellwein and Kligman 1979). Similarly, IPAs have been shown to be less costly to start up than group or staff model HMOs, but some have had difficulty in maintaining the initial cost advantage because of ineffective data-management systems and poor utilization controls.

It is impossible to predict HMO success on the basis of simple structural factors such as group, staff, or IPA model. Insufficient managerial expertise and control within various types of plans, however, is a variable that consistently appears in case studies of HMO failure (MacColl 1966; Lubalin et al. 1974; Lane 1979). HMO spokesmen have stated that a lack of good managers is the biggest problem facing the HMO industry (*American Medical News* 1980).

METHOD OF PAYING THE PHYSICIANS. Another key variable in the success of HMOs is the method of paying the physician. There are three basic ways to pay physicians: (1) fee-for-service; (2) straight salary; and (3) capitation, or a fixed amount per year per enrollee to accept responsibility for a specific range of services, e.g., all primary care. Straight salary is relatively uncommon except for a brief probationary period; instead salary is often combined with bonuses tied to productivity or cost effectiveness (Ellwein and Kligman 1979; Held and Reinhardt 1980). Some HMOs provide capitation payments to contracting medical groups which, in turn, pay their physician members using a modified salary or fee-for-service arrangement (Hartshorn 1979). (Note that this is also effectively the situation when a physician group owns the HMO.) A few HMOs make capitation payments directly to individual primary-care physicians who are than responsible for monitoring all patient care (Moore 1980).

Fee-for-service payments, such as those used by many IPAs, are likely to increase the number and cost of physician procedures. Even with a fixed fee schedule, the provider can increase income by reclassifying procedures into more complex (i.e., more expensive) categories. At the end of the year, if there is budget overrun, all parties suffer a proportionate cutback in funding or a withholding from plan reserves. In many cases the plan represents only a small fraction of the physicians' patients so, while a plan may be losing large sums of money, the impact on an individual physician's income is negligible (Meier and Tillotson 1978; Newhouse 1973).

Risk-sharing agreements; whereby physicians share in the HMO's potential gains and losses, may also influence HMO performance. Risk-sharing may involve withholding a certain percentage from fee-for-service physician payments or creating a reserve fund prior to establishing a capitation rate; sometimes risk-sharing is strictly dependent on the overall net revenue of the HMO. Physicians may be placed at risk for hospital use, for out-of-plan specialty referrals, or for ambulatory and inpatient physicians services. Generally, incentive payments are made from the reserve funds if the plan achieves certain predetermined financial goals (i.e., total annual hospital charges fall below specified levels). Conversely, if the plan fails to break even or if hospital charges or out-of-plan referrals exceed specified levels, funds are withdrawn from the reserve accounts to reimburse the health plan. To date, published studies have not found a strong link between different types of risk-sharing and HMO performance (Meier and Tillotson 1978). Also, risk-sharing is difficult to separate out from other structural factors which influence provider behavior. For instance, most IPAs and some PGPs which contract with medical groups allow their primary-care physicians to maintain private practices; in such situations, physicians may be tempted to shift costs from their own private patients to the HMO and to be less responsive to their HMO patients (Levy and Fein 1972; Health insurance plan 1979). Medical groups that contract with HMOs and continue to reimburse physicians for productivity without distinguishing between prepaid and fee-for-service patients may have difficulty controlling utilization of services (Aldrich and Shearer 1980).

PHYSICIAN STAFFING. In all situations, the success of an HMO is directly related to the recruitment of an initial core of primary-care physicians who are amenable to practicing cost-conscious medicine. Plans which begin operation with too many specialists and too few primary-care physicians are at a competitive disadvantage as specialists tend to rely more heavily on tests and procedures and to demand higher incomes. In small prepaid group practices, outside specialists are often used on a fee-for-service basis because the patient load is too small to justify a full-time staff. Unless the HMO physicians assure that referrals are appropriate and that patients are promptly returned to the original physician, the costs can be substantial. In the case of PGPs with full-time specialists, there may be a tendency to provide more specialty care than necessary unless new staff is not added until an adequate work load is present (Scitovsky and McCall 1979). For this reason, plans which begin operation with too many specialists and too few primary-care physicians, such as those IPAs which include nearly all of the physicians in an area or plans affiliated with medical schools or referral medical centers, are likely to encounter problems controlling utilization (Luft 1981).

In terms of the employment of allied health professionals (e.g., nurse practitioners, orthopedic technicians), large PGPs can more effectively integrate such personnel into their operations than smaller plans. However, there is no conclusive evidence that the use of such practitioners results in substantial savings (Hershey and Kropp 1979). Moreover, as discussed above, there is little evidence that PGPs differ from fee-for-service group practices in the use of allied health professionals.

CONTROL OF HOSPITAL SERVICES. An HMO can own its own hospital facility outright, can contract for a specific number of beds at a local facility, can negotiate a per diem room rate, or can buy services at prevailing community rates. If an HMO buys hospital days passively on an average cost basis, it will pay for all of the inefficiencies of the existing system. In contrast, fully utilizing a moderately sized hospital requires a patient pool of about a hundred thousand people and a high market penetration within a relatively densely populated area. Because as of June 1979 only twenty-one plans have such concentrated enrollments, many HMOs attempt to negotiate guaranteed rates with local hospitals. If the hospitals have high occupancy rates, HMOs may not be able to negotiate reduced rates. However, if HMOs approach hospitals with excess capacity and offer to quarantee a certain number of bed days in return for lower rates and possible controls on the purchase of new equipment, then there may be little advantage to purchasing a hospital outright.

The ability of HMOs to negotiate discounts is subject to great regional variation. In many large eastern and midwestern cities, Blue Cross/Blue Shield (BC/BS) plans dominate the insurance market and can command sizable discounts of up to 20 to 30 percent (ICF 1979). Some hospitals, fearful of jeopardizing their relationship with BC/BS, have been reluctant to grant the same discounts to HMOs. In contrast, the relative power of HMOs may be substantial in areas where BC/BS is not a dominant carrier and there are excess hospitals beds, as in southern California.

MARKETING OF SERVICES. No HMO can succeed without a good marketing strategy. A recent survey indicates that four of five Americans are not familiar with the HMO concept, including more than half of those eligible to join (Louis Harris and Associates 1980). The dual-choice requirements, as specified in Section 1310 under the HMO Act of 1973 and as established in some states, do not ensure that an HMO can gain access to an employee group. For instance, an HMO may use Section 1310 to require an employer to offer dual choice and discover that another federally qualified HMO is offered as the HMO option. Similarly, employers may not allow HMOs to make direct presentations to their employees or to distribute their own marketing literature. Thus, the success of an HMO in approaching an employer depends upon the ability of the sales staff to make a convincing and realistic presentation to benefit managers and company management. Because salesmen derive their income from commissions, they may tend to "oversell" plans—that is, to tell prospective enrollee groups that "full service is available any time" but to downplay the importance of the judicious use of services. Overselling may result in subscriber dissatisfaction with plan services. Similarly, overmarketing of the plan, without assessing the capability of contracting facilities to absorb the new enrollment, can lead to overcrowding or create long delays for appointments. In the case of Health Alliance of Northern California, premiums were kept at an artificially low level to make the plan competitive with the Kaiser Foundation Health Plan; when enrollment increased rapidly, the professional staff could not keep up and began to refer patients to noncontracting providers, thereby undermining the solvency of the plan.

Successful marketing of a health plan requires more than a well-trained and controlled sales staff. Because HMOs must compete with conventional health insurers for enrollees, HMO management must be able to make a careful assessment of the local market, taking into consideration the factors (e.g., location, premium, supplemental benefits) which influence consumer choice of particular plans.

External Factors

This section will examine the external environment in which HMOs operate, discussing the various sociodemographic, market, professional, legal, and regulatory factors which affect the structure and performance of HMOs.

LOCAL SOCIODEMOGRAPHIC MARKET CHARACTERISTICS. As indicated in the earlier discussion of self-selection, some HMOs are more attractive to certain types of people than to others. Similarly, areas with certain population groups appear more conducive than others to HMO development and growth. Large metropolitan areas, those with highly mobile population, a high physician-to-population ratio and a liberal political outlook are more likely to have HMOs and foster HMO growth (Keller 1979).

Most health insurance coverage is obtained through employer or employee groups which develop a set of options for their members. Thus, the interest of local employers in encouraging HMOs may be a crucial factor. In many instances, an HMO option has not been offered even when plans were available in the area (Gilmore 1979). For companies with relatively limited health benefit packages, introducing an HMO option with broad benefits may create pressures to upgrade existing conventional coverage—a costly proposition. For nationwide companies, the administrative process of reviewing a variety of locally based plans and negotiating HMO benefit packages may be expensive and tedious (Employee Benefit Plan Review 1979). Similarly, HMOs may find that marketing to employers headquartered outside of their region is time consuming and costly. Finally, a number of larger corporations have begun to self-insure—that is, to bear the financial risk which is usually assumed by the insurance firms. Community-rated HMO premiums are based upon the cost of services provided to members of the HMO. When the decision to self-insure is made by firms with a relatively young and healthy employee population, community-rated HMO premiums will be far more expensive—and therefore noncompetitive (Miller 1980).

The way in which employers structure premium subsidies and benefits packages is also important. Over the past two decades, the comprehensiveness of coverage under conventional health insurance packages has increased as has the proportional contribution by employers to premium costs. In many cases, particularly for union-negotiated plans, employers regularly pay the full premium for all health options, regardless of cost. In such a situation, HMOs no longer have a price advantage from the enrollee's perspective. The extent of the employer contribution and the health plan alternatives available can have a substantial influence on the selection of enrollees into various plans. In some cases when the enrollee has not had to pay higher premiums for more expensive plans, the result has been the selection of very high utilizers into certain IPA-type plans (Neilson 1979; Luft 1980b; Sorensen, Saward, and Wersinger 1980). In one instance, hospitalization rates experienced by an IPA were more than ten times those experienced by competing PGPs.

There may also be a "bandwagon" effect associated with HMO growth. As long as market penetration by HMOs within a local area remains relatively low (under 5 percent), most physicians are unlikely to notice any appreciable effect on their private practices. However, when market penetration begins to rise, physicians may see their case load diminish, and elect to affilliate with an HMO or to form a competitive IPA. Such was the case with the Physicians Health Plan in Minneapolis, which was developed by the medical society in 1975 to compete with the six other HMOs in the area (Physicians Health Plan of Minnesota Staff, 1980).

REGULATORY REQUIREMENTS. HMOs sometimes operate at a competitive disadvantage with traditional plans because of the requirements established under state HMO enabling acts and under the Federal HMO Act of 1973. A guide to state laws and regulations is available (Aspen Systems Corporation 1980), but an understanding of how these regulations are implemented requires in-depth case studies. For instance, some states require extensive utilization and quality audits to monitor HMO performance while traditional health insurance plans operating under the insurance code escape similar regulations. Moreover, in California there are two sets of HMO regulations, one for Blue Cross–sponsored HMOs and one for all others. Because states often do not coordinate the form and timing of their data requirements with those of the federal government, a substantial administrative burden is placed on the HMOs. In other states, insurance departments regulate HMO premiums, thereby hampering the ability of HMOs to compete for business against the commercial insurers (Zelten 1977). Other states continue to maintain capitalization and reserve requirements in excess of federal HMO standards for application to nonfederally qualified plans.

Even the process of federal qualification can work to the detriment of HMOs. Under the HMO Act of 1973 and subsequent revisions, HMOs are required to offer an extensive benefit package and to use a community rating formula for the pricing of premiums. In contrast, traditional insurers can tailor benefits and premiums to conform to the specific needs and expected utilization of each employee group. Also, employers with relatively young, healthy employees may opt for self-funding of insurance benefits rather than offering the more costly HMO option.

The federal qualification process and the state licensing process do not necessarily provide adequate protection for plan enrollees in case of HMO failure. For instance, HMOs may not have contractual agreements with referral specialists or adequate reinsurance to cover emergency care outside of the immediate service area. If an HMO fails, enrollees may find themselves being billed by noncontracting providers (physicians, hospitals, ambulance services, etc.). When this happened recently, Hewlett-Packard filed a lawsuit on behalf of its employees against providers associated with a defunct Colorado plan (*Hewlett-Packard Company* v. *Choicecare Health Services et al.*, Civil Action 80-CV-313, 24–26 August.

HMOs and Larger Public Policy Issues

The preceding sections focused on a variety of aspects of HMO performance. The implicit question behind this analysis is whether HMOs should be made available as an alternative method of health care financing and delivery. Recent public policy encouragment of HMO development is based upon the perception of HMOs not just as options but as answers to a set of questions arising from major policy issues, particularly access to care by underserved population groups and the rising costs of medical care. Thus we must consider some additional issues: the ability of HMOs to serve poor, aged, and rural populations; the performance of HMOs in controlling the rate of cost increases for enrollees; and the competitive effects of HMOs on other providers and insurers.

Meeting the Needs of the Underserved— the Poor, the Aged, and Rural Populations

THE POOR. In the late 1960s, the HMO concept was seen as a means of improving the health care of the poor while providing an alternative to the open-ended costs of the fee-for-service system (Columbo, Saward, and Greenlick 1969; Sparer and Anderson 1973). By 1973, some sixty-two prepaid health plans in twelve states were providing care to over two-hundred-thousand Medicaid-eligible individuals (Strumpf 1979). Then came a series of scandals associated with the Medicaid program. "Medicaid mills," operating on a fee-for-service basis in a number of large cities, were discovered to be delivering shoddy care and to be using fraudulent billing practices. In California, the Medicaid prepaid plans were accused of questionable marketing and enrollment procedures, delivering poor quality care, restricting access to medical personnel, and siphoning funds from nonprofit HMO entities into for-profit subsidiaries (Goldberg 1975; California Department of Health 1975; Chavkin and Treseder 1977). Analyses of the California situation revealed that the problem was not in the concept of capitation payment, but largely in the design and administration of the state Medicaid program. For instance, plans were not given lists of Medicaid eligibles so door-to-door marketing was done by salesmen paid on commission; plans were given overlapping market areas; no funding was provided for start-up costs and premiums were fixed by the state, so there were extreme pressures to underserve. The California experience, however, led to a major restructuring of Medicaid HMO contracts by Congress. In 1976, new legislation required that prepaid plans thereafter meet the standards of federally qualified HMOs (with certain exceptions granted to public agencies and rural facilities) and that private-pay enrollees (non-Medicare and non-Medicaid) had to make up at least 50 percent of the enrollees within a specified time period. Moreover, there have been several other important attempts to enroll the poor in HMOs. Multnomah County (Portland) Oregon acts as a broker for several HMOs (Lewis 1979). It allows certain poor people to enroll in any of several HMOs while paying premiums that reflect both family income and the costliness of the health plan option chosen. A California project (Prepaid Health Research Evaluation and Demonstration) has examined the feasibility of offering Medicaid eligibles the option of an HMO when they report to the welfare office (Owen 1980). HIP of Greater New York has had major enrollment of the poor since the early 1960s

(Shapiro and Brindle 1969). The evidence so far suggests that HMOs can enroll the poor and provide them with good quality care at reasonable cost. Moreover, the PGP structure does not seem to be a major deterrent to use by the poor.

To date, the number of Medicaid contracts has not increased significantly above the 1973 level, accounting for slightly less than 3 percent of all HMO enrollment in 1979 (U.S. Department of Health, Education and Welfare 1980). Few incentives exist for Medicaid recipients to seek out prepaid plans because Medicaid generally offers a broad benefit package and copayments are prohibited. Additionally, HMOs have few financial incentives to develop Medicaid contracts. Negative factors associated with an HMO Medicaid contract include increased costs associated with administration and marketing of the program, high turnover of Medicaid enrollees because of loss of Title XIX eligibility, unrealistic capitation rates, as well as the possibility of high utilization of medical services by the needy.

THE AGED. Most HMOs were designed primarily for middle-and working-class populations in urban or suburban environments. In 1979, only 4.3 percent of HMO enrollment was made up of Medicare beneficiaries, most of whom were HMO members while employed and retained coverage after retirement, although Medicare beneficiaries account for roughly 10 percent of the U.S. population (U.S. Department of Health, Education and Welfare 1980). This low participation rate is the result of two factors: (1) HMOs cannot use savings from lower hospitalization to attract Medicare beneficiaries through better coverage; and (2) complex Medicare reimbursement policies fail to provide HMOs with an incentive to seek out Medicare beneficiaries (Luft et al. 1980; Strumpf 1979). HMOs can receive payment from the Health Care Financing Administration of the Department of Health and Human Services according to a cost-reimbursement system or on a capitation basis. Cost reimbursement produces increased administrative costs for HMOs. Annual capitation rates for at-risk HMOs are based on the per capita cost for local Medicare beneficiaries receiving fee-for-service care. However, any savings generated by HMOs are shared with the government, while deficits must be absorbed by the HMO or carried forward to be offset against future savings. Therefore, it is not surprising that most HMOs are not at risk for their Medicare enrollees. The Health Care Financing Administration is currently sponsoring demonstration projects in which HMOs will receive capitation payments which are structured to allow the savings to be shared with the beneficiaries.

RURAL POPULATIONS. In rural areas the chief problem is often the availability and accessibility of any health providers. In particular, nonmetropolitan areas with stable or declining populations have the greatest difficulty attracting and retaining physicians (Cotteril and Eisenberg 1979). For the rural poor and aged, georgraphic access is further complicated by financial constraints and the problem is exacerbated when rural physicians are unwilling to accept Medicare and Medicaid patients. IPAs have been considered as a means of implementing prepaid coverage for rural populations. The IPA structure is proposed as a means to encourage more rural physicians to accept Medicaid eligibles by reducing state-imposed paperwork because the physicians deal with the IPA rather than the state. Another method calls for networks of primary-care physicians operating in conjunction with HMOs in urban settings. Some notable prepaid group practices have developed in rural areas, but in most instances their history reflects unique circumstances (e.g., United Mine Workers of America–sponsored clinics, and Two

Harbors Clinic serving steel workers in rural Minnesota). As in the case in urban settings, group practices in rural areas might find attractive the improved cash flow and altered financial incentives of capitation payments for hospital and physician services. By reducing the use of hospital services, HMOs can increase the share of health expenditures received by physicians. The higher physician income may help attract MDs to rural areas. However, little is known about the performance of different HMO models for financing and delivering medical care in rural areas.

Do HMOs Lower the Rate of Expenditure Increases for Enrollees?

Since the early 1960s, total expenditures for HMO enrollees have grown at only a slightly lower rate than expenditures for those with conventional insurance coverage (Luft 1980a). As indicated before, at any point in time the comparative advantage of HMOs vis-à-vis conventional providers is lower hospitalization rates. Over a twenty-year period a number of HMOs show substantial long-term reductions in hospitalization, but there is also evidence of long-term reductions in hospitalization for conventionally covered enrollees (Luft 1980a). Moreover, some apparent reductions in HMO utilization can be explained by the changing age-sex mix of the enrolled population. Costs per inpatient day in HMOs largely reflect changes in the costs of inputs and do not demonstrate differential increases in efficiency over time (Luft 1980a). Physician productivity in HMOs actually decreased over time, but this too seems to reflect a national pattern. Although the cost, utilization, and productivity in HMOs follow the same basic trends as the whole medical-care sector, this still implies lower HMO cost and utilization in each year. Throughout this period, however, HMOs have had only a very small segment of the medical-care market and have not drawn much attention. If their market share increases and results in substantial competition, then the cost trends may change.

The Competitive Impact of HMOs

Perhaps the most important potential role for HMOs is the possibility that they can promote beneficial competition in the health-care system. By stimulating conventional providers to restructure medical practice and insurance benefits, HMOs might function as catalysts for cost containment. Unfortunately, only a handful of studies address this crucial problem. While there are many reports of a competitive process developing in areas such as Minneapolis–St. Paul, the available evidence on the outcomes of competition is mixed (Luft 1980b).

A 1977 Federal Trade Commission study argues that the entry of HMOs is responsible for lowering the hospital utilization of people in conventional plans (Goldberg and Greenberg 1977). Unfortunately, these results are largely limited to the experiences of four states on the West Coast: California, Washington, Oregon, and Hawaii. If the experiences of these four states are omitted, the competitive effect of HMOs is no longer clearly evident. The study indicates clear competitive reactions by Blue Cross of Northern California to Kaiser's growth, beginning in the 1950s, but there is little supporting evidence in other areas. Moreover, the decline in hospital utilization in California, which appeared during a period of substantial HMO growth, cannot be used as convincing evidence of an "HMO effect" because of other developments in the California insurance market, such as the split between Blue Cross and Blue Shield (which now compete with each other, unlike the cooperation usual in most states), and the entrance of commercial insurers.

Other examples that have been used to support the notion of an HMO competitive effort also produce inconclusive results. For instance, in Rochester, New York, there has been intense competition between HMOs and the local Blue Cross/Blue Shield plan. The inpatient medical-surgical utilization rate for BC/BS members has fallen markedly in recent years, and much of this decline is attributed to a competitive effect (Finger Lakes Health System Agency 1980). There are a number of alternative explanations, however. Rochester has had aggressive health planning since the late 1940s, and traditionally has had a very low ratio of beds per capita. Additionally, a unique regional budgeting strategy is being implemented (Sorensen and Saward 1978). Changes in New York state policies toward nursing home reimbursement have hindered the transfer of Medicare and Medicaid recipients out of general hospitals. Thus the lower BC/BS utilization rate for the nonelderly, nonpoor population may be a reflection of the tight bed supply, rather than of competition with local HMOs.

Generally, the "HMO effect" has been discussed in terms of an impact upon hospitalization rates, insurance premium costs, and benefit packages. Little attention has been devoted to the issue of overall health expenditures. If competition between HMOs and conventional providers does have an effect on overall costs, one might expect this result to appear in California, with its large well-established Kaiser plans, its competing HMOs, and a documented history of Blue Cross concern. While by some standards the mix of medical services purchased by Californians may appear to be more efficient than elsewhere—namely, low hospital admissions and high physician use—there is no evidence that extensive HMO enrollment has resulted in overall cost containment. In fact, the share of per capita income allocated to medical-care expenditures by Californians is among the highest in the nation; the medical-care pie is no smaller in California, but the physician share is larger (Cooper, Worthington, and Piro 1975). While other factors may explain the high medical-care expenditures in California, this example suggests that the competitive effect of HMOs cannot be easily discerned.

Directions for Further Research

A careful reading of the existing research on HMOs quickly points out that there is a great deal that is not yet known about their performance. Merely listing the specific questions can take the better part of a chapter (Luft 1981). However, the most important unresolved issues can be grouped under three major headings: (1) what accounts for performance differences between HMOs and conventional providers; (2) what accounts for variations in performance among HMOs; and (3) what impact do HMOs have on the rest of the medical-care system? Although these issues are linked, they will be discussed separately because of differing research approaches needed for each set of problems. Ideally, to evaluate performance one would design large-scale studies incorporating many HMO and non-HMO settings and assess the relative importance of variables within and across groups. However, given time and budget constraints and problems related to data availability, it is likely that studies addressing the first set of questions will be undertaken in selected HMO sites while other, less detailed studies will be used to address the second set of issues. Addressing the third set of questions will be even more difficult because there are even fewer cases to observe and more variables to consider.

Differences Between HMOs and Conventional Providers

There is substantial evidence that HMO enrollees experience lower health-care costs, largely because they have less hospital use than people in conventional plans. The major unresolved question is understanding why and how this occurs. Several, not mutually exclusive, explanations, such as careful case management, preventive care, quality differences, and self-selection, were offered in the preceding discussion. Determining the relative importance of each should be high on the proposed research agenda.

The role of self-selection is crucial because HMOs essentially require voluntary participation by enrollees and physicians. At one extreme, if all the cost and utilization difference is attributable to selection, then HMOs achieve no true savings and a pro-HMO strategy merely transfers money from high to low utilizers of medical care. At the other extreme, if sicker people are attracted to HMOs, their true savings are even greater than the apparent cost difference.

As discussed earlier, there is clear evidence that in certain cases self-selection occurs among people newly offered a choice of health plans. Various factors, including prior physician relationships, the premiums, benefits, and delivery system structure of each health plan, and several personal characteristics influence choice of plan. For instance, when an employee group is offered a PGP and an IPA, each of which offers more comprehensive benefits at somewhat higher premiums than the conventional insurance alternative, the PGP seems to attract people who have a preference for preventive care, yet have no strong physician ties and are relatively low users of hospital care. These and other variables also may determine who switches *out* of each plan. The net result of the enrollment and disenrollment decisions is the mix of people in each plan. But examining people's medical-care use before and after switching plans provides only limited information concerning the long-run effects of selection. People who anticipate switching plans may move forward or postpone certain types of medical care, or they may switch plans just to receive specific services, such as maternity care, and then switch back. Thus, utilization patterns among "switchers" may be very different from the patterns of long-term enrollees. While there have been some studies of the utilization patterns of new enrollees, these studies have not focused on self-selection and preenrollment-use patterns, nor have they examined the impact of utilization by "switchers" on the overall costs of the plan.

Discussions about selection are often couched in terms of differences in health status or in expressed preferences for medical-care use (Blumberg 1980). Although such differences may be present, research also should focus on the role played by indifference. While some patients may clearly prefer a physician who is clinically aggressive and believes "the patient is ill until proven healthy," and other patients prefer physicians espousing a "wait-and-see" attitude, there may be a third group without strong preferences, the "whatever you say, Doc" group. The first and second groups are likely to select conventional fee-for-service and HMO options, respectively; but the third group may not feel strongly about practice styles even though they may have strong existing ties to a physician. It is this third group which offers the greatest potential for HMO savings, especially if they are relatively indifferent to large changes in practice style and a large fraction of the population falls within this group. In other words, the "wait-and-see" group are likely to be relatively low utilizers of care regardless of the system, and those who favor aggressive intervention will be highly resistant to more conservative practice styles. It is the group of relatively indifferent patients who are the primary candidates for accepting a major change in practice styles.

Patient preference and self-selection is only one part of the question; we know even less about how physician preferences and selection influence practice patterns. There is some evidence that physicians in various practice settings (and payment systems) have different orientations toward their work (Held and Reinhardt 1979; Mechanic 1975). However, probably even more important than understanding the physician's work orientation is an understanding of the ways in which different practice patterns are manifested at the clinical level. For instance, are patients with earaches, abdominal pain, or back pain "worked up" and treated differently in HMO and non-HMO settings? Are such differences more apparent in the diagnostic phase or in the treatment phase of patient care? Do HMO physicians use more stringent criteria in reaching a diagnosis? Does the HMO physician rely to a greater extent upon the patient rather than on laboratory tests to monitor signs and symptoms? What impact do the different practice patterns, if they exist, have on patient outcomes? For instance, it may be the case that an HMO physician can emphasize careful monitoring of abdominal pain and be able to achieve a much lower appendectomy rate with no increase in the rate or perforated appendices, that is, all the reduction takes place in the "false-positive rate."

If physician behavior is different in HMO and non-HMO settings, how does this occur? For instance, it may be the case that some medical students and residents are conservative users of medical technology and others are more aggressive in their diagnostic and treatment decisions. Are they differentially attracted to (or repelled from) HMO practice? Alternatively, do HMOs seek out certain types of new physicians and, if so, are they identified before joining the plan or during the initial probationary period? At the other extreme, HMO physicians may acquire their different practice habits only after joining the plan. If this is the case, what is the process? Are there explicit or implicit guidelines or decision rules set down by the HMO for the use of specific tests or procedures? Do more senior physicians explain what is considered to be appropriate practice? Or, do the different economic and organizational incentives in an HMO result in behavioral changes so subtle that no one notices them occurring?

Differences Among HMOs

The preceding questions have focused on the issue of HMO performance in general in contrast to the conventional fee-for-service system. However, not all HMOs are the same and, in fact, there is evidence of substantial variation in performance among HMOs. Some of this variation may be random or a function of idiosyncratic characteristics of the staff and mamagement of particular HMOs.

Other differences, however, may be consistently related to factors that either can be influenced by policy (e.g., profit/not-for-profit orientation) or should be taken into consideration when evaluating HMO performance (e.g., a hostile medical market environment). As suggested earlier, there has been very little research concerning the influence of the various organizational and environmental factors on HMO performance. Some future studies will probably focus on specific variables such as sponsorship or plan structure. However, some more ambitious studies should be undertaken to examine differences in HMO performance within the context of a broader model of health-care systems.

While the exposition of a complete model of health-care systems is well beyond the scope of this paper, some general ideas may help the reader understand the underlying concept. The performance of a specific HMO is the result of complex interactions among external environmental factors, internal characteristics of the HMO, and adaptive mechanisms of both the HMO and its local market. For instance, some medical-care markets will be more or less accepting of the general HMO concept. Moreover, acceptance may depend on the specific variety of the HMO—an area may allow a provider-sponsored plan to thrive yet offer strong opposition to a consumer cooperative. The relative abundance of physicians, hospitals, and other medical resources in the area may help determine some of the organizational characteristics of the local HMOs. For instance, in an area with many surplus hospital beds an HMO may be able to negotiate favorable rates from existing institutions while in an area with a tight bed supply an HMO may build its own facility. State laws may differentially encourage or hinder certain types of HMOs. At the same time, laws are not immutable and some HMOs or HMO sponsors may reshape the state laws to their own advantage.

The internal organizational characteristics of the HMO will influence and be influenced by its leadership, providers, and enrollees. A not-for-profit, consumer controlled plan is unlikely to attract a hard-driving entrepreneurial manager. Some types of physician payment schemes encourage more or less attention to productivity, and the choice of scheme will at least partially reflect the needs of the plan. Similarly, relationships with hospitals, laboratories, and other providers can be changed to reflect the needs of the organization. Researchers should not assume that there is one optimal design for an HMO or that organizational patterns can be easily "transplanted" to other settings. Thus, the organization of the HMO and its incentives are appropriately considered dependent, as well as explanatory, variables. Moreover, the broader model should also allow for an evaluation of the influence of the HMO on its environment, a subject discussed below.

While outlining such an ambitious approach, I would venture to add two additional and testable hypotheses. The first is that history, and especially local history, may have an important role in explaining current HMO performance. Plans may be structured in ways that currently appear irrational, yet are in direct response to historical factors such as the previous failure of a "more rationally designed plan." For instance, the relative lack of clinical innovation in many mature HMOs may be a direct result of accusations thirty years ago of providing cut-rate care. Although such charges might be easily rejected today, thirty years of organizational inertia can have a powerful influence.

The second hypothesis is that there may be large "gray areas" in medical care in which no particular organizational structure, delivery system, or clinical rule is clearly better than other, even substantially different, approaches. This hypothesis stems from the fact that health outcomes depend on such a wide range of factors, that clinical medicine is largely art, rather than science, and that in addition to the patient's physical state, the patient's psychological state (which is often unmeasured) may have a major influence on outcome. Moreover, our measures of performance, such as mortality, are extremely crude, so that even if two systems truly resulted in different outcomes, the investigator probably could not detect a significant difference. The relative lack of competition in the medical-delivery system compounds the importance of these gray areas so that one cannot rely upon the traditional economic assumptions that producers are using the best techniques and consumers have found the best delivery system. This implies that future analyses of performance should be designed not to search for optimal models, but to *explore and understand* differences with the goal of explaining why they occur and why some results may be better for some people and worse for others.

Impact of HMOs on the Total Medical-Care System

Until recently the major focus of research on HMOs has been on how they differ from conventional fee-for-service system with the expectation that the major benefits of HMOs accrue to their own members. In the last few years HMOs have become important in policy discussions because of their potential catalytic role in changing the rest of the system, particularly in terms of cost containment. In this view, if HMOs achieve a given market share, say, 15 percent, they will also help contain costs for the remaining 85 percent of the population. The section on organizational and environmental factors pointed out how inconclusive the evidence is on the competitive effects of HMOs and that several types of further research are necessary.

One line of future investigation is to measure the effect that increased HMO market share has on medical-care expenditures by non-HMO members in an area. The scantly research to date has emphasized changes in hospital use, yet if providers merely shift expenditures from hospitals to outpatient units and physicians, there may be no net savings. More important, studies of a competitive effect should examine *how* such an effect occurs and researchers should be alert to unanticipated consequences of competition. The logic behind the competitive model is that physicians and insurers in the conventional sector will constrain their costs in order to compete with HMOs. Counteracting this is the drive of existing providers to maintain their incomes. This may be done by squeezing certain providers, such as hospitals; by convincing patients that additional services are really necessary, especially in light of the difficulty in evaluating outcomes; by constraining costs for some groups sensitive to competition, such as the healthy middle class, while increasing costs for captive populations such as the sick and public patient; or by other, as yet unspecified, means. Rather than beginning with the view that a cost-containing competitive response will occur and searching for some confirmatory evidence, researchers should begin with Murphy's law—if something can go wrong, it will—and make sure that competition leads to overall cost containment, not just cost shifting (Luft 1982).

A second type of competitive impact may be much more important, yet is even more difficult to measure and evaluate. Trends in cost and utilization suggest that, while PGPs have consistently been less expensive than the conventional system, costs for enrollees in both settings have beeen rising at comparable rates over time. This similarity may be due, in part, to underlying forces such as the development of new technology, the shift toward inpatient-oriented practice, the substitution of tests and diagnostic procedures for "clinical judgment," and trends in medical education and practice. As HMOs and other alternative delivery systems grow and develop, some may challenge current practices and techniques. The large-scale long-term data base available in some HMOs has already been used to evaluate the effectiveness of selected procedures such as mammography and annual physical examinations. Much more can be done along these lines. Moreover, the prepayment concept can be used to cover a wide range of nonmedical alternatives to traditional practice, such as home care, nutritional supplements, and personal or life-style changes. Such innovations have the potential to alter substantially the future course of the medical-care system and HMOs can offer a means for exploring their implementation.

REFERENCES

ALDRICH, S., and SHEARER, W. 1980. HMO income distribution in fee for service medical groups: survey results and implications. Presentation at National Health Lawyers Meeting: HMOs: New Perspectives, New Dimensions, Los Angeles, Calif., 24–26 August 1980.

American Medical News. 1976. Are physicians overworked? *American Medical News Impact*, 23 August 1976, p. 5.

———. 1980. Lack of good managers called biggest problem facing HMO industry. *American Medical News*, 13 June 1980, P. 8.

ANDERSON, O. W., and SHEATSLEY, P. B. 1959. *Comprehensive medical insurance: a study of costs, use, and attitudes under two plans.* New York: Health Insurance Foundation, Research Series no. 9.

ASHCRAFT, M., et al. 1978. Expectations and experience of HMO enrollees after one year: an analysis of satisfaction, utilization and costs. *Medical Care* 16 (no. 1):14–32.

Aspen Systems Corporation. 1980. *Digest of state laws affecting the prepayment of medical care, group practice and HMOs.* Germantown, Md.: Aspen Systems Corporation, September 1980.

BARR, J. K., and STEINBERG, M. K. 1979. Organizational structure and the professions in an alternative health care system: physicians in health maintenance organizations. Paper presented at Annual Meeting of the Society for the Study of Social Problems, Boston, 24–27 August 1979.

BERKI, S. E., and ASHCRAFT, M. L. 1980. HMO enrollment: who joins what and why: A review of the literature. *Milbank Memorial Fund Quarterly/Health and Society* 58 (no. 4): 588–632.

BERKI, S. E., et al. 1977. Enrollment choice in a multi-HMO setting: the roles of health risk, financial vulnerability, and access to care. *Medical Care* 15 (no. 2): 95–114.

BLUMBERG, M. S. 1980. Health status and health care use by type of private health care coverage. *Milbank Memorial Fund Quarterly/Health and Society* 58 (no. 4): 633–55.

BROWN, E. C. 1976, The roots of RIGHA: a personal history of the Rhode Island Group Health Association. Providence, R.I.: Aloig Printing Co.

California Department of Health. 1975. Prepaid health plans: the California experience. In U.S. Senate, Committee on Government Operations, Permanent Subcommittee on Investigations, *Prepaid Health Plans*, Hearings, 13–14 March 1975, 94th Congress, 1st sess. Washington, D.C.: Government Printing Office.

CHAMBERLAIN, J. 1975. Screening for the early detection of diseases in Great Britain. *Preventive Medicine 4: 268.*

CHAVKIN, D. F., and TRESEDER, A. 1977. California's prepaid health plan program: can the patient be saved? *Hastings Law Journal* 28: 685–760.

COHN, V. 1976. Doctors in GHA want own firm. *Washington Post,* 17 March 1976. Reprinted in *Medical Care Review* 33 (no. 4) 406–407.

COLOMBO. T. J.; SAWARD, E. W.; and GREENLICK, M. R. 1969. Integration of an OEO health program into a prepaid comprehensive group practice plan. *American Journal of Public Health* 59 (no. 4): 641–50.

Columbia University School of Public Health and Administrative Medicine. 1962. *Prepayment for medical and dental care in New York State.* New York: Commissioner of Health and the Superintendent of Insurance.

Committee on the Costs of Medical Care. 1932. *Medical care for the American people: the final report of the committee on the costs of medical care.* Chicago: University of Chicago Press.

COOK, W. H. 1971. Profile of the Permanente physician. In *The Kaiser-Permanente medical care program: a symposium,* ed. A. R. Somers, pp. 97–105. New York: Commonwealth Fund.

COOPER, B. S.; WORTHINGTON, N. L.; and PIRO, P. A. 1975. *Personal health care expenditures by state.* DHEW pub. no. (SSA) 75–11906. Washington, D.C.: Government Printing Office.

COTTERIL, P. G., and EISENBERG, B. S. 1979. Improving access to medical care in underserved areas: the role of group practice. *Inquiry* 16:141–53.

CUNNINGHAM, F. C., and WILLIAMSON, J. W. 1980. How does the quality of health care in HMOs compare to that in other settings?—an analytic literature review: 1958 to 1979. *Group Health Journal* 1 (no. 1): 4–25.

DEFRIESE, G. H. 1975, On paying the fiddler to change the tune: further evidence from Ontario regarding the impact of universal health insurance on the organization and patterns of medical practice, *Milbank Memorial Fund Quartely/Health and Society* 53 (no. 2): 117–48.

DOZIER, D., et al. 1964. *Report of the medical and hospital advisory council to the board of administration of the California State employees' retirement system.* Sacramento, Calif., June.

——. 1973. *1970-71 survey of consumer experience report of the State of California employees' medical and hospital care program prepared under the policy direction of the medical advisory council to the board of administration of the public employees' retirement system.* Sacramento, Calif.: State of California.

ELLWEIN, L., and KLIGMAN, L. 1979. *An overview of group practice HMOs: survey results, March 1979.* Excelsior, Minn. InterStudy, September 1979.

Employee Benefit Plan Review. 1979. Offering an HMO if you have 144 health plans, 250 payroll systems, and 21 businesses. *Employee Benefit Plan Review* 34 (August 1979): 24–25.

Finger Lakes Health Systems Agency. 1980. *Health maintenance organizations in Rochester, New York: history, current performance, and future prospects.* Finger Lakes Health Systems Agency, Task Force on Prepaid Health Care, January 1980.

FOLTZ, A.-M., and KELSEY, J. 1978. The annual pap test: a dubious policy success. *Milbank Memorial Fund Quarterly/Health and Society* 56 (no. 4): 426–62.

FREELAND, M.; CALAT, G.; and SCHENDLER, C. E. 1980. Projections of national health expenditures, 1980, 1985, and 1990. *Health Care Financing Review* 1:1–27.

FREIDSON, E. 1973. Prepaid group practice and the new demanding patient. *Milbank Memorial Fund Quarterly* 51 (no. 4): 473–88.

GIBBENS, S. F. 1973. *Hospitalization savings under prepayment—California Medi-Cal* (an analysis of Consolidated Medical Systems Ltds. Operations), February 1973.

GIBSON, R. M. 1979. National health expenditures, 1978. *Health Care Financing Review* 1:1–36.

GILMORE, M. 1979. Santa Clara County employers: number offering fair economic choice of health benefits plan. Research paper no. 514, Graduate School of Business, Stanford University, 1 September 1979.

GOLDBERG, L. G., and GREENBERG, W. 1977. *The HMO and its effects on competition.* Washington, D.C.: Federal Trade Commission, Bureau of Economics.

GOLDBERG, V. P. 1975. Some emerging problems of prepaid health plans in the Medi-Cal system. *Policy Analysis* 1 (no. 1): 55–68.

GOLDSTEIN, G. S. 1978. *Consumer participation in UMWA-related health clinics.* Paper presented at the panel on Consumer Participation in a National Health Service, APHA Meetings, Los Angeles, Calif., 17 October 1978.

HARRELSON, E. F., and DONOVAN, K. M. 1975. Consumer responsibility in a prepaid group health plan. *American Journal of Public Health* 65 (no. 10): 1077–086.

HARTSHORN, T. O. 1979. Innovation in partnership, *Medical Group Management 26:34–36.*

HASTINGS, J. E. F., et al. 1973. Prepaid group practice in Sault Ste. Marie, Ontario—Part I: analysis of utilization records. *Medical Care* 11 (no. 2): 91–103.

Health insurance plan of New York and its affiliated medical groups. 1979. *Urban Health* 8: (no. 4): 18–37.

HELD, P. J., and REINHARDT, U. 1979. Analysis of economic performance in medical group practices. Final report. Princeton, N.J.: Mathematica Policy Research.

———. 1980. Prepaid medical practice: a summary of findings from a recent survey of group practices in the United States—a comparison of fee-for-service and prepaid groups. *Group Health Journal* 1:4–15.

HERSHEY, J. C., and KROPP, D. H. 1979. A reappraisal of the productivity potential and economic benefits of physician's assistants. *Medical Care* 17 (no. 6): 592–606.

HETHERINGTON, R. W.; HOPKINS, C. E.; and ROEMER, M. I. 1975. *Health insurance plans: promise and performance.* New York: Wiley-Interscience.

Hewlett-Packard Company v. Choicecare Health Services et al. 1980 Civil Action 80-CV-313, District Court for Larimer County, Colorado. Reprinted in *HMOs: New Perspectives, New Dimensions 1980,* proceedings of National Health Lawyers Association Conference, Los Angeles, Calif., 24–26 August 1980.

HOLLAND, W. 1974. Screening for disease: taking stock. *Lancet* 1:1494–97.

ICF. 1979. Proposal to study HMO development in three cities. Response to DHEW request for Proposal no. RFP-PL-79-36-GH. Washington D.C., September 1979.

Jurgovan and Blair, Inc. 1979. Health maintenance organization viability. Rockville: Jurgovan and Blair. DHEW Contract #100–77–0109.

Kaiser Foundation Health Plan. 1976. Health examinations: an important message. *Planning for Health* 19 (no. 1): 2–3.

KELLER, P. F. 1979. Environmental conduciveness to health maintenance organizations: a population ecology explanation. Ph.D. dissertation, School of Education, Stanford University, August 1979.

KORNFIELD, A. 1979. Patient satisfaction in pre-paid care—Health Insurance Plan of Greater New York (HIP) experience. In *Health handbook,* ed. G. K. Chacko, pp. 169–77. Amsterdam: North-Holland Publishing Co.

LANE, M. 1979. HMO health improving: growth stops. (Michigan) *State Journal,* 20 May 1979. Reprinted in *DHEW Green Sheet* 26:111 (6 June 1979), R19.

LEVY, H., and FEIN, O. 1972. Crippled H.I.P. *Health/PAC Bulletin* 45:15–22.

LEWIS, R. 1979. Oregon County buying prepaid care for the needy. *American Medical News,* 27 July 1979, pp. 1, 14, 50.

LOGERFO, J. P., et al. 1976. Quality of care. In *The Seattle prepaid health care project: comparison of health services delivery,* ed. W. C. Richardson. Seattle,: Wash. University of Washington, School of Public Health and Community Medicine.

Louis Harris and Associates. *Employers and HMO's: a nationwide survey of corporate employers in areas served by health maintenance organizations.* New York: Louis Harris and Associates.

LUBALIN, J. S., et al. 1974. *Evaluation of the accomplishments of selected HMOs-funded projects.* Draft Final Report, Contract HSA 105-74-10, May 1974.

LUFT, H. 1978a. Why do HMOs seem to provide more health maintenance services? *Milbank Memorial Fund Quarterly/Health and Society* 56:140-68.

———. 1978b. How do health maintenance organizations achieve their savings: rhetoric and evidence. *New England Journal of Medicine* 298:1336-43.

———. 1980a. Trends in medical care costs. Do HMOs lower the rate of growth? *Medical Care* 18:1-16.

———. 1980b. HMOs and the medical care market. In *Socioeconomic issues of health 1980,* ed. D. E. Hough and G. I. Misek, pp. 85-102. Monroe, Wis: Center for Health Services Research and Development, American Medical Association.

———. 1981. *Health maintenance organizations: dimensions of performance.* New York: Wiley-Interscience.

———. 1982. On the potential failure of good ideas: an interview with the originatior of Murphy's Law. *Journal of Health Politics, Policy, and Law* 7:45-53.

———, and CRANE, S. 1980. Regionalization of services within a multihospital health maintenance organization. *Health Services Research* 15:3.

LUFT, H. S.; FEDER, J.; HOLAHAN, J.; and LENNOX, K. D. 1980. Health maintenance organizations. In *National health insurance conflicting goals and policy choices,* ed. J. Feder, J. Holahan, and T. Marmor. Washington, D.C.: The Urban Institute.

MACCOLL, W. A. 1966. *Group practice and prepayment of medical care.* Washington, D.C.: Public Affairs Press.

McCAFFREE, K. M., et al. 1976. Comparative cost of services. In *The Seattle prepaid health care project: comparison of health services delivery,* ed. W. C. Richardson. National Technical Information Service, PB #267488-SET.

McELRATH, D. C. 1961. Perspective and participation in prepaid group practice, *American Sociological Review* 26: 596-607.

MECHANIC, D. 1975. The organization of medical practice and practice orientation among physicians in prepaid and nonprepaid primary care settings. *Medical Care* 13 (no. 3): 189-204.

Medical World News. 1978. Prepaid plan takes on New York City Medicaid. *Medical World News* 19, 6 March 1978, p. 29.

MEIER, G. B., and TILLOTSON, J. 1978. *Physician reimbursement and hospital use in HMOs.* Excelsior, Minn.: InterStudy, September 1978.

MEYER, L. 1978. Group health in trouble. *Washington Post, 2 January 1978. Reprinted in Medical Care Review* 35: 163-67.

MILLER, JOHN. 1980. Personal interview, 1, May 1980.

MOORE, S. 1980. The primary care network: a new type of HMO for private practice physicians. *Western Journal of Medicine* 132: 418-23.

National Association of Employees on Health Maintenance Organizations. 1979. *NAEHMO overview of annual survey of HMOs, 1978.* Minneapolis,: Minn. NAEHMO.

National Center for Health Services Research. 1980. Request for Proposal #233-80 -3004 for organizational structure of health maintenance organizations (HMOs). April 1980.

NEILSON, CHRIS. 1979. Personal communication. 26 September 1979.

NEWHOUSE, J. P. 1973. The economics of group practice. *Journal of Human Resources* 8 (no. 1): 37-56.

———. 1974. A design for a health insurance experiment. *Inquiry,* 11 (no. 1): 5-27.

OWEN, E. 1980. *Mainstreaming marketing for medicaid: what works, what doesn't (seems to), and why. A preliminary report on the marketing demonstration results from California's prepaid health research, evaluation and demonstration (PHRED) Project.* 1 February 1980.

OWENS, A. 1977. What doctors want most from their practices now. *Medical Economics* 54 (no. 5): 88-92.

————. 1978. What's behind the drop in doctors' productivity? *Medical Economics* 55 (no. 15): 102–5.

PAYNE, B. C., and LYONS, T. F. 1972. *Detailed statistics and methodologies for studies of personal medical care in Hawaii.* Ann Arbor, Mich.: University of Michigan School of Medicine, 1972.

PECK, R. L. 1978. The HMO that drove doctors to strike. *Medical Economics* 55 (no. 19): 142–60.

Physicians Health Plan of Minnesota Staff. 1980. *The physicians health plan of Minnesota: a case study of utilization controls in an IPA.* HHS pub. no. (PHS) 80–50128.

POLLACK, B. 1979. The evolution of an HMO. *Medical Group Management* 26:15–18.

RICHARDSON, W. C., et al. 1976. *The Seattle prepaid health care project: comparison of health services delivery.* Chapter 1: Introduction to the project, the study, and the enrollees. Grant no. R18 HS 00694—National Center for Health Services Research, HRA, DHEW, November 1976.

RICHARDSON W. C.; SHORTELL, S. M.; and DIEHR, P. K. 1976. Access to care and patient satisfaction. In *The Seattle prepaid health care project: comparison of health services delivery,* ed. W. C. Richardson. Seattle, Wash.: University of Washington School of Public Health and Community Medicine.

ROGHMANN, K. J.; SORENSEN, A.; and WELLS, S. M. 1980. Hospitalization in three competing HMOs during their first two years: a cohort study of the Rochester experience. *Group Health Journal* 1:26–33.

SACKETT, D. L. 1975. Screening for early detection of disease: to what purpose? *Bulletin of the New York Academy of Medicine* 51 (no. 1): 39–52.

SAGEL, S. S., et al. 1974. Efficacy of routine screening and lateral chest radiographs in a hospital based population. *New England Journal of Medicine* 291 (no. 19): 1001–4.

SCITOVSKY, A., and McCALL, N. 1979. Use of physician services under two prepaid plans. *Medical Care* 17:441–60.

SHAPIRO, S., and BRINDLE, J. 1969. Serving medicaid eligibles. *American Journal of Public Health* 59 (no. 4): 635–41.

SHAPIRO, S., et al. 1967. Patterns of medical use by the indigent aged under two systems of medical care. *American Journal of Public Health* 57 (no. 5): 784–90.

SHAPIRO, S., et al. 1960. Further observations on prematurity and perinatal mortality in a general population and in the population of a prepaid group practice medical care plan. *American Journal of Public Health* 50 (no. 9): 1307–17.

SHAPIRO, S.; WEINER, L.; and DENSEN, P. 1958. Comparison of prematurity and perinatal mortality in a general population and in the population of a prepaid group practice medical care plan. *American Journal of Public Health* 48 (no. 2): 170–87.

SLOAN, F. A. 1974. Effects of incentives on physician performance. In *Health manpower and productivity,* ed. J. Rafferty, pp. 53–84. Lexington, Mass.: D.C. Health.

SORENSEN, A., and SAWARD, E. 1978. An alternative approach to hospital cost control: the Rochester project. *Public Health Reports* 93 (No. 4): 311–17.

————; and WERSINGER, R. P. 1980. The demise of an individual practice association: a case study of health watch. *Inquiry* 17 (no. 3): 244–53.

SPARER, G., and ANDERSON, A. 1973. Utilization and cost experience of low income families in four prepaid group practice plans. *New England Journal of Medicine* 289 (no. 2): 67–72.

STARKWEATHER, D. 1970. The laws affecting health insurance in California. In *Health insurance plans: studies in organizational diversity,* ed. M. I. Roemer, D. M. DuBois, and S. W. Rich. Los Angeles, Calif.: University of California.

STEINBERG, M. K. 1976. Consumer participation in a health care organization: the case of the health insurance plan of greater New York. Ph.D. dissertation, City University of New York.

STRUMPF, G. B. 1979. Public payor participation in HMOs. Paper presented at ABT Associates, Inc., conference, Boston, 1–2 November 1979

——, and GARRAMONE, M. A. 1976. Why some HMOs develop slowly. *Public Health Reports* 91 (no. 6): 496–503.

TESSLER, R., and MECHANIC, D. 1975. Factors affecting the choice between prepaid group practice and alternative insurance programs. *Milbank Memorial Fund Quarterly/Health and Society* 53 (no. 2): 149–72.

THOMPSON, R. S. 1979. Approaches to prevention in an HMO setting. *Journal of Family Practice* 9 (no. 1): 71–82.

U.S. Department of Health, Education and Welfare. 1980. *National census of prepaid plans, 1979* Rockville, Md.: Public Health Service.

U.S. Department of Health, Education and Welfare, Office of Health Maintenance Organizations. 1979. *National HMO development strategy through 1988.* DHEW pub. no. (PHS) 79–50111, September 1979.

U.S. Health and Human Services, Office of Health Maintenance Organizations. 1979. *National HMO census update.*

WERSINGER, R., and SORENSEN, A. 1980. An analysis of the health status, utilization and cost experience of an HMO population compared to a Blue Cross/Blue Shield matched control group. University of Rochester School of Medicine and Dentistry, Department of Preventive, Family and Rehabilitation Medicine, Feburary 1980.

ZELTEN, R. A. 1977. *The study of enrollment in prepaid group practice plans. final report to the Robert Wood Johnson Foundation.* University of Pennsylvania, Leonard Davis Institute of Health Economics, August 1, 1977.

——. 1979. Alternative HMO models. University of Pennsylvania, National Health Care Management Center, Issue Paper no. 3, April 1979.

Chapter 15

Nursing Homes

Bruce C. Vladeck

NURSING HOMES are the most numerous health-care institutions in the United States, though hardly the most visible or best understood. There are roughly three times as many nursing homes as there are community hospitals, and on any given day nursing homes are serving almost twice as many people as hospitals. Nursing homes are much less expensive than hospitals—almost everything is—but they still consume in excess of $20 billion annually, and that amount has been growing at an extraordinary rate for most of the past decade. Yet remarkably little is known, in any systematic way, about nursing homes, the sorts of services they actually deliver (as opposed to the services they are required to deliver or report delivering), or the effects they have on their residents. Indeed, there is not even anyone in the United States who can claim with assurance to know precisely how many nursing homes there are.

Amid this prevailing ignorance and misapprehension, it has become increasingly apparent in recent years that the issues surrounding nursing-home care and especially nursing-home policy are among the most complex and troubling in the entire arena of social welfare policy. And attached to them is a special sense of urgency, since the population at risk for nursing-home care is growing so rapidly, expenditures are rising so uncontrollably, and consensus on how to deal with the problems is so weak.

This chapter can neither answer all the questions about nursing homes nor establish the missing consensus on policy. It has much more modest objectives: to provide a brief description of nursing homes and the nursing-home industry; to identify some of the major issues surrounding nursing-home care and nursing-home policy; and to make some suggestions about likely future directions. Because a central problem of nursing homes and thinking about nursing homes has been their isolation from the rest of the health-care system (to the extent there is a system), this discussion will also continually seek to identify linkages.

Vital Statistics

There are about eighteen thousand nursing homes in the United States, with between 1.3 and 1.5 million beds, using the standard definition of residential facilities providing some degree of nursing services over and above simple room and board, personal care, or "merely custodial" services. The average nursing home has between seventy-five and eighty beds. The modal facility is probably closer to a hundred beds, and very large nursing homes (more than two hundred beds) are relatively uncommon, confined to the Northeast and a number of public facilities elsewhere in the country. About three-quarters of all nursing homes, with about two-thirds of all beds, are proprietary—that is, operated for profit by private owners, whether individuals, partnerships, or corporations (See Table 15.1.). Fifteen percent of all nursing homes, with about 20 percent of all nursing-home beds, are operated by voluntary, private not-for-profit corporations. The balance—somewhat less than 10 percent of all facilities with something over 10 percent of all beds—are under direct government auspices, most commonly county governments, although the Veterans' Administration operates a number of nursing homes and every state has one or more state-operated veterans home (Vladeck 1980, pp. 8–9).

The supply of nursing homes is very unevenly distributed across the country. In proportion to population, nursing homes are most numerous in the upper Midwest (Minnesota, Wisconsin, Iowa, Nebraska, and the Dakotas) and least numerous in the Mid-Atlantic and southeastern states. The ratio of nursing-home beds to population sixty-five and over (the most commonly used measure of nursing-home availability) varies from over 100 per 1,000 in Wisconsin and Minnesota to less than 35 per 1,000 in New Jersey, Florida, and West Virginia. There is no apparent correlation between the absolute or relative size of a state's elderly population and the number of nursing-home beds. Public and voluntary nursing homes are concentrated both in states with high overall supplies of nursing homes (Minnesota, Wisconsin) and low supplies (New York) (Vladeck 1980, pp. 9–12).

For a variety of reasons, some of which will be discussed below, most nursing homes are relatively new. Most nursing homes currently in operation were constructed in the last twenty years, with the greatest boom in construction covering the period from the early 1960s through the early 1970s. That is not to say that there were no nursing homes before that time; indeed, the absolute number of facilities classified as nursing homes has grown much more slowly than the number of beds. Since 1965, the number of facilities has increased by about 25 percent while the number of beds has tripled (Vladeck 1980, pp. 102–3). Construction has primarily involved the replacement of older facilities, which generally had been converted to nursing-home care from other uses, with newer and much larger ones built for the sole purpose of nursing-home care. A rough estimate would be that nursing-home construction has cost more than $10 billion over the last two decades; the replacement cost of existing nursing-home facilities would be something on the order of $45 billion.

TABLE 15.1 Nursing Homes and Nursing-Home Beds by Auspice (approximate)

	PROPRIETARY	VOLUNTARY	GOVERNMENTAL
Nursing homes (pct.)	13,000 (77%)	3,000 (18%)	900 (5%)
Nursing home beds (pct.)	950,000 (68%)	300,000 (21%)	150,000 (11%)

Source: Derived from U. S. Department of Health, Education and Welfare 1975, and author's estimates.

To turn from bricks and mortar to flesh and blood, the typical nursing-home resident can be characterized as a poor white widow or spinster in her eighties with three or more significant chronic illnesses and substantial functional impairment. Nursing-home residents are very old, even in the context of an aging society. Eighty-five percent are over seventy-five, and more than 10 percent are over ninety. Three-quarters of nursing-home residents are women, and very few of those women have surviving spouses capable of caring for them. For the typical resident, a monthly social security check—generally at the level available to a survivor, rather than a retiree—is the sole significant source of income, and whatever assets were available prior to institutionalization have long since been liquidated. Blacks and Hispanics are substantially underrepresented in the nursing-home population, for reasons that have little to do with cultural preferences or family patterns, and much to do with continuing patterns of inequity in the distribution of services (Vladeck, 1980, pp. 13–17).

It is critically important to emphasize that, in terms of the overall need for long-term care of the frail elderly population, nursing homes serve only a very specific minority. The best estimates are that somewhere around a third of all elderly persons requiring regular continuous personal and medical care as a result of illness and functional disability receive such care in institutions. The rest are sustained in the community, most commonly by other family members (Dunlop 1976, pp. 75–87; Comptroller General 1977). Institutionalization in a nursing home is the result not solely of age and physical incapacity but of age, incapacity, and the absence of familial or other supports for the provision of care—along, in many instances, with the absence of sufficient purchasing power with which to buy noninstitutional care. In the sociological jargon, social isolation is as much a predictor of institutionalization as age or illness (Brody 1977, pp. 81–93).

These facts lead to an immediate conclusion of central significance to any understanding of nursing homes and public policy toward long-term care: The growth of nursing-home care simply can not be attributed to a generalized failure of family members to take care of their elderly relatives. To be sure, there are countless individual instances in which grandma has been "dumped" into an institution, and the availability of public reimbursement dollars may induce some families at the margin to use institutional services rather than provide care at home. But the great majority of elderly persons in need of long-term care are receiving such care from family members, and the great majority of those in institutions have no family members capable of providing them with the services they need. There is substantial evidence that families are more likely to attempt to continue providing care to elderly relatives long past the point when it is sensible for them to do so than they are to seek to escape their responsibilities prematurely (Brody 1977, p. 92).

The apparent explosion in the number of people in nursing homes arises not from changes in social attitudes or the willingness of family members to look after one another but from the enormous explosion in the number of very old people in the population, and from shifts among types of institutional care. The proliferation of nursing homes constitutes a response, however skewed and imperfect, to a situation that is literally without historical precedent. Never before in human history have there been so many of the very old in need of care (Cowgill 1974, pp. 1–18).

Taking care of nursing-home residents are approximately a million employees, the vast majority of whom are untrained and often unskilled nursing aides and attendants. The amount of direct, hands-on care by licensed nursing personnel is remarkably small; "nursing" homes merit the name, to the extent that they do, because patient care is supervised by registered nurses, and those unlicensed employees who work under their direction are categorized as givers of "nursing" service by definition. Every licensed nursing home must employ at least one full-time registered nurse, whose responsibilities are primarily supervisory and administrative. Many smaller nursing homes employ only that one. The best, largest nursing homes in states with the most stringent regulations rarely employ more than one registered nurse per shift per thirty- to sixty-bed unit.

Those who actually render most of the care in nursing homes—assisting patients into and out of bed; helping them dress; supervising their bathing and personal hygiene; dispensing medication (often illegally)—are aides and attendants without formal educational preparation, and customarily with only "on-the-job" training. In most of the country, nursing homes are a minimum-wage industry, and the jobs are difficult and frustrating. It is thus hardly surprising, though hardly conducive to optimal care, that the annual personnel turnover in nursing homes tends to run between 75 and 100 percent (Vladeck 1980, pp. 19–22).

Half of all nursing-home residents have major psychiatric diagnoses, most commonly senile dementia (for which the now receding euphemism is "organic brain syndrome," and the currently popular medical terminology "Alzheimer's disease"), although both reactive and endogenous depressions and psychotic illnesses are also widely prevalent. Yet only the most unusual nursing homes provide any formal psychiatric services at all, and the training of staff in psychosocial and psychiatric treatment ranges from minimal to nonexistent.

Nor do most nursing-home residents, despite their multiple medical conditions and residence in ostensibly health-care institutions, receive much in the way of physicians' services. The nation's sixteen to seventeen thousand nursing homes employ fewer than three hundred full-time physicians, and it has been argued that the typical frail older person with multiple chronic illnesses residing in the community receives substantially more time and attention from physicians than her counterpart who resides in a nursing home (Vladeck 1980, pp. 17–19).

In part, the limited supply of professional services in nursing homes simply reflects the chronic problems of inadequate quality that have always plagued the nursing-home industry in the United States. But they also reflect the fundamental paradox of service delivery in nursing homes. For above all else, nursing homes are primarily places where people live. Sixty-four percent of all nursing home stays last less than six months; but the median length of stay in nursing homes exceeds a year and a half, and the average is more than two and a half. More than 25 percent of nursing-home admissions initiate stays of three years or longer. For most nursing-home residents, their stays are terminal. For those who stay more than a year, "discharge" is either to a terminal hospital stay or "discharged dead" (Vladeck 1980, pp. 16–17, 221).

Indeed, if one could characterize the single most pervasive shortcoming of the typical nursing home, it would be in terms otherwise largely foreign to the health services. The principal problem with nursing homes for a large fraction of their residents a large fraction of the time is that they can be terribly boring places to be. Day follows day in the partially inevitable pattern of institutional routine, in which three meals provide the primary diversion and opportunity for social interaction, as well as nutrition, and television serves as the omnipresent source of entertainment, activity, and anesthesia. The best description is that nursing-home residents "spend most of their time (1) in the facility and (2) doing nothing" (Manard 1977, p. 22).

The quality of nursing-home services thus has two relatively distinct, if frequently intercorrelated, dimensions. The first is the appropriateness and skill with which the formal provision of professional or professionally supervised "services" is rendered: whether the right medications are administered at the right time; whether changes in patient status are quickly identified and quickly responded to; whether those who can benefit from habilitative or restorative care receive it. The second dimension might be characterized as the "quality of life": whether the food is palatable and tasty as well as minimally nutritious; whether the facility is clean and pleasant; whether there are activities that truly engage the residents' interest as well as meeting formal regulatory requirements; most crucially, perhaps, whether the paid staff are nice to and caring about the residents.

Nursing homes have frequently failed to meet minimal standards along either of these dimensions, and in some instances the acutal filth, physical danger, and physical and pharmaceutical abuse of residents has been quite literally scandalous. In part because of vigorous (though far from universal) governmental responses to the worst of such abuses, the most extreme cases are increasingly rare. But the majority of nursing homes meet minimal standards along the two dimensions of care only minimally, and the number that provide both excellent professional care and an excellent quality of life comprise a very small minority.

The Hospital Connection

If nursing-home services are inevitably, and perhaps self-defeatingly, dichotomous (being both quasi-medical and quasi-residential) then at least part of the problem may be attributed to the fact that the role of nursing homes in health and psychosocial care has rarely been directly defined in terms of the needs of a client population. Rather, the existing nursing-home industry, and the sort of facilities nursing homes are, is largely a side effect of policies and programs oriented to other concerns, most notably concerns with general hospitals. Only in the last few years has it been possible to talk sensibly about nursing-home policy or long-term care per se; until very recently, nursing homes were perceived, at least by health professionals, largely as a kind of curious and uncomfortable appendage to the hospital system. In at least one sense, nursing homes exist primarily to take care of people in whom general hospitals are not interested, or no longer interested. And we have so many nursing homes because, for a generation, policymakers have been trying to save on hospital expenditures.

The very physical configuration of most nursing homes derives, indeed, from the characteristic physical configuration of general hospitals in the 1950s and '60s for fairly straightforward historical reasons, even though such a layout may not be conducive—may be directly inimical—to a positive quality of life in institutions in which people live. When the federal government first became directly involved with nursing homes in the early 1950s, it found itself obligated to develop minimum physical standards for facilities to which it was going to give or lend construction funds. The nursing home as we know it today didn't exist at all at that time. Most of what were then called nursing homes were former dwellings converted to quasi–health-care uses. Since no one was entirely clear as to just what it was nursing homes were supposed to do, other than accepting patients hospitals wanted to get rid of or forgo admitting in the first place, government officials understandably modeled their nursing-home standards on those then in use for hospitals (Vladeck 1980, pp. 42–43).

Thus, we have rows of "semiprivate" rooms facing onto a wide corridor ending in, or centered on, a nurses' station. Public areas for dining, recreation, or just hanging out are concentrated in a central core, or placed as solaria or lounges at the end of the corridor. Such an arrangement may be efficient (or at least customary) in acute-care settings where patients stay an average of eight to ten days, are generally ill enough to spend most of their time in bed, and can make use of a central dining area only when they are well enough to go home, but you probably wouldn't want to live there.

Similarly, the administrative organization and structure of care mandated for nursing homes by both government regulation and professional standards are derived from the general hospital model despite its obvious inappropriateness to long-term care. Medical care is provided by "attending physicians" who are hardly ever in attendance; homes which are too small to employ a pharmacist, dietitian, physical therapist, or social worker must have organized departments of pharmacy, dietary, physical therapy, and social services. Sixty-eight percent of all nursing-home employees belong to the nursing staff (mostly, again, as aides and attendants) and most of the rest are engaged in maintenance, housekeeping, or cooking, yet the formal subservience of nursing to physicians that prevails in hospitals has been carried over to nursing homes, even though physicians are much less directly involved in directing nursing-home care.

Most important—in fact, of central importance—the growth of the nursing-home industry has been fueled largely by a concern with the placement problems of hospitals and the apparent costs of keeping in hospitals elderly patients who are no longer in need of acute services. For a generation, there has been widespread discontent with the quality of most nursing-home care, and a widespread belief that many of those in nursing homes could be cared for better, and perhaps less expensively, in noninstitutional settings. Yet health-care planners and public policymakers, almost in spite of themselves, have continued to encourage the proliferation of nursing homes, and to countenance the existence of substandard nursing homes, as a response to the "backlog" of elderly nonacute patients in hospitals.

If it now cost $200 to $300 a day for acute hospital care, and if nursing home care cost $40 to $50 a day, then every patient discharged from a hospital to a nursing home should save the health-care system between $150 and $260 for each day she would otherwise spend in the hospital. If there are 100 patients in a community occupying hospital beds when they could be served just as adequately in nursing homes, the annual excess costs exceeds $6 million. Or so it would appear. The logic of that argument is widely accepted, straightforward, and commonsensical. It is also wrong—demonstrably, irrefutably, and tragically wrong. Not only that, it has been recognized as wrong since at least 1970, and yet it has continued to drive much of public policy.

To begin with, the $200 or $300 per diem in the acute hospital is an average cost, calculated over-all patient days in the hospital in the course of a year. The $200 price charged to the elderly victim of stroke or congestive heart disease in the third week of waiting for a nursing-home placement is the same price charged to the cardiac surgery patient his first day out of intensive care, or the automobile accident victim after he has been patched up in the emergency room. From the point of view of resources actually consumed, patients awaiting nursing-home place-ment are probably the least expensive of any in the hospital, except perhaps for healthy newborns, who eat less. Depending on how one allocates hospital overhead, the actual cost of caring for such geriatric patients is probably pretty close to the average per diem cost in a nursing home. The marginal cost, in a hospital that would otherwise not be full, is probably still less. Yet patients awaiting nursing-home placement are clearly marginal in terms of the major ac-tivities of the hospital. And occupancy rates in American hospitals average less than 75 percent.

Further, people stay a lot longer in nursing homes than they stay in hospitals. To take the same hypothetical figures, a patient who stays in the hospital for twenty days, receiving acute services only in the first ten, and then goes home, in-curs lower costs, even when costs are set at an artificial average per diem, than the patient who leaves the hospital after ten days but then spends fifty or sixty days in a nursing home. The average length of stay in nursing homes exceeds two years. Of course, in this example, many of the people who would be discharged directly home from the hospital in the first case probably need more services than they could get at home. If they stay two years in the nursing home they will clearly re-ceive more service, as well as incur much more cost, than if they were home. But from the narrow perspective of health-care costs, they are still more expensive.

Finally, but perhaps most tellingly, every 100 nursing home beds added in a community free up far fewer than 100 hospital beds previously occupied by pa-tients in need of long-term care. Fewer than half of all nursing-home admissions come directly from a hospital. Within certain bounds, there appears to be an effec-tively infinite demand for nursing-home care among people residing in the com-munity, and nursing-home operators concerned with profit or even simple sol-vency prefer admissions from the community, all other things being equal, because those patients are less sick and therefore less expensive to care for. And again, nursing-home residents don't turn over very quickly, so that while many patients discharged from hospitals die or go home after relatively short nursing home stays, others occupy beds for several years. Thus, the addition of a hundred new nursing-home beds may reduce the hospital "backlog" by thirty or forty in the first year the new nursing home is in operation, but over time it will provide beds for only thirty or forty hospital discharges *a year*.

Nursing-home care seems to follow "Roemer's Law," that capacity generates use, even more than the hospital care Roemer was observing. Nursing-home occu-pancy rates are no higher in Florida, with 25 nursing-home beds per 1,000 elderly, than in Wisconsin or Minnesota, with four times as many beds. Within any rea-sonable range of nursing-home supply, new construction will never eliminate the backlog of patients in hospitals awaiting long-term–care placement. Whatever may cause such backlogs, it is not marginal shortages in the supply of nursing homes.

Yet a concern with hospital backlogs, largely because of the apparent, if illu-sory, resultant costs, has led public officials to support new nursing-home con-struction in the New York City area, for example, since the early 1950s (Thomas 1969, p. 97). Worse, it has affected the policies of those responsible for enforcing quality-of-care standards in existing nursing homes, because those officials have felt themselves constrained from closely even grossly inadequate and dangerous facilities, since doing so would increase the hospital backlog (Vladeck 1980, p. 163).

Dollars and Cents

So, through a variety of incentives direct and indirect, intentional and unintentional, policymakers have encouraged the addition of close to a million nursing-home beds in the last fifteen years. The cost has been staggering. (See Table 15.2.) In the twelve-month period ending with March 1981, total expenditures, public and private, for nursing-home care are estimated to have exceeded $21 billion. That represented an increase of 16.7 percent over the previous year, a growth rate consistent with the 15.6 and 16.1 percent increases in the years immediately preceding that (Health Care Financing Administration 1981, p. 2). Hospital costs make up, of course, the largest fraction of total health-care expenditures, and their rate of increase has been the cause of well-founded public and governmental alarm. But nursing-home costs, though starting from a much smaller base, have grown substantially faster than hospital costs since at least 1975. Indeed, they have grown faster than any other category of health-care expenditures.

Only a small part of this cost increase, it should be noted, is attributable to increased utilization of nursing-home services. The greatest growth in nursing-home use occurred in the decade prior to 1975, and utilization changes since then account for perhaps a third of the increase in expenditures. Much, but far from all, of the rest can be accounted for by the general level of inflation in the economy. In the period ending March 1981, for example, the prices nursing homes paid for the goods and services (including labor) they bought increased 10.2 percent, 6 percent less than the expenditure increase (Health Care Financing Administration 1981, p. 11).

Some of the increase since 1975 can be attributed to a conscious effort to improve the quality of nursing-home services by increasing reimbursement from Medicaid and better tying that reimbursement to the cost of high-quality services. Federal legislation enacted in 1972, but not fully implemented until 1978, required states to pay nursing homes "reasonable cost related" rates, in an explicit effort to improve the quality of services. No direct, one-to-one linkage between the level of payment and the quality of services has ever been established, and none probably exists. A reduction of $2 per day in reimbursement for nursing costs will probably reduce the level of nursing services provided by most facilities, but a doubling of

TABLE 15.2   Growth In Nursing-Home Expenditures

	1965	1970	1975	1978	1979	1980
Total national health expenditures (billions of $)	43.0	74.7	131.5	174.0	195.2	245.0
(Increase over previous year [%])	—	—	—	(12.9)	(12.1)	(14.6)
Total nursing home expenditures (billions of $)	2.1	4.1	9.9	13.7	15.8	20.7
(Increase over previous year [%])	—	—	—	(16.1)	(15.6)	(16.7)
Nursing homes as % of total national health expenditures	4.8	6.3	7.5	7.9	8.1	8.4

Sources: Freeland, Calat, and Schendler 1980, 1981.

reimbursement will not double nursing care. Nonetheless, many state Medicaid reimbursement systems were made substantially more generous in the 1975–80 period in compliance with federal mandates and a desire of state officials to pay more equitably and with more incentives for better care (Weiner and Lehrer, forthcoming).

Nursing-home costs have been the fastest-growing component of health-care costs; of more immediate practical relevance, they have also been far and away the fastest-growing component of the costs of Medicaid, which in most states has been the single fastest-growing object of expenditures, and which at the national level has been among the fastest growing of the "uncontrollable entitlement" programs which make the current director of the Office of Management and Budget unhappy. About 55 percent of all nursing-home expenditures are made by Medicaid; conversely, close to 40 percent of all Medicaid expenditures now go to nursing homes.

Just how a program originally designed to provide insurancelike coverage of acute medical expenses for the welfare population came to be dominated by expenditures for long-term care for the elderly, most of whom are not recipients of cash assistance, while at the same time the Medicare program of insurance for the health-care costs of the elderly pays for very little nursing-home care, is a long story, which can not be fully told here. But a couple of summary, capsulized points should be made. First, Medicare originally contained an "extended-care" benefit designed precisely to address the problems and save the associated costs of patients who needed some degree of postacute care before they went home in order to be promptly discharged from hospitals. But, for all the reasons enumerated above, the extended-care benefit, which was supposed to save money, in fact cost a lot (U.S. Congress, Senate Committee on Finance 1970, pp. 33–36), and while the coverage of extended care, narrowly defined, has not been modified since Medicare was enacted in 1965, the content of the benefit has been significantly reduced ever since 1970. Medicare will now pay for posthospital nursing-home care only under very limited circumstances. Thus, while more than 90 percent of nursing-home residents are Medicare beneficiaries, Medicare pays for less than 3 percent of total nursing-home expenses—although it does pay for at least a part of the expenses of about 10 percent of nursing-home admissions (Vladeck 1980, p. 72).

In contrast, the role of Medicaid in paying for nursing-home care arises from two rather contradictory but increasingly potent forces. The more important of the two is that hardly any elderly person who needs institutionalization can afford to pay annual costs now exceeding $15,000 for very long. Medicaid has, since its inception, excused relatives other than spouses from financial responsibility for health-care services to the elderly, and most state Medicaid programs provide that individuals can become eligible for benefits when medical expenses force them to "spend down" to income eligibility levels when the costs of service, such as nursing homes, exceeds their income. Thus many, perhaps most, of those for whom Medicaid is paying nursing-home costs were originally admitted to nursing homes as private patients, or recipients of the limited Medicare extended-care benefit, but subsequently exhausted their assets and their Medicare eligibility (Comptroller General 1979, pp. 43–53). Medicaid-reimbursed nursing-home services have thus become the largest "welfare" benefit available to formerly middle-class individuals and their families. People who would not otherwise qualify for any form of public

TABLE 15.3 Medicaid Nursing-Home Expenditures

	Calendar Year			Fiscal Year								
	1968	1969	1970	1971	1972	1973	1974	1975	1976	1977	1978	1979 *
												(est.)
Total nursing home expenditures (millions $)	1,050	1,381	1,666	2,211	2,214	3,019	3,587	4,661	5,279	6,392	7,583	8,800
Skilled nursing homes	1,050	1,286	1,362	1,674	1,471	1,959	2,002	2,446	2,488	2,808	3,203	3,600
Intermediate Care	—	95	304	537	743	1,060	1,585	2,215	2,791	3,584	4,380	5,200
Nursing home expenditures as % of total Medicaid expenditures	29.6	31.2	32.5	34.1	31.5	35.0	36.0	37.9	37.3	39.2	41.9	—
Skilled nursing homes	29.6	29.1	26.6	25.8	20.9	22.7	20.1	19.9	17.6	17.0	17.7	—
Intermediate care	—	2.1	5.9	8.3	10.6	12.3	15.9	18.0	19.7	22.0	24.2	—

Source: U. S. Department of Health, Education and Welfare 1979, p. 34.
* 1979 figures estimated by author on basis of Table 15.2 and relative growth rates of skilled and intermediate care.

assistance become impoverished merely by several months' residence in a nursing home.

On the other hand, state and local government have been paying for institutional care for otherwise homeless indigent elderly people since the early nineteenth century. Many existing county nursing homes, for example, are the direct institutional descendants of county almshouses. Since the 1950 Social Security Act Amendments first permitted federal matching for the cost of "vendor payments" for health services, states have sought to transfer more and more of the costs associated for caring with this and other residual populations to health-care programs for which federal matching funds were available. Thus, Medicaids's coverage of long-term–care services gradually expanded between 1965 and 1980. At first, it encompassed only "skilled nursing homes" (which were never statutorily defined). Thereafter, coverage was extended to intermediate-care facilities (defined as nursing homes providing care less intense than that in skilled nursing homes but more than "merely custodial"), then over-sixty-five inpatients in state mental hospitals, then to intermediate-care facilities for the mentally retarded (ICF-MRs). While the overall proportion of Medicaid expenditures going to long-term care has increased continually since 1966, expenditures within the area of long-term care have also shifted increasingly from presumably more intensive "skilled" services to larger and larger proportions of intermediate care and ICF-MR expenditures.

Future Directions

What really scares policymakers is not so much the alarming growth in nursing-home expenditures to date, but the prospect for still-larger future increases unless there are substantial shifts in policy. Those over seventy-five are the fastest-growing population group in society. Their numbers will double within the next twenty-five years. And something like 10 percent of all those now over seventy-five are in nursing homes. If current age-specific use rates are maintained, we will need more than a million *new* nursing-home beds before the end of the century, at a capital cost alone, in 1981 prices, in excess of $30 billion. In 1978 the Congressional Budget Office predicted that public expenditures for nursing-home care would *increase* by $11 billion between 1980 and 1985 (U.S. Congress, Congressional Budget Office 1977, p. 3). As of late 1981, expenditures remain on track with those predictions.

These are very large numbers. Yet they are conservative, at least to the extent that they fail to take into account increasing rates of marital dissolution, the growing differential in life expectancy between women and men, or the increasing life expectancy of the elderly. Nursing homes primarily serve socially isolated old women, and these projections probably underestimate the growth of that population group.

At the same time, however, they do not take into account the fact that almost no one wishes to see the existing nursing-home system expanded very much. Concerns about the quality of care of which most nursing homes will ever be capable rank right behind budgetary motives, and there is a growing consensus, in many areas of social welfare policy, that dependent persons should be served in the "least restrictive environment" practical. As a result of these concerns, and the availability of certificate-of-need laws with which to implement the resulting policies (and with which to protect the "franchises" of existing operators) the growth of the nursing-home industry has slowed quite markedly in the last several years, and will certainly continue to be slow so long as capital markets are in disarray.

Increasingly, there is consensus among policymakers and students of long-term care that the enormous projected future demand for long-term–care services can best be met through the expansion of home and community-based services. These would include home health care, homemaker/home health-aide services, personal-care services, medical and social day care, congregate housing, and a host of others. The expansion of these services is not, however, without problems of its own. The most important of those problems arises from the statistic that two-thirds of those in need of long-term care are not in institutions but are receiving uncompensated, unreimbursed help from families and friends. There is, in the jargon of policy economists, an astonishing, and frightening, degree of "latent demand" for in-home and in-community long-term–care services, one that would bust the budget of any new benefit entitlement. The Congressional Budget Office, for example, estimated that comprehensive public insurance for noninstitutional long-term–care services could cost as much as $25 billion over and above nursing-home expenditures by 1985 (U.S. Congress, Congressional Budget Office 1977, p. 43).

In an effort to address concerns of this kind, both public and private sponsors have supported a number of experiments and demonstrations to determine whether a community "channeling" or "gatekeeping" agency could match long-term–care clients with needed services without catastrophic budgetary consequences. Initial results from these demonstrations have been extremely encouraging, although few formal evaluations have been completed. It is clear, however, that, at a minimum, the "technology" for managing a long-term–care system that matches clients and services in an economical way is still in the process of development.

And in the meantime, the Omnibus Budget Reconciliation Act of 1981 and the philosophies it reflects have turned social policy on its ear, and begun an effort to enforce the most radical redirection in social services this country has experienced in at least forty-five years. In the course of the debate over President Reagan's budget proposals, it should be recorded, no issue appeared to trouble knowledgeable members of Congress and interest group representatives more than that of the financing of long-term care, and those parts of the Reconciliation Act which are furthest from the president's proposal on a major budgetary item are the revisions to Medicaid. Further efforts to reduce federal financial involvement in health care, including long-term care, have, however, been promised.

It is thus at least somewhat possible that nursing homes, as they are now known, will increasingly come to be seen as an anachronism, as state governments, which now clearly have the policy initiative, seek to channel ever more scarce dollars into noninstitutional services while discouraging private investment by reducing reimbursement rates for nursing homes. It is even possible to imagine a future in which nursing-home care is reserved for the very affluent elderly (those who do not have to rely on Social Security) while those in need of public support either receive minimal services in their communities or none at all.

But the population needing such services is not going to go away. Indeed, it will get larger and larger. There are rational strategies that might partially meet the needs of that population, although just laying them out would require another chapter. But there are already thousands of demented old women wandering the streets of New York City. And the back wards of state mental hospitals, while now largely vacant, are still standing. A generation from now, the inadequate and expensive provision of long-term–care services in nursing homes might look like a relatively good deal, at least in comparison to the worst one can imagine for the future. And a generation from now, it may be too late to finally begin the process of creating a humane, efficient, and effective long-term–care system. That process should have been begun a generation ago.

REFERENCES

BRODY, E. M. 1977. Environmental factors in dependency. In *Care of the elderly: meeting the challenge of dependency,* ed. A. N. Exton-Smith and J. Grimley Evans. New York: Grune and Stratton.

Comptroller General of the United States. 1977. *Home health—the need for a national policy to better provide for the elderly.* Washington, D.C.: General Accounting Office.

———. 1979. *Entering a nursing home — costly implications for Medicaid.* Washington, D.C.: General Accounting Office, Novermber 26,1979.

COWGILL, D. D. 1974. The aging of populations and societies. *The Annals* 415:1–18.

DUNLOP, B. D. 1976. Need for and utilization of long-term care among elderly Americans. *Journal of Chronic Diseases* 29:75–87.

FREELAND, M.; CALAT, G.; and SCHENDLER, C. E. 1980. Projections of national health expenditures, 1980, 1985, and 1990. *Health Care Financing Review,* Winter, pp. 16–17.

———. 1981. Projections of national health expenditures, 1980, 1985, and 1990. *Health Care Financing Trends,* Summer, p. 2.

Health Care Financing Administration, Office of Research, Demonstrations, and Statistics. 1981. *Health Care Financing Trends* 2:1–24.

MANARD, B. B.; WOCHLE, R. E.; and HEILMAN, J. M. 1977. *Better homes for the old.* Lexington, Mass.: Lexington Books.

THOMAS, W. C., JR. 1969. *Nursing homes and public policy: drift and decision in New York State.* Ithaca, N.Y.: Cornell University Press.

U.S. Congress, Congressional Budget Office. 1977. *Long-term care for elderly and disabled.* Washington, D.C.: Government Printing Office.

U.S. Congress, Senate Committee on Finance. 1970. *Medicare and Medicaid: problems, issues, and alternatives.* 91st Cong., 2d sess.

U.S. Department of Health, Education and Welfare. 1975. Public Health Service, National Center for Health Statistics. *Selected operating and financial characteristics of nursing homes, United States: 1973–74 national nursing home survey.* Rockville, Md.: National Center for Health Statistics.

———. 1979. Health Care Financing Administration, Medicaid/Medicare Management Institute. *Data on the Medicaid program: eligibility, services, expenditures.* 1979 ed., rev. Baltimore, Md.

VLADECK, B. C. 1980. *Unloving care: the nursing home tragedy.* New York: Basic Books.

WEINER, S. and LEHRER, S. S. The afterthought industry: developing reimbursement policy for nursing homes. *Milbank Memorial Fund Quarterly/Health and Society* (forthcoming).

Chapter 16

Long-Term Care:
Financing and Policy Issues

Diane Bolay Lawrence
Clifton R. Gaus

In 1950, the United States spent $12 billion or 4.6 percent of its gross national product (GNP) on health care. During the next three decades, the portion of resources devoted to health more than doubled so that by 1980, 9.4 percent of the GNP was health-care expenditures. This rapid rise in health-care spending is expected to continue and reach $757.9 billion, or 11.5 percent of the GNP, by 1990.

The private sector is still the major source of health-care expenditures, paying over two-thirds of the nation's health-care bill in 1980. However, the public sector is paying an increasingly larger share, especially for the age group sixty-five years and older. In 1980, it paid 63.9 percent of the health-care expenditures for the elderly, of which 45.0 percent was paid by Medicare, 14.3 percent by Medicaid, and 4.6 percent by other local, state, and federal programs. In contrast, the public sector paid only 28.6 percent of personal health-care expenditures for both the under nineteen years age group and the nineteen to sixty-four years age group.

One of the fastest growing components of health-care expenditures is long-term–care services for chronic diseases and conditions. In 1978, these long-term–care health expenditures totaled approximately $22 billion. Two-thirds of this total ($14.5 billion) was for nursing-home care, 29.6 percent was for long-stay hospitals, and 4.4 percent was for home health services.

The Long-term–Care Population and Its Problems

The increase in long-term–care expenditures is due mainly to the aging of the American population and the resulting increase in the number of people needing long-term–care services. Americans are living longer. At age sixty-five, Americans still have an average of sixteen years of life remaining. In 1980, there were

The authors are grateful to Diane Rowland for her careful and thoughtful contributions to the numerous drafts of this chapter.

25.7 million aged Americans. By the year 2035 the elderly population will more than double.

As the elderly population grows, however, it will tend to be older. Between 1970 and the year 2000, the eighty-five years and older age group will grow twice as fast as the seventy-five to eighty-four age group and four times as fast as the sixty-five to seventy-four age group. By the year 2035, one out of every ten Americans will be eighty-five years or older. They will also be mostly women living alone due to the difference in life expectancy between the sexes and the fact that 60 percent of the elderly population today are single, widowed, or divorced females.

As the American population ages, the number of persons with chronic conditions continues to increase since the risk of debilitating illness increases with age. In 1976, 30 million Americans were limited in their activities due to chronic conditions (those lasting three months or more). Although the percentage was equally divided between males and females and among the three age groups: under forty-five years, forty-five to sixty-four years, and sixty-five years and over, the rate per 1,000 population varied greatly. For the under forty-five years age group the rate per 1,000 population was 67 while for the forty-five to sixty-four and sixty-five and over age groups it was 242 and 453 respectively.

Moreover, the seriousness of chronic conditions is greater for the aged population. Visits to physicians as well as hospital days vary according to age group. Seventy-five percent of all physician visits for the sixty-five years and over age group were due to chronic conditions whereas only 41 percent were for chronic conditions in the under forty-five age group. With respect to hospitalization, 67 percent of hospital days for the aged were due to chronic conditions compared to 45 percent for the under forty-five age group. Chronic conditions account for nine out of ten of the deaths for the sixty-five and over age group but only four out of ten for the under forty-five age group. Chronic conditions also account for 81 percent of the days of restricted activity for aged Americans but only 35 percent for young Americans.

The morbidity costs resulting from chronic conditions are high. In 1975 they totaled $37.1 billion compared to only $20.7 billion for acute conditions. More than half the population with chronic conditions were unable to work compared to one-quarter of those with acute conditions. One-fifth were institutionalized.

Furthermore, the cost of treating chronic conditions is extremely expensive. This is due to the large portion of care that is provided in institutions. As the degree of impairment becomes more severe the full range of services required can most easily be provided in an institutional setting. In 1975, 62 percent of the $46.5 billion spent on hospital care was for chronic conditions while 84 percent of nursing-home expenditures were attributed to chronic problems. Chronic conditions also accounted for half the dollars spent on physician services and drugs.

Individuals who have a chronic condition that, combined with personal characteristics, renders them incapable of performing one or more daily activities require more than just episodic health-care services. They also require personal and support services. These types of services include physician care, nursing care, therapeutic care, nutrition counseling, homemaker or chore services, transportation, meals, vocational rehabilitation, and social services. In 1975, 8.1 million Americans required long-term–care services. This population includes the aged, physically disabled, the mentally ill, and the developmentally disabled.

The Long-term–Care Delivery System

The broad mix of health and social services required to meet the needs of the long-term–care population can be provided in the home, in ambulatory-care settings, or in institutions such as nursing homes. Most individuals requiring long-term–care services prefer to receive these services in their home. Visiting nurses associations and home health agencies are the major providers of in-home care. However, services at the community level are difficult to organize, usually not available, and often not reimbursed by state and federal programs.

Institutions, on the other hand, can easily provide a full range of health and social services to the long-term–care population. Furthermore, they are reimbursed by federal and state programs even though the care is more expensive. (The average yearly cost of a nursing-home patient is $12,000 to $15,000. Thus, although institutions account for only a small proportion of the long-term–care population (21 percent), they account for over two-thirds of the long-term–care dollars.

There are two major categories of long-term–care institutions: long-stay hospitals and nursing homes. Long-stay hospitals include, for example, psychiatric, rehabilitation, chronic disease, and tuberculosis facilities. In 1977 there were 597 long-stay hospitals with 277,278 beds. Of these totals, psychiatric facilities accounted for 61 percent of the hospitals and 77 percent of the beds. Federal, state, and local governments own 64 percent of these hospitals and control 90 percent of the beds. Nonprofit organizations own 24 percent of the hospitals and 8 percent of the beds, while proprietaries own only 12 percent of the hospitals and maintain 2 percent of the beds.

Nursing homes, however, account for 70 percent of the institutionalized population. In sharp contrast to long-stay hospitals, there are thirty-one times as many nursing homes (18,900) and five times as many nursing-home beds (1,402,400). Three-quarters of these facilities are proprietary. The large difference in the number of facilities is due to the difference in size. Nursing homes tend to be much smaller than long-stay hospitals with approximately 42.3 percent being under fifty beds and almost 75 percent being under a hundred beds. The geographic distribution of nursing home beds per 1,000 population sixty-five years and over includes a larger proportion of beds (80–120/1,000 population) in the Midwest and smallest proportion (22–39 beds/1,000 population) in the South.

Nursing homes can be classified according to different levels of care offered and whether they are certified for the Medicare and/or Medicaid programs. A skilled nursing facility (SNF) is an institution which provides inpatient skilled nursing and restorative/rehabilitative-care services. SNFs must provide twenty-four-hour nursing services on a daily basis, have transfer agreements with participating hospitals, and meet other specific regulatory requirements with respect to the types of services, the utilization of physicians and registered nurses, and the implementation of certain policies and procedures.

An intermediate-care facility (ICF) is an institution which provides inpatient health-related care and services to individuals who do not require the degree of care provided by SNFs. In 1977, 19 percent of the nursing homes were certified as SNFs, 32 percent as ICFs, 24 percent were certified as providing both levels of care, and 25 percent were not certified.

The primary source of payment for nursing-home residents is mainly split between own income and family support (38.4 percent) and the Medicaid program (47.8 percent). Other public-assistance or welfare programs pay 6.4 percent while Medicare accounts for only 2.0 percent of the payments.

Nursing-home costs vary by type of ownership and certification. In 1976 the average cost per patient day was $23.84. However, for SNFs it was $29.71, while those homes not certified cost only $16.98. Proprietary nursing homes were less expensive than voluntary nonprofit and government facilities, $21.97 compared to $27.56 and $29.54 respectively.

The variation in nursing-home costs is attributed to many factors. These include patient selection and mix (i.e., young, old, severely debilitated); the scope and quality of services provided; the age, location, and construction of the facility; management capabilities; institutional philosophy; return on equity; and regulatory intervention (i.e., fire and safety standards).

The elderly account for 87 percent of all nursing-home residents. Approximately 20 percent of the aged will enter a nursing home at some point in their life. Nursing-home residents are predominantly older, single women. The median age in a nursing home is eighty-one years. Almost one-quarter of the aged eighty-five years and older are in nursing homes. Three out of four nursing-home residents are women and nine out of ten are either single, widowed, or divorced.

The major diagnosis of nursing-home residents is disease of the circulatory system, which accounts for almost 40 percent of the population and includes arteriosclerosis, stroke, congestive heart failure, and hypertension. Twenty percent are diagnoses of mental disorders and senility including chronic brain syndrome, mental retardation, and psychoses. Other diagnoses of nursing-home residents include disease of the nervous system and sense organs (3.3 percent), cancer (2.2 percent), fractures (3.0 percent), arthritis and rheumatism (4.3 percent), and diabetes (5.5 percent).

Studies have shown, however, that many nursing-home residents (estimates range from 6 to 76 percent) are inappropriately placed and do not require the extensive services of the nursing home. Moreover, findings show that 5 to 20 percent of the elderly are admitted to institutions primarily for social and financial rather than strictly medical reasons.

The Governmental Programs of Long-term Care

Private insurance coverage for long-term–care services is minimal thus leaving the burden to the individual and his/her family or to the federal, state, and local governments. The government programs which provide various institutional and community services for the elderly and chronically impaired include Medicaid (Title 19 of the Social Security Act), Medicare (Title 18 of the Social Security Act), Social Services (Title 20 of the Social Security Act), Supplemental Security Income (Title 16 of the Social Security Act), the Administration on Aging, the Veterans Administration, and the Department of Housing and Urban Development (see Figure 16.1).

The *Medicaid* program is the main source of public spending for long-term care. It is a voluntary federal grant-in-aid program with states to finance health-care services for public-assistance recipients and other low-income individuals and

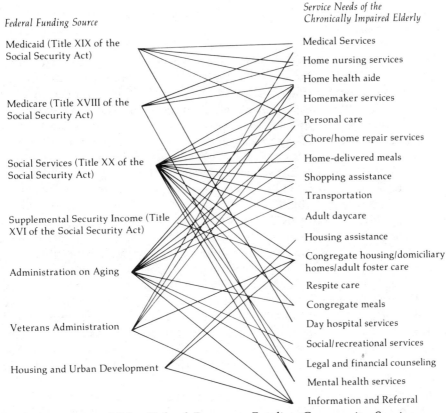

Federal Funding Source

Medicaid (Title XIX of the
Social Security Act)

Medicare (Title XVIII of the
Social Security Act)

Social Services (Title XX of the
Social Security Act)

Supplemental Security Income (Title
XVI of the Social Security Act)

Administration on Aging

Veterans Administration

Housing and Urban Development

*Service Needs of the
Chronically Impaired Elderly*

Medical Services
Home nursing services
Home health aide
Homemaker services
Personal care
Chore/home repair services
Home-delivered meals
Shopping assistance
Transportation
Adult daycare
Housing assistance
Congregate housing/domiciliary
homes/adult foster care
Respite care
Congregate meals
Day hospital services
Social/recreational services
Legal and financial counseling
Mental health services
Information and Referral

Figure 16.1 Major Federal Programs Funding Community Services
for the Elderly

families. Certain basic services must be offered in any state Medicaid program, including: inpatient hospital services, outpatient hospital services, laboratory and
X-ray services, physician services, family-planning services, rural health clinic services, early periodic screening, diagnosis and treatment for children, skilled nursing facility services and home health services, both for individuals age twenty-one
and over. In addition, states may provide a number of optional services including
long-term–care services such as SNF services for persons under age twenty-one,
intermediate-care facility services (ICF), care in mental institutions for individuals
age sixty-five and over, physicial therapy, and related services. Fifty of the fifty-
four state Medicaid plans reimburse for ICF services. The states, however, may
place limitations on the Medicaid benefits including the need for prior authorization, length of stay, the number of visits, the type of care setting, or the maximum
expenditure for a service. For example, twenty-six states require prior authorization for SNF services and twenty states require it for ICF services; four states limit
physicians to one nursing home visit per month. The Medicaid program, however,
is still the largest single government provider of long-term–care services. In 1978,
43.1 percent ($7.93 billion) of Medicaid expenditures were for long-term–care ser-
vices; the majority of which went for ICF services (24.2 percent), followed by SNF
services (17.7 percent) and home health services (1.2 percent).

The *Medicare* program is a federal health insurance program for persons sixty-
five years of age and over, and for disabled beneficiaries and persons with chronic
renal disorders. The emphasis of the program, however, is to reimburse for acute

episodic care (hospitals and physician services) rather than long-term–care services and management. The long-term–care aspects of the program include provisions for skilled nursing facility (SNF) care and home health services. The SNF care is limited to 100 days per benefit period. It is intended for short-term posthospital convalescence. Furthermore, the patient must pay a coinsurance ($22.50 per day in 1980) after an initial 20-day period. Although the home health benefit is no longer limited to 100 visits per benefit period, the care must still occur within one year following the most recent discharge from a hospital or SNF. Medicare does not reimburse for custodial care in nursing homes or related personal-care needs of those receiving home health services. In 1978, only 4 percent of Medicare expenditures were for long-term–care services. In addition, 1 million of the aged are not eligible for Medicare, because they are not entitled to social security benefits.

The *Social Services* program (Title 20 of the Social Security Act) is a block grant program to states to provide a variety of social and personal support services at the community level to achieve or maintain the functional independence of vulnerable populations and to prevent inappropriate institutionalizations. Services provided under Title 20 include such items as homemaker, chore, housekeeping, personal care, home management, day care, transportation, and counseling. The program does not provide for institutional care. In 1977, approximately $400 million or 16 percent of the total $2.5 billion Title 20 funds were for in-home services to about 1.6 million elderly and disabled. States must make SSI recipients eligible for Title 20 services; beyond this requirement, eligibility is left to the states. Thus, many marginally poor elderly are outside the scope of Title 20 coverage.

The *Supplemental Security Income* program (SSI) is a federal program of cash assistance for the aged, blind, and disabled poor. It is intended to provide sufficient resources for food, shelter, and related living expenses since individuals under SSI are eligible for Medicaid to pay for medical services. States may supplement the federal SSI payment. Thirty-one states do supplement primarily to help pay for "congregate" living arrangements in domiciliary, personal-care and board-and-care facilities. Although not specifically health-related care, congregate care does comprise long-term care in terms of protective and personal-care services. In 1976, $287 million in state and federal funds were specifically used to purchase congregate care.

The *Administration on Aging* under the Older Americans Act, as amended, funds a nationwide network of Area Agencies on Aging (AAA). These agencies serve as advocates and coordinative units for the development of comprehensive social and personal services for the aged. The major goals of the program are to secure and maintain maximum independence and dignity in a home environment for older individuals capable of self-care with appropriate supportive services and to prevent unnecessary or premature institutionalization. Types of services funded include meals, homemaker services, chore services, home health aids, nutrition education, transportation, information and referral services, advocacy, legal aid, protective services, case management, and counseling. AAA funds are frequently used to supplement direct services provided through Title 20, Medicaid, and other public programs. In 1975, $235 million were spent for services.

The *Veterans' Administration* operates a national network of hospitals as well as a series of long-term–care facilities for veterans. It also provides a monthly cash benefit for "aid and attendance" whereby housebound and bedbound veterans can purchase home care. Several thousand disabled veterans are serviced through these long-term–care efforts.

The *Department of Housing and Urban Development* (HUD) provides support for congregate housing and regular housing for the elderly and handicapped through insured mortgages, direct loans, rent subsidies, and public housing aid.

Finally, state and local governments support long-term–care services through their matching of federal program funds such as Medicaid, Title 20, and SSI supplementation. Many also operate public welfare programs that provide for people who are not eligible for federal programs.

Problems and Policy Issues

Although there are numerous programs which attempt to provide the necessary long-term–care services, public policies regarding long-term care have been criticized as leading to a system of service that is ineffective, inefficient, and inequitable. The major problems characterizing the current long-term–care system include service and eligibility gaps, inappropriate service mix, and fragmented, uncoordinated programs for the delivery of long-term care. For the individual in need of long-term–care services, this system often means that the individual is unable to receive the services needed to remain in the community and must be institutionalized to obtain care. From a societal perspective, this system leads to large expenditures for institutional services at the expense of less costly community care.

Less than one-third of the 5.5 to 9.9 million functionally disabled persons in the United States receive government assistance. Gaps in program eligibility and coverage create perverse incentives for individuals in need of care and can lead to impoverishment to obtain services. Most long-term care is provided informally by family and friends of the aged and disabled. Between 60 and 85 percent of disabled individuals receive such family assistance. While the government, through the Medicaid program, is the largest public financer of long-term–care services, most people become eligible for these services only after exhausting their personal resources. Long-term care, particularly nursing-home care, is the most significant catastrophic expense for the aged. As a result, most individuals become eligible entering a nursing home. The Medicare program, with its acute-care orientation, limits long-term–care coverage to skilled nursing care and rehabilitation services necessary to complete one acute-care episode and generally excludes most nursing-home care.

One of the most obvious problems of long-term care is the predominance of the nursing home and the lack of developed community-based care systems. The lack of financing for and availability of community-based care such as homemaker, home health, nutrition, and other services often creates an incentive to use nursing-home care, which covers all of the individual's basic needs, including food, and shelter. Thus, use of generally more costly and often less appropriate resources is encouraged by the absence of realistic alternatives. The Congressional Budget Office estimates that 10 to 20 percent of SNF patients and 20 to 40 percent of ICF residents are inappropriately placed.

Most of the aged would not choose the nursing home if they could avoid it, but at the crisis stage of an illness it is often easier to obtain care in a nursing home than to develop alternatives. The individual lacks basic control over use or cost of care, since utilization is controlled more by providers than by the individual. For example, physicians control entry into nursing homes, are the only ones legally authorized to prescribed Medicare and Medicaid home health services, and heavily influence discharge planning. There are few incentives to recommend less costly but harder to organize community care.

The current system of long-term care is a patchwork of separate public programs providing related services to similiar populations. Programs are skewed toward either health or social services. However, most long-term–care services incorporate both of these elements. It is nearly impossible to meet an individual's long-term–care service needs through a single provider or financing source. Each program has a different benefit, eligibility, and reimbursement structure which must be faced by each person in need. Even when one is eligible for services, the needed services are often difficult to coordinate into a meaningful package.

In summary, current program policies and benefit structures and difficulties in arranging home care probably lead to inefficient use of resources by fostering unnecessary institutional placement. Difficulties in locating home-care services and lack of coordination among the various providers make planning care for individuals and families seeking assistance difficult. Institutional care is all inclusive and does not present a coordination problem for the patient. The following are examples of the policies that contribute to this institutional bias in Medicaid, the major purchaser of long-term–care services:

- Medicaid will pay for certain services when provided in a nursing home. For instance, Medicaid will not reimburse for homemaker services, housekeeping, personal care, or counseling when provided at home or in the community but will reimburse for these services when provided as part of the nursing-home package.
- Income standards for Medicaid eligibility are often higher for persons in nursing homes than for persons living in their own homes or in congregate-care facilities. Thus, individuals with too much income cannot receive long-term–care services at the community level which may be more appropriate for their needs, but can receive long-term care in a nursing home. As a result, these people either go into an institution where they get medical assistance or do without the care they need.
- Individuals eligible for public programs who enter nursing homes must reduce their assets and have cash assistance reduced to levels so low that maintenance of their own home or return to independent living may be financially infeasible. For instance, if an SSI recipient enters a nursing home, his or her SSI payment is reduced to $25 after one month in the nursing home. Similarly, all income over $25 per month of persons who do not receive SSI must be used to help pay for the institutional care in order to receive Medicaid benefits. The reduction to $25 may make it impossible for the single recipient who enters the nursing home for a projected stay of only a few months to maintain a home to which he/she can return and thus becomes permanently institutionalized.
- Cash assistance to married recipients is also reduced when one spouse enters an institution. Thus, the noninstitutionalized spouse may be left with too little income to maintain the home; leading him or her to also enter a nursing home or move in with relatives or friends, either of which may make it more difficult for the institutionalized spouse to return to independent living.

• Cash support and Medicaid coverage is reduced if an individual lives with or receives support from families or friends who have no legal obligation to provide such support. Many elderly live with or receive voluntary cash or in-kind contributions from their adult children, siblings, or friends. SSI considers such voluntary contributions as income and reduces the recipient's SSI payment accordingly. If the recipient's income is high enough, eligibility to SSI and Medicaid is lost. The loss of these benefits results in two alternatives: either family and friends assume an additional financial burden, or the person needing care enters an institution in order to receive assistance with his or her medical-care costs.

From a policy perspective, the rising cost of long-term care and the growing population in need of long-term–care services, especially as the U.S. population ages, are major concerns. To redesign the current system to meet the broad needs of the long-term–care population requires major reform.

Several approaches that could be considered include: (1) expanding Medicare and Medicaid to cover more home-care services; (2) establishing a separate long-term–care entitlement with emphasis on home-and community-based services; (3) implementing a long-term–care voucher system to provide individuals with financial assistance to meet the cost of care while maintaining the individual's freedom to choose providers and arrange for services; (4) providing grants to states and localities to organize and coordinate the delivery of long-term–care services with regard to population characteristics and provider availability; (5) encouraging private insurance to cover long-term–care services; and (6) providing assistance to families to care for their disabled relatives. None of these approaches are exclusive of others. A brief discussion of these approaches is presented below.

Expand Medicare and Medicaid Coverage

Expanding coverage of community-based care under the Medicare program would require changes in benefits, eligibility, and/or financing. Benefits could be expanded by redefining home services to cover some types of nonmedical care. These services include personal-care services to assist in activities of daily living such as bathing, exercising, and personal grooming; household-care services such as maintaining a safe environment, light housekeeping, and purchase and preparation of food; respite care; foster care; expanded transportation services; and nutrition counseling. It would include payment for the services of home health aides, homemakers, social workers, technicians, and dietitians.

In order to increase use of in-home services under Medicaid, benefits could be expanded to allow short-stay nursing-home patients to retain the standard SSI or the noninstitutional income level necessary for Medicaid eligibility for up to three months so that they can maintain their homes in the community. Thus individuals who do not require extensive institutional care could return home after the need for institutional care has been met rather than becoming permanently institutionalized. For patients who are institutionalized for long periods of time (i.e., over three months) benefits could provide an extra cash payment upon being released to help finance the one-time cost of establishing a private residence.

Eligibility requirements could also be altered to remove the incentives for institutionalization and encourage community-based care. For example, income standards for eligibility for Medicaid for noninstitutional services could be set at the same level (or at a higher level) as that set for nursing-home care, thereby enabling individuals requiring community-based services to become eligible for Medicaid at a more accelerated spend-down rate than those individuals entering institutions. ("Spend-down" is the process of deducting medical expenses from income so that the income is reduced to meet eligibility standards. Thus, if higher income standards were used, community-based individuals would need to spend a lower amount of dollars on medical care to become eligible for Medicaid.) Likewise, in determining SSI or Medicaid eligibility for individuals not in institutions gifts up to $50 a month (or higher) in cash or in kind would be disregarded and not counted as income. In addition, the requirement to reduce the SSI payment by one-third when a recipient lives in the household of another and does not contribute a pro rata share toward household expenses could be eliminated.

Financing requirements could also be changed to encourage home care. Medicaid matching rates could be changed to provide a higher federal share for noninstitutional rather than institutional services. In addition, the Title 20 ceiling could be raised to expand coverage of in-house services for the aged and disabled.

The advantage to this approach of redesigning the current system to meet the broad needs of the long-term–care population is that it builds on an existing administrative and financial structure and avoids unforeseen adverse consequences which might result from any major restructuring at one time. In this approach, each modification could be phased in incrementally and evaluated before proceeding with the next step. It minimizes the impact of any program cost increases.

The disadvantage to this approach is that the current program structures are left intact thus continuing the split between medical services and social services. As a result the problems of fragmentation, poor coordination, inflexibility of benefits and gaps in eligibility and coverage would most likely remain. Consequently, the system would continue to meet poorly the fluctuating needs of individuals who are not in institutions.

Establish a Separate Entitlement

An entitlement program separate from Medicare and Medicaid could be established to provide both medical and social services to the long-term–care population. The focus would be on noninstitutional services. Eligibility requirements would be broader to include disabled persons who are not eligible for Medicare and do not meet Medicaid income standards as well as all individuals age sixty-five and over. The entitlement program could be funded through trust fund monies and/or general revenues. Federal costs could be reduced through deductibles or copayments.

The advantage to a separate entitlement program is that it would eliminate the problem of gaps in eligibility and coverage. It would help reduce the medical emphasis of long-term–care services, encourage a more efficient and effective mix of institutional and home-care resources, and ensure services for all elderly and disabled individuals.

The disadvantage to this approach is that the cost for long-term–care services would increase due to the broader eligibility and benefit coverage. Many individuals who now rely on family and friends for support and use private dollars to finance their care could be expected to take advantage of the new entitlement program. Thus, the costs of care now purchased privately would be shifted to the public sector. In addition, new administrative and financial structures would need to be established to operate the program.

Long-term–Care Voucher System

Establishment of a long-term–care voucher system would provide eligible individuals with an income supplement (voucher) to purchase a broad array of health and social services. Services could be provided in a variety of settings including nursing homes, domiciliary-care facilities, congregate living facilities or the individual's home. Vouchers would be issued on a monthly or quarterly basis. Under this system, the individual, rather than the government, would directly reimburse providers. In addition, the individual would be able to determine the range and scope of services needed as well as who provides those services. This approach allows the individual freedom of choice concerning his/her long-term–care needs.

The advantage of a voucher system is that it eliminates the maze of the current patchwork quilt of programs. Individuals would not have to contend with varying eligibility requirements, benefit limitations, or reimbursement structures. Cost could be controlled by controlling the dollar amounts of the vouchers. Furthermore, the voucher system would encourage competition by allowing individuals to make choices about services they prefer and bring market pressure to bear on providers to offer high quality services. Noninstitutional services might become more widely available if they could meet the market tests of reasonable cost and consumer preferences.

The disadvantage to this approach is that it would be extremely complex to design an equitable system. Determining who would be eligible and the amount of the voucher are two of the most difficult issues to be solved. For example, should the amount of the voucher be based on the extent of functional disability, the amount and types of services needed, the extent of family support, the individual's place of residence, or a combination of these factors. Each factor will have an impact on the effectiveness of the voucher and the cost of the program. Quality of care would also be extremely difficult to monitor under this program. Furthermore, the voucher would provide a limited benefit in that once the voucher has been used, the benefit would be exhausted for the quarter. If an individual misjudges his/her needs for the quarter, the voucher could fail to cover necessary services required by the individual at the end of the quarter.

Grants to States and Local Communities

Grants to states for long-term–care services would enable state and local communities to develop programs to meet the needs of their individual long-term–care populations. Programs could be devised to fit local circumstances with regard to population characteristics and provider availability. Under this approach federal funds from existing long-term–care programs would be consolidated into a single grant program. The total federal contribution would be determined by Congressional appropriation. Block grants could be allocated among the states by a formula which would reflect the number of aged and disabled population in the state as well as relative costs. The exact composition of the benefit package would be at state and local discretion, although emphasis would be on medical and social services at the community level.

The advantage to this approach is that the artificial division between health and social service programs could be eliminated. New programs adapted to local conditions and preferences could be devised. In addition, federal costs could be controlled directly through the appropriation process thus avoiding the large federal cost increases inherent in entitlement programs. Furthermore, budget constraints would encourage states to reduce the bias toward institutionalization and to maximize the number of persons served by making efficient service assignments through the use of noninstitutionalized services and appropriate nursing-home placement.

The disadvantage to this approach is that a cap on funding might result in increased financial burdens on the states as well as reduced availability of services if funding levels do not keep pace with inflation and increases in the needs of the long-term–care population. In addition, the allocation of resources between institutional and noninstitutional services could become a political battle between nursing-home operators and home-based providers and might result in the continued dominance of institutional providers. Furthermore, federal control over the quality of care in nursing homes and over other long-term–care providers would be reduced or eliminated. This could result in poor quality care if funding were severely limited. Finally, significant reallocations of funds among states would occur since a formula based on the long-term–care population would not match the current allocation for existing programs.

Encourage Private Insurance

Currently, private insurance for long-term–care services is almost nonexistent. Long-term care is a relatively uninsurable risk. In order for a private insurance plan to be financially viable, payment for long-term–care insurance would have to begin at a young age. There appears to be an insufficient young population who recognizes the risk of chronic disability and are willing to pay in advance to protect themselves. In addition, insurance companies are reluctant to set premiums that are level for life when prices and delivery modes are constantly changing and expenses decades in the future are almost impossible to predict accurately.

Under a private insurance approach, subsidies through the tax structure would be given to encourage development of long-term–care insurance plans. The benefit package would be broad and include both health and social services delivered in a variety of settings. Standards for minimum coverage could be established. Coinsurance and deductibles would be allowed.

The advantage to a broad benefit long-term–care insurance program is that with comprehensive coverage it would protect individuals against a significant risk and would eliminate fragmentation of benefits and reimbursement.

One disadvantage to this approach is the cost. Employers would be reluctant to offer a long-term–care policy without sufficient tax subsidies. (Currently, employment-related health insurance is subsidized at an average rate of 43 percent and does not include long-term–care coverage.) Consequently, revenue losses to the government might be high. Second, with private companies insuring individuals, there is no guarantee that all individuals would be assured full and comprehensive coverage. High-risk individuals may be screened out from purchasing the insurance. In order to prevent such selectivity from occurring, federal standards would need to be set.

Provide Assistance to Families

Most elderly individuals who need long-term care (numbers range between 60 and 80 percent) turn to their spouses, children, and other relatives for help. Institutionalization occurs when family supports either do not exist and/or are unwilling or unable to provide the necessary services. The great physical and mental burdens of providing care as well as the financial cost eventually motivates many families to institutionalize their elderly and /or disabled relatives.

Under this approach the government could provide a tax credit to families who provide care. Alternatively, the government could directly reimburse the family to cover the costs of the services provided.

The advantage to this approach is that by decreasing the financial burden it might encourage families to continue to care for their elderly and/or disabled relatives rather than institutionalizing them and would create circumstances under which more families could afford to do so.

The disadvantage to this approach is the uncertainty of increased costs. Whether substitution of family-provided services for professionally provided services would offset payments to families for services already provided without federal payments is difficult to determine.

Summary

Each of the aforementioned approaches to solving the problems of delivering services to the long-term–care population has its benefits as well as its drawbacks.

The goal of long-term–care policy must be to design a system of health, social, and medical services that will help people to remain as independent as possible by preventing the loss of functional abilities, minimizing the effect of loss when it occurs, and providing rehabilitation to the maximum extent feasible. To design and implement such a system without substantial increases in the federal budget during a time of fiscal constraint is the major challenge facing policymakers today.

BIBLIOGRAPHY

BINSTOCK, R. and SHAMAS, E., eds. 1976. *Handbook on aging and the social sciences*. New York: Van Nostrand Reinhold.

FISHER, C. 1980. Differences by age groups in health care spending. *Health Care Financing Review* 1 (no. 4).

FREELAND, M.; CALAT, G.; and SCHENDLER, C. 1980. Projections of national health expenditures, 1980, 1985 and 1990. *Health Care Financing Review* 1 (no. 3).

GIBSON, R. M. 1979. National health expenditures, 1978. *Health Care Financing Review* 1 (no. 1).

LA PORTE, V., and RUBIN, J., eds. 1979. *Reform and regulation in long term care*. New York: Praeger.

Lee, P., and Estes, C. 1979. Public policies, the aged and long term care. *Journal of Long Term Care Administration* 7 (no. 3).

Pollack, W. 1979. *Expanding health benefits for the elderly.* I: *Long Term Care.* Washington, D.C.: Urban Institute.

Scanlon, W.; Difederico, E.; and Stassen, M. 1979. *Long term care: current experience and a framework for analysis.* Washington, D.C.: Urban Institute.

Sherwood, S. ed. 1975. *Long term care: a handbook for researchers, planners and providers.* New York: Spectrum.

U.S. Congressional Budget Office. 1977. *Long term care for the elderly and disabled.* Washington, D.C.

U.S. Department of Health, Education and Welfare. 1977. Current estimates from the health interview survey: United States 1976. *Vital and Health Statistics,* series 1O (no. 119).

———. 1979. The national nursing home survey: 1977 summary for the United States. *Vital and Health Statistics.* series 13 (no. 43).

———. 1980. Office of Health Research, Statistics and Technology. *Health United States 1979. DHEW Publication No. (PHS) 80-1232.*

———. 1981. Health Care Financing Administration. The Medicare & Medicaid Data Book, 1981. Publication no. 03128.

U.S. Department of Health and Human Services. 1981. Health Care Financing Administration. Long term care: background and future issues. DHHS Publication No. (HCFA) 81-20047.

U.S. General Accounting Office. 1979. *Entering a nursing home: costly implications for Medicaid and the elderly.* Publication no. PAD 80-12.

Chapter 17

The Federal Health Structure

Gerald Rosenthal

ALTHOUGH THE FEDERAL GOVERNMENT has long been involved with health-related activities, the scale and variety of the involvement have increased considerably over the past three decades.

Stimulus for this involvement in health care has come from a wide variety of legislative and executive responses to new problems, obligations, and public expectations. Depressions, inflation, war, and the increased mobility of the American public have all contributed to the development of new public policies for health care. Each new policy, in turn, has stimulated the development or modification of organizations within the federal government to carry out and implement these new activities. It is the set of these organizational entities that constitutes the federal structure in health.

Because the policies that give rise to the organization have developed over time, it follows that the federal health structure has also developed over time and that it is subject to continuous change and modification as new legislation is passed, levels of funding are changed, or priorities are modified. It is important to recognize, therefore, that any description of the federal health structure is, at best, illustrative. This caveat is even more important at the present time since we are in a period characterized by significant changes in policies and associated changes in organization. This makes an understanding of the diversity, range, and variety of federal activities particularly important.

In some sense, it is simplistic to speak of a federal health structure. In fact, health and health-related activities make up part or all of the functions of many organizational units throughout the federal government. Although these activities may be interrelated, in many cases the organizations function quite independently within the overall federal structure. Because many such programs serve specific populations or implement single strategies specified in the legislation that created them, priorities can often be established internally and success or failure determined without reference to other federal programs.

The wide dispersion of health activities throughout the federal government is a reflection of the variety of stimuli that give rise to the development of all federal programs, diversity in the constituencies to be served by the programs, and the differences in the basis for the focus on health. For example, the health-care activities of a given organization may be its primary purpose, as in the Indian Health

Service, or only a support activity for an entirely different set of organizational objectives, as in the case of health services in the Department of Defense. Alternatively, the health focus may only characterize a small portion of a given organization's responsibility, as in the regulatory activities of the Federal Trade Commission, or represent the entire direction of effort, as in the regulatory activities of the Professional Standards Review Organizations (PSRO) program of the Health Care Financing Administration. The degree to which health goals are central will influence both structure and performance. It should be clear, however, that such diversity leaves much room for apparently conflicting policies within the federal health structure and for widely varying responses to central changes in "federal health policy."

Not only are the organizations that make up the federal health structure varied, but the health-related functions of the government are varied as well. In addition to numerous programs that provide health services directly, the federal government plays a major role in financing of health care through reimbursement for services and through direct and indirect subsidy to both users and providers. The federal government through its regulatory activities has responsibility for quality assurance of various aspects of health care and through research and education plays a major investment role.

Although organizations differ in their range of functions, the specificity of their areas of activity, and their degree of coordination with other organizational components within and outside of the federal system, these functions—provision of services, financing of care, regulation, and investment—characterize the entire federal health structure.

Because these functions are so widely dispersed throughout the federal government, it follows that elements of the federal health structure can be found within many departments and independent agencies. Nevertheless, the central organizational focus in the federal health structure is the Department of Health and Human Services (DHHS). The secretary of DHHS is the major adviser to the president on policies and programs in the areas of health, welfare, and income security and directs the department in carrying out and implementing programs in these areas. The DHHS is organized around four principal operating components: the Public Health Service (PHS), the Health Care Financing Administration (HCFA), the Social Security Administration (SSA), and the Office of Human Development Services (OHDS) (see Figure 17.1).

This structure, approved in 1979, represents only the current stage of an evolutionary process that began almost two hundred years ago and continues to the present. PHS had its beginnings in an act passed in 1798 that authorized the federal government to establish hospitals for the care of U.S. merchant seamen. Federal public health functions were consolidated and expanded with extensive legislation passed in 1944 and many times thereafter. The creation of a federal Department of Health, Education, and Welfare did not occur until 1953. HCFA, on the other extreme, was only established in 1977 to integrate and consolidate in a single organization major financing and quality assurance programs located in different organizations throughout the department. At the current time, most of the federal programs for which the health component is the central purpose are located in these organizations.

The PHS has had six operating agencies: the Alcohol, Drug Abuse, and Mental Health Administration (ADAMHA); the Center for Disease Control (CDC); the Food and Drug Administration (FDA); the Health Resources Administration

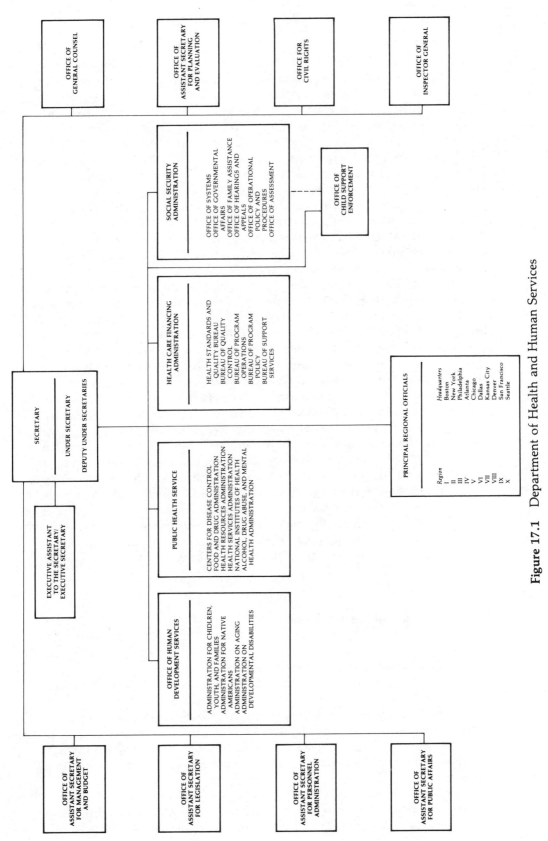

Figure 17.1 Department of Health and Human Services

381

(HRA); the Health Services Administration (HSA); and the National Institutes of Health (NIH). The HRA and HSA have recently been combined into a single operating unit. In addition to the agencies, the Office of the Assistant Secretary for Health includes three major operating centers: the National Center for Health Statistics (NCHS), the National Center for Health Services Research (NCHSR), and the National Center for Health Care Technology (NCHCT). Each of the operating agencies of PHS is organized into a number of bureaus or institutes which are each responsible for some component of the overall health programs. In some cases, these entities are established directly as part of the legislation that authorizes the program. In other cases, the organizational structure reflects an executive response to a legislated obligation. There are over forty such organizations within PHS, exclusive of support activities, sixteen of which are in NIH. The large number of operating organizations is a reflection of the tremendous diversity in function and target populations which characterizes federal health policy in general and PHS responsibilities in particular.

By way of contrast, HCFA, while representing a federal expenditure five times greater than that of PHS, is currently organized around five major bureaus: Health Standards and Quality, Quality Control, Program Operations, Program Policy, and Support Services. This simpler structure reflects a more focused set of operating responsibilities and reflects the fact that HCFA was established specifically to provide a more integrated focus for federal health-care financing and quality-assurance activities. It is important to note that, even where the organizational mission is straightforward, the actual activities incorporated within the structure of the organization may be quite diverse. For example, HCFA carried out an extensive program of research as part of its responsibility for operating the major federal financing programs. The Indian Health Services in PHS, in addition to the direct provision of care, also supports training and research. The integration of multiple functions within programs is typical of the federal health structure.

Because the functions, in a generic sense, have more stability than the organizations, a sense of the federal health structure is better derived from a discussion of them. As noted earlier, federal activities in health fall into four major areas: provision of services, financing of care, regulation, and investment. An examination of the activities in each of these areas and the organizations that carry them out follows.

Direct Provision of Health Services

Although the United States has a health-care system that is largely privately operated, the federal government has extensive responsibilities for the direct provision of health services by federal personnel in federal facilities. In most cases, these responsibilities are part of an overall federal responsibility for a given group of beneficiaries related to a unique status. Groups falling into this category include merchant seamen, Native Americans, federal prisoners, veterans, and military personnel. For each of these groups, federal organizations exist to meet the service obligations.

As noted earlier, the U.S. Public Health Service had its roots in legislation establishing hospitals for the care of merchant seamen. At the present time there are seven hospitals and twenty-eight clinics serving approximately 450,000 beneficiaries in this program. The hospitals are staffed primarily by personnel from the Commissioned Corps of the Public Health Service, one of the uniformed services of the federal government. The program has been operated by the Division of Hospitals and Clinics of HSA. In addition to the PHS hospitals and clinics, this unit also has operated the National Hansen's Disease Center. Although serving a designated set of beneficiaries, the PHS hospitals also provide training opportunities for residents and other health professionals and function in many ways like general community hospitals.

The Bureau of Medical Services also provides personnel and services to the Federal Bureau of Prisons to provide care for some 240,000 federal offenders in forty-three institutions and nine treatment centers, and to the U.S. Coast Guard. In addition, it provides on-site occupational health and safety services to federal employees at the workplace. In addition, personnel of the bureau have been called on to provide medical services in time of emergency and for special programs such as establishing health care for Cuban and Haitian refugees.

Another major provider of health services within the HSA is the Indian Health Service. This program, for which the Public Health Service took responsibility in 1955, provides comprehensive health services directly and through contract to over 802,000 American Indians and Alaskan Natives. To meet this obligation, the Indian Health Service (IHS) operates approximately forty-nine hospitals and outpatient departments, more than a hundred health centers, and over two hundred small satellite clinics and health stations in twenty-four states. These institutions together with contracted services accounted for over 400,000 inpatient days and 3,250,000 outpatient visits in 1981.

In addition to direct medical services, the IHS maintains an extensive program of preventive health services. Emphasis in this aspect of the program is in sanitation, public health nursing, and health education. As an overall responsibility, the IHS serves as an advocate for the health interests of Native Americans and provides support for training Indian health manpower and general community development and organization around health issues.

The PHS hospitals and the IHS represent the major direct service provision activities of DHHS. However, as part of its research support effort, the NIH operates a 541-bed clinical facility that serves as a major referral facility. Although not primarily operated to provide services, the clinical center does represent another federal institution involved in the direct provision of health services. In addition, ADAMHA has responsibility for St. Elizabeth's Hospital, a mental health facility in the District of Columbia which provides a broad range of inpatient and outpatient care for District residents and beneficiaries of the federal government. During 1980, the average daily inpatient load was over two thousand. This facility also serves as a clinical research setting for the National Institute of Mental Health.

While the provision of services in the DHHS are significant, they do not represent the major federal activities in this area. In fact, the largest medical-care delivery system in the United States is a federally operated system, the Veterans' Administration health-care program. The VA operates 172 hospitals with an average daily census of approximately 66,000 inpatients. It also operates 220 clinics, 16 domiciliary facilities, and 92 nursing homes. Facilities are located throughout the United States, Puerto Rico, and the Philippines and provide services to eligible veterans of military services in the armed forces. For 1982, these facilities anticipate providing 18.6 million outpatient medical and dental visits and serving 1.3 million patients in hospitals.

VA facilities provide a major medical resource in many areas of the country. Over the past ten years they have developed extensive affiliations with teaching institutions and a program of research and development. They represent a system of medical care larger than those of many countries where the responsibility for providing medical care for all is a federal one. It is important to emphasize that the VA health-care system serves a potential population of over 30 million that is often eligible for and uses other service delivery systems, both public and private. This gives it a functional interdependence with other providers even though there is no formal organizational interdependence.

In addition to DHHS and the VA, the other major health- and medical-care service provision activity is in the Department of Defense. DOD has the responsibility to provide medical care to all active and retired military. This represents more than 2 million people, a population approximately one-third that of Switzerland.

To meet this obligation through the individual services, DOD operates 167 hospitals throughout the world and provides ambulatory care in almost every location where military personnel are deployed. In addition, military facilities provide care to dependents when alternative services are not available or when the facilities have the capacity to provide services without significant added cost.

These three programs, DHHS, VA, and DOD, are the major institutions in the federal government with responsibility for the direct provision of medical care. It is of some interest that DHHS is the smallest program, although it is the major health-related setting. The importance of service provision as a federal activity accounts for the fact that approximately 5 percent of the physicians licensed in 1977 were federal employees, yet discussions of the American health-care system often fail to acknowledge the scope of these activities.

Even more important, the three organizations are operationally independent and not subject, often, to rules affecting nonfederal facilities. Each serves specific constituencies and is authorized to do so under different legislation developed by different legislative committees and supported by appropriations incorporated in separate budgets and approved by different appropriations subcommittees. Although the functions may interact and beneficiaries of one system may also be eligible for services from another as well, no process currently operates to integrate these institutions.

Financing of Health Care

If annual expenditures are a guide, the major health-related function of the federal government is the financing of health care. Such financing takes a number of forms: reimbursement for services, grants to support the service, and indirect subsidy of medical expenditures through tax offsets. Of the three, reimbursement for services is the most significant and represents the fastest-growing area.

The organizations responsible for operation of reimbursement programs were widely spread throughout the federal government, typically located within programs serving a constituency which acquires eligibility as part of a broader set of benefits such as those related to employment or public dependency. The federal role in reimbursement increased considerably in 1965 with the passage of two major financing programs, Titles 18 and 19 of the Social Security Act. This legislation created a program of health insurance for the elderly as part of social security and a program of grants to the states for payment for services to the needy and medically needy. Although both in the DHHS (then DHEW), each program was initially separately managed and each was located in a different organization in the department. In 1977, these programs were relocated within DHHS to form the core of a new organization, the Health Care Financing Administration (HCFA).

With an annual budget of almost $40 billion, HCFA is the major financing organization in the federal structure. The Medicare program of hospital insurance for the elderly and disabled paid almost $24 billion in benefits in 1980 and covered almost 39 million Americans. The Medicaid program of grants to the states for medical services to the needy and medically needy provided care for more than 17 million recipients and provided over $14.5 billion of federal funds as part of a total program expenditure of almost $26 billion. As the overall costs of medical care have risen the HCFA programs increase in costs. This has given HCFA a special role in federal efforts to reduce the costs of care and to control unnecessary utilization and expenditures.

The scale and magnitude of this program make its decisions on reimbursement and medical practice impact throughout the health-care system, even for activities not directly supported under HFCA reimbursement. This responsibility shapes the HFCA research and demonstration programs, much of which are legislatively mandated. The search for more effective payment strategies is a major goal of this program.

Although HCFA is the largest health-care financing program in the federal government, it is by no means the only one. The Department of Defense, through the office of Civilian Health and Medical Program of the Uniformed Services (CHAMPUS), provides for payment for care for spouses and dependent children of active duty, retired, and deceased military personnel as well as totally disabled veterans. In addition, CHAMPUS pays for services provided to services personnel from private providers when such services are not available from military facilities. This program paid over $700 million for care in 1980. The VA also paid for significant services from the private sector. This amounted to approximately 158,000 visits during 1980.

The federal government also operates significant financing programs on behalf of current and retired employees. The Federal Employees Health Benefits Fund, operated by the Office of Personnel Management, covers over 3.6 million persons. Two-thirds of those covered are active employees and one-third are annuitants. The fund amounted to more than $4 billion in 1981. In addition to financing health benefits for employees, the federal government also operates its own workman's compensation program. This program, established under the Federal Employees' Compensation Act, pays for medical care and income loss arising from job-related illness and injury. The Office of Workers' Compensation Programs, in the Department of Labor, manages this program along with the compensation programs covering injuries to maritime employees in the U.S. waters and the "black lung" program. Together, this agency managed programs which paid over $1.2 billion in 1981. Although all of this expenditure was not for direct medical care, the amount is still significant and growing.

While direct payment for services provided is the largest form of federal expenditure for the financing of care, significant programs operate which finance care through grants, general support, and subsidy. In the aggregate, such programs represent considerable resources managed by organizations widely dispersed throughout the federal system. The major setting for such programs is the Bureau of Community Health Services (BCHS) in the Health Services Administration. This agency provides funds for primary-care programs which supported over 870 centers serving 6.2 million users in 1981 as well as 56 black-lung centers serving 55,000 persons. BCHS also supported 122 migrant health centers throughout the country. In addition to grants to support health centers, the agency also managed a number of categorical programs which make funds available for special health needs. In 1980, such activities included 57 blood pressure screening and referral programs serving 7.8 million persons, genetic counseling and referral for 3.9 million persons, and similar programs in the areas of sudden infant death, hemophilia, and family planning. In addition, maternal and child health programs serving over 3 million children are supported through this arm of DHHS. In addition to categorical programs such as these, BCHS, through its emergency medical services program, has provided grants to 303 communities to design and implement community-based emergency medical systems.

Programs that provide support for health services are found in other components of the Public Health Service as well. The Center for Disease Control, through various operating components, provides support and technical assistance for immunization and disease surveillance and for the development of community-based health education programs as well as consultation and technical assistance to states and communities in improving the performance of clinical laboratories.

Through the various categorical research and training centers, the institutes of NIH provide referral and community education in areas of heart disease, arthritis, cancer, diabetes, and other diseases as part of their overall research activities.

Within the Alcohol, Drug Abuse, and Mental Health Administration (ADAMHA) are included a number of programs which provide grant support for improved and expanded services. In the area of mental health, almost $30 million were provided to states and communities in 1980 to develop comprehensive mental health programs, programs for the elderly, support for the chronic mentally ill, and prevention programs. Similar grants supported improved prevention and treatment networks in the areas of drug abuse and alcoholism. In 1980 over $600 million were spent to support such services through the grant mechanism by this agency of PHS.

Outside of DHHS, other components of the federal government provide support for direct service provision through grants and contracts, although these do not represent major areas of expenditure. The Department of Education, by virtue of its responsibility for support of Howard University, provides approximately 30 percent of the operating costs of Howard University Hospital, and the Department of the Interior is responsible for the operation of health services on American Samoa. The Appalachian Commission provided support in 1980 for 144 health-care and community health education projects in the region and Vista and the Older Americans Volunteers programs also staffed and supported health and nutrition programs at the local level. Other programs to provide direct patient care through local health centers are being funded by the Community Services Administration, part of the federal antipoverty programs, although this program is being phased out.

Although not truly part of the federal health structure, a major, often overlooked, source of federal financing of health services is found within the Internal

Revenue Service in the Treasury Department. This results from the tax treatment of medical expenditures. It has been estimated that itemized medical deductions reduced tax revenues in 1980 by more than $6 billion. The subsidy implicit in the treatment of health fringe benefits as nontaxable income to the employee is likely to be of even greater magnitude. The role of the Treasury Department will increase considerably if current plans to discontinue many of the categorical grant programs and substitute direct revenue sharing are implemented. Such a strategy would also have significant impacts on other parts of the federal health structure.

Regulation

The federal structure in the regulation of health and medical care refers to those organizations for which the regulatory function is primary. It is important to note, however, that much of the concern about "regulations" refers to the growing body of rules which establish the conditions of participation and entitlement in other federal programs. The regulations covering major financing programs, as they have become more significant in the overall financing of care, have the impact of shaping and influencing all of the activities of providers, not just those specifically covered by the program. As concerns about the costs of the federal programs increase, the "regulations" surrounding these programs have increased significantly. While this aspect of government regulation in the health area is important, it is not the type of regulation which is referred to in this paper.

The general regulation of certain aspects of the health system is a function of long standing in the federal government. Primary among the organizations with direct regulatory functions is the Food and Drug Administration (FDA) in the DHHS. The FDA is the agency with major responsibility for protecting the public from unsafe and impure foods, drugs, cosmetics, and medical devices. Many of its functions were established in 1908 after passage of the Food and Drug Act of 1906. Named as an organizational entity in 1930, FDA became part of the Public Health Service in 1968.

FDA is responsible for the establishment of standards for new drugs and biologicals, for the licensing of new products, for assessment of the safety and effectiveness of new drugs, and for monitoring the quality and labeling accuracy of marketed drugs. In addition, FDA establishes standards for classes of food, uses of food additives, and manufacturing practices to prevent food and cosmetic adulteration. It also inspects food and cosmetic processing plants to verify labeling accuracy and product safety and to ensure compliance. More recently, FDA has had responsibility for assessing and establishing standards for electronic product radiation and for developing methods to control unnecessary exposure. FDA also carries out these same regulatory functions for medical devices, evaluating safety, efficacy, and labeling, setting standards for new devices, operating a program of surveillance to assure compliance, and providing technical assistance to manufacturers. FDA also carries out an extensive program of research and review and, for many areas, initiates enforcement activities where evidence of noncompliance requires such action.

While FDA is the oldest and most well established federal regulatory program in health, other programs have been growing in importance. The Health Care Financing Administration (HCFA) is responsible for operation of the major quality-assurance program, the Professional Standards Review Organizations (PSRO). Under this program, DHHS has established a national network of local physician sponsored groups, PSROs, to provide ongoing peer review of inpatient services provided to beneficiaries of the Medicare, Medicaid, and Maternal and Child Health programs. These groups set standards for care and assess experience of users against those standards. The HCFA Office of Quality Assurance also develops and monitors safety standards for providers of care.

Similar oversight is carried out as part of the End-stage Renal Disease program. The law authorizes the secretary both to develop standards and to deny reimbursement to those facilities that do not meet them. While the regulatory device is the ability to deny payment for services covered under the programs for which HCFA has responsibility, the growing dependency of providers on this source of financing together with the acceptance of PSRO standards by other payers has made these activities, in fact, a form of general system-wide regulation. Through its Office of Long Term Care, HCFA also has responsibility for establishing standards for long-term care and developing means to monitor the degree to which providers meet these standards. Even where direct enforcement responsibility does not exist, the willingness of states to utilize HCFA developed standards provides a much broader impact of the federal program.

In recent years, the Federal Trade Commission (FTC) has directed its attention to a number of health-related activities. The FTC, an independent federal agency, is responsible for both consumer protection and the enhancement of competition. Its consumer protection activities include the prevention of untrue or deceptive advertising and other practices which limit the ability of consumers to make informed judgments. As part of its efforts to promote "free and fair" competition, FTC seeks to prevent price-fixing agreements, unfair and illegal restraints on trade, and unlawful price discrimination. Although efforts in each of these areas are of long standing, only recently has the FTC focused its competition-promoting efforts on the providers of health and medical care. Within the past few years, FTC has taken action against a number of hospital-based speciality groups—radiologists, anesthesiologists, and pathologists—for interfering with competition by restricting access to facilities and limiting competition.

As FTC has focused increasingly on the health sector, the potential for significant conflicts with other health policies is increased. Much of the federal effort to promote the more effective use of health services has taken the form of restricted competition through formal planning mechanisms and "franchising" type activities.

The dissonance between the planning focus of the health-related agencies and the general competition enhancing mandate of FTC is another example of the wide diversity of regulatory perspectives and strategies contained within the federal health structure. Similar problems occur in the areas of labor relations and interstate commerce where traditional medical care system strategies may conflict with general public policies as enforced by federal agencies with general regulatory responsibility.

The growth in economic importance of the health sector has been reflected in increasing involvement of federal agencies outside of the organizations where the health focus is primary. This will enhance the opportunities for conflict.

Investment in the Health System

While almost all federal programs in health and medical care have an element of investment, the major investment strategies operate through support of research, training, and construction, and programs in each of these areas are as widespread as federal health activities generally. Of the three, however, research is the most ubiquitous. Within DHHS, research is supported by virtually every major agency. Typically, such research is directed at improving the performance of the programs. There are however, organizations throughout the federal government whose central purpose is the support and carrying out of research. In the area of health, such research may be either directed at disease and disease processes or directed at factors influencing the utilization, production, and delivery of health and medical-care services.

In the area of biomedical research, the major federal activity is within the National Institutes of Health (NIH). NIH conducts and supports an extensive program of biomedical research organized, for the most part, around a number of separate institutes, each focusing on a specific set of categorical diseases or target groups such as children and the aged. In addition, NIH has responsibility for making medical information, developed through the research process available through the programs of the National Library of Medicine as well as through the individual institutes.

The programs of NIH include many activities of long standing in the federal government. The National Library of Medicine was originally established as the library of the Office of the Surgeon General (Army) in 1836 and was renamed the Army Medical Library in 1922. The first PHS research grants, for venereal disease studies, were made in 1891, a research laboratory to study Rocky Mountain spotted fever was established in 1921, and the National Cancer Institute was established in 1937.

Currently, NIH consists of twelve institutes, of which the National Library of Medicine (NLM), the National Cancer Institute (NCI), and the National Heart, Lung, and Blood Institute (NHLBI) are separate bureaus. NIH also operates a major clinical center drawing patients from throughout the world for clinical studies and controlled research and the Fogarty International Center, which promotes study and research through a number of international programs for advanced study in health sciences.

NIH supports research through grants to institutions, contracts, and an extensive intramural research effort. They also support a number of categorical centers around the country to serve as research, training, and referral resources. Both the scale of effort and the quality of the scientific staff have made NIH world renowned in the field of biomedical research as well as the major source of support for the research community in these areas. Other components of PHS also support research in areas of their categorical responsibility. An extensive program of research in mental health, alcoholism, and drug abuse is carried out by the Alcohol, Drug Abuse, and Mental Health Administration.

Here, as in NIH, research is carried out through both extramural grants and contracts and programs of intramural research and is organized around these major institutes: the National Institute of Mental Health (NIMH), the National Institute of Alcohol Abuse and Alcoholism (NIAAA), and the National Institute of

Drug Abuse (NIDA). The Food and Drug Administration, through the National Center for Toxicological Research, conducts research on the biological effects of toxic substances in the environment, and the Center for Disease Control, through the National Institute for Occupational Safety and Health (NIOSH), carries out research on factors in the work environment which are harmful to health and safety. NIOSH is also charged with developing safety standards for dissemination of information about workplace hazards.

Research has also been supported as part of the Maternal and Child Health program in the Health Services Administration. HSA also carried out research directly in the intramural programs of the Public Health Service hospitals. Within the Health Resources Administration (HRA), research in the area of health manpower utilization, methods for planning for health services, and nursing research has been supported through grants and contracts through each of the bureaus with operating responsibilities in these areas.

The other major research activities in PHS are currently located in the Office of the Assistant Secretary (OASH). Here is found the National Center for Health Services Research (NCHSR), which supports an extensive program of research and dissemination on all aspects of the organization and delivery of health and medical care through grants, contracts, and an intramural program. NCHSR was established in 1968 to provide a central research capacity in the department and to improve the secretary's policymaking capacity and serves as a source for the dissemination of health services research results throughout the world. Also in OASH is the recently established National Center for Health Care Technology (NCHCT), which carries out research to identify and assess the social, technical, and economic impacts of medical technology. NCHCT also provides advice to HCFA on the appropriateness of reimbursing for newly developed technologies through Medicare and organizes, often in conjunction with other agencies, conferences in which new technologies can be discussed and existing experience evaluated.

Outside of PHS, the Health Care Financing Administration (HCFA) supports an extensive program of research and demonstration related to improving the Medicare and Medicaid programs and other areas of their responsibility. Many of the demonstation programs are mandated by Congress to experiment with alternative strategies of reimbursement and organization to contain costs and improve incentives in these financing programs. HCFA also does analyses on data generated from Medicare and Medicaid to monitor program performance. Some health-related research is also supported through the DHHS Office of Human Development Services grants programs in aging, children and youth, and rehabilitation.

Outside of DHHS, significant research is supported which has a health focus. Life-sciences research is supported through the Department of Energy and the National Aeronautics and Space Administration and a broad range of research is funded through the biological, behavioral, and social science programs of the National Science Foundation. Research in health and health services is carried out as part of the health-care programs of the Veterans' Administration. The Department of Agriculture (DOA), through the land grant college funds, supports research in over 1,850 colleges and universities. Although not specifically identified, some portion of this research is focused on health issues. In addition, DOA supports directly research on various aspects of nutrition and health.

The support of training in health takes many forms, from academic and professional education to the development and extension of specific training in support of particular program goals. In addition to the support of individuals through scholarships, fellowships, and, increasingly, loans, many programs provide general support directly to the institutions which provide the training. The Bureau of Health Professions Education in HRA has been, until recently, the major source of support for health-related professional education. Programs operated from this bureau have included capitation payments to schools of medicine, dentistry, veterinary, osteopathy, nursing, and other allied health professional career areas. In more recent years, support for programs in administration, epidemiology, and biostatistics has also been included. In 1980, almost $500 million were spent through these programs to support students and institutions. The bureau also seeks to develop more effective ways to utilize human resources and provides special financial support directly to a few institutions currently training large numbers of minority students. A major financial activity has been the student loan guarantee program.

In addition to the HRA programs, training support is a function of many other PHS programs. NIH provides the major source of support for training in biomedical research fields, through extensive fellowship programs in universities and research facilities, through the various centers' programs, and through the opportunities for training incorporated into its own extensive intramural activities. HSA, through its newly established Bureau of Health Personnel Development and Service, operates a number of programs which provide scholarships or loans which are forgiven for physicians and nurses who serve specified lengths of time in designated underserved areas providing medical care. The Indian Health Service also has a recruitment and scholarship program for health professional training for Native Americans. The Maternal and Child Health program provided support for fifty-nine MCH training programs in 1980 and short-term training is also supported as part of many of the categorical programs of HSA.

Outside of DHHS, the Department of Defense provides scholarships through the Armed Forces Health Professions Scholarship program. Almost five thousand students were supported through this program in 1980 and approximately four hundred to five hundred medical officers are commissioned each year from this source. More recently, DOD has established the Uniformed Services University of the Health Sciences, a medical school which will train physicians and other health personnel for the military. The Department of Education through its general support of education and training and, directly, through its operating support of Howard University medical school, provides resources for health-related training. The VA, as part of its health services programs, provides and supports training through residency programs and medical school affiliations. In addition, it carries out training for staff within the VA system.

The other major investment function of the federal government is in the support of construction of health facilities. The major locus for this activity has been in the Bureau of Health Facilities Financing, Compliance, and Conversion in HRA. This program, and its predecessors, provide grants for the construction, modernization, and conversion of health facilities. In more recent years, there is a growing emphasis on loans rather than grants to support construction in part due to the ability to recover such costs through the reimbursement system. This trend, together with the increasing significance of proprietary facilities with their access to more traditional money markets, has reduced the importance of the grant programs. However, they continue to provide a measure of flexibility that makes these programs still a significant component of federal health policy.

Construction of facilities is also supported through those federal programs with direct responsibility for the provision of services such as the VA, the Indian Health Service, and DOD. The Appalachian Regional Development Commission supported over fifty construction projects in 1980, and the Department of the Interior, through its Office of Territorial Affairs, supported construction of health facilities in Saipan and the Virgin Islands. There is also considerable support for construction incorporated in research and training programs since awards for such activities often include the facilities in which to conduct them.

The preceding discussion has been an attempt to identify the organizations within the federal health structure engaged in each of the major functional areas of public policy in health. As should be clear, there is widespread involvement in health and health-related activities throughout the entire federal structure. Simply focusing attention on single agencies or even departments will yield a too narrow view of the extent and variety of such efforts. While reflecting a reality that has developed over time, the federal health structure and its diversity adds to complexity of policy discussion by making the step from concept to execution even more complicated and uncertain.

The federal health structure described here has the executive branch activities and organizations. Congress demonstrates a similar pattern, as might be expected. While major attention to health legislation is centered in two substantive committees in each chamber, virtually every committee has an interest that will often overlap into the health area. In some cases, the executive branch structure described in this chapter is a reflection of the source of original legislative interest.

A strong legislative interest in a particular program may argue for a special organization where other administrative criteria would suggest such activities might be integrated within existing settings. It is important to be aware of the implications of building policies and programs through legislation. The long-time duration of that activity and the ready opportunity to incorporate additional and occasionally diverse views of policy into a single piece of authorizing legislation contributes greatly to the dynamic nature of the federal health structure.

The above comment also reinforces a second important point. Although it is easy to speak of a federal health structure, that entity is not very centralized. Federal organizations with significant health responsibilities are found in many departments and extradepartmental components of the executive branch and even, as noted above, in the legislative branch. Since each setting is often tailored to serve a narrow set of functions or a specific constituency, the sum of those individual activities may not add up to a consistent federal strategy. It is far more likely, in such a system, that there will be numerous inconsistencies and conflicts. Many organizations, while effectively part of the federal health structure, may also be part of an organizational entity with different priorities and different criteria for success. (A simple contrast between espoused federal physician manpower policy and the health manpower development programs of DOD should be sufficient example.)

Because structure, ideally, bears some relationship to function, it is important to understand the wide variety of functions encompassed in the organizations which make up the federal health structure. This chapter has attempted to "map" some of the main components of that structure in each of the main functional areas of federal health activities. The "half-life" of such a descriptive exercise may be quite short, particularly in a period of potentially large change in the programs and legislation that is served by this structure. Nevertheless, the principle remains that a simplistic concept of a federal health structure will no more suffice to describe it than a simplistic view of federal health policy will suffice to describe that aspect of federal health activities. The federal responsibilities in health are generated by a process that is diverse, dynamic, and disaggregated. It is unrealistic to expect that the structure of the organizations that fulfill those responsibilities could be any different.

Chapter 18

Does Medical Care Do Any Good?

Sol Levine
Jacob J. Feldman
Jack Elinson

AT FIRST RHETORICALLY, and in recent years more seriously, a thesis has emerged that medical care has little or no impact on health. Here we examine this thesis critically, and raise some initial questions that have to be addressed to stimulate policy deliberation and more rigorous research on this topic.

In questioning the emerging thesis that medical care does no good, we do not wish to obscure such issues as resource allocation, methods of financing, organizational structures and incentives and methods of deploying personnel—all of which may influence the effectiveness of medical care, in particular, and health care, in general. Thus we state our biases and assumptions at the outset. We hold that:

1. Public health measures, social conditions, and personal health behavior are the main determinants of health.
2. Our health system is too heavily weighted in the direction of hospital-based medicine and that there is need to give greater emphasis to community-based ambulatory care with a strong preventive component.
3. Many medical measures and interventions are not effective by any criterion. Those measures or interventions that are proved to be ineffective should be abandoned.
4. Many services now provided by physicians can be performed by other health personnel.
5. Iatrogenic illness is fairly extensive and is a very serious concern.
6. Costs in the health sector have risen disproportionately and economies and cost controls are warranted.
7. Some health and human services which presently are not available should be provided.
8. There is need for more humane health care.

We wish to thank Robert H. Brook and John B. McKinlay for reading this chapter and providing helpful comments and suggestions.

In popular as well as in professional deliberations, the emerging argument that medical care does no good has become enjoined with an emphasis on the importance of other factors such as environment, accidents, and life-style as the main determinants of health. Why these factors, which have been recognized by public health professionals and epidemiologists for many years, are now receiving enthusiastic endorsement needs careful examination. As Starr notes: "Students of public health have long observed, without anyone's paying much attention, that the effect of environment and behavior on the health of populations is much greater than that of medical care. Suddenly this point is being treated, in influential circles, as if it were a major discovery" (Starr 1976).

While public health leaders have consistently stressed the importance of environmental social conditions and personal behavior, they have rarely coupled their emphasis with the assertion that medical care does no good nor with the implication that basic health-care services should be restricted. Quite the contrary; public health leaders devoted much of their efforts to making care more available and accessible to all segments of the population, particularly the poor. Public health leaders were among the first to criticize the priorities in our health system, our emphasis on the hospital "repair" system instead of preventive primary care, and the widespread diffusion of costly and ineffective interventions, but they have rarely permitted their critique to serve as a rationale for the restriction or curtailment of basic health services, particularly for the poor.

The writings of public health professionals contrast most sharply with the most extreme critic of medicine, Ivan Illich, who argues that to increase the access of the lower classes to health care "would only equalize the delivery of professional illusions and torts" (Illich 1975). Illich has even maintained that "less access to the present health system would, contrary to the political rhetoric, benefit the poor."

The extension of health services to the American population in the past two decades and the growing concern with the unprecedented rise in the costs of health care have provided the fertile context if not the impetus for the popularization of the thesis that medical care is not effective and that the individual must assume more responsibility for his health. There is no doubt that, in raising the question, various writers like McKeown (1976, 1978) and Fuchs (1975, 1978) (their writings are on a different plane from that of Illich) have directed our attention to the priorities of our health system, the separation of preventive services from curative services, the inordinate emphasis on tertiary care, the proliferation of various practices and the procedures that have not been properly evaluated and the burgeoning growth of what Lewis Thomas (1972) has described as halfway technologies.

A judicious and discriminating approach to this question, however, will require us to unravel and clarify conceptual and methodological issues and to attend to questions that have not as yet been addressed. How have they formulated their questions? What types of data have they used? What types of reasoning and evidence have they employed? What types of questions deserve to be addressed within this general rubric? Finally, is the criterion of mortality appropriate or sufficient in answering the question: Does medical care do any good?

A thoughtful assessment of the limits of medicine's contribution to human health has been made by Thomas McKeown (1976). He argues that society's investment in health is misdirected and is guided by an erroneous assumption about how health is achieved. "It is assumed that the body can be regarded as a machine whose protection from disease and its effects depends primarily on internal intervention" (p. 71). He asserts, however, that changes in nutrition, environment, and behavior were the major factors that led to improvements in health (McKeown equates "improvements in health" with declines in mortality) and that in the more developed countries personal behavior, especially, and environmental factors are the main determinants of health.

McKeown goes on to dismiss some conventional beliefs about the efficacy of medical services in the twentieth century. The decline in infant mortality, for example, owed much more to improvements in maternal nutrition and better infant care and feeding than to improvements in obstetric services. He argues further that declines in mortality from tuberculosis were evident long before the introduction of effective treatment in 1947. McKeown's thesis of the overwhelming primacy of social and environmental factors is also extended to explain the declines in such diseases as pneumonia, bronchitis, and influenza. "The infections were declining long before effective measures were introduced, and, since that time, with the notable exceptions of streptomycin and poliomyelitis vaccine, they have been less important than other influences" (p. 92).

McKeown himself explicitly grants a not inconsiderable role to medical care, though he constantly points out that it plays a lesser role than the social, behavioral, and environmental factors. He credits surgery with some of the decline in mortality from violence in the twentieth century and acknowledges the value of surgery in treating several digestive disorders. He also views the improvement in obstetric services as contributing partly to the decline in infant mortality and states that the national use of poliomyelitis vaccine played a significant role in reducing disability and death. He also notes that there have been advances in the treatment of many uncomfortable and disabling conditions such as hernias and arthritis.

Finally, the role McKeown assigns to medicine is "to assist us to come safely into the world and comfortably out of it, and during life to protect the well and care for the sick and disabled." If one accepts McKeown's definition of the major role of medicine, which we do, then we must question whether mortality alone is a sufficient or appropriate criterion to evaluate the effectiveness of medical care, however relevant it may be for assessing the impact of the overall health system. Despite his deep appreciation of the importance of social factors in the etiology of disease, McKeown's conception of health or health status is primarily biological, not social. He appears deeply wedded to the view that health is a biological-physical state, not a level of social functioning. It is this view which pervades the thinking of some writers, who allege that these health services may do all kinds of things, but they have "little to do with health."

Although, as we have already indicated, mortality may not be an appropriate criterion to assess the value of medical care, it should be noted that there have been marked changes in United States mortality rates during the past decade, which suggest that it may be necessary to reappraise the contribution of medical-care measures to longevity. Several of the most influential of the assessments that have relegated medicine to a tertiary role focused on mortality trends in the distant past and do not necessarily have relevance for present and future health policies (McKeown 1976; McKinlay and McKinlay 1977). Typically, it is argued that personal medical services contributed little to the decline in death rates during the latter half of the nineteenth century and the early part of the twentieth century. It is then generally noted that there has been little or no decline in mortality rates during the period since the mid-1950s, despite rapidly increasing expenditures for personal medical services. The latter observation is now (1982) seriously outdated. Some mortality rates have been declining extremely rapidly during the past decade; in the older age groups, more rapidly than recorded in any previous period. A wide variety of explanations for the decline have been put forward. In dealing with a particular historical trend, epistemological constraints preclude establishing definitely the relative importance of various factors in its initiation and maintenance. It is nevertheless plausible that medical advances, operating through personal health services, have played a significant role in the recent mortality declines and may continue to contribute to longevity.

Death rates due to stroke, particularly, have been decreasing rapidly. For instance, among sixty-five- to seventy-four-year-olds, provisional 1979 data indicate a 40 percent decline in death rates from stroke in the nine years since 1970. In a recent review of stroke epidemiology, Ostfeld (1980) concluded that the rather extensive diffusion during the early 1970s of more effective antihypertensive treatment might well have played a substantial role in the stroke mortality decline. Personal health services are the vehicles for antihypertensive treatment. Stroke has been a sufficiently common cause of death among the elderly in the United States to view a reduction as a major health improvement. Since a number of individuals with hypertension remain untreated, it would seem that further reductions in mortality could be achieved through additional medical intervention.

A striking decline has been taking place in mortality from heart disease, the leading cause of death among people over age fifty. Since the late 1960s, death rates have dropped by more than 20 percent in most age × sex × race subgroups. While there is a great deal of uncertainty and controversy over the factors primarily responsible for the decline (see Stallones 1980), there is at least a reasonable possibility that the improved management of hypertension and of heart disease itself have been involved (Feinleib, forthcoming).

In considering some illustrative writings of the economists, we must differentiate their work from that of the more extreme critics of medicine who deny the value of basic health services. Economists, in general, see significant health benefits derived from basic medical and health services. Indeed, as the economists Lee and Alexander Benham (1975) attest, "If all hospital and physician services were eliminated the health status of the population almost certainly would decline substantially."

Economists, in general, then, do not question the value of basic health services but, for the most part, are asking what impact on health would be produced by *additional increments* of health services, especially when compared with the value of such other possible inputs as nutrition and health education. For example, in 1969, Auster, Leveson and Sarachek wrote: "If the production process is viewed as one that changes the health status of the population, medical services must be considered an intermediate product in the 'production' of health . . . we would like to determine the benefits of medical care and compare them with cost, to arrive at judgments as to whether additional expenditures are warranted." Analyzing age-adjusted death rates and health expenditures, Auster et al. (1969) produced economic models which "indicate that a 1 percent increase in the quantity of medical services is associated with a reduction in mortality of 0.1 percent."

Other findings are in the same direction. On the basis of estimates of production function parameters derived from 1968–73 mortality data, Hadley (1981) concludes that increases in medical care result in some increased longevity. "For all age and sex groups other than middle-aged males, a 10 percent increase in medical care was estimated to reduce mortality rates by about 1.5 percent; for white males, 45 to 64 years old, the impact was about twice as large, and for black males, 45 to 64, about half as large."

Hadley further compares the effectiveness of medical care in reducing mortality rates with alternative interventions. He estimates that averting one death for at least one year by boosting medical expenditures would cost about $85,000 in 1970 dollars. By contrast, he calculates that reducing cigarette consumption via public and private programs would result in a cost per death averted of only $9,000.

Some economists, recognizing the limits of data based only on mortality, have attempted to employ more refined measures in assessing the impact of medical services on health. For example, Newhouse and Friedlander (1977) used six indicators of health including cholesterol level, blood pressure, and periodontal index and found no systematic relationship between these measures of health and the amount of health resources in some thirty-nine metropolitan areas in the United States.

Lee and Alexandra Benham (1975) also employed measures of health status other than mortality to appraise "The Impact of Incremental Medical Services on Health Status, 1963-1970." Using data from national surveys conducted by the Center for Health Administration Studies between 1963 and 1970, they related changes in medical utilization across population groups to changes in health status of those groups. Their findings, however, were "not consistent with the view that increased utilization of medical services was associated with improved health status from 1963 to 1970."

The Benhams were aware that the indexes they examined "measure only a part of health status and neglect some very important components." But it is not obvious that unmeasured components would show improvements with increments in medical care. Thus, their results were qualitatively similar to the earlier studies using mortality indexes as measures of health status. They conclude convincingly that their "results should tend to shift the burden of evidence more to those who argue, either explicitly or implicitly, that providing more medical services will raise health levels. While concern about equity of access might be satisfied, improvements in the level or distribution of health will not necessarily follow." Indeed, "increased expenditures by government or medical services can be further counterproductive in that they draw resources away from other more effective programs."

We agree that those who maintain that increments in medical care do good must provide the evidence for this popularly perceived proposition. But the use of easily available data such as mortality statistics and health survey data which were not collected to test the proposition at issue as a means of refuting that care has a beneficial impact is akin to looking for the lost wallet under the lamppost because that is where the light is.

In an effort to respond to the charge that medical care has little impact, Beeson reviewed changes in a host of medical therapeutic efforts during the past half century. He compared treatments recommended in the first (1927) and the fourteenth (1975) editions of the multiauthored *Textbook of Medicine* (Beeson 1980). He employed a ten-point rating scale running from 1 and 2, recommended treatments now regarded as valueless or no effective treatments available, to 9 and 10, effective treatments in most circumstances or effective preventive treatments. He found that the category 1 rating, where the mode of therapy was either useless or harmful, was eliminated in "no fewer than 74 instances." On the other hand, when compared to 1927, an appreciable number of interventions are reported to exhibit increased effectiveness. Beeson notes that the improvements range over the entire spectrum of internal medicine. "These improvements have resulted from various approaches, including better drugs, better surgery, and new therapies that depend on neither of these agencies." He concludes that "a patient today is likely to be treated more effectively, to be returned to normal activity more quickly, and to have a better chance of survival than fifty years ago. These advances are independent of such factors as better housing, better nutrition, or health education."

Beeson acknowledges that his method is largely subjective and that his assessments need to meet more rigorous and objective examination. Nonetheless, in focusing on specific therapies and in considering dependent variables other than mortality, with specific populations at risk, Beeson (1980) and McDermott (1978) are closer to the appropriate strategies for evaluating the effectiveness of medical care than those writers who have relied upon more gross, macro, demographic and historical types of data and who have focused on mortality and, only to a limited extent, used morbidity as a major criterion in assessing the impact of medical care.

Although some critics have made important contributions to our understanding of the relationship between medical care and health (McKeown 1976, 1978; Fuchs 1975, 1978; Benham 1975), there are several limitations to most of the existing literature which attempts to assess the contribution of health care to health. First, the analyses tend to be based on generic or macro levels of data in which attempts are made to ascertain whether there is a relationship between expenditures for utilization of services for an undifferentiated population and improvement in health without other variables being controlled. When there is focus upon a specific disease, the analyses tend to be gross and the particular populations at risk are not specified or delineated.

Logically, it is possible that medical care is in fact making an appreciable difference for some segments of the population even with regard to mortality and morbidity, but that the influence of social, environmental, and behavioral factors overwhelms those positive influences. It is not possible to ascertain whether this is true in most of the general historical and demographic analyses or the gross relationships relating expenditures and utilization with mortality and morbidity with little separation and control of the relevant variables. Assessing the impact of health care on health status requires much more rigorous prospective studies with clearly delineated populations, health indicators, and types of intervention. Gordis (1973), who compared different census tracts with special programs for children with census tracts without these programs, provides an example of one type of necessary investigation. Rheumatic fever decreased 60 percent in those tracts where the programs existed but remained unchanged in the areas where the programs were nonexistent.

Moreover, there is seldom effort to differentiate between the following four components of health care: (1) the technology of health care; (2) the intensity and quality of the technology; (3) the organization of health care; and (4) the methods of financing health care. Variation in these components of health care may produce variation in health status for some segments of the population. Although many of the critics are somewhat ambivalent about the value of health care—and at times make some very favorable assessments—they tend, as we have noted, to focus primarily on mortality outcomes. This criterion, as McDermott (1978) suggests, may be useful in assessing the overall impact of a society or large health system but may be less useful in assessing the patient-physician encounter. Aggregate national data are insensitive to the benefits of personal health services, and McDermott suggests examples of the benefits of medical interventions: The fifty-year-old man with rheumatoid arthritis who is spared pain and incapacity; the sixty-year-old man who has suffered cardiac failure who can live productively a few additional years; a seventy-year-old woman whose cataracts have been removed who achieves better vision; the forty-year-old salesman who no longer suffers pain, discomfort, and distraction from ear and sinus infection; the sixty-year-old woman who is living a productive life relatively free of discomfort even while she is afflicted with ovarian cancer; and the forty-five-year-old woman who has peace of mind in learning that the lump in her breast is benign.

Critics often misjudge the major function or contribution of health care. They are not sufficiently aware of its social dimension. In their avidity to advance biomedical research, the expansion of sophisticated technology and the extension of services, all kinds of people—physicians, legislators, health advocates, and government administrators—have made exaggerated claims about the ability of medicine to eradicate disease and extend life. In contrast, most serious students believe the gains have been more modest but that the capacity of health care to extend life, cure disease, and modify morbidity has expanded somewhat over the past few decades with regard to such specific conditions as kidney disease, hypertension, burns, and trauma. (It would be interesting to compare deaths from similar wounds among soldiers in the two world wars, the Korean War, and the Vietnam War.) A crucial criterion for evaluating medical or health care—and one which sociologists especially would embrace—is the contribution it makes to the individual's quality of life, level of functioning, or ability to perform his or her social roles (Najman and Levine). Rene Dubos (1981) stated this position most eloquently:

> What is Health? Theoretically, health is the complete absence of organic and mental disease. But for most of us, health is the ability to function. To be healthy does not mean that you are free of all disease; it means that you can function, do what you want to do and become what you want to become.

In keeping with a social rather than a distinctively biological view of health, we should ask the following types of questions:

To what extent does medical care provide palliative measures that reduce pain, suffering, and discomfort arising from illness?

To what extent does medical care provide reassurance to the patients and their families with respect to the presence or absence of a definitive diagnosis? Does reduction of uncertainty about the cause of illness have any health, let alone human, value?

To what extent is medical care able to maintain sick people at home with their families and in the community as against relegation to an institution? To what extent is medical care able to permit sick people to perform their normal social roles as workers, spouses, friends, citizens?

To what extent does medical care compensate for negative impacts of the larger social system, e.g., exposure to hazards of dangerous occupations, poor housing, automobile accidents, food and tobacco policies? To what extent does medical care provide useful advice and help to promote preventive health behavior with regard to smoking, diet, and exercise?

We are not concerned here with the social functioning of medical care, as elucidated by Judith Shuval (1970). Our concern is the manifest purposes of medical care as measured by the precise works of such investigators as Katz et al. (1972), Patrick and Bush (1973), Stewart et al. (1978), Donald et al. (1978), and Bergner and Gilson (1979) to maintain human functioning in the face of illness; and to the direct assessments of needs for medical care on a population basis in the work of Trussell and Elinson (1955) and Wolfe and Carr (1977). It may be that the reason the products of these investigators are not often used (and rarely even cited by critics of medical care) is that such data are not available on a national basis, since in the main they have developed in geographically defined communities or special population groups. Mortality statistics have the advantage of being available nationally and internationally, as well as for small geographic units.

From a policy point of view, there is danger that in identifying and constantly emphasizing the importance of social and behavioral factors in producing disease, without the necessary strong caveats and cautions, we give increased justification for neglecting the health-care needs of millions who suffer from poverty, chronic illness, and the infirmities which attend growing old (Knowles 1977; Strauss 1978). A more circumspect approach would be to continue to provide funds for the necessary services for the poor, the sick, the disabled and to decrease these funds slowly and gradually *as* and *if* the fruits of a new socially preventive policy became evident. As the new image emerges that medical care does no good, the preventive factors will be given lip service while the legitimate day-to-day health-care needs of the poor, the sick, and disabled will be neglected. Eisenberg (1977) posed the issue in explicit moral terms: "Even if we could deliver on the uncertain promises of prevention, we have not the right to abandon those who are already ill and in need of care that they cannot obtain."

If we expand the role of health practitioners to include health education, there may be need for more not less health care. But we should remember what we have learned from Dubos (1959)—that sickness and disability will, in varying degrees, always be with us and that health care in all societies will always have to address the negative consequences of adaptation to existing and new social and environmental influences. Even under optimal arrangements, even where preventive care is integrated with curative care, the overwhelming concerns of health-care providers will be providing not cure but care.

Sociologists have used their critical perspective in assessing the corporate invasion into the health field, in criticizing the allocation of resources, and in questioning the extent of medical dominance; they have noted the positive constructive problem-solving efforts which people pursue in their own self-help and mutual aid groups, their lay health culture, and even in disregarding the advice of health practitioners. It may also be time for us to ask whether we have probed deeply enough into the reasons behind the almost universal search for health care by sophisticated people throughout the world. Such persistence is evident in every developed society. Even refugees from the Soviet system, while critical of the system, value the accessibility of health care in that society. Kohn and White (1976) found, in their international study of health care, that despite enormous variations in the political and social complexion of such societies and their health systems as Yugoslavia, Argentina, Great Britain, Brazil, the United States and Canada, there is consistency in the population's search for the services of physicians and other health practitioners. While other factors played a part, perceived morbidity was the most important determinant of physician use.

While use alone is, of course, not sufficient evidence that medical care does any good, and a high percentage of physician visits have no discernible organic basis, we may not have given sufficient attention to the value people place on assurance, peace of mind, and other psychological and social benefits derived from medical care.

It is important to recognize the potentially human side of health care, as Fuchs, a critic of the system, does most lyrically in pointing up the analogy between medical care and religion. He states:

> The analogy I have drawn between medical care and religion may be regarded as disparagement of care by those who share Marx's opinion of religion as the "opium of the people." But it is well to remember that in the very same passage Marx also called religion the "heart of a heartless world . . . the spirit of spiritless conditions." Despite the many criticisms that can be raised about medicine today—its high cost, its preoccupation with technology, its fragmentation into specialties and subspecialties—the truth is that for many people it is the "heart of a heartless world . . . the spirit of spiritless condition."
> [Fuchs 1978, p. 13]

REFERENCES

ABEL-SMITH, B. 1976. *Value for money in health services.* New York: St. Martin's Press.

AIKEN, L. H., and FREEMAN, H. E. 1980. Medical sociology and science and technology in medicine. In *A guide to the culture of science, technology and medicine*, ed. P. T. Durbin, Chap. 8. New York: Free Press.

AUSTER, R.; LEVESON, I,; and SARACHEK, D. 1969. The production of health, an exploratory study, *Journal of Human Resources* 4: 412–36.

BEESON, P. B. 1980. Changes in medical therapy during the past half century. *Medicine* 59 (no. 2): 79–99.

BENHAM, L, and BENHAM, A. 1975. The impact of incremental medical services on health status, 1963–1970. In *Equity in health services: empirical analyses in social policy*, ed. R. Andersen, J. Kravits, and O. W. Anderson. Cambridge, Mass.: Ballinger.

BERGNER, M. et al. 1979. The sickness impact profile: conceptual formulation and methodology for the development of a health status measure. *Sociomedical Health Indicators*, ed. J. Elinson and A. E. Siegmann, Chap. 1. Farmingdale, N.Y.: Baywood.

BRADBURN, N. M. 1975. *The stucture of psychological well-being.* Chicago: Aldine.

———. 1977. The measurement of psychological well-being. In *Health goals and health indicators*, ed. J. Elinson, A. Mooney, and A. E. Siegmann, Chap. 6. Boulder, Colo.: Westview Press.

———, and CAPLOVITZ, D. 1965. *Reports on happiness: a pilot study of behavior related to mental health.* Chicago: Aldine.

CARLSON, R. J. 1975. *The end of medicine.* New York: Wiley.

CARR, W., and WOLFE, S. 1979. Unmet needs as sociomedical health indicators. In *Sociomedical health indicators*, ed. J. Elinson and A. E. Siegmann, Chap. 2. Farmingdale, N.Y.: Baywood.

COCHRANE, A. L. 1972. *Effectiveness and efficiency.* London: Nuffield Provincial Hospital Trust.

Commission on Chronic Illness 1957. *Chronic illness in a large city.* Chronic illness in the United States, vol. 6. Cambridge, Mass.: Harvard University Press.

DONALD, C. A.; WARE, J. E.; JR.; BROOK R. H.; and DAVIES-AVERY, A. 1978. *Conceptualization and measurement of health for adults in the health insurance study: social health*, vol. 4. Santa Monica, Calif.: Rand.

DUBOS, R. 1959. *The mirage of health.* New York: Harper and Row.

———. 1981. Interview reported in *Modern Maturity*, August–September 1981, p. 35.

Dupuy, H. J. 1973. Developmental rationale, substantive derivative and conceptual relevance of the general well-being schedule. Unpublished working paper. Hyattsville, Md.: National Center for Health Statistics.

Eisenberg, L. 1977. The perils of prevention: a cautionary note. *New England Journal of Medicine* 297 (no. 22): 1230–1232.

Elinson, J. 1974. Toward sociomedical health indicators. *Social Indicators Research* 1: 59–71.

———. 1977. Insensitive health statistics and the dilemma of the HSAs. *American Journal of Public Health* 67 (no. 5): 417–18.

———; Mooney, A.; and Siegmann, A. E., eds. 1977. *Health goals and health indicators: policy, planning and evaluation.* Boulder, Colo.: Westview Press.

Elinson, J., and Siegmann, A. E., eds. 1979. *Sociomedical health indicators.* Farmingdale, N.Y.: Baywood.

Erickson, P. *Clearinghouse on health indexes.* Hyattsville, Md.: National Center for Health Statistics.

Feinleib, M. The changing pattern of ischemic heart disease mortality and morbidity. *Journal of Cardiovascular Medicine,* forthcoming.

Fuchs, V. R. 1975. *Who shall live? Health, economics and social choice.* New York: Basic Books.

———. 1978. Economics, health and post-industrial society. The E. S. Woodward Lectures in Economics, University of British Columbia, Vancouver, B.C.

Gordis, L. 1973. Effectiveness of comprehensive-care programs in preventing rheumatic fever. *New England Journal of Medicine* 289 (no. 7): 331.

Hadley, J. 1981. Does medical care affect health? An economic analysis of geographic variations in mortality rates. Washington, D.C.: Urban Institute.

Horrobin, D. F. 1980. *Medical hubris: a reply to Ivan Illich.* Montreal: Eden Press.

Illich, I. 1975. *Medical nemesis: the expropriation of health.* New York: Random House.

Katz, S., and Akpom, C. A. 1979. A measure of primary sociobiological functions. In *Sociomedical health indicators,* ed. J. Elinson and A. E. Siegmann, Chap. 8. Farmingdale, N.Y.: Baywood.

Katz, S.; Ford, A. B.; Downs, T. D.; et al. 1972. *Effects of continued care: a study of chronic illness in the home.* DHEW pub. no. (HSM)73–3010. Rockville, Md.: Dept. of Health, Education and Welfare.

Knowles, J. H. 1977. Responsibility for health. Editorial, *Science* 198 (no. 4322): 1103.

———. 1978. Letter to the editor in response to letter of Anselm Strauss. *Science* 199 (no. 4329) 597–98.

Kohn, R., and White, K. L. 1976. *Health care: an international study.* London: Oxford University Press.

McDermott, W. 1978. Medicine: the public good and one's own. In *Perspectives in biology and medicine,* vol. 21, no. 2. pp. 123–32. Chicago: University of Chicago Press.

McKeown, T. 1976. *The role of medicine, dream, mirage or nemesis?,* London: Nuffield Provincial Hospital Trust.

———. 1978. Determinants of health. *Human Nature* 1 (no. 4): 60–67.

McKinlay, J. B. 1981. From "promising report" to "standard procedure": seven stages in the career of a medical innovation. *Milbank Memorial Fund Quarterly Health and Society* 59 (no. 3): 374–411.

———, and McKinlay, S. M. 1977. The questionable effect of medical measures on the decline of mortality in the United States in the twentieth century. *Health and Society* 55 (no. 3): 405–28.

———. 1979. Examining trends in the nation's health. Paper presented at APHA Annual Meeting, New York, 1979.

Najman, J., and Levine, S. A meta-analysis of studies which evaluate the impact of health care on the quality of life. *Social Science and Medicine,* forthcoming.

Newhouse, J. P., and Friedlander, M. J. 1977. *The relationship between medical resource and measures of health: some additional evidence.* Rand Corporation Document R–2066–HEW. Santa Monica, Calif.: Rand.

OSTFELD, A. M. 1980. A review of stroke epidemiology. *Epidemiological Reviews* 2: 136–52, 350.

PATRICK, D. L.; BUSH, J. W.; and CHEN, M. M. 1973a Toward an operational definition of health. *Journal of Health and Social Behavior* 14: 6–23.

———. 1973b. Methods for measuring levels of well-being for a health status index. *Health Services Research* 8 (no. 3): 228–45.

POWLES, J. 1973. On the limitations of modern medicine. *Social Science and Medicine* 1: 1–30.

SCHELLING, T. C. 1968. The life you save may be your own. In *Problems in public expenditure analysis*, ed. S. Chase, pp. 127–62. Washington, D.C.: Brookings Institution.

SHUVAL, J. T.; ANTONOVSKY, A.; and DAVIES, M. F. 1970. *Social functions of medical practice.* San Francisco, Calif.: Jossey-Bass.

STALLONES, R. A. 1980. The rise and fall of ischemic heart disease. *Scientific American* 243 (no, 5): 53–59.

STARR, P. 1974. *The discarded army: veterans after Vietnam.* New York: Charterhouse.

———. 1976. The politics of therapeutic nihilism. *Hastings Center Report,* October 1976, pp. 24–30.

STEWART, A. L.; WARE, J. E., JR.; BROOK, R. H.; and DAVIES-AVERY, A. 1978. *Conceptualization and measurement of health for adults in the health insurance study: physical health in terms of functioning,* vol. 2. Santa Monica, Calif.: Rand.

STRAUSS, A. L. 1978. Letter to the editor in response to John H. Knowles's editorial, "Responsibility for Health." *Science* 199 (no. 4329): 597.

THOMAS, L. 1972. *Aspects of biomedical science policy.* Washington, D.C.: Institute of Medicine.

TRUSSELL, R. E., and Elinson, J. 1955. Measuring needs for medical services. In *Fourth conference on administrative medicine,* ed. G. S. Stevenson. New York: Josiah Macy, Jr., Foundation.

———. 1959. *Chronic illness in a rural area.* Chronic illness in the United States, Vol. 3. Cambridge, Mass.: Harvard University Press.

WILLIAMS, R. L. 1979. Measuring the effectiveness of perinatal medical care. *Medical Care* 17 (no. 2): 95–110.

WOLFE, S.; CARR, W.; NESER, W. B.; and REVO, L. T. 1977. Unmet health care needs and health care policy. In *Health goals and health indicators,* ed. J. Elinson, A. Mooney and A. E. Siegmann, Chap. 3. Boulder, Colo.: Westview Press.

IV

THE HEALTH
OCCUPATIONS

Chapter 19

Nurses

Linda H. Aiken

OVER THE PAST 40 YEARS, rapidly increasing knowledge and new technologies have reshaped both medical and nursing practice. Nurses, traditionally concerned with the provision of comfort, psychological support, and assistance with activities of daily living, are increasingly involved in the direct application of complex modern medical technologies to patient care.

The institutions where most nurses practice have also been transformed, and nurses' roles and responsibilities have changed accordingly. Hospitals, the major employer of nurses, have evolved from small community institutions managed by nurses or voluntary groups to multimillion-dollar enterprises employing a broad array of personnel and providing a wide range of medical and social services. The nursing home, a relatively new health-care institution that has emerged over the past twenty-five years, also will present an increasing challenge to the nursing profession.

Disease patterns have shifted from a predominance of acute infectious diseases to chronic illnesses. New organizational arrangements are required to provide appropriate long-term care for these illnesses. As a result of this need, more autonomous roles have emerged for nurses, particularly in ambulatory settings, in the provision of care to the chronically ill and the increasing numbers of frail elderly.

These shifts in the patterns of medical care have occurred in the context of dramatic social change. Changing attitudes regarding women's participation in careers outside the home have resulted in significant modification of nurses' career expectations. Many nurses now view their employment as lifelong career commitments rather than as temporary work to generate a second income, and consequently the majority are seeking identification as professionals with career advancement opportunities.

Given these many changes in medicine and society, it is not surprising that nursing is in a state of ferment. New responsibilities for nurses, new career expectations, and the changing needs of sick people all require modifications in the traditional relationships between nurses and physicians, and within the institutions in which nurses work (Brown 1970). These changes will not come easily. Relationships between health professionals and organizational arrangements for the provision of health care are deeply embedded in traditions which are not easily modified. Many of the issues facing nursing can best be understood by examining nursing's origins and history, and its present position within the larger social context.

Historical Perspective

Modern nursing dates back to mid–nineteenth-century England. English voluntary hospitals of that time were disorganized, staffed by unskilled and undisciplined workers, and generally held in low esteem. Florence Nightingale accepted the challenge of recruiting, organizing, and training nurses as professionals who could bring order to the hospitals. Nightingale believed that nurses capable of skilled work and responsible ward management in hospitals would have to be recruited from the better educated classes (Woodham-Smith 1951). To legitimize the work of nursing, she drew heavily on the well-respected traditions of religious education and the military. Young nurses motivated by a sense of dedication and service to mankind worked long hours for few economic rewards under strict discipline with total obedience expected (Abel-Smith 1960; Jacox 1978).

Lavinia Dock, one of nursing's most distinguished early educators, stated in 1893:

> Absolute and unquestioning obedience must be the foundation of the nurse's work, and to this end complete subordination of the individual to the work as a whole is as necessary for her as for the soldier. [Dock 1966, p. 96]

The impact of these traditions can still be seen today in the organization of hospital nursing and in the interactions between nurses and physicians.

In the early medical division of labor, nurses had two primary responsibilities that have been carried forward over the years. First, nursing evolved as an ancillary medical occupation responsible for maintaining the comfort and well-being of the sick, as well as giving general assistance to physicians (Freidson 1970). Second, nursing was involved in the management of hospital wards (Reeder and Mauksch 1979).

Nightingale's reform of the English voluntary hospital had two major objectives—the training of nurses to provide skilled care and the creation of an efficient bureaucracy to manage the day-to-day operation of hospitals. Nightingale, borrowing from the organizational traditions of the military and religious orders, instituted a rigid bureaucracy in hospitals. The nursing hierarchy, headed by a matron, became the administrative structure (Glaser 1966). Physicians of the time did not pay much attention to the management of hospitals, and the occupation of hospital administration was not to develop until much later. Thus, the nursing hierarchy organized and administered the hospital in addition to caring for patients, giving nurses important responsibilities, particularly when considered in the context of the roles of women at the time. Nurses have retained many of the managerial functions in hospitals over the years, although the nurse matrons who once governed hospitals have now been replaced by hospital administrators with special training.

Nursing has been traditionally identified as women's work (Simpson and Simpson 1969). This is partly due to the caring nature of nursing, since caring is commonly believed to be a feminine quality. The connotations of service, charity, and obedience inherent in early nursing roles also fit the female stereotype

(Mauksch 1966). Sex-role stereotyping of nurses has persisted despite a shift in nursing roles from the nurturant to the more technological. In the view of many, sex discrimination is one of nursing's most pervasive problems (Cleland 1971).

In contrast to the entrepreneurial practice styles developed by the medical profession, nursing evolved as a salaried, institution-based occupation (Strauss 1966). Studies of nursing, as well as other predominantly female occupations such as teaching and social work, indicate that women have generally sought salaried employment in bureaucratic organizations (Simpson and Simpson 1969). Even women physicians have sought salaried employment in greater proportions than their male counterparts (Wunderman 1980). This preference has been attributed to women's interrupted career patterns, to their family responsibilities, and to prevailing social attitudes. As attitudes and realities have changed, nurses have demonstrated a greater interest in the establishment of entrepreneurial practices, but this has, in turn, created problems for them. Medicine's traditional dominance over access to diagnostic services, hospitals, referrals, and third-party reimbursement has created an inevitable area of conflict between medicine and nursing.

Four factors emerge from an analysis of nursing's history which influence nursing today and may continue to be important in the future:

- Nursing developed as an ancillary occupation supportive to physicians. Nurses gained much of their professional status and legitimacy from functions delegated by physicians, but nurses' dependence on physicians also hinders their quest for greater autonomy.
- Nursing is primarily an institution-based occupation—rather than an independent, entrepreneurial profession like medicine—and nurses answer not only to physicians but also to institution administrators.
- Nursing is predominantly a female occupation. Despite a shift from caring and nurturant functions to more technological functions akin to those associated with male roles in other occupations, nursing has retained a feminine image, and is subject to sex-role stereotyping and sex discrimination in professional relationships and labor practices.
- The association of early nursing education with religious orders has reinforced a continuing expectation of service, dedication, and charity. These attributes are no longer valued as highly in our culture, and no longer serve as sufficient motivating forces to recruit and retain professional nurses in today's world.

Nurses and Nursing Education

Nurses are the largest single health-provider group. There are close to 1.7 million licensed registered nurses in the United States—more than three times the number of practicing physicians. Most nurses are women. While the number of male nurses has doubled since 1972, men constitute only 2 percent of all nurses. Slightly more than 6 percent of nurses have minority racial or ethnic backgrounds (Moses and Roth 1979).

Contrary to popular opinion, most nurses are employed as nurses, and nursing has one of the highest labor force participation rates of any predominantly female occupation. The widespread belief that significant numbers of nurses are employed in nonnursing fields is not substantiated by employment surveys. Nationally, fewer than 57,000 nurses, representing less than 4 percent of all nurses, are working in nonnursing jobs (Johnson 1980, p. 6). Moreover, 75 percent of nurses are actively employed, an employment rate comparable to that for all American men, and considerably higher than the 50 percent employment rate for American women (U.S. Bureau of the Census 1980, p. 394).

Trends in labor force participation of nurses have generally paralleled changes in the work patterns of American women. Younger nurses are staying in the labor force longer; the median age of employed nurses is thirty-eight years. Most are married and half have children under seventeen years of age.

Nursing Education

Nurses are a heterogeneous group educationally. There are three generic education programs for registered nurses: three-year hospital diploma schools, two-year community college programs, and four-year baccalaureate degree programs in colleges and universities. In 1977, the highest educational credential of the majority of nurses (67 percent) was the hospital nursing school diploma. Close to 18 percent had baccalaureate degrees, and 11 percent held associate degrees. An additional 4 percent held master's or doctoral degrees. In addition, there were 550,000 licensed vocational or practical nurses who have had approximately one year of training. Over half of all practical-nurse training programs are conducted in trade, technical, or vocational schools, one-quarter in community colleges, and one-quarter in hospitals (National League for Nursing 1981).

There is little differentiation by employers among registered nurses from the three types of educational programs. And, while licensed practical nurses are required by law to work under the supervision of a registered nurse, it is difficult for consumers or other health professionals to distinguish registered nurses from practical nurses, or even aides, and to identify nurses with advanced preparation.

Without restrictions on licensure, employers are able to substitute one nurse for another without regard to educational preparation, resulting in continuing substitution from the least-educated group at a time when nursing is attempting to raise educational standards. For this reason, Freidson (1970, p. 66) has characterized nursing as an "incompletely closed" occupation.

Multiple educational levels within nursing have created a difficult problem for nurses as they seek increased responsibilities, greater autonomy, and higher status. It is almost impossible to differentiate nurses who have taken on the more technically based functions of medicine requiring considerable clinical judgment from those who are following orders without substantial independent decision-making.

In response, the nursing leadership has attempted to standardize nursing education by setting the minimum entry-level educational requirement for professional nurses at the baccalaureate level. This recommendation emerged as early as 1923 in the Goldmark Report,*The Study of Nursing and Nursing Education* (Committee for the Study of Nursing Education 1923) followed by other reports and commissions over the subsequent forty years (Brown 1948; ANA 1965; National Commission for the Study of Nursing and Nursing Education 1970; ANA 1979a).

The American Nurses' Association (ANA), the professional association representing nurses, has set 1985 as the target year for requiring the baccalaureate degree as the minimum education for professional nursing (American Nurses' Association 1979a). Since a minority of nurses hold baccalaureate degrees, this issue has been widely debated both within nursing and among employers of nurses.

Despite the controversy over entry-level education requirements, future patterns are emerging. Enrollments in hospital diploma programs have declined dramatically. By 1985, diploma schools will account for only 15 percent of new graduates, with associate degree programs and baccalaureate programs contributing 48 percent and 37 percent respectively (Johnson 1980). Given the phasing out of diploma schools, the debate now centers around the future of associate degree programs.

The closing of hospital diploma programs and the legitimization by the profession of the baccalaureate degree might have propelled nursing toward standardization of nursing credentials and the elimination of multiple training programs. However, largely unanticipated by the nursing establishment, the community college movement rapidly developed the capacity to train large numbers of nurses.

Proponents of associate degree education for nurses perceived a continuum of nursing functions, with a natural division between "semiprofessional or technical" functions and professional services (Montag 1951). The two-year associate degree graduate was prepared to provide bedside nursing care but not to take on administrative or teaching responsibilities.

The development of associate degree programs was a mixed blessing for advocates of professionalism. Although community colleges were numerous enough to provide a large supply of new nurses, and therefore to substitute for hospitals as the source of education for most nurses, community colleges were associated with vocational education. Although nursing labeled these graduates "technical" nurses to avoid confusion with professional nurses educated at the baccalaureate level, no changes have been made in eligibility for licensure. In addition, the designation "technical nurse" is not consistent with prevalent nursing roles. The present division of labor within nursing is not amenable to separating technical from professional tasks except in administrative roles (McClure 1978).

Baccalaureate graduates will still be in the minority in 1985, and the future of associate degree programs is unclear. Nevertheless, a national trend has been set in motion. The dominant training institution throughout nursing's history, the hospital, has been replaced by institutions of higher education. And, in 1977, one out of every ten nurses was working on a post-RN college degree (Moses and Roth 1979). Preliminary data from the 1980 national survey of nurses indicate that between 1977 and 1980 the number of nurses with baccalaureate degrees increased from 18 to 35 percent of the total as a result of practicing nurses continuing their education (Moses and Levine 1982). At this rate, nursing may reach its objective of baccalaureate education faster than has been anticipated.

A major problem in nursing is the failure of nurses to define clearly what they do and their contributions to patient care. Unlike physicians, who responded to the expansion of knowledge and technology by developing an elaborate structure of specialties and subspecialties, nurses have remained generalists and are perceived by employers as being interchangeable. This has created a twofold problem. First, it is becoming increasingly difficult to remain a generalist in medical care and to maintain sufficient expertise and command over the demands of professional nursing practice. Second, employers' assumptions about the substitutability of nurses across a wide range of tasks has resulted in staffing patterns which interfere with nurses establishing continuity of contact with their patients (Marram, Schlegel, Bevis 1974). The result has been that patients, and attending physicians, have contact with too many different nurses to develop an appreciation for their special expertise.

Nursing, like medicine, is beginning to institutionalize a specialty structure which will give nurses the opportunity to develop greater expertise in more limited specialty practices to facilitate the assumption of greater degrees of clinical decision-making. Specialty practice should lead to new arrangements for staffing institutions which will allow nurses to maintain greater continuing contact with patients. And formal certification, if successfully implemented, may result in improved remuneration and career advancement opportunities.

For the most part, nursing clinical specialties have been organized around medical specialties, but with a differentiation between hospital-based and ambulatory practice. Those in hospital practice are called clinical nurse specialists and usually have master's degrees (Lewis 1970). Their roles include direct care of patients with complex needs, collaborative practice with physicians, and provision of clinical consultation to staff nurses. Many hold academic appointments and clinical positions in nursing service. Clinical nurse specialists are concentrated in high-technology areas such as coronary care, heart surgery, renal dialysis and transplantation, and neonatology. In 1977, approximately eight thousand nurses were employed as clinical specialists (Moses and Roth 1979). This is a rapidly growing area, with almost 40 percent of all recent master's-prepared nurses choosing careers as clinical specialists.

Nurses in specialty practice in ambulatory care are usually nurse practitioners or nurse midwives. Many have master's degrees; all have advanced post-RN clinical training (Sultz, Henry, and Sullivan 1979; Bliss and Cohen 1977). There are currently twenty thousand nurse practitioners and approximately fifteen hundred certified nurse midwives.

Specialty certification was introduced to nursing as early as 1945 by the American Association of Nurse Anesthetists, but the ANA did not launch its certification program until 1973. The certification program of the ANA is the largest in nursing and currently certifies clinical proficiency in fifteen areas, including both nurse practitioners and clincial nurse specialists. Many nursing specialty associations have established their own mechanisms for awarding credentials, including the nurse midwives, critical-care nurses, and occupational-health nurses. The proliferation of certification programs reflects the fragmentation which pervades most aspects of nursing, and the certification process has been undermined to some degree by the lack of consistency with regard to eligibility, standards, and testing procedures.

The ANA is undertaking a major effort to gain control of certification with the intent of giving it greater legitimacy with employers (ANA 1979b). Nurse practitioners have received increased status and remuneration as a result of their specialty training, in addition to improving the quality of care provided to patients. However, legitimization of their advanced preparation may be more a response to changes in state nurse practice acts than to specialty certification. Certification of hospital-based nurse specialists has not, for the most part, been acknowledged by employers in terms of higher salaries or innovative roles. Even intensive-care nurses who are in short supply and by definition have special expertise receive salaries comparable to nurses in generalist roles (Donovan 1980). The development of a specialty structure in nursing should give nurses the opportunity to develop greater expertise in the care of patients. Greater expertise will lead to the assumption of more responsibility for clinical decision-making and improved remuneration and opportunities for career advancement necessary to attract and retain highly qualified nurses in the profession.

Nursing Practice In Hospitals

In 1859, Florence Nightingale defined nurses' major responsibility for personal health care as "putting the patient in the best condition for nature to act upon him" (Nightingale 1946 [facsimile of 1859 first edition]). More than a century later, a new definition has evolved which represents the changing nature of modern nursing practice: "Nursing is the diagnosis and treatment of human responses to actual or potential health problems" (ANA 1980). Although the underlying theme in both definitions is similar—protecting and enhancing the individual's natural defenses against illness—the recent definition reflects nurses' increasing responsibilities in clinical assessment and treatment which have developed since World War II.

In the late forties, the rapid growth of medical technology and knowledge resulted in the transfer of a significant amount of technologic practice and patient care responsibility from physicians to nurses. Nurses took primary responsibility for many diagnostic and therapeutic procedures formerly provided by physicians. Intramuscular injections, insertion of Foley catheters, and the administration of intravenous fluids and medications are but a few of the therapeutic procedures which have passed from medicine into the realm of standard nursing practice.

In Nightingale's era, visual observation, touch, sound, and smell were nurses' main assessment tools. Today, nurses monitor the electrical impulses of the heart, measure blood pressure through special lines placed in arteries and veins, assess intracranial pressure by special monitoring devices, examine chests and hearts with stethoscopes, the inner ear with the otoscope, and culture throats, wounds, and urine to determine the presence or absence of bacterial infections. Nurses are also increasingly involved in the direct application of modern medical technologies. They maintain the life support systems of tiny, immature babies in neonatal intensive-care units as well as those of comatose adults in the medical-surgical intensive-care units. They initiate cardiopulmonary resuscitation in the event of a cardiac arrest. Specially trained nurses administer anesthesia during surgery, manage renal dialysis units, and deliver babies.

Sixty-five percent of registered nurses are employed by hospitals; nurses make up almost 20 percent of all hospital employees. Nursing service personnel, including RNs, LPNs, and aides, constitute the largest single group within hospitals. They number 2.4 million and account for close to 40 percent of all hospital employees.

While nurses' first and foremost responsibility, historically, has been the care of individual patients, they have had a variety of other roles as well. Until recently, nurses also served as hospital administrators, the coordinators of housekeeping and dietary services, and managers of patient records, and took on a variety of other tasks necessary to operate a hospital. Habenstein and Christ (1963), in a study of small rural hospitals in the late fifties, even found nurses cutting the grass.

Patient assessment and implementation of the therapeutic plan of care is the most critical nursing responsibility. Although much of the therapeutic plan is developed by physicians and jointly implemented, other parts of the plan are designed and carried out by nurses themselves. Physicians' prescriptions tend to cover use of specific technologies and drugs. Nurses specify preventive care ranging from the maintenance of intact skin, mucous membranes, muscle tone, and maximum function during illness to the prevention of catastrophic complications such as cardiac arrest. Nurses are also concerned with alleviating pain, educating patients about caring for themselves, and preparing patients and families for hospital discharge.

Patient assessment has become the most challenging part of nursing. This process involves the integration of numerous sources of information; accurate nursing assessment may make profound differences in patient outcomes. Patients in today's hospitals are sicker than ever before. Many are older and have multiple chronic illnesses. They are at high risk of potentially fatal complications. Nurses are the only constant source of continuing professional surveillance in hospitals, and their ability to detect problems and prevent crises is of ever increasing importance.

Given nurses' central role in the hospital management of sick patients, it is not surprising to find that the quality of nursing care is one of the most important factors affecting patient outcomes in hospitals (Georgopoulos and Mann 1962). The importance of nurses in high-technology care is even more dramatic. Studies of differential postoperative mortality rates between hospitals point to the qualifications and experience of the nursing staff as a major variable in determining outcomes (Moses and Mosteller 1968; Scott et al. 1976).

The nature of hospital care has changed dramatically over the past thirty years. In 1958, only 25 percent of large tertiary-care hospitals had intensive-care units; by 1976, almost all large community hospitals and many small ones had medical-surgical intensive-care units as well as coronary-care units (Russell 1979). Between 1972 and 1979 alone, the number of intensive-care beds in community hospitals increased by more than 20 percent. Changes in medical practices have led to fewer hospitalizations for those less severely ill and shorter stays for all patients. On average, therefore, those in the hospital are sicker. Hospital staff involvement per patient day increased by 19 percent between 1971 and 1978, reflecting both the increased use of technology and the sicker patients in hospitals (National Center for Health Statistics 1980, p. 104).

Institutional mechanisms for professional surveillance and clinical decision-making have become increasingly important as a result of greater severity of patient problems managed in American hospitals. Over the past thirty years, as physicians have sought a life-style more comparable to that of other American professionals, there has been a steady reduction in their work week. There are more extended periods of time when physicians are not physically present in the hospital. Nurses have assumed increased responsibility for professional supervision of patients in the absence of physicians.

This problem has been compounded by the increasing number of physicians involved in each patient's care. Specialists, by definition, focus on specific problems and the array of diagnostic and therapeutic technologies applicable to those problems, and assume more limited responsibility for integrating all aspects of patients' care and the totality of needs of patients and families. The greater the involvement of multiple specialists in the care of a hospitalized patient, the greater the need for nurses to assume an integrating function to ensure that all parts of the medical regimen fit together and that patients' safety and well-being are assured. This has become particularly important in tertiary hospitals.

The increasing demands on nurses in hospitals, which have not been paralleled by organizational and managerial arrangements that clearly recognize the new role of nurses in modern medical practice, have led nurses to be increasingly dissatisfied with hospital practice (Wandelt 1980; Fagin 1980). Three issues are the major sources of contention (Aiken 1981a):

- What is the clinical decision-making authority of the nurse and how should it relate to that of the physician?
- What is nursing's proper role in the management of hospitals, including decisions relating to total hospital resource allocation?
- How can nursing salaries and the promotions structure within the hospital appropriately reflect nurses' specialization and experience?

Clinical Decision-Making

Clinical decision-making is the major source of continuing tension between nurses and physicians in the hospital context. Nurses have been cast in roles where they frequently must make clinical decisions, some of critical life-and-death significance, but they work under institutional rules that recognize only physicians as having authority to make independent professional decisions about patients. Stein (1971) refers to this phenomenon as the "doctor-nurse game," where the nurse is to take the initiative and be responsible for making important recommendations but in a manner which offers the appearance that the recommendation has come from the physician. Much of the continuing conflict between nurses and physicians could be reduced if better agreements regarding decision-making could be achieved which appropriately recognized nurses' levels of expertise and their particular responsibilities for seriously ill patients.

Management Responsibilities

Nurses have two major roles in hospitals. One is the caring role, which involves clinical decision-making on the individual patient level. The second is the integration role, which includes hospital management at the ward level (McClure and Nelson 1982). For patients to receive optimum care, the hotel services necessary in hospitals—including housekeeping, maintenance, security, and food service—must operate within reasonable standards. And to implement the plan of care, a number of nonnursing services are involved, including pharmacy, central supply, laboratories, radiology, respiratory therapy, and patient transport services.

Despite long-standing claims from nursing that ward management is not a nursing responsibility, there is an unfilled void. The only serious attempt to fill the management void has been the introduction of unit managers, persons who assumed overall responsibility for ward management including the support services and nonprofessional nursing staff (Mercadante 1962). Unit managers were intended to be an extension of the hospital's administrative management staff. However, the unit-manager concept has not diffused widely, and although hospitals employ clerical personnel, nurses remain hospital management's representatives at the ward level.

Nurses' clinical effectiveness depends upon the adequacy of hotel and ancillary support services. However, at the ward level nurses have no authority to influence the operation of support services, and at the institutional level they do not have a decision-making role in institutional governance and resource allocation that might help correct deficiencies in the support services. Hospitals already have two interdependent lines of authority—hospital administration and the medical staff (Smith 1958). Although the medical staff is primarily concerned with the process of diagnosis and treatment, physicians legitimately intercede in the diverse functions ascribed to and assumed by the hospital when matters of patient care for which they are accountable are concerned. Nurses, who now share the accountability for patients' welfare with physicians, are seeking similar authority.

The Economics of Hospital Nursing

The salary and promotions structure in hospitals has not kept pace with nurses' changing career expectations. Salary structures in hospitals reflect the common perception that most nurses are temporary workers (Friss 1981). A recent national survey of nurses found only a $2,000-a-year difference in average salaries of beginning nurses and those with twenty years of experience (Donovan 1980). Further, many hospitals require all nurses, irrespective of skills or seniority, to rotate shifts and work weekends. The economic incentives used in industry to attract personnel to work unpopular hours have been, until recently, largely absent in hospital settings.

Health economists have observed that the labor market for nurses does not respond to changes in supply and demand (Altman 1971; Yett 1975; Sloan 1978). In recent years the acute shortage of nurses in hospitals has been of particular interest because the shortage has persisted despite extraordinary increases in the supply of nurses. The economists have one potential answer.

Nursing is among a few occupations in the American economy affected by monopsony, meaning the presence of only a few firms who employ the vast majority in a particular occupation (Feldstein 1979). Sixty-six percent of nurses work in hospitals. In most communities there are fewer than ten hospitals; many communities have only one or two hospitals. It logically follows that if nurses want to work in health care, they must, for the most part, work in those hospitals. Further, the nature of nurses' education is such that it does not seem to allow them to move easily out of nursing or health care into other positions of comparable status. In short, nurses are in a captured labor market.

Because geographic mobility of many nurses is limited by family obligations, and because there is little competition for nurses elsewhere, hospitals have not competed with each other to any extent by increasing wages. It has been the conventional wisdom that such competition will not attract additional nurses to hospitals in the community but will only increase turnover of existing nurses, causing hospital costs to rise even faster without resolving the community's nursing shortage.

This belief has predominantly applied to nurses. It has not prevailed when hospitals have sought to fill other positions. Many hospital workers have employment options in alternative industries. When shortages occur elsewhere in the economy, hospitals must match the wage rates if they want the services. Computer experts, for example, are in high demand across many industries, and workers with these skills are recruited by those willing to offer the largest salaries. The same is true of managers, electricians, accountants, and even other health professionals such as pharmacists, physical therapists, dieticians, and social workers. All have employment options outside the hospital sector. To attract these workers, hospitals pay the market rate. For nurses, however, hospitals have been and remain the dominant employer, and thus are freer of pressures from other industries which might compete to push nurses' salaries upward.

This attitude on the part of those responsible for hospitals is understandable. In recent years, hospitals have been under enormous pressure to slow the growth of their costs. Since 1971, federal wage and price controls, state rate commissions, and the voluntary hospital cost-containment effort have all placed tremendous pressures on hospitals. Moreover, hospitals have been unable to control the costs of energy, supplies, the minimum wage, the growth of unions, or the salaries of other personnel whose rates are determined by competition in the economy as a whole. Thus, hospitals have sought to contain their costs any way they can, and nurses' salaries, which represent at least 25 percent of hospital costs, have been one area of focus.

The data available suggest, however, that limiting the growth of nurses' salaries relative to others is creating an artificial shortage of hospital nurses (Aiken, Blendon, and Rogers 1981). A comparison of nurses' incomes with those of LPNs and aides indicates that the gap between these groups is narrowing. Licensed practical nurses incomes are now 76 percent of nurses' incomes, and aides' incomes are 71 percent. In actual dollars, the differential amounts to only several thousand dollars. When the versatility of nurses is considered in addition to the high costs of supervision and continuing education for nonnurses, it is probably more economical to replace all nursing ancillary personnel with nurses given current nurse salaries.

At the same time, the income gap between nurses and other health professionals is widening. In 1945, nurses' incomes were one-third of physicians' incomes; now they are less than one-fifth. Health professionals, whose work and general responsibilities are roughly similar to nurses—social workers, physical therapists, occupational therapists, and pharmacists—all appear to be faring better in the current economic market than nurses. If it remains economical to use nurses to substitute for other health professionals as well as for lower level nursing ancillary personnel, it seems unlikely that the supply of nurses will ever be sufficient to meet increasing demands.

Nurses have been ambivalent about pursuing higher salaries. The tradition of service and charity is still deeply ingrained in the fabric of nursing. Although the ANA proposed an economic welfare program as early as 1937, the ANA was not a strong proponent of unionization. In addition, nurses employed in nonprofit hospitals were expressly exempt from the legal provisions of the National Labor Relations Act between 1947 and 1974, and did not, therefore, have legal protection to organize a union. Since the repeal of the provisions that excluded hospitals from the jurisdiction of the Taft-Hartley Act, organized labor has become very active in unionizing hospital workers, including nurses. In response, the ANA, which opposes nurses' participation in trade unions, has intensified its own economic welfare program. Approximately 29 percent of hospital nurses worked under collective-bargaining agreements in 1977 (Feldman and Lee 1980), compared to less than 10 percent in 1969 (U.S. Bureau of Labor Statistics 1971). Although a minority of hospital nurses are currently covered by collective bargaining agreements, the covered population is growing at a steady pace and the effects on nurses' salaries are likely to extend well beyond the nurses directly involved. Other hospitals will offer higher salaries in order to forestall the spread of collective bargaining (Feldstein 1979; Miller 1979).

Although there has been increased participation by nurses in collective-bargaining agreements in recent years, the salary gains nationally have not been substantial. Union organizers have found nurses unwilling to participate in strikes, which has reduced the negotiating power of the union. Furthermore, many nurses remain opposed to unionization and believe that collective bargaining will undermine efforts to attain professional status for nurses. It does not appear, therefore, that collective bargaining alone will lead to sweeping changes in hospital nurses' salaries and working conditions.

However, a new entrepreneurial nursing service organization has emerged in recent years which may have the potential to break hospitals' monopsonistic control over the nurse market (Yett 1975, p. 236). Temporary nursing personnel agencies provide hospitals (and nursing homes) with nurses on a per diem basis to supplement their existing permanent staff. The agencies are independent organizations, and many are proprietary. Nurses are employees of the agency, and the agency bills the hospital for each nurse's services plus a brokerage fee. Individual nurses define if, how, when, and where they will work. The agency negotiates the hourly wage with the hospital, which in many instances is significantly higher than the hourly wage paid to hospital employees.

The single most important reason nurses choose agency employment is the freedom to control basic working conditions—when and where they work (Prescott 1982). Hospitals' control over the nursing market has resulted not only in artificially low wages but in rigid scheduling of working hours and assignment of responsibilities without regard to expertise or preference. Temporary agencies offer nurses the opportunity to make their own choices.

Temporary personnel agencies have the potential for increasing hospital wages as well as for giving nurses greater control over working conditions by increasing competition among nurse employers for the available nurse supply. The effect of agencies on wages varies considerably depending upon local market conditions. In some urban areas where hospitals are experiencing an acute shortage of nurses, agencies are offering hourly wages up to 300 percent higher than competing hospitals. Hospitals are willing to pay considerably higher salaries for agency nurses than they offer their own staff. It seems to be more economical to invest in high salaries at the margin to reduce the hospital's nursing shortage than by raising the base salaries of all nurses. The effects of agencies on local salaries depend upon the rate of nurse participation. In communities where hospitals experience small nurse shortages which can easily be ameliorated by agency nurses, the impact may be to further depress hospital nurses' incomes. However, in some locales more than 50 percent of nurses are working for agencies, leaving hospitals with vacancy rates of 20 to 30 percent. When the marginal costs of employing agency nurses becomes too great, hospitals increase their own base salaries.

Recent national estimates indicate that 40 percent of hospitals employ agency nurses (Prescott 1982). In some areas of the country, particularly in California, almost all hospitals employ agency nurses. Thus, in the relatively short period of about five years, temporary nursing personnel agencies have become a major force in the nurse market, and may be a more effective force in the long term in improving nurses' salaries and working conditions than collective bargaining.

Long-Term Care

Registered nurses are the largest single group of professionals in long-term care. Over eighty thousand nurses are currently employed in nursing homes and extended-care facilities, and more than twenty thousand work in home health agencies. The demand for nurses in long-term care is increasing very rapidly. Employment of nurses in nursing homes has increased by 42 percent since 1972 (Moses and Roth 1979); the number of nurses in home health agencies has tripled (Division of Nursing 1981).

Recent projections estimate a serious impending shortage of nurses in long-term care (Reif and Estes 1982). The White House Conference on Aging (1981) projects a shortfall of seventy-five thousand nurses in nursing homes alone by the year 2030. There will be an average of sixty-two hundred new nursing positions created every year in nursing homes (Administration on Aging 1980). Overall estimates of future needs include twelve thousand to twenty thousand geriatric nurse practitioners by the year 2010, depending upon the extent of physician involvement in long-term care (Kane et al. 1980). Currently only about a thousand nurse practitioners have been prepared in geriatrics and related fields (Health Resources Administration 1980).

Nurses have not been attracted to long-term–care settings in large numbers. Numerous studies have underscored the generally negative view of health providers toward care of the elderly; the research question is not who likes to work with the aged most, but who dislikes it least (Feldbaum and Feldbaum 1981). The problems of the aged are often depressing, and there are few cures. Most health professionals, including nurses, are educated in tertiary-care centers where the challenges of acute care are emphasized and long-term care is all but forgotten. It is not surprising that a recent national survey of nursing students found that less than 5 percent were committed to working in nursing homes, and that geriatrics and long-term care were the least popular specialty choices (Feldbaum and Feldbaum 1981).

Nursing homes are probably the least satisfactory setting for nursing practice (Vladeck 1980). Nursing-home nurses are isolated from their peers and receive little status or recognition for their contributions. Only 15 percent of the staff in skilled nursing facilities are nurses, compared to 46 percent of the nursing staff in hospitals. Only 42 percent of skilled nursing facilities have twenty-four-hour nursing coverage; many nursing homes have only one nurse on duty at a time (National Center for Health Statistics 1979). Nursing-home nurses spend much of their time supervising untrained aides who provide most of the direct patient care. On average, a nurse in a skilled nursing facility is responsible for 49 patients at a time, compared to about 5 patients in a hospital setting. Even under the best circumstances, nurses can devote only an average of twelve minutes a day to each patient (Flagel 1978), which is hardly consistent with the values internalized by most nurses.

In addition to the isolation and low status accorded nursing-home nurses, long-term–care facilities pay lower salaries and give substantially fewer benefits than do hospitals and other employers. The result is high staff turnover, chronic shortages, and low morale.

Unless changes occur in nursing homes to ameliorate some of these problems, the shortage of nurses is likely to persist. A number of proponents of change suggest that nursing homes be formally affiliated with voluntary and teaching hospitals, and that the medical and nursing leaders in these institutions assume responsibility for care in nursing homes (Rogers 1978; Aiken 1981a; Butler 1981). The successful integration of nursing homes with hospitals could reduce the isolation of nurses and offer them opportunities for broader roles, continuing education, and greater potential for advancement. Disadvantages of such affiliations include the higher costs associated with hospital involvement and the potential for "overmedicalizing" the problems of the elderly.

A second strategy for motivating a greater number of nurses to choose careers in nursing homes is the development of expanded roles for nurses in the provision of general medical services (Kayser-Jones 1981; Smits 1981). Nursing homes report serious difficulties obtaining physicians to provide ongoing medical services. Only 17 percent of physicians report making nursing-home visits at all (Smits 1981), and adult primary-care physicians spend, on the average, less than two hours a month caring for their patients in nursing homes (Aiken 1981a). As a result, the quality of medical care is less than it could be, and the overall costs of care are increased by frequent hospitalizations for minor, preventable problems. On average, there is one hospital admission for every four skilled nursing beds annually costing billions of dollars (Williams 1981). Nurse practitioners might reduce this rate by half. In addition, the use of drugs in nursing homes vastly exceeds the estimated need. In a recent study of nursing homes in Tennessee, Ray and colleagues determined that 43 percent of Medicaid patients were receiving antipsychotic drugs (Ray, Federspiel, and Shaffner 1980). Nurse practitioners have historically used few drugs and technological interventions with patients in other settings, and they have the potential to reduce the use of unnecessary drugs in nursing homes.

Nurses are uniquely suited to provide expanded health services in nursing homes. They are well trained in the social and psychological aspects of care, which are of great importance in long-term–care settings. And a large proportion of the problems of nursing-home residents are basic nursing care problems—nutrition, skin care, ambulation. The development of more autonomous roles for nurse practitioners which allow nurses to assume some of physicians' mandated responsibilities accompanied by appropriate remuneration would increase the attractiveness of nursing-home practice significantly.

Nursing's future role in long-term care is highly dependent upon changes in physician practice and reimbursement policies. The Graduate Medical Education National Advisory Committee (GMENAC) predicts a surplus of 70,000 physicians by 1990, rising to 145,000 by the year 2000 (GMENAC 1980). Some manpower analysts predict that physicians will change their practice patterns to maintain income levels, and more physicians will begin to make nursing-home visits. If so, the resources available to support nurses in expanded roles may be reduced. However, many are skeptical that physicians will alter their practice patterns in ways that will significantly affect nursing-home care. In that case, nurses have considerable potential for role expansion in long-term care.

National policies for financing long-term–care services will also be an important determinant of nurses' future roles. Although national health-care expenditures for the elderly are considerable, the disproportionate expenditures for highly sophisticated technical care has left long-term care underfinanced. Medicare and other insurance plans have focused almost entirely on hospital care, physician services, and drugs. Only 2 percent of national health expenditures for the elderly are devoted to noninstitutional long-term care (Fox and Clauser 1980; Gibson 1979). Even nursing-home expenditures, which are now approaching $13 billion a year, are inadequate to provide high-quality long-term care in institutional settings. States, under the Medicaid program, bear the largest public share of long-term–care expenditures. At present, nursing home residents make up only 4 percent of the Medicaid-eligible population but account for more than 30 percent of total Medicaid expenditures. It is unlikely that states will continue to expand Medicaid-covered services for the elderly given the rapid rise in current program expenditures.

For the most part, current reimbursement policies do not recognize nurses' potential to assume major roles in long-term care. Nursing-home reimbursement rates are not high enough to permit many nurses to be employed. And most states do not reimburse nurse practitioners to provide substitutive medical services in nursing homes.

Nurses have the potential to make major contributions to the improvement of long-term care. The major impediments are professional indifference and inadequate resources. The impact of the projected physician surplus and future reimbursement policy will be major determinants in nursing's future involvement in long-term care.

Nurses In Noninstitutional Settings

Nurses practice in a variety of roles in ambulatory care (Aiken 1981b). Approximately 12 percent of nurses work in community health agencies or in physicians' offices. For the most part, jobs in ambulatory care are in high demand because the hours are regular and a greater degree of autonomy is possible. Most nurses who work in ambulatory settings are salaried employees of physicians or community agencies. Even home health services, once delivered by private-duty nurses, are now provided by community agencies as a result of recent changes in third-party reimbursement policies.

In response to a perceived shortage of generalist physicians in the mid-1960s, a new role for nurses emerged in ambulatory care. The new specialists, called nurse practitioners, received advanced clinical training in physical assessment, diagnosis, and medical management of commonly occurring problems. They provided much of the general medical care traditionally provided by physicians. Together physicians and nurse practitioners were able to provide a broader range of ambulatory services than was possible in traditional office-based medical practice, and the services were more accessible and less costly. Nurse practitioners were also more likely to settle in underserved areas than were physicians, thus helping to alleviate the geographic imbalance in health-care resource availability (Lewis, Fein, and Mechanic 1976).

The nursing profession had a special interest in the development of the nurse practitioner for reasons unrelated to the shortage of physicians. The nurse-practitioner role offered the promise of greater autonomy, higher status, and better economic rewards. Although physicians and public policymakers thought of nurse practitioners as physician substitutes or "extenders," the nurses themselves were interested in providing new types of services (Ford 1982). While physicians focused on diagnosis and disease, nurses' priorities were patients' problems, counseling, and the development of social support systems necessary to improve compliance with prescribed medical regimens.

By 1981, twenty thousand nurse practitioners had been trained, primarily in pediatrics, family practice, and adult medicine. Consumer acceptance of nurse practitioners has been high since their introduction in the late sixties (Linn 1976). Numerous studies indicate that the quality of care provided by nurse practitioners is comparable to care provided by physicians, and is frequently better in some areas including compliance, health education, and counseling (Sox 1979; Lawrence 1978). For example, in one randomized trial comparing the nurse practitioner with the physician, 1,529 patients of nurse practitioners and 2,796 patients of physicians had similar outcomes as judged by physical, social, and emotional status at the end of one year of study (Spitzer et al. 1974).

Nurse practitioners have been particularly successful in managing chronically ill patients. Lewis and colleagues compared the outcomes for stable chronically ill patients randomly assigned to nurse practitioners and traditional university hospital medical clinics. Patients in the nurse-practitioner clinics reported fewer symptoms, used fewer medical services, and returned to work in significantly greater numbers than patients in the medical clinic (Lewis et al. 1969). In a similar study comparing outcomes for patients with diabetes, hypertension, and cardiac disease, Runyan (1977) found that patients cared for by nurse practitioners were more likely to experience reductions in blood pressure and blood glucose, hospitalization rates, and morbidity than a control population cared for in conventional physician outpatient clinics.

The practice of nurse-midwifery began in the United States in 1925 with the introduction of English-trained nurse-midwives in Appalachia in the Frontier Nursing Service (Breckenridge 1952). The first American education program began in New York City in 1932. Nurse-midwives' practice consists of management of essentially normal women during the prenatal period, the delivery, their newborn infants, postpartum care, and continuing general gynecological care. Nurse-midwifery developed slowly in the United States until the 1960s when the "baby boom," a perceived shortage of obstetricians, and the increased employment opportunities in the Great Society programs came about (Hellman 1967). The number of nurse-midwives has doubled during each decade since the 1950s. There are currently about fifteen hundred certified nurse-midwives, and twenty-one educational programs (Varney 1980; Diers 1982).

Nurse-midwifery has been opposed by many physicians in the United States who believe that the quality of care provided by nurse-midwives is inferior to physician care. In recent years, medical opposition has increased as national concerns escalate about an impending oversupply of physicians (GMENAC 1980). Yet, performance data belie the contention that the quality of care provided by nurse-midwives is poor.

Research comparing the practices of nurse-midwives and obstetricians show the prenatal care by nurse-midwives is more comprehensive, the rates of prematurity and neonatal mortality are reduced, and that more mothers return for postpartum care and contraception (Diers 1982). A poignant example of both the effectiveness of nurse-midwives and the barriers to practice has been reported from Madera County, California (Levy, Wilkinson, and Marine 1971). After the introduction of nurse-midwives to care for poor women in a hospital clinic, prematurity decreased from 11 percent to 6.6 percent. More extensive prenatal care was given to a larger proportion of expectant mothers, neonatal mortality was halved from 23.9 per 1,000 to 10.3 per 1,000, and a greater proportion of expectant mothers returned for routine postpartum visits. The nurse-midwifery service ceased to exist after three years when the California Medical Association refused to support a permanent change in legislation allowing nurse-midwives to practice. Data for the two years following termination of the service showed prematurity had returned to preprogram levels (9.8 percent) and neonatal mortality had tripled to 32.1 per 1,000.

The costs of care delivered by nurse-midwives is less than one-third of the costs of obstetrical care (Lubic 1981). Most of the cost difference is attributable to the noninterventionist approach of nurse-midwives to childbirth. Obstetrical care often includes the use of fetal monitoring, labor-stimulating drugs, episiotomy, amniotomy, forceps, and ultrasound. Cesarean-section rates have increased as much as 30 percent in some areas over the past ten years (Bottoms, Rosen, and Sokol 1980). Nurse-midwifery care, by definition, is low-intervention practice with high priority placed on patient preferences (Diers 1982). A large part of the recent success of nurse-midwives in establishing practices has come from consumer demand, particularly from older, well-educated women who are seeking an alternative to the increased technological bias of physician-oriented obstetrical care (Arms 1975; Corea 1977).

Despite extensive evidence that the use of nurse practitioners and nurse-midwives is a cost-effective strategy to improve access to general medical care, reimbursement policy remains at odds with public- and private-sector efforts aimed at training and utilizing these individuals. The rapidly escalating costs of medical care have led to skepticism and the fear that extending reimbursement to yet another provider group, such as nurse practitioners, will only lead to increased overall expenditures. The dilemma for those shaping public policy is how to encourage the productive use of nurse practitioners and provide third-party reimbursement while containing the inflationary trend in medical-care expenditures. There is little direct reimbursement to nurse practitioners now. For the most part, physicians bill for reimbursable services of nurses under their supervision, and nurses work for an established salary.

Much of the public support for nurse practitioners emerged during a time of perceived shortage of primary-care physicians. It is unclear whether nurse practitioners can survive in their current roles if competition for patients among health professionals escalates (Lewis 1982; Budetti 1981). Even in health-maintenance organizations (HMOs), where economic incentives should encourage the effective use of nurse practitioners, future employment of nurse practitioners is questionable. For despite the ideology of HMOs, the care is focused on episodic illness rather than long-term health maintenance, where nurse practitioners make their greatest contribution (Luft 1981). Many HMO physicians prefer to employ additional physicians who can share hospital coverage and on-call hours instead of nurse practitioners (Barham and Steiger 1982). Thus, growth in HMOs will have little noticeable effect on nurses unless HMO attention is focused on nonacute health services. If they are to survive, nurse practitioners will have to develop competitive practice models where consumers benefit either by reduced costs, expanded scope of services, or increased access to health care.

Political Organization Of Nursing

Over the past twenty years, government involvement in health care has increased dramatically. Government policies have the potential to affect nurses directly, as in the case of explicit nurse manpower policies or state nurse practice acts, and indirectly through the implementation of broad health-care programs. Employer policies also have a major impact on the practice of nursing, particularly hospital policies governing employment and salaries. The potential influence of the decisions of federal, state, and local government, of employer groups, and of other health professionals has increased the need for strong, viable professional nursing organizations to represent the interests of nurses.

There are two major national nursing organizations. The American Nurses' Association (ANA), founded in 1896, is the national membership association for registered nurses, and represents nurses at the national, state, and local levels (see Flanagan 1976). The National League for Nursing (NLN), founded in 1952, includes not only nurses but also nonnurses, consumer representatives, and member agencies such as nursing service organizations and nursing schools. Nurses' rate of participation in either organization is low and declining. In 1958, ANA represented 41 percent of all practicing nurses; in 1980, ANA had 165,000 members representing only 13 percent of practicing nurses. The decline in ANA membership is attributed to two major factors: ANA's stand on baccalaureate education and collective bargaining. Many nurses without baccalaureate degrees feel disenfranchised and have left the association. Others disagree with ANA's direct involvement in collective bargaining. The National League for Nursing has a membership of 15,000 individual nurse and nonnurse members, and about 1,800 agency members.

The American Nurses' Association is generally recognized as the major professional and political organization representing American nurses. ANA maintains a full-time Washington office to lobby for national legislation favorable to nurses. Since 1965, federal support of nursing education under the Nurse Training Act and related nursing research and training programs has totaled more than $1.5 billion, about 10 percent of the total nursing education expenditures. ANA has successfully lobbied to retain federal nursing education subsidies despite opposition from Presidents Nixon, Ford, and Carter. Nurses have also benefited from the increased government involvement in health care. Medicare and Medicaid have been more liberal in their reimbursement policies regarding nurses than have physician- and hospital-dominated private insurance plans. Publicly funded programs for underserved groups, such as community health centers and rural health clinics, have offered nurses opportunities to practice in more autonomous roles. Thus, ANA's Washington lobby is perceived by nurses as one of its most important and successful functions.

The ANA also provides assistance to state nursing associations' legislative programs. The legal practice of nursing is structured by nurse practice acts in each state. As nurses have sought greater autonomy, there has been a need for state enabling legislation which has, in some states, engendered considerable opposition from physician groups. Many states have had bitter battles over amending nurse practice acts to enable nurse practitioners and nurse-midwives to practice. Although nurses have resorted, in some cases, to antitrust litigation, there has been little success in the absence of enabling legislation (Latanich and Schultheiss 1982). Given the importance of state legislation on nursing practice, state nurses' associations have become increasingly important in the political organization of nursing.

The ANA also carries out a broad program of professional and scholarly activities. ANA publishes a number of professsional journals, conducts continuing-education programs, and certifies nurses in advanced clinical specialties.

The most controversial function of ANA is its economic and general welfare program. Many nurses are opposed to collective bargaining because they believe it will detract from nurses' quest for professional status. And for years, nurses have debated whether ANA can be effective as a professional association while at the same time serving as a trade union. ANA provides funds for legal, educational, consultation, and public relations support for collective bargaining. Activities relating to unit organizing and negotiating are the functions of state nurses' associations. Until recently, ANA has been able to continue its economic welfare program with an investment of about 12 percent of its budget (Cleland 1982).

The major trade unions have begun to invest heavily in organizing nurses, and have been successful in drawing nurses away from state nurses' association bargaining units. The ANA currently represents 63 percent of all organized nurses but a recent study predicts that unless ANA finds an effective way to counter the organizing activities of trade and teachers unions soon, ANA will represent less than half of organized nurses and thereby lose much of its negotiating strength (Miller and Cameron 1981). Nurses do not have a strong tradition of participation in professional associations. ANA fears that nurses will not support both a union and a separate professional association. If the association abandons its economic welfare program, the overall decline in membership is likely to be greater than that already experienced because of opposition to collective bargaining. Further loss of membership will fiscally cripple ANA's other programs. However, competing successfully with major trade unions could require huge resources and detract from ANA's professional and legislative efforts. Thus, the ANA is caught in a major dilemma and the resolution of the collective bargaining issue will be an important determinant in the evolution of the political organization of nursing in the future.

The NLN is charged with accrediting nursing education programs for professional and practical nurses. Although the NLN also supports professional activities such as journals, continuing education, and lobbying, its influence derives from the accreditation function. The league accredits all three types of generic nurse education programs—diploma, associate degree, and baccalaureate—in addition to programs to prepare licensed practical nurses and graduate programs in nursing. Its membership includes constituencies interested in maintaining each type of nursing program, a source of increasing conflict with ANA.

The dispute over education has led ANA to take on an increasing number of functions relating to accreditation and certification. As 1985 approaches, the ANA target date for baccalaureate education, increased efforts may be made by ANA to gain control of accreditation, which if successful would significantly reduce the NLN's influence.

The Future

Nursing is an occupation in transition. It is attempting to emerge from a tradition-laden past which seems no longer functional in a world of high technology and changing social attitudes. Nurses are trying to sustain their traditional nursing contributions while at the same time achieving more autonomous roles in health care.

The major strategy pursued to date by nursing to achieve greater autonomy has been the pursuit of higher education. Collegiate education for nurses and faculty preparation in academic research disciplines have enhanced nursing's influence in health care. The emphasis on education at the expense of clinical training, however, has divorced many in nursing from their raison d'être and created serious problems that must receive high priority on nursing's agenda for the future.

While collegiate education has succeeded in attracting better-qualified and career-oriented applicants to nursing, it has not by itself enhanced the ability of graduates to function as clinicians, or to bring about the desired changes in nursing roles. Nurses from collegiate programs tend to have conceptions of the role of the professional nurse and standards of clinical care which differ from the realities of today's health-care institutions. This results in high levels of dissatisfaction, high job turnover, and in some cases abandonment of nursing as a career (Krammer 1974). The greater autonomy and more favorable employment conditions in universities has led many of nursing's more articulate and well-educated leaders to abandon practice settings and retreat to nursing schools. While these are the nurses who are most committed to the development of professional roles, they have been ineffectual in bringing about change because they lack responsibilities for practice settings and the opportunity to demonstrate superior clinical skills.

In this regard, nurses have behaved in ways which parallel those of talented secondary-school teachers. They have often moved out of the clinical arena into administrative positions as a way of circumventing the limits of career mobility found in clinical institutional settings. This course, however, does not offer a long-term solution. Nurses' professional legitimacy derives from what their clinical expertise can bring to patient care—not their administrative skills.

Nursing has undergone considerable change and still faces major problems. Practice conditions in most settings do not meet nurses' changing expectations for rewarding, challenging professional activity. Working conditions are poor (Wandelt 1980), lifetime earnings are low in comparison with other college-educated women (Yett 1968), and career mobility is limited. Nurses are dissatisfied and job turnover is high (Price and Mueller 1980). Since 1960, nursing school admissions as a proportion of all female high school graduates have persistently declined. Given the many career options available to women, it is not surprising that they are choosing fields with greater economic rewards and fewer constraints than nursing. Between 1970 and 1980, the number of women enrolled in law school increased from 7,000 to 42,000 (American Bar Association 1980); women medical students increased from 9 percent of the entering class in 1969 to 28 percent in 1979 (*Journal of the American Medical Association* 1980).

The real question for nursing will be whether nurses can reaffirm their commitment to clinical excellence and demonstrate its importance with sufficient persuasiveness to cause health-care institutions to restructure nursing responsibilities in ways that keep pace with nurses' career expectations. In the long run, new opportunities for nursing to play a broader, more satisfying role in the totality of health care seem good. Health care is a growing industry. The demand for nursing care can only increase in contrast to a decline in the demands for other kinds of trained people. Changing disease patterns, technological advancements in medicine, and the need for continuing health surveillance for those with long-term chronic illnesses should mean that nurses and nursing will be of even greater importance in the future.

REFERENCES

ABEL-SMITH, B. 1960. *A history of the nursing profession.* London: Heinemann.

Administration on Aging. 1980. *Human resource issues in the field of aging: the nursing home industry.* (DHEW pub. no. (OHDS)80–20093). Washington, D.C.: Office of Human Development Services, Dept. of Health and Human Services.

AIKEN, L. H. 1981a. Nursing priorities for the 1980's: hospitals and nursing homes. *American Journal of Nursing* 81 (no. 2):324–30.

———, (ed.) 1981b. *Health policy and nursing practice.* New York: McGraw-Hill.

———; BLENDON, R.; and ROGERS, D. 1981. The shortage of hospital nurses: a new perspective. *Annals of Internal Medicine.* 95 (no. 3):365–71.

ALTMAN, S. 1971. *Present and future supply of registered nurses.* DHEW pub. no. (NIH) 72–134. Washington, D.C.: Government Printing Office.

American Bar Association. 1980. *Review of legal education, 1980.* Chicago: American Bar Association.

American Nurses' Association. 1965. *Educational preparation for nurse practitioners and assistants to nurses: a position paper.* New York: American Nurses' Association.

———. 1979a. *A case for baccalaureate preparation for nursing.* Kansas City, Mo.: American Nurses' Association.

———. 1979b. *The study of credentialing in nursing: a new approach,* vol. 1 and 2. Kansas City, Mo.: American Nurses' Association.

———. 1980. *Nursing: a social policy statement.* Kansas City, Mo.: American Nurses' Association.

ARMS, S. 1975. *Immaculate deception: a new look at women and childbirth in America.* Boston: Houghton Mifflin.

BARHAM, V., and STEIGER, N. 1982. HMOs and nurse practitioners: the Kaiser experience. In *Nursing in the 1980s: crises, opportunities, challenges,* ed. L. H. Aiken. Philadelphia: Lippincott.

BLISS, A., and COHEN, E. D., eds. 1977. *The new health professionals.* Germantown, Md.: Aspen Systems Corp.

BOTTOMS, S.; MORTIMER, R.; and SOKOL, R. 1980. The increase in Cesarean birth rate. *New England Journal of Medicine* 302:559–63.

BRECKENRIDGE, M. 1952. *Wide neighborhoods: a story of the Frontier Nursing Service.* New York: Harper.

BROWN, E. L. 1948. *Nursing for the future.* New York: Russell Sage.

———. 1970. *Nursing reconsidered.* Philadelphia: Lippincott.

BUDETTI, P. P. 1981. The impending pediatric "surplus": causes, implications, and alternatives. *Pediatrics* 67 (5):597–606.

BUTLER, R. N. 1981. The teaching nursing home. *Journal of the American Medical Association* 245:1435–37.

CLELAND, V. 1971. Sex discrimination: nursing's most pervasive problem. *American Journal of Nursing* 71:1542–47.

———. 1979. Fee-for-visit concept. In *Nursing's influence on health policy for the eighties.* Kansas City, Mo.: American Academy of Nursing.

———. 1982. Collective bargaining in nursing. In *Nursing in the 1980s: crises, opportunities, challenges,* ed. L. H. Aiken. Philadelphia: Lippincott, 1982.

Committee for the Study of Nursing Education. 1923. *A report of a survey of nursing and nursing education,* ed. J. Goldmark. New York: Macmillan.

428 THE HEALTH OCCUPATIONS

CoReA, G. 1977. *The hidden malpractice: how American medicine mistreats women.* New York: Harcourt, Brace, Jovanovich.

Diers, D. 1982. The future of nurse midwives in American health care. In *Nursing in the 1980s: crises, opportunities, challenges,* ed. L. H. Aiken. Philadelphia: Lippincott.

Division of Nursing. 1981. Preliminary data from the 1979 survey of community health nursing. Washington, D.C.: Health Resources Administration, Dept. of Health and Human Services, unpublished data.

Division of Research in Medical Education, University of Southern California, L.A. 1981. *Health care needs of the elderly* (draft report). Paper presented to the White House Conference on Aging, Technical Committee on Health Services, February 1981.

Dock, L. 1966. Nurses should be obedient. In *Issues in nursing,* ed. B. Bullough and V. Bullough. New York: Springer.

Donovan, L. 1980. Survey of nursing incomes, part 2. What increases income most? *RN* 43:27–30.

Fagin, C. 1980. The shortage of nurses in the United States. *Journal of Public Health Policy* 1 (no. 4).

Feldbaum, E. G., and Feldbaum, M. B. 1981. Caring for the elderly: Who dislikes it least? *Journal of Health Politics, Policy and Law* 5:62–72.

Feldman, R., and Lee, L. 1980. *Hospital employees: wages and labor union organization.* Final report. Hyattsville, Md.: National Center for Health Services Research, Dept. of Health and Human Services, November 1980.

Feldstein, P. 1979. *Health care economics.* New York: Wiley.

Flagle, C. D. 1978. Issues of staffing long-term care activities. In *Nursing personnel and the changing health care system,* ed. M. L. Millman. Cambridge, Mass.: Ballinger.

Flanagan, L. 1976. *One strong voice: the story of the American Nurses' Association.* Kansas City, Mo.: American Nurses' Association.

Ford, L. 1982. Nurse practitioners: history of a new idea and projections for the future. In *Nursing in the 1980s: crises, opportunities, challenges.* ed. L. H. Aiken. Philadelphia: Lippincott.

Fox, P. D., and Clauser, S. B. 1980. Trends in nursing home expenditures: implications for aging policy. *Health Care Financing Review* 2 (no. 2):65–70.

Freidson, E. 1970. *Profession of medicine.* New York: Dodd, Mead.

Friss, L. O. 1981. Work force policy perspectives: registered nurses. *Journal of Health Politics, Policy and Law* 5:696–719.

Georgopoulos, B. S., and Mann, F. C. 1962. *The community general hospital.* New York: Macmillan.

Gibson, R. M. 1980. National health expenditures, 1979. *Health Care Financing Review* 2 (no. 1):1–36.

Glaser, W. 1966. Nursing leadership and policy. In *The nursing profession: five sociological essays,* ed. F. Davis. New York: Wiley.

Graduate Medical Education National Advisory Committee. 1980. *Report to the secretary.* Washington, D.C.: Dept. of Health and Human Services, September 30, 1980.

Habenstein, R. W., and Christ, E. A. 1963. *Professionalizer, traditionalizer and utilizer.* Columbia, Mo.: University of Missouri Press.

Health Resources Administration. 1980. *Health personnel issues in the context of long-term care in nursing homes.* Washington, D.C.: Public Health Service, Health Resources Administration, 18 August 1980.

Hellman, L. M. 1967. Nurse-midwifery in the United States. *Obstetrics and Gynecology* 30 (no. 6):883.

Institute of Medicine. 1978. *A manpower policy for primary care.* Washington, D.C.: Institute of Medicine.

Jacox, A. 1978. Professional socialization of nurses. In *The nursing profession: views through the mist,* ed. N. Chaska. New York: McGraw-Hill.

Johnson, W. L. 1980. Supply and demand for registered nurses: some observations on the current picture and prospects to 1985. *Nursing and Health Care,* September 1980, pp. 73–79.

Journal of the American Medical Association. Medical education in the United States 1979–1980. *Journal of the American Medical Association* 244 (no. 25):2814.

KANE, R. L.; SOLOMON, D. H.; BECK, J. C.; KEELER, E.; and KANE, R. A. 1980. *Geriatrics in the United States: manpower projections and training considerations,* (R2543–HJK). Santa Monica, Calif.: Rand Corporation.

KAYSER-JONES, J. S. 1981. A comparison of care in a Scottish and a United States facility. *Geriatric Nursing,* January/February 1981, pp. 44–50.

KRAMER, M 1974. *Reality shock: why nurses leave nursing.* St. Louis: C. V. Mosby.

LATANICH, T., and SCHULTHEISS, P. 1982. Competition and health manpower issues. In *Nursing in the 1980s: Crises, opportunities, challenges,* ed. L. H. Aiken. Philadelphia: Lippincott.

LAWRENCE, D. 1978. Physicians assistants and nurse practitioners: their impact on health access, costs, and quality. *Health and Medical Care Services Review* 1 (no. 2):1–12.

LEVY, B. S.; WILKINSON, F. S.; and MARINE, W. M. 1971. Reducing neonatal mortality rate with nurse-midwives. *American Journal of Obstetrics and Gynecology* 109 (no. 1):51–58.

LEWIS, C. E. 1982. Nurse practitioners and the physician surplus. In *Nursing in the 1980s: Crises, opportunities, challenges,* ed. L. H. Aiken. Philadelphia: Lippincott.

———; FEIN, R.; and MECHANIC, D. 1976. *A right to health: the problem of access to primary medical care.* New York: Wiley.

———; Resnick, B.; Schmidt, G.; and WAKMAN, D. 1969. Activities, events and outcomes in ambulatory care. *New England Journal of Medicine* 280:645–49.

LEWIS, E., (ed.) 1970. *The clinical nurse specialist.* New York: American Journal of Nursing Company.

LINN, L. S. 1976. Patient acceptance of the family nurse practitioner. *Medical Care* 14:337–64.

LUBIC, R. W. 1981. Evaluation of an out-of-hospital maternity center for low risk patients. In *Health policy and nursing practice,* ed. L. H. Aiken. New York: McGraw-Hill.

LUFT, H. S. 1981. *Health maintenance organizations: dimensions of performance.* New York: Wiley.

MARRAM, G. D.; SCHLEGEL, M. W.; and BEVIS, E. O. 1974. *Primary nursing.* St. Louis: C. V. Mosby.

MAUKSCH, H. O. 1966. The organizational context of nursing practice. In *The nursing profession: five sociological essays,* ed. F. Davis. New York: Wiley.

McCLURE, M. L. 1978. Entry into professional practice: the New York proposal. In *The nursing profession: views through the mist,* ed. N. Chaska. New York: McGraw-Hill.

———, and NELSON, J. 1982. The challenges of hospital nursing. In *Nursing in the 1980s: Crises, opportunities, challenges,* ed. L. H. Aiken. Philadelphia: Lippincott.

MERCADANTE, L. T. 1962. An organizational plan for nursing service. *Nursing Outlook,* May 1962, vol. 10.

MILLER, R. U. 1979. Hospitals. In *Collective bargaining: contemporary American experience,* ed. G. Somers. Madison, Wis.: Industrial Relations Research Association.

———, and CAMERON, K. 1981. *Study of ANA's Economic and General Welfare Program.* Madison, Wis.: Industrial Relations Research Institute, University of Wisconsin, 1981, unpublished.

MONTAG, M. L. 1951. *The education of nursing technicians.* New York: G. P. Putnam and Sons.

MOSES, E., and LEVINE, E. 1982. Registered nurses today: A statistical profile. In *Nursing in the 1980s: crises, opportunities, challenges,* ed. L. H. Aiken. Philadelphia: Lippincott.

MOSES, E., and ROTH, A. 1979. What do statistics reveal about the nation's nurses? *American Journal of Nursing* 79:1745–56.

MOSES, L., and MOSTELLER, F. 1968. Institutional differences in postoperative death rates. *Journal of the American Medical Association* 203:492–94.

National Center for Health Statistics. 1979. *The national nursing home survey: 1977 summary for U.S.* Hyattsville, Md.: Department of Health, Education, and Welfare.

———. 1980. *Health United States 1980.* DHHS pub. no. (PHS) 81–1232.

National Commission for the Study of Nursing and Nursing Education. 1970. *An abstract for action*, ed. J. Lysaught. New York: McGraw-Hill.

National League for Nursing. 1981. *NLN nursing data book, 1980*. New York: National League for Nursing.

NIGHTINGALE, F. 1946. *Notes on nursing: what it is and what it is not*. New York: Lippincott.

PRESCOTT, P. A. 1982. Supplemental agency employment of registered nurses in hospitals. In *Nursing in the 1980s: crises, opportunities, challenges*, ed. L. H. Aiken. Philadelphia: Lippincott.

PRICE, J., and MUELLER, C. 1980. *Professional turnover: the case of nurses*. Jamaica, N.Y.: Spectrum Publications.

RAY, W. A.; FEDERSPIEL, C. F.; and SCHAFFNER, W. 1980. A study of antipsychotic drug use in nursing homes: epidemiological evidence suggesting misuse. *American Journal of Public Health* 70 (no. 5):485–91.

REEDER, S., and MAUKSCH, H. 1979. Nursing: continuing change. In *Handbook of medical sociology*, 3d ed., ed. H. Freeman, S. Levine, and L. Reeder. Englewood Cliffs, N.J.: Prentice-Hall.

REIF, L., and ESTES, C. 1982. Long-term care: a policy perspective. In *Nursing in the 1980s: crises, opportunities, challenges*, ed. L. H. Aiken. Philadelphia: Lippincott.

ROGERS, D. E. 1978. *American medicine: challenges for the 1980s*. Cambridge, Mass.: Ballinger.

ROOKS, J. B., and FISCHMAN, S. H. 1980. American nurse-midwifery practice in 1976–1977: reflections of 50 years of growth and development. *American Journal of Public Health* 70 (no. 9):990–96.

RUNYAN, J. 1977. The Memphis chronic disease program: comparison in outcome and the nurses' extended role. In *The new health professionals*, ed. A. Bliss and E. Cohen. Germantown, Md.: Aspen.

RUSSELL, L. B. 1979. *Technology in hospitals: medical advances and other diffusion*. Washington, D.C.: Brookings Institute.

SCOTT, W. R.; FORREST, W. H.; and BROWN, B. W. 1976. Hospital structure and postoperative mortality and morbidity. In *Organizational research in hospitals*, ed. S. M. Shortell, and M. Brown. Chicago: Blue Cross Association.

SIMPSON, R. L., and SIMPSON, I. H. 1969. Women and bureaucracy in the semiprofessions. In *The semiprofessions and their organization: teachers, nurses, social workers*, ed. A. Etzioni. New York: Free Press.

SLOAN, F. A. 1978. *Equalizing access to nursing services*. DHEW pub. no. (HRA) 78–51. Washington, D.C.: Government Printing Office.

SMITH, H. L. 1958. Two lines of authority: the hospital's dilemma. In *Patients, physicians and illness*, ed. E. G. Jaco. New York: Free Press.

SMITS, H. L. 1981. Manpower for long-term care: two simple suggestions. *National Journal* 13 (no. 18):807–9.

SOX, H. 1979. Quality of patient care by nurse practitioners and physicians' assistants: a ten-year perspective. *Annals of Internal Medicine* 91:459–68.

SPITZER, W.; SACKETT, D.; SIBLEY, J.; et al. 1974. *New England Journal of Medicine* 290:251–56.

STEIN, L. 1971. The doctor-nurse game. In *New directions for nurses*, ed. B. Bullough and V. Bullough. New York: Springer.

STRAUSS, A. 1966. The structure and ideology of American nursing: an interpretation. In *The nursing profession*, ed. F. Davis. New York: Wiley.

SULTZ, H. A.; HENRY, M.; and SULLIVAN, J. 1979. *Nurse practitioners: U.S.A.* Lexington, Mass.: D. C. Heath.

U.S. Bureau of the Census. 1980. *Statistical abstract of the United States, 1980* (101st ed.). Washington, D.C.

U.S. Bureau of Labor Statistics. 1971. *Industry wage survey: hospitals, March 1969*. Washington, D.C.: Government Printing Office, bulletin no. 1688, pp. 219–21.

VARNEY, H. 1980. *Nurse midwifery.* Boston: Blackwell Scientific Publications.

VLADECK, B. 1980. *Unloving care: the nursing home tragedy.* New York: Basic Books.

WANDELT, M. A. 1980. *Conditions associated with registered nurse employment in Texas.* Austin, Center for Research, School of Nursing, University of Texas.

WILLIAMS, T. F. 1981. *An overall strategy for reducing the wait in hospitals for long term care.* Rochester, N.Y.: Center on Aging, University of Rochester Medical Center, unpublished manuscript, February 1981.

WOODHAM-SMITH, C. 1951. *Florence Nightingale 1820–1910.* New York: McGraw-Hill. 1951.

WUNDERMAN, L. 1980. Female physicians in the 1970s: their changing roles in medicine. In *Profile of medical practice 1980,* ed. G. Glandon and R. Shapiro. Chicago: American Medical Association.

YETT, D. E. 1968. Lifetime earnings for nurses in comparison with college trained women. *Inquiry* 5 (no. 4):35–70.

———. 1975. *An economic analysis of the nurse shortage.* Lexington, Mass.: D.C. Heath.

Chapter 20

Physicians

David Mechanic

THE ORGANIZATION OF PHYSICIANS reflects the character of the health-care delivery system of which they are a part, and their efforts are affected substantially by their specialty or subspecialty differentiation, by the type of individual or group organization under which they practice, and by existing modes of remuneration. The work of physicians is also a product of their personal and professional ideologies, the rapidly changing character of medical knowledge and technology, and the nature of external regulation of their activities by government and other groups such as insurance companies as well as by their own peers. Physicians in the United States, and in other Western countries, are experiencing considerable strain resulting from increasing public criticism, the growth of government involvement in their work, the rapidity of changing conditions of knowledge and practice, and the impact of increasing numbers of doctors.

Specialization

The most salient aspect of medical organization is the extent to which physicians have divided into specialties and subspecialties. A great deal of such specialization is a response to the development of new technology and the growth of scientific knowledge. Through specialization, the physician gains control over the uncertainty inherent in medical work and more competence in exercising skills. When the field of action is narrowly defined, control over the substance of work is more readily achieved. Specialization also brings political and economic advantages as well as greater control over scheduling of work and definition of responsibility.

There are twenty-two approved medical specialty boards (American Medical Association 1973), organizations that voluntarily certify physicians in specialties who attain a certain level of training and who pass specified examinations. Such board certification, which is carried out by the organized medical specialties themselves and not by government, often brings higher remuneration in salaried positions and may be a criterion for higher payment under various public and private insurance programs. The largest boards are internal medicine, surgery, pediatrics, obstetrics and gynecology, radiology, psychiatry and neurology, and

432

pathology. Family practice, the newest board, established in 1969, is growing rapidly. The large boards like internal medicine and surgery include many subspecialties, with opportunities to receive certification in a subspecialty like nephrology or cardiology. Other recognized subspecialties within internal medicine include allergy, gastroenterology, and pulmonary disease.

The establishment of boards and subspecialties is as much a political process through which physicians come to dominate a specified domain and restrict competition as it is a reaction to the mandates of an increasingly sophisticated technology (Stevens 1971). While the traditional concept of the specialist was as a consultant physician who assisted the generalist with problems that were puzzling or of greater complexity than he could handle, existing specialization is organized around population groups (pediatrics, adult medicine, geriatrics), types of technology (radiology, radiation therapy, anesthesiology), organ systems (nephrology, cardiology, dermatology), etiologies (infectious disease), and specific disease categories (pulmonary disease, psychiatry). The most recent distortion of the concept of the consulting physician was the development of the American Board of Family Practice, which in effect defines the generalist as another kind of specialist. This trend reflects a conference of status and privilege through a redefinition of terms to achieve greater political and economic power.

Many countries attempt to maintain a balance between the doctors of first contact (the general practitioners, family physicians, general internists, and general pediatricians) and those who are more limited in their scope of work. While no country has completely retained the traditional concept of the consulting specialist, those that organize medicine through the public service tend to restrict the number of specialist positions available. In many European countries there is a long and traditional division between the general practitioners who did their work in the community and the consultants who were based in hospitals. In countries where such traditions persist, generalists constitute a larger proportion of all doctors. Physicians cannot establish themselves as specialists unless hospital positions are available, and thus there are limits on the proliferation of specialists who are expensive.

Although there are many contentious issues among the numerous specialties, from a public policy viewpoint the major distinction is between physicians who engage in primary medical care and those who perform other medical tasks, such as providing specialty care on referral or providing more complex services in hospitals. Since the primary-care issue is so important in much that follows in this chapter, some extended discussion is necessary.

Primary Care

As the issue of primary care has become more politically important—not only in the United States but throughout the world—there has been considerable controversy as to its appropriate definition. Discussions of primary medical care tend to confuse three dimensions of the problem: the organizational dimension, the service aspect, and the manpower situation. The most typical definition is that primary care is the care given by certain types of practitioners who work as generalists: general practitioners, family practitioners, nurse practitioners, and so on. It is assumed that such practitioners' training prepares them adequately to provide first-contact care and to take continuing responsibilities for the health-care needs of the patient. Defining primary care, however, as what the practitioner of first contact does leads to a variety of absurdities, as when doctors of first contact carry out highly complex medical and surgical procedures usually requiring additional training. A considerable amount of major surgery in the United States, for example, is performed by general practitioners (Mechanic 1972a). In contrast, many specialists devote significant amounts of their time doing primary care, and thus the claim of a shortage of primary-care physicians may be seen as exaggerated (Aiken et al. 1979).

When the first definition fails to suffice, the suggestion is sometimes made to separate discrete medical services into those that are primary and those that are not. While this is possible, it is arbitrary, and the issue becomes less conceptual and more political. Moreover, most available data on how physicians are functioning are based on the International Classification of Disease, but this type of classification of diagnoses does not readily permit the classification of cases into primary versus nonprimary care. Diagnostic judgments have already filtered through the physician's understanding and perceptual selection. Varying physicians with diverse training perceive, evaluate, classify, and manage comparable patients differently. Even if presenting symptoms are used instead of diagnoses, as in the National Ambulatory Medical Care Survey (1974), the entries are likely to be distorted by the preexisting doctor-patient relationship and the manner in which the physician proceeds to elicit information from the patient. The key point here is that differences between primary and specialist practitioners are not simply a matter of what they do but also a matter of how they do it.

It is in examining the task of classifying discrete services into primary and non-primary that some extremely important issues begin to emerge. One important aspect of primary care is the attitude of the physician, his assumptions, use of information about the particular patient, and the way he goes about evaluating the patient's complaint. As Balint (1957) has so persuasively argued, many patients seeking the assistance of a physician are in a stage in which their symptoms are unorganized and fluid. What the physician sees as important, what he inquires about, and how he evaluates the patient are all dependent on his training and orientations (Beeson 1974). In understanding how varying types of general and subspecialty training affect medical practice, it is necessary to have better data on how patients with comparable presenting complaints are evaluated and managed differently by physicians with varying types of training and by physicians who have continuing relationships with these patients, as compared with those who only see such patients on an irregular basis and do not take continuing responsibility for their care. Are there differences, for example, between a family physician, a general internist, and a cardiologist in how they go about evaluating and managing varying types of chest pain? In short, the focus here moves away from simple and arbitrary attempts at classification toward understanding the strategies of evaluation used by different physicians and their implications for effective outcome, cost, and patient satisfaction.

A third approach to primary care—and one with more inherent logic—is based on the organization of care as a system. Here the emphasis is less on a particular type of practitioner and how the doctor is trained and more on how different levels of care are organized and how they relate to one another. For example, in most organized medical-care systems there are designated primary-care physicians who have responsibility for first-contact care, for assuming continued responsibility for an enrolled population, and for dealing with the more common and less complicated problems of their patients. These systems are often established so that patients are required to seek more specialized services through the referral of their primary physician. Similarly, secondary- and tertiary-care services are organized in relation to the system as a whole, and attempts are made to specify the conditions for coordination among varying levels of care. Although the particular type of practitioner used at varying levels of care is not an unimportant issue, the main focus shifts to defining responsibilities for care functions at each level of care. Thus, primary-care services, however they are defined by the system, may be organized in a variety of ways with alternative types of personnel as long as the necessary functions are performed. In this context, primary care is a level of service, not a particular type of practitioner. This concept is characteristic of the organization of primary care in England and is increasingly seen in the United States in large health-maintenance organizations (see Chapter 14).

Even when primary medical care is defined as part of a system, problems remain in the coordination between varying levels of the system. For example, the decision as to when referrals should take place from one level of care to another is left to the individual practitioner and is often affected by the implicit incentives built into the organization of health services or in how health personnel are paid. It is often argued, for example, that capitation payment tends to encourage unnecessary referral to secondary services when the functions can more properly be performed by the primary-care service. The development of an effective incentive system depends on having a clear definition of the epidemiology of complaints and what cases should be referred to specialty care.

Degree of Group Organization

The second crucial element defining the physician's work is the extent to which he operates as an independent practitioner in contrast to being part of a larger group organization. Although physicians have traditionally worked as independent practitioners out of their own offices or in people's homes, physicians' work is now more commonly based in group practices, health centers, or hospitals. In the United States, while physicians still mostly operate as individual entrepreneurs, selling their services on a fee-for-service basis, there has been a persistent trend toward group practice (McNamara and Todd 1970). The proportion of active physicians in group practice between 1969 and 1975 increased from 18 to 24 percent, and the trend has continued (Office of Health Research, Statistics, and Technology 1980, p. 162). Group practice also appears to be growing elsewhere in the world, stimulated by a willingness among young doctors to enter such practice and by the advantages of group organization for sharing responsibilities and providing greater opportunities for control over one's schedule. Most substantial group organization is found in countries that provide ambulatory care through health centers and polyclinics, either developed by the state or by large insurance funds. In the United States, the largest groups are more likely to be organized on a prepaid basis than the smaller groups; but the vast majority of groups of any size are largely engaged in fee-for-service practice (McNamara and Todd 1970).

Most of the advantages from group structure come from having a sufficient patient load to justify the acquisition of expensive facilities and equipment and the use of a variety of middle-level health practitioners who increase the physician's productivity and the scope of practice. Large groups facilitate the development of preventive programs, opportunities for continuing education, and control over schedules of work. But the larger the group, the greater the pressure is for physicians to adjust their practice style to others; and disputes develop over such issues as equitable remuneration, productivity, and administrative rules (Prybil 1970). Many physicians adapt to the need for economy of scale by developing independent arrangements with other physicians to share facilities and personnel, and even to cover for one another, without incurring the perceived disadvantages of accommodating to a formal organizational arrangement. Some of the new independent practice associations (one type of HMO) are a community-wide response of physicians to meet competition of prepaid group practices by offering consumers insurance for medical care on a prepaid basis but without requiring physicians to alter fundamentally their pattern of practice (see Egdahl 1973).

Observations of physicians practicing in large prepaid group practices suggest that, despite differences in organization, doctors do not fundamentally practice differently than in the traditional mode. Certainly mode of clinic organization, patient load, and types of remuneration have some impact on patterns of practice in a way I will review in detail later, but the amount of variance in practice behavior among doctors having the same roles in the same organizations is substantial (Greenlick and Freeborn 1971). Thus, it is clear that the physician's prior socialization and values have an important impact on style of practice independent of organizational factors; and such differences are supported by the widely shared norms of "medical responsibility" and "clinical experience" (Freidson 1976).

Systems of Remuneration

The effort and commitment physicians give to their work depends on the rewards received. Such rewards include income, status and esteem, appreciation of patients, and the satisfaction that comes from the knowledge of doing one's job well. Because of the lack of visibility of the office-based physician's work to the general public, or even to other doctors, the income earned by the physician tends to become an important symbol of success. Thoughtful physicians worry about the lack of a system of rewarding the physician in office-based patient care through means other than income, since this allows the economics of practice to have too large an effect on performance. Physicians may perform procedures that are remunerative, neglecting those for which payments are not made through insurance (such as patient education or listening to the patient). It is difficult to change the reward system and substitute other types of reward for income, since the physician's office work is not easily observable to anyone but patients; and patients are not usually a reference group for the physician since their judgments tend to be made primarily on the physician's manner as compared with technical criteria.

In part, because of the symbolic importance of income as an affirmation of the doctor's worth, physicians tend to be extraordinarily sensitive to how they are paid; and few other issues seem to arouse comparable emotion. The mode most doctors favor in the United States is the fee-for-service, which rewards them on a piecework basis in proportion to the work they do. Various studies indicate that doctors in office-based practice work longer hours and see more patients when they are paid on fee-for-service than when they are on salary or on capitation (receiving a fixed sum per patient per year) (Mechanic 1972a).

There are a remarkable number of variations in how physicians are remunerated from one country to another and under varying insurance mechanisms (Glasser 1970). In general, physicians tend to favor the system of remuneration they are most accustomed to, assuming that remuneration is adequate, and resist changes in it, fearing that structural changes will erode their economic position. Moreover, the evidence suggests that physicians adapt their behavior to whatever system of remuneration exists (Glaser 1970, p. 289), performing those procedures that are most likely to be rewarded by the scheme within which they work.

Basically, there are four major ways to remunerate physicians, with infinite variations and combinations. The first is the fee-for-service, where physicians receive an established amount for every specific procedure performed. Some fee schedules are highly specified; the relative value studies of the California Medical Association include thousands of procedures, although some six hundred entries account for most payments made to physicians (Crncich 1976). The second mode of paying doctors is on a salary—a fixed amount for specified hours or sessions. Third, doctors may be paid on capitation, a fixed amount per unit of time for each patient or family for whom the doctor takes responsibility. The amount of capitation can be adjusted by the characteristics of the patient, the attributes of the doctor, or the characteristics of the practice setting. Thus the amount of capitation per person may be higher if the patient is 65 or over, if the doctor has special training, or if the practice is located in a rural area. Finally, doctors may be paid on a case-payment method, fixed sums for giving patients all necessary care. Obstetricians often provide prenatal and delivery services to mothers on such a basis.

An important distinction is how the patient pays for care as compared with how the physician is paid. Patients, for example, may purchase a prepaid plan but the physicians may be paid on a salary, a capitation basis, or on a fee-for-service. Moreover, patients may purchase insurance on a service or indemnity basis. When the insurance is on a service basis, the physicians may have to negotiate the fee schedule with the health plan. In the indemnity situation the patient usually pays the doctor and is reimbursed at some level by insurance. Thus there is no direct relationship between the physician and the insurance plan. Some doctors refuse to accept patients on a service benefit plan or insist on charging the patient more for the service than the fee schedule established by the insurance plan.

Each form of payment tends to have distinct advantages and disadvantages, and it is difficult to achieve an effective balance among the competing payment mechanisms (Glaser 1970; Roemer 1962). Fee-for-service encourages the physician's hard work and commitment to the patient, and fee-for-service physicians tend to show greater responsiveness to their patients and interest in them (Mechanic 1976, pp. 99–118). Studies showing this, however, refer to the patient's direct payment to the physician, and we know very little about the consequences of fee-for-service when paid indirectly as in an independent practice association. The major disadvantage of fee-for-service is that it creates an incentive for unnecessary and sometimes dangerous procedures, particularly discretionary surgical interventions (Roemer 1962). Also, it tends to encourage the performance of technical procedures in contrast to communication, listening, and explanation.

Salary and capitation are seen as the payment methods most likely to direct the physician's attention to necessary medical tasks rather than to implicit economic incentives. Their advantage allegedly is that the revenue for care is known in advance and expenditures can be controlled, and that they require physicians to establish priorities in the use of their time and effort on the basis of need rather than on the patient's ability to pay. Fixed payment, however, provides little incentive for the physician to work long or irregular hours. Physicians on salary or capitation are more likely to decide what they regard as a reasonable work week for the remuneration received, and they are more likely to devote time to leisure and other personal activities. While the fee-for-service physician may be reluctant to make necessary referrals for fear of losing patients to competitors, it is alleged that capitation and salaried physicians refer too readily, placing an excessive burden on their colleagues and specialists (Forsyth and Logan 1968; Freidson 1976). Salary and capitation, in the absence of other incentives, provide no encouragement for careful, thorough, or responsive care. Patients are more likely to feel that physicians on salaries or capitation are less responsive, less interested in them, and more inflexible (Freidson 1961; Mechanic 1976). As Freidson (1970a, pp. 98–108) has noted, there is less client control in the encounter when the physician is less dependent on the patient's fee. Similarly, while case payment makes costs predictable for the patient or insurance plan, without careful monitoring there is no assurance that physicians will not provide less service than patients require.

A major problem in formulating an adequate remuneration system is the lack of clear standards of how much care is truly necessary. Much of medical care is discretionary and not easily demonstrated to have discernible influence on outcomes. With the lack of clear objective standards, political considerations determine the method of payment. In the United States physicians have been wedded traditionally to the fee-for-service method. Doctors know that this method is financially advantageous for them, amenable to their control, and most difficult for government to manipulate. Health-care plans and financing sources, however, dislike the open-ended nature of the fee-for-service system and the lack of control over expenditures for physician's services. Fixed payments allow them to predict and control costs more easily, although the actual cost depends on the size of salaries or capitation values. Because fixed-payment systems allow third parties greater potential control over amount of future remuneration, physicians are wary of them. They believe that such control would be used in fiscal crises, and they are probably correct in this assessment.

Physicians, on the whole, work long hours and have great responsibility. A majority of doctors have a strong belief that they should be rewarded in proportion to investments of their time and effort, and that the fee-for-service method is the fairest system to relate remuneration to effort. Increasing numbers of doctors, however, are acceptant of a fixed-payment system as long as the salaries are consistent with their aspirations. The tendency to favor fee-for-service found in the United States is not universal since its advantage depends on an affluent population willing and able to expend funds for physician services. In much of the world, where the population's income is too low to afford much private service, public subsidy of medical care through capitation or physician's salaries tends to increase physicians' total earnings, since they tend to be paid for many services that they previously provided free. Public programs even in the United States, such as Medicare, increased physicians' incomes since they paid for services that physicians were already providing without remuneration. Indeed, most systems of national health insurance, when first enacted, increase physicians' incomes unless stringent controls are put on types and amount of payment. But such controls are usually not adopted at first, since proponents wish to gain physicians' cooperation in enactment and implementation of new programs. Controls are usually added after the fact, and this is what particularly makes physicians fearful of government control over the means of remuneration.

A Social Profile

The role of the physician has exceedingly high prestige in American society and in most societies of the world (Hodge et al. 1965; Reiss 1961). In the United States it ranks with such lofty occupations as Supreme Court Justice and governor of a state, and has higher status than any other professional group. Medicine, thus, is attractive to recruits who value status and income, who seek a challenging and interesting occupation, who enjoy exercising judgment, and who seek to do good. Because of the preparation necessary for admission to medical school and the necessary long training and high costs of medical education, students from higher status families are disproportionately selected into the profession. Although more recent efforts have been made to select minority-group members, more women, and students from rural areas, medicine will remain disproportionately urban, white, male, and upper-middle class in its recruitment for a long time to come.

In the decades of the 1960s and 1970s there was a persistent perception of a doctor shortage. The growth of specialization and the geographic maldistribution of doctors, and the decline of numbers of primary-care physicians, convinced policymakers, legislators, and much of the public that we needed more doctors. Government policy, and the subsidies made available, encouraged the development of new medical schools and the expansion of existing ones. The result was a dramatic increase in the production of new doctors to the point that there is now a growing apprehension of an excess of medical manpower in the future. The number of physicians per 100,000 population increased from 144 in 1960 to almost 200 in 1980. Given the number of students being trained, it is projected that by 1990 we will have 242 physicians per 100,000 population, approximately one for every 400 people. It is now widely appreciated that the key issues are geographic distribution and specialty balance and not total medical manpower. Indeed, the knowledge that physicians generate costs for services many times their own remuneration is an alarming thought in light of anticipated increased numbers of doctors.

Selection into Medical Education

A great deal has been written about the attitudes and personality characteristics of students selected into medicine, but it is clear that there is tremendous diversity in this population and that the profile changes with modified social definitions over time (Funkenstein 1971). Studies have found that medical students are high on endurance and need for achievement, but lower on needs for change, succorance, and the like (Gough 1971). Some medical educators worry that the emphasis on hard scientific performance among medical admissions committees results in the selection of students whose interpersonal skills and human concerns are not as well developed as their scientific abilities. Others worry that medicine tends to attract students who may be more committed to economic incentives than to social concerns. While all of these tendencies may exist relative to students choosing some other fields, medical students still constitute a heterogeneous group. Greater personality and social selection probably occurs when the student decides on a specialty interest.

Socialization of the Physician

The process of medical education is demanding, and over a period of four years the student not only acquires massive amounts of information and a great variety of skills but also many attitudes and values that are shaped by the demands of medical work, a sense of confidence in his ability to take care of practical problems, and a repertoire of behavior shaped by clinical experience and responsibility (Becker et al. 1961). The applied character of clinical medical work, as Eliot Freidson (1970a, p. 78) has noted, "gives rise to a special frame of mind oriented toward action for its own sake, action based on a radical pragmatism. Such action relies on firsthand experience and is supported by both a will to believe in the value of one's actions and a belief in the inadequacy of general knowledge for dealing with individual cases."

A large number of students come to medical school with the intention of becoming primary-care physicians. Given the uncertainties of the role of the medical student during training, however, the student is very much influenced by the context and values dominant in the training situation. When students begin medical school they have only limited understanding of the nature of medical work or of the possible choices they will have. Medical school and even the early residency years confront them with a more complex reality to which they have to make a continuing series of personal, social, and academic adjustments (Becker et al. 1961; Miller 1970). As reality diminishes their naive idealism and makes them aware of the complexity of clinical problems, they begin to take on a more professional and limited perspective (Carlton 1978). Mastering the broad scope of medicine with a sense of competence and confidence is a very difficult task in the light of modern developments. Physicians who concentrate their efforts on a specialty have a much greater sense of mastery over the relevant material and can feel more secure that they know what they are doing. Thus young physicians aspiring to reduce anxiety about their own competence and performance are intuitively drawn to a more limited sphere of activity that provides a greater sense of self-confidence. Residency programs in family practice and primary care, which have developed substantially in recent years, must not only prepare physicians to exercise a wide variety of skills but also to live comfortably with uncertainty (Fox 1980).

Specialty Choice

The process by which a physician enters a particular specialty is a mixture of social selection, personal interest, accident, and opportunity, and also is dependent on the cast of characters who teach in the various specialties at a particular medical school. A student's interest in psychiatry, for example, might develop in a school where the department is strong and has high standing, but not in one where the psychiatrists are weak and poorly regarded. Similarly, the relative social standings of specialties change over time with changing economic opportunities, social definitions, and advances in science and technology. Thus it is difficult to speak in broad generalities about the selection process. Many students make definitive choices prior to medical school, while others may drift for several years of postgraduate education before finalizing their choice. Many students with defined preferences change them as they become aware of new fields and opportunities. Despite the idiosyncratic aspects of the process, both general impressions and empirical studies suggest that there are substantial differences among recruits to various specialties in social background, personality, and values (Coker et al. 1966). Such differences probably reflect both social selection and the influence of certain types of work on doctors' values, self-images, and presentations of self.

It might be useful to suggest some of the selective tendencies believed to be characteristic of varying specialties despite the changing character of the specialties over time. Some specialties, for example, tend to be almost exclusively male (surgery, radiology, urology), while others have much higher representation of women (pediatrics, anesthesiology, dermatology, psychiatry). Jews tend to be drawn disproportionately to psychiatry; and more politically liberal students to psychiatry and pediatrics. The image of the internist is that of the intellectual problem-solver, while the surgeon is seen as more aggressive and active. The family practitioner, in contrast, tends to be less conceptual and more gregarious than the internist. Psychiatry is seen to draw recruits who are abstract and playful about ideas, while surgeons tend to be more concrete and moralistic. Psychiatrists tend to be very high on Machiavellianism, while surgeons tend to be low (Christie and Geis 1970, pp. 346–47). Within-specialty variation, however, may far exceed the differences between specialties. Certain types of medical activities, like any other tasks, require certain skills and orientations. A physician who does not enjoy people, who is exceedingly exacting, and who has little tolerance for ambiguity would in all probability do better in pathology than in family medicine. Physicians sometimes choose specialties incompatible with their personal needs, and some resorting goes on throughout the careers of such persons.

We know relatively little about the factors that influence the types of practice physicians enter following their residency training. Practice location is affected by personal preferences, good economic opportunities, and the location of the institution where the student received his residency training (Steinwald 1974; Yett and Sloan 1974). Residents trained in a particular area become acquainted with it and with the medical community. Being on the spot, they often find a practice niche in an area nearby (Mumford 1970). Students trained in an area or institution in which they have had experience in a multispecialty group practice are more likely to enter such a practice (Prybil 1970). The probability that a resident will do primary care, establish a rural practice, or work in a health center is likely to depend on his having had a good experience as a resident in such a practice setting. To the extent that residency programs provide good models for such practices, there is increased likelihood that young doctors will see these as viable opportunities. Also, while general practitioners tend to be distributed more widely, specialists are more likely to locate in urban and suburban centers close to hospitals and other physicians.

Satisfactions and Dissatisfactions

In the United States physicians have not only maintained extremely high status and income but have also retained control over the work of other health professionals (Freidson 1970b). Thus, it is not surprising that there is relatively little literature dealing with dissatisfaction and identity problems of physicians in contrast to the literature on such problems among nurses and a variety of other professional groups such as priests, social workers, and teachers. The overwhelming majority of physicians appear to be extremely satisfied not only in general but also relative to most dimensions of their occupational role. This, too, is not surprising in that a number of studies have shown that job satisfaction is related to perceived status, although the appropriate reference group may vary from one study to another (Faich 1969). Physicians in the United States have been encouraged for the most part to organize and practice as they wish with extraordinary autonomy and control over their conditions of work. Moreover, the existing health-care system has been sufficiently flexible to allow physicians with varying personalties, interests, and personal goals to seek out specialized functions and practice settings consistent with their desires and without serious economic disadvantage; and thus it should be no surprise to us that the average physician has been relatively content with things as they are.

The literature on job satisfaction suggests that, although perceived adequate remuneration is an important condition for satisfaction, once a certain level of remuneration is reached, attention focuses on nonremunerative aspects of work satisfaction such as conditions of work, perceived autonomy, and opportunities for self-improvement and self-actualization (Faich 1969). Also, assessments of remuneration tend to be relative to remuneration of other colleagues in varying work settings and to the past history of remuneration (Mechanic and Faich 1970). Any changes that threaten the relative standing of the profession are vigorously resisted. Colombotos (1969, 1971), for example, found that prior to Medicare physicians were very much opposed to the program, but overwhelmingly supported it following its implementation. The key to this observation is that the Medicare program basically maintained the existing payment system and became a tremendous economic asset for physicians. In contrast, the Medicaid program—a federal-state matching program that in some states seriously attempts to regulate physicians' fees and conditions of reimbursement—has had more difficulty in achieving physician cooperation.

Physicians in the United States earn extremely high incomes. Although physicians feel threatened by impending national health legislation, the rise of malpractice insurance rates, the growing controls of governmental agencies over their activities, and criticisms in the mass media, the threat has yet to affect their earnings significantly. Indeed, most government programs that increase the insurance coverage of the population result in increases in physicians' incomes. Yet many physicians are worried about the future, and feel that the conditions of their work are being threatened by new government regulations and social changes. It is clear that medicine is in a process of transition and that physicians, while maintaining a great deal of autonomy, will no longer exercise the authority and control that they took for granted in the past. Moreover, the vast increases in the number of physicians relative to the population will contribute to diluting the economic power of the profession. To understand the effect of social trends on physician perceptions, it is necessary to examine the impact of the ferment of the 1960s and 1970s.

The Currents of Change and Physician Perceptions

The decades of the 1960s and 1970s brought many changes in medical care, as well as more generally. With Medicare and Medicaid and a vast array of other federal programs in the health services, government became intimately involved in both financing and regulating health care, establishing modes of payment, and providing incentives for changing organizational arrangements (Lewis, Fein, and Mechanic 1976). While medicine up to the 1960s maintained a united front in public despite internal cleavages between town and gown, among specialties, and between institutional and community care, the availability of public monies brought these strains into the open; and doctors began publicly debating—and sometimes debasing—one another. Thus organized medicine and medical schools fought over the structure of the Regional Medical Program, psychiatry opposed organized medicine on federal support for staffing mental health centers, and proponents and opponents fought bitterly over HMOs. While in prior decades malpractice litigation was made near impossible by the difficulty of locating physicians to testify against one another, physicians were now more likely to criticize one another in court as well as elsewhere. In short, there was no longer one voice speaking for medicine, and those that did were not singing the same song.

Recent decades also brought more challenge to the professional dominance of medicine relative to other health occupations (Freidson 1970b). In the 1960s there were massive increases in professional and technical manpower in health, and these groups increasingly organized and unionized. Nurses became more militant and fought more aggressively not only for improved wages and fringe benefits but also for more autonomy from physicians. Psychologists fought the dominance of psychiatrists over the services they could provide, and began to establish an independent domain. House staff began to bargain collectively, insisting that they be paid commensurately with the services they offered, and brought issues of quality of service, staffing, equipment provision, and related issues to the bargaining table. Hospital employees further eroded physician control through the provisions of contracts won through collective bargaining, creating pressure for more centralized administrative control. And court rulings in a variety of malpractice and other cases made it clear that hospitals were responsible for staff actions, building further incentives for administrative activity. As the organizational structures of medical practice became more varied, physicians frequently had conflicting interests among themselves and with other health providers that would surface in the public arena.

Existing evidence suggests that such fragmentation will increase and perhaps lead to greater acrimony within the profession itself. Certainly the extreme right and left wings of medicine are more polarized than ever before, and the American Medical Association has increasing difficulty in formulating policies that consolidate their membership. While in previous times, attack came exclusively from the left, now it comes from both extremes. Perhaps more ominous for the profession is that physicians are deeply divided on the need for national health insurance, and a majority hold their view strongly, making compromise more difficult. There is a growing gap between young and old physicians, between office-based and organizationally based doctors, and between general practitioners and surgeons as compared with other types of specialists such as pediatricians, psychiatrists, and internists (Colombotos, Kirchner and Millman 1975). Women in medicine tend to have less traditional views, and the proportions of women among younger doctors will increase.

Physicians feel besieged by new demands. Not only are the dilemmas in decision-making more complicated then ever before—decisions about extending life, providing heroic care, measuring large risks and costs against possible benefits—but they also take place in a context of monitoring, regulation, and public scrutiny. It is not too difficult to perceive why physicians feel uneasy and stressed, why they cope by restricting their efforts to small areas of expertise in which they feel they can master and control their work, and why they feel concerned about growing intrusions on their autonomy. One typical way physicians deal with their own uncertainty, anxiety, and fear about their own errors is to project an image of authority. But sophisticated consumers are critical of such behavior, viewing it as insensitive, arrogant, and callous, and the character of paternalism in doctor-patient relationships is itself under attack. Patients are demanding new types of relationships in which they share in decision-making, and doctors will have to adapt. Although definitive data are difficult to locate, the indications are that physicians have high rates of alcoholism, suicide, drug addiction, and marital disruption.

We have built increasingly complex expectations for the physician, demands that are increasingly difficult to meet. Doctors are expected to be technically proficient and to keep up with rapidly changing knowledge. They are to be warm, compassionate, responsive, and personally concerned. They should be sophisticated not only about narrow medical concerns but also about such varied areas as psychiatric illness, alcoholism, sexuality, the management of chronic disease, and the appropriate handling of death. They should be involved in changes in health-care delivery and responsive to research, and should participate in peer review and other quality of care efforts. They should be sensitive to informed consent and other ethical issues, but also should be productive, pursue cost-effective practice, and have a broad picture of social as well as medical needs. Even the very best can stagger under this load—perhaps some of the most conscientious do.

Given the demands on physicians, it seems evident that they will best be able to cope in organizational settings that can appropriately link their work with the efforts of other professionals, paraprofessionals, and administrative and managerial personnel and that provide the tools necessary for effective practice that are beyond the economic capacity of a single-handed or small practice. Younger doctors realize this and increasingly choose group settings, but older physicians—more set in their ways—find it difficult to make the accommodations to others that are more necessary in a group setting. It seems clear, however, that practice in organizations is the wave of the future, and both doctors and patients increasingly will have to work out appropriate relationships in such contexts.

The Social Role of the Physician and Orientations to Patients

As biomedical science and the specialization associated with medical advance have developed, physicians have come to view their work more narrowly. The flow of patients into medical care, however, reflects not only serious physical illness but social and psychological need, the desire to legitimate failure or diminished functioning, and search for secondary advantages through the certification of illness or disability. Illness remains one of the few acceptable means to escape or relieve ordinary responsibilities; and regardless of the physicians' technical training or interests, their roles are as much socially defined by the demands of patients as by their wishes.

The divergence in viewpoint of the technically oriented physician and the patient has contributed to much dissatisfaction with the organization of medical care (Mechanic 1976). Physicians, in general, prefer to deal with conditions that pose a diagnostic challenge and which they feel they can do something about. In contrast, they often feel uncomfortable with psychological or psychosocial problems, not only because they have no great efficacy in treating them but also because they have never been trained to feel comfortable in evaluating these problems and providing supportive care. Moreover, care for such problems—unlike the application of discrete technical procedures—is time-consuming and often increases the uncertainties of the physician's day. Thus, for the typical physician they constitute bottlenecks that increase the difficulties of handling one's practice. In recent years family practice residency programs have been training the physician to handle such problems with greater confidence and responsiveness.

One manifestation of the physician's tolerance for psychosocial problems is the tendency to characterize such patients as "trivial" or "crocks." The patients defined as trivial are those who have ordinary and common complaints such as upper respiratory infections, insomnia, fatigue, and the like. From the physician's perspective, many of these patients have either self-limited conditions or problems the physician can do nothing about, and thus consultation is unjustified. The crock, in contrast, tends to be a persistent complainer who has been evaluated repeatedly but with no observable organic basis of the complaint. Such attributions tell us more about how physicians define their work than about the needs of patients for assistance. There is little question that from a technical organic point of view most of these patients do not require sophisticated technical care. However, such patients are often fascinating from a psychosocial perspective. Exploration of their problems beyond the initial complaint frequently suggests that the initial presentation of symptoms is a means of justifying the consultation, and that the patient has a "hidden agenda" of problems really troubling him or her (Mechanic 1972b).

Physicians, of course, vary in their personalities, the organization of their practices, and the way they respond to patients. In a variety of studies of physicians in the United States and England, Mechanic found that attributions of triviality were related to the physician's concept of the appropriate range of medical complaints, to the method of payment, and to the intensity of patient demand (Mechanic 1976). British general practitioners, for example, who are paid on a capitation basis, appear to schedule their office hours in terms of some concept of what is reasonable, given their fixed level of remuneration. They then attempt to accommodate the patients who wish to consult them within these office hours. When physicians have a heavy patient load, they must keep their minds not only on the individual patient but also on keeping the queue moving. Patients with vague complaints, or psychosomatic or psychosocial problems, require considerable time to assess what their real problems are or to have an opportunity to talk. The doctor, however, who knows that many patients are waiting to see him feels pressure to move the patient along, and often treats the symptom rather than the "whole patient." The doctor often deals with his feelings of frustration and his knowledge that he really did not give the patient sufficient time by attributing triviality to the patient.

One solution to the pressure of patient load is to work longer hours, allocating more time to each patient. But physicians on a fixed salary or a capitation system have no economic incentive to do so, although they may do so because they are conscientious or otherwise want to do a good job. The system of remuneration is an important factor affecting style of practice. In contrast, American fee-for-service physicians tend to increase their hours of patient care more with increased demand, and are less likely to attribute triviality to their patients. Unlike their British counterparts, fee-for-service primary-care physicians are reinforced for every additional consultation and, thus, are less likely to feel frustrated by additional consultations. Doctors in large prepaid group practices who are paid on a salaried basis react more like the British general practitioners than their counterparts in fee-for-service practice (Mechanic 1975).

Although the structure of practice and the system of remuneration have an important influence, the doctor's attitudes and training also affect styles of practice. In a study of British general practitioners, Mechanic (1970) classified doctors into four groups based on their levels of use of diagnostic facilities and on the extent to which they were tolerant of broader functions such as dealing with birth control, marital difficulties, excessive drinking, anxieties about child care, and the like. Doctors who had a broad view and a high use of technical facilities were called "moderns" and those low on both dimensions were called "withdrawers." Those high only on diagnostic use were characterized as "technicians," and those who were high solely on perceived scope of practice were called "counselors." Moderns were less likely to characterize their patients as trivial, were more likely to do psychotherapy, and included a high proportion of members of the Royal College of General Practice. Moderns also seemed more intellectually active in other ways, as evidenced by a higher tendency to read the *Lancet*, a sophisticated medical journal. The withdrawers were most likely to attribute triviality to their patients, were the least likely to acknowledge responsibility for psychiatric patients or to do psychotherapy, gave the least time to their practices, were least satisfied, had least contact with other doctors, had least training in social aspects of medicine, and did the least reading of professional journals.

There were some major differences between the counselors and the technicians. Counselors were older doctors, were more likely to be in solo practice, were less likely to rely on an appointment system, and gave somewhat less effort on the average to their practices. Technicians, in contrast, reported greater professional contact and less satisfaction and were more likely to attribute triviality to patients. In general, the technicians included more of the younger doctors who had been trained to be more reliant on diagnostic technology and who also were more intolerant of nonmedical problems and supportive aspects of the physician's role. The counselors were more likely to be old-timers who depended on talking and supportive therapies and clinical judgment more than on the laboratory. The moderns, who seemed to combine the best of both groups, were not particularly distinctive from other doctors by age or practice organization. However, they appeared to be much more committed to continuing education.

Another way of viewing the practice style of the physician is described by Freidson (1976, pp. 44–48) in his depiction of physicians in fee-for-service and prepaid practice as the merchant, the expert, and the bureaucratic official. The merchant is the traditional entrepreneurial physician who sells his services in a market on a fee-for-service basis. Depending on the competitiveness of the marketplace, patients may have some control in these circumstances, demanding a certain flexibility and responsiveness from the doctor, and threatening to go elsewhere if the doctor is rigid or unresponsive. In the expert-layman relationship the client puts himself in the hands of the doctor on the assumption that the doctor knows best and implicitly agrees to comply with the doctor's advice; "analytically, expertise gains its authority by its persuasive demonstration of special knowledge and skill relevant to particular problems requiring solution. It is the antithesis of the authority of office" (Freidson 1976, pp. 46–47). The third style, characterized by many physicians in large bureaucratic organizations, is the official who controls access to services and client abuse. Patients have a contract entitling them to specified services which they may claim. The physician, however, is the official gatekeeper, who is expected to ration the use of scarce services in terms of patient need, itself an intangible concept. In this context the patient may demand services on the basis of his contractual rights, thus forcing the physician to play the role of the bureaucratic official. As Freidson notes, such patients—however uncommon they may be—may infuriate the physician because their claims challenge the physician's assumptions about his role which are based largely on the view of the physician as expert.

As medical settings are increasingly more organized and as financing on a prepaid, prospective, or global budget is more commonly instituted, physicians face increasing conflicts between their roles as agents of patients and as officials of health insurance plans (Mechanic 1976, pp. 49–57). In order to achieve controls over costs, organizational devices are developed to create tension between the physician's economic interests and providing care to patients. In many respects this situation is the obverse of the fee-for-service situation where it is in the physician's economic interest to use any procedure, and even unnecessary and possibly dangerous procedures as well, however small the clinical gain. In each of these examples appropriate controls are necessary to insure that economic incentives do not produce pathological practice tendencies (Mechanic 1979).

Physicians respond not only to the economic and organizational contexts of their practices and to their own personality needs but also to the characteristics and behavior of patients. Doctors can identify more easily with patients who share their cultural orientations and life-styles, and they tend to find such patients more attractive. But they respond as well to the interesting medical challenge, the nonroutine, the appreciative patient, and the patient who gives them proper deference. Like others in the society, physicians have concepts of more or less worthy patients, and may give varying effort to different patients. (In respect to resuscitation see Sudnow 1967; for a somewhat contrasting view, see Crane 1975, pp. 52–61.)

Physicians' Attitudes, Values, and Ideologies

Although physicians occupy positions on the entire political spectrum, a majority describe themselves as politically conservative and identify with the Republican party. Office-based, nongroup physicians tend to be more conservative than physicians in groups or in hospital-based practice; and doctors in prepaid practice and academic medicine are most likely to hold liberal attitudes (Colombotos et al. 1975; Mechanic 1974 pp. 69–87). General practitioners have more conservative attitudes than internists or pediatricians. These general descriptions do not control for varying ages among physicians in the different subgroups or for differences in social background. While interesting, none of these facts is particularly crucial. What is especially important is the fact that physicians' political views are highly correlated with how they view the organization and delivery of medical care.

In his study of receptivity to health-care delivery among a national sample of primary physicians, Mechanic (1974, pp.69–87) found that conservative doctors and those describing themselves as Republicans were more likely to oppose government financing, changes in organization (such as prepaid practice, remuneration by salary and neighborhood health centers), peer review, and the use of physician extenders. Using multiple regression techniques, he found that physicians' political-philosophical orientations were the most consistent and substantial predictors of attitudes toward changes in the delivery system. It was the only predictor, among thirty-eight different variables, that consistently achieved substantial correlations with varying measures of organizational change and between group and nongroup practitioners. Goldman (1974), studying a sample of graduates from the Yale University School of Medicine between 1930 and 1976, also found that political philosophy was the strongest predictor of attitudes toward medical care. Colombotos and colleagues (1975), in studying a national sample of physicians, interns, residents, and medical students, have also made similar observations. These studies suggest that the debates over medical care, which are often represented as technical issues for which medical training and expertise are especially relevant, are in fact predominantly political in nature.

The ideology of physicians depends on background characteristics, the nature of their work, and on their self-interest. In general, the physicians who tend to support social reform are those who appear to have the least to lose from it, although we must also take into account that physicians in part have preselected themselves into different types of work and practice settings on the basis of their social orientations.

The medical practitioner, whose social origins are largely bourgeoisie, has a strong commitment to independence, social and economic individualism, and class status (Freidson 1970a, pp. 172–73). A variety of studies over the years have indicated that medical students have strong economic motivations, although they also value working with people and being of service. In a 1970 survey of 21,000 college seniors, future medical students stood high relative to others on such values as "service to others," "working with people," "working independently," and "interest in work activities," but reported little interest in free time or travel. They were highest of any group on the value of security (Baird 1975). Also, as Freidson (1970a) has so nicely illustrated, medicine—being an applied activity involving emphasis on the individual case in contrast to more global concepts like mankind or the social good—results in a "special frame of mind." This perspective is reflected in what Fuchs (1968) has called the "technologic imperative"—the tendency to give the best care technically possible with the only recognized or legitimate constraint being the state of the art. These values, thus, have enormous consequences for the costs of medical care as well as other matters.

Political Organization of the Medical Profession

The American Medical Association constitutes the single largest medical professional organization and, generally, has the support of the rank-and-file physician despite the feelings of a significant minority that the AMA does not represent their views. Four-fifths of the physicians studied by Colombotos and associates (1975, p. 382) felt that doctors disagreeing with the policies of the AMA should work within the organization to change it rather than organize in other ways. Relatively small groups of doctors on the extreme right and on the extreme left have organized new groups, but they are relatively unimportant compared with the AMA. Greater competing power lies with various specialty associations and the Association of American Medical Colleges (AAMC), which represents academic medicine. As physicians are more specialized they see their welfare more dependent on the fate of their fellow specialists than on physicians in the aggregate. As medical policy and the economics of care have become more complicated, specialty groups and the AMA clash more frequently, or one specialty group comes into conflicts with others over the definition of a common domain. Many of the specialty groups have sufficient resources to maintain good communication with their members, to lobby for favorable legislation, to initiate litigation, and generally to support the interests of their members.

The stand of any group of doctors on a particular issue depends on a variety of factors. Most important is their stake in a particular controversy. The technical guidelines for the administration of the renal program may be emotional issues for transplant surgeons and nephrologists, but may be totally irrelevant for most other doctors. How hospital radiologists or anesthesiologists are remunerated may be crucial for them but of little concern to the office-based pediatrician. Federal financing for staffing of mental health centers may be an important economic issue for many psychiatrists, but may be opposed on purely philosophical grounds by other physicians who have no stake in the matter. In general, each medical subgroup pursues the issues of greatest importance for them with the tacit support of uninvolved doctors. The disputes become bitter when different groups of doctors have sharply conflicting interests, as occurred on such issues as the support of Regional Medical Programs, federal subsidy for medical students, differential fee schedules for generalists and specialists, and the like. Increasingly, the American Medical Association finds it difficult to mediate among all the conflicting groups it encompasses, and the AMA itself has become in recent years less monolithic, less united, and less powerful.

The American Medical Association is a national organization with affiliated state and county associations. Membership in the national organization is achieved only through membership at the local level, although local membership may or may not require membership in the national organization. Many physicians prefer local membership without national affiliation. Although local societies are highly autonomous and while election to state and AMA offices occurs through local and state election procedures, the types of physicians elected to the AMA House of Delegates tend to be "medical politicians" with a long involvement in local medicopolitical affairs. They tend to be exceedingly conservative and much involved with preserving the economic and political status of the medical profession.

The AMA is also a professional organization, and has an enormous range of publications dealing with general medicine, scientific matters in various specialties, and health economics as well as a widely distributed periodical dealing with health issues for the general public. Much of the budget and efforts of both national and local organizations are devoted to matters of medical-care standards, professional education, medical ethics, and the like. Unlike many other professional organizations, however, its unique influence comes through quasi-official functions such as approving medical schools, which it does jointly with the Association of American Medical Colleges and which is the criterion then used by state licensing boards in granting medical licenses. Similarly, the AMA jointly with the American Hospital Association (AHA) approves hospitals for postgraduate physician education. Since federal programs frequently use as criteria for reimbursement or federal support certification or approval by such organizations as the AMA, the AAMC, and the AHA, the standards promulgated by these interest groups have effects beyond the functions performed.

The state and local medical societies are highly autonomous and pursue issues of greatest concern at the grass-roots level. In addition, they often take on major responsibilities in sponsoring insurance plans and, more recently, medical foundation plans. Local societies in some states become competitors in selling insurance programs, and at times such competition has become acrimonious. Medical societies may differ a great deal in their programs, philosophy, and leadership, and it is naive to view the profession as a monolith without internal competing interests. Physician service programs are often jointly organized with Blue Cross plans, and relationships between these organizations may have great significance. There are no major sociological studies as yet of such relationships (for a definition of some of the issues, see Law 1974).

It has been argued that the center of power of the medical profession has shifted from the office-based practitioner to "professional monopolists" and "corporate rationalizers." Professional monopolists are mainly physicians in medical schools or large medical centers who "exploit organizational resources for their personal or professional interests," while "corporate rationalizers" are "hospital administrators, medical school directors, public health officials, directors of city health agencies, heads of quasi-public insurance (Blue Cross), state and federal health officials" who seek "to expand the powers of their home institutions" (Alford 1972, pp. 141, 143). Alford has argued, with very little evidence, that problems in health care result from competition and conflict between these two groups. Each manipulates the system to serve its own purposes, resulting in failure to meet basic needs, empire building, excessive expenditures, and waste. While there is little doubt that the influence of large medical organizations in medical affairs has grown very substantially in recent decades—particularly in large urban areas with many medical centers like New York and Boston—in much of the country power still very much resides with the local practitioners. While they may have little direct influence on federal policy or the development of new programs, the care given depends very substantially on how they define their work and on their medical and social orientations.

Control over the Physician's Work

There are many studies suggesting that the quality of medical practice departs significantly from the standards taught in medical schools, and even studies of performance in teaching hospitals suggest that these efforts leave much to be desired. There is abundant evidence of excessive and inappropriate surgery, inappropriate use of antibotics and other drugs, failure of follow-up, lack of coordination in care with duplication of service or conflicting therapies, and many other problems. Similarly, there have been many problems in the administration of health plans involving inappropriate and excessive utilization. The most pervasive view among doctors is that the remedy to these problems is in peer review and continuing education, and the Professional Standards Review Organization legislation is an attempt to make such review a more widespread process.

More than any other sociologist, Eliot Freidson (1976) has directed his attention to the processes of professional self-regulation, and although his excessive pessimism may be in part a product of his focus on ambulatory as compared with in-hospital care, he has been a keen observer of the difficulties. In essence, Freidson argues that effective peer review is extraordinarily difficult because of the acceptance among physicians of the values of autonomy and clinical judgment as a major aspect of dealing with the individual case, the limited observability of the actual performance of physicians, and the commonly shared notions that the individual physician ought to be trusted and that mistakes are an inevitable consequence deriving from medical work. Moreover, since all physicians are vulnerable to criticism, a rule of etiquette prevails which protects one's colleagues. Freidson observes that physicians distinguish between mistakes that are normalized and those that are seen as more deviant. In many situations, physicians make judgments that in retrospect appear not to have been optimal; normalization is seen as justifiable in that the decision when it was made appeared to be a reasonable one. Freidson notes that

> The ambiguity introduced into the idea of error or mistake by the idea of judgment is such that the possibility of utilizing consistent technical rules for evaluating and controlling mistakes seems to be very much reduced, if not precluded for all practical purposes. . . . With rules removed, the criteria for evaluating one's own and one's colleagues' work become so permissive as to allow extremely wide variation in performance. Only gross or blatant acts of ignorance or inattention which all physicians would be united in recognizing and condemning remain securely in the category of deviant mistakes. [Freidson 1976, pp. 136–37]

Bosk (1979), in a qualitative study of surgical training, found that while surgeons readily excused technical errors, they were much harsher in the case of moral errors—those involving failures to follow rules of conduct on which professional action is based. Bosk found that social control over deviants was quite strong in an individual sense, although there was an absence of corporate responsibility. Thus, while a surgeon who was deviant might be asked to leave the department or hospital, no one would take responsibility to exercise any control over the surgeon once he left the setting. Thus he could practice elsewhere with impunity.

The practical task even of establishing standards for hospital care to be used as part of a peer-review process is formidable. The development of Professional Standards Review Organizations was motivated by goals that may be contradictory—improving the quality of care and reducing the costs of care. Standards have the effect of reducing variance in behavior and, if the standard is higher than the statistical norm, it results in increased procedures and more care which may frustrate the goal of controlling costs. Medical care is very largely a matter of judgment, and most of the standards that presently exist are rules of process (rules about how the doctor should proceed, what tests he should order, and the like) and not decisions based on outcome experience. It is conceivable that standards established on the basis of medical judgments of reasonable process may substantially increase costs without materially affecting the welfare of patients.

The idea of peer review of hospital and medical work through agreed-upon process standards also is likely to reinforce a mode of decision-making based on individual patients in contrast to the needs of populations. In deciding on the allocation of limited resources—and medical resources, despite their abundance, are limited—it is necessary to consider not only the care received by those who find their way into treatment but also those not in treatment who should be. The focus of peer review is on the hospitalized patients and not on others who may need such care but were not hospitalized. Only a monitoring approach based on the study of populations can rectify such errors of omission.

The Future

The profession of medicine is in a state of active transition stimulated by the growth of science and technology, changing public expectations, increased government financing and regulation, and the dilemmas inherent in its existing forms of organization. Each year it becomes more difficult for the profession to maintain traditional organizational forms in face of the onslaught of new developments, new regulations, and changing public demands. While the profession has shown extraordinary adaptive capacities, as in the development of shared arrangements among independent practitioners, the growth of physician-run insurance plans, and more recently the organization of independent practice associations, these accommodations are slowly but surely changing the basic character of medical organization and the locus of control from the individual physician to physician administrators. Pressures for cost containment will be strong in coming years and are likely to have important effects on how medical care is perceived, organized, and delivered.

REFERENCES

Aiken, L. H., et al. 1979. The contribution of specialists to the delivery of primary care. *New England Journal of Medicine* 300: 1363–70.

Alford, R. 1972. The political economy of health care: dynamics without change. *Politics and Society* 2: 127–164.

American Medical Association. 1973. *The profile of medical practice.* Chicago: AMA Center for Health Services Research and Development.

Baird, L. L. 1975. The characteristics of medical students and their views of the first year. *Journal of Medical Education* 50: 1092–99.

Balint, M. 1957. *The doctor, his patient, and the illness.* New York: International Universities Press.

Becker, H. S.; Geer, B.; Hughes, E. C.; and Strauss, A. L. 1961. *Boys in white: student culture in medical school.* Chicago: University of Chicago Press.

Beeson, P. 1974. Some good features of the British National Health Services. *Journal of Medical Education* 49: 43–49.

Bosk, C. 1979. *Forgive and remember: managing medical failure.* Chicago: University of Chicago Press.

Carlton, W. 1978. *In our professional opinion: the primacy of clinical judgment over moral choice.* Notre Dame, Ind.: University of Notre Dame Press, 1978.

CHRISTIE, R., and GEIS, F. L. 1970. *Studies in Machiavellianism.* New York: Academic Press.

COKER, R., et al. 1966. Medical careers in public health. *Milbank Memorial Fund Quarterly* 44 (pt. 1): entire issue.

COLOMBOTOS, J. 1969. Physicians and medicare: a before-after study of the effects of legislation on attitudes. *American Sociological Review* 34: 318–34.

——. 1971. Physicians' responses to changes in health care: some projections. *Inquiry* 8: 20–26.

——; KIRCHNER, C.; and MILLMAN, M. 1975. Physicians view national health insurance: a national study. *Medical Care* 13: 369–96.

CRANE, D. 1975. *The sanctity of social life: physicians' treatment of critically ill patients.* New York: Russell Sage Foundation.

CRNCICH, J. 1976. The making of the California relative values studies: the ideology and administration of pricing policy in the fee-for-service medical market. Unpublished paper, Program in Health Administration, University of Wisconsin-Madison.

EGDAHL, R. 1973. Foundations for medical care. *New England Journal of Medicine* 288: 491–98.

FAICH, R. 1969. Social and structural factors affecting work satisfaction: a case study of general practitioners in the English National Health Service. Ph.D. dissertation, University of Wisconsin-Madison, 1969.

FORSYTH, G., and LOGAN, R. 1968. *Gateway or dividing line: a study of hospital out-patients in the 1960s.* New York: Oxford University Press.

FOX, R. 1980. *Essays in medical sociology.* New York: Wiley-Interscience.

FREIDSON, E. 1961. *Patients' views of medical practice.* New York: Russell Sage Foundation.

——. 1970a. *Profession of medicine: a study of the sociology of applied knowledge.* New York: Dodd-Mead.

——. 1970b *Professional dominance: the social structure of medical care.* New York: Atherton.

FREIDSON, R. 1976. *Doctoring together: a study of professional social control.* New York: Elsevier.

FUCHS, V. 1968. The growing demand for medical care. *New England Journal of Medicine* 279: 190–95.

FUNKENSTEIN, D. 1971. Medical students, medical schools, and society during three eras. In *Psychosocial aspects of medical practice,* ed. R. Coombs and C. Vincent, pp. 229–81. Springfield, Ill.: Thomas.

GLASER, W. A. 1970. *Paying the doctor: systems of remuneration and their effects.* Baltimore, Md.: Johns Hopkins Press.

GOLDMAN, L. 1974. Factors related to physicians' medical and political attitudes: a documentation of intraprofessional variations. *Journal of Health and Social Behavior* 15: 177–87.

GOUGH, G. 1971. The recruitment and selection of medical students. In *Psychosocial aspects of medical practice,* ed. R. Coombs and C. Vincent. Springfield, Ill.: Thomas.

GREENLICK, M., and FREEBORN, D. 1971. *Determinants of medical care utilization: on choosing the appropriate measure of utilization.* Henniker, N. H.; Engineering Foundation Conference on Qualitative Decision Making for Ambulatory Care.

HODGE, R. W.; SIEGEL, P. M.; and ROSSI, P. H. 1965. Occupational prestige in the United States, 1925-63. *American Journal of Sociology* 70: 286–302.

LAW, S. 1974. *Blue Cross: what went wrong?* New Haven, Conn.: Yale University Press.

LEWIS, C.; FEIN, R.; and MECHANIC, D. 1976. *A right to health.* New York: Wiley-Interscience.

McNAMARA, M., and TODD, C. 1970. A survey of group practice in the United States. *American Journal of Public Health* 60: 1303–13.

MECHANIC, D. 1970. Practice orientations among general medical practitioners in England and Wales. *Medical Care* 8: 15–25.

———. 1972a. General medical practice: some comparisons between the work of primary care physicians in the United States and England and Wales. *Medical Care* 10: 402–20.

———. 1972b. Social psychologic factors affecting the presentation of bodily complaints. *New England Journal of Medicine* 286: 1132–39.

———. 1974. *Politics, medicine, and social science.* New York: Wiley-Interscience.

———. 1975. The organization of medical practice and practice orientations among physicians in prepaid and nonprepaid primary care settings. *Medical Care* 13: 189–204.

———. 1976. *The growth of bureaucratic medicine: an inquiry into the dynamics of patient behavior and the organization of medical care.* New York: Wiley-Interscience.

———. 1979. *Future issues in health care.* New York: Free Press.

———, and FAICH, R. 1970. Doctors in revolt: the crisis in the English national health service. *Medical Care* 8: 442–55.

MILLER, S. J. 1970. *Prescription for leadership: training for the medical elite.* Chicago: Aldine.

MUMFORD, E. 1970. *Interns: from students to physicians.* Cambridge, Mass.: Harvard University Press.

Office of Health Research, Statistics, and Technology. 1980. *Health—United States, 1979.* DHEW pub. no. (PHS) 80-1232. Washington, D. C.: Government Printing Office.

PRYBIL, L. 1970. Physicians in large, multi-specialty groups: an investigation of selected characteristics, career patterns, and opinions. Ph.D. dissertation, University of Iowa Graduate Program in Hospital and Health Administration.

REISS, A. J., JR. 1961. *Occupations and social status.* New York: Free Press.

ROEMER, M. 1962. On paying the doctor and the implications of different methods. *Journal of Health and Social Behavior* 3:4–14.

STEINWALD, B. 1974. Physician location: behavior versus attitudes. In *Reference data on socioeconomic issues of health*, ed. B. Eisenberg, pp. 34–41. Chicago: Center for Health Services Research and Development, Americal Medical Association.

STEVENS, R. 1971. *American medicine and the public interest.* New Haven, Conn.: Yale University Press.

SUDNOW, D. 1967. *Passing on: the social organization of dying.* Englewood Cliffs, N.J.: Prentice-Hall.

YETT, D. E., and SLOAN, F. A. 1974. Migration patterns of recent medical school graduates. *Inquiry* 9:125–42.

Chapter 21

Medical and Nursing Education: Surface Behavior and Deep Structure

Donald W. Light

DURING THE PAST TWO DECADES, schools of medicine and of nursing have been in great turmoil over their purpose and how they influence their respective domains. According to the implicit social contract between any profession and society, professional schools should train practitioners to serve the needs of the people. Increasingly, however, public leaders became aware of serious breaches in this contract in the form of maldistribution by geography, specialty, social class, and race that left large groups underrepresented and underserved. Since the Health Professions Educational Assistance Act in 1963, Congress has passed a spate of bills designed to redirect professional schools in health so that they admit more women, blacks, and low-income students and train them for primary-care medicine among the economically and geographically underserved (Weisfeld 1980).

Aside from the large increase of women in medicine, these efforts have not been very successful and continue to be the focus of major study. During the past year in medicine alone, three large reports have appeared: the Graduate Medical Education National Advisory Committee report (1980), whose methodology tells us as much about professional bias as it does about the growing physician surplus; the Macy report (1980), which, among other things, continues to find curricular neglect of the social, psychological, and economic aspects of medical care; and the Association of American Medical Colleges report (1980), which documents the rough-hewn nature of graduate programs and is forced, like its forerunners, to discuss their uneven quality without any objective measures of quality. On the whole, the authors of this new generation of studies are less sanguine about using medical schools to redress imbalances, as well they might be if they had read sociological studies of medical schools. For medical schools, like other professional schools, are paradoxically the fountainhead of the profession and yet separate from it. On one hand, professional schools create and transmit the skills on which

I am indebted to Ernest M. May and William Lehrman for their assistance in preparing this chapter, to David Mechanic for his editorial advice, and to B. L. Cohen, R. F. Leedy, and N. V. Velez, without whose support this chapter would not have been possible.

the profession is based. Max Weber observed that professional skills are a form of property on which one can collect "rent" and develop new markets (Weber 1954, pp. 180–95). Thus medical and nursing educators disproportionately influence the way professional work is organized and carried out. On the other hand, medical and nursing schools are institutions with a concern for theory, research, academic prestige, and influence not necessarily compatible with the manpower needs of the nation.

The major studies which examine the educational experience of going through medical or nursing school are rarely cited in policy reports. Yet through their observation of what actually happens in classrooms and clinics, they separate the possible from the improbable. If read from a policy perspective, which they rarely take, these studies can begin to discern the goals of professional education. For example, a professor of internal medicine recently became a medical student again to observe medical education from the inside. In his final report, he felt it necessary to emphasize that the *"focus and first priority of medical-school education is the patient"* (Eichna 1980, p. 728, italics in original). Such studies also document how medical and nursing schools shape the values of their graduates and their style of patient care.

Continuity and Change in Medical Education

A revealing portrait of medical education which sheds light on a number of current issues is provided by the pioneering studies at mid-century of medical programs at Western Reserve, Cornell, and Colorado. These largely forgotten reports deserve attention both for what they neglected to look at and what they found. Although Bloom (1979) points out that investigations of medical education date back to 1834 in England and to the 1910 Flexner report in the United States, this burst of activity between 1955 and 1965 was the first time that well-trained social scientists analyzed experiments in medical education.

At all three medical schools, educators designed programs with "the goal of humanizing medicine to repair what were believed to be the dehumanizing effects of scientific specialization, but with the retention of the best of science. To achieve this goal, the behavioral sciences—psychology, sociology, and anthropology—were assigned for the first time a role in the contributing basic sciences of medicine" (Bloom 1979, p. 6). In an era of primary care, these experiments put in perspective current efforts to achieve similar goals.

Of the three, Western Reserve acted most boldly, "turning the standard curriculum upside down and shaking it out into a strikingly new form" (Bloom 1979, p. 6). Academic disciplines were integrated around subject committees, and clinical experience was integrated with scientific subjects throughout the entire four years. Students were given three and a half days of free time, and independent research studies were required (Horowitz 1964, chap. 3). Exams, grades, and invidious rankings were minimized. Underlying these changes was a shift in philosophy from the faculty *teaching* to the students *learning*. As the Faculty Committee on Medical Education put it in 1951, "It is essential that the M.D. student be treated as a maturing individual, as a colleague, and as a student in the graduate professional school who is given increasing responsibility for his own education, for a knowledge of medicine, and for the care of patients" (Horowitz 1964, p. 22).

A year earlier, a group at Cornell founded the Cornell Comprehensive Care and Teaching Program (CC&TP). Comprehensive care, they argued, "demands attention to emotional and social as well as physical factors and continuing supervision of the patient in the clinic, hospital or home during each episode of illness for sufficient time to bring him through convalescence and rehabilitation, if such is possible, to an optimal state of health and productivity and to maintain him in it" (Reader and Goss 1967, p. 2). The spokesmen talked about "compassionate care" and the "humane consideration for the patient as a person." More modest in scope than the reforms at Western Reserve, the program involved each half of the fourth-year class spending half the year in a comprehensive clinic where students were encouraged to consult with a comprehensive team of providers and were given a family to follow on a continuing basis.

Like the Cornell experiment, the General Medical Clinic (GMC) at Colorado used a separate, broadly trained and humanistic staff to change the values and attitudes of students during their fourth year (Hammond and Kern 1959; Merton et al. 1957). Close reading indicates that their patients were quite poor, while those in the Cornell program came more often from the working class. Nearly half of the former were either Spanish-speaking or black, and two-thirds received public assistance. But the clinic was organized to give these patients the time needed for comprehensive attention, and the staff emphasized the need for medical students to be exposed to as wide a range of people as pathologies (Hammond and Kern 1959, p. 24). As in the Cornell program, students were assigned to families during their time at the clinic. Unlike the Cornell program, members of each fourth-year class were randomly assigned to either an experimental group or a control group matched for class standing. Only the experimental group experienced the General Medical Clinic and "benefited" from comprehensive-care conferences, seminars on ambulatory care, psychosomatic conferences, and other special experiences

How were the studies carried out and what did they find? At Western Reserve, Horowitz had the first class rate their peers in terms of academic, professional, and social behavior. He then took the ten with the highest and with the lowest overall ratings and followed them through medical school and into practice five years after graduation. He carried out numerous in-depth interviews on their academic and personal development and their views of medicine as a field, of medical school, of their progress each year, and of the stresses they faced. A psychologist by training, Horowitz skillfully combined all this information with instructors' ratings and grades to identify patterns of going through medical school, styles of self-appraisal, and approaches to learning (Horowitz 1964, chaps. 6–8). He found that students fell into four patterns of response to medical school. Some entered with a clear goal, were well organized, and went through it with no difficult decisions facing them. Others had no clear plans but enjoyed the challenge of tough science problems. They liked the flexibility of the program because it allowed them to find their own interests and to pursue research questions that challenged them. A third group had no clear plans nor any particular enthusiasm for science; they discovered the pleasures of clinical work. Finally, a few students were heavily invested in outside commitments and did not get involved in medical school. They were married and regarded medical courses as assignments to be done. On the whole, Horowitz found that students felt they learned a lot and experienced significant personal growth.

What strikes the contemporary reader about Horowitz's report is how little it says about one of the most important and successful experiments in medical education. His study could have been done anywhere. His focus on social psychology and attitude change, moreover, is typical of most studies of medical and nursing education where both the educators running the schools and the social scientists they retain to study them ignore how the impact of structural features of the schools, their politics, and their economics may fundamentally affect the education of health professionals. For example, it has often been pointed out that university hospitals are designed to select and focus on unusual pathologies which in turn give medical trainees a skewed notion of medical practice (White 1973). It is important that evaluations of medical education be organizational as well as social psychological.

Another largely ignored dimension of medical and nursing education is the extent to which a given program improves patient care. While none of these studies evaluates patient care, one gathers from details of the research that many patients did not particularly want or like so much attention. If they had a fever or a pain, they wanted to get rid of it and go home. Such incidental observations implicitly raise questions about whether many poor people regard comprehensive care as intrusive.

The Colorado and Cornell studies did, however, take note of how students responded to their patients, and this is relevant to comtemporary programs for training physicians to practice in underserved, low-income areas. Faced with a predominantly white, female working-class population of which 40 percent had graduated from high school, the Cornell students reported no particular difficulties of rapport. On the other hand, the researchers did not measure student attitudes toward patients as they did at Colorado. Cornell students complained that they did not see enough patients and enough interesting pathologies, but they liked the greater degree of responsibility they had in patient care and thrived with it. This is a nearly universal finding of many studies about medical education—that students gain confidence and competence in direct relation to the amount of clinical responsibility they are given.

At Colorado, where patients were poorer and measurements better, the study portrays fouth-year students liking the greater responsibility they had at the General Medical Clinic but disliking their patients. They found barriers of language, ignorance, race and poverty more than they could handle. They considered many of these patients "crocks" with socioemotional problems they could not treat. These patients differed considerably from those seen by the control group in the regular rotations, so that the impact of the General Medical Clinic as an educational program was confounded by having such a different and difficult clientele. Under these circumstances, comprehensive care never had a chance, because it was associated with undesirable patients. One notes ironically how often humane, comprehensive-care training programs are established in low-income areas where patients resist so much attention and students resist the patients.

At Colorado, students liked the idea of comprehensive care but criticized the program and did not feel they benefited from the special conferences and seminars. They resented being pulled away from the hospital-based experience their classmates in the control group were having, and they complained about seeing too little pathology. This desire for pathology, for classic medical experience, and a dislike of emotional or social psychological problems is another nearly universal finding in numerous studies. Before students turn to the interpersonal subtleties of comprehensive care, they are most concerned that they become technically competent and do not miss a Level II lead poisoning or an ovarian cyst. By implication, training in comprehensive care that focuses on interpersonal skills and psychosomatic problems might be most effective during residency after students feel reasonably competent to diagnose and treat medical problems.

While the ideological bias of researchers at both programs led them to conclude that the programs worked, their findings indicate otherwise. At Colorado, with its superior research design and extensive tests, investigators found that compared to the control group of peers, the General Medical Clinic experimental group learned as much medicine and as many skills as their classmates in the hospital, even though they thought comprehensive care was impeding their medical education. As for attitudes, despite the frustrations and hostility, the experimental group registered a more positive attitude toward comprehensive care than the control group, but what this means is that they did not become quite so negative towards the experiment as the control group. Even this effect weakened as the experimental group approached graduation and began anticipating their new role as interns. Concerning the key area of social and psychological knowledge and skills, the two semesters in the comprehensive-care clinic did *not* increase them compared to the control group of seniors in the hospital. Nor did the comprehensive-care students develop better doctor-patient relationships. The evaluation team suggests two reasons for these negative findings: the patients' problems did not interest the student-physicians, and the cultural barriers frustrated them. Both studies suffered from unclear definitions of what "comprehensive care" meant and from an emphasis on humane and compassionate attitudes, as if patient-oriented general practitioners have a monopoly on humane and compassionate attitudes. Without behavioral measures, the distinction between comprehensive care and compassionate specialty care becomes difficult to defend, and one is not surprised to learn that both programs were eventually abandoned.

Some years later, Reader and Soave (1976) reflected on these and other experiments aimed at instilling an attitude of comprehensive care. They emphasized that the exposure had to be longer than half a year and in a nonhospital setting with the right atmosphere. They concluded that placing this experience in the fourth year as students are anticipating graduate training is a mistake, and they conceded that perhaps a team approach would be better than expecting each person to be skilled in medicine, social work, psychotherapy, and all else that comprehensive care orginally implied. But this view does not go far enough; for surface descriptions of these mid-century experiments tell us a great deal more about the deep structure of medical school as a social institution.

Starting with Johns Hopkins Medical School and solidified by the Flexner report, medical education in the United States evolved around a structure that rewards scientific expertise and research (Stevens 1971; Rothstein 1972; Light 1982). Although Flexner himself recommended the Hopkins model as a way to train first-rate general practitioners, and although he appreciated the importance of prevention and the expanded social role of the local physician (Jonas 1978, chap. 8), the model he chose was structured to engender increasing specialization, a near exclusive focus on the biomedical aspects of disease, and a faculty devoted to publishing research. The irony of the Flexner report is that it promoted a model that undermined its initial goal of training good general practitioners, because the internal dynamics of the model has led to a nation of specialists and subspecialists far beyond the proportions needed by the population (Stevens 1971; Jonas 1978).

This trend continued until public officials became concerned with the lack of primary care and intervened with large rewards to the medical schools if they would develop programs in primary care. The original goal of the reforms at Western Reserve to humanize medicine united with the values of the 1960s on personal care and community to promote community medicine and family care. Bloom considers the 1960s a watershed era in which "the established structure of medical education was shaken to its roots." He concludes that "it is difficult to conceive of either a full return to the traditional Flexnerian curriculum or a rejection of the main themes of the Western Reserve reforms" (Bloom 1979, p. 6). However, the traditional emphasis on research and specialization seems to have persisted, with primary care and family medicine as an overlay that has not significantly affected the underlying structure of medical education which undermined the experiments in comprehensive care at Cornell and Colorado. One case in point is faculty promotions. While the legislatures of many states want their medical schools to train primary-care physicians, the trustees of those schools establish rules of promotion that make it difficult to hire or promote primary-care faculty models because, in the Flexner-Hopkins tradition, they must publish research in refereed journals. External support for primary care is already dwindling, and the forces inherent in the Hopkins research model continue to assert themselves. Thus the emphasis in the Macy report (1980) on teaching the social, psychological, and economic aspects of medical care throughout residency training is unlikely to happen unless fundamental structural changes are made such as large-scale support for research and careers in those areas.

The enduring significance of the early experiments in comprehensive care is their detailed description of how the values and priorities of prevailing hospital-based, specialized, research institutions shaped the minds and actions of students involved in family-based primary care. As for Western Reserve, its experiment succeeded and has been imitated widely in part because it involved all the faculty in reforming the entire curriculum, and in part because it did not attempt to stem the tide of specialization so much as it aimed to integrate clinical and academic material. But if one were to attempt to build a medical school that would train physicians in community-based primary-care medicine, one would, as Alfred Gellhorn did at the Sophie Davis School for Biomedical Education in New York, admit students sympathetic to comprehensive care, and design an entire curriculum around this goal (Gellhorn and Scheuer 1978; Haglund 1981). Even then, one would still have to cope with a health-care system which underpays the physician who wants to help the needy and does not reimburse the time it takes to be compassionate or comprehensive.

Socialization and Alienation in Medical School

For over twenty years a debate has raged between Robert Merton and his followers who believe that professional training is the fountainhead of professional identity (Merton et al. 1957; Levinson 1967; Bloom 1979), and Howard Becker and his colleagues who believe that people adjust their values and attitudes to suit each new situation (Becker et al. 1961; Becker 1970; Freidson 1970). This debate has been analyzed in depth elsewhere (Light 1980, chap. 15; Simpson 1979, chap. 1), but the central conclusions can be quickly summarized. First, Becker's concept of socialization as situational adjustment is logically untenable because socialization means the development of attributes that transcend situations (Bloom 1979; Levinson 1967; Light 1975, 1980). Second, there is evidence for both camps depending on what dimensions one considers (Bloom 1979; Light 1980). (Ironically, the students in the Cornell experiment which Merton studied merely made a situational adjustment to the comprehensive-care clinic). Most important is the observation that as captains of the team, physicians have designed a world of practice which reflects values and practice skills they learned during their medical education so that to a great degree, *the structure of practice reflects the values of medical school.* It is for this reason that we have built up a health-care system designed to deliver and support acute intervention, treatment by specialists, and hospital care. From a larger historical and institutional perspective, socialization has shaped the work situation to which the Becker school says students adjust so that the debate is largely a quibble.

A corollary to the debate over the enduring impact of medical education is whether medical students are essentially acquiring a professional role as student-physicians who emulate their mentors (Merton et al. 1957), or whether they are boys dressed in white coats who react to medical school by forming a subculture with countervailing norms and techniques for coping with their powerful opponents, the faculty (Becker et al. 1961). While theoretically interesting to sociologists, this debate has less to do with medical education per se than with the role of student. The preponderance of subsequent studies (Reader and Goss 1967; Bloom 1973; Olesen and Whittaker 1968), including the studies of Cornell, support Becker's view. Moreover, no one seems to have pointed out that the "student-physician" was an ideological term used in the Cornell program to emphasize the collegial atmosphere it wanted to engender, and to some extent the Merton group became the theoretical legitimizer of that ideology. However, the two perspectives involve different variables, and Simpson (1979) correctly argues that *both* are part of socialization. One might add that some students are inclined toward accepting authority while others tend to resist it.

Whether students directly emulate their mentors or form their own subculture, in the end most become practicing physicians not unlike what their faculty expected to produce. Thus differences in surface behavior become less consequential than the underlying structural characteristics that led to a relatively uniform result. One reason, I believe, is that the student counterculture becomes progressively weaker the closer students get to specific training for their life's work. This would mean that it is weaker in the last two years of medical school than the first two (even in Kansas, where Becker did his study), and that it is weakest in residency—a hypothesis borne out in more recent studies of residency training (Bosk 1979; Bucher and Stelling 1977; Light 1980).

The most critical period of medical training occurs when students learn clinical skills in their advanced years, and a recently published study by Paul Atkinson closely scrutinizes this process at the Royal Infirmary at Edinburgh (1981). Following Goffman and the ethnomethodologists, Atkinson wanted to find out just how clinical knowledge and skills are reproduced in the next generation of physicians. First, he discovered that signs as well as symptoms of disease are ambiguous and need interpretation. Teachers try to get their students to "see" skin color they do not see and "feel" nodules they cannot feel, raising questions about the objective nature of medical knowledge. In the end, the students learn a language and set of perceptions that match those of their mentors; but given the amount of indeterminancy in this work, Atkinson argues that personal knowledge and assertion play a major role (Atkinson 1981, shap. 7). Independent verification is often not sought or available.

On the larger stage of medical training, the role of personal knowledge and assertion is also important, as reflected by a comprehensive assessment of a medical school (Bloom 1973). In 1962, the faculty and administration at Downstate Medical Center became so worried about student tension and anxiety that they asked Samuel Bloom to study the school. Using questionnaires, interviews, official records, and field notes, Bloom produced one of the most frank portraits in the literature (1973). He found that faculty and administrators, who were working furiously to up-grade what had been the Long Island College of Medicine into the Johns Hopkins of New York, emphasized research and academic learning. The students, on the other hand, were second-generation middle-class Europeans who wanted to be doctors and emphasized practical training in skills. They characterized the first two years as entailing fierce competition over seemingly irrelevant material, and they ranked memorization as the number-one skill needed to succeed in medical school. Yet no clear student culture developed, and students disinvested themselves through passive conformity with mottos such as, "Don't make waves," and "Play it safe."

Bloom concluded that, "The faculty and students, although they agree very strongly about what the educational goals of this institution should be, each perceives the other as being opposed to these goals" (Bloom 1973, pp. 141–42). This paradox came from the faculty defining competence in a narrow, technical way and from the students expressing their hostility through passive conformity. Bloom recommended a good deal more talk, self-study, and decision-making among all the faculty so that common values could develop. To his shock and surprise, the administration suppressed his report, and it became an underground best-seller.

Upon reflection, Bloom realized that his report had been a threat to the power and status of the dean and the executive faculty council (Bloom 1973, epilogue). His report had taken a functionalist perspective which assumed that students and faculty are (or ought to be) engaged in the same pursuit, rather than a conflict perspective which would have assumed countervailing forces in tension. By recommending that the administration and council be accountable to the rest of the school and share their power, Bloom's study had inadvertently exposed the latent organization of power in the school. Few studies have picked up Bloom's insights so that today, as twenty-five years ago, we know a good deal about the social psychology of medical training but little about the social structure of medical schools and their differential impact on the socialization of physicians.

Internship: Vestige of Apprenticeship

As medical education shifted from apprenticing with individual physicians to organized schools, many required a premedical apprenticeship where the prospective student could get some experience in the rudiments of practice. As the new Hopkins model of medical education took hold, and as the rapid expansion of surgery led to hundreds of new hospitals needing thousands of assistants, the idea of a year of supervised experience after graduation supplanted the earlier requirement. By 1904, half of all medical graduates took internships, and in time it became a requirement for licensure (Stevens 1971, pp. 116–20). Internship was regarded as part of undergraduate training, an experiential corollary to medical school; yet it was always plagued by structural ambiguity. It occurred in hospitals often unaffiliated with medical schools so that while interns were supposed to be students, they were treated like workers by hospital staff. Often internships lacked an educational rationale, so that finally this vestige of apprenticeship was blended into residency training (Stevens 1971, pp. 379–88; Macy 1980). Nevertheless, studies of internship were the first to recognize medical education beyond medical school, and they produced insights into the early postgraduate experiences of young physicians.

In one of the best studies of medical education, Emily Mumford wrote, "Yesterday's medical student becomes tomorrow's physician by traveling a long way through the looking glass of confirming experiences and disquieting threats to his self-image as a doctor" (Mumford 1970, p. 118). Mumford was one of the first researchers to analyze the impact of social structure on the educational process. Few other studies integrate field observations with quantitative data, and few uphold as she does the academic tradition of building on past theory and research.

Mumford's study rests on two premises: that internship significantly affects professional development and that the hospital is a major learning environment for professional values. Consequently, she compared internship at a community hospital and a university hospital. The latter is part of the unique arrangement in medical education created when American medicine combined European models of scientific education and hospital training to form the triangle of university, research lab, and hospital (Mumford 1970, pp. 2–3, 18–32). Mumford describes how community and university hospitals function rather differently and how selecting an internship in one or the other leads to quite different experiences and career opportunities. Essentially, university hospitals select patients with exotic problems for research purposes and carry out work in teams where the intern's performance as student is highly visible and where specialized expertise is esteemed (see Table 21.1). Community hospitals take a wide range of patients who are linked to the hospital as the outpatients of attending physicians, and they give interns a great deal of responsibility in a low-key, self-learning atmosphere where the attending physicians dominate but are not rated as up-to-date on new medical developments. Only in the community-based hospitals are psychological dimensions of medicine and outpatient care respected (Mumford 1970, chap. 8). Mumford's analysis of how hospital structure generates this respect is the missing element in recent reports urging attention to social psychological and ambulatory skills in graduate training, because most graduate education occurs in settings that are not conducive to them (Association of American Medical Colleges 1980; Macy 1980). If curricular changes lack organizational underpinnings, they are unlikely to succeed.

The other notable study of internships is weaker on structure but provides a useful description of the stages and process of what is now known as PGY 1, or the first post-graduate year of residency. Stephen J. Miller (1970) observed interns at Boston City Hospital on the Harvard unit. Miller provides a good description of what internship was like for his subjects, starting with their choice of Boston City Hospital because it was prestigious, had good teachers, and gave them lots of responsibility. The interns immersed themselves into their work and tried to "do everything"—diagnose their patients, carry out lab work, negotiate treatment

TABLE 21.1 Differences Between University Hospital and Community Hospital in Mumford's Study of Internship

University Hospital	Community Hospital
Colleague controlled	Client-responsive
Team care; work highly visible to teammates; shared responsibility	Work more alone; low visibility; individual responsibility
Long, meticulous charts (on which many others depend)	Short chart notes (on which few depend)
Screen patients for exotic problems, though have "ward problems"	Admit broad range of community patients
Interesting patients are those with exotic medical problems	Interesting patients are those with psychogenic problems, therapeutic problems, or who are rewarding to work with
Dull patients are those with psychogenic problems or who are "not really sick"	Dull patients are not much of an issue here
Patient compliance a minor issue, not a matter of concern	Patient compliance a matter of concern
Low regard for outpatient care or local physicians	Outpatient care valued; local physicians are central figures. Avoid arrogant university doctors
Student status constantly reinforced by one's teachers on the team	Physician status quickly attained
Uncertainty a legitimate norm; openly confess it and seek advice	Uncertainty not a norm; expected to resolve it somehow
Frequent consults; implicit in the organization of work	Infrequent consults; not implicit in the organization of work
Nurses not important; low status members of the team	Nurses have considerable power on the wards; significant teachers
Attending physicians are always learning; brushing up their knowledge with sharp residents	Attending physicians are the masters

plans, attend lectures, rounds, and seminars as well as keep up on their reading. Within a month or two they were overwhelmed. "I knew I had to work hard," said one intern, "but I didn't know what hard was, I just had no idea . . . I know there's a routine here somewhere, and once I learn it, everything will be O.K." (Miller 1970, p. 193).

The "routine" interns found, argues Miller, was a shift in perspective from doing everything to emphasizing clinical experiences. They cut down on lectures, conferences, and readings to focus on their patients. Miller closely follows *Boys in White* (Becker et al. 1961) in its emphasis on student perspectives for coping, and he argues that the clinical perspective continues for the rest of the year. But in a reanalysis of Miller's data, Light (1975) found two more stages of development. After six months the interns felt they had learned all they could from maximizing clinical experience, and they took on the more depressing perspective of merely Pushing Through to the end of the year. This continued for about three months, when the interns began to learn from the teaching staff how to discern the unique and subtle aspects of their largely routine cases so that they acquired the perspective of Learning from Each Patient.

Given the historical fate of internship, perhaps the most interesting part of

Miller's account concerns how little the work of internship had to do with being a physician—either academic or regular (Miller 1970, chaps 8, 10). Rather, it was "a particular kind of job" in a hospital (p. 91). As in the university internship studied by Mumford, ethical dilemmas and value conflicts between service, research, and education were common. Despite Miller's respect for Harvard, everyone, including senior physicians at this distinguished internship, appeared out for themselves, so that interns had to contrive "interesting" cases to keep a Visit occupied or get a Consult (chap. 7). The extent to which residencies today contain mixed agenda that compromise patient care or physician training has yet to be measured by the recent reports on graduate medical education.

Residency: The Core of Modern Training

Today almost all medical students enter residency training, so that medical school has become essentially a preparation for residency. As Samuel Bloom observed, "This is the crucial period when the values to which the individual has been exposed in the medical school and the hospital are most likely to find their final internalized form and become the basis upon which the new physician begins to make decisions for himself" (Bloom 1963, p. 87). Residency influences where a person will practice, how, and with whom.

The elite place of residency as the pinnacle of medical education echoes its origins at Johns Hopkins Hospital in the 1890s (Stevens 1971, p. 121). Based on the idea of the German university hospital "assistant," the program was designed to select the most able physicians and train them to be specialists or professors. Prior to World War I, this highly competitive system developed at leading American hospitals, and the imprint of these origins remains in residencies today even though residencies are now training almost every graduating physician. Whether it is reasonable or cost effective to have nearly all physicians trained at the residency level seems too radical a question to ask anymore. Yet given that 80 to 90 percent of all medical problems in a population do not require specialized treatment, the question is not unreasonable.

Studies of residency training by social scientists, however, have eschewed such basic issues and focused on the inner process of training itself. Medical educators and behavioral scientists commonly approach the training process in psychological terms, but one of the major accomplishments in recent years has been to show how trainees' behavior and responses are shaped by social forces (Bucher and Stelling 1977; Light 1980). The ground-breaking work by Stanton and Schwartz (1954), which demonstrated that disturbances of hospitalized mental patients reflect structural relations and stresses among the staff, also applies to the responses of residents (Light 1980, chaps. 11–12). Bucher and Stelling (1977, p. 21). investigate this relationship on a comparative basis and develop a useful framework for thinking about graduate medical education. Concerning structural variables, they ask, "What is the nature of the organization housing the training program and what sorts of affiliations does it have with other institutions?" What position does the professional staff have in the organization, and which segments or schools of thought hold various positions of power? The answers go far in explaining what gets taught to whom, how candidates are selected, and what collegial networks they will enter. Finally, there is the structure of the training program itself— its forms of teaching, its stages and rites of passage, and its ideology (pp. 22–25). Unfortunately, the authors do not apply this comparative framework systematically, in part because each program differs on so many variables that comparability dissolves into case studies. Nevertheless, one can glean certain relationships that are instructive and find support in other studies.

First, as Mumford and Miller observed, residencies vary in their organizational and professional affiliations, which in turn affects one's career and network of contacts. Second, the degree of homogeneity among the teaching staff not only affects the models whom trainees may emulate but also affects the modeling process. In a homogeneous program differentiations form around fine distinctions, ensuring that in the main trainees will become imbued with the prevailing school of thought (Light 1980). Moreover, the peer subculture will also echo prevailing values, while a heterogeneous staff leads to trainees each wokring out their own professional identity. Third, the number of role models affects socialization and can vary from one mentor who controls one's fate to a parade of role models from which one can selectively choose traits to admire or abhor.

Fourth, the clarity of assignments, pacing, and stages produces a more uniform identity. When any of these is clouded or uneven, trainees become preoccupied with strategies of coping with their confusion (Bucher and Stelling 1977, chap. 6). In particular, the authors note the exceptionally long period of confusion in psychiatric residencies. Although psychiatrists attribute this to the experience of confronting mental disorders, Bucher and Stelling think the confusion stems from structural ambiguities in the residencies themselves.

Finally, in all three clinical residencies studied by Bucher and Stelling, trainees resented any activity that impeded the growth of their autonomy. In particular, the latent or manifest challenges to autonomy in teamwork engendered discomfort if not avoidance.

The studies of residency are the richest in the literature on medical education and include useful material on the nature of supervision, the manipulation of supervisors and impression management, the influence of peers, relations with nonphysicians, tensions between education and service, organizational influences on diagnosis, and the selection of residents (Bucher and Stelling 1977; Bosk 1979; Coser 1979; Light 1980). Here we shall focus on one key topic shared by most of the studies and crucial to medical education: learning to cope with uncertainty, mistakes, and criticism. In a recent essay, Renée C. Fox eloquently describes the pervasive preoccupation with uncertainty brought on by the powerful advances in pharmacology, genetics, surgery, and biochemistry (1980). These require being open to criticism and learning from it throughout one's career, which David Rogers notes as being one of the two principle goals which medical educators emphasize (Rogers 1981, p. 10). On it rests the profession's capacity to regulate itself through criticism of self-performance and the performance of others. However, Bucher and Stelling's comparative, longitudinal study concludes that "there is nothing in our findings which would support the notion that socialization processes build in effective mechanisms for either individual internal control or colleague control among professionals. On the contrary, the experiences of trainees militate *against* the acquisition of such mechanisms" (Bucher and Stelling 1977, p. 281–82). In their study the authors identify several techniques residents use to discount criticism such as disparaging the source, dismissing the issue, or considering the issue a matter of style (pp. 171–73).

In this context Charles Bosk studied how errors were handled in a surgical residency (1979). He eloquently describes the complex nature of errors and identifies four kinds. *Technical errors* are a failure in skill—cutting too deep or tying a knot poorly. In surgery (but not in less precise specialities), these are quickly recognized, and Bosk identifies a number of social mechanisms to minimize them such as legitimating any request for help and emphasizing the speedy report of technical errors so their effects can be minimized (Bosk 1979, pp. 38–43). Not to report them quickly or to make many technical errors are examples of *normative error*, the failure to discharge role obligations conscientiously. *Judgmental errors* occur when an incorrect strategy is taken, and *quasi-normative errors* are committed largely by subordinates. Because Bosk does not examine errors among peers, it is not clear to what extent judgmental and quasi-normative errors differ from insubordination (Simmel 1950, part 3). To the extent that they are errors of subordinates, they may be regarded differently after graduation. Indeed Bosk discovers that what are treated in residency as judgmental or normative errors become considered after residency to be merely differences in style (Bosk 1979, pp. 46, 186). This is the profession's graceful way of *avoiding* criticism among colleagues. In a specialty like psychiatry where its weak paradigm means few errors can be recognized as being technical, residency training enables each psychiatrist to legitimate his or her personal style as professionally acceptable (Bucher and Stelling 1977, p. 221; Light 1980, chap. 15).

When technical and judgmental errors are too serious to regard as matters of style, the profession holds rituals of contrition and reconstitution such as mortality or morbidity conferences (Light 1972; Millman 1977; Bosk 1979; Light 1980). As Everett C. Hughes wrote in a classic essay, rituals "provide a set of emotional and even organizational checks and balances against both the subjective and the objective risks of the trade" (Hughes 1958, p. 97). It is surprising how similar these conferences in surgery and psychiatry were found to be. Bosk notes that "Grand Rounds celebrate the extraordinary successes of surgeons" while in morbidity and mortality conferences, surgeons "are able to use unexpected failure to serve the same end" through "the transformation of negative evidence into positive display of an attending's skill" (Bosk 1979, pp. 122, 127–28). He details the social and educational functions of the attendings putting on the hair shirt so that they "excuse their mistakes by admitting them" (p. 145). Bosk's discussion does not indicate whether the physicians learn from their mistakes. This research parallels Light's research on suicide reviews (1972, 1980). He notes that little is done to communicate the lessons of such conferences and concludes they are "a ritual designed to reaffirm the profession's worth after doubt was cast upon it" (Light 1980, p. 216).

Intertwined with handling criticism and error is training for uncertainty. First explored by Renée C. Fox (1957), this dimension of medical and residency training has received increasing attention in recent years (Bosk 1979; Light 1980; Fox 1980). The double bind for physicians is that uncertainty pervades their work and they must be open to it; yet their license and mandate from society presumes they know how to take care of problems which laymen are uncertain how to address. Thus Oliver Wendell Holmes wrote to a young physician, "Let me recommend to you, as far as possible, to keep your doubts to yourself, and give the patient the benefit of your decision" (in Mumford 1970, p. 163).

Based on student diaries and her own observations, Fox described a triology of uncertainties confronted in medical school which result from a limited mastery of available knowledge, the limitations of medical knowledge itself, and the difficulty of telling one kind of limitation from the other. From his research on residency training, Light (1980, chap. 13) developed a systematic analysis of uncertainty and classified Fox's triology as uncertainties of knowledge (see Table 21.2). He found in Fox's data and his own that as students do more clinical work, uncertainties arise around four other areas: diagnosis, treatment, collegial relations, and patient response. The issue is how residents are trained to cope with these various kinds of uncertainty.

In her comparative study of internships, Mumford had noted that the staff at university hospital fostered the norm of admitting uncertainty while the staff at community hospital did not (Mumford 1970, pp. 158–62). Recognizing uncertainty fit with the norm of scientific research and the organization of work into teams characteristic of university hospitals. This full and complex appreciation of uncertainty also characterizes research settings, where Renée Fox has devoted twenty years to examining its dimensions and consequences (1959, 1976, 1980; Fox and Swazey 1978). But for regular medical practice, residents must learn to control uncertainty, or they cannot get their work done. Based on his study of psychiatric residency, Light identified dominant and subordinate techniques of control which

TABLE 21.2   Kinds of Uncertainty and Their Control in Professional Training

KINDS OF UNCERTAINTY	FORMS OF CONTROL LEARNED
1. Of professional knowledge	*Mastering knowledge* Specializing Adopting a "school" of professional work
2. Of diagnosis	Mastering Knowledge Specializing Adopting a "school" of professional work *Deferring to clinical experience*
3. Of procedure or treatment	Mastering knowledge Specializing Adopting a "school" of professional work Deferring to clinical experience *Turning to technique*
4. Of collegial relations	Mastering knowledge Specializing Adopting a "school" of professional work Deferring to clinical experience Turning to technique *Gaining autonomy*
5. Of client response	Mastering knowledge Specializing Adopting a "school" of professional work Deferring to clinical experience Turning to technique Gaining autonomy *Maintaining a dominant class relationship* Institutionalizing authority Keeping clients ignorant

Source: Light 1980, p. 284.

residents learned for handling each area of uncertainty (see Table 21.2). From observations of surgeons, pediatricians, and anesthesiologists, Bosk identified other responses to uncertainty including requests for consultation, probablistic thinking, and deciding not to decide (1979).

Does the shape of uncertainty and residency training around it differ by paradigm strength? In a comparison of orthopedic surgery with psychiatry, Light (1980, chap. 13) found that residents and their mentors in both fields perceived a great deal of uncertainty, suggesting that a specialty will emphasize the gray areas and leading edges of its field whether they circumscribe a large or small body of established knowledge. Moreover, Light concludes, "regardless of how technically developed a professional field is, it will define the treatment of problematic cases as the true measure of its worth" (1980, p. 291).

While paradigm strength does not seem to affect the *amount* of uncertainty, the stronger the paradigm for a specialty the clearer are technical errors. More technically advanced specialties carry out their work in more visible settings where everyone quickly recognizes a mistake. By extension, mastering technical literature is an essential method for controlling uncertainty in orthopedic surgery, while ideology plays a larger role in psychiatry (Light 1980, chap. 13). What these findings imply is that medical educators should beware of residents in less technically developed fields prematurely closing themselves to uncertainties when they have the greatest need to remain open. Many observers express concern over premature closure, and the principle danger comes from a focus on technique as an end in itself. Because of their preoccupation with teaching specialized skills, residency programs must pay serious attention to this danger.

Nursing: Professional Training in Turmoil

While the danger of premature closure has not been a concern of nursing education, the uncertainty of procedures and collegial relations has. In her chapter on nurses, Linda Aiken (1982) describes the multiple issues and debates concerning the role of nursing and its relations to other members of the health-care team. Partly because of its ambivalent and semiprofessional status, and partly because the Merton-Becker debate focused on the meaning of socialization, the major longitudinal studies of nursing education have focused on the issue of professional identity. Ida Harper Simpson, in her six-year study of socialization into nursing at Duke University, begins by arguing that the Merton group and the Becker group were studying different variables and therefore do not hold incompatible perspectives. Simpson calls Merton's approach the "induction perspective," because the students are inducted by faculty into a role that is part of the nursing or medical profession as a whole. Becker used the "reaction perspective" because students react to being put in a subordinate position at a particular institution (the school) not necessarily connected to a larger profession. Given the disjunctures between nursing schools and the work of nurses, one might expect an emphasis on reactive behavior. However, Simpson thinks that socialization "adjusts students to their education, but unlike adjustments to specific situations, it persists. Its persistence across status transitions and situational changes is one of its distinguishing features" (1979, p. 6). Reactions to being a student occur and are a real part of the educational experience. Students' complaints represent reactions to tensions generated by the need to conform to program requirements and inform us of constraints within a program (Becker, et al. 1961, p. 21); Olesen and Whittaker 1968). Simpson argues that the complaints are short-lived and change as students progress through the program. But as we shall see, these student reactions to role models in the program influence long-term socialization more than faculty values.

Simpson has her own scheme for understanding professional education. Its three dimensions are knowledge and skills, identity and motivation, and occupational orientation. These dimensions can operate somewhat independently, though she emphasizes that "knowledge and skills are prerequisites for acquisition of enduring orientations and motivations" (Simpson 1979, p. 6). On its face, this assertion is debatable, because nursing (and medical) students enter programs with strong orientations and motivations before learning anything. In fact, a central focus of Simpson's study and most others is how these strong feelings get altered by faculty orientations and organizational constraints. These constraints are particularly pertinent to the semiprofessions, which Simpson says are distinguished by three characteristics: Their work is organized by bureaucracies, professions, and legal regulations; they lack an "authority base" to undergird their work; and their collegiality is weakened by the vertical differentiation of their work by organizations (pp. 24-25). Such limitations on autonomy had an interesting role in the socialization of the nursing students at Duke.

In order to study the multidimensional aspects of socialization, Simpson followed individuals in three panel groups through school and into their work after graduation. She used questionnaires, interviews, diaries, and faculty evaluations in a research design which assumed "socialization is individual change (Simpson 1979, p. 46). Simpson found that entering students (around 1960) were overwhelmingly white, Protestant, small-town and lower middle class, bringing with them a quasi-religious orientation toward personal service, taking responsibility, helping others, and not indulging in self-expression that was completely compatible with the values and orientation of the faculty (chaps. 5-6). In this sense, students were presocialized and basically needed the skills to carry out their goals.

However, the students confronted a series of contradictions in the program not irrelevant to the problems of nursing education today. On one hand, 90 percent of the faculty held a view of nurses as sophisticated social psychologists who were able to identify covert as well as overt patient needs, empathize with the patient, and be autonomous creative caretakers. Only 10 percent emphasized technical competence—another route toward higher professional status in an age of complex medical technology. While the faculty stressed patient care, they encouraged students toward administration, which takes one away from patient care. It would seem that at some level the faculty realized that their capable caretaker ideal did not have a complement in the practical world, and in fact nurses advanced professionally through administration. Finally, the teaching hospital was bureaucratically organized and emphasized "technical" and administrative nursing (Simpson 1979, chap. 8). The students responded to these conflicting elements in a pragmatic way; they abandoned faculty ideals about patient care and reoriented themselves to the hospital's bureaucratic approach. This meant they also did not embrace the faculty's ideals about teamwork because hospital training did not include it. Moreover, Simpson argues that the adjustment to the realities of clincial practice in the hospital was a permanent one: "No reversions to the idealistic orientations occurred among the graduates of the nursing school" (p. 127). As they became more committed to their new role, students' attraction to nursing steadily decreased. In short, young nurses realistically adjusted to a bureaucratic kind of nursing they did not like (chap. 10). Nursing became just a job, and personal fulfillment came from another set of values which they had had from the start—marriage and family (chaps. 5, 11). While most of them started promising careers, many expected to drop out as soon as family needs increased (chap. 14).

This important study is flawed. Simpson's emphasis on acquiring knowledge and skills as the key to professional socialization is not supported by her own account of how predisposing values and structural aspects of the program shaped the nurses' socialization. Nor did socialization turn out to be an individual phenomenon. Her conclusion that student culture is not very important stems, one gathers, from her relying on questionnaires and interviews with no field observations of student subculture. Her research design assumes Merton's induction perspective and is contaminated by the faculty having selected the students to be interviewed and helped write the interview items. Nevertheless, Simpson provides a tough, complex portrait of the countervailing forces in nursing education twenty years ago and how nursing students responded to them.

In many ways *The Silent Dialogue* by Olesen and Whittaker (1968) complements Simpson's study. Although published much earlier, *The Silent Dialogue* was also a longitudinal study done in the early sixties of nursing students at a university-based baccalaureate program. The methodological emphasis was the opposite of Simpson's: participant observation supplemented by questionnaires, interviews and the like. Like Simpson, Olesen and Whittaker found that most of the students entering the program at the University of California, San Francisco, came from the same backgrounds and had the same value orientations as Simpson found at Duke. Moreover, the faculty at San Francisco also emphasized the social psychological approach to nursing rather than physical and technical care. However, the dominance of a hospital in which students learned technical, administrative nursing is not found in Olesen and Whittaker's report.

Because the authors are masters of participant observation, new dimensions of nursing socialization are brought out that contrast with Simpson's findings. Olesen and Whittaker observed a vibrant, influential student subculture. consisting of "underground student behavior that plays a prominent part in shaping interactional styles, operational values, and staunchly-held attitudes among students" (Olesen and Whittaker 1968, p. 149). This student subculture orbited around faculty values and expectations but served as a buffer to them and a buffer among the students. Thus on one hand, the students would "psyche out" the instructors so they could give them what they wanted. On the other hand, students would harass peers who tried too hard or were too eager to please instructors. Thus outstanding performance was discouraged because it threatened the group. One effective vehicle for socialization was "fronting"—putting on an act to impress the teachers. The irony of fronting, of course, was that in time the front and the self merged so that in the end, "the instructors became embedded in the student view of self" (p. 205). At the same time, the student subculture retained and promoted the traditional values of womenhood and female identity lest they be forgotten in a program devoted to professional socialization. The power of the student subculture to legitimate the emergent professional self in its various stages is reflected in the authors' conclusion that dropouts failed because they were isolated from the subculture (p. 242).

The authors document the students' cycles of depression and elation, inadequacy and competence, which others have confirmed and amplified (Davis 1968; Light 1980, chap. 11). However, their view of the way socialization occurs is particularly subtle and echoes Auden's poem (1933–38) about how suffering takes place in unnoticed places at unnoticed times (Auden 1966). Olesen and Whittaker write:

> It was not in the high council of the curriculum planners, nor the skill of the most sophisticated and understanding instructor, nor in the late night cramming for exams that professional socialization occurred. Embedded in the frequently banal, sometimes dreary, often uninteresting work of everyday living, professional socialization was of the commonplace . . . the minute starts and stops, the bits of progress and backsliding, the moments of reluctant acquisition of a new self and the tenacious relinquishing of the old. . . . These matters constitute the silent dialogue wherein are fused person, situation, and institution. [Oleson and Whittaker 1968, pp. 296–297]

That fusion included traditional desires to be a wife and mother, to pursue nursing when it fit one's larger life plan rather than build a professional career. As for the unrealistic ideals of the faculty at Duke about psychological nursing that fell before the reality of clinical training in hospital nursing, Olesen and Whittaker report that while students admired staff nurses for their mastery of technique and physical nursing, they used the faculty's model of psychological nursing to criticize the staff nurses (pp. 226–31). This faculty model of nursing led students to prefer jobs in psychiatry and public health, though how many were able to find such jobs is another matter (Aiken 1982). Over the four years, psychological tests showed that the students had become less authoritarian, more emotionally expressive, more capable of complex thinking, and more open to novel ideas (Olesen and Whittaker 1968, pp. 133–34). The authors were optimistic that the graduates "would not be the victims of their new and different environments, for they had the awareness with which to liberate themselves and to regulate themselves in these new situations" (p. 298).

Much has changed for women and nursing since these two studies were done (Aiken 1982). From a national perspective, the warm optimism of Olesen and Whittaker would appear to need a cold splash of Simpson's realism about the limited power of a semiprofession to control its work. The number of jobs in psychiatry and public health that meet the faculty's ideals is small. Within a job, control is limited. For example, a recent study in San Francisco of a program to train nurse practitioners to deliver primary care to adults found that because the hospital where they worked reinforced traditional roles, and because nurses and doctors there resented any signs of autonomy, "the stuctural and situational constraints of the work setting were more powerful than the professional socialization of the program" (Lurie 1981, p. 45). Of course nurse practitioners in other settings work with considerable autonomy, but the national pattern for nurses is that five years after graduation 62 percent of the nurses with a B.S. are still working, compared to 68 percent with a diploma and 75 percent with an associate degree (Knopf 1975). Baccalaureate degree nurses are less likely to hold positions as head nurse or charge nurse than graduates with an associate or diploma degree (National League for Nursing 1980). In terms of socialization, these patterns may show the B.S. graduates' unwillingness to abandon their self-image as professionals when faced with low-paying bureaucratic work. In terms of education, it may reflect the gap between nursing educators' image of nursing and the prevalent demands for service (Institute of Medicine 1981, p. 28).

A central problem today is that the status of the three levels of nursing education in the eyes of nursing leaders—the subcollegiate diploma schools, the community-college associate programs, and the collegiate B.S. programs—do not coincide with differences in skills (Institute of Medicine 1981; American Nurses' Association 1979; National Commission on Nursing 1981). In fact, the lowly diploma schools spend more time on nursing skills (Ramphal 1981). These hospital-based programs are more interested in practice than theory, and their declining influence may be a loss to patient care. The same drive for theory and specialized knowledge evident in the development of medical education is now increasingly characteristic of nursing education.

The attempt to professionalize nursing has taken several forms. One effort has been to develop clinical specialists and nurse-administrators at the graduate level, and this strategy seems to be working well for a small number of nurses (Aiken 1982). Another, reflected in the studies of Duke and San Francisco, is to develop a body of theory that does not rest on medicine's body of knowledge but on the social psychology of patient care. A prominent book of such theory reflects the intellectual and sociological problems of this strategy (Stevens 1979). The "theories," however, are diffuse and consist of treatises not originally written as theory. To accommodate them, Stevens defines nursing as "an activity or occasion occurring where some agent of entity uses its power to aid or manipulate some other agent or entity in relation to some aspect of the latter's health status" (1979, p. 8). This is obviously too inclusive.

The effort by the nursing profession to upgrade educational qualifications has also run into trouble. Despite a resolution that every nurse by 1985 shall have a B.S.N. degree and despite fifteen years of effort, the American Nursing Association concedes that "little progress has been made in instituting the bachelor's degree in nursing as minimum preparation for professional nursing practice" (American Nurses' Association 1979, p. 5). The American Nurses' Association admits that it has yet to define what distinguishes a B.S. nurse from a diploma nurse (1979, p. 6), and commitment to nursing as a full-time career is declining (Rowland 1978, p. 131). These problems stem largely from employers not paying nurses well, not recognizing different grades of nurses, and keeping them in subordinate positions (Aiken and Blendon 1981; Aiken 1982; National Commission on Nursing 1981; Institute of Medicine 1981). Two useful suggestions are to commission a detailed comparative study of exactly what goes on in the three kinds of nursing programs and to merge diploma schools with collegiate programs so one benefits from the best of both (May 1981). One is struck with the paucity of imparital information about the educational process in nursing since the two studies in the early sixties and particularly with the lack of comparative analysis of the three types of school. The fact that nursing programs are in flux makes such research even more interesting, because one could study how the three programs absorb or resist forces of change. As for integration, Ernest May points out that the diploma schools are strong on practice and continuity of care, while the collegiate schools are strong on theory and concepts. One nursing school's dean has concluded, "It is a great pity—perhaps a profession-destroying tragedy—that the two kinds of strengths described, which are characteristic of diploma school education at its best and of university nursing education at its best, have been characterized by the profession as either/or propositions, both in terms of desirability and supposed feasibility" (Ramphal 1978, p. 769).

While the debate continues between more academic and more hands-on training, the overall pattern of nursing education shows increased enrollments and increased proportions of nurses receiving higher degrees. The number of annual graduates from nursing programs increased from 46,455 in 1970–71 to 75,523 in 1979–1980 (Levine and Moses 1982). All of this increase took place in associate and baccalaureate degree programs and increased the number of employed registered nurses. Nevertheless, nursing shortages arose, and approximately 100,000 vacancies in acute-care hospitals go unfilled. The percentage of registered nurses employed has risen steadily and stood at 76.4 percent in November 1980. Data analysis shows that the shortage is not due to nurses leaving to work in other fields, working part-time, or returning to school (Levine and Moses 1982). Thus the nursing shortage would appear to be caused by a rapidly increasing demand, which will increasingly be met by graduates of associate, baccalaureate, and master's degree programs that emphasize academic training.

Conclusion: Medical and Nursing Education and the Public Interest

The inadequate distribution of doctors and nurses by number and type is one part of a larger issue that underlies the shape of education for both physicians and nursing: the discrepency between professional ambitions and society's needs. Professions strive to gain a monopoly over a domain of services and a market of clients (Freidson 1970; Larson 1977). Unlike other industries, their schools are the lynchpins to this effort; by honing specialized skills and producing research they substantiate their claims for market control. The rising power of the AAMC (Association of American Medical Colleges) and the decline of the American Medical Association over the past fifty years attest to this argument (Stevens 1971). To return to the opening themes of this essay, the elite of a profession are its educators, and they attempt to shape schools to serve their ends. Through the education of their students and the influence of their graduates, they try to alter the structure of society in their domain.

Society's needs, in contrast, begin with the nature and distribution of disease and health problems. Most of these are minor, self-limiting, emotional and/or chronic. They require a large volume of primary care with a significant amount of counseling directed toward patient education and emotional problems. Physicians are usually not needed to do this work. Even the Graduate Medical Education National Advisory Committee report, assembled by physicians concerned about graduate medical education, concluded that 22 percent of all medical services could be rendered by nonphysicians (1980, vol. 2, p. 31). David Rogers recently concluded, on the basis of numerous studies comparing the performance of nurse practitioners and physicians assistants with that of physicians that in primary-care settings, the nonphysicians performed equally well (Rogers 1981; Lewis 1969; Sackett et al. 1974; Runyan 1975; Slome et al. 1976; Greenfield, et al. 1978; Edmunds 1978; Sox 1979; Lubic 1981). Thus subphysician programs are turning out graduates who perform well in general medicine.

This picture of health needs and the training needed to meet them contrasts sharply with the world view of the medical school faculty. They believe, as authorities in their respective specialties, that graduates from four years of medical school are barely competent and that licensed family practitioners are only adequate to handle elementary cases. They point out that even subspecialists have difficulty keeping up with advances. Yet most of these advances affect a small percentage of the population and do not significantly alter morbidity (Benham and Benham 1976) or mortality (McKinlay 1973; Levin and Idler 1981).

The current pattern of medical education is terribly expensive. Not only does it cost over $200,000 to train physicians today for eight years, but it costs even more to support their practice. Each new doctor probably generates an average of $350,000 of new costs to society every year of his or her career. In the coming decades, physician surplus will be one of the most important sources of increased medical cost, which is one reason why the Graduate Medical Education National Advisory Committee analyzed the problem (1980). Two features of its report stand out. The committee concluded that there would be an average of 7,000 surplus physicians per year through at least the year 2000 for a total surplus of 70,000 by 1990 and 145,000 by 2000 (vol. 1, p. 3). However, it recommended a 17 percent reduction in class size, which equals 3,403 students, not 7,000 (vol. 1, pp. 6, 21). To eliminate the surplus would require a 35 percent reduction. Second, the expert panels estimated that 22 percent of all visits could be handled by nonphysicians, but this figure was "adjusted" to 12 percent because "there would not be enough nonphysician personnel to handle all of the delegated visits" (vol. 2, p. 31). Although the committee's purpose was to identify manpower surpluses and shortages, in the case of nonphysician providers it simply made the service needs fit the projected supply and moved the balance (128.5 million visits) over to the physician column. The final report politely calls the trade-off between more physicians and more nonphysicians providers "a public policy dilemma" (vol. 1, p. 3). At stake, however, are large economic and educational issues about professional versus public priorities. To these the longitudinal studies of medical and nursing education contribute a richly detailed account of what is feasible and wherein lie the points of resistance to implementing policy directives. They affirm once again Michel's theory that the leaders of any organization will tend to become more preoccupied with consolidating their position and pursuing their interests than with the organization's original charter (1915). In the case of medical and nursing schools, these studies describe faculty pursuing educational goals not directly-aimed at the health needs of society.

REFERENCES

AIKEN, L. H. Nurses. 1983. In *Handbook of health, health care, and the health professions*, ed. D. Mechanic, Chap. 19. New York: Free Press.

——, and BLENDON, R. J. 1981. The national nurse shortage. *National Journal*, May 23, 1981.

American Nurses' Association. 1979. *A case for baccalaureate preparation in nursing*. American Nurses' Association.

Association of American Medical Colleges. 1980. *Graduate medical education: proposals for the eighties*. Washington, D. C.: Association of American Medical Colleges.

ATKINSON, P. 1981. *The clinical experience: the construction and reconstruction of medical reality*. Westmead, England: Gower.

AUDEN, W. H. 1966. Musée des beaux arts. In W. H. Auden, *Collected shorter poems 1927–1957*, pp. 123–24. New York: Random House.

BECKER, H. S. 1970. *Sociological work: method and substance*. Chicago: Aldine.

——; GEER, B.; HUGHES, E. C.; and STRAUSS, A. M. 1961. *Boys in white: student cultures in medical school*. Chicago: University of Chicago Press.

BENHAM, L., and BENHAM, A. 1976. The impact of incremental medical services on health status, 1963–1970. In *Equity in health services*, ed. R. Andersen, J. Dravits, and O. W. Anderson, pp. 217–28. Cambridge, Mass.: Ballinger.

BLOOM, S. W. 1963. The process of becoming a physician. *Annals of the American Academy of Political and Social Science* 346 (no. 87):77–87.

———. 1973. *Power and descent in the medical school.* New York: Free Press.

———. 1979. Socialization for the physician's role: a review of some contributions of research to theory. In *Becoming a physician: development of values and attitudes in medicine*, ed. E. C. Sharpiro and L. M. Loenstein, pp. 3–52. Cambridge, Mass.: Ballinger.

BOSK, C. A. 1979. *Forgive and remember.* Chicago: University of Chicago Press.

BUCHER, R., and STELLING, J. G. 1977. *Becoming professional.* Beverly Hills, Calif.: Sage Publications.

COSER, R. L. 1979. *Training and ambiguity: learning through doing in a medical hospital.* New York: Free Press.

DAVIS, F. 1968. Professional socialization as subjective experience: the process of doctrinal conversion among student nurses. In *Institutions and the person*, ed. H. S. Becker et al., pp. 235–51. Chicago: Aldine.

EDMUNDS, M. W. 1978. Evaluation of nurse practitioner effectiveness: an overview of the literature. *Evaluation and the Health Professions* 1:69.

EICHNA, L. W. 1980. Medical-school education, 1975–1979: a student's perspective. *New England Journal of Medicine* 303 (no. 13):727–34.

FREIDSON, E. 1970. *Profession of medicine.* New York: Dodd, Meade.

FOX, R. C. 1957. Training for uncertainty. In *The student-physician*, ed. R. K. Merton, G. G. Reader, and P. L. Kendall. Cambridge, Mass.: Harvard University Press.

———. 1959. *Experiment perilous: physicians and patients facing the unknown.* Glencoe, Ill.: Free Press.

———. 1976. Advance medical technology: social and ethical implication. *Annual Review of Sociology* 2:231–68.

———. 1980. The evolution of medical uncertainty. *Milbank Memorial Fund Quarterly/Health and Society* 58 (no. 1):1–49.

———, and SWAZEY, J. P. 1978. *The courage to fail: a social view of organ transplants and dialysis*, 2d ed. rev. Chicago: University of Chicago Press.

GELLHORN, A., M.D., and SCHEUER, R. 1978. The experiment in medical education at the City College of New York. *Journal of Medical Education* 53:574–82.

Graduate Medical Education National Advisory Committee. 1980. *Summary report.* Washington, D.C.: Dept. of Health and Human Services.

GREENFIELD, S.; KOMAROFF, A. L.; PASS, T. M.; ANDERSON, H.; and RESSIM, S. 1978. Efficiency and cost of primary care by nurses and physician assistants. *New England Journal of Medicine* 298:305–309.

HAGLUND, K. 1981. Taking it to the streets. *The New Physician* 30 (no. 3):26–31.

HAMMOND. K. R., KERN, F. G., JR. 1959. *Teaching comprehensive medical care.* Cambridge, Mass.: Harvard University Press.

HOROWITZ, M. 1964. *Educating tomorrow's doctors.* New York: Appleton-Century-Crofts.

HUGHES, E. C. 1958. *Men and their work.* Glencoe, Ill.: Free Press.

Institute of Medicine. *Six-month interim report by the committee of the Institute of Medicine for a study of nursing and nursing education.* Washington, D.C.: National Academy Press.

JONAS, S. 1978. *Medical mystery: the training of doctors in the United States.* New York: Norton.

KNOPF, L. 1975. *RN's: one year and five years after graduation.* New York: National League for Nursing.

LEVIN, L. S., and IDLER, E. L. 1981. *The hidden health care system: mediating structures and medicine.* Cambridge, Mass.: Ballinger.

LEVINE, E. and MOSES, E. B. 1982. A statistical profile of registered nurses in the United

States 1977–1980. In *Nursing in the 1980s: crises, opportunities, challenges,* ed. L. A. Aiken. Philadelphia: Lippincott.

LEVINSON, D. J. 1967. Medical education and the theory of adult socialization. *Journal of Health and Social Behavior* 8:253–65.

LEWIS, C. E.; RESNICK, B.; WAXMAN, D.; and SCHMIDT, G. Activities, events, and outcome in ambulatory care. *New England Journal of Medicine* 280:645–49.

LIGHT, D. W. 1972. Psychiatry and suicide: the management of a mistake. *American Journal of Sociology* 77:821–38.

———. 1975. The sociological calendar: and analytic tool for field work applied to medical and psychiatric training. *American Journal of Sociology* 80 (no. 5):1145–64.

———. 1980. *Becoming psychiatrists: the professional transformation of self.* New York: Norton.

———. 1982. The development of professional schools in America. In *The transformation of higher learning, 1840–1930,* ed. K. Jarausch. Stuggart: Klett Verlag.

LUBIC, R. W. Evaluation of an out-of-hospital maternity center for low-risk patients. In *Health policy and nursing practice,* ed. L. H. Aiken. New York: McGraw-Hill.

LURIE, E. E. 1981. Nurse practitioners: issues in professionalization socialization. *Journal of Medicine and Social Behavior* 22:31–48.

Macy Study Group. 1980. *Graduate medical education present and perspective: a call for action.* New York: Josiah Macy, Jr., Foundation.

MAY, E. M. 1981. Testimony to the Nurse Study Committee of the Institute of Medicine. 11 May 1981, typed.

MERTON, R. A.; READER, G.; KENDALL, P. L., eds. 1957. *The student-physician: introductory studies in the sociology of medical education.* Cambridge, Mass.: Harvard University Press.

McKINLAY, J. B., and McKINLAY, S. M. A refutation of the thesis that the health of the nation is improving. N.d., typed script.

MICHELS, R. 1949. *First lectures in political science (1915).* Trans. Alfred deGrazia. Minneapolis: University of Minnesota Press.

MILLER, S. J. 1970. *Prescription for leadership.* Chicago: Aldine.

MILLMAN, M. 1977. *The unkindest cut: life in the back rooms of medicine.* New York: William Morrow.

MUMFORD, E. 1970. *Interns: from student to physician.* Cambridge, Mass.: Harvard University Press.

National Commission on Nursing. 1981. *Initial report and preliminary recommendations.* Chicago: Hospital Research and Education Trust.

National League for Nursing. 1980. *Nursing data book, 1980.* New York: National League for Nursing.

OLESEN, V. L., WHITTAKER, E. W. 1968. *The student dialogue.* San Francisco, Calif.: Jossey-Bass.

RAMPHAL, M. 1978. Rethinking diploma school and baccalaureate education. *Nursing Outlook* 26:768–71.

———. 1981. Reported to Ernest M. May. 17 July 1981, typed.

READER, G. G., and Goss, M. E. W., eds. 1967. *Comprehensive medical care and teaching.* New York: Cornell University Press.

READER, G. G., and SOAVE, R. 1976. Comprehensive care revised. *The Milbank Memorial Fund Quarterly* 54:391–414.

ROGERS, D. E. 1981. Some musings on medical education: is it going astray? Princeton, N.J.: Robert-Wood-Johnson Foundation, typed script.

ROLAND, H. S., ed. 1978. *The nurse's almanac.* Germantown, Md.: Aspen Publications.

ROTHSTEIN, E. 1972. *American physicians in the 19th century: from sects to science.* Baltimore, Md.: Johns Hopkins University Press.

RUNYAN, J. W. 1975. The Memphis chronic disease program: comparisons in outcomes and nurse's extended role. *Journal of the American Medical Association* 231:27.

SACKETT, D. L.; SPITZER, W. O.; GENT, M.; ROBERTS, R. S. 1974. The Burlington randomized trial of the medical practitioner: health outcomes of patients. *Annals of Internal Medicine* 80:137.

SIMMEL, G. 1950. *The sociology of Georg Simmel.* Trans. and ed. Kurt H. Wolff. New York: Free Press.

SIMPSON, I. H. 1979. *From student to nurse: a longitudinal study of socialization.* New York: Cambridge University Press.

STANTON, A., and SCHWARTZ, M. 1954. *The mental hospital.* New York: Basic Books.

SLOME, C., et al. 1976. Effectiveness of certified nurse-midwives. *American Journal of Obstetrics and Gnyecology* 124:177–82.

Sox, H. C. 1979. Quality of patient care by nurse practitioners and physicians' assistants: a ten-year perspective. *Annals of Internal Medicine* 91:459.

STEVENS, B. J. 1971. *Nursing theory: analysis, applications, evaluation.* Boston: Little, Brown.

STEVENS, R. 1971. *American medicine in the public interest.* New Haven, Conn.: Yale University Press.

WEBER, M. 1954. Class, status, party. In *From Max Weber*, ed. H. Gerth and C. W. Mills, pp. 180–95. New York: Oxford University Press.

WEISFELD, N. 1980. Regulatory perspectives on national problems involving graduate medical education. *Graduate medical education present and perspective: a call for action,* Macy Study Group, pp. 148–84. New York: Josiah Macy, Jr., Foundation.

WHITE, K. 1973. Life and death and medicine. In *Life and death in medicine* by the editors of *Scientific American.* San Francisco, Calif.: W. H. Freeman.

Chapter 22

Allied Health Resources

Eli Ginzberg

At the turn of the twentieth century physicians accounted for about one out of every three health workers. At the beginning of the 1980s the comparable ratio is approximately one out of sixteen. If one considers all health workers except the physician (and the dentist) as "allied" then clearly the expansion of allied health manpower (AHM) has played a critical role in the evolution of twentieth-century medical care in the United States.

It is not customary, however, to include within the category AHM the following health practitioners: optometrists, pharmacists, podiatrists, veterinarians, and registered nurses. Less agreement exists whether to include licensed practical nurses and nurses aides, emergency medical technicians, and other health and health-related professionals and technicians including persons employed in environmental control, midwives, nutritionists, and medical secretaries.

The answer depends on whether the health-care industry is defined broadly or narrowly and secondly whether all persons within the industry irrespective of their occupational designations are included or whether only individuals in health-care occupations are counted. To illustrate: Is an accountant employed in a hospital to be included and a nurse employed by an insurance company excluded?

The principal reason for raising these classification issues is to emphasize the wide range of estimates about the total number of persons employed in health care—from a low of around 5.5 million to a high of close to 8.0 million and a correspondingly wide range in the numbers classified as AHM.

Since this chapter is analytical and policy-directed, not statistical and reporting-oriented, there is no gain in pursuing these classification issues further. The reader has been alerted to the ambiguities in the total number of AHM. This chapter will follow the conventions and the data presented in *A Report on Allied Health Personnel*, 26 November 1979, prepared by the Bureau of Health Manpower, HRA, PHS, for Committee on Interstate and Foreign Commerce, House of Representatives and the Committee on Labor and Human Resources, U.S. Senate (U.S. Dept. of Health, Education and Welfare 1979, hereafter HEW *Report*).

This report estimates the number of health workers employed in the United States in 1978 at 5.4 million distributed as follows:

Health practitioners	1.8
Allied health personnel	1.0
Other health personnel	2.6

TABLE 22.1   Allied Health Manpower: Key Groups

Laboratory workers	240,000
Medical technologists	125,000
Cytotechnologists	7,000
Medical laboratory technicians	12,000
Other laboratory workers	96,000
Dental auxiliaries	231,000
Hygienists	35,000
Assistants	149,000
Laboratory technicians	47,000
Radiologic service workers	104,000
Medical records	80,000
Administrators	12,000
Technicians	68,000
Respiratory therapy workers	52,000
Speech pathology-audiologists	36,000
Dieticians	28,000
Technicians	4,000
Physical therapists	30,000
Occupational therapists	15,000
Physicians assistants (primary care)	6,000
Other Allied Health	200,000
including assistants in optometry, orthopedics, podiatry, pharmacy, rehabilitation, etc.	

Over 60 percent of the last category consists of licensed practical nurses (500,000) and nursing aides and orderlies (1,100,000). Another sizable group consists of 270,000 emergency medical technicians. If these three groups are included within allied health the new subtotal comes to just under 3 million, or approximately 3 out of every 5 health workers, which is a reasonable measure of AHM in the United States at the beginning of the 1980s.

Table 22.1, adapted from the above report, sets out the principal categories of AHM about which there is no dispute.

Structure and Functions

Using the foregoing as a point of departure, one is led to the forces responsible for the rapid increase in AHM in recent decades. It also provides an insight into the multiple types of work setting in which AHM are employed and the relationships between AHM and physicians and dentists who continue to exercise primary responsibility for decisions affecting patient care.

The single largest group of AHM consists of laboratory workers, a reflection of the transformation of U.S. medicine from handholding to active intervention, based on advances in knowledge and technology, resulting in the heavy use of the laboratory for diagnosis and therapy. An additional factor speeding the expansion of laboratory personnel has been the growing importance of the hospital, which facilitated both heavy concentration of sophisticated equipment and the employment of persons with modest education and training able to carry out under supervision a wide array of standardized procedures. Since laboratory tests for inpatients are generally paid for in full by third parties, barriers to widespread use of tests have been largely removed.

Similar considerations, with some modification, help to explain the more than a hundred thousand radiologic workers. Here too technology has been in the driver's seat, a technology used not only for diagnosis but also for therapy both within the hospital setting and in physicians' offices. Physicians early discovered that they could train assistants who could prepare patients for radiologic examination as well as operate the machines. Radiologists recognized that their gross and net incomes could be substantially enlarged by their employing one or more trained assistants to perform these routine tasks so that they themselves could devote more time to reading the plates and determining appropriate therapeutic interventions for their patients.

Developments in instrumentation requiring close and continuing monitoring of intricate respiratory machines explains the large number of workers in respiratory therapy, one of the newer breakthroughs in contemporary medicine. Earlier, patients who had been placed in an oxygen tank or fitted with an oxygen mask required only periodic observation; the more advanced repiratory equipment requires full-time personnel capable of immediate responses to signals from the control mechanisms. Once again, advances in technology have made it possible for therapists to delegate responsibility for many of these procedures to assistants.

The large number of dental auxiliaries, about two for each dentist, reflects the widespread recognition on the part of the dental profession in the post–World War II era that dentists could substantially increase their productivity and earnings by using helpers. Moreover, dentists could also increase their work satisfaction by passing down to their assistants the cleaning of teeth and other routine activities. The almost fifty thousand laboratory technicians represent a related, but distinguishable specialization, once removed from direct patient treatment. Dental laboratories were established and technical personnel trained and employed to prepare dentures, crowns, and other special inlays at a volume that permits economies of scale, with one laboratory supporting a considerable number of dentists who practice within the same or adjacent areas.

How does one explain the different ratios of dental auxiliaries to dentists (2:1) and physicians assistants to primary-care physicians (1:9)? Several points suggest themselves: technical procedures play a larger role in the practice of dentistry than in medicine since in the latter history-taking and diagnosis are critical aspects of patient-physician interchange. The aforementioned ratios also hide the fact that physicians make use of large numbers of helpers in their office practice, roughly two for every physician and more if laboratory personnel involved in serving ambulatory patients are taken into account. Broad-scale consumer acceptance of physicians' assistants remains an open question while there is little or no reported resistance to the use of dental auxiliaries, at least not up to the point of their engaging in expanded functions.

The fact that during the course of a year approximately 39 million persons are admitted to a hospital (37 million to a short-term hospital) and that over $100 billion annually is expended on their care helps to explain the sizable number of AHM engaged in record keeping, either as administrators or staff. Since records are critical for physicians' decisions, reimbursement, quality control, and evidence in the event of malpractice suits, small wonder that the record-keeping function requires so many technicians and supervisors.

The concentration of large numbers of patients in hospitals, many of whom require special diets explains the sizable number of dieticians and dietetic technicians. While the total number looks sizable, it averages out to more than one dietician for 250 patients, a modest figure when one realizes the proportion of patients who have special needs and the further fact that dieticians frequently oversee the entire food service for patients and employees alike.

Physical and occupational therapists together with speech pathologists and audiologists represent a manpower response to the development of specialized therapeutics beyond the province of the medical practitioner but inside of modern medicine. These therapies required a considerable degree of technical skill but do not require the practitioner to be well versed, as physicians are, in the biomedical sciences. These therapists have considerable scope for independent judgment even though they depend on physicians to refer patients and to prescribe the type of treatment patients are to receive. While many of these practitioners are employed by institutions, particularly hospitals, many others treat mostly ambulatory patients in an office setting.

The large catch-all category, amounting to about one in five AHM, reflects the wide range of assistants who are closely linked to health practitioners in the fields of optometry, podiatry, pharmacy, and veterinary medicine as well as in certain specialized branches of medicine including pediatrics, orthopedics, rehabilitation and still others.

Between 1970 and 1978 total employment in the health-service industry increased from approximately 4.3 to 6.6 million, or by slightly more than 50 percent. Between 1966 and 1978 AHM (narrowly defined) grew from 442,000 to 1,026,000, or by 132 percent. Several inferences suggest themselves. First, the industry experienced a continuing rapid rate of employment growth during a decade when cost containment came center stage. Next, with the number of newly licensed physicians and dentists accounting for less than 10 percent of the total growth of employment, the importance of AHM and other health practitioners and personnel is clearly demonstrated. Third the responsiveness of the educational system and the market to the demands for new health personnel is impressive, the more so when one realizes that many, though by no means all, of the new workers had to undergo preemployment training.

The remainder of this chapter will explore the major dimensions of AHM with particular reference to recruitment, education and training, professionalization, income and careers, and public policy. The rapid changes in AHM that have taken place during the last decades underscore the importance of not seeing the future solely in terms of the current situation and recent trends. To avoid this trap requires that potential changes in AHM be set within a larger framework in which two major determinants are given heavy weight—the labor market and the health-care industry.

Recruitment, Education, and Training

Up to the mid-1960s employers, in the first instance, hospitals and, secondarily, physicians and dentists were the primary trainers of AHM. Hospitals had no alternative to undertaking the training of the increasing numbers of technicians to back up and assist physicians in the laboratory, in the X-ray department, and in operation of new equipment used to monitor seriously ill patients concentrated in intensive-care units. Most of these training programs were initially not accredited; the faculty consisted of knowledgeable hospital staff who were persuaded to take on the additional duty of instruction; the numbers trained, except in large institutions, were quite small since each hospital sought only to meet its own requirements; most trainees were employees who were already on the payroll.

But this long-established training pattern was radically altered in the sixties, which saw the proliferation of junior and community colleges whose primary claim for public financing was to provide students with a "salable" skill. The infusion of new money into the provision of health-care services precipitated a greatly increased demand for health workers which provided the community college movement with the incentive it needed to move into the breach.

And breach it was, because many hospitals were not in a position to expand their training and many smaller institutions were disinclined to start.

Economics played a role. Many hospitals that had long sponsored diploma schools of nursing discovered that the operation was costly and that they stood to gain if nurse training was moved into the postsecondary educational structure. The same thinking applied to AHM. Further, some of the educational leaders of AHM, convinced that the quality of student preparation could be significantly improved if training were centered in university health science centers, urged their states and the federal government to support this move. They argued that the university would provide an environment conducive to the development of core curricula and broad faculty competence in the training not only of AHM but of all health professionals.

The expansion of AHM at both junior and senior colleges appeared attractive for another reason. More and more young Americans were desirous of obtaining college degrees while at the same time strengthening their preparation for the labor market. The movement of education for AHM out of the hospital into academe appeared to provide an optimal solution. Many hospitals, freed of the necessity of expanding training for a wide array of AHM specialists and technicians, were agreeable to providing clinical work sites for the newly burgeoning college based programs.

Table 22.2 for 1975–76, shows the exent to which collegiate training of AHM has come to dominate both with respect to programs and graduates. Hospitals still perform a training mission but in terms of graduates they account for only one out of every six.

TABLE 22.2 AHM-Training Structure

SETTING	INSTITUTIONS	PROGRAMS	GRADUATES
Collegiate	1700	6900	145,000
Senior (4 year)			
Junior (2 year)			
Noncollegiate	2500	4700	75,000
Hospitals	1600	3300	35,000
Other nonmilitary	900	1300	20,000
Military	UNR	100	2,000
Total	4200	11,600	220,000

HEW *Report* III–2

Several additional facts: The 6,900 programs prepare students for 148 different occupations, mostly for entry-level assignments. The collegiate structure has 170,000 first-year places, for which they receive about 400,000 applications. Minorities account for about one in seven of the enrollees most of whom (three out of four) are women. School costs (excluding living expenses) varied from about $46 a month in public institutions, which account for two-thirds of the senior enrollment and over 90 percent of the junior enrollment, to $220 in private institutions.

The number of hospital programs with 35,000 graduates are heavily concentrated in clinical laboratory, radiologic technology, administration and planning, mental health, and dietetics.

The "Other nonmilitary" training institutions included in Table 22.2 refer primarily to vocational-technical schools, two-thirds public, one-third proprietary. The latter prepare students primarily for medical office assisting, dental assisting, nursing aid, dental laboratory, and medical laboratory.

The U.S. Office of Education Report to the Congress released early in 1980 (U.S. Dept. of Health, Education and Welfare 1980) provides additional data on enrollment in secondary schools in the health occupations (overlapping but not identical with AHM since 378,000 nursing personnel are included). Secondary school enrollments in health occupations increased from about 60,000 in 1972 to 132,000 in 1978, but with total enrollments in 1978 calculated at 759,000, secondary schools were clearly playing a minor training role accounting for no more than 17 percent of all students (p. 50).

The military has long been a trainer of the personnel it needs to perform essential functions. But many who are trained to serve in military institutitons leave after their initial tour of duty or after one or more reenlistments. Still relatively young, they need jobs after their return to cilvilian life. For those who were trained and employed in the military in health occupations who desire to find comparable jobs after discharge, the federal government has funded a series of "transition programs" to facilitate such conversion.

Professionalization

Physicians learned a long time ago that they could advance their professional interests and at the same time help to advance their economic well-being through organizing themselves to exercise leadership over medical education, graduate training, hospital appointments, and to deal with other groups in society, governmental and nongovernmental. Small wonder, therefore, that AHM groups have sought to follow the same model by organizing themselves into associations, with an aim of exercising control via accreditation over the educational and training structures through which students must pass and of establishing systems for registration, certification, or, where indicated, licensing as a precondition for entrance into the field. However, the tight training structure of medical education with only about 130 schools in comparison to no fewer than 4,200 institutions involved in AHM training suggests that the medical pattern is not directly applicable.

Nonetheless, an older and better organized group such as the American Medical Technologists, established in 1939, is engaged in the following range of activities: registering medical laboratory personnel at three different levels--medical assistant, medical laboratory technician, medical technologist, for each of which the AMT has specified the required level of education and experience. Next, the AMT through an autonomous agency is involved in accreditation, which means that the agency assesses the quality of the preparatory programs and approves those that meet its standards. The AMT has, in addition to a national structure, a regional and state structure, which enables members to engage in educational, public information, representational, and similar activities. The AMT publishes a bimonthly journal that features primarily scientific articles of interest to the membership but that also devotes space to economic, political, and organizational developments. Since its organization forty-one years ago, AMT has certified over 30,000 individuals, but, as its president recently noted, there remain about "120,000 laboratory workers in the U.S. not certified by any agency."

A scanning of the *Health Careers Guidebook* (U.S. Departments of Labor and Health, Education and Welfare 1979, hereafter *Guidebook*), calls attention to the muliple agencies that are involved in accreditation, examination, certification and licensing. To stay with medical laboratory technicians and technologists: The AMA's Committee on Allied Health, Education, and Accreditation approves training programs. Upon graduation, however, the successful candidate can be certified by different organizations and in a minority of states including Florida, Georgia, Pennsylvania, they must be licensed (*Guidebook*, p. 41).

If one stands back from the pulling and hauling that goes on within the broad domain of AHM as to the goals of professionalization and the best ways of accomplishing training, certification, or licensing, one can identify the following underlying forces, several of which operate at cross purposes. As noted earlier, the functions to be performed by different groups of health workers from the physician to the assistant are subject to continuing change in response to the dynamism of medicine, the incentives for physicians to delegate routine responsibilites to others so as to free their time for more complex tasks, the differing patterns for organizing the performance of routine tasks within and outside of institutions depending on the volume of work and availability of trained personnel, the ambivalence of the AMA about professional goals for AHM, the realization on the part of the AMA leaders that they must not assume a dominating role, and the stake that many medical and surgical specialty groups have in structuring the conditions under which AHM assists them.

Additional complications grow out of the tension between the federal government and the private sector. Picking up the steadily rising bills for Medicare and Medicaid, Washington is increasingly concerned about costs and quality. But the states have traditionally had primary responsibility for establishing standards for education and licensure.

Additional tension grows out of the inherent contradiction between the efforts of the several groups of AHM to gain optimal control over the qualifications of their members and the barriers to occupational mobility that accompany such efforts as each group seeks to delineate ever more explicitly the terms and conditions under which individuals are to be trained and employed.

The great variability that exists in the United States as to the size of hospitals, the availability of postsecondary education, the sophistication of medical practice, the breadth and depth of the labor market, and still other critical dimensions have made it difficult to resolve the overriding tension between movement toward a national standard of competence without jeopardizing the delivery of essential health services in communities facing constrained resources. Although HEW has taken small steps now and again in the direction of setting national standards for educational institutions, competency examinations, and licensing regulations, the members of Congress, especialy those from rural and low-income states, have seen to it that the status quo is altered, if at all, only at a rate at which institutions in their communities can accommodate. Nowhere is the gap between medical practitioners and AHM wider than in the arena of national standard setting.

A recent report of the comptroller general to the Congress provides a dramatic illustration of the conflicts that surface when the federal government seeks to bring about a major change in the ultilization of AHM (General Accounting Office 1980). The GAO report argues that there would be important gains to consumers, dentists, and taxpayers if the overwhelming number of states that now prohibit dental auxiliaries from completing restorations (fillings) permitted them to undertake such work. The evidence the GAO garnered in its review of the few states in which such expanded functions are permitted pointed to no loss in quality and significant reductions in costs and improved access to care.

But the dissenting submission of the American Dental Association has much to commend it since it argued cogently that permitting auxiliaries to do more was not the answer to restricted access because dentists avoided setting up practices in communities that could not support them. The ADA acknowledged that finances kept some people from seeking dental care but noted that many others saw no point to seeking dental care; they preferred to take their chances. Most important, the ADA argued that there was no shortage of dentists.

As of 1977, forty states had laws prohibiting auxiliaries from engaging in expanded functions. The nub of the issue is whether the critical GAO recommendation encourages early federal legislative action in the event that the states do not act quickly to permit auxiliaries to engage in expanded functions. We will reserve judgment until the last section, which deals with policy.

Jobs and Careers

In the *Guidebook* noted above there are several pages of graphs (pp. 27–30) which list a great many health occupations indicating the years of education and training beyond high school graduation required for entrance into the field. Most assistants and many technicians, such as certified laboratory assistants and histological technicians, can qualify on the basis of one year's instruction. At the opposite extreme are specialist in blood bank technology, five years; medical social worker, six years, speech pathologist and audiologist, six years. In between, one finds physical therapist assistant, two years; dispensing optician, two years, radiation therapy technologist, two years, cytologist, three years, prosthetist, four years, orthotist, four years. Even if human capital theory cannot by itself account fully for differences in lifetime earnings much of the variability in earnings among AHM workers that we will soon identify is linked to the time and expense that they have invested in their preparation.

On page 204 the *Guidebook* presents a salary chart developed by the University of Texas Medical Branch 1978 National Survey of Hospital and Medical School Salaries for a forty-hour week exclusive of fringe benefits. The chart presents ranges for starting and maximum rates. Certified laboratory assistants, dialysis technicians, EKG and EEG technicians, operating-room technicians, optometric assistants, radiologic technologists, and recreational therapists all have monthly starting salaries that at the lower end of the range fall between $500 and $600. However, at the upper end of the starting range some individuals may be offered as much as $1,200 or even $1,500 a month.

What is striking is the relatively small increase at both ends of the range between starting and maximum salaries. We find as little as $100 or $200 a month between a person's opening salary and what he or she is likely to earn after five or ten years on the same job.

With respect to those AHM workers with four to six years of formal preparation beyond high school, one finds a midpoint starting salary of around $1,200 a month with a midpoint maximum of around $2,000. Once again, one finds relatively little room for salary improvement over time when one compares the starting with maximum earnings. A spread of about $500 is characteristic for these better paying AHM positions.

The salary and career prospects of AHM are strongly affected by the following. The first is that the predominance of women in the field has a depressing influence on the salary structure. Discrimination against women in the labor market has been characteristic of our economy, and while recent legislation, administrative practices, and institutional arrangements have begun to shift in the direction of greater equity, women generally remain seriously disadvantaged with respect to salaries and promotional opportunities.

While there were a few years in the latter 1960s when many health-care institutions found themselves shorthanded with respect to AHM, the responsiveness of the educational and training structures prevented significant long-term shortages from developing which in turn weakened the ability of AHM to bargain for substantial increases in salaries. Unlike physicians, most of whom are able to bill on a fee-for-service basis, most AHM personnel, though not all, are employees of institutions. They have been poorly positioned to secure for themselves any appreciable part of the new flow of funds that followed the implementation of Medicare, Medicaid, and the growth of nonprofit and commercial insurance.

A considerable number of AHM not employed in hospitals work for physicians in private practice. The physician is in a relatively strong bargaining position since he determines the qualifications of those whom he selects to assist him and the functions which he delegates, and his employees face difficulties in organizing to press their demands.

A further salary depressive is the fact that since many women, although fewer than in past years, leave employment during their childbearing years, many employers can hire replacements at entrance-level salaries.

As noted earlier, one of the concomitants of the drive toward professionalization is the increasing control exercised by the more potent AHM organizations over their field, and the conditions of entrance and advancement. Each of the groups—assistants, technicians, technologists—seeks to build protective barriers, the consequence of which is to limit the occupational mobility open to members who are at a lower rung. While the American Medical Technologists have structured an occupational ladder that enables individuals at the bottom to advance through additional education, training, and experience, their approach is the exception. More often than not, both embryonic and established AHM professional associations place obstacles in the path of persons who seek to advance on the basis of experience by insisting that they scale specific educational hurdles which, for reasons of time and cost, many of the upwardly mobile are unable to accomplish.

One of the newer developments is the availability of continuing education courses to enable AHM personnel to keep abreast of rapid developments in their field. Quoting from the *Guidebook* (p. 48) for dental hygienists: "Continuing education courses are available in some states for hygienists who want to keep up with the latest techniques and materials. There may be regularly scheduled evening classes in local schools or 'refresher' courses running for a few days to several weeks sponsored by professional associations or educational institutions. In several states continuing education is required to maintain licensure."

Along these same lines the American Dietetic Association permits the continuing use of the designation RD (registered dietician) only for those members who pass an examination and maintain a given number of hours in continuing education every five years (*Guidebook*, p. 58).

While the acquisition of diplomas and degrees is definitely the preferred route to employment and advancement in some of the newer occupations, as well as in some of those that have been long established, opportunities exist for trading experience for education. To illustrate: biomedical equipment technician: "In some cases individuals with less than an associate degree may substitute experience for education requirements" (*Guidebook*, p. 137).

Policy Considerations

Before assessing the more important policy issues involving AHM currently on the nation's agenda or likely to be added in the near future, it may be useful to look back and sketch in broad outline what has been occurring on the policy front during the highly dynamic post-World War II era when health-care expenditures as a percentage of GNP increased from about 4.5 to over 9.0 percent. The pluralistic health-care system, often referred to disparagingly as a "cottage industry" or "nonsystem," has demonstrated great flexibility in meeting its expanded manpower requirements, including large increases in the number and types of AHM. Credit for coping goes first to the hospital sector, which early recognized that its only prospect for meeting its manpower requirements was through expanding its training activities.

The second principal contributor was state governments, which by the early 1960s were increasingly active in expanding their collegiate establishments, both at the junior and senior college level, which, sensitive to their students' vocational interests and goals, responded by instituting training opportunities for AHM occupations.

The federal government, at least in terms of its health manpower programming (HEW), was a latecomer. Its first modest appropriations date from 1966, and in the following thirteen years federal outlays for AHM totalled $276 million (HEW Report, pp. 1–7), or slightly over $20 million a year for construction, training, special projects and other designated objectives. The department's objectives were set out as follows:

—To assure an adequate supply
—To assure adequate quality
—To minimize costs of health services
—To increase opportunities for the disadvantaged
—To increase the effectiveness of education and training
—To optimize geographic and speciality distribution [HEW Report, pp. 1–4]

The weight of the evidence suggests that the principal leverage used by the federal government has been to encourage experimentation in the arena of education and training and new forms of service delivery. Most of the aforementioned goals were largely beyond the reach of the federal government as long as it limited severely its annual level of expenditures.

In sketching the evolution of AHM one must also take note of the striking changes which occurred in the role of women in the labor force. Between 1950 and 1980 the proportion of women aged sixteen and over in paid employment increased from about one-third to over one-half. Women accounted for approximately three out of every five new job holders during these decades. The large inflow of women into the world of work during a period when the health-care system was expanding rapidly was mutually supportive. Without the much enlarged supply of women workers, the health-care industry could not have moved forward so rapidly. And the rapid expansion of health care created a large number of relatively attractive employment opportunities for many female job seekers.

A more inclusive view of the role of the federal government's impact on AHM requires a broader angle of vision than its specific appropriations for health manpower. Large-scale federal funding for Medicare and Medicaid patients provided greatly enlarged revenues to hospitals and other providers, which in turn enabled them to increase their hiring of AHM. From this broadened vantage, it would be difficult to exaggerate the influence of the federal government on AHM.

The increasing importance of the federal government as the payor of bills—it currently covers over 25 percent of total annual expenditures of the health-care system—helps to explain its increasing concern with various aspects of AHM. In terms of staging, the federal government first became concerned about potential shortages of health manpower, including AHM; later about their quality; and still later about how more effective use of AHM could help to control total costs.

Congress having legislated and financed the broadened access of older persons and the poor to the health-care system could not ignore the threat of restricted access resulting from shortages of health personnel. Congress was loath, however, to become involved in the financing of junior and senior colleges and therefore limited its expenditures for AHM to selected projects and grants aimed at strengthening the educational and training infrastructure without becoming heavily involved in providing operational support. Moreover, Congress appreciated, even during the latter 1960s, when concern with shortages of health manpower was to the fore, that the preparation of AHM was so broadly diffused, involving so many different institutions, that general federal support was not an appropriate intervention.

The federal government, concerned over the significant shortage of physicians (estimated in the mid-1960s at fifty thousand) played a more active role in furthering the development of new training programs for physicians assistants or physician extenders, the first effort having been initiated at Duke University in the mid-1960s. Federal officials saw in the physician assistant a rapid and cost-efficient way of responding to the physician shortage. It also early encouraged the specialty societies to experiment with using extenders and helped to finance programs for physicians assistants in pediatrics, urology, allergy, orthopedics, and surgery in addition to assisting the establishment and expansion of programs for physicians assistants in primary care. More recently it has centered its support on the latter making funds available for about forty such programs.

Once the Washington officialdom decided (early 1970s) that the perennial physician shortage had been resolved federal policy with respect to physicians assistants faced a dilemma. Why continue to train PAs in the face of a possible surplus of physicians? The answer, at least up to the present, has been the PAs are used where physicians are unlikely to practice as in outlying areas and among urban concentrations of low income groups. In 1978, it was estimated that there were over six thousand PAs; the fifty programs or so graduated around twelve hundred graduates a year (1976), but no firm figure exists as to the numbers actively working as PAs.

It is difficult to see how the training of PAs can expand in the 1980s in the face of a substantially increased inflow of fully trained physicians. Some of the specialty societies, such as orthopedists, early concluded that the training of PAs was not desirable and terminated their programs. With the nurse leadership belatedly, but aggressively, pushing to expand the number of nurse practitioners the future role of the PAs becomes equivocal. Other issues that have never been adequately resolved affect the scope of practice of PAs when they are under the direct or indirect supervision of physicians and the reimbursement for their services under Medicare and Medicaid.

If one were forced to make a forecast of the future role of PAs it would be safer to assume that the training programs will shrink rather than expand; that among those currently employed as well as future graduates a significant minority will be lost through attrition; and that the total number of PAs a decade out will probably not exceed ten thousand to fifteen thousand. Their principal contribution will continue to be as auxiliary providers to members of disadvantaged groups that have difficulty on a regular basis of gaining access to physicians. It is highly unlikely that they will have any significant effect on altering the pattern of delivering health care to the population as a whole.

This brief discussion of the future of PAs helps to point up a generic issue about the effective deployment of AHM. From the vantage of a health planner one can identify a great many settings where the substitution of less for more trained personnel under appropriate supervision would be cost reducing without loss of quality. But these opportunities do not turn into realities because of the self-interest of affected practitioners, systems of reimbursement, legal constraints on practice, consumer preferences, and the absence in many cases of organizational structures necessary to take advantage of such potential efficiencies and economies. To drive the last point home: Even in the federal establishment—the armed forces, the Veterans Administration, the Public Health Service—there has been at best only modest progress in the effective utilization of AHM. There has been much talk about encouraging physicians to work with AHM as a "team," but the fact is that the organizational structures for the delivery of heatlh care in the United States are basically antagonistic to the optimal utilization of AHM even under prepayment plans and more so under fee-for-service.

One must not jump to the conclusion, however, that in other countries where governments play a more active role in the health-care system one finds greater utilization of AHM. The recent study of Milton and Ruth Roemer (1978), provides interesting insights. The Roemers point out in their conclusions that "In general . . . there are fewer categories and lesser relative numbers of other allied health personnel in all the study countries than in the United States" (p. 55).

Another unresolved and possibly unresolvable issue relates to the tradeoffs between the trend to professionalization, with its associated emphasis on educational standards, competence, and quality control and the fractionalization, short career ladders, and higher personnel costs that follow upon such specialization. The suggestion was advanced some years ago by Ruth Roemer and others to shift from licensing individuals to licensing institutions. She argued that placing responsibility for the quality of the output on the provider organization would encourage management to assign personnel with an aim to improving their utilization. The proposal, however, has never been adopted. In the United States, as in most other countries, the degrees of freedom in work granted a health professional are directly linked to the competence of the individual as measured by his educational achievements and by certification or licensing.

Several AHM groups have sought in recent years to provide opportunities for individuals who have acquired additional knowledge and competence on the job and through training programs to demonstrate this through a written examination after which, if they are successful, they can move up the job and career ladder. But the development of good testing instruments is a difficult and expensive undertaking, and most AHM groups continue to place primary emphasis for certification and licensure on the completion of formal educational requirements.

The training of "narrow specialists" is dysfunctional for many smaller and even medium-sized hospitals where in the face of an explosion in technical procedures their need is for personnel trained to handle a variety of machines and competent to perform several technical procedures. Canada, according to the Roemers (p. 36), is considering the training of such "critical care technologists" following upon its earlier combined training of laboratory and X-ray technicians and physical and occupational therapists (p. 56).

The relationship between raising the requirements for credentialling and licensing and improvements in the quality of the service remains obscure. The presumption is deeply ingrained that better educated and trained persons perform better, make fewer mistakes, are alert to idiosyncratic results, know when they need to seek help. It is therefore discouraging to discover that the Center for Disease Control has found no improvement over a ten-year period in the quality of independent laboratories in bacteriology, parasitology, virology and only marginal improvements in other areas (HEW Report, p. 50).

The scale of future training efforts for AHM as well as for other health personnel should be subject to continuing scrutiny. The *Guidebook* takes a distinctly optimistic stance toward future openings in most AHM occupations. If the assumption of a marked slowdown in new funding proves correct, it will be hard to justify its optimism about future manpower requirements.

A marked deceleration of new funds is likely to occur at the same time that the number of physicians per 100,000 is almost certain to increase by at least one-third (from 180 to 240) within a single decade. Physicians will be looking for ways to maintain their income in an environment in which dollars will be scarcer. It is likely that they will adopt a more restrictive stance toward others who see patients, especially PAs and nurse practitioners; they will seek to cut their overhead by reducing the number of helpers in their offices; and will return to doing work previously delegated to others.

To the extent that these forebodings are borne out, it is important for the states and the federal government to keep under close surveillance their appropriations for the training of AHM. There is no point in encouraging large numbers of young people to secure such training if the job market tightens appreciably. True, there will always be a reasonable number of replacement openings, and new breakthroughs in technology will create a demand for new specialists. But if containment rather than expansion in health care is the dominant theme, a cautionary training stance is indicated.

Even in the face of a general stringency of dollars it is likely that the 1980s will see a considerable effort made to improve the health-care services provided older persons, particularly on an ambulatory basis. It is too costly and too "unloving" to force more and more of the feeble aged into nursing homes. Accordingly, there should be expanding opportunities for a new type of combined social-health-geriatric worker to play a leading role in the delivery of such services.

The problem of adjusting the number and types of training programs in AHM to the changing realities of the labor market will be that much more difficult because the declining number of postsecondary students will put additional pressure on the educational establishment not to cut back until forced to do so. This presents an additional challenge to state legislators who appropriate most of the funds for AHM.

Although the role of the U.S. Department of Labor (CETA) has not previously been discussed it should be noted that this arm of the federal government has been a large trainer of health personnel for low level positions. The number of such positions is likely to shrink if health planners succeed in reducing the number of hospital beds they consider to be in oversupply by between 10 and 15 percent. Once again it will be important to align local training programs with employment opportunities.

The last decade has seen gains in the education of AHM, especially through the establishment of schools of allied health manpower in large academic health science centers. Important innovations occurred involving new core curriculum, faculty improvement, broadened opportunities for clinical experience. The leadership of AHM emphasizes the need for continuing such efforts to strengthen the educational base.

The last important policy issue involves the changing relations of the federal government to the states, remembering that it is the states that have primary responsibility for the licensing of health personnel and for the regulation of health providers. Although the federal government made several feints in the 1970s toward setting national standards for the certification and/or licensing of selected groups of AHM, a critical review suggests that such intervention is premature. The several professional associations, working separately and cooperatively, should be encouraged to move in the direction of the national standard setting. To the extent that they are successful the next logical step is for the states to adjust their rules and regulations accordingly. If the efforts of nonprofit organizations and the states show reasonable progress there is no reason for the federal government to take the lead. If they fail there is little prospect of the federal government's succeeding.

This is not to say that the federal government should play possum. Rather, it should explore its targets of opportunity carefully and seek to benefit from its recent experiences. There is every reason why the federal government should take the lead, surely within its own institutions, in exploring the more effective use of AHM. It faces no inhibitions of so doing in the use of PAs, nurse practitioners, and extended functions by dental auxiliaries. In addition, Congress has authorized the federal government to finance the use of extenders in providing direct care for patients in rural and inner-city community health centers. The federal government should test the limits of making gains through the improved utilization of AHM in a fashion that can serve as a model for other providers. If the federal government can point the way others are more likely to follow.

The federal government has also made funding available in recent years to encourage professional associations to develop competency examinations so as to broaden the opportunity of those who have been trained mostly on the job. This is clearly a desirable approach if opportunities for improved mobility are not to be limited solely to individuals who have had access to educational programs.

A third sensible line of activity for the federal government is to continue, and possibly expand, the efforts which it helped to initiate to encourage a large group of AHM societies to work cooperatively toward improved examination and certification standards (National Commission for Health Certifying Agencies).

During the expansionary 1960s, not only in health but across the gamut of social policy, the dominant style in the United States was for professors, politicians, and public interest groups to identify unsolved problems and then to advocate new federal interventions aimed at removing the deficiencies that had been identified. While many of these efforts proved more successful than fiscal conservatives are willing to acknowledge it is also true that loading all unfinished social reform on the federal government proved impractical for a great number of different reasons from increasing the inflationary potential in the economy to undermining the long-term relationships among the several levels of government.

In this context, we found that the expanding needs for AHM were met in the first instance by the shift in the locus of training from hospitals to higher education, a process serendipitously aided by the aggressive search of junior colleges for new vocational programs. The principal actors in shaping and reshaping curricula and strengthening quality assurance were the educational leadership and professional associations aided by financial support from both the federal and state governments. This loose, largely unarticulated process resulted in providing the much increased numbers of AHM that the health-care system required, not only in total but in almost every community in the United States.

One can also identify much that was not resolved, such as the optimal patterns of health manpower utilization, improved quality controls over the work performed by AHM; greater opportunities for occupational mobility for persons low on the totem pole, and reciprocity in licensing among the states.

These and other issues remain on the agenda. But if the recent past can provide guidance for the near future it should be that the accommodations between the supply and demand for AHM represent, unlike the case with physicians, a challenge to local institutions in which the principal actors have been and must continue to be individuals in search of jobs and careers; employers in search of workers; state governments involved in providing educational and vocational opportunities for the population; professional associations committed to improving the competence, status, and rewards of their members; and the federal government seeking to identify a limited number of frontiers where it can assume a leadership position. The future of AHM will depend more on the changes in the structure of health-care delivery than on the education and professionalization of the work force.

REFERENCES

FEIN, R., and BISHOP, C. 1976. *Employment impacts of heatlh policy developments.* Special Report no. 11, October 1976. Washington, D.C.: National Commission for Manpower Policy.

General Accounting Office. 1980. *Increased use of expanded function dental auxiliaries.* HRD 80–61. 7 March 1980. Washington, D.C.: Government Printing Office.

GINZBERG, E. 1978. *Health manpower and health policy.* Montclair, N.J.: Allanheld and Osmun.

GREENFIELD, H. I., and BROWN, C. 1969. *Allied health manpower: trends and prospects.* New York: Columbia University Press.

HIESTAND, D. L., and OSTOW, M. 1976. *Health manpower information for policy guidance.* Cambridge, Mass.: Ballinger.

National Advisory Council on Vocational Education. 1980. *The education of nurses: a rising national concern.* Issue Paper no. 2. Washington, D.C.: The Council.

ROEMER, M., and ROEMER, R. 1978. *Health manpower policies under five national health care systems.* U.S. Department of Health, Education and Welfare pub. no. (HRA) 78–43. Washington, D.C.: Government Printing Office.

U.S. Department of Health, Education and Welfare, 1979. Bureau of Health Manpower, HRA, PHS. *A report on allied health manpower,* 26 November 1979. Prepared for the Committee on Interstate and Foreign Commerce, House of Representatives, and the Committee on Labor and Human Resources, Senate. Washington, D.C.: Government Printing Office.

———. 1980. Office of Education. *Status of vocational education in 1978.* Washington, D.C.: Government Printing Office.

U.S. Departments of Labor and Health, Education and Welfare. 1979. *Health careers guidebook.* 4th ed. Washington, D.C.: Government Printing Office.

Chapter 23

Social Work
as a Health Profession

Rosalie A. Kane

THIS CHAPTER DISCUSSES the past, present, and future of professional social work in health care. The very presence of social workers in health-care settings attests to the truism that "patients are people." It reinforces the widely shared understanding that illness and disability may have a psychosocial etiology and certainly may carry profound psychosocial consequences for patients and their families. The social worker translates a theoretical understanding of the stresses associated with medical problems into interventions that help people cope, that assist them in making decisions occasioned by the health problem, or that necessitate environmental changes to meet human needs more adequately.

At a time when many health professionals rail against "the medical model," social work (the profession that most represents the interface of medicine and society) is in a complex and somewhat paradoxical position. Social workers chafe against medical dominance over their work; they have asserted their authority in the social sphere as much as the hierarchical delivery system allows. Social-work leaders protested using health programs and health dollars to solve social problems (Dinerman 1979). They have been even louder in asserting that professional social workers are not medical handmaidens (Hallowitz 1972; Pfouts and McDaniel 1977). But, at the same time, social workers have adapted to the health-care setting over the years by accepting some of its apparent values, by taking the facilitation of the medical plan as a major goal, and by struggling (with considerable success) for recognition as reimbursable health-care vendors. The tension of developing social services within an entrepreneurial system of health-care delivery is ever present.

Thus, while other health-care providers debate about the appropriate way to take cognizance of newly recognized social factors and forces, social workers raise questions about the proper role of a socially oriented profession in the delivery of health care. Are social workers professionals with a primary concern for social welfare who, for convenience, are housed in health settings? Or is health per se their primary concern? Should social workers accept the medical expansionism implicit in the World Health Organization's definition of health ("a state of complete physical, mental, and social well-being"), or should social-work practice rest on the assumption that health, along with justice, social relatedness, self-fulfillment, and economic self-sufficiency is just one aspect of social welfare (Kane 1979)? The point is more than semantic; the answer to that question will shape social-work practice in health settings for years to come.

Toward Definition

Social workers are found in all settings where health care is delivered, coordinated, or planned. Close to eighty thousand social workers with professional education at the master's level (MSWs) or at the bachelor's level (BSWs) are employed in health-care and mental health settings (Bracht 1978; Nacman 1977). This estimate excludes the larger number of social service personnel in health settings who lack formal social-work credentials or training; the latter may or may not act under social-work supervision and direction.

Despite the ubiquity of social workers, their purposes and functions in health organizations are not well understood by colleagues from other disciplines (Kane 1975a; Lister 1980) or by the general public (Condie et al. 1978). In a vague and general way, it is understood that social workers help patients and their families cope with the psychological and social adjustments demanded by the exigencies of disease and disability. Some recognize social workers as primary deliverers of mental health services, including psychotherapy with individuals, families, and groups. Others hold more constrained views of social workers' roles, pigeonholing them as members of the health team most suited for making practical arrangements and linking patients to community services, including income-maintenance programs. The traditional specializations within social work are social casework, social group work, community organization, research, and administration; because social work specializations are organized according to method of practice, a reading of the standard texts fails to explain the essential nature of social work practice in particular fields, such as health care.

Social workers themselves constantly struggle to identify the strands that hold social-work practitioners together despite the diverse populations they serve and the wide range of techniques they use. The organized profession has been perennially preoccupied with defining itself. (This collective introspection led an unidentified pundit to remark that social work is one of the few professions that keeps pulling itself up by the roots to see how it is growing.)

Most definitions of social work construe the "person-in-the-environment" as the appropriate unit for social-work attention. For example, a decade ago, Bartlett (1970) suggested that social functioning is the common theme in all social-work practice. According to her formulation, the social worker's task is to "improve the balance between people's coping efforts and the environmental demands." This requires "working with people or the environment but most frequently with both and always with concern for the interaction between them" (p. 103). Major variations among social workers can be attributed to differential emphasis on either the individual or the environment as the target for change.

More recently, a group of social-work leaders produced an updated statement of professional purpose:

> The purpose of social work is to promote or restore a mutually beneficial interaction between individuals and society in order to improve the quality of life for everyone. [Working Statement 1981, p. 6]

The statement went on to indicate six objectives compatible with this goal and consistent with the traditional focus on person-and-environment-in-interaction:

- Help people enlarge their competence and increase their problem-solving ability.
- Help people obtain resources.
- Make organizations responsive to people.
- Facilitate interaction between individuals and others in their environment.
- Influence interactions between organizations and institutions.
- Influence social and environmental policy.

Coulton (1981) aptly illustrated that social workers in the health field work toward each of these objectives.

In keeping with these general statements about social work, specific standards for social work in health and mental health care have been drafted. The following principle was held as central:

> Every health care organization shall have social work services as an integral part of the organization in order to provide comprehensiveness and continuity of health care. . . . The social work services are performed to alleviate the social or emotional impact of physical or mental illness or disability, enhance physical or social functioning, promote those conditions essential to assure maximum benefits from short- and long-term health care services, prevent illness, and promote and maintain health. [Health Quality Standards Committee, NASW 1981]

As befits a pronouncement of a professional association, this statement is ambitious and all-encompassing. Fortunately, the last ten years have seen a burgeoning of social-work knowledge and skills that assist the profession in living up to its own rhetoric about its role in health settings.

Historical Background

Social work in health care today is best understood in the context of the profession's evolution over the last century and the almost simultaneous development of what was then called medical social work.

Evolution of Social Work in the United States

Toward the end of the nineteenth century, public-minded citizens were preoccupied with identifying and responding to the urban problems created by the Industrial Revolution and the relentless immigration to overcrowded cities, with their inhumane living and working conditions. Heavily influenced by British examples, benevolent individuals founded "charity organization societies" to investigate the problems of the poor, to provide friendly visiting and advice, and to mete out tangible assistance in a rational way. From its beginnings in Buffalo in 1877, the charity organization movement spread rapidly. Charity organization societies were the precursors of today's family service associations and child welfare agencies. Such settings are still considered *primary* social-work settings because social workers are the dominant discipline, and the agencies tend to be managed by social-work administrators.

In the earliest charity organization societies, the "friendly visitors" were volunteers, supported by a paid "agent" or "secretary," who organized the day-to-day administration of the program. Gradually, however, the paid staff came to be the repository of expertise and decision-making. By the early 1900s, staff had developed educational programs for social-work practitioners and assumed responsibility for supervising and training the volunteers. One landmark in this progression occurred when the New York Charity Organization Society launched its Summer School in Philanthropy in 1889; in 1904, this became a year-long program and the precursor of Columbia University School of Social Work. Other charity organization societies organized similar ventures, which also were incorporated into the various universities.

Another landmark in the professionalization of social work was Mary Richmond's publication of *Social Diagnosis* (1917), a panegyric to the power of facts when carefully marshaled by an observant, sympathetic, and "scientific" social worker. From her experience in the charity organization movement in Baltimore from 1891 to 1900 and later in Philadelphia, she forged an early expression of the techniques of social casework, the method used most often by the majority of social workers. As social casework continued to evolve, it became less and less rooted in contemporary morality and more committed to nonjudgemental acceptance of human diversity. This transformation was assisted after World War I when social workers enthusiastically endorsed the insights of psychoanalysis with its belief that behavior is determined by unconscious motivations rooted in early childhood experience.

The social settlement house (also considered a primary social-work setting) was another early manifestation of charitable concern. In 1889, Jane Addams moved into Hull House and began her pioneering work among Chicago's poor. In 1893, Lillian Wald founded the Henry Street Settlement House on New York's Lower East Side. These are but two of the better-known examples of programs through which social workers took up residence among the poor as "neighbors." From that vantage point, settlement workers observed social problems, gave advice, organized communities, helped socialize immigrants to the American way of life, and developed vigorous platforms for social reform. Settlement leaders were indeed generalists; the leaders of the early settlements and community centers joined with leaders in the adult education movement to shape the contours of two other social-work methods—social group work and community organization.

At the turn of the century, the social-work world was small and rather unspecialized. Charity organization workers, settlement leaders, criminologists, public health advocates, and social reformers met regularly through the Association of Charities and Corrections. All shared a concern about health conditions and health problems. In 1893, Jane Addams opened a medical dispensary at Hull House. Lillian Wald, herself a nurse, organized home nursing services in the tenements of New York and campaigned for better sanitation regulations. As early as 1902, medical students at Johns Hopkins University were sent to the Baltimore Charity Organization Society to learn firsthand about the social side of medicine. Leaders in both the charity organization and the settlement movements became the pioneer faculty at schools of social work. Many were involved in the lobbying efforts that led to the creation of the Children's Bureau in 1912 and in early efforts to regulate the excesses of child labor.

In 1915 Abraham Flexner (the same commentator who critiqued medical education five years earlier), raised doubts about whether social work's knowledge and skills were sufficiently developed to qualify it as a profession. Social work responded to Flexner's criticism by efforts to build a body of distinctive social-work knowledge from raw material borrowed from medicine, psychology, psychiatry, sociology, education, and other social sciences. In more recent years, social work evolved and tested practice theories developed by, of, and for social workers. Social casework has been explicated as a problem-solving method (Perlman 1957) and as psychosocial therapy (Hollis 1964). Even more recently, social workers have refined the principles of time-limited casework directed toward specific goals agreed upon in advance by client and therapist. This "task-centered casework" (Reid and Epstein 1972), supported as it is by empirical evidence of its superiority over unfocused, open-ended counseling (Reid and Shyne 1969), has been influential for social workers in health settings. Similarly, social group work has had its practice theorists (Bernstein 1965; Glasser, Sarri, and Vinter 1974; Roberts and Northen 1976; Hartford 1971), who have shown that knowledge about human behavior in groups can be applied by social workers to bring about individual or community change. However, even as social-work knowledge has been refined, other voices have cautioned against the profession's replacing its idealism, its commitment to the poor and the disadvantaged (often members of minority groups), and its emphasis on social reform with a narrow preoccupation with professional status (Richan and Mendelsohn 1973; Howe 1980).

Evolution of Social Work in Health-Care Settings

> "Have some wine," the March Hare said, in an encouraging tone.
> Alice looked all around the table. "I don't see any wine," she remarked.
> "There isn't any," said the March Hare.

A misquoted version of this passage from *Alice's Adventures in Wonderland* was included in a 1906 report, entitled "Social Service Permitted at Massachusetts General Hospital" (Cannon 1954). Richard Cabot, the physician generally considered the founder of medical social work, used the quotation to emphasize the discrepancy between medical recommendations and their feasibility; it was a symbol of the distance between the world of medical practitioners and the realities of many of their impoverished patients. Medical social work was expected to bridge that gap, ensuring that the offer of wine be more than an empty invitation.

Cabot was an eloquent spokesman for teamwork between physician and social worker. He perceived the former as essentially "absent-minded"—unaware of the past and the future of the patients who "shoot by us like comets" (Cabot 1915, p. 20):

> The need, then, is for all-round human beings who can supplement the necessary and valuable narrowness of the physician. The physician is there because he has learned a great deal about one small aspect of human life. . . . But with the painful acquisition of the necessary habit of abstraction, he becomes a dangerous man . . . unless supplemented and balanced. Abstractedly he will give an appetizing, bitter tonic to a starving man, or break up a family some crowded Saturday morning, unless there is help at hand. [Cabot 1915, pp. 176–77]

Social workers were to be the supplementers and balancers. Not merely "all-round human beings," their expertise, in Cabot's view, was the "study of character under adversity," and their method was "psychical diagnosis and treatment."

In another insight that sounds contemporary, Cabot warned that physicians are often blind to the "backgrounds" and the "foregrounds" of their hospital patients. By backgrounds he meant the social, psychological, economic, cultural, and environmental factors that contribute to the etiology of disease and influence the course of recovery. Foregrounds were the observable needs or feelings of patients that might be overlooked by those bent on diagnosing and curing disease. Here Cabot anticipated the recent recognition that existential fears, anxieties, discomfort, and alienation may negatively affect compliance and health, and will certainly play havoc with the immediate quality of life.

This, then, was the mandate for medical social work, a vision that still sustains the profession to some extent. Hospitals became the first *secondary* practice settings for social workers in the United States. In contrast to primary settings, such as family service associations, a secondary setting is one where the major function is other than social-work practice; social workers then support the organization's primary function. The social-work literature often refers to such secondary settings as "host environments" for social work. Specialization within social work received its earliest expression in the hospitals, dispensaries and mental hospitals of the early twentieth century.

According to Lubove's analysis (1965), the entry of social workers into the hospitals hastened the infusion of science into philanthropy, presenting an opportunity to practice social casework along the empirical lines envisaged in Richmond's *Social Diagnosis* (1917). Although many of the first hospital social workers were nurses by training, they sought a role complementary to physicians rather than the subservient one they identified with nurses of that time. Cannon's early account of hospital social work (1913) stated issues that still reverberate in the social-work profession. She asserted that "human kindness cannot alone solve social problems"; she distinguished the social worker from the doctor or nurse (despite the "deep sympathy" the latter might feel for the patients), because, unlike them, "character, human relationships, and community life are her [the social worker's] field of study" (p. 98). Furthermore she warned about the tendency of patients, doctors, and even social workers themselves to confuse the essence of social-work practice with relief services. Advocating a thorough knowledge of community resources, a specific social-work record-keeping system, and social-work casefinding among private patients as well as charity cases, her views were modern indeed. These ideas also set the stage for the ambivalence toward concrete services that has characterized many social workers in health-care settings.

Shortly after social workers began practicing in hospitals, they entered other secondary settings, including mental hygiene clinics, psychopathic hospitals, schools, juvenile courts, and child guidance clinics. Social service was established in the Veterans Bureau in 1926; similarly, social workers became attached to public health programs at the state and local level. The March of Dimes began providing stipends for social-work education in 1946; a year later, the National Institute of Mental Health began awarding similar training stipends.

Hospital social workers were probably the first social workers to affiliate in a professional social-work organization. The American Society of Hospital Social Workers was founded in 1918; later it became known as the American Society of Medical Social Workers. (The *Hospital Social Work Service Journal* was published between 1919 and 1933, and the *Medical Social Work Journal* appeared for a brief time in the 1930s.) Other specialized social-work organizations followed suit, including, for example, the National Association of School Social Workers, 1919; the

American Society of Psychiatric Social Workers, 1926; and the American Association of Group Workers in 1946.

The terms *medical social worker* and *psychiatric social worker* came into prominence in the thirties to connote two distinct career paths, each with specialized knowledge, although based on a common core. That distinction and the myth that the "psychiatric" social worker was somehow more versed in psychodynamics and more capable of being a psychotherapist than the medical social worker still lingers.

In 1955, various specialized social-work organizations joined together to form the National Association of Social Workers (NASW), and the studies about the proper definition and scope for the profession continued with renewed vigor. NASW began publishing *Social Work*, a professional journal meant for a general social-work readership. At that time, the recognized basis for social-work specialization was methodological; social workers educated as caseworkers, group workers, or community organizers, for example, were seen as possessing a method that they could apply in any setting (for example, hospitals, schools, or prisons). As in many professions, the pendulum inexorably swings on this point. The seventies saw a resurgence of enthusiasm for a social worker who was a specialist in a problem area but a generalist in method. Many argue that social-work practice in health-care settings particularly requires a blend of services to individuals, groups, organizations, and communities. In 1976, NASW began publishing *Health and Social Work* as its first specialty journal, in official recognition of the burgeoning content in that field and the large number of members practicing in health care settings.

Current Practice

Settings

The approximately eighty thousand social workers in health care are dispersed across a wide variety of settings. These include general and specialty hospitals, community health and mental health settings, nursing homes, rehabilitation centers, hospices, residential centers for the developmentally disabled, day-care programs, home health programs, mental hospitals, public health departments, industrial and school health programs, health-maintenance organizations, health-planning agencies, and even private medical practice. But social workers are by no means distributed in equal numbers across these practice settings.

Mental health programs probably claim the largest number of social workers. (In some ways, all social workers are mental health professionals who share a focus on emotional well-being, but here the term is reserved for those employed in organizations with a primary focus on delivery of psychiatric or psychotherapeutic services.) Figures are difficult to come by, and estimated numbers of social workers in various psychiatric settings often are out-of-date. About 6,800 social workers were employed in federally funded community mental health centers in 1976 (Linn and Stein 1981). Social workers often hold top- or middle-management roles in community mental health centers. Nacman (1977) cites 1972 figures for social workers in mental health settings as follows: state mental hospitals, 5,324; private mental hospitals, 415; outpatient psychiatric clinics, 3,860; psychiatric units in general hospitals, 1,934; and Veterans Administration psychiatric services, 1,098. In 1976, social workers were said to contribute 3 percent of the full-time equivalent staff of psychiatric inpatient facilities. Most of these personnel are educated at the MSW level or beyond; for the estimated 30 percent with only bachelor's level training, however, it is impossible to determine what proportion hold BSW degrees.

The majority of social workers in health-care settings are based in hospitals. (This is especially true when freestanding psychiatric outpatient settings are dropped from consideration.) But even though social workers are overrepresented in hospitals compared to other health-care settings, some hospitals are under-served. Again, available figures are illustrative but outdated. Phillips (1977) reports that, in a 1970 survey of the 7,144 hospitals then registered in the United States, about 40 percent of the 6,651 responding hospitals had a social-work department. A 1971 Medicare report on participating providers (cited by Bracht 1978) listed 9,101 qualified social workers and 7,475 other social workers employed in the 6,935 participating hospitals. Berkman and Henley (1981) estimated that in 1980 there were about 15,000 social workers in acute medical hospitals; only half of these workers had MSWs. Those without MSWs were likely to have had no formal social-work training. The distribution of social workers is uneven; some hospitals have large departments (with more than fifty social workers), whereas other hospitals may have a single social worker to handle all the social work tasks arising from a hospital with two hundred or more beds. With the exception of the occasional small university-affiliated hospital, the smaller the hospital, the less likely it is to have social-work coverage.

Numbers of social workers in other health-care settings are even harder to estimate. Increasingly, social workers are developing the interest and the competence to work in long-term care (Brody 1974), but that general area is still underserved, partly because ready reimbursement is unavailable for many services that social workers could perform in this for-profit industry. The qualified social workers in long-term care are for the most part employed in the Veterans' Administration, in nonprofit nursing homes, and in some home health agencies. The vast majority of long-term–care facilities receive social services from "social-work designees," who have no formal training in social work (Mercer and Garner 1981; Gehrke and Wattenberg 1981). The facility and the designee may have access to the infrequent services of a qualified social-work consultant; these consultants, in turn, may be social workers in private practice or may be "moonlighting" in addition to their agency employment. Turning to home health services, Oktay and Sheppard (1978) found that, in the mid–70s, only about 25 percent of the 2,329 health agencies then certified by Medicare provided social services; about 75 percent of the hospital-based, home-service programs has social-work coverage in contrast to only 15 percent of those programs operating in health departments.

No satisfactory basis is available to estimate the number of social workers in local health departments or in primary-care settings. A survey published in 1976 indicated that almost 600 social workers held appointments in medical schools; quite often these individuals both delivered services and taught in departments of psychiatry or family medicine (Grinnell, Kyte, and Hunter 1976). A study of the academic backgrounds of professional staff in health-planning agencies (Finney, Pessin, and Matheis 1976) shows that social workers were the most numerous group among staff planners and the third most numerous at the director or assistant-director level. Despite the contention of social-work educators that health planning is an advanced skill requiring an MSW, a large number of the identified social workers were trained at the bachelor's level.

Social workers tend to gravitate to specialized health programs where grant funds may be available or where particular mandates for their services exist. Examples of such programs include neonatal units of hospitals, renal dialysis settings (social work is mandated for Medicare certification of End-Stage Renal Disease vendors), burn treatment centers, rape crisis centers, alcohol treatment centers, cancer care settings, or cardiac rehabilitation teams. Usually the social workers in the subspecialized setting enjoys a much smaller caseload than the worker who does a "general practice" on a medical, surgical, pediatric, or psychiatric service. The numbers of social workers affiliated with such areas are difficult to estimate.

Although social workers in health-care settings have skills that can be transferred from one patient population to the next, those who specialize in particular diseases often develop a deepened knowledge about the psychosocial concomitants of that disease and the psychosocial consequences of the characteristic medical interventions. Their smaller caseloads and the likelihood that they will screen patients for social services put them in a good postition to engage in research that will further refine social-work practice in health-care settings.

The majority of social workers in health care may be based in hospitals or free-standing medical or psychiatric clinics, but social workers are appearing in a wide variety of other niches. For example, social workers have taken leadership in industrially based employee health programs (Masi 1979), sometimes sponsored by management and sometimes by unions. Often the focus of industrial social work is treatment of alcohol-related problems, but increasingly the concept is expanded to include stress occasioned by the demands of the work place. In school and college health programs, social workers engage in diagnosis and treatment of emotional and social problems that create obstacles to learning; in prisons and other correctional settings, social workers are part of the rehabilitation team. Social-work statistics would likely allocate those workers respectively to industrial social work, school social work, or correctional social work; yet they, too, are involved in health care.

Finally, social workers are increasingly "hanging out their shingles" in private therapeutic or consultative practice. Sometimes social workers affiliate with medical or psychiatric group practices as a base for fee-for-service activities; other times they establish solo or group social-work practices. At times, the social worker in private practice offers a specialized service (e.g., sexual counseling, intergenerational counseling, play therapy for children, or consultation to nursing homes). The extent of the private-practice phenomenon is unknown at present; it occurs differentially across the country, and an accurate count is hampered because many private practitioners do so on a part-time basis, with or without other primary employment.

In summary, then a wide range of settings is embraced under the rubric of social work in health care. Statistics on where social workers practice are incomplete and inaccurate, partly because the situation is fluid but more tellingly because no taxonomy is available to categorize social-work settings in health care.

Tasks and Roles

The mix of social-work tasks and functions varies somewhat according to the type of setting, but a considerable range of activity can take place in any given setting.

The acutal performance depends on many things—the preference, skill, and philosophy of the social workers; the constraints or permissiveiness of the organization; and, of course, the amount of social-work coverage available.

INDIRECT PRACTICE ROLES. One classification by role or task distinguishes direct practice from "indirect" practice; the latter includes administration, resource development, program consultation, education and training, and research. Social workers who direct hospital social-work departments, community mental health programs, or home health agencies, to take a few examples, function solely in the indirect mode. Other social workers employed by federal or state monitoring organizations or resource groups also are squarely in the business of designing, implementing, and/or monitoring delivery systems or offering consultation to those in direct service. As an administrator or program manager, a social worker may well be responsible for nonsocial workers. In fact, a relatively recent trend finds some social workers at a level of administration within health-care organizations where their purview includes a variety of human and/or community services as well as the social-work department (Rosenberg and Weissman 1981). Similarly, those social workers who act exclusively as educators may be involved in translating their social work expertise well beyond social workers to a range of educational targets, including medical students, nurses, paraprofessional caregivers, or even patients and potential patients. For example, Levy, Lambert, and Davis (1979) strongly advocate using social workers in the basic training of dental students.

The social worker's role is often a mixture of indirect and direct services. Starting from a responsibility for a caseload, the social worker identifies gaps in resources and works to develop needed services. For example, Cacioppo and Andrews (1979) developed a respite care program for short-term relief of parents with multiple-handicapped children; essentially the project involved recruiting, training, and monitoring baby-sitters. Sometimes the social worker perceives that the health care organization itself is dysfunctional in meeting human needs and develops an educational or supportive program for other health care personnel. For example, social workers report developing multidisciplinary team training (Harris, Saunders, and Zasorin-Connors 1978), "race relations training" at military hospitals (Raglad, Furukawa, and Gardner 1976), assertiveness training for nurses (Numerof 1978), training for home health aides (Sterling 1978), and "humanistic" training for all hospital staff (McNamara 1976). In the same vein, assisting other members of the health-care team to cope with the stress of working with dying patients through formal or informal means has become part of the stock-in-trade of social workers in oncology departments or in hospices.

DIRECT SERVICE. Most social workers in health settings begin with the intent of serving individual patients and their families. Typically, they have been assigned responsibility for a caseload. When they act as community organizers, educators, or program administrators, these activities occur as an extension of their efforts to serve a particular population.

The social worker's direct services are sometimes subdivided into two general types: instrumental and affective-expressive (Schrager 1974). Stripped of jargon, this distinction separates concrete arrangements from psychotherapeutic work directed at helping people adjust to and cope with health problems. In practice, however, affective and instrumental functions overlap, despite efforts to divide them and assign their performance to different categories of personnel. The formulation is most useful because it reminds us of the great variety of social-work functions. It is a major challenge for a social-work department to handle, at times simultaneously for the same individual, tasks as disparate as conducting conjoint marriage counseling and helping establish welfare eligibility, as providing behavior therapy to modify a health habit and arranging for a hospital bed at home.

A psychosocial assessment triggers the social-work treatment plan. Doremus (1976) suggests that the basis for such assessments should be the "four R's"—roles, relationships, reactions (to the illness or hospital), and resources. Other social workers have moved to even greater specificity in an effort to create a uniform data base for establishing social-work treatment plans.

Once the assessment is performed, casework in health-care settings may be similar to casework in any other context. It is a "talking treatment" aimed at helping people ameliorate problems, combined with an effort to shape the environment to approximate more closely an individual's needs. In health settings, however, the profession-wide move to brief, goal-focused casework has been accelerated and intensified. At the same time, the social worker attempts to clarify to other members of the health team how the particular client's needs are shaped by social, psychological, and cultural factors.

Typically, for example, the social worker in a hospital performs time-limited casework focused on specific problems that have been mutually agreed upon by the client and the worker. Such "contracting" permits both the social worker and the client to evaluate the outcomes of the work; after the time has elapsed, a new contract might be formulated for further work. Contracting protects social workers from a grandiosity that would be doomed to failure, namely an open-ended responsibility for the amelioration of all identifiable problems in a particular client. Various problem classifications have been developed in departments of social work; the one that has been applied most widely across settings and studied most thoroughly is the Berkman/Rehr Social Problem-Outcome Classification System (Rehr 1979), a list of intrapsychic and social problems. Using this system, Berkman did a follow-up study of closed cases at six hospitals (1980), finding high concurrence between social workers and their clients on the problems that were worked on. She also found that the former clients were more likely than the social workers themselves to consider that the social work had been successful in resolving those identified problems.

Social workers in health-care settings often perceive their work as "crisis intervention," a short-term treatment in response to the disequilibrium created by illness or disability (Caplan 1970; Rapoport 1970). Crisis intervention is more directive than many other psychotherapies; it builds on the strength of the clients, helps the individual to marshal resources, contains an educational or didactic component, and allows the client to lean first on the therapist and then to resume control, all in a brief period of time. The successful resolution of certain specifiable crises are thought to have implications for preventive mental health. For example, the premature birth of a child may be a crisis, the resolution of which has implications for subsequent parenting. Diagnosis of a life-threatening illness, accidental trauma, disfiguring surgery, or bereavement are other examples of crises that appear in health-care contexts. Social workers in specialized treatment centers have endeavored to isolate the specific elements characteristic of a particular crisis (e.g., a mastectomy or coronary) so that they can anticipate the resultant psychosocial stress and develop formulas for educational and therapeutic approaches.

The social worker based in a health-care setting also encounters clients with longstanding psychosocial problems. Although such problems may not have been triggered by the illness, they can cause or exacerbate the physical problem or make satisfactory rehabilitation more difficult. (Examples are alcoholism, marital discord, or parent/child friction.) Social workers in health-care settings do not necessarily personally follow and treat such problems; more likely, they help the client with the immediate health-related problem and then make a referral to a community-based resource.

ENVIRONMENTAL MANIPULATION. A physical illness may require major life-style changes of a permanent or temporary nature. Social workers are intensively involved in facilitating the practical arrangements required. These "environmental manipulations" include arrangements for medical equipment, financial assistance, transportation, or posthospital placements in nursing homes, rehabilitation settings, or other congregate facilities. Discharge planning is often the common denominator for social workers in hospitals and is the social-work function most recognized by members of other disciplines. (Similarly, admission planning may require the development of a community-support system that permits a family member to enter the hospital.)

Social workers have at times denigrated discharge planning as a mechanical function unworthy of the expertise of a psychosocial therapist. Of late, however, social workers are recognizing that effective discharge planning (measured by client satisfaction with the plan or by placements in the "least restrictive" environment) requires a high degree of clinical skill and carries enormous ramifications for the subsequent lives of the clients served (Kane 1980a; Schrieber 1981; Lurie, Pinsky, and Tuzman, in press). A series of hospital-based studies (Berkman and Rehr 1972a, 1972b, 1973) suggests that one key to more effective discharge planning might be social-worker involvement earlier in the hospitalization or, alternatively, screening by social workers to identify those likely to need discharge planning or other psychosocial services. Although such screening produces some false positives, it identifies many complex situations where the lead time is needed to contact relatives and to help the client take responsibility for his or her decision, despite the enforced dependency of the hospital inpatient situation. Performing discharge planning and other concrete services has enabled social workers to note gaps in community-based services. For example, a study in nine Cleveland-area hospitals (Lindenberg and Coulton 1980) showed that patients eligible for nursing-home care were being discharged to the community with almost no formal service available to them. Social workers are increasingly generating such data, which, in turn, bring them into the role of advocate and lobbyist.

GROUP INTERVENTIONS. In the last ten years, group approaches to social-work practice in health-care settings have proliferated. Partly they are used as a way of more efficiently reaching clients with social-work services and partly as a strategy of choice. The rationale for choosing group methods is that persons with similar problems can effectively offer each other advice, encouragement, reassurance, and psychosocial support. Recently Northen (1981) reviewed more than a hundred examples of such groups described in the social-work literature of the last ten years. The groups blend didactic approaches and opportunities for group problem-solving and self-expression. Often social-work groups are diagnostically based, sometimes limited to the patients with the disease, sometimes designed for family members (especially parents when children are primary patients), and sometimes including both patients and family members.

To give an example of the potential volume of service, in a three-year period, the social-work department of a single hospital offered 32 different groups, involving 1,788 patients and about 1,800 sessions (Lonergan 1980). A burgeoning literature cites group approaches for patients with epilepsy (Lessman and Mollick 1978), stroke (Singler 1975), kidney disease (Leff 1975), parents of children with specific developmental diseases such as muscular dystrophy (Kornfeld and Siegel 1980), and spouses of patients with Alzheimer's disease (LaVorgna 1979), to give just a few examples. Sometimes the social worker establishes a regular meeting time, and all eligible inpatients are invited; at other times the membership is closed and the group is conducted with a specified number of sessions. Sometimes the common link for group members is a behavior each wishes to change (i.e., smoking, overeating, alcoholism), in which case the social-work group may be the primary health treatment.

A number of variations on the group theme have occurred. Some social workers report taking advantage of the "natural" groups that form in hospitals, using the group dynamics in the service of therapeutic goals. Placing a group leader in the waiting room of an intensive-care unit is one such example (Bloom and Lynch 1979). In other cases, the social worker attempts to stimulate the development of a natural support network independent of professional leadership—"stroke clubs" are examples of such self-help groups. In the same vein, Foster and Mendel (1979) describe a "mutual help group" for emphysema patients. In long-term–care settings, groups have been used in a variety of ways including traditional group psychotherapy, activity groups, organizing ongoing client governance structures, and a large variety of group approaches for families, including even "grandchildren" groups (Streltzer 1979).

If, as was suggested earlier, the particular crisis has common definable elements, a group can be an efficient educational medium. Social workers conduct educationally focused groups to prepare clients for a variety of life experiences, including parenthood, divorce, or retirement. A demonstration is currently under way in a heath maintenance organization (Burnell and Taylor, 1982) to determine whether groups led by social workers and others who focus on prevention (centered on topics like stress reduction, weight loss, or parenting skills) are associated with improved health status or lower health utilization. In some health clinics and outpatient settings, social workers offer such educational groups on a fee-for-service basis. Educational groups may be constituted as courses, as in Zelich's workshops for families of schizophrenics (1980). Classroom-style formats are often more acceptable to health consumers than an experience billed as psychotherapy.

The swift development of group activities and their application to new patient populations in new contexts has outpaced systematic evaluation of their effects. Research is now needed to examine the outcomes associated with social group work in health-care settings as well as to understand the extent to which self-selection operates to define and limit those accessible through group methods.

CASE MANAGEMENT. Short-term, problem-focused treatment of individual, family, or group counseling is a primary method by which social workers foster specific changes in the lives of clients or their families. But social workers in health settings are also increasingly engaged in case management, a longer-term process that includes screening or case finding, comprehensive assessment, case planning, monitoring, and reevaluation.

Case management implies a continuity of responsibility for a particular clientele; the concept is most relevant for populations that may predictably experience a sustained period of dependency. Dependent children in the custody of the state have traditionally constituted a population for case management by social workers. Typically, such children are under the purview of the child welfare agency for many years, with that agency taking responsibility for defining needs, planning services, supervising some components of a service system (e.g., foster care, group settings), purchasing other services (e.g., medical care, special schooling), and implementing as needed episodes of psychotherapeutic services for children, natural parents, and adoptive parents. Some social-work authors, particularly Morris (1977), strongly suggest that social workers assume responsibility for managing (and even delivering) care to other dependent populations such as the chronically mentally ill, the developmentally disabled, and the frail elderly.

Case managers are found in community mental health centers, health departments, or regional centers for the developmentally disabled. A series of case management programs for long-term care were also developed in the 1970s under Medicare or Medicaid waivers to test the cost-effectiveness of a variety of community-based services (Applebaum, Seidl, and Austin 1980; Eggert, Bowlyow, and Nichols 1980; Hodgson and Quinn 1980; Skellie and Coan 1980). In such programs, the case manager had responsibility for developing service packages for long-term care in the least restrictive environment, with recommendations tailored specifically to the assessment of functional abilities. Here, too, active involvement reveals gaps and discontinuities of service. For example, the articulation between the acute hospital and community-based programs is notoriously poor; the most superb case management system breaks down if pivotal management decisions are made in the acute hospital without reference to the case manager who, presumably, has a detailed longitudinal understanding of the clients, their support systems, and resources.

Issues for Social Workers in Health

Issues facing social workers in health-care settings mirror the concerns of all health-care providers. Like their colleagues in other disciplines, social workers are giving attention to the distribution, effectiveness, and cost of their services. The profession also faces internal issues about its roles and functions that are hardly unique to social work; these stem, in part, from that effort to increase access, effectiveness, and efficiency, and in part from the imperative for professional survival. Among the questions that recur are the following: the proper allocation of responsibility between the bachelor's-, master's-, and doctoral-level social worker; the degree to which specialized education, credentialing, and practice should be encouraged for social work; the role overlap between the social worker and other members of the health team; and role tensions within social work between psychotherapy and environmental manipulation or between individual treatment and social reform. Underlying all these issues is the question posed at the beginning of the chapter: How does social work fit into health-care delivery, given an assumption that social well-being is a broader construct than health? That philosophical question takes on practical significance because social workers are often torn between helping health providers (e.g., hospitals and physicians) achieve their goals and helping the patients achieve theirs.

The remainder of this chapter, discusses each of these topics separately.

Distribution of Social-Work Services

Concern that the appropriate clientele gain access to social-work services gives rise to two considerations: (1) improving social-work case finding from within the patient populations served by a particular health-care program; and (2) ensuring that social workers are strategically located in the proper settings for casefinding.

The most tangible efforts to improve casefinding have moved beyond using the referral as a trigger for social-work action to the development of screening tools to identify those "at social risk." Coulton (1979) reviewed twenty-seven exemplary quality-assurance programs in social-work departments, finding that twelve had introduced systems to ensure social-work access. Certain problems or diagnoses (e.g., suspected child abuse or failure to thrive in infants less than eighteen months old) automatically receive a social-work evaluation in most hospitals. Beyond that, various departments have identified specific factors in the patient or the situation that are considered "high social risk." Among the items often included are advanced age (especially in combination with living alone), serious injuries, disfigurement, presence of factors that are negatively linked to compliance (e.g., alcohol problems, mental illness, or history of noncompliance), recent bereavement, and the severity or life-threatening characteristics of the illness.

One such screening system developed at Mount Sinai Hospital in New York was recently tested against the criterion of professional social-work judgment about the need for social-work services (Berkman, Rehr, and Rosenberg 1980). In 618 successive admissions, the screening test identified about one-third as requiring social-work intervention; in-person assessment by a social worker verified that 58 percent of those screened were true positives, with a rather high (42 percent) false positive rate. The false negative rate was estimated by observing how many patients not picked up by the screen were later referred to social work. This produced the low figure of 3 percent; however, the number of false negatives would have been more accurately determined had social workers themselves evaluated the control group to assess their need for social services rather than monitoring the natural referrals.

Earlier studies (e.g., Berkman and Rehr 1973) have shown that when social workers do their own casefinding rather than relying on referrals from physicians and nurses they identify at least 10 percent more cases for social-work intervention, that they identify more problems of adjustment to illness, and that they identify more cases emanating from the private-pay sectors of the hospital. These findings make the development of sensitive and specific tools for screening an immediate practice priority (Kane and Kane 1981).

Social workers have recently begun to consider the trade-offs between specificity and sensitivity. In outpatient and primary-care settings, much more specific screening tools are needed (Ell and Morrison 1981) lest the volume of patients render follow-up of the patients with false positives prohibitively expensive. Because the screening procedures are themselves cumbersome and important variables are not always found in the records, some social workers have begun to test self-completed questionnaires as an aid to casefinding in outpatient settings.

Another approach to ensuring access to services is a more strategic distribution of social workers themselves. Social workers are disproportionately found in hospital inpatient units, where their services become part of the inpatient daily rate charge, or at least are justified by the potential cost-effectiveness of services that could reduce length of stay. This allocation of personnel, however, means that the resources may be clustered in the wrong place for identifying psychosocial needs and serving clients. Problems associated with rehabilitaion or with adjustment to chronic illness often express themselves after a patient is discharged. Problems surounding initial diagnois and treatment may manifest themselves in outpatient clinics. For example, a recent review of programs designed to improve management of breast cancer (Kane et al. 1981) found that social workers based in hospitals were poorly positioned to help women make presurgical decisions or to faciliatie their postdischarge adjustment.

Recently social workers have recognized the potential for a social-work presence in emergency rooms (Bergman 1976; Jacobsen and Howell 1978; Healy 1981); furthermore, such social workers are now available to emergency rooms in evenings and on the weekends. Although a wholesale redistribution of social workers is unlikely at present, even from a hospital base, social workers can develop innovative outreach programs or assume administrative responsibility for after-care programs. One such example, currently being tested, is an adult posthospital foster-care program operated by Johns Hopkins Medical Center (Oktay and Voland 1981). Another approach to getting the right services in the right place is the integration of a mental health team within the primary medical-care setting (Brockstein et al. 1979). Of course, professional social workers are a scarce resource in rural areas. As Horejsi (1979) points out, the social worker in some community hospitals is not only a one-person department but also has a limited repertoire of referral options. A widespread, extra-hospital focus, however, requires a payment system that recognizes the contribution of social workers in such roles.

Access to health-related social services is a different question from access to health care itself. Social workers have traditionally been concerned that underserved persons, including members of ethnic minority groups, have appropriate access to health care. Social work education has increasingly tried to sensitize workers to the "ethnic and cultural barriers to health care" (Watkins and Johnson 1979). Typically, a social worker in a health-care setting analyzes culturally based reasons why consumers might fail to follow through with care or seek it in the first place. An example is a progam that identified and counteracted barriers to effective contraception practices among "third-world males" (Norman 1977); target groups included black, Asian, Hispanic, and Native American youth in the Los Angeles area. Outreach efforts with certain populations at risk have been enhanced by vigorous affirmative action programs in schools of social work and by deployment of indigenous "community health aides" in many settings. Ironically, however, although the poor may have inadequate access to health-care services, middle-class clientele are less likely to gain access to the broad range of social services directed at their rehabilitation and adjustment to illness without a systematic process to identify those in need.

Effectiveness of Social-Work Services

Accountability was a buzzword in social work during the seventies. Social workers welcomed the advent of Professional Standards Review Organizations (PSROs) and applied its terminology and techniques to developing their own quality-assurance programs. Accordingly protocols began appearing for standard social-work procedures. Ferguson and her colleagues (1977) concentrated particularly on disease-specific social-work protocols (e.g., for mastectomy, rheumatoid arthritis, and pediatric cancer); in a later paper (1980), they claim that the existence of such procedures enabled social workers to participate in multidisciplinary diagnostically oriented audits. In any event, such protocols form the basis for a social-work department's own peer review and provide standards to use in explaining social-work practice to other personnel. For instance, standard, auditable protocols for procedures such as nursing-home placements provide the basis for requests for additional personnel and for earlier social-work involvement on the cases. Social-work audits are still rather dependent on professional judgment of colleagues' work; to the extent that explicit criteria have been developed, the audits can be performed by clerical personnel. For an example of a highly specific protocol, see Holland and Rogich's(1980) procedures for dealing with grief in the emergency room.

Coulton (1979) reports that a growing number of social-work departments are developing client-centered information systems; these tend to record information about the physical and social characteristics of the clients, the client's problems (or the goals of the social-work interventions), the social-work services received, and some indicator of the outcomes achieved. The latter is still at a rudimentary stage and may consist of a judgment about the extent to which the problems worked with were resolved or exacerbated. Examples of social-work information systems have been reported from New England Deaconess Hospital (La Bianca and Cubelli 1977) and Johns Hopkins Medical Center (Volland and German 1979).

Most significantly, social workers in health settings recently put renewed energy into examining the effects of their interventions. This welcome trend has been accelerated by the growing numbers of social workers educated at the doctoral level, the increasing interest in using single-subject designs to study the effects of clinical practice, and the recognition that social workers need an empirical basis for setting service priorities and for justifying their presence in the cost-conscious world of health care.

Research in social work is impeded by the common arguments that it detracts from the ability to give service and that randomization to control groups deprives clients of assistance. Furthermore, the social-work profession was traumatized by a small number of social experiments in the fifties and sixties that found social work to be ineffective or deleterious compared to control groups (Fischer 1973; Mullen and Dumpson 1972). Most of these studies concerned delinquency prevention or establishment of economic self-sufficiency; the particular example most relevant to health care was a randomized controlled trial of community-based protective services for the frail elderly (Blenkner, Bloom, and Neilson 1971), which found that the rates of institutionalization and subsequent mortality were higher for the experimental group receiving professional casework services than the control group receiving no systematic service. Critics of all these studies point out that the independent variables (social-work services) were poorly defined, that the outcomes examined were often inappropriate to the treatment, and that the experimental intervention sometimes did not even occur.

This history has sensitized social workers to the fallacy of testing global interventions labeled "social work" rather than specific, well-described techniques performed under consistent circumstances and designed to achieve specific results (Kane, 1982). With this frame of mind, social workers are now conducting more modest experiments and quasi-experiments in health settings. An illustration is a recent randomized, controlled experiment to test the effect of several types of social-work interviews in a pediatric cardiology clinic immediately after the physician's diagnosis was imparted to the parents (Blatterbauer, Kupst, and Schulman 1976). The social worker's interventions were: (1) a reexplanation in layman's terms of the medical advice; (2) an anticipatory review of the types of emotional reactions and social implications that might be expected; and (3) a combination of both approaches. The study was able to demonstrate that the latter two approaches led to parents becoming more vigorous, active consumers (measured by the activity and questions they initiated with the physicians). To take another example in a nursing-home context, a quasi-experiment showed that the patients' perceptions of an increased opportunity to make choices had a positive effect on their depression and activity levels (Mercer and Kane 1979). Social workers are coming to appreciate that the more carefully social-work interventions are described, the more amenable they are to testing.

In addition to experimental approaches, social workers are conducting other research to improve their effectiveness. Among the trends observed in the social-work literature are: follow-up studies of former clients; client satisfaction polls; cross-sectional and longitudinal studies designed to gather detail about the psychosocial concomitants of various health problems.

Cost and Efficiency

The cost-effectiveness of social work can be approached in two ways. The social worker can attempt to achieve the same effects at less cost or can attempt to provide expanded services (either more services to the same number of clients or similar services to a larger number of clients) at the same cost. Both approaches have been used; however, because the social worker in the majority of health settings is constantly required to make difficult choices about how much service to give and to whom, the latter approach is intrinsically more attractive.

Ways to increase the productivity of the social workers are myriad. They include using less expensive professional social workers for various procedures; using paraprofessionals, social-work aides, or student trainees; using group instead of individual counseling techniques; streamlining routine procedures such as screening, record-keeping, and administrative duties; and eliminating those practices that are ineffective or are extraneous to a positive effect. Ways to use the social service resource on behalf of more clients include: organizing a volunteer program; identifying and building on natural "helping networks," or capitalizing on modern communications technology to reach more people. To illustrate the latter, social workers who engage in reassuring patients prior to surgery might develop and test audiotaped or videotaped messages to reach more patients than could be done individually. In the same vein, social workers have developed booklets and brochures to explain psychosocial problems or describe available resources to particular audiences; Kaminsky and Shecter's (1979) approach to abortion counseling in a general hospital, for example, included dissemination of a brochure designed by the social worker.

Hospital social workers, in particular, seek a standard unit with which to express social-work productivity. A national study (Coulton et al. 1979) was conducted to describe the average time per client contact required for social-work services in various clinical departments of the hospital. An unanticipated finding was that social workers, in common with other health professionals, lacked an agreed-upon taxonomy for their services. Terms such as *open case* or *interview* were subject to widely varying definitions. Group interventions could not readily be incorporated into existing productivity measures based on the case. A joint committee of the Society for Hospital Social Work Directors and the National Association of Social Workers is presently considering the feasibility of developing a more uniform "social-work dictionary."

The social worker's efforts to demonstrate efficiency are plagued by a catch–22. The most visible social-work activity is performed with reference to the individual case. Most analyses of productivity to date count the amount of time spent in direct service to clients (e.g., Chernesky and Lurie 1976). Time that cannot be readily traced to any particular case (general team meetings, community-based meetings, education for other health care staff, or development of self-sustaining "clubs" for mutual self-help) quite often appears as unproductive administrative time. Yet efficient approaches to meeting a social worker's goals for clients demand more indirect approaches, more efforts to change the milieu in which care is delivered, more attempts to alter the perceptions of the care-giving staff, and more program development both within the institution and in the community. Thus, the more the social worker develops innovative ways to reach greater numbers, the less productive that worker may seem in terms of client contacts.

Differential Social-Work Manpower

Use of manpower is related to productivity. As yet, little empirical evidence is available to guide social-work personnel deployment. Because of its conscious effort to hire social workers at different levels, the Veterans Administration is perhaps the health organization with the most extensive information about the performance of BSW and other bachelor's-level workers. Engel (1977) found, however, that the roles of the bachelor's-level worker may be artificially constrained by the perceptions of their MSW supervisors. Earlier work (Barker and Briggs 1969; Carlsen 1969; Brieland, Briggs, and Leuenberger 1973) suggests the value of an intradisciplinary social-work team, led by an MSW, where the case responsibility is shared. Other working arrangements have designated bachelor's-level workers to specific tasks, for example arranging transportation, lodging, medical aids, welfare coverage, or even nursing-home placements. Because most hiring practices fail to differentiate the BSW from the general college graduate, proper test of the abilities of the former have not yet been conducted.

As Coulton and Butler (1981) suggest, the complexity of the social-work task is a logical basis for differential assignments; a system reported from a Canadian hospital introduced a complexity measure into the case statement (Farber and Sime 1979). Complexity, however, is notoriously difficult to predict at the beginning of a case. Moreover, some assumptions about complexity may be in error. Discharge planning, often perceived as routine, may be one of the most complex tasks performed by social workers in health settings. Discharge planning requires matching the person to the environment and doing so under conditions of great haste and tension. Properly performed, it requires assessment of the physical, emotional, and social needs of the patient and family, exploration of alternatives, helping all relevant parties sort out complex feelings of fear, guilt, and depression, expert knowledge of resources, and ability to communicate with the medical side of the team (Kane 1980a).

Social-work doctoral education has expanded enormously in the past decade, producing another level of social-work manpower in greater numbers than needed for faculty slots in schools of social work. Some DSWs have entered health-care settings; their roles include administration, research and evaluation, staff development, and program leadership. Often a doctorally trained social worker carries a joint appointment with a school of social work. This development has enhanced empiricism in health practice, faciliated descriptive and evaluative studies, and helped forge new relationships between schools of social work and teaching hospitals (Bracht and Briar 1979).

Specialization

The extent to which specialized education, credentialing, and practice is desirable for social work is a vexing question. The issue is relevant for social workers in health care on two levels. First, health practice is a social-work specialization, albeit one in search of delineated boundaries. Second, within health practice, numerous subspecialized groups have emerged; the latter are often referred to as "specialty interest areas."

HEALTH SPECIALIZATION IN SOCIAL WORK. Schools of social work have responded to the burgeoning knowledge in the health-care field by creating a cluster of course offerings, known as specializations or concentrations. (The term *concentration* is often used when the school already has specializations according to method of practice.) At least a quarter of the almost ninety MSW programs in the United States organize their curriculum primarily into practice specializations, and still others superimpose practice concentrations upon their method specializations.

Health curricula in schools of social work vary in intensity, duration (i.e., one year versus two years), and content. Some schools have developed separate concentrations in health and in mental health, whereas others subsume mental health within a health program. Joint degree programs with schools of public health are offered in several parts of the country, and elswhere social-work health majors are encouraged to take courses in epidemiology or health-care delivery with other health science students. At the moment, despite this activity, graduates of health concentrations are not credentialed in any identifying way (other than their transcripts), and it is not clear whether they enjoy a competitive edge for jobs in health settings.

Various efforts to delineate content for a social-work specialization in health have been undertaken. Formulating objectives is usually a joint undertaking of educators and practitioners (Caroff and Mailick 1980; Kumabe et al. 1977). The common content denominators include an introduction to the organization of health-care delivery and related policy issues and to health-related behavior; it is emphasized that the latter varies by age, geography, socioeconomic status, education, and ethnicity. Health concentrations generally include more medical information than does the social-work curriculum. Skills for multidisciplinary collaboration are stressed, sometimes in self-contained courses. From such a base, schools have developed their own formulations. For example, Rutgers built its health concentration in part around the needs of various frail and dependent populations. These courses also teach students to distinguish different types of "illness careers" based upon suddenness of onset, duration, severity, and prognosis; each pattern has different psychosocial implications for the patient and the family (Dinerman, Schlesinger, and Wood 1980). To take another example with particular reference to preparation for practice in maternal and child health settings, the University of Hawaii developed detailed content on illness-related tasks for individuals and their family members based on an understanding of normal tasks at different stages of the life cycle (Kumabe et al. 1977).

SPECIALTY INTERESTS. Simultaneously with the advent of curriculum to prepare neophyte workers for a health specialization, practitioners have developed specialty interest affiliations based on subspecialized areas of practice. Some such specialty interest groups have organized formal channels for communciation and collective action, whereas others are less channeled. Among the more active specialty interest practitioners are perinatal social workers, social workers in oncology, renal social workers, social workers in developmental disabilities, social workers in long-term care, social workers in maternal and infant health, social workers in community mental health, and social workers in primary care. With no claims to be exhaustive, *Health and Social Work* (1980) recently listed thirty such interest areas in a 1980 reader survey.

Specialty interest areas are not mutually exclusive; rather, they are comprised of overlapping categories of employment setting (e.g., hospitals, home health agencies, or hospices), medical specialties (e.g., renal social work or social work in oncology), problem classification (e.g., alcohol treatment), or skill mix (e.g., sex therapy). The affiliations of specialty practitioners are based both on common substantive interests (e.g., defining practice skills, sharing information, mutual support, basic or continuing education, or cooperative research) and on common political/administrative agendas (e.g., legislative lobbying, licensure, or securing reimbursement). Social workers in health care are presently examining the various specialty interest areas to determine the extent to which a subspecialized knowledge and skill base characterizes the various groups (Kane 1980b).

Role Overlap and Teamwork

Social workers are ubiquitous on the health-care team, but their roles overlap with a wide variety of other practitioners. This is especially true in an era when almost every health-care profession has discovered the psyche and when physicians and nurses are turning their focus outward to the community. In the mental health sphere, role overlap among psychiatrists, psychologists, nurses, and social workers has long been observable. In the general health-care setting, the social worker may at times overlap with the nurse (particularly clinical nurse specialists and public health nurses), the occupational therapist, the health educator, the pastoral counselor, the rehabilitation counselor, and many others. (Relatively new roles [such as ombudsman, patient representative, or case manager] confuse the picture more because they may be filled by members of many basic disciplines, who then may take on a new identity.) Although the broad mix of interests and skills of the social worker constitutes a distinctive blend, each particular interest or skill is likely to be shared by some colleague in another discipline.

Social-work educators have begun consciously preparing their students for the leadership roles they fill on multidisciplinary teams. The group work skills of the social worker are neatly transferable to facilitating the effectiveness of small task groups (Kane 1975b). On the other hand, because teamwork has become fashionable, social workers and others have recently begun to overemphasize the process rather than the goals; teams are more often evaluated by the satisfaction of the various members than by other indicators of achievement. The democratically satisfying tendency is to represent an increasingly large array of disciplines on the team and to involve most team members in most decisions (Kane 1980c). Having invested considerable collective energy in selling the team concept, social workers, especially those acting as team planners and leaders, are faced with determining more precisely when teamwork is preferable to the less-coordinated work of individual practitioners and which skills are needed on the "core team."

Social workers engage with members of other disciplines in many ways besides participation on formally constituted working teams (such as the rehabilitation team). They assemble ad hoc "teams" for a particular case. They offer and receive consultation from members of other disciplines. They are continually making referrals, a process which in itself involves communication skills across disciplines to ensure that both the client and the other providers follow through. Because the social worker has considerable expertise that would be useful to many health professions (e.g., skills in interviewing on sensitive topics, knowledge of community resources), they engage in formal and informal educational efforts. This gives rise to questions about the extent to which the social worker should focus such education on helping others acquire social work skills as opposed to informing others about those skills (Rehr 1974).

Role Tensions within Social Work

A key to competence on a multidisciplinary team is a clear delineation of role. Social workers have two disadvantages in this regard; their role is both broad and fluctuating, and historically it contains internal stresses and contradictions. As we have already illustrated, the social worker must deal with an ever-present tension between serving the individual, the family, and society; between social treatment and social reform; between psychotherapy and environmental modification.

In this time of methodological expansion, social-work techniques are advancing on all fronts. Interest in the intrapsychic needs of individuals is exemplified by new departures in family therapy, play therapy for children, hypnosis and systematic desensitization techniques, or bereavement therapy. The interest in social reform finds expression in increased emphasis on social-work roles of advocate or ombudsman. Environmental modification goals are currently illustrated by a range of techniques to identify and mobilize natural support systems or helping networks on behalf of clients (Katz 1979; Collins and Pancoast 1976). This profusion of interest and activity is valuable, but its difficulty arises if the profession needs to explain itself with a united voice.

Social Work and Health-Care Delivery

Perhaps the most critical issue (and one relevant to all others) is the appropriate stance of social work vis-à-vis the organizations in the health-care delivery system that employ them. Sometimes social-work effectiveness is expressed as enhancement of the goals of the organization. For example, Nacman (1980) points out that social workers can minimize the hospital's risk of law suits by ensuring that patients leave satisfied. Similarly, social workers have developed techniques to secure a truly informed consent in sensitive areas such as sterilization (Shapiro-Steinberg and Neamatalla 1979). Hookey (1979), among others, has argued that the social worker in primary care saves valuable physician time by working with the "worried well." Many authors have pointed to the value of social work to the hospital in the sense of "saved days" for utilization review. In other kinds of markets where bed census is down, social workers can demonstrate the opposite effect, recruiting patients for psychiatric and other services. These examples and many more illustrate ways that the social worker can prove valuable to the health-care organization and either prevent costs or produce revenues. An astute administrator creatively employs such strategies to expand the role of the profession (Rosenberg and Weissman 1981). Substantial energy, publication, and even research has been directed toward demonstrating that social work is useful to the health-care organization.

In a starkly contrasting point of view, Reichert (1977) rejects what he calls a "drift toward entrepreneurialism" in social work. More recently, he contrasts the classical public health and social reform stance of traditional social work with the newer "marketing approaches" (1981). The latter include not only examples of revenues generated by social workers for the "host" organization but also the trend of private voluntary agencies to contract for services, the trend toward private social-work practitioners, the quest for third-party vendorship status, and the vested interest that agencies have in growth and expansion of services rather than the content and direction of those services.

It is easier for purists to deplore this trend than to find a ready solution. Unlike the British system where social workers are employed by local welfare authorities and positioned in health-care settings, the social worker in the American health-care agency is in a more ambiguous position. In the United States, the more difficult strategy of merging a public service (social work) with a free enterprise system arises. Of course, social worker's goals are not invariably in conflict with those of physicians, hospitals, or other care-givers. For example, when social workers demonstrate an ability to increase compliance with medical regimens, they may well be meeting the goals of client, physician, and social worker (Kane and Glicken 1979). The point where the social worker's exploration with the client leads to a course of action at variance with medical advice or against the perceived best interest of the care system is the time of possible conflict. Sometimes the social worker is involved in facilitating a client's wishes to reject a surgical procedure or to become more autonomous in a long-term–care facility. Then the social worker's advocacy may come at the expense of his job (Berg 1981). The danger, of course, is that the social worker who becomes too invested in the goals of the organization may lose the ability to perceive any other purposes.

In words reminiscent of Cabot, sixty-five years earlier, Hoffman (1981), a hospital administrator, called social work "the conscience of the hospital." Applied more broadly to all health settings, this may be an accurate description of the challenge to the profession. The values of the social-work profession, firmly tied to the self-determination of the individual client, have historically been more precise than the profession's techniques. Now, however, those techniques are also becoming more exact and targeted, while the values must remain unchanged. The bioethical dilemmas posed by modern medical capabilites require social workers to address more complex value questions more systematically than ever before. The demand for cost-effectiveness requires a greater emphasis on demonstrated effectiveness than ever before. Social workers need to keep intact their humanistic values while continuing to develop their science.

REFERENCES

APPLEBAUM, R.; SEIDL, F. W.; and AUSTIN, C. D. 1980. The Wisconsin Community Care Organization: preliminary findings from the Milwaukee Experiment. *Gerontologist* 20:350–55.

BARKER, R., and BRIGGS, T. 1969. *Using teams to deliver social service.* Syracuse, N.Y.: University School of Social Work (Social Work Manpower Monograph #1).

BARTLETT, H. M. 1970. *The common base of social work practice.* New York: National Association of Social Workers.

BERG, W. 1981. Working with physically handicapped patients: advocacy in a nursing home. *Health and Social Work* 6:33–40.

BERGMAN, A. S. 1976. Emergency room: a role for social workers. *Health and Social Work* 1:32–44.

BERKMAN, B. 1980. Psychological problems and outcome: an external validity study. *Health and Social Work* 5:5–21.

———, and HENLEY, B. 1981. The social worker and medical surgical acute care. *Health and Social Work*, 6:225–75.

BERKMAN, B., and REHR, H. 1972a. Social needs of hospitalized elderly. *Social Work* 17:80–88.

———. 1972b. The sick role cycle and the timing of social work intervention. *Social Work Review* 46:567–80.

———. 1973. Early social service casefinding for hospitalized patients. *Social Service Review* 47:256–65.

———, and ROSENBERG, G. 1980. A social work department develops and tests and screening mechanism to identify high social risk situations. *Social Work in Health Care* 5:373–85.

BERNSTEIN, S. 1965. *Explorations in group work.* Boston: Boston University School of Social Work.

BLATTERBAUER, S.; KUPST, M.; and SCHULMAN, J. 1976. Enhancing the relationship between physician and patient. *Health and Social Work* 1:46–57.

BLENKNER, M.; BLOOM, M.; and NEILSEN, M. A. 1971. A research and demonstration project in protective services. *Social Casework* 52:483–89.

BLOOM, N., and LYNCH, J. 1979. Group work in a hospital waiting room. *Health and Social Work* 4:49–63.

BRACHT, N. 1978. *Social work in health care: a guide to professional practice.* New York: Haworth Press.

———, and BRIAR, S. 1979. Collaboration between schools of social work and univerisity medical centers. *Health and Social Work* 4:73–91.

BRIELAND, D.; BRIGGS, T.; and LEUENBERGER, P. 1973. *Team model of social work practice.* Syracuse, N.Y.: Syracuse School of Social Work (Social Work Manpower Monograph #5.

BROCHSTEIN, J.; ADAMS, G.; TRISTAN, M.; and CHENEY, C. 1979. Social work and primary health care: an integrative approach. *Social Work in Health Care* 5:71–81.

BRODY, E. A. 1974. *A social work guide for long-term care facilities.* Washington, D.C.: Government Printing Office.

BURNELL, G., and TAYLOR, P. 1982. Psychoeducational programs for problems in living. *Health and Social Work*, 7:7–13.

CABOT, R. 1915. *Social service and the art of healing.* New York: Moffat, Yard.

CACIOPPO, B., and ANDREWS, S. 1979. Respite care for parents of handicapped children. *Social Work in Health Care* 5:99–101.

CANNON, I. 1913. *Social workers in hospitals.* New York: Russell Sage.

———. 1954. *On the social frontier of medicine.* Cambridge, Mass.: Harvard University Press.

CAPLAN, G. 1970. *Principles of preventive psychiatry.* New York: Basic Books.

CARLSEN, T., ed. 1969. *Social work manpower in mental health programs.* Syracuse, N.Y.: University of Syracuse School of Social Work (Social Work Manpower Monographs #2.

CAROFF, P. and MAILICK, M. 1980. *Social work in health services: an academic practice partnership.* New York: Prodist.

CHERNESKY, R., and LURIE, A. 1976. The functional analysis. *Social Work in Health Care* 1:213–23.

COLLINS, A., and PANCOAST, D. 1976. *Natural helping networks.* New York: National Association of Social Workers.

CONDIE, D.; HANSEN, J.; LANE, N.; MOSS, D.; and KANE, R. A. 1978. How the public views social work. *Social Work* 23:47–53.

COULTON, C. J. 1979. *Social work quality assurance programs: a comparative analysis.* Washington, D.C.: National Association of Social Workers.

———. 1981. Person-environment fit as the focus in health care. *Social Work* 26:26–35.

———, and BUTLER, N. 1981. Measuring social work productivity in health care. *Health and Social Work,* 6:4–12.

COULTON, C.; PASCHALL, N.; FOSTER, D.; BOHNENGEL, A.; and SLIVINSKE, L. 1979. *Nationwide survey of hospital social work practice* Cleveland, Ohio: Case Western Reserve University School of Applied Social Sciences.

DINERMAN, M. 1979. In sickness and in health: future social work roles. *Health and Social Work* 4:5–23.

———; SCHLESINGER, E.; and WOOD, K. 1980. Social work roles in health care. *Health and Social Work* 5:13–20.

DOREMUS, B. 1976. The four R's: social diagnosis in health care. *Health and Social Work* 1:120–39.

EGGERT, G. M.; BOWLYOW, J. E.; and NICHOLS, C. W. 1980. Gaining control of the long-term care system: first returns from the ACCESS experiment. *Gerontologist* 20:356–63.

ELL, K. and MORRISON, D. 1981. Social work in primary medical care. *Health and Social Work,* 6:355–435.

ENGLE, P. 1977. *Supervision of the baccalaureate social worker.* Syracuse, N.Y.: University of Syracuse School of Social Work (Social Work Manpower Monograph #1.

FARBER, J. M., and SIME, K. C. 1979. A computerized department information system. Paper presented at the Second Annual Meeting of the Social Work Administrators in Health Facilities, Quebec, 11 October 1979.

FERGUSON, K.; BOWDEN, L.; HALMAN, M.; HUFF, A.; LANGLIE, J.; and MORGAN, G. 1980. Social work quality assurance based on medical diagnosis and task: a second stage report. *Social Work in Health Care* 6:63–72.

FERGUSON, K., BOWDEN, M. L.; LACHINET, D.; MALCOLM, A.; and MORGAN, G. 1977. Initiation of a quality assurance program for social work practice in a teaching hospital. *Social Work in Health Care* 2:205–18.

FINNEY, R.; PESSIN, R.; and MATHEIS, L. 1976. Prospects for social workers in health planning. *Health and Social Work* 1:7–26.

FISCHER, J. 1973. Is casework effective? *Social Work* 18:5–20.

FOSTER, Z., and MENDEL, S. 1979. Mutual help group for patients. *Health and Social Work* 3:83–98.

GEHRKE, J. R., and WATTENBERG, S. H. 1981. Assessing social services in nursing homes. *Health and Social Work* 6:14–35.

GLASSER, P.; SARRI, R.; and VINTER, R., eds. 1974. *Individual change through small groups.* New York: Free Press.

GRINNELL, R.; KYTE, N.; and HUNTER, S. 1976. Social workers teaching in medical schools. *Health and Social Work* 1:152–65.

HALLOWITZ, E. 1972. Innovations in hospital social work. *Social Work* 17:89–97.

HARRIS, J.; SAUNDERS, D.; and ZASORIN-CONNORS, J. A. 1978. Program for interprofessional health care teams. *Health and Social Work* 3:36–53.

HARTFORD, M. 1971. *Groups in social work.* N.Y.: Columbia University Press.

Health and Social Work. 1981. Reaction Form 5:n.p.

Health Quality Standards Committee, 1981. Proposed health and mental health care standards. *NASW News,* January 1981.

HEALY, J. 1981. Emergency rooms and psychosocial services. *Health and Social Work* 6:36–43.

HODGSON, J. H., and QUINN, J. L. 1980. The impact of the TRIAGE health care delivery system on client morale, independent living and the cost of care. *Gerontologist* 20:364–71.

HOFFMAN, P. B. 1981. The social work director's responsibility for contributing to knowledge: a hospital administrator's perspective. Paper presented at the 16th Annual Meeting of the Society for Hospital Social Work Directors of the American Hospital Association, Philadelphia, Pa. 3 April 1981.

HOLLAND, L., and ROGICH, L. E. 1980. Dealing with grief in the emergency room. *Health and Social Work* 5:12–17.

HOLLIS, F. 1964. *Casework: a psychosocial therapy.* New York: Random House.

HOOKEY, P. 1979. Cost-benefit evaluations in primary health care. *Health and Social Work* 4:152–67.

HOREJSI, G. 1979. Social work in the small hospital. *Health and Social Work* 4:9–25.

HOWE, E. 1980. Public professions and the private model of professionalism. *Social Work* 25:179–91.

JACOBSEN, P., and HOWELL, R. 1978. Psychiatric problems in emergency rooms. *Health and Social Work* 3:88–107.

JOHNSON, W. L. 1980. Supply and demand for registered nurses: some observations on the current picture and prospects to 1985, pt. 2 *Nursing and Health Care,* September.

KAMINSKY, B., and SCHECTER, L. 1979. Abortion counseling in a general hospital. *Health and Social Work* 4:93–103.

KANE, R. A. 1975a. *Interprofessional teamwork.* Syracuse, N.Y.: University of Syracuse School of Social Work (Social Work Manpower Monograph #8).

———. 1975b. The interprofessional team as a small group. *Social Work in Health Care* 1:19–31.

———. 1979. Social work, social values, and health. *Health and Social Work* 4:2–3,

———. 1980a. Discharge planning: an undischarged responsibility. *Health and Social Work* 5:2–3.

———. 1980b. Specialization and specialty interests. *Health and Social Work* 5:2–3.

———. 1980c. Multidisciplinary teamwork in the United States: trends, issues, and implications for the social worker. In *Teamwork in the personal social services and health care: British and American perspectives,* ed. S. Lonsdale, A. Webb, and T. L. Briggs. London: Croom Helm.

———. 1982. Lessons for social work from the medical model. *Social Work,* 27:315–321.

———, and GLICKEN, M. 1979. Compliance and consumerism: complementary goals of social work practice in health settings. In *Toward human dignity: social work in practice,* ed. J. Hanks. Washington, D.C.: NASW Publications.

KANE, R. A., and KANE, R. L. 1981. *Assessing the elderly: a practical guide to measurement.* Lexington, Mass.: D. C. Heath.

———; WILLIAMS, C. E.; HOPWOOD, M. D.; LINCOLN, T. L.; RETTIG, R. A.; and WILLIAMS, A. P. 1981. *The breast cancer network: organizing to improve management of a disease* (R–2789–NCI). Santa Monica, Calif.: Rand.

KATZ, A. 1979. Support systems, prevention, and health care. In *Social factors in prevention: proceedings of the 1978 Annual Public Health Institute*, ed. R. Jackson, J. Morton, and M. Sierra-Franco. Berkeley, Calif.: University of California Public Health Social Work Program.

KORNFELD, M., and SIEGEL, I. 1980. Parental group therapy in the management of two fatal childhood diseases: A Comparison. *Health and Social Work* 5:28–34.

KUMABE, K.; NISHIDA, C.; O'HARA, D.; and WOODRUFF, C. 1977. *A handbook for social work education and practice in community health settings.* Honolulu: University of Hawaii School of Social Work.

LaBIANCA, O., and CUBELLI, G. 1977. A new approach to building social work knowledge. *Social Work in Health Care* 2:139–52.

LaVORGNA, D. 1979. Group treatment of wives of patients with Alzheimer's disease. *Social Work in Health Care* 5:219–21.

LEFF, B. 1975. A club approach to social work treatment within a home dialysis program. *Social Work in Health Care* 1:33–40.

LESSMAN, S., and MOLLICK, L. 1978. Group treatment of epileptics. *Health and Social Work* 3:105–21.

LEVY, R.; LAMBERT, R.; and DAVIS, G. 1979. Social work and dentistry in clinical training, research, and collaboration. *Social Work in Health Care* 5:177–85.

LINDENBERG, R. E., and COULTON, C. 1980. Planning for posthospital care. *Health and Social Work* 5:12–17.

LINN, M., and STEIN, S. 1981. Social work practice and chronic adult mental illness. *Health and Social Work*, 6:545–615.

LISTER, L. 1980. Role expectations of social workers and other health professionals. *Health and Social Work* 5:41–49.

LONERGAN, E. C. 1980. Humanizing the hospital experience: report of a group program for medical patients. *Health and Social Work* 5:53–63.

LUBOVE, R. 1965. *The professional altruist.* Cambridge, Mass.: Harvard University Press.

LURIE, A.; PINSKY, S.; and TUZMAN, L. A practice model for the training of social workers in discharge planning. *Health and Social Work*, in press.

MASI, D. 1979. Combating alcoholism in the workplace. *Health and Social Work* 4:41–59.

McNAMARA, J. 1976. Social work designs a humanistic program to enhance patient care. *Social Work in Health Care* 1:145–54.

MERCER, S., and KANE, R. A. 1979. Helplessness and hopelessness in the institutionalized elderly. *Health and Social Work* 4:90–116.

MERCER, S., and GARNER, J. D. 1981. Social work consultation in long-term care facilities. *Health and Social Work* 6:5–13.

MORRIS, R. 1977. Caring for versus caring about people. *Social Work* 22:353–59.

MULLEN, E., and DUMPSON, T. R. 1972. *Evaluation of social intervention.* San Francisco, Calif.: Jossey-Bass.

NACMAN, M. 1977. Social workers in mental health services. In *Encyclopedia of social work*, 17th issue. New York: National Association of Social Workers.

———. 1980. Social work can eliminate potential risks. *Hospital* 54:189–92.

NORMAN, A. J. 1977. Family planning with third-world males. *Health and Social Work* 2:138–57.

NORTHEN, H. 1981. Social work with groups in health settings: promise and problems. Paper presented in the 75th Anniversary Series at Mount Sinai Hospital, New York, June, 1981.

NUMEROF, R. 1978. Assertiveness training for nurses in a general hospital. *Health and Social Work* 3:79–102.

OKTAY, J., and SHEPPARD, F. 1978. Home health care for the elderly. *Health and Social Work* 3:36–47.

OTKAY, J., and VOLLAND, P. 1981. Community care program for the elderly. *Health and Social Work* 6:41–47.

PERLMAN, H. H. 1957. *Social casework: a problem-solving process.* Chicago: University of Chicago Press.

Pfouts, J., McDaniel, B. 1977. Medical handmaidens or professional colleagues? *Social Work in Health Care* 2:275–84.

Phillips, B. 1977. Social work in health services. In *Encyclopedia of social work,* 17th issue. New York: National Association of Social Workers.

Ragland, S.; Furukawa, T.; and Gardner, L. 1976. Race relations training at Walter Reed Army Medical Center. *Health and Social Work* 1:138–49.

Rapoport, L. 1970. Crisis intervention as a mode of brief treatment. In *Theories of social casework,* ed. R. W. Roberts and R. Nee. Chicago: University of Chicago Press.

Rehr, H., ed. 1974. *Medicine and social work: an exploration in interprofessionalism. New York: Prodist.*

Rehr, H., ed. 1979. *Professional accountability for social work practice.* New York: Prodist.

Reichert, K. 1977. The drift toward entrepreneurialism in health and social welfare. *Administration in Social Work* 1:123–33.

———. 1981. Social work in the health field: the years ahead. Paper presented at Rutgers University School of Social Work, March 1981.

Reid, W. J., and Epstein, L. 1972. *Task-centered casework.* New York: Columbia University Press.

Reid, W. J. and Shyne, A. 1969. *Brief and extended casework.* New York: Columbia University Press.

Richan, W. C., and Mendelsohn, A. R. 1973. *Social work: the unloved profession.* New York: New Viewpoints.

Richmond, M. 1917. *Social diagnosis.* New York: Russell Sage Foundation.

Roberts, R., and Northen, H., eds. 1976. *Theory of social work practice with group.* New York: Columbia University Press.

Rosenberg, G., and Weissman, A. 1981. Marketing social work services in health care settings. *Health and Social Work* 6:4–12.

Schrager, J. 1974. *Social work departments in university hospitals.* Syracuse, N.Y.: Syracuse University School of Social Work (Social Work Manpower Monograph #6)

Schrieber, H. 1981. Discharge-planning: key to the future of hospital social work. *Health and Social Work* 6:48–53.

Shapiro-Steinberg, L., and Neamatalla, G. 1979. Counseling for women requesting sterilization: a comprehensive program designed to ensure informed consent. *Social Work in Health Care* 5:151–63.

Singler, J. 1975. Group work with hospitalized stroke patients. *Social Casework* 56:348–54.

Skellie, F. A., and Coan, R. E. 1980. Community-based long-term care and mortality: preliminary experimental findings. *Gerontologist* 20:372–79.

Sterling, M. 1978. Visiting aides training program. *Health and Social Work* 3:156–64.

Streltzer, A. 1979. A grandchildrens' group in a home for the aged. *Health and Social Work* 4:68–183.

Volland, P. and German, P. 1979. Development of an information system. *American Journal of Public Health* 69:335–39.

Watkins, E., and Johnson, A. 1979. *Removing ethnic barriers to health care.* Chapel Hill, N.C.: University of North Carolina School of Social Work.

Working statement on the purpose of social work. 1981. *Social Work* 26:6.

Zelich, S. 1980. Helping the family cope: workshops for families of schizophrenics. *Health and Social Work* 5:47–52.

Chapter 24

The Evolution in Health Services Management

Walter J. McNerney

TEN YEARS AGO, when alumni of graduate programs in health-services administration got together at their annual dinners or seminars, the common yardstick applied to measure the professional success of a colleague was institutional size. At five-hundred beds he or she was obviously doing well, especially if the institution was graced with an aura of scientific respectability through university affiliation. At two-hundred and fifty beds an administrator was on the way, if young, and an accepted member of the club at any age. Except at the age of a beginner, one hundred beds called for either explanation or apology. And those who had drifted into public health, planning agencies, or prepayment plans could expect only sidelong glances and remarks about the weather. Administrators of proprietary hospitals and nursing homes didn't come to the meetings.

Like everything else in the health field the management status scale has changed appreciably in the past decade. Among hospital executives, the question today isn't, "How big is your hospital?" It's, "How many hospitals in your system?" The once-honored title "administrator" is considered outmoded and demeaning. If your aren't either a president or a chief executive officer, always called CEO, you aren't really in the inner circles. The executives of planning or reimbursement agencies are no longer on the fringe; in many cases they're influential and respected figures. What used to be called proprietary hospitals are now dignified as "investor-owned," and the people who run them are seen almost as regulars, certainly not renegades. Guest speakers at the seminars are no longer strictly professors, they're also investment bankers and management consultants.

As an indication of the way things have been going, consider these advertisements that appeared on the same page in a recent edition of a metropolitan daily newspaper: "A federally funded health planning agency, operating budget in excess of $ one million, seeks candidates for the position of Executive Director," said one. "Responsibility for overall management and operation of the agency under direction of a governing body. Candidates should have proven leadership abilities and management experience, knowledge of the health care system, community dynamics, and health planning legislation. Experience with HSAs preferred. Minimum qualifications are a master's degree in planning, hospital, public, or

523

business administration, and five years of increasingly responsible professional experience. Salary range $35,000 to $45,000." And another: "We are a national health care organization seeking an individual who feels confident working with employee benefit consultants. Must be versatile enough to deal comfortably in both one-to-one supportive roles in presentations and selling situations. We require a highly motivated, creative self-starter with excellent written and verbal communication skills, and the ability to follow through on a rolling marketing plan. A degree in marketing would be a plus. $30,000 to $40,000, excellent fringe benefit package is included." or, "Director of planning for suburban 250 bed acute care hospital. Five years experience in hospital short and long range planning required. Familiar with laws and regulations related to national, state, and local planning agencies. Successful candidate will find position challenging and attractive with many employer paid benefits." These observations are not anomalous and the changes indicated by them are not unimportant. Rather, they are symptomatic of changing values among health-care institutions and agencies. Today's—and tomorrow's—health-services manager faces a set of complex tasks that will require not only considerable technical business expertise but also a firmly grounded sense of mission and purpose. For the really top-flight manager, neither attribute will, in itself, be sufficient.

Environmental Trends

Up to and pretty well through the 1930s, except in the armed services and in public health, which was almost wholly concerned with sanitation and immunization programs, the health services were relatively uncomplicated, consisting for the most part of the private practice of medicine in patients' homes, doctors' offices, and hospitals. Hospitals were constructed and maintained largely through voluntary efforts and services were paid for by patient themselves or, for those who couldn't afford to pay, by philanthropists or local tax sources. The 1930s also saw the beginnings of voluntary health-care prepayment plans, such as the Blue Cross and Blue Shield Plans, as sources of payment. Around the same time, prepaid group practice—notably the Kaiser-Permanente Medical Care Program and the federal employees' Group Health Association—were established as alternatives to fee-for-service practice, which was already divided into several major specialties, especially in hospital settings. Speeded up by the urgency of wartime needs and funding, scientific advance and specialization in medicine proliferated in the 1940s, the beginning of a period of industrial expansion, full employment, and prosperity. Labor unions grew in size and power, and health insurance benefits gradually became standard provisions in contracts negotiated through collective bargaining. Although hospital expansion had been restrained through years of depression and war, after World War II hospitals had to expand rapidly to meet the multiple requirements of new medical specialties and procedures coupled with increased demand fueled by expanding health insurance benefits. Philanthropic sources for funding expansion were available in most communities, and the federal Hill-Burton Act provided seed money for new hospitals in underserved areas to meet population growth. The wartime emergency act that provided federal assistance for maternal and infant care had broken the barrier of resistance to government participation in medical affairs, but Hill-Burton was the landmark legislation. With authority to approve hospital location and to specify construction standards for federally aided hospitals, the U.S. Public Health Service, as administrator of Hill-Burton grants, for the first time gave the government a real voice in medical care of the civilian population.

This was also a period of rapid change in the management of medical institutions. Hospital administrators in past decades had been a mixed lot: physicians retired or in part-time practice; up-from-the-ranks nurses; accountants and business managers; members of religious orders and retired clergymen; a few businessmen from other fields who became interested as trustees. The American College of Surgeons since 1918 had conducted a hospital standardization program including recommendations for medical staff organization and staff relationships with trustees and administrators, but the standards were concerned chiefly with patient safety. ACS approval was valued and sought after, but it signified only that minimum standards had been met, and it wasn't until after the college program had evolved into the Joint Commission on Accreditation of Hospitals that the slow and painful process of requiring medical staffs to monitor and upgrade patient care was undertaken in earnest.

The first viable graduate education program in hospital administration had been established in the mid-1930s. One or two others were initiated in the next few years. During the war the military services organized training programs for medical administrative officers, many of whom stayed in the field after the war, when the complexities of the management assignment began to multiply and the demand for training administrators grew accordingly. After the war, many new university programs were established in response to the perceived need. Most were in schools of business or schools of public health, and the relative merits of these jurisdictions were argued, at times vigorously, in the 1950s.

Those favoring the business environment liked to point out that course content depended more heavily on management, statistics, accounting, economics, and other faculties and resources of the business schools than it did on the medical and public health faculties, but others considered that the latter provided a background more appropriate to the hospital mission. Among the accredited graduate programs today, the numbers in these two schools are about the same, but more of the programs are independent of either one. In any case, it seems likely that the business school influence over the years has contributed to what some critics have seen as overemphasis on the business operations as opposed to the social purpose of medical institutions and programs. Whatever the shortcomings of the religious-nursing-up-from-the-ranks corps of administrators of prewar times, everybody knew their institutions were devoted wholly to the needs of doctors caring for patients, but this is not always evident in many of our hospitals today.

There were other, and probably more influential, factors contributing to the divergence of business operations and social purpose in medical institutions. These began to be apparent in the 1960s, when management had to comprehend two formidable forces that had not previously been serious concerns: the direct involvement of government as a party to the social contract in medical care and the organized consumer movement. The thin end of the wedge of federal participation in the health field had been perceived in Hill-Burton, but this had been limited to capital funding and was generally welcomed as an aid to needed expansion. The relatively few medical society officials and others who had warned that it was a dangerous precedent had usually been dismissed as conservative cranks. But worry about health care of the aged, especially the underprivileged aged, had begun in the late 1950s, and in 1960 the Congress passed the Kerr-Mills Act providing federal funds to the states for medical care of aged public-assistance recipients—a measure that was a compromise intended to resolve the conflicting demands of those who wanted all-out government support and those who insisted nothing of the kind was needed.

Kerr-Mills didn't satisfy either side, and the debate was intensified and prolonged. Eventually, it resulted in passage of the Social Security Amendments of 1965, including Medicare and Medicaid. In one legislative stroke, the federal government had become the largest single purchaser of medical care, and the cranks had been right in one important respect: Things would never be the same again.

But the cranks and critics were wrong when they said Medicare and Medicaid hadn't been needed. The Medicare program has been the means of providing needed medical care for millions of aged patients who would have had inadequate care without it, and the Medicaid program, unsatisfactory as it has been in many ways, has provided needed assistance to more millions. The basic problem in both programs has been that the cost, from the beginning, has far exceeded the early estimates, and most of the efforts to hold costs down, in the private sector as well as in the public programs, have proved inadequate. Critics of the private, voluntary health-care system, like critics of the public programs, have insisted that the failure to contain cost has been managerial failure. But this view seriously underestimates the effect on the rise in health-care costs of inflation in the general economy, which nobody has known how to control, and of the interaction of the accelerating rate of adoption of sophisticated medical equipment with rising public expectations undergirded by prepayment and insurance coverage.

Whatever the causes, most of the cures haven't worked. The efforts to control expenditures date back to the years immediately following introduction of Medicare and Medicaid, when the Congress passed the Comprehensive Health Planning and Partnership for Health Acts and the Regional Medical Program Act, all aimed at rationalizing use of voluntary health resources. None of these was notably successful, and the Social Security Amendments of 1972 followed up with stronger measures—the Professional Standards Review Organizations program and capital expenditure controls under section 1122. The first Health Maintenance Organization Act was an attempt to encourage the introduction of competitive options to fee-for-service medicine and insured hospitalization, and the National Health Planning and Resources Development Act in 1974, which established Health Systems Agencies, state planning agencies, and required states to adopt certification-of-need statutes, is credited at least with helping spur the movement of voluntary institutions into larger systems, where systematic interinstitutional planning and economies of scale will presumably emerge over time.

It is difficult to determine just how effective all these laws and their layers of regulations have been in curbing the growth of expenditures, but it is plain to see that the need to manage the complexities of the conditions of participation, entitlements, and reimbursement procedures of Medicare and Medicaid and assure compliance with all the control measures has added enormously to the responsibilities of health-care management. Estimates of what it costs hospitals to meet all the requirements of health-care legislation and regulations today vary widely, but the costs unquestionably are considerable. In spite of pressures to "deregulate" the health-care field, there is at least an even chance that there will be more legislation and regulation, not less, in the 1980s.

The failure of existing expenditure-control mechanisms has led, in a time of increased fiscal conservatism, to a renewed interest in restructuring the health-services market through statute. Currently in vogue are the so-called consumer choice proposals that call for increasing consumer involvement in medical decisions through increasing the patient's economic interest in those decisions. By requiring that employees have a choice among a range of competing coverage packages and by limiting the amount the employer can pay for those plans, theoreticians anticipate that the amount of cost sharing by patients will increase, with a concomitant reduction in demand.

One primary goal of these proposals is to increase competition among health insurance carriers and, through them, among providers of care. Attending regulation may be transferred from the providers to the carriers and aimed at structuring the conditions under which competition can occur. While passage of any complete consumer choice proposal is not likely in the near future, elements of the model may appear in other, more piecemeal, ways—as parts of other bills, for example. Managers of health-care institutions will have to be particularly wary of possible adverse effects on high-cost institutions, such as teaching hospitals or on rural hospitals, and on high-risk segments of the population who may find adequate coverage unaffordable unless specific provisions are written into consumer choice legislation.

Discussion of alternative approaches to structuring the health-services market is occurring at a time when significant changes in the capital financing market for hospitals are looming. Since the advent of Medicare and Medicaid, philanthropy and federal grant sources have played a smaller and smaller role in financing hospital capital projects. This has forced hospitals to turn to debt financing for such projects. In recent years, even with the availability of tax-exempt revenue bonds, rising interest rates in the capital market have greatly increased the costs of hospital capital projects. This is viewed by many in the field as a serious constraint on hospital management decisions. In fact, some who argue for the repeal of all capital expenditure controls argue that the natural operations of the commercial capital market will forestall any precipitous capital investment by hospitals.

Another new force that emerged in the 1960s and is likely to continue, although it has undergone several changes since it first appeared, is consumerism. Actually, there had been a consumers' movement since the depression years of 1930s—Consumers Union, Consumers Federation, and others. Some aspects of unionism were essentially consumer oriented, as were aspects of the drive for equal civil rights for minorities and women, and the youth movement. In the 1960s, a combination of these forces selected health care institutions and practices as one of their principal targets, especially in the large cities. The goals of these groups varied at different times and places. Elimination of discrimination in patient services and in employment were common objectives, and in many cases advocacy groups sought specific representation on the governing boards of hospitals, Blue Cross and Blue Shield plans, and planning agencies. There were some uncomfortable and challenging episodes, such as sit-ins at hospital administrative offices, demonstrations and picketing at public hospitals in several cities, strikes of house staffs and nurses hoping to achieve consumer-oriented objectives, demands by citizens to attend and be heard at meetings of boards of trustees, and, always, lots of publicity.

Like the "student revolution" on the college and university campuses, the hospital sit-ins and demonstrations subsided in the early 1970s, but the consumer movement in the health field has had some lasting results and is still alive. Unquestionably, for example, consumer pressure generally, and the recommendations of a Secretary's Commission on Medicaid and Related Programs in 1971 in particular, influenced the Congress to include in the health planning law the provision requiring consumer majorities on the boards of directors of Health Systems Agencies. The same and similar influences are visible in the fact that some Blue Cross and Blue Shield Plans now either have, or are moving toward having, consumer majorities on their governing boards. Many hospitals have added consumer members, including minorities and women, to boards of trustees that were traditionally male and elitist. Some city hospitals have established community or consumer advisory committees to add this dimension to board and management deliberations. Not all these attempts to add consumer representation have worked well; some have proved to be time-wasting or even disruptive, but in many cases consumer representatives have been able to point out needs for services, interpret neighborhood and community attitudes, and help avoid conflicts. The difference between the programs that have worked well and those that have failed has appeared to lie in the skill and sensitivity with which management has identified consumer representatives whose approach would be constructive, oriented the consumers to institutional goals, constraints, programs, and requirements, and guided their participation. These are arts that are rarely acquired in formal training programs, but which may have as much to do with management effectiveness in the years to come as anything in the graduate curriculum.

In the last half of the 1970s, an altogether new kind of consumer interest in health care arose, one that seems certain to intensify and to contribute another thread to the tangle of complexities with which managers of health-care enterprises will have to cope. This is industry's active concern about the cost of employees' health benefits, now paid for largely or wholly by employers. The concern is expressed in many ways. Some corporations have changed health insurers; some have become self-insured and in some cases sought to initiate their own health-care cost-containment systems; some have turned to HMOs, either through contract or sponsorship, with the expectation that an alternative to traditional fee-for-service medical care might be less costly. Many firms have become actively interested in the health of the work force, not just its medical bills, and have initiated programs of screening, prevention, health promotion and education, and physical fitness. Several large corporations—General Motors and Alcoa are examples—have encouraged their executives to become active in health affairs in their communities as trustees of hospitals or health-planning agencies and have conducted seminars aimed at making those executives informed, critical, and effective in these roles. These are all constructive interests and maneuvers which add another dimension to the responsibilities of health-care managers—the necessity for establishing productive liaisons with private business firms. One result of increasing cost pressures, a growing body of epidemiological evidence, and an increasingly sophisticated and involved public is the rising emphasis on health promotion and physical fitness in the general population. This trend is evidenced by the jogging and exercise phenomena, the rise of the "health food" industry, and the well-documented changes in national dietary, smoking, drinking, and exercise habits. While the full effects of this change have not been felt yet, managers in the health-care field need to be aware of the epidemiological potentials, as well as the revenue-producing opportunities of health-promotion services.

There is one other environmental trend—one which will undoubtedly have a profound effect on the organization and composition of our health-care delivery and financing systems—with which managers will have to deal in the coming decades. This is the aging population of the United States. The figures are staggering: in 1975, 22 million Americans were sixty-five or over, some 11 percent of the population; by 2000 those figures will be 31 million and 12 percent; and by 2030, when the "baby boom" reaches sixty-five, 46 million and 17 percent. Moreover, the composition of the elderly segment is itself aging. In 1975, 8.4 million persons were seventy-five or over, 38 percent of the sixty-five-plus age cohort; by 2000, those figures will be 21 million, 45 percent of the sixty-five-and-over group. When one considers that persons sixty-five and over currently account for one-third of all personal health-care expenditures and that those seventy-five and older have hospital admission rates 270 percent higher than those of the under-sixty-five age group, the potential impact of this aging population on our health-care system will require a degree of management expertise perhaps unmatched so far (Siegel 1976). Not only will services, facilities, and funding need to be restructured to meet this coming demand, but managers will have to seek ways to mobilize untapped resources—including the volunteer potential of the elderly themselves—in innovative service delivery and financing arrangements that may require a rethinking of the role of the hospital and other health-care delivery and financing organizations in relation to community social service agencies.

Trends in the Field

In response to the kinds of environmental forces discussed here, certain changes have been taking place extensively enough and long enough to be identified as trends likely to continue through the next decade. These can generally be grouped into three sets: the organization of hospitals into multi-institutional arrangements, the development of alternative delivery and financing systems, and a change in the perception of hospitals by management professionals in the field, from public service organizations to businesslike enterprises with social service products. These trends have had, and will continue to have, an effect on the practice of management in the health services and on the training appropriate to those new management roles.

The organization of hospitals into multi-institutional arrangements is hardly a new development. The beginnings of such arrangements can be traced back at least to World War II. Nor is there any set pattern for these arrangements. They vary all the way from federations, whose members may share some administrative services and join hands in coping with a hostile regulatory and economic environment, to the more or less integrated regional vertical systems with referral linkages from outpatient facilities and group practices to community hospitals and academic medical centers, offering a comprehensive range of services to defined regional populations. The organization of regionally linked clinical services has been envisioned by medical planners ever since the report of the first national Committee on the Cost of Medical Care in 1932, but progress in that direction has been negligible until fairly recently. In 1973, there were some 744 nongovernmental hospitals involved in multi-institutional arrangements (Barrett 1980). By 1980, there were 1,797 acute care, nongovernmental hospitals with over 340,000 beds arranged in multi-institutional systems, either under ownership or through management contracts (*Directory of Multihospital Systems* 1980).

Coupled with this dramatic growth has come increasing managerial and organizational sophistication of the arrangements themselves. These developments have been in response to: the changes in capital financing for hospitals; the pressures for economy of scale and expenditure controls; onerous regulation; excess bed capacity in many areas; the expectations of the public; the need to attract high-priced management talent and planning initiatives. But, the movement toward multi-institutional arrangements has been occurring primarily through voluntary initiatives among voluntary institutions without, for the most part, specific coercion from regulatory or planning agencies. This trend provides evidence counter to the assumption that only governmental action could produce regional coordination of services. One effect of the trend toward multi-institutional grouping is an increasing need for new management skills applicable to the larger, more complex organizations.

The second current trend is the accelerating emergence of so called alternative delivery systems (ADS), chiefly health-maintenance organizations and independent practice associations, offering consumers choices other than traditional fee-for-service medical and hospital care. This movement received some impetus from the federal government through the HMO Act. More recently, advocates of ADS have been supporters of various consumer choice legislative approaches. In what may be the most significant development, the last half of the 1970s saw an increasing amount of interest in ADs on the part of businesses seeking to control their employee health benefit outlays. As a part of this trend, sponsors of HMOs in many parts of the country have put their hospital business out for contract among local hospitals. In those circumstances, hospitals that desired the HMO patients had to submit competitive bids to the HMO. This approach to hospital pricing, which puts the hospital at partial risk, is relatively new to most administrators and requires a skillful management touch to be successful.

The third trend, which is reflected in the first two, is the growing tendency of the health enterprise, and particularly hospitals, to be thought of more as, and to act more like, businesses as opposed to social institutions. This is both good and bad. A major responsibility of the management of health related enterprise in the future is going to be to take full advantage of the many efficiencies of good business practice without sacrificing or diminishing the sense of social mission and the dedication to social purpose that have been the distinctive characteristics of health enterprise in the past. The recent increase in the number of investor-owned hospitals that exist in large measure to provide a return on equity to stockholders is evidence of the changing emphasis. Moreover, while many hospitals have not altered their not-for-profit status, they have contracted with management firms to supply administrative services. Managers in the for-profit segment of the hospital field argue persuasively that, given the current and anticipated environment, a sense of hospital mission is not in itself sufficient to assure survival. What is needed is a financially sound institution. Only from such a sound base will the kind of health care demanded by the community be assured.

While for-profit status is certainly not a prerequisite to sound business practice, hospitals are turning increasingly to the traditional business sector for organizational models. This is evident in the trend toward the adoption of innovative corporate structures in the hospital field, a trend accelerated by the movement toward multi-institutional arrangements. Many managers are sensing the advantages that can flow from diversifying the hospital's lines of business on the basis of incisive demographic, epidemiological, and financial analyses. Thus, for example, hospitals are establishing remote ambulatory surgical centers or outpatient departments in areas where data are indicative of a beneficial flow of patients. Other examples of diversification include services aimed at the elderly segment of the population, with hospital investment in such activities as retirement housing, home health-care services, nursing homes, and hospital services. In many cases, hospitals have found it advantageous to establish financially diversified services such as HMOs or for-profit subsidiaries, which can protect the hospital's not-for-profit status while allowing the hospital to take advantage of certain aspects of the reimbursement system. Moreover, a few multi-institutional systems have even established their corporate structures along the lines of holding companies, with control over the component institutions exercised, to varying degrees, from the central headquarters.

Trends in Health-Services Management

The journals and textbooks of management deal for the most part with principles that remain constant in all kinds of enterprise, and it is certainly true that wherever they may be found, managers are concerned with the formulation of policy, with organizational structure, plans, systems, controls, communications, and other activities that are common to all organizations, from churches to circuses. But this truth has given rise to many misconceptions. The fact that some successful executives move from one business environment to another without loss of stride does not mean that the same executives could necessarily transfer their talents easily or with the same success to a different environment, where the purpose is not to make money but to satisfy complex human needs, where outcomes are difficult to measure precisely, and where organizations are subject to pressures from a complex array of constituencies, many of which are responding to noneconomic as well as economic stimuli.

In the health-sevices field, managers who are not familiar with, and sensitive to, the sense of mission and the complexity of an organization's constituents will find it difficult to fulfill that mission or to satisfy those constituents. Any such failure will jeopardize the institution, regardless of the business knowledge and skills the manager may bring to the organization. Thus there are cases where successful managers in the for-profit field have been unable to achieve success in hospitals, and where persons who had little explicit business training, such as physicians or nurses, have been able to run viable hospitals because of their profound understanding of the hospital's mission and the people affected by it. One might conclude from such contrasting experiences that sensitivity to purpose and constituency are indispensable components of successful management of health enterprise, and management skills are nice to have around but not really necessary.

But, of course, that is not true either. There have been some notable failures caused by sensitive and well-meaning managers who did not have the business skills necessary to run an institution in today's increasingly complex environment. In the more complicated decade that lies ahead, as all the environmental trends continue, they will interact and beget their own complexities. The need will be for more and more sophisticated managers with more of both the technical skills *and* the sense of mission than has been required of successful managers in the health-care field in the past. The professional training of health-service managers has been carried on energetically in a number of leading universities ever since World War II and has kept pace with the demand over most of these years. Every year, the graduate programs turn out hundreds of young people with some knowledge of the principles of management and some understanding of how the principles may be applied in actual practice. These people then move into residency or preceptorship programs in health-care enterprise—hospitals, most commonly. If they are fortunate in their choice of preceptors and perceptive in their observations and judgments of the environment and the forces and influences at play within it, they add something to their knowledge of the principles and the practice, and the more thoughtful among them may begin to have some feeling for the nature of the responsibility that pervades the enterprise. Up to now, this sense of mission has been something the professors and visiting lecturers talked about, but it has to be felt to be understood—and there are some health-service administrators, including some who have achieved at least a measure of success, who haven't felt it yet. But there will be fewer of these in the future than there have been in the past as the environment becomes more demanding.

Inevitably, the management tasks will become more and more demanding in a new decade characterized by the accelerating movement of hospitals into systems, heightened and more varied competition, demanding regulation, changing capital constraints and more complex financing, continued public concern about cost, as well as security, especially on the part of industry and government, and rising public concern for positive health as well as sickness. Given this kind of revolving complexity, it goes without saying that the managers of health-care enterprise in the 1980s will have to understand both the capabilities and the limitations of the evolving management and information technology, and they must be familiar also with the risks and promises of such concepts as management by objectives, organizational development, participative management, and whatever new constructs of human relations or motivational theory may come along to capture the excitement of company psychologists and the pages of *Harvard Business Review*. They can always hire statisticians and financial specialists to manage the day-to-day tracking of operations and cash flow, but they had better know enough about trends in the hospital environment and the imperatives of the hospital and its constituencies to properly anticipate change and position their institutions accordingly.

Increasingly, the manager of health-service enterprise is becoming a facilitator and a coordinator of change for the governing board of health-services institutions, systems or programs; few board members today can have either the time or the specialized knowledge required to formulate policies, set goals, make plans, and evaluate performance without the guidance of a knowledgeable and forceful executive. Similarly, the executive must be the window to the world for the professional staff, whose preoccupation with professional care too often precludes much functional involvement with institutional or program direction. The manager, then, has a responsibility to encourage informed involvement by the professional staff and must also look out for, and look ahead to, the long-term health manpower needs of the community and the institution. The executive must also possess the technical knowledge and the moral courage to be an effective interpreter and arbiter of needs for professional personnel and resource allocation of all kinds—a function that often requires a tightrope act to avoid making business judgments that can damage quality of care on the one hand, or, using quality as a screen, can produce inefficiency or extravagance on the other.

With these and other requirements on management, which will only become more exacting with the increasing environmental pressures, it is likely that, during the coming decade, the graduate programs in health administration will have to change to include, among other provisions, the management specialties that are being increasingly adapted to the health services. Already the demand of the multihospital systems for specialists in financial management, computer systems design, organizational development, personnel, marketing and strategic planning, and other specialties has institutions and groups looking outside the health field for people with these particular skills. The entry of such individuals at advanced levels adds to the number of managers in the field who lack the understanding of institutional purpose that comes from extended familiarity with the professional environment. This might not be an important consideration in the performance of specialized assignments, but as more of these people succeed to policymaking positions over the years, it could have a lasting effect on the character of the health related services.

The adaptation of business expertise to the health services is complicated by the increasingly complex interrelationships between the delivery and financing systems. The diversity of financing sources—Blue Cross and Blue Shield Plans, commercial health insurers, governmental at all levels, and, increasingly, direct sponsorship by industrial firms—will persist in a pluralistic economy and the web of interdependencies will increase. In a sense, and this may be seen most clearly in vertically integrated delivery and financing arrangements such as the Kaiser-Permanente Medical Care Program, the delivery system has become a part of the financing system, and vice versa. This development has led to a broadening of the management perspective, so that increasingly the scope of the sophisticated health-services manager must encompass both the delivery and financing aspects simultaneously.

Imperatives for the Future

For the cited reason, one can calculate that environmental forces acting on the health field will require more sophisticated management responses. How education and other programs should be fashioned to meet the need is less apparent.

It is tempting to think of requiring additional semesters to qualify for a master's degree in health administration. But such a requirement would be expensive for the student and, perhaps, make the field less attractive in the light of other educational alternatives. There is growing interest in postmaster's degree residencies and fellowships. This path should be energetically pursued. It provides a modest income for the student and, if well designed, it joins effectively the influences of the faculty and the practicing administrator. It might be well also to formulate mid-career programs that could, but not necessarily, lead to a doctoral degree, through individual choice, with the expenses paid by the benefiting institution.

In any case, the postdegree experiences will need structure. This will call for a much closer relationship between management practitioners and the university than has existed in the recent years. The result should be an enriched curriculum and enriched cooperating institutions. The two have been apart for too long.

With the marked shifts under way in the job of the health administrator, it is important that the accreditation of university program be reasonably flexible in regard to course requirements and course/work experience mixtures. Currently, accreditations are being evaluated, and it appears as though there is a healthy interest in both flexible and outcome versus input measures.

Student demand is high and the quality is reasonably competitive. However, problems are emerging in the university. Hospitals and other institutions, public and private, are bidding high for new skills (e.g., financial management), making it difficult for the universities to recruit full-time faculty. Moreover, it is possible that the federal government will cut back on, or eliminate, support for health administration programs, placing up to a quarter of the program in jeopardy.

Neither problem is insurmountable. While certain faculty skills are in short supply, practitioner teachers can be used. And it can be argued that all would be served well if the weaker programs did terminate and resources were devoted to strengthening the surviving programs. In the light of the job requirements, too many existing university programs lack the rigor to do the job.

There is room, too, for a rich menu of in-service programs of short duration sponsored by professional organizations (e.g., the American College of Hospital Administrators), and by universities. But the menu needs to be changed. The needs of the field are vastly different from the time when such training became popular.

One of the major questions facing the field of health administration is what degree of emphasis should be put on administration per se versus the environment of which it is a part. In recent years, we have seen a swing to a greater emphasis on business courses. There are signs that the swing is slowing.

It would be fruitless here to weigh the proper balance, but it should be pointed out that in the health field, without doing a disservice to management courses, mission and objectives are of unique importance and goals and objectives are derived essentially from an understanding of environment. This is particularly so because of the lack of competitive lash among providers. For example, it is essential that the primary function of the health-care system be to improve health, not only provide medical care. While some leaders have seen and accepted the responsibility, others, concerned with short-term problems of survival in a difficult environment and preoccupied with technology, are reluctant to do so. It is encouraging that some delivery and financing organizations have viewed health in the context of total life-style and have begun to be critical of the effectiveness of various technologies and procedures, but, given the counter forces, the impulse needs strong leadership and education has a substantial role to play. To cite another example, the health administrator will need to understand not only the forces of competition and regulation but of voluntary effort. For years, voluntary effort and its corollary, self-regulation, have been the equilibratory force between competition and regulation, a major source of innovativeness and a major support for pluralism in the health field. Is voluntary effort out-of-date? Or is it an essential element of a public-private partnership? Here, again, the university should promote the debate. Whereas it is important for the health field to be efficient, it also needs direction. It needs to increase its productivity, but it also needs a North Star.

In essence, health administration is a facinating field under rapid change, animated in novel ways by demand and need, urgently seeking better management and deeply imbued through tradition with community service. It offers the younger generation an unparalleled challenge for both management and service.

REFERENCES

BARRETT, D. 1980. *Multihospital systems—the process of development.* Cambridge, Mass.: Oelgeschlager, Gunn, and Hair.

Directory of Multihospital Systems. 1980. Chicago: American Hospital Association.

SIEGEL, J. S. 1976. Demographic aspects of aging and the older population in the United States. *Current Population Reports: Special Studies,* Series P-23, No. 59. U.S. Department of Commerce–Bureau of the Census. Washington, D.C.: Government Printing Office.

V

HEALTH, ILLNESS, AND SOCIAL ADAPTATION: PSYCHOSOCIAL AND BEHAVIORAL ISSUES

Chapter 25

Models of Health-Related Behavior

Marshall H. Becker
Lois A. Maiman

THERE IS CONSIDERABLE ONGOING DEBATE about various aspects of health-services delivery, quality of care, and the value of different public health and medical-care recommendations. Nonetheless, it is apparent that the ultimate success of efficacious preventive and curative regimens is often dependent upon individuals' willingness to undertake and/or maintain the required health behaviors. Given the extensive documentation of suboptimal public participation in screening, immunization, and other preventive health efforts, as well as low levels of individual compliance with prescribed medical therapies (Becker and Maiman 1975; Sackett and Snow 1979), it is not surprising that behavioral scientists have devoted extensive conceptual and empirical effort toward the explanation and prediction of individuals' health-related decisions.

Individuals voluntarily elect to engage in health-related activities for three major classes of reasons (Kasl and Cobb 1966): (1) to prevent illness or to detect it at an asymptomatic stage ("health behavior"); (2) in the presence of symptoms, to obtain diagnosis and to discover suitable treatment ("illness behavior"); and (3) in the presence of defined illness, to undertake/receive treatment aimed at restoration of health or at halting disease progression ("sick-role behavior"). (It is important to note that, for any individual and/or illness episode, these activities need not directly involve advice from, or visits to, health-care professionals.) As will be apparent from later discussion, different investigators have focused their models and studies upon different classes of health-related behavior.

The determinants of these voluntary health behaviors are many, multifaceted, and complex. For example, McKinlay's (1972) review of the vast literature on the use of health services identified six major approaches: economic, sociodemographic, geographic, social-psychological, sociocultural, and organizational; eclectic reviews of research on health, illness, and sick-role behaviors have summarized findings across all or most of these perspectives (cf. Coe and Wessen 1965; Kasl and Cobb 1966; Anderson 1973; Jenkins 1979). Over the past two decades, a number of theoretical frameworks have appeared which attempt to account for individuals' health actions, each formulation encompassing some of the dimensions listed above. Most notable, in terms of predictive ability and frequency of citation, have been the models of health behavior proposed by Andersen (1968),

Anderson and Bartkus (1973); Antonovsky and Kats (1970); Fabrega (1973, 1974), Green (1975), Hochbaum (1958), Kasl and Cobb (1966a, 1966b) (actually two models, one for "health" and one for "illness" behaviors); Kosa and Robertson (1975), Langlie (1977), Mechanic (1968), Rosenstock (1966), and Suchman (1965a, 1965b, 1966). These models differ considerably with regard to theoretical perspective and type of health behavior to be explained; however, they appear to contain classes of similar variables. This chapter will summarize the most prominent models, and will conclude with an attempt to combine the major components of these approaches in a single conceptual scheme.

Suchman

Among efforts to adopt a *sociological* perspective in understanding individuals' decisions with respect to health-services utilization, Suchman's examination of health behaviors within their surrounding social and cultural contexts was seminal, and involved hypothesized links between specified health orientations/behaviors and social relationships/group structures.

The foci of Suchman's model were social patterns of illness behavior "accompanying the seeking, finding and carrying out of medical care" (Suchman 1965b, p. 114). The approach evolves from four elements presented as principal factors in illness behavior: (1) content; (2) sequence; (3) spacing; and (4) variability of behavior during different phases of medical care. The first element, content, provides a series of concepts facilitating description of alternative behaviors and their outcomes: (1) "shopping" (the seeking of medical care from different providers); (2) "fragmentation of care" (receiving medical care from different providers at the same source); (3) "procrastination" (delay in seeking care subsequent to the observation of symptoms); (4) "self-medication" (self-initiated use of therapies); and (5) "discontinuity" (interruptions in the treatment or process of care).

In Suchman's paradigm the sequence of medical events is divided into five transitional stages: (1) symptom experience; (2) assumption of the sick role; (3) medical-care contact; (4) dependent-patient role; and (5) recovery or rehabilitation. At each stage, the individual must make health-care decisions and undertake health-related behaviors. At the initial stage, three dimensions of the symptom experience enter into the individual's decision that something is wrong. First, the physical sensation of pain, discomfort, or abnormality is experienced. Next, the cognitive dimension of the symptom experience causes the individual to interpret and define the physical sensations or symptoms on the basis of their degree of interference with usual social functioning. Finally, the emotional dimension of the symptom experience produces fear or anxiety responses associated with the illness. It is recognized that outcomes at this stage (as in other stages of the sequence) can vary. While this theory moves from acceptance of the symptom-experience stage to assumption of the sick role, the individual may decide on alternatives to this progression, such as denying the presence of illness or delaying seeking medical care.

During the assumption of the sick role, the individual attempts to reduce or control symptoms of illness by self-initiated therapies or treatments. Simultaneously, family and friends are called upon to provide information and advice. The lay referral system influences entry to the sick role; discussions with significant others serve primarily to provide the "provisional validation" necessary to relinquish obligations and responsibilities. Next, in the medical-care contact stage, a physician is consulted to assist with the patient's organic and psychosocial needs, both by providing diagnosis and treatment for the symptoms and by legitimating the relinquishment of responsibilities and activities. As in the two previous stages, the individual may not believe the diagnosis or accept the recommended therapy, and may depart from the normal progression by seeking opinions and recommendations from other sources of medical care.

At the dependent-patient role stage, the individual diagnosed as ill enters into a relationship which entails acceptance of the prescribed regimen and transference of health-related decisions to the physician. Although the individual may not wish to waive all rights to health decision-making, the dependent-patient stage is accepted as necessary for regaining good health and returning to preillness roles and activities. It is recognized that physical, administrative, social, and psychological factors, as well as the quality of the doctor-patient communication, may interfere with adherence to the prescribed treatment.

Finally, the patient is called upon to relinquish the patient role and to enter the recovery stage (i.e., terminate medical care and reassume prior role as a healthy individual) or the rehabilitation stage (i.e., adopt a new role as a chronically ill individual or rehabilitee). In some instances, the patient returning to his/her former role is given an interval during which reduced social functioning is acceptable. With respect to the individual entering the rehabilitation stage, resocialization may be required to facilitate adoption of a new role.

Suchman (1965a) then formulates a theoretical statement concerning the relationship of social structure and medical orientation to individual variations in response to illness and medical care. In developing this portion of the model, Suchman elaborates the functions of the remaining factors (spacing and variations in response to illness and medical care) at the five transition stages of illness and the medical-care process.

Social structure of the group in which the person holds membership is determined by the social cohesion of three levels of group membership: community, friendship, and family. Degree of social organization is characterized by the level of ingroup attraction and exgroup exclusion as measured by "ethnic exclusivity" on the community level, "friendship solidarity" on the social level, and "orientation to family tradition and authority" on the family level. The three dimensions are combined in an index of cosmopolitan-parochial social structure, where parochialism is defined by high ethnic exclusivity, high friendship group solidarity, and high family orientation to tradition and authority. Health orientation of the individual is seen as a continuum, varying from scientific (objective, professional, impersonal) to popular (subjective, lay, personal) based on the level of "knowledge about disease," "skepticism of medical care," and "dependency in illness," where popular health orientation is identified by cognitive (low knowledge about disease), affective (high skepticism of medical care), and behavioral (high dependency in illness) dimensions.

Suchman hypothesized that medical behavior during the five stages of illness would reflect the individual's social group affiliation and health orientation. These variations in behavior would affect progression through the stages; for example, an individual with parochial group affiliation and popular health orientation would be likely to: exhibit delay in the recognition of, and underestimate the seriousness of, symptoms during the symptom-experience stage; seek repeated approval from others to abandon role obligations, try self-medication and home remedies, and display greater ambivalence in actions during assumption of the sick-role stage; delay in seeking medical care, "shop" for a group-approved physician, and be suspicious of the diagnosis during the medical-care contact stage; experience difficulty in assuming the sick role and fail to adhere to the therapeutic regimen during the dependent-patient role stage; and quickly relinquish the sick role (or, if chronically ill, deny continued illness and neglect rehabilitation).

Findings (Suchman 1965a, 1966) from a subsample of 137 subjects experiencing a serious illness during the two months prior to interview in a community health survey of Washington Heights (New York City) residents seem to support the proposed relationships among social structure, health orientation, and variations in response to illness. At the symptom-experience stage, only scientific-popular health orientation accounts for differential response to illness, with the "popular"-oriented individual less likely to be aware of the seriousness of symptoms and their potential adverse sequelae. At the remaining four stages, both social structure and health orientation appear to be related to differences in response to illness; parochial and popular group members are more likely to discuss symptoms with family and friends, delay seeking professional care, feel dependent on others during their illness, seek care from medical sources other than the physician involved in the initial diagnosis and treatment of the illness, and exhibit concern about the physical and social consequences of illness.

However, additional research using diverse ethnic groups has yielded results inconsistent with the hypothesized function of social group affiliation as a predictor of medical orientation. To test the replicability of Suchman's finding that individuals who are members of cosmopolitan social groups are relatively more scientific in their orientation to medical matters, Reeder and Berkanovic (1973) surveyed a multistage area probability sample of subjects (N = 1,026) living in the Los Angeles metropolitan area. The study employed Suchman's measures of medical orientation, but used different (although purportedly theoretically similar) items to measure social group orientation. In contrast to Suchman's results, the Los Angeles data provide moderate associations suggesting that individuals who belong to parochial social groups may actually be more scientific in their medical orientation. Similarly, when the relationship between social group orientation and medical orientation is analyzed by racial subgroups (black, Mexican-American, and white), the findings linking parochialism to scientific medical orientation are the reverse of those obtained by Suchman. Finally, while the Washington Heights data provided support for the influences of socioeconomic status (measured by education and income) and ethnicity on medical orientation, these variables were not predictive of differential medical orientation in the Los Angeles study.

Geertsen and associates (1975) also obtained partially divergent results from their study based in Salt Lake City, Utah. Using Suchman's original social group and medical-orientation indices, interviews were obtained from a representative cross-section of heads of household (N = 535). In the Salt Lake City study, family authority and friendship solidarity were significantly related to medical orientation (measured by knowledge of health and disease, skepticism of medical care, and dependency in illness). However, ethnic exclusivity (the measure of community social group structure) was not found to be significantly related to any of the three medical-orientation variables.

Finally, Farge (1978) was unable to replicate Suchman's findings for the three levels of group membership and health orientation. A random sample of 150 households was selected in Houston, Texas, from areas where a significant proportion of the population was Mexican-American. Findings from the Houston study revealed that, on the family and social group level, neither family authority nor friendship solidarity were significantly related to the three measures of medical orientation. In addition, the significant findings for ethnic exclusivity and the components of medical orientation differed in direction from Suchman's findings. High ethnic exclusivity was significantly associated with both a high level of knowledge of health and disease and with requiring less help from lay persons during sickness episodes.

A partial explanation of these contradictory results is that individuals' medical orientations reflect the specific subcultural beliefs and practices of their group, independent of group structure (i.e., cosmopolitan versus parochial). According to this subcultural argument, members of parochial social groups which possess a scientific orientation to medical care will respond in a manner consistent with that orientation, while members of parochial social groups possessing a skeptical view of medical care will be likely to have a popular medical orientation. The composition of the samples employed in Suchman's research, and the previously mentioned studies testing the Suchman model, support the interpretation that subcultural background influences the association of social group and medical orientation. The Washington Heights sample contained high percentages of Jews (27 percent), Catholics (20 percent), and Puerto Ricans (9 percent) (many of whom were immigrants) and blacks (25 percent) (who had migrated from the south). These groups have been characterized as distrusting of societal institutions, including the medical-care system (Geertsen et al. 1975; Lendt 1960), and as having strong traditions of folk medicine. In contrast, the Salt Lake City sample, which was 70 percent Mormon, is identified as exclusive (tradition-oriented) on the family level but also as displaying scientific orientations which include emphasizing good health and appropriate use of medical care. Further support for the consistency of medical orientation with group culture is provided by the Los Angeles sample. Although this population is heterogeneous, it differs from the Washington Heights sample in its ethnic variations (largely native-born American Protestant [47 percent] and Mexican-American [15 percent], fewer blacks [13 percent] and Jews [6 percent]).

Hochbaum/Kasl and Cobb/Rosenstock

Paralleling Suchman's sociological formulation was the development of a model that focused on individual (as opposed to contextual) variables. This Health Belief Model (HBM) was derived from well-established bodies of psychological and behavioral theory (particularly "value-expectancy" approaches and theories about "decision-making under conditions of uncertainty"), and was similar to the decision-making models of Lewin, Tolman, Rotter, Edwards, Atkinson and others (Maiman and Becker 1974).

As it was originally conceived, the HBM hypothesized that individuals will generally not seek preventive care or health screening unless they possess minimal levels of relevant health motivation and knowledge, view themselves as potentially vulnerable and the condition as threatening, are convinced of the efficacy of intervention, and see few difficulties in undertaking the recommended health behavior (Rosenstock 1974). Specifically, the model contains the following elements:

1. The individual's subjective state of readiness to take action, which is determined by both the individual's perceived likelihood of "susceptibility" to the particular illness and by his/her perceptions of the probable "severity" of the consequences (organic and/or social) of contracting the disease.
2. The individual's evaluation of the advocated health behavior in terms of its feasibility and efficaciousness (i.e., a subjective estimate of the action's potential "benefits" in reducing susceptibility and/or severity), weighed against perceptions of physical, financial, and other costs ("barriers") involved in the proposed action.
3. A "cue to action" must occur to trigger the appropriate health behavior, coming from either internal (e.g., symptoms) or external (e.g., interpersonal interactions, mass media communications) sources.

In the HBM context, it is understood that diverse demographic, personal, structural, and social factors are capable of influencing health behaviors; however, these variables are believed to work through their effects on the individual's health motivations and subjective perceptions rather than functioning as direct causes of health action (Becker et al. 1977).

The major modifications introduced by Kasl and Cobb (1966b) involve the likelihood of an individual's undertaking a specific behavior in the presence of symptoms; the pain and discomfort of the symptoms, psychological distress, personal tolerance for pain, disability and coping mechanisms, and sociodemographic characteristics become important. As with the basic HBM, it is hypothesized that behavior undertaken in the presence of symptoms is influenced directly by an individual's perception of the threat of the disease and belief concerning the value of the health action. However, pain and discomfort associated with symptoms are seen as influencing an individual's perceptions of threat, as well as acting directly upon behavior; social characteristics, personal pain tolerance level, disability, and coping mechanisms are hypothesized to have indirect affects on behavior.

A large body of evidence has accumulated in support of the HBM's ability to account for the undertaking of preventive health actions, seeking diagnoses, and following prescribed medical advice (cf. review by Becker 1979). However, several studies that included HBM variables have not yielded the anticipated results; only about half of the relevant studies have been prospective in design (i.e., with attitudes measured prior to the behaviors they are supposed to predict); and few attempts have been made to examine (through multiple regression analyses or similar techniques) how the model variables work in concert (cf. Becker et al. 1979; Langlie 1977).

Fabrega

A decision-theoretic, anthropological approach to understanding illness behavior, which focuses on "the information that a person might be expected to process during an occurrence of illness," provides the framework for Fabrega's (1973,

p. 473) model. ("Illness" refers to the *culturally* defined state that forms the basis of decisions about medical treatment; thus, the model has cross-cultural application.) This model tries to order and categorize the stages an individual passes through in recognizing and responding to illness by concentrating on: (1) the information to be evaluated and acted upon; (2) the time ordering of events in the decision process; and (3) reducing variation in processes and events of the health-illness-medical treatment cycle by providing constant and repetitive structure for channeling and processing medically relevant information.

Fabrega (1973, p. 473) posits that the individual has four connect systems which provide "coding units. . .[or] norms or experienced levels of variations," which permit continuous monitoring of health-related happenings and processes. Put another way, the four systems are involved in information processing: coding, classifying, and ordering events related to symptoms and to feelings of illness. The systems are both open and interjoined, each contributing to illness behavior: (1) the *biological system*, which focuses on chemical and physiologic processes; (2) the *social system*, which executes relationships with other individuals, groups, and institutions; (3) the *phenomenologic system*, which is concerned with the individual's state of awareness and self-definition; and (4) the *memory system*, which includes earlier illness occurrences and accompanying medical attitudes and beliefs, and which serves as a continual influence on the other three systems.

The model provides an abstract definition of illness behavior outlined in nine stages describing the sequence of decisions people make during illness. The first two stages reflect the individual's recognition and evaluation of symptoms. During the initial stage, "illness recognition and labeling," internal cues (biological system conjoined with phenomenologic system) or external cues (appraisal of others, i.e., social system) lead the individual to realize the presence of illness and/or deviant changes and to undertake action to alleviate the perceived changes. (Recognition of illness is a subjective judgment rather than the result of objective medical diagnosis.) Illnesses are subjected to an evaluation cycle which produces constant monitoring and relabeling, and which incorporates memories of past experiences with similar disease occurrences (e.g., a condition originally defined as a headache will be relabeled with the appearance of additional symptoms such as tiredness or nausea).

At the next stage of the decision-making trajectory, the negative components of the illness are evaluated on the bases of present situation and past experiences (personal, or those of others in the individual's social group). This assessment of the problem attaches an "illness disvalue" to the condition, which reflects the danger, disability, discomfort, social stigma, and sociopsychological disruption associated with the illness.

At the third stage, the individual considers a variety of mutually exclusive "treatment plans" which might be implemented; these actions, which are learned and evolve from the individual's prior experience with illness, include options ranging from self-care (e.g., use of home remedies and patent medicines, or modification of dietary intake) to consulting the lay referral system (i.e., advice of significant others) to obtaining formal medical care.

In the next four stages, the individual undertakes a series of comparisons concerning alternative treatment plans: (1) "assessment of treatment plans" (the estimation of the probability that each alternative action will reduce the "disvalue" or threat of the illness); (2) computation of "treatment benefits" (the amount of illness reduction that might potentially be derived from each treatment plan); (3)

computation of "disvalues of illness" (the costs, both personal and economic, of undertaking each action); and (4) determination of the utility of each alternative treatment plan by subtracting treatment costs from treatment benefits, thus obtaining a "net benefits or utility" for each plan. Information from the preceding comparisons leads to the eighth stage, "selection of treatment plan." In choosing the treatment plan to be implemented, the individual applies personal decision rules (e.g., to select the plan that is least costly, that has the highest net utility, etc.).

At the final (ninth) stage, new information resulting from the outcome of the treatment plan selected in stage eight provides an up-dated history for the individual, which is learned and stored in the memory system. Thus, at stage nine, the individual is defined as "set up for recycling," which entails an evaluation of the illness in terms of both the treatment plan selected and the remaining manifestations. If, after a suitable lapse of time, the illness is relabeled, or if there is onset of new disease, the initial stage of the sequence is reentered.

In order for the model of illness behavior to operate, Fabrega specifies three assumptions. First, illness must be recognized as undesirable; i.e., the model is not applicable to individuals who favor or who deny disease states and thus would not be motivated to undertake remedial action. Second, illness must be perceived as a discrete occurrence rather than an undifferentiated and constant state managed by habitual behaviors (which do not require decisions of illness definition and treatment selection). Finally, individuals must make their illness decisions based on rational evaluations of optimal treatment actions (rather than on random or irrational bases).

In summary, Fabrega has developed a behavioral framework to study how social and cultural behavior influences the individual's processing of information about illness and decisions about medical treatment; he suggests that the model be used in cross-cultural comparisons of the disvalues or costs of illness. Although difficulties in operationalizing the variables contained in the model are acknowledged, it is proposed that it be used as a rubric for empirical studies which would yield an "estimate" of the key variables. This approach to studying illness episodes was employed in a longitudinal study of a panel of families (N = 174) living in San Cristobal de las Casas, Mexico (Fabrega 1977a; 1977b). Interviews with female heads of household (five contacts during a one-year period) focused on actual occurrences of illness. Comparisons of two very distinct social-ethnic groups revealed important differences in perceived symptom and illness levels, as well as in the ultimate medical actions taken. However, the disparity between the illness indicators employed in the study (subjective reports of the frequency and duration of illness, and perceptions of frequency of physiological symptoms and amount of interference with work) and Fabrega's theoretical formulation illustrates the difficulties involved in assessing the elements of the nine stages of the model.

Mechanic

In a more recent presentation, Mechanic advances a model of factors affecting the ways in which symptoms "may be differently perceived, evaluated, and acted (or not acted) upon by different kinds of persons" (Mechanic 1962, p. 189). In developing a "general theory of help seeking," and stressing the importance of studying what occurs before an individual sees a health care provider, Mechanic

(1978, p. 268–269) enumerates ten types of variables as determinants of illness behavior: "(1) visibility, recognizability, or perceptual salience of deviant signs and symptoms; (2) the extent to which symptoms are perceived as serious (that is, the person's estimate of the present and future probabilities of danger); (3) the extent to which symptoms disrupt family, work, and other social activities; (4) the frequency of the appearance of deviant signs or symptoms, their persistence, or their frequency or recurrence; (5) the tolerance thresholds of those who are exposed to and evaluate the deviant signs and symptoms; (6) available information, knowledge, and cultural assumptions and understandings of the evaluator; (7) basic needs that lead to denial; (8) needs competing with illness responses; (9) competing possible interpretations that can be assigned to the symptoms once they are recognized; and (10) availability of treatment resources, physical proximity, and psychological and monetary costs of taking action (included are not only physical distance and costs of time, money, and effort, but also such costs as stigma, social distance, and feelings of humiliation)."

The variables are identified as "help-seeking" influences from the perspective of the patient, and Mechanic cautions that an individual's recognition of symptoms may not necessarily be correlated with their seriousness from a medical perspective. Variables "2," "3," "9," and "10" bear a close resemblance to the basic elements of the HBM; however, Mechanic goes well beyond that formulation by emphasizing the critical roles of symptoms (their salience, frequency, and persistence) and evaluators (their knowledge and discomfort levels, cultural backgrounds, and reality processes).

In discussing each of the factors through which symptoms are recognized and help-seeking is initiated, Mechanic distinguishes between "other-defined" and "self-defined" illness. Both situations involve the influences of lay referral systems and family pressures; they differ in that, with "other-defined" conditions, the definition of illness originates from others in the environment; the sick individual tends to resist the evaluation, and may have to be brought into treatment involuntarily. "Other-defined" illness frequently occurs with psychotic conditions, and also includes illnesses of children and adult physical conditions accompanied by denial of symptoms and/or the need for care. Mechanic (1968, 138–39) maintains that "the variables affecting definitions of a condition by the person himself or others in his social group are surprisingly similar, and that these variables equally pertain to the area of physical illness and to the mental disorders." Moreover, some of the help-seeking influences are viewed as interdependent, while others remain independent. Although systematic identification and discussion of the many possible relationships among the ten variables is not presented, illustrative examples are provided of the effects of persistent and frequent physical pain influencing perceptions of the seriousness of the pain, the ensuing disruption of activities, and the lowering of the individual's tolerance of the symptom (Mechanic 1968), and of the way in which, for a socially deviant behavior, perceived seriousness may (over time) come to overshadow perceived stigma (Mechanic 1978).

Andersen

A widely used conceptual approach in large-scale surveys of use of physician services is a behavioral model of health-services utilization developed by Andersen

(1968) and subsequently expanded by Andersen and colleagues (Andersen and Newman 1973; Aday and Andersen 1974; and Andersen et al. 1975). The original framework presented a sequence of individual determinants of health-services utilization by the family and stated that use is dependent upon: (1) the predisposition of the family to use services; (2) their ability to secure services; and (3) their need for such services (Andersen 1968). Each of the three components includes several dimensions or "subcomponents" which provide the theoretical and operational definitions of the model.

The "predisposing" component of the model includes family characteristics existing prior to the onset of illness which result in differences in propensity to use health services, including: demographic variables (e.g., age, sex, marital status); social structure variables (e.g., education and occupation of the family head, ethnicity); and health beliefs and attitudes about medical care, physicians, and disease (including health-related anxiety and stress). These predisposing variables are not seen as directly responsible for use of health services but rather as determinants of variation in "inclination" toward use; thus, Andersen suggests that patterns of utilization are affected by individuals in various age groups having different types and amounts of illness, by families with different social-structural characteristics having different life-styles (in terms of physical and social environment and behavior patterns), and by variations of belief in the efficacy of medical care (i.e., families with relatively stronger belief in the efficacy of medical treatment might seek care sooner and use more services).

The second model component refers to conditions which permit the use of health services, or which make them available. Andersen (1968, p. 16) notes that "even though families may be predisposed to use health services, some means must be available for them to do so." "Enabling" conditions include both family resources (e.g., family income and savings, health insurance or other source of third-party coverage, including use of welfare care, and whether or not the family has a regular source of care) and community resources (e.g., availability of health services and health personnel, travel times, waiting times).

When appropriate predisposing and enabling conditions are present, variations in perception of illness (or the probability of its occurrence) and the manner of response to illness (or potential illness) will determine the use of health services. The first subcomponent, perceived "need," is measured by: (1) *subjective* perceptions of illness (including reported disability days, number of symptoms experienced, and self-reported general state of health); and (2) *clinical* evaluation of illness (usually based on the weighing of reported symptoms for probability of need for care by age group) (Andersen and Newman 1973). Finally, reaction to illness is measured by pattern of seeing a doctor for symptoms (on a continuum from "doctor not seen for any symptoms" to "doctor seen for all symptoms") and by receipt of regular physical examinations.

In specifying hypotheses generated by the model, Andersen (1968, p. 19) states that "the amount of health services used by a family will be a function of the predisposing and enabling characteristics of the family and its need for medical care." The components of the model are hypothesized to contribute independently to the understanding of differential utilization of health services—and need, which represents factors most directly related to use, is expected to be more important than either predisposing or enabling components.

The model has been employed with varying degrees of explanatory success in several surveys of large national samples. In Andersen's (1968) original study, based on a 1964 national survey of 2,367 families, the model explains 43 percent of the variance in use of health services. Review of the relative contributions of predisposing, enabling and need components shows that:

1. Family size (15 percent) accounted for almost all the variance explained by predisposing factors, only a very small contribution was made by social structural variables, and health beliefs did not account for any of the difference in use.
2. Enabling conditions shown to influence use were health insurance (2 percent), use of welfare care (1 percent) and regular source of care (3 percent).
3. Need accounted for the greatest amount of variance (20 percent), with perceptions of illness (operationalized as disability days) the strongest contributor in this category (accounting for 14 percent of the variance).

Subsequent trials of the model were conducted in two national studies of determinants of health behavior, fielded in 1971 (Andersen et al. 1975) and in late 1975 through early 1976 (Andersen and Aday 1978). In the 1971 study of 3,880 families comprising 11,822 individuals, need variables were the most powerful predictors, accounting for 16 percent of the variance in physician contacts and 23 percent of the volume of physician visits. In the case of physician contacts, three indicators of perceptions of illness (disability days, number of symptoms experienced, and worry about health) accounted for 14 percent of the variance, and all but a negligible amount of the resulting variance in volume of physicians visits was due to both perceptions of illness (9 percent) and clinical evaluation of illness (11 percent). The second survey, based on a probability sample of 7,787 individuals, substantiated the findings of the previous studies concerning relationships of the predictive components of the model to physician utilization: the 22 percent of the variance explained by the model resulted mainly from perceptions of illness, with self-reported general state of health and number of symptoms experienced yielding standarized partial regression coefficients of .19 and .32, respectively.

Despite the prevailing concern about equal access to the medical-care system for all population subgroups, and the numerous programs designed to equalize such access, Aday and Andersen (1974) note that systematic conceptual and empirical definitions of "access" have not been developed. In response, an expanded formulation of Andersen's (1968) original framework was developed which considers the health-care system and the characteristics of the population at risk as indicators of the availability and utilization of health services for different population subgroups.

This systems model contains the process and outcome components of access; the former are characteristics of the population at risk, and of the delivery system, that affect both entry into the system and subsequent consumer satisfaction, while the latter components are utilization levels and consumer satisfaction. In addition, the model designates health policy (i.e., financing, education, manpower and health-care reorganization programs) as the starting point for considering access. Indicators of each of the process components vary in their ability to be modified by health policy; indicators which can be manipulated by health policy (e.g., medical manpower distribution, insurance coverage, ease of getting to care, general health-care beliefs and attitudes, knowledge and sources of health-care information) are described as "mutable" and are viewed as more significant indicators of the access concept than those indicators that cannot be altered by policy (e.g., age, sex, race) but which play an important role in defining the subgroups or target populations experiencing differential access and at whom policy should be directed.

The health-care delivery system includes both volume/distribution of resources (i.e., labor and capital designated for health care) and the means of entry to and structure of the organization. In the second process component (characteristics of the population at risk), Aday and Andersen (1974) incorporate the three basic components of Andersen's earlier model (i.e., predisposing, enabling and need factors). Indicators of predisposing and enabling factors also vary in terms of their potential modifiability by health policy. Mutable indicators of predisposing factors are the individual's health beliefs and attitudes about medical care, physicians, and diseases (including health-related anxiety and stress), while demographic variables and social structure variables are immutable. Mutable indicators of enabling factors include both family resources (such as income, health insurance coverage, and regular source of care) and community resources (such as availability of and ease of getting care), while the urban-rural nature of the community is immutable.

Outcome components serve as measures of the predictive validity of the indicators of access for the health-care delivery system and population at risk. Utilization of health services involves the type, site, purpose, and time interval of care, and outcome indicators of access are measures of the level and patterns of use. The second outcome component, consumer satisfaction, reflects consumer attitudes toward the medical-care system based on their system-related experiences. Such factors as convenience, cost, courtesy, and perceptions of the quality of care are indicators of consumer satisfaction.

Aday and Andersen propose that health policy indirectly affects utilization and consumer satisfaction through the two process components, and that characteristics of the health-care delivery system influence characteristics of the population at risk, utilization, and consumer satisfaction. Finally, characteristics of the population may directly affect use and satisfaction independent of features of the health delivery system. For example, a financing program may increase the volume of services available for a particular health condition and change an individual's insurance coverage to include payment for such services, thus influencing a mutable indicator of enabling factors. A corresponding education program for the same condition may alter an individual's knowledge about the condition, availability of services, and beliefs in the effectiveness of the service for the condition, and thereby affect mutable indicators of predisposing factors. In turn, these characteristics directly influence consumer satisfaction and utilization of services.

Although the systems approach provides a comprehensive model for considering the influence of access, the components have not yet been evaluated together as an explanation for access or utilization. A number of studies have focused on the influence of enabling and predisposing conditions, and the recent work of Dutton (1978) presents empirical evidence for remedying the various barriers and structural impediments of health-care systems in addition to eliminating enabling constraints and inadequate levels of predispositions to use health services in order to improve utilization.

Anderson and Bartkus

Another model of health-services utilization, incorporating elements from various theoretical frameworks (including those of Suchman [1965] and Andersen [1968]), was formulated to account specifically for choice of alternative health services following the decision to seek professional help. Anderson and Bartkus (1973) studied the extent to which students used outside care in lieu of university health services available through prepaid student fees; their interest in this population was based on the premise that students' decisions to use outside private care are similar to decisions made in the selection of alternative care by members of other prepaid medical programs (use of sources of care outside the university health center would result in greater demands on the community health system). Factors found in previous research to account for variations in utilization of services are combined in a model subsequently tested for its utility in predicting differential patterns of utilization of a university student health center.

The model attempts to link sociodemographic characteristics to need, economic, ecological, and social-psychological variables, and includes the following dimensions: (1) the individual's appraisal of the adequacy of health care provided by various sources; (2) perception of friends' appraisal of alternative care sources; (3) perception of medical symptoms, and orientation toward action in response to symptoms; (4) perception of need for health care; (5) economic factors (e.g., income, health insurance); (6) availability of health services (i.e., "access"); (7) sociodemographic factors; (8) symptom sensitivity (ability/propensity to recognize symptoms); and (9) organization of health care.

In their study, Anderson and Bartkus identify student perceptions of the health center and appraisals of other students concerning the health facility, and symptom perception and response to health problems, as determinants of utilization. Need for medical care was measured by designating disease categories and resultant need for hospitalization, physician care, diagnostic services, medicine, and other care. Economic factors were operationalized as ability to pay for health services (i.e., whether the student has health insurance in addition to the prepaid fee to the university health service). An ecological measure of the availability of health services involved the university health service being judged as less available to those students living off campus and located farther from the health center. Finally, sociodemographic factors thought to affect differences in health behavior were included in the study: a composite socioeconomic status score (Green 1970) based on weightings for education, income and occupational status; age; sex; marital status of the student; and presence of a regular family physician prior to attending the university.

When the model was applied to data from a random sample of students enrolled in a university health plan, medical need and additional insurance coverage for services not included in the basic student fee (e.g., hospitalization, extensive diagnostic services, and referral to outside specialists) were related to greater use of the university facilities. Social-psychological factors, friends' positive evaluations of services ("lay referral system") which affected the student's own view of these services, and increased symptom sensitivity, resulted in a higher probability that male students with health problems requiring medical attention would use the campus medical center, while female students tended to use outside medical services to a greater extent.

Increased medical need and the pressure of health insurance (in addition to the basic student plan) were directly related to student use of campus health services (as opposed to private physicians), the latter relationship suggesting that financial barriers are important when comprehensive coverage is not provided by a prepaid plan. Sociodemographic and ecological factors are seen as influencing utilization indirectly, through their influence on intervening social-psychological variables. Increased age was associated with decreased utilization through influences on economic, ecological, and social-psychological variables; older students were less likely to have additional health insurance, which resulted in lower use of the university health service; they were more likely to live off campus, and to perceive the attitudes of their friends toward the university health service as more negative. Different social-psychological processes intervene between marital status and utilization for females and males; increased utilization by married females was influenced by perceptions of their friends as having positive attitudes toward the university health service, and increased utilization by married males was influenced by increased symptom sensitivity.

Kosa and Robertson

Another attempt to understand health and illness behaviors from both the individual and social-context perspective is the model developed by Kosa and Robertson (1975). This formulation includes four major components: (1) assessment of a disturbance in (or a threat to) usual health and functioning: (2) arousal of anxiety by the perception of symptoms; (3) application of one's medical knowledge; and (4) performance of actions for removing anxiety and the disturbance. Thus (in common with Mechanic's model), behavior is motivated largely by the individual's basic psychological need to reduce the anxiety caused by the threat of illness.

Two classes of anxiety are described: "floating" anxiety, a kind of general anxiety "usually present in the psychological makeup of every person," and "preexistent to, and independent from, the morbid episode"; and "specific" anxiety, evoked as a psychological response to the expectation/experience of fever or pain, which "tends to be proportionate to the seriousness of the symptom or threat" (Kosa and Robertson 1975, p. 59). This model also makes a notable contribution to the study of health behaviors by distinguishing between actions on the basis of their goal orientation. "Therapeutic" manipulations are interventions which are rationally based and planned, and which are directed at the cessation or removal of a particular health disturbance and its concomitant anxiety-arousal. By contrast, "gratificatory" manipulations involve nonrational behaviors whose goal is something other than curing the health disturbances: "It may aim at a relief of the anxiety without arresting the underlying disturbances, or at the gratification of wishes and needs not directly related to the morbid episode" (Kosa and Robertson 1975, p. 65). Examples of gratificatory health behaviors might include the avoidance of threatening or painful therapy, or an unwillingness to cease a pleasurable activity deleterious to health (including situations in mental and psychosomatic illness where the patient wishes to perpetuate the symptom/s for reasons of pleasure and/or manipulation of others).

The framework is, then, a process model, with stages organized around the illness episode as a unit. Every state of the model is influenced by culture, situation, and interaction patterns in primary (i.e., the family) and secondary (the system of professional health care) groups. A special contribution of this approach is its focus on the degree to which health-related behavior depends upon psychological and social-interaction processes.

Antonovsky and Kats

In attempting to account for preventive health behavior, Antonovsky and Kats (1970) present an integrative model which purports to categorize different types of variables involved in specific actions or patterns of actions, and to specify linkages among these variables. Three classes of variables are identified as determinants of preventive (dental) health behavior (PDB) (including both one-time and repetitive actions): (1) predisposing motivation; (2) blockage variables; and (3) conditioning variables. As will be seen, these variables bear close resemblance to the main elements of Andersen's model as well as to the HBM.

"Predisposing motivation" constitutes the core of the model, as all behavior is viewed as motivated (i.e., goal-directed). Three types of mutually reinforcing goals related to PDB are assumed to be present to varying degrees in all people: (1) enhancement of health or avoidance of ill health; (2) achievement of approval by significant others; and (3) achievement of self-approval. Although variation in the salience of the three types of goals determines the individual's predisposing motivation, the presence of high motivation toward one or more of the goals does not assure that the recommended action will be undertaken. If the individual is motivated in terms of enhancing health or avoiding ill health, the action must be perceived as beneficial in achieving this goal; if the motivating intention is obtaining the approval of significant others or self-approval, then the action must be linked to group or self-approval. It is important that the individual acknowledge a *link* between the behavior and one of the goals. If a relationship is recognized, the individual is considered to be "effectively motivated."

"Blockage variables" permit or prevent the motivated individual from undertaking the health behavior. Blockage can occur both internally, such as lack of knowledge about the behavior or fear of the action (e.g., anxiety about pain involved in dental work), and externally, in terms of perceived lack of available resources (e.g., time, money, practitioners).

Finally, "conditioning variables" are assumed to modify ("condition") the motivating and blockage variables. Antonovsky and Kats (1970, p. 369) provide examples of the conditioning function: . . . "feeling susceptible to ill health is likely to intensify the salience of the goal of avoiding ill health. A high education level is likely to minimize the lack of knowledge block." Other conditioning variables might include prior health-related experiences and socioeconomic status. The model does not propose any necessary sequence among the three variables, but suggests that the predictor variables—effective motivation and blockage—are interactive, and also that they interact with the conditioning variables, each variable making an independent contribution to preventive health behavior and each having an influence on the others.

The model was tested for ability to predict the PDB of employees (N = 384) and their dependents (N = 200) at Hadassah Medical Organization in Jerusalem. The employees were stratified into five occupational groups, and each group was sampled to provide approximately seventy-five respondents. PDB was found to vary by social class and occupation, with doctors most prevention oriented, then nurses, and manual laborers least prevention oriented.

The study employed a single measure of predisposing motivation, the "salience" of dental health as a goal (salience was operationalized as the individual's willingness to spend a lot on health action, and the amount of discussion about health problems with friends and relatives). While salience was found to be related to PDB (among subjects exhibiting high levels of PDB, 40 percent of subjects were in the high salience group; 23 to 29 percent were in the intermediate salience group, and only 6 percent were in the low salience group), it did not account for a major part of the variance. Although a linear relationship did not appear between perceived benefits of PDB and actual behavior, subjects categorized as high on perceived benefits were most likely to engage in more PDB. Measures of internal blockage (i.e., knowledge and anxiety) and external blockage (i.e., financial difficulty) were also associated with PDB: (1) a minimum amount of knowledge was sufficient to enable PDB; (2) an inverse linear relationship obtained between anxiety and PDB; and (3) a weak, statistically significant association was found between perceptions of difficulty in paying for dental treatment and PDB.

Dependents formed a second group for the analyses. The relationships among salience, benefits of PDB, and knowledge were not as consistent for dependents as were the findings for employees. Almost half of the dependent sample consisted of dependent children rather than wives or parents of the employees. Within the framework proposed by Antonovsky and Kats, independent attitudes of the children were assessed, while a possibly significant intervening variable, the influence of parental authority in determining the health behavior of children, was not measured in the study.

In summary, each of the model variables appeared to make an independent contribution to PDB, although the associations were limited in strength and consistency. Analyses of the joint influence of variables in association with each other revealed that combining the variables increases predictive power.

Langlie

The preponderance of research aimed at discovering the determinants of (preventive) health behavior (PHB) has focused upon individuals' sociodemographic (e.g., Andersen) and sociopsychological (e.g., the HBM) characteristics. However, some studies approached PHB by concentrating on influences from various aspects of the individual's social milieu (e.g., Suchman). Langlie (1977) proposes a model of PHB that includes *both* the social-psychological variables of the HBM and the social-group characteristics of Suchman's formulation.

Before proceeding, it should be noted that this particular Suchman model (which Langlie terms the Social Network Model) was specifically directed toward explaining *illness* behavior (Rosenstock and Kirscht 1979); Suchman had proposed a separate model to explain *preventive* health behavior (Suchman 1967), which included the major components of the Health Belief Model. However, Langlie's adaptation of Suchman's work on illness behavior to preventive health behavior is sufficiently innovative to warrant separate consideration. First, preventive health behavior (PHB) is defined by Langlie as "any medically recommended action, voluntarily undertaken by a person who believes himself to be healthy, that tends to prevent disease or disability and/or detect disease in an asymptomatic state" (Langlie 1977, p. 247). She measures health beliefs by scales that tap "perceived vulnerability," "perceived benefits of PHB," "perceived barriers/costs of PHB," and three modifying variables ("saliency" of health, "perceptions of control" over health matters, and "attitudes towards providers of health services.") She measures social network variables by "family SES," "neighborhood SES," "kin interaction," "non-kin interaction," "conjugal structure," and "religious affiliation."

Before attempting to assess the explanatory value of the health beliefs and the social network variables in accounting for PHB, Langlie employs factor analysis to group eleven preventive health behaviors into two categories, one called Direct Risk and the other labeled Indirect Risk. Direct Risk PHB contains measures of four preventive behaviors classified as having "a direct potential for producing injury or disease": reckless driving and pedestrian behavior, poor personal hygiene, and smoking behavior. Indirect Risk PHB is measured by responses to seven items representing behaviors considered to be discursively hazardous to the individual failing to undertake these medically recommended actions: seat-belt use, exercise, nutrition behavior, medical checkups, dental care, immunizations, and miscellaneous screening examinations. Respondents were also identified as "behaviorally consistent" or "behaviorally inconsistent" on the basis of their overall scores on the eleven PHB items. Subjects were designated as "consistent" when scores on eight or more of the eleven behaviors were either above or below the mean for their gender or within one standard deviation of the mean, and as "inconsistent" when the scores were equally distributed above and below the mean or when a score was missing for more than one of the items. Study analyses were carried out to reflect the two-dimensional aspect of PHB and variations in the consistency of the indicator behaviors.

A survey of a systematic random sample of adults in Rockford, Illinois, yielded 383 respondents for the self-administered questionnaire (a response rate of 62 percent).

The interested reader should consult Langlie's article for details of the findings. For present purposes, it is sufficient to indicate that both health beliefs and social network variables help to explain various aspects of PHB, and that the two sets of variables taken together explain still more of the variance in PHB. As Langlie (1977, p. 254) summarizes, "since a substantial proportion of the variation in Indirect Risk PHB is accounted for by the *joint* effects of social-psychological and social-group characteristics, failure to include both in studies of PHB may distort the interpretation of the findings by attributing all of the explained variance to only one of the models." The explanation of Direct Risk PHB is somewhat more complex; while health beliefs and social network variables account for some of the variance, more is accounted for by age and sex (appropriate behaviors are associated with older age and female gender).

Langlie proposes a framework that combines health beliefs and social network factors into a causal model to account for adults' PHB. Some seventeen hypotheses are entered into this causal model, some of which are generated by Langlie or other investigators and supported by prior data, while others represent agendas for future research. The major variables in the model include the effects on PHB of socioeconomic status, parental relationships with kin and nonkin, locus of control, attitudes toward providers, and degree of cosmopolitaness. Langlie also attempts to explain the different causal sequences involved in Direct versus Indirect Risk behaviors.

Implicit in the proposed model is the placing of greater weight on social network factors than on health beliefs. Langlie (1977, p. 257) argues that "it makes no sense to think of [the HBM variables] as 'causes' of Social Network properties, but the reverse is plausible." Other social network factors, however, might well be influenced by beliefs (e.g., types and frequency of kin interaction). Moreover, while beliefs about one's vulnerability to disease can hardly "cause" socioeconomic status, it is not clear why socioeconomic status is regarded as a reasonable "cause" of beliefs about vulnerability to disease. Finally, it is possible that some beliefs and social network factors are spuriously related. For example, some third factor may cause both more frequent contacts with nonkin groups and beliefs about disease vulnerability.

The validity of Langlie's causal hypotheses is an empirical matter that is clearly worthy of further study; she is certainly to be commended for showing how social network and social-psychological characteristics may be *combined* to produce better explanations of PHB than either approach could accomplish separately. Her work is also noteworthy for making useful distinctions between different kinds of preventive health behavior.

Recent Approaches

A number of authors have, in recent years, advanced the understanding of health behaviors by modifying one or more of the traditional models and /or by placing the behaviors in a different context. For example, Green (1975) suggests that the undertaking of a health-related behavior constitutes the adoption of an innovation, and thus the behavior can be examined within the perspective of the rich literature on diffusion of innovations, which emphasizes characteristics of the adoptors, the innovation, and the setting in which adoption occurs (Becker 1970). The diffusion and adoption model includes three categories of factors that influence the acceptance of health practices: (1) environmental or system factors such as socioeconomic strata and social norms; (2) characteristics of the adoptor, such as contact and communications with individuals within and outside one's own social stratum and participation in social groups; and (3) characteristics of the innovation such as its relative advantages compared to other options, its compatability with existing values, its complexity, the degree to which it can be "tried out," and its observability by others. Such a model places great emphasis on the importance, in adopting a health behavior, of interpersonal interaction, social influences, and features of the particular health action to be undertaken.

In an approach directed at illustrating misinterpretations of utilization data due to the exclusion of important variables, Hershey and colleagues (1975) propose a model that combines multiple measures of utilization and an expanded set of independent variables. The central study hypothesis is that different independent variables will exhibit varying importance in predicting different types of utilization behavior (categorized as total office visits and hospital inpatient nights, patient-initiated [as distinct from physician-initiated] visits, and visits for physical checkups).

Data from interviews with a 10 percent simple random sample of 315 families (1,065 individuals) in the San Joaquin Valley of California are analyzed by regression equations for each type of utilization behavior. Independent variables measuring need (i.e., "health status") and presence of a usual source of care appear to be influential in determining all types of utilization. The coefficients for health status are more strongly related to the study's aggregate measures of total utilization (i.e., total number of physician visits and the sum of all physician visits and hospital inpatient nights) and to patient-initiated physician visits than to the study's measures of "access" to the medical system (i.e., whether a physician has been seen and whether the individual has had a physical checkup). Education and income were predictive of specific types of utilization, the former for checkups and the latter for patient-initiated physician visits and checkups. None of the attitude measures considered in the study (measures of "self-reliance," "fatalism," and "ethnocentricity") were related to any of the categories of utilization.

Berki and Ashcraft (1979) provide a valuable approach to understanding ambulatory health-service utilization through the disaggregation of the dependent variables into illness and preventive visits. The test of predictors of ambulatory health-service utilization employs variables similar to those included in Andersen's (1968) model:

1. "Need" is measured by reported number of acute and chronic conditions (including their duration, periodicity, degree of interference with usual work and leisure activities, and whether they required physician care or hospitalization) and by the individual's health concern (responses to a scale tapping the salience of the value of health).
2. "Access" is measured by having a usual source of care, identification of the source as either a private physician or a prepaid group health plan, and perceived convenience of the site of care.
3. "Cost" per visit is based on the number of reported physician visits and reported total nonreimbursed expenditures for the visits.

An additional distinction is made in the dependent variable with regard to whether the data are based on utilization averaged over family members or are independent, individual-specific data.

When the disaggregated model is applied to data collected by interviews with 626 families (with a subsample of 560 independent observations of adult members of married families), reported number of chronic and acute conditions, number of hospital days, and having a regular source of care are the strongest predictors in the 47 percent of variance explained in family-member illness visits, and number of chronic and acute conditions, perceived health status and number of hospital days are important in explaining the variance (34 percent) in individual illness visits. The effect of the predictors on family-member preventive visits is small: Neither need variables (as hypothesized) nor cost were predictive, while greater health concern, having a regular source of care, and membership in a prepaid health plan contribute to the variation. The variables yielded a stronger effect on the number of individual preventive visits: The majority of the 30 percent variance explained was attributable to number of acute conditions, health conditions, health concern, perceived health status, membership in a prepaid health plan, and perceived convenience of the site of care.

Finally, Young (1980) has constructed a model of choice-of-treatment behavior which is a cross-cultural adaptation of the Health Belief Model aimed at explaining treatment decision-making. Young's formulation includes four major elements:

1. "Gravity," which is the level of perceived severity of the illness *held by the individual's reference group* (this assumes that there exists, prior to onset of illness, some group consensus about the relative and/or absolute level of seriousness of various illnesses).

2. "Knowledge of a home remedy," derived from the lay referral system (if such a remedy is unknown, or if it is tried and found to be ineffective, the individual is then likely to turn to the professional referral system).
3. "Faith," or level of belief in the efficacy of different treatment options (especially folk remedies).
4. "Accessibility," the costs and availability of health services (similar to "perceived barriers" in the HBM, and to "enabling" factors in the Andersen model).

In a study conducted in a small Mexican community, Young was able to use this model to predict accurately 287 of 300 treatment choices.

A Unified Conceptual Framework

The models described differ considerably in their theoretical perspectives, in the types of health behavior they attempt to explain, and in the terms employed to label their respective dimensions and variables. Moreover, each formulation contains some variables whose explanatory/predictive value have not been supported empirically, and each omits significant variables acknowledged and examined in the other models. Finally, many investigators, noting an at least superifical similarity across the classes of factors included in the models, have felt that the actual number of truly distinct concepts relevant to explaining health-related behaviors is probably far smaller than the large number of variables which have been advanced in these models (Becker et al. 1977).

These considerations provide impetus to the development of a single, unified framework which might serve as a basis for further research on the determinants of health behavior. However, while the variables could be placed into a limited number of conceptual groupings solely on a "face validity" basis, it might be argued that the creators of the models would be aware of more subtle aspects and distinctions which, if made explicit, would require that these like appearing variables *not* be viewed as highly comparable. (Such an approach also constitutes a conservative test of intermodel comparability, since one would expect each model builder to wish to preserve what he/she felt to represent the unique characteristics and contributions of his/her model.) Thus, any attempt to reduce this great multiplicity of concepts and variables should be based upon data obtained from the various model builders themselves.

Such a project was, in fact, conducted in 1979 (Cummings et al. 1980). Eight of the eleven living (in the United States) authors of the various models described in this chapter agreed to serve as judges, comparing each of 109 variables extracted from the models and placing them into categories on the basis of their similarity. The name and definition (as they appeared in publications) of each variable were presented to the judges on individual cards in order to simplify the sorting task. A method of nonmetric multidimensional scaling, Smallest Space Analysis, employed aggregation, across judges, of the number of times a pair of variables was grouped together to approach, iteratively, that configuration of points in multidimensional space which best represents, simultaneously, all pairwise relations among variables. Thus, variables which were grouped together frequently (suggesting that they tap the same concept or highly related ones) are placed close to one another, and variables that are independent are placed far apart. Ultimately, ten of the rated variables were excluded from the analyses because they were classified as "miscellaneous" by five of the eight judges. The remaining 99 variables are presented in the Appendix, and the resultant spatial configuration yielded by the Smallest Space Analysis is displayed in Figure 25.1.

The variables appear to be arrayed in six distinct categories, and a label was assigned to each category in an attempt to represent the variables contained therein. These categories include the following clusters of variables: "perception of illness" and "threat of disease" variables located in the upper left portion of the figure, "knowledge of disease" variables located in the center, "social network" variables located in the upper right portion, "demographic" variables located to the right of center, "access to health care" variables located in the lower right portion, and "attitude toward health care" variables located in the lower left portion of the figure. Moreover, within several of these larger groupings there exist subclusters of items which help to define further the meanings of the underlying categories. For example, the cluster of "accessibility" variables can be subdivided into two distinct groups: (1) items on the financial costs of health care (v65,v81, v89) and (2) items on the availability of health services (v9,v26,v82). Similarly, the variables comprising the social network cluster can be further subdivided into three meaningful groups: (1) items dealing with social interaction patterns (v37,v95,v96,v98); (2) items on social structural characteristics (v16,v17,v18,v25, v38,v70,v72,v73); and (3) items pertaining to social norms (v57,v94). Finally, the variables included in the "health threat" cluster can be subdivided into two groups: (1) items on perception and evaluation of symptoms (v1,v2,v30,v31,v50, v55,v80,v90,v91) and (2) items on response to illness (v5,v7,v47,v48,v49).

The analyses revealed several items which did not fall into the six categories of variables just identified. With respect to the first two axes of the figure (i.e., the vertical and horizontal dimensions), it is apparent that the items dealing with support from friends and family (v13,v29,v68,v77,v85) are scattered about the right-center portion of the structure; however, they are highly related in the third dimension. Items pertaining to knowledge about health services (v14,v15) are located midway between the cluster of knowledge of disease variables and the cluster of access to health service variables in both the second and the third dimensions. On the third dimension (which runs "in front of" to "in back of" the plane of the figure), the locus of control (v35), cues to action (v36), need for medical care (v79), effective motivation (v86), and anxiety (v88) items are located outside and well back from the "evaluation" category, and general motivation (v34) and belief in value of good health (v60) items are located within the category but modestly back, while the competing needs item (v8) is located slightly in front of the other evaluation of health care variables. Items which remain substantially independent of other items in the figure include disruption of social activities (v3), sources of information (v19), topics on which information is sought (v20), past experience with illness and/or health action (v24), avoidance of ill health (v84), and compatability of an action with existing values (v99). Failure of these items to cluster with other items in the figure relfects disagreement among judges on where to categorize these variables.

The distance between clusters provides an indication of the degree of association obtained between categories of variables. For example, the knowledge of disease items are located more closely to items pertaining to perception and evaluation of symptoms than to items on access to health care. Items on evaluation of

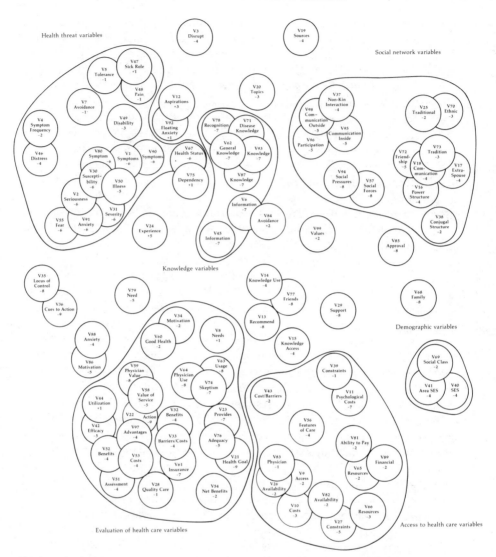

Figure 25.1 Three-Dimensional Structure of 99 Correlates of Individual Health-Related Behaviors

Note: Signed numbers indicate the position of the variable on the third dimension.

health care are located more closely to items on access to health care than to items dealing with social interactions, social structure, or social norms. Demographic variables are associated most closely with the accessibility items and are quite distinct from the cluster of variables dealing with perception of illness.

The basic similarities identified among the variables contained in the different models examined are important to the advancement of research on understanding individual health-related behaviors. Clearly, the models are far from independent; despite differences in the labeling and defining of variables contained in the different frameworks, there is considerable overlap, *as judged by the model builders themselves.* The results of combining the variables from the different models provide a more complete representation of the factors thought to influence health actions.

The set of major variable categories that emerged from these analyses (Cummings et al. 1980) includes: (1) items pertaining to *accessibility of health services*, such as the individual's ability to pay for health care and awareness of health services, and availability of health services; (2) items dealing with the individual's *attitudes toward health care*, such as beliefs in the benefits of treatment and beliefs about the quality of medical care provided; (3) items concerning the *threat of illness*, such as the individual's perception of symptoms and beliefs about susceptibility to, and consequences of, disease; (4) items pertaining to *knowledge about disease*; (5) items dealing with the individual's *social interactions, social norms, and social structure*; and (6) items on *demographic characteristics* (social status, income, and education).

Finally, the spatial representation of items provided information on the association between clusters of variables in three dimensions. The items pertaining to knowledge of disease were located in close proximity to the items dealing with perception and evaluation of symptoms and the items on social interactions. Although the specific causal linkages are unknown, one might reasonably speculate that knowledge about disease is exchanged through one's social interactions, and that this information is used in making judgments about symptoms and the threat of disease. Similarly, the close proximity of items dealing with the individual's attitudes toward health care and items on accessibility to health services suggests a relationship in which access factors affect and/or are affected by one's evaluation of health care. The close proximity between demographic variables and access to health service variables suggests a relationship in which accessibility is a function of an individual's social class (such a relationship has, of course, been frequently documented [McKinlay 1972; Anderson and Bartkus 1973; Anderson 1973]).

According to Leventhal (1978), models serve two functions: (1) to focus attention on certain factors while leading us to ignore others, usually factors that do not fit the model, and (2) to make predictions about what should happen in specific settings under certain conditions. This chapter has reviewed the elements of important extant models of health behavior and has attempted to lay the groundwork for further model construction and testing by presenting a general unified framework for describing such behavior. Further investigation is essential to (1) assess the value of this conceptualization in understanding different health behaviors in various populations and settings and (2) test, through the use of causal models, the processes and interrelationships among factors and variables which are implied by the various theories of health behavior.

Appendix. Model Variables and Their Definitions

1. Perceptual salience of symptoms—Perceived importance of symptoms.
2. Perceived seriousness of symptoms—Estimates of present and future probabilities of danger associated with symptoms.
3. Extent to which symptoms disrupt social activities—Symptoms which cause inconvenience, social difficulties, pain, and annoyance.
4. Frequency of occurrence and persistence of symptoms—Frequent and persistent symptoms are more likely to influence a person to seek help than occasional or recurring symptoms.

5. Tolerance threshold regarding deviant signs and symptoms—Person's tolerance for pain and discomfort and his values about stoicism and independence affect response to symptoms.

6. Available information, knowledge, and cultural assumptions—The sophistication of patients about medical matters varies from those who are aware of the latest therapeutic developments to those who hold very naive notions about bodily functioning.

7. Perceptual need which leads to avoidance—Extent to which denial tendencies, in part motivated by psychological need to maintain the situation under control, influence the recognition of symptoms and delay in seeking care.

8. Need competing with illness response—Behavior takes place within a context where motives are frequently competing or are in conflict.

9. Availability of treatment resources—Distance to health service, convenience, availability of particular practitioner.

10. Monetary costs of taking action—Financial costs associated with taking a particular health action.

11. Psychological costs of taking action—Acceptability of facilities, embarrassment or shame associated with taking action, cultural expectations, anticipation of humiliation resulting from treatment, degree of stigma or social threat implied in using service.

12. Aspiration for self—Individual's level of striving and aspirations for the future.

13. Willingness to recommend behavior to others—individual's willingness to recommend health action to family and friends.

14. Knowledge concerning health action—Awareness and understanding of health action, such as a particular method.

15. Knowledge of the availability of health service—Awareness of available health facilities which provide particular kinds of health service.

16. Conjugal power structure—Amount of influence assumed in family decision by either the husband or wife.

17. Extra-spouse communication—Extent to which the individual discusses specific problems with people other than his/her spouse.

18. Conjugal communication—Amount of discussion between husband and wife on specific issues such as expenditures, politics, and use of health services.

19. Sources of information—Individual's sources of information on different issues (e.g., interpersonal sources—friends and relatives; nonpersonal sources—mass media).

20. Topics on which information is sought—Types of information a person seeks out most frequently.

21. Attitudes toward health-related goal—Perception of norms associated with a particular health action.

22. Attitudes toward health action—Intention to take health action.

23. Attitudes toward providers of care—Perceptions concerning providers of care such as helpfulness and caring.

24. Past experience—Past experience with illness and/or health action.

25. Traditional/modern—Participation in social groups, use of modern technology.

26. Availability of health services—Perceived access to care.

27. Situational constraints—Factors which intervene between intention to take health action and behavior.
28. Quality of care—Satisfaction with health care received in the past.
29. Social support—Perceived approval of health action by spouse, other relatives and friends.
30. Perceived susceptibility—Individual's belief regarding the likelihood of a particular condition occurring.
31. Perceived severity—Individual's belief that the occurrence of a condition would have a moderately serious impact on life.
32. Perceived benefits—Individual's belief that there are actions which would be beneficial in reducing his susceptibility to and/or severity of the condition should it occur.
33. Perceived barriers/costs—individual's belief concerning the costs associated with taking a health action.
34. General health motivation—Individual's concern for health matters in general.
35. Internal/external locus of control—Individual's perception of his control over both personal health matters and life in general.
36. Cues to action—Stimulus or cue which may be internal or external to the individual which triggers appropriate health behavior.
37. Nonkin interaction—Frequency with which an individual interacts with people who live outside one's immediate residential area.
38. Conjugal structure—Sex role differentiation and influence in family decision-making.
39. Situation constraints—Number of dependents in a household and the number of instrumental tasks involving the respondent.
40. Socioeconomic status—Combined measure of the individual's educational level and family income.
41. Neighborhood socioeconomic status—Score reflecting socioeconomic status assigned to census tract where individual resides.
42. Perceived efficacy—Probability that health action will lead to the desired outcome.
43. Costs/Barriers—Unpleasantness or cost of taking the health action compared with taking no action and suffering the consequences.
44. Past utilization of medical services—Past use of health services in general.
45. Factual information—Information concerning the health action and health condition in question (e.g., danger of the disease, knowledge of the prescribed medical regimen).
46. Psychological distress—Feelings of distress and discomfort arising from the identification of symptoms.
47. Self-accepted—Willingness to adopt the sick role.
48. Threshold for pain—Individual's perception of pain sensations.
49. Tolerance of disability—Individual's willingness to accept disability associated with illness condition.
50. Illness disvalues—Individual's evaluation of the illness's meaning and/or significance. It is assumed that every illness is associated with a set of undersirable features or components (e.g., presumed danger to life, degree of disability).
51. Assessment of treatment plans—Estimate of the probability that a treatment plan will alleviate a negative component or disvalue of illness.

52. Treatment benefits—Assessment of the potential benefits that can be accrued from various treatment plans. Benefits are assumed to represent the amount of disvalue that is eliminated by a treatment plan.

53. Treatment costs—Estimate of the costs associated with a treatment plan (e.g., time lost from work, monetary costs, loss of personal control).

54. Net benefits or utility—Costs of treatment plan subtracted from the potential benefits of the same treatment plan.

55. Fear—Feelings of fear regarding specific features of the disease (e.g., discomfort, disfiguration) and subsequent consequences of the disease.

56. Features of the sources of care—Cost and location of service, individual's opinion concerning quality of medical care provided.

57. Social factors—Individual's perceptions of the attitudes of friends and relatives concerning a particular health action and knowledge of others past health behaviors.

58. Beliefs concerning the value of health services—Six-item Guttman scale with question on the individual's beliefs about value of home remedies, need for medical aid, assessment of modern medicine, individual's control over health.

59. Beliefs concerning the value of physicians—Five-item Guttman scale with question on the evaluation of care received from doctors, assessment of the status of the medical profession, importance of choosing a doctor, doctors' interest in their incomes.

60. Beliefs concerning the value of good health—Nine-item Guttman scale on the likelihood of making changes in life-style if doctors said it was necessary to protect health (e.g., stop eating favorite foods, get more exercise).

61. Beliefs concerning the value of health insurance—Two-item index including the individual's judgments concerning the value of health insurance which covers expenses only with participating hospitals and doctors and the value of some kind of insurance which covers all medical expenses.

62. Knowledge about disease in general—Ten-item index based on agreement that each of ten symptoms might be early signs associated with disease (e.g., shortness of breath related to heart disease, coughing and spitting up of blood related to tuberculosis).

63. Attitudes concerning the use of different health services—Six-item Guttman scale with questions on the individual's beliefs about when to seek medical care and avoiding seeing a doctor.

64. Attitudes concerning physician use—Six-item Guttman scale with questions on the individual's beliefs about seeing a doctor in the presense of symptoms such as diarrhea, high fever, loss of weight.

65. Family resources—Family's ability to pay for health services.

66. Community resources—Availability of health services, convenience, health education level in the community (e.g., scientific knowledge of medicine as opposed to folk knowledge of medicine).

67. Perception of health status—Individual's perception of physical condition which is considered less than optimal (e.g., recognition of symptoms, disability days).

68. Family composition—Age, sex, and marital status of the head of household, family size, age of the youngest and oldest family member.

69. Social structure—Characteristics of the family's main earners such as employment, social class, occupation, educational level, race and ethnicity.
70. Ethnic exclusivity—Refers to the tendency of an individual to interact with persons with the same ethnic and social background.
71. Knowledge about disease—Understanding of disease etiology, symptoms, and prognosis of various diseases.
72. Friendship solidarity—Refers to the degree to which the individual belongs to a close friendship group(s) of long duration.
73. Orientation to family tradition and authority—Refers to the importance placed on the individual's family upon customs, traditions, and the degree of authority possessed by the head of the household.
74. Skepticism of medical care—Doubts the individual has about the claims of professional medicine and his desire to check on who the doctor is and what he is doing.
75. Dependency in illness—Need of the sick individual to rely upon others for help and support during illness.
76. Appraisal of the adequacy of care provided by various health facilities—Individual's evaluation of different providers of medical care.
77. Perception of friend's appraisal of the adequacy of alternative health services—Individual's perceptions concerning what their friends' think about different health-care providers.
78. Recognition of medical symptoms—Awareness and knowledge about various disease symptoms.
79. Need for medical care—Individual's perceived need for medical advice and/or treatment.
80. Symptom sensitivity—Individual's belief that symptoms are serious enough to require consulting a doctor.
81. Ability to pay for health service—Indicated by whether an individual has health insurance.
82. Availability of health services—Distance an individual is from health-care facilities.
83. Regular family physician—Individual's report of having a regular family doctor.
84. Avoidance of ill-health—Willingness on the part of the individual to spend a lot of money on health care.
85. Approval of friends—Discussion with friends about health care.
86. Effective motivation—Belief that a particular health action would be effective in avoiding illness.
87. Knowledge—Awareness of certain facts about disease.
88. Anxiety—Hesitation about engaging in a health action because of possible pain or discomfort associated with that action.
89. Financial difficulty—Ability to pay for health care.
90. Assessment of symptoms—Difference between the present functioning of health and its previous or usual functioning. Any disturbance must reach a certain degree of seriousness or duration in order to be assessed as a symptom.
91. Specific anxiety—Anxiety aroused as a result of the assessment of specific symptoms.
92. Floating anxiety—Anxiety which is preexistent to , and independent from,

the morbid episode. Anxiety which is a function of psychological and social forces.

93. Pertaining knowledge—General body of knowledge about health; illness and therapy corresponding to the cultural, situational, and interaction patterns in the community.

94. Social pressures—Support in the form of social norms which affects one's decision to adopt certain health practices.

95. Contact and communication within one's own social strata—Amount of contact and/or communication with adopters or nonadopters within one's own social strata.

96. Social participation—Amount of participation with other people through social groups or informal relationships.

97. Relative advantages of action—Individual's judgment regarding the relative merits of a certain action compared to other actions.

98. Contact and communication outside one's own social strata—Amount of contact and/or communication with adopters or nonadopters outside one's own social strata.

99. Compatability with existing values, past experiences, and needs of the individual—Extent to which an action is compatible with the individual's values, past experiences, and needs.

REFERENCES

ADAY L. A., and ANDERSEN R. 1974. A framework for the study of access to medical care. *Health Services Research* 9:208–20.

ANDERSEN, R. 1968. *A behavioral model of families' use of health services.* Chicago: Center for Health Administration Studies, University of Chicago.

———; KRAVITS, J.; and ANDERSEN, O. W., eds. 1975. *Equity in health services: empirical analyses in social policy.* Cambridge, Mass.: Ballinger.

ANDERSEN, R., and NEWMAN, J. F. 1973. Societal and individual determinants of medical care utilization in the United States. *Milbank Memorial Fund Quarterly/Health and Society* 51:95–124.

ANDERSON, J. G. 1973. Demographic factors affecting health services utilization. *Medical Care* 11:104–20.

———, and BARTKUS, D. E. 1973. Choice of medical care: a behavioral model of health and illness behavior. *Journal of Health and Social Behavior* 14:348–62.

ANTONOVSKY, A., and KATS, R. 1970. The model dental patient: an empirical study of preventive health behavior. *Social Science and Medicine* 4:367–79.

BECKER, M. H. 1970. Factors affecting diffusion of innovations among health professionals. *American Journal of Public Health* 60:294–304.

———., ed. 1974. *The health belief model and personal health behavior.* Thorofare, N.J.: Slack Press.

———. 1979. Understanding patient compliance: the contributions of attitudes and other psychosocial factors. In *New directions in patient compliance*, ed. S. J. Cohen, pp. 1–31. Lexington, Mass.: D.C. Heath.

———; HAEFNER, D. P.; KASL, S. V.; KIRSCHT, J. P.; MAIMAN, L. A.; and ROSENSTOCK, I. M. 1977. Selected psychosocial models and correlates of individual health-related behaviors. *Medical Care* 15 (suppl.): 27–46.

Becker, M. H., and Maiman, L. A. 1975. Sociobehavioral determinants of compliance with health and medical care recommendations. *Medical Care* 13:10–24.

———; Kirscht, J. P.; Haefner, D. P.; Drachman, R. H.; and Taylor, D. W. 1979. Patient perceptions and compliance: recent studies of the health belief model. In *Compliance in health care*, ed. R. B. Haynes, D. W. Taylor, and D. L. Sackett, pp. 78–109. Baltimore, Md.: Johns Hopkins University Press.

Berki, S. E.; and Ashcraft, M. L. 1979. On the analysis of ambulatory utilization: an investigation of the roles of need, access and price as predictors of illness and preventive visits. *Medical Care* 17:1163–81.

Coe, R. M., and Wessen, A. 1965. Social-psychological factors influencing the use of community health resources. *American Journal of Public Health* 55:1024–31.

Cummings, K. M.; Becker, M. H.; and MAILE, M. C. 1980. Bringing the models together: an empirical approach to combining variables used to explain health actions. *Journal of Behavioral Medicine* 3:123–45.

Dutton, D. B. 1978. Explaining low use of health services by the poor: costs, attitudes or delivery systems? *American Sociological Review* 43:348–68.

Fabrega, H., Jr. 1973. Toward a model of illness behavior. *Medical Care* 11:470–84.

———. 1974. *Disease and social behavior: an interdisciplinary perspective.* Cambridge, Mass.: Massachusetts Institute of Technology Press.

———. 1977. Perceived illness and its treatment: a naturalistic study in social medicine. *British Journal of Preventive and Social Medicine* 31:213–19.

———, and Zucker, M. 1977. Comparison of illness episodes in a pluralistic setting. *Psychosomatic Medicine* 39:325–43.

Farge, E. J. 1978. Medical orientation among a Mexican-American population: an old and a new model reviewed. *Social Science and Medicine* 12:277–82.

Geersten, R.; Klauber, M. R.; Rindflesh, M.; Kane, R. L.; and Gray, R. 1975. A reexamination of Suchman's views on social factors in health care utilization. *Journal of Health and Social Behavior* 16:226–37.

Green, L. W. 1970. Manual for scoring socioeconomic status for research on health behavior. *Public Health Reports* 85:815–27.

———. 1975. Diffusion and adoption of innovations related to cardiovascular risk behavior in the public. In *Applying behavioral science to cardiovascular risk—proceedings of a conference*, ed. A. J. Enelow and J. B. Henderson. Washington, D. C.: American Health Association.

Hershey, J. C.; Luft, H. S.; and Gianaris, J. M. 1975. Making sense out of utilization data. *Medical Care* 13:838–53.

Hochbaum, G. M. 1958. *Public participation in medical screening programs: a sociopsychological study.* Washington, D.C.: Government Printing Office.

Jenkins, C. D. 1979. An approach to the diagnosis and treatment of problems of health related behavior. *International Journal of Health Education* 22 (suppl.) :3–24.

Kasl, S. V., and COBB, S. 1966a. Health behavior, illness behavior, and sick role behavior. I. Health and illness behavior. *Achives of Environmental Health* 12:246–66.

———. 1966. Health behavior, illness behavior and sick role behavior. II. Sick role behavior. *Achives of Environmental Health* 12:531–41.

Kosa, J., and Robertson, L. S. 1975. The social aspects of health and illness. In *Poverty and health: a sociological analysis*, ed. J. Kosa and I. K. Zola, pp. 40–79. Cambridge, Mass.: Harvard University Press.

Langlie, J. K. 1977. Social networks, health beliefs, and preventive health behavior. *Journal of Health and Social Behavior* 18:244–60.

Lendt, L. A. 1960. *A social history of Washington Heights, New York City.* New York: Columbia–Washington Heights Community Mental Health Project.

Leventhal, H.; Patient behavior. In *Patient education in the primary care setting—proceedings of the second conference.* Madison, Wis.: Center for Health Services, University of Wisconsin.

MAIMAN, L. A., and BECKER, M. H. 1974. The health belief model: origins and correlates in psychological theory. *Health Education Monographs* 2:336-53.

McKINLAY, J. B. 1972. Some approaches and problems in the study of the use of services—an overview. *Journal of Health and Social Behavior* 13:115-52.

MECHANIC, D. 1962. The concept of illness behavior. *Journal of Chronic Diseases* 15: 189-94.

———. 1978. *Medical sociology: a comprehensive text.* New York: Free Press.

———. 1968. *Medical sociology: a selective view.* New York: Free Press.

REEDER, L. G., AND BERKANOVIC, E.: Sociological concomitants of health orientations: a partial replication of Suchman. *Journal of Health and Social Behavior* 14:134-43.

ROSENSTOCK, I. M. 1966. Why people use health services. *Milbank Memorial Fund Quarterly* 44 (part 2):94-124.

———. 1974. The health belief model and prevention health behavior. *Health Education Monographs* 2:354-86.

———, and KIRSCHT, J. P. 1979. Why people seek health care. In *Health psychology —a handbook,* ed. G. C. Stone, F. Cohen, and N. E. Adler, pp. 161-88. San Francisco, Calif.: Jossey-Bass.

SACKETT, D. L., and SNOW, J. C. 1979. The magnitude of compliance and noncompliance. In *Compliance in health care,* ed. R. B. Haynes, D. W. Taylor, and D. L. Sackett, pp. 11-22. Baltimore, Md. Johns Hopkins University Press.

SUCHMAN, E. A. 1965a. Social patterns of illness and medical care. *Journal of Health and Social Behavior* 6:2-16.

———. 1965b. Stages of illness and medical care. *Journal of health and Social Behavior* 6: 114-28.

———. 1966. Health orientation and medical care. *American Journal of Public Health* 56: 97-105.

———. 1967. Preventive health behavior: a model for research on community health campaigns. *Journal of Health and Social Behavior* 8:197-209.

YOUNG, J. 1980. *Medical choice in a cultural context: treatment decision making in a Mexican town.* New Brunswick, N.J.: Rutgers University Press.

Chapter 26

Popular Health Care, Social Networks, and Cultural Meanings: The Orientation of Medical Anthropology

Noel J. Chrisman
Arthur Kleinman

FROM THE OUTSET medical anthropologists have studied patients' perspectives and experiences with health care. However, in keeping with anthropology's abiding core concern with culture, these perspectives and experiences are interpreted as the surface social and psychological reality of everyday life that expresses deep and tacit relationships among meanings, norms, and power that are the very stuff of cultural reality. Illness episodes—and the characteristic local ways in which they are conceived and coped with—are examples of how emotion, cognition, motivation, behavior, and social interaction are made *meaningful* in particular cultural contexts. Medical anthropologists have described and compared these local contexts as *systems* of health care (Fabrega and Silver, 1973; Good 1977; Kleinman et al. 1975; Leslie 1976; Lewis 1975; Press 1969; Schwartz 1969). Even when healers (folk or professional) have been the focus of anthropological analysis, they have been understood in their relation to popular health-care networks and shared cultural meanings. Medical anthropologists are especially interested in the personal interpretation of and response to illness, the search for help, communication between patient and healer, and the assessment of outcome.

Because most medical anthropological research has been conducted in non-Western societies or among the more traditional ethnic groups of Western society, concepts and findings are not well appreciated by other social scientists and health professionals whose primary concern is with health care in the mainstream of Western society. Hence the extensive anthropological materials on popular health care and lay networks are typically not taken into account when these subjects are reviewed by medical sociologists and health-service researchers. In this chapter we stress precisely those medical anthropological orientations that challenge customary ways of viewing these issues and taken-for-granted assumptions about them. Our approach is predicated upon the distinction between patient views of sickness as *illness* and biomedical views of sickness as *disease* (Eisenberg 1977). In this chapter we would like to stress that from an anthropological and cross-cultural perspective: (1) popular health care is the norm and professional health care is the exception; (2) lay treatment is a much more common function of social networks than lay referral; (3) *interpretation* is the core clinical activity requiring psychological, social, and cultural analysis for both lay people and practitioners; and (4) cultural processes are viewed as relating everyday reality with sickness through dominant idioms and metaphors concerning society, person, body, etiology, pathophysiology, and therapy (ethnopsychology and ethnomedicine).

Health Care as a Cultural System

Anthropological research supports a view of medicine in society as a *cultural system* (Kleinman 1980). Recent medical ethnographies and cross-cultural comparisons disclose how the health- and health-care-related aspects of society are culturally constituted and expressed (Comaroff 1980; Fabrega and Silver 1973; Good 1977; Janzen 1978; Kleinman 1980; Lindenbaum 1979; Sargent, in press; Young 1980). Of the various models of the cultural system of medicine that have been advanced (cf. Dunn 1976; Fabrega, in press; Leslie 1976), the most useful conceptualization, based on substantial cross-cultural findings, conceives of three distinctive and overlapping local arenas of health and health care: the *popular, folk* and *professional* sectors of care (see Figure 26.1).

The *popular sector* consists of diagnosis, triage, and care by sick persons, their families, social networks, and communities. The shared meanings of illness constitute what Polgar (1962) has called popular health culture (see also Weidman et al. 1978). Several decades of research now make it clear that in many societies most health maintenance and care are delivered in and by the popular sector (cf. Demers et al. 1980; Hulka et al. 1972; Kleinman 1980, pp. 179–202; White et al.

Figure 26.1   Local Health-Care System: Internal Structure
Source: Kleinman 1980, p. 50.

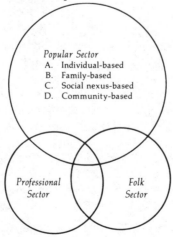

Popular Sector
A. Individual-based
B. Family-based
C. Social nexus-based
D. Community-based

Professional
Sector

Folk
Sector

1961; Zola 1972a, 1972b). In this sector illness is first perceived and labeled, treatment is first applied, and most illness episodes receive care. Demers et al. (1980) recently demonstrated that members of a prepaid health cooperative in Seattle reported symptoms as often as once every week. The great majority of these symptoms were either "normalized" (e.g., observed and interpreted as acceptable, minor, or unimportant problems) or self-treated.

Popular treatment includes a variety of remedies, such as diet, special foods, herbs, exercise, baths, massage, and rest; use of technical devices such as humidifiers, hot blankets, ice packs, braces, canes, patent medicines, prescription medicines which have been obtained from practitioners for past illnesses or are obtained from neighborhood pharmacists or family physicians on the patient's request or are received from family and friends; support and caring from members of one's social network; symbolic therapies such as prayer, religious rituals, charms, and secular rituals; and many other technical and nontechnical interventions (both part of mainstream and ethnic practices). As this list indicates, there is an ongoing reciprocal interaction between the different levels of popular care (self, family, network, neighborhood, community) and the folk and professional sectors of care. This interaction includes exchanges of knowledge and technical resources such that members of the popular sector gain access to and often control over treatments, while popular beliefs and practices become part of folk and professional practice (Gaines 1979; Helman 1978). Furthermore, the decisions to relate with other sectors, including decisions about whether or not to adhere to the medical regimen and how to assess outcome, are made largely in the popular sector, even though from the physician's perspective these are "professional" decisions. Negotiation of the sick role, an appropriate patient role, compensation benefits, and the like involve different subsectors of and interactions between popular and professional arenas of care.

Although families and social networks are the major social contexts where illness is interpreted, health care delivered, and utilization of professional services determined, this popular arena of care is commonly discounted by professional health planners and providers. Even social scientists tend to deprecate the therapeutic aspects of popular involvement in health and health care. Popular sector activities rarely are included in public health statistics. Little attempt has been made to examine critically how changes in resource allocation and control that favor family treatment might be instituted and evaluated in health-policy decision-making processes. This is an example of a general failure of researchers and planners to challenge the dominant professional orientation which views care largely or entirely in terms of the professional sector and plays down the importance of the popular sector.

The *folk sector* includes specialist, nonprofessional, nonbureaucratized, often quasi-legal and sometimes illegal forms of care based on various folk health cultures that shade imperceptibly into professional practice on the one side and popular care on the other. This sector, though it is also quite extensive, is frequently unlicensed or minimally regulated. In many non-Western societies it represents a substantially larger component of services than professional biomedicine. Even in late twentieth-century America, especially among ethnic minorities, it constitutes a not inconsiderable proportion of services (Chrisman and Kleinman 1980). Yet we do not possess a careful inventory of the kinds and numbers of folk healers in American society. Most psychotherapy in America is delivered by folk healers such as lay therapists, hypnotists, faith healers, and ethnic folk healers (curanderas, root workers, spiritists). But their contribution to general medical care is also considerable.

The WHO has supported the integration of folk healers into the orthodox health-service delivery system in developing societies, but such integration has not been examined for developed societies (for exceptions see Baer 1981; Harwood 1977; Snow 1978; Weidman et al. 1978). Indeed compared with the enormous and still rapidly growing body of research by medical anthropologists on folk healers in non-Western societies, there is an embarrassing lack of data on folk healers (especially urban ones) in developed Western societies. This is a key objective for future medical anthropological research. Moreover, while folk healers are usually studied solely as therapists, they deserve study as a key part of the nonprofessional referral system as well. A recent study comparing patients matched on various characteristics treated by folk healers and physicians in Taiwan disclosed that approximately 75 percent of patients in both groups improved and were generally satisfied with their treatment (Kleinman and Gale, in press). Neither group performed well in treating "somatization" and other types of "problem patients," suggesting that folk healing also shares problems with professional care. These data do not sustain the romantic and reverse ethnocentric assertions that folk healing is better than professional care. Nor do they sustain the argument that all folk healers are charlatans and quacks. But such research does make obvious how very little is presently known about this important arena of health care, especially in the United States and other Western societies.

The borderland between folk healing and popular care in American society includes a large number of local family and network "experts" in treating specific disorders such as self-help groups, religious networks and cults organized as living groups, and other primary ideological groups organized around publically articulated ideological models of particular illnesses or deviance (such as Schizophrenics Anonymous, victims of rape and wife abuse groups, and a wide variety of secular therapy systems such as community-based massage, dance, birthing, health foods, and related forms).

The *professional sector* of care includes the health-services professions and bureaucracies basing clinical practice on highly developed and complex professional health cultures. In many societies there are distinctive health professions, and these relate to the popular and folk sectors in different ways, such as in the case of Ayurvedic medicine and biomedicine in India, Chinese medicine and Western medicine in China, or chiropracty, optometry, osteopathy, naturopathy, and biomedicine in America.

As Unschuld (1979) demonstrates, analysis of the professional sector draws attention to the competition for limited resources (knowledge, techniques, patients, reimbursement) among distinctive providers. Unschuld also notes that medical professional group ethics sometimes function as ideological defenses against competitors, means of justifying established resource control, and as a blueprint for future expansion. In addition, Unschuld suggests that "medicalization" is a complex process of expansion and retreat among different subsectors and arenas of care. For example, the commercial pharmaceutical interests have been associated with expansion of pharmaceutical sales in developing countries independent of health professionals (cf. Ferguson 1981). In the mental health field, psychiatrists, psychologists, and social workers have openly competed for patients and dominance.

Most of the work in medical sociology and anthropology has focused only upon the helpers in the folk and professional sectors, and neglected family and community networks. In contrast to folk and professional helpers, however, those who participate in a patient's illness episode in the popular sector do so in the context of diffuse rather than specific institutionalized role relationships (Parsons 1951).

Health-Seeking Process

The second model influencing this discussion of illness behaviors in the popular sector is the health-seeking process (Chrisman 1977), a conceptual elaboration of the "natural history of an illness episode" in which the focus is on the individual and the ways the health-care system influences behavior (see Figure 26.2). The health-seeking process shares a great deal with Suchman's conception of stages of illness and medical care (1965), but builds on later work as well (e.g., Geertson et al. 1975).

An illness episode begins with an evaluation of the problem *(symptom definition)*. The most closely related element, *treatment action*, denotes suggestions directed toward resolving the problem. *Adherence* may follow treatment action; this element refers to the degree to which treatment suggestions are followed by the ill person. Two additional social processes are included in this health-seeking scheme: *role shift* (not considered here because of space limitations), involving changes in daily life behavior that result from sickness; and *lay consultation and referral*, involving discussion of the illness with others to negotiate a socially legitimate definition and choices among options for care. Underlying all the elements, but most visibly adherence, is a monitoring process in which illness categories, outcome, and social relations are evaluated. Hence Blumhagen (1980), Kleinman (1980), Good and Good (1981), and AmaraSingham (1980) have shown that patients (and families) routinely assess symptom change, treatment response, side effects, and satisfaction with professional care, and alter the explanatory models of sickness consistent with these responses, social relations, and environmental stressors. Health-seeking elements do not necessarily occur in a fixed sequence. Moreover, they can recur during an episode as new information stimulates recycling through the process.

Figure 26.2 Health-Seeking Process
Source: Chrisman 1977, p. 354.

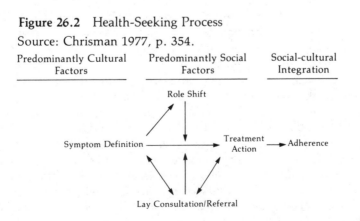

Prelude to Sickness

Sickness episodes begin with the perception of a "deviation from the culturally and historically variable standard of normality established by everyday experience" (Freidson 1970, p. 285). The crucial factors are the "variable standard of experience" and perception. Humans in all social groups monitor their physiological as well as their sociocultural systems for potential deviations (see Fabrega 1973) based on culturally established standards of normality and idiosyncratic perceptions. Standards of normality establish thresholds of severity and types of symptoms for potential attention.

For example, certain physiological reactions such as "fight" or "flight" responses of the autonomic nervous system may yield symptoms that are perceived as threatening signs of disorder among certain groups, even though from a biomedical perspective they are innocuous. Heart palpitations and "fright" in Iran (Good 1977; Good and Good 1981), nocturnal emissions of semen among adolescents in South India (Obeyeskere 1978), mild dizziness among Chinese believed to be susceptible to neurasthenia, and a benign small lump in the breast among middle-class Americans all are charged with fearsome cultural significance. Such symptoms are not likely to be normalized. The patient has a psychological set that sensitizes to such symptoms and results in strong reactions. Conversely, symptoms that are important for health professionals such as black stools, worms in the stool, excessive and easy bruising, whitish discoloration of the skin (say, in an area with endemic leprosy), may be seen as normal and indeed expectable symptoms in areas where such problems have such high prevalence that they are viewed as "natural." The poor urban elderly in America may be more likely to normalize failing vision as an expected part of aging, whereas the middle-class elderly may find even minimal change in vision as grounds to seek expert assistance. High stress, lack of social support, and a personality type obsessively focused on self and body may predispose to hypochondriacal fears such that normal bodily reactions are seen as peculiar or signs of "something wrong." Culturally informed perception may also lead to somatic preoccupation, complaints, illness labeling, and help seeking due to selective attention. Somatization, though it is often seen by mental health professionals as the result of a psychological problem or stress, can be viewed also as a culturally constituted idiom to express grievance, misfortune or distress in a socially acceptable way (Nichter, in press). The foundation of somatization is not conscious malingering in which symptoms are made up, but selective scanning of key bodily functions and structures that socially create illness experience (Katon and Kleinman, in press). For example, among Chinese it is permissible and expected to complain of body pains and weakness when under stress, but not psychological symptoms such as depression and anxiety. Moreover, certain complaints (dizziness, headaches, sourness in the stomach, lack of energy) are culturally marked among Chinese as conveying both somatic and psychic distress, and these are the symptoms preferentially attended to, communicated, and perhaps actively constructed (psychosomatically) in that society. As Nichter has shown in South India, semen loss, loss of appetite and weight, and gastrointestinal complaints play a similar role. Zola (1966) and Zborowski (1958) suggest that among certain Caucasian ethnic groups the complaint of pain may be used to communicate personal and interpersonal distress in a culturally acceptable way.

The articulation of private illness experience in public metaphors that make common sense and are part of the assumed world of everyday life is a related process. When symptoms are amplified in the process of labeling and explaining sickness, structures of relevance will determine whether they are further normalized or pathologized by the group. Structures of relevance are hierarchies or priority lists that encompass key values and that "define the situation." For example, stress has become a significant element of conventional wisdom in the United States that is used to explain heightened susceptibility to or the cause of a wide variety of illnesses. In turn, stress is seen to be the result of difficulties in such valued contexts as the family or occupational settings. After an illness episode, retrospective narratization (AmaraSingham 1980) will relate such illness to later episodes consistent with common sense (Zola 1972a).

Symptom Definition

Once an alteration in normal health status has been perceived, the individual begins to define symptoms. The key activity is relating cultural meanings to body experience. Beliefs and practices related to health, illness, and treatment in the popular sector of American society can be categorized as having originated from three principal sources: notions derived from American folk medicine, a tradition with its roots in beliefs brought to this country by the early waves of settlers and modified in interaction with Native American practices; beliefs that are part of the many folk medical traditions brought to and maintained within this country by the later and continuing immigrants from other nations; and medical ideas diffused to lay people from the professional biomedical sector. This diffusion, especially in commercial advertising and popularization, introduces a substantial distortion of scientific beliefs and clinical norms. Some have begun to talk of the commercial health sector as an important component linking popular and professional sectors and responsible for much of the popularization and distortion of biomedical knowledge (Ferguson 1981).

Crucial to understanding popular health culture is recognizing that diverse sources of health beliefs exist in particular combinations for each individual and group as a result of personal and group history. Members of disadvantaged ethnic groups probably exhibit a higher proportion of beliefs related to their homeland medical tradition; middle-class whites are likely to possess beliefs that strongly reflect those of the practitioners they visit for care. People learn, from an early age, how to categorize symptoms, to attach meaning to them, and to treat them. It is during socialization that basic cognitive perspectives and norms about illness are acquired. These perspectives include those in which individual, spiritual or magical power is related to sickness as among some blacks and Hispanic Americans; or Asian and Native American perspectives that relate cosmological harmonies to wellness and illness; or middle-class notions that germs and pollutants are the most likely culprits.

Over time, lay people build a repertoire of health beliefs and practices that is roughly integrated with the limited basic perspectives, but need not be completely consistent. The acquisition of new ideas about sickness occurs against the backdrop of existing health beliefs. Thus, ideas from professional health practitioners, for example, become modified by individuals as they are compared with existing notions. Discussions with social network members about health and illness produce the same effects. For example, Helman (in press) demonstrates that middle-class Londoners view the sedatives they take not as drugs in the biomedical sense or in the popular sense in which commonly abused narcotics are so labeled, but as "tonics," "fuels," and even "food."

One of the most significant basic perspectives of popular health culture derives from the ancient beliefs of humoral pathology, identified with Galen and Hippocrates in the West. Humoral pathology is based on the concept of balance; in this case balance between hot and cold, wet and dry, and among various bodily humors. Although this belief system is best known for its Asian and Latin American variants, it also is strongly represented in the United States and Britain (Foster 1979; Helman 1978; Logan 1977). Popular American ideas about "colds," for example, are directly related: going outside with wet hair or moving too quickly from heated to cooled spaces can "cause" congestion and other symptoms of a cold. The importance of humors, such as phlegm, seems to underlie the frequently found set of beliefs related to the accumulations of "slime" (Snow 1974) or "poisons" in the body. Regular bowel movements, or purgatives in some cases, are seen to be important preventive or curing procedures. Among Americans who devote extra attention to their dietary habits, particularly those who prefer organic foods, there is the belief that "junk foods" and food with artificial additives leave an undesirable residue in the body after elimination: the poisons. Recent concerns about environmental pollutants as disease agents build on this tradition. Illnesses ranging from headaches to breast cancer are sometimes explained in this way (Mauthe 1978).

A second set of perspectives implicates the supernatural world in illness in a variety of ways. The most pervasive of these supernatural explanations of illness is related to the will of God. Illness may be seen as punishment or a test of faith. God may remove His protection from the individual, substantially increasing one's susceptibility to evil influences from the devil or witchcraft, or susceptibility to germs (Snow 1974). Witchcraft or sorcery, documented among ethnic groups such as Filipinos, Native Americans, blacks, and Mexican Americans (Clark 1970; McKenzie and Chrisman 1977; Snow 1974), constitute another set of viable supernatural explanations in the popular health culture. Finally, spirits and ghosts are seen by Puerto Ricans and other Caribbean peoples, Chinese, and people from the Middle East to play a role in the cause and course of illness (Harwood 1977; Weidman et al. 1978; Kleinman 1980).

Humoral pathology, supernatural beliefs, germ theory, and other popular cultural explanations of illness are usually rooted in everyday life events. Common activities such as eating or ambulating are linked to symptoms with hot-cold or wet-dry implications. Similarly, the stresses and strains of interpersonal relationships within family, neighborhood, or work environment may be conceptualized as illness produced through the medium of supernatural causes or stress.

The importance of one's health culture during the symptom-definition stage of health seeking is that such beliefs provide the evaluative guidelines for decisions about what is wrong and what to do about it and the categories (illnesses) into which to class symptoms. Once meaning has been imputed, or at least hypothesized, decisions about what to do or not to do may be made.

The first step in the lay search for the meaning of symptoms is to classify the noticed discomforts roughly in terms of popular cultural perspectives. Thus complaints might be assigned to the general area of the respiratory system in the case of a cold or to the digestive system in the case of a stomachache or diarrhea. The process of relating meaning to symptoms involves hypotheses about likely cause(s). In most instances, the cause is located by retrospectively examining occurrences in previous days that might relate to the symptoms. It is at this point that cultural perspectives exert their strongest influence.

Memory is powerfully affected by cultural categories. For example, a digestive upset could be seen as resulting from the ingestion of spoiled food, meals in which a balance of "hot" and "cold" quality foods had not been achieved, the ingestion of foods whose unnatural additives had left toxic substances in the body, or stressful events in the person's life. Clearly any of these may have occurred in the recent past for an individual, but one's cultural perspective will single out only those that conform with previously existing beliefs about health and illness.

In each instance, a public "case" is socially created out of private experience, and in so doing illness receives a cultural stamp, a symbolic objectification of it into a "natural" thing, an "it" (Cassell 1976) that the sick person can communicate about with others, "bring" somewhere for treatment, and which he can reassure himself is understandable to others and hence to himself. Investing illness with meaning and interpreting its significance to others, and simultaneously to oneself, is central to the resolution of anxiety, which is a basic clinical component (Kleinman 1980). Building a case embeds illness in shared understandings and popular advice that carry with them treatment choices (AmaraSingham 1980).

Lay Consultation

The concept of social network is valuable for establishing the fact that illness episodes occur in social situations and are embedded in social relationships (Mitchell 1969, p. 1). However, greater descriptive and analytical depth is achieved through an examination of the Lay Referral System (Freidson 1970) using emerging anthropological techniques of network analysis (Mitchell 1969). The cultural dimension of the Lay Referral System—"the particular culture or knowledge people have about health or health agents" (Freidson 1970, p. 290)—is discussed in terms of health beliefs and practices in other sections of this chapter. The social dimension—"the interrelationships of the laymen from whom advice and referral are sought" (Freidson 1970, p. 290)—will be the subject of this section. The relevant question here is what people become coparticipants in an illness episode. What these individuals do, and why, is the subject of concern here.

The involvement of network members can be examined using both morphological and interactional criteria for describing networks. A critical morphological dimension is the degree of connectedness in a social network, i.e., the extent to which members know each other independently of the person on whom the network is anchored (Bott 1957). Connectedness is measured by density, "the extent to which links that could possibly exist among persons do in fact exist" (Mitchell 1969, p. 18), and reachability, the number of links needed for a person to reach others in the social network (Mitchell 1969, pp. 17–18). Density and reachability are related to the compactness of a network which in turn channels information, opinions, and judgments toward network members. In a compact network there are numerous routes by which information or influence can reach any member. A consequence of this structure is a higher degree of consistency in the opinions and actions of its members. Beliefs about illness and expectations of the most appropriate treatment responses are thus likely to be highly consistent within the group. Much less consistency is expected in the loose-knit network in which lower density and reachability of network linkages reduce intercommunication.

A second significant morphological variable is range: the number and social heterogeneity of individuals in a person's effective network (Wheeldon 1969). A network with high range—more people, more heterogeneity—possesses much more access to the society beyond the social network itself. Those with relatively small numbers of people who are socially homogeneous receive less information flow from the outside.

Joining range with compactness allows evaluation of a network's degree of insularity. The insular network with compact (highly interconnected) internal social ties and narrow range might be viewed, as its name implies, as an island set apart from the larger context of society. These structural qualities are associated with Suchman's (1965) social category of parochial—ethnocentric, traditional, and the like. In his discussion of the Italian-American working-class subculture, Gans (1962) noted that these people, whose compact social networks are composed of kin and neighbors, reinterpret outside events and beliefs in terms of their effects upon life within the group. The same can be expected for health-related events and beliefs (cf. Geertson et al. 1975).

High network insularity also has implications for the maintenance of particular sets of health beliefs and practices. If traditional beliefs are relevant to the network—as among ethnic minorities, for example—there is a higher likelihood that they will be validated and reinforced. Although contacts with formal health practitioners are unlikely to be less frequent than among people with noninsular networks, new ideas from these sources are likely to be reinterpreted according to the beliefs of the group.

The noninsular network with loose-knit ties and a wide range of outside contacts is better connected with the institutions of the wider society. Gans (1962) suggests in the case of middle-class subculture that no solid boundary is perceived between the central nuclear family organization and formal educational, governmental, economic, and health institutions. The wide range of network members provides numerous opportunities for new health-related information to be transmitted to any participant in the network. Moreover, the loose-knit social ties imply less consistency in opinion and less persuasive force to opinions. The noninsular network, allied with the cosmopolitan style, promotes a much more independent approach. For example, McKinlay (1973), Salloway and Dillon (1973), and, more recently, Horwitz (1977, 1978) document variations in help seeking between more compact family-based networks and less compact friendship networks.

A second significant set of descriptors of network composition include criteria such as content, directedness, durability, intensity, and frequency (Mitchell 1969, pp. 20–29). The latter four refer to relatively easily measured qualities such as the length of time a link has been in existence. For our meaning-centered approach, content is the most significant interactional criterion, "the meanings which persons in the network attribute to their relationships" (Mitchell 1969, p. 20). These meanings constitute a significant area of research in the health field since they include: dimensions of support such as personal or economic assistance; psychosocial activities such as comforting and affirmation of personal importance and role relationships (Chrisman 1970; Mitchell 1974; Tolsdorf 1976), and the nature of the information that is transferred among links (Garrison 1980). However, caution must be exercised so that morphological features such as density or number of people are not confused with support, which is an interactional criterion (Garrison 1980, pp. 32–33n; cf. Caplan 1974).

Social and cultural factors influence network construction among American

ethnic groups. Socially, socioeconomic position and discrimination constrain people's participation or predispose toward aversive interactions that may occur with
police and social workers (Hannerz 1969). Thus network range is narrowed, resulting in networks composed largely of coethnics (Chrisman 1981b). Culturally, social
bonds within the ethnic group are promoted because of the ease of and greater
satisfaction with interactions with people who share values and beliefs (Chrisman
1981b).

One's social network constitutes the resources available for lay consultation
and/or referral during illness. The people called upon to participate with the patient may do so in a variety of ways: e.g., providing reassurance or information,
suggestions for treatment, or referral to an expert for help. Face-to-face participation is characteristic of the person's illness-related *action set.* An action set is a
cluster of individuals recruited from the wider social network to serve a limited
purpose (Mayer 1966, pp. 97–98). Purposive selection implies that action-set
members may not know each other or even interact as a group when they have
been selected from diverse areas of a network. However, the action set drawn
from an insular network with its high interconnectedness retains previously existing close interaction patterns.

The size of an action set and the nature of its involvement with an illness depend both on the structural properites of the network and on the type of illness.
The extensive participation deriving from highly interconnected networks implies
similar participation in illness. In contrast, the member of a loose-knit (less interconnected) network possesses a greater range of choice about the degree of action-
set involvement. Severity and duration of the illness also influence action-set
involvement. For example, for minor illnesses, only the spouse or immediate family might be mobilized with extensions further into the network when severity is
moderate. Patients with chronic illness may experience an enlargement (during the
acute episode) of action-set size which diminishes as illness continues (Finlayson
1976).

Among some American ethnic groups such as Hispanics (Clark 1970; Harwood 1977) and blacks (La Fargue 1981; Chrisman 1981a), the illness-related action set occupies a central role in illness. When the action set takes significant
responsibility for shepherding the sick person through the activities of an entire illness, we are justified in using the concept of *therapy management group* (Janzen
1978). In introducing the concept, Janzen draws upon data from Zaire, where he
found that the family or clan, not the individual, acted as the decision-making
body which organized care for the sick person. In cases in which traditional healing was the option for care, the therapy management group was part of the ritual
healing group. With Western-style practitioners, this group receded only partly to
the background; it continued to aid the patient in decisions, but was less visible.

The presence of therapy management groups in American popular health care
is influenced by both socioeconomic and cultural factors. Cultural influences include the value placed on family and social-network decisions and the importance
of including others in discussions about the etiology and treatment of illness.
Therapy management groups in the professional health-care sector are evident
among Chicanos who rebel against the exclusion of family members from examination rooms and Gypsies who congregate in hospital lobbies when a kinsman
is hospitalized. In addition, LaFargue's data (1981) show that working-class black
women are reluctant to seek professional help without their "sisters" from the
church. Care for these women in the popular arena, in this case church prayer

meetings, was carried out with the "sisters" and others from the congregation. Both T. Y. Lin et al. (1978) and K. M. Lin et al. (nd) show that North American Chinese families of psychotic patients stay active in family care and help seeking much longer in the course of illness and exert greater control over it than do families of North American Anglo patients.

The group character of therapy management is greatly attenuated or absent in the action set composed from a noninsular network. The existence of loose-knit links implies that lay consultation for symptom definition may well be sporadic. Although the spouse or other coresident adult(s) is nearly always consulted, the individual frequently acts alone to make therapeutic decisions. Suggestions are less likely to be consistent across consultants. After the spouse, the most likely lay consultant, and not infrequently a source of treatment, is the person's mother or both parents. Although consultation of this sort depends upon proximity and frequency of visiting, middle-class people, particularly women, are likely to use the telephone. Other lay consultants include friends, neighbors, and coworkers. It must be remembered, however, that among cosmopolitans these consultants are usually not in contact with each other as commonly occurs among parochials.

A person's lay consultant action set, or more extended portions of the personal network, may also constitute a personal community (Henry 1958) and serve as the source of support such as reassurance, sharing of similar experiences, household help, or monetary assistance. The relationship of network and support has become the subject of growing research interest in the past decade (see McKinlay 1981 and Mueller 1980 for excellent reviews). However, we know little about who is involved in the provision of support and the cultural context or meanings of the support and why it is given (cf. MacElveen-Hoehn and Smith-DiJulio 1978). This is a consequence of the lack of ethnographic data. Without adequate descriptions of class or ethnic variations in network (or action set) structure and the cultural meanings of supportive activites, we do not have a complete picture of *how* support systems work. Moreover, anthropological descriptions make us aware of the potential of social networks to be stressful as well as supportive.

Treatment Action

Two significant functions of the illness-oriented action set are to provide the sick person with treatment suggestions and/or to help him select an appropriate source of treatment outside the action set. These activities take place as the sick individual constructs an illness action set through the consulting process. A necessary component of these interactions is obtaining aid in the construction of an explanatory model or validation of the patient's existing model. Joint symptom definition (or agreement on definition within insular networks) is an important aspect of the process because notions about cause and/or pathology imply a limited set of responses.

Treatment action must be broken into two constituent parts: the source of treatment and the type of treatment. Treatment sources include: (1) formal health practitioners, such as doctors or nurses; (2) licensed health practitioners, such as pharmacists, midwives, or chiropractors; (3) alternative or native health practitioners, such as herbalists, astrologers, curanderas, or spirit mediums; (4) lay consultants; and (5) self (Chrisman 1977, p. 368). Types of treatment include: (1) activity alterations such as exercise, bed rest, or sweat baths; (2) the application or ingestion (or injection) of substances such as poultices or pills; (3) verbal or ritual behaviors such as psychiatric therapy or prayer; and (4) physical interventions on the body such as surgery or cupping (Chrisman 1977, p. 368).

The complex interplay among treatment sources and treatment behaviors is strongly influenced by the experiences of the individual and his or her personal community. Once complaints have been categorized as deviant *and* needing attention, the demands of the problem must be weighed against the resources available. Demands may be seen in terms of the threat posed by the sickness (Becker 1974; Kasl and Cobb 1966), which includes an assessment of the degrees of danger and disability provoked by ill health (Chrisman 1977). In addition, children and the elderly, seen as more vulnerable, are more frequent recipients of formal care than adults (cf. Kleinman 1980 for the analogous situation in Taiwan). In his examination of Mexican data, James Young (1980) has outlined an approach to family decision-making about appropriate use of resources based on a configuration of knowledge about the illness and its degrees of threat, economic resources, and the putative power of the types of helpers available. Consistent with health-services research findings (e.g., Anderson and Newman 1973), Young identifies gravity of the illness as the primary determinant of choices among treatment sources; for grave illnesses, the choice will be the practitioner in whom the family has the most faith, usually the physician in a neighboring town, regardless of cost. For less serious and common illness, however, the family turns to its own resources—home remedies known by family members.

Helping resources available in the U.S. popular sector are varied in terms of both the kinds of illness for which they are relevant and the types of treatment offered (Gottlieb 1978). An important dimension along which these resources may be arrayed is the diffuseness or specificity of the relationship between the sick person and the helper. This continuum ranges from the diffuse, multiplex relationships among family and friends in which helping with illness is but one of a wide range of areas of reciprocity, to more specific single-stranded relationships in which the relationship is organized around a limited set of goals such as help with illness. Alternative health practitioners are an example of the specific end of this continuum. Arrayed along this axis are: (1) family-based neighborhood specialists such as "la que sabe" among Chicanos (Dorsey and Jackson 1978) or "granny" among blacks (Baer 1981); (2) religious and cult groups, such as churches and Dianic or Satanic witch cults (Moody 1966: Ness 1980; Shuman 1979); (3) soothsayers such as astrologers, palm readers, or fortune tellers (Snow 1978); (4) members of the various populist health movements such as health food movements, yoga or massage groups, or human potential movements such as Lifespring; and finally (5) the alternative therapists such as polarity therapists, reflexologists, massage therapists, or aura and lapidary diagnosticians (Byerly and Molgaard, in press) whose relationships with clients are single stranded and focused more directly on health issues.

A central feature of the social matrix in which health decisions are made is the dominant *world view* (cf. Jones 1976) of the family and associated social network. Building on Gans's contrast of working-class and middle-class subcultures and their varying degrees of boundary permeability between the family and the wider urban environment, we can contrast a *person-oriented* world view among the lower classes and an *institution-oriented* world view among the higher classes. These world views are related to the social adaptations of the two groups. Among the lower classses who, by definition, have fewer economic resources for coping with daily life, an investment must be made in *people* to ensure survivial. Many of the traits of the culture of poverty (Lewis 1966) result from such adaptive behavior. For example, expanding and contracting household composition and "present-oriented" spending patterns reflect the need to maximize close social links with people who are economically productive (Liebow 1967). The person orientation is seen in the elaborate kin networks of poor blacks (LaFargue 1981; Stack 1974). Among poor Italian-Americans, evaluations of neighbors are made more on the basis of past personal and family history than in regard to a particular behavior (Suttles 1968). The person-oriented world view is probably related to the persistence of health beliefs that relate sickness to the malevolent spiritual or occult powers of individuals (see Gaines 1979 for the notion of "enchanted" world view; Harwood 1977; Smith 1972; Snow 1974).

The middle-class, cosmopolitan, institution-oriented world view is related to a social adaptation dependent on an adequate level of financial resources. Rather than needing to use a personal reciprocity system for obtaining goods and services, most middle-class people use the market economy system (LaFargue 1981). They are more accustomed to interacting with representatives of institutions who behave in a distant bureaucratic fashion and find the process less objectionable. Thus, contacts with health professionals are more congruent with the middle-class world view, symbolically reflecting a shared view of social reality.

This institution-oriented world view also contributes to the help-seeking activities of middle-class individuals. Their explanatory models of illness rarely implicate the personal powers of other persons. When people or daily life activities are linked to illness, there is a higher likelihood that they will be conceptually related to illness through the concept of stress, an explanantory mechanism that seems to depersonalize the roles of persons in the illness process. Thus, it is not surprising that when middle-class people seek alternative helpers in the popular arena, the sources of care conform to the instrumental, segmental model of help seeking that characterizes other aspects of their lives (Leiberman and Glidewell 1978). For example, the range of group experiences available, ranging from the more esoteric new age movements to stress management groups or yoga sessions, tend to gather together people who were previously unknown to each other, expose them to particular health-promoting or illness-solving techniques, and then allow the individual to continue the practice in private. This contrasts with the healing practices among lower-class ethnics such as Puerto Ricans, whose spiritist seances include friends, kin, and neighbors (Garrison 1977; Harwood 1977). Encounters with practitioners among the middle class seem to be treated in a similar fashion. Visits to polarity therapists, specialists in massage, astrologers, naturopaths, chiropractors, and the like are made on an individual basis and segregated from the normal course of everyday events.

The person-oriented world view and the insular networks to which it is related tend to promote the use of helping resources within the local community setting and which involve interaction styles that are less formal and bureaucratic than those tolerated by people with an institution-oriented world view. Treatment suggestions are frequently home remedies passed from generation to generation within families. Ointments, tonics, and alterations in diet or behavior are legitimated not only by knowledge of their success through the generations but also by their logical relationship to culturally accepted explanatory models of illness. For example, among some blacks, spring cleaning must be accomplished for the body as well as the house. Impurities that have accumulated through the winter months may "rise" like the sap. Thus, treatments such as sulfur and molasses for purification and castor oil for lubrication may be taken as preventive measures (Snow 1974).

The experiential basis of treatments is important within these person-oriented personal communities. In addition to the structural influences to stay within a tightly interconnected network, there are also the knowledge resources to do so (e.g., the "granny"). Among middle-class people, there are likely to be fewer "knowledgeable people" as sources of help within the household and personal community. Over-the-counter preparations may be used for minor problems, but individuals tend to be quicker in their use of physicians. Their conceptualizations are more biomedical than those of ethnic groups with continuing folk medical traditions. When a strong ethnic healing tradition is present, fewer illnesses are obviously appropriate to bring to a physician.

The interaction styles of various kinds of providers also promote more family-based care among parochials. The emotionally distancing, "professional" interaction style of formal health practitioners contrasts strongly with the emotionally close, personal style of alternative and native practitioners and familial style (Friedl 1978). This class difference carries over to communication as well, with middle-class patients using elaborated codes that are more congruent with professional communication than the restricted code of lower-class patients (cf. Bernstein 1971). Among cosmopolitans, the bureaucratic interaction style of providers is more congruent with everyday experience. The meaning of these style variations goes much deeper than the simple, and widespread, distaste for impersonal physicians. Bureaucratic and familistic interaction styles are allied with differences in world view in lower- and working-class subcultures and contrast with middle-class subcultures, thus symbolizing different perspectives on human nature. They also involve different concepts of self and body, notions of personal and social efficacy, modes of interacting, affective distances, and norms guiding therapeutic expectations and styles.

Adherence and Evaluation

The cognitive and social events in illness are continuously evaluated by the sick person against both past personal experience and group standards. People attempt to determine whether explanatory models, recommended treatments, and the social interactions accompanying these suggestions "make sense" and whether the recommendations should be followed. One outcome of these evaluative processes is varying degrees of adherence to treatment suggestions.

In his discussion of healing praxis, Alan Young (1976) elaborates two evaluative processes involved in healing. Improvement in the health status of the individual is an obvious component. The second—culturally constructing the nature of the illness episode—is less obvious, in large measure due to researchers' use of the biomedical model as the explicit or implicit guide for examining health care. A third element that must be added is the sick person's evaluation of care-givers—lay or professional—in terms of their congruence with preferred styles of interaction and the nature of the personal commitment these styles imply.

The first evaluative process—problem relief—is a continuation of biobehavioral monitoring. A temporal link is forged between the particular treatments or other interventions attempted (including doing nothing, hoping the problem will resolve itself) and persistence or change in symptoms. Traditionally, this dimension has been seen as the only relevant evaluative element. Symptom monitoring is related to adherence in two ways. First, past experiences with successful problem resolution resulting from the same or similar treatments promotes adherence on the basis of judgments of the likelihood of success (or "frequency interpretation," Erasmus 1961). Secondly, during the illness episode, symptoms are closely monitored for expected changes during specific time periods. When temporal boundaries have been exceeded, adherence may decline or cease and stimulate a new symptom definition search, reactivating all or part of the health-seeking process.

A second aspect of illness behavior evaluation is related to the cultural construction of clinical reality (Kleinman 1980) that occurs in the symptom definition-treatment action process. Kleinman (1980) and Young (1976) have shown that labeling the illness is a central function of healing systems. Through this process, the etiological agents and/or pathologies are identified. For adherence to occur, the clinical reality implied by labeling and treatment must be congruent with the patients' sociocultural construction of reality (Berger and Luckman 1967), and the symbolic content within which symptoms are embedded (Geertz 1966). The probability that congruence will be present is much higher in the popular sector because of the degree of shared knowledge.

A third evaluative aspect involves an assessment of the social events that occur throughout the health-seeking process—role shift, lay consultation and referral, and choice among helpers. The basic dynamic in this evaluation is concerned with trust (cf. Chrisman and Baker 1977). Trust involves: (1) the nature of cultural rights and obligations in role relationships; and (2) situational "therapeutic alliances" generated during care-related encounters. Trust on the part of the patient is related to the degree of perceived helper commitment. In kinship/family systems the expected persistence of relationships and knowledge that obligations are deeply felt and usually honored contribute to trust (Jacobson 1973). Ethnicity, another "primordial" basis for role relationships, also contributes to trust (Chrisman 1981b). For the more insular parochials, trust decreases with an increase in distance from family and neighbors. Noninsular cosmopolitans thus tend to place more trust in people outside the family than parochials. Parochials are likely to evaluate the advice of personally known and trusted helpers positively, with a concomitantly higher probability of adherence. Cosmopolitans are more likely to be flexible in their judgments; adherence is determined to a greater extent by other factors.

The three aspects of illness behavior evaluation interact with each other. Lay consultants or other popular treatment sources will have been chosen in the first place on the basis of cultural congruence—the fit between the emerging personal explanation of the illness and the expected explanation by the helper; and on the basis of social congruence—trust, and interaction style. Moreover, problem resolution may well be linked with these social and cultural aspects insofar as the cognitive assessment of congruence may actually contribute to feeling better (Starfield et al. 1981). These evaluative processes underlie more diversity in adherence following physician consultations than health-services research on compliance has indicated. For example, preliminary analysis of Chrisman's data indicates that doctors contributed about half of the treatments used by primary-care patients. The remainder derived from the popular sector.

Conclusion and Implications

We have suggested that natural histories of illness episodes in the popular sector are complex and rich in their social and cultural meaning. The experience of illness in community settings is far more than the diagnosis of disease in the examination room (Eisenberg 1977). Social interactions among lay people involve far more than lay referral to medical care. Evaluations of events during illness imply more than deciding whether to comply with a medical regimen. Indeed, most health care occurs in the popular sector.

The evaluation process that underpins patient decisions during illness provides clues to practitioners about how to modify practice styles in ways more sensitive to the sociocultural needs of their clients. Clinical assessments of disease process resolution may well be unrelated to lay evaluations of "feeling better" (Knowles 1977). The symbolic ramifications of illness definitions on well-being (Good 1977) imply that illness resolution is as much or more dependent upon the reestablishment of harmony in cultural meanings, stable family or work relationships, or positive affective state as upon laboratory confirmation that a pathological process has been arrested. Professional discussion and examination of how symptoms have been defined signals to the patient (a) that the practitioner is concerned with the person and not just biology and (b) allows the practitioner an opportunity to assess the resolution of psychosocial and cultural complaints as well as biological ones.

Joint participation in symptom definition and treatment action is crucial to joint construction of clinical reality. Practitioner-patient collaboration in this process is not only indicative of success in the management of the case, it is also the opportunity for health-promoting patient education. Instead of hiding behind medical jargon that protects the physician from involvement in the patient's life (Chrisman and Baker 1978, p. 718), medical knowledge can be shared and negotiated: increasing the patient's repertoire of health beliefs and allowing for potentially maladaptive beliefs to be altered; and providing knowledge that gives the patient greater confidence in what symptoms to look for when deciding on future consultations.

Americans are well aware of the cool, detached, "professional" style of health practitioners and have learned to live with it. Some people in the professional middle-class may actually prefer such institutionalized impersonality because of its congruence with other aspects of their daily lives. This presentation of self, no matter how useful in promoting a necessary element of trust in scientific medicine (see Blumhagen 1979; Anderson and Helm 1979), is inconsistent with the preferences of some patients (Friedl 1978). It seems to us that flexibility in interaction style to more closely respond to patient desires results in greater satisfaction for both patient and provider. Some physicians, for example, openly negotiate a preferred style.

Mental health professionals also have begun to recognize the central importance of "natural support systems" in the community and the relationship of these to both primary prevention and receiving help (Gottleib 1976; Gourash 1978). Moreover, they have begun to create formal and informal collaborative relationships among health providers, support networks, and lay helpers, including folk health practitioners such as *espiritistas* (Garrison 1980; Gottlieb and Schroter 1978). We believe that similar initiative is necessary in medical primary care. This suggestion derives not only from the importance of illness-related action sets in the popular sector but also from the likelihood of a significant psychosocial component in the wide range of relatively benign physical complaints presented to family practitioners and others in primary care.

As these examples suggest, we see the need for a solid understanding of *illness in the popular sector* as an important aspect of clinical work (e.g., Good and Good 1981; Katon and Kleinman, in press; Katon and Kleinman 1981; Pfifferling 1981; Stoeckle and Barsky 1981), and a central element in the education of health practitioners. As educators, we must work to develop further a clinically applied social science that can be taught to practitioners as strategies for patient care (Chrisman and Maretzki, in press; Kleinman and Smilkstein 1980; Smilkstein et al. 1981). As health researchers, we need to devote much more attention to ethnographic description of illness in community settings and to clinical ethnographies that can inform us on how the popular sector interacts with and affects care in the professional sector.

Finally, for health-care planners, our remarks emphasize the importance of reconceptualizing health-care delivery systems as reciprocal arenas of care. The popular sector requires some hard thinking about education and planning so that the care delivered in this sector as well as the referral process are better rationalized, more effective, and more culturally appropriate (see Kleinman 1978; Kleinman 1980, pp. 375–87; Kleinman and Hahn 1980).

REFERENCES

AMARASINGHAM, L. R. 1980. Movement among healers in Sri Lanka: a case study of a Sinhalese patient. *Culture, Medicine, and Psychiatry* 4(no. 1):71–92.

ANDERSEN, R., and NEWMAN, J. F. 1973. Societal and individual determinants of medical care utilization in the United States. *Health and Society* 51(no. 1):95–124.

ANDERSON, W. T. and HELM D. T. 1979. The physician-patient encounter: a process of reality negotiation. *In Patients, Physicians, and Illness*, ed. E. G. Jaco, pp. 259–71. New York: Free Press.

BAER, H. A. 1981. Prophets and advisors in black spiritual churches: therapy, palliative or opiate? *Culture, Medicine, and Psychiatry* 5(no. 2):145–70.

BECKER, M., ed. 1974. The health belief model and personal health behavior. *Health Education Monographs* 2(no.4):405–20.

BERGER, P. L., and LUCKMAN, T. 1967. The social construction of reality. Garden City, N.Y.: Anchor Books.

BERNSTEIN, B. 1971. *Class, codes and control*. London: Routledge and Kegan Paul.

BLUMHAGEN, D. 1979. The doctor's white coat: the image of the physician in modern America. *Annals of Internal Medicine* 91(no. 1):111–16.

———. 1980. Hyper-tension: a folk illness with a medical name. *Culture, Medicine, and Psychiatry* 4(no. 3):197–229.

BOTT, E. 1957. *Family and social network*. London: Tavistock.

BYERLY, E., and MOLGAARD, C. Social institutions and disease transmission. In *Clinically applied anthropology: anthropologists in health science settings*, ed. N. Chrisman and T. Maretzki. Dordrecht, Holland: D. Reidel, in press.

CAPLAN, G. 1974. Support systems and community mental health. *Behavioral Publications*.

CASSEL, E. J. 1976. Disease as an "it": concepts of disease revealed by patients' presentation of symptoms. *Social Science and Medicine* 10(no. 3, 4):143–46.

CHRISMAN, N. J. 1970. Situation and social network in cities. *Canadian Review of Sociology and Anthropology* 7(no. 4):245–58.

———. 1977. The health seeking process: an approach to the natural history of illness. *Culture, Medicine, and Psychiatry* 1(no. 4):351–77.

———. 1981a. Folk beliefs, popular culture, and health care. *University of Washington Medicine* 8(no. 1):21–28.

———. 1981b. Ethnic persistence in an urban setting. *Ethnicity* 8:256–92.

———, and BAKER, R. M. 1978. Exploring the doctor-patient relationship: a sociocultural pilot study in a family practice residency. *Journal of Family Practice* 7(no. 4):713–19.

———, and KLEINMAN, A. 1980. Health beliefs and practices. In *Harvard encyclopedia of American ethnic groups*, ed. S. Thernstrom, A. Orlov and O. Handlin. Cambridge, Mass.: Harvard University Press.

———, and MARETZKI, T. eds. *Clinically applied anthropology: anthropologists in health settings*. Dordrecht, Holland: D. Reidel, in press.

CLARK, M. 1970. *Health in the Mexican-American culture*. Berkeley, Calif: University of California Press.

COMAROFF, J. 1980. Health and the cultural order: the case of the Barolong boo Ratshidi of Southern Africa. *American Ethnologist* 7:637–57.

DEMERS, R., et al. 1980. An Exploration of the depth and dimensions of illness behavior. *Journal of Family Practice* 11:1085–92.

DORSEY, P., and JACKSON, H. 1976. Cultural health traditions: the Latino/Chicano perspective. In *Providing safe nursing care for ethnic people of color*, ed. M. Branch and P. Paxton, pp. 41–80. New York: Appleton-Century-Crofts.

DUNN, F. L. 1976. Traditional Asian medicine and cosmopolitan medicine as adaptive systems. In *Asian medical systems*, ed. C. Leslie, pp. 133–58. Berkeley, Calif: University of California Press.

EISENBERG, L. 1977. Disease and illness: distinctions between professional and popular ideas of sickness. *Culture, Medicine, and Psychiatry* 1(no. 1):9–23.

ERASMUS, C. J. 1961. *Man takes control: cultural development and American aid*. Minneapolis, Minn.: University of Minnesota Press.

FABREGA, H. 1973. Toward a model of illness behavior. *Medical Care* 11(no. 6):470–84.

———. *A cultural approach to medicine*, Pittsburgh, Pa.: University of Pittsburgh Press, in press.

———, and SILVER, D. 1973. *Illness and shamanistic curing in Zinacantan*. Stanford, Calif.: Stanford University Press.

FERGUSON, A. 1981. The role of pharmaceuticals in the development of the commercial pharmaceutical sector of medical care and alternative medicalization: the case of El Salvador. *Culture, Medicine, and Psychiatry* 5(no. 2):105–134.

FINLAYSON, A. Social networks as coping resources. *Social Science and Medicine* 10:97–103.

FOSTER, G. 1979. Humoral traces in United States folk medicine. *Medical Anthropology Newsletter* 10(no. 2):17–20.

FREIDSON, E. 1970. *Profession of medicine: a study of the sociology of applied knowledge*. New York: Dodd, Mead.

FRIEDL, J. 1978. *Health care services and the Appalachian migrant*. Ohio State University. Prepared for Health Services Research, Health Resources Administration, Department of Health, Education, and Welfare.

GAINES, A. 1979. Definitions and diagnoses: cultural implications of psychiatric help-seeking and psychiatrists' definitions of the situations in psychiatric emergencies. *Culture, Medicine, and Psychiatry* 3(no. 4):381–418.

GANS, H. 1962. *The urban villagers: group and class in the life of Italian-Americans*. New York: Free Press.

GARRISON, V. 1977. Doctor, *espiritista* or psychiatrist? Health seeking behavior in a Puerto Rican neighborhood of New York City. *Medical Anthropology* 1(no. 2):65–180.

———, Folk healing systems as elements in the community support systems of psychiatric patients. 1980. Working paper 18b, Inner City Support Systems.

GEERTSEN, R., et al. 1975. A reexamination of Suchman's views on social factors in health care utilization. *Journal of Health and Social Behavior* 16(no. 2):226–37.

GEERTZ, C. 1966. Religion as a cultural system. In *Anthropological approaches to the study of religion*, ed. M. Banton, pp. 1–46. London: Tavistock.

GOOD, B. S. 1977. The heart of what's the matter. The semantics of illness in Iran. *Culture, Medicine, and Psychiatry* 1(no. 1):25–29.

——, and GOOD, M. D. 1981. The meaning of symptoms: a cultural hermeneutic model for clinical practice. In *The relevance of social science for medicine*, ed. L. Eisenberg and A. Kleinman, pp. 165–96. Dordrecht, Holland: D. Reidel.

GOTTLIEB, B. 1976. Lay influences on the utilization and provision of health services: a review. *Canadian Psychological Review* 17(no. 2):126–36.

——. 1978. The development and application of a classification scheme of informal helping behaviors. *Canadian Journal of Behavioral Science* 10(no. 2):105–15.

——, and SCHROTER, C. 1978. Collaboration and resource exchange between professionals and natural support systems. *Professional Psychology*, November 1978, pp. 614–22.

GOURASH, N. 1978. Help-seeking: a review of the literature. *American Journal of Community Psychology* 6(no. 5):413–23.

HANNERZ, U. 1969. *Soulside: inquiries into ghetto culture and community*. New York: Columbia University Press.

HARWOOD, A. 1977. *Rx: spiritist as needed*. New York: Wiley.

HELMAN, C. 1978. "Feed a cold, starve a fever"—folk models of infection in an English suburban community and their relation to medical treatment. *Culture, Medicine, and Psychiatry* 2(no. 2):107–39.

——. Patients' perceptions of psychotropic drugs. *Social Science and Medicine*, in press.

HENRY, J. 1958. The personal community. *American Anthropologist* 60(no. 5):827–32.

HORWITZ, A. 1977. Social networks and pathways to psychiatric treatment. *Social Forces* 56(no. 1):86–105.

——. 1978. Family, kin, and friend network in psychiatric help-seeking. *Social Science and medicine* 12:297–304.

HULKA, B., et al. 1972. Determinants of physician utilization. *Medical Care* 10:300–9.

JACOBSON, D. 1973. *Itinerant townsmen: friendship and social order in urban Uganda*. Menlo Park, Calif.: Cummings.

JANZEN, J. 1978. *The quest for therapy in lower Zaire*. Berkeley, Calif: University of California Press.

JONES, W. T. 1976. World-views and Asian medical systems: some suggestions for further study. In *Asian medical systems*, ed. C. Leslie, pp. 383–404. Berkeley, Calif: University of California Press.

KASL, S. U., and COBB, S. 1966. Health behavior, illness behavior, and sick role behavior. *Archives of Environmental Health* 12:246–66.

KATON, W. and KLEINMAN, A. Somatization and depression: a review, pts. 1 and 2. *American Journal of Medicine*, in press.

——. 1981. Doctor-patient negotiations and other social science strategies in patient care. In *The relevance of social science for medicine*, ed. L. Eisenberg and A. Kleinman, pp. 253–379. Dordrecht, Holland: D. Reidel.

KLEINMAN, A. 1978. International health care planning from an ethnomedical perspective. *Medical Anthropology* 2(no. 2):71–96.

——. 1980. *Patients and healers in the context of culture*. Berkeley, Calif: University of California Press.

——, and GALE, J. C. Comparative outcome study of patients treated by Western physicians and healers in Taiwan. *Culture, Medicine, and Psychiatry*, in press.

KLEINMAN, A., and HAHN, R. A. 1980. The sociocultural model of illness and healing: review and policy implications. Paper prepared for the Working Conference on Competing Definitions of Health, The Rockefeller Foundation, 11–12 January 1980.

KLEINMAN, A., and SMILKSTEIN, G. 1980. Psychosocial issues in assessment in primary care. In *Behavioral science in family practice*, ed. G. M. Rosen et al., pp. 95–108. N.Y.: Appleton-Century-Crofts.

KLEINMAN, A., et al. 1975. Medicine in Chinese cultures: comparative studies of health care in Chinese and other societies. DHEW pub. no. (NIH) 75–653.

KNOWLES, J. H., ed. 1977. *Doing better and feeling worse: health in the United States.* New York: Norton.

LAFARGUE, J. 1981. *Those you can count on: a social network study of family organization in an urban population.* Ph.D. dissertation, University of Washington.

LESLIE, C., ed. 1976. *Asian medical systems: a comparative study.* Berkeley, Calif: University of California Press.

LEWIS, G. 1975. *Knowledge of illness in a Sepik society.* London: Athlone Press.

LEWIS, O. 1966. *La vida: a Puerto Rican family in the culture of poverty.* New York: Random House.

LIEBERMAN, M. A., and GLIDEWELL, J. C. 1978. Overview: special issue on the helping process. *American Journal of Community Psychology* 6(no. 5):405–11.

LIEBOW, E. 1967. *Tally's Corner: a study of Negro streetcorner men.* Boston: Little, Brown.

LINDENBAUM, S. 1979. *Kuru sorcery: disease and danger in the New Guinea highlands.* Palo Alto, Calif. Mayfield Publishing Company.

LIN, K. M., et al. *Sociocultural determinants of the help seeking behaviors of patients with mental illness* (manuscript).

LIN, T. Y., et al. 1978. Ethnicity and patterns of help seeking. *Culture, Medicine, and Psychiatry* 2(no. 1):3–14.

LOGAN, M. H. 1977. Anthropological research on the hot-cold theory of disease: some methodological suggestions. *Medical Anthropology* 1(no. 4):88–112.

MACELVEEN-HOEHN, P., and SMITH-DEJULIO, K. Social network behavior in long-term illness: preliminary analysis. In *Networks for helping: illustrations from research and practice*, ed. C. Froland and D. Pancoast. Portland, Oreg.: Portland State University Press.

MAUTHE, J. 1978. *Health beliefs, social networks and breast self-examination.* M.N. thesis, University of Washington.

MAYER, A. C. 1966. The significance of quasi-groups in the study of complex societies. In *The social anthropology of complex societies*, ed. M. Banton. ASA Monograph #4. London: Tavistock.

MCKENZIE, J., and CHRISMAN, N. 1977. Healing herbs, gods and magic. *Nursing Outlook* 77(no. 5):326–29.

MCKINLAY, J. B. 1973. Social networks, lay consultation, and help-seeking behavior. *Social Forces* 51(no. 3):275–92.

———. Social network influences on morbid episodes and the career of help seeking. In *The relevance of social science for medicine*, ed. L. Eisenberg and A. Kleinman, pp. 77–107. Dordrecht, Holland: D. Reidel.

MITCHELL, J. C. 1969. The concept and use of social networks. In *Social networks in urban situations*, ed. J. C. Mitchell, pp. 1–50. Manchester: Manchester University Press.

———. 1974. Social networks *Annual Review of Anthropology* 3:279–99.

MOODY, J. 1966. Personal communication to Chrisman, San Francisco satanic witch cult.

MUELLER, D. P. 1980. Social networks: a promising direction for research on the relationship of the social environment to psychiatric disorder. *Social Science and Medicine* 14A:147–61.

NESS, R. C. 1980. The impact of indigenous healing activity: an empirical study of two fundamentalist churches. *Social Science and Medicine* 14B:167–80.

NICHTER, M. Idioms of distress: alternatives in expression of psychosocial distress: a case study from South India. *Culture, Medicine, and Psychiatry* 5(no. 4):in press.

OBEYESEKERE. G. 1978. Illness, culture and meaning. In *Culture and healing in Asian societies*, ed. A. Kleinman, pp. 253–63. Cambridge, Mass.: Schenkman.

PFIFFERLING, J. 1981. A cultural prescription for mediococentrism. In *The relevance of social science for medicine*, ed. L. Eisenberg and A. Kleinman, pp. 197–222. Dordrecht, Holland: D. Reidel.

POLGAR, S. 1962. Health and human behavior: areas of interest common to the social and medical sciences. *Current Anthropology* 3(no. 2):159–205.

PRESS, I. 1969. Urban illness: physicians, curers and dual use in Bogota. *Journal of Health and Social Behavior* 10:209–218.

SALLOWAY, J. C., and DILLON, P. B. 1973. A comparison of family networks and friend networks in health care utilization. *Journal of Comparative Family Studies* 4(no.1):131–42.

SARGENT, C. *The cultural context of therapeutic choice: obstetrical decisions among the Bariba of Benin.* Dordrecht, Holland: D. Reidel, in press.

SCHWARTZ, L. R. 1969. The hierarchy of resort in curative practices: the Admiralty Islands, Melanesia. *Journal of Health and Social Behavior* 10:201–8.

SHUMAN, D. 1979. Personal communication to Chrisman, Dallas Dianic witch cult.

SMILKSTEIN, G., et al. 1981. The clinical social science conference in biopsychosocial teaching. *Journal of Family Practice* 12(no. 2):347–53.

SMITH, M. E. 1972. Folk medicine among the Sicilian-Americans of Buffalo, New York. *Urban Anthropology* 1(no. 1):87–106.

SNOW, L. F. 1974. Folk medical beliefs and their implications for care of patients. *Annals of Internal Medicine* 81:82–96.

———. 1978. Sorcerers, saints and charlatans: black folk healers in urban America. *Culture, Medicine, and Psychiatry* 2(no. 1):69–106.

STACK, C. 1974. *All our kin.* New York: Harper Row.

STARFIELD, B., et al. 1981. The influence of patient-practitioner agreement on outcome of care. *American Journal of Public Health* 71(no. 2):127–31.

STOECKLE, J. D., and BARSKY, A. J. 1981. Attributions: uses of social science knowledge in the "doctoring" of primary care. In *The relevance of social science for medicine,* ed. L. Eisenberg and A. Kleinman, pp. 223–40. Dordrecht, Holland: D. Reidel.

SUCHMAN, E. 1965. Stages of illness and medical care. *Journal of Health and Human Behavior* 6:114–28.

SUTTLES, G. 1968. *The social order of the slum.* Chicago: University of Chicago Press.

TOLSDORF, C. 1976. Social networks, support and coping: an exploratory study. *Family Process* 15:407.

UNSCHULD, P. 1979. *Medical ethics in Imperial China: a study in historical anthropology.* Berkeley, Calif: University of California Press.

WEIDMAN, H. H., et al. 1978. *Miami health ecology project report,* Vol. 1. Miami, Fla.: University of Miami.

WHEELDON, P. D. 1969. The operation of voluntary associations and personal networks in the political processes of an inter-ethnic community. In *Social networks in urban situations,* ed. J. C. Mitchell, pp. 128–80. Manchester: Manchester University Press.

WHITE, K. T.; WILLIAMS, T.; and GREENBERG, B. G. 1961. The ecology of medical care. *New England Journal of Medicine* 265(no. 18):885–92.

YOUNG, A. 1976. Some implications of medical beliefs and practices for social anthropology. *American Anthropologist* 78(no. 1):5–24.

———. 1980. The discourse on stress and reproduction of conventional knowledge. *Social Science and Medicine* 14B:133–46.

YOUNG, J. 1980. A model of illness treatment decisions in a Tarascan town. *American Ethnologist* 7(no. 1):106–131.

ZBOROWSKI, M. 1958. Cultural components in response to pain. In *Patients, physicians and illness,* ed. E.G. Jaco. New York: Free Press.

ZOLA, I. 1966. Culture and symptoms: an analysis of patient's presenting complaints. *American Sociological Review* 3:615–30.

———. 1972a. The concept of trouble and sources of medical assistance. *Social Science and Medicine* 8:216–36.

———. 1972b. Studying the decision to see a doctor. *Advances in Psychosomatic Medicine* 8:216–36.

Chapter 27

The Experience and Expression of Distress: The Study of Illness Behavior and Medical Utilization

David Mechanic

ONE OF THE MOST VEXING PROBLEMS in the study of illness concerns the relationships among psychological discomforts, physical symptoms, and behavioral responses. Social and cultural expectations shape how we experience and interpret events, leaving many issues of scientific interest not only outside the direct scrutiny of the scientist but also outside the awareness of the respondent. Thus, it may be a formidable challenge to differentiate what people actually experience from what they are willing to acknowledge about their subjective states. The study of illness behavior involves a wide range of approaches that illuminate aspects of experience and response. Approaches from varying angles come together to provide a richer picture of the fascinating complexity of how people experience and express discomfort.

Although the concept of illness usually refers to a limited scientific concept denoting a constellation of symptoms or a condition underlying them (Mechanic, 1978), the term *illness behavior* describes the way persons respond to bodily indications which they experience as abnormal. Illness behavior thus involves the manner in which persons monitor their bodies, define and interpret their symptoms, take remedial actions, and utilize the health-care system. People differentially perceive, evaluate, and respond to bodily changes, and such behaviors have enormous influence on the extent of the interference of symptoms with usual life routines, the chronicity of the condition, the attainment of appropriate care, and the cooperation of the patient in the treatment situation.

Strategies for Studying Illness Behavior

People's responses to changes in bodily functioning come from prior learning and previous experience, from dominant cultural explanations of symptoms, from prior illness experience, and from their own intuitive models of body functioning and those of their closest intimates. In some cases, the occurrence of bodily changes may involve clearcut symptoms, be highly visible or unambiguously

591

observable, and be readily interpretable with existing and commonly shared schema of disease. For example, the person may have a severe cough, a high fever, and upper respiratory discomfort. Previous experience, observable symptoms, and readily available interpretations make the illness definition less problematic than if the symptoms are ambiguous, outside the person's usual experience, and not easily made sense of within readily available understandings. Many symptoms are diffuse. vague, and fluctuating, providing an opportunity for the respondent to consider alternative definitions, interpretations, and modes of action.

In the process of living their lives, people experience many troubles and tensions which may result in a wide variety of adaptations including physical illness, psychological disorder, and risk-taking behaviors of a variety of kinds. In these circumstances persons may or may not be aware of the degree of tension they are experiencing or its determinants. The factors shaping how tensions are expressed, and the conditions under which they become manifest as physical or psychological disorder, or both, are only poorly understood, and investigators working in psychiatric epidemiology are in a quandary as how best to aggregate varying types of expressive patterns. Are we to take the fact that women complain of depression and anxiety much more commonly than men as indicative that they have more such disorder (Weissman and Klerman 1977), or are we also to take into account the higher prevalence of excessive drinking, drug use, and violence among men (Dohrenwend 1976)? Similarly, does the fact that Chinese rarely complain of depression and show little depressed affect suggest the absence of such disorder, or are common complaints among Chinese of physical symptoms frequently accompanying depression among Westerners indicative of the fact that they are indeed depressed but do not manifest such disorder on a psychological level (Kleinman and Mechanic 1979)? While there are a variety of clinical theories in psychosomatic medicine that speak to the interrelationships among the sociocultural, psychological, and physical subsystems, the absence of a successful methodological strategy for attacking such questions leaves much of the work in this area at a descriptive level. Thus, while clinicians may illustrate the conversion of psychological tensions to bodily symptoms or to disturbing behavior, we have made little progress in explaining or predicting the conditions under which one or another adaptive response will occur.

Since the major way of enhancing understanding is to develop research strategies that allow amplification of issues, it is often the case that indirect approaches, however incomplete, allow us to push our understanding forward. While each approach may be limiting in some fashion, the synthesis of information from alternative strategies helps us to piece together a more comprehensive picture. In the study of illness behavior, one can focus on modes of interpreting symptoms as an acquired disposition, view such behavior as part of a complex interaction between personal and situational factors shaped by a particular sociocultural milieu, or conceptualize it as a process of information processing and decision-making. Before considering these strategies, however, let us consider how the larger sociocultural setting limits expressive modes.

The Sociocultural Context

Even a cursory reading of medical history reveals a remarkable shift in the manner in which expressions of illness are transformed from one era to another. Female hysteria, for example, characterized by fainting, conversion reactions, and "kicking about" have virtually disappeared in the urban modern environment although vestiges of the disorder are still occasionally seen in isolated rural cultures that are relatively unsophisticated and psychologically repressive. One interpretation of the disappearance of hysteria is that it no longer brings a sympathetic response from the social environment and is suspect not only among physicians but among sophisticated persons more generally (Veith 1970). But while the dramatic histrionics of hysteria are rarely seen, more mundane expressions of the somatization of distress are ubiquitous and constitute a major demand on the medical-care system.

In any historical period the normative and ideological opportunities and constraints influence the selection among alternative modes of tension reduction. People facing personal troubles can draw on existing sociocultural conceptions of the nature of these troubles and what one might do about them. At any point in time there may be more or less social consensus surrounding the definition of the problem, attribution of the cause, and conceptions of possible remedies. These shape how people view their troubles and what actions they contemplate. Personal tension, for example, alternatively may be defined as resulting from personality deficiencies, moral dilemmas, social or cultural constraints, or exploitation. The availability of reference groups that adhere to particular definitions and provide social support is essential to maintaining particular interpretations (Greenley and Mechanic 1976; Kadushin 1969). The development of women's consciousness groups is a case in point. Prior to such developments many women experiencing distress and dissatisfaction came to psychiatrists complaining of unhappiness and feelings of inadequacy as wives, mothers, and women. The problem was viewed primarily as a unique personal problem resulting from the client's personality and social development. With the growth of the women's movement, such feelings are increasingly explained as a consequence of constraining role expectations, exploitative role relationships, and blocked opportunities to achieve aspirations; and it is not difficult to find many women reinforcing this conception and providing social support. Thus such personal distress is increasingly being redefined as a commonly shared social problem. Similar redefinitions are increasingly applied by the aged, the handicapped, and homosexuals.

The Dispositional Approach

The dispositional approach assumes that persons have a fairly stable orientation to respond to illness in particular ways and seeks to identify differences in these response patterns and the ways they develop. While some persons tend to be stoic in the face of illness, others are matter-of-fact or hypochondriacal. While some patients seek care readily for even minor symptoms, others are reluctant to seek care for even life-threatening illnesses. The point to remember is that the disposition is a research assumption and not necessarily a reality. There is considerable variability in people's responses from one situation to another and over time, and we have insufficient evidence demonstrating the stability of health and illness behavior patterns over time to feel fully confident in the dispositional assumption (Mechanic 1979b). It is simply a convenience for the purposes of acquiring more knowledge.

Reactions to pain or dispositions to use various kinds of medical services may be measured by verbal reports of what respondents would do in hypothetical situations or by their actual behavior such as consulting a psychiatrist, joining a self-help group, or practicing transcendental meditation. The fact of having used one of these approaches may serve as a proxy for the disposition, and the investigator then tries to identify the factors associated with the response of interest.

Most dispositional studies are efforts to understand the development of the behavior pattern. For example, many studies of illness show that women report symptoms more frequently than men do and that they use physicians and psychiatrists more frequently as well (Lewis and Lewis 1977; Mechanic 1976b). A variety of interpretations have been posited to account for these findings, but none that adequately explains all of the available data. Interpretations for the sex differences include the hypothesis that there are real differences in the prevalence of disorder. Other explanations are that characteristics of the measures used and judgments made reflect sex biases, women's lower thresholds to perceive symptoms, women's greater willingness to acknowledge symptoms and seek care, women's greater knowledge and interest in health matters, and different role responsibilities between the sexes that affect the use of services. Differences in prevalence of symptoms are sometimes explained by differential stress among men and women, by different vulnerabilities to stressors, varying levels of coping resources and skills, and different networks of social support. Although each of these interpretations is given from time to time, few studies successfully compare competing explanations (Mechanic 1976b).

Significant differences in responses to pain and illness between the sexes are already apparent by the fourth grade and increase with age (Mechanic 1964). Aggregate data on sex and use of medical care suggest that women have higher rates of utilization at all ages, except during childhood when the mother probably makes most of the decisions for both boys and girls. Lewis and his colleagues (1975), however, have shown that sex differences in using a school health service were apparent among young children in an experimental child-initiated help-seeking system. How these differences arise, how they are sustained, and how they might be modified are important research issues, an area to which I now turn.

Acquisition of Health Attitudes and Behavior

The large range of variations in health and illness behavior from one culture to another and among varying ethnic groups suggests that these are largely learned differences, but we understand relatively little about how these patterns are taught and acquired and how the health education of children can successfully be altered. In trying to explain the cultural differences he observed, Zborowski (1952) reported that Jewish and Italian patients related that their mothers showed overprotective and overconcerned attitudes about the children's health and participation in sports, and that they were constantly warned of the advisability of avoiding colds, fights, and other threatenting situations. Zborowski suggested that this overprotective attitude fostered complaining and anxieties about illness. Schachter (1959) executed an impressive series of experiments of affiliation under stress and found that firstborn and only children were more likely than others to want to be in the presence of another person when facing stress in adult life. Schachter hypothesized that the attention given to the first child and the inexperience of the parents in child rearing are likely to result in a greater dependence among such children as compared with later-born children. Consistent with Schachter's hypothesis, Tessler (1980) found in a study of 1,665 children from 587 families that early-born children were more frequent users of physician services than later-born, even controlling for variation in family size.

However simple the notion of cultural acquisition of illness behavior may appear, it is difficult to demonstrate empirically the processes of transmission. Mechanic (1964), using data acquired in 1961 from 350 children, their mothers, teachers, school records, and family illness diaries, found that the best predictors of children's illness responses were sex and age. By the fourth grade, girls were more likely to express pain and fear than boys, and these differences increased with age, although both older boys and girls were more stoic than younger children. Although the mothers' illness behavior patterns were predictive of decisions they made about the children's health, they did not successfully predict the children's response patterns in 1961.

In a sixteen-year follow-up of these children, we had an opportunity to examine developmental influences on syndromes of symptom reporting in young adulthood (Mechanic 1979a, 1980). The first measure—an index of psychological distress—is a summative measure of seven symptoms depicting anxiety and depression; the second, a summary measure of fifteen common physical complaints. These two measures are correlated .42, and neither are associated with sex in this sample. Since the results are similar for the two dependent variables, I focus on the former but will later briefly note some differences in determinants of the two types of complaining.

These dependent variables, typical of measures used in psychiatric epidemiology, are important because they are associated with measures of functioning, and persons with high scores on such scales are disproportionately seen in general medical settings, psychiatric outpatient clinics, and other agencies providing assistance. While these measures do not denote illness as such, there is considerable disagreement as to what they actually represent. It has been suggested that they reflect demoralization, self-dissatisfaction or a quasineurosis, and may either accompany or be independent of tangible illness (Dohrenwend et al. 1980). High scores on these measures appear to tap the diffuse neuroses that have been of particular interest to psychodynamically oriented ego psychologists and psychiatrists. The index used in our study had an average correlation of .56 with five other variables denoting low psychological well-being: self-description of unhappiness (.46); description of low spirts (−.44); degree of worry about eight specified life problems (.56); high neuroticism on the Eysenck scale (.77); and low self-esteem (−.59). It was also correlated .41 with respondents' reports in 1977 that they had emotional problems, nervous trouble, or chronic nerves.

One deterrent to predictions of distress in young adulthood using childhood measures is instability in the dependent measure. Studies of the Langer twenty-two-item scale or subsets of items from this scale suggest that the three-to-four-year correlation of scores on such scales is approximately .5 to .6 (Wheaton 1978). The size of the correlation will be affected by both reliability problems and lack of stability. While we do not know the degree of stability for a period as long as sixteen years, it is unlikely to be as high as .5, thus making it difficult to identify 1961 predictors of distress in 1977.

The theoretical approach used in this developmental study was that the sense of distress measured by our index was shaped by three aspects: (1) body sensations, symptoms, or feelings different from those ordinarily experienced; (2) social stress; and (3) cognitive definitions suggesting organizing hypotheses about what a person is feeling (Mechanic 1972). Changes in body sensations increase self-awareness, and stress contributes to body arousal and psychological disorientation that further motivate attention to inner feelings. The findings are consistent with the conclusion that factors that focus the child's attention on internal states and that teach a pattern of internal monitoring contribute to a distress syndrome. Respondents with such syndromes were more likely to come from families in which the mother was more upset and symptomatic, the child had more common physical symptoms such as colds and sore throats, and attention was directed to such symptoms by keeping the child home from school. Moreover, the data do not support the hypothesis that adulthood distress syndromes are simply a continuous pattern of illness from childhood to young adulthood. Although learned internal monitoring appears to be an important aspect of distress, it is only a vulnerability factor. The regression model based on the four most influential 1961 predictors of distress characterizing childhood physical symptoms, school absence, and two maternal measures explain only 9 percent of the variance. Whether a distress syndrome will develop depends on many additional influences, such as the degree of psychological and bodily dysfunction, adverse life experience, and influences that reinforce a focus on internal feeling states.

There is increasing experimental evidence that simply drawing a subject's attention to some aspect of bodily functioning results in an increased prevalence of symptom reporting (Pennebaker & Skelton 1978), and experimentally induced self-awareness most commonly results in negative evaluation (Wicklund 1975). Thus, it is plausible that persons who focus on feelings and bodily changes will be more likely to experience discomforting states than those who do not. In an earlier epidemiological study of Wisconsin students, Greenley and Mechanic (1976) found that respondents high on a scale of identification with introspective others not only reported more psychological symptoms but also were more likely to use medical, counseling, and other formal helping services. In the child follow-up, introspectiveness was measured by a scale in which respondents indicated the degree to which they were "sensitive and introspective," "worried about meaning in life," and "interested in psychology." Scores on this scale are correlated .47 with the distress measure despite the fact that the items do not directly measure symptoms and describe everyday concerns. The effect is approximately the same for each item in the scale. When added to various regression models of distress, introspectiveness retains its strength as a predictor, overshadowing all other predictors.

When psychological orientations, such as introspectiveness, persist into adulthood, they affect the interpretation of life experience and illness. In a recent study of psychological reactions to the nuclear accident at Three Mile Island, persons high on a measure of introspectiveness were more upset, reported more physical and behavioral symptoms, and had higher levels of psychological distress than those with lower scores. Since we studied a cohort of the same individuals following the accident, and again nine months later, we also examined to what degree distress persisted over time, when the initial level of distress following the accident is taken into account. Introspective persons not only were more distressed initially, but were also more likely to remain distressed over time, relative to their initial reactions.

As one might anticipate, the introspectiveness score is related to parental variables similar to those predicting adult distress, particularly measures of parental negative behavior toward the child. It is conceivable that such a pattern of concern with self and self-scrutiny results when familial patterns are disrupted and such self-appraisal usually culminates in negative self-evaluation.

As noted earlier, our scales of psychological distress and reporting of common physical symptoms are substantially correlated, have many similar predictors, and are amenable to a common theoretical interpretation (Mechanic 1980). Two possible important determinants differentiating whether persons favor psychological or physical complaining are actual adult experience with symptoms and illness on the one hand, and cultural influences on the definition of illness on the other. While reporting physical symptoms is culturally more neutral, reporting psychological symptoms is more dependent on social acceptability. Social desirability response bias was significantly associated with reporting psychological symptoms ($-.18$) but was not significantly associated with reporting physical symptoms ($-.06$). In contrast, reports of chronic illness, bed disability days, and tendency to get sick were more highly correlated with physical symptoms than with psychological reports. In short, it is my hypothesis that the types of processes of perception and definition that have been described are filtered through objective physical experience and cultural influences.

The Broad Epidemiological Survey

The most typical approach to studying illness behavior is to carry out epidemiological surveys and identify those using or not using certain types of care or those who engage in particular health and illness practices. Other data from the surveys are then used to account for these differences. Such surveys typically examine sociodemographic factors, distress, life-change events, and attitudes toward medical care. Among factors commonly found to be associated with utilization of medical care are quality and severity of physical symptoms, levels of distress, sex, inclination to use medical facilities, skepticism of medical care, and faith in doctors.

A major problem with most epidemiological studies of help seeking is that they fail to differentiate the extent to which various independent predictors affect utilization through their influence on the occurrence of symptoms and the extent to which they have an independent effect on the help-seeking pattern (Mechanic 1976c). Moreover, in concentrating on studying only one source of assistance, such as general physician services or a psychiatric clinic, these studies cannot differentiate factors that predict help seeking in general as compared with those that predict the use of a specific type of service. Studies of use of multiple agencies by a specified population are extremely difficult to execute because of the complexity of the American health-care system and modes of payment. These studies usually require an enrolled population using a defined set of helping agencies.

Gurin and associates (1960), in a national survey of definitions and reactions to personal problems, suggested that different types of factors influence various aspects of the help-seeking process, such as identification of the problem, the decision to seek care, and the type of practitioner consulted. Greenley and Mechanic (1976) studied the patterns of use of helping facilities for psychological distress syndromes among a large student population. Among the types of sources of help studied were psychiatrists, counseling services, religious counselors, general physicians, and other agencies on campus. There was considerable overlap in the problems brought to different sources of help, and most predictors of help seeking were specific to particular sources of assistance.

It was difficult to identify factors predicting help seeking in general as compared with those specifically predicting going to a psychiatrist, a clergyman, or to a general physician. Students with a tendency to seek help for psychological problems as measured by hypothetical items, women, and those with introspective orientations were more inclined to use most types of helping services including psychiatrists, counseling, and general physicians. In contrast, most other predictors were linked specifically to certain types of providers. A disproportionate number of women, Jewish students, students with no religious affiliation, those from the eastern United States, and those from more educated and affluent families were more likely to use psychiatric services. Students who were high on countercultural orientations were much more likely to use psychiatry than other sources of assistance. Catholics and students with more religious participation went to religious counselors. Younger students, unmarried students, and those with less distinctive social and cultural orientations were more likely to use student counseling than student psychiatry. However, the characteristics of students using any of a variety of sources of help were not very different than the characteristics of the population as a whole. Sociocultural characteristics, attitudes, knowledge, reference group orientations, and degree of psychological distress all had independent effects on the use of helping services. In sum, it appears that symptoms and distress are triggers that initiate the patient's search and evaluation process. Social and cultural attitudes and orientations tend to shape this evaluative process and the decisions made about appropriate ways of coping. This can be investigated through studies of symptom attribution.

Symptom Attribution

A third approach to studying illness behavior, thus, is to focus on the processes through which persons identify and evaluate symptoms, make interpretations of their causes and implications, and decide on the types of help to seek. Persons experiencing changes in their feeling states and physical functioning attempt to make sense of what is happening, and they tend to examine different intuitive hypotheses about the seriousness of their problems and the need for assistance. A major dimension of this process is the way people evaluate the causes of a problem and the extent to which they attribute the problem to external factors, internal difficulties, or moral and existential issues. An important function of health education is to shape such processes of evaluation and attribution so that they culminate in an effective pattern of care. Understanding attribution processes and the ways to modify them has many rehabilitative implications (Mechanic 1977).

For example, during World War II soldiers who experienced "breakdowns" in combat were evacuated to the back lines, and their disorganized behavior was interpreted as a product of early childhood socialization. This provided the soldier with an excuse for maintaining his behavior, and one that made it difficult to return him to a functioning role. The military later developed a policy that defined combat stress reactions as transient responses. Although soldiers were given opportunities to rest, the behavior was defined as a normal reaction to prolonged stress, and most soldiers were expected to return to active duty. As a result, there were many fewer psychiatric losses (Glass 1958). These policies are now used in community care of the mentally ill, and it is clear that patients suffering from considerable distress and impairment can continue to cope in many realms of their lives. Although such "normalization" can be carried too far, the evidence is that the encouragement of continued coping and activity often protects the patient from further deterioration and despair, and that patients are very much influenced by social expectations (Brown et al. 1966).

Influence of the Health-Care Services System

A fourth way of studying illness behavior is to examine the influence of varying features of the health-care system on the responses of the patient. One crucial determinant of help seeking among patients is the accessibility of medical care (Lewis, Fein, and Mechanic 1976); and barriers to care may develop because of location, financial requirements, bureaucratic responses to the patient, social distance between client and professional, the lack of a regular or continuing relationship with an appropriate therapist, and stigma in seeking assistance. The point is that the problem can often be attacked more effectively by modifying the way agencies and professionals organize to deal with a problem than by attempting to change patient behavior. Organizational barriers affect patients differently (Mechanic 1976a). Coinsurance and deductibles inhibit the poor more than the affluent; and aggressive, educated, and sophisticated patients can get what they want from medical bureaucracies more readily than can passive and less informed patients. Similarly, such factors as distance to the site of care, waiting time, and a personal and continuing interest in the patient have different significance for varying population groups, and these must be understood for the effective organization of medical services.

Vocabularies of Distress

It is apparent that social learning affects the vocabularies that people use to describe their problems and complaints. It is reasonable to anticipate that persons from origins in which the expression of symptoms and a desire for help are permissible will be more likely to voice such feelings than those who are socialized in cultural settings that encourage denial of such feelings. Moreover, social groups differ in the extent to which they use and accept psychological and psychodynamic vocabularies, and these are likely to shape the way people conceptualize and deal with their distress. Kadushin (1969) found, for example, that persons who were receptive to psychotherapy were part of a loose social network of friends and supporters of psychotherapy, They shared the same life-styles, liked the same music, and had many social and political ideas in common. Such networks tend to support and encourage psychological conceptualizations of problems just as certain families do. In contrast, other families and subgroups disapprove of such patterns of expression and tend to sanction them. Zborowski (1952), for example, in describing the "Old American" family stressed the tendency of the mother to teach the child to take pain "like a man," not to be a sissy, and not to cry. Such training, he argued, does not discourage use of the doctor, but implies that such use will be based on physical needs rather than emotional concerns.

It might be anticipated that persons from subgroups that discourage the expression of psychological distress will be inhibited from showing such distress directly but will mask it with the presentation of more acceptable symptoms. Kerckhoff and Back (1968), in a study of the diffusion among women employees of a southern mill of an hysterical illness alleged to be caused by an unknown insect, found that the prevalence of the condition was high among women under strain who could not admit that they had a problem and who did not know how to cope with it. Bart (1968), in comparing women who entered a neurology service but who were discharged with psychiatric diagnoses with women entering a psychiatric service of the same hospital, found that they were less educated, more rural, of lower socioeconomic status, and less likely to be Jewish. Of these women, 52 percent had had a hysterectomy as compared with 21 percent of women on the psychiatric service. Bart suggests that such patients may be expressing psychological distress through physical attributions, thus exposing themselves to unnecessary medical procedures.

Illness Behavior as a Means of Coping

It has already been noted that psychological distress increases the probability of use of medical care. Illness behavior is part of a socially defined status and may serve as an effective means of achieving release from social expectations, as an excuse for failure, or as a way of obtaining a variety of privileges including monetary compensation. Moreover, the physician and other health personnel may be an important source of social support and may be particularly important for patients lacking strong social ties. A vague complaint of illness may be one way of seeking reassurance and support through a recognized and socially acceptable relationship when it is difficult for the patient to confront the underlying problem in an unambiguous way without displaying weaknesses and vulnerabilities contrary to expected and learned behavior patterns. Balint (1957) and others have noted that the presenting symptoms may be of no special importance, but serve to establish the relationship between the patient and the doctor.

There are many ways in which adaptive needs interact with responses to symptoms and illness. A vast number of doctor-patient contacts involve symptoms and illnesses that are widely distributed in the population and that are more frequently untreated than treated (White, Williams, and Greenberg 1961). Thus the decision to seek care is frequently a result of contingencies surrounding the perception of symptoms. Perceptions of oneself as ill and seeking care may provide self-justification when potential failure poses much greater symbolic threats to the person's self-esteem than the process of being ill or dependent (Cole and Lejeune 1972).

A related issue is the difficulty some patients have in differentiating symptoms of psychological origin from symptoms of particular diseases. Many illnesses or medications prescribed for dealing with them produce feelings that are comparable to those associated with stress and psychopathology. Such symptoms as fatigue, restlessness, and poor appetite, for example, may result either from depression or from an acute infectious disease. When both occur concurrently, patients may attribute the effects of one to another. There is indication, for example, that long convalescence from acute infectious disease may result from the attribution of symptoms caused by depression to the acute condition (Imboden, Canter, and Cluff 1961). This complicates not only the patient's recovery but also the physician's perception and management of the patient.

Factors Affecting Symptom Definition and Patient Response

There is a wide variety of influences on the way people evaluate and make decisions in respect to their symptoms (Mechanic 1978). It is useful to classify these, although the categories overlap to some degree. Three categories describe the characteristics of the symptoms: their visibility or recognizability, their frequency of occurrence, and the extent to which they are amenable to varying interpretive schemes. Symptoms that are frequent or occur visibly are more likely to be identified and result in some tangible response. However, although some symptoms are only amenable to an illness interpretation, such as a high fever or an acute and persistent chest pain, other symptoms, such as a depressed feeling, may be interpreted as a religious, social, or medical issue. Similarly, while some physical symptoms allow for varying possible hypotheses about cause and seriousness, such as fatigue or poor appetite, others do not. Two types of variables define the person's estimate of the impact of symptoms: perceived seriousness and extent of disruptiveness. Although physicians ordinarily focus more on symptoms that are serious in their implications for future health, patients often focus more on symptoms that interfere in some obvious way with usual routines.

There are three classes of variables that define the person and his/her evaluative process: (1) tolerance thresholds; (2) the information, knowledge, understanding, and cultural assumptions of the evaluator; and (3) the extent to which he/she has needs that interfere with an acceptance of an illness definition. People seem to vary a great deal in their subjective response to pain and discomfort, although there appears to be much less difference in physical thresholds. Much research has demonstrated that pain has an important subjective component, and there is no clear relationship between the amount of tissue damage and the degree of discomfort reported by the patient (Beecher 1959). What people know, believe, and think about illness, of course, affects what symptoms they think are important, what is viewed as more or less serious, and what one should do. However, because of their social roles or personal desires, some persons deny illness. Often people wait until a convenient time to allow themselves to be ill and may ignore symptoms for long periods before taking action. There are some patients who have sufficient fear about particular illnesses or doctors so that they deny danger even when they fear they may have a particular problem such as cancer. These denial processes may be highly dysfunctional and result in more serious problems but appear to be deeply rooted in some people's psychological responses (Janis and Mann 1977). Such denial processes seem to be associated with high levels of fear but inadequate defense and coping skills to deal with the degree of threat experienced. While threat motivates individuals to take action when they feel they can do something and know what to do, fear without coping capacity increases the chances of denial. An important function of health education is to short-circuit dysfunctional attribution and defensive processes in the face of illness threats and to provide individuals with more functional types of interpretations and pathways to effective response.

Models of Physician Utilization: Multivariate Approaches

In addition to the types of approaches already discussed, another major emphasis has been on explaining physician utilization using a multivariate schema based on assessments of need, predisposing variables, and enabling factors (Aday and Eichhorn 1972; Andersen, Kravits, and Anderson 1975; Kohn and White 1976; Wolinsky 1978). Andersen and his coworkers, for example, define predisposing variables as those that exist prior to the onset of illness and include demographic factors (age and sex, for example), social structural variables (ethnicity, occupation, and education), and beliefs about medical care, physicians, and disease. Enabling factors "include family resources such as income and level of health insurance coverage or other source of third party payment, and the existence, nature and accessibility of a regular source of health care" (p. 6). Community characteristics such as number of health facilities and personnel, region, or rural-urban nature of the community may also be relevant as enabling variables. Need may be divided into perceived need and evaluated need. For example, Anderson and colleagues measure perceived need by: (1) the number of reported bed days and other restricted activity days resulting from injury or illness; (2) number of symptoms reported from a checklist including such symptoms as "sudden feeling of weakness or faintness," "getting up some mornings tired and exhausted even with a usual amount of rest," "feeling tired for weeks at a time for no special reason," and "frequent headaches" (Aday and Andersen 1975; Andersen, Kravitz, and Anderson, 1975); and (3) self-perceived general state of health. Evaluated illness includes symptom scores weighted by the extent to which physicians indicated that persons should see a doctor for these symptoms and physicians' ratings of the medical severity of the diagnoses reported in the interview.

Typically, such studies explain a modest amount of variance in physician contact (16 to 25 percent) using many predictors, and almost all of the variance explained is accounted for by "need" or "illness" variables. In Andersen's (1975) 1971 national study of health services utilization, for example, 85 percent of the variance in physician contact explained is accounted for by three perceived illness variables: worry about health (7.6 percent), disability days (4.8 percent), and symptoms (1.4 percent). In the case of volume of visits, diagnostic severity and perceived illness account for almost all of the 23.4 percent of variance explained: severity of diagnosis (14 percent), disability days (4.6 percent), symptoms (1.9 percent), perceived health (1 percent), worry about health (0.7 percent), and pain frequency (0.7 percent). Even less success in predicting utilization has been achieved in the International Collaborative Study (Kohn and White 1976) (explaining 4 to 10 percent of the variance in adult utilization across geographic areas), and the variance explained was almost totally accounted for by "illness" variables.

The results of these multivariate studies can be attributed in part to gross measurement of subtle processes of response by summary measures that are not specific enough to capture important variations among respondents. Moreover, the variance attributed to "illness" in multivariate models that have only a very general theoretical rationale often masks the effects of important psychosocial processes. What are called "illness" and "need" in these studies are usually summary measures of illness behavior that incorporate psychological and attitudinal components and are correlated at a zero-order level with many relevant psychosocial measures. The introduction of the global illness measures in a regression equation simultaneous with other social and behavioral measures will often reduce the betas of such variables correlated with it to insignificance. From a theoretical standpoint, however, one should have a model that posits the interrelationships between the global illness behavior measures and other psychosocial factors.

The large-scale study of utilization is useful, however, because it allows the examination of many variables simultaneously and facilitates testing for spurious correlations. For such studies to be more valuable, however, specific theoretical models are required that hypothesize as clearly as possible the processes through which utilization is determined. Measurement must also be specific, must involve relatively short recall periods, and ideally should be sequential over some prospective time frame, capturing more closely important variations in illness response (Gortmaker, Eckenrode, and Gore 1982). Whenever possible, studies should be prospective, involving repeated measurements and/or linking data obtained during the interview with subsequent behavior as measured independently through observation, medical records, or other official documents. It is prudent to measure dependent variables independent of respondent reports if possible, because this limits distortions resulting from memory, the respondents' needs, or retrospective reconstruction.

Some Other Approaches to Physician Utilization

In addition to these multivariate approaches, other models have been suggested that focus to a larger degree on sociocultural and social-psychological issues. Antonovsky (1972), for example, suggests a model in which he includes host characteristics, characteristics of the medical institutions, and characteristics of the larger sociocultural environment. Host characteristics include latent need, intolerance of ambiguity of symptoms, and an orientation toward the use of professionals; medical system variables include availability of facilities, the ability to be responsive to various latent functions, and the degree of receptivity of physicians; and the sociocultural environment variables include organizational facilitation in using medical services, absence of stigma for such use, cultural pressures to have problems diagnosed, and the degree of availability of functional alternatives.

Antonovsky's model takes account of the fact that medical care constitutes a small social system that may be used to deal with diffuse social and psychological needs when the system is available, when its use is socially encouraged, and when it is receptive to peoples' needs and orientations. One study examining some aspects of this model in Israel, which has a population with high social need and a high physician-patient ratio, found that higher levels of need for catharsis, legitimation of failure, and the resolution of the magic-science conflict were associated with higher levels of utilization (Shuval 1970). Another study in Israel by Mann and colleagues (1970) found that latent social need was influential in the long-term pattern of use of health services. Persons who had been in concentration camps had much higher levels of utilization over a period of years that could not be accounted for solely on the basis of illness patterns.

The research on social need points to the fact that the provision of medical care is not simply an economic process but is also an important aspect of social adaptation. We have ample evidence that there is large overlap between the occurrence of illness in populations that does not result in utilization of the physician and the most common presenting complaints seen by the physician of first contact. The main task for the behavioral scientist is to understand why persons with similar complaints behave so differently and why the same person with comparable symptoms at varying times chooses to seek medical care on one occasion but not on another (Mechanic 1978). Such processes depend on a wide range of factors, as the medical sociology literature suggests, including the organization of physician services and the receptivity of health personnel to varying types of problems and to sociocultural alternatives to medical care. A much more careful dissection is required of the ways in which people perceive their bodies, make sense of their symptoms, and come to depend on the medical-care system.

Implications for Health Care, Medical Research, and Medical Education

Illness behavior is a dynamic process through which the person defines the problems, struggles with them, and attempts to achieve a comfortable accommodation. Such processes of adaptation are partly learned and partly shaped by the social situation and influences in the immediate environment. The health worker thus can help guide the process by suggesting constructive alternatives for the patient and by avoiding the reinforcement of distorted meanings and maladaptive responses. Treatment personnel have considerable choice as to whether they encourage realistic understanding and coping efforts among patients or whether they encourage dependence and helplessness. Much of medical care has encouraged the patient to assume a dependent stance relative to the professional and has failed to support the patient's ability to struggle for mastery over his/her problems. This problem is particularly evident in chronic illness in which the degree of social disability characterizing many patients far exceeds that required by the physical condition of the patient. While myocardial infarction patients, for example, may be troubled by the way their condition affects their ability to work and their family life, the physician frequently focuses too narrowly on minor variations in cardiac output (Aiken 1976; Reif 1975). Constructive illness behavior and the patient's coping capacities may be more influential on outcomes than many of the biological indicators on which physicians focus.

Illness behavior may seriously affect the way the physician comes to define the patient. The assessment of patients' conditions is more than a physical diagnosis; it is a construction of the totality of events shaping their reactions and reflects not only evident physical symptoms and signs but also cultural patterns, peer pressures, self-identity, life difficulties, attitudes toward the value of medical care, and many other factors. Zola (1963), for example, studied a group of patients who were evaluated at various outpatient clinics at the Massachusetts General Hospital but for whom no medical disease was found. Zola found that psychogenesis was implied in the medical evaluation of eleven of the twelve Italian patients evaluated, but in only four of the thirteen other cases. On the basis of a psychosocial study there was no evidence that the Italian patients had more life difficulties or psychological problems, but their mode of expressing distress was extremely different. Zola hypothesizes that the emotionality of the Italian patients was interpreted by the residents evaluating the patients as indicators of psychiatric disturbance. Thus the behavioral pattern of expressing distress was confused with the patients' symptoms.

Much research in medicine and public health is based on populations selected from clinics, outpatient departments, and hospitals. Such populations, however, are the culmination of a selective flow determined by not only the nature, quality, and severity of the symptoms but also patients' sociocultural orientations and environmental pressures. Moreover, such populations are shaped as well by the special interests and attitudes of the personnel who operate these facilities, and they often select out patients of interest to them or with whom they most like to deal. Many such samples thus are highly biased representations of the population of patients with comparable illnesses, and attributions to the illness process that really reflect the biases of the sample are quite common. For example, it is frequently found that patients with particular diseases have high levels of stress, and it is often suggested that stress plays a role in the development of the condition. If stress, however, is an important factor triggering help seeking, it is inevitable that treated populations will have higher stress levels than the population as a whole quite independent of any effect of stress on disease (Mechanic 1963). Or, to cite another example, the factors sometimes identified as predictors of disease in treated populations are associated with seeking care from a particular type of practitioner, such as a psychiatrist, and are not necessarily related to either the particular disease state at issue or the help-seeking process in general. In researching particular populations of patients seeking care from a single source of care, one can mistakenly attribute to the illness process certain features of response characteristic of the particular pathway into care or place undue emphasis on the significance of particular symptoms (Shepard, Oppenheim, and Mitchell 1966).

Finally, illness behavior is an important consideration in planning medical education. The patients treated in teaching hospitals are highly selected populations of sick persons not only in respect to the types of illnesses they have but also in terms of social and cultural factors that lead them to such care. Although most physicians are trained in such contexts, they will primarily have to work in more mundane settings in which the majority of patients have more limited problems. The strategies of approach to both health and illness must be different in these settings, and yet the models used for dealing with severe and acute illness are too commonly applied to patients with psychosocial problems, with chronic disabilities, and with self-limited acute illness. This results often in reinforcement of dysfunctional illness behavior and poor skills in coping. Recognition of the implications of illness behavior and social adaptation for health provides the young health professional and researcher with a perspective to deal with illness not only as an individual affliction but also as part of a social process.

REFERENCES

ADAY, L. A., and ANDERSEN, R. 1975. *Development of indices of access to medical care.* Ann Arbor, Mich.: Health Administration Press.

ADAY, L. A., and EICHHORN, R. 1972. *The utilization of health services: indices and correlates. A research bibliography, 1972.* DHEW pub no. (HSM) 73–3003. Rockville, Md.: National Center for Health Services Research and Development.

AIKEN, L. H. 1976. Chronic illness and responsive ambulatory care. In *The growth of bureaucratic medicine: an inquiry into the dynamics of patient behavior and the organization of medical care,* ed. D. Mechanic. New York: Wiley-Interscience.

ANDERSEN, R.; KRAVITS, J.; and ANDERSON, O. W., eds. 1975. *Equity in health services: empirical analyses in social policy.* Cambridge, Mass.: Ballinger.

ANTONOVSKY, A. 1972. A model to explain visits to the doctor: with specific reference to the case of Israel. *Journal of Health and Social Behavior* 13: 446–54.

BALINT, M. 1957. *The doctor, his patient and the illness.* New York: International Universities Press.

BART, P. B. 1968. Social structure and vocabularies of discomfort: what happened to female hysteria? *Journal of Health and Social Behavior* 9: 188–93.

BEECHER, H. K. 1959. *Measurement of subjective responses: quantitative effects of drugs.* New York: Oxford University Press.

BROWN, G. W.; BONE, M.; DALISON, B.; and WING, J. K. 1966. *Schizophrenia and social care: a comparative follow-up study of 339 schizophrenic patients.* New York: Oxford University Press.

COLE, S., and LEJEUNE, R. 1972. Illness and the legitimation of failure. *American Sociological Review* 37: 347–56.

DOHRENWEND, B. P., and DOHRENWEND, B. S. 1976. Sex differences and psychiatric disorders. *American Journal of Sociology* 81: 1447–54.

DOHRENWEND, B. P.; SHROUT, P. E.; EGRI, G.; and MENDELSOHN, F. S. 1980. Nonspecific psychological distress and other dimensions of psychopathology. *Archives of General Psychiatry* 37: 1229–36.

GLASS, A. 1958. Observations upon the epidemiology of mental illness in troops during warfare. *Symposium on preventive and social psychiatry.* Walter Reed Army Institute of Research, Washington, D.C.: Government Printing Office.

GORTMAKER, S. L.; ECKENRODE, J.; and GORE, S. 1982. Stress and the utilization of health services. *Journal of Health and Social Behavior* 23: 25–38.

GREENLEY, J. R., and MECHANIC, D. 1976. Social selection in seeking help for psychological problems. *Journal of Health and Social Behavior* 17: 249–62.

GURIN, G.; VEROFF, J.; and FELD, S. 1960. *Americans view their mental health.* New York: Basic Books.

IMBODEN, J. B.; CANTER, A.; and CLUFF, L. 1961. Symptomatic recovery from medical disorders. *Journal of the American Medical Association* 178: 1182–84.

JANIS, I. L., and MANN, L. 1977. *Decision making: a psychological analysis of conflict, choice, and commitment.* New York: Free Press.

KADUSHIN, C. 1969. *Why people go to psychiatrists.* New York: Atherton.

KERCKHOFF, A. C., and BACK, K. W. 1968. *The June Bug: a study of hysterical contagion.* New York: Appleton-Century-Crofts.

KLEINMAN, A., and MECHANIC, D. 1979. Some observations of mental illness and its treatment in the People's Republic of China. *Journal of Nervous and Mental Disease* 167: 267–74.

KOHN, R., and WHITE, L., eds., 1976. *Health care—an international study: report of the World Health Organization/international collaborative study of medical care utilization.* London: Oxford University Press.

LEWIS, C. E.; FEIN, R.; and MECHANIC, D. 1976. *A right to health: the problem of access to primary medical care.* New York: Wiley-Interscience.

LEWIS, C., E., and LEWIS, M. A. 1977. The potential impact of sexual equality on health. *New England Journal of Medicine* 297: 863–69.

———; LORIMER, A,; and PALMER, B. B. 1975. *Child-initiated care: a study of the determinants of the illness behavior of children.* Unpublished report, Center for Health Sciences, University of California, Los Angeles.

MANN, K. J.; MEDALIE, J. H.; LIEBER, E.; GROEN, J. J.; and GUTTMAN, L. 1970. *Visits to doctors.* Jerusalem: Jerusalem Academic Press.

MECHANIC, D. 1963. Some implications of illness behavior for medical sampling. *New England Journal of Medicine* 269: 244–47.

———. 1964. The influence of mothers on their children's health attitudes and behavior. *Pediatrics* 33: 444–53.

———. 1972. Social psychological factors affecting the presentation of bodily complaints. *New England Journal of Medicine* 286: 1132–39.

———. 1976a. *The growth of bureaucratic medicine: an inquiry into the dynamics of patient behavior and the organization of medical care.* New York: Wiley-Interscience.

———. 1976b. Sex, illness, illness behavior, and the use of health services. *Journal of Human Stress* 2: 29–40.

———. 1976c. Stress, illness, and illness behavior. *Journal of Human Stress* 2: 2–6.

———. 1977. Illness behavior, social adaptation, and the management of illness: a comparison of educational and medical models. *Journal of Nervous and Mental Disease* 165: 79–87.

———. 1978. *Medical sociology.* 2d ed. New York: Free Press.

———. 1979a. Development of psychological distress among young adults. *Archives of General Psychiatry* 36: 1233–1239.

———. 1979b. The stability of health and illness behavior: results from a 16-year follow-up. *American Journal of Public Health* 69: 1142–45.

———. 1980. The experiences and reporting of common physical complaints. *Journal of Health and Social Behavior* 21: 146–55.

PENNEBAKER, J. W., and SKELTON, J. A. 1978. Psychological parameters of physical symptoms. *Personality and Social Psychology Bulletin* 4: 524–30.

REIF, L. J. 1975. *Cardiacs and normals: the social construction of a disability.* Doctoral dissertation, University of California, San Francisco.

SCHACHTER, S. 1959. *The psychology of affiliation: experimental studies of the sources of gregariousness.* Stanford, Calif.: Stanford University Press.

SHEPHERD, M.; OPPENHEIM, A. N.; and MITCHELL, S. 1966. Childhood behavior disorders and the child-guidance clinic: an epidemiological study. *Journal of Child Psychology and Psychiatry* 7: 39–52.

SHUVAL, J. T., in collaboration with ANTONOVSKY, A., and DAVIES, A. M. 1970. *Social functions of medical practice.* San Francisco, Calif.: Jossey-Bass.

TESSLER, R. 1980. Birth order, family size, and children's use of medical services: a research note. *Journal of Health Services Research* 15: 55–62.

VEITH, I. 1970. *Hysteria: the history of a disease.* Chicago: University of Chicago Press.

WEISSMAN, M. M., and KLERMAN, G. L. 1977. Sex differences and the epidemiology of depression. *Archives of General Psychiatry* 34: 98–111.

WHEATON, B. 1978. The sociogenesis of psychological disorder: reexamining the causal issues with longitudinal data. *American Sociological Review* 43: 383–403.

WHITE, K. L.; WILLIAMS, T. F.; and GREENBERG, B. G. 1981 The ecology of medical care. *New England Journal of Medicine* 265: 885–92.

WICKLUND, R. 1975. Objective self-awareness. In *Advances in experimental social psychology* ed. L. Berkowitz, vol. 8. New York: Academic Press.

WOLINSKY, F. D. 1978. Assessing the effects of predisposing, enabling, and illness-morbidity characteristics on health service utilization. *Journal of Health and Social Behavior* 19: 384–96.

ZBOROWSKI, M. 1952. Cultural components in responses to pain. *Journal of Social Issues* 8: 16–30.

ZOLA, I. K. 1963. Problems of communication, diagnosis, and patient care: the interplay of patient, physician and clinic organization. *Journal of Medical Education* 38: 829–38.

Chapter 28

Coping and Adaptation in Health and Illness

Frances Cohen
Richard S. Lazarus

IN RECENT YEARS there has been considerable interest in the role that coping plays in facilitating adjustment in health-care settings and in buffering the potentially deleterious effects of stress. Important questions include: (1) What is adaptive coping in situations of illness and medical treatment? (2) What role does coping play in the etiology of physical disease? Before addressing these issues, we will outline our theoretical framework and discuss some definitional issues, namely, how coping is defined, classified, and assessed, and the assessment problems that impede research efforts. Finally, we review some research on coping and illness which we believe begins to suggest answers to the questions posed above.

Theoretical Framework

Cognitive Appraisal

Our view is that cognitive factors play a central role in determining the effect of stressful life events. More specifically, the ways individuals appraise a situation affect the stressful impact of the event, how people cope with it, and the emotional, physiological, and behavioral reactions. (This framework has been described in detail elsewhere; see Lazarus 1966, 1981; Lazarus, Averill, and Opton 1970, 1974; Lazarus and Launier 1978). Cognitive appraisal is the mental process of judging events with respect to their significance for the person's well-being (primary appraisal) or the resources and options available for coping (secondary appraisal). *Primary appraisals* can be one of three types: (1) irrelevant; (2) benign-positive; or (3) stressful.

If an event is appraised as irrelevant, the person does not consider it to have any implications for his or her well-being. A benign-positive appraisal means that the event signifies a positive situation. An appraisal of stress requires a judgment that environmental or internal demands tax or exceed one's adaptive resources. Stress appraisals are of three types: (1) harm-loss; (2) threat; or (3) challenge.

Harm-loss and threat connote a negative evaluation of one's present or future state of well-being. Harm-loss refers to damage that has already occurred, as when one suffers an injury, loses a job, or finds an option closed. Threat refers to the possibility of future harm. Sometimes harm and threat appraisals are mixed as when severely injured patients must deal with the reality of their injury (e.g., pain, loss of function, interruption of work) and with the implications for the future (e.g., Hamburg, Hamburg, and deGoza 1953; Visotsky et al. 1961).

An important concept for stress and health is the distinction between threat and challenge. Situations of challenge present opportunities to overcome hardship and achieve growth and mastery but demand more than routine resources. Whether situations involving challenge have different adaptive consequences than those involving threat has not been established. However, we would expect challenged people to have better morale, but it is an empirical question, as yet untested, what the effects of challenge are on social functioning and somatic health. The Holmes and Rahe (1967) life-change approach implies that *any* type of life change has damaging consequences for health regardless of how it is appraised. However, Selye (1974) has recently made the distinction between harmful and constructive stress, although he has not specified whether the disease-creating General Adaptation Syndrome occurs in both. Research should determine whether the same somatic reaction occurs to situations of threat and challenge. Recent life-events research suggests that the links between life changes and illness are greater for events viewed by the person as undesirable than for those viewed as desirable (e.g., Vinokur and Selzer 1975).

Secondary appraisal refers to an evaluation of coping resources and options. This judgment does not necessarily follow primary appraisal in time and it can utilize cognitions about resources that are stored in memory. Examples of secondary appraisals include: I have no way to cope; If I practice I can do it; I know someone who could help me; If this method does not work I know others I can try; I need to figure out a way around that person's ill-will.

Primary and secondary appraisals are interdependent in any given encounter. The person's resources are balanced cognitively against the harms being faced to determine whether a threat exists, and what to do. For example, people who think they have no coping options feel threatened by a potential stressor if it endangers them in some way. In contrast, people who have an available repertoire of coping options potentially to master the problem and grow or gain may interpret a similar situation as challenging rather than threatening. Cognitive appraisals are continually changing, a process that has been labeled reappraisal (Lazarus 1966). Appraisal processes may be conscious, unconscious, or at the fringe of consciousness (e.g., what Weisman [1972] refers to as "middle knowledge"). They change in response to feedback from the environment and from the person's own thoughts, feelings, and actions. They can also be defensive and distort reality.

FACTORS INFLUENCING APPRAISALS. Both situational and person factors influence the type of appraisals that are made (Lazarus 1966). Situational factors that influence primary appraisal include: (1) the strength of the external demands; (2) the imminence of the anticipated confrontation; and (3) ambiguity. Person factors include: (1) motivational characteristics; (2) belief systems; and (3) intellectual resources and skills. For example, challenge appraisals probably depend in part on the person's beliefs about the potential for mastery. Some persons exhibit a style of thinking that disposes them to challenge rather than threat appraisals, as in people who have very high self-esteem, or who consider themselves lucky and can therefore "put a good face on things." Degree of stress also depends on how much is at stake in the transaction (which would take account of a person's commitments and motives). Both situational and person factors also influence secondary appraisals. With respect to the former, the type of harm, the viability of alternative actions to prevent harm, situational constraints, and environmental resources are important; with respect to the latter, pattern of motivation, ego resources, coping dispositions, and general beliefs about the environment are relevant factors. See Lazarus (1966; Lazarus and Folkman in press) for further discussion of these factors.

RESEARCH ON COGNITIVE APPRAISAL. Numerous laboratory studies have investigated the role of cognitive appraisals in mediating the response to stressors. This literature has been reviewed elsewhere (e.g., Lazarus 1968; Lazarus et al. 1970). We illustrate this literature by describing one important early experiment (Speisman, Lazarus, Mordkoff, and Davison 1964) carried out by Lazarus and his associates to investigate stress processes using distressing motion pictures. Autonomic nervous system and organ reactions were recorded continuously as subjects watched films and a report of distress was also obtained repeatedly. The stressful movie was *Subincision*, which showed a rite of passage among Australian aborigine adolescent boys in which sharpened stones were used to cut the penis and scrotum. In order to manipulate appraisals experimentally, three different sound tracks were employed: (1) a trauma sound track that focused on the main sources of threat in the film; (2) a denial sound track that characterized the procedures as without pain and even a source of inspiration; and (3) an intellectualization sound track that engendered detached observation of the film. It was found that the trauma sound track increased subjective distress and autonomic disturbances, as compared to a control film, while denial and intellectualization sound tracks reduced them. The magnitude of the reduction depended on personality characteristics. Subjects who generally employed denial coping strategies showed less reduction of stress if given the intellectualizing passage rather than the denial passage; the reverse was true for intellectualizers. Thus, although the appraisal process could be influenced by the cognitive context, the magnitude of the effect was greatest if the experimental manipulation was compatible with coping predispositions.

The Concept of Coping

Coping can be defined as the process of managing demands (external or internal) that are appraised as taxing or exceeding the resources of a person (Lazarus and Folkman in press). This definition emphasizes five distinct perspectives. It: (1) does not make a sharp distinction—as is often done—between "coping" and "defensive" processses; (2) focuses on *process* rather than trait; (3) speaks of *management* rather than mastery; (4) underlines the central role of psychological mediation (through the concept of *appraisal*); and (5) emphasizes the *relational* character of stress and coping, that is, they depend on both the demands placed on the organism and the resources one has available for dealing with those demands.

We do not make a distinction between coping and defensive processes (cf. Haan 1977) or rank strategies into a hierarchy with mature processes distinguished from immature ones (e.g., Vaillant 1977). These common distinctions involve a value judgment made solely on the basis of the coping mode employed without considering the situation in which the strategy is used (Lazarus 1966) or the effects of the strategy on the total psychological economy of the person (Lazarus 1981). In hierarchical definitions, defense is inappropriately equated with pathology. Further, both defensive and coping processes may interweave as people confront stressful situations and it is difficult to separate these two strands (Murphy 1974; White 1974). In this chapter, "coping" or "coping processes" refer to any efforts at stress management regardless of their effectiveness, including processes that could be called defenses.

Furthermore, coping processes refer to what the person actually does in a particular stressful encounter, and how this changes over time, in contrast with coping traits which refer to a stable set of dispositions to respond but which may or may not be activated in any stressful encounter. Notice too that we speak of stress management rather than mastery. Many human problems cannot be overcome but must be adapted to, tolerated, or accepted (see, e.g., White 1974). We also emphasize the importance of psychological mediation and the relational nature of stress and coping; if environmental or internal demands are not appraised as stressful, or if a person has the resources to meet these demands fully, a stress appraisal may not be made and no coping efforts elicited.

COPING AS DISTINGUISHED FROM ADAPTATION. Coping and adaptation are often treated as synonymous terms, but important distinctions exist. First, to many theorists adaptation is a broader concept that includes routine or automatized actions while coping always involves some type of stress (e.g., Lazarus et al. 1974; Murphy 1974; White 1974). It is the special mobilization of effort and the drawing upon unused resources or potentials, then, that distinguishes coping. Automatic actions, such as turning off burners after cooking, driving defensively, checking the gas gauge, and verifying bus timetables normally take little energy or conscious attention. To include them as coping would broaden considerably the activities to be studied and would encompass almost everything we do in living. Although we consider these activities (which could be called adaptive behaviors rather than coping behaviors) to fall outside of the rubric of coping, they nonetheless may form an important repertoire of behaviors that can prevent unnecessary crises (such as kitchen fires, running out of gas, missed buses) and even facilitate one's ability to cope in situations of crisis.

Second, we use the word adaptation in the psychological, not biological, sense. In biology, adaptation refers to a *species'* ability to survive through mechanisms that result from the evolutionary process (Lazarus 1968). However, in psychology, adaptation refers to *individual* survival, as well as to the capacity to sustain a high quality of life and to function effectively on a social level. In this use of the word, the focus is on outcome from an evaluative perspective—adaptive or maladaptive. As we will discuss in detail later, determining the adaptiveness of behaviors is not a straightforward process, and different evaluations may result when long-term versus short-term measures or psychological rather than physiological outcomes are considered. The adaptiveness of behaviors always involves a focus on outcomes (which may be referred to as adaptational outcomes).

Functions of Coping

Coping efforts may serve one of two major functions—problem solving or emotion-regulating (Hamburg, Coelho, and Adams 1974; Lazarus 1975b; Lazarus et al. 1974; Lazarus and Launier 1978; Mechanic 1962; Murphy 1974). Problem-solving functions involve efforts to deal with environmental or internal demands or obstacles that create threat. Seeking medical treatment, quitting a stressful job, or studying for an exam all represent efforts to alter the troubled person-environment transaction. Emotion-regulating functions involve efforts to regulate the emotional distress that is a consequence of threat, e.g., by avoiding unpleasant news, drinking excessively, minimizing the danger, or learning biofeedback (Lazarus 1975a).

Emotion-regulating functions are often thought of as ineffective and inappropriate. In our culture there is a bias against solutions that merely make us feel better in favor of actually doing something about our problems. As Robert White describes it:

> In the psychological and psychiatric literature there lies a concealed assumption. . . that any delay, avoidance, retreat, or cognitive distortion of reality is in the end a reprehensible piece of cowardice. We must march forward, ever forward, facing our problems, overcoming all obstacles, masters of our fate. . . .
> In actuality, of course, there are many situations that can be met only by compromise or even resignation. . . . adaptation often calls for delay, strategic retreat, regrouping of forces, abandoning of untenable positions. . . . recovery from a personal loss or disaster requires a long period of internal readjustment that may not be well served at the start by forceful action or total clarity of perception. [White 1974, p. 50]

Although Freud regarded denial as a psychotic process, there are numerous studies in which under some circumstances, deniallike forms of coping are associated with positive adaptive outcomes (see Lazarus's [in press] review). Such modes can also have maladaptive consequences (e.g., Goldstein 1980). Lazarus (in press) and Mechanic (1974) have both discussed the importance of illusion in sustaining human functioning. As Mechanic describes it:

> This brings me to consideration of a serious misconception that appears to run throughout the stress literature—the notion that successful adaptation requires an accurate perception of reality. There is perhaps no thought so stifling as to see ourselves in proper perspective. We all maintain our sense of self-respect and energy for action through perceptions that enhance our self-importance and self-esteem, and we maintain our sanity by suppressing the tremendous vulnerability we all experience in relation to the risks of the real world. . . . [Mechanic 1974, pp. 37–38]

Although we distinguish two functions of coping, they can facilitate each other, as when reducing feelings of anxiety gives one the ability to face threats and do something about them more effectively. On the other hand, one function can interfere with the other as when denial processes are acted out by engaging in strenuous physical activity during a heart attack to reassure oneself that nothing is seriously wrong (Hackett and Cassem 1975). Emotion-focused coping that involves reality distortion may appear "irrational" to health professionals but may fulfill the other important function of maintaining one's emotional equilibrium.

There are two subtypes of problem-solving coping. One focuses on changing internal or external obstacles, for example, by building needed skills to overcome them (such as studying in preparation for an exam), or by undergoing unpleasant medical treatments in order to halt a disease process. The second addresses the satisfaction of personal needs that are threatened by stressors rather than the removal of obstacles per se. For example, the need to maintain close social relationships may be threatened by hospitalization and illness and can be coped with by babyish or demanding behavior to elicit increased attention and reassurance of affection or approval. As another example, attempts to remain physically active even under orders for complete bed rest may result from the individual's need to maintain self-esteem. Brehm (1966) has suggested that if people feel their sense of freedom and control is challenged, a negative state of "reactance" develops and results in efforts to regain a sense of control. Patients may sign out against medical advice and forgo necessary treatments or rehabilitation efforts if they feel their freedom is compromised. Thus an active coping strategy used by the patient to restore a sense of control may interfere with medical treatment (see Janis and Rodin's [1979] discussion).

People use both emotion-focused and problem-focused coping simultaneously in dealing with daily stressors. For example, in their study of middle-aged men and women, Folkman and Lazarus (1980) found that in 98 percent of the coping episodes studied, both modes were utilized. Thus coping frameworks that overemphasize either emotion-regulation (e.g., Haan 1977; Vaillant 1977) or problem-focused coping (e.g., Janis and Mann 1977) are dealing with only a limited number of the coping processes people use in dealing with stressful life experiences.

Modes of Coping

We identify five modes of coping: information-seeking, direct action, inhibition of action, intrapsychic (or cognitive) processes, and turning to others for support (Cohen and Lazarus 1979). *Information-seeking* involves trying to learn more about the problem and what can be done to deal with it. In the context of illness there are considerable individual differences in the degree to which people use this mode. *Direct actions* include any concrete act such as taking drugs, running away, cleaning a wound, or arguing with opponents. The opposite of direct action— *inhibition of action*—is also a mode of coping, since refraining from impulsive action, as in the expression of anger, may often be the best way to deal with a situation. *Intrapsychic processes* involve ways of reappraising the situation, deploying attention, or seeking alternate routes for gratification; this category includes those processes traditionally viewed as defenses, such as denial and intellectualization. *Turning to others* for support is another mode of coping (Mages and Mendelsohn 1979) that may enhance one's efforts to deal with stressful events (Cobb 1976; Dimsdale et al. 1979; Kaplan, Cassel, and Gore 1977), or one's feeling of well-being (Schaefer, Coyne, and Lazarus, 1981).

The five modes listed above are broad strategies that can be elicited in many types of stressful situations. Other classification schemes identify coping modes specific to a particular situation (e.g., Davis 1963; Katz et al. 1970; Lipowski 1970; Moos and Tsu 1977; Weisman and Worden 1976–77) or restrict their scheme to intrapsychic processes (e.g., Haan 1977; Menninger 1963).

Assessment of Coping

PROCESS VERSUS TRAIT OR STYLE.   There are two ways to assess coping—as a trait or style, or as a process (Averill and Opton 1968). Coping traits refer to a disposition to respond in a specific way in situations that are stressful. Coping traits are thus stable characteristics of the person that transcend classes of situations. Although the terms coping trait and coping style are often used synonymously, style tends to imply a broader, more encompassing disposition. For example, the cognitive style research of Gardner and his colleagues (Gardner et al. 1959) emphasizes broad perceptual styles that pervade the way a person relates to the world. Shapiro (1965) has also outlined broad cognitive styles such as the obsessive-compulsive, hysterical, and paranoid. The strategy of insulating or distancing oneself from others—found in hypertensives (Weiner, Singer, and Reiser 1962) and in people who may be at lower risk of becoming physically ill (Hinkle 1974)—is also a broad style which influences interpersonal transactions in emotional contexts.

Coping process refers either to (1) what the person actually does in a particular encounter (what Averill and Opton [1968]call episodic coping); or (2) how what is done changes (over time). What the person actually does in a particular stressful encounter may be unrelated to the coping traits he or she is said to possess. Further, the coping processes actually used, rather than the trait measure, may be stronger predictors of outcome (Cohen and Lazarus 1973). There is increasing recognition that in studying how individuals deal with complex situations, coping must be viewed as a process that changes over time.

Many studies of the relationship between coping and health outcomes assess only coping traits. If coping traits were good predictors of what the person actually does in a situation of threat, this approach would be quite adequate. However, the empirical evidence suggests that so-called coping traits are not significantly related to the coping processes people actually employ. For example, in a study by Cohen and Lazarus (1973) people were interviewed in the hospital the evening before surgery, and an assessment of process made on an avoidance-vigilance dimension. At one end were people who knew little and did not want to know more about their operation while at the other end were those who knew much and sought more information. Two parallel trait measures of represssion-sensitization were also administered. The results showed that the correlations between the trait measures and the actual coping processes used were quite low. Thus the trait measures were not able to predict how people actually coped with the imminent surgery. Further, studies using trait or process measures of depression as predictors of recovery from illness show different predictive validity for state and process measures (Cohen and Lazarus 1979).

Coping trait measures are further limited by their assumption of consistency in coping behaviors over time and situation. There is increasing evidence that there may be little or at best very modest consistency in the coping strategies employed (Aldwin et al. 1980) and that time frame, context, and other factors strongly influence coping. For example, Visotky et al. (1961) and Hamburg et al. (1953) found different coping strategies were used at different stages of adjustment to poliomyelitis or severe burns. Mages and Mendelsohn (1979) suggest that adjustment to cancer is a developmental process which changes over the course of the disease. Horowitz (1976) describes opposing patterns of denial and intrusive thought which may alternate over the course of responding to stressful life events. Bereavement is also a complex process which changes greatly over time (Parkes

1972). The first reactions may involve shock and disbelief, coupled with efforts to deny the loss. Later reactions may include frantic activity to regain the lost person, depression, and disengagement. The entire process may take several years and be characterized by many different emotional reactions and modes of coping.

Context also influences the types of strategies employed. For example, Folkman and Lazarus (1980), in a study of the stress and coping experiences of 100 middle-aged men and women, found that work-related stressors more commonly elicited problem-focused modes of coping while health stressors were more often associated with emotion-focused modes. In summary, there is considerable evidence that traits may not be an accurate measure of the way individuals are dealing with the stresses associated with illness and that studying the coping processes people use, and how they change over time and situation, may be a more revealing research strategy than using coping trait measures.

COPING TRAIT MEASURES. The investigation of coping is hampered by lack of adequate instruments for its measurement. Moos (1974) reviews trait measures that have been used to assess coping. Coping trait measures include repression-sensitization (Byrne 1961, 1964); repression-isolation (Gardner et al. 1959; Levine and Spivack 1964), avoidance-coping (Andrew 1970; Goldstein 1959); measures of defense, coping, and ego fragmentation (Haan 1977); and a defense mechanisms inventory (Gleser and Ihilevich 1969). Information on validity and reliability is far from adequate (e.g., Lazarus et al. 1974). Although the theoretical basis of some of the dimensions listed above appears to be similar, research reveals low or nonsignificant correlations among them (Cohen and Lazarus 1973; Levine and Spivack 1964). We have earlier discussed the problems with the assumption of consistency in the coping modes used over time and across situations. In addition, persons reporting their coping habits may be unaware of the strategies they actually are using (cf. Kasl 1978). Further, since most coping trait measures tap only one or a few coping traits, they cannot reflect the complexity of the processes used in stressful encounters.

Pearlin and Schooler (1978) have developed survey questions to measure the ordinary stresses of living that arise from four social roles—marriage partner, household economic manager, parent, and coworker—and the types of coping strategies used in response. It is one of the few current approaches that measures the ordinary problems of living (see also Kanner, Coyne, Schaefer, and Lazarus, 1981). It also adopts a trait definition of coping—subjects were asked how they usually coped with general types of stress rather than how they actually coped in specific encounters. Pearlin and Schooler found that although people used many diverse coping strategies, some were consistent across all social roles while others were specific to a given context. By focusing on persistent life strains, that is, those that subjects have not been able to resolve, their findings perforce exclude the domain of coping responses that may have been effective in altering stressful life situations.

COPING AS A PROCESS. There are a number of problems in trying to assess coping as a process (Cohen and Lazarus 1979; Folkman and Lazarus 1980). First, we need to develop better ways to obtain information about such processes. There is the perennial problem of an unknown relationship between self-reports of coping processes and observer-based assessments. However, clinical evidence suggests that people tend to be more aware of coping strategies they are struggling to use, or ones that are problematic, than they are of strategies they are successfully using or that have already accomplished their purpose (Horowitz and Wilner 1980). In other words, effective strategies may not be reported. Guidelines can be developed for observers to make judgments about coping based on reports of what individuals did in a particular situation. Process ratings can be made with good reliability between raters if clear criteria are established for them (Cohen 1975; Cohen and Lazarus 1973). Researchers must continue to explore the relationship between observer-based and self-report measures of coping and to determine which are most successful in predicting outcome measures under given conditions.

Second, coping is most often a constellation of many acts and thoughts and ways must be found to categorize the complex pattern used in any given encounter. To date, our measures have not tapped the rich panoply of coping strategies people use in their struggles with stressful experiences, especially how these progress and change as the encounter unfolds. More sophisticated efforts than have been made thus far are urgently needed before we will be able to understand more fully how coping affects health and health behaviors.

Third, we need to develop more accurate and reliable ways to define and assess specific coping processes. The mechanism of denial illustrates the problem (Lazarus, in press). There are many varieties of what is called denial, each involving quite different cognitive-affective properties. For example, denial of fact and denial of implications must be distinguished because they probably have different sequellae. As cancer progresses, denial of the fact of the illness may no longer be tenable; however, it may still be possible to deny successfully the future implications of the illness (Weisman 1972). As another example, some polio patients have been observed to deny the implications of their illness for a year or more after it was diagnosed (Visotsky et al. 1961). In situations involving high degrees of ambiguity, denying negative implications may sustain feelings of hope. But one cannot deny what is not known, and when the situation is ambiguous, knowledge is uncertain. If denial is used to refer to a benign appraisal of ambiguous information, it would be equivalent to optimism rather than the distortion of reality.

Certain strategies of coping appear similar to denial but involve different cognitive processes. Denial, for example, is easily confused with avoidance and minimization (Lipowski 1970). To Anna Freud (1946) and others (e.g., Hackett and Cassem 1974) denial can be achieved in many ways, such as by not talking or thinking about a threat (avoidance) or by minimizing how badly off one is. However, one can avoid talking about unpleasant events without negating their reality. Two different processes are involved, and it is erroneous to infer denial without evidence of such negation. Yet Hackett and Cassem's (1974) denial scale, developed to assess coping in patients recovering from myocardial infarction, intermingles a host of processes such as minimization, avoidance, nonchalance, and delay in seeking treatment. This overextends the meaning of denial and impairs understanding of the role of diverse processes in coping.

The tendency to treat coping as a fixed cognitive achievement rather than as a constant changing process also creates difficulties. To do the former prematurely freezes people into immutable styles—we speak of deniers rather than denying— that do not accurately represent the ongoing struggle to interpret what is happening. Knowing that a coping strategy typifies the person's response to the stressful situation, that is, is well established or stable, requires the individual be studied more than once and across diverse circumstances and times. More often than not, coping processes are transient processes, changing in response to changing conditions (see further discussion of these issues in Cohen and Lazarus 1979).

Fourth, we need to consider new ways of conceptualizing coping variables. For example, it may not be important whether individuals utilize one coping strategy rather than another but whether they can draw on many different ones adaptively, depending on the requirements of a situation. It may be more important that a particular individual uses strategies that are inappropriate to or counterproductive in the specific situation of stress, and that this individual cannot shift to another, more functional approach in coping.

Outcomes of Coping

Types of Outcome. Coping can have effects on three kinds of outcome—psychological, social, and physiological. From a *psychological perspective*, coping could affect psychological morale (that is, the way one feels about oneself and one's life), emotional reactions (e.g., level of depression or anxiety, or the balance between positively toned and negatively toned feelings [Bradburn 1969]), performance, or the incidence of psychiatric disorders. From a *social perspective*, one can measure its impact on functioning effectiveness, such as employability, community involvement, and sociability (e.g., Renne 1974); the effectiveness of interpersonal relationships; or the degree to which useful social roles are filled (and acting out, antisocial behavior, etc., are avoided). See fuller discussion of these variables in Lazarus and Folkman (in press). From a *physiological perspective*, outcomes include short-term physiological reactions and long-term health consequences such as the development and progression of particular diseases. Space limitations do not permit a discussion of *how* coping might influence psychological, social, and illness outcomes. For a discussion of these issues see Lazarus (in press), Cohen (1979), and Cohen and Lazarus (1979).

Issues in Physiological Outcome. The complexity of the issues involved in analyzing physiological outcome measures needs to be underlined (Cohen 1979; Elliott and Eisdorfer 1982). Physiological responses to stressors include autonomic nervous system, hormonal, immunological, and neuroregulator (both neurotransmitter and neuromodulator) reactions. As examples, one might measure heart rate and blood pressure; secretion of cortisol, epinephrine, and norepinephrine; changes in cell mediated and humoral immune responses; and changes in particular neurotransmitters such as dopamine and norepinephrine, and neuromodulators such as serotonin and endorphins. Within each physiological system not all indicators respond in similar fashion, making it difficult to draw conclusions from the response of just one physiological indicator (Mason 1974; Rogers, Dubey, and Reich 1979).

Another issue concerns the relationship between acute responses and long-term disease outcomes. Because behavioral stimuli can produce acute physiological changes, such as increases in heart rate or blood pressure or increased secretion of hormones, does not establish a cause-and-effect relationship between the stimulus and subsequent disease. We still do not know how or whether acute physiological responses can lead to permanent changes in a person's health. There is a normal variation in most physiological systems; they fluctuate in relation to time of day, sleep patterns, diet, etc. We need to determine at what point and in what forms variations can be pathological. There could even be positive consequences of physiological activation. For example, some studies show that those who habitually secrete high levels of epinephrine have higher IQ and better school performance, are rated as happier and livelier, achieve higher scores of ego strength and perform better on laboratory tasks (Frankenhaeuser 1975, 1976). Gal and Lazarus (1975) and Frankenhaeuser (1976) also suggest that rather than using the magnitude of response as a measure of adaptive outcome, a more appropriate measure might be the time it takes for the return to baseline levels. Successful adaptation may involve both efficient mobilization and demobilization of physiological systems.

Adaptiveness of Coping

One of the thorniest problems in coping theory and research is how to determine whether coping behavior is adaptive. This is partly a question of values and encompasses three factors: (1) the domain of outcome; (2) the point in time; and (3) the context. Adaptiveness can be assessed in psychological, physiological, or social *domains* as we have earlier described. Most studies evaluate functioning in only one (Cohen and Lazarus 1979), yet adaptiveness may differ with the domain being judged. For example, in situations of stress, many people prefer to be active. However, being active may reduce psychological distress at the cost of increasing the physiological disturbance (Gal and Lazarus 1975; Singer 1974). Type A behavior provides another example. It has been linked to increased risk of coronary heart disease, but the Type A pattern may also be associated with greater personal satisfaction and greater work achievements (e.g., Burke and Weir 1980). Is increased risk of disease a more important outcome than psychological morale and community accomplishment? Any answer requires a choice between values. Furthermore the impact of coping behavior on outcomes in each of these three domains must be specified for a thorough understanding.

A second important problem is to distinguish *long-run from short-run* outcomes of coping. For example, denial defenses may be useful for parents whose child is dying of leukemia *during* the time period before the child dies (Wolff, Friedman, Hofer, and Mason 1964), but its use may cause increased psychological problems after the death of the child (Chodoff, Friedman, and Hamburg 1964). Hydrocortisone levels which were reduced in the parents using denial mechanisms prior to the child's death were found to increase sharply after the child died (Hofer, Wolff, Friedman, and Mason 1972a, 1972b). Thus the long-term and short-term effects of the denial process were quite different. In other studies, though denial defenses were associated with lower hydrocortisone levels *before* a breast biopsy (Katz et al. 1970), they were also associated with a dangerous delay in seeking treatment for the breast lump (Cameron and Hinton 1968); this delay could increase the risk of progression of the disease in the event the lump were malignant. Denial has also been found to be associated with decreased mortality in the coronary care unit (Hackett, Cassem, and Wishnie 1968), but also with decreased compliance with medical treatment one year later (Croog, Shapiro, and Levine 1971).

Third, the adaptiveness of any coping strategy can only be determined by taking *context* into account. A strategy may work well in one situation but not in another. For example, Cohen and Lazarus (1973) suggest that denial may be an effective mechanism for patients about to undergo elective hernia or gallbladder surgery. But Layne and Yudofsky (1971) suggest that it may be a maladaptive strategy for patients facing life-threatening operations such as open-heart surgery, where its use may result in increased postoperative delirium (however, see Morse and Litin 1969). Likewise, the expression of emotion may exacerbate physical symptoms for patients suffering from irreversible diffuse obstructive pulmonary syndrome (Dudley, Verhey, Masuda, Martin, and Holmes 1969), but is related to longer survival for patients with cancer (Derogatis, Abeloff, and Melisaratos 1979; Stavraky et al. 1968). It begins to look as though a coping process is not always either constructive or destructive in consequence, but its costs and benefits depend on the person, its timing, and the stress context.

Adaptiveness of Coping Behavior in Situations of Illness

In a previous paper we have extensively reviewed research seeking to answer the question, What is adaptive coping in situations of illness and medical treatment (Cohen and Lazarus 1979)? Looking at recovery from illness or recovery from surgery as the outcome variable, we noted inconsistent results that defied simple generalizations about coping strategies that are most adaptive. The nature of the disease, whether trait or process measures of coping were used, and the type of outcome variable all influenced the direction of results (see Cohen and Lazarus [1979] for discussion of the issues involved). There were some consistent findings, however, and these will be the focus of our discussion below. The variables of concern here include: (1) active participant coping strategies, including avoidant versus vigilant coping modes; (2) personal control; (3) expression versus inhibition of emotion; and (4) specific negative affects such as depression and anxiety.

ACTIVE PARTICIPANT COPING STRATEGIES. In a number of studies of *recovery from illness*, adopting an involved, active role appears to aid long-term rehabilitation after serious illnesses but also results in more adjustive difficulties during the stay in the hospital. Andreasen, Noyes, and Hartford (1972) found that patients with severe burns who took an active, involved coping role had a smoother psychological and physiological course of recovery. The original expectation had been that the opposite would be true, i.e., that the qualities of independence and aggressiveness would prove ineffective in coping with the forced dependency and passivity of prolonged patienthood. Similar results have been reported for patients' long-term rehabilitation from reconstructive vascular surgery (Boyd, Yeager, and McMillan 1973). Still another study showed that tuberculosis patients who are active make the easiest community adjustment after release from the hospital, though they have more difficulty in the hospital setting (Vernier et al. 1961). This latter finding is consistent with the observation that patients who prefer hospital staff to act in an authoritarian manner show the best emotional response to hospitalization (DeWolfe, Barrell, and Cummings 1966). On the other hand, autonomous, independent women delay longer than more passive ones in seeking treatment for symptoms of breast or cervical cancer (Fisher 1967; Hammerschlag et al. 1964). This series of studies illustrates the importance of situations as a factor affecting whether particular processes of coping are adaptive. They show that qualities of independence and autonomy can result in delay in seeking treatment for needed medical problems and greater distress in the hospital, but these same outlooks can facilitate efforts by patients to hasten their rehabilitation.

Similar though somewhat different dimensions have been examined with respect to *recovery from surgery*. If we regard dominance and self-assuredness, and vigilance in seeking information about the surgery, as an expression of the desire for active involvement, research by Kornfeld, Heller, Frank, and Moskowitz (1974) fits this theme. They found that patients who were dominant and self-assured had a greater incidence of delirium after open-heart surgery. The authors consider this style to be maladaptive in the postoperative setting because the environment of the intensive-care unit prevents patients from active participation in their treatment. And in an investigation of the hypothesis that patients can develop effective ways to cope with the threats involved in surgery by gaining information about what to expect, Cohen and Lazarus (1973) found that patients who knew the most about their operations and had sought out information (vigilant coping) had the slowest and most complicated recovery (see also Cohen [1975] for a replication). Cohen and Lazarus suggest that vigilant patients were trying actively to master the situation by seeking information. In the postoperative situation, however, they argue that there is nothing patients can do to "master" the situation actively, which may have a negative influence on their recovery processes.

Using a similar approach, George, Scott, Turner, and Gregg (1980) investigated the relationship between avoidant-vigilant coping and the outcome of dental surgery. These researchers found that vigilant copers have an overall slower healing rate, and that of the psychological variables examined, vigilance was the strongest (negative) predictor of overall healing after the degree of physical trauma induced by the surgery was statistically partialed out. Although in a number of studies vigilant behaviors have been linked to more complicated recovery from surgery, this variable shows no significant relationships with the number of pain medications taken (Cohen 1975; Cohen and Lazarus 1973; George et al. 1980; Sime 1976) indicating that postsurgical complications and pain medications are two very different indicators of recovery.

PERSONAL CONTROL. There has been considerable interest in the extent to which people believe they can control their fate as a factor in adaptational outcomes. Stemming from social learning theory and Rotter's work (1966) on locus of control (see also Lefcourt 1973, 1976), researchers have examined the differences between people who believe that they can control outcomes by virtue of their own efforts (internal locus) versus people who believe that fate, luck, and external powers control outcomes (external locus). Several other versions of the measure have been developed to test locus of control beliefs in health settings (Wallston, Wallston, and DeVellis 1978; Wallston et al. 1976). Most studies have focused on preventive health behaviors, and the magnitude of the effects obtained is small (Strickland 1978). Since most studies involve correlational analyses, cause-and-effect interpretations cannot be readily made. In a review of such research, Strickland (1978) has summarized the overall findings and the cautions that must be considered:

> Although results are not altogether clear, convincing, and as free of conflict as one might hope, the bulk of the research is consistent in implying that when faced with health problems, internal individuals do appear to engage in more generally adaptive responses than do externals. These range from engagement in preventive and precautionary health measures through appropriate remedial strategies when disease or disorder occurs. . . . One must be quite cautious, however, in assuming that internal beliefs are always facilitative. The continued alertness of internals and their attempts at mastery behavior is

most appropriate when events are actually controllable. When individuals persist in efforts that bring no relief, then they may find themselves to be actually exacerbating the undesirable characteristics of the situation in which they find themselves. [Strickland 1978, pp. 1204–1205]

Averill (1973) and Janis and Rodin (1979) have also elaborated on these issues. For example, Averill (1973) argues that the effects of personal control in reducing stress responses depend mainly on the meaning that the control response has for the person. The sense of control may enhance stress if the person believes there are actions he or she should be taking but is not, or if the person tries to control processes that are uncontrollable. Others have suggested that exercising control over an event may decrease anxiety only when the control is easy to achieve (Solomon, Holmes, and McCaul 1980).

Health locus of control has been shown to be significantly related to the outcome of dental surgery, with internals showing the *slowest* healing rate (George et al. 1980). However, mixed results have also been found in locus of control research on recovery from surgery (Johnson, Leventhal, and Dabbs 1971; Smith 1974).

The issues concerning personal control have many implications for the health-care arena. Being sick or being hospitalized places patients into situations where control may be difficult or impossible to achieve. For those who desire control, stress reactions may result. Those who do not feel that control is within their capability or who readily relinquish efforts at control may do better, not worse, in such situations. This theoretical perspective is congruent with the findings, described earlier, that dominant, autonomous, active, and vigilant patients have more difficulties adjusting to the hospital environment. Health-care professionals might seek ways to modify the health-care environment in order to allow these patients some degree of control or to develop interventions to aid those who seek control to make a better adjustment in a situation where control is not possible.

EXPRESSION VERSUS INHIBITION OF EMOTION. The adaptiveness of being emotionally expressive varies with the type of illness and the outcome measure used. More frequent expression of hostility and other negative affects and less inhibition and defensiveness seem to be associated with longer survival rates from cancer (Blumberg, West, and Ellis 1954; Derogatis et al. 1979; Klopfer 1957; Rogentine et al. 1979; Stavraky et al. 1968; cf. Krasnoff 1959). Calden and associates (1960) found that patients rated as nonconforming and recalcitrant had a faster recovery from tuberculosis than patients rated as cooperative (cf. Cuadra 1953).

However, for patients with irreversible diffuse obstructive pulmonary syndromes, successful use of denial and repression, which reduced strong emotional reactions, was associated with better psychological and physiological adjustment. And emotional expressiveness increased respiratory symptoms and physiological decompensation (Dudley et al. 1969).

Both asthma patients and tuberculosis patients who were emotionally labile required longer hospitalization and, in the case of asthma patients, more steroid drugs after hospital discharge (Dirks, Jones, and Kinsman 1977; Dirks et al. 1977; Kinsman et al. 1977). However, in the asthma patient group, those both high and low on this dimension were rehospitalized more than those in the middle (Dirks et al. 1978). These latter authors have suggested that patients high on this dimension may exaggerate their symptoms, leading physicians to decide to rehospitalize them. On the other hand, as noted earlier, those low on the dimension, who minimize their symptoms, may allow symptoms to develop unchecked to the point that rehospitalization would be necessary.

Thus, in some cases the expression of emotion can directly exacerbate symptoms and hasten degeneration. However, in other cases it may draw physicians' attention to patients and their symptoms which could result in more frequent hospitalization and drug treatment and increased survival, since the disease process could then be treated before excessive deterioration had occurred. Depending on the particular outcome—hospitalization or survival—different conclusions about the adaptiveness of emotional expression would have to be drawn.

SPECIFIC NEGATIVE AFFECTS: DEPRESSION AND ANXIETY. Displaying symptoms of depression or anxiety is often viewed as an indicator that the person is using inadequate coping strategies in dealing with situations of illness. We shall discuss each of these affects in turn.

Several studies using the *Depression (D)* scale of the Minnesota Multiphasic Personality Inventory (MMPI) have been reported in which those who are depressed take longer to recover from brucellosis, tuberculosis, and influenza (Calden et al. 1960; Imboden, Canter, and Cluff 1961; Imboden et al. 1959); have more complications during hospitalization after a myocardial infarction (Pancheri et al. 1978); and are less likely to survive a myocardial infarction for at least five years (Bruhn, Chandler, and Wolf 1969). In the case of infectious diseases, a physiological link is not necessarily involved. Depressivelike symptoms such as tiredness may merge with the transient symptoms associated with infectious diseases, making it difficult for patient and physician to determine when the disease has run its course (Imboden, Canter, and Cluff 1961).

Although the *D* scale consistently is associated with longer and more complicated recovery from illness, it does not show a significant relationship to recovery from *surgery*. Patients high on the *D* scale do not show greater mortality from open-heart surgery (Gilberstadt and Sako 1967; Henrichs, MacKenzie, and Almond 1969; Kilpatrick et al. 1975). A personality trait factor loading high on the Well-being scale of the California Psychological Inventory (Gough 1956), reflecting a minimization of worries and complaints, has been related to more minor medical complications, not less, after gallbladder and hernia surgery (Cohen 1975).

Clinical ratings of depression do show some relationship to surgery outcome variables. In one study, those rated as depressed display greater mortality after open-heart surgery (Kimball 1969). In another study, patients who showed optimism and confidence (the opposite of depression) before a retinal operation healed more quickly (Mason et al. 1969). On the other hand, ratings of depression were not related to a more difficult hospital course of recovery after myocardial infarction (Rosen and Bibring 1966).

The inconsistency of these results suggests that there are important differences between trait and process (rating) measures of depression. Process measures of depression may be confounded by the physical condition of the patient, the severity of the illness, or preoperative organicity, which could directly influence medical outcomes postoperatively (Kornfeld et al. 1974). These confounding variables must be controlled when process measures are used.

Anxiety is often used as another indicator of inadequate coping, and its physiological concomitants are thought to have negative effects on bodily processes.

However, there is no consistent evidence that anxiety is linked to slower recovery from illness (see Pancheri et al. 1978; Rosen and Bibring 1966; Vetter et al. 1977).

In a series of studies of asthma patients, state and trait measures of anxiety showed quite different relationships to outcome (Kinsman et al. 1980). For the *trait* measures of anxiety, both high and low levels of anxiety were associated with rehospitalization rates two to three times higher than for patients falling in the middle on the scale. A measure that tapped anxiety *specifically focused on the illness* showed that high levels of anxiety were related to increased use of as-needed medications, vigilance toward symptoms, and lower rates of rehospitalization as compared to those with low illness-focused anxiety (Dahlem, Kinsman, and Horton 1977; Staudenmayer et al. 1979). Those patients who were vigilant became fearful at symptom onset and took early preventive action (e.g., using an inhalator), whereas avoiders did nothing in the hope that the attack would not materialize. In the latter group, the asthmatic attacks often progressed too far to treat without hospitalization. Kinsman and his colleagues conclude that whereas *both* high and low levels of trait anxiety are maladaptive, high levels of illness-related anxiety *are* adaptive and that anxiety-reduction procedures should not be used to try to alter this type of anxiety. They state:

> Thus, anxiety reduction procedures should never address illness-focused anxiety alone, for this is an appropriate and adaptive anxiety. A lack of anxiety about breathing difficulties may lead the patient to forego expeditious action to resolve the distress associated with acute episodes of asthma. In effect, illness-specific anxiety acts like a signal energizing the patient to act. . . . Psychological intervention should leave the appropriate symptoms vigilance, associated with illness-focused anxiety, intact. [Kinsman et al. 1980, p. 402]

Kinsman et al. (1980) also conclude that anxiety-reduction techniques should not be used with all asthmatic patients and that such across-the-board treatments are premature and may be harmful for some types of patients.

On the other hand, there is consistent evidence that high levels of anticipatory fear, assessed with questionnaire or self-report measures, are related to postoperative emotional difficulties in general surgery patients (Cohen and Lazarus 1973; Janis 1958; Johnson et al. 1971; Sime 1976; Wolfer and Davis 1970). Contradictory results have been found with open-heart surgery patients (Layne and Yudofsky 1971; Morse and Litin 1969) and when self-report measures are related to physical rather than psychological outcomes of recovery (Cohen and Lazarus 1973; Johnson et al. 1971; Sime 1976). Clinical reports have also suggested that patients high in anxiety have the worst postoperative adjustment (Kimball 1969; Eisendrath 1969; cf. Kornfeld et al. 1974).

Overall, most state measures of anxiety show a positive linear relationship to postoperative emotional difficulties (cf. Janis 1958). This may be due merely to the same personality state or response style manifesting itself in two different time periods.

Our review of the literature in these four areas suggests that there is no simple answer to the question, What is adaptive coping behavior in situations of illness and treatment? The nature of the disease, the type of outcome variable examined, the time frame, and the way that coping is measured all affect the results. The nature of the illness and whether hospitalization is required appear to be especially important factors, and these factors may explain why different results are found for studies looking at short-term recovery from surgery as compared to longer term recovery from illness. The restrictions of the hospital setting, the absence of opportunities for personal involvement, and the uncontrollability of one's physical progress and day-to-day routines may induce greater stress for certain types of people or increase their sense of vulnerability. In future research efforts it would be useful if both trait and process measures were employed and if measures of both in-hospital and post-hospital outcomes were utilized. This should yield a better understanding of the adaptiveness of particular coping strategies over time and situation.

Relationship of Coping to the Etiology of Physical Disease

Although in recent years much attention has been focused on the role that stress plays in the etiology of physical illness (for reviews see Cohen 1979, 1981; Elliott and Eisdorfer 1982), there is a growing recognition that the link between stress and illness is not simple and depends on how individuals appraise the stressor, how they cope, the context, and the personal and social resources available. An examination of the research on modifiers of stress is beyond the scope of this chapter (see Cohen 1979, 1981; Cohen et al. 1982). We focus here on the research related to coping.

There is increasing agreement that the way one *copes* with stress is an important modifier of the stress-disease relationship (e.g., Jenkins 1979; Lazarus 1981; Rahe and Arthur 1978). For example, many studies have shown that the way an individual copes may reduce the physiological response to stressful events (see Rose's review, 1980). "Successful" defenses lower levels of 17-hydroxycorticosteroids in patients anticipating surgery, in parents whose child is dying of leukemia, and in soldiers facing combat (Bourne, Rose and Mason 1967; Friedman, Mason, and Hamburg 1963; Katz et al. 1970; cf. Gorzynski et al. 1980). However, actively engaging in overt motoric activity in situations of threat results in increased physiological arousal, especially of the adrenal cortical hormones (Gal and Lazarus 1975). The cardiovascular and psychoneuroendocrine systems show increased physiological reactivity in situations where people are "engaged" (Singer 1974). Further, animal work suggests that the inability to cope with an environmental stressor may influence immunological response (Sklar and Anisman 1979).

Engel and Schmale (Engel 1968; Engel and Schmale 1967; Schmale 1972) suggest that those who are unable to cope may give up, thereby increasing their susceptibility to disease. They believe that giving-up and the consequent feelings of helplessness increase susceptibility in those who are biologically predisposed (see also Seligman 1975). Although the animal studies tend to support the hypothesized relationships, there are serious methodological problems with the human studies, including lack of truly predictive studies, lack of control groups, and other alternative explanations (Cohen 1979).

Some aspects of personality that may influence coping have been related to decreased incidence of disease. Although the research has serious methodological problems, Kobasa (1979) found that those who did not get ill after undergoing many stressful life events were those who had a stronger sense of meaningfulness and commitment to self, a vigorous attitude to life, and an internal locus of control—a constellation she called "hardiness." On the other hand, Hinkle (1974) has argued from his observations that those who remain healthy may be those who are emotionally insulated and less involved with others.

The results described above suggest that how one copes with stress is linked to short-term physiological changes. However, the role that coping plays in increasing or decreasing long-term health consequences such as the incidence of illnesses has not been thoroughly studied except in the case of the so-called psychosomatic illnesses where the research studies are seriously flawed and show few consistencies (see Weiner's review, 1977). Research is needed to examine the direct link between coping and the etiology of physical disease as well as to investigate its role in modifying the relationship between stressors and illness. Sound methodological principles need to be followed, including use of prospective—not retrospective—designs, and adequate measures of illness, not illness behavior (Cohen 1979).

Of the coping variables investigated in etiological studies, the only one with strong research support from methodologically sound studies is Type A behavior. We turn our attention now to a discussion of this work.

Type A Behavior Pattern

There is considerable evidence that Type A behavior is linked to increased risk of coronary heart disease (e.g., Jenkins 1976; Rosenman et al. 1975; Rosenman et al. 1964) and fairly consistent evidence that it may be associated with the process of coronary atherosclerosis (Blumenthal et al. 1978; Frank et al. 1978; Williams et al. 1980; Zyzanski et al. 1976; cf. Dimsdale et al. 1978; Dimsdale et al. 1979; Krantz et al. 1979). Type A is a pattern of behavior with which people respond to environmental circumstances, and thus might be considered a coping style: "It is a particular complex of personality traits, including excessive competitive drive, aggressiveness, impatience, and a harrying sense of time urgency. . . . They also frequently exhibit a free-floating but well-rationalized form of hostility" (Friedman and Rosenman 1974, p. 4). The psychological components that are involved in the Type A behavior pattern and that might result in pathophysiological processes are still poorly understood. Some suggest that the need for control is a primary component of the Type A personality, and that Type A persons engage in exaggerated struggles to master encounters with others, feeling helpless and distressed when their efforts at control are unsuccessful (Glass 1977). However, contradictory data also exist (Lovallo and Pishkin 1980). Others believe that it is specifically the Type A person's hostility, and the way he or she handles it, that is the most damaging component of the behavior pattern (Williams et al. 1980). Other studies report that Type A persons use excessive denial and suppression (Pittner and Houston 1980) which may lead them to deny subjective distress and feelings of fatigue and to endure stresses longer than Type B's (Carver, Coleman, and Glass 1976; Pittner and Houston 1980). Such a coping style could ultimately have a long-term effect on the cardiovascular system.

Further work is needed to determine the essential psychological components of Type A behavior that are related to increased coronary heart disease risk. We also need to learn more about the physiological mechanisms that might link Type A behavior to long-term health reactions. Friedman and Rosenman (1974) suggest that the catecholamines may be the central biological mechanisms influenced by Type A behavior and through their effects (e.g., increasing the blood level of cholesterol and other lipids, increasing the tendency for the clotting elements of the blood to precipitate out, thus building up the plaques) increasing the risk of heart disease. Further work is needed to substantiate these relationships among Type A individuals.

A further question concerns whether Type A/Type B is really a typology or whether it represents a continuous dimension. To force people into a typology when a dimension is involved can distort the relationships that may exist and impedes our gaining understanding of the psychological and physiological components that play a role in this relationship.

The Type A work illustrates that it is possible to investigate the influence of coping in the etiology of physical disease using prospective designs and adequate illness indicators. The main weakness of this approach is the poor conceptualization of the critical psychological dimensions. Work in this area is ongoing. We also need to understand more about the physiological mechanisms that link this style of coping to long-term health consequences, and about the effects of this behavior pattern on measures of psychological and social functioning. To justify efforts to change Type A behavior in order to decrease risk of disease, evaluation must also be made of the negative consequences which might result in other areas of adaptive functioning.

Summary and Conclusions

In this chapter we have described a theoretical framework for viewing coping in general and in health-care settings in particular. If the study of coping is to be of practical value in guiding interventions to help people to cope more effectively, then we must be able to assess it successfully, and we have outlined some of the main problems and possibilities inherent in this task. Above all we have pointed out that the same coping process will produce positive outcomes under some conditions and negative ones under other conditions. Our review of research suggests that the following conditions must be taken into account:

First, the *point in time* at which a particular kind of outcome is assessed affects the relationship. Thus, studies have shown that avoidance and denial *prior* to a biopsy and *during* a heart attack may be counterproductive because they lead the person to delay seeking medical attention with the consequent increased risk of mortality or a worsening of the disease process. On the other hand, avoidance and denial seem also to be associated with more favorable surgical outcomes and better and more rapid return to normal functioning *after* a coronary attack.

Second, the *context of coping* also makes a big difference in adaptational consequences. Consistently, for example, research suggests that active, vigilant copers have more difficulties while still in the hospital setting, yet have better long-term rehabilitation after hospital discharge. Moreover, if this generalization were used to suggest interventions, e.g., to modify the hospital environment to allow greater autonomy and control for patients who seek it, one must take into account ever-present *individual differences;* some patients seem to do better through more passive forms of coping, or may reject efforts to provide autonomy and control because these conditions are more threatening to them.

Third, the *type of illness* may also be an important factor affecting the role of coping in outcomes. Thus, if we consider the tendency to express or inhibit emotional expression as a feature of coping, studies show that such expression is associated with a worsening of some medical problems and improvement in others. For example, the expression of anxiety is associated with poor psychological, but not physical, recovery, and in some diseases, such as asthma, it may be adaptive because it encourages patients to initiate needed treatment which aborts a severe attack leading to hospitalization. Techniques designed to reduce anxiety, therefore, should probably not focus on illness-focused anxiety for asthmatics, since this kind of anxiety might have utility.

Fourth, *different domains of adaptational outcomes are sometimes affected differently* by coping and thus require an evaluation of values, one value being bought at the expense of another. This is illustrated by the research on Type A behavior which adds to the risk of coronary heart disease but which also involves behaviors and attitudes that are personally and socially valued and associated with positive morale and functioning. The dilemma is that reducing physical risk might also be psychologically and socially destructive, unless a way can ultimately be found to change the former without impairing the latter (cf. Roskies 1980).

Aside from the obvious need for further research on coping and adaptational outcomes which takes into account all of these moderating conditions, the prime lesson is that we should not expect any given pattern of coping to work in the same way in all circumstances. Coping *is* an important factor in health and illness because it affects adaptational outcomes. However, in reaching toward health-care interventions, we must guard against a simplistic approach and work toward recognizing those conditions that make a difference in the coping/adaptational outcome relationship. In this chapter we have discussed four, namely, the time factor, the coping context, the type of illness, and the particular adaptational outcome which implies a value-laden choice.

The reader-practitioner who perceives that our message emphasizes individual variation and a host of circumstances that qualify broad general principles on which clinical intervention could depend should carefully consider what we have discussed. What has been said is that we should not expect a simple, one-to-one relationship between any form of coping, or coping-relevant intervention, and good adaptational outcomes. On the contrary, to help people cope better means that we also have to take into account the *classes* (or groups) of persons who can profit from a particular coping strategy, as well as the *classes* of situational contexts mediating adaptational outcomes. Although we have seemed to emphasize variation, we are not implying that the study of coping and adaptation, or the interventions potentially capable of benefitting people, need be chaotic, which would mean that we could have as many principles, concepts, or descriptions of coping and adaptation as there are people. As Lewin so aptly put it:

> A law is expressed in a equation which relates certain variables. Individual differences have to be conceived of as various specific values which these variables have in a particular case. In other words, general laws and individual differences are merely two aspects of one problem: they are mutually dependent on each other and the study of the one cannot proceed without the study of the other. [Lewin 1946, p. 794]

The task of coping research, therefore, is to find the laws of coping and adaptation that are serviceable, and classify or group people and situational contexts on variables that really make a difference. In this way we will learn what these variables are and how they work, ultimately to try to influence them in favorable directions.

Even the limited research we have examined suggests that the coping process is a powerful factor in morale, social functioning, and somatic health, and that by understanding how this process functions in health and illness settings we will be better able to help troubled and ill people manage more effectively. Coping is relevant in both treatment and prevention areas. In regards to coping with illness or medical treatment, people can be offered training in coping skills and learn to substitute effective forms of coping for counterproductive ones (e.g., Bowers and Kelly 1979; Roskies and Lazarus 1980). Whenever one talks about health maintenance, coping processes are always involved, whether directly or indirectly. As our knowledge about coping develops and becomes more specific, this should contribute significantly to our efforts in prevention and treatment.

REFERENCES

ALDWIN, C.; FOLKMAN, S.; SCHAEFER, C.; COYNE, J.; and LAZARUS, R. 1980. Ways of coping: a process measure. Paper presented at American Psychological Association, Montreal, September 1980.

ANDREASEN, N. J. C.; NOYES, R., JR.; and HARTFORD, C. E. 1972. Factors influencing adjustment of burn patients during hospitalization. *Psychosomatic Medicine* 34:517–25.

ANDREW, J. M. 1970. Recovery from surgery, with and without preparatory instruction, for three coping styles. *Journal of Personality and Social Psychology* 15:223–26.

AVERILL, J. R. 1973. Personal control over aversive stimuli and its relationship to stress. *Psychological Bulletin* 80:286–303.

———, and OPTON, E. M., JR. 1968. Psychophysiological assessment: rationale and problems. In *Advances in psychological assessment*, ed. P. McReynolds, vol. 1. Palo Alto, Calif.: Science and Behavior Books.

BLUMBERG, E. M.; WEST, P. M.; and ELLIS, F. W. A possible relationship between psychological factors and human cancer. *Psychosomatic Medicine* 16:277–86.

BLUMENTHAL, J. A.; WILLIAMS, R. B.; KONG, Y.; SCHANBERG, S. M.; and THOMPSON, L. W. 1978. Type A behavior pattern and coronary atherosclerosis. *Circulation* 58:634–39.

BOURNE, P. G.; ROSE, R. M.; and MASON, J. W. 1967. Urinary 17–OHCS levels. *Archives of General Psychiatry* 17:104–10.

BOWERS, K. S., and KELLY, P. 1979. Stress, distress, psychotherapy, and hypnosis. *Journal of Abnormal Psychology* 88:490–505.

BOYD, I.; YEAGER, M.; and McMILLAN, M. 1973. Personality styles in the post-operative course. *Psychosomatic Medicine* 35:23–40.

BRADBURN, N. 1969. *The structure of well-being.* Chicago: Aldine.

BREHM, J. W. 1966. *A theory of psychological reactance.* New York: Academic Press.

BRUHN, J. G.; CHANDLER, B.; and WOLF, S. 1969. A psychological study of survivors and nonsurvivors of myocardial infarction. *Psychosomatic Medicine* 31:8–19.

BURKE, R. J., and WEIR, T. 1980. The Type A experience: Occupational and life demands, satisfaction and well-being. *Journal of Human Stress* 6(4):28–38.

BYRNE, D. 1961. The repression-sensitization scale: rationale, reliability, and validity. *Journal of Personality* 29:334–49.

———. 1964. Repression-sensitization as a dimension of personality. In *Progress in experimental personality research*, ed. B. A. Maher, vol. 1. New York: Academic Press.

CALDEN, G.; DUPERTUIS, C. W.; HOKANSON, J. E.; and LEWIS, W. C. 1960. Psychosomatic factors in the rate of recovery from tuberculosis. *Psychosomatic Medicine* 22:345–55.

CAMERON, A., and HINTON, J. 1968. Delay in seeking treatment for mammary tumors. *Cancer* 21:1121–26.

CARVER, C. S.; COLEMAN, A. E.; and GLASS, D. C. 1976. The coronary-prone behavior pattern and the suppression of fatigue on a treadmill test. *Journal of Personality and Social Psychology* 33:460–66.

CHODOFF, P.; FRIEDMAN, S. B.; and HAMBURG, D. A. 1964. Stress, defenses, and coping behavior: observations in parents of children with malignant disease. *American Journal of Psychiatry* 120:743–49.

COBB, S. 1976. Social support as a moderator of life stress. *Psychosomatic Medicine* 38:300–14.

COHEN, F. 1975. Psychological preparation, coping, and recovery from surgery. Unpublished Ph.D. dissertation, University of California, Berkeley, 1975.

——. 1979. Personality, stress, and the development of physical illness. In *Health psychology—a handbook*, ed. G. C. Stone, F. Cohen, and N. E. Adler. San Francisco, Calif: Jossey-Bass.

——. 1981. Stress and bodily disease. *Psychiatric Clinics of North America*, 4(2):269–86.

——; HOROWITZ, M. J.; LAZARUS, R. S.; MOOS, R. H.; ROBINS, L. N.; ROSE, R. M.; and RUTTER, M. 1982. Panel report on psychosocial assets and modifiers of stress. In *Stress and human health*, ed. G. R. Elliott and C. Eisdorfer. New York: Springer.

COHEN, F., and LAZARUS, R. S. 1973. Active coping processes, coping dispositions, and recovery from surgery. *Psychosomatic Medicine* 35:375–89.

——. 1979. Coping with the stresses of illness. In *Health psychology—a handbook*, ed. G. C. Stone, F. Cohen, and N. E. Adler. San Francisco, Calif.: Jossey-Bass.

CROOG, S. H.; SHAPIRO, D. S.; and LEVINE, S. 1971. Denial among male heart patients: an empirical study. 1971. *Psychosomatic Medicine* 33:385–97.

CUADRA, C. A. 1953. A psychometric investigation of control factors in psychological adjustment. Unpublished Ph.D. dissertation, University of California, Berkeley.

DAHLEM, N. W.; KINSMAN, R. A.; and HORTON, D. J. 1977. Panic-fear in asthma: requests for as-needed medications in relation to pulmonary function measurements. *Journal of Allergy and Clinical Immunology* 60:295–300.

DAVIS, F. 1963. *Passage through crisis*. Indianapolis: Bobbs-Merrill.

DEROGATIS, L. R.; ABELOFF, M. D.; and MELISARATOS, N. 1979. Psychological coping mechanisms and survival time in metastatic breast cancer. *Journal of the American Medical Association* 242:1504–8.

DEWOLFE, A. S.; BARRELL, R. P.; and CUMMINGS, J. W. 1966. Patient variables in emotional response to hospitalization for physical illness. *Journal of Consulting Psychology* 30:68–72.

DIMSDALE, J. E.; ECKENRODE, J.; HAGGERTY, R. J.; KAPLAN, B. H.; COHEN, F.; and DORNBUSCH, S. 1979. The role of social supports in medical care. *Social Psychiatry* 14:175–80.

DIMSDALE, J. E.; HACKETT, T. P.; HUTTER, A. M.; BLOCK, P. C.; and CATANZANO, D. 1978. Type A personality and extent of coronary atherosclerosis. *American Journal of Cardiology* 42:583–86.

——; and WHITE, P. J. 1979. Type A behavior and angiographic findings. *Journal of Psychosomatic Research* 23:273–76.

DIRKS, J. F.; JONES, N. F.; and KINSMAN, R. A. 1977. Panic-fear: a personality dimension related to intractability in asthma. *Psychosomatic Medicine* 39:120–26.

DIRKS, J.F.; KINSMAN, R.A.; JONES, N.F.; SPECTOR, S.L.; DAVIDSON, P.T.; and EVANS, N.W. 1977. Panic-fear: a personality dimension related to length of hospitalization in respiratory illness. *Journal of Asthma Research* 14:61–71.

DUDLEY, D. L.; VERHEY, J. W.; MASUDA, M.; MARTIN, C. J.; and HOLMES, T. H. 1969. Long-term adjustment, prognosis, and death in irreversible diffuse obstructive pulmonary syndromes. *Psychosomatic Medicine* 31:310–25.

EISENDRATH, R. M. 1969. The role of grief and fear in the death of kidney transplant patients. *American Journal of Psychiatry* 126:381–87.

ELLIOTT, G. R., and EISDORFER, C., eds. 1982. *Stress and human health*. New York: Springer.

ENGEL, G. L. 1968. A life setting conducive to illness: the giving up–given up complex. *Bulletin of the Menninger Clinic* 32:355–65.

——, and SCHMALE, A. H. 1967. Psychoanalytic theory of somatic disorder. *Journal of the American Psychoanalytic Association* 15:344–63.

FISHER, S. 1967. Motivation for patient delay. *Archives of General Psychiatry* 16:676–78.

FOLKMAN, S., and LAZARUS, R. S. 1980. An analysis of coping in a middle-aged community sample. *Journal of Health and Social Behavior* 21:219–39.

FRANK, K. A.; HELLER, S. S.; KORNFELD, D. S.; SPORN, A. A.; and WEISS, M. D. 1978. Type A behavior pattern and coronary angiographic findings. *Journal of the American Medical Association* 240:761–63.

FRANKENHAEUSER, M. 1975. Sympathetic-adrenomedullary activity, behavior, and the psychosocial environment. In *Research in psychophysiology*, ed. P. H. Venables and M. J. Christie. New York: Wiley.

——. 1976. The role of peripheral catecholamines in adaptation to understimulation and overstimulation. In *Psychopathology of human adaptation*, ed. G. Serban. New York: Plenum Press.

FREUD, A. 1946. *The ego and the mechanisms of defence.* New York: International Universities Press.

FRIEDMAN, M., and ROSENMAN, R. H. 1974. *Type A behavior and your heart.* New York: Knopf.

FRIEDMAN, S. B.; MASON, J. W.; and HAMBURG, D. A. 1963. Urinary 17–hydroxycorticosteroid levels in parents of children with neoplastic disease: a study of chronic psychological stress. *Psychosomatic Medicine* 25:364–76.

GAL, R., and LAZARUS, R. S. 1975. The role of activity in anticipating and confronting stressful situations. *Journal of Human Stress* 1(4):4–20.

GARDNER, R. W.; HOLZMAN, P. S.; KLEIN, G. S.; LINTON, H. B.; and SPENCE, D. P. 1959. Cognitive control: a study of individual consistencies in cognitive behavior. *Psychological Issues* 1(4).

GEORGE, J. M.; SCOTT, D. S.; TURNER, S. P.; and GREGG, J. M. 1980. The effects of psychological factors and physical trauma on recovery from oral surgery. *Journal of Behavioral Medicine* 3:291–310.

GILBERSTADT, H., and SAKO, Y. 1967. Intellectual and personality changes following openheart surgery. *Archives of General Psychiatry* 16:210–14.

GLASS, D. C. 1977. *Behavior patterns, stress, and coronary disease.* Hillsdale, N.J.: Erlbaum.

GLESER, G. C., and IHILEVICH, D. 1969. An objective instrument for measuring defense mechanisms. *Journal of Consulting and Clinical Psychology* 33:51–60.

GOLDSTEIN, A. M. 1980. The "uncooperative" patient: self-destructive behavior in hemodialysis patients. In *The many faces of suicide: Indirect self-destructive behavior*, ed. N. L. Farberow. New York: McGraw-Hill.

GOLDSTEIN, M. J. 1959. The relationship between coping and avoiding behavior and response to fear-arousing propaganda. *Journal of Abnormal and Social Psychology* 58:247–52.

GORZYNSKI, J. G.; HOLLAND, J.; KATZ, J. L.; WEINER, H.; ZUMOFF, B.; FUKUSHIMA, D.; and LEVIN, J. 1980. Stability of ego defenses and endocrine responses in women prior to breast biopsy and ten years later. *Psychosomatic Medicine* 42:323–28.

GOUGH, H. G. 1956. *California psychological inventory.* Palo Alto, Calif.: Consulting Psychologists Press.

HAAN, N. 1977. *Coping and defending: processes of self-environment organization.* New York: Academic Press.

HACKETT, T. P., and CASSEM, N. H. 1974. Development of a quantitative rating scale to assess denial. *Journal of Psychosomatic Research* 18:93–100.

——. 1975. Psychological management of the myocardial infarction patient. *Journal of Human Stress* 1(3):25–38.

——; and WISHNIE, H. A. 1968. The coronary-care unit: an appraisal of its psychologic hazards. *New England Journal of Medicine* 279:1365–70.

HAMBURG, D. A.; COELHO, G. V.; and ADAMS, J. E. 1974. Coping and adaptation: steps toward a synthesis of biological and social perspectives. In *Coping and adaptation*, ed. G. V. Coelho, D. A. Hamburg, and J. E. Adams. New York: Basic Books.

HAMBURG, D. A.; HAMBURG, B.; and DEGOZA, S. 1953. Adaptive problems and mechanisms in severely burned patients. *Psychiatry* 16:1–20.

HAMMERSCHLAG, C. S.; FISHER, S.; DeCOSSE, J.; and KAPLAN, E. 1964. Breast symptoms and patient delay: psychological variables involved. *Cancer* 17:1480–85.

HENRICHS, T. F.; MACKENZIE, J. W.; and ALMOND, C. H. 1969. Psychological adjustment and acute response to open-heart surgery. *Journal of Nervous and Mental Disease* 148:158–64.

HINKLE, L. E., JR. 1974. The effect of exposure to culture change, social change, and changes in interpersonal relationships on health. In *Stressful life events: their nature and effects*, ed. B. S. Dohrenwend and B. P. Dohrenwend. New York: Wiley.

HOFER, M. A.; WOLFF, C. T.; FRIEDMAN, S. B.; and MASON, J. W. 1972a. A psychoendocrine study of bereavement: Part 1. 17–hydroxycorticosteroid excretion rates of parents following death of their children from leukemia. *Psychosomatic Medicine* 34:481–91.

——. 1972b. A psychoendocrine study of bereavement: Part 2. Observations on the process of mourning in relation to adrenocortical function. *Psychosomatic Medicine* 34:492–504.

HOLMES, T. H., and RAHE, R. H. 1967. The social readjustment rating scale. *Journal of Psychosomatic Research* 11:213–18.

HOROWITZ, M. J. 1976. *Stress response syndromes*. New York: Aronson.

——, and WILNER, N. 1980. Life events, stress and coping. In *Aging in the 1980's: selected contemporary issues*, ed. L. Poon. Washington, D.C.: American Psychological Association.

IMBODEN, J. B.; CANTER, A.; and CLUFF, L. E. 1961. Convalescence from influenza. *Archives of Internal Medicine* 108:393–99.

——; and TREVER, R. W. 1959. Brucellosis: III. Psychologic aspects of delayed convalescence. *Archives of Internal Medicine* 103:406–14.

JANIS, I. L. 1958. *Psychological stress: psychoanalytic and behavioral studies of surgical patients*. New York: Wiley.

——, and MANN, L. 1977. *Decision making: a psychological analysis of conflict, choice and commitment*. New York: Free Press.

JANIS, I. L., and RODIN, J. 1979. Attribution, control, and decision making: social psychology and health care . In *Health Psychology—a handbook*, ed. G. C. Stone, F. Cohen, and N. E. Adler. San Francisco, Calif.: Jossey-Bass.

JENKINS, C. D. 1976. Recent evidence supporting psychologic and social risk factors for coronary disease. *New England Journal of Medicine* 294:987–94, 1033–38.

——. 1979. Psychosocial modifiers of response to stress. *Journal of Human Stress* 5(4):3–15.

JOHNSON, J. E.; LEVENTHAL, H.; and DABBS, J. 1971. Contribution of emotional and instrumental response processes in adaptation to surgery. *Journal of Personality and Social Psychology* 20:55–64.

KANNER, A. D.; COYNE, J. J. C.; SCHAEFFER, C.; and LAZARUS, R. S. 1981. Comparison of two modes of stress measurement: daily hassles and uplifts versus major life events. *Journal of Behavioral Medicine*, 4:1–39.

KAPLAN, B. H.; CASSEL, J. C.; and GORE, S. 1977. Social support and health. *Medical Care* 15(5,suppl,):47–58.

KASL, S. 1978. Epidemiological contributions to the study of work stress. In *Stress and Work*, ed. C. L. Cooper, and R. Payne. New York: Wiley.

KATZ, J. L.; WEINER, H.; GALLAGHER, T. G.; and HELLMAN, L. 1970. Stress, distress, and ego defenses. *Archives of General Psychiatry* 23:131–42.

KILPATRICK, D. G.; MILLER, W. C.; ALLAIN, A. N.; HUGGINS, M. B.; and LEE, W. H., JR. 1975. The use of psychological test data to predict open-heart surgery outcome: a prospective study. *Psychosomatic Medicine* 37:62–73.

KIMBALL, C. P. 1969. Psychological responses to the experience of open-heart surgery: I. *American Journal of Psychiatry* 126:348–59.

KINSMAN, R. A.; DAHLEM, N. W.; SPECTOR, S.; and STAUDENMAYER, H. 1977. Observations on subjective symptomatology, coping behavior, and medical decisions in asthma. *Psychosomatic Medicine* 39:102–19.

KINSMAN, R. A.; DIRKS, J. F.; JONES, N. F.; and DAHLEM, N. W. 1980. Anxiety reduction in asthma: four catches to general application. *Psychosomatic Medicine* 42:397–405.

KLOPFER, B. 1957. Psychological variables in human cancer. *Journal of Projective Techniques* 21:331–40.

KOBASA, S. C. 1979. Stressful life events, personality, and health: an inquiry into hardiness. *Journal of Personality and Social Psychology* 37:1–11.

KORNFELD, D. S.; HELLER, S. S.; FRANK, K. A.; and MOSKOWITZ, R. 1974. Personality and psychological factors in postcardiotomy delirium. *Archives of General Psychiatry* 31:249–53.

KRANTZ, D. S.; SANMARCO, M. I.; SELVESTER, R. H.; and MATTHEWS, K. A. 1979. Psychological correlates of progession of atherosclerosis in men. *Psychosomatic Medicine* 41:467–75.

KRASNOFF, A. 1959. Psychological variables and human cancer: A cross-validational study. *Psychosomatic Medicine* 21:291–95.

LAYNE, O. L., JR., and YUDOFSKY, S. C. 1971. Postoperative psychosis in cardiotomy patients. *New England Journal of Medicine* 284:518–20.

LAZARUS, R. S. 1966. *Psychological stress and the coping process.* New York: McGraw-Hill.

———. 1968. Emotions and adaptation: conceptual and empirical relations. In *Nebraska symposium on motivation*, ed. W. J. Arnold. Lincoln, Nebr.: University of Nebraska Press.

———. 1975a. A cognitively oriented psychologist looks at biofeedback. *American Psychologist* 30:553–61.

———. 1975b. The self-regulation of emotion. In *Emotions—their parameters and measurement*, ed. L. Levi. New York: Raven Press.

———. 1981. The stress and coping paradigm. In *Theoretical bases for psychopathology*, ed. C. Eisdorfer, D. Cohen, and A. Kleinman. New York: Spectrum.

———. The costs and benefits of denial. In *Denial of stress*, ed. S. Breznitz. New York: International Universities Press, in press.

———; Averill, J. R.; and OPTON, E. M., JR. 1970. Towards a cognitive theory of emotion. In *Feelings and emotions*, ed. M. B. Arnold. New York: Academic Press.

———. 1974. The psychology of coping: issues of research and assessment. In *Coping and adaptation*, ed. G. V. Coelho, D. A. Hamburg, and J. E. Adams. New York: Basic Books.

LAZARUS, R. S., and FOLKMAN, S. Coping and adaptation. In *The handbook of behavioral medicine*, ed. W. D. Gentry. New York: Guilford Press, in press.

LAZARUS, R. S., and LAUNIER, R. Stress-related transactions between person and environment. In *Perspectives in interactional psychology*, ed. L. A. Pervin and M. Lewis. New York: Plenum Press.

LEFCOURT, H. 1973. The functions of illusions of control and freedom. *American Psychologist* 28:417–25.

———. 1976. *Locus of control: current trends in theory and research.* New York: Halstead.

LEVIN, K. 1946. Behavior and development as a function of the total situation. In *Manual of child psychology*, ed. L. Carmichael. New York: Wiley.

LEVINE, M., and SPIVACK, G. 1964. *The Rorschach index of repressive style.* Springfield, Ill.: Thomas.

LIPOWSKI, Z. J. 1970. Physical illness, the individual, and the coping process. *Psychiatry in Medicine* 1:91–102.

LOVALLO, W. R., and PISHKIN, V. 1980. Performance of type A (coronary-prone) men during and after exposure to uncontrollable noise and task failure. *Journal of Personality and Social Psychology* 38:963–71.

MAGES, N. L., and MENDELSOHN, G. A. 1979. Effects of cancer on patients' lives: a per-
sonological approach. In *Health psychology—a handbook,* ed. G. C. Stone, F. Cohen,
and N. E. Adler. San Fransciso, Calif.: Jossey-Bass.

MASON, J. W. 1974. Specificity in the organization of neuroendocrine response profiles. In
Frontiers in neurology and neuroscience research, ed. P. Seeman and G. M. Brown. First
International Symposium of the Neuroscience Institute. Toronto, Ontario: University
of Toronto.

MASON, R. C.; CLARK, G.; REEVES, R. B.; and WAGNER, B. 1969. Acceptance and healing.
Journal of Religion and Health 8:123–42.

MECHANIC, D. 1962. *Students under stress.* New York: Free Press.

————. 1974. Social structure and personal adaptation: some neglected dimensions. In *Coping and adaptation,* ed. G. V. Coelho, D. A. Hamburg, and J. E. Adams. New York:
Basic Books.

MENNINGER, K. 1963. *The vital balance: The life process in mental health and illness.* New
York: Viking.

MOOS, R. H. 1974. Psychological techniques in the assessment of adaptive behavior. In *Coping and adaptation,* ed. G. V. Coelho, D. A. Hamburg, and J. E. Adams. New York:
Basic Books.

————, and TSU, V. 1977. The crisis of physical illness: an overview. *Coping with physical
illness,* ed. R. H. Moos. New York: Plenum Press.

MORSE, R. M., and LITIN, E. M. 1969. Postoperative delirium: a study of etiologic factors.
American Journal of Psychiatry 126:388–95.

MURPHY, L. B. Coping, vulnerability, and resilience in childhood. In *Coping and adaptation,* ed. G. V. Coelho, D. A. Hamburg, and J. E. Adams. New York: Basic Books.

PANCHERI, P.; BELLATERRA, M.; MATTEOLI, S.; CRISTOFARI, M.; POLIZZI, C.; and PULETTI, N.
1978. Infarct as a stress agent: life history and personality characteristics in improved
versus non-improved patients after severe heart attack. *Journal of Human Stress*
4(1):16–22, 41–42.

PARKES, C. M. 1972. *Bereavement: studies of grief in adult life.* New York: International
Universities Press.

PEARLIN, L., and SCHOOLER, C. 1978. The structure of coping. *Journal of Health and Social
Behavior* 19:2–21.

PITTNER, M. S., and HOUSTON, B. K. 1980. Response to stress, cognitive coping strategies,
and the Type A behavior pattern. *Journal of Personality and Social Psychology*
39:147–57.

RAHE, R. H., and ARTHUR, R. H. 1978. Life change and illness studies. *Journal of Human
Stress* 4(1):3–15.

RENNE, K. S. 1974. Measurement of social health in a general population survey. *Social
Science Research* 3:25–44.

ROGENTINE, G. N.; VAN KAMMEN, D. P.; FOX, B. H.; DOCHERTY, J. P.; ROSENBLATT, J. E.;
BOYD, S. C.; and BUNNEY, W. E. 1979. Psychological factors in the prognosis of malignant melanoma: a prospective study. *Psychosomatic Medicine* 41:647–55.

ROGERS, M. P.; DUBEY, D.; and REICH, P. 1979. The influence of the psyche and brain on immunity and disease susceptibility: a critical review. *Psychosomatic Medicine* 41:147–64.

ROSE, R. M. 1980. Endocrine responses to stressful psychological events. *Psychiatric Clinics
of North America* 3:251–76.

ROSEN, J. L., and BIBRING, G. L. 1966. Psychological reactions of hospitalized male patients
to a heart attack: age and social-class differences. *Psychosomatic Medicine* 28:808–21.

ROSENMAN, R. H.; BRAND, R. J.; JENKINS, C. D.; FRIEDMAN, M.; STRAUSS, R.; and WURM, M.
1975. Coronary heart disease in the western collaborative group study: final follow-up
experience of 8½ years. *Journal of the American Medical Association* 233:872–77.

ROSENMAN, R. H.; FRIEDMAN, M.; STRAUS, R.; WURM, M.; KOSITCHEK, R.; HAHN, W.; and
WERTHESSEN, N. T. 1964. A predictive study of coronary heart disease: the western collaborative group study. *Journal of the American Medical Association* 189:15–22.

ROSKIES, E. 1980. Considerations in developing a treatment program for the coronary-prone

(Type A) behavior pattern. In *Behavioral medicine: changing health life styles*, ed. P. O. Davidson and S. M. Davidson. New York: Brunner/Mazel.

——, and LAZARUS, R. S. 1980. Coping theory and the teaching of coping skills. In *Behavioral medicine: changing health life styles*, ed. P. O. Davidson and S. M. Davidson. New York: Brunner/Mazel.

ROTTER, J. B. 1966. Generalized expectancies for internal versus external control of reinforcement. *Psychological Monographs* 80(1): No. 609.

SCHAEFER, C., COYNE, J. C.; and LAZARUS, R. S. 1981. The health-related functions of social support. *Journal of Behavioral Medicine* 4:381–406.

SCHMALE, A. H., JR. 1972. Giving up as a final common pathway to changes in health. *Advances in Psychosomatic Medicine* 8:20–40.

SELIGMAN, M. E. 1975. *Helplessness*. San Francisco, Calif.: W. H. Freeman.

SELYE, H. 1974. *Stress without distress*. Philadelphia, Pa.: Lippincott.

SHAPIRO, D. 1965. *Neurotic styles*. New York: Basic Books.

SIME, A. M. 1976. Relationship of preoperative fear, type of coping, and information received about surgery to recovery from surgery. *Journal of Personality and Social Psychology* 34:716–24.

SINGER, M. T. 1974. Engagement-involvement: a central phenomenon in psychophysiological research. *Psychosomatic Medicine* 36:1–17.

SKLAR, L. S., and ANISMAN, H. 1979. Stress and coping factors influence tumor growth. *Science* 205:513–15.

SMITH, L. S. 1974. An investigation of pre- and postsurgical anxiety as a function of relaxation training. Unpublished Ph.D. dissertation, University of Southern Mississippi.

SOLOMON, S.; HOLMES, D. S.; and McCAUL, K. D. 1980. Behavioral control over aversive events: Does control that requires effort reduce anxiety and physiological arousal? *Journal of Personality and Social Psychology* 39:729–36.

SPEISMAN, J. C.; LAZARUS, R. S.; MORDKOFF, A. M.; and DAVISON, L. A. The experimental reduction of stress based on ego-defense theory. *Journal of Abnormal and Social Psychology* 68:367–80.

STAUDENMAYER, H.; KINSMAN, R. A.; DIRKS, J. F.; SPECTOR, S. L.; and WANGAARD, C. 1979. Medical outcome in asthmatic patients: effects of airways hyperreactivity and symptom-focused anxiety. *Psychosomatic Medicine* 41:109–18.

STAVRAKY, K. M., et al. 1968. Psychological factors in the outcome of human cancer. *Journal of Psychosomatic Research* 12:251–59.

STRICKLAND, B. R. 1978. Internal-external expectancies and health-related behaviors. *Journal of Consulting and Clinical Psychology* 46:1192–1211.

VAILLANT, G. 1977. *Adaptation to life*. Boston: Little, Brown.

VERNIER, C. M.; BARRELL, R. P.; CUMMINGS, J. W.; DICKERSON, J. H.; and HOOPER, H. E. 1961. Psychosocial study of the patient with pulmonary tuberculosis: a cooperative research approach. *Psychological Monographs* 75(6):1–32.

VETTER, N. J.; CAY, E. L.; PHILIP, A. E.; and STRANGE, R. C. 1977. Anxiety on admission to a coronary care unit. *Journal of Psychosomatic Research* 21:73–78.

VINOKUR, A., and SELZER, M. L. 1975. Desirable versus undesirable life events: their relationship to stress and mental distress. *Journal of Personality and Social Psychology* 32:329–37.

VISOTSKY, H. M.; HAMBURG, D. A.; GOSS, M. E.; and LEBOVITZ, B. A. 1961. Coping under extreme stress: observations of patients with severe poliomyelitis. *Archives of General Psychiatry* 5:423–48.

WALLSTON, B. S.; WALLSTON, K. A.; KAPLAN, G. D.; and MAIDES, S. A. 1976. Development and validation of the health locus of control (HLC) scale. *Journal of Consulting and Clinical Psychology* 44:580–85.

WALLSTON, K. A.; WALLSTON, B. S.; and DEVELLIS, R. 1978. Development of multidimensional health locus of control (MHLC) scales. *Health Education Monographs* 6:160–70.

WEINER, H. 1977. *Psychobiology and human disease*. New York: American Elsevier.

——; SINGER, M. T.; and REISER, M. F. 1962. Cardiovascular responses and their psychological correlates. I. A study in healthy young adults and patients with peptic ulcer and hypertension. *Psychosomatic Medicine* 24:477–98.

WEISMAN, A. D. 1972. *On dying and denying: a psychiatric study of terminality.* New York: Behavioral Publications.

———, and WORDEN, J. W. 1976–77. The existential plight in cancer: significance of the first 100 days. *International Journal of Psychiatry in Medicine* 7:1–15.

WHITE, R. W. 1974. Strategies of adaptation: an attempt at systematic description. In *Coping and adaptation*, ed. G. V. Coelho, D. A. Hamburg, and J. E. Adams. New York: Basic Books.

WILLIAMS, R. B.; HANEY, T.L.; LEE, K. L.; KONG, Y.; BLUMENTHAL, J. A.; and WHALEN, R. E. 1980. Type A behavior, hostility, and coronary atherosclerosis. *Psychosomatic Medicine* 42:539–49.

WOLFER, J. A., and DAVIS, C. E. 1970. Assessment of surgery patients' preoperative emotional condition and postoperative welfare. *Nursing Research* 19:402–14.

WOLFF, C. T.; FRIEDMAN, S. G.; HOFER, M. A.; and MASON, J. W. 1964. Relationship between psychological defenses and mean urinary 17–hydroxycorticosteroid excretion rates: I. A predictive study of parents of fatally ill children. *Psychosomatic Medicine* 26:576–91.

ZYZANSKI, S. J.; JENKINS, C. D.; RYAN T. J.; FLESSAS, A.; and EVERIST, M. 1976. Psychological correlates of coronary angiographic findings. *Archives of Internal Medicine* 136:1234–37.

Chapter 29

Social Adaptation of the Chronically Ill

Margaret Dimond

CHRONIC ILLNESS is a twentieth-century phenomenon. Prior to this time illness was generally acute in nature and limited in duration. Advances in sanitation; recognition of the importance of adequate nutrition; improved living conditions and personal hygiene; breakthroughs in the biological sciences in terms of vaccines, antibiotics, and other treatment and preventive technologies; as well as other advances in medical knowledge and management of illness, have resulted in impressive gains over the infectious and parasitic diseases. Regimens for curing or preventing previously irreversible or fatal diseases are currently available that could not have been imagined a century ago. These gains have not been entirely free of problematic consequences. The successful treatment of acute life-threatening illnesses has resulted in an increase in the numbers of individuals with residual limitations and chronic physical or emotional problems. The difficulties attending many chronic conditions continue long after the acute stage of the illness has been successfully managed.

Neither the incidence nor the prevalence of chronic conditions is a sufficient indication of the magnitude of the problem. The real measure is the extent to which individuals with chronic illness and their families are functioning in ways that are acceptable to them. The consequences of chronic illness can range from relatively minor inconveniences to what Katz and Capron (1975, p. 8) describe as catastrophic, or those that "radically alter a person's existence and accustomed way of life, disable him from pursing his accustomed work and activities, and leave his private affairs in disorder."

The extent to which individuals are able to manage the consequences of chronic illness depends upon factors ranging across the biological, psychological, interpersonal, and sociocultural spheres of life. Any comprehensive analysis of the process of adaptation to stressful situations includes at least five major classes of variables: (1) objective social conditions conducive to stress; (2) individual perceptions of stress; (3) individual responses to perceived stress; (4) long-term outcomes of perceived stress and responses to it; and (5) individual and situational variables that influence the relationships among the first four classes of variables (House 1974, p. 13).

In order to review, integrate, and evaluate the "state of knowledge" on social adaptation of the chronically ill, a modified version of House's (1974) model has been used to organize this chapter. I will first consider the concept of adaptation as it is discussed in the literature on chronic illness. Then, four major factors that influence social adaptation among the chronically ill will be considered: (1) nature of the illness; (2) definitions and meaning of the illness; (3) responses to chronic illness; and (4) the environment and illness.

Social Adaptation

The concept of adaptation implies a balance between the demands and expectations of a given situation and the capacities of an individual to respond to those demands. Failure to adapt, therefore, is a discrepancy between demands and capabilities. The magnitude of the discrepancy determines, in part, the stress experienced by the individual (Mechanic 1977). All of life is an adaptive process. Man is, as Masi (1978) suggests, an adaptive organism in a changing environment. The states of health or disease are the expressions of the success or failure experienced by individuals in their efforts to respond adaptively to environmental challenges (Dubos 1965, p. xvii). However, the capacity for adaptation is not limitless; adaptive responses are characterized by dynamic flux within finite limits (Dubos 1965; Goosen and Bush 1979; Thompson 1980). Toffler described the limits of capacity as follows:

> When we alter our life style, when we make and break relationships with things, places or people . . . we adapt; we live. Yet there are finite boundaries, we are not infinitely resilient. Each adaptive reaction exacts a price, wearing down the body's machinery bit by minute bit . . . Thus man remains a biosystem with a limited capacity for change. [Toffler 1970, p. 324]

Everyone has achieved some measure of life adaptation; chronic illness disrupts this achievement. The demands of life for the chronically ill remain the same or greater than those present before illness, but often the capacity to respond in a satisfying way is diminished.

To define the concept of adaptation is difficult for several reasons. First, adaptation is dynamic. It is a continuous round of negotiation between the individual and the environment. There is no point at which to declare the achievement of adaptation. With respect to adaptation to chronic illness there are periods of progress and periods of regress depending on changes in the illness and changes in response patterns of the individual. Second, adaptation to chronic illness is influenced by multiple forces and achieved by individual creativity.

> The response that a particular person makes to a given situation is conditioned by his past . . . . But experience shows that human beings are not passive components in adaptive systems. Their responses commonly manifest themselves as acts of personal creation. [Dubos 1965, p. xviii]

To capture the many factors involved and the infinite variety of individual creativity in a single definition is impossible. Third, adaptation takes place at an uneven pace within multiple spheres of life. The chronically ill individual may be functioning well physiologically but be unable to come to terms with necessary changes required by the illness in the social sphere; or the individual may be psychologically "together" but biochemically out of balance. It is not inconceivable that the individual is integrated at one level and disintegrating at another. Fourth, adaptation is evaluated from many perspectives and by many persons. The client, his/her family, friends, employers, health-care providers, and funding agencies (e.g., Workmen's Compensation) may each have different sets of criteria for measuring different sets of expectations. To declare one perspective to be representative of adaptation is neither appropriate nor justified.

So what is adaptation to chronic illness? In a very broad sense it can be defined as Feldman has suggested:

> Coming to terms existentially with the reality of chronic illness as a state of being, discarding both false hope and destructive hopelessness, restructuring the environment in which one must now function. Most importantly, adaptation demands the reorganization and acceptance of the self so that there is a meaning and purpose to living that transcends the limitations imposed by the illness. [Feldman 1974, p. 290]

This definition includes both a psychological and a behavioral component. The emphasis is on the individual's ability to resolve the chronicity or "long-termness" of the situation, balance hope against despair, and find purpose and quality in life. There is also recognition of the necessity to organize the environment in ways that will accommodate changes in the individual.

There is little disagreement over the appropriate conceptualization of adaptation. Descriptions such as the one by Feldman (1974) represent the concept very well. For practitioners or others who are concerned with day-to-day functioning of the chronically ill, a more operational definition is necessary. How is existential acceptance measured or evaluated? What are the indicators of hope or despair? How is the environment to be restructured? There is considerable variation in the range of empirical indicators of adjustment found in the literature.

Some of the earliest work in rehabilitation focused on very basic skills necessary for daily living: eating, dressing, toileting, ambulation within the living facility, and fundamental communication skills (Katz et al. 1963). Achieving functional independence, as measured by these basic skills, is still a part of programs for assisting the chronically ill or disabled. Increasingly the dimensions of adjustment have been broadened to include psychological and sociobehavioral aspects of life. Vocational activities, particularly paid employment, have become primary indicators of adjustment. Morrow, Chiarello, and Derogatis (1978) included indicators of job disruption, changes in performance and job satisfaction. Other measures of changes in work habits have included quitting, working fewer hours, missing work, working slowly, or avoiding parts of the job (Carlson 1979; Garrity 1973a, 1973b; Goldberg 1974; Holcomb and MacDonald 1973; Hyman 1975; Reif 1975; Smith 1979). Adjustment to chronic illness among children has been measured in terms of school activities and enjoyment of peers (Sullivan 1979a, 1979b).

Ability to function in the family has also become a common indicator of adjustment to chronic illness. Household activities, communication with family members, participation in and enjoyment of family life, and the quality of sexual activities are some of the major dimensions used to assess adjustment to chronic illness within a family context (Gilson, Gilson, and Bergner 1975; Morrow et al. 1978).

Other social relationships (friends and work colleagues) and leisure pursuits have more recently been used as empirical indicators of social adjustment to chronic illness (Benoliel, McCorkle, and Young 1980; Gilson et al. 1975). Concern for these dimensions of life indicates that care-givers and investigators are beginning to recognize the need for a more holistic approach to chronic illness which incorporates the important concept of quality of life.

Psychological dimensions of adaptation are closely related to social adjustment. Some of the psychological concepts treated as dependent or outcome variables in the literature are: denial, displacement, and projection (Christopherson and Gonda 1973; DeNour, Shaltiel, and Czaczkes 1968; Short and Wilson 1969); depression (Buchanan and Abram 1975); anger (Arnaud 1959); anxiety, frustration, body image (Arnaud 1959; Buchanan and Abram 1975). In more recent times, problem-solving skills and learning abilities (Worden and Sobel 1978); psychological well-being and life satisfaction (Carlson 1979; Holcomb and MacDonald 1973; Simmons, Klein, and Simmons 1977); and morale (Dimond 1979, 1980; MacElveen 1972) have more frequently been used as indicators of psychological adjustment.

There are also physiological dimensions to adaptation which have to do with general physical well-being, physiological stability, complications and exacerbations of the underlying pathology. The measurement and evaluation of these dimensions is specific and different for each type of long-term illness.

The Nature of the Illness

Adaptation to chronic illness is determined, in part, by the character of the specific illness in question. There are at least three major characteristics of illness that are critical to the long-term adaptive responses that a chronically ill person achieves: (1) the type of onset and expected course of the illness; (2) the nature and extent of limitation; and (3) the type and extent of changes in physical appearance and bodily functions (Haber and Smith 1971; Melvin and Nagi 1970; Moos 1977; Safilios-Rothschild 1970).

The type of onset and expected course of an illness is likely to influence the kind of adaptive response to it. Distinctions may be made between chronic conditions that are congenital and those that are acquired. The latter involves the experience of adjusting to a loss of function, the former requires adjustment to diminished or absent function without the experience of loss. Sudden versus gradual onset is another important distinction. The opportunity for gradual adjustment to diminishing body function, a kind of anticipatory socialization to the role of the chronically ill, may be a very different phenomenon from the experience of sudden, unexpected changes in function. A third distinction is whether the chronic condition is the result of accident, pathology, genetic defect, or some other cause. The way an individual responds initially; the sense of hope or despair; feelings of anger, guilt, frustration; the ability or willingness to accept assistance from others; and other initial responses are apt to be different depending on the identified cause of illness.

Chronic illnesses vary widely in expected course. Some are quite stable once the acute phase is over; some involve periods of remission followed by exacerbation; and some are continuously progressive and deteriorating. The element of certainty or predictability is a key factor in the management of chronic illness. Unforeseen, unpredicted complications can be distressing and discouraging. Experiences with sudden and unexpected problems such as seizures, loss of bowel control, loss of recent memory, or severe pain may be major factors in determining the nature and extent of return to social roles.

The management of the treatment regimen is also a factor in adaptation. Some regimens are extremely time-consuming and tedious (dialysis); some are physically painful (injections); and some require major modification in life-style (diet, smoking, exercise, climate changes, various kinds of employment change). The perceived cost-benefit ratio of the treatment may seem (or actually be) marginal, and thus influence the response to chronic illness.

The nature and extent of limitations is somewhat difficult to describe in a "pure" sense since some of the limitations of chronic illness are those perceived as such by the patient but which have no physiological or anatomical basis. Obviously there will be differences in response options and capabilities depending on the body system(s) affected by disease. Sensory problems (vision-hearing) require different adaptive responses from problems associated with mobility, cognition, and speech. Also, it must be remembered that multiple impairments are relatively common among the chronically ill, particularly the elderly chronically ill. Knowledge of the system affected and the nature of the disease process is necessary but not sufficient to determine the extent of the limitations in activities that will occur. Melvin and Nagi (1970) point out the problems encountered when assessing the perceived need for restricted activity among the chronically impaired. Physicians, insurance companies, sometimes employers, and others may base the perception of need for restricted activity primarily on the anatomic and physiological deficiencies apparent in the disease. The criteria used by the individual may be quite different, and often is based on the experience of pain, anxiety, depression or worry. Frequently, but not always, family and friends will relate to the reported experience of the patient. These differences in criteria for assessment and evaluation create ambiguities for the patient as well as conflict between and among groups of people concerned about the chronically ill person.

Type and extent of changes in physical appearance and bodily functions is a third major characteristic of illnesses. Adaptation to chronic illness is likely to be associated with visibility and disfigurement as well as annoying or embarrassing changes in bodily functions. Visible disfigurement, particularly that affecting the face, may result in complete withdrawal from social interaction, while for objectively more functionally limiting conditions such as quadraplegia there may be no major change in social behavior. Changes in bodily functions may also bear on the extent to which individuals engage in social or public activities. Odors, sounds, visible equipment, or appliances draw unwanted attention to the individual with a chronic impairment. Discomfort and embarrassment is often experienced when others interact with persons who are visibly disfigured or who have noticeable differences in body functions. Such strained interpersonal interactions may have the effect of reducing the extent to which the chronically ill person will engage in gainful employment or social and recreational activities.

The type of onset and course of illness, kinds of limitations, and the changes in physical appearance and bodily functions will impact upon the long-term adaptive responses of individuals with chronic illness. These factors also have a powerful influence on the way the illness is defined and the meanings attached to it.

Definitions and Meaning of Illness

The way ill persons define chronic illness depends on the extent of abnormality of biological structure and function; the nature and severity of symptoms; competence and skill to manage or control symptoms; and the values, norms, and expectations of others. Except for the anatomical or structural changes caused by the disease process itself, most of the factors that determine the meaning of illness are related in some way to the sociocultural world of the ill person.

The world of the chronically ill is made up of family, friends, and health-care professionals, each with a personal perspective on the meaning of the illness and each, therefore, with a framework or rationale for responding to the ill person. Differences in perspectives and expectations between and among these sets of individuals create ambiguities, confusion, tension, and sometimes distress for the individual with a chronic illness.

Professional care-givers (physicians, nurses) frequently have treatment goals that are at odds with those of patients. Professionals may define illness only, or primarily, in terms of physiological deviations from normal (elevated blood gases, diminished breath sounds, sugar in the urine, low hemoglobin) and plan treatment to manage these abnormalities with little concern for broader aspects of the patient's life. The individual with a chronic illness may, on the other hand, define the situation primarily in terms of his/her quality of life and establish goals related primarily to social functioning (eating out, entertaining friends, spending time with children, maintaining some level of gainful employment).

The achievement of both sets of goals (professional and personal) may be incompatible and the potential for tension and misunderstanding between patient and care-giver is great. Unless steps are taken to change or modify goals, the final outcome may be discouragement, disappointment, and perhaps "giving-up" on the part of both the professional and the patient. What is needed is communication and negotiation to achieve a compromised, but common, goal. Sharing a common goal, professionals and patients can establish reasonable criteria for judging the success of treatment. It may be that the most appropriate and humane criteria for success is measured in terms of the clients' ability to function at some acceptable level of social intercourse and not in terms of "near normal" body chemistries.

Communication between health-care providers and the chronically ill is a critical factor in determining the way the ill person assesses his/her situation. It is generally recognized that individuals define situations through some cognitive process and that, based on this assessment, they determine the appropriate management strategies (Chrisman 1977; Lazarus 1966; Lazarus and Cohen 1977; Mechanic 1974; Shalit 1977).

One assumption that is made in most discussions of cognitive appraisal is that the individual has the "facts" about the situation being appraised, i.e., there is no ambiguity. On the contrary, in many instances of chronic illness there is considerable uncertainty and lack of information. For example, the symptoms of a disease, although perhaps not life-threatening, may be confusing, unexpected, and frightening. Physicians who tell patients not to worry, to relax, to reduce their activity, or to call back later if the symptoms persist, without giving any rationale for their advice, may only add to the uncertainty and fear.

Ambiguity may be the result of the client's inability to "hear" what is being said, or the failure of the clinician to communicate in a clear and unambiguous manner (Davis 1963; Roth 1963). There are many reasons why clinicians might communicate in a manner that leaves clients perplexed. The obvious reason may be that the clinician does not know exactly what to do or how to predict outcomes, simply because of the lack of medical knowledge and technology about a specific disease and its sequelae. Second, it may be that all known treatments have been exhausted and nothing more can be done. Failure is difficult to acknowledge and some clinicians are not able to face the patient and family and admit that every treatment has been tried. Contrary to some opinions, many patients have sufficient personal and social resources to handle this kind of information. A third reason for ambiguous communication from clinicians may be the fact that as a result of treating some symptoms additional problems arise ("iatrogenic disease"). Fox (1959) has recorded the agony of well-intentioned and sincere clinicians who vigorously treat disease only to have the treatment create unresolvable complications. The "facts" of the situation might be improved through frank, though perhaps painful, discussions between patient and professional. Appraisal processes may then be more accurate and selection of management strategies by the client will be more appropriate. Obviously, open communication is not the only factor in determining the way a situation is defined and managed, but it is a key factor.

If ambiguity persists, for whatever reason, individuals may seek to reduce it and increase the accuracy of their appraisals by some form of comparison with other patients. It is not uncommon to find patients in hospitals or clinics comparing symptoms, remedies for relief of symptoms, and progress toward stabilization of the illness.

Increasingly, support groups for the chronically ill are functioning as settings for comparison activities as well as opportunities for giving and receiving support and encouragement. The growth of the self-help movement over the past twenty years is part of what Vickers (1971, p. 439) has called "the search for an appreciative system sufficiently widely shared to mediate communication, sufficiently apt to guide action and sufficiently acceptable to make personal experience bearable." While the self-help movement has been steadily proliferating, health-care professionals have given it only scant attention either from the perspective of systematic investigation or as a potential alternative or enhancer of organized health care.

The benefits of self-help groups apply both to patients and their families. Their success can be attributed to several characteristics of these groups. First, the members and their families *share a common experience*. Recognition that others share what was believed to be a unique experience can be a very encouraging and strengthening experience. Second, members of self-help groups provide *mutual help and support* to one another. A third characteristic of self-help groups which accounts for their success is what Riessman (1965) calls the *helper principle*. The experience of reciprocating help received from others provides reassurance of one's own competence and usefulness. The likelihood of *gaining information* is a fourth characteristic of self-help groups. In the course of interacting with individuals with similar conditions, circumstances, or problems each member is likely to gain factual information and/or workable solutions and alternatives for the management of the exigencies of a given chronic illness.

Mechanic (1977) has suggested that it is probably very useful for persons with serious disabilities to have the opportunity to interact with others in similar circumstances. When, in the course of any specific chronic illness, is the most beneficial time for this opportunity is a matter for individual consideration. However, given the range of opportunities in self-help groups, it may be that individuals and their families benefit in different ways at different times; sometimes receiving support, information, and validation, sometimes providing this for others, yet always sharing the common experience of trying to manage life with an irreversible illness. This latter factor may make the difference between a life of despair and one of hope.

To summarize, the personal definition and meaning attached to any given chronic illness may be facilitated in a positive way through open, informative communication with professional care-givers as well as through participation in the many facets of appropriate self-help groups.

Responses to Chronic Illness

Living with a chronic illness requires management expertise in many areas. Some of these have been identified as preventing or managing medical crises, managing regimens which require extensive changes in life-style, reordering time, managing upsetting feelings, managing family relationships, maintaining adequate relations with health-care providers, and controlling symptoms (Moos 1977; Strauss and Glaser 1975). Other aspects of living with chronic illness may include managing a new identity, balancing the need for help from family and friends with the need for personal control and self-sufficiency, and the need to reciprocate (Dimond and Jones, forthcoming). Most of these management tasks have less to do with the disorder itself than with the consequences of the management of symptoms or the management of social relationships.

The way individuals cope with difficult situations has been conceptualized in a variety of ways (Averill 1973; French, Rodgers, and Cobb 1974; Levine and Scotch 1970; Mechanic 1968, 1970, 1974). There is general agreement and substantial support for the idea that significant life changes are stressful and affect the psychological, social, and physical well-being of the individual who experiences them (Dohrenwend and Dohrenwend 1974).

If we define stress simply as an imbalance between the demands of the environment and the capacity of the individual to respond to those demands (Mechanic 1974), then whether or not any given experience is stressful depends on two factors: (1) the meaning of the experience to the individual (to which allusion has already been made); and (2) the repertoire of balance-restoring or maintaining mechanisms available to the individual (Antonovsky 1979). There have been attempts to separate responses to stressful situations into those that are principally cognitive and those that are behavioral. Averill (1973, p. 295) speaks of cognitive control mechanisms as "the processing of potentially threatening information in such a manner as to reduce the net long-term stress or cost of adaptation." Behavioral control of the situation involves direct actions to modify the environment, or "the availability of a response which may directly influence or modify the objective characteristics of a threatening event" (Averill 1973, p. 296).

Pearlin and Schooler (1978, p. 3) define coping as "any response to external life strains that serves to prevent, avoid or control emotional distress," and propose two major types of coping: (1) responses that change the situation; and (2) responses that function to control meaning ("cognitive neutralization'). Others have defined responses to stress similarly (Kiely 1972; Lipowski 1970; Mechanic 1978; Turk et al. 1980).

Two characteristics which enter into most strategies for overcoming stress and which presumably are predictive of effectiveness are flexibility and farsightedness (Antonovsky 1979). The characteristic of flexibility refers to the ability to plan multiple approaches to a given problem and, assuming the availability of such contingencies, the willingness to consider and act out such strategies. This notion is quite commonly accepted, and there is some evidence to support the idea that a particular response may be less effective than having a variety of responses in one's repertoire (Pearlin and Schooler 1978).

Farsightedness, as conceived by Antonovsky (1979), is the ability to project or anticipate how the environment will respond to a given strategy. Standard problem-solving techniques frequently employ the procedure of specifying the possible consequences of proposed actions and then taking the action with the most positive consequences.

An important issue in the area of stress response is whether or not any category or type of response is more effective than another for managing stressful situations. This issue can only be definitively addressed with empirical evidence from many and varied situations. However, it is generally agreed that an active response by the individual is of great importance. By definition, as House (1974, p. 14) notes, coping (action) is potentially more successful than defenses (cognitions) in relieving stress since it acts on the objective source of stress.

Coping is clearly not a unidimensional concept. It functions at many levels and is achieved through multiple means, sometimes with actions, sometimes by cognitions and perceptions. Lazarus and Cohen summarize the diversity and complexity of coping as follows:

> Most persons utilize a variety of coping strategies, anticipating and evaluating what might happen and what has to be done, planning and preparing, changing the environment, retreating when necessary, postponing action for maximum effort, tolerating frustration and pain, and even deceiving themselves in order to feel better and to maintain hope and a sense of self-worth. [Lazarus and Cohen 1977, p. 112]

Certainly the above comments are applicable to individuals with chronic illnesses, who must manage daily stresses that interfere with ordinary life activities. Davis (1972, p. x) has referred to the ill individual as a "perplexed coper" who is "a well-intentioned character groping among alternatives . . . He sees none of the alternatives as ideal, although he reasons that one must after all be better than all the rest. The object of his quest is to decide on that alternative."

The literature is replete with discussions of responses by individuals to specific chronic illnesses. It is beyond the scope of this chapter to review this literature in detail. Instead several representative works will be presented to illustrate current work and provide direction for future investigative efforts.

While psychological attitudes and strategies are important factors in adaptation to chronic illness, they do not, as some would suggest, spell the difference between rehabilitation and chronic invalidism (DeNour and Czaczkes 1976). Adaptation is much too complex a process to be attributed only to a single factor or set of factors. A more reasoned approach is to suggest that the individual needs to develop psychological responses sufficient to control distressing emotions and to facilitate the tasks of adjustment (Mechanic 1977, p. 84).

Perhaps the most widely reported psychological response to stressful situations, and chronic illness particularly, is denial. This concept conjures up nearly universal negative definitions among those whose theoretical perspectives are rooted in the psychoanalytic tradition. There is, however, a sense in which denial is a positive force. Lipowski (1970) uses the term *minimization* and Lazarus (1974) speaks of *palliation*. Both refer to psychological strategies of ignoring, denying, selective attention, and rationalization. Neither writer declares these cognitive processes to be negative. In fact, Lazarus (1974) states that palliation is sometimes necessary initially to prepare for more active responses. There are instances where actions may not be possible and the only responses available are those Mechanic (1968) referred to as "comforting cognitions."

Anxiety and anger are common psychological responses to the onset of serious or disabling illness (Pritchard 1974a). The individual may be anxious about the extent of disability that will occur, anxious because of uncertainty about the course and outcome of the illness, fearful about the possibility of death. None of these feelings are abnormal nor are they particularly useful when considered in isolation. But they may in fact be necessary precursors to the initiation of certain active responses.

Other psychological responses less commonly reported are reordering priorities to match changed capabilities (Pearlin and Schooler 1978; Worden and Sobel 1978); assuming personal responsibility for managing the consequences of the illness (Dimond 1978); suppression of feelings in order to perform daily functions (Worden and Sobel 1978); making positive comparisons, e.g., taking account of successes over time, or comparing self with others who have the same illness (Dimond 1980).

There are some responses which seem to be primarily negative or at least not useful: hopeless defeat (Pritchard 1974b); depression (Sullivan 1979a, b); shame, guilt, and self-blaming (Kiely 1972); fatalistic acceptance (Worden and Sobel 1978); and giving up (Schmale 1972). Until there are longitudinally designed studies to investigate the onset and course of these kinds of responses, it is premature to label them as maladaptive. It may be that they serve some need for withdrawal and self-preservative purpose in a similar way suggested for denial; a kind of time-out or respite period.

One of the most predominant behavioral strategies reported in the literature is information seeking (Caplan 1964; Dimond 1978; Moos 1977; Pritchard 1974a; Sidle, Moos, and Adams 1969; Worden and Sobel 1978). Knowledge about the illness, the expected course and prognosis, how to manage symptoms, how to perform the technical skills necessary to control the disease, all depend on information. Thus, a necessary first step toward reducing ambiguity, anxiety, and fear and gaining control over the illness situation is acquiring information about the illness.

There are many sources of information that can be used: family and friends, physicians, nurses, other health-care workers and organized self-help groups. One of the most important sources of information is the physician. Unfortunately, obtaining accurate information from this source is sometimes possible only through determined and persistent effort. In a recent best seller, Martha Lear (1980) details the frustration, anger, and sometimes despair she and her husband experienced following his myocardial infarction. This is a moving and poignant account of one man's monumental efforts to cope with extreme mental and physical disability in spite of medical mismanagement and almost total absence of communication from physicians. As noted earlier, most patients are able to manage truthful, even if unpleasant, information about their condition much better than misinformation or no information.

Another category of behavioral response has to do with planning, partitioning, and pacing activities. Sidle, Moos, and Adams (1969) and Antonovsky (1979) speak of making alternate plans and being flexible in one's willingness to adopt such plans. For the chronically ill, the ability to plan daily activities and set reasonable and attainable short-term goals is very important for the achievement of social adaptation (Dimond 1980). One strategy for achieving this end is to break tasks or problems into manageable parts and concentrate on one part at a time (Caplan 1964; Moos 1977); another is consciously to pace oneself in order to control fatigue, which is a factor in many chronic illnesses and which can be psychologically demoralizing when it predominates. Still another strategy is to do what Goode (1960) suggested when he wrote of managing role strain, to compartmentalize, i.e., to set aside for the moment the role demands which one has been meeting and attend only to the one relevant at the present moment. To an observer, compartmentalizing may appear to be eliminating social roles or social withdrawal, but in some chronic illnesses where fatigue and/or time are factors, the ability to alter or eliminate selected social roles has been shown to be strongly related to social adaptation (Dimond 1980).

A variety of other strategies has been reported in the literature, many of which are not yet tested. For example, activities to reduce tension include biofeedback, yoga, relaxation exercises, hypnosis, use of drugs and alcohol, eating, smoking, and physical exercise (Lazarus 1974; Sidle, Moos, and Adams 1969). Although these activities have been reported as in use or suggested for use as tension reducers, obviously not all are "healthy" activities. None of the writers cited are advocating the use, for example, of smoking, but merely noting that it is used by many persons to reduce tension. Other intriguing coping strategies are the use of laughter (Cousins 1977) and humor (Worden and Sobel 1978). Finally, perhaps one of the most useful techniques is to draw on the past, review previous difficult situations and repeat those strategies that were successful in the past and appropriate for the present situation.

The Environment and Illness

The final set of factors which influence's social adaptation to chronic illness can be loosely classified as environmental. An ecological system may be thought of as consisting of four components: (1) the individual: age, sex, race, personality traits, stage of physical, cognitive, and psychosocial development; (2) the physical environment; (3) the personal environment: family, friends, authority figures; and (4) the sociocultural environment: norms, values, socioeconomic resources, religion. The extent to which any aspect of environment has an influence on the individual is related to the degree of competence of the individual (Lawton 1970). Lawton and Simon (1968) have proposed an "environmental docility hypothesis" which states that the greater the degree of competence of the organism, the less will be the proportion of variance in behavior due to environmental factors. Conversely, limitations in health, cognitive skills, ego strength, status, social role performance, or degree of cultural evolution will tend to heighten the docility of the person in the face of environmental constraints and influences (Lawton 1970, p. 40).

Environmental factors can have an impact on all aspects of chronic illness: its occurrence and characteristics, the way it is perceived and the meaning it has to the individual, the response options and opportunities, and finally the kind of long-term adaptive response that is formulated. The extent of the influence of environmental factors will depend on the particular capacities and resources of the chronically ill individual.

The way individuals respond to chronic illness and disability has been shown to be determined in part by their social group membership, e.g., age, sex, ethnicity, socioeconomic status and religious orientation (Graham and Reeder 1972; Kutner and Kutner 1979; Safilios-Rothschild 1970). However, the findings reported on demographic variables and adaptation to long-term illness are inconsistent. For example, Ludwig and Adams (1968) report that children, women over sixty years of age, nonwhites, and unemployed are more likely to complete formal rehabilitation programs. Croog, Levine, and Lurie (1968) cite studies indicating an advantage to white-collar over blue-collar workers for returning to work after illness. Others report greater likelihood of return to work among those with jobs requiring high skill levels (Acker 1968), and high prestige occupations (Garrity 1973b; Shapiro, Weinblatt, and Frank 1972). Still another group of studies provides evidence that being white, male, and married will predict return to work (Freeman and Simmons 1963; Kir-Stiman 1963; Weiner 1964).

Two comments can be made about studies of demographic indices and adaptation. First, most of these investigations have dealt with adaptation to long-term illness in general. We know enough about chronic illness to recognize that the requirements for adaptation are unique for specific kinds of conditions. For example, it takes different management skills to cope with maintenance hemodialysis, postmyocardial infarct life-style changes, or an above-the-knee amputation. Second, most of the studies have used return to work as the indicator of adaptation. Recently, as noted earlier, adaptation has been measured along multiple dimensions, e.g., household activities, employment, social involvement with family and friends, personal satisfaction with life, morale, and many others.

There is a rich literature which deals with a variety of psychological factors and personality characteristics as contributors to the management of an adjustment to chronic illness. Most of this literature represents reports of correlational studies, and some is theoretical speculation. There are few definitive studies. However, the value of these works lies in the direction they provide for future investigations. Some examples will illustrate the scope of work done in terms of the personality characteristics considered and the chronic conditions studied.

For persons whose life is maintained on the artificial kidney, one of the major sources of stress comes from the severe fluid and dietary restrictions. High tolerance for frustration and mild obsessive-compulsive traits characterize dialysis patients who manage these restrictions with little difficulty. Denial of the sick role and introjection of aggression (manifested by suicidal tendencies) have been shown to correlate with poor fluid and dietary management among dialysis patients (Abram 1970; DeNour and Czaczkes 1976).

Self-esteem is commonly believed to be a factor in adjustment to chronic illness. Sullivan (1979b) reports that among adolescent diabetics high self-esteem predicts normal peer and family relationships and better resolution of dependence-independence conflicts associated with this chronic illness. Self-esteem has been shown to correlate positively with rehabilitation success among individuals with various long-term conditions (Hyman 1975). Worden and Sobel (1978) demonstrated a negative correlation between ego-strength and hopelessness, frustration and denial, and a positive correlation with successful problem-solving among cancer victims.

An intriguing study done by Carlson (1979), in which she formulated a measure of belief systems based on the theoretical work on conceptual styles of Harvey, Hunt, and Schrodes (1961), showed that a high level of abstractness was associated with life satisfaction among persons with spinal cord injuries. Operationally, abstractness was indicated by high task orientation, risk-taking, and capacity for integrating multiple points of view.

Locus of control, a personality construct derived from Rotter's (1966) social learning theory, has been widely used in studies to predict patient responses in health and illness (Wallston and Wallston 1978). The evidence on sick role and locus of control is quite inconclusive. Weaver (1972) has shown that internality correlates with compliance among dialysis patients. However, locus of control was not predictive of compliance among black female hypertensives (Key 1975) or among postmyocardial infarct patients (Marston 1970).

It is probably correct to attribute the discrepant and inconsistent findings in the literature on demographic and personality variables and adjustment to long-term illness to the fact that adaptation to chronic illness is a much more complex, dynamic, and multidimensional process than can be captured by demographics or personality characteristics alone.

Perception of and adaptive responses to chronic illness are more completely understood by considering sociocultural factors. Individuals with chronic illnesses are likely to be able to minimize the stresses of their situation if they have appropriate skills and competencies to meet the demands imposed by the illness, if they are motivated to do so, and if they can establish and maintain a sufficiently balanced psychological state which allows them to pursue the task of managing the illness.

An as yet unexplored area in the study of adaptation to stressful situations is the influence of sociocultural factors. To a large extent the success of individual adaptive strategies is determined by "the efficacy of the solutions that the culture provides" (Mechanic 1974, p. 33). Whether an individual is able to muster appropriate skills and problem-solving capacities or generate the motivational forces necessary to cope depends partly on the institutions developed for learning and the values, norms and practices, and rewards and punishments promulgated by a society (Jenkins 1979; Mechanic 1968, 1974). Unfortunately, the relationship between individual personal responses to stress and the institutional or societal solutions available remains a major unknown in the field of stress research.

In recent times considerable attention has been given to social support as an important, and perhaps critical, variable influencing adaptation to stressful situations. One of the difficulties in determining the precise role of social support in relation to stress and illness has been the lack of a unifying or common definition (either conceptual or operational). Several definitions are beginning to emerge. Social support has been defined as:

- information that tells a person that he/she is loved, valued and is part of a network of communication and mutual obligation (Cobb 1976, p. 300).
- an interpersonal transaction that consists of the expression of positive affect toward another person, the affirmation or endorsement of certain behaviors or attributes of another person, or the giving of material or symbolic aid to the other (Kahn 1978, p. 4).

- a set of personal contacts through which the individual maintains his social identity and receives emotional support, material aid and services, information and new social contacts (Walker, McBride, and Vachon 1977, p. 35).

The accumulated studies over the past several years are strongly indicative of social support as a major factor in health and illness. As Cassel (1976, p. 121) notes, "Taken alone, no one study is entirely convincing. Taken together the results are more impressive . . . . In each case a positive finding in the predicted direction has been discovered . . . . [This is] sufficiently encouraging to warrant further research."

In an extensive review of the literature on social support Hamburg and Killilea (1979) note a number of studies that relate to the management of long-term illness. An expanded version of their review shows that social support:

- aids recovery from congestive heart failure (Chambers and Reiser 1953); tuberculosis (Roth and Eddy 1967).
- reduces the need for steroid therapy in adult asthmatics in periods of life stress (De Araujo et al. 1973).
- protects against clinical depression in the face of adverse events (Brown, Bhrolchain, and Harris 1975).
- helps keep patients in needed medical treatment and promotes adherence to medical regimens (Baekeland and Lundwall 1975; MacElveen 1972).

Most of the studies cited in the literature suggest that social support has a positive impact in situations of long-term illness or stress. There is, however, a small but impressive collection of studies in which the findings are not congruent with this interpretation. For example, Litman (1966) found no difference in rehabilitation progress based on perceived family support; Lewis (1966) and Garrity (1973b) showed that behaviors of significant others generally considered to be supportive were related inversely to the extent of return to work among men recovering from congestive heart failure and myocardial infarction. Reif (1975) reported an increase in perceived disability among men recovered from myocardial infarction when the behaviors of expressed concern and warnings of caution were engaged in by the subjects' spouses, friends, and employers.

These apparent contradictory findings in the literature can be partially understood as conceptual or methodological issues. The way the network functions is determined in part by the nature of the stressful situation and the time factor. "To suggest that one specific type of network is universally most supportive in a crisis is to ignore the diversity of needs that can be experienced by an individual under stress" (Walker et al. 1977, p. 37). For example, the need to maintain social identity is probably most effectively done in a small, high-density network with strong ties between members; on the other hand, when seeking new information, or trying to establish new social contacts, a network with some bridging ties to other groups may be most useful (Walker et al. 1977). Weiss (1976) remarks that people in crisis (acute, short term) probably require different kinds of assistance from those who are managing a transition (longer period of adjusting to disrupted personal and/or social life). Individuals in crisis need emotional support primarily, and may not be able to use any other form of help, while individuals in transition need orientation, guidance, and concrete help with problem-solving (Hirsch 1980; Mueller 1980; Walker et al. 1977; Weiss 1976).

Coming to terms with the realities of a chronic illness is a long-term process.

Surviving the initial shock, assessing remaining capabilities, and planning strategies to cope with limitations take time. Because of the uncertain course of many chronic conditions, it is often necessary periodically to reassess and reorganize one's life to meet the requirements of the changing situation. The social network most appropriate at the onset of a chronic illness may not be as appropriate when the individual progresses beyond this stage and begins to negotiate and renegotiate life-style changes to meet the demands of the illness. We know very little about the way social support systems function over time to sustain the chronically ill person.

If social support is as critical a factor in the management of stressful situations as the evidence suggests, and if, as Cassel (1976) notes, the task of improving and strengthening social supports is more feasible than eradicating or dramatically reducing stressors, then it is clear that social scientists need to place considerable emphasis on the continuing investigation of social support. Sound programs could then be tailored to meet the changing needs for support as individuals and families reorganize their lives to live with chronic illness.

Summary

Chronic illness is a major health problem. The cost in terms of health-care dollars and loss of employment is staggering; but the cost to individual lives in terms of pain, distress, despair, and disruption of families is overwhelming. Social adaptation to chronic illness is therefore an important economic as well as social and psychological problem. An analysis of the social and psychological factors that influence successful adaptation has been the focus of this chapter.

From the perspective of the chronically ill person, social adaptation is a series of challenges which must be met daily or at least regularly. There are the challenges of the disease itself: managing expected and unexpected symptoms; performing treatments which may be painful, time-consuming, repugnant, or in some other way distressing. Closely related are the challenges of achieving a workable relationship with health professionals; one which allows questioning, exchange of information, mutual understanding and agreement on the mode of treatment, and shared plans for meeting long-term treatment goals. Finally, successful adaptation depends on the sustained support of family and friends. For the chronically ill person the challenge is to achieve a satisfying balance between the need for, and acceptance of, help from family and friends, and the need for personal control and self-sufficiency. In sum, the ultimate measure of achievement of successful adaptation to a chronic illness is found in a way of life that sustains hope, diminishes fear, and preserves a quality of living that takes account of, perhaps transcends, but is not controlled by, the limitations of the illness.

REFERENCES

ABRAM, H. 1970. Survival by machine: the psychological stress of chronic hemodialysis. *Psychiatry and Medicine* 1: 37–51.

ACKER, J. E. 1968. Factors affecting the employment of patients treated in coronary care units for myocardial infarction. *Journal of the Tennessee State Medical Association* 61: 1200–1201.

ANTONOVSKY, A. 1979. *Health, stress, and coping.* San Francisco, Calif.: Jossey-Bass.

ARNAUD, S. 1959. Some psychological characteristics of children of multiple sclerotics. *Psychiatry in Medicine* 21: 8–22.

AVERILL, J. 1973. Personal control over aversive stimuli and its relationship to stress. *Psychological Bulletin* 80: 286–303.

BAEKELAND, F., and LUNDWALL, L. 1975. Dropping out of treatment: a critical review. *Psychological Bulletin* 82: 738–83.

BENOLIEL, J.; MCCORKLE, R.; and YOUNG, K. 1980. Development of a social dependency scale. *Research in Nursing and Health* 3: 3–10.

BROWN, G.; BHROLCHAIN, M,; and HARRIS, T. 1975. Social class and psychiatric disturbance among women in an urban population. *Sociology* 9: 225–31.

BUCHANAN, D., and ABRAM, H. 1975. Psychological adaptation to hemodialysis. *Dialysis and Transplantation* 1: 36–41.

CAPLAN, G. 1964. *Principles of preventive psychiatry.* New York: Basic Books.

CARLSON, C. 1979. Conceptual style and life satisfaction following spinal-cord injury. *Archives of Physical Medicine and Rehabilitation* 60: 346–52.

CASSEL, J. 1976. The contributions of the social environment to host resistance. *American Journal of Epidemiology* 104: 107–23.

CHAMBERS, W., and REISER, M. 1953. Emotional stress in the precipitation of congestive heart failure. *Psychosomatic Medicine* 15: 38–60.

CHRISMAN, N. 1977. The health seeking process: An approach to the natural history of illness. *Culture, Medicine, and Psychiatry* 1: 351–77.

CHRISTOPHERSON, L., and GONDA, T. Patterns of grief: end-stage renal failure and kidney transplantation. *Transplantation Proceedings* 5: 1051–57.

COBB, S. 1976. Social support as a moderator of life stress. *Psychosomatic Medicine* 38: 300–314.

COUSINS, N. 1977. Anatomy of an illness. *Saturday Review,* 28 May 1977, pp. 4–51.

CROOG, S.; LEVINE, S.; and LURIE, Z. 1968. The heart attack patient and the recovery process. *Social Science and Medicine* 2:111–64.

DAVIS, F. 1963. *Passage through crisis.* Indianapolis: Bobbs-Merrill.

———. 1972. *Illness, interaction, and the self.* Belmont, Calif.: Wadsworth.

DE ARAUJO, G.; VAN ARSDAL, R.; HOLMES, T.; and DUDLEY, D. 1973. Life change, coping ability and chronic intrinsic asthma. *Journal of Psychosomatic Research* 17: 359–63.

DENOUR, A., and CZACZKES, J. 1976. The influence of patient personality in adjustment to chronic dialysis. *Journal of Nervous and Mental Disease* 162: 323–33.

DENOUR, A.; SHALTIEL, J.; and CZACZKES, J. 1968. Emotional reactions of patients on chronic hemodialysis. *Psychosomatic Medicine* 30: 521–33.

DIMOND, M. 1978. Social support and adaptation to long-term illness. Doctoral dissertation, University of Wisconsin, Madison, 1978. *Dissertation Abstracts International* 39 1869A (University Microfilms No. 78–11717).

———. 1979. Social support and adaptation to chronic illness: the case of maintenance hemodialysis. *Research in Nursing and Health* 2: 101–8.

———. 1980. Patient strategies in managing maintenance hemodialysis. *Western Journal of Nursing Research* 2: 555–74.

———, and JONES, S. *Chronic illness across the life span.* New York: Appleton Century Crofts, forthcoming.

DOHRENWEND, B., and DOHRENWEND, B. 1974. *Stressful life events: their nature and effects.* New York: Wiley.

DUBOS, R. *Man adapting.* New Haven, Conn.: Yale University Press.

ELTON, D.; STANLEY, G.; and BURROWS, G. 1978. Self-esteem and chronic pain. *Journal of Psychosomatic Research* 22: 25–30.

FELDMAN, D. 1974. Chronic disabling illness: a holistic view. *Journal of Chronic Disease* 27: 287–91.

Fox, R. 1959. *Experiment perilous.* New York: Free Press.

Freeman, H., and Simmons, O. 1963. *The mental patient comes home.* New York: Wiley.

French, J.; Rodgers, W.; and Cobb, S. 1974. Adjustment as person-environment fit. In *Coping and adaptation,* ed. G. Coelho, D. Hamburg, and J. Adams. New York: Basic Books.

Garrity, T. 1973a. Social involvement and activeness as predictors of morale six months after first myocardial infarction. *Social Science and Medicine* 7: 199–207.

———. 1973b. Vocational adjustment after first myocardial infarction: comparative assessment of several variables suggested in the literature. *Social Science and Medicine* 7: 705–17.

Gilson, B.; Gilson, J.; and Bergner, M. 1975. The sickness impact profile: development of an outcome measure of health care. *American Journal of Public Health* 65: 1304–10.

Goldberg, R. 1974. Vocational rehabilitation of patients on long-term hemodialysis. *Archives of Physical Medicine and Rehabilitation* 55: 60–65.

Goode, W. 1960. A theory of role strain. *American Sociological Review* 25: 483–96.

Goosen, G., and Bush, H. 1979. Adaptation: a feedback process. *Advances in Nursing Science* 1: 51–65.

Graham, S., and Reeder, L. 1972. Social factors in the chronic diseases. In *Handbook of medical sociology,* 2d ed., ed. H. Freeman, S. Levine, and L. Reeder. Englewood Cliffs, N.J.: Prentice Hall.

Haber, L., and Smith, R. 1971. Disability and deviance: Normative adaptations of role behavior. *American Sociological Review* 36: 87–97.

Hamburg, B., and Killilea, M. 1979. Relation of social support, stress, illness, and use of health services. In *Healthy people: the surgeon general's report on health promotion and disease prevention.* U.S. Department of Health, Education and Welfare, pub. no. 79–55071A.

Harvey, D.; Hunt, D.; and Schroder, H. 1961. *Conceptual systems and personality organization.* New York: Wiley.

Hirsch, B. 1980. Natural support systems and coping with major life changes. *American Journal of Community Psychology* 8: 159–71.

Holcomb, J., and MacDonald, R. 1973. Social functioning of artificial kidney patients. *Social Science and Medicine* 7: 109–119.

House, J. 1974. Occupational stress and coronary heart disease: a review and theoretical integration. *Journal of Health and Social Behavior* 15: 12–27.

Hyman, M. 1975. Social psychological factors affecting disability among ambulatory patients. *Journal of Chronic Disease* 28: 199–216.

Jenkins, C. 1979. Psychosocial modifiers of response to stress. *Journal of Human Stress* 5: 3–15.

Kahn, R. 1978. Aging and social support. Paper presented at the meeting of the American Association for the Advancement of Science, Washington, D.C., May 1978.

Katz, J., and Capron, A. 1975. *Catastrophic diseases: who decides what?* New York: Russell Sage Foundation.

Katz, S.; Ford, A.; Moskowitz, R.; Jackson, B.; and Jaffe, M. 1963. The index of ADL: a standardized measure of biological and psychosocial function. *Journal of American Medical Association* 185: 914–19.

Key, M. 1975. Psychosocial and education factors surrounding compliance behavior of hypertensives. Doctoral dissertation, George Peabody College, Nashville, Tennessee, 1975. *Dissertation Abstracts International* 36, 2524B (University Microfilms No. 75–22, 274).

Kiely, W. 1972. Coping with severe illness. *Advances in Psychosomatic Medicine* 8: 105–18.

Kir-Stimon, W. 1963. *Discards on trial.* Chicago: Rehabilitation Institute.

Kutner, N., and Kutner, M. 1979. Race and sex as variables affecting reactions to disability. *Archives of Physical Medicine and Rehabilitation* 60: 62–66.

Lawton, M. Ecology and aging. In *Spatial behavior of older people,* ed. L. Pastalan and D. Carson. Ann Arbor, Mich.: University of Michigan Press.

———, and Simon, B. 1968. The ecology of social relationships in housing for the elderly. *Gerontologist* 8: 108–15.

Lazarus, R. 1966. *Psychological stress and coping process.* New York: McGraw-Hill.

———. 1974. Psychological stress and coping in adaptation and illness. *International Journal of Psychiatry in Medicine* 5: 321–33.

Lazarus, R., and Cohen, J. 1977. Environmental stress. In *Human behavior and environment,* ed I. Altman and J. Wohlwill. vol. 2. New York: Plenum.

Lear, M. *Heartsounds.* 1980. New York: Simon and Schuster.

Levine, S., and Scotch, N. 1970. *Social stress.* Chicago: Aldine.

Lewis, C. 1966. Factors influencing the return to work of men with congestive heart failure. *Journal of Chronic Disease* 19: 1193–1209.

Lipowski, Z. 1970. Physical illness, the individual and the coping process. *Psychiatry and Medicine* 1: 91–102.

Litman, T. 1966. The family and physical rehabilitation. *Journal of Chronic Disease* 19: 211–17.

Ludwig, E., and Adams, S. 1968. Patient cooperation in a rehabilitation center: assumption of the client role. *Journal of Health and Social Behavior* 9: 328–36.

MacElveen, P. 1972. Cooperative triad in home dialysis care and patient outcomes. In *Communicating nursing research,* vol. 9, ed. M. Batey. Boulder, Colo.: WICHEN Publication.

Marston, M. 1970. Compliance with medical regimens: a review of the literature. *Nursing Research* 19: 312–23.

Masi, A. 1978. An holistic concept of health and illness: a tricentennial goal for medicine and public health. *Journal of Chronic Disease* 31: 563–72.

Mechanic, D. 1968. *Medical sociology.* New York: Free Press.

———. 1970. Some problems in developing a social psychology of adaptation to stress. In *Social and psychological factors in stress.* ed. J. McGrath. New York: Holt, Rinehart and Winston.

———. 1974. Social structure and personal adaption: some neglected dimensions. In *Coping and adaption,* ed. G. Coelho, D. Hamburg, and J. Adams. New York: Basic Books.

———. 1977. Illness behavior, social adaptation, and the management of illness. *Journal of Nervous and Mental Disease* 165: 79–87.

———. 1978. Effects of psychological distress on perceptions of physical health and use of medical psychiatric facilities. *Journal of Human Stress* 4: 26–32.

Melvin, J., and Nagi, S. 1970. Factors in behavioral responses to impairments. *Archives of Physical Medicine and Rehabilitation* 51: 552–57.

Moos, R., ed. 1977. *Coping with physical illness.* New York: Plenum Medical Book Company.

Morrow, G.; Chiarello, R.; and Derogatis, L. 1978. A new scale for assessing patients' psychosocial adjustment to medical illness. *Psychological Medicine* 8: 605–10.

Mueller, D. 1980. Social networks: a promising direction for research on the relationship of the social environment to psychiatric disorder. *Social Science and Medicine* 14A: 147–61.

Pearlin, L., and Schooler, C. 1978. The structure of coping. *Journal of Health and Social Behavior* 19: 2–21.

Pritchard, M. 1974. Reaction to illness in long-term hemodialysis. *Journal of Psychosomatic Research* 18: 55–67.

———. 1974b. Meaning of illness and patients response to long-term hemodialysis. *Journal of Psychosomatic Research* 18: 457–64.

Reif, L. 1976. Cardiacs and normals: the social construction of a disability. Doctoral dissertation, University of California, San Francisco, 1975. *Dissertation Abstracts International* 36, 7003A (University Microfilms No. 76–8246).

Riessman, F. 1965. The "helper" therapy principle. *Social Work* 10: 27–32.

Roth, J. 1963. *Timetables.* New York: Bobbs-Merrill.

———, and Eddy, E. 1967. *Rehabilitation for the unwanted.* New York: Atherton.

ROTTER, J. 1966. Generalized expectancies for internal vs. external control of reinforcement. *Psychological Monographs* 80: 1–28.

SAFILIOS-ROTHSCHILD, C. 1970. *The sociology and social psychology of disability and rehabilitation.* New York: Random House.

SCHMALE, A. 1972. Giving up as a final common pathway to changes in health. *Advances in Psychosomatic Medicine* 8: 20–40.

SHALIT, B. 1977. Structural ambiguity and limits to coping. *Journal of Human Stress* 3: 32–45.

SHAPIRO, E., WEINBLATT, E.; and FRANK, C. 1972. Return to work after first myocardial infarction. *Archives of Environmental Health* 24: 17–26.

SHORT, M., and WILSON, W. 1969. Roles of denial in chronic hemodialysis. *Archives of General Psychiatry* 20: 433–37.

SIDLE, A.; MOOS, R.; and ADAMS, J. 1969. Development of a coping scale. *Archives of General Psychiatry* 20: 226–32.

SIMMONS, R.; KLEIN, S.; and SIMMONS, R. 1977. *The gift of life.* New York: Wiley Interscience.

SMITH, R. 1979. Disability and the recovery process: role of social networks. In *Patients, physicians, and illness,* 3d ed., ed. E. G. Jaco. New York: Free Press.

STRAUSS, A., and GLASER, B. 1975. *Chronic illness and the quality of life.* St. Louis, Mo.: C. V. Mosby.

SULLIVAN, B. 1979a. Adjustment in diabetic adolescent girls: development of the diabetic adjustment scale. *Psychosomatic Medicine* 41: 119–26.

———. 1979b. Adjustment in diabetic adolescent girls: adjustment, self-esteem, and depression in diabetic adolescent girls. *Psychosomatic Medicine* 41: 127–38.

THOMPSON, J. 1980. Adaptation in health and illness: a conceptual approach to illness onset and progress. University of Utah College of Nursing.

TOFFLER, A. 1970. *Future shock.* New York: Random House.

TURK, D.; SOBEL, H.; FOLLICK, M.; and YOUKILIS, H. 1980. A sequential criterion analysis for assessing coping with chronic illness. *Journal of Human Stress* 6: 35–40.

VICKERS, G. 1971. Institutional and personal roles. *Human Relations* 24: 433–47.

WALKER, K.; McBRIDE, A.; and VACHON, M. 1977. Social support network and the crisis of bereavement. *Social Science and Medicine* 11: 35–41.

WALLSTON, B.; and WALLSTON, K. 1978. Locus of control and health: A review of the literature. *Health Education Monographs* 6: 107–17.

WEAVER, R. 1972. Internality, externality, and compliance as related to chronic home dialysis patients. Unpublished master's thesis. Emory University, Atlanta.

WEINER, H. 1964. Characteristics associated with rehabilitation success. *Personnel and Guidance Journal* 42, 687–694.

WEISS, R. 1976. Transition states and other stressful situations: their nature and programs for their management. In *Support systems and mutual help: multidisciplinary explorations,* ed. G. Caplan and M. Killilea. New York: Grune and Stratton.

WORDEN, J., and SOBEL, H. 1978. Ego strength and psychosocial adaptation to cancer. *Psychosomatic Medicine* 40: 585–92.

VI

EMERGING PERSPECTIVES IN HEALTH-CARE RESEARCH AND ANALYSIS

Chapter 30

A Marxist View of Health and Health Care

Howard Waitzkin

THIS CHAPTER SURVEYS the growing Marxist literature in health and health care. The purpose is first to give a critical review of recent theoretical and empirical developments. Intensive-care technology is then emphasized as an empirical application of Marxist perspectives to current medical issues. One thrust of this field—an assumption also accepted by many non-Marxists—is that the problems of the health system reflect the problems of our larger society and cannot be separated from those problems.

Marxist analyses of health care have burgeoned in the United States during the past decade. However, it is not a new field. Its early history and the reasons for its slow growth, until recently, deserve attention.

Historical Development of Marxist Studies in Health Care

The first major Marxist study of health care was Engels's *The Condition of the Working Class in England* (1845), originally published three years before Engels coauthored with Marx *The Communist Manifesto* (1848). This book described the dangerous working and housing conditions that created ill health. In particular, Engels traced such diseases as tuberculosis, typhoid, and typhus to malnutrition, inadequate housing, contaminated water supplies, and overcrowding. Engels's analysis of health care was part of a broader study of working-class conditions under capitalist industrialization. But his treatment of health problems was to have a profound effect on the emergence of social medicine in Western Europe, particularly the work of Rudolf Virchow.

Virchow's pioneering studies in infectious disease, epidemiology, and "social medicine" (a term Virchow popularized in Western Europe) appeared with great rapidity after the publication of Engels's book on the English working class. Virchow himself acknowledged Engels's influence on his thought (1879). In 1847, based on an investigation of a severe typhus epidemic in rural East Prussia, Virchow recommended a series of profound changes that included increased employment, better wages, local autonomy in government, agricultural cooperatives, and a more progressive taxation structure. Virchow advocated no strictly medical solutions, such as more clinics or hospitals. Instead, he saw the origins of ill health in societal problems. The most reasonable approach to epidemics, then, was to change the conditions that permitted them to occur (1868).

During this period Virchow was committed to combining his medical work with political activities. In 1848 he joined the first major working-class revolt in Berlin. During the same year he strongly supported the short-lived spring uprising in Paris (Virchow 1907). In his scientific investigations and in his political practice, Virchow expressed two overriding themes. First, the origin of disease is multifactorial. Among the most important factors in causation are the material conditions of people's everyday lives. Second, an effective health-care system cannot limit itself to treating the pathophysiologic disturbances of individual patients. Instead, to be successful, improvements in the health-care system must coincide with fundamental economic, political, and social changes. The latter changes often impinge on the privileges of wealth and power enjoyed by the dominant classes of society and encounter resistance. Therefore, in Virchow's view, the responsibilities of the medical scientist frequently extend to direct political action.

During the late nineteenth century, with the work of Ehrlich, Koch, Pasteur, and other prominent bacteriologists, germ theory gained ascendancy and created a profound change in medicine's diagnostic and therapeutic assumptions. A unifactorial model of disease emerged. Medical scientists searched for organisms that caused infections and single lesions in noninfectious disorders. The discoveries of this period undeniably improved medical practice. Still, as numerous investigators have shown, the historical importance of these discoveries has been overrated. For example, the major declines in mortality and morbidity from most infectious diseases preceded rather than followed the isolation of specific etiologic agents and the use of antimicrobial therapy. In Western Europe and the United States, improved outcomes in infections occurred after the introduction of better sanitation, regular sources of nutrition, and other broad environmental changes. In most cases, improvements in disease patterns antedated the advances of modern bacteriology (Cochrane 1972; McKeown 1977; Powles 1973).

Why did the unifactorial perspective of germ theory achieve such prominence? And why have investigational techniques that assume specific etiology and therapy retained a nearly mythic character in medical science and practice to the present day? A serious historical reexamination of early twentieth-century medical science, which attempts to answer these questions, has begun only in the past few years. Some preliminary explanations have emerged; they focus on events that led to and followed publication of the Flexner report (Flexner 1910).

Until recently, the Flexner report held high esteem as the document that helped change modern medicine from quackery to responsible practice. One underlying assumption of the report was that laboratory-based scientific medicine, oriented especially to the concepts and methods of European bacteriology, produced a higher quality and more effective medical practice. Although the comparative effectiveness of various medical traditions (including homeopathy, traditional folk healing, chiropractic, and so forth) had never been subjected to systematic test, the report argued that medical schools not oriented to scientific medicine fostered mistreatment of the public. The report called for the closure or restructuring of schools that were not equipped to teach laboratory-based medicine. The report's repercussions were swift and dramatic. Scientific, laboratory-based medicine became the norm for medical education, practice, research, and analysis.

Historical studies cast doubt on assumptions in the Flexner report that have comprised the widely accepted dogma of the past half century. They also document the uncritical support that the report's recommendations received from parts of the medical profession and the large private philanthropies (Berliner 1975; Brown 1979; Kleinbach [Ziem] 1974; Kunitz 1974). The Flexner report and its supporters exerted a profound impact on the intellectual horizons of twentieth-century medicine. The multifactorial vision of medical problems which Virchow and his contemporaries set forth fell into obscurity, and the Marxist orientation that guided social medicine in the mid-nineteenth century remained in eclipse.

Perhaps reflecting the political ferment of the late 1960s and widespread dissatisfaction with various aspects of modern health systems, serious Marxist scholarship of health care has grown rapidly. Recent work began in Western Europe and quickly spread to the United States (Kelman 1971; Polack 1970; Rossdale 1965). The following sections of this chapter give an overview of current research and analysis.

Class Structure

Class structure has been a primary focus of analysis and research throughout the history of Marxist scholarship. Marxist studies in medicine address the interrelationships between class structure and the health-care system. Marx's definition of social class emphasized the social relations of economic production. Although a brief summary perhaps oversimplifies, Marx noted that one group of people, the capitalist class, or bourgeoisie, own or control (or both) the means of production: the machines, factories, land, and raw materials necessary to make products for the market. The working class, or proletariat, who do not own or control the means of production, must sell their labor for a wage. But the value of the product that workers produce is always greater than their wage. Workers must give up their product to the capitalist; by losing control of their own productive process, workers become "alienated" from their labor. "Surplus value," the difference between the wage paid to workers and the value of the product they create, is the objective basis of the capitalist's profit. Surplus value also is the structural source of exploitation; it motivates the capitalist to keep wages low, to change the work process (by automation and new technologies, close supervision, lengthened work day or overtime, speed-ups, and dangerous working conditions), and to resist workers' organized attempts to gain higher wages or more control in the workplace (Marx 1963 [1890], 1964, 1971 [1859]).

Although they acknowledge the historical changes that have occurred since Marx's time, recent Marxist studies have reaffirmed the presence of highly stratified class structures in advanced capitalist societies and Third World nations. Another topic of great interest is the persistence or reappearance of class structure, usually based on expertise and professionalism, in countries where socialist revolutions have taken place. These theoretical and empirical analyses show that relations of economic production remain a primary basis of class structure and a reasonable focus of strategies for change.

Miliband's definitions of social class have provided a framework for Marxist research on class structure in the health system (Miliband 1969). This research has shown that the health system mirrors the class structure of the broader society.

The "corporate class" includes the major owners and controllers of wealth (U.S. Department of Commerce 1980). They make up 1 percent of the population and own 80 percent of all corporate stocks and state and local government bonds; their estimated median annual income in 1979 was $137,000 to $170,000. The "working class," at the opposite end of the scale, makes up 49 percent of the population. It is composed of manual laborers, service workers, and farm workers, who generally earn $9,100 per year or less. Between these polar classes are the "upper middle class" (professionals like doctors, lawyers, and so forth, making up 14 percent of the population and earning about $44,600; and middle-level business executives, 6 percent of the population and earning about $28,400) and the "lower middle class" (shopkeepers, self-employed people, craftsmen, artisans, making up 7 percent of the population, earning about $13,700; and clerical and sales workers, 23 percent of the population, earning about $11,700 per year). Although these definitions provide summary descriptions of a very complex social reality, they are useful in analyzing manifestations of class structure in the health system.

CONTROL OVER HEALTH INSTITUTIONS. Navarro (1975, 1976) has documented the pervasive control that members of the corporate and upper middle classes exert within the policy-making bodies of American health institutions (Table 30.1). These classes predominate on the governing boards of private foundations in the health system, private and state medical teaching institutions, and local voluntary hospitals. Only on the boards of state teaching institutions and voluntary hospitals do members of the lower middle class or working class gain any appreciable representation; even there, the participation from these classes falls far below their proportion in the general population. Community-based research has documented corporate control of health institutions in many parts of the United States. Navarro has argued, based partly on these observations, that control over health institutions reflects the same patterns of class dominance that have arisen in other areas of North American economic and political life.

TABLE 30.1   Social Class Composition of U.S. Labor Force and Boards of U.S. Health Institutions

| | CLASS * (%) | | | |
	CORPORATE	UPPER MIDDLE	LOWER MIDDLE	WORKING
U.S. labor force	1	20	30	40
Board members				
Foundations	70	30	—	—
Private medical teaching institutions	45	55	—	—
State medical teaching institutions	20	70	10	—
Voluntary hospitals	5	80	10	5

* See text for definitions.
Source: Navarro 1975.

STRATIFICATION WITHIN HEALTH INSTITUTIONS. As members of the upper middle class, physicians occupy the highest stratum among workers in health institutions. Composing 7 percent of the health labor force, physicians receive a median net income (approximately $61,200 in 1977) that places them in the upper 5 percent of the income distribution of the United States. Under physicians and professional administrators are members of the lower middle class: nurses, physical and occupational therapists, and technicians. They make up 29 percent of the health labor force, are mostly women, and earn about $12,000. At the bottom of institutional hierarchies are clerical workers, aides, orderlies, and kitchen and janitorial personnel, who are the working class of the health system. They have an income of about $8,100 per year, represent 54 percent of the health labor force, and are 84 percent female and 30 percent black.

Recent studies have analyzed the forces of racism, sexism, and professionalism that divide health workers from each other and prevent them from realizing common interests. These patterns affect physicians, nurses, and technical and service workers who comprise the fastest growing segment of the health labor force. Bureaucratization, unionization, state intervention, and the potential "proletarianization" of professional health workers may alter future patterns of stratification (Boston Nurses Groups 1978; Brown 1973; Ehrenreich and Ehrenreich 1973; McKinlay 1978; Stevenson 1976; Waitzkin and Waterman 1974).

OCCUPATIONAL MOBILITY. Class mobility into professional positions is quite limited. Investigations of physicians' class backgrounds in both Britain and the United States have shown a consistently small representation of the lower middle and working classes among medical students and practicing doctors (Simpson 1972; Ziem 1977). In the United States, historical documentation is available to trace changes in class mobility during the twentieth century. As Ziem has found, despite some recent improvements for other disadvantaged groups like blacks and women, recruitment of working-class medical students has been very limited since shortly after publication of the Flexner report. In 1920, 12 percent of medical students came from working-class families, and this percentage has stayed almost exactly the same until the present time.

In summary, class structure in the health system parallels the class structure of the entire society. Members of the corporate and upper middle classes predominate in the decision-making bodies of North American health institutions. Within those institutions, workers are highly stratified. Mobility into the medical profession by individuals from working-class or lower-middle-class families remains limited. Strategies for changing the health-care system must take into account the broader class structure of the society.

Emergence of Monopoly Capital in the Health Sector

During the past century, economic capital has become more concentrated in a smaller number of companies, the monopolies. Monopoly capital has emerged in essentially all advanced capitalist nations, where the process of monopolization has reinforced private corporate profit. Monopoly capital has become a prominent feature of most capitalist health systems and is manifested in several ways.

MEDICAL CENTERS. Since about 1910, a continuing growth of medical centers has occurred, usually in affiliation with universities. Capital is highly concentrated in these medical centers, which are heavily oriented to advanced technology. Practitioners have received training where technology is available and specialization is highly valued. Partly as a result, health workers are often reluctant to practice in areas without easy access to medical centers. The nearly unrestricted growth of medical centers has contributed to the maldistribution of health workers and facilities throughout the United States and within regions (Kelman 1971; Waitzkin and Waterman 1974).

FINANCE CAPITAL. Monopoly capital also has been apparent in the position of banks, trusts, and insurance companies, the largest profit-making corporations under capitalism. For example, in the late 1970s, the flow of health-insurance dollars through private insurance companies was more than $30 billion, about half of the total insurance sold. Among commercial insurance companies, capital is highly concentrated; about 60 percent of the health-insurance industry is controlled by the ten largest insurers. Metropolitan Life and Prudential each control more than $30 billion in assets, more than General Motors, Standard Oil of New Jersey, or International Telephone and Telegraph (Navarro 1975).

Finance capital figures prominently in current health-reform proposals (Salmon 1975). Most plans for national health insurance would permit a continuing role for the insurance industry. Moreover, corporate investment in health-maintenance organizations is increasing, under the assumption that national health insurance, if and when enacted, will assure the profitability of these ventures.

THE MEDICAL-INDUSTRIAL COMPLEX. The "military-industrial complex" has provided a model of industrial penetration in the health system, popularized by the term "medical-industrial complex." Investigations by the Health Policy Advisory Center and others have emphasized that the exploitation of illness for private profit is a primary feature of the health systems in advanced capitalist societies. Many reports have criticized the pharmaceutical and medical equipment industries for advertising and marketing practices, price and patent collusion, marketing of drugs in the Third World before their safety is tested, and promotion of expensive diagnostic and therapeutic innovations without controlled trials showing their effectiveness (Ehrenreich and Ehrenreich 1970; Kotelchuck 1976; Rodberg and Stevenson 1977).

The State and State Intervention

The state (although difficult to define simply, because of its complexity) comprises the interconnected public institutions that act to preserve the capitalist economic system and the interests of the capitalist class. This definition includes the executive, legislative, and judicial branches of government; the military; and the criminal justice system—all of which hold varying degress of coercive power. It also encompasses relatively noncoercive institutions within the educational, public welfare, and health-care systems. Through such noncoercive institutions, the state offers services or conveys ideologic messages that legitimate the capitalist system. Especially in periods of economic crisis, the state can use these same institutions to provide public subsidization of private enterprise.

The Private-Public Contradiction

The health system has two subsectors. The "private sector" is based in private practice and companies that manufacture medical products or control finance capital. The "public sector," as part of the state, operates through direct public expenditures and employs health workers in public institutions. Examples of institutions in the public sector are the Public Health Service, Indian Health Service, the Veterans' Administration hospitals, county and municipal hospitals, public mental hospitals, and the Medicare and Medicaid systems. Nations vary greatly in the private-public duality. In the United States, a dominant private sector coexists with an increasingly large public sector. The public sector is even larger in Great Britain and Scandinavia. In Cuba and China, the private sector essentially has been eliminated.

A general theme of Marxist analysis is that the private sector drains public resources and health workers' time, on behalf of private profit and to the detriment of patients using the public sector. This framework has helped explain some of the problems that have arisen in such countries as Great Britain and Chile, where private sectors persisted after the enactment of national health services. In these countries, practitioners have faced financial incentives to increase the scope of private practice, which they often have conducted within public hospitals or clinics. In the United States, the expansion of public payment programs such as Medicare and Medicaid has led to increased public subsidization of private practice and private hospitals, as well as abuses of these programs by individual practitioners (Modell and Waitzkin 1974; Waitzkin and Modell 1974; Waitzkin and Waterman 1974).

Similar problems have undermined other public health programs (Law 1976). These programs frequently have obtained finances through regressive taxation, placing low-income taxpayers at a relative disadvantage. Likewise, the deficiencies of the Blue Cross and Blue Shield insurance plans have derived largely from the failure of public regulatory agencies to control payments to practitioners and hospitals in the private sector. If enacted, national health insurance also would use public funds to reinforce and strengthen the private sector, by assuring payment for hospitals and individual physicians and possibly by permitting a continued role for commercial insurance companies.

Throughout the United States the problems of the private-public contradiction are becoming more acute. In most large cities, public hospitals are facing cutbacks, closure, or conversion to private ownership and control. This trend heightens low-income patients' difficulties in finding adequate health care and reinforces private hospitals' tendency to "dump" low-income patients to public institutions (Blake and Bodenheimer 1975; Roemer and Mera 1973).

General Functions of the State Within the Health System

The state's functions in the health system have increased in scope and compexity. In the first place, through the health system, the state acts to legitimate the capitalist economic system based in private enterprise (Navarro 1976; Renaud 1975). The history of public health and welfare programs shows that state expenditures usually rise during periods of social protest and decrease as unrest becomes less widespread. In the early 1970s a Congressional committee summarized public opinion surveys that uncovered a profound level of dissatisfaction with government and particularly with the role of business interests in government policies: ". . . citizens who thought something was 'deeply wrong' with their country had become a national majority. . . . And, for the first time in the ten years of opinion sampling by the Harris Survey, the growing trend of public opinion toward disenchantment with government swept more than half of all Americans with it" (Committee on Government Operations 1973). Under such circumstances, the state's predictable response is to expand health and other welfare programs. These incremental reforms, at least in part, reduce the legitimacy crisis of the capitalist system by restoring confidence that the system can meet the people's basic needs. The cycles of political attention devoted to national health insurance in the United States appear to parallel cycles of popular discontent. Recent cutbacks in public health services to low-income patients follow the decline of social protest by low-income groups since the 1960s.

The second major function of the state in the health system is to protect and reinforce the private sector more directly. As previously noted, most plans for national health insurance would permit a prominent role and continued profits for the private insurance industry, particularly in the administration of payments, record-keeping, and data collection. Corporate participation in new health initiatives sponsored by the state—including health-maintenance organizations, preventive screening programs, computerized components of professional standards review organizations, algorithm and protocol development for paraprofessional training, and audiovisual aids for patient education programs—is providing major sources of expanded profit (Salmon 1977).

A third (and subtler) function of the state is the reinforcement of dominant frameworks in scientific and clinical medicine that are consistent with the capitalist economic system and the suppression of alternative frameworks that might threaten the system. The U.S. government has provided generous funding for research on the pathophysiology and treatment of specific disease entities. As critics even within government have recognized, the disease-centered approach has reduced the level of analysis to the individual organism and, often inappropriately, has stimulated the search for unifactorial rather than multifactorial causation. More recently, analyses emphasizing the importance of individual lifestyle as a cause of disease have received prominent attention from state agencies in the United States and Canada (Fuchs 1974; Illich 1976; Lalonde 1974). Clearly, individual differences in personal habits do affect health in all societies. On the other hand, the life-style argument, perhaps even more than the earlier emphasis on specific cause, obscures important sources of illness and disability in the capitalist work process and industrial environment; it also puts the burden of health squarely on the individual rather than seeking collective solutions to health problems.

The issues that the state has downplayed in its research and development programs are worth noting. For example, based on available data, it is estimated that in Western industrialized societies environmental factors are involved in the etiology of approximately 80 percent of all cancers (Higginson 1974). The American Public Health Association (1975) has produced an exhaustive documentation of common occupational carcinogens. A task force for the Department of Health, Education, and Welfare on *Work in America*, published by a nongovernmental press in 1973, reported:

> In an impressive 15-year study of aging, the strongest predictor of longevity was work satisfaction. The second best predictor was overall "happiness." . . . Other factors are undoubtedly important—diet, exercise, medical care and genetic inheritance. But research findings suggest that these factors may account for only about 25 percent of the risk factors in heart disease, the major cause of death. [Special Task Force to the Secretary of Health, Education and Welfare 1973]

Occupational and environmental health problems often persist or arise anew in socialist societies. While socialism clearly is no panacea, several socialist countries have made advances in the recognition and amelioration of these problems (Witt 1981; Waitzkin 1982, in press). Yet such findings are particularly threatening to the current organization of capitalist production. They have received little attention or support from state agencies. A framework for clinical investigation that links disease directly to the structure of capitalism is likely to face indifference and active discouragement from the state.

Limits and Mechanisms of State Intervention

State intervention faces certain structural limits. Simply summarized, these limits restrict state intervention to policies and programs that will not conflict in fundamental ways with capitalist economic processes based on private profit, or with the concrete interests of the capitalist class during specific historical periods.

"Negative selection mechanisms" are forms of state intervention that exclude innovations or activities that challenge the capitalist system (Navarro 1976; Offe 1975). For example, agencies of the state may enact occupational health legislation and enforcement regulations. However, such reforms generally will not reach a level strict enough to interfere with profitability in specific industries. Nor will state ownership of industries responsible for occupational or environmental hazards occur to any major degree. State ownership per se does not eradicate these hazards in socialist countries. In fact, the quest for high economic productivity has created major environmental and occupational health problems, particularly in the Soviet Union. However, state ownership does eliminate private profit as a disincentive to safe working conditions and permits rapid improvements when problems are recognized (Waitzkin 1983, in press). Under capitalism, negative selection tends to exclude state ownership from serious consideration as a policy option in environmental and occupational health.

Negative selection also applies to the potential nationalization of the health system as a whole. In most capitalist societies, the state generally has opposed structural changes that infringe on private medical practice, private control of most hospitals, and the profitability of the pharmaceutical, medical equipment, insurance, and other industries operating in the health system. While excluding nationalization through negative selection, the state sponsors incremental reforms that control excesses in each of these spheres, thus maintaining the legitimacy of the whole. As an example of negative selection, Congressional deliberations in the United States systematically exclude serious consideration of a national health service (as opposed to national health insurance) that might question the appropriateness of private medical practice or the nationalization of hospitals.

Another example is governmental regulation of the drug and insurance industries; aside from its erratic effects, state regulation rules out public ownership of these industries.

The state also can use "positive selection mechanisms" that promote and sponsor policies strengthening the private enterprise system and the interests of capital. As discussed earlier, positive selection has involved sponsorship of biomedical research that assumes unifactorial etiology or, more recently, the life-style analysis. Most importantly, state agencies tend to favor financial reforms like health insurance, that would assure the stability of the private sector in the health system. The state's positive selection of financial reforms contrasts sharply with the exclusion of organizational reforms that potentially might change the broader political and economic structures of the present system.

A Unifying Example: Coronary Care Technology

The financial burden of health care has become a major issue of social policy. From the Marxist perspective, costs cannot be divorced from the structure of private profit. Incredibly enough, most non-Marxist analyses of costs either ignore the contradictions of capitalism or accept them as given. But the crisis of health costs intimately reflects the more general fiscal crisis that advanced capitalism is facing worldwide. In considering costs, it is foolhardy to overlook the connections between the health sector and the structure of the capitalist system. Wearing blinders that limit the level of analysis to a specific innovation or practice, while not perceiving the broader political-economic context in which costly and ineffective procedures are introduced and promulgated, will only obscure potential solutions to the difficulties that confront us. Coronary care technology is a particularly revealing example of apparent irrationalities of health policy that make sense when seen from the standpoint of capitalist profit structure. However, the overselling of numerous other technologic advances—such as computerized axial tomography, new laboratory techniques, fetal monitoring, and many surgical procedures—reflects very similar structural problems.

Early Claims

Intensive care for patients suffering heart attacks emerged rapidly during the 1960s. The first major reports of coronary care units (CCUs) were written by Day, who developed a so-called coronary care area at the Bethany Hospital in Kansas City, with financial help from the John A. Hartford Foundation (Day 1963). From these early articles until the mid-1970s, claims like Day's were very common in the literature. Descriptions of improved mortality and morbidity appeared, based totally on uncontrolled data from patients with myocardial infarction (MI) admitted before and after the introduction of a CCU. Until the 1970s, no major study of CCUs included a randomized control group.

However, Day's enthusiasm spread to many others. In 1967, the classic descriptive study by Lown's group at the Peter Bent Brigham Hospital in Boston appeared (Lown et al. 1967). This study was supported by the U.S. Public Health

Service, the Hartford Foundation, and the American Optical Company, which manufactured the tape-loop recall memory system that was being used in the CCU. The CCU's major objective, as the article pointed out, was to anticipate and to reduce early heart rhythm disturbances, thereby avoiding the need for resuscitation. The paper cited several other articles showing before-after decreases in mortality with a CCU, but never with randomization or other forms of statistical control introduced, and certainly never with a random controlled trial.

This publication led to a conference in 1968, sponsored by the Department of Health, Education and Welfare (HEW), in which greater development and support of CCUs were advocated, despite clear-cut statements within the conference that the effectiveness of CCUs had not been demonstrated. For example, at the conference the chief of the Heart Disease Control Program of the Public Health Service claimed: "An attempt was made a few years ago to make some controlled studies of the benefits of CCU efforts, but it was not possible to carry out those investigations for many reasons, some of them fiscal. Therefore, we do not have proper studies for demonstrating the advantages of CCUs. But now that these opportunities and occasions to prevent heart rhythm disturbances have become a great deal more common, we can be assured that our efforts are worthwhile. ... Upon advice of our colleagues in the profession, we have not considered it ethically acceptable, at this time, to make a controlled study which would necessitate shunting of patients from a facility without a CCU (but with the support that CCUs provide) to one with a CCU" (U.S. Department of Health, Education and Welfare 1968a).

So, despite the lack of controlled studies showing effectiveness, there were many calls for the expansion of CCUs to other hospitals and increased support from the federal government and private foundations. In 1968 HEW also issued a set of guidelines for CCUs (U.S. Department of Health, Education and Welfare, 1968b). Largely because of these recommendations, CCUs grew rapidly in the following years. Table 30.2 shows the expansion of CCUs in the United States between 1967 and 1974 (Metropolitan Life Insurance Company 1977). Although some regional variability was present, a large increase in the proportion and an even larger increase in the absolute number of hospitals with CCUs occurred during this period—still, without demonstration of effectiveness.

TABLE 30.2 Growth of Coronary Care Units in the United States, by Region, 1967–74

	CORONARY CARE UNITS (% OF HOSPITALS)	
	1967	1974
United States	24.3	33.8
New England	29.0	36.8
Mid-Atlantic	33.8	44.2
East North Central	31.0	38.2
West North Central	17.0	25.3
South Atlantic	23.3	38.2
East South Central	13.4	30.1
West South Central	15.3	24.3
Mountain	21.4	29.3
Pacific	32.7	37.8

Source: Metropolitan Life Insurance Company 1977.

Later Studies of Effectiveness

Serious research on the effectiveness of CCUs did not begin until the 1970s. As several critics have pointed out, the "before-after" studies done during the 1960s simply could not lead to valid conclusions about effectiveness, since none of these studies had adequate control groups or randomization (*Lancet* Editorials 1979; Martin et al. 1974; Peterson 1978; Waitzkin 1978).

Several later studies compared treatment of MI patients in hospital wards versus CCU settings (Astvad et al. 1974; Christiansen et al. 1971; Hill et al. 1977; Hofvendahl 1971). Patients were "randomly" admitted to the CCU or the regular ward, simply based on the availability of CCU beds. Ward patients were the "control" group; CCU patients were the "experimental" group. Table 30.3 reviews the findings of these studies, which are very contradictory. From this research it is unclear, at this late date, that CCUs improve in-hospital mortality.

More recent research contrasted home versus hospital care (Table 30.4) (Colling 1978; Dellipiani et al. 1977; Hill et al. 1978; Mather et al. 1971). One major study was the prospective, random controlled trial by Mather and his colleagues in Great Britain. This was an ambitious and courageous study, of the type that was not considered possible by HEW in the 1960s. Although some methodologic problems arose concerning the randomization of patients to home versus hospital care, the cumulative one-year mortality was not different in the home and hospital groups, and there was no evidence that MI patients did better in the hospital. A second random controlled trial of home versus hospital treatment tried to correct the methodologic difficulties of the Mather study by achieving a higher rate of randomization and strict criteria for the entry and exclusion of patients from the trial. The preliminary findings of this later study, conducted by Hill's group in Great Britain, confirmed the earlier results; the researchers concluded that for the majority of patients with suspected MI, admission to a hospital "confers no clear advantage." A third study of the same problem used an epidemiologic approach in the Teesside area of Great Britain. This investigation was not a random controlled trial but simply a twelve-month descriptive epidemiologic study of the incidence of MIs, how they were treated in practice, and the outcomes in terms of mortality. Both the crude and age-standardized mortality rates were better for patients treated at home.

In summary, these issues are far from settled even now. The thrust of available

TABLE 30.3   Recent Studies Comparing Coronary Care Unit and Ward Treatment for Myocardial Infarction

	No CCU		CCU	
	N	% Mortality	N	% Mortality
Prospective				
Hofvendahl (1971)	139	35	132	17
Christiansen (1971)	244	41	171	18
Hill (1977)				
< 65 yrs	186	18	797	15
≥ 65 yrs	297	32	200	31
Retrospective				
Astvad (1974)	603	39	1108	41

TABLE 30.4   Recent Studies Comparing Hospital and Home Care for Myocardial Infarction

	HOSPITAL		HOME	
Prospective Randomized	N	% Mortality	N	% Mortality
Mather (1976)				
< 60 yrs	106	18	117	17
≥ 60 yrs	112	35	103	23
Total	218	27	220	20
Hill (1978)	132	11	132	13

	HOSPITAL CCU		HOSPITAL WARD		HOME	
Epidemiologic	N	% Mortality	N	% Mortality	N	% Mortality
Dellipiani (1977)	248	13	296	21	193	9

research indicates that home care is a viable treatment alternative to hospital or CCU care for many patients with MI. Early CCU promotion used unsound clinical research. More adequate studies have not confirmed CCU effectiveness. One other question is clear: If intensive care is not demonstrably more effective than simple rest at home, how can we explain the tremendous proliferation during the past two decades of this very expensive form of treatment?

From a Marxist viewpoint, these events cannot be chance phenomena. Nor are they simply another expression of the Pollyanna-like acceptance of high technology in industrial society. The enormously costly development of CCUs occurred without any demonstration of their effectiveness. Therefore, one must search for the social, economic, and political structures that fostered their growth.

The Corporate Connection

To survive, capitalist industries must produce and sell new products. Expansion is an absolute necessity for capitalist enterprises. The economic surplus (defined as the excess of total production over "socially essential production") must grow continually larger. Medical production also falls in this same category, although it is seldom viewed in this way. The economist Mandel emphasizes the contradictions of the economic surplus: "For capitalist crises are incredible phenomena like nothing ever seen before. They are not crises of scarcity, like all pre-capitalist crises; they are crises of overproduction" (Mandel 1970). This scenario also includes the health-care system, where an overproduction of intensive-care technology contrasts with the fact that many people have little access to the most simple and rudimentary medical services.

Large profit-making corporations in the United States participated in essentially every phase of CCU research, development, promotion, and proliferation. Many companies involved themselves in the intensive-care market. Here I consider the activities of two such firms: Warner-Lambert Pharmaceutical Company and the Hewlett-Packard Company. I selected these corporations because information about their participation in coronary care was relatively accessible and because they have occupied prominent market positions in this clinical area.

However, many other firms, including at last eighty-five major companies, also have been involved in coronary care (DeSalvo 1978).

Warner-Lambert Pharmaceutical Company (W-L) is a large multinational corporation, with $2.1 billion in assets and over $2.5 billion in sales annually during the late 1970s. The corporation comprises a number of interrelated subsidiary companies: Warner-Chilcott Laboratories, the Parke-Davis Company, and Warner-Lambert Consumer Products, which makes Smith Brothers cough drops, Bromo-Seltzer, Chiclets, DuBarry, Richard Hudnut, Rolaids, Dentyne, Certs, Cool-Ray Polaroid (sunglasses), and Oh! Henry (candy). Warner-Lambert International operates in more than forty countries. Although several divisions of the W-L conglomerate participated actively in the development and promotion of coronary care, the most prominent division has been the American Optical Company (AO), which W-L acquired during 1967 (W-L 1969).

By the early 1960s AO already had a long history of successful sales in such fields as optometry, ophthalmology, and microscopes. The instrumentation required for intensive coronary care led to AO's diversification into this new and growing area. The profitable outcomes of AO's research, development, and promotion of coronary care technology are clear from AO's 1966 annual report: "In 1966, the number of American Optical Coronary Care Systems installed in hospitals throughout the United States more than tripled. Competition for this market also continued to increase as new companies, both large and small, entered the field. However, we believe that American Optical Company will continue a leader in this evolving field" (American Optical Company 1966).

After purchasing AO in 1967, W-L maintained AO's emphasis on CCU technology and sought wider acceptance by health professionals and medical centers. Promotional materials contained the assumption, never proven, that the new technology was effective in reducing morbidity and mortality from heart disease. Early products and systems included the AO Cardiometer, a heart-monitoring and resuscitation device; the first direct-current defibrillator; the Lown Cardioverter; and an Intensive Cardiac Care System that permitted the simultaneous monitoring of sixteen patients by oscilloscopes, recording instruments, heart-rate meters, and alarm systems (W-L 1967). In 1968 the company introduced a new line of monitoring instrumentation and implantable demand pacemakers. Regarding the monitoring systems, Warner-Lambert reported that "acceptance has far exceeded initial estimates" and that "to meet the increased demand for its products" the medical division was doubling the size of its plant in Bedford, Massachusetts (W-L 1968). By 1969 the company introduced another completely new line of Lown Cardioverters and Defibrillators (W-L 1969). The company continued to register expanding sales throughout the early 1970s.

Despite this growth, W-L began to face a typical corporate problem: the potential saturation of markets in the United States. Coronary care technology was capital-intensive. The number of hospitals in the United States that could buy coronary care systems, though large, was finite. For this reason, W-L began to make new and predictable initiatives to assure future growth. First, the company expanded coronary care sales into foreign markets, especially the Third World. Subsequently W-L reported notable gains in sales in such countries as Argentina, Canada, Colombia, France, Germany, Japan, and Mexico, despite the fact that during the 1970s "political difficulties in southern Latin America slowed progress somewhat, particularly in Chile and Peru" (W-L 1970).

A second method to deal with market saturation was further diversification within the coronary care field with products whose intent was to open new markets or to create obsolescence in existing systems. For example, in 1975 the AO subsidiary introduced two new instruments. The Pulsar 4, a lightweight portable defibrillator designed for local paramedic and emergency squads, created "an exceptionally strong sales demand." The Computer Assisted Monitoring System used a computer to anticipate and control changes in cardiac patients' conditions and replaced many hospitals' CCU systems that AO had installed but that lacked computer capabilities. According to the 1975 annual report, these two instruments "helped contribute to record sales growth in 1975, following an equally successful performance in the previous year" (W-L 1975).

A third technique to assure growth involved the modification of coronary care technology for new areas gaining public and professional attention. With an emphasis on preventive medicine, AO introduced a new line of electrocardiogram telemetry instruments, designed to provide early warning of MI or rhythm disturbance in ambulatory patients. In addition, AO began to apply similar monitoring technology to the field of occupational medicine after the passage of the Federal Occupational Safety and Health legislation in 1970 (W-L 1970).

W-L is only one of many companies cultivating the coronary care market. Another giant is the Hewlett-Packard Company (H-P), a firm that in 1977 held more than $1.1 billion in assets and reported over $1.3 billion in sales. Since its founding in 1939, H-P grew from a small firm, manufacturing analytical and measuring instruments mainly for industry, to a leader in electronics. Until the early 1960s H-P's only major product designated for medical markets was a simple electrocardiogram machine. Along with pocket computers, medical electronic equipment became the most successful of H-P's product groups. During the 1960s H-P introduced a series of innovations in coronary care (as well as perinatal monitoring and instrumentation for respiratory disease) that soon reached markets throughout the world.

Initially the company focused on the development of CCU technology. H-P aggressively promoted CCU equipment to hospitals, with the consistent claim that cardiac monitors and related products were definitely effective in reducing mortality from MI and rhythm disturbances. Such claims as the following were unambiguous: "In the cardiac care unit pictured here at a Nevada hospital, for example, the system has alerted the staff to several emergencies that might otherwise have proved fatal, and the cardiac mortality rate has been cut in half" (H-P 1966). Alternatively, "hundreds of lives are saved each year with the help of Hewlett-Packard patient monitoring systems installed in more than 1,000 hospitals throughout the world. . . . Pictured here is an HP system in the intensive care ward of a hospital in Montevideo, Uruguay" (H-P 1969).

Very early, H-P emphasized the export of CCU technology to hospitals and practitioners abroad, anticipating the foreign sales that other companies like W-L also later enjoyed. In 1966 the H-P annual report predicted that the effects of a slumping economy would be offset by "the great sales potential for our products, particularly medical instruments, in South American, Canadian and Asian markets. These areas should support substantial gains in sales for a number of years" (H-P 1966). In materials prepared for potential investors, H-P made explicit statements about the advantages of foreign operations. For example, because H-P subsidiaries received "pioneer status" in Malaysia and Singapore, income generated in these countries remained essentially tax-free during the early 1970s: "Had their income been taxed at the U.S. statutory rate of 48 percent in 1974, our net earnings would have been reduced by 37 cents a share" (H-P 1974). By the mid-1970s, H-P's international medical equipment business, as measured by total orders, surpassed its domestic business. More than a hundred sales and service offices were operating in sixty-four countries.

Like W-L, H-P also diversified its products to deal with the potential saturation of the coronary care market. During the late 1960s the company introduced a series of complex computerized systems that were designed as an interface with electrocardiogram machines, monitoring devices, and other CCU products. For example, a computerized system to analyze and interpret electrocardiograms led to the capability of processing up to five hundred electrocardiograms per eight-hour day: "This and other innovative systems recently introduced to the medical profession contributed to the substantial growth of our medical electronics business during the past year. With this growth has come increasing profitability as well" (H-P 1971). Similar considerations of profitability motivated the development of telemetry systems for ambulatory patients with heart disease and battery-powered electrocardiogram machines designated for regions of foreign countries where electricity was not yet available for traditional machines. In 1973 H-P provided a forthright statement of its philosophy: "Health care expenditures, worldwide, will continue to increase significantly in the years ahead, and a growing portion of these funds will be allocated for medical electronic equipment. Interestingly, this growth trend offers the company. . . the unique opportunity to help shape the future of health care delivery" (H-P 1973). From the corporate perspective, spiraling health-care expenditures, far from a problem to be solved, are the necessary fuel for desired profit.

The Academic Medical Center Connection

Academic medical centers have played a key role in the development and promotion of costly innovations like those in coronary care. This role seldom has attracted attention in critiques of technology, yet both corporations considered here obtained important bases at medical centers located in geographic proximity to corporate headquarters. Academic cardiologists participated in the proliferation of CCU equipment. Their work was doubtless motivated in part by a belief that the new technologies would save lives and help patients, rather than by a desire for personal profit. Yet their uncritical support for these innovations fostered CCUs' widespread acceptance without documented effectiveness.

Before its purchase by W-L, AO—with headquarters in Southbridge, Massachusetts—established ties with the Peter Bent Brigham Hospital in Boston. Specifically, the company worked with Bernard Lown, an eminent cardiologist who served as an AO consultant, on the development of defibrillators and cardioverters. Lown pioneered the theoretical basis and clinical applications of these techniques; AO engineers collaborated with Lown in the construction of working models. As previously discussed, AO marketed and promoted several lines of defibrillators and cardioverters that bore Lown's name.

AO's support of technologic innovation at the Peter Bent Brigham Hospital was clear. The CCU developed in the mid-1960s received major grants from AO that Lown and his group acknowledged (Lown et al. 1967). AO also used data and pictures from the Brigham CCU in promotional literature distributed to the medical profession and potential investors. Lown and his group continued to influence the medical profession through a large number of publications—in both the general medical and cardiologic literature—that discussed CCU-linked diagnostic and therapeutic techniques (Table 30.5). In these papers Lown emphasized the importance of automatic monitoring. He also advocated the widespread use of telemetry for ambulatory patients and computerized data-analysis systems, both areas into which AO diversified during the late 1960s and early 1970s. AO's relationship with Lown and his colleagues apparently proved beneficial for all concerned. The dynamics of heightened profits for AO and prestige for Lown were not optimal conditions for a detached, systematic appraisal of CCU effectiveness.

H-P's academic base has been the Stanford University Medical Center, located about one-half mile from corporate headquarters in Palo Alto, California. For many years William Hewlett, H-P's chief executive officer, served as a trustee of Stanford University. In addition, as discussed later, a private philanthropy established by Hewlett was prominent among the university's financial benefactors.

Since the late 1960s Donald Harrison, professor of medicine and chief of the division of cardiology, has acted as H-P's primary consultant in the development of coronary care technology. Harrison and his colleagues at Stanford collaborated with H-P engineers in the design of CCU systems intended for marketing to both academic medical centers and community hospitals. H-P helped construct working models of CCU components at Stanford University Hospital, under the direction of Harrison and other faculty members. Stanford physicians introduced these H-P systems into clinical use.

Innovations in the treatment of patients with heart disease had a profound impact on the costs of care at Stanford. As documented in a general study of the costs of treatment for several illnesses at Stanford, Scitovsky and McCall stated: "Of the conditions covered by the 1964–1971 study, the changes in treatment in myocardial infarction had their most drastic effect on costs. This was due principally to the increased costs of intensive care units. In 1964, the Stanford Hospital had a relatively small Intensive Care Unit (ICU). It was used by only three of the 1964

TABLE 30.5 Publications Concerning Coronary Care from Peter Bent Brigham Hospital and Stanford University Medical Center Groups, 1965–75

Year	Peter Bent Brigham Hospital	Stanford University Medical Center
1965	1	1
1966	3	1
1967	3	4
1968	7	4
1969	11	3
1970	6	1
1971	7	2
1972	3	4
1973	4	5
1974	3	5
1975	2	4

Source: Index Medicus, citations listing B. Lown or D. C. Harrison as author or co-author and dealing specifically with diagnostic or therapeutic techniques in coronary care units.

coronary cases. . . . By 1971, the hospital had not only an ICU but also a Coronary Care Unit (CCU) and an intermediate CCU. Of the 1971 cases, only one did not receive at least some care in either the CCU or the intermediate CCU" (Scitovsky and McCall 1977).

Many articles from the Harrison group described new technical developments or discussed clinical issues tied to intensive-care techniques (Table 30.5). Several papers directly acknowledged the use of H-P equipment and assistance. These academic clinicians also participated in continuing medical education programs on coronary care, both in the United States and abroad. The Stanford specialists thus played an important role in promoting technology in general and H-P products in particular.

Private Philanthropies

Philanthropic support figured prominently in the growth of CCUs. Humanitarian goals doubtless were present, but profit considerations were not lacking, since philanthropic initiatives often emerged from the actions of corporate executives whose companies produced medical equipment or pharmaceuticals.

Primary among the philanthropic proponents of CCUs was the American Heart Association (AHA). The AHA sponsored research that led to the development of CCU products, especially monitoring systems. In addition, the AHA helped finance local hospitals establishing CCUs. The "underlying purpose" of these activities, according to the AHA's 1967 annual report, was "to encourage and guide the formation of new [CCU] units in both large and small hospitals." Justifying these expenditures, the AHA cited some familiar "data": "Experience with the approximately 300 such specialized units already established, mostly in large hospitals, indicated that a national network of CCUs might save lives of more than 45,000 individuals each year" (American Heart Association 1967). The source for this projected number of rescued people, though uncited, presumably was a "personal communication" from an HEW official to which Day referred in his 1963 article. Later in the 1960s, the AHA's annual number of estimated beneficiaries rose still higher, again with undocumented claims of effectiveness. According to the 1968 annual report, "only about one third of hospitalized heart attack patients are fortunate enough to be placed in coronary care units. If all of them had the benefits of these monitoring and emergency service facilities, it is estimated that 50,000 more heart patients could be saved yearly" (American Heart Association 1968). This unsubstantiated estimate, raised from the earlier unsubstantiated figure of forty-five thousand, persisted in AHA literature into the early 1970s. During this same period the AHA cosponsored, with the U.S. Public Health Service and the American College of Cardiology, a series of natonal conferences on coronary care whose purpose was "the successful development of the CCU program" in all regions of the United States.

Other smaller foundations also supported CCU proliferation. For example, the John A. Hartford Foundation gave generous support to several hospitals and medical centers during the early 1960s to develop monitoring capabilities. The Hartford Foundation's public view of CCU effectiveness was unequivocal; the Kansas City coronary care program "has demonstrated that a properly equipped and designed physical setting staffed with personnel trained to meet cardiac emergencies will provide prophylactic therapy which will materially enhance the survival of these patients and substantially reduce the mortality rates" (John A. Hartford Foundation 1963). Another foundation that supported CCU growth, though somewhat less directly, was the W. R. Hewlett Foundation, founded by H-P's chief executive officer. The Hewlett Foundation earmarked large annual grants to Stanford University, which, after an undoubtedly fierce competitive evaluation of alternatives, chose H-P equipment for its CCU and other intensive-care facilities (W. R. Hewlett Foundation 1967, 1971).

The commitment of private philanthropy to technologic innovations is a structural problem that transcends the personalities that control philanthropy at any specific time. The bequests that create philanthropies historically come largely from funds generated by North American industrial corporations, which are highly oriented to technologic advances. Moreover, the investment portfolios of philanthropic organizations usually include stocks in a sizable number of industrial companies. These structural conditions encourage financial support for technical advances, like those in coronary care. The same conditions tend to discourage philanthropic support for new programs or organizational changes that would modify the overall structure of the health-care system. Occasionally, private philanthropies underwrite efforts in preventive and community medicine that do not involve technical innovations, but these initiatives are more the exception than the rule.

In addition, it is useful to ask which people made philanthropic decisions to fund CCU development. During the mid-1960s the AHA's officers included eight physicians who had primary commitments in cardiology, executives of two pharmaceutical companies (L. F. Johnson of American Home Products Corporation's drug subsidiaries and Ross Reid of Squibb Corporation), a metals company executive (A. M. Baer of Imperial Knife Associated Companies), a prominent banker (W. C. Butcher, president of Chase Manhattan Bank), and several public officials (including Dwight Eisenhower). At the height of CCU promotion in 1968, the chairman of the AHA's annual Heart Fund was a drug company executive (W. F. Laporte, president of American Home Products Corporation, former chief of its pharmaceutical subsidiaries, and director of several banks). During the 1960s and early 1970s, bankers and corporate executives also dominated the board at the Hartford Foundation. The Hewlett Foundation remained a family affair until the early 1970s, when R. W. Heyns—former chancellor of the University of California, Berkeley, and also a director of Norton Simon, Inc., Kaiser Industries, and Levi-Strauss—assumed the foundation's presidency. It is not surprising that philanthropic policies supporting CCU proliferation showed a strong orientation toward corporate industrialism.

The Role of the State

Agencies of government played a key role in CCU growth. The U.S. Public Health Service gave substantial financial support to clinicians in the early 1960s for CCU development. An official of HEW provided an "estimate" of potential lives saved by future CCUs (Day 1963); without apparent basis in data, this figure became a slogan for CCU promotion. Conferences and publications by HEW during the late 1960s specified guidelines for adequate CCU equipment, even though the effectiveness of this approach admittedly remained unproven by random controlled trial.

In these activities, as noted earlier, three common functions of the state in capitalist societies were evident. First, in health policy the state generally supports private enterprise by encouraging innovations that enhance profits to major industrial corporations. The state does not enact policies that limit private profit in any serious way. Recognizing the high costs of CCU implementation, state agencies could have placed strict limitations on their number and distribution. For example, HEW could have called for the regionalization of CCU facilities and restrictions on their wider proliferation. Subsequently, studies of CCU mortality rates generally have shown better outcomes in larger, busier centers and have suggested the rationality of regionalized policies (Bloom and Peterson 1973). HEW's policies supported just the opposite development. By publishing guidelines that called for advanced CCU technology and by encouraging CCU proliferation to most community hospitals, HEW assured the profitability of corporate ventures in the coronary-care field.

A second major function of the state is its legitimation of the capitalist political-economic system. The decade of the 1960s was a time of upheaval in the United States. The civil rights and black power movements called into question basic patterns of injustice. Opposition to the war in Indochina mobilized a large part of the population against government and corporate policies. Labor disputes arose frequently. Under such circumstances, when government and corporations face large-scale crises of legitimacy, the state tends to intervene with health and welfare projects. Medical technology is a "social capital expenditure" by which the state tries to counteract the recurrent legitimacy crises of advanced capitalism (O'Connor 1973). Technologic innovations like CCUs are convenient legitimating expenditures, since they convey a message of deep concern for the public health while also supporting new sources of profit for large industrial firms.

Thirdly, government agencies provide market research that guides domestic and foreign sales efforts. The Global Market Survey, published by the U.S. Department of Commerce, gives a detailed analysis of changes in medical facilities, hospital beds, and physicians throughout the world. The survey specifies those countries that are prime targets for sales of biomedical equipment. For example, the 1973 survey pointed out that "major foreign markets for biomedical equipment are expected to grow at an average annual rate of 15 percent in the 1970s, nearly double the growth rate predicted for the U.S. domestic market" (U.S. Department of Commerce, Domestic and International Business Administration 1973). The same report predicted that West Germany (which would emphasize CCU construction), Japan, Brazil, Italy, and Israel would be the largest short-term markets for products manufactured in the United States. According to the report, "market research studies identified specific equipment that present [sic] good to excellent U.S. sales opportunities in the 20 [foreign] markets"; "cardiologic-thoracic equipment" headed the list of products with high sales potential. Market research performed by state agencies has encouraged the proliferation of CCUs and related innovations, whose capacity to generate profits has overshadowed the issue of effectiveness in government planning.

Changes in the Health-Care Labor Force

Intensive care involves workers as well as equipment. Throughout the twentieth century, a process of deskilling has occurred, by which the skilled trades and professions have become rationalized into simpler tasks that can be handled by less skilled and lower paid workers (Braverman 1974). In medicine, paraprofessionals take on jobs that can be specified by algorithms covering nearly all contingencies. This deskilling process applies equally to CCUs and other intensive-care facilities, where standard orders—often printed in advance—can deal with almost all situations that might arise.

The deskilling of the intensive-care labor force has received support from professional, governmental, and corporate planners. During the late 1960s and early 1970s, the training of allied health personnel for intensive-care technology became a priority of educators and administrators. According to this view, it was important to train a "cadre of health workers capable of handling routine and purely functional duties" (Rosinski 1969). The linkage between allied health workers and new technology was a clear assumption in this approach. There were limits on "the extent to which a markedly greater delegation of tasks can be achieved without the introduction of new technology" that compensates for aides' lack of "decisional training" (Moore 1970). The availability of monitoring equipment in CCUs made this setting adaptable to staffing partly by technicians who could receive lower wages than doctors or nurses. Paramedical training programs, focusing on intensive care, became a goal of national policymakers, even though they recognized the "built in obsolescence of monitoring equipment" and the tendency of industrial corporations to "capitalize" in this field (Barnett and Robbins 1969; Foster et al. 1969; Sanazaro 1970).

Conclusion: Health Care, Cost Containment, and Capitalism

The Marxian framework is not a conspiratorial model. The very nature of capitalist production necessitates the continuing development of new products and sales in new markets. From the standpoint of potential profit, there is no reason that corporations should view medical products differently from other products. The commodification of health care and its associated technology is a necessary feature of the capitalist political-economic system. Without fundamental changes in the organization of private capital, costly innovations of dubious effectiveness will continue to plague the health sector. It is the structure of the system, rather than decision-making by individual entrepreneurs and clinicians, that is the appropriate level of analysis.

Cost-containment activities that do not recognize the structure of the capitalist system will remain a farce. During the last decade, sophisticated methodologies to analyze costs and effectiveness have emerged in medical care research. These techniques include clinical decision analysis and a variety of related methods (Abrams and McNeil 1978; Bunker et al. 1977; McNeil et al. 1975; Schoenbaum et al. 1976). Ironically, economists first developed this type of analysis at the Pentagon, to evaluate technologic innovations like new missiles (Hitch and McKean 1967). The methodology led to disastrous policy decisions in Indochina, largely because the cost-effectiveness approach did not take into account the broader, so-called imponderable context. This analysis did not predict accurately the political response of the Indochinese people to such technologies as napalm and mechanized warfare. Even more ironically, many of the same people who developed cost-effectiveness research at the Defense Department now are moving into the health field, where this approach has become quite fashionable (Enthoven 1978).

In health care as in other areas, cost-effectiveness methodology restricts the level of analysis to the evaluation of specific innovations. Studies using this framework generally ignore, or make only passing reference to, the broader structures of capitalism (Cochrane 1972; Illich 1976; Mechanic 1978; Rose 1975; Stevenson 1978; U.S. Congress, Office of Technology Assessment 1976). As a result this approach obscures one fundamental source of high costs and ineffective practices: the profit motive. Apparent methodologic sophistication masks the analytic poverty of research that evaluates many different innovations while overlooking their common origins in the drive for profit. Because of this deficiency, cost-effectiveness analysis mystifies the roots of costly, ineffective practices in the very nature of the political-economic system.

Defects of research, however, are less dangerous than defects of policy. Cost containment has become a highly touted national priority. In a climate of fiscal crisis, an ideology of austerity is justifying cutbacks in health and welfare programs. Services whose effectiveness is difficult to demonstrate by the new methodologies are prime candidates for cutbacks and therefore face a bleak future. Poor people and minority groups, historically victimized by the free-enterprise system, will be the first to suffer from this purported rationalization of policy. Meanwhile, private profit in health care, a major fuel for high costs, continues unabated. Just as it eludes serious attention in research, the structure of profit evades new initiatives in health policy.

Cost containment will remain little more than rhetoric unless we begin to address the linkages between cost and profit. An initial step involves support for policies that curtail private profit. Unlimited corporate involvement in medicine must end. The corporations that develop and successfully promote ineffective innovations like those in coronary care must cease these activities. Because this will not happen voluntarily, compulsory restriction of profit in health care and eventual public ownership of medical industries must occur, especially in pharmaceutical and medical equipment manufacturing. A national formulary of permitted drugs and equipment, like that established in several socialist countries, would reduce costs by eliminating the proliferation of unneeded products. Socialization of medical production is no more fanciful than public ownership of utilities, transportation facilities, or schools.

In summary, the development and promotion of high technology in medicine may seem irrational when analyzed in terms of proven medical effectiveness. These trends appear considerably more rational when viewed from the needs of a capitalist system in crisis. By questioning what capitalism does with our hearts, we get closer to the heart of many of our other problems.

REFERENCES

ABRAMS, H. L., and McNEIL, B. J. 1978. Medical implications of computed tomography (CAT scanning). *New England Journal of Medicine* 298:310–18.

AMERICAN HEART ASSOCIATION. 1967; 1968. *Annual report*. New York, 1967, 11; 1968, 2, 13–14.

AMERICAN OPTICAL COMPANY. 1966. *Annual report*. Southbridge, Mass. 9.

AMERICAN PUBLIC HEALTH ASSOCIATION. 1975. *Chart book, health and work in America*. Washington, D.C.: American Public Health Association.

Astvad, K.; Fabricius-Bjerre, N.; Kjaerulff, J.; et al. 1974. Mortality from acute myocardial infarction before and after establishment of a coronary care unit. *British Medical Journal* 1:567–69.

Barnett, G. O., and Robbins, A. 1969. Information technology and manpower productivity. *Journal of the American Medical Association.* 209:546–48.

Berliner, H. 1975. A larger perspective on the Flexner Report. *International Journal of Health Services* 5:573–92.

Blake, E., and Bodenheimer, T. 1975. *Closing the doors to the poor.* San Francisco, Calif.: Health Policy Advisory Center.

Bloom, B. S., and Peterson, O. L. 1973. End results, cost and productivity of coronary-care units. *New England Journal of Medicine* 288:72–78.

Boston Nurses Group. 1978. *The false promise: professionalism in nursing.* Somerville, Mass.: New England Free Press.

Braverman, H. *Labor and monopoly capital.* 1974. New York: Monthly Review Press.

Brown, C. A. 1973. The division of laborers: allied health professions. *International Journal of Health Services* 3:435–44.

Brown, E. R. 1979. *Rockefeller medicine men: medicine and capitalism in the Progressive Era.* Berkeley, Calif: University of California Press.

Bunker, J. P.; Barnes, B. A.; and Mosteller, F. eds. 1977. *Costs, risks, and benefits of surgery.* New York: Oxford University Press.

Christiansen, E.; Iversen, K.; and Skouby, A. P. 1971. Benefits obtained by the introduction of a coronary care unit: a comparative study. *Acta Medica Scandinavica* 189:285–91.

Cochrane, A. L. 1972. *Efficiency and effectiveness: random reflections on health services.* London: Nuffield Hospitals Trust.

Colling, A.; Dellipiani, A. W.; and Donaldson, R. J. 1976. Teesside coronary survey: an epidemiological study of acute attacks of myocardial infarction. *British Medical Journal* 2:1169–72.

Day, H. W. 1963. An intensive coronary care area. *Diseases of the Chest* 44:423–27.

Dellipiani, A. W.; Colling, W. A.; Donaldson, R. J.; et al. 1977. Teesside coronary survey—fatality and comparative severity of patients treated at home, in the hospital ward, and in the coronary care unit after myocardial infarction. *British Heart Journal* 39:1172–78.

DeSalvo, R. J. 1978. Medical marketing mixture—update. *Medical Marketing and Media* 13 (September): 21–35.

Ehrenreich, B., and Ehrenreich, J. eds. 1970. *The American health empire.* New York: Vintage.

Ehrenreich, B., and Ehrenreich, J. 1973. Hospital workers: a case study of the new working class. *Monthly Review* 24 (January):12–27.

Engels, F. 1968 (1845). *The condition of the working class in England in 1844,* trans. and ed. by W. O. Henderson and W. H. Chaloner. Stanford, Calif.: Stanford University Press.

Enthoven, A. C. 1978. Consumer-choice health plan. *New England Journal of Medicine* 298:650–58, 709–20.

Flexner, A. 1910. *Medical education in the United States and Canada.* New York: Carnegie Foundation.

Foster, F. L.; Casten, G. G.; and Reeves, T. J. 1969. Nonmedical personnel and continuous ECG monitoring. *Archives of Internal Medicine* 124:110–12.

Fuchs, V. R. 1974. *Who shall live? Health, economics, and social choice.* New York: Basic Books.

Hartford Foundation. 1963. *Annual report.* New York. 58.

Hewlett Foundation. 1967; 1971. *Annual report to the Internal Revenue Service.* Palo Alto, Calif.

Hewlett-Packard Company. 1966; 1969; 1971; 1973. *Annual report.* Palo Alto, Calif. 1966, 11, 4; 1969, 11; 1971, 5; 1973, 18–19; 1974, 2.

HIGGINSON, J. 1974. Developments in cancer prevention through environmental control. In *Cancer detection and prevention*, ed. C. Maltoni, vol. 2, pp. 3–18. New York: American Elsevier.

HILL, J. C.; HAMPTON, J. R.; and MITCHELL, J. R. A. 1978. A randomised trial of home-versus-hospital management for patients with suspected myocardial infarction. *Lancet* 1:837–41.

HILL, J. C.; HOLDSTOCK, G.; and HAMPTON, J. R. 1977. Comparison of mortality of patients with heart attacks admitted to a coronary care unit and an ordinary medical ward. *British Medical Journal* 2:81–83.

HITCH, C. J., and McKEAN, R. N. 1967. *The economics of defense in the nuclear age.* New York: Atheneum.

HOFVENDAHL, S. 1971. Influence of treatment in a CCU on prognosis in acute myocardial infarction. *Acta Medica Scandinavica* (suppl.) 519:1–78.

ILLICH, I. 1976. *Medical nemesis.* New York: Pantheon.

KELMAN, S. 1971. Towards a political economy of health care. *Inquiry* 8:30–38.

KLEINBACH, G. (Ziem). 1974. Social structure and the education of health personnel. *International Journal of Health Services* 4, 297–317.

KOTELCHUCK, D., ed. 1976. *Prognosis negative.* New York: Vintage.

KUNITZ, S. J. 1974. Professionalism and social control in the progressive era: the case of the Flexner Report. *Social Problems* 22:16–27.

LALONDE, M. *A new perspective on the health of Canadians.* Ottawa: Information Canada.

LANCET EDITORIAL. 1979. Antidysrhythmic treatment in acute myocardial infarction. *Lancet* 1:193–94.

LANCET EDITORIAL. 1979. Coronary-care units—where now? *Lancet* 1:649–50.

LOWN, B.; FAKHRO, A. M.; HOOD, W. B.; et al. 1967. The coronary care unit: new perspectives and directions. *Journal of the American Medical Association* 199:188–98.

MARTIN, S. P.; DONALDSON, M. C.; LONDON, C. D.; et al. 1974. Inputs into coronary care during 30 years: a cost effectiveness study. *Annals of Internal Medicine* 81:289–93.

MARX, K. 1963 (1890). *Capital*, vol. 1. Moscow: Progress Publishers.

——. 1964. *The economic and philosophic manuscripts of 1844.* New York: International.

——. 1971 (1859). *A contribution to the critique of political economy.* New York: International.

——, and ENGELS, F. 1948 (1848). *The communist manifesto.* New York: International.

MATHER, H. G.; MORGAN, D. C.; PEARSON, N. G., et al. 1976. Myocardial infarction: a comparison between home and hospital care for patients. *British Medical Journal* 1:925–29.

MATHER, H. G.; PEARSON, M. G.; READ, K. L. Q.; et al. 1971. Acute myocardial infarction: home and hospital treatment. *British Medical Journal* 3:334–38.

McKEOWN, T. 1977. *The modern rise of population.* New York: Academic Press.

McKINLAY, J. B. 1978. The changing political and economic context of the patient-physician encounter. In *The doctor-patient relationship in the changing health scene*, ed. E. B. Gallagher. DHEW pub. no. (NIH) 78-183. Washington, D.C.: Government Printing Office.

McNEIL, B. J.; KEELER, E.; and ADELSTEIN, S. L. 1975. Primer on certain elements of medical decision making. *New England Journal of Medicine* 293:211–15.

MECHANIC, D. 1978. Approaches to controlling the costs of medical care: short-range and long-range alternatives. *New England Journal of Medicine* 298:249–54.

METROPOLITAN LIFE INSURANCE COMPANY. 1977. Geographical distribution of coronary care units in the United States. *Statistical Bulletin* 58 (July–August):7–9.

MILIBAND, R. 1969. *The state in capitalist society.* New York: Basic Books,

MODELL, H., and WAITZKIN, H. 1974. Medicine and socialism in Chile. *Berkeley Journal of Sociology* 19:1–35.

MOORE, F. J. 1970. Information technologies and health care: the need for new technologies to offset the shortage of physicians. *Archives of Internal Medicine* 125:351–55.

NAVARRO, V. 1975. Social policy issues: an explanation of the composition, nature, and functions of the present health sector of the United States. *Bull. N.Y. Acad. Med.* 51:199–234.

———. 1976a. *Medicine under capitalism.* New York: Prodist.

———. 1976b. Social class, political power and the state and their implications in medicine. *Social Science and Medicine* 10:437-57.

O'Connor, J. 1973. *The fiscal crisis of the state.* New York: St. Martin's Press.

Offe, C. 1975. The theory of the capitalist state and the problem of policy formation. In *Stress and contradiction in modern capitalism,* ed. L. Lindberg, R. Alford, C. Crouch, and C. Offe. Lexington, Mass.: Lexington Books.

Peterson, O. L. 1978. Myocardial infarction: unit care or home care? *Annals of Internal Medicine* 88:259-61.

Polack, J. C. 1970. *La médecine du capital.* Paris: Maspero.

Powles, J. 1973. On the limitations of modern medicine. *Science, Medicine and Man* 1:1-30.

Renaud, M. 1975. On the structural constraints to state intervention in health. *International Journal of Health Services* 5:559-71.

Rodberg, L., and Stevenson, G. 1977. The health care industry in advanced capitalism. *Review of Radical Political Economics* 8 (spring):104-15.

Roemer, M. I., and Mera, J. A. 1973. "Patient dumping" and other voluntary agency contributions to public agency problems. *Medical Care* 11:30-39.

Rose, G. 1975. The contribution of intensive coronary care. *British Journal of Preventive and Social Medicine* 29:147-50.

Rosinski, E. F. 1969. Impact of technology and evolving health care systems on the training of allied health personnel. *Military Medicine* 134:390-93.

Rossdale, M. 1965. Health in a sick society. *New Left Review* 34 (November–December):82-90.

Salmon, J. W. 1975. Health maintenance organization strategy: a corporate takeover of health services. *International Journal of Health Services* 5:609-24.

———. 1977. Monopoly capital and its reorganization of the health sector. *Rev. Radical Political Economics* 8 (Spring):125-33.

Sanazaro, P. J. 1970. Physician support personnel in the 1970s. *Journal of the American Medical Association* 214:98-100.

Schoenbaum, S. C.; McNeil, B. J.; and Kavet, J. 1976. The swine-influenza decision. *New England Journal of Medicine* 295:759-65.

Scitovsky, A. A., and McCall, N. 1977. *Changes in the costs of treatment of selected illnesses, 1951-1964-1971.* DHEW pub. no. (HRA) 77-3161, Washington, D.C.: Government Printing Office.

Simpson, M. A. 1972. *Medical education: a critical approach.* London: Butterworths.

Special Task Force to the Secretary of Health, Education, and Welfare. 1973. *Work in America.* Cambridge, Mass.: MIT Press. 73-79.

Stevenson, G. 1976. Social relations of production and consumption in the human service occupations. *Monthly Review* 28 (July–August):78-87.

———. 1978. Laws of motion in the for-profit health industry: a theory and three examples. *International Journal of Health Services* 8:235-56.

U.S. Congress, Office of Technology Assessment. 1976. *Development of medical technology: opportunities for assessment.* OTA publication, unnumbered. Washington, D.C.: Government Printing Office.

U.S. Department of Commerce, Domestic and International Business Administration. 1975. *Global market survey: biomedical equipment.* USDC Publication, unnumbered. Washington, D.C.: Government Printing Office.

U.S. Department of Commerce. 1980. *Statistical abstracts of the United States 1980.* Washington, D.C.: Government Printing Office. 413, 424.

U.S. Department of Health, Education and Welfare. 1968a. *Proceedings of the national conference on coronary care units.* DHEW pub. no. 1764. Washington, D.C.: Government Printing Office.

———. 1968b. *Guidelines for coronary care units.* DHEW pub. no. 1824. Washington, D.C.: Government Printing Office.

U.S. Senate, Committee on Government Operations. 1973. *Confidence and con-*

cern: citizens view American government: a survey of public attitudes. Washington, D.C.: Government Printing Office.

VIRCHOW, R. 1868. Ueber den Hungertyphus und einige verwandte Krankheitsformen. Berlin: Hirschwald.

——. 1879. Gesammelte Abhandlungen aus dem Gebiet der oeffentlichen Medicin und der Seuchenlehre, vol. 1, pp. 305, 321–34. Berlin: Hirschwald.

——. 1907. Briefe an seine Eltern, pp. 121–64. Leipzig: Engelmann.

WAITZKIN, H. 1978. How capitalism cares for our coronaries: a preliminary exercise in political economy. In The doctor-patient relationship in the changing health scene, ed. E. B. Gallagher. DHEW pub. no. (NIH) 78–183. Washington, D.C.: Government Printing Office.

——. 1980. Medical philanthropies. The Sciences (New York Academy of Sciences) 20 (no. 6):25–28.

——. 1983. The second sickness: contradictions of capitalist health care. New York: Free Press.

——, and MODELL, H. 1974. Medicine, socialism, and totalitarianism: lessons from Chile. New England Journal of Medicine 291:171–77.

WAITZKIN, H., and WATERMAN, B. 1974. The exploitation of illness in capitalist society. Indianapolis, Ind.: Bobbs-Merrill.

WARNER-LAMBERT PHARMACEUTICAL COMPANY. 1967; 1968; 1970; 1975. Annual report. Morris Plains, N.J., 1967, 7; 1968, 25; 1969, 8, 18–19, 1970, 16, 19; 1975, 5.

WITT, M. 1981. Production with safety? Cubatimes 1 (no. 4):3–5.

ZIEM, G. 1977. Medical education since Flexner. Health/PAC Bulletin 76:8–14, 23.

Chapter 31

Social and Psychological Factors Affecting the Course of Disease: An Epidemiological Perspective

Stanislav V. Kasl

THE STUDIES WHICH WILL BE EXAMINED in this chapter fall into an ill-defined domain of collaboration between social-behavioral science and medicine. This domain has ambiguous boundaries and encompasses a multiplicity of theoretical and disciplinary approaches. Accordingly, the first step must be to set up some approximate boundaries and to explicate the perspective from which the studies will be discussed.

In epidemiology, the conventional definition of the *incidence* rate of a specific disease is the number of *new* cases of a disease, in a defined population at risk, over a period of time. The theoretically preferred method for determining incidence is a prospective surveillance of a cohort, initially free of the disease, who are assessed for a variety of possible risk factors and are monitored for the development of cases of the disease.

If the monitoring of the new cases of disease were to continue for additional medical outcomes, it would become a study of *course of disease*. The outcomes of interest would include: (1) case fatality: frequency with which individuals with the disease die of the disease during a stated period; (2) repeat episodes: additional events, such as myocardial infarction, among those who have already experienced the initial event; (3) exacerbations: for example, periods of dyspepsia among patients with a documented history of ulcer; (4) length of recovery: this might include length of hospitalization following a surgical procedure or the length of time before white blood cell and lymphocyte counts return to normal in infectious mononucleosis; (5) amount of residual morbidity; for example, among patients recovering from stroke, the range of motion left in the affected limb.

In terms of the above distinction, this chapter is concerned with the social and psychological factors which influence the course of disease; conversely, it is *not* concerned with factors which relate to incidence of new disease.

In an ideal world (for the reviewer), this should be enough to define the boundaries and the goals of this chapter. In reality, however, it only serves to provide the reviewer's approximate intent. Fundamentally, the distinction between incidence and course presupposes a discontinuity which may not be defensible, either from the medical-biological perspective or the social-psychological one. Furthermore, the specific methodology of many a study may make such a distinction impossible. Let us examine these complexities.

The ideal of a prospective incidence study is heavily dependent on the presence of one or more clinical features of the disease such as: (1) dramatic, sudden onset (such as an attack of gout) which can be adequately recalled; (2) severity of episode which almost always leads to some medical attention (such as myocardial infarction, MI); (3) an irreversible diagnostic sign (such as a characteristic EKG pattern after a "silent" MI). However, intermittent conditions with gradual onset and full remission of signs and symptoms are most difficult to study prospectively; these include such diseases as rheumatoid arthirits, asthma, and peptic ulcer. The consequence is that studies of course of disease for these conditions have an ambiguous initial point of assessment: not at the beginning of the initial episode, but anywhere along the temporal dimension of "disease in progress," depending on the method of identifying cases for study. Combining subjects who are highly heterogeneous with respect to previous medical history, and not knowing where exactly in the temporal dimension one is examining the effect of psychosocial variables on further changes in morbidity, can certainly lead to difficult to interpret results.

Another problem is that the distinction between overt, diagnosable disease and the underlying disease process is arbitrary, a matter of convention and convenience. For example, in cardiovascular epidemiology we avoid defining the disease in terms of atherosclerosis, and the resulting vascular stenosis and occlusion, and accept a definiton of disease in terms of the consequences of atherosclerosis, such as heart attack, because of the major difficulties of studying the former (Kuller 1976). Yet it should be of considerable interest for this review that Type A behavior is related to amount of occlusion (Dembroski, Weiss, and Shields 1978; Williams et al. 1980) as well as to progression of atherosclerosis (Krantz et al. 1979). Similarly, it appears somewhat arbitrary whether infectious mononucleosis (IM) is defined (a) in terms of presence of infection due to Epstein-Barr virus (EBV), documented by sero-conversion and the presence of antibody to EBV, or (b) by the clinical picture and laboratory findings for only those with overt clinical IM. In the former case, the difference between subclinical and clinical IM is an inidicator of course of disease, whereas in the latter, only such data as length of hospitalization among those with apparent illness indicate course of disease. In a prospective study with full serological monitoring (Kasl, Evans, and Niederman 1979), the arbitrary distinction can be bypassed and psychosocial variables for both types of indicators of course of illness can be examined and compared.

Mortality studies pose another problem to defining the scope of this review. In cardiovascular epidemiology, estimating mortality following hospitalization with a diagnosis of MI represents a study of case fatality, an eminently worthwhile indicator of course of illness. However, when death is the first manifestation of coronary heart disease (CHD), then we are, by convention, dealing with incidence; such deaths include instantaneous death, those on the way to the hospital, and, presumably, those during the acute phase in the coronary care unit. Calculations of changes in case fatality versus in incidence, in order to understand the recent decline in CHD mortality (Proceedings 1979), are affected by these arbitrary distinctions. General mortality data, without previous medical history, do not allow one to distinguish incidence from course of disease. For example, most of the evidence on mortality after bereavement (Cottington et al. 1980; Jacobs and

Ostfeld 1977; Helsing and Szklo 1981) deals with subjects on whom previous medical history data were not available. Thus it is impossible to tell whether the elevated mortality is due primarily to increased case fatality (a more adverse course among subjects with previous disease) or to a more severe initial manifestation of a disease (incidence).

Finally, it is necessary to note that the distinction between incidence and course of illness—which at the level of research is based on classifying subjects before versus after they satisfy a set of diagnostic criteria—may or may not represent a corresponding social reality for the patient. The major formulations in medical sociology, health psychology, and psychosomatic medicine (e.g., Jaco 1979; Lipowski, Lipsitt, and Whybrow 1977; Mechanic 1978; Stone, Cohen, and Adler 1979) emphasize the role of the symptom experience, the nature of the contact with health professionals, the demands of the treatment regimen, the impact of physical morbidity on social functioning, the relevance of previous symptom and medical-care experience, and so on. The process of diagnostic labeling (which is communicated to the patient) does not play a major role in these formulations and it is not clear what separate impact it may have on the individual. For example, the nature and the severity of the signs and symptoms suggestive of rheumatoid arthritis may determine the impact on the patient much more than the physician's statement that he was or was not able to arrive at a diagnosis of rheumatoid arthritis.

Whether the risk-factor picture for incidence and for course of disease will be similar or different appears to be specific to the disease and the variables under study. A dynamic continuity between incidence and course of disease is suggested by such findings as: (1) Type A behavior is a risk factor for initial MI as well as for recurrence of later MIs (Dembroski et al. 1978; Jenkins, Zyzanski, and Rosenman 1976); (2) higher body weight is a risk factor for initial diagnosis of breast cancer as well as for recurrence after radical mastectomy (Donegan, Hartz, and Rimm 1978). On the other hand, discontinuity is suggested by the comparison of minimization of symptoms (denial) after a heart attack with presentation of symptoms at the initial point of seeking medical care. In a study of prevalence of denial by ethnic origin among male patients with a first diagnosis of MI (Croog, Shapiro, and Levin 1971), high rates of denial were found among Jewish and Italian patients, and low rates, among Irish and British patients. This appears to be a reversal of ethnic differences found by Zborowski (1969) and Zola (1966): Their work on pain and presentation of symptoms (prediagnosis illness behavior stage) revealed the Jewish and the Italian subjects to be high on emotional description of pain and its intensity and to present a greater variety of symptoms in contrast to the Irish and Anglo-Saxon groups who tended to de-emphasize pain and under-report symptoms. Other results of the Croog and Levine study also point to different dynamics of incidence versus course of illness (Croog and Fitzgerald 1978); the impact of the MI on the stress level of the wife did not occur following the initial event, but later on and only for wives whose husbands experienced a poorer course of disease, as measured by additional hospitalizations.

Some Conceptual and Methodological Considerations

In the prospective study of incidence of disease, the problem of measuring health status is usually equivalent to having agreed upon diagnostic criteria which are adequately operationalized. When the incidence study deals with psychosocial risk factors, we generally wish to show that such factors have an effect in addition to (or in interaction with) known biological risk factors. For example, a recent analysis of CHD mortality in British civil servants (Marmot et al. 1978) showed that men in the lowest grades have higher rates of risk factors and adverse life-style habits, but that adjusting for these, their excess mortality persists. When the risk factor picture is unclear, such as in general cancer mortality (Shekelle et al. 1981), one does the best one can with statistical controls for smoking, alcohol consumption, occupational exposure, and so on to show that the risk factor being studied—in this case depression—persists in its effect. And when the study involves mortality for all causes, then the goal of prior control on biological risk factors, before examining the role of psychosocial risk factors, becomes quite unattainable and one falls back on some broad additive index of health status, encompassing symptoms, chronic conditions, and disability indices in order to try to control for prior health status (e.g., Berkman and Syme 1979).

In the study of course of disease there are many complications, which are absent—or, at least, not as intrusive—in the study of incidence. The ones which loom particularly large are:

1. We need to quantify the severity of the disease episode (and any comorbidity) which is the starting point of the course of disease study; if this is not a first episode, we need to quantify previous medical history in order to establish level of health status at inception of study.
2. We need to establish the impact of treatment(s), particularly when patients are heterogeneous with respect to treatments received; if this is not a first episode, treatment history is also needed.
3. We need to select indices of health status which denote course of illness, appropriate for the disease or condition under study.
4. We need an analytic schema in which measurements of 1 and 2, above, prognostically link 3, the outcomes; then within this schema, psychosocial factors can be introduced and examined for impact.

The measurement issues under point 3 above are particularly troublesome and much literature has been devoted to it. Obviously, we need a broad range of indicators so that we may adequately reflect the course of disease, both at the biological level and the psychosocial level; such indicators tend to be relatively independent of each other (e.g., Albrecht and Higgins 1977). However, such a broad range of indicators enormously complicates the task of controlling for extraneous (or spurious) influences and of interpreting the possible underlying mechanisms which may be involved. For example, outcomes such as return to work or length of hospitalization are "contaminated" indicators which may need considerable refinement before they are an interpretable index in a particular study. For example, failure to return to work may reflect primarily local labor economic conditions and the patient's prior skill level and have little to do with health status at the end of the recovery period.

The above represents a general discussion of methodological issues intended to set the framework for more detailed comments later when specific types of studies are reviewed. The methodological issues are certainly complex to the point of appearing sometime intractable; moreover, they tend to be specific to a particular disease under study. For the area of cancer, Fox (1981a) and Morrison and Paffenbarger (1981) offer an excellent and detailed critique of the studies of the role of psychological factors in the rate of progression of cancer. Their compelling conclusion, incidentally, is that methodological weaknesses preclude any positive statements regarding the role of psychological factors.

In this chapter we shall give greater emphasis to studies in which the indices of recovery reflect a long-term rather than acute outcome and include some biomedical aspects of health status. Less emphasis will be given to studies of acute effects measured in purely behavioral terms. This selective emphasis is a reflection of the epidemiological orientation of this chapter as well as an attempt to reduce overlap with other chapters in this handbook.

From the perspective of this chapter, certain studies are designed to yield only trivial findings. Specifically, they correlate, cross-sectionally or over time, two or more measures which essentially tap the same underlying psychological or behavioral construct. A few examples will suffice:

1. Quality of life among former coronary artery bypass surgery patients is explored by correlating work status with desire to work or with perceptions of physical limitations (LaMendola and Pellegrini 1979).
2. Ego strength assessed at time of initial cancer diagnosis is associated with later ratings of the patient's use of effective coping strategies (Worden and Sobel 1978).
3. Self-reported expectations of family and friends regarding social functioning are correlated (cross-sectionally and over time) with self-reported social functioning among chronic dialysis patients (O'Brien 1980).

The point is that such correlations tell us very little beyond the temporal stability and "validity" (in the sense of alternate measures of the same broad construct) of such indicators. We would need several comparison groups—healthy subjects, patients with other diseases, individuals undergoing other crises—before we can begin to have faith that the findings have anything to do with the disease under study.

Survival Studies

It was already noted that data on broad social predictors of mortality, such as social class (Kitagawa and Hauser 1973; Syme and Berkman 1976) or bereavement (Jacobs and Ostfeld 1977; Helsing and Szklo 1981) do not provide enough information to rule out differences in risk factors, health habits, incidence, and medical care so that one can retain the one interpretation of interest, an independent psychosocial effect on case fatality. Mortality analyses in which there is a stratification on initial health status can be somewhat more informative; if the effect of the social variable is primarily among those with previous illnesses or disability, then it is more suggestive of the case fatality interpretation than if the effect is a broad one, showing up among the relatively healthy subjects as well. The Berkman and Syme (1979) report shows that the mortality gradient associated with their social network index is considerably steeper for those with disability, chronic conditions, or symptoms than for those with no health problems. This trend thus suggests that social networks may influence survival (case fatality). An analysis of follow-up mortality data from the Manitoba Aging Study (Mossey and Shapiro, 1982) has revealed that positive, global self-assessments of health are associated with lower mortality, after the contribution of a broad index of health status (based on self-reports of medical conditions, medical-care contacts, and objectively rated severity of conditions revealed by such contacts) had been partialed out. However, the protective effect appears to be similar in strength at different levels of health status, thus not encouraging a case fatality interpretation. The third set of analyses, not yet published (Zuckerman, Kasl, and Ostfeld 1981), come from a study of relocation among the elderly (Kasl et al. 1980); the results revealed a protective effect of religiousness (both feelings and behavior) on follow-up mortality, partialing out the effects of prior health status, based on a detailed medical history. Furthermore, this effect was only seen among those in poor health, thus supporting a case fatality interpretation. This interpretation is further strengthened by the finding that religiousness was not associated with the risk of hospitalizations during the follow-up period. Overall, these three studies suggest that social networks and religiousness, but not self-perceived health status, may act in a specific way to influence survival after illness.

The other reports reviewed in this section are more direct case fatality studies, as conventionally conceived, and of the role psychosocial factors may play in survival; they deal with cancer, open heart surgery, and survival after MI.

The early work on cancer progression-survival (Fox 1981a; Morrison and Paffenbarger 1981) is methodologically flawed (as noted earlier) and cannot generate positive conclusions. Two more recent studies are somewhat more promising (Derogatis, Ableoff, and Melisartos 1979; Gorzynski et al. 1980) and both suggest that breast cancer patients who express more emotional distress and have higher levels of anxiety and hostility (at the beginning of chemotherapy or prior to breast biopsy) have a longer survival. The biological mechanism involved is unclear, but at least one report clearly shows (Gorzynski et al. 1980) that the emotional expressiveness is a stable trait, not an acute reaction to the breast biopsy. Two other reports of cancer survival (Linden 1969; Lipworth, Abelin, and Connelly 1970) show a protective effect of a higher socioeconomic status. However, the proper interpretation of the results appears to be in terms of differential medical care rather than some characteristic of the patients themselves; social status does not influence survival except via differential medical care.

There are several reports on survival after open-heart surgery (Kilpatrick et al. 1975; Kimball 1969; Tufo and Ostfeld 1968) which suggest that higher levels of depression and impaired performance on the Digit Span subtest of the WAIS preoperatively are related to greater mortality after the surgery. It is not clear from these reports to what extent the degree of preoperative cardiac impairment and general poor health status can account for these results.

Survival after myocardial infarction has been examined in a number of studies (Bruhn, Chandler, and Wolf 1969; Doehrman 1977; Garrity 1981; Garrity and Klein 1971, 1975; Hrubec and Zukel 1971; Shapiro et al. 1970) and a reasonable pattern of results emerges. Those with longer survival time are more likely to be of higher socioeconomic status, white-collar (versus blue-collar) workers, married (rather than single), and lower on depression; during the acute phase, they show less evidence of behavioral disturbance and emotional upset, together with somewhat greater denial of illness. Some studies control for severity of the MI and history of coronary events (e.g., Garrity and Klein 1971, 1975), while many others do not appear to do so. Controlling for risk factors and medical status not only reduces the chances of confounding or spurious associations but may reveal interesting interactions as well. For example, Shapiro et al. (1970) found that when they stratified on presence versus absence of hypertension, excess mortality among blue-collar workers was observed to be only among the hypertension subjects.

The literature also contains one report on survival in myasthenia gravis (Meyer 1969); the results suggest a higher mortality among patients with emotional or psychiatric problems, with the increased risk particularly notable among the younger patients. However, lack of detail regarding methodology makes it difficult to evaluate the results.

Delayed Recovery in Infectious Conditions

Most of the studies in this section date from the 1950s and 1960s and are understandably vulnerable to methodological criticisms, such as their use of projective techniques and unstructured clinical asessments. But they have two advantages in comparison to studies of chronic conditions: (1) the acute onset tends to reduce the concern over possible confounding due to initial health status; and (2) biological, laboratory-based criteria of recovery are generally available and these tend to be independent (i.e., unconfounded) of psychosocial processes involving the patient and the care-givers; for example, conversion from positive to negative bacteriology among tuberculosis patients (Moran et al. 1956) and reduction in white blood cells and lymphocyte counts in infectious mononucleosis (Greenfield, Roessler, and Crosley 1959).

The bulk of the studies in this area (Brodman et al. 1947; Calden et al. 1960; Eifrig et al. 1961; Greenfield et al. 1959; Imboden 1972; Imboden, Canter, and Cluff 1961a; Imboden et al. 1959; Moran et al. 1956) tend to generate a consistent picture. Those who show delayed recovery tend to be higher on depression, hypochondriasis, and a variety of other clinical scales on the Cornell Service Index, the Cornell Medical Index, and the Minnesota Multiphasic Personality Inventory; their scores on self-esteem and ego strength are correspondingly lower. Sometimes greater life stress at time of acute infection is also found to delay recovery (Imboden et al. 1959). Some inconsistency is found in the two studies of tuberculosis patients with respect to the issue of adaptation to the hospital setting; one study (Moran et al. 1956) refers to the "docile amiability" of those who recover fastest, while the other (Calden et al. 1960) found that fast recoverers were rated by the nurses as less "cooperative" or "good" patients. The Brodman et al. (1947) study of military personnel found that their findings of greater personality disturbance among the delayed recoverers applied to white, but not black patients; also they noted that ward officers had considerable influence on the average length of hospitalization and such influence interacted with personality characteristics of the patients.

These findings do not particularly clarify the biological and/or behavioral mechanisms which may be involved. Imboden, Canter, and Cluff (1961b) offer a useful discussion of the possible ways emotional status or disturbance could influence recovery: (1) lack of cooperation and adherence; (2) elevating physiological parameters of "stress"; (3) as a direct influence on the disease process (unspecified); and (4) giving rise to its own symptoms (such as reports of listlessness and fatigue) which mask the illness or merge with it. It is particularly important for the reader to avoid making any facile connections between stress or distress and heightened susceptibility or immonosuppression. Recent reviews (e.g., Ader 1981; Fox 1981b; Rogers, Dubey, and Reich 1979) are in complete agreement on the conclusion that "stress" may enhance as well as decrease suscep- tibility to disease; the immune system is much too complex a network and a vari- ety of factors in the host, in the challenge to the host, and in the chronicity and in- tensity of the challenge must also be considered.

Course of Illness in Remitting (Mostly Chronic) Conditions

Weiner's (1977) comprehensive and scholarly review of a number of chronic diseases clearly reveals that we know very little about psychosocial factors which affect course of illness. There seems little doubt that attacks of asthma or hay fever show some temporal coexistence with emotional conditions (see also Backus and Dudley 1977), but it is difficult to be more precise about such a conclusion and to extend it to other diseases. The studies briefly discussed below reveal that there is no systematic and comprehensive research effort to deal with psychosocial in- fluences on the course of specific diseases; asthma is one possible exception. Con- sequently, the studies present a most fragmentary picture.

A few studies have concerned themselves with short-term fluctuations in emo- tional or behavioral factors and in disease condition. Moldovsky and Chester (1970) have observed a synchronicity in daily mood ratings of anxiety and hostil- ity with degree of pain, using a dolorimeter (an instrument which is a modified strain gauge and measures the pressure inducing joint tenderness when applied to the peripheral joints of the upper limb). On the other hand, Weisman (1956) was unable to link duodenal ulcer exacerbations with changes in depression or any other emotional factor. A couple of reports (Bradley 1979; Grant et al. 1974) have linked fluctuations in the condition of diabetics to levels of stressful life events; the voluminous research on behavioral factors in control of diabetes (Hamburg et al. 1980; Johnson 1980), suggests that the link with stressful life events operates via the mechanism of inadequate adherence to medical regimen.

Luborsky et al. (1976) studied recurrent herpes labialis (RHL) in nursing students. They found that the general unhappiness factor on the Clyde Mood Scale predicted the frequency of RHL during a one-year follow-up. However, in a daily follow-up of mood fluctuations, the onset of RHL was quite unrelated to any kinds of mood changes. It thus appears that subjects who had stable unhappy dispositions were at greater risk of RHL; but actual fluctuations in unhappiness were not associated with onset of RHL, which was just as likely to take place when students were relatively happy as unhappy. This is an unusually clear demonstra- tion of the significance of the state versus trait distinction.

In addition to acute fluctuations, studies have also examined course of illness from a longer term perspective. A couple of reports dealing with rheumatoid ar- thritis (Moos and Solomon 1964, 1965) suggest that rapid disease progression may be related to higher levels of anxiety and depression; patients whose disease pro- gressed more slowly, on the other hand, scored higher on scales relfecting com- pliance, conscientiousness, social responsibility, and denial of hostility. More anxious and depressed patients also have a higher level of functional incapacity for a given level of "objective" signs of disease. One study (Rogentine et al. 1979) has reported on relapse among patients with clinical Stage I or II malignant melanoma who were apparently disease free. Ratings of the amount of adjustment needed to cope with the illness were related to later relapse, with high scores (i.e., a lot of adjustment needed) being predictive of less relapse. This study involves careful methodology, including cross-validation of the prediction formula and controls on known biological prognostic factors. The finding is difficult to interpret but certainly appears consistent with the previously mentioned reports (Derogatis et al. 1979; Gorzynski et al. 1980) linking survival to greater emotional expressiveness. There is also a study of the natural history of multiple sclerosis (Kurtzke et al. 1977); the results indicate that the demographic and sociological variables which are known to be related to MS did not predict the subsequent course of illness over the next fifteen years. Symptoms at onset and laboratory findings at time of diagnosis also had no predictive power. Since neurologic and clinical status at five years after onset were highly predictive of course of illness during the next ten years, this suggests that the course of disease during the first five years is crucial, but unaccounted for by any of the data collected at time of diagnosis.

Many of the studies of course of illness deal with asthma patients, both children and adults. The role of family dynamics in the child's asthma has not been clearly pinned down. Two reports (Dubo et al. 1961; Pinkerton and Weaver 1970) reveal no association between the degree of disturbance in the family and the clinical course of the child's asthma, its symptomatology, or the response to medical treatment. However, a third report (Matus and Bush 1979) showed that attack frequency in a pediatric sample of asthmatics was predicted, in part, from a family adjustment rating (independently of pulmonary parameters, such as maximal midrespiratory flow rate). A fourth report (Purcell et al. 1969) also suggests an effect of the family, albeit somewhat indirectly; the specific experimental intervention of separation of the asthmatic children from the family (but caring for them in their own homes by a substitute parent) led to clinical improvement, but only—as predicted—for those children for whom the parents had listed various emotions as precipitants of asthma attacks.

A number of studies of adult asthmatics (Dirks et al. 1978; Dirks et al. 1977; Kinsman et al. 1977; Standenmayer et al. 1979) have utilized a new, MMPI-derived personality scale labeled Panic-Fear. A high score indicates a fearful emotional individual whose feelings are easily hurt, who feels helpless and is likely to give up. Asthmatics with high scores: (1) receive a more intensive oral corticosteroid regimen at time of discharge from a residential treatment facility (unrelated to pulmonary function differences); and (2) experience a longer hospitalization before eventual discharge. The latter finding was also observed for tuberculosis patients (Dirks et al. 1977) and was independent of bacteriological type and drug resistance. Panic-Fear scores also predict rehospitalization (Dirks et al. 1978); however, both very high and very low scores were associated with increased rates of rehospitalizations. This is a puzzling finding, but the ad hoc interpretation in terms of symptom exaggeration and helplessness, on the one hand, and symptom minimization and denial, on the other hand, with both leading to poor adherence, is not unconvincing. In any case, the best prediction of rehospitalization comes from utilizing both the Panic-Fear symptomatology and airways hyperreactivity data (Standenmayer et al. 1979). An earlier report (DeAraujo et al. 1973) revealing higher doses of steroids among asthmatics reporting more life events and scoring low on the Berle Index (of assets and adjustment) is broadly consistent with the Panic-Fear data, both suggesting level of distress influencing medication prescribing.

Many of the studies reviewed in this section, particularly those dealing with acute fluctuations and the work on asthma, are vulnerable to two serious disclaimers: (1) many indicators of health status and course of illness (such as length of hospitalization, rehospitalization, and strength of medication) may in fact be properly interpreted as indices of illness behavior, the results of blatant, or subtle, processes of influence and "negotiation" between the patient and the caregiver; (2) direction of causality between mood, distress, or psychological impairment, on the one hand, and adverse course of disease, on the other, is difficult to establish, particularly with naturalistic observations on "disease in progress."

Recovery in Cardiovascular Disease

A good deal of the literature considered in this section concerns recovery from CHD and several useful reviews are available (Croog, Levine, and Lurie 1968; Doehrman 1977; Garrity 1981; Krantz 1980). Least illuminating of the studies are those which focus on return to work. One finds that those likely to return to work are: younger; of higher social status; with previously sedentary white-collar jobs (rather than physically demanding blue-collar jobs); those who don't have to change place of employment; with good self-perception of health status; deniers; and those who are lower on anxiety and depression (Croog and Levine 1977; Doehrman 1977; Garrity 1981; Kellerman et al. 1968; Krantz 1980; Stern, Pascale, and McLoone 1976). Certainly many of these predictors are of general labor-economic significance and predict reemployment after job loss for a variety of reasons, such as plant closing or geographic mobility (Cobb and Kasl 1977; Sheppard, Belitsky, and Harvey 1966); they are particularly significant for the older workers (Parnes and King 1977). Even self-perceived status and anxiety-depression are general predictors of reemployment (Cobb and Kasl 1977), whether or not one has experienced an MI. Interestingly, the role of medical status variables after the MI is not clear; Doehrman (1977) suggests in his review that they are relatively unimportant in vocational adjustment, while Croog and Levine (1977) view them as crucially important, particularly among patients who experienced additional hospitalization during the first year after their initial MI.

The role of denial appears to be both important and complex. It seems to have broad benefits, going beyond vocational adjustment (Stern et al. 1976); it seems to have little effect on certain aspects of rehabilitation, such as exercise tolerance (Soleff and Bartel 1979); and it seems to interfere with compliance with medical advice regarding rest or smoking (Croog et al. 1971). In a way, denial appears to function similarly to strong work orientation (Davis and Eichhorn 1963; Willis and Dunsmore 1967); it promotes social role performance and psychological well-being but reduces compliance with medical regimen.

Return to work has also been studied in controlled trials with impressive and clean results (Block et al. 1974; Harpur et al. 1971); instituting early mobilization within two to three days of admission, rather than insisting on bed rest for several weeks, is associated with higher rates of returning to work after hospitalization.

There are also several follow-up studies of open-heart surgery patients, but problematic operationalizations of crucial variables make it hard to interpret such studies. Heller et al. (1974) measured one year postoperative outcome by having psychiatrists and surgeons rate "psychological hindrance to recovery" (i.e., the extent to which emotions and attitudes interfered with optimal convalescence); these ratings, they then report, are substantially correlated with patient's anxiety and depression. Brown and Rawlinson (1975, and 1977) measured rejection of the sick role, their central outcome variable, by determining from a semantic differential instrument the degree of similarity between the concepts "most persons who are sick" and "myself after heart surgery." Since the behavioral validity of this index is unclear, it is difficult to understand and interpret their findings, such as the greater similarity of the two concepts for female (versus male) patients or for patients who were more depressed and had a longer-lasting illness prior to surgery. Brown and Rawlinson (1976) have also examined the correlates of morale (life satisfaction) of open-heart surgery patients one year or later after surgery. Such cross-sectional analyses revealed associations with marital status, self-reports of physical symptoms, predisposition to depression, coping style, and so on. Since these are mostly general correlates of life satisfaction in any unselected population (e.g., Larson 1978), it is difficult to see how such data say anything specific about open-heart surgery.

One study has addressed the issue of predicting relief from angina among coronary artery bypass surgery patients (Pilowski, Spence, and Waddey 1979). Complete relief from angina at follow-up was associated with several attitudinal variables, assessed preoperatively: high responsiveness to reassurance, low interpersonal discord and irritability, low pain-related illness anxiety, and low health concern. These are interesting findings even though it is impossible to rule out possible confounding due to underlying traits which influence both the experiencing and reporting of angina pain, on the one hand, and the preoperative variables, on the other hand.

In general, many of the results in this section are of rather limited value when viewed from the perspective of the aims of this chapter. The outcome variables tend to be purely behavioral or psychological and data analysis does not resemble the kind of analytical schema (discussed in the section on Methodological Considerations) which would permit an assessment of the impact of psychosocial variables on health status, additive to the prognostic role of medical history and treatment variables.

Rehabilitation Process and Outcomes

Even though the general rehabilitation literature is quite large, much of it is not relevant to the aims of this chapter. The comments in this section are intended to convey the flavor of the studies which are at least indirectly relevant to our general concern, that of understanding the role of psychosocial factors in the course of disease.

This literature has its share of studies of return to work (e.g., Daughton et al. 1979; el Ghatit and Hanson 1978; Levenson and Green 1965) and, like those in the previous section, they contain few surprises. Postrehabilitation employment is related to: younger age, better education, higher IQ, being able to return to previous place of employment, engaging in an active job search, and being able to engage in crucial needed self-care activities.

If one assumes that rehabilitation treatment is effective in bringing about a higher level of health and functioning, then variables which influence the decision to enter a rehabilitation program, or the level of cooperation, should be distally related to such outcomes. Gray, Kesler, and Newman (1964) studied the decision of severely disabled older persons to participate in a free rehabilitation program and found that refusals were more likely to be: better off economically but with lower education; to have an unhappy family situation or unhappy marriage and to report little affection from spouse. Other variables, such as number of friends and frequency of contacts with them, or self-assessment of health status, showed no association with refusal of treatment. Ludwig and Adams (1968) found higher levels of cooperation in a rehabilitation center among subgroups whom they viewed as reflecting normal role relationships and social position which already contained elements of dependency or subordination: women, blacks, the unemployed, and those with more severe handicaps.

Rehabilitation outcomes tend to be better among those who have fewer psychological symptoms of depression and anxiety (Agle et al. 1973) and who have maintained a positive conception of self (Litman 1962). The role of social isolation in poor rehabilitation performance appears to be a strong one (Heyman 1972; Litman 1962); the best response is seen among those who are married, with children at home, receiving family encouragement and acceptance, and with a history of a high level of social participation in various organizations. The Hyman (1972) article contains a particularly useful discussion of the various possible links between social isolation and poor performance in rehabilitation.

The studies considered above included a mixture of conditions, and it is likely that specific conditions introduce additional and unique influences and contingencies affecting the rehabilitation process. For example, Gray, Reinhardt, and Ward (1969) compared two samples of severely disabled persons: those with cardiovascular disease (CVD) and those with a variety of other disabilities. The CVD were found to be higher on denial of illness and more reluctant to accept the illness realistically or to adopt the sick role. Such a finding makes it likely that different dynamics of rehabilitation success apply to the two groups.

Reactions to Surgery and Postsurgical Outcomes

Our coverage of the studies reviewed here will be brief and selective for two reasons: (1) the bulk of them deal with short-term acute effects in the psychological-behavioral area and their significance for long-term physical health status outcomes is generally not demonstrated; and (2) they are likely to receive extensive coverage in other chapters of this handbook.

A good deal of research in this area is concerned with coping with the stress and fear of surgery and with psychological preparation for it (Cohen and Lazarus 1979; Leventhal, Meyer, and Nerenz 1980; Reading 1979). Comparison of studies of recovery from illness with studies of recovery from surgery (Cohen and Lazarus 1979) would suggest that, for the latter, the role of anxiety and depression and additional life stresses is much less clearly demonstrated. When anxiety is the postsurgical outcome variable, then one generally sees a linear association with presurgical levels (Reading 1979), revealing a less than exciting temporal stability of this trait-state variable. The curvilinear association reported by Janis (1958, 1977), which showed the benefits of moderate levels of preoperative anxiety, has been difficult to replicate.

Above all, one sees a great specificity of findings which preclude broad generalizations and amply justify Reading's (1979) conclusion: "It seems likely that the effects of psychological preparation will vary according to the nature of the situation as well as the personality of the patient. It is necessary for studies to attend more clearly to individual differences" (p. 641). Here's a sampling of such specificity of results:

1. Patients with internal locus of control show better adjustment to dental surgery when given specific information, while those with external locus of control do better with general information (Auerbach et al. 1976).
2. Subjects who tend to deny or repress anxiety-provoking stimuli respond more poorly when given preparatory information than do those who tend to be sensitized to stressful stimuli (Shipley et al. 1978).
3. Patients with high levels of preoperative fear who reported receiving little information about surgery had poorer outcome (as measured by length of hospital stay, number of analgesics, postoperative negative affect), than patients with moderate levels of preoperative fear who received much information (Sime 1976).
4. Among patients awaiting hernia surgery, the benefits of receiving the experimental intervention of preparatory instruction were found to be strongest for those whose coping style was classified as "neutral," rather than for either sensitizers or repressors (Andrew 1970).
5. In a study of recovery from oral surgery (George et al. 1980) it was found that different outcome variables—postoperative pain, swelling and healing, interference with sleep and various activities—were explained by different sets of predictors.

It is interesting to note that so much of the research on surgical patients deals with preparatory information. However, one study which compared medical and surgical patients on "hospital stress" (Volicer, Isenberg, and Burns 1977) found that lack of information represented higher stress for medical patients than surgical ones. The latter group were more concerned with unfamiliarity of surroundings, loss of independence, and threat of severe illness. This would suggest that investigators have misplaced the emphasis in their research.

In general, it appears that the theoretical analysis of the issues in coping with illness and surgery is much richer and subtler (Cohen and Lazarus 1979; Leventhal, Meyer, and Nerenz 1980; Moos and Tsa 1977; Reading 1979) than the actual empirical studies. Important distinctions are being made with respect to types of coping (e.g., with fear versus with danger), varieties of coping skills, and the dynamics of different types of information (e.g., about disease and reasons for treatment, about procedures, about sensations and side effects, and about effective coping strategies). Actual studies have not yet operationalized these distinctions, either in their specific experimental manipulations or in their assessment procedures. And the close confounding between measuring coping styles and measuring psychological outcomes remains a serious problem. For example, there is a strong association between the sensitizer-repressor distinction and the reporting of symptoms of distress. Similarly, the marital coping style of advice seeking (versus self-reliance) in the work of Pearlin and Schooler (1978) is confounded with having or admitting to maritial problems.

There are a few studies which have looked at postoperative course from a somewhat longer term perspective. Stevenson et al. (1979) observed an associa⁺ tion between greater number of reported life events after surgery among duodenal ulcer patients and the greater severity of postoperative symptoms. However, the totally retrospective nature of these reports (going back as much as eight years) and the low participation rates make it difficult to accept the findings at face value. Another study of surgical outcomes among duodenal ulcer patients (Pascal and Thoroughman 1964) observed a link between poor surgical outcomes and a history of emotional deprivation in childhood; here, the retrospective method- ology is equally problematic. Two other studies have utilized prospective methodology. In one (Parbrook, Dalrymple, and Steel 1973), preoperatively assessed high scores on the Eysenck Neuroticism scale showed substantial relation- ships to such outcomes as percentage of vital capacity impairment and a chest complication score (based on such data as antibiotics prescribed, positive bacteriological examination of sputum, new and/or increased sputum production, and so on). The other study (Rundall 1978) examined the role of life change in recovery from a variety of surgical procedures; the results revealed extremely weak and inconsistent effects which did not offer clear support for the role of life events in either physiological arousal or sensitization to existing symptoms.

Modifying Factors and Mediating Processes

The studies which have been discussed present a very fragmentary picture. However, they are also rather unsatisfactory in that they give an incomplete pic- ture of the underlying processes and mechanisms. A better picture of such mechanisms permits more secure interpretations, suggests needed controls for confounded associations, and points toward possible therapeutic interventions. In this section we shall consider two topics briefly: (1) the role of significant others as a source of modifying factors; and (2) adherence to medical regimen as a prototype of mediating processes.

The role of significant others is a neutral label intended to encompass the cur- rently "hot" topics of social support and social networks as well as the older work on social isolation and referral networks. There is no dearth of recent publications which lay out the argument for the importance of this set of constructs and offer theoretical and methodological refinements (Berkman 1980; Cobb 1976; Dean and Lin 1977; Kaplan, Cassel, and Gore 1977; Levin and Idler 1981; Lin et al. 1979; McKinley 1980; Mueller 1980; Porritt 1979; Walker, McBride, and Vachon 1977).

The role of significant others appears particularly important in serious chronic illnesses where the postacute recovery phase takes place outside of formal medical- care settings; for example, Croog, Lipson, and Levine (1972) found that patients after first MI made minimal use of institutional and professional services and relied instead on family, kin, and friends. The home may be the preferred setting for long-term care (Mitchell 1978), but the benefits in specific instances may be primarily social-behavioral rather than clinical-biological (Hill, Hampton, and Mitchell 1978). However, certain chronic conditions may put too much burden on the family and the home setting becomes less preferred; Marshall et al (1975) found that dialysis home training may represent too much of stress and demand for older couples. They also report the paradoxical finding that some level of hostility and anger in spouse may enhance patient adaptation to training.

The role of significant others in the course of brief illnesses or acute, episodic contacts with the medical-care system may be smaller. For example, Petroni (1969, 1971) found no associations between support from spouse in illness and sick role and reports of illnesses, frequency of seeing a doctor, or length of illness episodes. However, episodic contacts under threatening emergency circumstances may still reveal the benefit of social support; Linn, Ware, and Greenfield (1980) reported that relief from chest pain following emergency care was greater for patients who shared the decision to seek care with the spouse or relative and were accompanied to the emergency room by them.

There are several points worth making with respect to the social support literature and its relevance to course of disease. One is that the currently dominant formulations give too much emphasis to social support as a protective buffer or as a facilitation of "good" outcomes and not enough emphasis to social support as part of a broader process of social influence. As such, social influence may direct people in diverse directions, with either beneficial or adverse consequences for health status. Integration in social networks can interfere with medical treatment (e.g., McKinley 1973; Nall and Speilberg 1968) if one belongs to social groups which discourage participation. Social support may also delay the giving up of the sick role. Hyman (1975) observed greater levels of social disability among those who got preferential treatment in social relationships because of their condition. Cobb and Kasl (1977) found that among men who lost their jobs, the association between initially poor health and longer unemployment after plant closing was considerably stronger among men who reported high levels of social support.

The second point to be made is that there is still much to be learned about how social support versus isolation may operate (e.g., Hyman 1972), and why one or another aspect of the social relationship may or may not have a particular effect. For example, Litman (1962, 1974) has noted that family solidarity, marital happiness, egalitarianism, and close ties do not necessarily represent a special buffer against the disruptive effects of a family member's severe illness. The role of the mother-wife appears crucial and her illness is more disruptive; the wife's social support appears to influence the husband's illness and illness behavior more than the husband's support influences the wife. Other work also suggests complexity of the social support dynamics; control of tuberculosis is particularly poor among social isolates (Berry, Ross, and Deuschle 1963; Pragoff 1962), but the data on diabetes (Williams et al. 1967) seem to suggest just the opposite. Social support may also have a small role to play in facilitating alterations of intractable health habits, such as smoking and overeating (Kasl 1975); social support from friends for quitting smoking or the number of friends who are trying to quit does not seem to facilitate smoking cessation, while having nonsmokers (who may or may not be supportive) among one's friends does help.

The final point to be made regarding the research on social support is that we need a greater appreciation of the possible individual differences in the need to be part of social networks, in the need for social support. Social support, after all, implies reciprocal obligations and one may not wish to enter a network of such relationships. A life-long pattern of social isolation is quite different from recent, involuntary reductions in social interaction (Lowenthal and Boler 1965) and one must try to distinguish types of social isolation. We must also attempt to assess the extent of adaptation to isolation, even if involuntary. Rosow (1967), for example, found that complaints of the elderly about care when ill were not related to density of age peers or to socialization, suggesting perhaps that solitary elderly may develop more independence, as well as lower expectations of help.

Let us now turn briefly to the second topic of this section, adherence to medical regimen. To the extent that medical regimens influence the course of disease, the study of compliance or adherence is probably the most fruitful examination of mediating processes which take place at the behavioral level. The compliance literature is one of the most exhaustively reviewed and indexed areas of sociomedical research (Becker 1974; Blackwell 1972; Haynes, Taylor, and Sackett 1979; Kasl 1975; Kirscht and Rosenstock 1979; Marston 1970; Sackett and Haynes 1976; Wilson 1973) and there would be no point in attempting to summarize it here. Compliance includes a great variety of behaviors which are poorly related to each other and not particularly stable over time. A great deal of specificity of results exists which is due to the type of disease or condition. Adherence issues in controlling high blood pressure (Kasl 1978), a paradigmatic "at-risk" role (Baric, 1969), are vastly different from issues in chronic hemodialysis (De-Nour and Czaczkes 1972; Goldstein 1976; Marshall et al. 1975; Procci 1978; Yanagida, Strelzer, and Siemsen 1981).

We must also remember that biological outcomes need not be closely associated with level of adherence; psychosocial variables may influence adherence itself as well as the link between adherence and biological status. For example, there are several reports (Finnerty, Shaw, and Himmelsback 1973; Haynes et al. 1976; Henderson et al. 1974; Syme 1978) which suggest that stepped-up care appears to attain better blood pressure control above and beyond better compliance with medication; this may be interpretable in terms of some reduction in general distress if the stepped-up care is a fairly broad social intervention as well (Brody 1980).

The compliance literature has obvious general relevance to course of disease, though its precise relevance is difficult to pin down. Close adherence is needed in hemodialysis or diabetes, but noncompliance with medication involved in prophylactic treatment may have consequences for only a few. Adhering to regularly scheduled clinic visits among arthritis patients (Geersten, Gray, and Ward 1973) is likely to have little influence on the long term course of the illness; sign-outs against medical advice from a coronary care unit (Baile et al. 1979) may have few adverse consequences, particularly since it is done by the less seriously ill patients. More serious consequences can be expected for those with irregular discharge from a tuberculosis hospital (Moran, Fairweather, and Morton 1956; Rorabaugh and Guthrie 1953).

Sociodemographic characteristics and stable personality traits have traditionally explained a limited amount of variance in adherence behavior; and a good deal of specificity of results is evident. For example, the dimension of internal versus external locus of control interacts with the nature of regimen and the specific behaviors it calls for; only when the control orientation is congruent with the behavioral demands of the regimen is this dimension related to adherence (e.g., Best and Steffy 1975; Kirscht and Rosenstock 1977; Lewis, Morisky, and Flynn 1978).

The role of significant others is evident in much of the compliance work. Such varied behaviors as medication errors (Schwartz et al. 1962), drug defaulting

(Porter 1969), dietary abuse in hemodialysis (Procci 1978), and adherence to a hand resting splint regimen among arthritics (Oakes et al. 1970) are all sensitive to social isolation or social support influences. Inability to establish friendship networks in a hospital setting is predicitve of irregular discharge among tuberculosis patients (Calden et al. 1956). An intriguing finding has been recently reported by Brody (1980), who interviewed patients immediately after they saw their physicians, and determined errors made by patients in recalling the therapeutic regimens; patients living alone made more errors (above and beyond the effect of numbers of medications and ancillary measures). This suggests that social network variables may exert their influence in settings that intuitively would seem rather remote.

Seriousness of the disease and level of knowledge about the regimen and/or the illness have also been extensively examined in the compliance literature, and a picture of complex relationships again emerges. In general, perceiving one's condition as serious and/or having a serious condition is related to better compliance; however, serious conditions tend to call for more complex and demanding regimens which result in lower compliance (e.g., Charney 1972; Davis 1968; Marston 1970). Of course, perceived seriousness is a central concept in the Health Belief Model and its role continues to be extensively studied. The role of knowledge in compliance suggests again a complex picture, similar to that which emerged in our review of role of information in reactions to surgery. Certainly, specific information about the regimen is helpful in compliance (Kirscht and Rosenstock 1979); often, this is simply a necessary, logical relationship. However, for relatively simple and not exceedingly demanding regimens, such as those involved in control of high blood pressure, knowledge of regimen may be of dubious value (Taylor et al. 1978). Knowledge about disease tends to make relatively little difference, particularly among those who have a rich previous experience with their own condition, its management, and the relevant medical-care system (e.g., Tagliacozzo and Ima 1970). In a way, level of knowledge about illness is a byproduct of the illness experience rather than an independent variable influencing the course of disease and its management. For example, one study (Williams et al. 1967) found poorer control of diabetes among those with better knowledge of the disease and of the required regimen; surely, this surprising finding is because inadequate control precipitates medical crises which become compelling opportunities for learning about the disease.

Concluding Comment

The topic of this chapter encompasses a large and varied area of research which offers an exquisite challenge to the *methodologist*. The most fundamental and persistent problem is the need to have an adequate assessment of health status (at the initial point from which course of disease is examined) and an analytical schema, which controls for the effect of initial status on later outcome, thereby allowing for a relatively convincing demonstration of the role of psychosocial factors. Failing to address this problem raises the possibility that the psychosocial factors are mere epiphenomena, byproducts of the changes taking place at the biological level but with no causal influence on biological functioning. Such broad criticism has to be tempered by the acknowledgment that existing assessment methodologies are as yet inadequate to the task of quantifying disease-specific health status, severity of illness and comorbidity. Even at the broad level of general research design, easy solutions are unavailable. For example, the theoretically ideal design of a prospective study of incidence which is then converted into a course of disease study would have the great advantage of a predisease assessment of psychosocial factors. However, this is an infeasible and/or very expensive solution for most of the chronic diseases. In spite of the difficulty of improving existing methodology, the impression remains, from reviewing such studies, that investigators are inadequately sensitive to how damaging the confounding problem can be. A typical example: The Linn et al. (1980) study showed greater relief from chest pain following emergency care for those who shared the decision to seek care with spouse or relative and were accompanied to the ER by them. However, if patients without social support delay seeking care until their condition is considerably worse, then the finding obtained cannot be interpreted as the effect of social support on relief of chest pain.

The topic of this chapter also offers a challenge to the *theorist*, albeit a different kind of challenge. Any fondness for developing broad principles of human functioning has to be suppressed in order to pay attention to the specific dynamics of a particular disease situation or a particular treatment setting. The great need is to develop a better appreciation of individual differences in crucial characteristics of patients and to develop interactive rather than univariate formulations. Low level constructs are useful, while higher order constructs (such as adherence, which encompasses a variety of behaviors) get us in trouble since they represent a premature commitment to some functional equivalence of the various behaviors subsumed under the higher order construct. The need for interactive formulations and low level constructs can be seen in the following example. The effect of providing information depends on, at least, the following: the role expectations of the patient (about patient and doctor roles), previous disease and treatment history, level of anxiety, coping style, perceived control (locus of control), type of information, the behaviors the situation calls for, and the link of these behaviors to health status.

REFERENCES

ADER, R. 1981. Behavior influences on immune responses. In *Perspectives on behavioral medicine*, ed. S. M. Weiss, J. A Herd, and B. H. Fox. New York: Academic Press.

AGLE, D. P.; BAUM, G. L.; CHESTER, E. H.; and WENDT, M. 1973. Multidiscipline treatment of chronic pulmonary insufficiency. I. Psychologic aspects of rehabilitation. *Psychosomatic Medicine* 35: 41–49.

ALBRECHT, G. L., and HIGGINS, P. C. 1977. Rehabilitation success: the interrelationships of multiple criteria. *Journal of Health and Social Behavior* 18: 36–45.

ANDREW, J. M. 1970. Recovery from surgery, with and without preparatory instruction, for three coping styles. *Journal of Personality and Social Psychology* 15: 223–26.

AUERBACH, S. M.; KENDALL, P. C.; CUTTLER, H. F.; and LEVITT, N. R. 1976. Anxiety, locus of control, type of preparatory information, and adjustment to dental surgery. *Journal of Consulting and Clinical Psychology* 44: 809–18.

BACKUS, F. I., and DUDLEY, D. L. 1977. Observations of psychosocial factors and their relationship to organic disease. In *Psychosomatic medicine: current trends and clinical applications*, ed. Z. J. Lipowski, D. R. Lipsitt, and P. C. Whybrow. New York: Oxford University Press.

BAILE, W. F.; BRINKER, J. A.; WACHSPRESS, J. D.; and ENGEL; B. T. 1979. Signouts against medical advice from a Coronary Care Unit. *Journal of Behavioral Medicine* 2: 85–92.

BARIC, L. 1969. Recognition of the "at-risk" role: a means to influence health behavior. *International Journal of Health Education* 12: 24–34.

BECKER, M. H., ed. 1974. The health belief model and personal health behavior *Health Education Monographs* 2: 326–473.

BERKMAN, L. F. 1980. Physical health and the social environment: a social epidemiological perspective. In *The relevance of social science for medicine*, ed. L. Eisenberg and A. Kleinman. Boston: Reidel.

————, and SYME, S. L. 1979. Social networks, host resistance, and mortality: a nine-year follow-up of Alameda County residents. *American Journal of Epidemiology* 109: 186–204.

BERRY, D.; ROSS, A.; and DEUSCHLE, K. 1963. Tuberculous patients treated at home. *American Review of Respiratory Diseases* 88: 769–72.

BEST, J. A., and STEFFY, R. A. 1975. Smoking modification procedures for internal and external locus of control. *Canadian Journal of Behavioral Science* 7: 155–65.

BLACKWELL, B. 1972. The drug defaulter. *Clinical Pharmacology and Therapeutics* 13: 841–48.

BLOCH, A.; MAEDER, J.; HAISSLY, J.; FELIX, J.; and BLACKBURN, H. 1974. Early mobilization after myocardial infarction: a controlled study. *American Journal of Cardiology* 34: 152–57.

BRADLEY, C. 1979. Life events and the control of diabetes mellitus. *Journal of Psychosomatic Research* 23: 159–62.

BRODMAN, K.; MITTELLMANN, B.; WECHSLER, D.; WEIDER, A.; and WOLFF, H. G. 1947. The relation of personality disturbances to duration of convalescence from acute respiratory infections. *Psychosomatic Medicine* 9: 37–44.

BRODY, D. S. 1980a. An analysis of patient recall of their therapeutic regimens. *Journal of Chronic Diseases* 33: 57–63.

————. 1980b. Psychological distress and hypertension control. *Journal of Human Stress* 6: 2–6.

BROWN, J. S., and RAWLINSON, M. 1975. Relinquishing the sick role following open-heart surgery. *Journal of Health and Social Behavior* 16: 12–27.

————. 1976. The morale of patients following open-heart surgery. *Journal of Health and Social Behavior* 17: 135–45.

————. 1977. Sex differences in sick role rejection and in work performance following cardiac surgery. *Journal of Health and Social Behavior* 18: 276–92.

BRUHN, J. G.; CHANDLER, B.; and WOLF, S. 1969. A psychological study of survivors and nonsurvivors of myocardial infarction. *Psychosomatic Medicine* 31: 8–19.

CALDEN, G.; DUPERTUIS, C. W.; HOKANSON, J. E.; and LEWIS, W. C. 1960. Psychosomatic factors in the rate of recovery from tuberculosis. *Psychosomatic Medicine* 22: 345–55.

CALDEN, G.; THURSTON, J. R.; LEWIS, W. C.; and LORENZ, T. H. 1956. A psychological scale for predicting irregular discharge in tuberculosis patients. *American Review of Tuberculosis* 73: 338–50.

CHARNEY, E. 1972. Patient-doctor communication: implications for the clinician. *Pediatric Clinics of North America* 19: 263–79.

COBB, S. 1976. Social supports as a moderator of life stress. *Psychosomatic Medicine* 38: 300–14.

————., and KASL, S. V. 1977. *Termination: the consequences of job loss.* U.S.D.H.E.W., Career Development Center: DHEW Pub. no. (NIOSH) 76–1261.

COHEN, F., and LAZARUS, R. S. 1979. Coping with the stress of illness. In *Health psychology*, ed. G. C. Stone, F. Cohen, and N. E. Adler. San Francisco, Calif.: Jossey-Bass.

COTTINGTON, E. M.; MATTHEWS, K. A.; TALBOTT, E.; and KULLER, L. H. 1980. Environmental events preceding sudden death in women. *Psychosomatic Medicine* 42: 567–74.

CROOG, S. H., and FITZGERALD, E. F. 1978. Subjective stress and serious illness of a spouse: wives of heart patients. *Journal of Health and Social Behavior* 19: 166–78.

CROOG, S. H., and LEVINE, S. 1977. *The heart patient recovers.* New York: Human Sciences Press.

———; and LURIE, Z. 1968. The heart patient and the recovery process. *Social Science and Medicine* 2: 111–64.

CROOG, S. H.; LIPSON, A.; and LEVINE, S. 1972. Help patterns in severe illness: the roles of kin network, non-family resources, and institutions. *Journal of Marriage and the Family* 34: 32–41.

CROOG, S. H.; SHAPIRO, D. S.; and LEVINE, S. 1971. Denial among heart patients: an empirical study. *Psychosomatic Medicine* 33: 385–97.

DAUGHTON, D. M.; FIX, A. J.; KASS, I.; PATIL, K. D.; and BELL, C. W. 1979. Physiological-intellectual components of rehabilitation success in patients with chronic obstructive pulmonary disease (COPD). *Journal of Chronic Diseases* 32: 405–9.

DAVIS, M. S. 1968. Physiologic, psychological, and demographic factors in patient compliance with doctors' orders. *Medical Care* 6: 115–22.

———., and EICHHORN, R. L. 1963. Compliance with medical regimens: a panel study. *Journal of Health and Human Behavior* 4: 240–49.

DEAN, A., and LIN, N. 1977. The stress-buffering role of social support: problems and prospects for systematic investigation. *Journal of Nervous and Mental Disease* 165: 403–17.

DEARAUJO, G.; VANARSDEL, P. P.; HOLMES, T. H.; and DUDLEY, D. L. 1973. Life change, coping ability and chronic intrinsic asthma. *Journal of Psychosomatic Research* 17: 359–63.

DEMBROSKI, T. M.; WEISS, S. M.; and SHIELDS, J. L., eds. 1978. *Coronary-prone behavior.* New York: Springer-Verlag.

DE-NOUR, A. K., and CZACZKES, J. W. 1972. Personality factors in chronic hemodialysis patients causing noncompliance with medical regimen. *Psychosomatic Medicine* 34: 333–44.

DEROGATIS, L. R.; ABELOFF, M. D.; and MELISARTOS, N. 1979. Psychological coping mechanisms and survival time in metastatic breast cancer. *Journal of the American Medical Association* 242: 1504–8.

DIRKS, J. F.; KINSMAN, R. A.; HORTON, D. J.; FROSS, K. H.; and JONES, N. F. 1978. Panic-fear in asthma: rehospitalization following intensive long-term treatment. *Psychosomatic Medicine* 40: 5–13.

DIRKS, J. F.; KINSMAN, R. A.; JONES, N. F.; SPECTOR, S. L.; DAVIDSON, P. T.; and EVANS, N. W. 1977. Panic-fear: a personality dimension related to length of hospitalization in respiratory illness. *Journal of Asthma Research* 14: 61–71.

DOEHRMAN, S. R. 1977. Psychosocial aspects of recovery from coronary heart disease: a review. *Social Science and Medicine* 11: 199–218.

DONEGAN, W. L.; HARTZ, A. J.; and RIMM, A. A. 1978. The association of body weight with recurrent cancer of the breast. *Cancer* 41: 1590–94.

DUBO, S.; MCLEAN, J. R.; CHING, A. Y. T.; WRIGHT, H. L.; KAUFMAN, P. E., and SHELDON, J. M. 1961. A study of the relations between family situation, bronchial asthma, and personal adjustment in children. *Journal of Pediatrics* 59: 402–14.

EIFRIG, D. E.; IMBODEN, J. B.; MCKUSICK, V. A.; and CANTER, A. D. 1961. Constrictive pericarditis: psychological aspects of convalescence following pericardectomy. *Journal of Chronic Diseases* 13: 52–58.

EL GHATIT, Z. A., and HANSON, R. W. 1978. Variables associated with obtaining and sustaining employment among spinal cord injured males: a follow-up of 760 veterans. *Journal of Chronic Diseases* 31: 363–69.

FINNERTY, F. A.; SHAW, L. W.; and HIMMELSBACK, C. K. 1973. Hypertension in the inner city. II. Detection and follow-up. *Circulation* 47: 76–78.

FOX, B. H. 1981a. A psychological measure as a predictor in cancer. In *Psychological aspects of cancer,* ed. J. Cohen, W. Cullen, and L. R. Martin. New York: Raven Press.

———. 1981b. Psychosocial factors and the immune system in human cancer. In *Psychoneuroimmunology,* ed. R. Ader. New York: Academic Press.

GARRITY, T. F. 1981. Behavioral adjustment after myocardial infarction: a selective review of recent descriptive, correlational, and intervention research. In *Perspectives on behavioral medicine*, ed. S. M. Weiss, J. A. Herd, and B. H. Fox. New York: Academic Press.

———., and KLEIN, R. F. 1971. A behavioral predictor of survival among heart attack patients. In *Prediction of life span*, ed. E. Palmore and F. C. Jeffers. Lexington, Mass.: D.C. Heath.

———. 1975. Emotional response and clinical severity as early determinants of six month mortality after myocardial infarction. *Heart and Lung* 4: 730–37.

GEERTSEN, H. R.; GRAY, R. M.; and WARD, J. R. 1973. Patient non-compliance within the context of seeking medical care for arthritis. *Journal of Chronic Diseases* 26: 689–98.

GEORGE, J. M.; SCOTT, D. S.; TURNER, S. P.; and GREGG, J. M. 1980. The effects of psychological factors and physical trauma on recovery from oral surgery. *Journal of Behavioral Medicine* 3: 291–310.

GOLDSTEIN, A. M. 1976. Denial and external locus of controls as mechanisms of adjustment in chronic medical illness. *Essence* 1: 5–22.

GORZYNSKI, J. G.; HOLLAND, J.; KATZ, J. L.; WEINER, H.; ZUMOFF, B.; FUKUSHIMA, D.; and LEVIN, J. 1980. Stability of ego defenses and endocrine responses in women prior to breast biopsy and ten years later. *Psychosomatic Medicine* 42: 323–28.

GRANT, I.; KYLE, G. C.; TEICHMAN, A.; and MENDELS, J. 1974. Recent life events and diabetes in adults. *Psychosomatic Medicine* 36: 121–28.

GRAY, R. M.; KESLER, J. P.; and NEWMAN, W. R. E. 1964. Social factors influencing the decision of severely disabled older persons to participate in a rehabilitation program. *Rehabilitation Literature* 25: 162–67.

GRAY, R. M.; REINHARDT, A. M.; and WARD, J. R. 1969. Psychosocial factors involved in the rehabilitation of persons with cardiovascular diseases. *Rehabilitation Literature* 30: 354–59.

GREENFIELD, N. S.; ROESSLER, R.; and CROSLEY, A. P., JR. 1959. Ego strength and length of recovery from infectious mononucleosis. *Journal of Nervous and Mental Disease* 128: 125–28.

HAMBURG, B. A.; LIPSETT, L. F.; INOFF, G. E.; and DRASH, A. L., eds. 1980. *Behavioral and psychosocial issues in diabetes*. NIH Pub. no. 80–1993. Washington, D.C.: Government Printing Office.

HARPUR, J.; KELLETT, R.; CONNER, W.; GALBRAITH, H.; HAMILTON, M.; MURRAY, J.; SWALLOW, J.; and ROSE, G. 1971. Controlled trial of early mobilization and discharge from hospital in uncomplicated myocardial infarction. *Lancet* 2: 1331–34.

HAYNES, R. B.; GIBSON, E. S.; HACKETT, B. C.; SACKETT, D. L.; TAYLOR, D. W.; ROBERTS, R. S.; and JOHNSON, A. L. 1976. Improvement of medication compliance in uncontrolled hypertension. *Lancet* 1: 1265–68.

HAYNES, R. B.; TAYLOR, D. W.; and SACKETT, D. L., eds. 1979. *Compliance in health care*. Baltimore, Md.: Johns Hopkins University Press.

HELLER, S. S.; FRANK, K. A.; KORNFELD, D. S.; MALM, J. R.; and BOWMAN, F. O., JR. 1974. Psychological outcome following open-heart surgery. *Archives of Internal Medicine*. 134: 908–14.

HELSING, K. J., and SZKLO, M. 1981. Mortality after bereavement. *American Journal of Epidemiology* 114: 41–52.

HENDERSON, M.; APOSTOLIDES, A.; ENTWISLE, G.; and HEBEL, R. 1974. A study of hypertension in a Black urban community: preliminary epidemiologic findings. *Preventive Medicine* 3: 334–43.

HILL, J.; HAMPTON, J.; and MITCHELL, J. 1978. A randomized trial of home-versus-hospital management for patients with suspected myocardial infarction. *Lancet* 2: 837–41.

HRUBEC, Z., and ZUKEL, W. I. 1971. Socioeconomic differentials in prognosis following episodes of coronary heart disease. *Journal of Chronic Diseases* 23: 881–89.

HYMAN, M. D. 1972. Social isolation and performance in rehabilitation. *Journal of Chronic Diseases* 25: 85–97.

——. 1975. Social psychological factors affecting disability among ambulatory patients. *Journal of Chronic Diseases* 28: 199–216.

IMBODEN, J. B. 1972. Psychosocial determinants of recovery. In *Psychosocial aspects of physical illness*, ed. Z. J. Lipowski. Vol. 8: *Advances in psychosomatic medicine*. Basel: S. Karger.

——; CANTER, A.; and CLUFF, L. E. 1961a. Convalescence from influenza. *Archives of Internal Medicine* 108: 393–99.

——. 1961b. Symptomatic recovery from medical disorders. *Journal of the American Medical Association* 178: 1182–84.

——; and TREVER, R. W. 1959. Brucellosis: III. Psychologic aspects of delayed convalescence. *Archives of Internal Medicine* 103: 406–14.

JACO, E. G., ed. 1979. *Patients, physicians, and illness: a sourcebook in behavioral science and health*. 3d ed. New York: Free Press.

JACOBS, S., and OSTFELD, A. 1974. An epidemiological review of the mortality of bereavement. *Psychosomatic Medicine* 39: 344–57.

JANIS, I. L. 1958. *Psychological stress*. New York: Wiley.

——. 1977. Adaptive personality changes. In *Stress and coping: an anthology*, ed. A. Monat and R. S. Lazarus. New York: Columbia University Press.

JENKINS, C. D.; ZYZANSKI, S.; and ROSENMAN, R. 1976. Risk of new myocardial infarction in middle-aged men with manifest coronary heart disease. *Circulation* 53: 342–47.

JOHNSON, S. B. 1980. Psychosocial factors in juvenile diabetes: a review. *Journal of Behavioral Medicine* 3: 95–116.

KAPLAN, B. H.; CASSEL, J.; and GORE, S. 1977. Social support and health. Medical Care 15 (suppl. to no. 5): 47–58.

KASL, S. V. 1975a. Issues in patient adherence to health care regimens. *Journal of Human Stress* 1: 5–17, 48.

——. 1975b. Social-psychological characteristics associated with behaviors which reduce cardiovascular risk. In *Applying behavioral science to cardiovascular risk*, ed. A. J. Enelow and J. B. Henderson. New York: American Heart Association.

——. 1978. A social-psychological perspective on successful community control of high blood pressure: a review. *Journal of Behavioral Medicine* 1: 347–81.

——; EVANS, A. S.; and NIEDERMAN, J. C. 1979. Psychosocial risk in the development of infectious mononucleosis. *Psychosomatic Medicine* 41: 445–66.

KASL, S. V.; OSTFELD, A. M.; BRODY, G. M.; SNELL, L.; and PRICE, C. A. 1980. Effects of "involuntary" relocation on the health and behavior of the elderly. In *Second conference on the epidemiology of aging*, ed. S. G. Haynes and M. Feinleib. NIH pub. no. 80–969. Washington, D.C.: Government Printing Office.

KELLERMAN, J. J.; MODAN, B.; LEVY, M.; FELDMAN, S.; and KARIV, I. 1968. Return to work after myocardial infarction. *Geriatrics* 23: 151–56.

KILPATRICK, D. G.; MILLER, W. C.; ALLAIN, A. N.; HUGGINS, M. B.; and LEE, W. H., JR. 1975. The use of psychological test data to predict open-heart surgery outcome: a prospective study. *Psychosomatic Medicine* 37: 62–73.

KIMBALL, C. P. 1969. Psychological responses to the experience of open-heart surgery. *American Journal of Psychiatry* 126: 348–59.

KINSMAN, R. A.; DAHLEM N. W.; SPECTOR, S.; and STAUDENMAYER, H. 1977. Observations on subjective symptomatology, coping behavior, and medical decisions in asthma. *Psychosomatic Medicine* 39: 102–19.

KIRSCHT, J. P., and ROSENSTOCK, I. M. 1977. Patient adherence to antihypertensive medical regimens. *Journal of Community Health* 3: 115–24.

——. 1979. Patients' problems in following recommendations of health experts. In *Health psychology*, ed. G. C. Stone, F. Cohen, and N. E. Adler. San Francisco, Calif.: Jossey-Bass.

KITAGAWA, E. M., and HAUSER, P. M. 1973. *Differential mortality in the United States*. Cambridge, Mass.: Harvard University Press.

KRANTZ, D. S. 1980. Cognitive processes and recovery from heart attack: a review and theoretical analysis. *Journal of Human Stress* 6: 27–38.

———; SANMARCO, M. I.; SELVESTER, R. H.; and MATTHEWS, K. A. 1979. Psychological correlates of progression of atherosclerosis in men. *Psychosomatic Medicine* 41: 467–75.

KULLER, L. H. 1976. Epidemiology of cardiovascular diseases: current perspectives. *American Journal of Epidemiology* 104: 425–56.

KURTZKE, J. F.; BEEBE, G. W.; NAGLER, B.; KURLAND, L. T.; and AUTH, T. L. 1977. Studies on the natural history of multiple sclerosis-8. Early prognostic features of the later course of the illness. *Journal of Chronic Diseases* 30: 819–30.

LaMENDOLA, W. F., and PELLEGRINI, R. V. 1979. Quality of life and coronary artery bypass surgery patients. *Social Science and Medicine* 13A: 457–61.

LARSON, R. 1978. Thirty years of research on the subjective well-being of older Americans. *Journal of Gerontology* 33: 109–25.

LEVENSON, B., and GREEN, J. 1965. Return to work after severe disability. *Journal of Chronic Diseases* 18: 167–80.

LEVENTHAL, H.; MEYER, D.; and NERENZ, D. 1980. The common sense representation of illness danger. In *Medical psychology*, ed. S. Rachman, vol. 2. New York: Pergamon Press.

LEVIN, L. S., and IDLER, E. L. 1981. *The hidden health care system: mediating structures and medicine.* Cambridge, Mass.: Ballinger, 1981.

LEWIS, F. M.; MORISKY, D. E.; and FLYNN, B. S. 1978. A test of the construct validity of health locus of control: effects on self-reported compliance for hypertensive patients. *Health Education Monographs* 6: 138–48.

LIN, N.; SIMEONE, R. S.; ENSEL, W. M.; and KUO, W. 1979. Social support, stressful life events, and illness: a model and an empirical test. *Journal of Health and Social Behavior* 20: 108–19.

LINDEN, G. 1969. The influence of social class in the survival of cancer patients. *American Journal of Public Health* 59: 267–74.

LINN, L. S.; WARE, J. E.; and GREENFIELD, S. 1980. Factors associated with relief from chest pain following emergency care. *Medical care* 18: 624–34.

LIPOWSKI, Z. J.; LIPSITT, D. R.; and WHYBROW, P. C., eds. 1977. *Psychosomatic medicine: current trends and clinical applications.* New York: Oxford University Press.

LIPWORTH, L.; ABELIN, T.; and CONNELLY, R. R. 1970. Socioeconomic factors in the prognosis of cancer patients. *Journal of Chronic Diseases* 23: 105–16.

LITMAN, T. J. 1962. The influence of self-conception and life orientation factors in the rehabilitation of the orthopedically disabled. *Journal of Health and Human Behavior* 3: 249–57.

———. 1974. The family as a basic unit in health and medical care: a social behavioral overview. *Social Science and Medicine* 8: 495–519.

LOWENTHAL, M. F., and BOLER, D. 1965. Voluntary vs. involuntary social withdrawal. *Journal of Gerontology* 20: 363–71.

LUBORSKY, L.; MINTZ, J.; BRIGHTMAN, V. J.; and KATCHER, A. H. 1976. Herpes simplex virus and moods: a longitudinal study. *Journal of Psychosomatic Research* 20: 543–48.

LUDWIG, E. G., and ADAMS, S. D. 1968. Patient cooperation in a rehabilitation center: assumption of the client role. *Journal of Health and Social Behavior* 9: 328–36.

McKINLAY, J. B. 1973. Social networks, lay consultation, and help-seeking behavior. *Social Forces* 51: 275–92.

———. 1980. Social network influences on morbid episodes and the career of help-seeking. In *The relevance of social science for medicine*, ed. L. Eisenberg and A. Kleinman. Boston: Reidel.

MARMOT, M. G.; ROSE, G.; SHIPLEY, M.; and HAMILTON, P. J. J. 1978. Employment grade and coronary heart disease in British civil servants. *Journal of Epidemiology and Community Health* 32: 244–49.

MARSHALL, J. R.; RICE, D. G.; O'MERA, M.; and SHELP, W. D. 1975. Characteristics of couples with poor outcome in dialysis home training. *Journal of Chronic Diseases* 28: 375–81.

MARSTON, M. V. 1970. Compliance with medical regimens: a review of the literature. *Nursing Research* 19: 312–23.

MATUS, I., and BUSH, D. 1979. Asthma attack frequency in a pediatric population. *Psychosomatic Medicine* 41: 629–36.

MECHANIC, D. 1978. *Medical sociology*. 2d ed. New York: Free Press.

MEYER, E. 1966. Psychological disturbances in myasthemia gravis: a predictive study. *Annals of the New York Academy of Sciences* 135: 417–23.

MITCHELL, J. B. 1978. Patient outcomes in alternative long-term care settings. *Medical Care* 16: 439–52.

MOLDOFSKY, H., and CHESTER, W. J. 1970. Pain and mood patterns in patients with rheumatoid arthritis: a prospective study. *Psychosomatic Medicine* 32: 309–18.

MOOS, R. H., and SOLOMON, G. F. 1964. Personality correlates of the rapidity of progression of rheumatoid arthritis. *Annals of Rheumatic Diseases* 23: 145–51.

———. 1965. Personality correlates of the degree of functional incapacity of patients with physical disease. *Journal of Chronic Diseases* 18: 1019–38.

MOOS, R. H., and TSU, V. D. 1977. The crisis of physical illness: an overview. In *Coping with physical illness*, ed. R. H. Moos. New York: Plenum.

MORAN, L. J.; FAIRWEATHER, G. W.; FISHER, S.; and MORTON, R. B. 1956. Psychological concomitants to rate of recovery from tuberculosis. *Journal of Consulting Psychology* 20: 199–203.

MORAN, L. J.; FAIRWEATHER, G. W.; and MORTON, R. B. 1956. Some determinants of successful and unsuccessful adapation to hospital treatment of tuberculosis. *Journal of Consulting Psychology* 20: 125–31.

MORRISON, F. R., and PAFFENBARGER, R. A., JR. 1981. Epidemiological aspects of biobehavior in the etiology of cancer: a critical review. In *Perspectives on behavioral medicine*, ed. S. M. Weiss, J. A. Herd, and B. H. Fox. New York: Academic Press.

MOSSEY, J. M., and SHAPIRO, E. 1982. Self-rated health: a predictor of mortality among the elderly. *American Journal of Public Health* 72: 800–08.

MUELLER, D. P. 1980. Social networks: a promising direction for research on the relationship of the social environment to psychiatric disorder. *Social Science and Medicine* 14A: 147–61.

NALL, F. C., II., and SPEILBERG, J. 1968. Social and cultural factors in the response of Mexican-Americans to medical treatment. *Journal of Health and Social Behavior* 8: 299–308.

OAKES, T. W.; WARD, J. R.; GRAY, R. M.; KLAUBER, M. R.; and MOODY, P. M. 1970. Family expectations and arthritis patient compliance to a hand resting splint regimen. *Journal of Chronic Diseases* 22: 757–64.

O'BRIEN, M. E. 1980. Effective social environment and hemodialysis adaptation: a panel analysis. *Journal of Health and Social Behavior* 21: 360–70.

PARBROOK, G. D.; DALRYMPLE, D. G.; and STEEL, D. F. 1973. Personality assessment and post-operative pain and complications. *Journal of Psychosomatic Research* 17:277–85.

PARNES, H. S., and KING, R. 1977. Middle-aged job losers. *Industrial Gerontology* 4: 77–95.

PASCAL, G. R., and THOROUGHMAN, J. C. 1964. Relationship between Bender-Gestalt test scores and the response of patients with intractable duodenal ulcer to surgery. *Psychosomatic Medicine* 26: 625–27.

PEARLIN, L. I., and SCHOOLER, C. 1978. The structure of coping. *Journal of Health and Social Behavior* 19: 2–21.

PETRONI, F. A. 1969. Significant others and illness behavior: a much neglected sick role contingency. *Sociological Quarterly* 10: 32–41.

———. 1971. Preferred right to the sick role and illness behavior. *Social Science and Medicine* 5: 645–53.

PILOWSKI, I.; SPENCE, N. D.; and WADDY, J. L. 1979. Illness behavior and coronary artery by-pass surgery. *Journal of Psychosomatic Research* 23: 39–44.

PINKERTON, P., and WEAVER, C. M. 1970. Childhood asthma. In *trends in psychosomatic medicine*, ed. O. W. Hill. New York: Appleton-Century-Crofts.

PORRITT, D. 1979. Social support in crisis: quantity or quality? *Social Science and Medicine* 1: 218–22.

PORTER, A. M. W. 1969. Drug defaulting in general practice. *British Medical Journal* 1: 218–22.

PRAGOFF, H. 1962. Adjustment of tuberculosis patients one year after hospital discharge. *Public Health Reports* 77: 671–9.

PROCCI, W. R. 1978. Dietary abuse in maintenance hemodialysis patients. *Psychosomatics* 19: 16–24.

Proceedings of the Conference on the Decline in Coronary Heart Disease Mortality. 1979. NIH pub. no. 79–1610. Washington, D.C.: Government Printing Office.

PURCELL, K.; BRADY, K.; CHAI, H.; MUSER, J.; MOLK, L.; GORDON, N.; and MEANS, J. 1969. The effect on asthma in children of experimental separation from the family. *Psychosomatic Medicine* 31: 144–64.

READING, A. E. 1979. The short-term effects of psychological preparation for surgery. *Social Science and Medicine* 13A: 641–54.

ROGENTINE, G. N.; vanKAMMEN, D. P.; FOX, B. H.; DOCHERTY, J. P; ROSENBLATT, J. E.; BOYD, S. C.; and BUNNEY, W. E., JR. 1979. Psychological factors in the prognosis of malignant melanoma: a prospective study. *Psychosomatic Medicine* 41: 647–55.

ROGERS, M. P.; DUBEY, D.; and REICH, P. 1979. The influence of the psyche and the brain on immunity and disease susceptibility: a critical review. *Psychosomatic Medicine* 41: 147–64.

RORABAUGH, M., and GUTHRIE, G. 1953. The personality characteristics of tuberculous patients who leave the tuberculosis hospital against medical advice. *American Review of Tuberculosis* 67: 432–39.

Rosow, I. 1967. *Social integration of the aged.* New York: Free Press.

RUNDALL, T. G. 1978. Life change and recovery from surgery. *Journal of Health and Social Behavior* 19: 418–27.

SACKETT, D. L., and HAYNES, R. B., eds. 1976. *Compliance with therapeutic regimens.* Baltimore, Md.: John Hopkins University Press.

SCHWARTZ, D.; WANS, M.; ZEITZ, L.; and GOSS, M. E. W. 1962. Medication errors made by elderly, chronically ill patients. *American Journal of Public Health* 52: 2018–29.

SHAPIRO, S.; WEINBLATT, E.; FRANK, C. W.; and SAGER, R. V. 1970. Social factors in the prognosis of men following first myocardial infarction. *Milbank Memorial Fund Quarterly* 48: 37–50.

SHEKELLE, R. B.; RAYNOR, W. J.; OSTFELD, A. M.; GARRON, D. C.; BIELAUSKAS, L. A.; LIU, S. C.; MALIZA, C.; and PAUL, O. 1981. Psychological depression and 17-year risk of death from cancer. *Psychosomatic Medicine* 43: 117–25.

SHEPPARD, H. L.; BELITSKY, A.; and HARVEY, A. 1966. *The job hunt.* Baltimore, Md.: Johns Hopkins University Press.

SHIPLEY, R. H.; BUTT, J. H.; HOROWITZ, B.; and FARBRY, J. E. 1978. Preparation for a stressful medical procedure: effect of amount of stimulus pre-exposure and coping style. *Journal of Consulting and Clinical Psychology* 46: 499–507.

SIME, A. M. 1976. Relationship of pre-operative fear, type of coping, and information received about surgery to recovery from surgery. *Journal of Personality and Social Psychology* 34: 716–24.

SOLOFF, P. H., and BARTEL, A. G. 1979. Effects of denial on mood and performance in cardiovascular rehabilitation. *Journal of Chronic Diseases* 32: 307–13.

STAUDENMAYER, H.; KINSMAN, R. A.; DIRKS, J. F.; SPECTOR, S. L.; and WANGAARD, C. 1979 Medical outcome in asthmatic patients: effects of airways hyperreactivity and symptom-focused anxiety. *Psychosomatic Medicine* 41: 109–18.

STERN, M. J.; PASCALE, L.; and McLOONE, J. B. 1976. Psychosocial adaptation following an acute myocardial infarction. *Journal of Chronic Diseases* 29: 513–26.

STEVENSON, D. K.; NABSETH, D. C.; MASUDA, M.; and HOLMES, T. H. 1979. Life change and the postoperative course of duodenal ucler patients. *Journal of Human Stress* 5:19–28.

STONE, G. C.; COHEN, F.; and ADLER, N. E., eds. 1979. *Health psychology.* San Francisco Calif.: Jossey-Bass.

SYME, S. L. 1978. Drug treatment of mild hypertension: social and psychological considerations. *Annals of the New York Academy of Sciences* 304: 99–106.

———, and BERKMAN, L. F. 1976. Social class, susceptibility, and sickness. *American Journal of Epidemiology* 104: 1–8.

TAGLIACOZZO, D. M., and IMA, K. 1970. Knowledge of illness as a predictor of patient behavior. *Journal of Chronic Diseases* 22: 765–75.

TAYLOR, D. W.; SACKETT, D. L.; HAYNES, R. B.; JOHNSON, A. L.; GIBSON, E. S.; and ROBERTS, R. S. 1978. Compliance with antihypertensive drug therapy. *Annals of The New York Academy of Sciences* 304: 390–403.

TUFO, H. M., and OSTFELD, A. M. 1968. A prospective study of open-heart surgery. *Psychosomatic Medicine* 30: 552–53 (abstract).

VOLICER, B. J.; ISENBERG, M. A.; and BURNS, M. W. 1977. Medical-surgical differences in hospital stress factors. *Journal of Human Stress* 3: 3–13.

WALKER, K. N.; MACBRIDE, A.; and VACHON, M. L. S. 1977. Social support networks and the crisis of bereavement. *Social Science and Medicine* 11: 35–41.

WEINER, H. 1977. *Psychobiology and human disease.* New York: Elsevier.

WEISMAN, A. D. 1956. A study of the psychodynamics of duodenal ulcer exacerbations with special reference to treatment and the problem of specificity. *Psychosomatic Medicine* 18: 2–42.

WILLIAMS, R. B.; HANEY, T. L.; LEE, K. L.; KONG, Y.-H.; BLUMENTHAL, J. A.; and WHALEN, R. E. 1980. Type A behavior, hostility, and coronary atherosclerosis. *Psychosomatic Medicine* 42: 539–49.

WILLIAMS, T. F.; MARTIN, D. A.; HOGAN, M. D.; WATKINS, J. D.; and ELLIS, E. V. 1967. The clinical picture of diabetic control, studied in four settings. *American Journal of Public Health* 57: 441–51.

WILLIS, F. N., and DUNSMORE, N. M. 1967. Work orientation, health attitudes, and compliance with therapeutic advice. *Nursing Research* 16: 22–25.

WILSON J. T. 1973. Compliance with instructions in the evaluation of therapuetic efficacy. *Clinical Pediatrics* 12: 333–40.

WORDEN, J. W., and SOBEL, H. J. 1978. Ego strength and psychosocial adaptation to cancer. *Psychosomatic Medicine* 40: 585–92.

YANAGIDA, E. H.; STRELTZER, J.; and SIEMSEN, A. 1981. Denial in dialysis patients: relationship to compliance and other variables. *Psychosomatic Medicine* 43: 271–80.

ZBOROWSKI, M. 1969. *People in pain.* San Francisco, Calif.: Jossey-Bass.

ZOLA, I. K. 1966. Culture and symptoms—an analysis of patients' presenting complaints. *American Sociological Review* 31: 615–30.

ZUCKERMAN, D. M.; KASL, S. V.; and OSTFELD, A. M. 1981. Psychosocial predictors of mortality among the elderly poor: the role of religion, well-being, and social contacts. Unpublished manuscript, Department of Epidemiology and Public Health, Yale University School of Medicine.

Chapter 32

Behavioral Medicine: Psychology in Health Care

Howard Leventhal

BEHAVIORAL MEDICINE is in a state of explosive growth. The rate and diversity of its growth are reflected in new organizations (the Academy of Behavioral Medicine Research, the Division of Health Psychology of the American Psychological Association, Division 38), journals (*Behavioral Medicine, Health Psychology*), and behavioral medicine programs in departments of psychology and psychiatry. These developments result from an increased awareness of the importance of behavior in the delivery of health care as well as the need for a disciplinary label to integrate behavioral research and practice in the medical area. The use of the label also reflects the desire of behavioral investigators and practitioners to relate behavioral research to a publicy perceived need, in addition to conferring upon it the status and financial support accorded to medical research. The goal of this chapter is to review a few of the past contributions and future directions that psychological research has made and will make to behavioral medicine and to look at the future directions of the field. This is no simple task as both behavioral medicine and psychology are extremely complex. Indeed, it may help to enumerate a few of the subdisciplines of behavioral medicine lest we underestimate the difficulty of organizing the past and anticipating the future contributions of so heterogeneous a group of practitioners and investigators.

The first claim to membership in behavioral medicine is likely to come from the investigators and practitioners of psychotherapy. While they have traditionally sought to develop techniques for the treatment of mental illness, they are now transferring many of them to the prevention and treatment of cigarette smoking (Leventhal and Cleary 1980; Lichtenstein and Danaher 1975), hypertension (Seer 1979; Schwartz et al. 1979), stress (Meichenbaum 1975; Suinn and Bloom 1978), and the control of diet and weight (Leon 1976; Stunkard 1977, 1979). A second claim to membership might come from investigators and practitioners concerned with rehabilitation following the occurrence and treatment of catastrophic illnesses such as stroke and spinal injury. These individuals are using and testing methods developed in studies of behavioral management with humans and animals.

A third claim to the title will come from the investigators and practitioners studying the syndrome and treatment of chronic pain (Fordyce 1976) and pain behavior (Wooley, Blackwell, and Winget 1978). This third group includes investigators of treatments for headache (Blanchard, Ahles and Shaw 1980; Young and Blanchard 1980), lower back pain (Humphrey 1980), and menstrual pain (Tasto and Insel 1977). A fourth group, one which should be better integrated with pain researchers, has investigated the preparation of patients for stressful medical procedures. This work was initially focused on patient response to postsurgical stress (Egbert et al. 1964; Janis 1958; Johnson, Dabbs, and Leventhal 1970; Sime 1976) but now includes research on a variety of problems such as preparing adults for diagnostic examinations (Johnson and Leventhal 1974; Johnson 1975; Wilson 1981) and childbirth (Skipper and Leonard 1968), and preparing children for both cast removals (Johnson, Kirchoff, and Endress 1975; Johnson et al. 1978) and hospitalization (Melamed 1977; Skipper and Leonard 1968).

A fifth claim to the title of behavioral medicine comes from investigators studying the delivery and use of health services. This group includes social psychologists and epidemiologists interested in the processes underlying symptom awareness (Leventhal, Meyer, and Nerenz 1980; Pennebaker, in press; Pennebaker and Skelton 1978), the appraisals that lead to seeking medical care (Mechanic 1972; Robinson 1971; Safer et al. 1979; Suchman 1965; Zola 1973), and the cultural, interpersonal, and economic factors that affect the use of the medical-care system (McKinlay 1972; Kasteler et al. 1976; Sanne 1979).

Despite the omission of many lines of investigation and practice that comprised psychology's earliest contributions to behavioral medicine, e.g., neuropsychology and motor skill training (Stone 1979), the diversity of problems and expertise subsumed by this disciplinary label should be evident. It would be impossible to review the latest contributions of psychological theory and research to each of these areas within the confines of the present chapter. Instead I will first identify what seems to be the most recent conceptual approach of psychologists working in behavioral medicine. I will then examine how this conceptual approach is influencing current research and is likely to influence future investigations.

A Conceptual Approach to Behavioral Medicine: Systems Theory

Schwartz (1977, 1979) suggests that systems theory offers an ideal integrative framework for research in behavioral medicine. Systems theory views behavior as a product of multiple, interacting variables. The variables in a system may be at different levels of abstraction, yet they form a set in which every factor affects every other factor, though to different degrees (Lazarus and Launier 1978). For example, an individual's weight is clearly a product of an interacting system of variables which range from the number of fat cells in the body to motivational and decisional factors determining diet. The variables in a system framework can be independent, mediating, or dependent, depending on the experimental situation. Hence, the same factor may be an independent variable in one study and a dependent variable in another; the choice is determined by theoretical interest and experimental convenience.

Four important themes in systems theory will have an increasing impact on theory and research in behavioral medicine: (1) descriptions occur on multiple levels; (2) systems provide control through feedback; (3) systems are organized in hierarchies that are integrated within and across levels and (4) regulatory systems have a developmental history. I will discuss each briefly.

Multiple Levels of Description

Research in behavioral medicine is inherently multilevel. People's health and illness behavior take place within a social context, and that context changes markedly when they enter the medical-care system. We cannot understand health and illness behavior without understanding its context. At a cognitive, psychological level, an individual's health and illness behavior is affected by his or her sensations, symptoms, and moods. These experiences change with variation in the external and internal environments that affect the individual's physiological functioning. Hence, to identify the variables affecting an illness episode we must attend not only to physiological factors but to psychological and social factors as well (Engel 1977; Fabrega 1975; Schwartz 1979). Behavioral medical research demands, therefore, the rejection of simpleminded reductionistic thinking. We cannot account for health and illness behaviors unless we develop differentiated and coherent theories at each level of description and recognize that descriptions at one level of a system cannot be reduced to those at another. If we adopt a systems approach our goal will be to link concepts at different levels of description. How well this can be done is a theoretical and empirical question (Hempel 1966). The search for correlations may stimulate the development of a truly integrative bio-socio-psychological theory (Leventhal and Nerenz, in press).

Feedback and Control

Cannon's (1936) concept of homeostasis, the idea that our neurohumoral system operates to maintain a balance in the internal milieu during variations in the external environment, can be extended to every level of psychobiological function (Arbib 1972; Carver 1979; Carver and Schier 1981; Hebb 1949; Lazarus 1966; Leventhal 1970; Miller, Galanter, and Pribram 1960; Powers 1973a, 1973b). The systems emphasis on control or feedback is compatible with the movement toward cognitive theories in both clinical and social psychology (Carver and Scheier 1981; Goldstein 1968; Kanfer 1977, 1980; Leventhal and Nerenz, in press; Mahoney 1974; Meichenbaum 1975). Each of these theoretical systems uses a systems approach in which behavior is regulated by three components: (1) a mechanism for the representation of goals; (2) a mechanism for generating coping responses; and (3) a mechanism for comparing or evaluating the fit between coping responses and goals (Kanfer 1980; Leventhal and Nerenz, in press). Although we tend to think of the three components as working in a fixed, linear sequence, any of the three steps of regulation can take the role of independent, mediating, or dependent variables depending upon the particulars of the experimental situation. The system focus on comprehensive, multivariate methods for research and practice clearly encourages the move away from single-factor explanations of behavior.

Control theory also emphasizes that behavior is goal-directed: it moves toward anticipated outcomes rather than being controlled by past history (Lewin

1935). According to this theory, any particular behavior is a function of an implicit or explicit goal which is actively generated by the individual. An understanding of the individual's goals is necessary when treating illness, since the individual's health and illness behaviors will be guided by them. Because these goals are a product of the individual's current symptom experience as well as his or her past illness history, both of which may be idiosyncratic, the individual's representation of his or her illness problem may be unique as well as private.

Finally, the control or feedback approach views people as actively involved in maintaining a balanced relationship with their environments; it is process-oriented. This has important implications for both research and practice as it suggests that one should understand the individual's goals, skills, and appraisal strategies before attempting a behavioral intervention. The intervention would then focus on the known contents of one of these three components of the regulative mechanism: goal change, response (skill) instruction, or redefinition of the criteria for response evaluation. Medical models, by contrast, encourage practitioners to describe their patients with disease or personality trait labels. This categorical approach has two unfortunate consequences. First, it views the patient as a passive entity who must be pushed into action with warnings and assumes he or she will then follow medical prescriptions (Engel 1977; Leventhal, Meyer, and Gutmann 1980). As we shall see, this assumption is untrue (e.g., Becker and Maiman 1975). Second, it treats illness as unique or discontinuous with normal biological process. This may be appropriate in some instances, as in treating infections or a biochemically based mood disorder, but it gives less emphasis to the possibility that illness can be cured or health restored by strengthening existent biological processes through change in diet, reduced exposure to stress, and reduced smoking (Schwartz 1979). Emphasis upon self-regulation may correct both of the above biases as it will focus investigators and practitioners on the assessment of systems and the design of interventions to achieve long-term alterations of health behavior (Kirschenbaum and Tomarken, in press) and encourage the use of nonpharmacological methods for treatment.

Hierarchical Integration

The need to correlate theories formulated at the social, psychological, and biological levels is only one of several ways in which different levels of theory will be related to one another in behavioral medicine. The relationship between different types of theory must take into account dynamic or causal relationships across levels. Structure at one level may set limits on the operations of another, in the way that biological factors limit our perception and memory, and social and institutional factors limit our interpretations and coping skills. We may also find that control processes operating at one level regulate, i.e., drive and inhibit, those at another. This includes the effects of biological needs such as hunger or pain on psychological decisions (to eat, to lie still, or to seek medical care) and the effects of the social system in moderating and/or directing individuals' behavior in ways counter to their immediate (or long-term) desires. For example, if a person is sick and expresses distress and seeks care, the expectations of the sick role may require reducing work stress, although that would not otherwise be done. In summary, hierarchical integration across levels refers to the long- and short-term impact of changes at one level on processes at another. We have barely begun the task of describing such causal relationships.

Integration occurs within levels as well as across them. Processes such as the effects of hormones from the adrenal cortex on cerebral activity or the effects of concrete imagery on abstract thinking are examples. In both cases a more microscopic process alters a macroscopic one, and both examples refer to processes at the same level of conceptual language—physiological in the first instance and psychological in the second. To understand behavior during illness episodes, we must recognize that the patient's cognitive processes are both abstract or conceptual and concrete or perceptual. Cancer, for instance, might be conceptualized by a patient as a local, mechanical disease and completely identified with the lump that is its concrete presence. Or, the patient might conceptualize cancer as a systemic disease, with loss of stamina as its physical expression. We need to develop theoretical propositions to understand the integration of these levels. Questions about the type of information that must be coded at macroscopic levels to control microscopic ones have been addressed in control theory (Carver and Scheier 1981; Powers 1973a, 1973b).

Ontogenesis of Health Actions

Control systems operate over time. They also have a history which is recorded in memory systems at the social, psychological, and physiological levels. Hence, the behavior of the system changes over time. Cigarette smoking provides a clear example of developmental change in the area of health and risk behaviors. Smoking the first experimental cigarette is not the same as the ten thousandth. The experiences are different, the determinants are different, and the consequences, both social and physiological, are different. Initial exposure may be determined by social pressures and the experience is as likely to be negative as positive (Gilbert 1979). Indeed, nicotine level is very likely the source of negative affective reactions to initial smoking, particularly in females. Repeated exposure leads to tolerance for these pharmacological effects. After smoking and inhaling thousands of cigarettes the decline in nicotine level produced by the cessation of smoking is clearly a cause for negative bodily sensations or craving (Schachter 1977; Shiffman 1979). Hence, the withdrawal of the substance responsible for the distress during initial smoking episodes is partly responsible for the craving experienced during later cessation. The social system's response to the smoker will also change over time. The individual's smoking may be accepted and even encouraged, or the norms for smoking may change due to new perceptions of the harmfulness of the behavior for the smoker or others in the smoker's environment.

There are at least three important ways in which a behavioral system can change over time. First, the behavior may become more automatic, requiring less attention and effort. One consequence of this may be a reduction in the ease with which the behavior is accessed and changed. A second type of change would be structural. For example, there may be an increase in the number of concrete, perceptual memories that are tightly linked to one another which could strengthen the degree to which this set of cognitive material can provoke strong emotional reactions and direct behavior. Associations of concrete perceptual memories and their motor elements may also generate new emotional structures or blends, changing the type of behavior visible in situations which provoke this amalgam of concrete memories (Izard 1971; Leventhal 1980; Tomkins 1962; Ekman, Friesen, and Ellsworth 1972). For example, gastrointestinal nausea, pain and distress may be integrated with emotional reactions of fear and affection stimulated by parental responses to illness during early childhood. This entire emotional schema, a fearful affectionate pleading, will be reactivated in later illness episodes of this type. Structural change may also involve the formation and matching of abstract, volitionally controllable memory codes to concrete, perceptual memories. This match may serve to inhibit impulsive, emotional reactions (Leventhal 1980; Levy 1981). For example, a hostess of a formal affair may thoroughly rehearse and become so skilled at voluntarily emitting greetings and gracious smiles that she overrides both feelings of annoyance and feelings of joy and pleasure on encountering guests she dislikes or likes. Her voluntary smiles are felt as a sequence of intentional movement that produce an even set of external greetings devoid of internal, emotional substance. Finally, change over time may lead to opponent emotional reactions in which positive or negative changes in affect will be followed by a swing in the opposite affective direction. These reactions serve to maintain emotional equilibrium, a process which may be important for addictive behavior. (For a further elaboration of this theory, see Leventhal and Cleary 1980; Solomon and Corbit 1974; Tomkins 1968). It is clear that control systems change over time and that it is a serious error to assume that the same variables are involved in the control system in the early and late history of a behavior. This error is very easy to make, given that we use the same verbal label to describe a behavior irrespective of the stage of its development.

Summary

The four dimensions of systems theory I have outlined will influence health research in many specific areas, although the impact will be more apparent for some problems than for others. For example, the ontogenetic theme may prove most important for research in prevention, and the hierarchical integration theme may prove most important for the problem of self-regulation through biofeedback. Regardless of the differences in emphasis, using these themes to guide research in behavioral medicine will have lasting impact on psychological theory by forcing broader, more integrative conceptualizations in what is currently an excessively fragmented area.

Substantive Topics in Behavioral Medicine

The topics selected for discussion are as follows: (1) the use of the medical-care system: delay in seeking care and treatment compliance; (2) prevention; (3) self-regulation under stressful circumstances; and (4) individual differences in response to stress and health threats. These topics by no means exhaust the areas of active research in behavioral medicine. For more comprehensive coverage one should examine Melamed's (1980) recent textbook of behavioral medicine, Rachman's (1977, 1980) two volumes of behavioral medicine, Stone's (1979) *Health Psychology*, reviews in the *Psychological Bulletin* and the *Journal of Behavioral*

Medicine, and the new *Journal of Health Psychology*. My aim is simpler: It is to highlight the way self-regulation (systems) theory will impact on each of the above-mentioned topics.

Compliance with Medical-Care Regimes

Much of the psychological research on the use of the medical-care system focuses on the determinants of delay in seeking care and the determinants of compliance with medical treatment. The two problems are usually approached from a biomedical perspective which assumes that an underlying disease generates symptoms followed by awareness of symptoms, seeking or delay in seeking help followed by diagnosis, and compliance or noncompliance with a prescribed regimen (Dunbar and Stunkard 1979; Leventhal and Hirschman 1982; Leventhal, Zimmerman, and Gutmann, in press; Stimson 1974; Stunkard 1979; Zola 1973). This orientation led to the selection of dependent variables that measured the performance of prescribed actions and change in health indicators (blood pressure, mortality rates, etc.) and to the selection of independent variables that described the intellectual (education, income), motivational (Type A behavior) and emotional (anxious versus nonanxious) characteristics of the patient. Stimson (1974) and Stunkard (1975) argue that focusing on compliance to prescribed behaviors made noncompliance a fault of the patient and stimulated a futile search for the profile of the noncompliant patient. Restricting attention to prescribed actions and to medical endpoints may also have led investigators to view health and illness behavior in a framework more appropriate to acute infectious illness than to chronic illness.

THE ADHERENCE APPROACH TO HEALTH BEHAVIOR. Failure to isolate noncompliant types moved the focus of investigation from the patient to the situation (Leventhal, Meyer, and Gutmann 1980). Medically trained investigators looked at factors such as complexity of regimen (Blackwell 1979; Haynes 1979), individual appointments (Finnerty, Mattie, and Finnerty 1973; Haynes 1979), and continuity of care (Becker, Drachman, and Kirscht 1974). Because the medical model does not provide theoretical guidance for the analysis of behavioral problems, the consequence was a proliferation of empirical studies with inconsistent outcomes (Haynes 1979). This should not surprise us as there are very few situational factors that can be expected to have consistent main effects on compliance (hence on medical outcomes) if the mechanisms underlying behavior generate complex interactions between situational and personal factors.

Behaviorally trained investigators, on the other hand, moved toward even more detailed description of the environmental determinants of specific behaviors and paid little attention to medical endpoints. Sociologists found that stressful life situations initiated seeking medical care, i.e., illness behavior (Mechanic and Volkart 1961), and listed factors, such as interpersonal crises, interference with work or social relations, individuals sanctioning or encouraging one another's help seeking, etc., as determinants of seeking medical care or delay (Zola 1973). Behaviorally trained psychologists generated an extensive literature on the use of antihypertensive medications, weight control, and quitting smoking. In the latter two instances they examined when, how, and how much a person eats or smokes, the variables provoking or regulating these behaviors, and the development of tactics for controlling them. By contrast, earlier medically related studies had looked primarily at blood pressure, pounds lost, and change in lung function. These are important endpoints, but not the first to which we must attend if we are to achieve long-term adherence to new behavioral regimens. (For a review of studies on weight control see Stunkard 1977, 1979; and for a review of studies on smoking see Leventhal and Cleary 1980.)

Research guided by behavioral theory has clearly added to our understanding of behavior and increased success rates in weight- and smoking-reduction programs. But complete success has eluded us due to one critical factor: The typical curve for adherence for any one of these behaviors, whether those which are treatments (taking blood pressure medication) or those which are preventive (weight loss and quitting smoking), shows very high rates of success at the end of the intervention program (sometimes as high as 90 or 95 percent) falling off to relatively low rates (10 to 30 percent) within three to six months following the end of treatment (Hunt and Bespalec 1974; Hunt and Matarazzo, in press; Leventhal and Cleary 1980; McFall 1980). Focusing on the behavior, and on the environmental and attitudinal conditions preceding and supporting it, has proven insufficient to generate change for the long term. The initial attempts to cope with the problem added factors to the treatment regimen, such as combinations of treatments, booster sessions, or social support networks. When these tactics proved insufficient, investigators examined the conditions associated with adherence failures and tried to develop techniques to help individuals anticipate and manage delayed threats to behavioral change (Marlatt and Gordon 1980).

While the behavioral approach clearly represented a major step forward in our understanding of utilization and adherence problems (Stunkard 1975), success in promoting durable behavior change still eludes behavioral technology. Part of the failure may stem from the conceptual orientation of the behavioral approach. Behavior theory views responses as products of immediately antecedent and currently sustaining stimulus conditions (Zifferblatt 1975). It does not view behavior as moving toward goals constructed by the actor. The behavioral approach is essentially linear with antecedent, situational events provoking responses that may or may not be rewarded. The behavior reacts to its past (past rewards) and is blind to its future. A mechanical framework of this sort may be too limited to effect lasting behavioral change.

THE CONTROL THEORY APPROACH. The key proposition of self-regulation (control) theory is that the individual generates or constructs a representation of an illness problem to guide and evaluate his or her coping behaviors. Delay in use or failure to comply with prescribed health services will be affected by the way the individual represents the problem and the health-care system. The representation of the episode can be thought of as a hierarchical goal structure. It includes social aims (goals defined by the sick role and the practitioner-patient relationship) and aims defined by the illness representation, the label, and symptoms. These representations stimulate the individual to construct coping plans and provide the criteria (e.g., returning to work or symptom removal) for evaluating outcomes.

Since the representation of illness directs coping and evaluation, it is indeed important to understand how representations are generated. The major shift in focus introduced by control and cognitive theory is to the processes involved in generating representations of health problems and behavioral plans for coping: outcome expectations, behavioral skills, self-effectance, etc. It has been shown that symptoms and symptom interpretation play a major role in the construction of illness representations. (See, for example, Chrisman 1977; Hayes-Bautista 1976, 1978; Leventhal 1975; Meyer, Leventhal, and Gutmann, in press.) However, other factors, ranging from demographic variables (Robinson 1971) to life stress and emotional states (Mechanic 1966, 1972) modify the way symptoms are interpreted and inferences are made about the condition of one's body.

Control theory raises a number of critical questions about the way illness representations are constructed. Current research strongly suggests that representations of illness are generated by fitting current symptoms to schemata or memory representations of past illness episodes (Chrisman 1977; Hayes-Baustista 1976, 1978; Leventhal, Meyer, and Nerenz 1980; Leventhal and Nerenz, in press; Meyer, Leventhal, and Gutmann, in press). The representation of the ongoing episode emerges from the coding of inputs (body sensations, information from practitioners, etc.) in a schema. The input is checked against previous schemata and is then combined with a particular schema to form the representation of the current episode. The representation is enriched, therefore, by the expectations or features built into the schema.

Illness schemata are characterized by at least four features: (1) an identity, consisting of a symptom pattern and an illness label; (2) a perceived cause; (3) expectations about the severity or consequences of the illness; and (4) time lines or expectations about the duration of the illness (i.e. acute, cyclic, or chronic) and the other features, such as how long it takes the cause to operate and consequences to develop. Symptoms and labels are closely linked both in the schema and in the representation of the current episode. As a consequence, people seek labels (diagnoses or explanations) for symptoms, and when they are told they have a specific illness (hypertension, for example) they search for symptoms even if they have been told the condition is asymptomatic (Meyer, Leventhal, and Gutmann, in press). Data also suggest that patients initially represent illness episodes as acute diseases. Thus, whether the patient is diagnosed with cancer or hypertension, he or she is likely to assume the problem is caused by an external agent (stress, food, poisons, etc.; Herzlich 1973), that the consequences will be limited, and that he or she will return to health in a short period of time (Meyer 1981; Nerenz 1980; Ringler 1981).

Expectations about the severity of illness are clearly linked to the label (for instance, cancer is expected to be painful), to personal experience and observation of disease in others, and to symptoms. For example, direct observation of illness in friends and/or relatives seems especially important in generating an image of cancer as a highly malevolent disease (Ringler 1981). The perceived seriousness of the disease also depends on the severity of the disease symptoms (Suchman 1965; Safer et al. 1979; Zborowski 1969). But the impact of many symptoms depends on how they are interpreted. For example, fatigue and tiredness are the most threatening and distressing symptoms to cancer patients with metastatic disease. Patients in chemotherapy for preventive reasons (i.e., following "successful" surgery) attribute these symptoms to the treatment and are less likely to see them as implying severe consequences such as return of the disease.

The representation is important because it arouses emotional reactions and because it affects coping. At least three studies show that patients guide their coping on the basis of illness representations. For example, hypertensive patients monitor their symptoms and may drop out of treatment or vary their medications in conformity with the symptoms or cues they assume are indicators of the disease

(Meyer 1981). Cancer patients seem to follow a similar pattern; they can better understand and tolerate their chemotherapy treatment when it is minimizing bodily symptoms. When there is no "rational" relationship between the treatment and the disease, such as when patients are treated with chemotherapy which makes them feel ill although they have no clear symptoms of disease (as when their lumps are gone), they become distressed and want to drop treatment (Nerenz 1980; Ringler 1981). Cancer patients receiving preventive treatments seem more likely to have reductions in therapy for nonmedical reasons than patients receiving treatment for metastatic disease. These reductions may risk recurrence of their disease (Ringler 1981). Doctor shopping (Kasteler et al. 1976) is another response that may be accounted for, at least in part, by illness representation.

It is important to recognize that none of these responses is necessarily medically rational but that the responses are consistent with the patient's representation of the medical problem. Psychological consistency is not equivalent to objective validity.

SUMMARY AND REMAINING QUESTIONS. A significant segment of the research on compliance has moved from this initial focus on compliance to the question of adherence, and finally to self-regulation. The shift involved a change in theoretical orientation from models of compliance or rule following, through models of behavioral shaping, to models of self-regulation based on control or systems theory. In systems theory behavior moves or is pulled toward goals rather than pushed from behind by environmental stimuli (Powers 1973a, 1973b). Research shows that patients generate goals or representations of their illness episodes, and generate coping responses on the basis of these representations. The representation forms an interpretive framework for the generation and appraisal of coping responses. The hierarchical structure of the patient's representation includes both abstract (illness label) and concrete (symptom) features. Indeed, the presence of either one strongly implies and initiates a search for the other.

The data pointing to the way patients interrelate abstract labels and concrete symptoms provide new possibilities for understanding how cultural and social factors affect the way the individual represents an illness episode. Cultural factors have long been recognized as important determinants of responses to stress and the utilization of health services (Chrisman 1977; Hayes-Bautista 1976, 1978; Zborowski 1969; Zola 1973). Behavior theory and control theory make different suggestions, however, on how cultural factors influence individual actions. Behavior theory treats cultural factors as a collection of individual habits which are generated and steered by norms acting directly on behavior. Control theory suggests that social norms (and supports) act on the individual's self-regulatory system, that is, on the representation, coping skills, and evaluation criteria. This difference has important consequences, as it suggests that individuals will appraise and evaluate normative information in relationship to their ongoing behavioral systems. For example, suppose that community norms assert that high blood pressure is caused by stress. This interpretation seems especially congenial to well-educated people in independent, professional careers; stress clearly emerges as one of the major factors in commonsense views of disease causation (Meyer 1981; Nerenz 1980) and in epidemiological data (Friedman and Rosenman 1974). However, an individual who is diagnosed as hypertensive does not automatically accept that hypothesis as true in his or her individual case. The cultural norm orients the individual to check the relationship between the stressful events and body cues. One might check body symptoms that are considered signs of blood pressure elevation (heart throbbing, headache, etc.) to see if the symptoms appear under appropriate environmental conditions, such as having headaches when under stress. If the cultural hypothesis checks against private experience, it is more likely to be accepted.

We have inadequate data to support the sequence described above. We know, however, that face-to-face contacts provide abundant opportunity for checking the cause and meaning of symptoms. Thus, individuals regularly compare symptoms with friends and family, and when there is similarity they usually conclude that a benign, external condition is the cause (Safer et al. 1979). Social comparison also allows the individual to evaluate the effectiveness of coping reactions, for example, checking to see if one's symptoms clear as rapidly as one's friends' symptoms. These are only some of the many ways that social factors alter the illness representation and influence behavior.

The interaction between the practitioner and the patient provides another opportunity for social factors to influence individual representations and the way this happens is best understood from a control theory framework. For example, David Steele, Mary Gutmann, and I have observed that practitioners who know and tell patients that hypertension is asymptomatic act as though they do not believe their own assertions when they interview the individual patient. When facing the individual they allow clinical (case) experience to override their knowledge, thinking that at least "this particular patient" may indeed detect blood pressure swings. There is a clear contrast, therefore, between the practitioners' conceptual knowledge on the one hand and their case and personal knowledge on the other. They communicate their personal beliefs while quizzing the patient about symptoms. This questioning covers a wide range of symptoms, including some that are suspected correlates of blood pressure and others that are suspected consequences of the medication or of other, unrelated diseases. The questioning procedure follows the form of a medical inquiry which assumes that each underlying condition will manifest itself in specific, overt symptoms. Unfortunately, the practitioner seldom, if ever, tells the patient why questions are asked about specific symptoms, failing to recognize that patients are searching for information to evaluate their medical status and to guide later private evaluations of treatment. Hence, the patient is likely to believe that all or at least one of these symptoms is a valid indication of blood pressure. Unfortunately, the patients' search for a symptomatic indicator is virtually doomed to failure. The quest is biased by the assumption that the indicator must be aversive if hypertension is a disease, most likely a pain or a negative mood, and the tendency to recall positive instances of associations between symptoms and elevated pressure (I recall that I had a headache at my last high reading) and to forget negative instances (the times before and after when my pressure was high and I had no headache or had a headache and no elevation in pressure). These expectations and biases in recall lead to the illusion of predictable association of cues such as headache and feelings of stress and tension with blood pressure and the use of these symptoms as guides to seeking medical care and the use of medications. (In an ongoing study, David Steele and the author have observed that patients may ultimately persuade their providers that symptoms are caused by hypertension, though there is no evidence to confirm the hypothesis. We have observed this by listening to tape recordings of practitioner-patient interactions made over a nine-month period.)

Communications between doctor and patient can generate outcomes such as those described above when the participants use different and unshared models of the illness. One curious feature of this process, which Meyer (1981) has documented, is that patients develop one representation of an illness appropriate for public display and another for private use. For example, 80 percent of Meyer's hypertensives agreed that people could not tell when their blood pressure was elevated; 90 percent, however, believed they were exceptions to that rule. They not only believed their own experience differed from that of other people, they were also deceptive; 67 percent asked the interviewer not to tell the practitioner what they, the patients, were doing. The patients were clearly checking out and rejecting the physicians' statements about symptomatology and were developing their private representation of illness. However, their conception of the practitioner-patient relationship prevented the communication of the information to the physician.

Differences in the representation of the illness are but one of many communication barriers between practitioner and patient. Our research group has found that cancer chemotherapy patients are unwilling to communicate fear and despair to their doctors, perhaps out of fear that it will lead to rejection, or at least that it will discourage attention and active treatment of the patients' illness. While these fears are infrequently tested and possibly invalid, they are encouraged by a medical model which forces the practitioner-patient relationship into that of active, expert practitioner and passive, dependent patient. If the relationship were modeled on control theory, practitioner and patient could recognize other roles and problems. Patients need help in attempting to regulate their lives, including their feelings, as well as their illness; practitioners can also help to clarify when and how illness would and would not interfere with life, and when fears are reasonable with respect to the reality of the disease process. Such a change of role would require new skills and appraisal criteria as well as a new representation of the practitioner-patient relationship and the goals of treatment.

One of the most interesting of the many problems remaining to be explored respecting representations and coping concerns the conditions (type of symptoms, focus of attention, and social information, etc.) which influence the individual's interpretations of symptoms as due to acute, remediable illness or to chronic dispositions, such as a terminal disease, or to stable attributes such as aging (Rodin 1978). Vague symptoms appear more likely to generate stable attributions. For example, when patients describe the onset of emotional disturbances they search much further back in time than when describing the onset of physical illnesses (Mosbach 1982). Chronic or stable self-attributions are also likely to be associated with depressive emotion and disruption of coping (Abramson, Seligman, and Teasdale 1978). It is also important to note that breakdowns in coping appear to generate vague symptomatology similar to that associated with stable self-attribution (Pennebaker et al. 1977). Hence, feelings of fatigue and depression may be self-reinforcing if they disrupt coping and they can easily confirm the belief that one is in a state of chronic failure. A systems approach may provide new insights into the internal, cognitive-affective, and the external social-psychological components affecting these attributions.

Prevention

From the perspective of the medical model, inoculation is the ideal preventive; a chemical technology is used to counter a specific, external cause of disease. Inoculation is also inexpensive and, in many cases, effective for a lifetime. Unfortunately, inoculations are simply unavailable for most of the top ten causes of morbidity and mortality, and physicians who believe in this highly focused technological approach to medical problems regard prevention as a goal for the future and an impossibility in the present (Bennett 1977; Thomas 1977).

Their pessimistic outlook is at odds with past history. Not one of the infectious diseases, such as pneumonia and tuberculosis, that were among the ten major causes of morbidity and mortality in 1900 were among the ten major "ills of man" in 1970 (Dingle 1973; McKinlay and McKinlay 1981; White 1973). This change was largely due to major improvements in diet and community and personal hygiene; medical technologies, e.g., innoculations, played little or no role in bringing it about (Mckinlay and McKinlay 1981).

THE BEHAVIORAL APPROACH TO PREVENTION. History may validate the importance of social and psychological factors for prevention but neither sociological nor psychological theory offers a coherent and differentiated view (or model) of prevention. Targets for prevention such as cessation of cigarette smoking and reductions in dietary salt and cholesterol levels are selected on the basis of epidemiological and biomedical data. Once a behavioral target is chosen investigators and practitioners proceed first to describe it in great detail and then to propose a behavioral technology to "modify" it (Leventhal and Cleary 1979, 1980). The aim is to match the appropriate technology to the appropriate behavior. This seemingly rational approach often ignores a number of critical steps. For example, the history of the behavior and the degree to which it is part of a larger control system are typically overlooked. Smoking may not only be linked to a large number of other specific actions, such as drinking coffee and alcoholic beverages, it may also be part of a control system for regulating distress or for defining oneself in social contexts. Hence, changing the behavior may prove a formidable task. Investigators also sometimes overlook whether changing a risk behavior will necessarily lead to improved health status. Even if a behavior is linked to morbidity and mortality in prospective and retrospective epidemiological studies, we cannot be sure it causes illness, nor can we be certain that reversal will lead to reductions in illness and illness consequences (Sackett 1978).

Given the above cautionary note, let us turn to a very abbreviated summary of the major contributions of social-psychological research to prevention. Two major lines of theory dominate prevention research. The first is concerned with the motivational and decisional factors leading people to develop skills for risk reduction. The second focuses on the development of skills themselves. Both types of study have been carried out in laboratory and field settings (for a more extensive review see Leventhal and Hirschman, in press). Research on the decisional or motivational component is illustrated by the literature on fear communications (Kirscht et al. 1978; Janis 1962; Leventhal 1970; Ley 1977; Rogers 1975). These studies demonstrated that increasing the vividness of threat information (pictures of surgery, death, and mutilation) increased the favorableness of attitudes toward risk-reducing behavior. But increasingly favorable attitudes and intentions did not necessarily ensure healthful behavior. A change toward healthful behavior required giving people specific instructions on how, when, and where to act, providing an opportunity for the rehearsal of the responses and the cues producing them, and developing a sense of self-confidence in controlling both the threatening event and one's emotional reactions to it (Bandura 1977; Leventhal 1970; Rogers, in press; Rosen, Terry, and Leventhal 1982). Other motivational factors that have been studied include emotional role-playing (Janis and Mann 1965; Mausner and Platt 1971) and the individual's values and commitment to change (Mausner 1971).

The investigation of skills training has proceeded largely within the framework of theories of behavior modification. The behavior modifier focuses on the action to be changed, not a medical endpoint. Hence, subjects in studies or therapeutic treatment are typically asked to monitor the behavior in various ways, such as, to keep records of the time and place of its occurrence and to plot these on graphic displays (see Stunkard 1979), to complete questionnaires describing the satisfaction the subjects achieve from the behavior (McKennell 1968; Tomkins, 1968; U.S. Department of Health Education and Welfare 1973), and to describe the way in which the behavior is performed. The behavior is changed by varying the rewards following it, or having the participant model other people's actions, practice new behaviors, and so on. As I have already indicated in the discussion of compliance with medical regimens, behavioral procedures have proved extremely powerful in generating short-term change. But none meet the acid test of producing lasting, let alone permanent, change; by three to six months after any intervention program, a substantial majority of those treated, sometimes 80 percent, will return to baseline values for the treated behavior (Hunt and Bespalec 1974; Hunt and Matarazzo 1981; Marlatt and Gordon 1979).

Two different types of hypotheses have been offered to account for the failure of behavioral risk-reduction programs. The first is that internal conditions (e.g., biologically based regulators) pose insuperable barriers to change. For example, smokers are said to be chemically addicted, a notion that "explains" their inability to stop smoking and helps to rationalize their failures to do so. Or obese people are seen as fighting a constitutionally determined (by genetics and early feeding) set point (Keesey 1978; Knittle and Hirsch 1970) or to be externally cue sensitive (Rodin and Slochower 1976; Schachter and Rodin 1974). These hypotheses take a dim view of the possibility of risk reduction *after* the risk behavior is establishd. Instead, they generate a great deal of pressure for primary behavioral prevention, such as health education in the early years, in order to block the behavior before it can occur. While primary prevention arouses the enthusiasm of health professionals, the low correlation between various health behaviors (Langlie 1977) and the substantial behavior changes which occur with growth and social development cast doubt on the appropriateness of excessive reliance on early intervention (Leventhal 1973).

The second type of hypothesis focuses on the external environment. One view is that the individual fails to maintain new behaviors because an unaltered environment continues to provoke earlier habits. Tactics for dealing with unchanged environments range from preparation for unanticipated threats (identifying situations likely to provoke risk behaviors and rehearsal of coping responses to manage these situations) to booster sessions and development of social support networks (see Kirschenbaum and Tomarken, in press). All of these tactics, however, are therapeutic in concept. Their aim is to improve the external behavioral supports for a single person. Changes in cultural and social norms respecting risk behaviors, perhaps the most important aspect of environmental control, have been given far less attention. For example, there has been a downward trend in adult smoking since the publication of the surgeon general's report in 1964 (Warner 1977). The change appears to reflect the impact of antismoking media campaigns and changed cultural mores (e.g., no-smoking sections on airplanes and in restaurants) which have greatly reduced the social support for smoking. These effects are entirely in keeping with Fishbein and Ajzen's (1975; Ajzen and Fishbein 1973) position that cultural norms play a central role in determining whether an attitude will be expressed in behavior.

Perhaps the most important development in the area of environmental change has been the effort to develop psychologically sophisticated school or community health promotion programs. Early efforts in this area were disappointing. In a succinct review of a hundred and fifty or more school-based antismoking programs Thompson (1978) declared smoking a clear winner; there was virtually no evidence of successful primary prevention. More recent programs hold forth greater hope (Evans et al. 1979) but the verdict is still out regarding long-term behavior change. Community-wide programs have been carried out in California (see Meyer et al. 1980), and elsewhere (Levens 1970). The Stanford program for heart disease control (Farquhar 1978; Farquhar et al. 1978; Meyer et al 1980) took an innovative, quasi-experimental approach to investigate the joint effects of an individualized behavioral program and environmental control. In one of three communities the behavioral risk-modification program was available to high-risk individuals and their families along with a community-wide mass media campaign for risk reduction. A second community was exposed only to the media program, and the third was an unexposed control. The samples were compared on knowledge about risk behaviors, reported change in diet, reported smoking behavior, blood pressure, blood lipid levels, and other measures of cardiac risk. The comparison showed favorable changes in knowledge of risk factors and reports of dietary practices for the samples in the communities exposed to the media programs. In addition, a fairly high proportion of the smokers exposed to the behavioral program (50 percent) quit smoking and maintained the change for a period of two years (Meyer et al. 1980).

Community studies represent the latest effort to modify risk behaviors and reduce premature morbidity and mortality from chronic illness. While these investigations have been hailed by some as the solution to our major health problems, they have also elicited considerable skepticism (see Kasl 1980; Leventhal et al. 1980). When the success rates in these programs are compared to those in recent behavior modification studies lacking the community component or those from the Multiple Risk Factor Intervention Trials (Benfari 1979), they prove less impressive than claimed by their partisans. But many of the shortcomings of these studies are due less to their community focus than to their medical and behavioral orientation in the absence of a systems-oriented view of the prevention process.

A CONTROL (SYSTEMS) THEORY APPROACH TO PREVENTION. Control (systems) theory highlights both the gaps and future possibilities for prevention programs and research. This is particularly true for community studies. A systems approach would ask how processes at the social level affect those at the individual level and would raise questions about whether these cross-level effects are important for the maintenance of behavioral change. For example, how did community process (media campaigns, reference and face-to-face groups) affect the individuals in the Stanford study? Did they impinge directly on the participants in the intensive behavioral treatments or did they affect peers or significant others who then pressured the individual to initiate and maintain risk reduction? No community

studies of risk behavior have investigated this, though such research has been conducted for the adoption of agricultural innovations (see Rogers 1962).

A systems approach would also ask how new behavioral patterns develop. But
none of the community studies tell us how the individuals decided to participate in
their program or whether the way the decision was made affected later participation. We do not even know if exposure to mass media affected the decision to participate, reinforced it after it was made, or sustained change after the individual
left the program. Moreover, we do not know if the participant's conception of his
or her risk changed because of media exposure or from participation in the
behavioral program. We also do not know how communities involve existent
organizations and develop new ones to conduct prevention programs.

Systems theory raises still more fundamental issues about prevention. If
behavior is goal-directed, as system theory argues, what is the goal of prevention?
Is it disease avoidance? If so, is it avoidance of known illness threats or is it the
avoidance of prior (or imagined) symptom experiences? Is there a goal of positive
health? If so, can it be represented in concrete form, or can it only exist as an
abstraction? If positive health can be defined only in abstract terms, can we expect
it to guide preventive health action when we know that illness representations are
powerful guides to coping because they include both concrete (symptomatic) and
abstract features? If we cannot create an integrated, hierarchical goal structure,
can we expect risk avoidance to persist? Behavioral interventions achieved short-
term behavioral control by focusing on specific actions, but they failed to examine
the network of goals or reference values that regulate actions over the longterm
and failed to maintain their short-term successes (Powers 1973a, 1973b). Change
in this network, including change in self-definition (Sarbin and Nucci 1973), may
be essential for sustaining risk-avoidant activity.

A relatively little explored approach to the establishment of new behavioral
systems involves attaching opposite emotional reactions to both the performance
and the *nonperformance* of specific actions. For example, it is possible that people
can readily reduce their food intake by experiencing disgust or anxiety to food-
related cues, such as the sweetness of desserts, and by experiencing positive affects
when eating low-calorie foods at the appropriate place and time. Similarly, addicted joggers may experience emotional distress when inactive and use exercise to
replace distress with positive affect (Solomon and Corbit 1974; Tomkins 1980).
The attachment of opposing affects to the presence or absence of specific activities
appears to be the key to the establishment of stable, addictive behaviors. We need
to learn more about how to establish healthful addictions in natural environments,
and to find out how addictions are affected. For example, social support may be
important to create and attach negative emotional responses to undesirable
behaviors, and positive emotional responses to desired behaviors (Leventhal and
Cleary, 1980). Little is known about this problem.

The importance of examining the way individuals generate their own, hierarchical goal systems to direct, evaluate and sustain behaviors is also suggested by
the comparison between success rates in risk-reduction programs and self-
initiated, risk-reduction efforts. Evidence in the risk-reduction literature for smoking (Leventhal and Cleary 1980) and weight control (Dunbar and Stunkard 1979;
Stunkard, 1979) and newly collected data from Schachter's laboratory (Schachter
1977) suggest that self-initiated risk reduction can produce high rates of long-term
success. Schachter reported that 67 percent of his sample succeeded in quitting
smoking and maintaining desired weights for periods of seven and more years. Of

course, the difference between self-initiated and therapeutic programs could reflect sampling differences, with persons who failed at self-control coming to therapy. On the other hand, the therapy setting may be a poor place for developing and internalizing a self-regulating goal structure because going to an expert for help may create a barrier to seeing oneself as competent to generate long-term behavioral change.

Control theory raises yet another question about the relationship between the social context and internal controls; how does the individual go about constructing an appropriate external, social support network? There is abundant attention to the impact of the social network on the individual. For instance, people are more likely to become smokers if friends and members of their families smoke, and it is easier to quit smoking if a spouse or friend also quits (Leventhal and Cleary 1980). What is given less attention is the way people go about constructing a social environment to support healthful behaviors. An example would be the person who moves to a community to make new friends and acquaintances in order to promote a healthy life-style. This may seem extreme, but moving to a new community has been a traditional way for Americans to alter their life-styles. If is difficult enough to change a complex behavior pattern without having to struggle with friends and family who insist we maintain established role relationships. The adolescent becomes an adult by moving out of the parental home and forming a new family unit. Changing the support network, literally changing its members or changing the attitudes and role behaviors of existent members, is a major aspect of altering life-style and health promotion.

It is difficult to tell which of the above issues will be developed in the coming decade. Each offers room for imaginative development in social psychological theory.

Self-Regulation under Stressful Circumstances

Life is filled with surprises—some pleasant, some not so pleasant. Unpleasant surprises and the excessive effort demanded by everyday high-pressure routines are sources of subjective distress and very possibly sources of psychological and biological illness (Levi 1971). Whether or not this distress actually causes illness, it is clearly noticed, and disliked, and is a target for intervention. Indeed, we categorize stress or distress with pain. Both are believed to be signs of affliction and treated as experiences we can do without. Evidence that stress is held in low regard can be found in any bookstore whose psychology and health section is filled with volumes on stress control, stress management, and stress and illness. The titles suggest our cultural motto is "Out, damned stress."

The popular literature is matched by a rapidly expanding technical literature on stress control. I will very briefly review the background assumptions underlying stress research and then reexamine the issue both from the perspective of control theory and from the accumulating literature of psychology and psychophysiology which will lead us to a far more differentiated view of stress and stress management.

EARLY APPROACHES TO STRESS. Selye (1956, 1976) laid the groundwork for research on stress. Stress is a patterned response of a specific set of organs over time. The temporal pattern involves three stages: an alarm reaction to the onset of stressful or disturbing conditions, a defense response to combat the environmental insult, and a stage of exhaustion where the defense process weakens and disappears. The specific organs involved are the pituitary, adrenal-cortical axis (the pituitary hormone stimulating the adrenal cortex to generate corticoids) which produce ulceration of the gut, and shrinkage of the thymus and lymph nodes (Selye 1973).

Selye argued that any demand or adaptive effort, regardless of its quality, evokes the stress response. Hence, the stress response is specific (patterned over time and organ systems) but the stressor is nonspecific, such that "it is even immaterial whether the agent or situation we face is pleasant or unpleasant; all that counts is the intensity of the demand for readjustment or adaptation" (1973, p. 693). This view of stressful events stimulated Holmes and Rahe (1978) and others to develop life-event scales. These are lists of events, ranging from minor irritations to major cataclysms (death of a spouse) that demand adaptive effort. Each event is given a weight for the amount of effort it demands (as rated by a group of judges), and a respondent's score is the sum of the items checked as having happened during a specific period of time (Dohrenwend and Dohrenwend 1974). Both retrospective and prospective studies have been conducted to relate life-event scores to the onset of physical (Holmes and Masuda 1974) and mental health problems (Brown and Harris 1978; Paykel 1979).

Selye's psychobiological hypothesis and the supporting evidence from life-event studies provide at least some support for the commonly held cultural belief that stress causes illness (see, for example, Friedman and Rosenman 1974). While Selye may have viewed stress as a process and wished us to be more tolerant of stress as part of normal living (Selye 1956, 1976), the culture appears to view stress as an entity to be extirpated to enhance survival. The methods of stress removal can range from relaxation, exercise, and reduced work schedules to various self-indulgent practices such as cigarette smoking and inappropriate eating patterns. Essentially, therefore, Selye's description of physiological process was reified by psychological investigators and laymen alike, and stress control procedures were applied in an ad-hoc manner. The pattern is identical to that followed in the early period of research on compliance to treatment regimens. It is little wonder that the stress control literature has generated a host of inconsistent findings and has failed to generate adequate theoretical models.

SYSTEMS THEORY AND STRESS. Words are not things, and the term *stress* refers to a process, not to an entity. Moreover both psychological and biological processes are involved in stress, as are the interactions between the processes at these two levels of description. To understand the full import of the above statement, we need to consider in some detail both the psychological and biological systems involved in stress reactions. As we explore the details of this statement we will better understand the future directions of stress research, including the way in which specific procedures such as biofeedback meld with other types of stress interventions.

1. The psychological level. It is clear that some kind of noxious stimulus event is necessary to arouse stress, but it is not sufficient (Steptoe 1980). Not even the venerable electrical shock automatically gives rise to subjective feelings of dysphoria or distress. As Lazarus (1966, 1968, 1980) and others have suggested (Janis 1958, 1962; Janis and Leventhal 1968; Leventhal 1970; Withey 1962), an interpretive step intervenes between stimulation and stress. This initial or primary appraisal (Lazarus 1966, 1980) process need not be conscious or deliberate; the stressed person does not need to talk to him or herself and say, "That situation is

dangerous." Threat interpretations can be fully automatic (Leventhal and Nerenz, in press) and are more likely to be so if the stimuli involved are peripheral to the focus of attention (see Bowlby 1973, chap. 11). Interpretations can be changed to decrease the impact of the stressor (Lazarus 1980), and interpretations can enhance or interfere with stress reduction, as when the use of threat warnings interferes with adaptation to threat stimuli (Epstein 1973; Leventhal et al. 1979).

Interpretation has been recognized as a significant step in the life-event literature (Brown 1974). It appears that negative life events rather than life events in general account for the major portion of variance in the association of life events and illness (see Paykel 1979; Rahe 1974). More important, it is becoming clear that specific kinds of life events may be responsible for particular kinds of illness. Loss, for instance, is crucial for the onset of depressive illness (Brown and Harris 1978). Time-urgent demands seem peculiarly suited to evoking the Type A behavior pattern linked to cardiovascular disease (Krantz et al. in press; Matthews, in press). The association of different life events with different illness problems is bringing the life-event literature into contact with the psychosomatic literature, which long emphasized that specific attitudes, or interpretations and coping patterns, were linked to particular, somatic illnesses (see Graham's [1972] excellent summary). It is unclear how this particular differentiation will continue. For example, it is possible that a variety of qualitative categories, such as loss, time urgency, etc., will emerge to account for the linkage of life events to various types of illnesses. On the other hand, a dimensional approach may also prove useful, with stress linked to factors such as the predictability versus the uncertainty of life events. Uncertainty clearly plays a major role in the onset of stress-induced disorders in animals (Weiss 1972) and humans (Glass and Singer 1972).

Recent research on the stress experienced by cancer patients during chemotherapy suggests that meaning and uncertainty are integrally related in human distress. Nerenz (1980) and Ringler (1981) have found that many cancer patients pay close attention to body symptoms to assess the progress of treatment and the likelihood they are winning the battle against this dread disease. They become severely distressed, however, if the symptoms they are monitoring abruptly disappear, leaving them with no clue as to the impact of continuing treatment on the disease status. What is curious about this finding is that the sudden, indeed abrupt, disappearance of symptoms might be interpreted as a sign that one is cured! But in the face of a continuing symptomatic treatment, the patient does not look with favor on his or her dramatic change. Treatment in the absence of symptoms makes no sense, and there is no clear way of interpreting what is happening. Thus, while uncertainty about the meaning of treatment and of disease status may be mediating distress, it is clear that the uncertainty arises out of deeper expectations about the relationship between symptoms and illness and illness and treatment. One is symptomatic if ill and one is treated only when ill (symptomatic). The continuation of treatment in the absence of symptoms violates the underlying schematic expectation. Uncertainty can only be understood in terms of the specific content of the interpretation given these environmental events (Leventhal, Meyer, and Nerenz 1980). Expectations about the self in relation to others as well as expectations about illness will also condition interpretation in the medical-care setting and determine the appearance of feelings of uncertainty, depersonalization and dehumanization (Leventhal 1975; Leventhal, Nerenz, and Leventhal 1982). Understanding uncertainty means understanding the content of specific cognitive schemata.

The possibilities for coping and the appraisal of the outcomes of coping responses (secondary appraisal—Lazarus 1966), form the second and third set of factors in a model of psychological distress (Leventhal and Nerenz, in press). If psychological stress reflects an imbalance between demands and coping, stress will be minimal even for severe threats if the individual's coping resources ensure that he or she can be protected from harm (Withey 1962). Coping can be problem- or danger-oriented, as when one takes inoculations to eliminate the possibility of contracting tetanus. Or, coping can be focused on the control of emotion, as when one denies danger to minimize fear or withdraws from a stressful setting to regain composure (Folkman and Lazarus 1980; Leventhal 1970; Rosen, Terry, and Leventhal 1982). Coping also includes use of environmental and social resources. Evidence exists showing the positive effects of social support in reducing coronary heart disease (Bruhn et al. 1966), eliminating postpartum complications (Nuckolls, Cassel, and Kaplan 1972), and cushioning stress reactions in a wide variety of life situations (Cobb 1976). Coping is so important in determining the stressfulness of a stimulus that subjects exposed to repeated shocks in a laboratory study will rate shocks as less distressing when they believe they have control over shock intensity (Geer, Davidson, and Gatchel 1970) or believe they can escape shock (Klemp and Leventhal 1974) even when their beliefs are false!

Research with animals underlines yet more forcefully the intimate association between coping and stress. In a series of elegant experiments, Weiss (1972) has demonstrated that coping can virtually eliminate the physiological impact of a noxious stressor. Weiss used a design in which two of three animals, all in identical cages containing a wheel, receive identical amounts of electrical shock. One of the two could terminate the shock by wheel turning while his yoked partner could not. The third animal received no noxious stimulation. Although the two shocked animals received identical shocks, the animal with control (whose wheel turning terminated the shock) showed no more psychophysiological distress (ulceration of the gut) than did the unshocked animal; the yoked animal showed extensive ulceration. The same shock had very different effects depending on the animal's ability to cope. As control theory would predict, the process underlying the stressful experience involves not just coping, but the appraisal of coping in relation to the representation or experience of the danger. Among the yoked animals, those who showed the most ulceration were the most active. Repeated responding (wheel turning) was associated with high levels of ulceration if the response was ineffective! This point was repeated in studies where animals received a mild shock after making an escape response; these animals showed very extensive ulceration. Noxious stimulation after a response eliminated the sense of safety or efficacy in escaping. Taken together the findings strongly suggest that effective coping reduces distress while ineffective coping, or coping that is ambiguous in effectiveness, may be the source of distress. The animal who is least harmed is the animal who can act to avoid or the animal who remains passive.

Weiss's findings emphasize the importance of the total coping mechanism, i.e., the representation of the stressor, the coping response, and the experience or appraisal of outcome as a determinant of stress. Being able to match response to expectation not only reduces the actor's sense of helplessness (Seligman 1975), it allows him or her to perceive the objective features of the situation and experience it as an event that is understandable. This appears to facilitate the adaptation of intense emotional reactions. What is most important about these findings is the suggestion that awareness of stress and acceptance and objective perception of the stress episode can actually protect against its stressful impact. Knowing when not to struggle, i.e., knowing when an event is uncontrollable, when to rest and restore, and when it is time to give control to others may be equal in importance to the exercise of problem-centered coping.

The conclusion is supported by laboratory and field studies showing that knowledge of the sensory experiences associated with a stressor along with information on how and when to cope facilitates distress reduction and adaptation (Johnson 1975; Johnson and Leventhal, 1974; Leventhal et al. 1981). Suls and Mullen (in press) conducted a meta-analysis and found that assimilative strategies, such as taking in information about the details of stressful situations, were most effective for long-term adaptation. They also found that self-awareness or sensitivity to subjective states was associated with lower levels of stress and illness in response to negative life events. Further, Suls and Mullen found higher levels of reported illness for negative life events of doubtful controllability than for life events clearly uncontrollable.

A similar picture appears for Type A persons who are more likely to develop serious cardiovascular disease when exposed to stressful situations (Friedman and Rosenman 1974). These persons become highly self-involved in threat situations (Scherwitz, Berton, and Leventhal 1978) and relatively insensitive to their internal stress states (Carver, Coleman, and Glass 1976; Glass 1977). Type A persons are also likely to delay seeking care for coronary symptoms; at least they show long delays between "noticing" symptoms and paying sufficient attention to them to decide they may be serious (Matthews et al. 1981). All of the above data support the general hypothesis that control involves a fit between representation, coping, and appraisal (Schwartz 1977, 1979), and that stress is minimized when fit is high.

2. Physiological aspects of stress. Stress theory at the physiological level is undergoing change and differentiation even more dramatically than that taking place at the psychological level. In a detailed review of this literature, Mason (1972) suggests the physiological stress pattern is extremely complex and differentiated across situations rather than relatively constant, as Selye (1973) claimed. A rather astonishing variety of hormones and neuropeptides (McGeer and McGeer 1980) are brought into play under stress situations and at the termination of these situations. Some of the after-effects, i.e., hormonal responses appearing when stress terminates, last far longer than do responses to the stressor itself (Mason 1972). This variety and durability of response and the likelihood that variation in response is associated with specific types of stress situations may help explain why different types of disease appear in different individuals and in different types of stress situations. Patterns of interpretation, coping, and appraisal may be linked to patterns of neuroendocrine response and have specific consequences for illness (Graham 1972).

Of course, not all of the illness following stress need be a direct consequence of the stressor, the interpretation of it, the coping response selected to deal with it, or the appraisal of coping. The self-regulative process may include a number of reactions which have unexpected health consequences. For example, if stress increases smoking and consumption of foods high in calories and fats (Conway et al. 1981), changes in these health behaviors may be disease inducing or may interfere with the body's ability to restore homeostasis after intense exertion.

Differentiation at the physiological level is important for yet another reason; different patterns of physiological change may be more or less detectable as mood states and/or feelings of sickness and distress. Differential detectability means differential modification of coping—variations in seeking release from pressure and use of social support or other resources to alleviate affect and change the environment. The risk of disabling illness will be greater, therefore, for some patterns of stress-induced disturbance than others. The degree to which changes at one level can drive or inform changes at another is a clear challenge to psychological research in behavioral medicine.

STRESS REDUCTION—RELAXATION TO BIOFEEDBACK. From the perspective of control theory, all forms of stress control are forms of biofeedback (Schwartz 1977, 1979). The individual who modulates his or her behavior, e.g., works less or eats less when feeling distress or gastric upset, is using a biological signal to guide coping. On the other hand, systems theory also focuses attention on the important differences between various methods of stress control. Biofeedback procedures use information to modify highly specific target responses. A light or other type of signal may come on whenever blood pressure (heart rate, frontalis or zygomatic muscle tension, capillary blood flow, etc.) drops below or exceeds a specified level. The hypothesis is that the signal can reward, or inform the human subject to regulate a specific visceral response in a particular direction (Yates 1980).

Relaxation training (Jacobson 1938), meditation (Benson 1975), and other forms of stress management training (Meichenbaum 1975; Suinn and Bloom 1978) target a more global set of reactions. For example, stress-management training may include reinterpretation of demand situations, developing of coping skills (assertion training, work planning, etc.), and tactics for coping with emotional arousal such as relaxation, exercise, and so forth (Meichenbaum 1975). Biofeedback appeals to the careful experimentalist; it is precise in target, and failure and success can be attributed to feedback in a well-designed study eliminating confounds. Stress management appeals to the practitioner; it is global and complex, requires little equipment, and can be performed by the client in life situations which are stress inducing. What are the relative merits of these various control procedures? How will they benefit practice and theory?

Both the more global relaxation and stress control procedures and the more specific biofeedback methods initially held out high promise as nonpharmacological methods of managing a variety of difficult to control disorders. Biofeedback was initially the most electrifying of these methods as the paradigm suggested that an individual could attain virtually unlimited voluntary control over highly specific, supposedly automatic, body response processes. Studies with animals showed that rewards—e.g., terminating electrical shocks or stimulating so-called reward centers of the brain, which systematically followed rises or falls in heart rate, blood pressure, stomach motility, electroencephalographic activity (increase or decrease in alpha frequency), changes in blood flow to the animal's ear, etc.—could train or shape these reactions leading to further increases or decreases in the response amplitude or frequency (Miller 1969). Could we not adapt these same procedures for the control of blood pressure, alertness, stomach disorders, headache, a variety of peripheral vascular conditions and cardiac problems such as premature ventricular contractions? Unfortunately, early enthusiasm has been followed by later disappointment. The animal research proved extremely difficult to replicate (Miller and Dworkin 1974) and the same has been true with the efforts to generalize these expectations to humans. As Young and Blanchard (1980) point out, to evaluate the effects of biofeedback, one must demonstrate that providing information about change in the direction of a response, e.g., drop in blood pressure, adds to therapeutic effectiveness above and beyond the effect obtained from the other procedures combined with biofeedback in the treatment package; nearly all clinical and many experimental uses of biofeedback combine it with relaxation, systematic desensitization, or other procedures. In addition, Blanchard (1979; Young and Blanchard 1980) points to several criteria for evaluating biofeedback (and indeed any therapeutic regimen) before it is accepted as a standard practice procedure. The most important of these is to demonstrate that effects can be obtained which are clinically significant. Clinically significant means the effect must be seen in abnormal and not just normal populations. For instance, normotensive persons might be more responsive than hypertensives to biofeedback training for blood pressure reductions. Furthermore, the size of the change, as with blood pressure reduction, must be sufficient to reduce the risk of heart attack, stroke, and other such complications. In addition, the effects must be repeatable, durable, and transfer to the patient's natural environment. After reviewing the many studies in the area of hypertension, Young and Blanchard (1980) concluded that "direct biofeedback of blood pressure offers little in the way of applicability in the treatment of hypertension" (p. 223). Their conclusion in respect to the control of hypertension using biofeedback to enhance relaxation is more optimistic. Research by Patel (Patel 1973, 1975; Patel and North 1975) created a relaxation package using a yogic exercise combined with biofeedback for a galvanic skin response and produced substantial and sustained reductions in blood pressure. Young and Blanchard (1980) qualify their endorsement by pointing out that it seems premature to recommend such treatments as an alternative to drug regimens of known effectiveness.

Biofeedback appears more successful in dealing with more specific problems, such as premature ventricular contractions, and specific types of abnormally high heart rate, such as sinus tachycardia. The greater success with these more specific cardiac problems may reflect differences between these behaviors and behaviors such as heart rate and blood pressure in that the latter may be responsive to a much wider variety of environmental and biological factors. The system controlling them may be more responsive to stresses induced by effort, emotion, and a variety of other conditions. Indeed, control theory suggests we need to limit severely our expectations with regard to success in directly influencing specific behaviors through biofeedback (information for voluntary control) when these behaviors are part of a larger control system and the treatment does not address other components in the system. It is not surprising to find, therefore, a somewhat more promising record for global, intervention therapies such as desensitization treatment, relaxation training, or stress-management training, as these packages target multiple parts of the control system. Unfortunately, the components of these complex packages are often assembled in an atheoretical, ad-hoc manner, and their use does little to advance our understanding of therapy, human behavior, or stress.

There are two important ideas which may help us understand the potential for success of biofeedback and other self-regulation procedures. First, the utility of a procedure appears to depend on the degree to which the information to guide response performance is readily available to the subject. Relaxation and stress control procedures target experiences that are highly available. The individual knows what external situations must be reinterpreted, and he or she can feel the anxiety and tension which signal the need to relax. Second, it must be possible to perform the required response. Many reactions are simply not accessible to volitional or controlled processing (Furedy 1979, 1973; Leventhal 1980; Riley and Furedy, in press; Shiffrin and Schneider 1977). These two important qualifiers make clear that our current understanding of self-control processes is not very different from that described by Bair (1901) in his paper on teaching people how to wiggle their ears! His procedure required: information to make salient the feeling of the appropriate muscle contracting; performing a volitional or controllable response which would also produce the ear wiggle such as jaw clenching or biting; and rehearsal of and attention to the sensation of the muscle action so as to gradually eliminate unwanted reactions to produce only the desired response. (It is also important to be sure the subject can perform the volitional response without embarrassment in public settings [Miller and Dworkin 1980]. Biofeedback practitioners may have overlooked these important factors because biofeedback practice shares many features of medically oriented treatments—a patient comes for help and is treated by a practitioner who uses an instrument to give information about a response which is gradually reinforced by an externally controlled source. The approach is similar to the medical approach to compliance with medication; in both instances control remains exclusively if not primarily in the hands of the practitioner and not the patient. The patient cannot access the necessary information nor can he or she perform the desired responses without the aid of instruments or an external expert observer. It should come as no surprise, therefore, that patients fall back on more readily available cues (symptoms) and regulate their performance in the simplest manner possible regardless of the validity of their strategies.

Riley and Furedy (in press) describe procedures for achieving control over simple visceral reactions that allow the individual to detect the conditions for response performance, to perform a controllable response, and allow the response process to become automatic. For example, if a violinist becomes excessively nervous at performances, he or she quickly becomes aware of both the external cues and internal changes signaling excessive levels of activation. By performing a controllable response, such as taking a deep breath, the performer can induce a reduction in heart rate, the outcome of which is likely to reduce the noxiousness of subsequent environmental stimuli (Schwartz et al. 1974). If this sequence is repeated over a number of occasions, the heart rate slowing produced by the controllable reaction will be conditioned to the performance situation: outer, performance-related cues will automatically provoke heart rate slowing. The performance setting can be said to elicit a schemata which includes components of the relaxation response (see Leventhal 1980; in press).

Research in biofeedback and stress control offers enormous potential for deepening our understanding of self-regulative processes. Important theoretical contributions have already been made (see Brener 1974) and procedures developed to ensure greater uniformity in outcome of therapeutic practice (Lang 1979). Most important, however, is that theory and empirical findings in this area are of direct relevance to theory in the wider sociobehavioral context discussed in the prior sections.

Summary and Conclusions

We can see control theory at work in each of the three areas reviewed. Whether the issue is use of the medical-care system, prevention, or regulation of stress or specific cardiovascular performance, we must consider the following factors: (1) the reference value (goal or target) guiding the response; (2) the response itself (is it volitional, automatic, etc.?); and (3) the information obtained respecting response outcomes (did the response fall short, reach or overshoot the target?). The feedback will reflect the target selected and the criterion for appraisal as well as the nature of the coping response. The ability to apply the control model to each of the three problem areas we have discussed should come as no surprise since the model is relatively open and can accept any number of contents. More important, however, is that it focuses on similar conceptual issues across these separate, substantive problems.

Perhaps the most important issue addressed by control theory is the origin of the reference values. Precisely how are reference values established, and how does their origin affect commitment to short- and long-term action? The investigations reviewed under utilization of the health-care system and prevention show that people often select goals or reference values different from those practitioners select, since patients concentrate on concrete, readily available cues for guiding action. Part of the problem with biofeedback and other strategies for controlling autonomic functions and emotional experience is selecting an appropriate reference value for self-regulation. It is clear that imposing reference values from the outside rather than helping the individual shape and formulate his or her own reference values is likely to undercut long-term compliance. Selecting reference values or choosing goals appears critical for developing a sense of self-control or effectance (Bandura 1977) and sustaining behavior over the long term.

Control theory makes clear the need for conceptual and empirical work investigating the impact the practitioner-patient relationship has on the way people represent the possibilities for health, the presence of illness, and their role in stress reduction and risk management. The medical relationship is built on an acute-disease model where the physician is active in diagnosis and treatment and the patient a passive recipient of information. Whether the information is used is indeed up to the patient, but neither the decision nor the patient's actions are typically issues of discussion. The form of the relationship discourages sharing information and the development of a sense of effectance in regulating outcomes.

Control theory also makes clear that reference values change over time, hence so too will the skills needed for effective self-regulation. Recognizing the separation between the underlying control system and overt behavior also makes clear that similarity of response (over time) does not require identity in the underlying control variables. The underlying factors (reference values and skills) can change while maintaining what superficially appears to be the same behavior.

Control theory also emphasizes the hierarchical nature of reference values (Powers 1973a, 1973b; Carver and Scheier 1981). The same behavior can be regulated on abstract (volitional or rules-based) grounds, concrete or schematic grounds, and still more primitive, sensory-motor conditions (Leventhal 1980; in press). The data from each of the three areas I have reviewed suggest that people tend to select a reference value in the hierarcy which requires the least effortful attention and allows for the most rapid switch to automatic regulation of behavior. This could lead to efficient, long-term maintenance of desirable health behaviors, whether these behaviors were prescribed by practitioners or rewarded by biofeedback, if the reference values in the hierarchy were linked to a common action that had beneficial effects on the individual's health status. As we have seen it is frequently the case that neither condition is met; symptoms may maintain action for the short term—e.g., take medication till the headache goes away—while the abstract representation, hypertension, demands long-term use of medication. If the two levels were tightly linked, i.e., all high blood pressure readings were accompained by headache, there would be no problem; but the linkage is weak if not nonexistent.

It is also clear that some people are more likely to construct goals or reference values using information from the external environment while others are more attentive to inner, symptomatic information. Differences in this area affect use of health services, participation in preventive behavior, and ability to benefit from biofeedback instruction. Responsiveness to inner cues will further subdivide into responsiveness to symptomatology and/or responsiveness to emotional states. The degree to which such differences reflect biological factors, socialization, or immediate environmental demands remains to be determined.

It is important to emphasize that not all people, patients or otherwise, actively construct complex representations of potential or current illness threats. Many people are passive, accepting externally imposed definitions of their lives and health status. Others may be active but accepting of socially defined goals. In either case the individual avoids conflict and stress. As I pointed out earlier, defining and struggling to reach one's own goals can be more stressful than accepting socially defined goals and coping strategies. Acceptance is particularly likely when the individual lacks the social supports and competence to effect change. It is important to recognize, however, that the phenomenon of passive acceptance is not incompatible with control theory: It is one state of a control system. Hence, control theory should illuminate the problems that will arise in attempting to move from passive to active states. One such problem will be the appearance of distress as initial efforts at goal attainment are likely to fall short of expectations. Setting realistic or attainable expectations will be an important prerequisite for change. Individual differences, established by biology, by culture, by social class, or by other more idiosyncratic features of personal history, form a challenge to control concepts; they do not negate them. Behavioral medicine provides an exciting arena for the inquiring investigator and a special challenge to those interested in developing theoretical models to describe both the parallel and interactive processes at the biological and psychological levels. But wherever we choose to probe the control system, it is important to develop sound theory. If control theory provides even a modest approximation to the structure underlying overt behavior, it is clear we cannot expect to find stable relationships between simple environmental and response measures. The mediating system is dynamic. Our studies must recognize this and conceptualize and investigate change.

REFERENCES

ABRAMSON, L. Y.; SELIGMAN, M. E. P.; AND TEASDALE, J. D. 1978. Learned helplessness in humans: critique and reformulation. *Journal of Abnormal Psychology* 87: 49–74.

AJZEN, I., and FISHBEIN, M. 1973. Attitudinal and normative variables as predictors of specific behaviors. *Journal of Personality and Social Psychology* 27: 41–57.

ARBIB, M. A. 1972. *The metaphorical brain.* New York: Wiley-Interscience.

BAIR, J. H. 1901. Development of voluntary control. *Psychological Review* 8: 474–510.

BANDURA, A. 1977. Self efficacy: toward a unifying theory of behavioral change. *Psychological Review.* 84: 191–215.

BECKER, M. H.; DRACHMAN, R. H.; and KIRSCHT, J. P. 1972. Predicting mother's compliance with pediatric medical regimes. *Journal of Pediatrics* 81: 843–45.

BECKER, M. H., and MAIMAN, L. A. 1975. Sociobehavioral determinants of compliance with health and medical care recommendations. *Medical Care* 13: 10–24.

———; KIRSCHT, J. P.; HAEFNER, D. P.; and DRACHMAN, R. H. 1977. The health belief model and dietary compliance: a field experiment. *Journal of Health and Social Behavior* 18: 348–66.

BENFARI, R. C. 1979. Lifestyle alternation and the primary prevention of CHD: the multiple risk factor intervention trial (MRFIT). In *Heart disease and rehabilitation*, ed. M. L. Pollack and D. H. Schmidt. Boston: Houghton Mifflin.

BENNETT, I. L. JR. 1977. Technology as a shaping force. In *Doing better and feeling worse: health in the United States*, ed. J. H. Knowles. New York: Norton.

BENSON, H. 1975. *The relaxation response.* New York: William Morrow.

BLACK, A. H.; BRENER, J.; and DiCARA, L. V., eds. 1974. *Cardiovascular psychophysiology.* Chicago: Aldine.

BLACKWELL, B. 1979. The drug regime and treatment compliance. In *Compliance in health care*, ed. R. B. Haynes, D. W. Taylor, and D. L. Sackett. Baltimore, Md.: Johns Hopkins University Press.

BLANCHARD, E. B. Biofeedback and the modification of cardiovascular dysfunctions. In *Clinical applications of biofeedback: appraisal and status*, ed. R. V. Gatchel and K. P. Price. New York: Pergamon Press.

———; AHLES, A., and SHAW, E. R. 1980. Behavioral treatment of headache. Unpublished manuscript. State University of New York at Albany.

BOWLBY, J. 1973. *Separation: anxiety and anger.* New York: Basic Books.

BRENER, J. 1974. A general model of voluntary control applied to the phenomena of learned cardiovascular change. In *Cardiovascular psychophysiology*, ed. P. A. Obrist, H. A. Black, J. Brener, and L. V. DiCara. Chicago: Aldine.

BROWN, G. W. 1974. Meaning, measurement and stress of life-events. In *Stressful life events: their nature and effects*, ed. B. S. Dohrenwend and B. P. Dohrenwend. New York: Wiley.

———, and HARRIS, T. 1978. *Social orgins of depression: a study of psychiatric disorder in women.* London: Tavistock.

BRUHN, J. G.; CHANDLER, B.; MILLER, M. C.; WOLF, S.; and LYNN, T. N. 1966. Social aspects of coronary heart disease in two adjacent, ethnically different communities. *American Journal of Public Health* 56: 1493–506.

CANNON, W. B. 1936. *Bodily changes in pain, hunger, fear and rage.* 2d ed. 1936. New York: Appleton-Century-Crofts.

CARVER, C. S. 1979. A cybernetic model of self-attention processes. *Journal of Personality and Social Psychology* 37: 125–81.

———; COLEMAN, A. E.; and GLASS, D. C. 1976. The coronary-prone behavior pattern and the suppression of fatigue on a treadmill test. *Journal of Personality and Social Psychology* 33: 460–66.

CARVER, C. S. and GLASS, D. C. 1978. Coronary-prone behavior pattern and interpersonal aggression. *Journal of Personality and Social Psychology* 36: 361–66.

CARVER, C. S., and SCHEIER, M. F. 1981. *Attention and self-regulation: a control-theory approach to human behavior.* New York: Springer-Verlag.

CHRISMAN, N. J. 1977. The health seeking process: an approach to the natural history of illness. *Culture, Medicine, and Psychiatry* 1: 351–77.

COBB, S. 1976. Social support as a moderator of life stress. *Psychosomatic Medicine* 38: 300–14.

CONWAY, T. L.; VICKERS, R. R., JR.; WARD, H. W.; and RAHE, R. H. 1981. Occupational stress and variation in cigarette, coffee, and alcohol consumption. *Journal of Health and Social Behavior* 22: 155–65.

DINGLE, J. H. 1973. The ills of man. *Scientific American* 229: 77–84.

DOHRENWEND, B. P. 1961. The social psychological nature of stress: a framework for causal inquiry. *Journal of Abnormal and Social Psychology* 62: 294–302.

DOHRENWEND, B. S., and DOHRENWEND, B. P., eds. 1974. *Stressful life events: Their nature and effect.* New York: Wiley.

DUNBAR, J. M., and STUNKARD, A. J. 1979. Adherence to diet and drug regime. In *Nutrition, lipids, and coronary heart disease,* ed. R. Levy, B. Rifkind, B. Dennis, and N. Ernest. New York: Raven Press.

EGBERT, L. D.; BATTIT, G. E.; WEBB, C. E.; and BARTLETT, M. K. 1964. Reduction of postoperative pain by encouragement and instruction of patients. *New England Journal of Medicine* 240: 825–27.

EKMAN, P.; FRIESEN, W. V.; and ELLSWORTH, P. 1972. *Emotion in the human face.* New York: Pergamon Press.

ENGEL, G. L. 1977. The need for a new medical model: a challenge for biomedicine. *Science* 196: 129–36.

EPSTEIN, S. 1973. The self-concept: or, a theory of a theory. *American Psychologist* 28: 404–16.

EVANS, R. I.; HENDERSON, A. H.; HILL, P.; and RAINES, B. E. 1977. Smoking in children and prevention strategies. In *Smoking and health: a report of the surgeon general* [U.S. Department of Health, Education, and Welfare pub. no. (PSH) 79–50066]. Washington, D.C.: Government Printing Office.

FABREGA, H., JR. 1975. The need for an ethnomedical science. *Science* 189: 969–75.

FARQUHAR, J. W. 1978. The community-based model of life style intervention trials. *American Journal of Epidemiology* 108: 103–11.

——; WOOD, P. D.; BREITROSE, H.; HASKELL, W. L.; MEYER, A. J.; MACCOBY, N.; ALEXANDER, J. K.; BROWN, B. W.; JR., McALISTER, A. L.; NASH, J. D.; and STERN, M. P. 1977. Community education for cardiovascular health. *Lancet* 1 (no. 8023): 1192–95.

FINNERTY, R.; MATTIE, E.; and FINNERTY, F. 1973. Hypertension in the inner city: 1. Analysis of clinic dropouts. *Circulation* 47: 73–75.

FISHBEIN, M., and AJZEN, I. 1975. *Belief, attitude, intention and behavior: an introduction to theory and research.* Reading, Mass.: Addison-Wesley.

FOLKMAN, S., and LAZARUS, R. S. 1980. An analysis of coping in a middle-aged community sample. *Journal of Health and Social Behavior* 21: 219–39.

FORDYCE, W. 1976. Behavioral concepts in chronic pain and illness. In *The behavioral management of anxiety, depression and pain,* ed. P. O. Davidson. New York: Brunner-Mazel.

FRIEDMAN, M., and ROSENMAN, R. 1974. *Type A behavior and your heart.* New York: Knopf.

FUREDY, J. J. 1973. Some limits of the cognitive control of conditioned autonomic behavior. *Psychophysiology* 10: 108–11.

——. 1979. Teaching self-regulation of cardiac function through imaginational Pavlovian and biofeedback conditioning: Remember the response. In *Biofeedback and self-regulation,* ed. N. Birbaumer and H. D. Kimmel. New Jersey: Pergamon Press.

GEER, J.; DAVISON, G. C.; and GATCHEL, R. J. 1970. Reduction of stress in humans through nonveritical perceived control of aversive stimulation. *Journal of Personality and Social Psychology* 16: 731–38.

GILBERT, D. G. 1979. Paradoxical tranquilizing and emotion-reducing effects of nicotine. *Psychological Bulletin* 86: 643–61.

GLASS, D. C. 1977. *Behavior patterns, stress, and cornary disease.* Hillsdale, N.J.: Erlbaum.

——, and SINGER, J. E. 1972. Behavioral aftereffects of unpredictable and uncontrollable aversive events. *American Scientist* 60: 457–65.

GOLDSTEIN, M. L. 1968. Physiological theories of emotion: a critical historical review from the standpoint of behavior theory. *Psychological Bulletin* 69: 23–40.

GRAHAM, D. 1972. Psychosomatic medicine. In *Handbook of psychophysiology,* ed. N. S. Greenfield and R. A. Sternbach. New York: Holt, Rinehart, and Winston.

HAYES-BAUTISTA, D. E. 1976. Modifying the treatment: patient compliance, patient control and medical care. *Social Science and Medicine* 10: 233–38.

———. 1978. Chicano patients and medical practitioners: a sociology of knowledge paradigm of lay-professional interaction. *Social Science and Medicine* 12: 83–90.

HAYNES, R. B. 1978a. Strategies to improve compliance with referrals, appointments, and prescribed medical regimes. In *Compliance in health care*, ed. R. B. Haynes, D. W. Taylor, and D. L. Sackett. Baltimore, Md.: Johns Hopkins University Press.

———.1978b. Determinants of compliance: the disease and the mechanics of treatment. In *Compliance in health care*, ed. R. B. Haynes, D. W. Taylor, and D. L. Sackett. Baltimore, Md.: Johns Hopkins University Press.

HEBB, D. O. 1949. *The organization of behavior*. New York: Wiley.

HEMPEL, C. G. 1966. *Philosophy of natural science*. Englewood Cliffs, N. J.: Prentice-Hall.

HERZLICH, C. 1973. *Health and illness: a social psychological analysis*. New York: Academic Press.

HOLMES, T. H., and MASUDA, M. 1974. Life changes and illness susceptibility. In *Stressful life events: their nature and effects*, ed. B. S. Dohrenwend and B. P. Dohrenwend. New York: Wiley.

HOLMES, T. H., and RAHE, R. H. 1967. *Schedule of recent experiences*. Seattle, Wash.: School of Medicine, University of Washington.

HUMPHREY, M. 1980. The problem of low back pain. In *Contributions to medical psychology*, ed. S. Rachman, vol. 2. New York: Pergamon Press.

HUNT, W. A., and BESPALEC, D. A. 1974. An evaluation of current methods of modifying smoking behavior. *Journal of Clinical Psychology* 30: 431–38.

HUNT, W. A. and MATARAZZO, J. D. Changing smoking behavior: a critique. In *Behavioral medicine and clinical psychology: overlapping disciplines*, ed. J. R. Gatchel, A. Baum, and J. E. Singer. Hillsdale, N.J.: Erlbaum, in press.

IZARD, C. E. 1971. *The face of emotion*. New York: Appleton-Centruy-Crofts.

JACOBSON, E. 1938. *Progressive relaxation*. Chicago: University of Chicago Press.

JANIS, I. L. 1958. *Psychological stress*. New York: Wiley.

———. 1962. Psychological effects of warnings. In *Man and society in disaster*, ed. C. W. Baker and D. W. Chapman. New York: Basic Books.

———, and LEVENTHAL, H. 1968. Human reactions to stress. In *Handbook of personality theory and research*, ed. E. F. Borgatta and W. W. Lambert. Chicago: Rand McNally.

JANIS, I. L., and MANN, L. 1965. Effectiveness of emotional role-playing in modifying smoking habits and attitudes. *Journal of Experimental Research on Personality* 1: 84–90.

JOHNSON, J. E. 1975. Stress reduction through sensation information. In *Stress and anxiety*, ed. I. C. Sarason and C. O. Speilberger vol. 2. Washington: Hemisphere Publishing Corporation.

———; DABBS, J. M.; and LEVENTHAL, H. 1970. Psychosocial factors in the welfare of surgical patients. *Nursing Research* 19: 18–29.

JOHNSON, J. E.; KIRCHOFF, K. T.; and ENDRESS, M. P. 1975. Deferring children's distress behavior during orthopedic cast removal. *Nursing Research* 75: 404–10.

JOHNSON, J. E., and LEVENTHAL, H. 1974. Effects of accurate expectations and behavioral instructions on reactions during a noxious medical examination. *Journal of Personality and Social Psychology* 29: 710–18.

JOHNSON, J. E.; RICE, V. H.; FULLER, S. S.; and ENDRESS, M. P. 1978. Sensory information instruction in a coping strategy and recovery from surgery. *Research Nursing Health* 1: 4–17.

KANFER, F. H. 1977. The many faces of self-control, or behavior modification changes its focus. In *Behavioral self-management: strategies, techniques and outcomes*, ed. R. B. Stuart. New York: Brunner-Mazel.

———. 1980. Self-management methods. In *Helping people change*, ed. F. H. Kanfer and A. P. Goldstein. 2d ed. New York: Pergamon Press.

KASL, S. V. 1980. Cardiovascular risk reduction in a community setting: some comments. *Journal of Consulting and Clinical Psychology* 48: 143–49.

Kasteler, J.; Kane, R. L.; Olsen, D. M.; and THETFORD, C. 1976. Issues underlying prevalence of "Doctor Shopping" behavior. *Journal of Health and Social Behavior* 17: 328–39.

KEESEY, R. E. 1978. Set-point and body weight regulation. *Psychiatric Clinics of North America* 1: 523–43.

KIRSCHENBAUM, D. S., and TOMARKEN, A. J. On facing the generalization problem: The study of self-regulatory failure. In *Advances on cognitive-behavioral research and theory*, ed. P. C. Kendall, vol. 1. New York: Academic Press, in press.

KIRSCHT, J. P.; BECKER, M. H.; HAEFNER, D. P.; and MAIMAN, L. A. 1972. Effects of threatening communications and mother's health belief on weight change in obese children. *Journal of Pediatrics* 81: 843–48.

KLEMP, G. O., and LEVENTHAL, H. 1974. Self-persuasion and fear reduction from escape behavior. In *Thought and feeling: cognitive alternation of feeling states*, ed. H. London and R. E. Nisbett. Chicago: Aldine.

KNITTLE, J. L., and HIRSCH, J. 1968. Effect of early nutrition on the development of rat epididymal fat pads: cellularity and metabolism. *Journal of Clinical Investigation* 47: 2091–98.

KRANTZ, D. S.; GLASS, D. C.; SCHAEFFER, M. A.; and DAVIA, J. E. Behavior patterns and coronary disease: a critical evaluation. In *Focus on cardiovascular psychophysiology*, ed. J. T. Cacioppo and R. E. Petty. New York: Guilford Press, in press.

LANG, P. J. 1979. A bio-informational theory of emotional imagery. *Psychophysiology* 16: 495–512.

LANGLIE, J. 1977. Social networks, health beliefs, and preventive health behavior. *Journal of Health and Social Behavior* 18: 244–60.

LAZARUS, R. S. 1966. *Psychological stress and the coping process.* New York: McGraw-Hill.

——. 1968. Emotions and adaption: conceptual and empirical relations. In *Nebraska symposium on motivation*, ed. W. J. Arnold, pp. 175–266. Lincoln: University of Nebraska Press.

——. 1980. The stress and coping paradigm. In *Theoretical bases for psychopathology*, ed. C. Eisdorfer, D. Cohen, A. Klienman, and P. Maxim. New York: Spectrum.

——, and LAUNIER, R. 1978. Stress-related transactions between person and environment. *Perspectives in interactional psychology*, ed. L. A. Pervin and M. Lewis New York: Plenum Press.

LEON, G. R. 1976. Current directions in the treatment of obesity. *Psychological Bulletin* 86: 557–78.

LEVENS, P. 1970. The Oslo diet—heart study. *Circulation* 42: 935–42.

LEVENTHAL, H. 1970. Findings and theory in the study of fear communication. In *Advances in experimental social psychology*, ed. L. Berkowitz, vol. 5. New York: Academic Press.

——. 1973. Changing attitudes and habits to reduce risk factors in chronic desease. *American Journal of Cardiology* 31: 571–80.

——. 1975. The consequences of depersonalization during illness and treatment. In *Humanizing health care*, ed. J. Howard and A. Strauss. New York: Wiley.

——. 1980. Toward a comprehensive theory of emotion. In *Advances in Experimental Social Psychology*, ed. L. Berkowitz. New York: Academic Press.

——. 1982. The integration of emotion and cognition: examples from illness thinking. In *Affect and cognition: the 17th annual Carnegie-Mellon symposium on cognition*, ed. M. S. Clarke and S. J. Fiske. Hillsdale, N. J.: Lawrence Erlbaum.

——; BROWN, D.; SHACHAM, S.; and ENGQUIST, G. 1979. Effects of preparatory information about sensations, threat of pain and attention on cold pressor distress. *Journal of Personality and Social Psychology* 37: 688–714.

LEVENTHAL, H., and CLEARY, P. D. 1979. Behavioral modification of risk factors: technology or science? In *Heart disease and rehabilitation: state of the art*, ed. M. L. Pollock and D. A. Schmidt. New York: Houghton Mifflin.

——. 1980. The smoking problem: a review of the research and theory in behavioral risk reduction. *Psychological Bulletin* 88: 370–405.

LEVENTHAL, H., and HIRSCHMAN, R. S. 1982. Social psychology and prevention. In *Social psychology of health and illness.* ed. G. S. Sanders and J. Suls. Hillsdale, N. J.: Erlbaum.

LEVENTHAL, H.; MEYER, D.; and GUTMANN, M. 1980. The role of theory in the study of compliance to high blood pressure regimes. In *Patient compliance to prescribed antihypertensive medication regimes: a report to the National Heart, Lung, and Blood Institute,* ed. R. B. Haynes, M. E. Mattson, and T. O. Engebeton. U.S. Department of Health and Human Services, N. I. H. pub. no. 81–2102, October 1980.

LEVENTHAL, H.; MEYER, D.; and NERENZ, D. 1980. The common sense representation of illness danger. In *Medical Psychology,* ed. S. Rachman, vol. 2. New York: Pergamon Press.

LEVENTHAL, H., and NERENZ, D. A model for stress research and some implications for the control of stress disorders. In *Stress prevention and management: A cognitive behavioral approach,* ed. D. Meichenbaum and M. Jaremko. New York: Plenum Press, in press.

LEVENTHAL, H.; NERENZ, D.; and LEVENTHAL, E. 1982. Feelings of threat and private views of illness: factors in dehumanization in the medical care system. In *Advances in environmental psychology,* eds. A. Baum and J. E. Singer. Hillsdale, NM.J.: Erlbaum.

LEVENTHAL, H.; SAFER, M. A.; CLEARY, P. D. and GUTMANN, M. 1980. Cardiovascular risk modification by community-based programs for life-style change: comments on the Stanford study. *Journal of Consulting and Clinical Psychology* 48: 150–58.

LEVENTHAL, E.; SHACHAM, S.; BOOTHE, L. S.; and LEVENTHAL, H. 1981. The role of attention in distress control during childbirth. Unpublished manuscript. University of Wisconsin, Madison.

LEVENTHAL, H.; ZIMMERMAN, R.; and GUTMANN, M. Compliance: a topic for behavorial medicine research. In *Handbook of behavioral medicine,* ed. D. Gentry. New York: Guilford Press, in press.

LEVI, L. 1971. *Society, stress and disease*: Vol. 1. *The psychosocial enviroinment and psychosomatic disease.* London: Oxford University Press.

LEVY, J. 1971. Lateral specialization of the human brain: behavioral manifestations and possible evolutionary basis. In *The biology of behavior,* ed. J. A. Kiger, Jr. Corvalis: Oregon State University Press.

LEWIN, K. 1935. *A dynamic theory of personality.* New York: McGraw-Hill.

LEY, P. 1977. Psychological studies of doctor-patient communication. In *Contributions to medical psychology,* ed. S. Rachman. vol. 1. New York: Pergamon Press.

LICHTENSTEIN, E., and DANAHER, B. G. 1975. Modification of smoking behavior: a critical analysis of theory, research and practice. In *Progress in behavior modification,* ed. M. Hersen, R. M. Eisler, and P. M. Miller. vol. 3. New York: Academic Press.

MAHONEY, M. J. 1974. Cognition and behavior modification. Cambridge, Mass.: Ballinger.

———.1974. Self-reward and self-monitoring techniques for weight control. *Behavior Therapy* 5: 549–72.

MARLATT, G. A., and GORDON, J. R. 1980. Determinants of relapse: implications for the maintenance of behavior change. In *Behavioral medicine: changing health lifestyles,* ed. P. O. Davidson and S. M. Davidson. New York: Brunner-Mazel.

MASON, J. W. 1972. Organization of psychoendocrine mechanisms: a review and reconsideration of research. In *Handbook of psychophysiology,* ed. N. S. Greenfield and R. A Sternbach. New York: Holt, Rinehart, and Winston.

MATTHEWS, K. A. What is the type A behavior pattern? A critical review from a psychological perspective. *Psychological Bulletin,* in press.

———; SIEGEL, J. M.; KULLER, L. H.; THOMPSON, M.; and VARAT, M. 1981. Determinants of seeking medical care by myocardial infarction victims. Paper presented at American Psychological Association, Los Angeles.

MAUSNER, B. 1973. An ecological view of cigarette smoking. *Journal of Abnormal Psychology* 81: 115–26.

———, and PLATT, E. S. 1971. *Smoking: a behavioral analysis.* New York: Pergamon Press.

McFall, R. 1970. Effects of self-monitoring on normal smoking behavior. *Journal of Consulting and Clinical Psychology* 35: 135–42.

McGeer, P. L., and McGeer, E. G. 1980. Chemistry of mood and emotion. *Annual Review of Psychology* 31: 273–307.

McKennell, A. C. 1968. British research into smoking behavior. In *Smoking, health, and behavior*, ed. E. F. Borgatta and R. R. Evans. Chicago: Aldine.

McKinlay, J. B. 1972. Some approaches and problems in the study of the use of services. *Journal of Health and Social Behaviors* 13: 115–52.

——, and McKinlay, S. M. 1981. Medical measures and the decline of mortality. In *The Sociology of health and illness: critical perspectives*, ed. P. Conrad and R. Kern. New York: St. Martins Press.

Mechanic, D. 1966. Response factors in illness: the study of illness behavior. *Social Psychiatry* 1: 11–20.

——. 1972. Social psychological factors affecting the presentation of bodily complaints. *New England Journal of Medicine* 286: 1132–39.

——, and Volkart, H. 1961. Stress, illness behavior, and the sick role. *American Sociological Review* 26: 51–58.

Meichenbaum, D. 1975. Self-instructional methods. In *Helping people change*, ed. F. H. Kanfer and A. P. Goldstein. New York: Pergamon Press.

Melamed, B. C. 1977. Psychological preparation for hospitalization. In *Contributions to medical psychology*, ed. S. Rachman, vol. 1. New York: Pergamon Press.

Meyer, A. J.; Nash, J. D.; McAlister, A. L.; Maccoby, N.; and Farquhar, J. W. 1980. Skills training in a cardiovascular health education campaign. *Journal of Consulting and Clinical Psychology* 48: 129–42.

Meyer, D. L. 1981. The effects of patients' representations of high blood pressure on behavior in treatment. Unpublished doctoral dissertation, University of Wisconsin-Madison.

——; Leventhal, H., and Gutmann, M. Symptoms in hypertension: How patients evaluate and treat them. *New England Journal of Medicine*, in press.

Miller, G. A.; Galenter, E.; Pribram, K. H. 1960. *Plans and the structure of behavior.* New York: Holt.

Miller, N. E. 1969. Learning of visceral and glandular responses. *Science* 163: 434–45.

Miller, N. E., and Dworkin, B. R. 1974. Visceral learning: recent difficulties with curarized rats and significant problems for human research. In *Cardiovascular psychophysiology*, ed. P. A. Obrist, A. H. Black, J. Brener, and C. V. DiCara. Chicago: Aldine.

——. 1980. Different ways in which learning is involved in homeostasis. *Neural mechanisms of goal-directed lerarning*. New York: Academic Press.

Mosbach, P. 1982. Factors associated with delay in seeking mental health care. Unpublished master's thesis, University of Wisconsin, Madison.

Nerenz, D. R. 1980. Control of emotional distress in cancer chemotherapy. Unpublished doctoral dissertation, University of Wisconsin-Madison.

Nuckolls, K. B.; Cassel, J.; and Kaplan, B. H. 1972. Psychosocial assets, life crisis and the prognosis of pregnancy. *American Journal of Epidemiology* 95: 431–41.

Patel, C. H. 1975. Twelve month follow-up of yoga and biofeedback in the management of hypertension, *Lancet* 1: 62–67.

——. 1980. Yoga and biofeedback in the management of hypertension. *Lancet* 2: 1053–55.

——, and North, W. R. S. 1975. Randomized controlled trial of yoga and biofeedback in management of hypertension. *Lancet* 2: 93–99.

Paykel, E. S. 1979. Recent life events in the development of the depressive disorders. In *The psychobiology of the depressive disorders: implications for the effects of stress*, ed. R. A. Depue. New York: Academic Press.

Pennebaker, J. W. Social and perceptual factors affecting symptom reporting and hysterical contagion. In *Psychogenic illness*, ed. M. Colligan, J. Pennebaker and L. Murphy. Hillsdale, N. J.: Erlbaum, in press.

————; BURNAM, M. A.; SCHAEFFER, M. A.; and HARPER, D. C. 1977. Lack of control as a determinant of perceived physical symptoms. *Journal of Personality and Social Psychology* 35: 167–74.

PENNEBAKER, J. W., and SKELTON, J. A. 1978. Psychological parameters of physical symptoms. *Personality and Social Psychology Bulletin* 4: 524–30.

PLATT, E. S.; KRASSEN, E.; and MAUSNER, B. 1969. Individual variation in behavioral change following role playing. *Psychological Reports* 24: 155–70.

POWERS, W. J. 1973a. Feedback: beyond behaviorism. *Science* 179: 351–56.

————. 1973b. *Behavior: the control of perception*. Chicago: Aldine.

RACHMAN, S., ed. 1977. *Contributions to medical psychology*, vol. 1. New York: Pergamon Press.

————. 1980. *Contributions to medical psychology*, vol. 2. New York: Pergamon Press.

RAHE, R. H. 1974. The pathway between subjects' recent life changes and their near-future illness reports: representative results and methodological issues. In *Stressful life events: their nature and effects*, ed. B. P. Dohrenwend and B. S. Dohrenwend. New York: Wiley.

RILEY, D. M., and FUREDY, J. J. Psychological and physiological systems: modes of operation and interaction. In *Psychological and physiological interactions in the response to stress*, ed. S. R. Burchfield. Washington, D.C.: Hemisphere, in press.

RINGLER, K. 1981. Process of coping with cancer chemotherapy. Unpublished doctoral dissertation, University of Wisconsin-Madison.

ROBINSON, D. 1971. *The process of becoming ill*. London: Routledge and Kegan Paul.

RODIN, J. 1978. Somatopsychics and attribution. *Personality and Social Psychology Bulletin* 4: 531–40.

————, and SLOCHOWER, J. 1976. Externality in the nonobese: effects of environmental responsiveness on weight. *Journal of Personality and Social Psychology* 33: 338–44.

ROGERS, E. M. 1962. *Diffusion of innovations*. Glencoe, Ill.: Free Press.

ROGERS, L. S. 1968. Public health asks sociology. *Science* 159:506–8.

ROGERS, R. W. 1975. A protection motivation theory of fear appeals and attitude change. *Journal of Psychology* 91: 93–114.

————. Cognitive and physiological processes in fear appeals as attitude change: a revised theory of protection motivation. In *Social psychophysiology*, ed. J. Cacioppo and R. Petty. New York: Guilford Press, in press.

ROSEN, T. J.; TERRY, N. S.; and LEVENTHAL, H. 1982. The role of esteem and coping in response to a threat communication. *Journal of Research in Personality*, 16: 90–107.

SACKETT, D. L. 1978. Patients and therapies: getting the two together. *New England Journal of Medicine* 298: 278–79.

SAFER, M. A.; THARPS, Q. J.; JACKSON, T. C.; and LEVENTHAL, H. 1979. Determinants of three stages of delay in seeking care at a medical care clinic. *Medical Care* 17: 11–29.

SANNE, H. 1979. Risk factor modification studies in Europe. In *Heart disease and rehabilitation*, ed. M. L. Pollock and D. H. Schmidt. Boston: Houghton Mifflin.

SARBIN, T., and NUCCI, L. P. 1973. Self-reconstruction processes: a proposal for reorganizing the conduct of confirmed smokers. *Journal of Abnormal Psychology* 81: 182–95.

SCHACHTER, S. 1977. Nicotine regulation in heavy and light smokers. *Journal of Experimental Psychology: General* 106: 5–12.

————, and RODIN, J. 1974. *Obese humans and animals*. Washington, D.C.: Erlbaum-Halsted.

SCHERWITZ, L., BERTON, K., and LEVENTHAL, H. 1977. Type A assessment and interaction in the behavior pattern interview. *Psychosomatic Medicine* 39: 229–40.

————. 1978. Type A behavior, self-involvement, and cardiovascular response. *Psychosomatic Medicine* 40: 593–609.

SCHWARTZ, G. E. 1977. Psychosomatic disorders and biofeedback: a pyschobiological model of disregulation. In *Psychopathology: experimental models*, ed. J. D. Maser and M. E. P. Seligman. San Francisco, Calif.: W. H. Freeman, 1977.

------. 1979. The brain as a health system. In *Health psychology: a handbook*, ed. G. C. Stone, F. Cohen, and N. E. Alder. San Francisco, Calif.: Jossey-Bass.

------; SHAPIRO, A. P.; REDMOND, D. P.; FERGUSON, D. C. E.; RAGLAND, D. R.; and WEISS, S. M. 1979. Behavioral medicine approaches to hypertension: an integrative analysis of theory and research. *Journal of Behavioral Medicine* 2: 311-63.

SEER, P. 1979. Psychological control of essential hypertension: review of the literature and methodological critique. *Psychological Bulletin* 86: 1015-43.

SELIGMAN, M. E. P. 1975. *Helplessness: on depression, development and death*. San Francisco, Calif.: W. H. Freeman.

SELYE, H. 1956/76. *The stress of life*. New York: McGraw-Hill.

------. 1973. The evolution of the stress concept. *American Scientist* 61: 692-99.

SIME, A. M. 1976. Relationship of preoperative fear, type of coping and information received about surgery to recovery from surgery. *Journal of Personality and Social Psychology* 34: 716-24.

SHIFFMAN, S. M. 1979. The tobacco withdrawal syndrome. In *Cigarette smoking as a dependence process*, ed. N. Krasnegor.Washington, D.C.: Department of Health Education and Welfare, NIDA Research Monograph 23.

SHIFFRIN, R. N., and SCHNEIDER, W. 1977. Controlled and automatic human information processing: II. Perceptual learning, automatic attending and a general theory. *Psychological Review* 84: 127-90.

SIROTA, A. D.; SCHWARTZ, G. E.; and SHAPIRO, D. 1974. Voluntary control of human heart rate: effect on reaction to aversive stimulation. *Journal of Abnormal Psychology* 83: 261-67.

SKIPPER, J. K., and LEONARD, R. C. 1968. Children, stress, and hospitalization: a field experiment. *Journal of Health and Social Behavior* 9: 275-87.

Smokers self-testing, I and II. 1973. *Smoking research—San Diego*. Washington, D.C.: Public Health Service, Center for Disease Control, U.S. Department of Health, Education, and Welfare, DHEW pub no. (CDC) 75-876, December 1973.

SOLOMON, R. L., and CORBIT, J. D. 1974. An opponent-process theory of motivation: I. Temporal dynamics of affect. *Psychological Review* 81: 119-45.

STEPTOE, A. 1980. Stress and medical disorders. In *Contributions to medical psychology*, ed. S. Rachman, vol. 2. New York: Pergamon Press.

STIMSON, G. V. 1974. Obeying doctor's orders: a view from the other side. *Social Science and Medicine* 8: 97-104.

STONE, G. C.; COHEN, F.; and ADLER, eds. 1979. *Health psychology: a handbook*. San Francisco, Calif.: Jossey-Bass.

STUNKARD, A. J. 1975. From explanation to action in psychosomatic medicine: the case of obesity. *Psychosomatic Medicine* 37: 195-236.

------. 1977. Behavioral treatment for obesity: failure to maintain weight loss. In *Behavioral self-control*, ed. R. B. Stuart New York: Brunner/Mazel.

------. 1979. Behavioral medicine and beyond: the example of obesity. In *Behavioral medicine: theory and practice*, ed. O. F. Pomerleau and J. P. Brady. Baltimore, Md.: Williams and Wilkins.

SUCHMAN, E. A. 1965. Stages of illness and medical care. *Journal of Health and Social Behavior* 6: 114.

SUINN, R. M., and BLOOM, L. 1978. Anxiety management training for pattern A behavior. *Journal of Behavioral Medicine* 1: 25-36.

SULS, J., and MULLEN, B. Life events, perceived control and illness: the role of uncertainty. *Journal of Human Stress*, in press.

TASTO, D. L., and INSEL, P. M. 1977. The premenstrual and menstrual syndromes—a psychological approach. In *Contributions to medical psychology*, ed. S. Rachman, vol. 1. New York: Pergamon Press.

THOMAS, L. 1977. On the science and technology of medicine. In *Doing better and feeling worse: health in the United States*, ed. J. H. Knowles. New York: Norton.

THOMPSON, E. L. 1978. Smoking reduction programs 1960–1976. *American Journal of Public Health* 68: 250–55.

TOMKINS, S. S. 1962. *Affect, imagery, consciousness: vol. 1. The positive affects*. New York: Springer-Verlag.

———. 1968. A modified model of smoking behavior. In *Smoking, health, and behavior*, ed. E. F. Borgatta and R. R. Evans. Chicago: Aldine.

———. 1980. Affect as amplification: some modifications in theory. In *Emotion: theory, research, and experience*, ed. R. Plutchik and H. Kellerman, vol. 1. New York: Academic Press.

WARNER, K. E. 1977. The effects of the anti smoking campaign on cigarette consumption. *American Journal of Public Health* 67: 645–50.

WEISS, J. M. 1972. Psychological factors in stress and disease. *Scientific American* 266 (no 6): 104–13.

WHITE, K. L. 1973. Life and death and medicine. *Scientific American* 229: 23–33.

WILSON, J. F. 1981. Behavioral preparation for surgery: benefit or harm? *Journal of Behavioral Medicine* 4: 79–102.

WITHEY, S. 1962. Reaction to uncertain threat. In *Man and society in disaster*, ed. G. Baker and D. Chapman. New York: Basic Books.

WOOLEY, S. C.; BLACKWELL, B.; and WINGET, C. 1978. A learning theory model of chronic illness behavior: theory, treatment, and research. *Psychosomatic Medicine* 40: 379–401.

YATES, A. J. 1980. Biofeedback and the modification of behavior. New York: Plenum Press.

YOUNG, L. D., and BLANCHARD, E. B. 1980. Medical applications of biofeedback training: a selective review. In *Contributions to medical psychology*, ed. S. Rachman, vol. 2. New York: Pergamon Press.

ZBOROWSKI, M. 1969. *People in pain*. San Francisco, Calif.: Jossey-Bass.

ZIFFERBLATT, S. M. 1975. Increasing patient compliance through the applied analysis of behavior. *Preventive Medicine* 4: 173–82.

ZOLA, I. 1966. Culture and symptoms: an analysis of patients presenting complaints. *American Sociological Review* 31: 615–30.

———. 1973. Pathways to the doctor—from person to patient. *Science and Medicine* 7: 677–89.

Chapter 33

Health Education and
Health Promotion

Lawrence W. Green
Katrina W. Johnson

THIS CHAPTER OFFERS a broad framework for the continuing analysis and application of the research and professional literature pertaining to health education. The social purposes of health education will be the focal point for consideration of planning, administration, practice, and evaluation in this field. At the onset, we present health education as an informal process of learning in individuals and families. Personal and family histories result in the development of attitudes and behavior among people learning to make sense of and maintain life in a changing environment. A second level of review concerns health education programs as part of a community or societal effort to improve health: i.e., the social organization of formal health education. Finally, a third level of analysis anticipates the social supports and individual adaptations of behavior required to protect, maintain, and promote health in a time of social and environmental change. Implications for government and private sector policies and programs in health education of the public will be proposed for both national and local planning.

Definitions and Biases

Health education refers here to any combination of learning experiences designed to facilitate voluntary adaptations of behavior conducive to health in individuals, groups, or communities. Health education strives to help people control their own health by predisposing, enabling, and reinforcing decisions and actions consistent with their own values and goals.

Acknowledgments: Preparation of this manuscript was supported in part by the University of Texas Center for Health Promotion Research and Development; the Office of Health Information, Health Promotion, and Physical Fitness and Sports Medicine and the National Heart, Lung and Blood Institute, U.S. Department of Health and Human Services; and the Division of Health Policy Research and Education, Harvard University.

744

Health promotion is any combination of educational, organizational, economic, and environmental supports for behavior conducive to health. Health promotion is more aggressive than health education in that it preselects the behavioral goals on the basis of epidemiological assessment. It also adds to the voluntary commitment of health education a dimension of economic and environmental intervention, sometimes through taxation, regulation of commerce, or legal enforcement, in order to support a specific behavior known to be conducive to health. Health promotion usually is targeted on one or more of the behaviors associated with lifestyle—smoking, alcohol and drug misuse, nutrition, exercise, stress management, and safety practices.

Our assumptions, if we differ at all from other analysts and commentators on this subject are the following:

1. That the analysis of health education must be contextual and sociological as well as personal and psychological. Health promotion will be required to contend with the broad economic and organizational contexts in which health behavior and learning are conditioned. Ultimately, however, health education must be delivered and supported at the level of the local community and the family.

2. That the philosophical roots and ethical tenets of health education are related to individual rights and the empowerment of people to determine their own behavior in relation to their own goals for health and quality of life. Nevertheless, it is also understood that the individual in increasingly complex societies does not act without direct influence from others or without consequences for others.

3. That health education is effective in varying degrees depending on circumstances, but in the long run is potentially more cost-effective, humane, and therefore more socially acceptable than most other technologies in the prevention of anticipated health problems.

4. That in order to serve its main function of anticipating health problems or needs, the analysis of health education must be prospective in addressing the health problems, the future health-care system conditions, and educational programs of the future.

Our analysis then proceeds from a review of highly individualistic and tailored health education interventions at the level of primary social groups such as family and friendship networks to an assessment of the macrosocial levels of mass media, community organization, and national points of future intervention for health education and health promotion.

Health Education in Personal History

The first and most fundamental health education takes place for each person in the family. No matter how *family* is defined, all children have early experiences in which those around them shape and contribute to their health beliefs and health behavior. This primary level of health education, whether intentional or happenstance, consists of that time in personal history in which an individual learns and is reinforced in acquisition of the basic attitudes and life habits that may persist for the rest of that person's life. Personal beliefs or attitudes, learned behavior, and cultural norms are intertwined within an individual's experience. The influence of attitude, modeled behavior, and norms, however, will be considered here separately as each contributes to the personal history of health education.

Development of Personal Beliefs and Attitudes Toward Health and Health Practices

Socialization theorists recognize the initial influence of the family unit on a child's beliefs about self and others (Lindesmith, Denzin, and Strauss 1975). Yet the process itself has been relatively neglected in health research. In the development of personal identity (Kuhn 1964; Johnson 1980) the child initially identifies strongly with his or her role as a child in a particular family and only later begins to build a complex identity when his or her social world expands beyond primary relationships. Yet there is relatively little research that traces the influences of the family or household unit on attitudes toward health (Litman 1974).

Within the framework of social learning theory, the role of parents as early models for children's health beliefs and behavior is undisputed (Mechanic 1964; Gochman 1972; Marshall 1970; Green 1970a; Brodie 1974). The family is the locus of daily habits that relate to adult health. One study (Pratt 1976) indicated that a large majority of mothers and fathers attempt specific health education activities with their children, suggesting that basic health habits are considered a proper realm for family-based education. In time of illness, it is within the family that most people discuss symptoms and talk over appropriate action before seeking medical care (Suchman 1965; Richardson 1970). Parent education in the home has been found effective in achieving improvements in child development (Gutelius 1972; Jason and Kimbrough 1974; Schaefer 1972).

On a psychological level, early experiences and perceptions of the world around structure personal beliefs and shape attitudes. When the child successfully or unsuccessfully responds to its environment the child will recall that experience the next time he or she is faced with a similar challenge or similar circumstances in the environment. Recall may be conscious or unconscious, reflective or reflexive, in that it occurs in thought or in action, or both. We may refer to this adaptative response in the specific instance as *attitude formation* (Abelson 1968; Festinger 1957). A learning situation may be based on a biological need, such as the hunger for food; how that need is fulfilled (potato chips or a nutritious meal) is part of personal experience and social learning. Beliefs about reality and beliefs about the consequences or risks of certain actions become the highly personal world of perception that make the values and attitudes of each individual unique (Fishbein and Ajzen 1975).

Development of Health Behavior

Individual health histories include translation of personal attitudes, values, and beliefs into health behavior. While the certainty of the link between a predisposing attitude and consequent behavior is unclear, health behavior and responses to health education are correlated with specific beliefs concerning personal susceptibility to and severity of consequences, the efficacy of recommended practices (Becker et al. 1974; Cummings et al. 1978; Maiman et al. 1977) and with beliefs concerning whether health is an outcome under a person's control (Hall 1971; Jeffrey 1974). The Health Belief Model and locus of control are specific examples of constructs that convert personal history into behavior related to health. The concept of locus of control for health behavior (Wallston and Wallston 1978) has been investigated as a variable to account for differing levels of medical compliance or health habits, even though the concept was originally developed to describe a relatively constant personality trait which would be based in an individual's belief system and not readily amenable to change (Rotter 1966). Health education interventions that have sought to change the locus of control of individuals in regard to health usually have attempted to modify basic belief structures concerning one's ability to control illness or health (see Wallston and Wallston 1978).

While there is little research on the specific ways health behavior is passed from parent to child or from sibling to sibling, there is evidence that informal health education does take place in family life in a way that affects specific health behaviors in adulthood. Habitual teeth brushing, recreational and exercise activities, eating patterns, and readiness to seek medical care are examples of health-related behavior learned in family life (Lewis et al. 1977; Haggerty et al. 1975). Behavior as amorphous and complex as eating patterns that lead to obesity (Garn, Cole, and Bailey 1976; Eppright et al. 1969) and as specific as smoking are related to the presence or absence of that behavior in parents and family members (Green and Green 1977).

Pratt (1976) presented evidence that health practices and illness behavior in a family are related to family interaction patterns. The "energized family" model was presented as conducive to the encouragement of good health by emphasizing family patterns of individual freedom, personal fulfillment, and flexible role relationships. Pratt's research suggested that such general open patterns of relationships among family members are correlated with specific health behavior in the areas of sleep, exercise, elimination, dental hygiene, smoking, alcohol, and nutrition. Results supported the conclusion that "combined health behavior of all family members may be regarded as a further dimension of the family's pattern of living" (p. 100). Pratt's research proposed strategies to increase the power of families to influence and deal with the medical-care system. The specific kinds of behavior such as regular eating, regular and adequate sleep, and moderate drinking, which, as Pratt suggested, are learned in early family life, are the same kinds believed to contribute to increased longevity and lower morbidity (Belloc and Breslow 1972).

Other research indicates that health may also be linked to family and early learning in still another way. Reexamination of data from the Alameda County study (Berkman and Syme 1979) suggested that the social supports available through the family and primary friendship groups may be as significant in life expectancy as specific health practices. People without close kin do not seek aid in time of illness from other relatives, friends, or neighbors. Those who are socially well intergrated (with friends or kin) have an underlying emotional support network to help in emotional or illness crises. From these findings the indication is that close family relationships, ability to handle stress, and a pattern of healthful living habits learned in early life are significant for later health. Early beliefs, attitudes, and behavior are related to eventual health responses. Some learned behaviors, however, such as overeating as a response to emotional problems, heavy salting of food, and a tendency to disregard symptoms of ill health, may not be conducive to adult health.

Because the behavior learned in childhood and practiced in the intimate environments of the family becomes part of an individual's cognitive mode and affective personality, it is often resistant to any reeducative intervention that requires a change in complex personal activities. Studies of medical compliance have emphasized that the behaviors least likely to be changed with a prescribed regimen are those that require family interaction or change of habits established early in life (Haynes et al. 1979). Eating patterns (salt reduction), change of life-style (increased or decreased activity), or elimination of established habits (smoking and drinking) are difficult to modify even under the threat of shortened life or illness (Sackett and Haynes 1976). Interventions to change health or illness behavior need to take into account the social context in which the behavior takes place (Green et al. 1980). Cooperation of other family members, particularly if combined with a means of self-monitoring of activity or health, has been shown to be an effective aid in securing compliance with medical regimens (Becker and Green 1975; Levine et al. 1979; Baranowski 1980).

We see from the foregoing that the microsocial forces of family and personal history are powerful determinants of health and illness behavior. Learned behavioral patterns from early life that are conducive to health tend to resist peer pressure and media persuasion to convert to unhealthy practices. Similarly, learned behavioral patterns from early life that are not conducive to health tend to resist reeducative attempts by health professionals and teachers. The natural allies required to modify behavior patterned by the family are the family members themselves.

Health Education in Social History

Beliefs and personal attitudes formed in early family life are not isolated from social and cultural influences; behavior learned at home is affected by the economic, ethnic, and cultural history of that family.

Cultural Influence on Individual Attitudes and Behavior

The learning of health behavior is influenced by more than isolated personal experience. Personal and family history are modified or pressured by generalized expectations for behavior that we label "norms" for a particular culture or subculture (Green 1970b). When these norms are stable and transmitted from one generation to another or are codified in formal or informal rules of behavior for a group, they become a part of the enduring value system of a culture or subculture. Expectations (norms) and cultural values influence individual attitudes and predispose behavior. Individual beliefs in the form of attitudes relate to more specific objects and behaviors. They represent the ad-hoc translation of values into specific propensities toward action or behavior.

Individual attitudes may represent an internalization of the generalized cultural values about health, about the appropriate use and efficacy of professional medical care, about the worth of health in comparison to other things valued in life such as economic independence or security, personal relationships, and temporary inconvenience. Eventual behavior is related to beliefs and attitudes, but is not necessarily a conscious extension of them. Behavior may be either an intentional outgrowth of beliefs and attitudes (voluntary decision), or may be a habitual response that still has its basis in early life values and subgroup acceptance of the habitual activity. In this way, health behavior is sometimes inconsistent with knowledge, attitudes, and even values developed later in life.

Personal health behavior is thus the combined result of isolated experiences and uniquely formed beliefs and the individual's incorporation of values common to his or her economic, racial, ethnic, or community subculture. Anthropologists have reminded us that the very perception of one's body, the sense of self, is a product of a particular cultural belief system (Idler 1979). Beliefs about the causes of health and illness vary widely between cultures. Health practices and medical-care organization are dependent on whether a culture has a belief system based on the notion of illness as caused by an impersonal disease event or based on the assumption that illness is most likely the result of sin, witchcraft, transgression of a group norm, or individual action (Manning and Fabrega 1973). Even within a society that relies on an objective etiology of illness and a "scientific, rational" approach to health, lay knowledge and health practices are not homogeneous.

Through the family as a health education medium, ethnic subcultures influence individuals in the recognition and expressions of pain. Socialization and early childhood experience for the subcultures of Italian, Jewish, and Old American groups have been shown to vary and produce distinct behavioral patterns in times of illness. Zola (1976) found that Irish Americans and Italian Americans described medically similar illness in different ways and tended to complain of symptoms in different parts of the body. The ethnic variations were both in perception and presentation of illness.

Socioeconomic Determinants of Health Attitudes and Behavior

Individual health attitude and behavior are similarly shaped by economic factors. Low-income individuals have been found to perceive themselves to be in poor health more consistently than higher income individuals (Randall and Wheeler 1979). Because of subcultural norms and beliefs about illness, family members in blue-collar families may be less likely to recognize particular physical symptoms as "illness" such as chronic backache, fatigue, or emotional difficulties than a member of a white collar family (Koos 1954).

Lower income families are less likely to have a regular source of medical care so that their access to care is reduced. Thus, economic differences in beliefs about health and illness can combine with the barriers to care caused by financial difficulties to produce an identifiably different pattern of preventive care use (Randall and Wheeler 1979).

The social influences of occupational, educational, and economic identity shape attitudes toward health, illness, and behavior concerning both health and illness. Patterns of expected *individual* behavior associated with these social identities are communicated through the family and other media as norms of health behavior. In this circular manner, the personal history of an individual is largely a function of social structure and culture (Green 1970a, 1970b, 1976; Mechanic 1974). As we shall show in a later section, health education can succeed in relation to complex individual health behavior only if it works with and through these webs of social, economic, and cultural support for the individual at the primary group and family levels of organization.

The Social Organization of Health Education

Traditional health education, even when directed at changing personal habits, infrequently sought to change the social context in which the individual holds or forms private beliefs and values (Mauksch 1974). Health education programs attempted more often to modify personal health behavior by influencing community organization or by communicating with an individual directly, circumventing the family or primary groups. For the most part, mass media messages and institutional programs structured their products for individuals, not for the subcultural groups or families as a composite or intermediate audience. The schoolteacher or nurse who prepares a lesson on smoking, for example, has little firsthand knowledge of the personal circumstances of the thirty or so students or patients with regard to their home, family, and peer relationships concerning smoking (Green and Green 1977; Green and Kansler 1980). Similarly, the federal agency or national organization that prepares radio and television public service announcements to persuade individuals to use seat belts has no possibility of tailoring that message to the varying social and cultural reasons people have for not using seat belts (Lau et al. 1980; Marshall et al. 1977; McAlister et al. 1976; Robertson et al. 1974; Salzer, Marshall, and Glazer 1977; Schmeling and Wotring 1976; Warner 1977). Thus, a commonly observed pattern of health education is that of persuasive efforts structured to communicate on an individual level without a wide range of contextual variation.

A second common pattern of intervention through health education is also individually oriented but not directed at beliefs or attitude change. These efforts have been directed at individual skills and resources that might *enable* the already motivated individual to pursue a behavior conducive to health. Examples of this type of health education include tutorial and training programs, referral to community resources, or encouraging organizational efforts to redistribute or allocate resources for individuals.

There is potential for conflict created when these efforts direct individuals away from their primary groups for support, usurping the role of family and friends and substituting an external agency or organization as a surrogate parent, spouse, or friend. In such instances the individual approach may successfully initiate a health behavior but loses the context of family and peer support to continue the behavior. The behavior enabled by these maneuvers must be supported by primary groups because formal organizations cannot sustain health behavior with sufficient continuity and social reinforcement (Haggerty et al. 1975; Becker, Drachman, and Kirscht 1974; Levin, Katz, and Holst 1976; Green and Kansler 1980).

A third type of intervention for health education is directed through significant others who can provide the continuing social support and reinforcement of the behavior. These interventions are especially effective in accomplishing and maintaining the types of complex and continuous health behavior associated with lifestyle. The hallmark of such programs is their active involvement of family, peers, employers, friends or colleagues of the people whose behavior is in question.

With this background on the individual's learning process in regard to health and common patterns of intervention variously combined in programmatic approaches to health education, we turn to specific examples of health education and the implications of these illustrative efforts.

Examples of Evaluative Research on Health Education, Health Promotion, and Self-Care

The two subjects in which the most extensive and fruitful research and evaluation have been conducted to test the efficacy and cost-effectiveness of health education are hypertension and smoking cessation. A set of eleven recent hypertension studies will be reviewed here to illustrate the major conclusions that can be drawn from patient education research. A set of forty-three smoking cessation studies will be summarized to illustrate the major conclusions that can be drawn concerning the relative cost-effectiveness of health promotion methods in clinical and community settings.

Patient Education Strategies in Hypertension

The National Heart, Lung, and Blood Institute sponsored eleven studies to test various strategies for improving compliance of patients with blood pressure control, as shown in Table 33.1 (Garrity 1980). All were randomized clinical trials and all used blood pressure measures in addition to the behavioral compliance measures shown in Table 33.1. Several generalizations can be drawn from these studies with general applicability to patient education for various conditions.

INCREASED CONTACT TIME WITH HEALTH-CARE PROVIDERS. In all eleven studies it was found that short-term improvement in blood pressure control can be achieved by almost any intervention that provides more time for discussion between a health-care provider and a patient. This finding suggests that intensive patient counseling, even without a highly structured educational or behavioral intervention, can be a cost-beneficial activity for patients with chronic conditions or risks. We offer this possibility with trepidation in view of the various designs of the studies on which it is based. Nevertheless, there are theoretical explanations for the phenomenon of reduced blood pressure resulting from such generalized interventions. Most such explanations can be categorized as experimental effects or placebo effects (Green 1977). Insofar as the studies from which this observation was drawn were experimental, reduced blood pressure could result from the patients knowing that they were being observed and therefore taking greater care to bring their pressure down by compliance only during the period of the study.

Some of the studies, however, used resident staff of the clinical setting rather than research staff to conduct the interventions, thereby minimizing the possibility that the patients would respond on the basis of knowing they were part of an experiment. An alternative explanation is that the mere process of being under more intensive care and observation resulted in a reduction of blood pressure without necessarily increasing compliance or other behavioral changes. Such a placebo effect is well documented in relation to a wide range of phenomena, including blood pressure control.

TABLE **33.1** A Listing of National High Blood Pressure Education Research Program Projects by Sample Size, Design, Type of Intervention, Time from Intervention to Last Followup and Type of Compliance Measure

PROJECT	SAMPLE SIZE	DESIGN	INTERVENTION	FOLLOWUP TIME	MEASURE OF COMPLIANCE
Brucker I	44	RCT*	Contracting without reward	6 months	Both experiments report drop-outs from care but other measures not reported
Brucker II	38	RCT	Contracting with material and social rewards	6 months	
Caplan	238	RCT	Social support from nurse or partner	12 months	Appointment-keeping records, and self-reports of various types of adherence, medication-taking, prescription-filling, dietary behavior, appointment-keeping
Chadwick	Not available	RCT	Individual patient education and counseling	Not available	Seeing physician after referral other measures not reported
Earp	218	RCT	Social support from significant other and health professional; home visits	24 months	Self-report measures not yet reported
Green	400	RCT	Individual patient education, social support from significant other, group support for patient activation	18 months	Appointment-keeping records and self-report of medication-taking and appointment-keeping

Kelley	212	RCT	Home BP monitoring by family member or patient	12 months	Records of appointment-keeping and dropping out of care
Powers	160	RCT	Fear-arousing messages, patient activation, nurse directiveness, more visits with nurse	3 months	Records of appointment-keeping, nurse subjective judgment of patient adherence in 16 areas of lifestyle and compliance
Rosenstock	432	RCT	Fear-arousing (and reassuring) messages, phone reminders, BP and diary self-monitoring, social supports from partner	12 months	Self-report of medication-taking and dietary behavior, pharmacy records of prescription-buying, records of appointment-keeping
Solomon	296	RCT	Nursing intervention, tangible rewards, group education, patient home BP monitoring	Not available	Self-report of medication-taking, records of appointment-keeping and dropping out of care
Swain	115	RCT	Individual patient education booklets, contingency contracting with rewards	30 months	Self-report of adherence to contracted behavior, record of dropping out of care
Syme	244	RCT	Group education and support sessions, home visits	7 months	Self-report of medication-taking, record of appointment-keeping and dropping out of care

Source: Garrity 1980.
* Randomized controlled trial.

INCREASED NUMBER OF CONTACTS.   A second observation from many of the studies was that the frequency and continuity of contact between patient and health-care provider resulted in greater blood pressure control. This observation is similar but it is in partial contrast to the first observation, which was concerned more with amount of time and intensity of each contact as opposed to the number and variety of contacts. But it was not the number of contacts alone that accounted for this effect; rather, it was the combination of content and contacts resulting in more opportunities for and types of repetition and reinforcement of behavioral changes. In both the Johns Hopkins study and the University of California study in Oakland, the combination of increased contact and enriched content accounted for the differences in blood pressure control between patients receiving supplementary home visits and those having regular contacts with clinic personnel (Chwalow et al. 1978; Green et al. 1975; Syme 1976; Fisher et al. 1977).

ACTIVE PATIENT PARTICIPATION.   A third generalization drawn from these eleven studies was that they achieved varying levels of blood pressure control depending on the extent to which patients were actively rather than passively involved in setting goals for their own blood pressure control or behavioral change. Some of the most dramatic effects were achieved, for example, in small studies in which each patient literally contracted with the health-care provider for behavioral and blood pressure achievements that would be rewarded by the provider with tangible goods such as trading stamps, a book, or a ticket to a sporting event (Brucker 1977; Steckel and Swain 1977; Swain 1978). In the Johns Hopkins study it was noted that of three kinds of intervention the one that required the greatest amount of participation by the patients, as distinct from provider-initiated contact, resulted in the greatest reduction in blood pressure (Levine et al.1979).

SOCIAL SUPPORT.   A fourth common observation in most of the eleven studies was that the involvement of a significant other person in addition to the patient and the provider was helpful in reducing blood pressure, at least temporarily. As in early personal history and development of health behavior, family and subcultural support is significant in changing illness behavior. Two of the University of Michigan studies were designed specifically to test the hypothesis that the enlistment of a partner in blood pressure control would have this effect. Perceived social support was significantly increased, and blood pressure control correlated with social support (Caplan et al. 1976; Flowers 1978; Kirscht and Rosenstock 1977; and personal communication about NIH grant No. HL18418 from R. D. Caplan, Research Center for Group Dynamics, Institute for Social Research, Ann Arbor, Michigan). The North Carolina study at Chapel Hill successfully mobilized the effect of social support through family members or friends who were trained to measure the patient's blood pressure and by home visits by a pharmacist or nurse (Earp and Ory 1978). The Johns Hopkins study also stimulated such social support through home visits (Fass et al. 1977). The worksite as a more convenient place than the home to mobilize social support for blood pressure control suggests an even greater potential for achieving this effect with coworkers in occupational health programs (Alderman et al. 1980).

SELF-MONITORING.   Some of the studies found an added effect when patients were given the opportunity to monitor their blood pressure and to keep records of changes (Steckel and Swain 1977; Kirscht and Rosenstock 1977; Earp and Ory

1978; Chadwick et al. 1977; Soloman 1978). This effect is believed to operate through another form of direct feedback and reinforcement. When the changes in blood pressure are more visible and accessible to patients, they can adjust a variety of life-style habits according to the patterns in their blood pressure. Some of these changes may not have been so obvious to the health-care provider, much less the patient, without direct feedback. The resources needed for the development of self-monitoring skills can be made more accessible and affordable in the worksite than in most medical sites or homes (Chadwick et al. 1970; Alderman et al. 1980).

In summary, programs that include some form of long-term contact with patients appear to be successful in achieving voluntary behavioral adaptations conducive to health. The success of programs is enhanced by contact with the patient's home or by the provision of services for the patient at the worksite, or both. The findings on the effectiveness of increased intensity, variety, and number of contacts and on the effectiveness of social support are consistent in the several studies of patient education strategies.

The experiences of the patient education programs reviewed afford some warnings and some encouragement. The cautionary conclusions come from the poor results and short-lived effects of simplistic educational programs that have no followup and reinforcement over time. The encouraging signs come from patient education and worksite programs that are more intensive, that involve patients in their own care and vigorously maintain contact wth these people over time. The cost-effectiveness and cost-benefit potential of such efforts have been reported (e.g., Alderman et al. 1980; Green and Kansler 1980) but can be more readily illustrated from the smoking cessation literature.

Smoking Cessation and Cost-Effectiveness of Health Education

The second illustrative body of literature describing the state of the art in health education and health promotion concerns smoking. The study designs, measurement procedures, and analytic methods have been sufficiently rigorous and consistent in this body of research and evaluation to allow comparative analysis of the cost-effectiveness of educational and related methods used to influence a specific behavior conducive to health (Green, Rimer, and Bertera 1978).

Some eighty-nine studies of smoking cessation were reviewed from the literature of the past decade, identified largely in the reviews of Bernstein and McAlister (1976), Best and Block (1978), Danaher (1977), Hunt and Bespalac (1974), Lichtenstein and Danaher (1977), and Schwartz (1969). Of these, only forty-three contained sufficient information on methods and results to permit analysis of their cost-effectiveness. The studies were grouped according to the primary method of intervention in six major classes of treatment methods: drugs, hypnosis, behavior modification, education and group support, aversive conditioning (including such techniques as rapid smoking, covert sensitization, electric shock and stimulus satiation), and self-control or combination methods. Studies excluded from the original eighty-nine were those with inadequate information to allow even reasonable assumptions concerning number of sessions and total hours of contact, type of professional or communicator conducting the intervention, or success rates.

Cost was defined as the dollars expended on contacts with smokers, based on the duration and number of contacts multiplied by the national average hourly salary or fees of workers of the kind used in the contact. Effectiveness was defined as the proportionate reduction in smoking as measured by the percentage of participants who remained abstinent at specific points in the months following the intervention. A composite, standardized measure of "person-months of smoking averted" was computed from the sample size times the proportion not smoking at three months, six months, or one year, times three, six, or twelve respectively.

The review of data, program descriptions, and intervention procedures in the forty-three usable studies enabled cost-effectiveness analyses in those with positive results as follows: six studies using hypnosis, twenty-four studies using aversive conditioning, six studies using behavior modification, six studies using education and group support, and one study using drugs. The total in each category is based on the classification of studies according to the primary method of interest in the study. Self-control and combination methods were not separately analyzed for cost-effectiveness, even though several of the studies included them, because cost elements could not be identified or isolated. Table 33.2 illustrates the analysis as applied to the fourteen studies reporting sufficient cost and abstinence data at six months to compute comparable cost-effectiveness values.

A particular feature of all six studies of behavior modification included in the

TABLE 33.2   Cost Effectiveness of Selected Methods from Studies Providing Sufficient Information to Compute Cost per Person—Month of Smoking Averted Six Months after Formal Intervention

TYPE OF INTERVENTION, AUTHOR (DATE)	AT 6 MONTHS	PERSON-MONTHS OF ABSTINENCE (N × p × 6)	ESTIMATED Cost	COST Effect.
	% ABSTINENT			
Aversive Conditioning				
Best (1975)	89 50	267.0	$ 779	$ 2.92
Best, Bass, and Owen (in press)	21 50	63.0	1,280	20.32
Chapman et al. (1971)	11 55	36.3	3,431	94.52
Dawley and Sardenga (1977)	12 25	18.0	6,840	380.00
Delahunt and Curran (1976)	49 56	164.6	25	0.15
Lichenstein et al. (1973)	10 60	36.0	103	2.86
Russell (1970)	9 43	23.2	3,850	165.81
Schmahl et al. (1972)	16 50	48.0	85	1.78
Suedfeld and Ikard (1974)	20 35	42.0	3,216	76.57
		Mean cost-effectiveness =		$ 82.77
Behavior Modification				
Lando (1975)	34 76	155.0	$ 441	$ 2.84
Winett (1973)	49 50	147.0	56	.38
		Mean cost-effectiveness =		$ 1.61
Education/Group				
Lawton (1967)	9 29	15.7	$ 400	$ 25.54
Hypnosis				
Nuland and Fuld (1970)	50 60	180.0	$ 13,440	$ 74.67
Watkins (1976)	36 67	144.7	9,600	66.33
		Mean cost-effectiveness =		$ 70.50

*N is the actual or interpolated number of subjects remaining in the study at six months. See text for explanation of other computations.

analysis is that they were carried out exclusively in group educational sessions. As others have noted, the effects of both educational and behavioral methods are enhanced by group cohesiveness (Lando 1975) and the advantage of group methods is particularly likely to show up in cost-effectiveness criteria of success (Green 1977). In addition, a majority of the most cost-effective aversive conditioning interventions were also conducted in groups (Lichtenstein and Danaher 1977; Berecz 1972; Delahunt and Curren 1976; Relinger et al. 1977; Wagner and Bragg 1970).

One of the most striking observations on the twenty-two studies that were most cost-effective, according to our calculations, is that the majority had multiple intervention points in the cessation process. For example, aversive conditioning may be provided in a group context, with considerable social reinforcement and followed by self-control or self-management techniques (Relinger et al. 1977; Wagner and Bragg 1970; Delahunt and Curran 1976). Apparently, combinations of techniques can enhance the cost-effectiveness of each (Lando 1975; Green 1977).

The large variance in effectiveness among experimental studies within each of the four classes of interventions analyzed makes any assertion of significant differences between methods premature. When therapeutic or problem-solving methods have no inherent or universal advantage over each other, then policymakers, practitioners, and consumers must make their selection of methods to support, promote, or consume on the basis of criteria other than simple probabilities of effectiveness.

Four criteria are likely to be predominant in the choice of methods for smoking cessation until more definitive evidence of their relative efficacy is established: accessibility, situational advantage, consumer preference, and cost. Clearly, these criteria are not entirely independent of efficacy and are inextricably related to each other. In the end, the first three will be dictated by a combination of cost and effectiveness. Accessibility, for example, is limited largely by the marketing and promotion of most methods, or by the availability of trained therapists in some, such as hypnosis. But these limitations could be overcome if the cost-effectiveness of the method were clearly shown to be superior to that of other methods, of if third-party payers would reimburse it.

Situational advantages will make some methods more effective or less costly, or both, for some smokers. For example, some methods can be applied in the home or workplace, others require clinical facilities. Similarly, consumer preferences will make some methods more acceptable, but these too will be determined ultimately by situational advantages in cost and effectiveness.

The best hopes, then, for the expansion of smoking cessation beyond the experimental programs for highly motivated subjects, and beyond the commercialized programs for affluent subjects, is to identify situational advantages of one method over another and to relate these advantages to cost and effectiveness. The form that programs and experiments based on this approach should take is a "broad spectrum behavioral approach" such as that of Lando (1975), but with greater differentiation of experimental treatments matched with subjects. The design and results of such an approach have been demonstrated in clinical trials of broad spectrum educational and behavioral programs for hypertensive and asthmatic outpatients (Levine et al. 1979). A threefold advantage in cost-effectiveness was estimated when educational methods were matched with patients according to selected patient characteristics that predict situational advantages.

There is still no clear evidence of the inherent or universal superiority of one method of smoking cessation over another. The potential advantages of different methods therefore lie in their cost-effectiveness under different circumstances. Comparing the cost-effectiveness of four types of interventions showed a clear disadvantage for hypnosis and a superiority of group methods, especially when the focus of the group is on education of smokers in behavior modification skills.

The circumstances under which these results were obtained are likely to change as new cohorts of smokers ready to quit, and the old cohorts who failed to quit before, submit themselves to the next generation of experiments and programs (Green and Green 1977). If the earlier studies had used factorial designs with as much attention to differentiating types of smokers and circumstances (situational variables) as they did to the fine distinctions in types of methods, we would be in a better position today to extrapolate to the future. We may expect a new generation of studies emphasizing self-control, relaxation and meditation methods. We may hope for greater economies of scale as the methods are applied on a community basis.

Current Options for Future Health Education

There are several options for organization of health education. A first option is to attempt, as in many health education programs in medical settings, to change attitudes, individual by individual, and consequently to modify individual behavior. It is possible to change a social norm by incrementally changing the attitudes of individuals in a social group. This individual approach is principally educational in character and depends more on voluntary change and targeted programs than on legislative or regulatory interventions which attempt to interrupt the behavior through coercion.

An individual educational approach to health policy is most acceptable when the behavior in question is not harming other people. Even when a self-injurious behavior is common, it cannot be easily legislated out of existence by arguing that it is in the common good to abolish the behavior. People will argue that it is their right to do with their bodies as they see fit. They will reject the attempt of legislators to tell them how to behave when the behavior is personal and even more especially when it is fun. Where behaviors are perceived as a private matter of individual choice, coercive measures are resisted, as in the case of alcohol prohibition and seat belt laws, whereas mandatory immunization for school entrance, no less coercive but more clearly related to the health of others, was successful.

A second option to support individuals in making life-style adaptations that are conducive to health is the implementation of laws or regulations that prohibit personal behavior. When a society decides that a particular health behavior is dangerous to the safety of others or that too many people are killing or injuring themselves and hence incurring costs to others with such behavior, society may decide that the only course of action is to compel behavior change with policies that proscribe the behavior. The Clean Indoor Air legislation, for example, addresses both the environmental and the social issue of passive smoking. Although this second option appears on the surface to be an alternative to health education, in fact it requires public health education no less than the first option. Without public education, the laws to compel behavior would not pass, of if passed would not long remain (as with crash helmet requirements for motorcyclists.).

Return to the Definitions

From these descriptions and options a return to our definitions of health education and health promotion suggests points of intervention to enhance the process of learning and behavior change to improve the health of people.

We have defined health education as any combination of learning opportunities designed to facilitate voluntary adaptations of behavior conducive to health. One condition of health education is the element of voluntary behavior. An insistence on self-determination recognizes that the adaptation takes place at the level of individual decision making, in the personal history of health attitudes and behavior. Personal history includes the less acknowledged influence of family and subcultural influence on adult health behavior and propensity to change. In consideration of personal history, opportunities for choice are necessary to set some humanitarian limit and political restraint on the application of education as a tool of social engineering, propaganda, or commerical exploitation. It also implies the freedom to choose unwisely, to act in congruence with subcultural beliefs, to pursue or continue a more familiar or minority normative behavior or attitude at the possible risk of personal health (Green 1970b).

By the above definition, we have insisted that effective health education must combine interventions in order to avoid the frustration or confusion that will result if pressure on individuals does not take into account the context of personal and social history in which health decisions are made. Failure to understand the context of primary relationships has resulted in some of the most embarrassing failures of health programs, especially in cross-cultural situations, because not only did the programs fail to achieve their intended results but they often aroused an antagonistic backlash as a result of heightened expectations that could not be fulfilled or insults to the integrity of cultural groups by ignoring their constraints or values.

Environmental impact, economic impact, and now family impact statements must be filed with many proposals for social intervention. Minority groups are recognized as needing attention in media and educational materials. Family and peer support for behavioral change are necessary for continued reinforcement. Citizen participation in health planning and in other aspects of policy development and program evaluation is increasingly accepted as a safeguard against insensitive or simplistic solutions that fail to recognize the need to combine or integrate interventions and to balance centrally defined goals against local perceptions of needs and barriers (Steckler et al. 1980).

With these constraints and professional commitments attached to the definition of health education, it enters the policy arena with notable handicaps. Its potency as a tool of social problem-solving is necessarily limited in two ways, both inherent in the definition. First, it cannot trespass the voluntary choices people might make to pursue a course of behavior that is not necessarily conducive to their own health. The government cannot do much about that limitation except to go beyond health education where the behavior of an individual or organization causes sufficient damage or threat to the health or well-being of other people to warrant more coercive means of control.

The second inherent limitation of health education by itself as a tool of health policy and government programs is the complexity of the deterrents to health behavior other than the motivation and ability of the individual. Health-related behavior is determined also by forces of the environment that may limit the choices available to the individual including economics, organizational arrangements, accessibility of other resources or technologies, and a variety of social forces in the family and friendship networks and community settings. With all of these environmental forces limiting or pushing individual choices, health education without the support of other interventions may frustrate people by increasing their motivation to take actions that are not possible in their circumstances, or actions that will be punished or ridiculed in their social environment.

National Planning for Health Education and Health Promotion

Recognizing that these limitations of health education apply particularly to the types of life-style behavior associated with the leading causes of disability and death, a definition and strategy for *health promotion* has been proposed to include health education *in combination with other interventions directed at organizations, economics, and the environment* to support behavior conducive to health. In developing a national media campaign for health promotion, for example, special arrangements with intermediary organizations at the national and community levels are made to assure the local development of resources or programs to suppport the behavior recommended through the mass media. The emphasis in health promotion is still on behavior, but the interventions have been diversified. Channels of communication have been sought through the media and through organizations that would reach not only the individuals whose behavior would be at risk of causing health problems but also the employers, teachers, family, and friendship networks of such people to build a supportive social climate for behavior more conducive to health.

The other element of national policy for health education is the negotiation and coordination with various agencies of government and the private sector to bring about some of the other environmental supports and organizational or economic changes necessary to support health behavior. For example, arrangements have been made with the President's Council on Wage and Price Stability to exempt employers from limitations under the 7 percent wage guidelines on development of health promotion programs as an employee benefit. Many of the major health and life insurance companies have given special consideration to premium reductions or benefits related to healthful practices, particularly blood pressure control and smoking. The United Way and the American Red Cross both have announced plans to shift economic and organizational resources in the direction of health education and health promotion.

The operational terms in the definitions of health education and health promotion for government action at the *program* level are "combination" and "designed." How can learning opportunities, organizations, economics, and the environment be designed and combined to support health actions most efficiently without coercing behavior? For *policy*, the issues are less with methods and design than with selecting those areas of health in which behavioral, environmental, and organizational changes can have the greatest payoff in cost-benefit terms for individuals and for society, and among those health actions the ones in which health education and health promotion can be most effective. These questions were addressed by the U.S. Public Health Service in a systematic process of policy analysis and consensus development in disease prevention and health promotion between 1977 and 1980 (Office of the Assistant Secretary of Health 1979), following passage of the National Disease Prevention and Health Promotion Act of 1976 which created the Office of Health Information and Health Promotion.

Having concluded that federal policy should seek a shift in some of the resources from future expenditure in medical care to increase current investments in disease prevention and health promotion, the questions posed by Congress and addressed by the Public Health Service have focused on selection of program elements and amounts required in times of severely limited spending. Two conclusions were possible: (1) not everyone benefits equally from a given health behavior; and (2) spending on health promotion need not be regarded as a bottomless pit. Stated more positively and specifically, high-risk groups and optimum age ranges could be clearly identified for most preventive and self-care actions that health education and health promotion can facilitate. Hence, it is possible to target scarce educational resources on those problems, settings and populations where impact and payoff will be greatest. This step of targeting and developing quantified objectives was completed with the publication of *Healthy People: The Surgeon General's Report on Health Promotion and Disease Prevention (1979) and Promoting Health/Preventing Disease: Objectives for the Nation (1980).*

Five age groups were delineated according to the predominant illness, injury, and mortality patterns of each. Quantified goals for reduction of morbidity and mortality were established by professional consensus and specific objectives for behavior and public awareness were specified for each goal. The quantified objectives for the nation should make it possible to identify the point of diminishing returns in health promotion expenditures in some types of programs. Additional research is needed on this, but the implication of existing evidence is that government investments in health education can be both focused and contained. Unfortunately, many past efforts in health education have been diffuse and unevaluated, making it difficult to account for their costs or their effects. The *Objectives for the Nation* also pointed the way for a sharing of the burden between government and the private sector, among different levels of government, and among various departments of the federal government.

Conclusion

The prospects are that health education and health promotion, even in an inflationary economy, will receive increasing attention and support from both public and private sectors. The scientific base for the effective and efficient practice of health education is still tenuous, but a growing body of literature, as illustrated here by the reviews of hypertension and smoking cessation studies, is taking shape. Research and evaluation is needed to temper or justify the growing enthusiasm for health promotion.

REFERENCES

ABELSON, R. P., ed. 1968. *Theories of cognitive consistency: a sourcebook.* Chicago: Rand McNally.

ALDERMAN, M.; GREEN, L. W.; and FLYNN, B. S. 1980. Hypertension control programs in occupational settings. *Public Health Reports* 95:158–63.

BARANOWSKI, T. 1980. *Utilization and medication compliance for high blood pressure: An experiment with family involvement and self-blood pressure monitoring in a rural population.* Paper presented at the Third Annual Symposium on Patient Education, Johns Hopkins University, Baltimore, Md., March 1980.

BECKER, M. H., and GREEN, L. W. 1975. A family approach to compliance with medical treatment—a selective review of the literature. *International Journal of Health Education* 18:1–11.

BECKER, M. H.; DRACHMAN, R. H.; and KIRSCHT, J. P. 1974. A field experiment to evaluate various outcomes of continuity of physician care. *American Journal of Public Health* 64:1062.

BELLOC, N. B., and BRESLOW, L. 1972. Relationship of physical health status and practices. *Preventive Medicine* 1:415–21.

BERECZ, J. 1972. Modification of smoking behavior through self-administered punishment and imagined behavior. *Journal of Consulting and Clinical Psychology* 38:244–50.

BERKMAN, L. F., and SYME, S. 1979. Social networks, host resistance and mortality: a nine year follow-up study of Alameda County residents. *American Journal of Epidemiology* 109:186–204.

BERNSTEIN, D., and McALISTER, A. 1976. The modification of smoking behavior: progress and problems. *Addictive Behavior* 1:89–102.

BEST, J. 1975. Tailoring smoking withdrawal procedures to personality and motivational differences. *Journal of Consulting and Clinical Psychology* 43:1–3.

———; BASS, F.; and OWEN, L. *Mode of successful delivery in a smoking cessation program.* *Canadian Journal of Public Health,* in press.

BEST, J., and BLOCH, M. 1978. *On improving compliance: cigarette smoking.* Unpublished manuscript, University of British Columbia.

BRODIE, B. 1974. Views of healthy children toward illness. *American Journal of Public Health.* 64:1156.

BRUCKER, C. 1977. *Assuring patient compliance by health care contracts.* Final summary report to the National High Blood Pressure Education Program on NIH grant No. HL17230.

CAPLAN, R. D., et al. 1976. *Adhering to medical regimens: pilot experiments in patient education and social support.* Ann Arbor, Mich.: Institute for Social Research.

CHADWICK, J. H.; CHESNEY, M. A.; and JORDAN, S. C. 1979. *Blood pressure education in an industrial setting.* Final progress report to the National High Blood Pressure Education Program on NIH grant No. HL18424. Menlo Park, Calif.: Stanford Research Institute.

CHAPMAN, R.; SMITH, J.; and LAYDEN, T. 1971. Elimination of cigarette smoking by punishment and self management training. *Behaviour Research and Therapy* 9:255–64.

CHWALOW, A. J.; GREEN, L. W.; LEVINE, D. M.; and DEEDS, S. G. 1978. Effects of the multiplicity of interventions on the compliance of hypertensive patients with medical regimens in an inner city population. *Preventive Medicine* 7:51.

CUMMINGS, K. M.; JETTE, A. M.; and ROSENSTOCK, I. M. 1978. Construct validation of the Health Belief Model. *Health Education Monographs* 6:394–405.

DANAHER, B. 1977. Research on rapid smoking: interim summary and recommendations. *Addictive Behavior* 2:151–66.

DAWLEY, H., and SARDENGA, P. 1977. Aversion cigarette smoking as a smoking cessation procedure. *Journal of Clinical Psychology* 33:234–39.

DELAHUNT, J., and CURRAN, J. 1976. Effectiveness of negative practice and self-control techniques in the reduction of smoking behavior. *Journal of Consulting and Clinical Psychology* 44:1002–7.

EARP, J. L., and ORY, M. G. 1978. *The effects of social support and health professional home visits on patient adherence to hypertension regimens.* Abstract based on year three progress report to the National High Blood Pressure Education Program on NIH grant No. HL18414.

EPPRIGHT, E.; FOX, H.; FRYER, B.; LAMKIN, G.; and VIVIAN, N. 1969. Eating behavior of preschool children. *Journal of Nutrition Education* 1:16–19.

FASS, M. F.; GREEN, L. W.; and LEVINE, D. M. 1977. *The effect of family education on adherence to antihypertensive regimens.* Paper presented at the National High Blood Pressure Control Conference, Washington, D.C.

FESTINGER, L. 1957. *A theory of cognitive dissonance.* Stanford, Calif.: Stanford University Press.

FISHBEIN, M., and AJZEN, I. 1975. *Belief, attitude, intention, and behavior.* Reading, Mass.: Addison-Wesley.

FISHER, A. A.; HUSSIEN, C. A.; and SYME, S. 1977. Congruence between self-reported and staff perception of compliance. *Hypertension management.* Berkeley, Calif.: School of Public Health, University of California.

FLOWERS, R. V. 1978. *Effects of social support on adherence to therapeutic regimens.* Doctoral dissertation, University of Michigan.

GARN, S. M.; COLE, P. E.; and BAILEY, S. M. 1976. Effect of parental fatness levels on the fatness of biological and adoptive children. *Ecology of Food and Nutrition* 6:1–6.

GARRITY, T. F. 1980. A review of preliminary intervention results from the National High Blood Pressure Education Research Program. In *Patient compliance to prescribed antihypertensive medication regimens: a report to the National Heart, Lung, and Blood Institute,* ed. R. B. Haynes et al. (NIH pub. no. 81–2101). Bethesda, Md.: U.S. Department of Health and Human Services, Public Health Service, October 1980.

GOCHMAN, D. S. 1972. Development of health beliefs. *Psychological Reports* 31:259–66.

GREEN, L. W. 1970a. Status identity and preventive health behavior. *Pacific Health Education Reports No. 1.* Berkeley, Calif: University of California.

———. 1970b. Should health education abandon attitude change strategies? Perspectives from recent research. *Health Education Monographs* 30:25–48.

———. 1977. Evaluation and measurement: some dilemmas for health education. *American Journal of Public Health* 67:155–61.

———, and GREEN, P. F. 1977. Intervening in social systems to make smoking education more effective. *Proceedings of the Third World Conference on Smoking and Health,* vol. 2 (U.S. Department of Health, Education, and Welfare pub. no. [NIH] 77–1413). Washington, D.C.: Government Printing Office.

GREEN, L. W., and KANSLER, C. C. 1980. *The professional and scientific literature on patient education.* Health Affairs Information Series, vol. 5. Detroit, Mich.: Gale Research Company.

GREEN, L. W.; KREUTER, M. W.; DEEDS, S. G.; and PARTRIDGE, K. B. 1980. *Health education planning: a diagnostic approach.* Palo Alto, Calif.: Mayfield.

GREEN, L. W.; LEVINE, D. M.; and DEEDS, S. G. 1975. Clinical trials of health education for hypertensive outpatients: design and baseline data. *Preventive Medicine* 4:417–25.

GREEN, L. W.; RIMER, B.; and BERTERA, R. 1978. How cost-effective are smoking cessation methods? *World Smoking and Health* 3:33–40.

GUTELIUS, J, et al. 1971. Promising results from a cognitive stimulation program in infancy. *Clinical Pediatrics* 11:585–93.

HAGGERTY, J.; ROGHMANN, K. J.; and PLESS, B. 1975. *Child health and the community.* New York: Wiley.

HALL, S. M. 1972. Self-control and therapist control in the behavioral treatment of overweight women. *Behavioral Research and Therapy* 10:59–68.

HAYNES, R. B.; TAYLOR, D. W.; and SACKETT, D. L., ed. 1979. *Compliance in health care.* Baltimore, Md.: Johns Hopkins University Press.

HUNT, W. and BESPALEC, D. 1974. An evaluation of current methods of modifying smoking behavior. *Journal of Clinical Psychology* 30:431–38.

IDLER, E. 1979. Definitions of health and illness and medical sociology. *Social Science and Medicine* 13A:723–31.

JASON, L., and KIMBROUGH, C. 1974. A preventive educational program for young economically disadvantaged children. *Journal of Community Psychology* 2:134–39.

JEFFREY, D. B. 1974. A comparison of the effects of external control and self-control on the modification and maintenance of weight. *Journal of Abnormal Psychology* 83:404–10.

JOHNSON, K. W. 1980. *Parents of diabetic children and medical compliance.* Unpublished doctoral dissertation, University of Notre Dame.

KIRSCHT, J. P.; HAEFNER, D. P.; KEGELES, S. S.; and ROSENSTOCK, I. M. 1966. A national study of health beliefs. *Journal of Health and Human Behavior* 7:248–54.

KIRSHT, J. P.; and ROSENSTOCK, I. M. 1977. Patient adherence to antihypertensive medical regimens. *Journal of Community Health* 3:115–24.

KUHN, M. 1964. The reference group reconsidered. *The Sociological Quarterly* 5 (Winter):6–21.

KOOS, E. L. 1954. *The health of regionville.* New York: Columbia University Press.

LANDO, H. 1975. Successful treatment of smokers with a broad-spectrum behavioral approach. *Journal of Consulting and Clinical Psychology* 43:350–55.

LAU, R.; KANE, R.; BERRY, S.; WARE, J.; and ROY, D. 1980. Channeling health: a review of the evaluation of televised health campaigns. *Health Education Quarterly* 7:56–89.

LAWTON, M. 1967. Group methods in smoking cessation. *Archives of Environmental Health* 14:248–65.

LEVIN, L. S.; KATZ, A. H.; and HOLST, E. 1976. *Self-care: lay initiatives in health.* New York: Prodist.

LEVINE, D. M.; GREEN, L. W.; DEEDS, S. G.; et al. 1979. Health education for hypertensive patients. *Journal of the American Medical Association* 241:1700–3.

LEWIS, E., et al. 1977. Child-initiated care: the use of school nursing services by children in an "adult-free" system. *Pediatrics* 60:499–507.

LICHTENSTEIN, E., and DANAHER, B. 1977. Behavior therapy and the control of cigarette smoking. *Proceedings of the Third World Conference on Smoking and Health*, vol. 2 (U.S. Department of Health, Education, and Welfare pub. no. [NIH] 77–1413). Washington, D.C.: Government Printing Office.

LICHTENSTEIN, E.; HARRIS, D.; BIRCHLER, G.; WAHL, J.; and SCHMAHL, D. 1973. Comparison of rapid smoking, warm smoky air, and attention placebo in the modification of smoking behavior. *Journal of Consulting and Clinical Psychology* 40:92–98.

LINDESMITH, A.; STRAUSS, A. L.; and DANZIN, N. K. 1975. *Social psychology.* Hinsdale, Ill.: Dryden Press.

LITMAN, T. J. 1971. Health care and the family: a three-generational analysis. *Medical Care* 9(no. 1):67–81.

MAIMAN, L. A., et al. 1977. Scale for measuring Health Belief Model dimensions: a test of predictive value, internal consistency, and relationship among beliefs. *Health Education Monographs* 5:215–30.

MANNING, P. K., and FABREGA, H. 1973. The experience of self and body: health and illness in the Chiapas Highlands. In *Phenomenological sociology*, ed. G. Pathas. New York: Wiley.

MARSHALL, C. L., et al. 1970. Attitudes toward health among children of different races and socioeconomic status. *Pediatrics* 46:422–26.

MAUKSCH, H. O. 1974. A social science basis for conceptualizing family health. *Social Science and Medicine* 8:521–28.

McALISTER, A. L.; FARQUHAR, J. W.; THORESON, C. E.; and MACCOBY, N. 1976. Behavioral science applied to cardiovascular health: progress and research needs in the modification of risk-taking habits in adult populations. *Health Education Monographs* 4:45–74.

MECHANIC, D. 1974. Social structure and personal adaptation: Some neglected dimensions. In *Coping and adaptation*, ed. G. V. Coelho, D. A. Hamburg, J. E. Adams. New York: Basic Books.

———, and VOLKART, E. 1960. Illness behavior and medical diagnoses. *Journal of Health and Human Behavior* 1:86.

NULAND, W., and FULD, P. 1970. Smoking and hypnosis: a systematic clinical approach. *International Journal of Clinical and Experimental Hypnosis* 18:290–306.

Office of the Assistant Secretary for Health. 1979. *Healthy people: the surgeon general's report on health promotion and disease prevention* (Stock No. 017-001-00416-2). Washington, D.C.: Government Printing Office.

PRATT, L. 1976. *Family structure and effective health behavior: The energized family.* Boston: Houghton Mifflin Company.

RANDALL, T., and WHEELER, J. R. C. 1979. The effect of income on use of preventive care: an evaluation of alternative explanations. *Journal of Health and Social Behavior* 20:397–406.

RELINGER, H.; BORNSTEIN, P. H.; BUGGE, I. D.; CARMODY, T. P.; and ZOHN, C. J. 1977. Utilization of adverse rapid smoking in groups: efficacy of treatment and maintenance procedures. *Journal of Consulting and Clinical Psychology* 45:245–49.

RICHARDSON, W. C. 1970. Measuring the urban poor's use of physician services in response to illness episodes. *Medical Care* 8:132–42.

ROBERTSON, L.S.; KELLEY, A.B.; O'NEIL, B.; WIXON, C.W.; EISWIRTH, R.S.; HADDON, W., JR. 1974. A controlled study of the effect of television messages on safety belt use. *American Journal of Public Health* 5:363–78.

ROTTER, J. B. 1966. Generalized expectancies for internal versus external control of environment. *Psychological Monographs* 80(no. 1):1–28.

RUSSELL, M. 1970. Effect of electric aversion on cigarette smoking. *British Medical Journal* 1:82–86.

SACKETT, D., and HAYNES, R. B. 1976. *Compliance with therapeutic regimens.* Baltimore, Md.: Johns Hopkins University Press.

SALZER, E., JR.; MARSHALL, C. L.; and GLAZER, E. R. 1977. The use of cable television as a tool in health education of the elderly. *Health Education Monographs* 5:363–78.

SCHAEFER, E. 1972. Parents as educators: evidence from cross-sectional, longitudinal and intervention research. *Young Children* 27:227–39.

SCHMAHL, D.; LICHTENSTEIN, E.; and HARRIS, D. 1972. Successful treatment of habitual smokers with warm, smoky air and rapid smoking. *Journal of Consulting and Clinical Psychology* 38:105–11.

SCHMELING, D., and WOTRING, E. 1976. Agenda setting effects of drug abuse public service ads. *Journalism Quarterly* 53:743–46.

SCHWARTZ, J. 1969. A critical review and evaluation of smoking control methods. *Public Health Reports* 84:483–506.

SOLOMON, H. S. 1978. *Hypertension—educational models to improve adherence.* Final progress report to the National High Blood Pressure Education Program on NIH grant No. HL18423-03. Boston: Peter Bent Brigham Hospital.

STECKEL, S. B., and SWAIN, M. A. 1977. Contracting with patients to improve compliance. *Hospitals* 51:81–84.

STECKLER, A. B.; DAWSON, L.; and HERNDON, S. 1980. Analysis of health education sections of health systems plans. *Health Education Quarterly* 7:186–202.

SUCHMAN, E. A. 1965. Social patterns of illness and medical care. *Journal of Health and Human Behavior* 6 (Spring):2–16.

SUEDFELD, P., and IKARD, F. 1974. Use of sensory deprivation in facilitating the reduction of cigarette smoking. *Journal of Consulting and Clinical Psychology* 42:888–95.

SWAIN, M. A. 1978. *Experimental interventions to promote health among hypertensives.* Paper presented at the American Psychological Association annual convention, Toronto.

SYME, S.L. 1979. *Hypertension education program in a low income community.* Final report to the National High Blood Pressure Education Program on NIH grant No. HL16959.

WAGNER, M., and BRAGG, R. 1970. Comparing behavior modification approaches to habit decrement—smoking. *Journal of Consulting and Clinical Psychology* 34:258–63.

WALLSTON, K. A., WALLSTON, B. S., eds. 1978. Locus of control and health: a review of the literature. *Health Education Monographs* 6, 107–17.

WARNER, K. E. 1977. The effects of the anti-smoking campaign on cigarette consumption. *American Journal of Public Health* 67:645–50.

WATKINS, H. 1976. Hypnosis and smoking: a five session approach. *International Journal of Clinical and Experimental Hypnosis* 24:381–90.

WINETT, R. 1973. Parameters of deposit contracts in the modification of smoking. *Psychological Record* 23:49–50.

ZOLA, I. K. 1966. Culture and symptoms—an analysis of patients presenting complaints. *American Sociological Review* 33:615–30.

Chapter 34

Multivariate Analysis:
Basic Approaches to Health Data

Paul D. Cleary

WITHIN THE PAST DECADE or so there has been an explosion of developments in multivariate statistical theory and data analysis techniques. It is virtually impossible, because of limitations in background and time constraints, for most health researchers to stay abreast of current developments in both their substantive areas and in statistics and methodology. Thus, it is necessary for researchers to seek and rely on the advice of experts in various analytical techniques and methodological approaches. However, for any given theoretical or exploratory problem it is important for the researcher to have a sense of the strengths and limitations of the available analytical strategies. A statistician or methodologist who acts as a consultant to a research project cannot be fully aware of the substantive issues involved and is not necessarily the best person to make the final decision concerning analysis strategy.

Even if a researcher has little statistical knowledge he/she should not allow a statistician to make design or analysis decisions without discussing the substantive issues involved. The theoretical perspective and practical background that a researcher has will almost always be at least as important in determining the design of a study and the types of analysis to be done as any set of statistical assumptions. The researcher has a responsibility to become involved in the statistical decision process and make sure that the analyses are appropriate to the theory being tested and not vice-versa.

This chapter will present an overview of some of the considerations that should be taken into account in collecting and analyzing health data. Rather than catalog and describe in detail the almost endless list of available "techniques," I will emphasize the basic features of various methods and describe some of the central issues in analyzing data. Although most descriptions of statistical techniques outline extremely fine distinctions and subtle assumptions, usually very basic considerations determine one's approach. Once a general strategy is selected, it is easy to allow one's statistician to make fine distinctions and choose the "best" technique or computer program. No set of elegant and elaborate techniques will compensate

Work on this chapter was supported by grants from the Center for Epidemiologic Studies of the National Institute of Mental Health and the Robert Wood Johnson Foundation.

for the lack of a good theory or deficient study design, but sometimes knowledge of available analytical strategies allows a researcher to test a hypothesis or clarify an empirical relationship that might otherwise remain elusive.

It is difficult to cover a broad range of topics in the limited space of a chapter and explain technical terms as clearly as would be desirable. An effort has been made, however, to provide numerous references for the techniques and procedures referred to. Thus, this chapter should serve primarily as a starting point for a more careful consideration of approaches to health data and the references should act as a guide to the information available on various statistical methods.

Planning

The analysis process should start well before data are collected. Usually substantive concerns and practical limitations determine most of the features of a study design, but initial consultation with a methodologist will help avoid many problems. Considerations such as sampling strategy, sample size, and necessary control variables often turn out to be critical for the proper interpretation of data (Hess, Riedel, and Fitzpatrick 1975; Levy and Lemshow 1980). For example, let us say a hospital is interested in factors influencing utilization patterns in its outpatient department. It would seem that a reasonable sample for such a study would be all patients coming to the outpatient department over several months. However, the researcher should always ask two basic questions: "Do the people in this sample represent the population about which I want to make inferences?" and "Are there some people who are more likely than others to fall into the sample?" In our example, although a sample of consecutive attenders would draw people from the population of interest (all outpatient users), people who frequently come to the outpatient department are more likely to fall into the sample (for example, Albee 1976; Shepard and Neutra 1977). Thus, a sample of consecutive users over a limited portion of the year would overrepresent high users. In addition, seasonal variations in patient characteristics might result in other biases. For example, in the winter months a sample of patients will overrepresent persons with upper-respiratory problems. Awareness of such potential problems before data are collected often allows the researcher to gather additional information for assessing the adequacy of such a sample and statistically correct for certain biases. Awareness of such problems after a study is conducted only results in frustration. It is usually possible to avoid many sources of sample bias, and the time and effort spent consulting with someone familiar with sampling techniques are investments that will usually pay off.

Sample Size

The amount of information collected in a study is partially a function of sample size, and inadequate samples are frequently the reason that studies yield inconclusive results. The statistician faces the same dilemma as the hematologist; he/she must usually make inferences from a small sample. How big a sample is big enough? The "necessary" sample size will vary for each statistical test. The researcher will probably have to determine the sample size necessary for the typical analysis and analyses of particular importance and then make a decision based on cost and logistical considerations.

There are numerous rules of thumb concerning the number of subjects needed for different types of analyses. For example, it is commonly asserted that in most social science applications, using multiple regression techniques, the sample size should be about twenty-five times as large as the number of predictor variables (Cohen and Cohen 1976). Kerlinger and Pedhazur (1973, p. 446) argue that any multiple regression analysis should have at least a hundred subjects and preferably two-hundred or more. In factor analysis, it has been suggested that one have at least four (Cattell 1952) to five (Bentler 1976) cases per variable (see also Kim and Mueller 1978, p. 76); and for discriminant analysis it has been proposed that about three times as many observations as there are parameters to estimate in each group is satisfactory (Krzanowski 1968; Lachenbruch 1975; Lachenbruch and Goldstein 1979).

There have also been studies of the number of subjects necessary for special types of analysis. Thus, Lunney (1979) has shown that one can use analysis of variance when the dependent variable is dichotomous if there are from twenty to forty more subjects (more observations are necessary when less than 20 percent of the subjects have one of the values of the dependent variable) than parmaeters estimated. A common rule of thumb for analysis of contingency tables is that the expected number of cases in each cell should be at least five and a minimun of ten if there is only one degree of freedom (Hays and Winkler 1971); however, in some cases this has been shown to be overly restrictive (Camilli and Hopkins 1979).

As useful as these guidelines are, they are usually too crude to be used alone in determining sample size (Cohen and Cohen 1976). A researcher should consider carefully what the typical analysis will entail and whether there are any analyses of special interest, and then determine the minimum sample size necessary to detect important effects. A researcher must specify three things in order to determine desired sample size: how confident he/she wants to be that when the null hypothesis is rejected this is the right decision; how big an effect he/she is interested in detecting; and with what probability such an effect should be detected. Once these decisions are made it is relatively easy to determine the number of subjects needed. Although this process sounds formidable, it is really quite straightforward. The concepts on which these calculations are based have their origins in elegant statistical theory, but in practice they are only conventions. For example, the decision concerning the confidence necessary for rejecting the null hypothesis has essentially been made for the researcher. Although there is some controversy over this issue (Morrison and Henkel 1970), almost all researchers reject the null hypothesis if the probability of its being true is less than .05 or .01.(This value is also known as "alpha" (α) or the Type I Error Rate. In biomedical and epidemiologic terms, $1 - \alpha$ is analogous to the specificity of a test.)

In determining the size of the effect to be detected or the expected proportion of variance to be explained, the researcher need rely on nothing more sophisticated than the amount of variance "typically" explained in the literature concerning the topic of interest. Usually investigators have a sense of how big an effect must be to be considered substantively important. Researchers should always remember, of course, that certain variables that are extremely "important" (e.g., adequate breathing air) may not vary in a particular study and consequently will not help explain variation in the dependent variable.) For example, most health researchers can specify approximately how much variance must be explained by a variable before they consider it "important." Similarly, if some test shows a great deal of variability among patients, the researcher will give less importance to a certain change in the value of that test than a test known to usually have little variability.

The third decision that must be made is how certain the researcher wants to be that an effect of this size will be detected if present; for any given effect or relationship, the larger the sample, the more likely is the effect or relationship to be detected. Once again, convention is probably the safest rule for the typical applied researcher. Thus, a reasonable choice for this confidence level is .80 (Cohen 1969). This is also known as the "power" of a statistical test. This is analogous to what biomedical researchers and epidemiologists refer to as the sensitivity of a test.

These rules mainly serve the purpose of making results from different studies and analyses comparable. In fact, the "significant at the .05 level" of one study usually means something very different from the same finding in another study. However, by following certain conventions, it is possible to be more confident of the comparability of one's results.

Once the researcher has decided on, for example, a Type I error rate (α) of .05, a power of .80 and the size of effect to be detected, it is easy to determine the appropriate sample size. Jacob Cohen (1969; Cohen and Cohen 1975) provides extensive tables for making power and sample size determinations in numerous situations. These references are designed for applied researchers and are easy to use (see also Feinstein 1977, chap. 22; Fleiss 1973; Stevens 1980).

An important fact to keep in mind when determining sample size is whether one's research is confirmatory or exploratory; that is, is one testing a priori hypotheses or looking "to see what's in the data"? Although most social research is exploratory in some sense (Borgatta 1961), necessary sample size and meaning of significance levels change substantially in purely exploratory research (see for example, Wilkinson 1979). For example, if twenty tests are done, one is likely to be significant at the .05 level by chance. Thus, in exploratory research, a more stringent criteria for significance should usually be used. There are both simple and complicated methods of determining what significance levels should be used (see Kirt 1968, pp. 82–98, for a lucid description of these issues). A stricter criterion for significance will of course affect the desired sample size. An appropriate sample size is a necessary condition for detecting effects at a given power level. Only by taking all the above factors into account when planning a study will a researcher be assured of having the "horsepower" to test his/her hypotheses.

Weighting

Often a situation arises where a particular group of people is included in a sample more frequently than another. For example, perhaps the utilization patterns and characteristics of mothers with large families are of particular interest. In such a situation, one might decide to sample *all* mothers with more than four children but only take every fourth parent from the rest of the population. Such a procedure obviously results in a sample which overrepresents mothers of large families. In some analyses it is necessary to take account of this fact. Thus, to estimate the average age of all clinic users (the summary statistic for the population of interest), it would be necessary to adjust for the fact that mothers with large families were overrepresented in the sample. One solution to this is to "weight" mothers in large families by one-fourth. This procedure will yield an unbiased estimate of the average age of the population from which the sample was drawn. When estimating more complicated statistics, such as regression coefficients, the considerations are more complicated and there is disagreement about how to proceed (DuMouchel and Duncan 1976; Klein and Morgan 1951; Porter 1973; and Konijn 1962). Often one can make the decision to weight or not to weight on fairly straightforward criteria. Let us call groups with different probabilities of being included in the sample "strata." If the relationship being estimated is the same in each strata, unweighted analysis will yield an unbiased estimate. For example, if the relationship between perceived health and ulitization is the same for mothers of large families and other patients, then estimating the regression equation without taking into account the sampling proportion will yield unbiased estimates of the coefficients. If, however, the relationship is not the same, neither weighted nor unweighted analysis will necessarily yield unbiased estimates and it is impossible to say which method will provide an estimate with the least bias. Thus, in the case that the relationship is different for different groups of subjects (strata), one must explicitly take this into account when developing the model and derive separate estimates for the different strata (Smith 1976).

Data Reduction

A basic motivation for multivariate analysis is to represent the complex associations among numerous variables in as parsimonious a manner as possible. A first step in this process is to decrease the dimensionality of the data and to combine measures to form scales representing specific constructs. Two types of scales are typically used: those containing counts of different events, and those containing several items measuring the same construct. An example of the first type is an index of chronic disease, which can be based on a count of the number of chronic health conditions experienced by a person. The domain of health conditions of interest is specified a priori and one would not necessarily expect that a person with one problem would be likely to have other problems (although this may be the case); that is, the components of the scale would not necessarily be correlated. In the second type of scale a researcher might wish to measure a subjective feature (such as satisfaction with care) and to tap different aspects of such satisfaction. Even if one postulated that there are different dimensions of satisfaction, one might wish to ask numerous questions about each dimension. In this situation, one would expect that measures of each aspect of satisfaction would be correlated; including several measures reflecting each dimension would increase the reliability of the subscales.

Given a group of variables, a researcher is faced with three decisions. First, he/she must decide how many constructs the variables represent. Second, it is necessary to specify which variables are most related to which constructs. Third, it is necessary to decide how the variables are to be combined to form a scale measuring the construct. Thus, if a researcher has data on patient responses to twenty questions concerning satisfaction with different aspects of care, he/she must first determine whether satisfaction is a single characteristic (i.e., unidimensional); if a patient is satisfied with some aspects of care, does this mean that he/she is also likely to be satisfied with all aspects of care, or are there distinct aspects of satisfaction? For example, perhaps satisfaction with the technical aspects of the medical setting is independent of satisfaction with the personal aspects of the care received. Once this decision is made the researcher must determine which items best measure each dimension. The final decision is how to combine the items.

There is an almost endless variety of methods and techniques for combining items to form a scale (Wang and Stanley 1970), and a choice among these techniques must be made. Although the simplest method of combining items is often the best, the researcher should be aware that there are numerous techniques that might suit his/her needs better than a simple unweighted combination of items. Sometimes these decisions can and should be made on substantive rather than methodological grounds. For example, if a person's history of chronic disease is to be measured it is possible to specify a priori what specific chronic diseases are of interest and thus include only those in a scale. In addition, there may be substantive reasons for making separate scales of chronic diseases. Thus, one may wish to distinguish between chronic diseases which are associated with high levels of disability and those with less impact (Benjamin 1965; 566). These decisions are based on knowledge of the diseases rather than some statistical technique. As was mentioned earlier, the fact that certain diseases are similar in some ways does not mean that they are more likely to occur together (i.e., their occurrence in the population is not necessarily correlated).

In the situation where a researcher has several items concerning a general substantive area (e.g., satisfaction with care) and wants to determine if they represent several, more specific aspects, numerous exploratory techniques are available for examining the data for patterns of association. The assumption behind these techniques is that the responses to different items representing the same construct will be more similar (e.g., correlated) than the responses to items representing different constructs. There are numerous techniques based on this principle, but only principal components analysis, factor analysis, multidimensional scaling, and cluster analysis will be reviewed here. These techniques are by far the most widely used and will meet the needs of the researcher in almost all circumstances. Despite the differences among these techniques, they all serve a common function: to explore associations among variables in an effort to detect groups of variables sharing common sources of variance, to determine the number of constructs giving rise to the observed pattern of responses, and to estimate the importance of each item in measuring each dimension.

Factor Analysis

Several models and analysis techniques fall under the rubric of "factor analysis" (Rummel 1970), but the focus here will be on the two most widely used techniques and some general considerations important for their application. These two models are referred to as principal components analysis and principal factor analysis. Both models assume that there are a number of unmeasured constructs that explain observed responses. The purpose of both techniques is to detect such dimensions and to determine the degree to which each measured variable is associated with each construct. In our satisfaction example, the purpose of using factor analytic techniques would be to determine how many dimensions of satisfaction were present in the responses and to what degree each question reflected each dimension of satisfaction. The measure of association on which factor analysis is based is the correlation coefficient (in certin circumstances, such as in comparing the factor structure in different populations, it may be desirable to analyze the covariance matrix; Kim and Mueller 1978). The main difference between the two methods is that the principal components model simply assumes that each dimension is represented by a linear combination of the question responses and does not allow for the possibility of measurement error in the responses to the question. Principal factor procedures, on the other hand, allow for both error (unique variance) and variation due to the construct being measured. In most social research the principal factor procedure is decidedly preferable to the principal components model because it allows for a much more reasonable model of the expected sources of variation in responses (c.f. Kaiser 1970). This procedure requires estimates of how much of each variable's variation is due to underlying factors (i.e., one must provide estimates of commonality). Although there are numerous ways of estimating this quantity (Rummel 1970), a simple and reasonable estimate of the commonality of a variable is the multiple correlation between a given variable and the other variables. Most factor analysis procedures routinely estimate this quantity for the researcher.

Despite the many technical presentations in the statistical literature, choosing the number of factors is as much an art as a science. Although there are both subjective (Rummel 1970) and objective criteria (Lawley and Maxwell 1971) for choosing the number of factors, the decision is most often made on the basis of the investigator's knowledge of the data and the substantive area under investigation. Two statistical criteria for determining the number of factors are statistical tests associated with certain techniques that determine how well the factor model reproduces the observed correlations and various criteria based on the relative importance (i.e., eigenvalue) of each factor (Kim and Mueller 1978). Because some of the considerations underlying use of these rules are complex, the researcher without statistical background should consult with someone knowledgeable in statistics about their application. However, there are several subjective criteria that most researchers can use and interpret quite readily. These are the patterns of statistical "importance" of the factors, the substantive "interpretability" of the factors, and the consistency of different criteria. Statistical importance means the proportion of variance explained by the factors (or, alternately, the size of the eigenvalues associated with the factors). By plotting the variance explained as a function of the number of factors in the model a researcher can identify visually the point of diminishing returns. That is, it is easy to see the point at which adding more factors yields little additional information. A second criterion for determining how many factors to extract is the degree to which the factors "make sense." Thus, even if a factor explains a large proportion of the variance in a correlation matrix, it is of little use to the researcher if it has no substantive interpretation. The third criterion of consistency is the ability of different techniques to yield the same answer. One should use different techniques, apply different criteria and accept those solutions that are supported by several independent decision rules (Harris 1967).

One convenient feature of factor analysis solutions is that they can be "rotated" to be more easily interpreted. Especially useful are methods of rotation known as oblique rotations that allow the factors to be correlated. In our satisfaction example, even though we think that satisfaction with the technical and personal aspects of care are distinct, we might also expect that satisfaction on these two dimensions is correlated. When one has decided to rotate factor analysis results and allow the factors to be correlated, there is almost an infinite number of "solutions" and results. The best guide here is consistency using different methods and substantive meaning. That the results of a factor analysis indicate satisfaction with the X-ray equipment at a hospital and satisfaction with the courtesy of the intake staff load on the same factor does not mean that they reflect similar concepts. In all exploratory analyses, such as the use of factor analysis described here, the researcher is the final judge of an acceptable solution. Theoretical considerations should guide interpretation of results and not vice-versa.

Although most statistical program "packages" calculate factor solutions by determining certain characteristics of the correlation matrix (eigenvectors and eigenvalues), maximum-likelihood factor analysis is increasingly considered by many to be the method of choice. Maximum-likelihood techniques determine parameter estimates that are most likely to have yielded the sample being analyzed. Despite the theoretical elegance of maximum-likelihood techniques, they usually yield almost identical results to more conventional techniques. It is frequently impossible to maximize the likelihood function without getting problematic solutions, and they are typically ten times more expensive than more traditional methods (Jackson and Chan 1980). Thus, unless the researcher has very specific questions or models that can be addressed only with these newer techniques, the recommendation is to use the standard methods.

It was previously mentioned that factor analysis is intended for the analysis of correlation or covariance. In fact, factor analysis can be applied to any measure of association and often the results are heuristic. However, dichotomous or ordinal measures violate the assumptions on which factor analysis was developed and, in cases where one is concerned with precise results, other techniques should be considered (Kim and Mueller [1978] present a very clear discussion of the advisability of analyzing measures other than correlation coefficients). In such circumstances multidimensional scaling and cluster analysis are the most commonly used alternatives.

Multidimensional Scaling

Although many researchers have only recently become aware of multidimensional scaling techniques, they have a long history in the psychometric literature (Shepard 1972b). The major trends in this area have been the classical, metric, or "Torgerson" approach (Torgerson 1952, 1958), methods developed by Coombs (1964), and the nonmetric approach developed and described primarily by Shepard and Kruskal (Shepard et al. 1972; Romney et al. 1972). The procedures developed by Shepard, Kruskal, and others have overtaken other types of multidimensional scaling and are currently the most popular techniques after factor analysis for analyzing patterns of association. The appeal of these methods is that they capture the best of both worlds: They can be used with nonmetric (ordinal) data, yet yield a metric representation. Thus, nonmetric multidimensional scaling is similar in purpose to factor analysis but is appropriate for a much wider range of data. The basic input used in nonmetric multidimensional scaling is a "distance" measure. This can be any index or measure of how similar or "close" two variables or subjects are. While factor analysis makes quite rigorous assumptions about the meaning of a correlation coefficient (i.e., the correlation between two items is equal to the cosine of the angle between the vectors connecting these items to the origin of the space), multidimensional scaling only assumes that the distance measure is related to how far apart those items are when arranged on their theoretical dimensions. Although a correlation can be used as a distance measure, other measures are also acceptable: ratings of similarity, measures of association based on dichotomous or ordinal data, difference scores, etc. The computer programs for conducting this type of analysis are increasingly available at different institutions and are relatively easy to use. The criteria for determining the number of dimensions are similar to those for determining the number of dimensions from a factor analysis; the measure of poor fit (stress) should not drop too sharply when further dimensions are added, the results should be reliable, and the solution should be readily visualized and interpreted (Kruskal 1964a, 1964b). One limitation of nonmetric multidimensional scaling techniques is that the dimensions or factors are necessarily uncorrelated. Although the solution from these techniques may be rotated, easy to use techniques analogous to the oblique rotation techniques used with factor analysis are not readily available.

In general, however, nonmetric multidimensional scaling procedures are relatively easy to use and have fascinating applications (see for example, Romney et al. 1972). The applied researcher should consider using this technique when his/her data are not appropriate for factor analysis. There is a multitude of techniques and programs for conducting these types of analyses but as Shepard notes, "when they are applied to the same data, the various methods of this general type—whether they are called 'proximity analysis' (Shepard), 'smallest space analysis' (Guttman and Lingoes), or simply 'nonmetric multidimensional scaling' (Kruskal and others)—usually yield virtually indistinguishable results." (Shepard 1972a p. 8).

Cluster Analysis

In cluster analysis techniques (Everitt 1977), one also attempts to define spaces common to variables by analyzing distance or similarity measures. Clustering techniques have a long history in the behavioral sciences (Cronbach and Gleser 1953), and since the 1960s there have been hundreds of studies published by researchers in all fields on typing and taxonomic grouping (Lorr 1976). However, despite this widespread interest in classification problems, there is no consensus on what the definition of a cluster should be (Sokal 1977). The only common ground these techniques share is that elements of a cluster are "closer" to each other than to other elements, but "closer" is operationalized in different ways by various researchers. The most commonly used techniques are hierarchical, and clusters of progressively larger size are formed by joining similar entities (e.g., variables) and then by joining similar clusters.

A concise, nontechnical overview of these techniques is provided by Lorr (1976), who lists five main approaches to clustering: in *single link* procedures, entities are merged on the basis of the distance between the two closest members of clusters; in *complete link* procedures, single entities are merged on the basis of distance between the most distant pair; the *average link* procedure defines the distance between groups as the average distance between all pairs of entities in two clusters; and in *centroid cluster* analysis, the two clusters at each stage with the most similar means are merged, and a procedure developed by Ward and Hook (1963) seeks to minimize the loss of information that results from combining entities into clusters. Current research in clustering is focused on understanding the relationships between different techniques and in developing tests of significance of classifications (Sokal 1977; Van Ryzin 1977).

The similarity among these data reduction techniques is that they all attempt to find commonalities among groups of variables or people. Although each represents a sophisticated statistical model and has quite distinct assumptions, each is basically providing a method of grouping "similar" variables. In most situations where numerous variables are analyzed for underlying structure and where correlation coefficents are used as indices of association, these techniques will yield similar results.

The assumptions underlying each of the techniques discussed above are specific and important, but most applied researchers cannot make statements about their data that are precise enough to help choose among techniques. An assumption necessary for factor analysis techniques is that the measured variables are related linearly to the unmeasured construct. However, it is that rare applied researcher who can specify with assurance that the response to a questionnaire item coded using a five-point scale is linearly related to some hypothetical construct. In addition, as Overall (1964) and others have shown, if the measured variables are related to the underlying constructs in a complicated way, these techniques will not reveal the basic structure.

There are substantial differences between clustering techniques and multidimensional scaling techniques (Kruskal 1977). For example, multidimensional scaling provides a spatial representation of the data whereas clustering techniques provide a "tree" representation. Nevertheless, many researchers find it useful to apply both techniques to the same proximities. Multidimensional scaling appears to be more sensitive to large dissimilarities in the data, and clustering techniques more sensitive to small dissimilarities. Thus, it is appropriate to use both techniques in many situations and to examine the similarities and differences in the results (Kruskal 1977, p. 34). Often, more can be gained from using different techniques and looking for commonalities than by going to great effort to use an esoteric procedure that has been determined to be "theoretically correct."

Once a researcher has used data reduction techniques such as factor analysis to determine how many constructs the analyzed items represent, it is necessary to combine the responses from those items to form scores for each dimension. Thus, if the health-care researcher has decided that the satisfaction items he/she has included in a questionnaire reflect satisfaction with technical aspects and satisfaction with personal aspects of care, it must be determined how responses to those items are to be combined to form two satisfaction scores. Although it is not necessary to do so, most researchers include a particular item in only one scale for conceptual clarity. For example, although it is possible that a particular question about satisfaction may reflect satisfaction with several dimensions of care, it is common practice to make a decision about the dimension to which it is most related and to include it in only that scale. If one's reduction technique is cluster analysis, this decision is relatively easy; either an item is or is not in a particular cluster. If techniques such as factor analysis or multivariate scaling are used, the decision is more difficult because an item may represent more than one dimension.

Common practice is to combine empirical criteria with substantive input. One may determine on which dimension an item loads most heavily and consider it a measure of that construct, or set an arbitrary cutoff point for loadings and include only items that reach a particular value. Several techniques should be used. Once a preliminary decision has been made as to which items tap which constructs, further calculations can be done to help refine a scale.

A key concept in scale construction is reliability; given that a person's attitude or characteristic is constant, how consistent is one's measure of that characteristic or attitude? One can talk of the consistency of a scale over time or the consistency of different items (internal consistency). Because of the practical and theoretical problems of measuring a characteristic that is known to be consistent at two points in time, reliability is most often estimated on the basis of internal consistency. There are various definitions of reliability and numerous formulae for calculating reliability (Bohrnstedt 1970 gives an excellent description of various reliability formulae), but the most common approach is the Coefficient Alpha, developed by Cronback (1951). Cronbach's Alpha, as this measure sometimes is called, is the expected correlation of a scale with another scale of the same length measuring the same thing.

Alpha will increase as a function of both the inter-item correlations and as a function of the length of the scale. In our satisfaction example, if a scale had a high Coefficient Alpha, this would imply that people who answered positively (in terms of satisfaction) to one item on the scale would also be likely to answer positively to other items. Most of the computer programs that calculate Coefficient Alpha also calculate the correlation between a particular item and the total score (usually correcting for the fact that that item is contributing to the total score). By examining item-to-total correlations one can see which items are less consistent with the overall pattern of responses to scale items. A low item-to-total correlation may indicate a "bad" item that should be dropped from the scale.

Scaling

The discussion up to this point has not considered whether different items should be given differential importance when creating a scale. For example, in a hypothetical scale of satisfaction with the personal aspects of care, should more importance be given to an item about physicians than to an item about nurses? Once again, if one has used cluster analysis, the answer is relatively simple: either a variable is or is not in a cluster, and thus simply summing the variables will result in a scale that incorporates the information from the analyses. If nonmetric multidimensional scaling analyses or factor analyses are conducted, one has information on relative weightings of different dimensions or factors. In the case of nonmetric multidimensional scaling, one can determine the projection of different variables on different dimensions. In factor analysis, there are several procedures for calculating factor scores from the weights derived from the analyses (Harman 1967; Rummel 1970).

There are three central points to be emphasized here. First, the results of a factor analysis, a multidimensional scaling program, or a clustering program are estimates of population characteristics. They are not the "truth." It is discouraging to read papers in which researchers use a scale that has been developed over many years in many samples but disregard available procedures for scaling the results. Often the paper will report that the scale was used, a factor analysis of one type was done, and since the results were different from the original, a new factor score was calculated on the basis of the coefficients derived in this new sample. There is no justification for such a procedure. If results and scaling procedures are available from other studies on a general population, those should be used. A researcher may wish to do a thorough job of developing a new scale because of a difference in populations, inclusion of new items, changes in circumstances, etc. However, development of a new scale is *not* calculating one factor analysis in a small sample and then using those results. All estimators show variation across samples, and unless one is confident that particular parameters are relatively stable, calculating a linear composite using coefficient estimates from the sample capitalizes on chance.

The second point is that there are important distinctions between the different coefficients generated from a factor analysis. Factor loadings, structure loadings, and factor score coefficients are not the same and should not be used for the same thing. More specifically, factor loadings represent the correlations between the variables and the factors. Factor score coefficients indicate the relationship between the variables and a new scale (Horn 1965; Glass and Maguire 1966; Harris 1967). It is beyond the scope of this chapter to describe the various methods of calculating factor scores, but Alwin (1973) provides an excellent overview of this issue.

The third point is that deriving weights may not be necessary in any case. As Alwin has stated, "it is unclear whether differential weighting schemes will make a difference in the performance of the complete score, either in terms of changing the essential definition of the construct involved or in terms of external prediction" (Alwin 1973, p. 206; see also Wainer 1976). McKennell (1977) has suggested a three-stage process of attitude scale development: a qualitative pilot, a scale development pilot study, and then a main survey. The problem of scaling and weighting items to form a scale is thus complicated, both in terms of the process involved (see for example, Thurstone 1928; Guttman 1944; Likert 1932; Summers 1970; Nunnally 1967) and in terms of the theoretical and empirical utility of the end result. For example, in health research the question of how to combine items to form a life-events scale has generated an enormous amount of debate among researchers (cf. Dohrenwend et al. 1978, 1979; Lorimenr et al. 1979; Dohrenwend 1980; Kessler 1980; Mirowski and Ross 1980; Ross and Mirowski 1979).

Given the amount of effort and expertise involved in scaling and the suggestion by some that the effort is not justified, how might the health researcher decide on the best way to combine items? The easiest answer, of course, is "it depends," but differential weighting usually does not improve the reliability or validity of a scale over what is obtained when items are simply summed or averaged. If scaling is of particular concern, Wang and Stanley (1970) present one of the most comprehensive reviews and evaluations of differential weighting techniques. The interested reader will find many approaches to the problems in that review but in summary, Wang and Stanley (1970, p. 699) note that "The effectiveness of weighting depends on the number of measures to be combined, their intercorrelations, and certain characteristics of the weights. Weighting is most effective when there are but a few relatively independent variables in the composite. With a large number of positively correlated variables . . . the correlation between two randomly weighted composites rapidly approaches unity." Thus, instead of using factor analysis to estimate coefficients to be used in calculating linear composites, the results can be used to determine simply whether or not an item is to be included in a scale; once included, that item is given a weight of 1. A common procedure is to include all items that have a coefficient that is above some arbitrary cutoff value. In practice, this procedure becomes very subjective, but it is surprising how informative and substantively meaningful scales derived in this way can be.

Even if factor coefficients are used only as a guide to what variables are to be included in a scale, there may be such gross differences among the variables that the researcher feels some differential weighting is mandatory. For example, if one item in an exercise scale is "Do you walk up stairs or take the elevator" and another is "How many miles do you run per day," there is clearly a difference between these items in the amount of information they yield concerning exercise. Two approaches are suggested. One is to use an intuitively reasonable scaling. For example, if one question is about how far one swims per day, and another is about how far one runs per day, one can determine a rough translation so that values of each are transformed into generally equivalent amounts of exercise. Another procedure is to standardize the items before summing them. Certain computer programs calculate Coefficient Alpha (internal consistency) for both the raw data and the standardized variables. Analyses of this sort can be used as a guide to the usefulness of some standarization procedure.

It must be remembered that this chapter is necessarily limited in its treatment of most topics. Consequently, much information on scaling has been omitted, or only briefly mentioned. However, the reader should not misinterpret this overview as supporting a "quick and dirty" approach to scaling. On the contrary, this is one area to which researchers should devote much more of their time. However, if it is not possible to follow carefully a rigorous procedure in developing and validating scales, one should not calculate detailed coefficients and use complicated weighting procedures that imply more precision than is warranted.

Modeling the Data

Whether research is exploratory or confirmatory, a common approach to the data is to develop models and test their appropriateness using the data collected. If one has temporally prior independent variables or data collected in a randomized experiment, patterns of association can argue quite strongly for causality. If the data are cross-sectional and "correlational" in nature, one is interested in providing supportive evidence for particular hypotheses or models. In any case, the basic approach is to attempt to detect patterns of association between the dependent variable of interest and one or more independent variables. Theoretically, an infinite variety of models is possible. Practically, however, most researchers have restricted themselves to two general classes of models. In the first, *Linear Models*, one assumes that the relationship between the dependent variable and the independent variable(s) is linear and of the form:

$$Y = a + bX \qquad (1)$$

In the second class of models, one assumes that the relationship is S-shaped (see Figure 34.1) and has the following form:

$$Y = [1 + e^{-[a + bx]}]^{-1} \qquad (2)$$

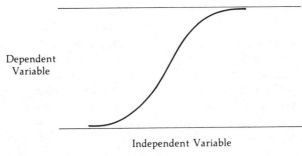

Independent Variable

Figure 34.1 *S-spaced Model*

Although this point may seem obvious and simplistic to many readers, it is surprising how few researchers fully appreciate the importance of this distinction. These models are relatively easy to choose between in most circumstances; once this decision is made, many of the problems associated with the "what technique to use" decision are solved. In order to simplify discussion of various models, let us choose a substantive example and assume that we are interested in testing several hypotheses concerning the relationship between physician utilization (the dependent variable) and illness and access (two independent variables). Physician utilization is an interesting variable because it can be treated as a continuous variable (number of visits per year) or as a dichotomous variable (did use/did not use). Although there are theoretical frameworks that suggest how utilization should be viewed (e.g., Aday, Anderson, Fleming 1980), for illustration purposes I will first describe multivariate approaches when it is considered as a continuous variable and next give an overview of the multivariate approaches available for the case when it is treated as a dichotomous variable.

When the dependent variable is continuous, the most parsimonious and intuitively plausible model is a linear one. That is, we assume that utilization is linearly related to the independent variables. The best approach at this point is to look at the data. Examine scattergrams of the joint distributions and examine the scattergrams for any unusual patterns of extreme values. Multivariate techniques can be extremely informative if one is familiar with the data, but generating a large multiple regression model and looking at coefficient estimates without having a sense of the data can lead one totally astray in interpreting results. Thus, after carefully looking at marginals and joint scattergrams, one might decide that utilization is not linearly related to illness but goes up dramatically at a particular level of illness, and therefore it is unreasonable to treat the items in the illness scale as forming an interval scale. Although analysis of cross-sectional survey data has come to be called "correlational analysis," using the correlation coefficient to summarize a relationship may gloss over important aspects of the data and indeed, as Tukey once commented, "most correlation coefficients should never be calculated" (Tukey 1954, p. 38). Although there is not space here to describe Tukey's suggested procedures for exploratory data analysis in more detail (Tukey 1977), it is recommended that researchers become as familiar as possible with the characteristics of their data before proceeding with more complicated multivariate techniques.

The General Linear Model (GLM) is, as the name implies, a general statistical formulation for modeling the linear relationship between a dependent variable and one or more independent variables. The GLM covers such techniques as linear regression, analysis of variance (ANOVA), analysis of covariance (ANCOVA) and Multiple Classification Analysis (Cohen 1968; Darlington 1968; Fennessey 1968; Gordon 1967; Gujarati 1970). Although there are numerous differences between the models and techniques mentioned, it is important to emphasize the similarities. All of these techniques follow the same formulation. For example, the results obtained from each can be derived using multiple regression. Thus, one can represent "groups" in analysis of variance as independent variables in multiple regression, and by appropriate coding can obtain the adjusted means of Multiple Classification Analysis (Melicar 1965, Overall and Spiegel 1969). There are, of course, different ways of estimating the coefficients in a linear model (e.g., least squares, weighted least squares, maximum-likelihood estimation, and analytical solutions based on orthogonal data sets), but all are based on the same principle: one estimates the conditional mean of the dependent variable using information from the independent variable, whether it be an interval variable or group classification.

The simplest way to describe the differences among linear techniques is that typically multiple regression is used in the situation where the dependent variable is continuous, and the independent variables are continuous and correlated. Analysis of variance typically refers to the situation where the dependent variable is continuous and the independent variables are categorical and independent (orthogonal). Analysis of covariance typically refers to the situation where the dependent variable is continuous, some of the variables are categorical and independent, and some of the variables (covariates) are continuous. However, various mixtures of types of variables do occur. For example, categorical variables are frequently used in a multiple regression framework using a technique known as "dummy variable regression." Computational algorithms make the results seem different; for example, ANOVA will generate effect coefficients representing estimated deviation from the grand mean while dummy variable regression will yield coefficients representing deviations from an omitted category, but the basic approach is the same. Understanding this basic similarity will give researchers a better feeling for the analyses that they are doing and provide more flexibility. For example, it is possible to test certain interaction effects, test the extent to which a particular variable or set of variables improves a model, and test certain contrasts of cells more easily using dummy variable regression than ANOVA programs.

The area most ripe for confusion when trying to switch from ANOVA to multiple regression, or vice-versa, is in testing the statistical importance of particular variables or groups of variables. If the independent variables are independent, regression and ANOVA will yield the same results in many situations. If they are correlated, however, different approaches to significance testing can produce dramatically different results. There are basically two methods of testing effects: (1) one may test each effect, after controlling for all other effects in the model, or (2) one may specify an a priori ordering of terms in the model and test for the importance of each effect controlling only for those preceding it in the ordering. The first approach is the one typically adopted in regression analysis. For example, if physician utilization is the dependent variable and access and physical health are the independent variables, the importance of access is tested controlling for health and the importance of health is tested controlling for access. The second approach is more typically adopted in ANOVA, but can also be accomplished using stepwise regression. In this case one might wish to test the im-

portance of health by itself, then control for health and test the residual importance of access. Both approaches to testing the "importance" of a variable can be
utilized in either regression or analysis of variance programs, but the researcher
must be able to specify what he/she means by the importance of a variable: its importance by itself, its importance in combination with other variables, or its importance over and above other variables. Overall and Spiegel (1969) present a
detailed discussion of these issues (cf. Cramer and Appelbaum 1980; Joe 1971;
Rawlings 1972). For those more familiar with analysis of variance, Edwards (1979)
presents a clear development of the correspondence between the analysis of
variance and multiple regression analysis of experimental data.

Treatments of regression analysis, analysis of variance, and multiple classification analysis usually are dominated by discussions of assumptions. However, the
meaning of certain assumptions is often misunderstood. For example, many people probably would be concerned about using physician utilization as a dependent
variable because it is not normally distributed. It is true that some estimation procedures such as maximum-likelihood require knowledge of variable distributions,
but neither the level of measurement of a variable (Stevens 1946) nor the distrubution of the variable necessarily determine what type of technique should be used
(Lord 1953). Usually the only assumptions concern the distribution of the error
term. Thus, as Gaito (1980) has so clearly pointed out, the assumptions for these
techniques are based on their mathematical properties and do not necessarily dictate the use of particular scale types.

The most common way of estimating a linear relationship is called ordinary
least squares. That is, this procedure fits a linear function to the data that
minimizes the squared deviations of the data points from the line. One can use this
procedure to fit a straight line to *any* data. The problem comes in making inferences about the characteristics of that line to the population. That is, when we
estimate the slope of the line in a sample, how confident can we be that the slope
on the population is close to the estimated slope? This is both a theoretical and
practical question. There are certain theoretical conditions which should be met,
but the real issue is to what extent deviations from such ideal conditions affect
one's inferences. Probably the most comprehensive and readable treatment of this
subject is "Robustness in Regression Analysis" by Bohrnstedt and Carter (1971).
They conclude that regression analysis is adequately robust except in the presence
of measurement error and incorrect choice of variables. They argue that problems
of unequal variances and nonnormality do not generally cause serious distortions.

In cases where one must deal with extreme violations of assumptions, one can
use various techniques such as transforming the data or using a solution that takes
into account unusual characteristics of the data (Aitken 1935; McGillivray 1970;
Theil 1971). These techniques are fairly sophisticated, and statistical advice should
be sought about how and when to use them. One should be careful not to assume
that a more "sophisticated" model will yield better results, however. For example,
Kobashigawa and Berki (1977) investigated several regression approaches to the
analysis of medical care data where utilization was the dependent variable and
found that several alternative analytic techniques provided only marginal gains
over the standard least squares technique. Thus, before abandoning the simplest
techniques for more elaborate procedures one should think carefully about what
the problem is, if it really is a problem, and the possible solutions.

The second class of models, S-shaped models, has generated a great deal of
confusion and technical discourse in the literature but can be summarized quite

simply. The main situation where one can postulate such a functional relationship would be where the dependent variable is dichotomous. For example, let us say that instead of being concerned with how many times a person used a medical clinic, we want to determine the factors related to whether or not he/she used the clinic at all. Thus, the dependent variable can only take on two values representing use and nonuse. In this situation, a linear relationship is intuitively unreasonable (Cox 1970, pp. 17–18; Walker and Duncan 1967). First, we know that the function has limits to it. If we are predicting use/nonuse, the dependent variable is really the probability of using the clinic. Since we know that a probability cannot be smaller than 0 nor larger than 1, the function must stop at 0 and 1. Also, it is reasonable to assume that as one approaches a high probability of using the clinic, variations in the independent variables will have less and less impact; that is, the function will flatten out and gradually approach 1. This, of course, describes the S-shaped curve. Convenient and theoretically tractable S-shaped curves are the cumulative logistic distrubution and the cumulative Normal distribution. Often an argument is made for using these distributions because having a dichotomous variable violates the assumptions of homoscedasticity of the error term (Goldberger 1964). Sometimes theoretical motivations are given for such distributions (Finney 1952; Tobin 1958; Warner 1967), but the researcher should keep in mind that he/she is trying to predict an outcome and usually the real reason that such a curve is used is because it is more likely to approximate the process modeled.

In situations where the independent variables are continuous, there are three main S-shaped models: two-group discriminant function analysis, Logit analysis, and Probit analysis. There are also techniques for improving the "performance" of linear models when the dependent variable is dichotomous (e.g., Grizzle, Starmer, and Koch 1969; Johnson and Koch 1971; Theil 1971). However, the real question is functional form and if one is interested in maintaining the S-shaped form, then the decision is among discriminant analysis, Logit and Probit. This statement may surprise the reader because there is a widespread assertion that discriminant analysis is "the same as" multiple regression analysis. It is true that when certain assumptions are met, the coefficients of the discriminant function are linear functions of multiple regression coefficients (Ladd 1966), but if one reformulates the discriminant function so that probability is the dependent variable, then the equation takes on the form described in equation 2: an S-shaped function. (The function in equation 2 also describes the situation in which the log of the odds of an event occurring is linearly related to the independent variables.) What then is the difference or utility of one of these techniques versus the other? The answer is that unless one can be extremely precise about the nature of the data, or one can make extremely specific assumptions, they will yield similar results and are theoretically similar.

Several persuasive arguments can be made for the theoretical and empirical superiority of Logit analysis (Press and Wilson 1978), but limited availability of computer programs may restrict the researcher's options. The results of a large number of empirical studies indicate that even in the case where various assumptions of certain models are violated, the results are often strikingly similar (e.g., Efran 1975; Gillespie 1977; Halperin, Blackwelder, and Verter 1971; McFadden 1976; Moore 1973; Nerlove and Press 1973; Press and Wilson 1978). Similarly, if the distribution of the dependent variable is not extremely skewed (i.e.,

.25 < p < .75), even fitting linear functions yield reasonable coefficients (Lunney 1970; Knoke 1975; Goodman 1975).

Theoretical considerations aside, the researcher has constraints on his time and computer facilities. Discriminant analysis is the technique for which there is most likely readily available computer programs and in most situations provides good information concerning the relationships under investigation. If independent variables are not approximately normally distributed and one is concerned with precise parameteer estimates and statistical tests, one should investigate the possibility of conducting Logit analysis. The presentation by Nerlove and Press (1973) is one of the clearest discussions of this issue and Press and Wilson (1978) have written an excellent but more technical article on the choice between logistic regression and discriminant analysis. The differences between the functions estimated by Probit analysis and Logit analysis are usually quite small (Cox 1970, p. 28), and if programs are available only for Probit analysis, they will usually yield results similar to Logit analysis.

It was mentioned at the beginning of this discussion that we were assuming that the independent variables were continuous. In addition, some of the techniques are based on the assumption of multivariate normality. When distribution assumptions are violated (such as when some of the independent variables are categorical and others are continuous), there is a sizable amount of work indicating that the methods we have discussed still yield reasonable results (Bahadur 1961: Chang and Afifi 1974; Gilbert 1968; Krzanowski 1975; Truett, Cornfield, and Kannel 1967). However, if all the independent variables are categorical in nature, there are several techniques for estimating Logit functions (Swafford 1980). In addition, there are techniques called loglinear modeling that provide a coherent framework and statistical theory based only on the assumption of a multinomial distribution for testing various models (Goodman 1971, 1972). This method will be discussed in more detail shortly.

A class of models not yet considered involves dependent variables that are categorical in nature and have more than two categories. Let us say, for example, that we wanted to predict whether a person with cancer received chemotherapy, radiation therapy, or no therapy. There are three categories of patients with no logical ordering to them. Three approaches to this problem are multiple group discriminant analysis, analyzing a series of dichotomies, and contingency table analysis. Although multiple group discriminant analysis is theoretically correct in such a situation and is usually easy to do because of available computer programs, we recommend against use of this procedure. The theory for discriminant analysis when the dependent variable consists of more than two groups is poorly developed and the results are usually difficult to interpret. Similarly, interpreting the analyses of a series of dichotomies can often be difficult (see Swafford 1980, p. 681 for a good discussion of this approach).

The third alternative mentioned involves forming cross-tabulations of the data and then analyzing the patterns of association in the table (Haberman 1978, 1979). Because of the way these tables are modeled, this method is usually referred to as loglinear analysis (Bishop, Fienberg, and Holland 1975; Fienberg 1977; Goodman 1971, 1972; Payne 1972; Reynolds 1977). This name comes from the fact that in such analyses one predicts the number of people in a given cell by multiplying the odds of being in the appropriate cell on the different marginals. When the log of such a formulation is taken, the prediction of the number of people in a cell becomes a linear function of the log of certain marginal or combination of marginal odds. Although this sounds intimidating and foreign, this technique is only a generalization of the familiar chi-square test of association in a two-dimensional table. The popularity and power of loglinear analysis arises from the unified formulation and ability to statistically test specific models. The most common computer program for calculating estimates and tests based on such models is called ECTA (Everyman's Contingency Table Analysis) and is now available at many institutions. The main constraint on loglinear analyses is that all the variables are categorical. If one has continuous independent variables, they must be categorized. This can be done on the median, or on quartiles, etc., and if one wishes to include some of the information from the interval nature of the scale in the model, it is possible to test for the significance of linear patterns in independent variables (Duncan and McRae 1978).

Estimates of Sampling Variability

No mention has been made up to this point of the consequences of using data from different types of samples. Early in the chapter, the possibility of weighting the data to compensate for certain sampling strategies was mentioned but the effect of such weighting on calculation of statistics was not. Unfortunately, although few studies use simple random sampling, most analyses in the literature assume random sampling when determining significance of results. When proper weighting techniques are used or when nonrandom representative samples are selected, the widely used statistical computer programs provide unbiased estimates of most parameters but generally give inaccurate estimates of the statistics' variances. For example, if stratified sampling is used, these programs will overestimate the statistic variability (Kish 1965; Smith 1976). This topic is much too involved to be covered here, but one should be aware that when any sampling strategy other than simple random sampling is used the classical textbook formulae and the calculations of most statistical "packages" will not yield correct results. In such a situation, a methodologist should be consulted as to analytical (see for example, Williams 1962; Kish 1965) or empirical methods (Finifter 1972; Kaplan, Francis, and Sedransk 1979) to determine the magnitude of such effects.

Conclusion

Space constraints have required that this review of approaches to data analysis be superficial and selective. Certain techniques such as nonparametric statistical methods (Bradley 1968), more general formulations for analyzing correctional data (e.g., Lisrel: Joreskog 1970; Joreskog 1973), Canonical Correlation Analysis (e.g., McKeon 1967; Laessig and Duckett 1979), Path Analysis (Duncan 1971; Berki and Kobashigawa 1976), Automatic Interaction Detection (AID: Sonquist and Morgan 1964), and special statistical problems such as case control studies (Breslow et al. 1978) and models predicting how soon an event happens (e.g., Dyer 1975; Myers, Hankey, and Mantal 1973) have not been covered. In addition, I have not mentioned how demographic techniques such as direct and indirect standardization relate to the techniques discussed (Kitogawa 1964; Fleiss 1973). Although some have argued that these standardization techniques are descriptive techniques made obsolete by newer techniques such as loglinear analysis of contingency tables (Fienberg 1977, p. 5), they are common in morbidity and mortality analyses and there are interesting comparisons to be made among methods of correcting for differences between populations.

The purpose of this chapter was certainly not to review all multivariate techniques or list all considerations determining analytic approach. Rather, it was to touch briefly on as many central points as possible to emphasize how often many of the analysis decisions to be made are based on substantive considerations and the experience of the researcher as opposed to complicated statistical considerations. The purpose of statistics is to summarize data in a parsimonious and informative way and to inform about the generalizability of results. If the basic features of a technique or model are incomprehensible to an applied researcher, it is not likely to be useful in explaining the data to colleagues. Although some subtle relationships must be pried from the data with "powerful" techniques, in general the best rule to follow is to use the simplest, most straightforward, and most comprenhensive method possible.

REFERENCES

ADAY, L. A.; ANDERSEN, R.; and FLEMING, G. V. 1980. *Health care in the United States. Equity for whom?* Beverly Hills, Calif.: Sage Publications.

AITKEN, A. C. 1935. On least squares and linear combination of observations. *Proceedings of the Royal Society of Edinburgh* 55: 42–48.

ALBEE, G. W. 1976. Into the valley of therapy rode the six thousand. Review of *Psychiatrists and their patients: a national study of private office practice*, by J. Marmor. *Contemporary Psychology* 21: 525–27.

ALWIN, D. F. 1973. The use of factor analysis in the construction of linear composites in social research. *Sociological Methods and Research* 2: 191–214.

BAHADUR, R. R. 1961. A representation of the joint distribution of responses to dichotomous items. In *Studies in item analysis and prediction*, ed. H. Solomon, pp. 158–68. Stanford: Stanford University Press.

BENJAMIN, B. 1965. *Social and economic factors affecting mortality.* The Hague: Moutin.

BENTLER, P. M. 1976. Factor analysis. In *Data analysis strategies and designs for substance abuse research. Research Issues, No. 13.* ed. P. M. Bentler, D. J. Lettieri, and G. A. Austin, pp. 139–58. Rockville, Md,: National Institute of Drug Abuse.

———; LETTIERI, D. J.; and AUSTIN, G. A., eds. 1976. *Data analysis strategies and designs for substance abuse research. Research Issues, No. 13.* Rockville, Md.: National Institute of Drug Abuse.

BERKI, S. E., and KOBASHIGAWA, B. 1976. Socioeconomic and need determinants of ambulatory care use: path analysis of the 1970 health interview survey data. *Medical care* 14: 405–21.

BISHOP, Y. M. M.; FIENBERG, S. E.; and HOLLAND, P. W. 1975. *Discrete multivariate analysis theory and practice.* Cambridge, Mass.: MIT Press.

BOHRNSTEDT, G. W. 1970. Reliability and validity assessment in attitude measurement. In *Attitude measurement*, ed. G. F. Summers. Chicago: Rand McNally.

———, and CARTER, M. T. 1971. Robustness in regression analysis. In *Sociological methodology.* San Francisco, Calif.: Jossey-Bass.

BORGATTA, E. F. 1961. Toward a methodological codification: the shotgun and the salt-shaker. *Sociometry* 24: 432–35.

BRESLOW, N. E.; DAY, N. E.; HALVORSEN, K. T.; PRENTICE, R. L.; and SABAI, C. 1978. Estimation of multiple relative risk functions in matched case-control studies. *American Journal of Epidemiology* 108: 299–307.

BRADLEY, J. V. 1968. *Distribution-free-statistical tests.* Englewood Cliffs, N.Y.: Prentice-Hall.

CAMILLI, G., and HOPKINS, K. D. 1979. Tests for association in 2 × 2 contingency tables with very small sample sizes. *Psychological Bulletin* 86: 1011–14.

CATTELL, R. B. 1952. *Factor analysis: an introduction and manual for the psychologist and scientist.* New York: Harper and Row.

CHANG, F. C., and AFIFI, A. A. 1974. Classification based on dichotomous and continuous variables. *Journal of American Statistical Association* 69: 336–39.

COHEN, J. 1968. Multiple regression as a general data-analytic technique. *Psychological Bulletin* 70: 426–43.

———. 1969. *Statistical power analysis for the behavioral sciences.* New York: Academic Press.

———, and COHEN, P. 1975. *Applied multiple regression/correlation analysis for the behavioral sciences.* New York: Wiley.

———. 1976. General multiple regression and correlation analysis. In *Data analysis strategies and designs for substance abuse research. Research Issues, No. 13,* ed. P. M. Bentler, D. J. Lettieri, and G. A. Austin, pp. 159–78. Rockville, Md.: National Institute of Drug Abuse.

COOMBS, C. H. 1964. *A theory of data.* New York: Wiley.

COX, D. 1970. *The analysis of binary data.* London: Methuen.

CRAMER, E. M., and APPELBAUM, M. I. 1980. Nonorthogonal analysis of variance—Once again. *Psychological Bulletin* 87: 51–57.

CRONBACH, L. J. 1951. Coefficient alpha and the internal structure of tests. *Psychometrica* 16: 297–334.

———, and GLESER, G. C. 1953. Assessing similarity between profiles. *Psychological Bulletin* 50: 456–73.

DARLINGTON, R. B. 1968. Multiple regression in psychological rsearch and practice. *Psychological Bulletin* 69: 161–82.

DOHRENWEND, B. S. 1980. The conflict between statistical and theoretical significance. *Journal of Health and Social Behavior* 21: 291–93.

———; KRASNOFF, L.; ACKENASY, A. R.; and DOHRENWEND, B. P. 1978. Exemplification of a method for scaling life events: the PERI life events scale. *Journal of Health and Social Behavior* 19: 205–29.

———. 1979. Reply to comment by Lorimor et al. *Journal of Health and Social Behavior* 20: 308.

DUNCAN, O. D. 1971. Path analysis: sociological examples. In *Causal models in the social sciences,* ed. H. M. Blalock, Jr. Chicago: Aldine.

———, and McRAE, J. A., JR. 1978. Multiway contingency analysis with a scaled response or factor. In *Sociological methodology,* ed. K. F. Schuessler, pp. 68–75. San Francisco, Calif.: Jossey-Bass.

DuMOUCHEL, W. H., and DUNCAN, G. T. 1976. *Using sample survey weights to test for misspecification in a linear regression model* (Department of Statistics Technical Report No. 72). Michigan: University of Michigan, October 1976.

DYER, A. R. 1975. An analysis of the relationship of systolic blood pressure, serum cholesterol, and smoking to 14-year mortality in the Chicago Peoples Gas Company study. *Journal of Chronic Diseases* 28: 571–78.

EDWARDS, A. L. 1979. *Multiple regression and the analysis of variance and covariance.* San Francisco, Calif.: W. H. Freeman.

EFRAN, B. 1975. The efficiency of logistic regression compared to normal discriminant analysis. *Journal of the American Statistical Association* 70: 892–98.

———. 1978. Regression and ANOVA with zero-one data: measures of residual variation. *Journal of the American Statistical Association* 73: 113–21.

EVERITT, B. S. 1977. Cluster analysis. In *The analysis of survey data*, ed. C. R. O'Muircheartaigh and C. Payne. Vol. 1: *Exploring data structures*, pp. 63–68. New York: Wiley.

FEINSTEIN, A. R. 1977. *Clinical biostatistics*. St. Louis, Mo.: C. V. Mosby.

FENNESSEY, J. 1968. The general linear model: a new perspective on some familiar topics. *American Journal of Sociology* 74: 1–27.

FIENBERG, S. E. 1977. *The analysis of cross classified categorical data*. Cambridge, Mass.: MIT Press.

FINIFTER, B. M. 1972. The generation of confidence: evaluating research findings by random subsample replication. In *Sociological methodology*, ed. H. L. Costner. San Francisco, Calif.: Jossey-Bass.

FINNEY, D. J. 1952. *Probit analysis*. (2d ed.) Cambridge, England: Cambridge University Press.

FLEISS, J. L. 1973. *Statistical methods for rates and proportions*. New York: Wiley.

GAITO, J. 1980. Measurement scales and statistics: resurgence of an old misconception. *Psychological Bulletin* 87: 564–67.

GILBERT E. S. 1968. On discrimination using qualitative variables. *Journal of the American Statistical Association* 63, 1399–1412.

GILLESPIE, M. W. 1977. Log-linear techniques and the regressional analysis of dummy dependent variables. *Sociological Methods and Research* 6: 103–22.

GLASS, G. V., and MAGUIRE, T. O. 1966. Abuses of factor scores. *American Educational Research Journal* 3: 297–304.

GOLDBERGER, A. S. 1964. *Econometric theory*. New York: Wiley.

GOODMAN, L. A. 1971. The analysis of multidimensional contingency tables: stepwise procedures and direct estimation methods for building models for multiple classifications. *Technometrics* 13: 33–61.

———. 1972. A modified multiple regression approach to the analysis of dichotomous variables. *American Sociological Review* 37: 28–46.

———. 1975. The relationship between modified and usual multiple-regression approaches to the analysis of dichotomous variables. In *Sociological Methodology*, ed. D. Heise, pp. 83–110. San Francisco, Calif.: Jossey-Bass.

GORDON, R. A. 1967. Issues in multiple regression. *American Journal of Sociology* 73 (no. 5): 592–616.

GRIZZLE, J. E.; STARMER, C. F.; and KOCH, G. G. 1969. Analysis of categorical data by linear models. *Biometrics* 25: 489–504.

GUJARATI, D. 1970. Use of dummy variables in testing for equality between sets of coefficients in linear regressions: a generalization. *American Statistician*, December 1970: 18–22.

GUTTMAN, L. 1944. A basis for scaling qualitative data. *American Sociological Review* 9: 139–50.

HABERMAN, S. J. *Analysis of qualitative data* (Vol. 1: *Introductory topics*, 1978; Vol 2: *New developments*, 1979). New York: Academic Press.

HALPERIN, M.; BLACKWELDER, W. C.; and VERTER, J. I. 1971. Estimation of the multivariate logistic risk function: A comparison of the discriminant function and maximum likelihood approaches. *Journal of Chronic Diseases* 24: 125–58.

HARMAN, H. H. 1967. *Modern factor analysis*. Chicago: University of Chicago Press.

HARRIS, C. W. 1967. On factors and factor scores. *Psychometrics* 32: 363–79.

HAYS, W. L., and WINKLER, R. L. 1971. *Statistics. Probability, inference and decision*. New York: Holt, Rinehart, and Winston.

HESS, I.; RIEDEL, D. C.; and FITZPATRICK, T. B., eds. 1975. *Probability sampling of hospitals and patients*. Ann Arbor, Mich.: Health Administration Press.

HORN, J. L. 1965. An empirical comparison of methods for estimating factor scores. *Educational and Psychological Measurement* 25: 313–22.

JACKSON, D. N., and CHAN, D. W. 1980. Maximum-likelihood estimation in common factor analysis: a cautionary note. *Psychological Bulletin* 88: 502–8.

JOE, G. W. 1971. Comment on Overall and Spitegel's least squares analysis of experimental data. *Psychological Bulletin* 71: 364–66.

JOHNSON, W. D., and KOCH, G. G. 1971. A note on the weighted least squares analysis of the Ries-Smith contingency table data. *Technometrics* 13: 438–47.

JORESKOG, K. G. 1970. A general method of analysis of covariance structures. *Biometrika* 57: 239–51.

———. 1973. Analysis of covariance structures. In *Multivariate analysis III*, ed. P. R. Krisnaiah, pp. 263–85. New York: Academic Press.

KAISER, H. F. 1970. A second generation little jiffy. *Psychometrika* 35: 401–15.

KAPLAN, B.; FRANCIS, I.; and SEDRANSK, J. 1979. A comparison of methods and programs for computing variances of estimates from complex sample surveys. In *American Statistical Association 1979 Proceedings of the Section on Survey Research Methods*, pp. 97–100. Washington, D. C.: American Statistical Association.

KERLINGER, F. N., and PEDHAZUR, E. J. 1973. *Multiple regression in behavioral research.* New York: Holt, Rinehart, and Winston.

KESSLER, R. C. 1980. A comment on "A comparison of life event-weighting schemes." *Journal of Health and Social Behavior* 21: 293–96.

KIM, J., and MUELLER, C. W. 1978. Factor analysis, statistical methods and practical issues. In *Quantitative Applications in the Social Sciences* (Sage University Paper Series, 07–014). Beverly Hills, Calif., and London: Sage Publications.

KIRT, R. E. 1968. *Experimental design procedures for the behavioral sciences.* Belmont, Calif.: Wadsworth.

KISH, L. 1965. *Survey sampling.* New York: Wiley.

KITAGAWA, E. M. 1964. Standarized comparisons in population research. *Demography* 1: 296–315.

KLEIN, L. R., and MORGAN, J. N. 1951. Results of alternative statistical treatments of sample survey data. *Journal of the American Statistical Association* 46: 442.

KNOKE, P. 1975. A comparison of log-linear and regression models for systems of dichotomous variables. *Sociological Methods and Research* 3: 416–34.

KOBASHIGAWA, B., and BERKI, S. E. 1977. Alternative regression approaches to the analysis of medical care survey data. *Medical Care* 15: 396–408.

KONIJN, H. S. 1962. Regression analysis in sample surveys. *Journal of the American Statistical Association* 57: 590.

KRUSKAL, J. B. 1964a. Multidimensional scaling by optimizing goodness of fit to a nonmetric hypothesis. *Psychometrika* 29: 1–27.

———. 1964b. Nonmetric multidimensional scaling: a numerical method. *Psychometrika* 29: 115–29.

———. 1977. The relationship between multidimensional scaling and clustering. In *Clustering and classification*, ed. J. Van Ryzin, pp. 17–44. New York: Academic Press.

KRZANOWSKI, W. J. 1975. Discrimination and classification using both binary and continous variables. *Journal of the American Statistical Association* 70: 782–90.

———. 1968. On expected values of probabilities of misclassification in discriminant analysis, necessary sample size, and a relation with the multiple correlation coefficient. *Biometrics* 24: 823.

LACHENBRUCH, P. A. 1975. *Discriminant analysis.* New York: Hofner Press.

———, and GOLDSTEIN, M. 1979. Discriminant analysis. *Biometrics* 35: 69–85.

LADD, G. W. 1966. Linear probability functions and discriminant functions. *Econometrica* 34: 873–85.

LAESSIG, R. E., and DUCKETT, E. J. 1979. Canonical correlation analysis potential for environmental health planning. *American Journal of Public Health* 69: 353–59.

LAWLEY, D. N., and MAXWELL, A. E. 1971. *Factor analysis as a statistical method.* New York: American Elsevier.

LEVY, P. A., and LEMSHOW, S. 1980. *Sampling for health professionals*. Belmont, Calif.: Lifetime Learning Publications.

LIKERT, R. 1932. A technique for the measurement of attitudes. *Archives of Psychology* 22: 1–55.

LORD, F. M. 1953. On the statistical treatment of football numbers. *American Psychologist* 8: 750–51.

LORIMOR, R. J.; JUSTICE, B.; McBEE, G. W.; and WEINMAN, M. 1979. Weighting events in life events research. *Journal of Health and Social Behavior* 20: 306–8.

LORR, M. 1976. Cluster and typological analysis. In *Data analysis strategies and designs for substance abuse research. Research Issues No. 13*, ed. P. M. Bentler, D. J. Lettieri, and G. A. Austin, pp. 103–24. Rockville, Md.: National Institute of Drug Abuse.

LUNNEY, G. H. 1970. Using analysis of variance with a dichotomous dependent variable: an empirical study. *Journal of Educational Measurement* 7: 263–69.

McFADDEN, D. 1976. A comment on discriminant analysis versus logit analysis. *Annals of Economic and Social Measurements* 5: 511–23.

McGILLIVRAY, R. G. 1970. Estimating the linear probability function. *Econometrica 38*: 775–766.

McKENNELL, A. C. 1977. Attitude scale construction. In *The analysis of survey data*, ed. C. A. O'Muircheartaigh and C. Payne. Vol. 1: *Exploring data structures*, pp. 183–220. New York: Wiley.

McKEON, J. J. 1967. Canonical analysis: some relations between canonical correlation, factor analysis, discriminant function analysis and scaling theory. *Psychometric Monographs, No. 13*. Chicago: University of Chicago Press.

MELICAR, E. 1965. Least squares analysis of economic survey data. *Proceedings of the Business and Economic Statistics Section of the American Statistical Association* pp. 1–13.

MIROWSKI, J., II, and Ross, C. E. 1980. Weighting life events: a second look. *Journal of Health and Social Behavior* 21: 296–300.

MOORE, D. M., II. 1973. Evaluation of five discrimination procedures for binary variables. *Journal of the American Statistical Association* 68: 399–404.

MORRISON, D. E., and HENKEL, R. E., eds. 1970. *The significance test controversy*. Chicago: Aldine.

MEYERS, M. H.; HANKEY, B. F.; and MANTEL, N. 1973. A logistic-exponential model for use with response-time data involving regressor variables. *Biometrics* 29: 257–69.

NERLOVE, M., and PRESS, S. J. 1973. *Univariate and multivariate loglinear and logistic models*. Santa Monica, Calif.: Rand.

NUNNALY, J. C. 1967. *Psychometric theory*, New York: McGraw-Hill.

OVERALL, J. E. 1964. Note on the scientific status of factors. *Psychological Bulletin*, 1964, *61*, 270–276.

———, and SPIEGEL, D. K. 1969. Concerning least squares analysis of experimental data. *Psychological Bulletin* 72: 311–22.

PAYNE, C. 1977. The log-linear model for contingency tables. In *The analysis of survey data*, ed. C. A. O'Muircheartaigh and C. Payne. Vol. 2: *Model Fitting*. New York: Wiley.

PORTER, R. D. 1973. On the use of survey sample weights in the linear model. *Annals of Economic and Social Measurement* 2: 141.

PRESS, S. J., and WILSON, S. 1978. Choosing between logistic regression and discriminant analysis. *Journal of the American Statistical Association* 73: 699–705.

RAWLINGS, R. R. 1972. Note on nonorthogonal analysis of variance. *Psychological Bulletin* 77: 373–74.

REYNOLDS, H. T. 1977. *The analysis of cross-classifications*. New York: Free Press.

ROMMEY, A. K.; SHEPARD, R. N.; and NERLOVE, S. B., eds. 1972. *Multidimensional scaling*, vol. 2. New York: Seminar Press.

Ross, C. E., and MIROWSKI, J., II. 1979. A comparison of life-event-weighting schemes: change, undesirability, and effect-proportional indices. *Journal of Health and Social Behavior* 20: 166–77.

SHEPARD, D. S., and NEUTRA, R. 1977. A pitfall in sampling medical visits. *American Journal of Public Health* 67: 743–50.

SHEPARD, R. N. 1972a. Introduction to Vol 1. In *Multidimensional scaling,* ed. R. N. Shepard, A. K. Romney and S. A. Nerlove, Vol. 1, pp. 1–20. New York: Seminar Press.

———. 1972b. A taxonomy of some principal types of data and of multidimensional methods for their analysis. In *Multidimensional Scaling,* ed. R. N. Shepard, A. K. Romney and S. B. Nerlove, vol. 1, pp. 21–47. New York: Seminar Press.

———; ROMNEY, A. K.; and NERLOVE, S. B., eds. 1972. *Multidimensional Scaling,* vol. 1. New York: Seminar Press.

SMITH, K. W. 1976. Analyzing disproportionately stratified samples with computerized statistical packages. *Sociological Methods and Research* 5: 207–30.

SOKAL, R. R. 1977. Clustering and classification: background and current directions. In *Classification and clustering,* ed. J. Van Ryzin. New York: Academic Press.

SONQUIST, J. A., and MORGAN, J. N. 1964. *The detection of interaction effects.* Ann Arbor, Mich.: Institute for Social Research.

STEVENS, J. P. 1980. Power of the multivariate analysis of variance tests. *Psychological Bulletin* 88: 728–37.

STEVENS, S. S. 1946. On the theory of scales of measurement. *Science* 103: 677–80.

SUMMERS, G. F. 1970. *Attitude measurement.* Chicago: Rand McNally.

SWAFFORD, M. 1980. Three parametric techniques for contingency table analysis: a nontechnical commentary. *American Sociological Review* 45: 664–90.

THEIL, H. 1971. *Principles of econometrics.* New York: Wiley.

THURSTONE, L. L. 1928. Attitudes can be measured. *American Journal of Sociology* 33: 529–54.

TOBIN. J. 1958. Estimation of relationships for limited dependent variables. *Econometrica* 26: 24–36.

TORGERSON, W. S. 1952. Multidimensional scaling: I. Theory and method. *Psychometrika* 17: 401–19.

———. 1958. *Theory and methods of scaling.* New York: Wiley.

TRUETT, J.; CORNFIELD, J.; and KANNEL, W. 1967. A multivariate analysis of the risk of coronary heart disease in Framingham. *Journal of Chronic Diseases* 20: 511–24.

TUKEY, J. W. 1954. Causation, regression, and path analysis. In *Statistics and mathematics in biology,* ed. O. Kempthorne. Ames, Iowa: University of Iowa Press.

———. 1977. *Exploratory data analysis.* Reading, Mass.: Addison-Wesley.

VAN RYZIN, J., ed. 1977. *Classification and clustering.* New York: Academic Press.

WAINER, H. 1976. Estimating coefficients in linear models: It don't make no nevermind. *Psychological Bulletin* 83: 213–17.

WALKER, S. H., and DUNCAN, D. B. 1967. Estimation of the probability of an event as a function of several independent variables. *Econometrica* 54: 167.

WANG, M. W., and STANLEY, J. C. 1970. Differential weighting: a review of methods and empirical studies. *Review of Educational Research* 40: 653–705.

WARD, J. R., JR., and HOOK, M. E. 1963. Application of a hierarchical grouping procedure to a problem of grouping profiles. *Educational and Psychological Measurement* 23: 69–81.

WARNER, S. L. 1967. Multivariate regression of dummy variables under normality assumptions. *Journal of the American Statistical Association* 58: 1054–63.

WILKINSON, L. 1979. Tests of significance in stepwise regression. *Psychological Bulletin* 86: 168–74.

WILLIAMS, W. H. 1962. The variance of an estimator with post-stratified weighting. *Journal of the American Statistical Association* 57: 622–27.

Index